Features

5th Edition

State and Metropolitan Area Data Book 1997-98

A Statistical Abstract Supplement

Issued April 1998

U.S. Department of Commerce
William M. Daley, Secretary
Robert L. Mallett, Deputy Secretary

Economics and Statistics Administration
Lee Price, Acting Under Secretary
for Economic Affairs

BUREAU OF THE CENSUS
James F. Holmes, Acting Director

ECONOMICS
AND STATISTICS
ADMINISTRATION

**Economics and Statistics
Administration**
Lee Price, Acting Under Secretary
for Economic Affairs

BUREAU OF THE CENSUS
James F. Holmes, Acting Director
Bradford R. Huther, Deputy Director

Nancy A. Potok, Principal Associate Director and Chief
Financial Officer
Michael S. McKay, Acting Associate Director for
Administration

ADMINISTRATIVE AND CUSTOMER SERVICES DIVISION
Walter C. Odom, Chief

ACKNOWLEDGMENTS

Wanda K. Cevis was responsible for the technical supervision and coordination of this volume under the general direction of **Glenn W. King**, Chief, Statistical Compendia Branch. Subject development and analytical review were provided by **Lars B. Johanson**, **Rosemary E. Clark**, **Edward C. Jagers**, and **David J. Fleck**. **Kathleen A. Siemer** was responsible for computer operations and data processing, assisted by **Mary Grace Lynch**. **Alice M. Novy** was responsible for text preparation and processing of state tables. Data compilation and review were provided by **Mary Grace Lynch** and **Kristen M. Barrack**. Data entry and other support activities were provided by **Juanita B. Anderson**, **Kristen M. Barrack**, **Catherine L. Crusan**, and **E. Fae Kesterson**.

The staff of the Administrative and Customer Services Division, **Walter C. Odom**, Chief, performed publication planning, design, composition, editorial review, and printing planning and procurement. **Cynthia G. Brooks** provided publication coordination and editing.

The cooperation of many contributors to this volume is gratefully acknowledged. The source notes below each table and in Appendix A credit the various government and private agencies which have furnished information for the **State and Metropolitan Area Data Book**. In a few instances, contributors have requested that their data be designated as subject to copyright restrictions, as indicated in the source notes. Permission to use copyright material should be obtained directly from the copyright owner.

Library of Congress Card No. 52-4576

SUGGESTED CITATION

U.S. Bureau of the Census. State and Metropolitan Area Data Book 1997-98
(5th edition.) Washington, DC, 1998

Reprinted without alteration on acid-free paper
National Technical Information Service
Springfield, Virginia
June 1998
ISBN 0-934213-54-2

219722

Preface

The *State and Metropolitan Area Data Book* (SMADB), published intermittently since 1979, is a local area supplement to the *Statistical Abstract of the United States*. This 1997-98 edition is the fifth; the book was also published in 1979, 1982, 1986, and 1991. The SMADB is a convenient summary of statistics on the social, political, and economic organization of the states and metropolitan areas (MAs) of the United States. It is designed to serve as a statistical reference and guide to other statistical publications and sources. The latter function is served by the source citations appearing below each table and in Appendix A, Source Notes and Explanations.

This volume includes a selection of data from many statistical publications and electronic sources, both government and private. Publications cited as sources usually contain additional detail and more comprehensive discussions of definitions and concepts than can be presented here. Data not available in publications issued by the contributing agency but obtained from unpublished records are identified in the source notes as "unpublished data." More information on the subjects covered in the tables so noted may generally be obtained from the source.

Except as indicated, figures are for the states and metropolitan areas of the United States as presently constituted. Although emphasis in this Data Book is primarily given to state and metropolitan area (MA) data, Table A includes U.S. totals and Tables B and C present data for the component counties and central cities of MAs, respectively. As an aid in locating data for counties and cities, Appendixes D and E present listings of these areas in alphabetic order by state with relevant MA code; these codes appear on Tables B-1, C-1, and D.

Changes in this edition. The order of tables has been changed in this volume. The state tables appear first as Tables A-1 through A-56 instead of as Table E in the previous edition. Metropolitan area data are covered in three tables in this edition: Metro areas, metro counties, and central cities. Selected state and metro area rankings can be found in Tables A and B; additional rankings may be found on the Census Bureau's Internet site.

We have changed the presentation of state data to an alphabetic one. The presentation of the various MA tables has been changed such that one data table for all MAs is shown before the next data table; earlier editions presented all the data tables for a specific group of MAs before

being repeated for the next group of MAs. This change has enabled us to include metropolitan area references in the index for ease in locating these data.

Source notes now appear at the bottom of each table page, as well as in the source notes and explanations appendix. Some citations provide Internet addresses either as the sole citation or as a supplement to the printed or electronic source. In addition, we now include a Telephone Contact List which provides a guide to federal agencies with major statistical programs, their mailing address, phone number, and Internet address.

Statistics in this edition. Data are generally shown for the most recent year or period available by fall 1997; some later data are included.

States. Data are presented for the United States, the 50 states, and the District of Columbia. 869 data items are presented for these areas in 56 tables, A-1 through A-56. The states and the District of Columbia are presented in alphabetic order under the U.S. total.

Metropolitan areas. Data for metropolitan areas (MAs) are for those areas defined by the Office of Management and Budget (OMB) as of June 30, 1996. The MAs presented in table sets B and C of this publication include 245 metropolitan statistical areas (MSAs), 17 consolidated metropolitan statistical areas (CMSAs) and their 58 primary metropolitan statistical areas (PMSAs) located outside New England; as well as 12 New England county metropolitan areas (NECMAs). These MAs are also presented in Table D but exclude the 58 PMSAs and the NECMA used as a substitute for the 5 PMSAs in the Connecticut portion of the New York-Northern New Jersey-Long Island, NY-NJ-CT-PA CMSA. For this reason, this CMSA is listed as CMSA/NECMA in this publication to alert users to this substitution. No data are presented for the 10 MSAs, 1 CMSA, and 15 PMSAs in New England. The guidelines for establishing metropolitan areas are presented in Appendix B, Geographic Concepts and Codes.

Table B. Metro areas. 159 data items are presented for all metro areas in 10 Tables, B-1 through B-10. The MSAs, CMSAs, and NECMAs are presented in alphabetic order, with PMSAs presented under the related CMSA. For an alphabetic listing of PMSAs along with their CMSA, see Appendix C.

Table C. Metro counties. 43 data items are presented for all metro areas found in Table B and their 844 component counties in three tables, C-1 through C-3. The MSAs, CMSAs, and NECMAs are presented in alphabetic order, with PMSAs presented under the related CMSA; component counties are presented under the appropriate MA. If you know the name of a county but not the MA in which it is located, see Appendix D for an alphabetic listing of metropolitan counties by state with the area's four-digit MSA/CMSA/NECMA code; this code is shown in the first column of Table C-1 in ascending order.

Table D. Central cities. Three population items are presented for the MSAs, CMSAs, and NECMAs found in Table B and their 538 central cities in Table D. The MSAs, CMSAs, and NECMAs are presented in alphabetic order, with central cities presented alphabetically under the appropriate MA. If you know the name of a central city but not the MA in which it is located, see Appendix E for an alphabetic listing of central cities by state with the area's four-digit MSA/CMSA/NECMA code; this code is shown in the first code column to the left of the area name in Table D.

Statistical reliability and responsibility, The contents of this volume were taken from many sources. All data from either censuses and surveys or from administrative records are subject to error arising from a number of factors: sampling variability (for statistics based on samples), reporting errors in the data for individual units, incomplete coverage, nonresponse, imputations, and processing errors. The Bureau of the Census cannot accept the responsibility for the accuracy or limitations of the data presented here, other than those for which it collects. The responsibility for selection of the material and for proper presentation, however, rests with the Bureau.

Maps. For a map of the United States with the 50 states and the District of Columbia, as well as census regions and divisions, see the inside of the front cover. For a map of MSAs, CMSAs, and PMSAs, see pages xii and xiii. For a map showing NECMAs, see page xiv. A wall-size version of the MA map, may be ordered through the Products and Services Staff, Geography Division, U.S. Bureau of the Census, at 301-457-1128.

Appendixes. Appendix A presents a discussion of source notes and explanations for the data items in Tables A through D. Appendix B presents a discussion of the geographic concepts and codes relevant to this volume, as well as the official standards for establishing metropolitan areas. Appendix C is an alphabetic listing of PMSA's showing the CMSA of which they are a part. Appendix D presents an alphabetic listing of component counties of MAs by state, with codes for the MSA, CMSA, or NECMA in which the county is located. Appendix E is an alphabetic listing of central cities of MAs, with codes for the MSA, CMSA, or NECMA in which the central city is located.

For additional information on data presented. Please consult the source publications available in local libraries, write to the agency indicated in the source notes, or visit the Internet site listed. Contact the Bureau of the Census only if it is cited as the source.

Statistics for the nation. Extensive data at the national level can be found in the *Statistical Abstract of the United States 1997,* an annual national data book, released each fall. *USA Statistics in Brief,* a pocket-size pamphlet highlighting many statistical series in the Abstract, is available separately; single copies of this pamphlet can be obtained free from U.S. Bureau of the Census, Customer Services, Washington, DC 20233 (telephone 301-457-4100).

Statistics for counties and cities. Data for all counties and cities of 25,000 or more population may be found in the *County and City Data Book 1994* and its forthcoming 1999 edition and related CD-ROMs. In addition, over 4,000 data items for all counties can be found on the forthcoming USA Counties 1998 CD-ROM. For information on ordering these products, see the inside back cover of this volume.

Suggestions and comments. Users of the *State and Metropolitan Area Data Book* and related publications (see inside back cover) are urged to make their data needs known for consideration in planning future editions. Suggestions and comments for improving coverage and presentation of data should be sent to the Director, U.S. Bureau of the Census, Washington, DC 20233.

Contents

States—Con.

Metro Areas

Metro Counties

Central Cities

Appendixes

Guide to Tabular Presentation

EXAMPLE OF TABLE STRUCTURE FROM:

Table B-8. Metro Areas – **Personal Income Projections and Civilian Labor Force**

[MSA = Metropolitan statistical area.CMSA = Consolidated MSA.PMSA = Primary MSA. NECMA = New England county metropolitan area.All areas defined as of June 30, 1996.Table includes 245 MSAs, 17 CMSAs, and 58 PMSAs not in New England; as well as 12 NECMAs.Table excludes 12 MSAs, 1 CMSA, and 15 PMSAs in New England]

| Metropolitan areas | Personal income projections (constant (1987) dollars) | | | | | | | | Civilian labor force | | | | | |
| | Total (mil dol) | | | | Per capita[2] (dollars) | | | | Total (1,000) | | | Unemployed (1,000) | | |
	2010	2005	2000	1993 esti-mate[1]	2010	2005	2000	1993 esti-mate[1]	1996	1995	1994	1996	1995	1994
Abilene, TX MSA........	2 296	2 122	1 947	1 671	17 366	16 402	15 358	13 762	60.5	59.6	58.1	3.0	3.1	3.0
Albany, GA MSA	2 054	1 881	1 711	1 472	15 539	14 765	13 934	12 680	55.7	53.5	54.5	3.3	3.3	4.8
Albany-Schenectady-Troy, NY MSA	20 165	18 594	16 980	14 825	20 400	19 444	18 397	16 958	446.8	450.9	455.5	20.4	22.5	22.3
Albuquerque, NM MSA ..	14 509	12 955	11 408	9 295	17 908	17 013	16 056	14 754	345.1	340.0	333.2	18.5	13.8	14.7
Alexandria, LA MSA	2 164	1 999	1 836	1 621	16 042	15 177	14 242	12 946	59.0	58.5	57.1	4.0	3.9	4.1
Allentown-Bethlehem-Easton, PA MSA	13 547	12 474	11 426	10 034	19 948	18 954	17 853	16 470	303.7	301.4	300.8	16.6	16.8	17.6

[1] Latest estimate available when projections were prepared.

[2] Based on resident population projected as of July 1 for 2010, 2005, and 2000 by the Bureau of Economic Analysis or estimated as of July 1, 1993 by the Bureau of the Census; 1993 estimate excludes subsequent census revisions.

Source: Personal Income Projections—U.S. Bureau of Economic Analysis, "Regional Economic Information System (REIS) 1969-1994" on CD-ROM; Civilian Labor Force—U.S. Bureau of Labor Statistics, Local Area Unemployment Statistics Time Series, Internet site %20Statistics/Data for each state (accessed April 1997), BLS gopher service discontinued October 31, 1997 (related BLS Internet site).

Headnotes immediately below table titles provide information on the geographic areas presented in the table.

Unit indicators show the specified quantities in which data items are presented. They are used for two primary reasons. Sometimes data are not available in absolute form. Other times we round the numbers in order to save space to show more data, as in the case above.

If no unit indicator is shown, data presented are in absolute form (see Table B-1 for an example). When needed, unit indicators are found in the column or spanner headings for the data items as shown above.

Footnotes below the bottom rule of table pages give information relating to specific data items or figures within the table.

Examples of Unit Indicator Interpretation From Table

Metropolitan area	Year	Item	Unit indicator	Number shown	Multiplier
Abilene, TX MSA..................	2010	Personal income projection	(mil dol)	2,296	$1,000,000
Abilene, TX MSA..................	1996	Civilian labor force.................	(1,000)	60.5	1,000

To Determine the Figure it is Necessary to Multiply the Number Shown by the Unit Indicator:

Personal income projection, 2010 = 2,296 * 1,000,000 or 2,296,000,000 (over 2 billion dollars).
Civilian labor force, 1996 = 60.5 * 1,000 or 60,500 (over 60 thousand).

In many tables, details will not add to the totals shown because of rounding.

EXPLANATION OF SYMBOLS AND TERMS

The following symbols, used in the tables throughout this book, are explained in condensed form in footnotes on the tables where they appear:

–	Represents zero or rounds to less than half the unit of measurement shown.
B	Base figure too small to meet statistical standards for reliability of a derived figure.
D	Figure withheld to avoid disclosure pertaining to a specific organization or individual.
NA	Data not enumerated, tabulated, or otherwise available separately.
S	Figure does not meet publication standards for reasons other than that covered by symbol B, above.
X	Figure not applicable because column heading and stub line make entry impossible, absurd, or meaningless.
Z	Entry would amount to less than half the unit of measurement shown.

The following terms are also used throughout this publication:

Averages. An average is a single number or value that is often used to represent the "typical value" of a group of numbers. It is regarded as a measure of "location" or "central tendency" of a group of numbers.

The *arithmetic* mean is the type of average used most frequently. It is derived by summing the individual item values of a particular group and dividing the total by the number of items. The arithmetic mean is often referred to simply as the "mean" or "average."

The *median* of a group of numbers is the middle number or value when each item in the group is arranged according to size (lowest to highest or visa versa); it generally has the same number of items above it as well as below it. If there is an even number if items in the group, the median is taken to be the average of the two middle numbers.

Rates. A rate is a quantity or amount of an item measured in relation to a specified number of units of another item. For example, unemployment rate is the number of unemployed persons per 100 persons in the civilian labor force. Examples of other rates found in this publication include birth rate, which is the number of births per 1,000 population; infant death rate, the number of infant deaths per 1,000 live births; and crime rate, which is the number of serious offenses per 100,000 population.

A *per capita* figure represents a specific type of rate computed for every person in a specified group (or population). It is derived by taking the total for a data item (such as income, taxes, or retail sales) and dividing it by the number of persons in the specified population.

Ranks. Various data items in Table A, States and Table B, Metro Areas of this publication are ranked from highest to lowest with a rank of 1 representing the highest rank. In both tables, when areas share the same rank, the next lower rank is omitted.

In Table A, only the 50 states are ranked; the District of Columbia is not included in the state rankings. In Table B, only 245 metropolitan statistical areas (MSAs), 17 consolidated MSAs (CMSAs), and 11 of the 12 New England county metropolitan areas (NECMAs) are ranked. Not ranked are the 58 primary MSAs (PMSAs), which make up the 17 CMSAs, and the one NECMA used as a PMSA substitute for the Connecticut portion of the New York-Northern New Jersey-Long Island, NY-NJ-CT-PA CMSA. Areas not ranked are indicated by an "X" in the data cell.

Index numbers. An index number is a measure of difference or change, usually expressed as a percent, relating one quantity (the variable) of a specified kind to another quantity of the same kind. Index numbers are widely used to express changes in prices over periods of time but may also be used to express differences between related subjects for a single point in time.

To compute a price index, a base year or period is selected. The base year price (of the commodity or service) is then designated as the base or reference price to which the prices for other years or periods are related. Many price indexes use the year 1987 as the base year; in tables, this is shown as "1987=100". A method of expressing the price relationship is: The price of a set of one or more items for a related year (e.g., 1990) divided by the price of the same set of items for the base year (e.g., 1987). The result multiplied by 100 provides the index number. When 100 is subtracted from the index number, the result equals the percent change in price from the base year.

Current and constant dollars. Statistics in some tables are expressed in both current and constant dollars (see, for example, Table A-23). Current dollar figures reflect actual prices or costs prevailing during the specified year(s). Constant dollar figures are estimates representing an effort to remove the effects of price changes from statistical series reported in dollar terms. In general, constant dollar series are derived by dividing current dollar estimates by the appropriate price index for the appropriate period (for example, the Consumer Price Index). The result is a series as it would presumably exist if prices were the same throughout, as in the base year; in other words, as if the dollar had constant purchasing power. Any changes in this constant dollar series would reflect only changes in real volume of output, income, expenditures, or other measure.

Telephone Contacts List

To help users find more data and information about statistical publications, we are issuing this list of contacts for Federal agencies with major statistical programs. The intent is to give a single, first-contact point-of-entry for users of statistics. These agencies will provide general information on their statistical programs and publications, as well as specific information on how to order their publications. We are also including the Internet (World Wide Web) addresses for these agencies.

Executive Office of the President

Office of Management and Budget

Administrator
Office of Information and Regulatory Affairs
Office of Management and Budget
Washington, DC 20503
Information: 202-395-3080
Publications: 202-395-7332
Internet address:
  http://www.whitehouse.gov/WH/EOP/omb

Department of Agriculture

Economic Research Service

Reading Information Center
U.S. Department of Agriculture
Room 3098
1800 M St., N.W.
Washington, DC 20036-5831
Information and Publications: 202-694-5050
Internet address: http://www.econ.ag.gov/

National Agricultural Statistics Service

National Agricultural Statistics Service
U.S. Department of Agriculture
1400 Independence Ave., S.W.
Washington, DC 20250
Information hotline: 1-800-727-9540
Internet address: http://www.usda.gov/nass/

Department of Commerce

Bureau of the Census

Customer Services Branch
Bureau of the Census
U.S. Department of Commerce
Washington, DC 20233
Information and Publications: 301-457-4100
Internet address: http://www.census.gov/

Bureau of Economic Analysis

Current Business Analysis Division, BE-53
Bureau of Economic Analysis
U.S. Department of Commerce
Washington, DC 20230
Information and Publications: 202-606-9900
Internet address: http://www.bea.doc.gov/

Department of Commerce—Con.

International Trade Administration

Trade Statistics Division
Office of Trade and Investment Analysis
International Trade Administration
Room 2814 B
U.S. Department of Commerce
Washington, DC 20230
Information and Publications: 202-482-2185
Internet address: http://ita.doc.gov/tradestats/

National Oceanic and Atmospheric Administration

National Oceanic and Atmospheric Administration
 Library
U.S. Department of Commerce
1315 East-West Highway
2nd Floor
Silver Spring MD 20910
Library: 301-713-2600
Internet address: http://www.noaa.gov/

Department of Defense

Department of Defense

Office of the Assistant to the Secretary of Defense
 (Public Affairs)
Room 1E794
Attention: Directorate for Communications
1400 Defense Pentagon
Washington, DC 20301-1400
Information: 703-697-5737
Internet address:
  http://web1.whs.osd.mil/mmid/mmidhome.htm

Department of Education

Office of Information Services

Statistical Information Office
U.S. Department of Education
555 New Jersey Ave., N.W.
Washington, DC 20208-5641
Information and Publications: 1-800-424-1616
Internet address: http://www.ed.gov/NCES/

Department of Energy

Energy Information Administration
National Energy Information Center
U.S. Department of Energy
1000 Independence Ave., SW
1F048, E1-30
Washington, DC 20585
Information and Publications: 202-586-8800
Internet address: http://www.eia.doe.gov/

Department of Health and Human Services

Health Resources and Services Administration
HRSA Office of Communications
5600 Fishers Lane
Room 14-15
Rockville, MD 20857
Publications: 301-443-3376
Internet address: http://www.hrsa.dhhs.gov/

*Substance Abuse Mental Health Services
Administration*
U.S. Department of Health and Human Services
5600 Fishers Lane
Room 12C105
Rockville, MD 20857
Information: 301-443-4795
Publications: 1-800-729-6686
Internet address: http://www.samhsa.gov/

Centers for Disease Control and Prevention
Office of Information
Centers for Disease Control
21600 Clifton Road, N.E.
Atlanta, GA 30333
Public Inquiries: 404-639-3534
Internet address: http://www.cdc.gov/cdc.html

Health Care Financing Administration
Office of Public Affairs
Health Care Financing Administration
U.S. Department of Health and Human Services
Room 403B, Humphrey Building
200 Independence Ave., S.W.
Washington, DC 20201
Media Relations: 202-690-6145
Internet address: http://www.hcfa.gov/

National Center for Health Statistics
Scientific and Technical Information Branch
National Center for Health Statistics
U.S. Department of Health and Human Services
6525 Belcrest Rd. Rm. 1064
Hyattsville, MD 20782
Information and Publications: 301-436-8500
*Internet address:
http://www.cdc.gov/nchswww/nchshome.htm*

Department of Health and Human Services—Con.
Social Security Administration
Office of Research Evaluation and Statistics
Social Security Administration
Division of Publications
Intl. Trade Commission Bldg.
500 E St., S.W.
Washington, DC 20254
Information and Publications: 202-282-7138
*Internet address:
http://www.ssa.gov/statistics/ores_home.html*

Department of Housing and Urban Development
*Assistant Secretary for Community Planning and
Development*
Office of the Assistant Secretary for Community
Planning and Development
U.S. Department of Housing and Urban
Development
451 7th St., S.W.
Washington, DC 20410-0555
Information: 202-708-2690
Publications: 1-800-245-2691
Internet address: http://www.huduser.org/

Department of the Interior
Geological Survey
Earth Science Information Center
Geological Survey
U.S. Department of the Interior
507 National Center
Reston, VA 20192
Information and Publications: 703-648-6045
*Internet address for minerals:
http://minerals.er.usgs.gov:80/minerals/*
*Internet address for other USGS materials:
http://www.usgs.gov/*

Department of Justice
Bureau of Justice Statistics
Statistics Division
U.S. Department of Justice
1110 Vermont Ave., NW, 10th Fl.
Washington, DC 20005
Information and Publications: 202-307-0765
Internet address: http://www.ojp.usdoj.gov/bjs/
National Criminal Justice Reference Service
Box 6000
Rockville, MD 20850
Information and Publications: 301-251-5500
Publications: 1-800-732-3277
Internet address: http://ncjrs.org/
Federal Bureau of Investigation
National Crime Information Center
Federal Bureau of Investigation
U.S. Department of Justice
935 Pennsylvania Ave., N.W.
Washington, DC 20535
Information and Publications: 202-324-3691
Publications: 202-324-5611
Internet address: http://www.fbi.gov/

Department of Justice—Con.

Immigration and Naturalization Service
Statistics Branch
Immigration and Naturalization Service
U.S. Department of Justice
425 I St., NW, Rm. 5309
Washington, DC 20536
Attention: Tariff Bldg. Rm. 235
Information and Publications: 202-305-1613
Internet address: http://www.usdoj.gov/ins/index.html

Department of Labor

Bureau of Labor Statistics
Office of Publications and Information Services
Bureau of Labor Statistics
U.S. Department of Labor
2 Mass. Ave., N.E., Room 2860
Washington, DC 20212
Information and Publications: 202-606-5886
Internet address: http://stats.bls.gov/

Employment and Training Administration
Office of Public Information
Employment and Training Administration
U.S. Department of Labor
200 Constitution Ave., N.W., Room S4206
Washington, DC 20210
Information and Publications: 202-219-6871
Internet address: http://www.doleta.gov/

Department of Transportation

Federal Aviation Administration
Public Inquiry Center
APA 200
Federal Aviation Administration
U.S. Department of Transportation
800 Independence Ave., S.W.
Washington, DC 20591
Information and Publications: 202-267-3484
Internet address: http://www.faa.gov/
Bureau of Transportation Statistics
Internet address: http://www.bts.gov/

Federal Highway Administration
Office of Public Affairs
Federal Highway Administration
U.S. Department of Transportation
400 7th St., S.W.
Washington, DC 20590
Information: 202-366-0660
Internet address: http://fhwa.dot.gov/

National Highway Traffic Safety Administration
Office of Public Affairs
National Highway Traffic Safety Administration
U.S. Department of Transportation
400 7th St., S.W.
Washington, DC 20590
Information: 202-366-9550
Publications: 202-366-2587
Internet address: http://www.nhtsa.dot.gov/

Department of the Treasury

Internal Revenue Service
Statistics of Income Division
Internal Revenue Service
Attn: Beth Kilss
P.O. Box 2608
Washington, DC 20013-2608
Information and Publications: 202-874-0410
Internet address:
http://www.irs.ustreas.gov/cover.html

Department of Veterans Affairs

Department of Veterans Affairs
Office of Public Affairs
Department of Veterans Affairs
810 Vermont Ave., N.W.
Washington, DC 20420
Information: 202-273-5400
Internet address: http://www.va.gov/

Independent Agencies

Environmental Protection Agency
Information Resource Center, Rm. MC3404
Environmental Protection Agency
401 M St., S.W.
Washington, DC 20460
Information: 202-260-5922
Internet address: http://www.epa.gov/

Federal Reserve Board
Division of Research and Statistics
Federal Reserve Board
Washington, DC 20551
Information: 202-452-3301
Publications: 202-452-3245
Internet address: http://www.bog.frb.fed.us/

National Science Foundation
Office of Legislative and Public Affairs
National Science Foundation
4201 Wilson Boulevard
Arlington Virginia 22230
Information: 703-306-1234
Publications: 703-306-1134
Internet address:
http://www.nsf.gov:80/sbe/srs/stats.htm

Securities and Exchange Commission
Office of Public Affairs
Securities and Exchange Commission
450 5th St., N.W.
Washington, DC 20549
Information: 202-942-0020
Publications: 202-942-4040
Internet address: http://www.sec.gov/

Metropolitan Areas of the United States: 1996

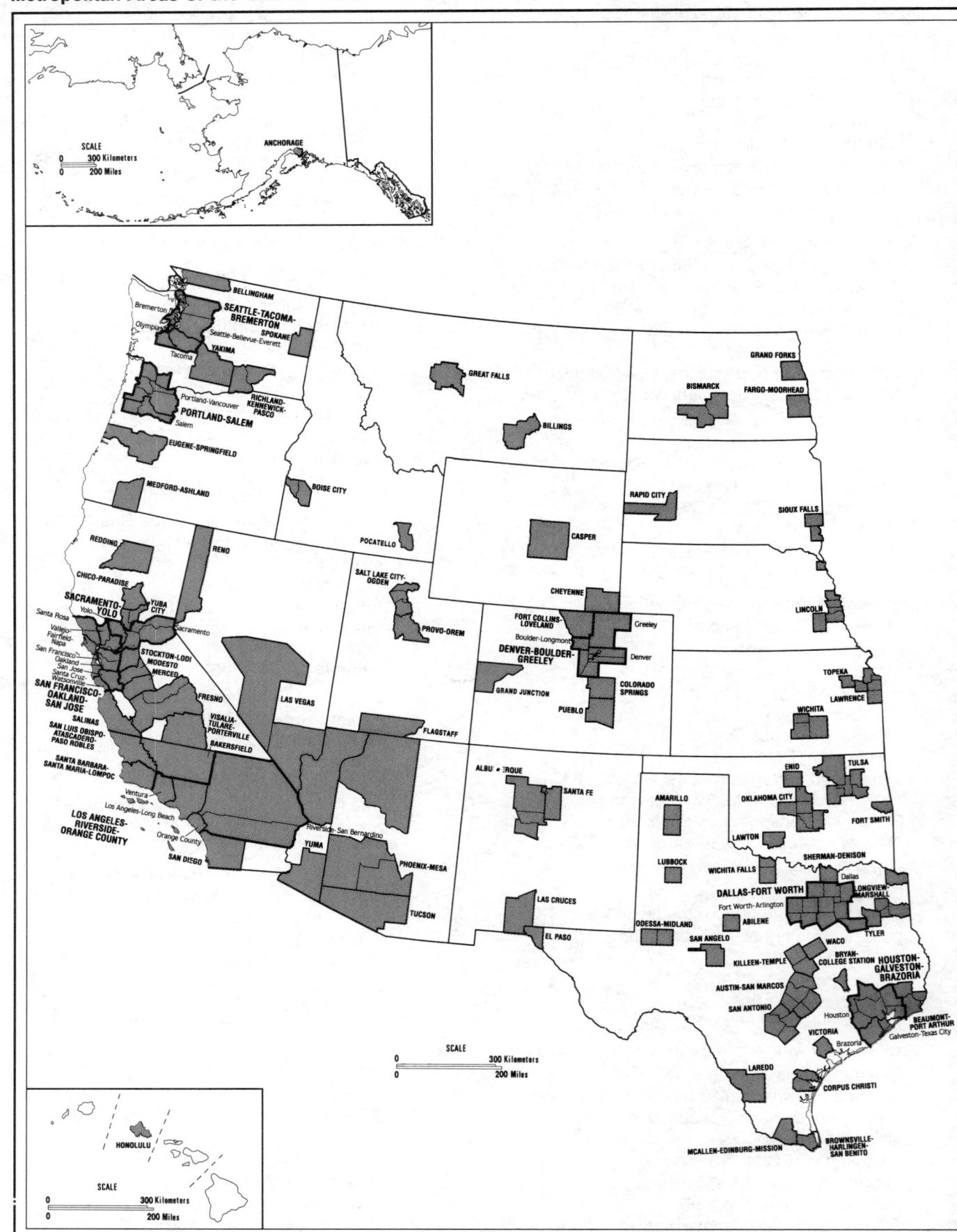

ANCHORAGE

SCALE
0   300 Kilometers
0   200 Miles

BELLINGHAM
Bremerton
SEATTLE-TACOMA-BREMERTON
Olympia
SPOKANE
Seattle-Bellevue-Everett
YAKIMA
Tacoma
RICHLAND-KENNEWICK-PASCO
Portland-Vancouver
PORTLAND-SALEM
Salem
EUGENE-SPRINGFIELD
MEDFORD-ASHLAND
GREAT FALLS
BILLINGS
BOISE CITY
POCATELLO

GRAND FORKS
BISMARCK
FARGO-MOORHEAD

REDDING
RENO
CHICO-PARADISE
SALT LAKE CITY-OGDEN
RAPID CITY
SIOUX FALLS
CASPER
SACRAMENTO-YOLO
Yolo
YUBA CITY
Santa Rosa
Sacramento
Vallejo
Fairfield-Napa
San Francisco
Oakland
San Jose
Santa Cruz-Watsonville
SAN FRANCISCO-OAKLAND-SAN JOSE
STOCKTON-LODI
MODESTO
MERCED
PROVO-OREM
SALINAS
FRESNO
SAN LUIS OBISPO-ATASCADERO-PASO ROBLES
LAS VEGAS
VISALIA-TULARE-PORTERVILLE
BAKERSFIELD
GRAND JUNCTION
SANTA BARBARA-SANTA MARIA-LOMPOC
FLAGSTAFF
Ventura
Los Angeles-Long Beach
LOS ANGELES-RIVERSIDE-ORANGE COUNTY
Orange County
Riverside-San Bernardino
SAN DIEGO
YUMA
PHOENIX-MESA
TUCSON

CHEYENNE
FORT COLLINS-LOVELAND
Greeley
Boulder-Longmont
DENVER-BOULDER-GREELEY
Denver
COLORADO SPRINGS
PUEBLO

LINCOLN
TOPEKA
LAWRENCE
WICHITA

ALBUQUERQUE
SANTA FE
LAS CRUCES
EL PASO

AMARILLO
LUBBOCK
WICHITA FALLS
LAWTON
ODESSA-MIDLAND
SAN ANGELO
ABILENE

ENID
TULSA
OKLAHOMA CITY
FORT SMITH
SHERMAN-DENISON
Dallas
DALLAS-FORT WORTH
Fort Worth-Arlington
LONGVIEW-MARSHALL
WACO
TYLER
BRYAN-COLLEGE STATION
KILLEEN-TEMPLE
HOUSTON-GALVESTON-BRAZORIA
AUSTIN-SAN MARCOS
Houston
BEAUMONT-PORT ARTHUR
Galveston-Texas City
SAN ANTONIO
VICTORIA
Brazoria
LAREDO
CORPUS CHRISTI
MCALLEN-EDINBURG-MISSION
BROWNSVILLE-HARLINGEN-SAN BENITO

SCALE
0   300 Kilometers
0   200 Miles

HONOLULU

SCALE
0   300 Kilometers
0   200 Miles

U.S. DEPARTMENT OF COMMERCE   Economics and Statistics Administration   Bureau of the Census

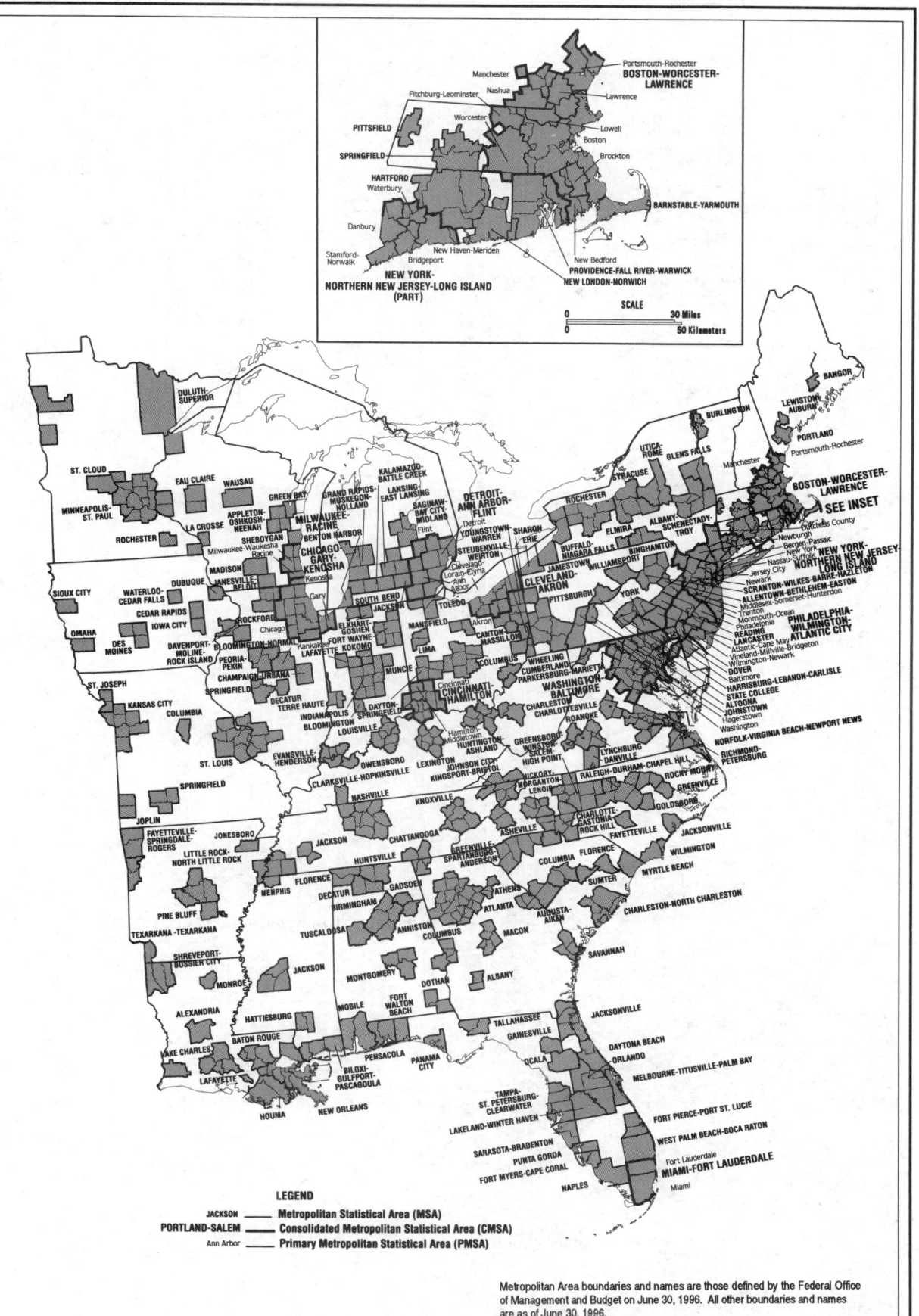

NEW YORK-NORTHERN NEW JERSEY-LONG ISLAND (PART)

BOSTON-WORCESTER-LAWRENCE

Portsmouth-Rochester
Manchester
Nashua
Fitchburg-Leominster
Worcester
Lawrence
Lowell
Boston
Brockton
PITTSFIELD
SPRINGFIELD
HARTFORD
Waterbury
BARNSTABLE-YARMOUTH
Danbury
Stamford-Norwalk
Bridgeport
New Haven-Meriden
New Bedford
PROVIDENCE-FALL RIVER-WARWICK
NEW LONDON-NORWICH

SCALE
0   30 Miles
0   50 Kilometers

BANGOR
LEWISTON-AUBURN
BURLINGTON
PORTLAND
Portsmouth-Rochester
UTICA-ROME
GLENS FALLS
Manchester
BOSTON-WORCESTER-LAWRENCE
SEE INSET
DULUTH-SUPERIOR
ST. CLOUD
EAU CLAIRE
WAUSAU
GREEN BAY
KALAMAZOO-BATTLE CREEK
LANSING-EAST LANSING
SYRACUSE
ROCHESTER
SCHENECTADY-TROY
ALBANY-
MINNEAPOLIS-ST. PAUL
APPLETON-OSHKOSH-NEENAH
GRAND RAPIDS-MUSKEGON-HOLLAND
SAGINAW-BAY CITY-MIDLAND
DETROIT-ANN ARBOR-FLINT
Detroit
ELMIRA
BINGHAMTON
Dutchess County
Newburgh
ROCHESTER
SHEBOYGAN
Flint
Detroit
YOUNGSTOWN-WARREN
SHARON
ERIE
BUFFALO-NIAGARA FALLS
WILLIAMSPORT
Bergen-Passaic
New York
NEW YORK-NORTHERN NEW JERSEY-LONG ISLAND
LA CROSSE
MILWAUKEE-RACINE
BENTON HARBOR
Milwaukee-Waukesha
Racine
Steubenville-Weirton
Cleveland
Lorain-Elyria
JAMESTOWN
Nassau-Suffolk
Jersey City
Newark
ROCHESTER
SIOUX CITY
CHICAGO-GARY-KENOSHA
Kenosha
Ann Arbor
Toledo
CLEVELAND-AKRON
PITTSBURGH
YORK
SCRANTON-WILKES-BARRE-HAZLETON
ALLENTOWN-BETHLEHEM-EASTON
Trenton
Monmouth-Ocean
WATERLOO-CEDAR FALLS
DUBUQUE
JANESVILLE-BELOIT
SOUTH BEND
JACKSON
Akron
Philadelphia
PHILADELPHIA-WILMINGTON-ATLANTIC CITY
CEDAR RAPIDS
IOWA CITY
ROCKFORD
Chicago
Gary
MANSFIELD
CANTON-MASSILLON
READING
LANCASTER
OMAHA
ELKHART-GOSHEN
FORT WAYNE
Atlantic-Cape May
DAVENPORT-MOLINE-ROCK ISLAND
BLOOMINGTON-NORMAL
Kankakee
LAFAYETTE
KOKOMO
COLUMBUS
WHEELING
Vineland-Millville-Bridgeton
Wilmington-Newark
DES MOINES
PEORIA-PEKIN
MUNCIE
LIMA
CUMBERLAND
PARKERSBURG-MARIETTA
Baltimore
HARRISBURG-LEBANON-CARLISLE
DOVER
ST. JOSEPH
CHAMPAIGN-URBANA
Cincinnati
CINCINNATI-HAMILTON
WASHINGTON-BALTIMORE
STATE COLLEGE
ALTOONA
SPRINGFIELD
DECATUR
TERRE HAUTE
DAYTON-SPRINGFIELD
JOHNSTOWN
KANSAS CITY
COLUMBIA
INDIANAPOLIS
BLOOMINGTON
Hamilton-Middletown
CHARLESTON
CHARLOTTESVILLE
ROANOKE
Hagerstown
Washington
NORFOLK-VIRGINIA BEACH-NEWPORT NEWS
ST. LOUIS
LOUISVILLE
HUNTINGTON-ASHLAND
GREENSBORO-WINSTON-SALEM-HIGH POINT
LYNCHBURG
DANVILLE
RICHMOND-PETERSBURG
SPRINGFIELD
EVANSVILLE-HENDERSON
OWENSBORO
LEXINGTON
CLARKSVILLE-HOPKINSVILLE
KINGSPORT-BRISTOL
JOHNSON CITY
ROCKY MOUNT
GREENVILLE
JOPLIN
NASHVILLE
HICKORY
MORGANTON-LENOIR
RALEIGH-DURHAM-CHAPEL HILL
GOLDSBORO
FAYETTEVILLE-SPRINGDALE-ROGERS
JONESBORO
JACKSON
CHATTANOOGA
KNOXVILLE
ASHEVILLE
CHARLOTTE-GASTONIA-ROCK HILL
FAYETTEVILLE
JACKSONVILLE
LITTLE ROCK-NORTH LITTLE ROCK
HUNTSVILLE
GREENVILLE-SPARTANBURG-ANDERSON
COLUMBIA
FLORENCE
WILMINGTON
FLORENCE
SUMTER
MYRTLE BEACH
MEMPHIS
DECATUR
GADSDEN
ATHENS
PINE BLUFF
BIRMINGHAM
AUGUSTA-AIKEN
CHARLESTON-NORTH CHARLESTON
TEXARKANA-TEXARKANA
ATLANTA
TUSCALOOSA
ANNISTON
COLUMBUS
MACON
SHREVEPORT-BOSSIER CITY
JACKSON
SAVANNAH
MONROE
MONTGOMERY
ALBANY
ALEXANDRIA
HATTIESBURG
DOTHAN
FORT WALTON BEACH
TALLAHASSEE
JACKSONVILLE
LAKE CHARLES
BATON ROUGE
MOBILE
PENSACOLA
PANAMA CITY
GAINESVILLE
DAYTONA BEACH
LAFAYETTE
BILOXI-GULFPORT-PASCAGOULA
OCALA
ORLANDO
MELBOURNE-TITUSVILLE-PALM BAY
HOUMA
NEW ORLEANS
TAMPA-ST. PETERSBURG-CLEARWATER
FORT PIERCE-PORT ST. LUCIE
LAKELAND-WINTER HAVEN
WEST PALM BEACH-BOCA RATON
SARASOTA-BRADENTON
PUNTA GORDA
FORT MYERS-CAPE CORAL
Fort Lauderdale
MIAMI-FORT LAUDERDALE
NAPLES
Miami

LEGEND

JACKSON ——— Metropolitan Statistical Area (MSA)

PORTLAND-SALEM ——— Consolidated Metropolitan Statistical Area (CMSA)

Ann Arbor ——— Primary Metropolitan Statistical Area (PMSA)

Metropolitan Area boundaries and names are those defined by the Federal Office of Management and Budget on June 30, 1996. All other boundaries and names are as of June 30, 1996.

NEW ENGLAND COUNTY METROPOLITAN AREAS: 1996

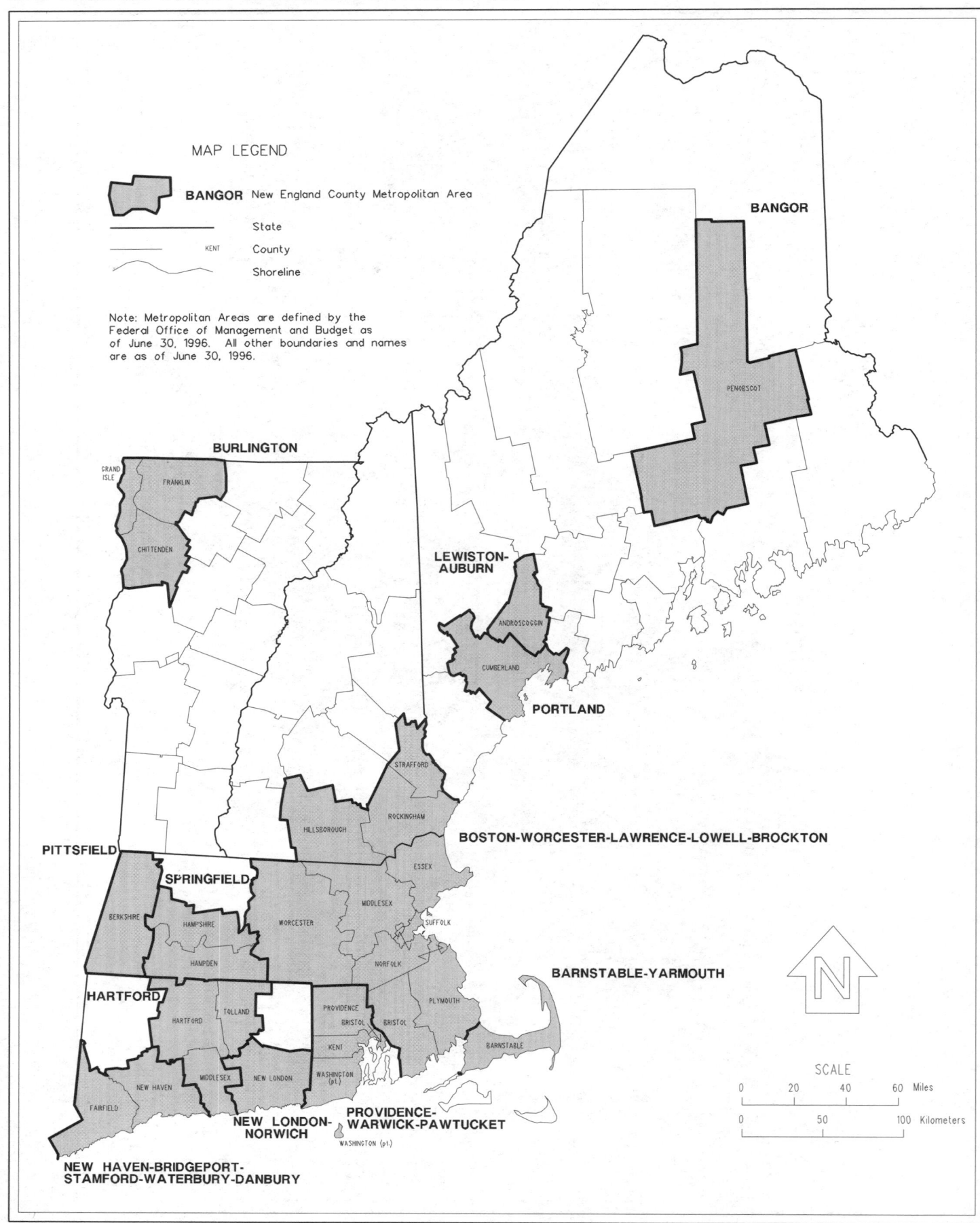

MAP LEGEND

BANGOR New England County Metropolitan Area

State

KENT County

Shoreline

Note: Metropolitan Areas are defined by the
Federal Office of Management and Budget as
of June 30, 1996. All other boundaries and names
are as of June 30, 1996.

BANGOR

PENOBSCOT

BURLINGTON

GRAND ISLE

FRANKLIN

CHITTENDEN

LEWISTON-AUBURN

ANDROSCOGGIN

CUMBERLAND

PORTLAND

STRAFFORD

ROCKINGHAM

HILLSBOROUGH

BOSTON-WORCESTER-LAWRENCE-LOWELL-BROCKTON

ESSEX

PITTSFIELD

SPRINGFIELD

BERKSHIRE

HAMPSHIRE

WORCESTER

MIDDLESEX

SUFFOLK

HAMPDEN

NORFOLK

BARNSTABLE-YARMOUTH

HARTFORD

TOLLAND

PLYMOUTH

HARTFORD

PROVIDENCE

BRISTOL

BRISTOL

KENT

BARNSTABLE

NEW HAVEN

MIDDLESEX

NEW LONDON

WASHINGTON (pt.)

FAIRFIELD

NEW LONDON-NORWICH

PROVIDENCE-WARWICK-PAWTUCKET

WASHINGTON (pt.)

NEW HAVEN-BRIDGEPORT-STAMFORD-WATERBURY-DANBURY

N

SCALE

0   20   40   60 Miles

0   50   100 Kilometers

U.S. DEPARTMENT OF COMMERCE Economics and Statistics Administration Bureau of the Census

States

Note:

Table A presents data for the United States, states, and the District of Columbia.

Data are presented for 869 items with the states listed in alphabetic order.

For a more detailed listing of subjects covered in this table, see subject index.

Table A–1. States — Area and Population

Geographic area	Area, 1990 (sq mi) Total	Land[1]	Water[2]	Population 1997 (1,000)	1995 (1,000)	1990[3] (1,000)	1980[4] (1,000)	Rank 1997	Rank 1990	Per square mile of land area 1997	Per square mile of land area 1990	Net change (1,000)	Net migration[5] (1,000) International	Net migration[5] (1,000) Domestic	Percent change	Percent change 1980-1990
United States	3 717 796	3 536 278	181 518	267 636	262 761	248 765	226 546	X	X	75.7	70.3	18 870.9	5 626.8	–	7.6	9.8
Alabama	52 237	50 750	1 486	4 319	4 262	4 040	3 894	23	22	85.1	79.6	278.8	10.1	100.9	6.9	3.8
Alaska	615 230	570 374	44 856	609	602	550	402	48	49	1.1	1.0	59.3	6.2	−17.1	10.8	36.8
Arizona	114 006	113 642	364	4 555	4 308	3 665	2 718	21	24	40.1	32.3	889.6	86.6	452.1	24.3	34.9
Arkansas	53 182	52 075	1 107	2 523	2 481	2 351	2 286	33	33	48.4	45.1	172.2	7.4	97.9	7.3	2.8
California	158 869	155 973	2 895	32 268	31 558	29 786	23 668	1	1	206.9	191.0	2 482.4	1 788.6	−1 962.1	8.3	25.8
Colorado	104 100	103 729	371	3 893	3 742	3 294	2 890	25	26	37.5	31.8	598.2	46.8	320.0	18.2	14.0
Connecticut	5 544	4 845	698	3 270	3 267	3 287	3 108	28	27	674.9	678.5	−17.3	51.4	−192.4	−.5	5.8
Delaware	2 396	1 955	442	732	716	666	594	46	46	374.2	340.8	65.4	6.7	26.5	9.8	12.1
District of Columbia	68	61	7	529	552	607	638	X	X	8 615.0	9 884.4	−77.9	24.1	−127.7	−12.8	−4.9
Florida	59 928	53 937	5 991	14 654	14 181	12 938	9 746	4	4	271.7	239.9	1 715.9	415.5	925.1	13.3	32.8
Georgia	58 977	57 919	1 058	7 486	7 192	6 478	5 463	10	11	129.3	111.8	1 008.1	73.9	514.0	15.6	18.6
Hawaii	6 459	6 423	36	1 187	1 179	1 108	965	41	41	184.7	172.5	78.4	39.1	−65.3	7.1	14.8
Idaho	83 574	82 751	823	1 210	1 165	1 007	944	40	42	14.6	12.2	203.5	13.7	120.2	20.2	6.6
Illinois	57 918	55 593	2 325	11 896	11 795	11 431	11 427	6	6	214.0	205.6	465.2	272.3	−435.6	4.1	–
Indiana	36 420	35 870	550	5 864	5 788	5 544	5 490	14	14	163.5	154.6	320.0	19.4	74.2	5.8	1.0
Iowa	56 276	55 875	401	2 852	2 841	2 777	2 914	30	30	51.1	49.7	75.6	15.3	−10.3	2.7	−4.7
Kansas	82 282	81 823	459	2 595	2 570	2 478	2 364	32	32	31.7	30.3	117.3	20.7	−23.6	4.7	4.8
Kentucky	40 411	39 732	679	3 908	3 856	3 687	3 661	24	23	98.4	92.8	221.2	10.6	78.6	6.0	.7
Louisiana	49 651	43 566	6 085	4 352	4 329	4 222	4 206	22	21	99.9	96.9	129.9	20.2	−105.8	3.1	.4
Maine	33 741	30 865	2 876	1 242	1 234	1 228	1 125	39	38	40.2	39.8	14.1	2.2	−14.6	1.2	9.1
Maryland	12 297	9 775	2 522	5 094	5 027	4 781	4 217	19	19	521.2	489.1	313.5	93.1	−39.3	6.6	13.4
Massachusetts	9 241	7 838	1 403	6 118	6 061	6 016	5 737	13	13	780.5	767.6	101.1	112.2	−220.8	1.7	4.9
Michigan	96 705	56 809	39 895	9 774	9 655	9 295	9 262	8	8	172.0	163.6	478.6	68.7	−161.5	5.1	.4
Minnesota	86 943	79 617	7 326	4 686	4 607	4 376	4 076	20	20	58.9	55.0	309.9	38.1	66.1	7.1	7.4
Mississippi	48 286	46 914	1 372	2 731	2 691	2 575	2 521	31	31	58.2	54.9	155.0	4.7	34.8	6.0	2.2
Missouri	69 709	68 898	811	5 402	5 325	5 117	4 917	16	15	78.4	74.3	285.2	26.8	85.6	5.6	4.1
Montana	147 046	145 556	1 490	879	869	799	787	44	44	6.0	5.5	79.7	1.9	49.4	10.0	1.5
Nebraska	77 358	76 878	481	1 657	1 636	1 578	1 570	38	36	21.6	20.5	78.5	11.3	5.3	5.0	.5
Nevada	110 567	109 806	761	1 677	1 530	1 202	800	37	39	15.3	10.9	475.1	33.8	349.1	39.5	50.2
New Hampshire	9 283	8 969	314	1 173	1 146	1 109	921	42	40	130.8	123.7	63.5	4.4	12.5	5.7	20.4
New Jersey	8 215	7 419	796	8 053	7 956	7 748	7 365	9	9	1 085.4	1 044.3	305.1	288.5	−305.0	3.9	5.2
New Mexico	121 598	121 364	234	1 730	1 686	1 515	1 303	36	37	14.3	12.5	214.7	35.0	62.2	14.2	16.3
New York	53 989	47 224	6 766	18 137	18 146	17 991	17 558	3	2	384.1	381.0	146.4	840.7	−1 513.5	.8	2.5
North Carolina	52 672	48 718	3 954	7 425	7 187	6 632	5 882	11	10	152.4	136.1	792.7	42.1	430.1	12.0	12.8
North Dakota	70 704	68 994	1 710	641	641	639	653	47	47	9.3	9.3	2.1	3.5	−24.6	.3	−2.2
Ohio	44 828	40 953	3 875	11 186	11 133	10 847	10 798	7	7	273.2	264.9	339.2	39.4	−106.7	3.1	.5
Oklahoma	69 903	68 679	1 224	3 317	3 271	3 146	3 025	27	28	48.3	45.8	171.5	21.1	38.4	5.5	4.0
Oregon	97 132	96 002	1 129	3 243	3 143	2 842	2 633	29	29	33.8	29.6	401.2	48.7	244.3	14.1	8.0
Pennsylvania	46 058	44 820	1 239	12 020	12 046	11 883	11 864	5	5	268.2	265.1	136.8	83.7	−169.9	1.2	.2
Rhode Island	1 231	1 045	186	987	990	1 003	947	43	43	944.9	960.3	−16.0	12.0	−65.6	−1.6	6.0
South Carolina	31 189	30 111	1 078	3 760	3 683	3 486	3 122	26	25	124.9	115.8	273.9	11.5	90.7	7.9	11.7
South Dakota	77 121	75 896	1 225	738	735	696	691	45	45	9.7	9.2	42.0	3.3	9.4	6.0	.7
Tennessee	42 146	41 219	926	5 368	5 235	4 877	4 591	17	17	130.2	118.3	491.0	20.9	300.8	10.1	6.2
Texas	267 277	261 914	5 363	19 439	18 738	16 986	14 229	2	3	74.2	64.9	2 453.0	598.3	461.4	14.4	19.4
Utah	84 904	82 168	2 736	2 059	1 974	1 723	1 461	34	35	25.1	21.0	336.3	21.3	87.2	19.5	17.9
Vermont	9 615	9 249	366	589	583	563	511	49	48	63.7	60.8	26.2	3.0	5.3	4.7	10.1
Virginia	42 326	39 598	2 729	6 734	6 601	6 189	5 347	12	12	170.1	156.3	544.8	106.1	70.0	8.8	15.8
Washington	70 637	66 581	4 055	5 610	5 436	4 867	4 132	15	18	84.3	73.1	743.7	98.4	352.4	15.3	17.8
West Virginia	24 231	24 087	145	1 816	1 822	1 793	1 950	35	34	75.4	74.5	22.3	3.0	11.0	1.2	−8.0
Wisconsin	65 499	54 314	11 186	5 170	5 113	4 892	4 706	18	16	95.2	90.1	277.9	18.7	84.8	5.7	3.9
Wyoming	97 818	97 105	714	480	479	454	470	50	50	4.9	4.7	26.2	1.6	1.3	5.8	−3.5

X Not applicable.
– Represents or rounds to zero.

[1]Dry land and land temporarily or partially covered by water.
[2]Comprises Great Lakes, inland, and coastal water. Data for prior years cover inland water only.
[3]April 1, 1990, census counts include count resolution corrections processed through December 1996 and do not include adjustments for census coverage errors.
[4]Total population count has been revised since the 1980 census publications. Numbers by age, race, Hispanic origin, and sex have been corrected.
[5]Excludes net movement of federal employees (both military and civilian) and their dependents.

Source: Area–U.S. Bureau of the Census, 1990 Census of Population and Housing, series CPH-2; and unpublished data from the TIGER/Geographic Information Control System (TIGER/GICS) computer file. Population–U.S. Bureau of the Census, 1990 Census of Population and Housing, Population and Housing Unit Counts (CPH-2); Current Population Reports, P25-1127; and ST-97-1 Estimates of the Population of States: Annual Time Series, July 1, 1990, to July 1, 1997, Internet site <http://www.census.gov/population/estimates/state/ST9097T1.txt> (accessed 31 December 1997); Population change–ST-97-3 Estimates of the Population of States: Annual Time Series, July 1, 1990, to July 1, 1997, and Demographic Components of Population Change, Annual Time Series July 1, 1990, to July 1, 1997, Internet site <http://www.census.gov/population/estimates/state/STCOM97R2.txt> (accessed 4 February 1998).

Table A–2. States — Population by Residence and Projections

Geographic area	Metropolitan area[1] population 1994[2] (1,000)	1990[3] (1,000)	Percent of total, 1994	Percent change, 1990-1994	Nonmetropolitan area population 1994[2] (1,000)	1990[3] (1,000)	Percent change, 1990-1994	Population projections (1,000) Series A[4] 2000	2005	2010	Series B[5] 2000	2005	2010
United States	207 654	198 023	79.8	4.9	52 687	50 696	3.9	274 634	285 981	297 716	274 634	285 981	297 716
Alabama	2 847	2 710	67.5	5.1	1 371	1 331	3.1	4 451	4 631	4 798	4 436	4 617	4 802
Alaska	254	226	41.8	12.1	353	324	8.9	653	700	745	632	659	690
Arizona	3 557	3 202	87.3	11.1	518	463	11.9	4 798	5 230	5 522	4 838	5 432	6 025
Arkansas	1 103	1 040	45.0	6.1	1 350	1 311	3.0	2 631	2 750	2 840	2 623	2 757	2 887
California	30 388	28 797	96.7	5.5	1 043	961	8.4	32 521	34 441	37 644	32 423	33 511	34 968
Colorado	3 086	2 779	84.4	11.0	570	515	10.6	4 168	4 468	4 658	4 154	4 510	4 837
Connecticut	3 133	3 148	95.7	-.5	142	140	2.0	3 284	3 317	3 400	3 286	3 291	3 303
Delaware	584	553	82.7	5.7	122	113	7.9	768	800	817	758	793	823
District of Columbia	570	607	100.0	-6.6	X	X	X	523	529	560	530	542	572
Florida	12 970	12 024	93.0	7.9	982	915	7.4	15 233	16 279	17 363	15 250	16 273	17 299
Georgia	4 804	4 351	68.1	10.4	2 251	2 127	5.8	7 875	8 413	8 824	7 893	8 540	9 167
Hawaii	874	836	74.2	4.6	304	272	11.9	1 257	1 342	1 440	1 238	1 297	1 367
Idaho	348	296	30.7	17.6	785	711	10.5	1 347	1 480	1 557	1 332	1 489	1 637
Illinois	9 879	9 574	84.1	3.2	1 873	1 857	.9	12 051	12 266	12 515	12 069	12 314	12 601
Indiana	4 124	3 962	71.7	4.1	1 628	1 582	2.9	6 045	6 215	6 318	6 060	6 301	6 532
Iowa	1 246	1 200	44.0	3.8	1 584	1 577	.4	2 900	2 941	2 968	2 891	2 939	2 992
Kansas	1 402	1 333	54.9	5.2	1 152	1 145	.7	2 668	2 761	2 849	2 675	2 788	2 908
Kentucky	1 848	1 780	48.3	3.8	1 979	1 907	3.8	3 995	4 098	4 170	3 990	4 109	4 220
Louisiana	3 240	3 160	75.1	2.6	1 075	1 061	1.3	4 425	4 535	4 683	4 445	4 558	4 687
Maine	445	443	35.9	.5	795	785	1.3	1 259	1 285	1 323	1 250	1 259	1 268
Maryland	4 641	4 438	92.7	4.6	365	343	6.6	5 275	5 467	5 657	5 261	5 426	5 577
Massachusetts	5 807	5 788	96.1	.3	234	229	2.4	6 199	6 310	6 431	6 224	6 361	6 498
Michigan	7 837	7 698	82.5	1.8	1 659	1 598	3.9	9 679	9 763	9 836	9 711	9 835	9 966
Minnesota	3 172	3 011	69.4	5.3	1 395	1 364	2.3	4 830	5 005	5 147	4 822	5 014	5 212
Mississippi	935	874	35.0	6.9	1 734	1 701	2.0	2 816	2 908	2 974	2 826	2 949	3 072
Missouri	3 591	3 491	68.1	2.9	1 686	1 626	3.7	5 540	5 718	5 864	5 547	5 750	5 953
Montana	204	191	23.8	6.7	652	608	7.3	950	1 006	1 040	937	998	1 056
Nebraska	823	787	50.7	4.5	800	791	1.1	1 705	1 761	1 806	1 700	1 766	1 837
Nevada	1 243	1 014	85.3	22.6	214	188	13.9	1 871	2 070	2 131	1 863	2 130	2 355
New Hampshire	677	659	59.6	2.8	460	450	2.0	1 224	1 281	1 329	1 217	1 267	1 307
New Jersey	7 904	7 730	100.0	2.2	X	X	X	8 178	8 392	8 638	8 185	8 387	8 594
New Mexico	932	842	56.4	10.7	722	673	7.2	1 860	2 016	2 155	1 858	2 035	2 223
New York	16 666	16 516	91.7	.9	1 503	1 475	1.9	18 146	18 250	18 530	18 174	18 227	18 363
North Carolina	4 708	4 380	66.6	7.5	2 362	2 253	4.9	7 777	8 227	8 552	7 789	8 312	8 780
North Dakota	269	257	42.1	4.5	369	381	-3.2	662	677	690	657	677	701
Ohio	9 016	8 826	81.2	2.2	2 086	2 021	3.2	11 319	11 428	11 505	11 352	11 534	11 726
Oklahoma	1 960	1 870	60.2	4.8	1 298	1 276	1.7	3 373	3 491	3 639	3 370	3 471	3 578
Oregon	2 162	1 985	70.1	8.9	924	858	7.8	3 397	3 613	3 803	3 397	3 625	3 837
Pennsylvania	10 206	10 084	84.7	1.2	1 846	1 799	2.6	12 202	12 281	12 352	12 220	12 329	12 443
Rhode Island	935	938	93.8	-.4	62	65	-5.1	998	1 012	1 038	989	986	986
South Carolina	2 555	2 422	69.7	5.5	1 109	1 064	4.2	3 858	4 033	4 205	3 852	4 015	4 169
South Dakota	238	221	33.0	8.0	483	475	1.6	777	810	826	770	811	853
Tennessee	3 509	3 298	67.8	6.4	1 666	1 579	5.5	5 657	5 966	6 180	5 668	6 039	6 385
Texas	15 455	14 166	84.1	9.1	2 923	2 821	3.6	20 119	21 487	22 857	20 178	21 635	23 158
Utah	1 475	1 341	77.3	10.0	433	382	13.3	2 207	2 411	2 551	2 216	2 477	2 738
Vermont	158	152	27.2	4.3	422	411	2.6	617	638	651	607	623	636
Virginia	5 091	4 775	77.7	6.6	1 461	1 414	3.3	6 997	7 324	7 627	6 965	7 234	7 474
Washington	4 428	4 036	82.9	9.7	915	830	10.2	5 858	6 258	6 658	5 829	6 184	6 524
West Virginia	762	748	41.8	1.9	1 060	1 045	1.4	1 841	1 849	1 851	1 833	1 842	1 852
Wisconsin	3 452	3 331	67.9	3.6	1 630	1 561	4.4	5 326	5 479	5 590	5 324	5 502	5 682
Wyoming	142	134	29.8	5.6	334	319	4.6	525	568	607	519	559	598

X Not applicable.

[1] Metropolitan refers to 253 metropolitan statistical areas and 18 consolidated metropolitan areas as defined by U.S. Office of Management and Budget, June 30, 1995.
[2] As of July 1.
[3] As of April 1.
[4] Series A is the preferred series model and uses state-to-state migration observed from 1975-76 through 1993-94.
[5] Series B is the economic model which uses the Bureau of Economic Analysis employment projections.

Source: Metropolitan areas–U.S. Bureau of the Census, 1990 Census of Population and Housing, Supplementary Reports, Metropolitan Areas as defined by the Office of Management and Budget, June 30, 1993, (CPH-S-1-1); Current Population Report, National and State Population Estimates: 1990 to 1994, P25-1127; and Population Paper Listing, Resident Population and Change for Metropolitan Areas in the United States: April 1, 1990 to July 1, 1994, PPL-27. Projections–U.S. Bureau of the Census, Population Paper Listing, Population Projections for States by Age, Sex, Race, and Hispanic Origin: 1995 to 2025; PPL-47, October 1996.

Population by Age Group and Sex

Geographic area	Population by age, 1996 (1,000)										Percent of population by age						Males per 100 females, 1996
	Under 5 years old	5 to 17 years old	18 to 24 years old	25 to 34 years old	35 to 44 years old	45 to 54 years old	55 to 64 years old	65 to 74 years old	75 to 84 years old	85 years old and over	Under 18 years old			65 years old and over			
											1996	1990	1980	1996	1990	1980	
United States	**19 286**	**49 762**	**24 882**	**40 368**	**43 393**	**32 370**	**21 361**	**18 669**	**11 430**	**3 762**	**26.0**	**25.7**	**28.1**	**12.8**	**12.5**	**11.3**	**95.8**
Alabama	296	780	436	629	670	528	376	312	185	60	25.2	26.3	29.8	13.0	12.9	11.3	92.6
Alaska	50	135	65	86	117	83	41	21	9	2	30.4	31.4	32.6	5.2	4.0	3.0	111.0
Arizona	343	807	429	677	704	524	358	332	199	56	26.0	26.9	29.1	13.2	13.0	11.3	98.1
Arkansas	175	484	249	340	369	304	226	195	125	42	26.3	26.5	29.4	14.4	14.8	13.6	93.7
California	2 736	6 131	3 003	5 394	5 266	3 634	2 198	1 961	1 180	375	27.8	26.2	27.0	11.0	10.5	10.2	100.3
Colorado	270	728	355	561	695	521	308	218	125	42	26.1	26.2	28.0	10.1	10.0	8.5	98.4
Connecticut	223	575	262	504	556	419	265	246	166	57	24.4	22.9	26.5	14.3	13.5	11.7	94.6
Delaware	50	126	65	122	123	88	59	54	30	9	24.3	24.6	27.9	12.8	12.1	9.9	95.1
District of Columbia	34	75	46	110	89	67	46	41	25	9	20.2	19.5	22.4	13.9	12.7	11.4	88.1
Florida	956	2 467	1 167	2 001	2 199	1 675	1 277	1 452	925	281	23.8	22.3	24.2	18.5	18.2	17.3	94.4
Georgia	552	1 401	733	1 224	1 243	916	555	414	240	75	26.6	26.8	30.1	9.9	10.0	9.5	95.0
Hawaii	91	215	116	168	198	149	93	89	49	14	25.9	25.4	28.6	12.9	11.2	8.0	101.9
Idaho	90	258	130	150	186	143	96	72	47	15	29.3	30.7	32.5	11.4	12.0	9.9	100.0
Illinois	915	2 241	1 098	1 806	1 930	1 424	947	803	510	172	26.6	25.9	28.4	12.5	12.5	11.1	95.4
Indiana	410	1 089	573	871	952	723	488	406	246	82	25.7	26.3	29.5	12.6	12.5	10.7	95.1
Iowa	182	537	271	386	448	345	250	219	153	61	25.2	25.9	28.3	15.2	15.3	13.3	95.0
Kansas	180	507	246	364	417	302	203	182	122	48	26.7	26.8	27.5	13.7	13.8	12.9	97.0
Kentucky	259	710	398	568	625	492	342	274	161	54	24.9	26.0	29.6	12.6	12.6	11.2	94.5
Louisiana	328	906	460	615	677	514	354	283	161	52	28.4	29.2	31.6	11.4	11.1	9.6	93.1
Maine	71	228	111	177	216	163	103	94	58	21	24.1	25.3	28.6	13.9	13.3	12.5	95.5
Maryland	360	927	427	837	897	653	393	329	190	59	25.4	24.4	27.7	11.4	10.8	9.4	94.9
Massachusetts	391	1 031	515	1 046	1 017	759	474	452	301	106	23.3	22.6	26.0	14.1	13.5	12.7	93.3
Michigan	672	1 865	904	1 423	1 587	1 188	763	666	400	126	26.4	26.5	29.7	12.4	11.9	9.8	95.1
Minnesota	316	931	420	695	797	562	359	298	202	78	26.8	26.7	28.8	12.4	12.5	11.8	97.4
Mississippi	204	552	300	385	407	310	224	184	111	39	27.8	29.1	32.3	12.3	12.4	11.5	92.4
Missouri	367	1 027	495	771	858	644	454	398	251	93	26.0	25.8	27.7	13.8	14.0	13.2	94.1
Montana	56	177	86	102	146	118	79	61	41	14	26.5	27.9	29.4	13.2	13.3	10.8	99.3
Nebraska	113	329	162	225	265	195	134	117	79	33	26.8	27.2	28.5	13.8	14.1	13.1	96.0
Nevada	124	293	134	256	267	206	141	115	56	13	26.0	24.8	27.0	11.4	10.5	8.3	104.0
New Hampshire	76	220	94	189	215	146	84	76	47	16	25.5	25.2	28.1	12.0	11.2	11.1	97.0
New Jersey	572	1 415	665	1 195	1 352	1 021	668	604	376	119	24.9	23.4	27.0	13.8	13.3	11.7	94.3
New Mexico	136	365	171	230	277	206	138	109	61	19	29.3	29.6	32.1	11.0	10.7	8.9	97.4
New York	1 322	3 219	1 605	2 862	2 939	2 267	1 537	1 335	815	284	25.0	23.9	26.7	13.4	13.0	12.3	93.0
North Carolina	513	1 321	703	1 157	1 180	911	621	527	298	92	25.0	24.4	28.2	12.5	12.1	10.3	94.5
North Dakota	41	127	66	88	102	73	53	46	34	13	26.2	27.5	29.2	14.5	14.2	12.3	99.8
Ohio	759	2 089	1 051	1 634	1 823	1 379	942	834	502	161	25.5	25.9	28.7	13.4	12.9	10.8	93.9
Oklahoma	228	653	330	445	506	401	293	242	149	54	26.7	26.7	28.3	13.5	13.4	12.5	95.8
Oregon	212	597	289	439	541	434	263	228	152	50	25.2	25.6	27.5	13.4	13.7	11.5	97.7
Pennsylvania	761	2 133	1 041	1 710	1 958	1 497	1 044	1 037	667	208	24.0	23.6	26.3	15.9	15.3	12.9	92.8
Rhode Island	63	172	85	160	162	117	75	82	55	19	23.8	22.6	25.7	15.8	14.9	13.3	92.8
South Carolina	254	684	378	569	593	464	310	261	144	42	25.4	26.5	30.2	12.1	11.3	9.2	93.5
South Dakota	51	153	73	94	114	82	59	54	37	15	27.9	28.6	29.7	14.4	14.7	13.2	97.2
Tennessee	364	958	511	804	862	686	468	375	220	73	24.9	25.1	28.3	12.5	12.6	11.3	93.6
Texas	1 583	3 869	1 970	2 935	3 129	2 247	1 444	1 112	627	212	28.5	28.6	30.3	10.2	10.1	9.6	97.7
Utah	188	490	262	289	276	194	125	97	60	19	33.9	36.5	37.0	8.8	8.7	7.5	99.3
Vermont	35	111	52	88	105	80	46	39	24	9	24.9	25.5	28.4	12.1	11.7	11.4	97.1
Virginia	455	1 177	649	1 116	1 141	860	530	428	243	76	24.4	24.4	27.6	11.2	10.7	9.4	96.1
Washington	386	1 051	509	835	973	719	419	346	223	72	26.0	26.0	27.6	11.6	11.8	10.4	99.2
West Virginia	107	315	187	233	284	244	178	156	93	29	23.1	24.8	28.7	15.2	14.9	12.2	93.3
Wisconsin	337	1 006	482	749	856	627	417	361	238	87	26.0	26.4	28.9	13.3	13.3	12.0	96.9
Wyoming	31	102	51	56	82	63	41	31	17	6	27.7	30.0	31.1	11.2	10.4	7.9	101.4

Source: Age–U.S. Bureau of the Census, press release CB97-64 and Current Population Report, State Population Estimates by Age and Sex: 1980 to 1992, P25-1106; 1980 Population for computation–U.S. Bureau of the Census, 1990 Census of Population and Housing Unit Counts (CPH-2); Sex–U.S. Bureau of the Census, Internet site <http://www.census.gov/population/estimates/state/96agesex.txt> (accessed 21 July 1997).

Table A–4. States — Series A Population Projections by Age Group

Geographic area	Under 5 years old (1,000) 2000	2005	5 to 17 years old (1,000) 2000	2005	18 to 44 years old (1,000) 2000	2005	45 to 64 years old (1,000) 2000	2005	65 to 74 years old (1,000) 2000	2005	75 to 84 years old (1,000) 2000	2005	85 years old and over (1,000) 2000	2005	Percent of population in 2000 Under 18 years old	65 years old and over
United States	18 986	19 127	51 796	52 837	108 151	106 738	60 991	71 113	18 136	18 369	12 315	12 898	4 259	4 899	25.8	12.6
Alabama..................	290	285	815	834	1 731	1 696	1 033	1 203	317	330	198	209	67	74	24.8	13.1
Alaska.....................	57	62	143	151	278	286	137	155	25	29	11	14	2	3	30.6	5.8
Arizona...................	348	371	965	1 004	1 812	1 859	1 038	1 289	339	371	226	248	70	88	27.4	13.2
Arkansas.................	169	167	484	484	977	958	624	739	200	216	130	135	47	51	24.8	14.3
California	2 678	2 782	6 672	7 164	13 260	13 412	6 524	7 629	1 757	1 742	1 226	1 254	404	458	28.8	10.4
Colorado	276	290	773	788	1 694	1 714	973	1 153	246	279	152	176	54	68	25.2	10.8
Connecticut	213	204	578	573	1 283	1 234	749	850	224	209	173	172	64	75	24.1	14.0
Delaware	50	50	141	141	311	307	169	201	51	51	35	37	11	13	24.9	12.6
District of Columbia	37	37	88	93	215	212	114	122	36	33	24	23	9	9	23.9	13.2
Florida	904	922	2 603	2 641	5 425	5 443	3 546	4 362	1 384	1 405	1 028	1 091	343	415	23.0	18.1
Georgia	544	558	1 526	1 597	3 301	3 326	1 725	2 080	429	468	263	282	87	102	26.3	9.9
Hawaii......................	98	103	230	251	495	505	277	319	83	80	56	60	18	24	26.1	12.5
Idaho.......................	97	107	281	293	516	537	296	361	82	96	55	61	20	25	28.1	11.7
Illinois	867	858	2 274	2 293	4 807	4 665	2 619	2 956	767	755	529	532	188	207	26.1	12.3
Indiana	401	396	1 117	1 128	2 396	2 330	1 368	1 567	402	407	268	282	93	105	25.1	12.6
Iowa	183	182	523	509	1 091	1 052	661	746	217	218	158	160	67	74	24.3	15.2
Kansas	183	187	515	513	1 036	1 026	575	669	179	179	128	131	52	56	26.2	13.5
Kentucky	251	244	712	707	1 577	1 516	946	1 093	279	293	173	183	57	62	24.1	12.7
Louisiana	320	320	894	884	1 722	1 678	966	1 098	289	299	176	190	58	66	27.4	11.8
Maine	77	74	216	210	485	462	309	366	89	87	61	63	22	23	23.3	13.7
Maryland	358	353	961	980	2 174	2 131	1 193	1 392	312	313	211	220	66	78	25.0	11.2
Massachusetts	400	382	1 096	1 106	2 499	2 429	1 361	1 566	413	384	311	309	119	134	24.1	13.6
Michigan..................	668	647	1 827	1 808	3 817	3 641	2 170	2 456	627	607	427	439	143	165	25.8	12.4
Minnesota	320	326	916	890	1 935	1 906	1 063	1 256	296	307	211	218	89	102	25.6	12.3
Mississippi	200	196	567	573	1 096	1 068	609	708	187	196	116	122	41	45	27.2	12.2
Missouri...................	365	366	1 027	1 024	2 146	2 099	1 247	1 455	391	393	263	272	101	109	25.1	13.6
Montana	61	65	179	177	348	345	234	276	66	74	45	47	17	22	25.3	13.5
Nebraska.................	116	119	327	323	654	646	369	425	120	121	83	88	36	39	26.0	14.0
Nevada....................	119	128	331	340	738	754	464	591	129	147	72	86	18	24	24.1	11.7
New Hampshire	80	79	224	224	503	494	275	336	72	71	51	55	19	22	24.8	11.6
New Jersey	548	535	1 456	1 489	3 216	3 136	1 868	2 139	565	543	395	403	130	147	24.5	13.3
New Mexico..............	145	155	389	413	717	737	403	483	114	124	70	77	22	27	28.7	11.1
New York	1 268	1 211	3 352	3 399	7 101	6 817	4 067	4 502	1 239	1 176	826	835	293	310	25.5	13.0
North Carolina..........	483	481	1 425	1 453	3 083	3 065	1 795	2 147	539	572	341	375	111	134	24.5	12.7
North Dakota............	43	44	125	119	253	249	142	162	48	48	35	36	16	19	25.4	15.0
Ohio	748	730	2 069	2 036	4 411	4 214	2 566	2 894	795	775	547	567	183	212	24.9	13.5
Oklahoma	220	224	641	628	1 265	1 242	775	893	249	262	160	172	63	70	25.5	14.0
Oregon	211	219	599	602	1 277	1 273	839	997	236	258	173	186	62	78	23.8	13.9
Pennsylvania............	759	730	2 143	2 115	4 582	4 363	2 819	3 206	956	883	709	715	234	269	23.8	15.6
Rhode Island............	65	63	180	181	390	374	215	251	70	62	57	57	21	24	24.5	14.8
South Carolina..........	255	248	715	732	1 513	1 479	897	1 057	263	277	165	178	50	62	25.1	12.4
South Dakota	55	58	155	153	293	292	164	193	54	54	39	41	17	19	27.0	14.2
Tennessee...............	359	362	1 017	1 046	2 238	2 225	1 336	1 573	382	407	242	258	83	95	24.3	12.5
Texas......................	1 545	1 629	4 163	4 347	8 122	8 251	4 188	4 963	1 154	1 234	704	784	243	279	28.4	10.4
Utah	192	209	527	550	896	941	390	477	107	122	71	80	24	32	32.6	9.2
Vermont	38	38	114	112	245	238	147	173	38	39	25	27	10	11	24.6	11.8
Virginia....................	451	444	1 246	1 284	2 912	2 876	1 600	1 875	422	439	276	297	90	109	24.3	11.3
Washington	388	402	1 071	1 094	2 346	2 351	1 368	1 654	350	384	248	265	87	108	24.9	11.7
West Virginia	104	99	300	295	679	636	471	523	155	156	100	105	32	35	21.9	15.6
Wisconsin	345	347	999	975	2 090	2 045	1 187	1 382	357	360	250	259	98	111	25.2	13.2
Wyoming	36	40	103	106	201	205	123	146	34	37	21	25	7	9	26.5	11.8

Note: Series A is the preferred series model and uses state-to-state migration observed from 1975-76 through 1993-94.

Source: U.S. Bureau of the Census, Population Paper Listing, Population Projections for States by Age, Sex, Race, and Hispanic Origin: 1995 to 2025, PPL-47, October 1996.

Table A–5. States — Population by Race

Geographic area	White (1,000)			Black (1,000)			Asian and Pacific Islander (1,000)			American Indian, Eskimo, and Aleut (1,000)			Percent of total, 1996			
	1990	1996	2000 proj.[1]	1990	1996	2000 proj.[1]	1990	1996	2000 proj.[1]	1990	1996	2000 proj.[1]	White	Black	Asian and Pacific Islander	American Indian, Eskimo, and Aleut
United States	208 704	219 749	225 533	30 483	33 503	35 456	7 458	9 743	11 246	2 065	2 288	2 402	82.8	12.6	3.7	.9
Alabama.....................	2 981	3 126	3 262	1 021	1 104	1 137	22	28	34	17	15	18	73.2	25.8	.7	.4
Alaska.......................	421	462	486	23	23	29	20	26	46	86	95	93	76.2	3.8	4.3	15.7
Arizona......................	3 277	3 937	4 252	115	154	177	58	89	107	214	248	262	82.7	3.5	2.0	5.6
Arkansas....................	1 951	2 076	2 186	374	403	409	13	17	19	13	13	15	82.7	16.1	.7	.5
California	24 241	25 492	25 517	2 290	2 371	2 425	2 943	3 712	4 289	285	303	292	80.0	7.4	11.6	1.0
Colorado	3 066	3 536	3 823	136	164	196	62	87	108	31	36	41	92.5	4.3	2.3	.9
Connecticut	2 946	2 895	2 873	282	298	324	52	73	80	7	8	8	88.4	9.1	2.2	.2
Delaware	541	573	603	113	136	147	9	13	15	2	2	2	79.0	18.8	1.9	.3
District of Columbia	191	185	184	402	341	321	12	16	15	2	2	–	34.0	62.7	3.0	.3
Florida	10 972	11 931	12 588	1 772	2 172	2 326	156	245	267	37	52	51	82.9	15.1	1.7	.4
Georgia	4 636	5 131	5 436	1 752	2 075	2 279	77	131	142	14	17	17	69.8	28.2	1.8	.2
Hawaii.......................	379	396	423	28	36	31	696	746	796	5	7	6	33.5	3.0	63.0	.6
Idaho........................	979	1 154	1 300	4	6	8	10	13	17	15	16	21	97.1	.5	1.1	1.3
Illinois.......................	9 407	9 640	9 736	1 707	1 807	1 865	292	374	423	24	26	26	81.4	15.3	3.2	.2
Indiana......................	5 059	5 297	5 466	434	478	502	38	51	60	13	14	16	90.7	8.2	.9	.2
Iowa.........................	2 695	2 754	2 786	48	55	62	26	34	43	8	8	9	96.6	1.9	1.2	.3
Kansas......................	2 277	2 355	2 419	145	152	173	32	42	50	23	23	27	91.6	5.9	1.6	.9
Kentucky....................	3 398	3 573	3 671	264	280	287	18	25	29	6	6	6	92.0	7.2	.6	.2
Louisiana....................	2 858	2 884	2 895	1 302	1 394	1 448	42	53	62	19	19	20	66.3	32.0	1.2	.4
Maine	1 210	1 224	1 238	5	6	5	7	8	9	6	6	6	98.4	.5	.7	.4
Maryland	3 430	3 495	3 546	1 197	1 373	1 489	141	188	223	13	15	16	68.9	27.1	3.7	.3
Massachusetts	5 530	5 500	5 523	327	378	417	146	201	246	13	14	14	90.3	6.2	3.3	.2
Michigan.....................	7 833	8 024	8 021	1 298	1 369	1 435	106	142	163	58	59	61	83.6	14.3	1.5	.6
Minnesota	4 149	4 361	4 469	96	128	158	79	112	139	51	57	64	93.6	2.7	2.4	1.2
Mississippi	1 636	1 702	1 774	916	987	1 012	13	18	19	9	10	8	62.7	36.3	.6	.4
Missouri	4 505	4 685	4 825	550	598	628	42	55	63	20	20	24	87.4	11.2	1.0	.4
Montana	744	817	879	2	3	3	4	5	7	48	54	61	92.9	.4	.6	6.2
Nebraska	1 495	1 552	1 595	58	65	72	13	20	23	13	15	16	94.0	3.9	1.2	.9
Nevada	1 061	1 389	1 619	80	118	138	39	68	85	21	28	31	86.6	7.4	4.2	1.8
New Hampshire	1 090	1 139	1 199	7	8	9	9	13	14	2	2	2	98.0	.7	1.1	.2
New Jersey	6 370	6 415	6 442	1 067	1 157	1 239	277	395	475	16	21	20	80.3	14.5	4.9	.3
New Mexico..................	1 331	1 490	1 615	32	43	48	15	23	29	138	157	169	87.0	2.5	1.3	9.2
New York.....................	14 150	13 992	13 747	3 065	3 198	3 299	709	922	1 028	66	73	73	76.9	17.6	5.1	.4
North Carolina...............	5 034	5 519	5 851	1 461	1 624	1 738	53	86	96	81	94	94	75.4	22.2	1.2	1.3
North Dakota................	606	605	617	4	4	5	4	5	5	26	29	32	94.0	.6	.8	4.6
Ohio.........................	9 575	9 767	9 835	1 160	1 264	1 320	92	119	140	21	22	22	87.4	11.3	1.1	.2
Oklahoma....................	2 617	2 746	2 759	236	253	282	35	42	51	258	261	281	83.2	7.7	1.3	7.9
Oregon	2 685	3 006	3 167	47	58	65	70	96	116	41	44	51	93.8	1.8	3.0	1.4
Pennsylvania................	10 621	10 690	10 741	1 105	1 162	1 224	140	186	218	15	17	18	88.7	9.6	1.5	.1
Rhode Island................	937	917	911	43	47	54	19	21	28	4	5	4	92.6	4.8	2.2	.5
South Carolina	2 414	2 544	2 660	1 041	1 116	1 156	23	30	33	8	9	8	68.8	30.2	.8	.2
South Dakota	639	666	706	3	5	5	3	4	5	51	57	60	91.0	.6	.6	7.8
Tennessee...................	4 056	4 385	4 658	779	875	929	32	48	57	10	12	12	82.4	16.4	.9	.2
Texas	14 535	16 204	16 920	2 048	2 336	2 543	331	498	562	72	90	95	84.7	12.2	2.6	.5
Utah	1 651	1 908	2 087	12	17	22	34	47	62	25	28	37	95.4	.8	2.4	1.4
Vermont	556	578	606	2	4	2	3	5	6	2	2	2	98.2	.6	.9	.3
Virginia	4 843	5 111	5 295	1 168	1 323	1 416	161	224	267	16	18	19	76.6	19.8	3.3	.3
Washington..................	4 411	4 945	5 200	153	189	192	215	300	358	87	99	107	89.4	3.4	5.4	1.8
West Virginia	1 727	1 757	1 769	56	58	58	7	9	11	2	3	2	96.2	3.2	.5	.1
Wisconsin	4 550	4 756	4 853	247	284	326	54	74	100	40	45	49	92.2	5.5	1.4	.9
Wyoming	437	463	501	4	4	6	3	4	4	10	11	13	96.2	.8	.8	2.2

– Represents or rounds to zero.

[1]Series A is the preferred series model and uses state-to-state migration observed from 1975-76 through 1993-94.

Source: Race–U.S. Bureau of the Census, Estimates of the Population of States by Race and Hispanic Origin: July 1, 1996, Internet site <http://www.census.gov/population/estimates/state/srh/srhus96.txt> (accessed 04 March 1998); Projections–U.S. Bureau of the Census, Population Paper Listing, Population Projections for States by Age, Sex, Race, and Hispanic Origin: 1995 to 2025, PPL-47, October 1996.

Table A–6. States — Hispanic Origin, Immigrants Admitted, and Households

Geographic area	Hispanic origin[1] (1,000) 1990	1996	2000, proj.[2]	Non-Hispanic White (1,000) 1990	1996	2000, proj.[2]	Percent of total, 1996 Hispanic origin[1]	Non-Hispanic White	Immigrants admitted 1995	1994	1990	Households Number (1,000) 1996	1990	Percent change, 1990-1996	Persons per household 1996	1990
United States	22 354	28 269	31 366	188 300	193 978	197 062	10.7	73.1	709 200	789 688	1 525 656	98 751	91 946	7.4	2.62	2.63
Alabama	25	36	37	2 961	3 096	3 231	.8	72.4	1 900	1 837	1 775	1 624	1 507	7.8	2.56	2.62
Alaska	18	22	31	407	444	461	3.7	73.2	1 049	1 129	1 207	214	189	13.4	2.76	2.80
Arizona	688	941	1 071	2 630	3 056	3 254	21.3	69.0	7 700	9 141	23 737	1 687	1 369	23.3	2.59	2.62
Arkansas	20	41	33	1 933	2 040	2 155	1.6	81.3	934	1 031	1 245	951	891	6.7	2.51	2.57
California	7 688	9 630	10 647	17 065	16 480	15 562	30.2	51.7	166 482	208 498	682 979	11 101	10 381	6.9	2.79	2.79
Colorado	424	536	594	2 663	3 032	3 268	14.0	79.3	7 713	6 825	9 125	1 502	1 282	17.1	2.47	2.51
Connecticut	213	253	288	2 757	2 672	2 622	7.7	81.6	9 240	9 537	10 678	1 231	1 230	–	2.65	2.59
Delaware	16	23	25	528	553	582	3.1	76.4	1 051	984	868	276	247	11.4	2.62	2.61
District of Columbia	33	38	40	166	155	152	6.9	28.5	3 047	3 204	5 467	231	250	-7.3	2.24	2.26
Florida	1 574	2 022	2 390	9 482	10 051	10 405	14.0	69.8	62 023	58 093	71 603	5 648	5 135	10.0	2.45	2.46
Georgia	109	187	189	4 545	4 968	5 270	2.5	67.6	12 381	10 032	10 431	2 723	2 366	15.1	2.65	2.66
Hawaii	81	93	107	349	350	363	7.9	29.5	7 537	7 746	8 441	389	356	9.0	2.97	3.01
Idaho	53	81	96	929	1 079	1 211	6.8	90.7	1 612	1 559	1 815	430	361	19.1	2.68	2.73
Illinois	904	1 136	1 267	8 556	8 576	8 553	9.6	72.4	33 898	42 400	83 858	4 352	4 202	3.6	2.65	2.65
Indiana	99	129	140	4 967	5 179	5 338	2.2	88.7	3 590	3 725	3 392	2 209	2 065	6.9	2.57	2.61
Iowa	33	50	54	2 665	2 709	2 737	1.7	95.0	2 260	2 163	2 252	1 103	1 064	3.6	2.51	2.52
Kansas	94	125	138	2 192	2 242	2 293	4.9	87.2	2 434	2 902	3 925	982	945	3.9	2.54	2.53
Kentucky	22	29	32	3 379	3 549	3 643	.7	91.4	1 857	2 036	1 365	1 478	1 380	7.1	2.55	2.60
Louisiana	93	110	119	2 778	2 790	2 792	2.5	64.1	3 000	3 366	4 024	1 572	1 499	4.8	2.67	2.74
Maine	7	8	8	1 204	1 216	1 230	.7	97.8	814	829	883	483	465	3.8	2.54	2.56
Maryland	125	170	214	3 328	3 353	3 371	3.4	66.1	15 055	15 937	17 106	1 871	1 749	7.0	2.70	2.67
Massachusetts	288	348	437	5 298	5 224	5 182	5.7	85.7	20 523	22 882	25 338	2 322	2 247	3.3	2.61	2.58
Michigan	202	242	261	7 654	7 809	7 790	2.5	81.4	14 135	12 728	10 990	3 576	3 419	4.6	2.66	2.66
Minnesota	54	76	95	4 103	4 295	4 387	1.6	92.2	8 111	7 098	6 627	1 763	1 648	7.0	2.58	2.58
Mississippi	16	20	21	1 624	1 686	1 755	.7	62.1	757	815	931	979	911	7.4	2.66	2.75
Missouri	62	77	90	4 450	4 618	4 745	1.4	86.2	3 990	4 362	3 820	2 052	1 961	4.6	2.51	2.53
Montana	12	15	20	734	805	861	1.7	91.5	409	447	484	341	306	11.3	2.50	2.53
Nebraska	37	63	61	1 461	1 495	1 540	3.8	90.5	1 831	1 595	1 573	631	602	4.8	2.54	2.54
Nevada	124	226	277	947	1 183	1 366	14.1	73.8	4 306	4 051	8 270	619	466	32.8	2.53	2.53
New Hampshire	11	16	17	1 080	1 125	1 184	1.4	96.8	1 186	1 144	1 191	439	411	6.7	2.62	2.62
New Jersey	740	920	1 044	5 725	5 622	5 558	11.5	70.4	39 729	44 083	52 670	2 889	2 795	3.4	2.75	2.70
New Mexico	579	677	736	767	840	912	39.5	49.1	2 758	2 936	8 840	619	543	14.1	2.64	2.74
New York	2 214	2 538	2 805	12 475	12 075	11 640	14.0	66.4	128 406	144 354	189 589	6 737	6 639	1.5	2.65	2.63
North Carolina	77	134	121	4 972	5 404	5 748	1.8	73.8	5 617	6 204	5 387	2 796	2 517	11.1	2.53	2.54
North Dakota	5	6	6	602	600	611	1.0	93.2	483	635	448	247	241	2.4	2.51	2.55
Ohio	140	169	183	9 450	9 617	9 672	1.5	86.1	8 585	9 184	7 419	4 260	4 088	4.2	2.54	2.59
Oklahoma	86	115	124	2 549	2 650	2 653	3.5	80.3	2 792	2 728	5 274	1 265	1 206	4.9	2.50	2.53
Oregon	113	177	195	2 581	2 843	2 990	5.5	88.8	4 923	6 784	7 880	1 249	1 103	13.2	2.51	2.52
Pennsylvania	232	292	334	10 427	10 445	10 460	2.4	86.6	15 065	15 971	14 757	4 594	4 496	2.2	2.58	2.57
Rhode Island	46	59	76	901	870	851	6.0	87.8	2 609	2 907	3 683	378	378	-.1	2.56	2.55
South Carolina	31	41	42	2 391	2 510	2 624	1.1	67.9	2 165	2 110	2 130	1 376	1 258	9.4	2.64	2.68
South Dakota	5	7	8	635	660	698	1.0	90.2	495	570	287	273	259	5.4	2.56	2.59
Tennessee	33	52	57	4 029	4 341	4 607	1.0	81.6	3 392	3 608	2 893	2 041	1 854	10.1	2.52	2.56
Texas	4 340	5 503	5 875	10 308	10 894	11 273	28.8	57.0	49 963	56 158	174 132	6 894	6 071	13.6	2.69	2.73
Utah	85	122	138	1 572	1 795	1 961	6.1	89.7	2 831	2 951	3 335	639	537	19.0	3.06	3.15
Vermont	4	6	6	552	573	600	1.0	97.3	535	658	614	227	211	7.5	2.57	2.57
Virginia	160	224	269	4 704	4 916	5 061	3.4	73.6	16 319	15 342	19 005	2 511	2 292	9.6	2.61	2.61
Washington	215	322	360	4 225	4 660	4 881	5.8	84.2	15 862	18 180	15 129	2 139	1 872	14.2	2.53	2.53
West Virginia	8	10	11	1 719	1 748	1 758	.5	95.7	540	663	552	714	689	3.7	2.50	2.55
Wisconsin	93	123	136	4 466	4 646	4 732	2.4	90.0	4 919	5 328	5 293	1 943	1 822	6.6	2.61	2.61
Wyoming	26	28	35	413	437	469	5.7	90.9	252	217	542	184	169	8.8	2.55	2.63

– Represents or rounds to zero.

[1]Persons of Hispanic origin may be of any race.
[2]Series A is the preferred series model and uses state-to-state migration observed from 1975-76 through 1993-94.

Source: Hispanic origin–U.S. Bureau of the Census, Estimates of the Population of the States by Race and Hispanic Origin: July 1, 1996 Internet site <http://www.census.gov/population/estimates/state/srh/srhus 96.txt> (accessed 04 March 1998). Projections–U.S. Bureau of the Census, Population Paper Listing, Population Projections for States by Age, Sex, Race, and Hispanic Origin: 1995 to 2025, PPL-47, October 1996; Immigrants–U.S. Immigration and Naturalization Service, Statistical Yearbook, annual; Households–U.S. Bureau of the Census, Population Paper Listing, Estimates of Housing Units and Households of States: 1990 and 1996, PPL-73.

Table A–7. States — Live Births and Birth Rates

Geographic area	Total 1996, prel.	Total 1990	Total 1980	Rate[1] 1996, prel.	Rate[1] 1990	Rate[1] 1980	Pct low birth weight[2] 1996, prel.	Pct low birth weight[2] 1990	Pct teenage mothers 1996, prel.	Pct teenage mothers 1990	Pct unmarried women 1996, prel.	Pct unmarried women 1990	1996, prel. White	1996, prel. Black	1996, prel. Hispanic[3]
United States	**3 914 953**	**4 158 212**	**3 612 258**	**14.8**	**16.7**	**15.9**	**7.4**	**7.0**	**12.9**	**12.8**	**32.4**	**28.0**	**3 113 014**	**596 039**	**697 829**
Alabama	61 477	63 487	63 503	14.4	15.7	16.3	9.3	8.4	18.3	18.2	33.5	30.1	40 943	19 833	937
Alaska	10 161	11 902	9 529	16.7	21.6	23.7	5.5	4.8	11.2	9.7	31.3	26.2	6 930	425	673
Arizona	79 590	68 995	50 048	18.0	18.8	18.4	6.6	6.4	15.0	14.2	39.0	32.7	69 869	2 447	29 217
Arkansas	36 418	36 457	37 278	14.5	15.5	16.3	8.5	8.2	19.8	19.7	31.6	[4]31.6	27 915	7 921	1 315
California	539 789	612 628	402 949	16.9	20.6	17.0	6.0	5.8	12.0	11.6	31.6	[4]31.6	440 213	37 695	251 123
Colorado	55 840	53 525	49 730	14.6	16.2	17.2	8.8	8.0	11.9	11.3	24.8	21.2	51 100	2 579	12 380
Connecticut	44 312	50 123	38 781	13.5	15.2	12.5	7.2	6.6	8.2	8.2	31.3	[4]26.6	37 755	5 224	5 614
Delaware	10 243	11 113	9 413	14.1	16.7	15.8	8.5	7.6	13.7	11.9	35.5	29.0	7 620	2 391	666
District of Columbia	8 336	11 850	9 361	15.3	19.5	14.7	14.2	15.1	16.8	17.8	66.0	64.9	2 062	6 123	772
Florida	189 458	199 339	131 795	13.2	15.4	13.5	7.9	7.4	13.4	13.9	36.0	31.7	142 670	42 288	35 708
Georgia	114 848	112 666	92 313	15.6	17.4	16.9	8.5	8.7	15.9	16.7	35.0	32.8	73 762	38 777	6 312
Hawaii	18 334	20 489	18 161	15.5	18.5	18.8	7.3	7.1	10.3	10.5	30.2	24.8	4 790	508	2 151
Idaho	19 059	16 433	20 167	16.0	16.3	21.4	5.7	5.7	13.5	12.3	21.3	16.7	18 446	76	2 220
Illinois	184 369	195 790	190 058	15.6	17.1	16.6	8.0	7.6	12.7	13.1	33.7	31.7	141 603	36 499	33 040
Indiana	83 303	86 214	88 440	14.3	15.6	16.1	7.7	6.6	14.5	14.5	32.6	26.2	73 237	9 024	3 036
Iowa	37 120	39 409	47 814	13.0	14.2	16.4	6.4	5.4	11.0	10.2	26.3	21.0	35 125	1 047	1 481
Kansas	39 734	39 020	40 716	15.4	15.7	17.2	6.9	6.2	13.1	12.3	26.9	21.5	35 518	3 006	3 504
Kentucky	52 632	54 362	59 582	13.6	14.8	16.3	7.8	7.1	17.0	17.5	29.8	23.6	47 243	4 862	558
Louisiana	66 178	72 192	82 163	15.2	17.1	19.5	9.8	9.2	18.9	17.6	43.4	36.8	37 983	26 860	1 288
Maine	13 775	17 359	16 461	11.1	14.1	14.6	5.9	5.1	9.7	10.3	28.7	22.6	13 461	85	115
Maryland	69 696	80 245	59 932	13.7	16.8	14.2	8.5	7.8	10.3	10.5	33.4	[4]29.6	44 763	22 349	3 146
Massachusetts	80 457	92 654	72 632	13.2	15.4	12.7	6.3	5.9	7.3	8.0	25.6	24.7	69 418	7 329	7 737
Michigan	137 471	153 700	145 509	14.3	16.5	15.7	7.6	7.6	12.2	13.5	33.8	[4]26.2	109 200	24 873	5 197
Minnesota	63 779	68 013	67 773	13.7	15.5	16.6	5.8	5.1	8.5	8.0	24.4	20.9	57 003	3 034	2 287
Mississippi	41 662	43 563	47 845	15.3	16.9	19.0	9.9	9.6	21.3	21.3	45.1	40.5	21 801	19 288	283
Missouri	73 782	79 260	78 934	13.8	15.5	16.1	7.5	7.1	14.1	14.4	33.1	28.6	61 277	11 091	1 516
Montana	10 707	11 613	14 206	12.2	14.5	18.1	6.4	6.2	12.5	11.5	27.8	[4]23.7	9 390	37	299
Nebraska	23 321	24 380	27 352	14.1	15.4	17.4	6.3	5.3	10.6	9.8	24.7	20.7	21 373	1 203	1 866
Nevada	26 034	21 599	13 320	16.2	18.0	16.6	7.5	7.2	13.3	12.6	42.7	[4]25.4	22 262	1 972	6 946
New Hampshire	14 548	17 569	13 745	12.5	15.8	14.9	4.8	4.9	7.4	7.2	23.4	16.9	14 252	112	232
New Jersey	113 902	122 289	96 866	14.3	15.8	13.2	7.6	7.0	7.7	8.4	27.9	24.3	86 407	20 101	19 458
New Mexico	27 235	27 402	26 115	15.9	18.1	20.0	7.5	7.4	17.9	16.3	42.1	35.4	23 193	467	13 250
New York	271 458	297 576	239 011	14.9	16.5	13.6	7.6	7.6	9.2	9.1	38.8	[4]33.0	197 275	55 805	53 024
North Carolina	105 741	104 525	84 496	14.4	15.8	14.4	8.7	8.0	15.0	16.2	32.0	29.4	74 710	27 462	5 500
North Dakota	8 358	9 250	11 982	13.0	14.5	18.4	5.7	5.5	9.6	8.4	25.2	18.4	7 416	87	137
Ohio	152 664	166 913	169 148	13.7	15.4	15.7	7.3	7.1	13.3	13.8	32.9	[4]28.9	128 739	21 705	2 992
Oklahoma	46 209	47 649	52 106	14.0	15.1	17.2	7.4	6.6	17.2	16.2	30.9	25.2	36 642	4 486	2 882
Oregon	43 677	42 891	43 127	13.6	15.1	16.4	5.3	5.0	13.2	12.0	29.7	25.7	40 456	893	5 464
Pennsylvania	149 962	171 961	158 823	12.4	14.5	13.4	7.5	7.1	10.6	10.9	32.3	28.6	125 639	20 791	6 811
Rhode Island	12 514	15 195	12 188	12.6	15.1	12.9	6.9	6.2	10.3	10.5	32.9	26.3	11 049	931	1 633
South Carolina	50 807	58 610	51 978	13.7	16.8	16.6	9.2	8.7	16.8	17.1	37.2	32.7	32 197	17 861	960
South Dakota	10 475	10 999	13 276	14.3	15.8	19.2	5.8	5.1	11.5	10.8	29.5	22.9	8 662	83	146
Tennessee	73 779	74 962	69 219	13.9	15.4	15.1	8.8	8.2	16.8	17.6	33.4	30.2	56 539	16 029	1 425
Texas	327 163	316 423	273 580	17.1	18.6	19.2	7.2	6.9	16.2	15.6	30.5	[4]17.5	278 760	38 708	140 539
Utah	41 388	36 277	41 797	20.7	21.1	28.6	6.5	5.7	10.6	10.3	16.0	13.5	39 291	331	3 865
Vermont	6 745	8 273	7 884	11.5	14.7	15.4	6.2	5.3	8.9	8.5	26.4	20.1	6 666	17	39
Virginia	92 400	99 352	78 443	13.8	16.1	14.7	7.7	7.2	11.0	11.7	28.8	26.0	67 359	20 920	5 158
Washington	79 959	79 251	67 858	14.5	16.3	16.4	5.6	5.3	11.3	10.8	27.3	23.7	69 329	3 187	9 183
West Virginia	20 704	22 585	29 464	11.3	12.6	15.1	7.9	7.1	16.8	17.8	31.4	25.4	19 808	744	122
Wisconsin	67 094	72 895	74 825	13.0	14.9	15.9	6.2	5.9	10.6	10.2	27.4	24.2	57 936	6 425	3 099
Wyoming	6 285	6 985	10 562	13.1	15.4	22.5	8.4	7.4	14.4	13.6	27.0	19.8	5 956	49	523

[1] Per 1,000 population estimated as of July 1 for 1996 and enumerated as of April 1 for 1990 and 1980.
[2] Less than 2,500 grams (5 pounds 8 ounces).
[3] Persons of Hispanic origin may be of any race.
[4] Marital status of mother is inferred.

Source: 1996, prel.—U.S. National Center for Health Statistics, Monthly Vital Statistics Report, Births and Deaths: United States, 1996, Vol 46, No. 1, Supplement 2, September 11, 1997; 1990 and 1980—U.S. National Center for Health Statistics, Vital Statistics of the United States, Vol I, Natality, annual.

Table A–8. States — Deaths and Death Rates

	Number (1,000)			Rate[1]			Infant deaths[2] Number			Rate[3] All races			White		Black	
	1996 prel.	1990	1980	1996 prel.	1990	1980	1995	1990	1980	1995	1990	1980	1995	1990	1995	1990
United States	2 322	2 148	1 990	8.8	8.6	8.8	29 583	38 351	45 526	7.6	9.2	12.6	6.3	7.7	15.1	18.0
Alabama	43	39	36	10.0	9.7	9.1	592	688	962	9.8	10.8	15.1	7.1	8.3	15.2	16.0
Alaska	3	2	2	4.3	4.0	4.3	79	125	117	7.7	10.5	12.3	6.1	8.5	S	S
Arizona	39	29	21	8.8	7.9	7.9	547	610	620	7.5	8.8	12.4	7.2	8.2	17.0	20.6
Arkansas	27	25	23	10.6	10.5	9.9	309	336	472	8.8	9.2	12.7	7.2	8.0	14.3	13.9
California	231	214	187	7.2	7.2	7.9	3 487	4 844	4 454	6.3	7.9	11.1	5.8	7.6	14.4	16.8
Colorado.................	26	22	19	6.8	6.6	6.6	352	472	501	6.5	8.8	10.1	6.0	8.4	16.8	19.4
Connecticut	30	28	27	9.0	8.4	8.8	317	398	433	7.2	7.9	11.2	6.5	6.6	12.6	17.6
Delaware	7	6	5	9.0	8.7	8.5	77	112	131	7.5	10.1	13.9	6.0	7.3	13.1	20.1
District of Columbia...........	7	7	7	12.1	12.0	11.1	146	245	234	16.2	20.7	25.0	S	12.1	19.6	24.6
Florida	154	134	105	10.7	10.4	10.7	1 420	1 918	1 921	7.5	9.6	14.6	6.0	7.6	13.0	16.8
Georgia	59	52	44	8.0	8.0	8.1	1 057	1 392	1 337	9.4	12.4	14.5	6.5	9.1	15.1	18.3
Hawaii	8	7	5	6.7	6.1	5.2	107	138	187	5.8	6.7	10.3	S	5.1	S	S
Idaho	9	7	7	7.3	7.4	7.2	110	143	216	6.1	8.7	10.7	5.8	8.7	S	S
Illinois	106	103	103	9.0	9.0	9.0	1 744	2 104	2 812	9.4	10.7	14.8	7.2	7.7	18.7	22.4
Indiana	55	50	47	9.3	8.9	8.6	692	831	1 050	8.4	9.6	11.9	7.3	8.9	17.5	17.4
Iowa......................	28	27	27	9.7	9.7	9.3	301	319	565	8.2	8.1	11.8	7.8	7.8	21.2	21.9
Kansas	24	22	22	9.3	9.0	9.3	262	329	424	7.0	8.4	10.4	6.2	7.7	17.6	17.7
Kentucky	37	35	34	9.6	9.5	9.2	400	461	766	7.6	8.5	12.9	7.4	8.0	10.7	14.3
Louisiana	40	38	36	9.3	8.9	8.5	644	799	1 178	9.8	11.1	14.3	6.2	7.3	15.3	16.7
Maine	11	11	11	8.9	9.0	9.6	90	108	152	6.5	6.2	9.2	6.3	6.2	S	S
Maryland	42	38	34	8.2	8.0	8.1	647	766	842	8.9	9.5	14.0	6.0	6.5	15.3	17.1
Massachusetts	55	53	55	9.1	8.8	9.6	421	650	763	5.2	7.0	10.5	4.7	6.7	9.0	11.9
Michigan	84	79	75	8.7	8.5	8.1	1 114	1 641	1 862	8.3	10.7	12.8	6.2	7.9	17.3	21.6
Minnesota	37	35	33	8.0	7.9	8.2	426	496	678	6.7	7.3	10.0	6.0	6.7	17.6	23.7
Mississippi	27	25	24	9.8	9.8	9.4	436	529	814	10.5	12.1	17.0	7.0	8.5	14.7	16.2
Missouri	54	50	50	10.1	9.8	10.1	541	748	980	7.4	9.4	12.4	6.4	7.8	13.8	18.2
Montana	8	7	7	8.7	8.6	8.5	78	105	176	7.0	9.0	12.4	7.0	8.6	S	S
Nebraska	16	15	14	9.4	9.4	9.2	173	202	314	7.4	8.3	11.5	7.3	7.2	S	18.9
Nevada	13	9	6	8.2	7.8	7.4	144	181	143	5.7	8.4	10.7	5.5	8.1	S	14.2
New Hampshire.............	9	8	8	8.1	7.7	8.3	81	125	136	5.5	7.1	9.9	5.5	7.2	S	S
New Jersey	72	70	69	9.0	9.1	9.4	761	1 102	1 215	6.6	9.0	12.5	6.3	6.8	13.3	18.4
New Mexico	13	11	9	7.3	7.0	7.0	166	246	301	6.2	9.0	11.5	6.1	9.3	S	S
New York	163	169	173	8.9	9.4	9.8	2 085	2 851	2 994	7.7	9.6	12.5	6.2	7.7	13.9	18.1
North Carolina	66	57	48	9.1	8.6	8.2	933	1 109	1 224	9.2	10.6	14.5	6.7	8.3	15.9	16.5
North Dakota	6	6	6	9.3	8.9	8.6	61	74	145	7.2	8.0	12.1	6.7	7.9	S	S
Ohio	105	99	98	9.4	9.1	9.1	1 346	1 640	2 160	8.7	9.8	12.8	7.3	8.2	17.5	19.5
Oklahoma	33	30	28	10.0	9.7	9.3	380	438	663	8.3	9.2	12.7	8.0	9.4	15.1	14.3
Oregon	29	25	22	9.0	8.8	8.3	262	354	525	6.1	8.3	12.2	5.9	8.1	S	S
Pennsylvania	130	122	124	10.7	10.3	10.4	1 185	1 643	2 101	7.8	9.6	13.2	6.2	7.8	17.6	20.5
Rhode Island	10	10	9	9.6	9.5	9.8	92	123	134	7.2	8.1	11.0	7.0	8.3	S	S
South Carolina...........	34	30	25	9.3	8.5	8.1	488	683	812	9.6	11.7	15.6	6.7	8.3	14.6	17.3
South Dakota	7	6	7	9.3	9.1	9.5	99	111	145	9.5	10.1	10.9	7.9	8.6	S	S
Tennessee	51	46	41	9.7	9.5	8.9	677	771	935	9.3	10.3	13.5	6.8	8.0	17.9	17.9
Texas	138	125	108	7.2	7.4	7.6	2 114	2 552	3 326	6.5	8.1	12.2	5.9	7.1	11.7	14.7
Utah	11	9	8	5.5	5.3	5.6	213	271	436	5.4	7.5	10.4	5.3	7.4	S	S
Vermont	5	5	5	8.3	8.2	9.0	41	53	84	6.0	6.4	10.7	6.2	6.5	S	S
Virginia	53	48	43	7.9	7.8	8.0	723	1 013	1 067	7.8	10.2	13.6	5.7	7.5	15.3	19.5
Washington	42	37	32	7.6	7.6	7.7	453	621	798	5.9	7.8	11.8	5.6	7.6	16.2	20.6
West Virginia	20	19	19	11.2	10.8	9.9	168	223	348	7.9	9.9	11.8	7.6	9.6	S	S
Wisconsin	45	43	41	8.7	8.7	8.7	494	598	770	7.3	8.2	10.3	6.3	7.2	18.6	19.0
Wyoming...................	4	3	3	7.5	7.1	6.9	48	60	103	7.7	8.6	9.8	6.8	8.8	S	S

S Figure suppressed; does not meet publication standards.

[1]Per 1,000 resident population estimated as of July 1 for 1996 and enumerated as of April 1 for 1990 and 1980.
[2]Deaths of infants under 1 year old, exclusive of fetal deaths.
[3]Infant deaths per 1,000 live births.

Source: Deaths 1996, prel.—U.S. National Center for Health Statistics, Monthly Vital Statistics Report, Births and Deaths: United States, 1996, Vol. 46, No. 1, Supplement 2, September 11, 1997; 1990 and 1980 deaths—U.S. National Center for Health Statistics, Vital Statistics of the United States, Vol II, Mortality, annual; Infant deaths and rates, 1995—U.S. National Center for Health Statistics, Monthly Vital Statistics Report, Report of Final Mortality Statistics, 1995, Vol. 45, No. 11, Supplement 2, June 12, 1997; Infant deaths and rates, 1990 and 1980—U.S. National Center for Health Statistics, Vital Statistics of the United States, Vol II, Mortality, annual.

Table A–9. States — Death Rates by Cause: 1994

Geographic area	HIV[1]	Malignant neoplasms	Diabetes mellitus	Alzheimer's disease	Diseases of the heart	Cerebro-vascular diseases	Pheumonia and influenza	Chronic obstructive pulmonary diseases[2]	Chronic liver diseases and cirrhosis	Accidents and adverse effects — Total	Accidents and adverse effects — Motor vehicle	Suicide	Homicide and legal intervention	Injury by firearms
United States	**16.2**	**205.2**	**21.8**	**7.1**	**281.3**	**58.9**	**31.3**	**39.0**	**9.8**	**35.1**	**16.3**	**12.0**	**9.6**	**14.8**
Alabama	[3]9.4	[3]223.0	[3]25.3	[3]8.1	[3]312.2	[3]62.0	[3]33.8	[3]42.7	9.6	[3]51.3	[3]26.8	[3]12.6	[3]14.2	[3]22.4
Alaska	[3]3.3	[3]93.7	[3]7.9	S	[3]88.4	[3]20.3	[3]8.2	[3]16.5	[3]6.8	[3]53.8	[3]13.9	[3]20.0	[3]5.9	[3]22.6
Arizona	10.6	195.5	18.8	8.3	245.0	52.3	29.6	46.0	13.7	44.9	21.6	18.8	11.2	22.1
Arkansas	6.2	241.1	21.9	8.2	340.6	88.9	41.2	47.9	8.9	46.5	26.7	14.8	13.1	20.5
California	21.5	163.7	15.7	4.9	218.9	50.2	32.6	35.2	11.6	30.1	14.3	11.8	12.5	16.5
Colorado	10.5	148.5	12.6	7.4	173.2	42.2	24.1	41.5	9.0	37.2	17.7	16.8	5.7	14.0
Connecticut	17.2	217.6	19.1	7.9	297.4	55.9	35.7	36.1	9.3	30.8	10.0	9.9	6.4	9.1
Delaware	19.4	230.2	23.5	6.8	281.7	49.3	28.3	37.9	8.2	39.9	17.3	11.3	4.2	9.3
District of Columbia	116.8	274.0	34.2	7.2	306.9	66.5	34.4	30.0	18.4	28.8	11.6	5.1	61.4	49.6
Florida	29.8	263.3	24.1	9.2	348.7	68.8	27.2	51.4	13.6	36.5	19.4	14.9	9.5	15.9
Georgia	20.4	175.0	15.4	7.2	241.4	55.2	29.2	34.7	8.6	40.0	21.1	11.8	11.6	18.0
Hawaii	[3]11.0	[3]149.8	[3]13.2	[3]4.1	[3]192.9	[3]49.6	[3]23.7	[3]17.8	[3]7.5	[3]28.5	[3]10.8	[3]11.7	[3]3.8	[3]6.7
Idaho	2.7	163.1	17.8	7.6	214.0	56.6	30.4	43.7	6.4	46.1	22.5	17.7	3.4	14.8
Illinois	12.0	213.9	22.0	8.0	301.1	62.0	33.1	36.6	10.4	34.4	15.0	9.1	12.4	13.6
Indiana	5.5	210.4	24.3	9.2	302.2	69.9	30.9	42.2	7.7	34.1	17.2	12.5	7.9	14.0
Iowa	2.9	233.6	21.9	11.6	326.8	74.5	43.2	46.5	5.8	39.9	18.5	11.4	2.3	8.0
Kansas	4.2	210.1	19.9	8.5	291.0	68.9	37.1	43.3	7.2	37.6	18.7	11.4	7.3	13.3
Kentucky	4.9	232.5	24.6	9.0	320.0	64.9	39.3	49.4	8.2	44.3	20.7	13.5	6.1	15.8
Louisiana	14.9	207.6	33.5	7.7	277.4	55.1	25.1	33.9	8.5	41.9	20.2	12.8	21.1	28.4
Maine	5.9	240.0	25.6	11.4	288.4	61.4	28.5	50.9	9.7	33.5	16.6	13.5	2.7	9.6
Maryland	24.2	201.2	26.4	6.4	240.5	50.3	23.7	33.0	8.3	27.6	13.2	10.5	13.0	15.5
Massachusetts	15.6	230.0	22.4	10.6	280.1	55.3	43.6	39.0	9.8	21.8	8.0	8.5	3.9	5.1
Michigan	8.0	205.0	23.5	5.7	297.5	60.0	30.3	36.4	10.9	31.5	15.6	10.9	10.9	14.7
Minnesota	5.6	187.7	18.7	9.0	225.7	63.5	31.9	34.3	6.7	35.6	15.8	10.8	3.3	7.8
Mississippi	10.1	210.5	18.7	6.2	361.8	66.7	34.8	35.6	8.8	57.2	31.8	11.8	17.2	24.2
Missouri	8.6	227.2	22.6	7.7	345.7	72.5	42.6	46.8	8.3	43.3	20.9	13.8	11.6	18.8
Montana	3.0	204.0	25.1	10.9	224.5	67.1	34.2	56.9	8.2	46.1	22.7	18.5	4.1	17.6
Nebraska	5.1	202.0	17.4	8.1	310.1	70.2	38.0	46.3	6.0	35.4	16.9	11.6	3.3	9.5
Nevada	15.3	203.6	13.1	5.5	236.6	44.3	21.9	53.2	14.3	36.2	19.4	23.4	11.3	25.7
New Hampshire	3.8	199.6	22.5	11.3	248.3	51.5	22.7	42.5	8.0	23.8	10.4	12.1	1.9	8.3
New Jersey	[3]29.5	[3]232.5	[3]27.6	[3]5.6	[3]299.4	[3]51.9	[3]29.0	[3]33.5	[3]11.1	[3]28.8	[3]9.8	[3]7.3	[3]5.4	[3]5.5
New Mexico	8.3	157.2	25.2	5.6	185.2	46.8	25.0	39.5	14.0	51.2	25.5	18.3	11.1	19.6
New York	44.5	215.6	20.1	3.2	347.9	45.3	34.5	33.7	10.1	27.4	10.1	8.2	11.3	11.6
North Carolina	13.8	206.4	22.6	8.1	272.6	73.3	31.3	36.3	9.9	41.3	20.7	12.7	11.6	18.1
North Dakota	S	212.9	27.0	6.6	302.7	79.8	31.8	36.5	7.7	36.4	13.5	12.5	S	8.9
Ohio	7.1	224.7	28.3	8.2	313.0	57.8	29.8	43.4	7.6	29.5	12.6	9.9	5.1	10.6
Oklahoma	7.9	216.9	19.5	6.5	342.5	65.9	42.8	47.8	8.8	45.0	22.6	13.8	8.6	16.7
Oregon	9.8	211.9	20.6	11.9	240.8	77.3	29.1	46.3	8.4	40.9	15.8	16.6	5.8	14.5
Pennsylvania	10.7	251.9	27.3	6.7	365.8	70.1	35.2	43.5	9.6	36.1	12.9	11.0	6.3	10.9
Rhode Island	11.5	243.7	24.3	10.0	319.0	59.6	30.0	38.1	10.8	22.2	7.5	8.2	4.9	5.6
South Carolina	14.3	202.3	25.4	6.8	270.8	69.4	23.1	35.8	9.6	44.2	22.6	12.8	10.8	17.8
South Dakota	S	204.1	24.0	8.3	316.8	68.8	39.4	41.6	11.9	41.9	22.0	13.5	3.3	11.8
Tennessee	8.8	219.8	20.5	8.2	312.9	76.9	39.3	42.0	9.6	46.4	24.6	12.8	10.6	18.9
Texas	14.9	171.0	23.8	6.6	226.5	50.3	21.3	34.0	10.2	34.5	18.1	12.7	11.7	18.5
Utah	4.2	109.6	17.8	6.4	148.0	37.6	24.6	23.7	4.3	33.9	19.0	15.3	3.3	11.7
Vermont	6.2	199.4	23.4	9.8	262.3	60.0	30.0	46.0	8.1	29.8	12.4	10.0	–	7.6
Virginia	11.1	192.7	17.2	7.2	243.3	55.8	26.8	33.3	6.8	33.5	14.0	12.5	8.9	15.8
Washington	11.3	181.6	18.3	9.2	209.7	58.2	27.3	41.6	9.0	33.2	13.4	14.2	6.0	12.7
West Virginia	3.3	259.8	34.1	8.2	377.2	67.2	37.3	58.6	9.6	41.2	20.6	14.2	6.3	16.2
Wisconsin	4.0	205.0	21.3	8.9	282.8	69.2	34.4	38.1	6.7	34.1	14.7	11.6	4.4	10.3
Wyoming	S	163.2	16.4	7.1	202.7	46.0	25.0	56.7	10.5	47.3	25.0	22.5	5.5	20.8

– Represents zero.
S Figure suppressed; does not meet publication standards.

[1] Human immunodeficiency virus.
[2] Includes allied conditions.
[3] Excludes some amended records for selected external causes.

Note: Deaths by cause per 100,000 resident population estimated as of July 1.

Source: U.S. National Center for Health Statistics, Monthly Vital Statistics Report, Advance Report of Final Mortality Statistics, 1994, Vol. 45, No. 3, Supplement, September 30, 1996.

Table A–10. States —Community Hospitals

Geographic area	Number 1995	Number 1990	Beds (1,000) 1995	Beds (1,000) 1990	Patients admitted (1,000) 1995	Patients admitted (1,000) 1990	Average daily census[1] (1,000) 1995	Average daily census[1] (1,000) 1990	Personnel[2] (1,000) 1995	Personnel[2] (1,000) 1990	Outpatient visits (milions) 1995	Outpatient visits (milions) 1990	Average cost per day[3] (dollars) 1995	Average cost per day[3] (dollars) 1990	Average cost per stay[3] (dollars) 1995	Average cost per stay[3] (dollars) 1990
United States	5 194	5 384	872.7	928.1	30 945	31 181	548.3	619.3	3 714	3 420	414.3	301.3	968	687	6 216	4 947
Alabama	115	120	18.3	18.6	642	597	10.8	11.7	67	59	6.4	4.6	819	588	5 028	4 175
Alaska	17	16	1.3	1.2	40	37	.7	.6	5	4	.8	.4	1 341	1 070	8 282	6 249
Arizona	61	61	9.9	9.9	427	396	5.6	6.2	43	36	4.0	2.7	1 191	867	5 613	4 877
Arkansas	85	86	10.1	10.9	342	347	6.0	6.7	38	33	3.6	2.2	704	534	4 459	3 730
California	424	445	75.0	80.5	3 029	3 063	45.1	51.3	323	311	39.5	29.7	1 315	939	7 111	5 709
Colorado	69	69	9.3	10.4	340	335	5.4	6.6	42	39	5.5	3.5	1 069	725	6 289	5 209
Connecticut	34	35	7.5	9.6	338	355	5.5	7.4	40	44	5.7	4.2	1 264	825	7 358	6 238
Delaware	8	8	1.9	2.0	81	84	1.5	1.5	10	10	1.4	1.0	1 058	771	7 298	5 112
District of Columbia	12	11	3.8	4.5	154	158	2.7	3.4	19	20	1.2	1.3	1 346	995	8 632	7 876
Florida	212	224	49.7	50.7	1 772	1 639	29.4	31.3	199	172	16.9	11.6	1 004	769	6 040	5 312
Georgia	160	163	26.1	25.7	859	888	15.8	16.8	101	89	9.6	6.8	836	630	5 618	4 303
Hawaii	21	18	3.0	2.9	97	96	2.4	2.5	14	12	2.1	1.8	956	638	8 445	6 048
Idaho	41	43	3.4	3.2	104	97	2.1	1.8	12	10	1.7	1.1	719	547	4 686	3 701
Illinois	207	210	42.0	45.8	1 452	1 499	25.1	30.3	183	174	20.6	16.4	1 050	717	6 584	5 253
Indiana	115	113	19.4	21.8	699	727	11.3	13.2	89	84	11.8	8.7	963	667	5 610	4 390
Iowa	116	124	12.6	14.3	361	385	7.1	8.8	47	44	6.2	4.1	702	495	5 049	4 135
Kansas	132	138	10.8	11.8	291	305	5.7	6.6	38	35	4.0	2.9	732	532	5 308	4 161
Kentucky	104	107	15.1	15.9	534	532	9.0	9.8	57	50	6.1	4.4	795	563	4 838	3 762
Louisiana	130	140	19.1	19.1	622	607	10.7	11.0	77	63	8.0	5.4	902	701	5 612	4 575
Maine	39	39	4.0	4.5	142	146	2.6	3.2	18	18	2.5	1.9	916	574	6 083	4 604
Maryland	50	52	12.6	13.6	574	562	8.8	10.6	62	59	4.9	4.6	1 064	678	5 899	4 640
Massachusetts	96	101	18.9	21.7	751	811	13.0	16.2	106	101	13.5	9.9	1 157	788	7 099	5 709
Michigan	167	176	29.6	33.9	1 120	1 069	19.3	22.2	147	135	19.2	15.3	994	716	6 218	5 358
Minnesota	142	152	17.4	19.4	496	530	11.3	13.0	58	56	5.7	4.4	736	536	6 241	4 782
Mississippi	97	103	12.6	12.9	388	396	7.7	7.7	42	34	3.2	2.2	584	439	4 265	3 116
Missouri	126	135	21.9	24.3	714	737	12.6	15.0	95	89	9.9	6.5	967	679	6 228	5 022
Montana	55	55	4.2	4.6	96	105	2.7	2.8	13	11	1.3	.8	493	405	3 973	4 675
Nebraska	91	90	7.9	8.5	183	188	4.5	5.0	29	24	2.5	1.6	661	490	5 880	5 184
Nevada	20	21	3.6	3.4	149	116	2.2	2.0	14	11	1.4	1.1	1 072	854	6 014	5 511
New Hampshire	29	27	3.4	3.5	110	125	2.1	2.3	15	14	1.8	1.6	915	671	6 188	4 544
New Jersey	92	95	29.9	28.9	1 068	1 132	21.4	23.1	121	108	12.8	9.7	962	613	7 007	4 573
New Mexico	36	37	3.7	4.2	156	153	2.1	2.4	19	14	2.5	1.8	1 073	734	5 358	4 172
New York	230	235	73.9	74.7	2 398	2 322	59.1	64.0	325	310	38.9	29.3	909	641	8 077	6 397
North Carolina	119	120	22.7	22.0	833	784	15.5	16.0	102	88	8.8	6.1	832	595	5 631	4 408
North Dakota	43	50	4.2	4.4	89	96	2.7	2.8	13	11	1.3	.5	521	427	5 589	4 468
Ohio	180	190	37.8	43.1	1 375	1 512	22.2	27.9	178	172	22.0	17.1	1 061	720	6 141	4 801
Oklahoma	110	111	11.5	12.4	368	382	6.1	7.2	47	42	3.8	2.3	861	632	5 188	4 302
Oregon	64	70	7.2	8.1	296	302	3.8	4.6	34	33	5.8	3.4	1 141	800	5 325	4 432
Pennsylvania	225	238	48.5	52.6	1 810	1 796	33.8	38.2	216	211	26.9	21.2	963	662	6 482	5 120
Rhode Island	11	12	2.7	3.2	119	127	1.8	2.5	15	15	1.7	1.2	1 092	663	6 202	4 839
South Carolina	66	69	11.3	11.3	410	413	7.3	8.0	48	41	4.7	3.4	923	590	5 935	4 168
South Dakota	50	53	4.6	4.2	94	94	3.0	2.6	12	11	1.0	.7	476	391	5 494	3 905
Tennessee	126	134	20.9	23.6	740	798	12.5	15.1	83	80	7.4	5.2	871	633	5 355	4 340
Texas	416	428	57.2	59.2	2 029	1 986	31.2	34.0	239	203	22.7	13.6	1 063	752	5 879	4 663
Utah	42	42	4.2	4.4	171	175	2.2	2.6	21	18	3.2	2.4	1 213	832	5 676	4 409
Vermont	14	15	1.8	1.7	55	58	1.3	1.2	8	6	1.0	.7	714	598	5 883	4 343
Virginia	96	97	18.6	20.0	699	706	11.5	13.5	74	71	7.2	5.8	901	635	5 423	4 408
Washington	88	91	10.8	12.0	467	492	6.1	7.5	56	49	8.4	4.9	1 318	817	6 180	4 519
West Virginia	59	59	8.1	8.4	271	277	4.9	5.3	31	28	4.0	2.8	763	565	4 974	3 918
Wisconsin	127	129	17.0	18.6	550	597	10.3	12.1	65	62	8.2	5.9	794	554	5 679	4 083
Wyoming	25	27	2.0	2.2	43	48	1.1	1.2	6	5	.7	.5	545	462	4 817	3 990

[1]Inpatients receiving treatment each day; excludes newborn.
[2]Includes full-time equivalents of part-time personnel.
[3]Total cost per patient based on total hospital expenses (payroll, employee benefits, professional fees, supplies, etc.). Data have been adjusted for outpatient visits.

Note: Covers non-Federal short-term general or special hospitals (excluding psychiatric or tuberculosis hospitals and hospital units of institutions). Data subject to copyright; see below for source citation.

Source: Healthcare InfoSource, Inc., a subsidiary of the American Hospital Association, Chicago, IL, Hospital Statistics, 1996-97 edition and prior editions (copyright).

Table A–11. States — Physicians, Nurses, Health Insurance, and AIDS

Geographic area	Physicians[1] 1995 Total	Rate[2]	1992 Total	Rate[2]	1990 Total	Rate[2]	Nurses[3] (Dec. 31) 1995 Total	Rate[2]	1992 Total	Rate[2]	Persons not covered by health insurance 1995 Number (1,000)	Percent	1990 Number (1,000)	Percent	AIDS[4] cases reported Total, 1981-96	Percent
United States	617 362	236	568 132	224	532 638	215	2 116 000	809	1 907 000	752	40 582	15.4	34 719	13.9	562 166	100.0
Alabama	7 814	184	6 913	168	6 464	160	32 300	763	28 900	703	595	13.5	710	17.4	4 266	.8
Alaska	890	153	748	133	734	139	5 900	1 011	3 600	640	79	12.5	77	15.4	363	.1
Arizona	8 315	198	7 461	196	6 961	191	31 900	760	28 300	742	885	20.4	547	15.5	5 038	.9
Arkansas	4 246	171	3 855	161	3 595	153	17 100	690	15 600	653	454	17.9	421	17.4	2 158	.4
California	75 496	241	73 713	241	70 062	237	180 300	574	175 800	574	6 601	20.6	5 683	19.1	98 157	17.5
Colorado	8 425	227	7 431	217	6 894	211	30 800	830	27 800	812	564	14.8	495	14.7	5 755	1.0
Connecticut	10 919	334	10 383	318	9 820	300	33 700	1 032	31 800	973	289	8.8	226	6.9	8 517	1.5
Delaware	1 546	217	1 420	207	1 329	200	7 600	1 067	6 300	920	112	15.7	96	13.9	1 777	.3
District of Columbia	3 623	662	3 908	677	3 674	616	9 300	1 699	9 000	1 559	96	17.3	109	19.2	9 414	1.7
Florida	31 053	220	28 379	212	26 123	202	115 200	818	97 000	723	2 628	18.3	2 376	18.0	58 911	10.5
Georgia	13 984	196	12 000	179	11 144	173	52 300	733	44 700	668	1 301	17.9	971	15.3	17 004	3.0
Hawaii	2 812	248	2 740	250	2 491	236	8 700	766	8 300	756	106	8.9	81	7.3	1 993	.4
Idaho	1 583	137	1 366	129	1 259	125	6 900	595	6 300	594	161	14.0	159	15.2	366	.1
Illinois	28 765	244	26 396	228	24 680	216	102 200	866	94 000	812	1 294	11.0	1 272	10.9	18 571	3.3
Indiana	10 426	180	9 318	165	8 764	158	45 500	784	40 900	724	716	12.6	587	10.7	4 424	.8
Iowa	4 703	166	4 393	156	4 280	154	28 200	992	26 400	940	327	11.3	225	8.1	983	.2
Kansas	4 961	195	4 549	183	4 360	177	20 700	814	19 900	799	316	12.4	272	10.8	1 846	.3
Kentucky	7 416	193	6 644	178	6 202	169	29 000	756	26 200	704	567	14.6	480	13.2	2 224	.4
Louisiana	9 604	222	8 526	201	8 173	195	31 300	724	24 700	582	885	20.5	797	19.7	9 126	1.6
Maine	2 449	198	2 325	189	2 155	176	13 100	1 059	10 800	878	166	13.5	139	11.2	755	.1
Maryland	17 463	349	16 695	343	15 484	326	42 700	854	39 100	803	783	15.3	601	12.7	15 298	2.7
Massachusetts	23 471	387	21 129	353	19 910	332	72 500	1 195	66 200	1 106	671	11.1	530	9.1	12 067	2.1
Michigan	20 061	210	18 265	194	17 129	184	78 300	820	68 200	724	938	9.7	865	9.4	8 386	1.5
Minnesota	11 007	239	10 379	232	9 574	218	44 000	955	41 600	930	370	8.0	389	8.9	2 999	.5
Mississippi	3 703	138	3 539	136	3 455	135	19 000	709	14 000	539	531	19.7	531	19.9	2 861	.5
Missouri	11 594	218	10 722	207	10 100	198	49 900	940	40 800	788	756	14.6	665	12.7	7 259	1.3
Montana	1 569	181	1 359	166	1 263	159	6 500	751	6 000	733	111	12.7	115	14.0	227	Z
Nebraska	3 236	199	2 964	186	2 741	175	15 300	940	13 400	842	149	9.0	138	8.5	789	.1
Nevada	2 391	157	1 928	146	1 746	144	9 300	611	7 700	582	292	18.7	201	16.5	3 068	.5
New Hampshire	2 451	214	2 324	209	2 199	198	11 400	993	10 600	952	114	10.0	107	9.9	712	.1
New Jersey	21 895	276	20 277	260	18 971	246	67 400	850	67 700	868	1 121	14.2	773	10.0	32 926	5.9
New Mexico	3 320	199	2 987	191	2 768	184	11 400	683	10 600	677	463	25.6	339	22.2	1 442	.3
New York	65 299	361	60 171	333	56 395	314	165 700	915	161 600	895	2 779	15.2	2 176	12.1	106 897	19.0
North Carolina	15 159	214	13 332	198	12 262	187	58 200	820	50 200	746	996	14.3	883	13.8	7 313	1.3
North Dakota	1 291	204	1 157	185	1 102	175	6 900	1 090	6 000	957	53	8.3	40	6.3	78	Z
Ohio	24 402	219	22 709	207	21 379	197	99 800	896	92 000	837	1 336	11.9	1 123	10.3	8 743	1.6
Oklahoma	5 203	160	4 865	153	4 697	151	19 200	591	17 100	538	615	19.2	574	18.6	2 731	.5
Oregon	6 648	212	6 234	210	5 778	202	25 300	806	23 700	797	403	12.5	360	12.4	3 862	.7
Pennsylvania	32 919	273	30 090	251	28 293	238	122 800	1 018	116 300	971	1 195	9.9	1 218	10.1	17 423	3.1
Rhode Island	2 942	298	2 680	269	2 515	252	11 200	1 136	9 500	954	124	12.9	105	11.1	1 590	.3
South Carolina	6 904	190	6 091	172	5 541	161	25 700	707	20 800	588	546	14.6	550	16.2	6 273	1.1
South Dakota	1 206	166	1 062	151	992	144	7 800	1 077	7 000	996	67	9.4	81	11.6	118	Z
Tennessee	11 846	226	10 396	208	9 619	198	45 500	869	37 000	740	814	14.8	673	13.7	5 536	1.0
Texas	35 100	189	31 374	179	29 451	174	120 400	647	95 200	542	4 615	24.5	3 569	21.1	39 871	7.1
Utah	3 766	194	3 384	187	3 145	182	12 600	647	10 200	565	235	11.7	156	9.0	1 385	.2
Vermont	1 577	270	1 503	263	1 432	254	5 400	924	5 200	910	79	13.2	54	9.5	298	.1
Virginia	14 676	227	13 366	215	12 615	209	52 700	816	45 400	731	862	13.5	996	15.7	9 104	1.6
Washington	12 032	224	11 054	217	10 006	207	42 900	798	40 000	786	676	12.4	557	11.4	7 591	1.4
West Virginia	3 582	196	3 240	179	3 086	172	14 500	793	12 800	709	276	15.3	249	13.8	745	.1
Wisconsin	10 903	213	9 733	195	9 172	187	45 200	882	41 800	837	391	7.3	321	6.7	2 786	.5
Wyoming	716	150	644	140	654	145	3 800	798	3 200	695	77	15.9	58	12.5	140	Z

Z Less than 500.

[1]As of December 31 for 1995; as of January 1 for 1992 and 1990. Includes physicians not classified according to activity status. Excludes doctors of osteopathy, federally employed persons, and physicians with addresses unknown. Data subject to copyright; see below for source citation.
[2]Per 100,000 civilian population estimated as of July 1 for years shown by the U.S. Bureau of the Census.
[3]Active, registered.
[4]Acquired immune deficiency syndrome.

Source: Physicians–American Medical Association, Chicago, IL, Physician Characteristics and Distribution in the U.S., annual (copyright); Nurses–U.S. Dept. of Health and Human Services, Health Resources and Services Administration, unpublished data; Persons not covered by Health Insurance–U.S. Bureau of the Census, Health insurance coverage: 1995, Table 2, published 26 September 1996, (related Internet site <http://www.census.gov/hhes/hltins/cover95/c95tab2.html>); AIDS–U.S. Centers for Disease Control and Prevention, Atlanta, GA, unpublished data.

Table A–12. States — **Public School Fall Enrollment**

Geographic area	Total (1,000)				Kindergarten through grade 8[1] (1,000)				Grades 9 through 12 (1,000)				Enrollment rate[2]			
	1994, prel.	1993	1990	1980	1994, prel.	1993	1990	1980	1994, prel.	1993	1990	1980	1994, prel.	1993	1990	1980
United States	**44 109**	**43 465**	**41 217**	**40 877**	**31 894**	**31 504**	**29 878**	**27 647**	**12 214**	**11 961**	**11 338**	**13 231**	**91.3**	**91.7**	**91.3**	**86.2**
Alabama	736	734	722	759	535	536	527	528	201	199	195	231	94.7	95.3	93.3	87.6
Alaska	127	126	114	87	94	94	85	60	33	32	29	26	93.6	95.4	97.4	94.0
Arizona	737	709	640	514	543	526	479	357	195	183	161	157	92.8	93.1	93.3	88.9
Arkansas	448	444	436	448	319	318	314	310	128	127	123	138	95.6	95.7	95.9	90.3
California	5 407	5 327	4 950	4 076	3 955	3 903	3 615	2 730	1 452	1 424	1 336	1 347	92.5	92.9	92.8	87.1
Colorado	641	625	574	546	470	460	420	374	171	165	154	172	91.5	92.3	94.6	92.2
Connecticut	507	496	469	531	376	369	347	364	131	128	122	168	91.0	91.1	90.2	83.3
Delaware	107	106	100	99	77	77	73	62	30	29	27	37	86.3	86.5	87.4	79.5
District of Columbia	80	81	81	100	62	61	61	71	18	19	19	29	106.1	107.6	100.9	91.8
Florida	2 109	2 041	1 862	1 510	1 567	1 515	1 370	1 042	542	526	492	468	91.7	91.5	92.6	84.4
Georgia	1 271	1 235	1 152	1 069	935	910	849	742	336	325	303	327	94.6	94.4	93.6	86.8
Hawaii	184	180	172	165	134	132	123	110	50	49	49	55	87.9	88.0	87.6	83.4
Idaho	240	237	221	203	169	167	160	144	72	70	61	59	95.5	96.6	96.9	95.4
Illinois	1 916	1 893	1 821	1 983	1 368	1 356	1 310	1 335	548	537	512	649	88.4	88.3	86.9	82.6
Indiana	969	966	955	1 056	679	679	676	708	290	287	279	347	90.9	91.0	90.4	88.0
Iowa	500	499	484	534	345	348	345	351	155	151	139	183	92.3	93.0	92.1	88.4
Kansas	461	458	437	415	329	330	320	283	132	128	117	133	91.0	92.1	92.6	88.7
Kentucky	658	655	636	670	467	467	459	464	191	188	177	206	92.8	92.9	90.5	83.7
Louisiana	798	801	785	778	584	587	586	544	214	213	199	234	88.9	89.6	88.2	80.2
Maine	213	217	215	222	156	157	155	153	57	60	60	70	93.2	96.0	96.5	91.6
Maryland	791	773	715	751	581	569	527	493	210	203	188	258	89.5	89.4	89.1	83.9
Massachusetts	894	878	834	1 022	659	646	604	676	235	232	230	346	89.3	89.7	88.8	88.6
Michigan	1 615	1 599	1 584	1 797	1 170	1 160	1 145	1 227	445	439	440	570	88.5	89.0	90.3	86.9
Minnesota	822	810	756	754	581	577	546	482	240	233	211	272	89.9	90.7	91.2	87.2
Mississippi	506	506	502	477	367	369	372	330	139	137	131	147	92.2	92.8	91.3	79.6
Missouri	879	866	817	845	628	622	588	567	250	244	228	277	87.6	89.0	86.5	83.8
Montana	164	163	153	155	117	117	111	106	48	46	42	50	92.0	93.7	93.8	92.9
Nebraska	287	285	274	280	203	203	198	189	84	82	76	91	88.1	88.8	88.7	86.6
Nevada	251	236	201	149	185	175	150	101	65	61	51	49	96.0	95.9	98.7	93.4
New Hampshire	189	185	173	167	139	136	126	112	50	49	46	55	89.5	90.0	89.1	85.3
New Jersey	1 174	1 151	1 090	1 246	862	844	784	820	312	308	306	426	86.9	86.8	86.1	81.5
New Mexico	327	322	302	271	229	226	208	186	98	96	94	85	91.5	92.9	94.3	89.5
New York	2 766	2 734	2 598	2 872	1 949	1 921	1 828	1 838	817	813	770	1 033	88.4	88.4	86.6	80.8
North Carolina	1 157	1 133	1 087	1 129	847	828	783	786	309	305	304	343	92.8	93.3	94.8	90.1
North Dakota	119	119	118	117	83	84	85	77	36	35	33	40	92.6	93.1	92.8	85.9
Ohio	1 814	1 807	1 771	1 957	1 295	1 290	1 258	1 312	519	517	514	645	87.6	88.2	88.0	84.8
Oklahoma	610	604	579	578	443	441	425	399	167	163	154	179	94.9	95.4	95.1	92.9
Oregon	522	517	472	465	372	368	340	319	150	148	132	145	91.0	91.6	90.7	88.5
Pennsylvania	1 766	1 744	1 668	1 909	1 244	1 233	1 172	1 231	522	511	496	678	84.1	84.4	83.6	80.4
Rhode Island	147	146	139	149	108	107	102	98	40	39	37	51	87.4	88.3	87.3	80.1
South Carolina	649	644	622	619	469	467	452	426	180	177	170	193	95.6	95.8	94.0	88.1
South Dakota	143	143	129	129	102	102	95	86	42	41	34	42	93.0	94.0	89.7	87.4
Tennessee	881	867	825	854	641	630	598	602	241	237	226	252	94.7	95.1	93.5	87.8
Texas	3 677	3 608	3 383	2 900	2 721	2 681	2 511	2 049	957	927	872	851	98.3	98.6	98.4	92.4
Utah	475	471	447	344	328	330	325	250	146	141	122	93	96.8	97.8	97.7	98.2
Vermont	105	103	96	96	76	75	71	66	29	28	25	29	97.2	96.9	93.9	87.9
Virginia	1 061	1 045	999	1 010	774	767	728	703	286	278	270	307	93.6	93.8	94.2	90.7
Washington	938	916	840	758	673	660	613	515	265	256	227	242	92.6	92.5	94.0	91.7
West Virginia	311	314	322	384	213	216	224	270	98	99	98	113	96.7	97.3	95.7	92.6
Wisconsin	861	844	798	830	601	596	566	528	259	248	232	303	86.4	86.0	86.0	82.1
Wyoming	100	101	98	98	70	71	71	70	30	29	27	28	96.2	98.0	97.3	97.3

[1]Data include a small number of pre-kindergarten students.
[2]Percent of persons 5-17 years old. Based on resident population enumerated as of April 1 for 1980 and 1990 and resident population estimated as of July 1 for other years. Data not adjusted for revisions based on the 1980 Census of Population.

Source: U.S. National Center for Education Statistics, Digest of Education Statistics, annual.

Table A–13. States — Public Elementary and Secondary Schools

Geographic area	Revenues (mil dol) 1993-1994 Total[1]	By source Federal	By source State	By source Local	Revenues 1990-1991	Expenditures 1993-1994 (mil dol) Total[2]	Current[3] Total[2]	Current[3] Instruction	Current[3] Student services	Expenditures 1990-1991 (mil dol)	Per capita[4] (dollars) 1993-1994	Per capita[4] (dollars) 1990-1991	Teachers[5], 1994-1995 Number[6] (1,000) Elementary	Number[6] (1,000) Secondary	Average salary ($1,000) Elementary	Average salary ($1,000) Secondary
United States	**260 142**	**18 336**	**117 462**	**117 424**	**223 341**	**265 285**	**231 522**	**141 599**	**79 407**	**229 430**	**1 029**	**922**	**1 535.2**	**1 011.7**	**36.3**	**37.6**
Alabama	3 121	346	1 851	667	2 705	3 140	2 810	1 757	830	2 743	751	679	23.8	19.6	31.1	31.1
Alaska	1 159	138	777	218	1 021	1 136	1 003	517	454	975	1 901	1 773	4.6	2.5	48.0	48.0
Arizona	3 550	332	1 474	1 662	3 004	3 820	2 911	1 680	1 041	3 185	966	869	29.8	8.9	32.2	32.2
Arkansas	2 015	177	1 164	577	1 645	1 991	1 783	1 117	545	1 678	820	714	13.0	13.6	28.1	29.7
California	29 050	2 572	16 325	9 824	25 267	28 681	25 141	15 028	9 061	25 821	920	868	162.8	58.9	40.6	42.7
Colorado	3 369	186	1 467	1 600	2 893	3 648	2 955	1 815	1 028	3 062	1 023	929	17.7	17.2	34.2	35.0
Connecticut	4 103	163	1 654	2 176	3 801	4 224	3 944	2 501	1 253	3 741	1 290	1 138	25.4	10.1	49.6	51.6
Delaware	684	54	441	179	576	725	644	399	218	598	1 037	898	3.2	3.2	38.6	39.6
District of Columbia	736	79	X	653	674	748	713	351	333	704	1 292	1 159	3.6	2.3	44.2	45.0
Florida	11 927	921	5 945	4 610	10 417	12 725	10 332	5 971	3 856	11 338	928	876	65.6	53.7	32.6	32.6
Georgia	6 631	518	3 361	2 618	5 418	6 686	5 644	3 474	1 823	5 595	968	864	56.6	21.3	32.6	32.6
Hawaii	1 128	84	1 014	9	945	1 174	998	615	323	961	1 012	867	6.0	4.7	38.5	38.5
Idaho	955	81	577	279	796	978	859	543	274	809	887	804	6.5	6.1	29.7	29.9
Illinois	11 323	744	3 196	7 116	9 314	11 117	10 077	6 065	3 670	9 879	953	864	78.8	33.8	37.7	43.5
Indiana	5 919	300	3 097	2 337	5 305	6 011	5 065	3 121	1 722	5 124	1 053	924	29.6	25.6	36.8	36.8
Iowa	2 783	147	1 340	1 141	2 212	2 769	2 527	1 558	856	2 364	981	851	14.9	17.0	30.5	32.4
Kansas	2 695	148	1 558	920	2 208	2 554	2 325	1 345	866	2 115	1 009	854	16.5	14.1	34.7	34.7
Kentucky	3 194	330	2 106	733	2 730	3 190	2 952	1 768	1 030	2 671	841	724	25.3	10.6	31.5	33.9
Louisiana	3 608	439	1 913	1 161	3 240	3 611	3 309	1 967	1 045	3 314	842	785	33.2	14.1	26.5	26.5
Maine	1 328	79	641	593	1 192	1 328	1 208	809	356	1 240	1 072	1 010	9.5	5.4	31.5	33.1
Maryland	5 145	268	2 002	2 715	4 622	5 240	4 783	2 891	1 650	4 649	1 058	972	25.5	19.8	39.6	41.8
Massachusetts	6 227	335	2 125	3 652	5 274	5 823	5 637	3 399	2 042	5 082	968	845	26.0	34.5	42.2	42.2
Michigan	11 134	715	3 201	7 007	9 054	11 410	9 817	5 692	3 840	9 830	1 207	1 058	48.3	20.4	47.4	47.4
Minnesota	5 160	237	2 841	1 887	4 301	5 352	4 328	2 758	1 396	4 482	1 183	1 024	24.2	23.4	35.7	36.2
Mississippi	1 879	307	1 025	479	1 599	1 928	1 725	1 066	521	1 658	731	644	16.0	13.1	26.4	27.4
Missouri	4 527	297	1 734	2 308	3 969	4 602	3 982	2 416	1 390	4 085	879	798	29.6	26.9	30.4	32.1
Montana	878	85	451	306	787	899	822	514	273	803	1 068	1 005	7.0	3.1	28.5	29.5
Nebraska	1 675	107	548	917	1 470	1 710	1 514	941	444	1 456	1 059	923	11.2	8.3	30.9	30.9
Nevada	1 269	59	416	747	1 007	1 345	1 099	654	407	1 220	971	1 015	7.6	5.7	34.4	35.5
New Hampshire	1 097	35	90	946	978	1 071	1 007	647	325	1 005	954	906	8.3	4.0	34.7	34.7
New Jersey	11 302	406	4 565	6 049	9 628	11 324	10 448	6 261	3 853	9 286	1 441	1 201	54.7	30.6	45.1	47.9
New Mexico	1 562	189	1 154	184	1 322	1 515	1 323	775	472	1 290	936	852	13.0	5.5	27.6	28.4
New York	23 775	1 473	9 090	12 979	21 363	24 981	22 060	14 884	6 549	22 115	1 375	1 229	94.8	95.6	46.1	49.1
North Carolina	5 560	455	3 560	1 321	5 057	5 844	5 145	3 161	1 592	5 447	840	821	44.4	26.3	30.7	31.0
North Dakota	563	67	241	226	515	585	522	320	157	491	918	769	5.0	2.8	26.4	26.2
Ohio	10 499	668	4 281	5 121	9 116	11 068	9 613	5 717	3 541	9 334	1 001	861	69.7	35.1	36.3	37.7
Oklahoma	3 078	263	1 811	871	2 385	2 875	2 659	1 552	884	2 347	889	746	20.8	18.5	27.5	28.9
Oregon	3 075	212	1 215	1 550	2 687	3 160	2 853	1 709	1 047	2 658	1 040	935	17.1	9.9	38.2	39.4
Pennsylvania	12 601	724	5 076	6 558	11 064	12 680	11 236	7 145	3 665	10 758	1 054	905	53.1	49.9	43.8	45.2
Rhode Island	1 023	60	399	552	866	1 028	990	660	305	857	1 028	854	5.5	4.6	40.7	40.8
South Carolina	3 200	295	1 478	1 286	2 862	3 183	2 791	1 652	963	2 934	877	842	26.5	12.2	30.0	30.9
South Dakota	647	70	169	390	532	666	585	361	192	557	928	800	6.2	2.7	25.7	25.9
Tennessee	3 650	348	1 708	1 345	3 034	3 687	3 306	2 125	999	3 286	724	674	34.6	13.9	32.4	33.6
Texas	18 744	1 517	7 542	9 174	15 408	19 919	16 194	9 602	5 621	16 148	1 103	951	123.1	111.1	30.5	32.0
Utah	1 786	126	981	581	1 420	1 848	1 511	1 014	405	1 423	993	826	10.8	9.1	29.4	29.1
Vermont	704	36	221	433	615	718	644	420	203	649	1 247	1 153	3.8	3.7	35.4	35.5
Virginia	6 163	371	1 895	3 672	5 529	6 276	5 441	3 275	1 884	5 774	969	933	42.6	27.9	33.0	35.5
Washington	5 724	334	3 988	1 225	4 699	5 961	4 893	2 921	1 746	4 885	1 133	1 004	27.1	19.3	35.9	36.5
West Virginia	1 879	151	1 214	486	1 600	1 865	1 664	1 035	535	1 599	1 025	892	12.1	8.8	31.6	32.4
Wisconsin	5 661	250	2 188	3 110	4 636	5 849	5 170	3 285	1 730	4 818	1 159	985	36.7	19.2	37.2	39.1
Wyoming	674	39	351	273	580	619	558	345	194	586	1 319	1 293	3.4	3.3	31.2	31.4

X Not applicable.

[1] Includes revenue from gifts, and tuition and fees from patrons not shown separately.
[2] Includes other items not shown separately.
[3] Excludes capital outlay and interest on school debt.
[4] Based on resident population estimated as of July 1 for 1993 and enumerated as of April 1 for 1990 by the U.S. Bureau of the Census.
[5] Data subject to copyright; see below for source citation.
[6] Full-time equivalent.

Source: Revenues and expenditures–U.S. National Center for Education Statistics, Digest of Education Statistics, annual; Teachers–National Education Association, Washington, DC, Estimates of School Statistics, 1995-96 (Table 5). (Copyright by the National Education Association. All rights reserved.)

Educational Attainment and Institutions of Higher Education

Geographic area	Public high school graduates[1] (1,000)				Educational attainment, 1990 Percent of persons 25 years and over, by highest level completed							Institutions of higher education (fall)		
	1996, est	1995	1990	1980	Not a high school graduate	High school graduate	Some college, but no degree	Asso-ciate's degree	Bache-lor's degree	Advanced degree	Drop-outs[2], 1990 (percent)	1994	1993	1990
United States	**2 304.7**	**2 287.7**	**2 320.3**	**2 747.7**	**24.8**	**30.0**	**18.7**	**6.2**	**13.1**	**7.2**	**11.2**	**[3]3 688**	**[3]3 632**	**[3]3 559**
Alabama	36.4	36.3	40.5	45.2	33.1	29.4	16.8	5.0	10.1	5.5	12.6	80	80	87
Alaska	6.3	5.8	5.4	5.2	13.4	28.7	27.6	7.2	15.0	8.0	10.9	9	8	7
Arizona	30.4	29.5	32.1	28.6	21.3	26.1	25.4	6.8	13.3	7.0	14.4	43	42	38
Arkansas	26.4	26.0	26.5	29.1	33.7	32.7	16.6	3.7	8.9	4.5	11.4	35	35	35
California	261.8	257.4	236.3	249.2	23.8	22.3	22.6	7.9	15.3	8.1	14.2	336	328	310
Colorado	33.4	32.4	33.0	36.8	15.6	26.5	24.0	6.9	18.0	9.0	9.8	61	59	57
Connecticut	26.4	26.3	27.9	37.7	20.8	29.5	15.9	6.6	16.2	11.0	9.0	43	42	47
Delaware	5.5	5.2	5.6	7.6	22.5	32.7	16.9	6.5	13.7	7.7	10.4	9	9	10
District of Columbia	2.7	3.0	3.6	5.0	26.9	21.2	15.6	3.1	16.1	17.2	13.9	19	18	17
Florida	90.6	89.8	88.9	87.3	25.6	30.1	19.4	6.6	12.0	6.3	14.3	111	108	101
Georgia	59.4	59.7	56.6	61.6	29.1	29.6	17.0	5.0	12.9	6.4	14.1	119	116	95
Hawaii	10.0	10.0	10.3	11.5	19.9	28.7	20.1	8.3	15.8	7.1	7.5	16	16	15
Idaho	14.5	14.2	12.0	13.2	20.3	30.4	24.2	7.5	12.4	5.3	10.4	11	11	11
Illinois	105.1	105.2	108.1	135.6	23.8	30.0	19.4	5.8	13.6	7.5	10.6	167	169	170
Indiana	57.7	56.6	60.0	73.1	24.4	38.2	16.6	5.3	9.2	6.4	11.4	78	77	80
Iowa	31.6	31.2	31.8	43.4	19.9	38.5	17.0	7.7	11.7	5.2	6.6	60	61	58
Kansas	26.0	26.4	25.4	30.9	18.7	32.8	21.9	5.4	14.1	7.0	8.7	52	51	53
Kentucky	36.2	36.7	38.0	41.2	35.4	31.8	15.2	4.1	8.1	5.5	13.3	62	62	62
Louisiana	35.6	36.7	36.1	46.3	31.7	31.7	17.2	3.3	10.5	5.6	12.5	35	33	36
Maine	11.3	13.0	13.8	15.4	21.2	37.1	16.1	6.9	12.7	6.1	8.3	33	31	31
Maryland	41.6	41.8	41.6	54.3	21.6	28.1	18.6	5.2	15.6	10.9	10.9	57	57	57
Massachusetts	49.7	49.1	55.9	73.8	20.0	29.7	15.8	7.2	16.6	10.6	8.5	118	117	116
Michigan	87.4	84.1	93.8	124.3	23.2	32.3	20.4	6.7	10.9	6.4	10.0	109	106	97
Minnesota	51.6	49.7	49.1	64.9	17.6	33.0	19.0	8.6	15.6	6.3	6.4	109	98	78
Mississippi	23.1	23.7	25.2	27.6	35.7	27.5	16.9	5.2	9.7	5.1	11.8	46	47	46
Missouri	49.2	48.9	49.0	62.3	26.1	33.1	18.4	4.5	11.7	6.1	11.4	102	98	93
Montana	10.3	10.0	9.4	12.1	19.0	33.5	22.1	5.6	14.1	5.7	8.1	21	20	19
Nebraska	16.2	18.0	17.7	22.4	18.2	34.7	21.1	7.1	13.1	5.9	7.0	35	33	34
Nevada	10.6	10.0	9.5	8.5	21.2	31.5	25.8	6.2	10.1	5.2	15.2	10	9	9
New Hampshire	8.8	9.1	10.8	11.7	17.8	31.7	18.0	8.1	16.4	7.9	9.4	30	30	28
New Jersey	69.5	68.6	69.8	94.6	23.3	31.1	15.5	5.2	16.0	8.8	9.6	61	61	59
New Mexico	15.0	14.9	14.9	18.4	24.9	28.7	20.9	5.0	12.1	8.3	11.7	35	32	28
New York	137.2	135.5	143.3	204.1	25.2	29.5	15.7	6.5	13.2	9.9	9.9	314	314	324
North Carolina	56.4	59.3	64.8	70.9	30.0	29.0	16.8	6.8	12.0	5.4	12.5	123	122	125
North Dakota	7.9	7.8	7.7	9.9	23.3	28.0	20.5	10.0	13.5	4.5	4.6	20	20	20
Ohio	110.2	109.4	114.5	144.2	24.3	36.3	17.0	5.3	11.1	5.9	8.9	157	156	154
Oklahoma	32.9	33.4	35.6	39.3	25.4	30.5	21.3	5.0	11.8	6.0	10.4	46	46	48
Oregon	27.1	26.9	25.5	29.9	18.5	28.9	25.0	6.9	13.6	7.0	11.8	44	44	46
Pennsylvania	108.5	105.4	110.5	146.5	25.3	38.6	12.9	5.2	11.3	6.6	9.1	218	219	220
Rhode Island	7.6	7.8	7.8	10.9	28.0	29.5	15.0	6.3	13.5	7.8	11.1	13	14	12
South Carolina	32.5	33.3	32.5	38.7	31.7	29.5	15.8	6.3	11.2	5.4	11.7	59	59	64
South Dakota	8.7	8.4	7.7	10.7	22.9	33.7	18.8	7.4	12.3	4.9	7.7	21	20	19
Tennessee	43.5	40.6	44.6	48.4	32.9	30.0	16.9	4.2	10.5	5.4	13.4	78	78	87
Texas	168.5	169.1	172.5	171.4	27.9	25.6	21.1	5.2	13.9	6.5	12.9	178	178	172
Utah	27.9	29.1	21.2	20.0	14.9	27.2	27.9	7.8	15.4	6.8	8.7	16	16	15
Vermont	5.3	5.6	6.1	6.7	19.2	34.6	14.7	7.2	15.4	8.9	8.0	22	22	22
Virginia	59.6	59.6	60.6	66.6	24.8	26.6	18.5	5.5	15.4	9.1	10.0	93	87	83
Washington	50.8	48.8	45.9	50.4	16.2	27.9	25.0	7.9	15.9	7.0	10.6	62	62	57
West Virginia	20.7	20.6	21.9	23.4	34.0	36.6	13.2	3.8	7.5	4.8	10.9	28	28	28
Wisconsin	52.8	51.8	52.0	69.3	21.4	37.1	16.7	7.1	12.1	5.6	7.1	65	64	61
Wyoming	6.1	5.9	5.8	6.1	17.0	33.2	24.2	6.9	13.1	5.7	6.9	9	9	9

[1]For school year ending in year shown.
[2]For persons 16 to 19 years old. A dropout is a person who is not in regular school and who has not completed the 12th grade or received a general equivalency degree.
[3]Includes military academies not distributed by state.

Source: Public high school graduates and institutions of higher education–U.S. National Center for Education Statistics, Digest of Education Statistics, annual; Education attainment–U.S. Bureau of the Census, 1990 Census of Population, CPH-L-96.

Institutions of Higher Education

Geographic area	Fall enrollment (1,000) Total			Public			Private			Public institutions current funds Revenue (mil dol) 1993-1994 Total	Tuition and fees	State appropriations	Federal appropriations	1990-1991, total	Expenditures (mil dol) 1993-1994 Total	Education and general	1990-1991, total
	1994	1993	1990	1994	1993	1990	1994	1993	1990								
United States	**14 280**	**14 305**	**13 820**	**11 134**	**11 189**	**10 845**	**3 145**	**3 116**	**2 975**	**112 968**	**20 825**	**40 536**	**12 465**	**94 905**	**109 310**	**87 139**	**92 961**
Alabama	230	234	219	207	210	196	23	23	23	2 614	388	829	273	2 131	2 510	1 711	2 055
Alaska	29	31	30	28	29	28	1	2	2	343	42	185	56	292	336	317	290
Arizona	275	272	264	252	247	248	23	26	16	1 834	391	630	259	1 597	1 755	1 524	1 587
Arkansas	96	99	90	86	88	79	11	11	12	1 037	153	411	81	818	1 003	707	797
California	1 836	1 836	1 809	1 583	1 604	1 595	253	232	214	13 869	1 809	5 001	1 402	12 282	13 244	10 735	12 023
Colorado	241	240	227	210	210	201	32	30	26	1 804	500	489	332	1 484	1 761	1 529	1 452
Connecticut	160	162	169	102	105	110	58	57	59	1 020	212	382	72	890	1 027	772	887
Delaware	44	44	42	36	36	34	8	8	8	471	161	135	43	389	442	388	367
District of Columbia	78	82	80	11	11	13	67	71	68	107	10	X	14	110	105	103	111
Florida	634	623	589	528	518	489	106	105	100	3 412	617	1 819	309	2 945	3 409	3 101	2 896
Georgia	309	303	252	244	240	196	65	63	55	2 494	401	1 183	235	1 954	2 453	2 038	1 930
Hawaii	64	63	56	52	51	46	13	12	11	628	51	400	96	497	613	557	498
Idaho	60	59	52	49	48	41	11	11	11	456	75	209	42	360	445	375	354
Illinois	731	734	729	546	550	551	185	184	178	4 101	744	1 428	408	3 566	4 054	3 397	3 529
Indiana	292	295	285	228	231	224	64	63	61	3 010	633	990	230	2 494	2 859	2 106	2 391
Iowa	172	173	171	122	122	118	50	51	53	2 014	292	625	282	1 775	1 981	1 355	1 734
Kansas	171	170	164	153	154	149	18	16	15	1 470	249	510	137	1 219	1 429	1 134	1 191
Kentucky	183	187	178	152	156	147	31	31	31	1 656	288	691	127	1 451	1 578	1 255	1 401
Louisiana	204	202	187	175	174	158	28	28	29	1 844	354	654	110	1 448	1 835	1 339	1 439
Maine	57	56	57	39	40	42	18	16	16	399	93	176	39	374	388	339	355
Maryland	266	268	260	224	227	221	43	41	39	1 984	501	733	233	1 778	1 940	1 673	1 684
Massachusetts	417	420	418	180	181	186	237	239	232	1 492	476	602	133	1 457	1 497	1 339	1 435
Michigan	551	568	570	467	483	487	85	85	82	5 530	1 272	1 497	547	4 648	5 095	3 886	4 417
Minnesota	289	268	254	227	207	199	62	61	55	2 494	437	905	269	2 081	2 459	1 938	2 012
Mississippi	121	122	123	108	109	109	12	13	14	1 216	210	440	156	1 005	1 200	919	978
Missouri	294	297	290	192	198	200	102	99	90	1 805	411	615	112	1 517	1 694	1 340	1 454
Montana	40	40	36	35	34	32	5	5	4	363	72	130	64	258	351	303	254
Nebraska	116	116	113	96	96	95	20	20	18	1 034	137	366	83	870	1 004	706	849
Nevada	64	64	62	63	63	61	1	1	Z	413	65	202	50	337	416	379	331
New Hampshire	63	64	60	35	36	32	28	29	27	373	148	82	39	304	361	296	282
New Jersey	336	343	324	272	278	262	63	65	63	2 921	603	1 126	182	2 414	2 810	2 237	2 310
New Mexico	102	101	86	97	98	83	5	3	2	1 191	110	387	211	944	1 143	807	896
New York	1 058	1 063	1 048	604	605	617	453	458	431	6 574	1 334	2 739	448	5 424	6 482	5 398	5 606
North Carolina	369	371	352	304	304	285	66	68	67	3 299	377	1 618	380	2 650	3 192	2 671	2 581
North Dakota	40	40	38	37	37	35	4	4	3	431	84	136	67	378	432	344	368
Ohio	549	562	558	418	430	428	132	133	130	4 896	1 274	1 411	338	4 185	4 640	3 363	4 085
Oklahoma	185	183	173	162	161	151	23	22	22	1 258	200	563	186	1 073	1 214	953	1 057
Oregon	164	166	166	141	143	144	23	22	21	1 687	281	448	239	1 358	1 624	1 195	1 330
Pennsylvania	611	621	604	343	352	343	269	269	261	4 424	1 295	1 113	471	3 693	4 240	3 281	3 603
Rhode Island	75	77	78	39	41	42	35	37	36	329	109	116	41	292	331	286	292
South Carolina	173	174	159	149	149	131	25	25	28	1 925	334	597	152	1 503	1 767	1 245	1 475
South Dakota	38	38	34	31	31	27	7	7	8	261	62	105	36	199	259	229	198
Tennessee	243	245	226	191	194	175	52	51	51	1 961	306	802	179	1 634	1 912	1 478	1 586
Texas	955	942	901	843	835	802	111	107	99	7 688	1 087	3 363	784	6 016	7 414	6 352	5 960
Utah	146	138	121	109	100	86	38	38	35	1 308	171	381	172	1 021	1 261	921	994
Vermont	35	36	36	21	21	21	15	15	15	317	138	47	40	282	306	271	275
Virginia	354	349	353	293	294	291	61	55	62	3 323	709	871	288	2 903	3 301	2 125	2 812
Washington	285	280	263	245	242	228	40	38	36	2 744	453	1 005	453	2 188	2 640	2 074	2 157
West Virginia	88	89	85	76	78	74	12	11	11	666	165	314	63	564	651	560	549
Wisconsin	304	309	300	250	257	254	54	52	46	2 955	502	948	363	2 488	2 872	2 394	2 469
Wyoming	31	31	31	30	30	31	1	1	1	278	37	125	37	252	271	231	240

X Not applicable.
Z Less than 500.

Note: Totals include U.S. military academics not distributed by state except for state apropriations.

Source: U.S. National Center for Education Statistics, Digest of Education Statistics, annual.

Table A–16. States — Crimes and Crime Rates

Geographic area	Number of offenses known to the police (1,000)				Offenses per 100,000 population[1]			Offenses by type per 100,000 population[1], 1995								
	1995							Violent crimes					Property crimes			
	Total	Violent	1994	1990	1995	1994	1990	Total	Murder[2]	Forcible rape	Robbery	Aggravated assault	Total	Burglary	Larceny/theft	Motor vehicle theft
United States	13 867	1 799	13 990	14 476	5 278	5 374	5 820	685	8.2	37.1	221	418	4 593	988	3 045	561
Alabama..................	206	27	207	199	4 848	4 903	4 915	632	11.2	31.7	186	404	4 216	1 025	2 844	347
Alaska....................	35	5	35	28	5 754	5 708	5 153	771	9.1	80.3	155	526	4 983	837	3 624	522
Arizona..................	346	30	323	289	8 214	7 925	7 889	714	10.4	33.6	174	496	7 500	1 417	4 926	1 158
Arkansas.................	117	14	118	114	4 691	4 799	4 867	553	10.4	37.2	126	380	4 138	997	2 815	325
California	1 842	305	1 940	1 965	5 831	6 174	6 604	966	11.2	33.4	331	590	4 865	1 120	2 857	888
Colorado.................	202	16	194	199	5 396	5 318	6 054	440	5.8	39.5	96	299	4 956	934	3 635	388
Connecticut	147	13	149	177	4 503	4 548	5 387	406	4.6	23.7	163	214	4 097	888	2 669	540
Delaware.................	37	5	35	36	5 159	4 890	5 360	725	3.5	80.2	199	443	4 434	905	3 114	414
District of Columbia ...	67	15	63	65	12 174	11 085	10 774	2 661	65.0	52.7	1 239	1 305	9 512	1 838	5 834	1 840
Florida	1 091	152	1 151	1 140	7 702	8 250	8 811	1 071	7.3	48.6	300	715	6 631	1 522	4 322	786
Georgia	432	47	424	438	6 004	6 010	6 764	657	9.5	35.3	205	407	5 347	1 060	3 678	608
Hawaii....................	85	4	79	68	7 199	6 681	6 107	296	4.7	28.3	131	132	6 903	1 165	5 047	691
Idaho.....................	51	4	46	41	4 402	4 077	4 057	322	4.1	28.4	24	266	4 079	780	3 058	242
Illinois..................	[3]645	[3]118	[3]661	678	[3]5 456	[3]5 626	5 935	[3]996	10.3	[3]36.5	331	619	4 460	918	3 019	523
Indiana...................	269	30	264	260	4 632	4 593	4 683	525	8.0	33.3	135	348	4 107	822	2 820	466
Iowa	117	10	103	114	4 102	3 655	4 101	354	1.8	21.8	53	278	3 748	758	2 767	223
Kansas	125	11	124	129	4 887	4 847	5 193	421	6.2	36.6	108	270	4 466	1 068	3 074	324
Kentucky	129	14	128	122	3 352	3 337	3 299	365	7.2	31.9	104	222	2 987	736	1 992	259
Louisiana................	290	44	288	274	6 676	6 671	6 487	1 007	17.0	42.7	269	679	5 669	1 232	3 839	598
Maine.....................	41	2	41	45	3 285	3 273	3 698	131	2.0	21.4	27	81	3 153	726	2 292	135
Maryland..................	317	50	306	279	6 295	6 123	5 830	987	11.8	42.2	423	510	5 308	1 058	3 533	718
Massachusetts	264	42	268	319	4 342	4 441	5 298	687	3.6	29.0	150	504	3 654	818	2 232	605
Michigan..................	495	66	517	557	5 183	5 445	5 995	688	8.5	62.0	187	430	4 495	910	2 940	646
Minnesota................	207	16	198	199	4 497	4 341	4 539	356	3.9	56.2	124	172	4 141	797	3 003	342
Mississippi..............	122	14	129	100	4 515	4 837	3 869	503	12.9	39.1	131	320	4 012	1 131	2 520	361
Missouri	273	35	280	262	5 121	5 308	5 121	664	8.8	32.1	204	419	4 457	933	3 051	473
Montana...................	46	1	43	36	5 305	5 019	4 502	171	3.0	25.9	33	109	5 134	721	4 106	308
Nebraska.................	74	6	72	66	4 545	4 440	4 213	382	2.9	19.4	65	295	4 163	632	3 179	351
Nevada...................	101	14	97	73	6 579	6 677	6 064	945	10.7	61.2	325	549	5 634	1 323	3 566	745
New Hampshire	30	1	31	40	2 655	2 741	3 645	115	1.8	29.0	27	56	2 541	419	1 977	145
New Jersey	374	48	368	421	4 704	4 661	5 447	600	5.1	24.3	283	287	4 104	875	2 597	632
New Mexico...............	108	14	102	101	6 428	6 188	6 684	819	8.8	56.6	155	599	5 609	1 447	3 649	513
New York.................	827	153	921	1 145	4 564	5 071	6 364	842	8.5	23.7	400	410	3 718	808	2 344	566
North Carolina...........	406	47	398	364	5 640	5 625	5 486	646	9.4	32.2	179	426	4 993	1 418	3 265	311
North Dakota.............	18	1	17	19	2 866	2 736	2 922	87	.9	22.8	10	53	2 780	351	2 250	179
Ohio	491	54	495	525	4 405	4 461	4 843	483	5.4	43.4	179	255	3 923	839	2 669	415
Oklahoma	183	22	181	176	5 597	5 570	5 599	664	12.2	44.6	116	492	4 933	1 272	3 164	496
Oregon	206	16	194	160	6 564	6 296	5 646	522	4.1	41.7	138	339	6 042	1 103	4 237	702
Pennsylvania.............	406	52	394	413	3 365	3 272	3 476	427	6.3	25.2	189	207	2 938	562	1 963	413
Rhode Island.............	42	4	41	54	4 245	4 119	5 353	368	3.3	27.0	92	245	3 877	933	2 503	441
South Carolina	223	36	220	211	6 064	6 001	6 045	982	7.9	47.3	176	751	5 082	1 255	3 442	385
South Dakota.............	22	2	22	20	3 061	3 102	2 909	208	1.8	41.0	26	139	2 853	541	2 192	121
Tennessee................	282	41	265	246	5 363	5 120	5 051	772	10.6	47.1	223	491	4 591	1 143	2 800	649
Texas	1 064	124	1 079	1 329	5 684	5 872	7 827	664	9.0	45.7	180	429	5 021	1 082	3 378	560
Utah	119	6	101	98	6 091	5 301	5 660	329	3.9	42.7	67	215	5 762	801	4 572	389
Vermont	20	1	19	24	3 434	3 250	4 341	118	2.2	28.2	11	77	3 315	761	2 419	136
Virginia.................	264	24	265	275	3 989	4 048	4 441	362	7.6	27.2	132	195	3 628	595	2 740	293
Washington...............	341	26	322	303	6 270	6 028	6 223	484	5.1	59.2	133	287	5 786	1 091	4 140	554
West Virginia............	45	4	46	45	2 458	2 528	2 503	210	4.9	21.2	43	141	2 248	565	1 517	166
Wisconsin................	199	14	200	215	3 886	3 944	4 395	281	4.3	23.3	105	148	3 605	613	2 628	364
Wyoming	21	1	20	19	4 320	4 290	4 211	254	2.1	34.4	18	200	4 066	612	3 286	168

[1]Based on resident population estimated as of July 1 for 1995 and 1994 and enumerated as of April 1 for 1990.
[2]Includes non-negligent manslaughter.
[3]Forcible rape figures for 1994 and 1995 were estimated using the national rate of forcible rapes when grouped by like agencies, as the figures were not in accordance with Uniform Crime Reporting program guidelines.

Source: U.S. Federal Bureau of Investigation, Crime in the United States, annual (related Internet site <http://www.fbi.gov/publish.htm>).

Table A–17. States — Law Enforcement

Geographic area	State and local government employment						Prisoners under jurisdiction of federal and state authorities (Dec. 31)				Prisoners executed		Prisoners under death sentence	
	Police protection 1995			Corrections 1995			1995							
	Number	Rate[1]	1990	Number	Rate[1]	1990	Number	Percent change, 1990-1995	Rate[1]	1990	1995	1977 to 1995	1995	1990
United States	**778 756**	**296**	**697 974**	**614 975**	**234**	**503 181**	[2]1 126 287	[2]45.5	[2]428	[2]773 919	56	313	[2]3 054	2 346
Alabama	10 891	256	10 023	6 760	159	6 053	20 718	32.3	488	15 665	2	12	143	117
Alaska	1 772	294	1 533	1 296	215	1 310	3 522	34.3	585	2 622	(3)	(3)	(3)	(3)
Arizona	12 751	296	10 887	12 324	286	8 880	21 341	49.6	496	14 261	1	4	117	87
Arkansas	6 293	253	4 984	4 627	186	3 097	9 411	28.5	379	7 322	2	11	38	33
California	90 484	287	85 514	70 854	224	63 989	135 646	39.4	430	97 309	–	2	[4]420	280
Colorado	10 608	283	9 012	7 108	190	5 431	11 063	44.2	295	7 671	–	–	4	3
Connecticut	9 625	294	9 423	7 443	228	5 364	14 801	41.0	453	10 500	–	–	5	2
Delaware	2 000	279	1 874	1 840	257	1 687	4 802	38.3	670	3 471	1	5	14	6
District of Columbia	4 490	810	5 591	4 185	755	4 392	9 800	–1.5	1 767	9 947	(3)	(3)	(3)	(3)
Florida	48 669	343	43 685	44 315	312	38 663	63 879	43.9	450	44 387	3	36	366	291
Georgia	21 151	293	18 182	25 355	352	16 751	34 266	52.9	475	22 411	2	20	98	99
Hawaii	3 291	279	3 149	2 131	181	1 501	3 560	40.5	302	2 533	(3)	(3)	(3)	(3)
Idaho	3 334	286	2 600	2 342	201	1 328	3 328	69.7	285	1 961	–	1	19	19
Illinois	43 120	366	39 346	21 757	185	18 650	37 658	36.9	319	27 516	5	7	154	128
Indiana	14 440	249	12 888	10 116	175	8 238	16 125	26.6	278	12 736	–	3	46	48
Iowa	6 633	233	6 043	3 234	114	2 785	5 906	48.9	208	3 967	(3)	(3)	(3)	(3)
Kansas	7 552	295	6 631	5 510	215	4 150	7 054	22.1	275	5 775	–	–	–	(3)
Kentucky	7 706	200	7 418	7 507	195	6 568	12 060	33.7	313	9 023	–	–	28	27
Louisiana	13 436	310	11 752	9 377	216	9 052	25 195	35.5	581	18 599	1	22	57	32
Maine	2 818	228	2 888	1 818	147	1 656	1 396	–8.3	113	1 523	(3)	(3)	(3)	(3)
Maryland	15 728	312	14 630	13 125	260	11 340	21 453	20.2	426	17 848	(3)	1	13	17
Massachusetts	18 320	302	17 556	11 097	183	8 555	11 687	40.0	193	8 345	(3)	(3)	(3)	(3)
Michigan	23 338	245	21 884	21 226	223	18 917	41 112	20.0	431	34 267	(3)	(3)	(3)	(3)
Minnesota	9 869	214	8 884	7 161	155	4 953	4 846	52.6	105	3 176	(3)	(3)	(3)	(3)
Mississippi	7 514	279	5 551	4 731	175	3 675	12 684	51.5	470	8 375	–	4	49	46
Missouri	16 283	306	14 459	8 984	169	8 498	19 134	28.0	360	14 943	6	17	92	71
Montana	2 130	245	1 932	1 170	134	1 061	1 999	40.3	230	1 425	1	1	6	6
Nebraska	4 140	253	3 780	2 728	166	2 493	3 074	27.9	188	2 403	–	1	10	11
Nevada	4 672	305	4 341	4 181	273	2 795	7 713	44.9	503	5 322	–	5	[4]75	59
New Hampshire	3 043	265	2 997	1 543	134	1 370	2 014	50.1	175	1 342	–	–	–	–
New Jersey	32 185	405	31 660	16 125	203	17 547	27 066	28.1	340	21 128	–	–	10	10
New Mexico	4 955	293	4 466	5 187	307	3 438	4 078	28.0	241	3 187	–	–	3	1
New York	76 593	421	66 348	58 067	319	59 157	68 489	24.8	377	54 895	–	–	–	(3)
North Carolina	19 827	275	16 850	15 922	221	13 704	29 253	58.9	406	18 411	2	8	139	84
North Dakota	1 338	209	1 311	717	112	495	608	25.9	95	483	(3)	(3)	(3)	(3)
Ohio	29 635	266	26 716	22 215	200	15 351	44 663	40.4	401	31 822	–	–	155	104
Oklahoma	9 548	292	8 520	8 875	271	5 062	18 151	47.7	554	12 285	3	6	129	117
Oregon	7 397	235	6 515	5 708	181	5 088	7 886	21.5	250	6 492	–	–	20	10
Pennsylvania	31 486	261	29 602	23 498	195	16 946	32 410	45.4	269	22 290	2	2	196	122
Rhode Island	2 879	290	2 989	1 655	167	1 742	2 902	21.3	293	2 392	(3)	(3)	(3)	(3)
South Carolina	10 770	294	8 485	10 075	275	8 181	19 611	13.2	535	17 319	1	5	67	40
South Dakota	1 574	216	1 471	1 001	137	746	1 841	37.3	252	1 341	–	–	2	–
Tennessee	13 562	258	12 333	11 332	216	10 281	15 206	46.4	290	10 388	–	–	96	85
Texas	56 794	302	43 802	63 917	340	37 429	127 766	155.3	680	50 042	19	104	404	323
Utah	4 663	238	3 720	3 196	163	2 488	3 452	38.3	176	2 496	–	4	10	11
Vermont	1 278	219	1 223	868	148	681	1 279	21.9	219	1 049	(3)	(3)	(3)	(3)
Virginia	16 710	253	14 992	18 926	286	14 869	27 415	55.8	414	17 593	5	29	56	45
Washington	12 410	228	10 456	10 944	201	8 445	11 608	45.2	213	7 995	–	2	9	10
West Virginia	3 240	178	2 898	1 204	66	1 327	2 512	60.5	138	1 565	(3)	(3)	(3)	(3)
Wisconsin	14 201	277	12 603	8 888	174	6 115	11 199	50.0	219	7 465	(3)	(3)	(3)	(3)
Wyoming	1 610	336	1 577	810	169	887	1 395	25.7	291	1 110	–	1	–	2

– Represents zero.

[1] Per 100,000 resident population estimated as of July 1 for 1995 and enumerated as of April 1 for 1990 by the U.S. Bureau of the Census.
[2] Includes federal prisoners not distributed by state.
[3] State did not have death penalty as of December 31 of year shown.
[4] One inmate who was previously in the custody of Nevada has been transferred to California where he is being held under a separate sentence of death.

Source: Employment–U.S. Bureau of the Census, Public Employment 1990, series GE, no.1 Internet site <http://www.census.gov/govs/apes/95stlus.txt> (accessed 26 June 1997); Prisoners– U.S. Bureau of Justice Statistics, Prisoners, annual; Capital punishment–U.S. Bureau of Justice Statistics, Capital Punishment, annual (related Internet site <http://www.ojp.usdoj.gov/bjs/correct.htm>).

Table A–18. States — Housing Starts, Sales, Vacancy Rates, and Ownership

Geographic area	Housing starts (1,000) 1996 Number	Housing starts 1996 Percent single family units	Housing starts 1995	Housing starts 1994	Housing starts 1990	Existing home sales[1] (1,000) 1997, prel.	Existing home sales 1996	Existing home sales 1995	Existing home sales 1990	Vacancy rates Rental[2] 1996	Rental 1990	Homeowner[3] 1996	Homeowner 1990	Homeownership rate[4] 1996	1995	1990
United States	1 451.0	79.0	1 354.0	1 457.0	1 193.0	[5]4 731.0	[5]4 559.0	[5]4 240.0	[5]3 211.0	7.8	7.2	1.6	1.7	65.4	64.7	63.9
Alabama.................	21.9	80.8	21.2	23.7	16.6	83.2	78.5	74.6	61.1	8.7	8.1	1.8	1.5	71.0	70.1	68.4
Alaska....................	2.7	66.7	2.5	2.2	1.0	NA	NA	NA	NA	5.9	6.8	1.7	2.6	62.9	60.9	58.4
Arizona..................	57.7	78.5	53.5	52.9	23.0	143.2	133.1	122.0	86.3	10.2	10.7	1.7	2.5	62.0	62.9	64.5
Arkansas................	13.2	77.3	12.2	15.1	8.8	58.8	58.5	55.3	44.8	7.2	7.9	1.4	2.5	66.6	67.2	67.8
California...............	95.3	82.8	86.9	97.6	171.9	[6]555.4	[6]505.4	[6]425.4	[6]452.1	7.2	6.0	2.0	1.8	55.0	55.4	53.8
Colorado	41.7	76.7	39.7	41.6	12.9	88.1	84.3	76.9	54.2	6.1	10.2	.9	2.2	64.5	64.6	59.0
Connecticut	9.8	94.9	9.1	9.7	8.4	55.5	49.2	51.4	34.3	10.7	7.5	2.0	2.4	69.0	68.2	67.9
Delaware................	4.9	95.9	5.3	5.7	5.8	NA	NA	10.3	9.7	7.7	6.0	1.4	2.1	71.5	71.7	67.7
District of Columbia	–	–	.1	.2	.4	14.4	11.1	11.7	13.1	13.4	7.7	3.5	2.4	40.4	38.2	36.4
Florida	122.8	74.3	123.4	131.0	134.1	238.0	229.7	220.8	183.3	9.0	9.0	2.4	2.7	67.1	66.6	65.1
Georgia	79.8	82.5	77.2	69.4	45.6	NA	NA	NA	73.2	11.6	9.4	2.0	1.8	69.3	66.6	64.3
Hawaii...................	3.9	66.7	6.9	6.6	6.5	11.8	10.1	10.0	19.2	6.0	6.6	1.4	.8	50.6	50.2	55.5
Idaho....................	9.4	87.2	9.5	13.3	6.4	21.3	23.4	22.8	18.1	5.8	5.4	1.1	1.5	71.4	72.0	69.4
Illinois..................	49.9	81.8	48.8	53.7	39.0	199.3	189.8	181.2	160.9	7.9	6.1	1.4	1.3	68.2	66.4	63.0
Indiana..................	40.3	87.1	36.8	38.1	29.9	111.1	103.0	100.3	80.1	6.9	5.3	1.1	1.5	74.2	71.0	67.0
Iowa	11.0	70.0	9.4	13.3	9.1	57.3	55.3	51.3	51.9	5.5	7.8	.8	.8	72.8	71.4	70.7
Kansas..................	14.6	66.4	11.0	14.6	9.8	61.5	57.9	54.2	38.8	9.9	7.8	1.8	2.0	67.5	67.5	69.0
Kentucky...............	20.2	83.2	18.9	21.5	15.0	82.5	80.2	78.2	66.4	5.8	5.8	1.2	1.7	73.2	71.2	65.8
Louisiana..............	16.5	85.5	14.4	16.4	7.9	54.2	51.9	50.1	41.6	7.8	13.1	1.1	1.7	64.9	65.3	67.8
Maine	4.6	95.7	4.2	4.9	5.2	15.5	14.2	13.1	NA	7.2	9.7	1.1	1.0	76.5	76.7	74.2
Maryland	27.7	89.9	28.9	30.8	32.4	66.9	61.6	59.2	67.1	6.7	5.2	2.3	1.7	66.9	65.8	64.9
Massachusetts........	16.6	94.0	16.3	18.3	15.0	93.1	82.2	68.1	44.0	5.8	6.9	1.1	1.4	61.7	60.2	58.6
Michigan................	53.7	84.2	47.6	49.2	41.4	182.0	182.5	176.3	145.0	10.2	7.3	1.4	1.1	73.3	72.2	72.3
Minnesota..............	24.7	87.4	25.0	27.6	22.6	91.8	88.4	78.5	64.8	5.5	6.5	1.1	1.2	75.4	73.3	68.0
Mississippi	13.6	73.5	12.2	13.2	7.9	49.1	45.0	43.8	34.7	13.2	8.7	1.0	1.6	73.0	71.1	69.4
Missouri	28.6	83.9	25.6	30.9	17.5	116.1	114.0	108.3	84.1	8.6	9.6	2.0	1.8	70.2	69.4	64.0
Montana................	2.8	64.3	3.1	3.9	1.7	15.6	15.8	14.8	12.7	5.1	8.1	1.4	3.0	68.6	68.7	69.1
Nebraska...............	9.7	60.8	8.0	8.5	7.5	23.3	20.1	21.0	19.3	6.6	6.5	2.0	1.6	66.8	67.1	67.3
Nevada..................	41.0	65.4	33.8	31.1	24.3	31.0	35.4	31.9	26.2	7.1	8.4	2.0	2.7	61.1	58.6	55.8
New Hampshire	4.5	82.2	4.3	4.6	4.5	NA	NA	NA	7.9	5.6	9.7	1.6	1.7	65.0	66.0	65.0
New Jersey	25.8	90.3	25.3	25.5	19.7	157.2	147.9	138.3	114.8	7.7	5.9	1.6	1.8	64.6	64.9	65.0
New Mexico............	9.2	79.3	9.7	9.3	4.7	26.6	27.4	28.9	23.6	7.1	13.7	1.3	2.4	67.1	67.0	68.6
New York...............	28.6	62.6	23.4	29.1	34.5	172.1	165.8	150.4	125.5	6.9	4.9	1.7	1.8	52.7	52.7	53.3
North Carolina........	67.6	81.2	64.4	66.9	46.7	231.4	219.7	200.1	135.9	8.0	7.2	1.4	1.6	70.4	70.1	69.0
North Dakota..........	2.0	80.0	3.2	3.8	1.8	11.9	12.0	10.6	10.4	8.5	8.0	1.8	3.6	68.2	67.3	67.2
Ohio	49.0	81.0	43.6	50.4	42.9	187.3	190.9	181.4	151.6	8.1	5.5	1.1	1.2	69.2	69.0	68.7
Oklahoma..............	13.4	81.3	11.8	12.7	8.1	64.9	62.0	58.1	53.4	11.0	14.6	1.6	3.1	68.4	69.8	70.3
Oregon..................	26.9	68.8	25.0	24.6	23.0	62.9	60.6	57.7	56.6	5.9	3.3	1.4	.8	63.1	63.2	64.4
Pennsylvania..........	32.2	88.5	31.1	40.7	38.1	234.5	222.8	217.2	182.7	8.7	7.2	1.6	1.1	71.7	71.5	73.8
Rhode Island..........	2.6	92.3	2.5	2.6	3.2	14.4	13.2	11.9	7.8	7.2	9.6	1.6	2.1	56.6	57.9	58.5
South Carolina	30.3	76.9	26.1	25.6	22.4	83.0	76.2	69.1	57.8	14.1	8.4	1.7	1.0	72.9	71.3	71.4
South Dakota	4.3	65.1	3.9	4.7	3.1	15.9	14.5	13.2	11.6	9.9	5.3	1.7	1.2	67.8	67.5	66.2
Tennessee.............	40.3	76.9	36.4	35.5	25.2	151.4	145.3	133.2	92.7	5.4	9.5	1.6	2.4	68.8	67.0	68.3
Texas	122.2	77.8	112.5	118.6	55.1	295.1	284.4	260.2	240.0	8.0	9.7	1.4	2.5	61.8	61.4	59.7
Utah	21.6	72.7	20.7	21.6	7.7	31.4	37.1	33.8	22.1	13.4	12.6	1.0	1.9	72.7	71.5	70.1
Vermont	2.1	90.5	2.0	2.5	2.6	8.1	8.4	9.0	6.1	4.2	6.2	1.4	1.9	70.3	70.4	72.6
Virginia	48.7	77.2	45.2	47.4	44.5	100.0	95.8	94.0	96.9	7.4	5.8	2.2	1.7	68.5	68.1	69.8
Washington	43.4	73.0	37.9	43.7	45.6	123.0	101.7	95.5	87.7	5.6	3.3	1.4	.8	63.1	61.6	61.8
West Virginia	4.6	89.1	4.8	5.3	2.9	46.2	44.5	44.5	42.0	5.8	8.2	2.2	2.9	74.3	73.1	72.0
Wisconsin	29.7	69.7	27.1	34.1	27.5	97.1	97.4	93.2	71.7	5.5	3.3	1.0	.9	68.2	67.5	68.3
Wyoming	2.5	80.0	1.9	2.8	1.0	10.7	10.5	10.5	7.4	6.4	7.9	1.4	2.0	68.0	69.0	68.9

NA Not available.
– Represents zero.

[1]Data are subject to copyright, see below for source citation.
[2]Proportion of the rental inventory which is vacant for rent.
[3]Proportion of the homeowner inventory which is vacant for sale.
[4]Proportion of owner households to occupied households.
[5]U.S. totals are derived independently and, therefore, are not equal to the sum of the states.
[6]Provided by the California Association of Realtors.

Source: Housing starts–National Association of Home Builders, Economics Division, Washington, DC. Data provided by Econometria Forcasting Service; Existing home sales–National Association of REALTORS, Washington, DC, Real Estate Outlook: Market Trends & Insights (copyright); Vacancy and homeownership rates–U.S. Bureau of the Census, Housing Vacancy Survey Annual Statistics: 1996, Internet site <http://www.census.gov/hhes/www/housing/hvs/annual96> (accessed 15 Sept 1997).

Civilian Labor Force and Employment

Geographic area	Civilian noninstitutional population 16 years old and over (1,000)					Civilian labor force (1,000)									
						Total					Employed				
	1996			1995	1990[1]	1996			1995	1990[1]	1996			1995	1990[1]
	Total	Male	Female			Number	Male	Female			Number	Male	Female		
United States	200 591	96 206	104 385	198 584	189 164	133 943	72 087	61 857	132 304	125 840	126 708	68 207	58 501	124 900	118 793
Alabama	3 285	1 527	1 758	3 253	3 072	2 088	1 099	989	2 060	1 889	1 981	1 045	936	1 930	1 759
Alaska	426	211	215	418	372	316	169	147	304	270	291	154	137	282	251
Arizona	3 385	1 637	1 748	3 254	2 767	2 249	1 233	1 017	2 207	1 800	2 125	1 168	958	2 095	1 701
Arkansas	1 907	910	997	1 886	1 778	1 234	652	582	1 222	1 126	1 168	617	550	1 163	1 048
California	23 797	11 667	12 130	23 562	22 633	15 596	8 750	6 846	15 427	15 193	14 470	8 119	6 351	14 217	14 319
Colorado	2 905	1 450	1 455	2 835	2 484	2 102	1 146	956	2 091	1 764	2 013	1 096	917	2 004	1 675
Connecticut	2 521	1 199	1 322	2 523	2 572	1 720	894	826	1 713	1 833	1 621	842	779	1 618	1 739
Delaware	558	263	295	549	519	382	194	188	383	359	363	183	180	366	340
District of Columbia	428	194	234	436	484	272	131	141	285	329	249	120	129	260	307
Florida	11 196	5 308	5 888	11 038	10 238	6 938	3 710	3 227	6 849	6 468	6 586	3 533	3 053	6 473	6 078
Georgia	5 533	2 598	2 935	5 410	4 868	3 753	1 986	1 767	3 627	3 300	3 580	1 907	1 673	3 450	3 118
Hawaii	865	402	463	858	808	591	304	286	577	550	553	283	270	543	534
Idaho	880	443	437	858	728	619	345	275	601	493	587	327	260	569	463
Illinois	8 902	4 271	4 631	8 868	8 683	6 100	3 291	2 809	6 055	5 916	5 778	3 115	2 663	5 743	5 547
Indiana	4 440	2 158	2 282	4 400	4 179	3 072	1 660	1 412	3 131	2 794	2 945	1 595	1 351	2 985	2 645
Iowa	2 174	1 046	1 128	2 158	2 087	1 599	830	769	1 561	1 448	1 539	801	738	1 508	1 386
Kansas	1 912	927	985	1 896	1 823	1 340	717	622	1 333	1 276	1 279	688	591	1 274	1 219
Kentucky	2 987	1 421	1 566	2 954	2 798	1 867	989	878	1 861	1 767	1 762	935	827	1 760	1 662
Louisiana	3 217	1 500	1 717	3 196	3 071	1 997	1 050	947	1 956	1 837	1 863	991	872	1 822	1 721
Maine	969	470	499	961	939	669	352	317	642	635	635	333	302	605	602
Maryland	3 870	1 862	2 008	3 846	3 691	2 786	1 445	1 341	2 721	2 609	2 650	1 375	1 275	2 582	2 487
Massachusetts	4 726	2 268	2 458	4 701	4 708	3 189	1 678	1 512	3 176	3 228	3 052	1 596	1 456	3 006	3 033
Michigan	7 247	3 459	3 788	7 190	7 013	4 807	2 586	2 220	4 734	4 596	4 572	2 454	2 118	4 480	4 246
Minnesota	3 493	1 722	1 771	3 451	3 267	2 609	1 393	1 216	2 599	2 386	2 505	1 326	1 179	2 502	2 269
Mississippi	2 025	951	1 074	2 000	1 894	1 262	675	588	1 260	1 184	1 185	639	545	1 182	1 094
Missouri	4 037	1 913	2 124	4 002	3 857	2 898	1 490	1 407	2 828	2 594	2 765	1 418	1 347	2 692	2 443
Montana	671	327	344	660	596	447	238	208	438	401	423	224	199	412	377
Nebraska	1 231	594	637	1 217	1 161	913	482	431	900	814	886	469	417	876	796
Nevada	1 221	607	614	1 167	935	844	471	373	804	665	798	448	350	761	632
New Hampshire	888	426	462	875	847	624	333	291	634	628	598	320	278	609	592
New Jersey	6 136	2 932	3 204	6 114	6 046	4 124	2 217	1 908	4 067	4 067	3 869	2 083	1 786	3 806	3 861
New Mexico	1 270	613	657	1 247	1 117	800	437	363	792	708	735	400	335	743	662
New York	14 014	6 558	7 456	14 026	14 062	8 639	4 621	4 018	8 537	8 843	8 100	4 320	3 780	7 996	8 375
North Carolina	5 544	2 663	2 881	5 451	5 083	3 796	2 025	1 771	3 639	3 468	3 631	1 939	1 692	3 482	3 324
North Dakota	477	232	245	474	463	343	181	163	336	318	333	175	158	325	305
Ohio	8 515	4 072	4 443	8 465	8 230	5 643	3 038	2 605	5 583	5 409	5 365	2 886	2 479	5 317	5 099
Oklahoma	2 469	1 160	1 309	2 445	2 345	1 577	846	730	1 548	1 514	1 513	816	696	1 475	1 428
Oregon	2 484	1 220	1 264	2 437	2 192	1 721	935	786	1 656	1 490	1 619	879	741	1 576	1 407
Pennsylvania	9 288	4 385	4 903	9 283	9 197	5 903	3 176	2 727	5 842	5 791	5 590	2 988	2 602	5 499	5 476
Rhode Island	755	353	402	756	774	496	259	237	488	519	470	246	224	454	484
South Carolina	2 825	1 347	1 478	2 787	2 611	1 848	987	861	1 858	1 739	1 737	930	807	1 764	1 656
South Dakota	539	265	274	533	501	390	207	183	384	347	377	200	177	373	334
Tennessee	4 106	1 965	2 141	4 041	3 762	2 751	1 450	1 301	2 707	2 387	2 609	1 379	1 230	2 567	2 261
Texas	14 120	6 843	7 277	13 844	12 600	9 748	5 403	4 345	9 613	8 616	9 200	5 119	4 080	9 034	8 071
Utah	1 400	684	716	1 357	1 156	998	557	441	974	816	964	539	425	940	781
Vermont	453	215	238	448	430	324	167	158	320	304	310	159	150	306	289
Virginia	5 039	2 373	2 666	4 982	4 655	3 389	1 769	1 621	3 491	3 239	3 240	1 694	1 546	3 333	3 098
Washington	4 193	2 034	2 159	4 118	3 675	2 887	1 568	1 319	2 817	2 538	2 699	1 475	1 224	2 637	2 413
West Virginia	1 452	676	776	1 448	1 399	808	437	370	787	761	747	401	346	725	697
Wisconsin	3 906	1 927	1 979	3 865	3 674	2 918	1 540	1 378	2 851	2 581	2 815	1 481	1 333	2 745	2 467
Wyoming	363	176	187	358	329	258	139	119	256	236	245	132	113	244	223

[1]1990 data not strictly comparable to other years; based on unrevised population controls.

Note: National totals are derived independently and differ from the sum of the states.

Source: Civilian noninstitutional population, civilian labor force, and employed for 1996 and 1995 data–U.S. Bureau of Labor Statistics, Internet site <http://stats.bls.gov/news.release/srgune.t01.htm> (accessed 8 July 1997); Male, female, and 1990 data–U.S. Bureau of Labor Statistics, unpublished data; related publication, Employment and Earnings, monthly, May 1997.

Table A–20. States — Civilian Labor Force and Unemployment

Geographic area	Employment/ population ratio[1], 1996		Unemployment										Participation rate[4], 1996	
			Total (1,000)					Rate[3]						
			1996			1995	1990[2]	1996			1995	1990[2]		
	Male	Female	Total	Male	Female			Total	Male	Female			Male	Female
United States	**70.9**	**56.0**	**7 236**	**3 880**	**3 356**	**7 404**	**7 047**	**5.4**	**5.4**	**5.4**	**5.6**	**5.6**	**74.9**	**59.3**
Alabama	68.4	53.2	107	54	53	129	130	5.1	4.9	5.4	6.3	6.9	71.9	56.3
Alaska	73.0	63.7	25	15	9	22	19	7.8	9.1	6.3	7.3	7.0	80.3	68.2
Arizona	71.4	54.8	124	65	59	112	99	5.5	5.3	5.8	5.1	5.5	75.3	58.2
Arkansas	67.8	55.2	67	35	31	59	78	5.4	5.4	5.4	4.9	7.0	71.7	58.4
California	69.6	52.4	1 126	632	495	1 211	874	7.2	7.2	7.2	7.8	5.8	75.0	56.4
Colorado	75.6	63.0	89	50	39	88	89	4.2	4.4	4.0	4.2	5.0	79.0	65.7
Connecticut	70.2	58.9	99	51	47	94	95	5.7	5.7	5.7	5.5	5.2	74.5	62.5
Delaware	69.6	61.0	20	11	9	17	19	5.2	5.8	4.5	4.3	5.2	73.9	63.7
District of Columbia	61.9	55.1	23	11	12	25	22	8.5	8.7	8.4	8.9	6.6	67.8	60.1
Florida	66.6	51.9	352	177	175	376	390	5.1	4.8	5.4	5.5	6.0	69.9	54.8
Georgia	73.4	57.0	173	79	94	177	182	4.6	4.0	5.3	4.9	5.5	76.4	60.2
Hawaii	70.4	58.3	38	21	17	34	16	6.4	6.9	5.8	5.9	2.9	75.7	61.9
Idaho	73.8	59.5	32	18	15	32	29	5.2	5.1	5.4	5.4	5.9	77.7	62.9
Illinois	72.9	57.5	322	176	146	312	369	5.3	5.3	5.2	5.2	6.2	77.1	60.7
Indiana	73.9	59.2	127	65	62	146	149	4.1	3.9	4.4	4.7	5.3	76.9	61.9
Iowa	76.6	65.4	60	29	31	54	62	3.8	3.5	4.1	3.5	4.3	79.4	68.1
Kansas	74.2	60.0	60	29	31	59	57	4.5	4.1	5.0	4.4	4.5	77.4	63.2
Kentucky	65.8	52.8	105	53	52	100	104	5.6	5.4	5.9	5.4	5.9	69.6	56.1
Louisiana	66.1	50.8	135	59	75	135	117	6.7	5.6	8.0	6.9	6.3	70.0	55.2
Maine	70.9	60.5	34	19	15	37	33	5.1	5.4	4.8	5.7	5.2	74.8	63.5
Maryland	73.8	63.5	136	70	66	139	122	4.9	4.9	4.9	5.1	4.7	77.6	66.8
Massachusetts	70.4	59.2	137	82	56	170	195	4.3	4.9	3.7	5.4	6.0	74.0	61.5
Michigan	70.9	55.9	234	132	102	253	350	4.9	5.1	4.6	5.3	7.6	74.8	58.6
Minnesota	77.0	66.6	104	67	37	96	117	4.0	4.8	3.1	3.7	4.9	80.9	68.7
Mississippi	67.2	50.7	77	35	42	77	90	6.1	5.2	7.2	6.1	7.6	70.9	54.7
Missouri	74.1	63.4	132	72	60	135	151	4.6	4.9	4.3	4.8	5.8	77.9	66.3
Montana	68.5	57.8	24	14	10	26	24	5.3	5.9	4.6	5.9	6.0	72.9	60.6
Nebraska	79.0	65.5	27	13	14	24	18	2.9	2.7	3.2	2.6	2.2	81.1	67.7
Nevada	73.8	57.0	46	23	23	43	33	5.4	4.8	6.2	5.4	4.9	77.5	60.8
New Hampshire	75.1	60.2	26	13	13	25	36	4.2	3.9	4.5	4.0	5.7	78.2	62.9
New Jersey	71.0	55.7	255	134	122	261	206	6.2	6.0	6.4	6.4	5.1	75.6	59.5
New Mexico	65.3	51.0	64	37	28	50	46	8.1	8.4	7.6	6.3	6.5	71.3	55.2
New York	65.9	50.7	540	301	238	541	467	6.2	6.5	5.9	6.3	5.3	70.5	53.9
North Carolina	72.8	58.7	165	86	79	158	144	4.3	4.3	4.5	4.3	4.2	76.1	61.5
North Dakota	75.4	64.5	11	6	5	11	13	3.1	3.1	3.0	3.3	4.0	78.0	66.4
Ohio	70.9	55.8	278	152	126	266	310	4.9	5.0	4.8	4.8	5.7	74.6	58.6
Oklahoma	70.3	53.2	64	30	34	73	86	4.1	3.6	4.6	4.7	5.7	72.9	55.8
Oregon	72.0	58.6	102	56	46	80	83	5.9	6.0	5.8	4.8	5.6	76.6	62.2
Pennsylvania	68.1	53.1	313	188	125	343	315	5.3	5.9	4.6	5.9	5.4	72.4	55.6
Rhode Island	69.7	55.7	25	13	13	34	35	5.1	4.9	5.4	7.0	6.8	73.3	58.9
South Carolina	69.0	54.6	111	57	54	94	83	6.0	5.8	6.2	5.1	4.8	73.3	58.2
South Dakota	75.5	64.6	13	7	6	11	13	3.2	3.2	3.2	2.9	3.9	78.0	66.7
Tennessee	70.2	57.4	142	71	71	140	126	5.2	4.9	5.4	5.2	5.3	73.8	60.8
Texas	74.8	56.1	549	284	265	579	544	5.6	5.3	6.1	6.0	6.3	79.0	59.7
Utah	78.8	59.4	35	18	16	35	35	3.5	3.3	3.7	3.6	4.3	81.4	61.6
Vermont	74.0	63.0	15	7	7	14	15	4.6	4.5	4.6	4.2	5.0	77.5	66.3
Virginia	71.4	58.0	149	75	74	157	141	4.4	4.2	4.6	4.5	4.3	74.5	60.8
Washington	72.5	56.7	188	93	94	179	125	6.5	5.9	7.2	6.4	4.9	77.1	61.1
West Virginia	59.3	44.6	61	36	24	62	64	7.5	8.3	6.6	7.9	8.4	64.6	47.7
Wisconsin	76.9	67.4	103	59	44	106	114	3.5	3.8	3.2	3.7	4.4	79.9	69.6
Wyoming	75.0	60.4	13	7	6	12	13	5.0	5.1	5.0	4.8	5.5	78.9	63.5

[1]Civilian employment as a percent of civilian noninstitutional population.
[2]1990 data not strictly comparable with other years; based on unrevised population controls.
[3]Percent unemployed of the civilian labor force.
[4]Percent of civilian noninstitutional population of each specified group in the civilian labor force.

Note: National totals are derived independently and differ from the sum of the states.

Source: Male, female, and 1990 data–U.S.Bureau of Labor Statistics, unpublished data; related publication, Employment and Earnings, monthly, May 1997. Unemployment totals for 1996 and 1995 data–U.S. Bureau of Labor Statistics, Internet site <http://stats.bls.gov/news.release/srgune.t01.htm> (accessed 8 July 1997).

Table A–21. States — Employment and Average Annual Pay by Industry

Geographic area	Nonfarm employment[1], 1996 (1,000) — Private industry								Government	Average annual pay[4], 1996 prel. (dollars) — Private industry								Government
	Total[2]	Construction	Manufacturing	Transportation and public utilities	Wholesale trade	Retail trade	FIRE[3]	Services	Government	Total[2]	Construction	Manufacturing	Transportation and public utilities	Wholesale trade	Retail trade	FIRE[3]	Services	Government
United States	100 093	5 407	18 282	6 316	6 483	21 625	6 977	34 359	19 461	28 581	30 340	36 235	36 095	37 527	15 215	41 728	27 213	30 878
Alabama	1 483	94	383	90	94	325	82	406	342	24 592	24 981	28 705	34 253	31 076	13 663	31 292	24 319	27 835
Alaska	190	13	16	23	9	46	12	62	73	30 548	45 427	29 205	39 558	33 761	18 325	31 563	25 128	37 783
Arizona	1 575	127	200	92	101	365	115	561	321	25 923	26 726	37 168	33 141	34 065	16 075	33 528	24 186	28 954
Arkansas	906	47	254	65	49	199	43	247	179	21 832	23 318	24 811	30 103	28 540	13 828	27 793	20 576	24 760
California	10 658	511	1 853	642	745	2 228	733	3 917	2 117	31 183	32 636	39 810	38 543	39 433	17 276	43 306	31 794	34 945
Colorado	1 588	111	196	120	98	367	118	565	309	28 182	29 870	37 080	39 290	37 788	15 528	35 976	27 212	30 334
Connecticut	1 359	52	275	73	81	266	131	481	224	36 439	37 777	47 045	41 246	49 449	17 806	57 686	32 272	37 539
Delaware	324	21	58	16	14	70	44	102	53	30 592	31 445	50 692	34 738	36 082	14 993	36 109	25 963	31 476
District of Columbia	382	9	13	19	5	45	28	263	241	40 195	34 814	52 970	55 710	51 434	16 260	56 463	41 075	51 008
Florida	5 253	324	490	314	331	1 276	394	2 118	929	25 045	26 184	31 946	32 933	35 783	15 621	34 918	24 961	29 093
Georgia	2 959	165	585	222	236	661	180	903	569	27 611	27 758	30 595	39 981	39 620	14 848	38 526	26 970	26 852
Hawaii	419	5 24	17	41	22	114	37	166	110	26 371	42 365	29 884	34 429	31 312	16 849	33 162	26 369	31 346
Idaho	395	30	73	23	29	96	25	115	98	23 047	25 910	32 274	28 434	26 074	13 783	28 522	22 261	24 703
Illinois	4 866	221	972	331	341	963	386	1 640	810	31 130	38 031	38 343	37 676	41 233	15 668	45 427	28 447	32 256
Indiana	2 419	132	674	139	139	541	135	653	394	26 379	29 997	36 328	31 928	32 946	13 394	30 541	22 586	27 116
Iowa	1 149	59	247	63	82	259	78	359	232	23 160	28 295	31 707	29 449	29 141	12 422	30 950	19 988	26 420
Kansas	993	57	196	70	75	229	59	301	235	24 574	26 762	32 967	32 095	33 238	13 396	30 174	22 281	24 764
Kentucky	1 382	77	312	93	81	320	68	408	290	24 130	25 446	31 631	32 272	30 104	13 190	29 994	21 881	26 167
Louisiana	1 449	113	188	108	92	331	83	486	361	24 732	26 753	35 137	32 570	30 592	13 168	29 442	22 626	23 685
Maine	447	23	88	22	26	111	27	150	93	23 288	26 005	30 521	29 159	30 532	14 126	32 153	21 970	26 686
Maryland	1 784	130	174	107	108	422	128	715	422	28 945	31 072	38 074	36 925	39 392	16 365	38 925	29 511	36 145
Massachusetts	2 636	94	444	129	167	530	209	1 063	400	33 765	37 618	42 635	37 303	45 641	16 853	51 310	32 613	35 135
Michigan	3 702	168	967	168	218	807	201	1 165	643	31 406	33 587	46 739	37 407	41 621	14 560	34 646	26 866	32 244
Minnesota	2 052	89	428	120	149	444	143	672	380	28 554	35 176	37 250	35 038	39 899	14 497	40 437	25 282	30 822
Mississippi	872	49	246	53	45	188	41	247	218	21 461	23 233	24 334	30 634	28 274	12 747	26 835	20 978	23 349
Missouri	2 165	116	414	160	146	467	150	708	400	26 551	31 194	34 315	34 103	34 901	14 243	33 657	24 545	26 926
Montana	282	17	24	21	18	79	16	102	77	20 082	25 433	26 856	29 134	26 612	12 382	25 988	18 999	25 440
Nebraska	683	37	114	50	53	154	53	220	152	22 823	28 049	28 857	30 460	27 459	12 627	30 433	21 964	25 461
Nevada	741	75	39	42	33	137	38	364	101	26 931	34 507	31 905	32 039	34 805	17 574	33 259	25 647	34 190
New Hampshire	481	21	105	20	26	118	28	162	79	27 648	30 053	36 378	34 326	42 392	15 535	35 338	25 911	27 972
New Jersey	3 073	123	485	254	269	587	232	1 122	567	35 351	38 510	44 126	43 381	45 641	18 366	50 391	33 082	39 194
New Mexico	523	43	46	31	27	137	32	192	171	22 604	23 392	29 630	30 431	28 215	13 884	26 336	23 907	27 700
New York	6 535	254	922	402	426	1 195	721	2 610	1 382	36 714	36 856	41 843	41 922	44 171	16 890	75 051	31 555	37 405
North Carolina	2 994	189	847	168	178	633	154	822	561	25 168	25 199	29 110	34 985	34 319	14 352	35 939	23 743	26 718
North Dakota	238	15	22	18	21	59	14	85	71	20 754	26 587	26 569	29 954	27 337	11 859	25 776	19 357	23 421
Ohio	4 544	213	1 094	232	284	1 016	277	1 415	752	27 448	30 703	38 356	33 329	36 423	14 126	33 157	24 238	29 848
Oklahoma	1 083	50	174	77	65	254	67	364	272	22 901	23 408	29 740	32 912	28 023	13 012	27 450	20 838	25 043
Oregon	1 229	78	235	73	89	276	91	385	246	26 434	33 009	34 870	33 556	36 962	15 857	32 445	23 608	30 321
Pennsylvania	4 587	202	929	272	263	943	309	1 651	721	28 369	31 710	36 328	36 124	36 291	14 515	38 056	27 083	32 909
Rhode Island	381	14	82	15	19	80	25	146	61	26 129	31 086	31 250	32 396	36 360	14 665	35 115	25 661	33 895
South Carolina	1 377	94	365	73	67	331	72	373	299	23 637	26 050	30 085	31 239	31 719	13 725	28 579	21 811	26 001
South Dakota	279	15	48	16	20	68	20	90	70	20 111	23 503	24 882	26 357	26 037	11 942	25 091	19 303	23 705
Tennessee	2 151	113	522	143	140	456	117	656	383	25 724	27 223	30 790	32 259	33 417	15 018	33 939	24 489	27 347
Texas	6 788	436	1 054	488	476	1 513	444	2 221	1 454	28 421	28 912	36 163	36 678	37 914	15 341	36 479	26 662	26 765
Utah	788	60	129	54	48	182	50	256	167	24 103	25 092	30 196	32 556	31 539	14 237	29 562	23 091	26 867
Vermont	230	13	46	12	13	52	12	82	45	24 040	25 471	30 616	30 341		13 998	32 166	22 225	26 786
Virginia	2 533	175	399	162	143	570	162	911	597	27 315	26 786	31 999	37 330	38 341	14 746	35 759	28 602	30 986
Washington	1 961	127	344	123	145	446	124	649	450	28 217	30 696	39 086	35 881	34 880	16 083	34 430	28 057	31 961
West Virginia	560	34	82	39	30	130	27	191	139	23 724	25 747	33 678	33 090	29 181	12 295	24 591	20 907	25 500
Wisconsin	2 218	105	601	121	129	466	138	655	383	25 505	31 902	33 464	29 983	32 787	12 916	31 811	22 558	29 365
Wyoming	163	14	11	14	7	45	8	48	59	22 264	24 634	29 486	31 664	27 793	12 372	27 247	18 048	24 708

[1]National totals are derived independently and differ from the sum of the state.
[2]Includes mining, not shown separately.
[3]Finance, insurance, and real estate.
[4]For workers covered by state unemployment insurance laws and for federal workers covered by unemployment compensation for federal employees.
[5]Hawaii includes mining with construction.

Source: Employment–U.S., Bureau of Labor Statistics, Employment and Earnings, monthly, May issue, compiled from data supplied by cooperating state agencies; Wholesale and retail employment–Bureau of Labor Statistics, Internet site <http://www.bls.gov/cgi-bin/dsrv> (accessed 10 October 1997); Average annual pay–U.S. Bureau of Labor Statistics, Internet site <ftp://stats.bls.gov/pub/news.release/annpay.toc.htm> (accessed 11 September 1997).

Employment, Average Annual Pay, and Union Membership

Geographic area	Nonfarm employment[1] (1,000)		Average annual pay[2] (dollars)		Labor union membership[3]									
					Union members (1,000)		Workers covered by union (1,000)		Percent of workers					
									Union members		Covered by union		Private manufacturing sector union members	
	1996	1990	1996, prel.	1990	1996	1985	1996	1985	1996	1985	1996	1985	1996	1985
United States	**119 554**	**109 419**	**28 945**	**23 602**	**16 269.4**	**16 996.1**	**18 158.1**	**19 358.1**	**14.5**	**18.0**	**16.2**	**20.5**	**17.2**	**24.8**
Alabama	1 825	1 636	25 180	20 468	200.7	226.6	226.2	254.9	11.4	15.7	12.8	17.6	16.5	25.2
Alaska	263	238	32 461	29 946	54.7	47.7	60.5	53.4	22.5	25.0	24.9	28.0	7.2	18.9
Arizona	1 896	1 483	26 387	21 443	106.8	115.6	135.9	145.7	5.9	9.5	7.5	12.0	3.9	7.8
Arkansas	1 086	924	22 294	18 204	74.4	91.6	88.4	108.4	7.1	11.2	8.4	13.3	12.5	20.4
California	12 775	12 500	31 773	26 180	2 060.6	2 123.1	2 339.9	2 485.8	16.5	20.4	18.8	23.9	9.2	18.6
Colorado	1 897	1 521	28 520	22 908	167.1	165.2	185.2	191.1	9.7	11.8	10.8	13.7	9.4	9.3
Connecticut	1 583	1 624	36 579	28 995	239.5	306.5	250.5	325.9	16.5	20.9	17.2	22.2	10.6	20.4
Delaware	377	348	30 711	24 423	40.0	45.6	45.2	50.9	12.4	16.6	14.0	18.5	16.2	23.5
District of Columbia	623	686	44 458	33 717	39.5	45.2	44.5	58.2	17.2	16.5	19.4	21.2	14.9	24.5
Florida	6 183	5 387	25 640	21 030	429.8	395.2	568.4	515.7	7.5	9.1	9.9	11.9	8.0	8.2
Georgia	3 528	2 992	27 488	22 115	242.1	239.5	285.5	273.1	7.7	10.0	9.1	11.4	8.7	13.8
Hawaii	529	528	27 363	23 167	111.9	109.6	118.3	121.2	23.2	27.8	24.5	30.8	18.8	34.8
Idaho	492	385	23 353	18 991	42.5	41.7	52.1	48.4	8.7	11.7	10.7	13.6	11.2	21.5
Illinois	5 676	5 288	31 285	25 312	1 043.1	1 031.7	1 124.8	1 124.9	20.0	22.2	21.5	24.3	23.6	30.9
Indiana	2 813	2 522	26 477	21 699	395.2	476.7	427.8	524.4	14.9	21.3	16.1	23.4	29.6	42.0
Iowa	1 380	1 226	23 679	19 224	168.7	181.7	203.0	212.8	13.0	17.0	15.7	20.0	21.5	37.7
Kansas	1 228	1 089	24 609	20 238	105.8	129.0	134.7	157.3	9.6	12.8	12.3	15.6	20.0	23.7
Kentucky	1 671	1 471	24 462	19 947	198.8	219.2	220.5	250.8	12.7	16.5	14.1	18.8	22.6	37.1
Louisiana	1 811	1 590	24 528	20 646	133.4	147.9	164.7	172.8	8.1	9.6	10.0	11.2	19.0	21.4
Maine	540	535	23 850	20 154	77.4	77.5	87.8	90.0	14.5	17.1	16.4	19.8	23.6	26.5
Maryland	2 206	2 171	30 293	24 730	353.5	329.9	415.4	412.9	14.8	16.7	17.4	20.9	22.0	28.7
Massachusetts	3 036	2 985	33 940	26 699	415.0	495.4	455.0	548.4	15.4	18.5	16.8	20.4	10.2	20.2
Michigan	4 345	3 970	31 522	25 376	983.3	1 004.5	1 042.2	1 071.0	24.0	28.4	25.4	30.3	34.9	42.3
Minnesota	2 432	2 127	28 869	23 121	437.4	407.5	457.9	452.7	20.3	22.6	21.2	25.1	17.0	23.1
Mississippi	1 090	937	21 822	17 718	62.0	81.3	86.4	94.5	5.8	9.3	8.1	10.8	10.7	15.0
Missouri	2 564	2 345	26 608	21 716	375.2	378.3	408.9	418.9	15.4	18.7	16.8	20.7	26.2	32.0
Montana	359	297	21 146	17 895	52.0	57.3	56.6	66.9	15.6	19.4	16.9	22.7	13.9	38.2
Nebraska	834	730	23 291	18 577	62.9	78.8	90.4	99.0	8.6	12.7	12.4	16.0	10.6	22.4
Nevada	843	621	27 788	22 358	147.3	89.7	175.7	102.1	20.4	21.6	24.3	24.6	9.6	13.7
New Hampshire	560	508	27 691	22 609	57.4	48.8	64.8	54.8	11.2	10.7	12.6	12.0	4.9	9.3
New Jersey	3 640	3 635	35 928	28 449	768.0	821.0	832.4	937.2	21.8	24.9	23.7	28.4	20.6	28.4
New Mexico	694	580	23 716	19 347	52.6	49.4	67.3	62.4	8.4	10.0	10.8	12.7	8.9	15.2
New York	7 917	8 212	36 831	28 873	1 942.0	2 102.3	2 041.9	2 298.3	26.8	30.2	28.2	33.0	19.6	28.7
North Carolina	3 555	3 118	25 408	20 220	134.0	167.0	161.3	209.5	4.1	6.4	5.0	8.0	2.5	7.0
North Dakota	309	266	21 242	17 626	24.4	27.9	28.1	34.2	9.1	11.4	10.5	14.0	17.8	17.4
Ohio	5 296	4 882	27 775	22 844	933.2	999.0	997.6	1 090.9	19.5	23.6	20.8	25.7	31.3	39.3
Oklahoma	1 354	1 196	23 329	20 288	135.5	128.4	161.6	151.0	10.4	10.5	12.4	12.3	16.4	21.0
Oregon	1 475	1 247	27 027	21 332	246.2	231.6	266.8	260.8	18.0	22.7	19.5	25.6	19.7	26.9
Pennsylvania	5 308	5 170	28 973	23 457	885.8	1 055.4	978.3	1 174.7	17.7	22.8	19.5	25.4	22.9	35.1
Rhode Island	442	451	27 194	22 388	81.0	90.2	85.3	97.7	19.1	21.1	20.1	22.9	11.0	16.2
South Carolina	1 676	1 545	24 039	19 668	58.2	58.8	78.7	72.5	3.7	4.5	5.0	5.6	4.3	6.7
South Dakota	349	289	20 724	16 430	23.0	27.9	28.6	34.5	7.4	11.2	9.2	13.8	9.7	19.3
Tennessee	2 534	2 193	25 963	20 611	219.2	236.8	254.2	281.8	9.6	13.1	11.1	15.6	14.8	18.9
Texas	8 242	7 095	28 129	22 700	527.7	474.8	645.8	626.2	6.6	7.4	8.0	9.7	8.5	9.8
Utah	955	724	24 572	20 074	71.1	69.9	94.2	91.9	8.4	11.4	11.1	14.9	5.4	8.6
Vermont	275	258	24 480	20 532	24.9	28.5	29.0	35.4	9.7	12.8	11.3	15.9	8.2	14.9
Virginia	3 130	2 896	28 001	22 750	200.8	236.0	236.5	296.7	6.8	9.7	8.0	12.2	11.8	18.7
Washington	2 412	2 143	28 881	22 646	464.2	405.8	511.3	469.2	19.8	25.0	21.8	28.9	29.0	37.8
West Virginia	698	630	24 075	20 715	109.7	134.7	124.7	148.3	15.7	22.7	17.9	25.0	29.2	40.3
Wisconsin	2 602	2 292	26 021	21 101	469.7	435.9	493.2	463.9	18.8	22.3	19.8	23.8	23.9	36.5
Wyoming	221	199	22 870	20 049	20.1	26.8	23.9	34.2	9.7	13.8	11.6	17.6	12.0	15.0

[1]National totals are derived independently and differ from the sum of the states.
[2]For workers covered by state unemployment insurance laws and for federal workers covered by unemployment compensation for federal employees.
[3]Annual averages of monthly figures. For wage and salary workers in agriculture and nonagriculture. Data represent union members by place of residence.

Source: Employment–U.S. Bureau of Labor Statistics, Employment and Earnings, monthly, May issues, compiled from data supplied by cooperating state agencies; Average annual pay, 1996–U.S. Bureau of Labor Statistics, State and Industry Average Annual Pay for 1995 and 1996 Percent Change in Pay for All Covered Workers, (related Internet site <http://stats.bls.gov/news.release/annpay.t04.htm>); Average annual pay, 1990–U.S. Bureau of Labor Statistics, USDL 92-631, October 1992; Union members–The Bureau of National Affairs, Inc., Washington, DC, Union Membership and Earnings Data Book: Compilations from the Current Population Survey; 1997 edition (copyright by BNA PLUS), authored by Barry Hirsh and David Macpherson of Florida State University (related Internet site <http://www.bna.com/bnaplus>).

Table A–23. States — **Personal Income**

Geographic area	Personal income (bil dol) Current dollars 1996, prel.	1995	1990	Constant (1992) dollars 1996, prel.	1995	1990	Percent change, 1990-1996	Percent distribution 1996	1990	Personal income per capita (dollars) Current dollars 1996, prel.	1995	1990	Constant (1992) dollars 1996, prel.	1995	1990	Percent change, 1990-1996
United States	6 428.1	6 098.0	4 774.0	5 852.3	5 669.9	5 138.3	13.9	100.0	100.0	24 231	23 196	19 142	22 060	21 568	20 603	7.1
Alabama	85.7	81.6	61.6	78.0	75.9	66.3	17.6	1.3	1.3	20 055	19 212	15 225	18 258	17 863	16 387	11.4
Alaska	14.9	14.5	11.6	13.6	13.5	12.5	8.8	.2	.2	24 558	24 045	21 048	22 358	22 357	22 654	-1.3
Arizona	92.9	86.4	60.9	84.6	80.4	65.5	29.2	1.4	1.3	20 989	20 074	16 539	19 109	18 665	17 801	7.3
Arkansas	47.5	45.0	33.0	43.3	41.8	35.6	21.6	.7	.7	18 928	18 093	14 032	17 232	16 823	15 103	14.1
California	801.5	760.4	636.6	729.7	707.0	685.2	6.5	12.5	13.3	25 144	24 091	21 290	22 891	22 400	22 915	-.1
Colorado	95.9	89.8	63.5	87.3	83.5	68.4	27.6	1.5	1.3	25 084	23 954	19 224	22 837	22 272	20 691	10.4
Connecticut	108.7	104.1	86.7	98.9	96.8	93.4	5.9	1.7	1.8	33 189	31 814	26 376	30 216	29 581	28 389	6.4
Delaware	20.0	18.8	14.5	18.2	17.5	15.6	16.7	.3	.3	27 622	26 279	21 695	25 147	24 434	23 351	7.7
District of Columbia	19.0	18.5	15.5	17.3	17.2	16.6	4.2	.3	.3	34 932	33 435	25 620	31 803	31 088	27 575	15.3
Florida	347.1	326.7	248.7	316.0	303.7	267.7	18.0	5.4	5.2	24 104	23 030	19 107	21 945	21 413	20 565	6.7
Georgia	167.0	156.6	113.1	152.0	145.6	121.7	24.9	2.6	2.4	22 709	21 718	17 377	20 675	20 193	18 703	10.5
Hawaii	29.8	29.2	23.7	27.1	27.1	25.6	5.9	.5	.5	25 159	24 749	21 337	22 905	23 012	22 965	-.3
Idaho	23.2	22.0	15.5	21.2	20.4	16.7	26.9	.4	.3	19 539	18 860	15 316	17 789	17 536	16 485	7.9
Illinois	315.1	298.4	234.6	286.9	277.5	252.5	13.6	4.9	4.9	26 598	25 310	20 496	24 215	23 533	22 060	9.8
Indiana	131.1	124.4	95.4	119.3	115.7	102.7	16.2	2.0	2.0	22 440	21 457	17 174	20 430	19 951	18 485	10.5
Iowa	64.3	59.5	47.1	58.6	55.3	50.7	15.6	1.0	1.0	22 560	20 911	16 959	20 539	19 443	18 253	12.5
Kansas	59.9	56.0	44.6	54.5	52.1	48.0	13.5	.9	.9	23 281	21 855	17 988	21 195	20 321	19 361	9.5
Kentucky	76.5	72.8	55.7	69.6	67.7	60.0	16.0	1.2	1.2	19 687	18 866	15 087	17 923	17 542	16 238	10.4
Louisiana	86.2	82.4	62.3	78.5	76.6	67.0	17.2	1.3	1.3	19 824	19 000	14 761	18 048	17 666	15 887	13.6
Maine	25.9	25.0	21.1	23.6	23.2	22.8	3.5	.4	.4	20 826	20 150	17 167	18 960	18 735	18 477	2.6
Maryland	138.1	132.8	107.9	125.7	123.5	116.1	8.3	2.1	2.3	27 221	26 352	22 484	24 782	24 502	24 200	2.4
Massachusetts	179.4	170.2	139.6	163.3	158.2	150.3	8.6	2.8	2.9	29 439	28 032	23 203	26 802	26 064	24 974	7.3
Michigan	238.0	228.4	174.2	216.7	212.3	187.5	15.6	3.7	3.6	24 810	23 943	18 711	22 587	22 262	20 139	12.2
Minnesota	119.1	110.5	85.0	108.5	102.7	91.5	18.6	1.9	1.8	25 580	23 944	19 374	23 288	22 263	20 852	11.7
Mississippi	47.5	45.0	32.8	43.2	41.8	35.3	22.4	.7	.7	17 471	16 690	12 710	15 906	15 518	13 680	16.3
Missouri	122.5	116.2	90.5	111.5	108.0	97.4	14.5	1.9	1.9	22 864	21 836	17 656	20 816	20 303	19 003	9.5
Montana	16.7	16.1	12.0	15.2	14.9	12.9	17.8	.3	.3	19 047	18 443	15 042	17 341	17 148	16 190	7.1
Nebraska	38.1	35.2	27.9	34.7	32.7	30.0	15.7	.6	.6	23 047	21 450	17 624	20 982	19 944	18 969	10.6
Nevada	40.8	37.3	24.5	37.1	34.7	26.4	40.5	.6	.5	25 451	24 336	20 123	23 171	22 628	21 659	7.0
New Hampshire	30.8	29.4	23.0	28.1	27.3	24.7	13.8	.5	.5	26 520	25 587	20 672	24 144	23 791	22 249	8.5
New Jersey	248.1	237.2	192.9	225.8	220.5	207.6	8.8	3.9	4.0	31 053	29 833	24 927	28 271	27 739	26 829	5.4
New Mexico	32.2	30.7	21.9	29.3	28.5	23.6	24.2	.5	.5	18 770	18 158	14 440	17 088	16 883	15 542	9.9
New York	523.4	502.0	448.2	476.5	466.7	448.2	6.3	8.1	8.7	28 782	27 595	23 131	26 204	25 658	24 896	5.3
North Carolina	161.2	151.8	110.9	146.7	141.2	119.4	22.9	2.5	2.3	22 010	21 082	16 663	20 038	19 602	17 935	11.7
North Dakota	13.3	11.9	9.8	12.1	11.1	10.5	15.2	.2	.2	20 710	18 621	15 324	18 855	17 314	16 493	14.3
Ohio	263.0	251.0	196.9	239.4	233.4	211.9	13.0	4.1	4.1	23 537	22 547	18 126	21 428	20 964	19 509	9.8
Oklahoma	63.9	60.9	49.0	58.2	56.6	52.8	10.2	1.0	1.0	19 350	18 596	15 583	17 617	17 291	16 772	5.0
Oregon	72.6	67.9	49.8	66.1	63.1	53.6	23.3	1.1	1.0	22 668	21 554	17 435	20 637	20 041	18 765	10.0
Pennsylvania	297.4	284.4	230.4	270.8	264.4	247.9	9.2	4.6	4.8	24 668	23 580	19 365	22 458	21 925	20 843	7.7
Rhode Island	24.5	23.6	19.8	22.3	21.9	21.3	4.7	.4	.4	24 765	23 798	19 690	22 546	22 127	21 193	6.4
South Carolina	73.1	69.8	54.0	66.5	64.9	58.1	14.5	1.1	1.1	19 755	19 031	15 420	17 985	17 695	16 597	8.4
South Dakota	15.8	14.3	10.8	14.3	13.3	11.6	23.3	.2	.2	21 516	19 564	15 537	19 588	18 191	16 723	17.1
Tennessee	115.8	110.6	79.7	105.4	102.8	85.8	22.8	1.8	1.7	21 764	21 076	16 294	19 814	19 596	17 537	13.0
Texas	421.7	397.1	293.5	383.9	369.2	315.9	21.5	6.6	6.1	22 045	21 119	17 218	20 070	19 636	18 532	8.3
Utah	38.3	35.6	24.6	34.9	33.1	26.4	32.2	.6	.5	19 156	18 167	14 204	17 440	16 892	15 288	14.1
Vermont	13.0	12.4	10.0	11.9	11.5	10.7	11.2	.2	.2	22 124	21 231	17 692	20 142	19 741	19 042	5.8
Virginia	166.4	158.7	124.3	151.5	147.5	133.7	13.3	2.6	2.6	24 925	23 985	19 997	22 692	22 301	21 523	5.4
Washington	137.4	129.1	96.0	125.1	120.1	103.3	21.1	2.1	2.0	24 838	23 701	19 583	22 613	22 037	21 077	7.3
West Virginia	33.7	32.3	25.4	30.7	30.1	27.3	12.5	.5	.5	18 444	17 714	14 177	16 792	16 470	15 259	10.0
Wisconsin	120.1	114.0	86.9	109.3	106.0	93.5	16.9	1.9	1.8	23 269	22 265	17 720	21 184	20 702	19 072	11.1
Wyoming	10.2	9.9	7.7	9.3	9.2	8.3	12.0	.2	.2	21 245	20 727	17 062	19 342	19 272	18 364	5.3

Source: 1996 and 1995–U.S. Bureau of Economic Analysis, Survey of Current Business, Volume 77, Number 5, May 1997; 1990–U.S. Bureau of Economic Analysis, Survey of Current Business, Volume 76, Number 10, October 1996.

Table A–24. States — Household and Family Income and Poverty

Geographic area	Median household income — Current dollars			Median household income — Constant (1995) dollars[1]			Median income for 4-person family — Current dollars		Median income for 4-person family — Constant (1995) dollars[1]		Persons below poverty level — Number (1,000)				Persons below poverty level — Percent			
	1995	1994	1990	1995	1994	1990	1995	1990	1995	1990	1995 Total	1995 Children[2]	1994	1990	1995 Total	1995 Children[2]	1994	1990
United States	34 076	32 264	29 943	34 076	33 178	34 914	49 687	41 451	49 687	48 333	36 425	9 583	38 059	33 585	13.8	19.0	14.5	13.5
Alabama	25 991	27 196	23 357	25 991	27 967	27 235	42 617	35 937	42 617	41 904	882	198	704	779	20.1	22.6	16.4	19.2
Alaska	47 954	45 367	39 298	47 954	46 653	45 823	56 045	51 538	56 045	60 095	45	10	61	57	7.1	6.7	10.2	11.4
Arizona	30 863	31 293	29 224	30 863	32 180	34 076	44 526	38 799	44 526	45 241	700	199	673	484	16.1	24.2	15.9	13.7
Arkansas	25 814	25 565	22 786	25 814	26 290	26 569	38 520	31 913	38 520	37 211	376	108	369	472	14.9	21.7	15.3	19.6
California	37 009	35 331	33 290	37 009	36 332	38 817	51 519	45 184	51 519	52 686	5 342	1 456	5 658	4 128	16.7	23.4	17.9	13.9
Colorado	40 706	37 833	30 733	40 706	38 905	35 836	50 941	41 803	50 941	48 744	335	82	335	461	8.8	10.7	9.0	13.7
Connecticut	40 243	41 097	38 870	40 243	42 262	45 324	62 157	53 931	62 157	62 885	318	120	344	196	9.7	17.8	10.8	6.0
Delaware	34 928	35 873	30 804	34 928	36 890	35 918	54 519	46 524	54 519	54 248	74	23	57	48	10.3	16.6	8.3	6.9
District of Columbia	30 748	30 116	27 392	30 748	30 969	31 940	49 837	38 824	49 837	45 270	122	27	129	120	22.2	31.5	21.2	21.1
Florida	29 745	29 294	26 685	29 745	30 124	31 115	44 626	38 438	44 626	44 820	2 321	540	2 128	1 896	16.2	22.1	14.9	14.4
Georgia	34 099	31 467	27 561	34 099	32 359	32 137	48 850	41 184	48 850	48 022	878	218	1 012	1 001	12.1	15.6	14.0	15.8
Hawaii	42 851	42 255	38 921	42 851	43 453	45 383	54 749	50 234	54 749	58 574	122	31	97	121	10.3	14.2	8.7	11.0
Idaho	32 676	31 536	25 305	32 676	32 430	29 506	42 142	34 091	42 142	39 751	167	39	137	157	14.5	16.7	12.0	14.9
Illinois	38 071	35 081	32 542	38 071	36 075	37 945	53 807	44 220	53 807	51 562	1 459	467	1 464	1 606	12.4	20.3	12.4	13.7
Indiana	33 385	27 858	26 928	33 385	28 647	31 399	47 465	39 700	47 465	46 291	545	153	816	714	9.6	14.5	13.7	13.0
Iowa	35 519	33 079	27 288	35 519	34 016	31 819	47 314	38 090	47 314	44 414	352	98	302	289	12.2	15.5	10.7	10.4
Kansas	30 341	28 322	29 917	30 341	29 125	34 884	46 611	40 576	46 611	47 313	273	51	375	259	10.8	10.7	14.9	10.3
Kentucky	29 810	26 595	24 780	29 810	27 349	28 894	40 587	36 348	40 587	42 383	572	139	710	628	14.7	19.3	18.5	17.3
Louisiana	27 949	25 676	22 405	27 949	26 404	26 125	41 442	36 510	41 442	42 572	849	205	1 117	952	19.7	24.4	25.7	23.6
Maine	33 858	30 316	27 464	33 858	31 175	32 024	45 507	38 848	45 507	45 298	138	31	113	162	11.2	14.3	9.4	13.1
Maryland	41 041	39 198	38 857	41 041	40 309	45 308	60 239	53 385	60 239	62 248	520	119	541	468	10.1	13.3	10.7	9.9
Massachusetts	38 574	40 500	36 247	38 574	41 648	42 265	59 191	52 171	59 191	60 833	665	170	585	626	11.0	16.8	9.7	10.7
Michigan	36 426	35 284	29 937	36 426	36 284	34 907	52 955	43 545	52 955	50 775	1 174	292	1 347	1 315	12.2	14.8	14.1	14.3
Minnesota	37 933	33 644	31 465	37 933	34 597	36 689	54 396	43 031	54 396	50 175	427	101	523	524	9.2	10.4	11.7	12.0
Mississippi	26 538	25 400	20 178	26 538	26 120	23 528	37 328	30 242	37 328	35 263	630	212	515	684	23.5	36.4	19.9	25.7
Missouri	34 825	30 190	27 332	34 825	31 046	31 870	45 795	39 766	45 795	46 368	484	89	797	700	9.4	9.8	15.6	13.4
Montana	27 757	27 631	23 375	27 757	28 414	27 264	42 987	35 105	42 987	40 933	133	31	97	134	15.3	19.0	11.5	16.3
Nebraska	32 929	31 794	27 482	32 929	32 695	32 045	44 886	39 664	44 886	46 249	159	41	146	167	9.6	11.9	8.8	10.3
Nevada	36 084	35 871	32 023	36 084	36 888	37 340	50 064	41 629	50 064	48 541	173	33	168	119	11.1	11.1	11.1	9.8
New Hampshire	39 171	35 245	40 805	39 171	36 244	47 580	54 492	49 088	54 492	57 238	60	8	87	68	5.3	4.3	7.7	6.3
New Jersey	43 924	42 280	38 734	43 924	43 478	45 165	61 409	56 436	61 409	65 806	617	127	730	711	7.8	9.5	9.2	9.2
New Mexico	25 991	26 905	25 039	25 991	27 667	29 196	37 365	32 941	37 365	38 410	457	150	356	319	25.3	34.9	21.1	20.9
New York	33 028	31 899	31 591	33 028	32 803	36 836	50 672	44 200	50 672	51 538	3 020	805	3 097	2 571	16.5	23.6	17.0	14.3
North Carolina	31 979	30 114	26 329	31 979	30 967	30 700	47 367	39 718	47 367	46 312	877	233	980	829	12.6	20.2	14.2	13.0
North Dakota	29 089	28 278	25 264	29 089	29 079	29 459	43 483	36 127	43 483	42 125	76	17	65	87	12.0	13.2	10.4	13.7
Ohio	34 941	31 855	30 013	34 941	32 758	34 996	50 893	42 821	50 893	49 931	1 285	380	1 571	1 256	11.5	17.1	14.1	11.5
Oklahoma	26 311	26 991	24 384	26 311	27 756	28 432	42 124	34 141	42 124	39 809	548	151	540	481	17.1	24.2	16.7	15.6
Oregon	36 374	31 456	29 281	36 374	32 347	34 142	46 229	39 653	46 229	46 237	360	92	373	267	11.2	16.2	11.8	9.2
Pennsylvania	34 524	32 066	29 005	34 524	32 975	33 821	50 884	40 892	50 884	47 681	1 464	369	1 496	1 328	12.2	16.5	12.5	11.0
Rhode Island	35 359	31 928	31 968	35 359	32 833	37 276	51 362	44 598	51 362	52 003	102	27	99	71	10.6	16.4	10.3	7.5
South Carolina	29 071	29 846	28 735	29 071	30 692	33 510	44 048	38 797	44 048	45 238	744	249	501	548	19.9	31.7	13.8	16.2
South Dakota	29 578	29 733	24 571	29 578	30 576	28 650	44 292	34 632	44 292	40 382	103	25	107	93	14.5	17.3	14.5	13.3
Tennessee	29 015	28 639	22 592	29 015	29 451	26 343	44 312	34 279	44 312	39 970	846	204	779	833	15.5	19.6	14.6	16.9
Texas	32 039	30 755	28 228	32 039	31 627	32 915	43 977	37 789	43 977	44 063	3 270	887	3 603	2 684	17.4	23.1	19.1	15.9
Utah	36 480	35 716	30 142	36 480	36 728	35 146	45 611	38 632	45 611	45 046	168	43	154	143	8.4	8.4	8.0	8.2
Vermont	33 824	35 802	31 098	33 824	36 817	36 261	47 376	41 312	47 376	48 171	61	16	45	61	10.3	13.0	7.6	10.9
Virginia	36 222	37 647	35 073	36 222	38 714	40 896	50 032	44 597	50 032	52 001	648	154	710	705	10.2	14.5	10.7	11.1
Washington	35 568	33 533	32 112	35 568	34 483	37 444	51 415	44 306	51 415	51 662	677	156	614	434	12.5	16.6	11.7	8.9
West Virginia	24 880	23 564	22 137	24 880	24 232	25 812	39 731	33 666	39 731	39 256	300	71	336	328	16.7	25.8	18.6	18.1
Wisconsin	40 955	35 388	30 711	40 955	36 391	35 810	50 628	43 182	50 628	50 351	449	123	453	448	8.5	11.2	9.0	9.3
Wyoming	31 529	33 140	29 460	31 529	34 079	34 351	45 925	36 796	45 925	42 905	59	11	45	51	12.2	10.6	9.3	11.0

[1]Constant (1995) dollars computed using the Consumer Price Index (CPI-U-X1) deflator from the Bureau of Labor Statistics.
[2]Related children under 18 years.

Source: Median household income–U.S. Bureau of the Census, Current Population Report, Money Income in the United States: 1995 P60-193; Median income for 4-person family–U.S. Bureau of the Census, Internet site <http://www.census.gov/hhes/income/4-person.html> (accessed 3 July 1997); Persons below poverty level–U.S. Bureau of the Census, Current Population Report, Poverty in the United States: 1995, P60-194.

Table A–25. States — **Energy Consumption**

Geographic area	1994 Total[1] (tril Btu)	1994 Per capita[2] (mil Btu)	1994 Percent change, 1990-1994	1993 (tril Btu)	1990 (tril Btu)	End-use sector, 1994 (tril Btu) Residential	Commercial	Industrial	Transportation	Selected source, 1994 (tril Btu) Petroleum	Natural gas (dry)	Coal	Hydroelectric power	Nuclear electric power
United States	88 788.6	341.0	5.8	87 006.9	83 952.6	17 623.2	13 431.2	[3]34 161.9	23 572.2	34 733.9	21 361.8	19 511.1	2 923.3	6 837.3
Alabama	1 882.4	446.6	9.8	1 821.0	1 714.9	318.1	166.4	957.2	440.7	563.1	297.5	770.6	117.4	218.6
Alaska	633.3	1 053.0	8.1	602.7	585.9	46.9	60.0	375.7	150.7	200.2	403.6	12.6	13.8	–
Arizona	1 033.3	252.5	9.9	981.6	940.3	237.3	219.2	206.4	370.3	386.1	137.1	402.3	78.8	247.4
Arkansas	956.5	389.6	12.8	923.7	848.2	177.0	110.2	408.7	260.6	308.8	249.8	221.9	35.6	148.6
California	7 554.8	240.9	–1.7	7 423.1	7 682.1	1 353.5	1 174.0	2 268.9	2 758.4	3 265.8	2 172.1	58.0	257.4	360.3
Colorado	1 049.0	286.4	13.6	1 034.8	923.7	229.6	221.8	283.7	313.8	383.8	277.1	349.1	17.0	–
Connecticut	796.9	243.5	4.0	799.5	766.1	246.2	183.3	159.6	207.8	381.5	123.6	22.5	11.3	215.2
Delaware	265.4	375.0	9.2	268.0	243.0	53.7	38.1	109.8	63.9	137.0	50.4	57.5	–	–
District of Columbia	176.0	309.8	2.9	180.3	171.1	35.5	110.0	3.5	26.9	37.7	31.2	1.2	–	–
Florida	3 382.1	242.2	7.2	3 228.6	3 155.4	919.6	719.6	554.2	1 188.6	1 686.1	392.5	641.7	2.8	284.9
Georgia	2 377.6	336.6	9.1	2 367.5	2 180.1	487.1	352.7	775.8	762.1	916.8	351.6	691.9	50.5	308.8
Hawaii	259.6	221.4	–13.5	244.6	300.2	23.4	25.4	75.2	135.5	237.2	2.9	1.8	1.5	–
Idaho	441.2	388.2	11.9	425.7	394.4	84.9	77.3	173.6	105.4	137.6	59.1	9.7	82.6	–
Illinois	3 694.7	314.9	3.1	3 673.3	3 583.4	898.3	682.4	1 322.0	792.0	1 228.3	1 046.4	818.9	1.3	775.7
Indiana	2 523.6	438.9	2.7	2 536.0	2 457.2	460.7	284.7	1 169.0	609.2	878.4	526.1	1 299.0	4.2	–
Iowa	1 030.0	363.7	13.6	994.5	906.5	222.0	146.1	409.8	252.0	371.4	250.3	346.9	11.0	43.9
Kansas	1 071.6	420.2	3.6	1 041.8	1 034.4	190.8	167.1	461.9	251.7	359.8	417.2	300.0	.1	91.1
Kentucky	1 704.6	445.6	15.4	1 652.5	1 476.7	300.5	187.9	802.1	414.2	608.7	221.3	897.5	41.2	–
Louisiana	3 817.0	884.7	5.7	3 673.8	3 612.4	303.9	216.5	2 515.3	781.2	1 554.2	1 688.7	230.8	10.1	136.4
Maine	546.9	441.8	7.8	536.6	507.2	85.6	53.4	299.9	108.0	249.2	5.1	11.6	58.4	70.8
Maryland	1 283.0	256.6	3.3	1 275.6	1 241.5	356.1	214.3	366.6	346.0	526.0	189.4	268.9	20.6	119.9
Massachusetts	1 487.5	246.2	5.5	1 484.0	1 410.0	433.7	351.9	304.9	397.0	712.8	346.1	100.7	28.5	41.2
Michigan	3 085.5	325.3	8.6	3 003.3	2 841.0	734.9	538.5	1 060.8	751.2	973.2	945.5	794.0	52.4	151.0
Minnesota	1 553.1	339.7	12.2	1 508.1	1 384.5	339.9	199.2	590.8	423.2	594.3	327.4	332.1	59.9	130.5
Mississippi	1 062.6	398.3	5.7	1 044.8	1 005.7	187.0	105.9	432.7	337.1	416.4	277.9	97.3	–	102.6
Missouri	1 611.1	305.4	7.9	1 583.7	1 492.8	413.7	307.8	361.3	528.2	681.3	269.2	542.3	18.9	106.8
Montana	368.8	430.6	6.9	365.7	344.9	61.6	53.4	156.2	97.6	159.4	53.3	189.3	84.5	–
Nebraska	558.7	343.7	9.1	534.8	512.1	130.1	116.8	154.1	157.7	215.7	124.8	160.3	13.5	67.7
Nevada	514.4	351.4	23.9	482.7	415.1	100.4	80.0	178.8	155.2	191.1	105.4	180.1	19.3	–
New Hampshire	285.5	251.5	3.1	282.1	276.9	76.5	53.3	77.4	78.3	149.4	20.0	33.5	21.8	66.2
New Jersey	2 546.6	322.1	10.7	2 446.5	2 300.9	552.5	497.6	648.3	848.2	1 259.1	607.7	52.4	1.6	236.3
New Mexico	590.4	355.8	–1.5	601.3	599.3	80.5	96.3	198.0	215.6	228.3	221.4	278.3	2.2	–
New York	3 867.4	212.5	3.9	3 854.9	3 723.5	1 054.4	1 051.2	874.4	887.4	1 513.8	1 040.8	297.3	356.5	312.1
North Carolina	2 214.2	312.8	9.4	2 186.1	2 024.1	508.2	371.8	747.9	586.2	795.9	194.6	578.8	78.0	345.3
North Dakota	344.0	537.8	11.5	332.5	308.5	54.5	40.0	175.2	74.4	120.9	45.3	402.4	24.2	–
Ohio	3 954.1	356.3	4.3	3 871.5	3 790.0	867.0	601.4	1 634.5	851.2	1 191.2	874.5	1 377.1	2.0	116.9
Oklahoma	1 381.6	424.6	.6	1 379.6	1 373.4	251.8	179.9	567.9	381.9	478.9	588.1	307.0	25.3	–
Oregon	1 038.2	335.5	4.1	1 032.0	997.7	220.7	169.7	349.9	297.9	362.6	152.3	44.6	345.5	–
Pennsylvania	3 830.7	317.7	4.6	3 782.4	3 662.3	897.4	572.4	1 464.8	896.2	1 348.3	723.3	1 357.8	19.6	717.5
Rhode Island	248.1	249.1	21.9	249.7	203.6	69.1	50.2	72.4	56.5	101.7	73.3	.1	3.6	–
South Carolina	1 359.6	373.2	7.6	1 361.7	1 263.7	257.5	174.7	604.6	322.8	428.3	149.0	330.7	24.8	474.7
South Dakota	231.1	319.1	12.1	221.8	206.1	54.8	36.9	59.9	79.5	113.9	31.3	39.2	54.9	–
Tennessee	1 953.2	377.4	7.6	1 896.2	1 815.6	432.4	126.4	886.6	507.8	654.9	254.0	622.9	117.6	127.4
Texas	10 387.6	563.5	5.3	10 121.1	9 869.2	1 195.8	1 027.7	5 929.2	2 234.9	4 811.1	3 802.0	1 382.8	15.7	306.9
Utah	594.8	311.5	8.6	584.5	547.5	110.2	99.8	215.1	169.6	216.6	146.3	376.5	7.7	–
Vermont	152.6	262.8	12.0	153.5	136.2	44.0	25.8	34.2	48.6	78.9	7.3	.1	20.4	46.1
Virginia	1 996.0	304.7	5.7	1 969.6	1 888.2	471.7	411.4	520.6	592.3	770.5	239.3	326.5	4.2	271.5
Washington	2 082.6	389.2	.7	2 072.0	2 068.0	397.2	297.6	781.8	606.1	817.5	221.5	106.9	657.2	72.0
West Virginia	817.1	448.4	.1	791.1	816.0	141.2	90.3	407.7	177.9	271.6	154.7	870.3	11.9	–
Wisconsin	1 713.4	337.0	10.8	1 654.7	1 545.8	372.6	251.4	703.6	385.8	531.1	359.9	426.0	30.2	122.9
Wyoming	410.3	862.4	2.5	408.7	400.4	36.3	41.4	245.9	86.7	127.9	112.3	489.5	9.2	–

– Represents zero.

[1]Sources of energy include geothermal, wood and waste, and net interstate sales of electricity, including losses, not shown separately.
[2]Based on resident population estimated as of July 1.
[3]Includes 149.3 trillion Btu of net imports of electricity generated from nonrenewable energy sources not shown by state.

Source: U.S. Energy Information Administration, State Energy Data Report, annual.

STATE AND METROPOLITAN AREA DATA BOOK

Table A–26. States — Energy Expenditures

Geographic area	Current dollars 1994 Total (mil dol)	Current dollars 1994 Per capita[1] (dollars)	Current dollars Percent change, 1990-1994	Current dollars 1993 (mil dol)	Current dollars 1990 (mil dol)	Constant (1992) dollars[2] 1994 (mil dol)	Constant 1993 (mil dol)	Constant 1990 (mil dol)	End-use sector 1994 Residential	End-use 1994 Commercial	End-use 1994 Industrial	End-use 1994 Transportation	Selected source 1994 Petroleum product Total	Motor gasoline	Natural gas	Coal	Electric purchasers
United States	[3]504 688	1 938	7.0	[3]491 801	[3]471 586	497 230	486 932	476 831	126 859	89 423	[3]108 465	179 941	229 040	129 900	77 753	27 251	200 894
Alabama	8 912	2 114	6.4	8 771	8 378	8 780	8 684	8 472	2 047	1 046	2 443	3 376	3 978	2 393	1 052	1 292	3 560
Alaska	1 765	2 934	-16.9	1 838	2 124	1 739	1 819	2 148	311	338	159	957	1 140	360	193	33	462
Arizona	7 545	1 844	15.8	7 351	6 518	7 434	7 279	6 590	1 972	1 586	957	3 030	3 280	2 265	523	563	3 748
Arkansas	5 147	2 097	9.7	5 081	4 694	5 071	5 030	4 746	1 245	656	1 201	2 044	2 351	1 392	791	357	2 003
California	50 216	1 601	3.3	48 542	48 612	49 474	48 061	49 153	11 587	10 723	7 625	20 281	22 118	14 658	8 708	110	20 662
Colorado	6 100	1 665	16.3	5 868	5 247	6 010	5 810	5 305	1 366	1 184	873	2 678	3 051	2 035	943	374	2 076
Connecticut	6 620	2 023	8.1	6 584	6 124	6 523	6 518	6 192	2 235	1 573	790	2 022	2 983	1 773	864	41	2 852
Delaware	1 510	2 133	6.8	1 494	1 414	1 487	1 480	1 429	428	244	312	526	761	415	196	92	627
District of Columbia	1 241	2 184	14.6	1 224	1 082	1 222	1 212	1 094	258	717	17	248	293	206	222	2	731
Florida	21 654	1 551	3.7	21 161	20 875	21 334	20 952	21 107	6 657	4 294	1 950	8 754	10 404	6 637	1 198	1 144	11 103
Georgia	13 777	1 951	6.7	13 835	12 918	13 574	13 698	13 061	3 461	2 402	2 708	5 206	5 994	3 708	1 758	1 176	5 873
Hawaii	2 065	1 761	-3.7	1 970	2 145	2 034	1 951	2 169	339	346	404	976	1 275	554	37	4	936
Idaho	2 176	1 915	18.4	2 073	1 838	2 144	2 052	1 859	417	331	507	921	1 114	655	230	18	796
Illinois	22 632	1 929	1.7	22 844	22 263	22 297	22 618	22 510	6 332	4 363	5 275	6 663	8 570	5 235	4 966	1 301	8 953
Indiana	12 825	2 230	5.8	12 298	12 116	12 635	12 176	12 251	2 902	1 561	3 913	4 448	5 497	2 841	2 597	1 749	4 356
Iowa	5 944	2 099	15.2	5 791	5 158	5 856	5 734	5 216	1 444	797	1 635	2 068	2 831	1 551	1 081	368	1 957
Kansas	5 391	2 114	2.1	5 218	5 278	5 311	5 166	5 337	1 215	952	1 444	1 779	2 353	1 267	1 133	309	1 947
Kentucky	8 046	2 103	10.3	7 885	7 293	7 927	7 807	7 374	1 617	899	2 392	3 137	4 010	2 116	814	1 091	3 059
Louisiana	13 320	3 087	-2.2	12 925	13 617	13 123	12 797	13 768	2 097	1 416	5 491	4 316	6 850	2 168	2 899	357	4 103
Maine	2 807	2 267	8.0	2 722	2 598	2 765	2 695	2 626	749	418	674	965	1 581	718	32	26	1 119
Maryland	8 692	1 738	10.3	8 527	7 882	8 563	8 443	7 969	2 691	1 353	1 561	3 087	3 951	2 536	999	413	3 846
Massachusetts	11 580	1 917	9.6	11 288	10 563	11 409	11 176	10 680	3 706	2 795	1 575	3 504	5 040	2 853	2 223	171	4 611
Michigan	17 777	1 874	6.8	17 387	16 642	17 514	17 214	16 828	4 534	3 459	3 964	5 820	7 234	4 607	3 918	1 217	6 423
Minnesota	8 502	1 859	13.2	8 290	7 507	8 376	8 208	7 591	2 017	1 034	1 970	3 481	4 305	2 600	1 270	406	2 852
Mississippi	5 282	1 979	5.2	5 173	5 022	5 204	5 122	5 078	1 205	683	1 216	2 177	2 617	1 498	650	154	2 139
Missouri	9 856	1 868	4.8	9 590	9 402	9 711	9 495	9 506	2 620	1 731	1 506	3 999	4 775	2 894	1 294	606	3 749
Montana	1 918	2 239	13.7	1 834	1 688	1 890	1 816	1 706	338	257	431	891	1 085	583	226	140	585
Nebraska	3 279	2 017	5.3	3 161	3 113	3 230	3 129	3 148	721	593	617	1 349	1 670	870	509	129	1 090
Nevada	3 099	2 117	28.6	2 732	2 411	3 053	2 705	2 438	675	484	687	1 254	1 445	861	459	259	1 253
New Hampshire	2 180	1 920	9.7	2 088	1 987	2 148	2 067	2 009	708	468	300	704	1 057	626	121	51	1 013
New Jersey	17 190	2 174	8.0	16 282	15 916	16 936	16 121	16 093	4 689	3 958	2 735	5 808	7 575	3 780	3 095	95	6 636
New Mexico	3 113	1 876	5.1	3 179	2 961	3 067	3 148	2 994	577	631	1 391	514	1 689	1 054	380	392	1 100
New York	31 041	1 706	12.6	30 288	27 562	30 582	29 988	27 869	10 303	8 949	3 972	7 818	10 818	6 147	6 366	455	14 320
North Carolina	13 677	1 932	9.1	13 557	12 542	13 475	13 423	12 681	3 791	2 250	2 790	4 846	5 987	3 802	915	980	6 611
North Dakota	1 645	2 571	4.4	1 630	1 575	1 620	1 614	1 593	307	204	532	602	824	402	120	474	443
Ohio	22 892	2 063	9.2	22 415	20 971	22 553	22 193	21 205	5 995	3 909	5 841	7 146	8 871	5 402	4 248	1 999	9 476
Oklahoma	6 450	1 982	3.9	6 405	6 209	6 354	6 341	6 278	1 562	979	1 292	2 617	3 074	1 781	1 367	321	2 391
Oregon	5 528	1 786	10.2	5 385	5 019	5 446	5 332	5 074	1 155	816	1 033	2 524	2 843	1 784	603	52	2 070
Pennsylvania	23 542	1 952	5.8	22 897	22 099	23 194	22 670	22 345	7 050	4 050	5 226	7 216	9 506	5 304	3 833	2 038	9 617
Rhode Island	1 894	1 902	17.5	1 912	1 612	1 866	1 893	1 630	589	407	367	532	784	447	432	-	674
South Carolina	7 245	1 989	4.9	7 124	6 907	7 138	7 053	6 983	1 797	1 043	1 909	2 496	2 981	1 909	618	528	3 510
South Dakota	1 429	1 973	5.2	1 388	1 358	1 407	1 374	1 374	334	202	251	642	841	458	129	48	444
Tennessee	10 203	1 972	5.1	9 895	9 711	10 052	9 797	9 819	2 409	742	3 037	4 015	4 694	2 917	1 071	799	4 265
Texas	47 246	2 563	8.7	45 210	43 468	46 548	44 763	43 952	8 686	6 332	16 749	15 480	25 473	10 276	7 800	1 860	16 149
Utah	2 959	1 550	7.7	2 926	2 748	2 916	2 897	2 779	606	480	540	1 333	1 496	912	458	450	945
Vermont	1 158	1 994	9.4	1 154	1 058	1 141	1 143	1 070	364	204	151	439	649	345	39	-	462
Virginia	11 858	1 811	5.2	11 770	11 270	11 683	11 653	11 395	3 390	2 225	1 582	4 662	5 559	3 491	1 107	497	5 075
Washington	9 185	1 716	7.1	8 664	8 578	9 049	8 578	8 673	1 923	1 315	1 593	4 354	4 836	2 916	822	156	3 446
West Virginia	3 858	2 117	-.5	3 772	3 876	3 801	3 734	3 919	849	497	1 123	1 389	1 896	1 025	513	1 213	1 290
Wisconsin	8 956	1 761	10.8	8 696	8 085	8 823	8 610	8 174	2 398	1 346	1 901	3 311	4 191	2 526	1 634	540	3 001
Wyoming	1 672	3 515	9.0	1 655	1 534	1 647	1 639	1 551	191	184	640	657	841	349	296	405	487

– Represents or rounds to zero.

[1]Based on resident population estimated as of July 1.
[2]Constant (1992) dollars computed by using personal consumption expenditures price index for energy from the Bureau of Economic Analysis.
[3]Includes net imports of coal coke not shown separately by state.

Source: U.S. Energy Information Administration, State Energy Price and Expenditure Report, annual.

Table A–27. States — Electric and Gas Utilities

Geographic area	Electric utility industry												Gas utility industry[1]			
	Sales to customers (mil kWh)			Revenue from sales (mil dol)			Net generation				Net summer capability (1,000 kWh)		Sales to customers[2] (tril btu)		Revenue from sales (mil dol)	
	1995		1990	1995		1990	1995			1990	1995	1990	1995	1990	1995	1990
	Total	Residential		Total	Residential		Total (bil kWh)	Coal (Percent)	Nuclear (Percent)	(bil kWh)						
United States	3 013 287	1 042 501	2 712 555	207 717	87 610	178 243	2 994.5	55.2	22.5	2 808.2	706 111	690 465	9 094	9 846	46 381	45 174
Alabama	70 007	24 314	59 926	3 831	1 631	3 338	99.6	68.8	20.8	76.2	20 463	20 023	107	111	583	542
Alaska	4 632	1 713	4 254	471	192	403	4.8	6.4	–	4.5	1 732	1 542	27	40	91	128
Arizona	48 589	18 036	41 470	3 700	1 640	3 215	69.0	46.0	39.1	62.3	15 221	14 906	56	80	331	380
Arkansas	34 671	12 417	27 365	2 174	991	1 833	39.5	54.4	29.5	37.1	9 639	9 641	89	84	390	358
California	212 605	68 783	211 093	21 070	7 983	18 664	121.9	–	24.8	114.5	43 302	43 681	733	1 337	4 297	6 158
Colorado	35 317	11 307	30 795	2 162	839	1 814	32.7	92.7	–	31.3	6 647	6 633	60	165	774	699
Connecticut	27 970	10 760	27 187	2 938	1 286	2 489	26.9	8.4	69.6	32.2	6 722	7 141	103	92	740	611
Delaware	9 580	3 168	8 284	662	288	535	8.3	50.8	–	7.1	2 239	1 965	29	22	127	101
District of Columbia	10 316	1 608	9 848	735	123	585	.2	–	–	.4	806	806	28	31	199	204
Florida	167 492	85 770	143 535	11 745	6 711	10 098	147.2	42.0	19.5	123.6	35 857	32 714	83	222	454	734
Georgia	96 192	35 812	80 440	6 363	2 811	5 275	102.0	64.6	30.1	97.6	22 290	20 731	230	204	1 201	1 091
Hawaii	9 188	2 606	8 311	1 038	347	750	6.2	–	–	8.0	1 602	1 487	3	3	45	43
Idaho	19 620	6 193	18 003	802	330	685	10.1	–	–	8.6	2 559	2 282	24	17	124	75
Illinois	126 231	38 386	111 577	9 712	3 982	8 361	145.2	43.2	54.1	127.0	33 139	32 602	599	621	2 722	2 871
Indiana	87 006	26 560	73 982	4 557	1 790	3 964	105.2	98.7	–	97.7	20 712	20 588	276	262	1 318	1 275
Iowa	34 301	11 640	29 437	2 069	959	1 745	33.5	84.8	11.1	29.0	8 237	7 952	137	149	652	613
Kansas	30 357	10 356	27 149	1 992	820	1 785	38.2	67.7	26.3	33.9	9 675	9 578	126	134	553	539
Kentucky	74 548	20 537	61 097	3 034	1 155	2 737	86.2	95.8	–	73.8	15 425	15 511	127	103	569	463
Louisiana	72 827	24 116	63 826	4 189	1 744	3 830	65.6	28.9	23.9	58.2	17 019	16 751	385	211	1 046	754
Maine	11 561	3 629	11 529	1 097	454	882	2.7	–	7.4	9.1	2 432	2 407	5	4	31	26
Maryland	56 158	22 234	49 534	3 964	1 875	3 121	44.7	61.3	29.0	31.5	10 957	9 758	141	129	778	700
Massachusetts	46 510	15 993	45 442	4 705	1 800	4 020	27.0	39.3	16.6	36.5	9 288	9 910	229	239	1 606	1 391
Michigan	94 701	28 623	82 367	6 679	2 387	5 850	92.5	70.7	26.4	89.1	21 981	22 315	525	481	2 303	2 198
Minnesota	53 959	16 974	47 167	3 011	1 217	2 516	42.5	63.1	31.2	41.6	8 923	8 834	253	224	1 058	917
Mississippi	37 868	14 181	32 127	2 265	991	1 963	26.4	35.1	30.4	22.9	7 170	7 016	82	76	312	299
Missouri	62 259	25 409	53 925	3 892	1 843	3 485	65.4	81.9	12.6	59.0	15 724	15 180	188	195	934	934
Montana	13 419	3 640	13 125	624	222	520	25.4	57.7	–	25.7	4 943	4 912	33	39	167	151
Nebraska	20 892	7 597	17 868	1 128	484	996	25.3	63.6	29.6	21.6	5 529	5 452	84	90	353	365
Nevada	20 659	6 655	16 352	1 260	473	880	20.0	69.9	–	19.3	5 556	4 944	37	36	224	171
New Hampshire	9 007	3 364	8 980	1 056	454	816	13.9	24.2	60.1	10.8	2 506	2 638	18	16	101	103
New Jersey	66 754	22 470	62 857	6 972	2 692	5 707	27.1	18.8	62.0	36.5	13 817	13 730	480	354	2 542	1 947
New Mexico	16 416	4 124	13 821	1 112	368	981	29.4	88.8	–	28.5	5 078	5 042	52	53	218	256
New York	130 471	39 887	129 324	14 435	5 544	12 119	101.2	19.7	26.0	128.7	32 147	31 224	593	571	4 350	3 647
North Carolina	104 673	39 506	89 924	6 885	3 207	5 740	96.1	58.0	37.4	79.8	20 597	20 190	140	130	702	565
North Dakota	7 883	3 384	7 014	450	211	403	28.8	91.3	–	26.8	4 485	4 525	23	18	94	79
Ohio	158 626	44 010	142 465	9 906	3 784	8 393	137.9	87.1	12.2	126.5	27 365	26 996	549	491	2 762	2 362
Oklahoma	41 392	16 319	42 504	2 306	1 113	2 328	48.0	62.0	–	45.1	12 928	12 769	153	217	637	633
Oregon	45 725	16 315	42 977	2 135	895	1 797	44.0	5.3	–	49.2	10 446	11 236	71	56	368	282
Pennsylvania	126 251	42 802	114 751	10 006	4 161	8 782	168.9	57.3	39.3	165.7	33 698	33 440	477	410	2 684	2 416
Rhode Island	6 636	2 472	6 419	689	283	587	.7	–	–	.6	442	263	33	31	231	206
South Carolina	65 074	21 392	55 652	3 703	1 611	3 113	78.4	32.9	62.7	69.3	16 701	14 908	117	96	528	422
South Dakota	7 414	3 268	6 334	460	231	388	8.8	30.9	–	6.4	2 950	2 708	26	21	118	92
Tennessee	82 030	30 967	77 145	4 274	1 832	4 096	82.3	70.5	19.1	73.9	16 144	16 996	161	159	763	645
Texas	263 279	92 831	237 415	16 066	7 162	13 715	261.7	46.7	13.8	234.0	64 424	62 034	641	1 173	2 608	3 702
Utah	18 460	5 041	15 402	979	350	841	32.1	94.3	–	32.3	4 927	4 805	81	73	324	328
Vermont	5 104	1 973	4 716	483	208	390	4.8	–	79.7	5.0	1 090	1 065	8	7	41	34
Virginia	85 162	33 472	72 696	5 331	2 626	4 386	52.7	46.4	47.7	47.2	14 342	13 661	135	119	796	633
Washington	88 353	30 147	91 046	3 626	1 497	3 092	95.7	6.1	7.3	100.5	24 277	24 173	138	134	629	478
West Virginia	25 977	9 166	23 132	1 386	596	1 095	77.3	99.2	–	77.4	14 451	14 435	99	64	446	341
Wisconsin	57 967	18 635	49 198	3 106	1 298	2 641	51.0	72.3	21.5	45.6	11 536	10 558	279	230	1 354	1 112
Wyoming	11 199	1 939	11 769	484	118	495	39.7	97.8	–	39.4	5 970	5 809	19	23	104	100

– Represents zero.

[1]Data subject to copyright; see below for source citation.
[2]Excludes sales for resale.

Source: Electric utility industry–U.S. Energy Information Administration; Electric Power Annual, Electric Sales and Revenue, annual and Inventory of Power Plants in the United States as of January 1, annual; Gas utility industry–American Gas Association, Arlington, VA, Gas Facts, annual (copyright).

Geographic area	Motor vehicle registrations[1] 1995									Motor-cycle[1] registra-tions, 1995 (1,000)	Highway mileage, 1995					State gasoline tax rate, 1995 (cents per gal)
	Number (1,000)			Per 1,000 population			Number (1,000)				Total	Inter-state[2]	Other arterial	Col-lector	Local	
	Total	Auto-mobile	Trucks	Total	Auto-mobile	Trucks	Total	Auto-mobile	Trucks							
United States	201 530	136 066	64 778	766.6	512.8	246.4	188 798	143 550	44 479	3 728	3 912 226	54 714	376 405	793 124	2 687 983	X
Alabama....................	3 553	1 842	1 702	836.7	430.3	400.9	3 744	2 733	1 003	37	93 313	925	8 673	20 325	63 390	18.0
Alaska......................	542	305	236	899.5	502.9	391.1	477	302	173	13	13 486	1 086	1 511	2 444	8 445	8.0
Arizona....................	2 873	1 881	988	667.4	433.2	229.5	2 825	2 002	819	68	54 561	1 250	4 701	8 721	39 889	18.0
Arkansas..................	1 613	807	800	649.2	321.2	322.1	1 448	934	508	17	77 222	646	6 739	20 120	49 717	18.7
California.................	22 432	14 850	7 539	710.6	465.0	238.8	21 926	16 972	4 914	519	170 389	3 750	26 754	32 206	107 679	18.0
Colorado	2 812	1 705	1 101	750.4	452.3	293.9	3 155	2 300	850	88	84 499	1 170	8 134	16 566	58 629	22.0
Connecticut	2 622	2 079	534	801.7	632.3	163.3	2 623	2 472	143	49	20 500	542	2 851	2 945	14 162	34.0
Delaware	592	405	185	825.6	555.1	258.0	526	406	118	9	5 631	51	615	943	4 022	23.0
District of Columbia	243	206	34	438.2	364.3	61.1	262	245	14	1	1 421	31	248	152	990	20.0
Florida	10 369	7 595	2 734	731.0	529.0	192.8	10 950	8 695	2 218	185	113 778	1 861	11 933	15 344	84 640	12.3
Georgia	6 120	4 226	1 879	849.0	583.0	260.7	5 489	3 834	1 641	71	111 273	1 413	12 998	23 093	73 769	7.5
Hawaii......................	802	533	265	680.1	446.9	224.4	771	672	95	13	4 133	77	754	792	2 510	16.0
Idaho.......................	1 043	587	453	894.4	498.2	388.6	1 054	636	413	33	59 733	613	3 580	9 647	45 893	21.0
Illinois.....................	8 973	6 612	2 345	761.0	555.8	198.9	7 873	6 300	1 556	184	137 413	2 245	13 872	21 429	99 867	19.0
Indiana	5 072	3 370	1 677	874.9	577.7	289.4	4 366	3 197	1 148	96	92 780	1 303	7 912	22 598	60 967	15.0
Iowa	2 814	1 829	976	989.8	639.1	343.2	2 632	1 880	743	111	112 702	781	9 412	31 488	71 021	20.0
Kansas	2 085	1 086	995	813.3	420.5	388.2	2 012	1 405	604	43	133 323	1 008	9 167	33 201	89 947	18.0
Kentucky	2 631	1 630	990	682.2	417.2	256.7	2 909	1 915	984	33	72 998	855	5 418	17 610	49 115	16.4
Louisiana	3 286	1 958	1 307	757.5	444.2	301.3	2 995	1 998	977	36	60 119	929	5 289	12 545	41 356	20.0
Maine	967	624	340	780.7	499.0	274.5	977	742	232	26	22 577	383	2 300	5 917	13 977	19.0
Maryland	3 654	2 705	938	725.2	534.2	186.1	3 607	2 970	625	39	29 680	711	3 551	4 987	20 431	23.5
Massachusetts	4 502	3 507	984	741.5	575.0	162.1	3 726	3 224	491	74	30 751	762	5 628	5 454	18 907	21.0
Michigan	7 674	5 315	2 335	804.6	552.5	244.8	7 209	5 613	1 573	127	117 611	1 458	12 150	25 847	78 156	15.0
Minnesota	3 882	2 552	1 314	841.2	550.6	284.8	3 508	2 742	752	118	130 391	1 042	12 260	29 345	87 744	20.0
Mississippi	2 144	1 408	726	795.2	518.5	269.1	1 875	1 434	433	30	73 102	726	7 018	15 554	49 804	18.4
Missouri	4 255	2 747	1 496	790.9	514.9	281.3	3 905	2 760	1 133	55	122 616	1 460	9 276	25 072	86 808	15.0
Montana	968	538	427	1 112.2	611.2	490.6	783	457	324	21	69 537	1 190	6 003	16 428	45 916	27.0
Nebraska	1 467	849	612	894.9	511.8	373.4	1 384	913	466	19	92 755	497	7 877	20 747	63 634	25.4
Nevada	1 047	593	452	682.8	380.2	295.0	853	592	260	21	44 936	586	2 729	4 895	36 726	24.0
New Hampshire	1 122	731	389	977.1	634.0	338.6	946	751	193	49	15 086	266	1 545	2 713	10 562	18.7
New Jersey	5 906	4 689	1 198	742.9	583.3	150.7	5 652	5 180	455	88	35 646	728	5 154	4 544	25 220	10.5
New Mexico	1 484	832	648	878.2	484.7	383.6	1 301	806	492	31	61 289	1 003	4 509	6 811	48 966	18.0
New York	10 274	7 917	2 311	564.8	431.4	127.0	10 196	8 831	1 332	168	112 193	2 328	13 690	20 496	75 679	21.9
North Carolina	5 682	3 685	1 962	788.9	507.1	272.4	5 162	3 677	1 451	67	96 809	1 237	8 850	17 788	68 934	21.6
North Dakota.............	695	372	321	1 083.4	573.7	500.1	630	372	256	17	86 830	570	5 870	11 372	69 018	18.0
Ohio........................	9 810	7 193	2 584	881.1	642.6	232.1	8 410	6 818	1 562	218	114 563	1 937	10 616	22 097	79 913	22.0
Oklahoma.................	2 856	1 629	1 212	872.1	494.4	370.0	2 649	1 711	925	55	112 517	1 064	7 832	25 349	78 272	17.0
Oregon	2 785	1 629	1 144	884.4	510.0	363.4	2 445	1 839	596	60	83 944	780	6 510	18 429	58 225	24.0
Pennsylvania.............	8 481	6 014	2 433	703.2	495.2	201.7	7 971	6 384	1 557	170	118 648	2 087	13 284	19 747	83 530	22.4
Rhode Island.............	699	545	152	704.8	546.5	153.6	672	563	107	17	5 893	137	751	818	4 187	29.0
South Carolina	2 833	1 865	953	772.6	506.1	259.9	2 521	1 878	628	34	64 293	894	6 802	13 390	43 207	16.0
South Dakota	709	380	326	971.9	514.1	447.5	704	425	277	25	83 360	681	6 284	19 272	57 123	18.0
Tennessee................	5 400	3 935	1 448	1 029.2	746.0	275.9	4 444	3 553	877	70	85 599	1 176	8 580	18 078	57 765	20.0
Texas	13 682	8 605	5 005	727.7	448.2	266.2	12 800	8 714	4 024	126	296 186	4 474	28 121	63 174	200 417	20.0
Utah	1 447	800	646	738.9	403.4	329.8	1 206	789	415	22	41 044	948	3 333	7 714	29 049	19.0
Vermont	492	317	173	841.3	537.0	296.1	462	342	119	18	14 184	339	1 300	3 110	9 435	16.0
Virginia	5 613	3 976	1 620	848.5	595.9	244.9	4 938	3 776	1 146	58	69 142	1 329	8 073	14 226	45 514	17.5
Washington	4 503	2 960	1 535	826.6	540.0	281.8	4 257	2 979	1 270	95	79 710	1 079	7 282	16 791	54 558	23.0
West Virginia	1 425	857	565	780.7	459.7	309.6	1 225	753	468	18	35 110	560	3 236	8 802	22 512	25.4
Wisconsin	3 993	2 424	1 557	779.6	470.7	303.9	3 815	2 757	903	168	111 489	830	11 767	21 421	77 471	23.4
Wyoming..................	601	368	231	1 254.2	759.6	481.7	528	309	217	17	35 461	916	3 663	10 567	20 315	9.0

X Not applicable.

[1]Includes official vehicles but excludes those owned by military services.
[2]Also includes freeways and expressways.

Source: U.S. Federal Highway Administration, Highway Statistics, annual.

Table A–29. States — Driver Licenses and Traffic Fatalities

Geographic area	Driver licenses (1,000) 1995	1990	Traffic fatalities 1995	1990	Fatality rate[1] 1995	1990	Persons killed in alcohol-related crashes 1995	1990	Percent of all persons killed in crashes 1995	1990	By highest BAC[2] in crash 0.01 to 0.09 1995	1990	0.10 or more 1995	1990	Vehicles involved in fatal crashes, 1995 Total	Large trucks Number	Percent of total
United States	176 628	167 015	41 798	44 599	1.7	2.1	17 274	22 084	41.3	49.5	3 710	4 434	13 564	17 650	56 485	4 453	7.9
Alabama	3 456	2 753	1 113	1 121	2.2	2.6	462	553	41.6	49.4	81	99	381	454	1 528	144	9.4
Alaska	434	314	87	98	2.1	2.5	48	48	54.5	48.4	11	8	37	40	109	8	7.3
Arizona	2 626	2 393	1 031	869	2.6	2.5	447	436	43.4	50.2	100	65	347	371	1 410	78	5.5
Arkansas	1 769	1 722	631	604	2.4	2.9	217	339	34.3	56.0	69	71	148	268	802	96	12.0
California	20 140	19 846	4 192	5 192	1.5	2.0	1 720	2 601	41.0	50.1	412	560	1 308	2 041	5 508	364	6.6
Colorado	2 728	2 043	645	544	1.8	2.0	294	253	45.6	46.5	68	61	226	192	849	51	6.0
Connecticut	2 349	2 214	317	385	1.1	1.5	155	216	48.8	56.0	25	39	130	177	406	25	6.2
Delaware	525	485	121	138	1.6	2.1	51	86	41.5	62.7	13	14	38	72	172	9	5.2
District of Columbia	339	412	58	48	1.7	1.4	31	31	54.7	65.3	6	9	25	22	82	1	1.2
Florida	11 024	9 231	2 805	2 891	2.2	2.6	1 110	1 399	39.6	48.3	237	256	873	1 143	4 002	282	7.0
Georgia	4 840	4 478	1 488	1 562	1.7	2.2	522	706	35.1	45.3	122	137	400	569	2 108	189	9.0
Hawaii	733	678	130	177	1.6	2.2	64	89	49.3	50.0	23	27	41	62	159	3	1.9
Idaho	806	704	262	244	2.1	2.5	88	139	34.0	56.8	19	33	69	106	330	29	8.8
Illinois	7 211	7 295	1 586	1 589	1.7	1.9	681	802	42.9	50.5	130	172	551	630	2 170	159	7.3
Indiana	3 706	3 601	960	1 049	1.5	2.0	330	471	34.4	44.9	67	76	263	395	1 383	160	11.6
Iowa	1 905	1 872	527	465	2.0	2.0	220	225	41.6	48.4	61	44	159	181	714	68	9.5
Kansas	1 771	1 715	442	444	1.8	1.9	179	225	40.4	50.6	27	44	152	181	577	59	10.2
Kentucky	2 535	2 402	849	849	2.1	2.5	287	353	33.8	41.7	60	81	227	272	1 122	101	9.0
Louisiana	2 594	2 575	883	959	2.3	2.5	470	552	53.2	57.6	117	116	353	436	1 096	85	7.8
Maine	864	887	187	213	1.5	1.8	52	93	27.7	43.8	8	24	44	69	259	22	8.5
Maryland	3 344	3 362	671	707	1.5	1.7	233	302	34.8	42.8	57	64	176	238	942	49	5.2
Massachusetts	4 211	4 229	444	605	.9	1.3	203	346	45.7	57.2	55	87	148	259	605	33	5.5
Michigan	6 659	6 440	1 530	1 571	1.8	1.9	616	758	40.3	48.2	133	134	483	624	2 258	163	7.2
Minnesota	2 761	2 529	597	566	1.4	1.5	265	254	44.3	44.8	50	52	215	202	823	76	9.2
Mississippi	1 693	1 885	868	750	2.9	3.1	361	391	41.6	52.1	55	88	306	303	1 155	103	8.9
Missouri	3 587	3 688	1 109	1 097	1.9	2.2	572	590	51.6	53.8	122	140	450	450	1 432	93	6.5
Montana	574	604	215	212	2.3	2.5	91	119	42.5	55.9	12	18	79	101	253	26	10.3
Nebraska	1 152	1 089	254	262	1.6	1.9	93	109	36.7	41.6	29	20	64	89	346	41	11.8
Nevada	1 045	846	313	343	2.2	3.4	154	196	49.4	57.3	27	29	127	167	397	32	8.1
New Hampshire	901	843	118	158	1.1	1.6	46	79	39.1	50.1	16	15	30	64	170	8	4.7
New Jersey	5 404	5 585	773	886	1.3	1.5	316	349	40.9	39.3	73	87	243	262	1 075	84	7.8
New Mexico	1 173	1 074	485	499	2.3	3.1	244	315	50.2	63.3	42	50	202	265	577	40	6.9
New York	10 474	10 254	1 674	2 217	1.5	2.1	543	890	32.4	40.1	138	218	405	672	2 276	148	6.5
North Carolina	5 028	4 551	1 448	1 385	1.9	2.2	488	628	33.7	45.4	89	105	399	523	1 982	178	9.0
North Dakota	449	425	74	112	1.1	1.9	42	59	57.9	52.2	10	8	32	51	98	8	8.2
Ohio	7 773	7 427	1 366	1 638	1.4	1.8	439	700	32.2	42.7	95	144	344	556	1 896	201	10.6
Oklahoma	2 156	2 278	669	641	1.7	1.9	251	269	37.5	42.0	46	51	205	218	904	83	9.2
Oregon	2 542	2 212	572	579	1.9	2.2	237	274	41.4	47.4	61	63	176	211	741	66	8.9
Pennsylvania	8 154	7 899	1 480	1 646	1.6	1.9	610	817	41.2	49.6	125	150	485	667	2 042	184	9.0
Rhode Island	670	671	69	84	1.0	1.1	29	49	41.6	58.0	7	8	22	41	89	3	3.4
South Carolina	2 542	2 373	881	979	2.3	2.8	280	497	31.8	50.9	51	104	229	393	1 171	89	7.6
South Dakota	516	492	158	153	2.1	2.2	71	80	45.0	51.8	8	10	63	70	194	15	7.7
Tennessee	3 739	3 334	1 259	1 177	2.2	2.5	512	581	40.7	49.4	92	127	420	454	1 701	115	6.8
Texas	12 369	11 137	3 181	3 250	1.8	2.1	1 782	2 038	56.0	62.7	375	383	1 407	1 655	4 268	333	7.8
Utah	1 255	1 046	326	272	1.7	1.9	86	65	26.3	23.8	17	12	69	53	437	29	6.6
Vermont	456	412	106	90	1.7	1.5	44	52	41.4	57.3	11	11	33	41	134	12	9.0
Virginia	4 629	4 389	900	1 079	1.3	1.8	358	527	39.8	48.8	86	119	272	408	1 201	93	7.7
Washington	3 765	3 377	653	825	1.3	1.8	316	473	48.5	57.3	68	92	248	381	847	65	7.7
West Virginia	1 305	1 284	376	481	2.2	3.1	160	227	42.7	47.0	28	38	132	189	493	50	10.1
Wisconsin	3 602	3 328	745	769	1.4	1.7	317	360	42.6	46.9	54	57	263	303	1 020	85	8.3
Wyoming	346	334	170	125	2.4	2.1	83	75	48.9	59.8	20	15	63	60	172	15	8.7

[1]Traffic fatalities per 100 million vehicle miles traveled.
[2]Blood alcohol concentration.

Source: Driver licenses–U.S. Federal Highway Administration, Highway Statistics, annual; Traffic fatalities and persons killed by alcohol-related crashes–National Highway Traffic Safety Administration, Traffic Safety Facts 1995; Vehicles involved in fatal crashes –National Highway Traffic Safety Administration, Traffic Safety Facts 1995, Large Trucks.

Business Failures and Starts, Patents, and Bankruptcies

Geographic area	Business failures[1]				New business starts[1] (1,000)							Patents		Bankruptcy cases (1,000)	
					Total				Employment						
	1996, prel.	1995	1994	1990	1995	1994	1993	1990	1995	1994	1990	1996	1990	1995	1990
United States	71 811	71 128	71 558	60 747	168.2	188.4	166.2	158.9	738 606	758 134	827 012	[2]69 390	52 958	[3]1 042.1	[3]725.5
Alabama	538	547	668	678	2.2	2.6	2.0	2.3	11 616	13 193	11 928	336	364	29.3	24.7
Alaska	182	124	112	124	.3	.3	.3	.3	944	803	1 189	50	30	1.0	1.2
Arizona	1 012	1 410	1 407	1 090	3.1	3.3	3.3	2.9	11 940	14 376	13 968	1 153	738	18.0	17.7
Arkansas	1 003	737	366	266	1.2	1.2	1.2	.9	5 401	6 264	4 476	164	151	11.2	6.8
California	16 871	16 307	16 796	8 968	23.6	27.2	25.6	23.8	96 842	98 912	121 944	11 957	7 935	164.3	103.2
Colorado	2 243	1 481	1 315	2 091	3.1	3.4	2.9	2.4	12 723	11 707	14 008	1 320	830	14.9	17.1
Connecticut	534	485	577	435	2.3	3.0	2.4	2.6	9 308	9 268	13 672	1 685	1 512	10.2	4.4
Delaware	49	45	88	80	.5	.6	.4	.4	2 363	2 491	2 112	472	434	1.9	.9
District of Columbia	123	155	168	100	.7	.9	.6	.5	3 701	3 542	2 452	42	48	1.6	1.0
Florida	2 655	2 904	3 609	3 665	12.3	14.0	12.5	10.7	55 761	56 781	57 145	2 509	1 905	51.9	31.9
Georgia	1 308	1 481	1 961	1 944	5.5	6.1	5.0	4.4	25 983	28 606	24 035	1 135	724	50.9	38.7
Hawaii	396	270	259	149	.6	1.0	.8	1.0	2 715	2 654	5 606	104	85	2.4	.9
Idaho	535	388	276	312	.6	.8	.6	.5	3 026	2 591	2 247	393	192	4.8	4.1
Illinois	2 557	1 696	1 757	2 149	7.2	8.1	7.9	7.3	32 269	31 666	39 273	3 674	2 939	48.5	35.8
Indiana	843	798	908	1 171	2.7	3.0	2.8	2.4	12 534	13 976	15 669	1 417	1 050	26.0	22.2
Iowa	453	573	473	553	1.2	1.3	1.1	1.1	6 386	6 329	5 326	485	388	7.6	5.5
Kansas	1 089	947	871	763	1.3	1.4	1.3	1.4	6 772	6 943	7 806	348	328	10.1	8.1
Kentucky	638	659	707	1 063	1.5	1.6	1.5	1.6	8 552	8 304	9 878	397	310	16.6	13.6
Louisiana	271	456	656	1 152	2.0	2.1	1.7	1.8	11 299	10 984	10 006	444	506	17.1	12.9
Maine	299	317	335	199	.8	.7	.7	.6	3 161	2 969	3 202	113	115	2.6	1.5
Maryland	1 620	1 804	1 610	693	3.1	4.0	3.2	3.2	12 225	14 648	17 189	1 208	900	20.4	9.2
Massachusetts	1 607	1 927	2 100	1 913	4.4	5.1	4.0	3.6	19 083	16 310	18 752	2 713	2 112	15.9	7.6
Michigan	1 558	1 681	1 955	2 109	5.4	5.6	5.2	5.2	22 357	21 542	24 791	3 457	2 707	28.0	18.8
Minnesota	593	903	722	529	2.3	2.5	2.4	2.2	10 996	11 952	13 470	2 000	1 476	16.3	14.0
Mississippi	184	232	249	453	1.0	1.2	.9	1.0	5 658	8 400	6 075	167	130	13.3	10.6
Missouri	1 054	1 109	1 059	1 221	2.9	3.0	2.9	2.5	14 437	16 009	13 835	762	704	19.8	13.4
Montana	179	152	181	191	.5	.5	.4	.4	1 395	2 070	1 862	141	74	2.5	1.8
Nebraska	390	323	314	358	.6	.8	.7	.6	2 947	4 803	3 030	187	145	4.6	3.8
Nevada	474	453	446	255	1.4	1.5	1.4	1.1	6 327	6 713	6 350	233	128	8.9	6.2
New Hampshire	374	389	416	279	.9	.9	.9	.9	3 504	3 628	3 613	468	328	3.4	1.8
New Jersey	2 451	2 779	2 190	1 265	7.5	7.9	6.7	6.4	26 592	27 178	29 089	3 385	3 112	30.6	12.6
New Mexico	428	405	330	319	1.0	1.2	.9	1.0	4 099	3 752	4 343	242	205	5.2	4.0
New York	4 931	5 060	5 540	3 284	15.7	16.2	14.8	14.2	51 805	54 378	64 623	5 816	4 525	56.1	29.0
North Carolina	1 041	962	1 046	1 026	4.0	4.3	3.4	3.7	16 806	19 515	20 482	1 454	848	18.9	10.7
North Dakota	80	98	90	144	.2	.3	.2	.2	1 159	1 395	885	72	51	1.5	1.1
Ohio	2 274	2 141	1 987	2 262	5.4	6.9	5.7	5.4	25 456	25 465	28 320	3 173	2 729	38.8	36.8
Oklahoma	1 559	1 311	1 168	1 597	1.5	1.8	1.6	1.4	8 322	8 738	8 062	542	633	16.1	14.3
Oregon	834	795	1 027	591	1.9	2.3	2.2	2.2	8 096	8 823	7 838	965	640	15.1	11.3
Pennsylvania	2 915	2 756	2 742	2 228	6.8	8.1	6.7	6.9	31 602	29 368	34 020	3 226	2 825	28.2	15.8
Rhode Island	134	129	213	183	.6	.8	.6	.6	2 692	3 115	3 075	291	181	3.8	1.7
South Carolina	375	490	498	415	2.0	1.9	1.6	1.8	10 548	9 249	10 316	518	409	8.5	4.8
South Dakota	158	182	168	271	.3	.4	.3	.3	1 711	2 460	1 791	49	41	1.7	1.4
Tennessee	1 329	991	956	1 475	2.9	2.8	2.5	2.6	15 708	13 931	15 753	719	565	43.7	34.2
Texas	6 086	6 152	5 835	6 743	11.8	13.2	10.8	11.1	58 944	56 398	62 986	4 511	3 191	54.2	41.7
Utah	378	344	260	372	1.1	1.2	1.1	.9	5 494	5 705	5 775	603	369	8.0	8.0
Vermont	107	148	130	78	.3	.4	.4	.4	1 285	1 469	1 550	282	144	1.2	.5
Virginia	1 064	1 713	1 459	1 597	3.5	4.1	3.9	3.8	17 570	18 998	19 003	967	831	31.7	19.3
Washington	2 687	2 384	2 005	860	2.9	3.2	2.7	3.3	13 108	12 961	16 854	1 330	953	25.0	17.0
West Virginia	294	287	296	240	.6	.7	.6	.7	2 010	2 962	4 336	139	166	4.9	3.5
Wisconsin	935	1 140	1 175	666	2.6	3.2	2.8	2.2	12 467	12 762	12 208	1 522	1 215	14.4	10.2
Wyoming	119	108	82	178	.3	.3	.2	.2	907	1 078	794	45	37	1.5	1.5

[1]Data subject to copyright; see below for source citation.
[2]Includes data not distributed by state.
[3]Includes outlying areas.

Source: Business failures–The Dun and Bradstreet Corporation, Murray Hill, NJ, Business Failure Record, (copyright); Business starts–The Dun and Bradstreet Corporation, Murray Hill, NJ, Business Starts Record (copyright) and A Decade of Business Starts, Historical Statistics (by States and Industries) 1985-1996, (copyright); Patents–U.S. Patent and Trademark Office, Patent Counts by County/State and Year, All Patents, All Types, January 1, 1977-December 31, 1996, (related Internet site <http://www.uspto.gov/web/offices/ac/ido/oeip/taf/cst_all.pdf>); Bankruptcy cases–Administrative Office of the U.S. Courts, unpublished data, (related Internet site <http://www.uscourts.gov/Press_Releases/bkpr.html>).

Private Nonfarm Establishments, Employment, and Payroll

Geographic area	Establishments							Employment[1] (1,000)						Annual payroll (bil dol)	
			Net change, 1990-1994	By employment-size class of establishment, 1994						By employment-size class of establishment, 1994					
	1994	1990		Under 20	20 to 99	100 to 499	500 or more	1994	1990	Under 20	20 to 99	100 to 499	500 or more	1994	1990
United States	6 509 276	6 175 563	333 713	5 661 525	704 499	127 676	15 576	96 733	93 476	25 373	28 138	24 048	19 175	2 488.2	2 104.1
Alabama....................	94 219	86 537	7 682	81 450	10 502	1 982	285	1 479	1 343	378	416	381	303	32.3	25.7
Alaska.....................	16 916	14 773	2 143	15 293	1 374	228	21	179	158	64	52	45	17	5.7	4.7
Arizona....................	97 007	86 489	10 518	83 915	11 033	1 863	196	1 415	1 236	382	435	347	251	33.1	25.0
Arkansas..................	59 021	53 409	5 612	51 913	5 847	1 090	171	843	751	230	233	214	166	16.8	13.1
California	735 570	745 686	−10 116	636 707	83 774	13 617	1 472	10 625	11 319	2 816	3 356	2 533	1 920	301.4	283.2
Colorado	114 069	96 828	17 241	100 517	11 459	1 891	202	1 481	1 248	427	453	343	257	37.0	27.5
Connecticut	90 789	92 816	−2 027	79 537	9 194	1 842	216	1 385	1 482	350	374	349	312	44.0	40.5
Delaware	20 479	18 761	1 718	17 983	2 059	375	62	307	311	78	81	71	77	8.7	7.5
District of Columbia	19 315	19 587	−272	16 237	2 477	533	68	411	427	79	100	105	127	13.9	12.4
Florida	392 762	361 330	31 432	348 083	37 387	6 624	668	4 984	4 607	1 466	1 496	1 188	834	110.8	89.6
Georgia	173 316	157 667	15 649	148 969	19 988	3 887	472	2 754	2 499	675	802	753	525	67.5	52.5
Hawaii.....................	29 995	29 313	682	25 962	3 478	483	72	426	433	126	138	89	73	10.6	9.3
Idaho......................	31 882	26 513	5 369	28 544	2 866	420	52	368	300	126	109	73	59	7.9	5.6
Illinois	288 689	272 738	15 951	247 700	33 498	6 619	872	4 802	4 647	1 127	1 357	1 243	1 075	134.6	114.5
Indiana	138 699	128 311	10 388	118 377	16 649	3 301	372	2 315	2 150	570	669	610	466	55.9	45.1
Iowa	77 764	73 130	4 634	68 127	8 092	1 383	162	1 090	1 008	314	324	257	195	23.3	18.6
Kansas....................	69 822	65 858	3 964	60 903	7 560	1 230	129	954	894	278	299	220	157	21.2	17.5
Kentucky	84 163	79 006	5 157	72 529	9 649	1 767	218	1 293	1 186	340	385	337	231	28.3	22.6
Louisiana	95 138	88 290	6 848	81 975	11 072	1 872	219	1 425	1 271	388	441	350	247	31.6	25.5
Maine	35 590	34 840	750	31 995	3 011	516	68	420	424	134	119	94	74	9.3	8.2
Maryland	120 378	114 874	5 504	104 468	13 345	2 319	246	1 752	1 811	485	536	428	303	46.1	41.1
Massachusetts	158 072	158 329	−257	136 314	17 532	3 774	452	2 661	2 772	608	712	722	619	77.3	68.7
Michigan	222 689	210 303	12 386	192 187	25 420	4 505	577	3 542	3 412	912	1 010	846	775	99.5	83.2
Minnesota	123 442	112 187	11 255	106 146	14 216	2 775	305	1 995	1 832	491	569	530	405	50.4	40.3
Mississippi	56 150	52 888	3 262	49 230	5 626	1 120	174	835	723	219	223	213	180	16.4	12.3
Missouri	138 274	130 287	7 987	119 987	15 119	2 830	338	2 101	2 014	539	603	528	432	50.2	42.1
Montana	28 358	25 028	3 330	25 783	2 319	238	18	250	222	106	88	41	14	4.8	3.7
Nebraska..................	46 640	43 749	2 891	40 894	4 856	773	117	648	587	186	192	139	131	13.5	10.5
Nevada....................	35 643	29 932	5 711	30 929	3 908	675	131	628	537	139	155	124	209	15.0	11.2
New Hampshire	33 865	33 249	616	29 915	3 309	572	69	446	440	130	133	108	75	10.9	9.5
New Jersey	217 506	214 076	3 430	191 201	21 503	4 269	533	3 125	3 220	795	870	812	648	97.9	85.4
New Mexico	40 001	35 700	4 301	35 146	4 210	592	53	489	418	158	162	109	60	10.3	7.9
New York	462 392	466 762	−4 370	409 521	43 429	8 158	1 284	6 665	7 075	1 661	1 724	1 576	1 703	211.1	191.8
North Carolina.............	176 803	165 076	11 727	152 652	19 650	3 978	523	2 855	2 679	697	797	785	576	64.8	51.4
North Dakota..............	20 129	18 979	1 150	17 898	1 935	275	21	221	197	78	77	47	19	4.2	3.3
Ohio	260 775	248 694	12 081	222 638	31 300	6 115	722	4 386	4 246	1 068	1 266	1 150	901	110.6	93.9
Oklahoma	80 519	74 663	5 856	70 630	8 508	1 252	129	1 025	941	313	335	235	143	22.0	18.7
Oregon	91 468	81 077	10 391	80 496	9 408	1 431	133	1 129	1 017	355	367	269	139	27.1	20.7
Pennsylvania..............	281 913	279 595	2 318	243 854	30 908	6 343	808	4 584	4 598	1 140	1 241	1 207	997	116.8	101.4
Rhode Island..............	27 467	27 726	−259	24 152	2 774	478	63	370	393	100	109	90	71	9.0	8.2
South Carolina	85 929	79 743	6 186	74 777	9 152	1 745	255	1 348	1 266	344	367	348	289	29.2	23.6
South Dakota	22 377	20 492	1 885	19 964	2 074	315	24	256	215	86	82	58	30	4.7	3.4
Tennessee.................	122 015	113 292	8 723	104 397	14 379	2 865	374	2 042	1 869	485	581	553	424	47.1	36.8
Texas	429 971	394 482	35 489	372 048	48 406	8 481	1 036	6 453	5 865	1 694	1 913	1 595	1 251	160.9	129.8
Utah	43 739	36 586	7 153	37 599	5 150	885	105	700	571	179	203	166	151	15.3	11.1
Vermont	20 321	19 839	482	18 347	1 709	240	25	219	215	76	66	46	30	4.7	4.1
Virginia	159 026	149 695	9 331	138 011	17 473	3 142	400	2 393	2 322	643	696	605	449	59.3	49.2
Washington	149 616	131 919	17 697	131 975	15 202	2 210	229	1 895	1 762	578	598	397	321	49.8	40.2
West Virginia	40 231	37 687	2 544	35 597	3 921	639	74	511	483	162	155	116	78	11.4	9.7
Wisconsin	131 614	122 142	9 472	112 868	15 408	2 984	354	2 100	1 949	532	617	571	380	50.5	40.3
Wyoming	16 748	14 630	2 118	15 185	1 381	175	7	154	132	64	52	33	5	3.3	2.6

[1]Employment for pay period including March 12.

Source: Establishments, employment, and annual payroll–U.S. Bureau of the Census, County Business Patterns on diskette, annual (related Internet site <http://www.census.gov/epcd/cbp/view/cbpview.html>); Employment-size class, 1994–U.S. Bureau of the Census, County Business Patterns on CD-ROM, annual.

STATE AND METROPOLITAN AREA DATA BOOK

Geographic area	Merchandise exports[1]						Foreign direct investment in the United States					International visitor travel impact					
	1996				1995 (mil dol)	1991 (mil dol)	Gross book value of property[2] (mil dol)		Total employment			Expenditures (mil dol)		Generated employment (1,000)		Generated payroll (mil dol)	
	Total (mil dol)	Percent change, 1991-1996	Percent to Canada	Percent to Mexico			1994	1990	1994 Total (1,000)	1994 Percent of all businesses	1990 (1,000)	1994	1990	1994	1990	1994	1990
United States	568 732	56.6	21.3	8.7	539 050	363 063	716 032	552 902	4 828.2	4.9	4 704.4	58 092	40 926	947.9	767.6	15 771	10 854
Alabama	3 702	52.4	31.8	8.8	3 587	2 430	10 058	7 300	60.6	4.2	55.7	111	72	2.1	1.6	25	16
Alaska	850	−20.0	21.3	.2	892	1 062	24 399	19 435	8.8	4.6	13.2	116	59	2.3	1.2	49	19
Arizona	9 938	119.4	9.8	16.3	8 403	4 529	5 681	7 234	50.1	3.4	57.1	1 297	1 090	23.5	21.7	331	247
Arkansas	1 997	137.8	30.8	5.1	1 794	840	3 554	2 344	31.6	3.6	29.2	55	38	1.2	.9	13	9
California	98 634	67.1	10.7	7.9	92 038	59 037	92 367	75 768	552.4	5.2	555.9	11 530	8 814	187.2	162.3	3 353	2 497
Colorado	10 065	65.4	6.1	9.0	9 689	6 085	8 250	6 544	65.3	4.3	56.3	501	453	10.6	10.7	165	146
Connecticut	13 052	93.9	12.3	4.0	12 942	6 731	8 137	5 357	76.5	5.6	75.9	379	253	5.9	4.5	97	66
Delaware	4 584	29.6	16.1	6.2	4 397	3 538	6 679	5 818	33.7	10.7	43.1	59	33	1.0	.7	13	8
District of Columbia	5 085	1 089.3	2.0	.2	5 324	428	4 966	3 869	11.1	2.7	11.4	1 314	6 535	15.3	124.3	297	1 640
Florida	19 618	55.2	8.3	3.8	18 564	12 643	23 488	18 659	198.2	3.9	205.7	11 962	363	194.9	8.5	3 002	137
Georgia	8 618	65.0	22.0	6.0	8 627	5 224	21 272	16 729	173.7	6.2	161.0	744	3 410	14.8	54.4	300	854
Hawaii	295	34.8	23.7	.3	256	219	16 482	11 830	51.0	11.5	53.0	5 680	53	77.5	1.4	1 371	12
Idaho	1 610	59.3	17.2	2.3	1 893	1 011	937	776	11.8	3.1	11.7	57	1 081	1.4	21.7	13	319
Illinois	32 225	96.9	21.0	5.7	30 478	16 363	31 994	23 420	229.0	4.8	245.8	1 426	142	23.2	3.3	394	36
Indiana	12 119	81.6	38.2	20.9	11 052	6 675	17 032	13 426	129.0	5.4	126.9	214	63	4.5	1.6	55	13
Iowa	2 695	94.4	47.4	4.1	2 578	1 386	4 329	2 712	35.4	3.1	32.8	78	91	1.6	1.9	16	18
Kansas	4 971	70.2	14.0	12.9	4 461	2 922	2 952	5 134	31.5	3.2	29.6	104	78	2.2	2.1	23	26
Kentucky	5 824	75.5	32.7	4.8	5 030	3 318	14 993	9 229	78.7	5.8	65.7	122	376	3.1	7.8	41	96
Louisiana	4 731	51.1	11.5	3.1	4 581	3 131	23 475	17 432	59.4	4.2	61.4	496	210	9.0	4.6	123	45
Maine	1 249	26.9	39.2	1.0	1 318	984	2 692	2 080	24.8	5.5	26.6	260	191	5.4	3.9	58	54
Maryland	3 510	30.2	15.8	5.0	3 439	2 696	7 342	5 713	78.9	4.4	79.6	273	985	4.9	17.1	77	253
Massachusetts	15 368	37.6	22.7	2.5	14 396	11 167	11 878	8 890	124.8	5.0	131.2	1 520	465	23.2	11.6	397	132
Michigan	38 128	102.3	57.6	12.3	37 102	18 850	17 224	12 012	159.4	4.4	139.6	587	197	12.7	5.4	167	76
Minnesota	13 884	75.7	20.6	6.1	12 404	7 900	8 506	11 972	82.9	4.1	89.8	368	43	8.8	1.1	144	10
Mississippi	1 222	54.9	31.7	7.5	1 369	789	3 958	2 989	24.0	2.8	23.6	57	108	1.2	2.5	14	33
Missouri	6 590	54.1	19.5	16.5	5 690	4 276	7 922	5 757	80.4	3.7	73.7	198	151	4.0	4.0	62	33
Montana	341	110.0	47.1	13.5	279	162	2 434	2 181	5.0	1.8	5.1	151	41	3.5	1.1	34	9
Nebraska	2 453	253.4	17.1	6.8	2 255	694	1 183	776	17.2	2.6	14.9	44	1 072	1.0	19.5	10	281
Nevada	692	64.3	38.4	1.3	711	421	8 315	5 450	22.8	3.4	22.7	1 791	95	29.7	2.0	506	22
New Hampshire	1 745	87.0	36.8	3.6	1 479	933	2 136	1 446	29.6	6.4	25.9	152	687	2.9	10.5	35	173
New Jersey	18 458	34.5	18.3	3.7	18 369	13 724	25 757	18 608	211.2	6.9	227.0	749	49	9.7	1.0	189	10
New Mexico	917	288.6	5.6	10.9	427	236	4 717	4 312	18.4	3.6	17.4	107	5 741	1.9	90.5	23	1 570
New York	44 965	20.0	19.9	2.9	44 080	37 462	49 588	36 424	356.0	5.4	347.5	7 583	260	101.6	6.3	2 040	87
North Carolina	11 587	86.0	30.4	8.0	10 567	6 229	22 718	15 234	221.8	7.6	181.0	313	114	6.8	3.5	109	25
North Dakota	576	108.3	65.7	2.0	489	277	1 210	1 251	3.8	1.6	3.1	61	385	1.8	8.8	15	99
Ohio	22 555	65.5	42.5	6.0	20 926	13 625	27 249	20 549	209.4	4.7	219.1	451	54	8.8	1.4	116	23
Oklahoma	2 538	4.7	22.5	7.0	2 467	2 423	5 849	6 049	37.9	3.6	43.6	89	198	2.1	4.7	38	50
Oregon	8 481	68.5	10.5	.6	9 902	5 033	5 449	3 427	47.0	4.0	39.1	272	657	5.6	13.5	71	174
Pennsylvania	17 446	42.8	27.4	5.0	17 680	12 217	23 256	16 587	233.1	5.1	221.6	769	56	14.4	1.0	217	13
Rhode Island	955	37.4	33.8	2.4	957	695	2 131	1 120	16.5	4.3	13.3	109	204	2.0	4.7	27	48
South Carolina	4 925	151.3	30.0	13.4	4 498	1 960	13 966	10 067	112.4	8.3	104.7	309	32	6.3	1.0	80	8
South Dakota	397	122.4	41.3	2.0	349	179	671	553	5.4	2.0	4.5	57	158	1.5	4.1	15	59
Tennessee	9 328	86.8	23.6	9.8	9 461	4 993	16 373	10 280	131.4	6.2	116.9	235	2 962	5.0	58.8	93	715
Texas	48 252	51.4	13.7	32.3	45 193	31 869	68 601	57 079	320.1	4.9	299.5	3 004	291	53.5	7.6	908	85
Utah	2 768	64.2	16.0	2.8	2 313	1 686	5 620	3 918	27.7	3.8	21.0	469	161	10.5	3.3	145	37
Vermont	2 611	32.8	91.1	.3	2 684	1 966	907	631	7.8	3.5	7.7	192	252	3.5	5.7	43	75
Virginia	10 926	23.7	12.4	3.1	10 425	8 836	16 635	10 702	131.6	5.3	113.3	418	672	8.8	14.8	133	177
Washington	25 498	−6.7	9.6	1.0	22 032	27 338	10 817	7 985	78.5	4.0	77.5	805	37	15.2	.9	218	9
West Virginia	1 218	38.1	31.0	1.6	1 098	882	9 230	7 975	34.6	6.4	34.9	30	137	.6	3.5	7	33
Wisconsin	8 410	70.3	31.9	4.2	8 004	4 937	7 110	5 088	74.9	3.4	81.4	305	165	6.8	3.9	72	37
Wyoming	124	137.0	56.1	2.8	101	52	3 544	2 782	5.8	3.5	5.8	124	1 093	2.9	14.5	30	247

[1]Excludes exports not allocated or reported by state.
[2]Includes property, plant, and equipment.

Source: Exports–U.S. International Trade Administration, Office of Trade and Economic Analysis, Internet site <http://www.ita.doc.gov/industry/otea/state> (accessed 8 September 1997); Foreign direct investment–U.S. Bureau of Economic Analysis, Survey of Current Business, May 1995, and Foreign Direct Investment in the United States, Operations of U.S. Affiliates of Foreign Companies, annual; and Foreign Direct Investment in the United States, 1992 Benchmark Survey; International visit travel impact–U.S. International Trade Administration, Tourism Industries, Impact of International Spending on State Economies, 1994, Internet site <http://www.tinet.ita.doc.gov/imp/imp_tab.htm> (accessed 30 January 1997), and unpublished data.

Geographic area	Farms (USDA) (as of June 1)								Value of farm land and buildings (USDA)					Farm earnings (BEA) (mil dol)		
	Number (1,000)			Land in farms (mil acres)			Average acreage per farm		Total value (mil dol)			Average value per acre (dollars)				
	1996	1995	1990	1996	1995	1990	1996	1990	1996	1995	1990	1996	1990	1995	1994	1990
United States	2 063	2 072	2 146	968	972	987	469	460	¹859 711	¹807 017	¹671 419	¹890	¹683	33 882	43 990	44 729
Alabama	45	47	47	10	10	10	218	215	13 594	12 875	8 989	1 387	890	845	1 171	892
Alaska	1	1	1	1	1	1	1 804	1 707	NA	NA	NA	NA	NA	12	11	8
Arizona	8	7	8	35	35	36	4 720	4 641	14 125	12 282	9 665	399	267	651	352	501
Arkansas	43	43	47	15	15	16	349	330	14 836	14 747	12 338	989	796	1 315	1 335	929
California	82	80	85	30	30	31	366	362	72 105	66 456	58 027	2 404	1 884	6 031	5 933	6 603
Colorado	25	25	27	33	33	33	1 327	1 249	18 150	17 020	12 379	558	374	431	472	830
Connecticut	4	4	4	Z	Z	Z	100	108	2 588	2 495	2 114	6 810	5 033	193	165	176
Delaware	3	3	3	1	1	1	226	207	1 643	1 533	1 328	2 907	2 214	127	143	168
District of Columbia ...	X	X	X	X	X	X	X	X	X	X	X	X	X	X	X	X
Florida	40	39	41	10	10	11	258	266	23 752	22 860	22 563	2 306	2 070	1 898	1 645	2 054
Georgia	43	45	48	12	12	13	274	260	16 025	15 076	13 488	1 358	1 079	1 937	2 005	1 237
Hawaii	5	5	5	2	2	2	346	357	NA	NA	NA	NA	NA	161	182	219
Idaho	22	22	22	14	14	14	614	628	12 223	11 286	9 015	905	658	678	691	968
Illinois	76	77	83	28	28	28	370	342	58 000	52 346	39 902	2 064	1 405	113	1 775	1 450
Indiana	60	62	68	16	16	16	265	240	28 642	26 302	20 440	1 801	1 254	87	634	780
Iowa	98	100	104	33	33	34	339	322	47 876	44 786	36 515	1 442	1 090	1 220	2 594	2 184
Kansas................	66	66	69	48	48	48	724	694	26 417	25 573	21 555	553	450	687	1 352	1 493
Kentucky..............	88	89	93	14	14	14	159	152	19 283	17 498	13 790	1 377	978	814	1 085	984
Louisiana.............	27	27	32	9	9	9	322	278	10 234	9 199	8 233	1 176	925	506	501	353
Maine	7	8	7	1	1	1	181	201	1 730	1 681	1 556	1 291	1 073	112	112	157
Maryland	14	14	15	2	2	2	153	148	8 034	8 155	5 767	3 826	2 563	227	286	360
Massachusetts.........	6	6	6	1	1	1	92	100	3 190	3 077	2 705	5 597	4 227	154	154	152
Michigan..............	53	54	54	11	11	11	200	200	15 579	14 219	10 854	1 470	1 005	540	381	730
Minnesota.............	87	87	89	30	30	30	343	337	29 079	27 907	24 300	976	810	641	1 283	2 007
Mississippi...........	44	42	40	13	13	13	286	325	11 557	11 432	9 568	917	736	522	706	362
Missouri..............	104	105	108	30	30	30	288	281	28 445	26 411	21 310	948	701	84	707	653
Montana...............	22	22	25	60	60	61	2 714	2 449	17 273	16 529	13 431	289	222	332	387	378
Nebraska..............	56	56	57	47	47	47	839	826	29 695	28 074	24 680	632	524	1 259	1 788	2 272
Nevada................	3	3	3	9	9	9	3 520	3 560	2 925	2 543	1 842	332	207	45	59	73
New Hampshire	2	2	3	Z	Z	Z	179	163	1 109	1 094	998	2 578	2 269	50	52	43
New Jersey............	9	9	8	1	1	1	91	107	6 865	6 844	4 780	8 172	5 494	284	268	235
New Mexico............	14	14	14	44	44	45	3 237	3 296	11 287	9 883	8 233	258	185	289	308	372
New York..............	36	36	39	8	8	8	214	218	10 266	10 628	8 518	1 333	1 014	500	528	735
North Carolina	58	58	62	9	9	10	159	156	18 120	16 092	13 144	1 970	1 355	2 883	2 989	2 255
North Dakota	31	32	34	40	40	41	1 300	1 209	15 417	15 041	13 001	383	321	229	719	632
Ohio	72	74	83	15	15	16	210	188	30 033	27 359	19 859	1 989	1 273	725	1 017	1 106
Oklahoma	72	71	70	34	34	33	472	471	18 609	18 609	16 203	547	491	373	867	850
Oregon	39	39	37	18	18	18	455	488	16 239	14 776	10 199	928	573	540	710	688
Pennsylvania..........	50	50	53	8	8	8	154	153	19 292	18 013	15 625	2 505	1 929	608	754	906
Rhode Island	1	1	1	Z	Z	Z	90	95	454	438	389	7 204	5 564	40	34	34
South Carolina	22	22	25	5	5	5	233	208	6 816	6 749	5 257	1 363	1 011	369	494	280
South Dakota	33	33	35	44	44	44	1 354	1 266	14 038	13 306	12 891	319	291	506	1 088	1 015
Tennessee.............	80	81	87	12	12	12	148	139	18 006	16 035	12 911	1 526	1 067	321	563	355
Texas.................	205	202	196	127	129	132	620	673	71 894	70 968	66 924	566	507	2 142	2 769	2 708
Utah..................	13	13	13	11	11	11	821	856	7 671	6 731	4 497	697	398	180	239	247
Vermont...............	6	6	7	1	1	1	225	222	2 070	2 026	1 817	1 534	1 262	107	120	109
Virginia..............	48	47	46	9	9	9	179	193	16 557	15 232	14 819	1 925	1 665	474	564	639
Washington............	36	36	37	16	16	16	436	432	17 538	16 825	13 136	1 117	821	1 247	1 231	1 125
West Virginia.........	20	20	21	4	4	4	185	180	3 570	3 368	2 457	965	664	9	52	34
Wisconsin.............	79	80	80	17	17	18	213	220	19 741	18 004	14 098	1 175	801	298	609	1 247
Wyoming...............	9	9	9	35	35	35	3 802	3 899	7 118	6 633	5 309	206	153	86	108	142

NA Not available.
Z Rounds to less than half the unit of measure shown.
X Not applicable.

¹Excludes Alaska and Hawaii.

Source: Farms and acreage–U.S. Department of Agriculture, National Agricultural Statistics Service, Farms and Land in Farms, Final Estimates, 1988-1992 and Farms and Land in Farms, July releases; Value of farm land and buildings–U.S. Department of Agriculture, Economic Research Service, AREI Updates, Number 17: Agricultural Land Values, annual; Farm earnings–U.S. Bureau of Economic Analysis, Survey of Current Business, Volume 76, Number 10, October 1996.

Table A–34. States — Farm Finances and Income

Geographic area	Balance sheet of farming sector (USDA)						Farm income (USDA)									
	Assets (mil dol)			Debt (mil dol)			Gross farm income[1] (mil dol)			Farm marketings cash receipts					Net farm income[1] (mil dol)		
										Total (mil dol)			Crops as percent of total, 1995				
	1995	1994	1990	1995	1994	1990	1995	1994	1990	1995	1994	1990		1995	1994	1990
United States	977 986	938 141	839 870	150 769	146 800	137 962	210 399	215 840	198 196	185 750	180 775	169 517	53.2	34 819	48 396	44 798
Alabama	13 970	13 567	10 130	1 553	1 466	1 378	3 622	3 726	3 259	2 908	2 951	2 766	25.5	946	1 269	908
Alaska	578	593	581	12	16	26	37	36	34	30	28	27	81.1	12	11	8
Arizona	14 513	12 832	11 232	1 209	1 241	1 386	2 390	2 026	2 028	2 256	1 854	1 930	64.1	715	466	612
Arkansas	17 496	17 482	15 628	3 609	3 398	3 027	5 843	6 047	4 949	5 066	5 395	4 254	40.3	1 363	1 480	890
California	76 083	71 002	68 298	14 307	13 927	13 151	23 462	22 741	20 437	22 261	21 282	19 214	75.1	4 347	5 575	5 700
Colorado	20 455	19 682	17 391	3 281	3 055	2 872	4 707	4 657	4 851	3 985	4 051	4 227	34.2	444	625	1 071
Connecticut	2 403	2 359	2 074	199	199	216	548	537	501	485	478	439	47.0	168	170	156
Delaware	1 689	1 592	1 361	313	305	316	766	734	722	676	658	636	23.5	132	163	194
District of Columbia	X	X	X	X	X	X	X	X	X	X	X	X	X	X	X	X
Florida	25 977	25 429	24 813	3 945	4 058	3 641	6 143	6 306	5 952	5 849	5 984	5 697	80.7	1 705	2 219	2 110
Georgia	17 694	16 993	15 416	3 143	2 852	2 751	5 986	5 680	4 435	5 166	4 689	3 855	46.0	2 016	2 139	1 233
Hawaii	4 516	4 223	4 043	203	259	350	517	552	653	484	508	610	85.1	22	45	130
Idaho	14 187	13 262	11 446	2 599	2 589	2 377	3 555	3 451	3 291	3 166	2 955	2 830	61.4	606	712	1 022
Illinois	64 464	58 816	49 269	8 079	7 797	7 107	8 035	9 790	8 973	7 887	7 946	7 779	78.3	445	2 017	1 494
Indiana	31 817	29 608	25 055	4 744	4 661	4 494	5 297	5 707	5 566	4 982	4 664	4 904	65.0	298	782	822
Iowa	59 313	56 163	50 776	10 933	10 725	9 647	11 992	13 166	11 925	10 959	9 999	10 275	53.8	1 768	2 976	2 317
Kansas	31 988	31 877	28 380	6 017	5 929	5 552	8 574	9 052	8 690	7 521	7 626	6 992	37.6	889	1 705	1 677
Kentucky	20 945	19 826	16 683	2 861	2 758	2 573	3 729	3 906	3 605	3 060	3 220	3 099	47.2	953	1 210	1 028
Louisiana	9 224	8 413	8 715	1 609	1 604	1 711	2 435	2 490	2 209	2 025	2 029	1 907	68.9	521	506	321
Maine	2 061	2 025	1 819	337	324	309	567	546	555	479	458	489	41.4	80	87	131
Maryland	7 967	8 116	5 898	964	1 014	930	1 658	1 602	1 567	1 402	1 339	1 359	40.8	242	302	353
Massachusetts	3 124	3 041	2 862	238	289	298	507	529	484	430	460	412	76.0	124	154	132
Michigan	17 838	16 676	14 761	2 712	2 633	2 629	4 059	3 877	3 723	3 521	3 381	3 171	62.4	449	217	587
Minnesota	37 705	35 942	35 011	7 691	7 306	6 433	8 364	8 971	8 610	7 002	6 408	6 894	50.7	974	1 545	2 130
Mississippi	13 091	12 964	11 346	2 496	2 414	2 454	3 574	3 688	2 912	3 126	2 871	2 405	46.1	593	728	335
Missouri	32 616	31 172	27 647	5 199	4 848	4 443	5 071	5 482	4 812	4 399	4 562	3 940	48.5	322	872	742
Montana	19 907	19 490	16 434	2 565	2 613	2 518	2 407	2 424	2 129	1 845	1 885	1 609	56.8	392	487	421
Nebraska	37 376	36 132	33 267	7 697	7 466	6 352	9 660	9 988	10 410	8 690	8 525	8 715	42.7	1 572	2 193	2 483
Nevada	2 978	2 712	2 484	235	235	254	342	364	332	286	299	301	42.7	39	61	78
New Hampshire	1 053	1 051	1 012	75	75	71	181	180	166	152	151	136	58.0	43	47	37
New Jersey	6 608	6 596	5 502	417	416	412	927	904	760	773	770	649	74.1	250	259	194
New Mexico	12 380	11 240	10 497	1 181	1 123	1 088	1 585	1 778	1 644	1 415	1 528	1 500	31.9	255	362	420
New York.................	12 513	13 045	12 100	2 171	2 150	2 169	3 251	3 160	3 229	2 878	2 868	2 926	35.2	364	420	603
North Carolina	20 065	18 241	15 160	3 273	2 970	2 577	7 996	7 804	6 154	6 987	6 439	5 230	46.5	2 880	3 076	2 197
North Dakota	21 240	21 006	18 923	3 719	3 608	3 351	3 572	3 981	3 441	3 154	3 028	2 373	82.1	398	859	664
Ohio	31 749	29 771	24 875	3 431	3 329	3 172	5 404	5 512	5 245	4 576	4 438	4 386	65.3	950	1 179	1 169
Oklahoma	21 497	22 253	19 940	3 845	3 886	3 746	4 333	4 793	4 421	3 705	3 899	3 598	30.6	498	1 086	943
Oregon	16 861	15 731	12 180	2 182	2 157	2 385	3 583	3 587	2 980	2 720	2 651	2 395	75.5	381	620	546
Pennsylvania	20 906	20 057	18 526	2 486	2 458	2 255	4 265	4 232	4 140	3 738	3 769	3 725	31.7	543	711	822
Rhode Island	426	412	349	61	39	34	91	90	78	80	80	70	87.5	43	43	34
South Carolina	7 449	7 420	6 698	842	847	937	1 645	1 673	1 332	1 441	1 383	1 190	57.6	389	528	264
South Dakota	19 152	18 824	18 335	3 711	3 670	3 256	3 725	4 250	3 814	3 384	3 336	2 963	50.5	673	1 276	1 074
Tennessee	19 078	17 919	15 484	2 070	1 993	2 002	2 628	2 749	2 430	2 127	2 172	1 995	59.2	464	676	425
Texas	80 434	81 649	76 770	10 149	9 909	9 513	15 706	15 347	14 463	13 288	12 930	11 791	36.4	2 419	3 737	3 051
Utah	7 894	6 946	5 403	688	669	662	993	1 029	903	815	827	744	27.3	181	248	257
Vermont.................	2 447	2 424	2 270	347	344	349	540	533	503	472	479	466	19.5	100	112	100
Virginia..................	17 302	16 614	14 416	1 836	1 879	1 914	2 599	2 603	2 556	2 248	2 194	2 138	38.0	531	632	677
Washington	19 141	18 663	16 257	3 052	3 031	2 899	5 962	5 608	4 544	5 158	4 769	3 740	69.1	915	1 080	869
West Virginia	3 570	3 525	2 870	390	402	398	479	507	417	386	400	318	19.2	36	77	46
Wisconsin	26 160	25 013	22 763	5 176	4 969	4 740	6 181	6 532	6 485	5 582	5 379	5 682	29.7	284	540	1 173
Wyoming	8 078	7 748	6 714	918	899	838	914	915	880	726	783	769	25.1	89	115	152

X Not applicable.

[1]Farm income data are after inventory adjustment and include income and expenses related to the farm operator's dwelling.

Source: U.S. Department of Agriculture, Economic Research Service, Farm Business Economic Report, annual.

Table A–35. States — Construction

Geographic area	Nonfarm employment (1,000)			Earnings (BEA) (mil dol)			Establishments		Contracts[1] (mil dol)			New private housing units authorized by building permits[2] (1,000)		
	1996	1995	1990	1995	1994	1990	1994	Net change, 1990-1994	1996	1995	1990	1996	1995	1990
United States	[3]5 407	[3]5 158	[3]5 120	235 315	226 432	204 504	620 852	42 477	330 073	305 464	246 022	1 425 616	1 332 549	1 110 766
Alabama	94	87	83	3 283	3 125	2 649	8 837	1 414	4 794	4 311	2 939	19 868	20 114	12 525
Alaska	13	13	11	929	942	703	1 909	384	983	1 660	1 919	2 640	2 164	732
Arizona	127	117	83	4 395	3 843	2 659	9 613	1 472	9 795	8 787	4 553	53 715	52 714	23 030
Arkansas	47	44	38	1 731	1 611	1 248	5 329	1 107	2 795	2 903	1 438	11 144	11 707	5 915
California	511	488	562	26 888	26 213	30 340	60 363	-8 271	31 758	28 919	37 318	92 060	83 864	163 175
Colorado	111	103	64	4 591	4 424	2 511	12 425	3 897	7 973	6 476	3 235	41 135	38 622	11 897
Connecticut	52	51	62	3 148	3 118	3 328	8 983	-1 419	3 414	3 124	3 058	8 537	8 550	7 584
Delaware	21	19	20	1 072	988	850	2 200	-16	800	871	787	4 370	4 608	5 142
District of Columbia	9	9	14	368	370	525	324	-94	1 162	656	795	-	35	368
Florida	324	304	323	11 470	10 984	10 372	36 321	844	22 323	21 534	16 975	125 020	122 903	126 347
Georgia	165	152	147	6 360	5 816	5 059	15 841	1 782	12 320	12 161	7 120	74 874	72 225	41 251
Hawaii	[4]24	[4]26	[4]32	1 677	1 821	1 681	2 527	164	1 805	2 273	2 831	3 927	6 614	8 718
Idaho	30	30	19	1 411	1 360	844	4 809	2 053	1 879	1 864	986	10 755	10 666	5 703
Illinois	221	216	220	11 660	11 327	10 319	26 668	2 948	12 614	11 736	10 796	49 592	47 467	38 255
Indiana	132	130	116	5 655	5 436	4 243	14 830	2 489	8 927	7 896	6 350	37 219	35 715	25 002
Iowa	59	55	45	2 493	2 361	1 718	7 541	1 396	2 795	2 883	2 034	12 027	11 341	7 637
Kansas	57	52	42	2 191	2 097	1 541	6 695	1 019	3 770	3 264	2 193	14 676	12 655	8 454
Kentucky	77	73	67	2 872	2 868	2 204	8 218	1 057	4 702	4 457	3 174	18 778	17 625	11 810
Louisiana	113	105	92	3 811	3 688	2 956	7 197	1 182	4 874	4 354	3 191	17 998	14 723	6 451
Maine	23	22	29	1 000	980	1 137	4 104	-436	983	1 076	897	4 685	4 417	4 757
Maryland	130	128	156	5 367	5 243	5 790	14 309	-126	6 480	6 299	6 056	25 108	26 576	32 004
Massachusetts	94	90	101	5 525	5 355	5 092	14 050	-2 311	7 679	7 411	5 135	17 261	16 428	14 290
Michigan	168	154	142	7 834	7 290	6 306	22 243	3 897	10 796	9 946	7 646	52 355	47 226	38 871
Minnesota	89	83	79	4 500	4 350	3 630	11 785	1 453	5 429	5 607	4 953	27 043	25 494	23 473
Mississippi	49	45	37	1 650	1 608	1 146	4 445	625	3 563	2 718	1 569	10 367	10 753	5 923
Missouri	116	111	98	5 151	4 927	3 658	14 571	2 190	6 050	6 440	3 833	26 298	24 282	15 284
Montana	17	16	10	726	692	421	3 119	1 254	916	865	332	2 678	3 064	1 191
Nebraska	37	34	27	1 415	1 351	937	4 774	668	1 870	1 694	1 318	10 091	8 164	6 750
Nevada	75	62	47	2 709	2 448	1 813	3 694	575	7 026	5 555	3 334	37 242	32 804	25 096
New Hampshire	21	19	23	1 075	1 005	1 036	3 502	-727	1 211	1 039	1 021	4 926	4 423	4 126
New Jersey	123	124	146	6 908	6 968	7 281	21 193	-751	7 134	6 457	6 141	24 173	21 521	17 524
New Mexico	43	46	30	1 545	1 432	863	4 604	878	2 227	2 108	1 124	10 180	11 009	5 988
New York	254	251	320	12 766	12 668	14 168	36 587	-3 909	13 891	13 456	14 137	34 895	28 060	34 950
North Carolina	189	174	164	6 800	6 360	5 243	20 680	1 745	12 448	10 574	6 614	66 997	60 923	40 777
North Dakota	15	14	10	521	479	346	1 876	206	656	791	506	2 324	3 185	1 512
Ohio	213	207	195	9 433	9 184	7 714	25 576	2 805	14 021	12 407	9 885	49 280	44 812	38 491
Oklahoma	50	48	40	1 945	1 910	1 599	6 512	1 271	3 184	2 967	2 164	10 640	10 066	5 284
Oregon	78	68	52	3 336	2 932	2 267	10 866	3 406	5 411	4 965	3 101	27 814	26 201	22 858
Pennsylvania	202	201	227	10 506	10 576	10 118	26 740	-1 212	9 406	9 326	10 117	37 895	36 250	37 204
Rhode Island	14	14	19	662	660	818	2 985	-285	658	465	594	2 462	2 331	3 042
South Carolina	94	87	102	3 185	3 018	3 185	9 261	891	5 457	4 580	3 664	29 403	23 959	21 251
South Dakota	15	14	12	578	566	405	2 318	730	814	706	468	3 648	3 832	2 830
Tennessee	113	108	92	4 801	4 484	3 395	10 482	1 185	8 273	7 167	4 388	40 522	35 096	20 194
Texas	436	409	336	17 752	16 590	12 911	33 234	5 034	25 017	22 988	13 197	118 823	105 102	47 103
Utah	60	54	28	2 079	1 823	1 054	5 676	2 058	3 756	3 725	1 884	23 481	20 898	7 324
Vermont	13	12	15	580	554	575	2 490	-383	588	484	515	2 070	2 269	2 370
Virginia	175	168	182	6 358	6 065	6 113	18 521	-12	9 213	8 794	7 180	45 919	43 129	42 116
Washington	127	123	117	5 967	5 919	4 781	19 594	4 345	8 539	7 330	6 185	39 597	38 160	48 447
West Virginia	34	33	27	1 225	1 289	940	4 193	948	1 258	1 215	1 253	3 616	3 691	1 766
Wisconsin	105	100	87	4 889	4 796	3 637	14 284	2 424	5 994	5 649	4 654	33 296	32 403	27 282
Wyoming	14	14	11	519	514	373	1 954	633	642	532	462	2 192	1 709	692

– Represents zero.

[1]Data are subject to copyright, see below for source citation.
[2]1990 based on 17,000 permit-issuing place universe; beginning 1995, based on 19,000 place universe.
[3]National totals are derived independently and differ from the sum of the states.
[4]Includes mining.

Source: Employment–U.S. Bureau of Labor Statistics, Employment and Earnings, monthly, May issue, compiled from data supplied by cooperating state agencies; Earnings–U.S. Bureau of Economic Analysis, Survey of Current Business, Volume 76, Number 10, October 1996; Establishments, County Business Patterns, on diskette, annual (related Internetsite <http://www.census.gov/epcd/cbp/view/cbpview.html>); Contracts–F.W. Dodge, McGraw-Hill, Inc., New York, NY, (copyright); Building permits–U.S. Bureau of the Census, Construction Reports, Series C40, annual, from source diskette state file.

Geographic area	Nonfarm employment (1,000)			Earnings (BEA) (mil dol)			Establishments		Average hourly earnings of production workers (dollars)			Value of shipments (mil dol)		
	1996	1995	1990	1995	1994	1990	1994	Net change, 1990-1994	1996	1995	1990	1995	1994	1990
United States	[1]18 282	[1]18 468	[1]19 076	796 685	760 619	664 475	386 868	8 781	1 2.78	12.37	10.83	3 589 157	3 348 019	2 873 502
Alabama	383	391	385	13 129	12 537	10 498	6 670	472	11.53	11.14	9.39	65 481	59 433	48 748
Alaska	16	17	17	663	634	593	549	51	11.14	11.00	12.46	3 994	3 686	3 676
Arizona	200	193	185	8 483	7 876	6 382	4 956	473	11.49	11.16	10.21	35 185	30 631	22 886
Arkansas	254	259	233	7 619	7 263	5 661	4 148	553	10.41	10.05	8.51	42 929	39 519	30 493
California	1 853	1 790	2 069	84 363	80 798	80 864	49 897	–1 797	12.83	12.55	11.48	348 765	321 789	293 190
Colorado	196	191	193	8 133	7 531	6 535	5 623	619	12.82	12.51	10.94	37 538	34 301	27 701
Connecticut	275	280	341	15 144	14 690	14 366	6 162	–312	14.01	13.71	11.53	44 102	41 522	39 898
Delaware	58	62	72	4 051	3 907	3 715	735	36	14.00	14.20	12.39	14 469	15 054	12 901
District of Columbia	13	13	16	911	865	820	441	–18	13.68	13.66	12.51	2 051	1 978	2 152
Florida	490	482	522	18 296	17 806	16 143	16 770	619	10.54	10.18	8.98	73 574	68 217	60 750
Georgia	585	588	561	20 485	19 156	15 339	10 103	624	11.17	10.71	9.17	112 023	102 674	83 997
Hawaii	17	17	21	798	802	779	983	–40	12.79	12.82	10.99	3 440	3 337	4 203
Idaho	73	71	63	2 897	2 732	1 928	2 004	260	12.15	11.46	10.60	16 484	14 792	9 184
Illinois..................	972	967	983	43 529	41 747	35 625	18 981	241	13.03	12.64	11.44	193 095	182 095	156 675
Indiana.................	674	684	638	29 696	27 963	22 145	9 461	369	14.33	13.91	12.03	130 899	122 566	98 619
Iowa....................	247	250	236	9 368	8 988	7 422	3 976	306	13.13	12.73	11.27	59 003	55 863	45 927
Kansas..................	196	192	186	7 201	6 835	5 734	3 517	150	12.88	12.39	10.94	42 641	39 267	26 349
Kentucky................	312	314	288	11 652	10 988	8 981	4 493	384	12.70	12.22	10.70	79 406	69 649	53 777
Louisiana................	188	188	184	8 040	7 697	6 332	4 109	255	13.66	13.43	11.61	74 493	64 988	65 807
Maine...................	88	92	102	3 284	3 172	3 085	2 258	43	12.71	12.39	10.59	14 477	12 917	12 477
Maryland................	174	176	206	7 873	7 707	7 339	4 269	–39	13.71	13.49	11.57	34 478	32 356	30 679
Massachusetts...........	444	445	521	22 012	21 128	20 489	10 086	–637	13.04	12.79	11.39	75 250	69 929	63 796
Michigan................	967	975	944	55 608	52 380	40 433	16 513	779	16.67	16.31	13.86	204 018	199 131	153 386
Minnesota...............	428	426	401	18 175	17 307	14 325	8 349	724	13.18	12.79	11.23	69 419	64 414	55 244
Mississippi..............	246	258	247	7 273	7 125	5 671	3 860	272	10.19	9.76	8.37	39 547	38 401	30 313
Missouri.................	414	421	438	17 097	15 968	14 031	8 055	378	12.54	12.16	10.74	82 557	78 621	67 355
Montana	24	23	22	808	788	661	1 426	213	13.00	12.94	11.51	4 899	4 700	4 040
Nebraska................	114	112	98	3 784	3 553	2 726	2 080	182	11.51	11.19	9.66	24 425	24 023	20 370
Nevada..................	39	37	26	1 326	1 188	790	1 464	316	13.59	12.62	11.05	5 445	4 799	2 925
New Hampshire	105	102	106	4 292	4 091	3 679	2 406	90	12.24	11.94	10.83	15 437	13 574	9 727
New Jersey..............	485	500	597	25 690	25 148	23 966	12 901	–1 035	13.86	13.56	11.76	92 383	89 555	87 498
New Mexico..............	46	45	43	1 666	1 582	1 228	1 647	251	10.97	10.68	9.04	12 561	12 465	5 548
New York................	922	944	1 131	46 445	45 494	44 853	25 971	–2 318	12.78	12.50	11.11	162 945	159 879	154 714
North Carolina	847	861	862	29 005	27 722	22 755	12 068	352	10.96	10.56	8.79	152 709	142 054	116 245
North Dakota	22	21	17	664	619	426	714	88	10.94	10.75	9.27	4 382	3 757	3 013
Ohio	1 094	1 101	1 112	51 343	48 946	41 672	18 406	389	14.69	14.42	12.64	222 923	207 541	177 787
Oklahoma	174	170	169	6 519	6 468	5 502	4 256	372	11.77	11.52	10.73	33 165	32 491	28 010
Oregon	235	228	220	9 377	8 664	7 179	7 029	429	13.01	12.75	11.15	42 338	38 177	31 073
Pennsylvania............	929	939	1 019	40 941	39 277	35 107	17 904	–249	13.39	12.81	11.04	164 879	151 750	136 526
Rhode Island	82	85	100	3 025	2 962	2 886	2 667	–86	10.94	10.62	9.45	10 074	9 911	9 761
South Carolina	365	378	383	13 101	12 591	10 544	4 986	239	10.26	10.16	8.84	66 903	62 044	46 734
South Dakota	48	46	34	1 328	1 204	796	952	153	9.59	9.36	8.48	9 213	8 258	4 533
Tennessee	522	542	520	19 165	18 521	14 557	7 937	592	11.28	10.78	9.55	96 208	91 194	67 404
Texas...................	1 054	1 030	997	48 653	45 461	37 327	22 568	1 787	11.82	11.47	10.47	265 092	241 348	210 584
Utah....................	129	124	107	4 259	3 867	3 074	2 737	427	12.22	11.62	10.32	20 089	17 862	13 950
Vermont.................	46	45	46	1 737	1 655	1 551	1 369	67	12.42	12.21	10.52	8 888	7 434	5 592
Virginia.................	399	402	426	15 272	14 714	13 070	6 656	255	12.19	11.72	10.07	75 762	71 529	61 042
Washington	344	332	369	15 458	14 990	13 849	8 848	561	14.70	14.73	12.61	69 062	66 452	67 538
West Virginia	82	82	88	3 349	3 200	2 999	1 870	147	12.96	12.64	11.53	17 765	15 702	12 938
Wisconsin	601	601	559	23 367	21 981	17 767	10 454	717	13.14	12.76	11.11	109 593	101 851	83 013
Wyoming	11	10	10	330	331	278	584	77	13.16	11.96	10.83	2 705	2 538	2 756

[1]National totals are derived independently and differ from the sum of the states.

Source: Employment and average hourly earnings–Bureau of Labor Statistics, Employment and Earnings, monthly, May issues, compiled from data supplied by cooperating state agencies; Earnings–Bureau of Economic Analysis,Survey of Current Business, Volume 76, Number 10, October 1996; Establishments–U.S. Bureau of the Census, County Business Patterns, on diskette, annual (related Internet site <http://www.census.gov/epcd/cbp/view/cbpview.html>); Value of shipments–U.S. Bureau of the Census, Annual Survey of Manufactures, M95(AS)-3 and M91(AS)-3.

Geographic area	Nonfarm employment (1,000)			Earnings (BEA) (mil dol)			Establishments,[1] 1994		Commodity transportation, 1993			
									Commodity shipments		Percent going out of state	
	1996	1995	1990	1995	1994	1990	Total	Net change, 1990-1994	Value (mil dol)	Weight (1,000 tons)	Value	Weight
United States	[2]4 038.0	[2]3 904.0	[2]3 511.0	156 576	148 307	122 440	208 380	30 746	5 846 334	9 688 493	X	X
Alabama	NA	NA	NA	1 871	1 720	1 339	3 095	518	88 845	218 864	66.2	28.8
Alaska	NA	NA	NA	808	802	610	1 081	236	8 120	23 479	19.2	17.4
Arizona	58.9	55.1	45.6	2 000	1 814	1 356	2 635	659	68 569	84 035	57.3	23.0
Arkansas	45.3	43.6	35.7	1 633	1 465	1 180	2 401	554	66 954	100 215	73.7	41.0
California.................	414.3	400.1	374.7	17 815	17 042	14 798	21 178	1 253	638 523	706 554	38.8	8.8
Colorado	NA	NA	NA	2 376	2 315	1 884	3 016	595	58 765	93 674	57.6	23.8
Connecticut	42.6	41.2	40.9	1 653	1 503	1 369	2 452	260	71 357	44 208	79.2	23.0
Delaware	10.6	10.3	10	367	350	473	675	94	16 140	24 326	85.2	72.2
District of Columbia	7.2	7.7	9.3	309	305	487	486	48	NA	NA	NA	NA
Florida	206.3	196.7	170.6	7 163	6 679	5 326	12 285	3 360	172 045	345 980	36.8	18.2
Georgia	134.5	131.9	117.6	5 752	5 500	4 295	5 385	1 383	210 143	262 173	66.8	28.3
Hawaii	30.9	30.7	31.8	1 138	1 122	960	1 250	157	11 462	24 748	7.4	10.8
Idaho	15.8	15.2	12.5	579	532	426	1 227	260	16 518	48 583	68.2	35.5
Illinois	NA	NA	NA	9 254	8 943	7 128	10 081	1 376	346 604	525 176	66.0	42.6
Indiana	NA	NA	85.8	3 633	3 384	2 721	4 617	851	178 704	285 805	71.6	43.9
Iowa	NA	NA	NA	1 532	1 416	1 158	3 138	488	79 900	164 544	64.9	39.6
Kansas...................	NA	NA	NA	1 628	1 635	1 412	2 357	145	70 519	134 545	74.7	46.2
Kentucky	66.1	63.8	51.8	2 484	2 325	1 751	3 215	423	112 047	353 170	75.6	51.0
Louisiana.................	67.4	66	66.7	2 588	2 459	2 163	3 723	687	96 194	359 855	50.7	33.6
Maine...................	NA	NA	NA	480	455	399	1 477	268	20 233	42 461	65.5	27.2
Maryland	62	61.4	56.8	2 282	2 171	1 874	3 747	485	98 508	123 215	69.0	43.4
Massachusetts	80.1	77.8	73.7	2 964	2 828	2 403	4 462	240	111 722	73 075	66.5	28.3
Michigan	NA	NA	NA	4 368	4 091	3 242	5 524	968	256 289	323 807	52.1	26.1
Minnesota	85	83.4	74.8	3 478	3 196	2 828	4 253	662	110 180	189 909	60.0	41.3
Mississippi	32.1	31	25.6	1 125	1 027	814	2 177	523	56 268	117 790	71.3	43.9
Missouri	NA	NA	NA	3 798	3 646	3 324	5 477	899	136 929	195 212	73.5	36.6
Montana	13.1	13.1	12.3	526	514	433	1 090	177	10 167	82 845	47.0	57.8
Nebraska.................	38.9	38	33.4	1 630	1 532	1 256	1 925	259	42 534	97 992	70.9	51.0
Nevada	27.1	25.2	18.7	868	778	557	1 046	265	19 597	30 871	74.1	19.0
New Hampshire	11.2	10.7	NA	390	362	280	919	127	16 465	S	77.8	S
New Jersey	162.2	158.4	144.2	6 190	6 052	5 047	8 194	775	252 790	179 510	68.7	40.6
New Mexico	NA	NA	NA	659	619	502	1 074	276	11 794	61 410	51.7	40.3
New York.................	NA	NA	NA	9 654	9 344	9 021	14 854	748	261 894	219 772	58.8	23.8
North Carolina	NA	NA	NA	4 105	3 796	3 115	5 234	932	209 398	205 317	61.9	30.4
North Dakota	10.7	10.6	8.9	410	392	297	1 003	192	10 528	60 768	62.5	43.9
Ohio	150.7	147.6	126.6	5 729	5 386	4 241	7 676	1 116	325 626	469 652	62.5	30.0
Oklahoma	46.7	45	40	1 851	1 766	1 502	2 242	454	48 702	119 595	65.5	45.1
Oregon	50.7	49.6	43	1 962	1 842	1 525	3 036	266	81 939	204 624	58.5	19.8
Pennsylvania	173.4	171.7	160.4	7 035	6 789	5 636	7 862	305	248 758	416 918	64.7	38.1
Rhode Island	9.4	9.1	8.7	289	269	245	689	28	19 475	14 670	79.1	45.8
South Carolina	NA	NA	NA	1 442	1 327	1 077	2 282	491	83 621	117 146	69.5	36.5
South Dakota	10.7	10.4	8	441	408	315	1 044	247	9 585	25 160	59.9	44.9
Tennessee	113.6	110.4	88.3	4 495	4 103	3 123	3 992	507	170 056	174 549	74.4	39.2
Texas...................	NA	NA	NA	13 101	12 290	9 244	13 645	3 055	451 847	882 021	40.0	16.3
Utah....................	NA	NA	NA	1 267	1 213	945	1 243	236	35 599	156 825	63.8	19.2
Vermont	7.6	7.3	6.4	240	220	186	622	73	8 599	12 271	65.8	31.9
Virginia..................	NA	NA	NA	3 517	3 363	2 743	5 025	754	114 590	289 195	63.5	28.4
Washington...............	85.8	83.5	78.3	3 373	3 174	2 735	4 734	718	123 245	259 359	44.2	16.2
West Virginia	NA	NA	NA	763	740	600	1 546	344	34 924	234 215	74.6	63.7
Wisconsin	NA	NA	NA	3 167	2 908	2 153	5 430	894	143 318	166 044	64.9	30.5
Wyoming	8.7	8.4	8.7	390	385	334	559	115	9 012	292 352	70.8	84.3

X Not applicable.
NA Not available.
S Data suppressed.

[1]Excludes railroad transportation and pipelines included in nonfarm employment and earnings.
[2]National totals are derived independently and differ from the sum of the state.

Note: Transportation includes railroad, passenger, water, and air transportation; trucking and warehousing; pipelines, except natural gas; and transportation services.

Source: Employment–Bureau of Labor Statistics, Employment and Earnings, monthly, May issues, compiled from data supplied by cooperating state agencies; Earnings–Bureau of Economic Analysis, Survey of Current Business, Volume 76, Number 10, October 1996; Establishments–U.S. Bureau of the Census, County Business Patterns, on diskette, annual (related Internet site <http://www.census.gov/epcd/cbp/view/cbpview.html>); Commodity transportation–U.S. Department of Transportation, Bureau of Transportation Statistics, Commodity Flow Survey, (related Internet site <http://www.bts.gov/ntda/cfs/cfsfutr.htm>).

STATE AND METROPOLITAN AREA DATA BOOK

Table A-38. States — Wholesale and Retail Trade and Shopping Centers

Geographic area	Wholesale and retail nonfarm employment (1,000)			Wholesale trade					Retail trade					Shopping centers[1]			
				Earnings (BEA) (mil dol)			Establishments		Earnings (BEA) (mil dol)			Establishments		Retail sales (mil dol)		Retail sales per square foot[2] (dollars)	
	1996	1995	1990	1995	1994	1990	1994	Net change, 1990-1994	1995	1994	1990	1994	Net change, 1990-1994	1996	1990	1996	1990
United States	[3]28 184	[3]27 585	[3]25 774	273 968	254 075	221 120	512 489	36 134	399 957	376 811	319 936	1 564 175	34 468	933 918	706 381	183	161
Alabama	419	411	355	3 323	3 035	2 504	7 346	611	5 483	5 148	4 000	25 192	1 253	14 245	11 166	200	172
Alaska	55	54	46	349	340	296	964	209	1 137	1 083	877	3 956	486	1 774	1 265	234	177
Arizona	466	449	367	3 598	3 191	2 357	7 131	1 045	6 583	6 060	4 541	22 682	1 511	22 123	16 168	190	162
Arkansas	247	242	206	1 666	1 528	1 216	4 409	351	3 436	3 200	2 362	15 713	798	6 904	5 466	200	177
California	2 973	2 927	2 993	33 988	31 487	29 866	60 303	3 948	50 308	47 692	44 773	161 127	-3 357	112 575	83 519	174	163
Colorado	465	458	372	4 068	3 698	2 867	8 230	1 065	6 687	6 138	4 474	24 798	2 524	20 454	15 134	223	177
Connecticut	347	341	360	4 692	4 322	4 143	6 348	113	5 847	5 657	5 436	21 057	-1 081	16 446	12 022	182	154
Delaware	84	83	76	589	543	475	1 135	107	1 203	1 121	963	4 915	236	3 848	2 821	191	164
District of Columbia.........	50	52	62	313	310	384	475	-60	903	897	953	3 762	-96	1 553	1 212	177	156
Florida......................	1 607	1 548	1 444	12 895	11 817	9 765	32 222	5 070	22 666	21 511	18 156	91 251	3 202	83 341	60 561	207	168
Georgia.....................	897	865	745	9 972	9 292	7 789	15 631	1 548	11 142	10 239	8 042	42 890	1 732	28 668	21 548	178	159
Hawaii......................	135	136	136	803	792	740	2 216	117	2 654	2 556	2 276	7 978	295	3 598	2 511	198	176
Idaho.......................	125	121	97	856	793	601	2 381	228	1 689	1 578	1 154	7 562	858	3 042	2 377	168	147
Illinois......................	1 304	1 317	1 264	16 408	15 334	13 861	24 946	699	18 208	17 118	14 692	66 426	1 068	37 606	28 818	153	141
Indiana.....................	680	669	600	5 178	4 793	3 903	10 595	848	8 471	7 879	6 377	34 459	895	19 565	15 339	168	147
Iowa........................	341	341	310	2 890	2 674	2 204	7 004	162	4 080	3 877	3 144	19 938	88	6 828	5 391	178	161
Kansas......................	303	296	269	2 894	2 590	2 224	6 021	308	3 831	3 591	2 891	16 839	-6	10 583	8 220	196	172
Kentucky....................	401	396	351	2 747	2 479	2 019	6 118	444	5 227	4 888	3 845	22 503	120	12 673	9 937	194	164
Louisiana...................	423	417	369	3 151	2 917	2 486	7 535	373	5 335	4 946	4 097	23 589	806	16 996	13 332	209	175
Maine......................	136	139	134	855	793	759	2 068	203	2 000	1 920	1 696	9 456	19	3 645	2 662	210	184
Maryland....................	529	530	531	4 627	4 347	3 971	7 443	496	8 100	7 778	7 255	28 249	172	22 534	16 909	191	159
Massachusetts...............	697	688	700	8 386	7 668	6 970	11 330	281	10 646	10 100	9 496	39 001	-639	20 859	15 602	191	163
Michigan....................	1 025	1 000	949	10 025	9 228	7 502	15 534	932	13 816	12 990	10 989	55 346	2 807	22 923	17 737	177	152
Minnesota...................	593	577	520	6 289	5 872	4 599	10 738	922	7 582	7 187	5 836	28 486	823	12 595	9 592	195	173
Mississippi..................	233	228	198	1 455	1 374	1 108	3 929	176	3 086	2 868	2 246	15 576	235	7 664	6 155	193	174
Missouri....................	613	603	562	5 912	5 468	4 852	11 489	567	8 063	7 613	6 129	32 932	-12	20 644	15 954	192	165
Montana....................	98	96	79	562	533	420	1 901	213	1 313	1 248	930	7 288	1 191	1 818	1 411	195	175
Nebraska....................	208	205	188	1 716	1 610	1 471	4 057	202	2 397	2 236	1 806	11 565	7	5 226	4 083	158	147
Nevada.....................	170	157	124	1 191	1 059	800	2 308	517	2 682	2 430	1 800	8 086	941	5 975	4 310	154	167
New Hampshire..............	145	141	129	1 312	1 068	851	2 291	280	2 248	2 109	1 784	8 722	17	3 742	2 590	172	154
New Jersey	855	851	864	13 417	12 816	11 418	19 289	1 394	12 791	12 317	11 296	49 664	155	26 204	18 747	163	148
New Mexico.................	164	164	138	898	846	660	2 637	252	2 393	2 204	1 634	9 978	1 004	5 847	4 447	204	182
New York...................	1 621	1 614	1 692	21 279	20 338	19 744	42 146	809	24 448	23 592	21 887	110 921	-1 591	40 440	31 248	177	160
North Carolina..............	811	799	716	7 009	6 439	5 241	13 850	1 243	11 067	10 179	8 188	45 591	982	26 328	19 944	164	150
North Dakota................	80	79	70	713	672	548	2 097	95	877	832	660	4 887	-66	1 921	1 496	204	172
Ohio.......................	1 300	1 276	1 172	11 411	10 591	8 937	19 796	1 030	16 829	15 770	12 880	64 678	786	37 889	29 547	161	150
Oklahoma...................	319	312	280	2 265	2 078	1 846	6 082	344	4 190	3 971	3 276	20 076	672	12 233	9 769	207	180
Oregon.....................	365	359	313	3 649	3 236	2 597	6 790	806	5 349	5 020	3 885	20 518	1 896	8 378	6 342	155	141
Pennsylvania................	1 205	1 197	1 179	11 368	10 684	9 609	20 333	331	17 983	17 004	14 854	71 764	-789	36 335	27 921	155	146
Rhode Island................	98	98	98	757	694	675	1 819	56	1 390	1 340	1 278	6 560	-247	3 405	2 587	193	165
South Carolina..............	398	384	349	2 341	2 071	1 792	5 767	557	5 455	5 018	4 046	23 576	1 189	14 269	10 934	190	159
South Dakota................	88	88	76	630	583	465	1 827	177	1 101	1 033	806	5 772	532	1 173	914	176	152
Tennessee..................	596	588	517	5 380	4 970	3 972	9 585	495	8 637	7 958	6 014	31 836	1 135	20 847	15 990	163	140
Texas......................	1 988	1 949	1 721	20 141	18 600	15 373	37 804	3 025	27 942	26 102	21 119	102 950	5 010	79 374	60 172	230	192
Utah.......................	231	220	173	1 607	1 443	1 152	3 485	445	2 925	2 607	1 794	10 046	1 313	5 983	4 616	192	169
Vermont	65	64	60	484	457	362	1 149	112	918	873	762	5 281	120	1 563	1 092	191	178
Virginia	714	700	658	6 007	5 516	4 478	9 606	664	9 755	9 258	8 003	38 541	1 149	28 440	21 032	180	156
Washington	591	583	522	5 817	5 392	4 295	11 289	1 596	9 013	8 536	6 768	33 075	3 348	15 950	11 870	170	149
West Virginia	160	159	145	983	946	824	2 463	-7	1 974	1 874	1 558	10 812	103	3 477	2 847	158	143
Wisconsin	595	587	542	4 865	4 524	3 704	9 600	671	7 399	7 002	5 683	32 322	277	13 164	10 058	177	151
Wyoming	52	52	45	236	220	190	977	64	698	663	524	3 983	597	1 249	996	209	179

[1]Data are subject to copyright; see below for source citation.
[2]Gross leasable area.
[3]National totals are derived independently and differ from the sum of the states.

Source: Employment–U.S. Bureau of Labor Statistics, Employment and Earnings, monthly, May issues, compiled from data supplied by cooperating state agencies; Earnings–U.S. Bureau of Economic Analysis, Survey of Current Business, Volume 76, Number 10, October 1996; Establishments–U.S. Bureau of the Census, County Business Patterns, on diskette, annual (related Internet site <http://www.census.gov/epcd/cbp/view/cbpview.html>); Shopping centers–National Research Bureau, Chicago, IL, data for 1996 published by International Council of Shopping Centers in Shopping Centers Today, April issue (copyright - Interactive Markets Systems, Inc.); data for 1990 published by Monitor Publishing, Clearwater, FL, in Monitor Magazine, November/December 1991 (copyright).

Table A–39. States — **Retail Sales**

Geographic area	Total[1] (mil dol)			Sales per household[2]			Food stores (SIC 54) (mil dol)		General merchandise stores (mil dol) Total (SIC 53)		Department stores (SIC 531)		Automotive dealers (SIC 55, ex. 554) (mil dol)		Eating and drinking places (SIC 58) (mil dol)	
	1995	1994	1990	1995 (dollars)	Percent change, 1994-1995	1990 (dollars)	1995	1994	1995	1994	1995	1994	1995	1994	1995	1994
United States	2 355 242	2 241 319	1 807 183	24 120	3.9	19 655	409 318	406 018	297 878	285 351	230 899	219 239	569 571	521 583	241 780	229 542
Alabama	35 946	33 586	26 373	22 430	6.0	17 504	6 138	6 200	5 180	4 881	4 122	3 838	9 377	8 102	3 168	3 033
Alaska	6 405	6 041	4 669	30 199	5.2	24 713	1 357	1 333	900	850	638	606	1 162	1 082	728	674
Arizona	39 322	36 517	26 137	24 544	4.4	19 094	7 862	7 604	5 023	4 665	3 779	3 456	8 572	7 934	5 342	4 629
Arkansas	20 999	19 091	15 386	22 099	8.5	17 266	3 432	3 275	3 370	3 127	2 716	2 511	5 990	5 193	1 672	1 537
California	257 662	247 689	225 066	23 427	3.0	21 681	47 256	46 882	31 892	30 960	21 645	20 786	56 523	53 675	26 812	24 113
Colorado	36 808	35 670	24 383	24 823	1.1	19 012	6 783	6 894	4 521	4 394	3 481	3 358	7 805	7 568	5 145	4 672
Connecticut	31 844	32 224	27 729	25 847	-1.5	22 535	6 293	6 433	3 414	3 501	2 681	2 726	6 015	5 747	2 663	3 135
Delaware	7 545	6 578	6 041	28 050	12.7	24 409	1 235	1 109	1 140	1 000	892	773	1 650	1 363	714	641
District of Columbia	3 760	3 762	3 815	16 406	1.3	15 284	631	641	224	224	195	193	162	146	1 065	1 080
Florida	145 665	137 812	105 304	25 688	4.0	20 508	23 421	22 700	17 155	16 437	12 697	12 047	41 680	37 383	14 261	13 812
Georgia	65 389	60 877	46 748	24 643	5.4	19 755	11 162	10 710	8 641	8 125	6 926	6 466	16 396	14 460	6 760	6 433
Hawaii	12 806	12 685	11 204	32 911	.2	31 447	2 209	2 272	2 115	2 142	888	862	1 951	1 934	1 951	1 817
Idaho	10 766	10 489	6 004	25 309	–	16 645	2 160	2 211	1 214	1 178	900	869	2 692	2 644	1 227	1 129
Illinois	104 528	99 964	83 479	24 093	3.8	19 865	15 348	15 534	12 536	11 963	10 357	9 819	26 068	24 157	11 703	11 111
Indiana	53 056	49 462	37 574	24 264	5.9	18 193	7 698	7 624	7 182	6 720	5 836	5 435	13 224	11 962	5 706	5 294
Iowa	26 968	25 538	18 818	24 536	4.7	17 681	5 219	5 036	3 490	3 300	2 884	2 712	7 030	6 525	2 539	2 347
Kansas	22 943	22 506	16 656	23 371	1.6	17 630	4 137	4 141	3 203	3 144	2 460	2 406	6 119	5 895	2 293	2 172
Kentucky	33 020	30 968	23 861	24 663	5.4	17 292	5 760	5 800	4 847	4 531	4 053	3 771	9 567	6 538	3 314	3 152
Louisiana	37 668	35 422	28 778	24 271	5.3	19 195	7 268	7 117	5 584	5 382	4 383	4 168	9 523	8 462	3 661	3 501
Maine	11 568	11 681	10 399	24 348	-1.6	22 349	2 612	2 689	1 199	1 225	740	747	2 092	1 982	899	1 069
Maryland	45 644	44 184	36 837	24 552	2.1	21 065	8 558	8 518	5 375	5 249	4 081	3 952	10 644	9 698	4 640	4 623
Massachusetts	53 873	52 466	50 757	23 652	1.7	22 588	10 714	10 564	5 566	5 483	3 995	3 904	9 988	9 160	5 779	6 476
Michigan	91 524	87 884	67 785	25 867	3.3	19 824	12 127	12 396	14 541	13 997	12 744	12 193	24 771	23 010	9 284	8 852
Minnesota	44 277	42 137	33 315	25 371	4.1	20 216	7 179	6 995	5 390	5 140	4 397	4 184	10 847	10 121	4 270	3 941
Mississippi	19 109	17 619	13 803	19 763	7.0	15 145	3 716	3 687	3 166	2 939	2 421	2 234	4 737	4 041	1 549	1 467
Missouri	52 511	48 783	36 032	25 589	6.7	18 373	9 080	8 636	7 392	6 875	6 361	5 876	13 840	12 697	5 606	5 030
Montana	7 831	7 592	5 333	23 181	1.5	17 417	1 507	1 535	887	866	636	613	1 731	1 680	1 123	1 027
Nebraska	15 731	15 227	10 313	25 073	2.4	17 120	2 773	2 760	1 945	1 899	1 542	1 485	3 844	3 633	1 627	1 533
Nevada	16 678	14 898	9 630	26 900	5.8	20 655	3 243	3 039	2 085	1 872	1 675	1 493	3 288	2 941	2 262	1 899
New Hampshire	12 997	12 761	11 860	30 239	.4	28 843	2 807	2 818	1 754	1 754	1 182	1 163	2 526	2 349	960	1 105
New Jersey	74 425	72 315	63 431	25 979	2.4	22 697	13 283	13 654	7 567	7 412	5 986	5 807	18 433	17 432	6 378	6 140
New Mexico	14 634	14 092	9 378	24 021	2.2	17 267	2 706	2 741	1 864	1 804	1 497	1 432	3 012	2 915	2 053	1 871
New York	137 771	134 422	124 479	20 759	2.5	18 748	24 651	25 391	13 792	13 467	10 839	10 432	26 921	25 411	14 415	13 856
North Carolina	65 781	60 196	45 756	23 698	7.1	18 179	11 888	11 199	7 804	7 182	6 264	5 703	16 423	14 030	6 462	6 448
North Dakota	6 381	6 182	4 467	25 898	2.2	18 546	1 009	1 001	946	924	769	753	1 780	1 695	593	559
Ohio	104 900	98 330	73 206	24 837	6.0	17 910	16 896	16 808	13 938	13 086	11 447	10 684	26 058	23 645	11 827	11 039
Oklahoma	25 998	25 620	20 218	20 727	1.1	16 763	4 318	4 457	3 740	3 780	3 007	3 018	7 699	7 237	2 564	2 577
Oregon	31 193	29 609	22 417	25 416	3.6	20 318	5 049	4 978	4 952	4 738	3 445	3 289	7 655	7 232	2 899	2 589
Pennsylvania	104 471	101 141	82 990	22 749	3.1	18 458	17 841	18 329	11 736	11 370	9 777	9 365	25 873	24 290	9 379	9 080
Rhode Island	7 359	7 538	7 325	19 766	-2.0	19 379	1 551	1 610	782	813	573	591	1 249	1 193	794	945
South Carolina	31 320	29 754	23 754	23 205	4.4	18 888	5 981	5 871	3 762	3 613	3 068	2 917	7 550	6 795	3 233	3 158
South Dakota	7 244	6 853	4 649	26 603	4.8	17 947	1 211	1 178	892	849	698	663	1 969	1 831	697	647
Tennessee	49 132	45 897	32 422	24 299	5.3	17 490	7 695	7 705	6 977	6 565	5 529	5 156	13 377	11 587	4 861	4 689
Texas	165 526	153 303	120 459	24 665	6.2	19 842	28 491	27 363	22 564	21 503	17 630	16 652	46 063	40 416	16 621	15 600
Utah	15 331	14 268	10 581	24 920	4.6	19 695	3 196	3 110	1 969	1 834	1 494	1 379	3 428	3 173	1 838	1 590
Vermont	5 144	5 125	4 512	23 129	-1.1	21 419	1 214	1 241	358	357	262	261	1 013	950	443	514
Virginia	66 648	62 293	47 472	26 932	5.7	20 712	12 560	12 105	8 098	7 616	5 842	5 543	15 386	13 584	6 294	6 017
Washington	49 551	48 468	36 762	23 562	.2	19 633	9 004	9 065	6 457	6 345	4 633	4 525	11 117	10 822	4 873	4 461
West Virginia	13 616	13 056	10 060	19 193	3.5	14 610	2 826	2 809	1 975	1 903	1 561	1 488	3 307	2 997	1 136	1 116
Wisconsin	49 473	46 358	36 031	25 738	5.8	19 774	7 451	7 419	6 204	5 811	4 859	4 538	12 481	11 343	5 082	4 781
Wyoming	4 501	4 385	2 726	24 785	1.6	16 146	813	830	569	556	412	400	944	925	615	559

[1]Includes other types of stores not shown separately.
[2]Based on number of households estimated as of January 1 for years shown by source.

Note: Data are subject to copyright; see below for source citation.

Source: Market Statistics, New York, NY, annual (copyright).

STATE AND METROPOLITAN AREA DATA BOOK

Geographic area	Finance, insurance, and real estate								Insured savings institutions (as of December 31)				Credit unions			
	Nonfarm employment (1,000)			Earnings (BEA) (mil dol)			Establishments		Number		Assets (mil dol)		Number		Assets (mil dol)	
	1996	1995	1990	1995	1994	1990	1994	Net change, 1990-1994	1996	1990	1996	1990	1995	1990	1995	1990
United States	[1]6 977	[1]6 830	[1]6 709	324 524	305 108	230 096	617 374	72 638	1 919	2 802	1 027 563	1 253 577	11 655	12 849	306 233	223 213
Alabama	82	77	74	2 746	2 596	1 978	7 870	909	14	30	1 971	7 877	197	227	5 310	3 939
Alaska	12	12	10	425	426	302	1 125	147	2	2	243	212	16	18	2 236	1 376
Arizona	115	107	94	4 524	4 142	2 638	9 934	1 885	2	2	515	220	74	81	4 112	3 070
Arkansas	43	42	38	1 398	1 324	979	4 839	795	16	20	3 403	2 582	91	107	854	561
California	733	737	809	39 127	38 370	30 212	74 572	1 711	66	138	248 032	325 596	754	879	43 653	37 240
Colorado	118	113	97	4 716	4 363	2 899	12 306	3 084	15	20	2 519	9 855	189	208	5 738	4 482
Connecticut	131	133	152	8 513	7 891	6 350	8 355	349	57	84	39 594	47 501	231	291	3 664	3 574
Delaware	44	41	32	1 659	1 453	920	3 212	931	5	6	2 162	2 119	50	55	727	508
District of Columbia...........	28	30	34	1 668	1 600	1 366	2 223	27	1	3	261	1 661	84	102	2 504	1 964
Florida	394	376	371	16 061	14 966	10 802	41 666	5 837	57	114	16 806	53 642	276	232	14 969	9 138
Georgia	180	174	165	7 906	7 288	5 431	15 962	2 462	35	62	5 834	17 730	251	224	6 506	3 737
Hawaii	37	37	37	1 591	1 589	1 093	3 897	171	5	6	6 567	7 314	116	133	3 439	2 965
Idaho	25	24	20	734	685	432	2 706	600	4	5	589	926	64	70	998	655
Illinois	386	384	379	18 509	17 475	12 758	28 693	3 682	141	195	49 828	53 822	654	830	10 350	7 790
Indiana	135	131	123	4 721	4 709	3 325	12 153	2 018	76	96	15 329	13 545	274	324	7 124	5 908
Iowa......................	78	77	70	2 852	2 691	1 997	7 185	1 061	30	37	5 906	5 819	218	252	2 539	2 170
Kansas	59	58	58	2 220	2 126	1 660	6 636	979	22	36	7 785	8 943	157	119	2 068	1 425
Kentucky	68	65	61	2 425	2 287	1 698	6 997	1 139	46	61	7 035	7 854	151	181	2 351	1 819
Louisiana	83	80	79	2 880	2 680	2 082	9 135	1 141	38	47	4 958	8 154	312	358	3 378	2 397
Maine	27	26	25	969	946	743	2 618	246	28	33	7 562	7 258	95	115	2 050	1 887
Maryland	128	128	133	6 019	5 930	4 401	11 485	1 346	71	93	9 807	21 561	141	168	6 634	5 059
Massachusetts	209	204	213	11 581	10 599	8 235	13 208	923	208	249	53 387	54 621	327	278	10 095	6 510
Michigan	201	196	191	8 173	7 735	5 746	17 552	2 332	26	42	26 474	32 709	524	600	15 684	11 027
Minnesota	143	138	125	6 454	6 163	4 239	11 549	2 155	23	27	6 093	7 127	214	244	5 194	3 837
Mississippi	41	40	39	1 354	1 277	998	5 113	446	14	26	2 642	2 923	143	166	1 328	937
Missouri	150	146	139	5 725	5 443	4 235	12 563	1 662	49	69	15 346	18 134	211	194	4 012	1 881
Montana	16	16	13	514	487	328	2 371	528	10	10	1 827	1 199	88	99	1 126	751
Nebraska	53	52	48	1 879	1 750	1 362	4 457	633	13	17	8 735	9 062	97	112	1 390	1 108
Nevada	38	36	28	1 551	1 351	741	4 204	1 178	1	5	2 772	4 599	25	30	1 277	845
New Hampshire.............	28	29	32	1 195	1 115	918	2 686	264	25	42	9 272	10 225	36	46	1 486	1 313
New Jersey	232	228	239	12 465	11 714	9 135	18 966	1 136	92	130	48 622	53 407	343	437	5 060	3 703
New Mexico	32	30	26	977	912	610	3 651	685	10	14	1 433	1 458	62	70	2 073	1 347
New York	721	724	781	58 167	52 814	41 880	54 599	3 243	105	151	121 296	152 971	719	861	15 756	12 984
North Carolina	154	144	135	6 234	5 636	4 015	14 840	1 852	60	123	7 733	19 276	204	251	8 304	5 848
North Dakota	14	14	13	451	427	311	1 985	270	3	5	5 569	5 237	69	84	733	538
Ohio......................	277	270	256	10 409	9 889	7 437	22 898	2 296	159	207	51 881	46 671	569	673	8 305	6 575
Oklahoma.................	67	65	60	2 100	2 047	1 568	7 530	1 317	13	27	6 204	6 724	105	118	3 740	3 024
Oregon	91	87	76	2 923	2 787	1 827	8 410	1 940	9	11	14 283	7 212	133	154	4 733	3 190
Pennsylvania	309	303	302	13 411	12 724	9 729	23 496	1 940	122	163	45 207	45 083	901	1 094	11 819	8 926
Rhode Island	25	25	27	1 003	979	873	2 014	111	6	8	5 569	7 143	45	35	1 590	1 030
South Carolina............	72	69	67	2 422	2 242	1 703	7 557	1 279	34	46	7 721	10 882	111	131	3 080	2 455
South Dakota.............	20	19	16	613	559	405	2 155	476	5	12	844	1 351	67	71	617	487
Tennessee	117	110	103	4 452	4 121	2 898	10 567	1 025	24	49	3 961	10 863	278	160	5 816	2 631
Texas....................	444	437	433	18 467	17 569	13 139	40 454	6 262	52	80	62 309	58 587	819	673	22 976	16 153
Utah.....................	50	48	34	1 648	1 469	874	4 242	961	2	8	571	3 851	150	171	3 764	2 643
Vermont	12	12	13	463	438	366	1 513	132	7	9	2 358	2 221	49	61	643	399
Virginia	162	161	155	6 810	6 543	4 737	14 927	1 449	31	56	15 472	26 781	279	309	18 218	11 267
Washington	124	122	116	5 198	4 981	3 497	14 189	2 821	21	39	36 654	28 642	126	130	8 018	4 717
West Virginia	27	27	25	791	749	616	3 176	509	9	15	1 106	1 918	141	143	1 283	820
Wisconsin	138	136	121	5 155	4 762	3 429	11 618	1 933	51	65	25 175	17 596	386	441	6 429	4 308
Wyoming..................	8	8	7	277	291	177	1 315	360	4	7	340	913	39	39	481	296

[1]National totals are derived independently and differ from the sum of the states.

Source: Employment–Bureau of Labor Statistics, Employment and Earnings, monthly, May issues, compiled frm data supplied by cooperating state agencies; Earnings–U.S. Bureau of Economic Analysis, Survey of Current Business, Volume 76, Number 10, October 1996; Establishments–U.S. Bureau of the Census, County Business Patterns on diskette, annual (related Internet site <http://www.census.gov/epcd/cbp/view/cbpview.html>); Insured savings institutions–U.S. Federal Deposit Insurance Corporation, Statistics on Banking, annual, Internet file <http://www.fdic.gov/databank/sob/his96/si12.html> (accessed 21 August 1997); Credit unions–National Credit Union Administration, Annual Report of the National Credit Union Administration, and unpublished data.

Table A–41. States — **Commmercial Banks and Insurance**

Geographic area	Number 1996	Number 1990	Assets (mil dol) 1996	Assets (mil dol) 1990	Deposits (mil dol) 1996	Deposits (mil dol) 1990	Equity capital (mil dol) 1996	Equity capital (mil dol) 1990	Net income (mil dol) 1996	Net income (mil dol) 1990	Total value (bil dol) 1996	Total value (bil dol) 1990	Average per household (dollars) 1996	Average per household (dollars) 1990	Automobile insurance avg exp 1995	Automobile insurance avg exp 1991
United States	9 508	12 325	4 547 519	3 369 558	3 175 039	2 633 001	372 931	217 274	52 059	15 872	13 761	9 393	139 353	98 400	666	596
Alabama	183	220	63 220	38 903	45 477	31 881	4 995	3 001	772	380	201	150	123 768	97 100	549	475
Alaska	8	8	5 816	4 450	4 202	3 494	754	499	87	63	27	19	126 168	96 000	730	643
Arizona	35	38	48 052	32 652	28 221	28 394	4 316	2 287	514	96	175	113	103 734	79 100	727	647
Arkansas	233	256	30 633	21 501	26 453	19 053	2 883	1 797	385	212	99	61	104 101	65 000	500	398
California	360	482	417 223	345 361	321 517	279 707	38 875	21 980	3 952	3 355	1 422	1 041	128 097	95 900	831	787
Colorado	223	446	41 013	26 917	34 319	22 724	3 212	1 877	554	31	223	138	148 469	103 600	722	588
Connecticut	28	66	10 875	36 070	8 639	31 698	1 005	1 624	97	707	266	202	216 084	153 200	881	841
Delaware	39	47	115 166	74 320	40 148	34 314	12 359	6 823	2 207	1 444	60	41	217 391	157 000	784	718
District of Columbia	8	26	3 411	18 103	2 550	15 411	307	729	36	357	73	68	316 017	244 400	959	863
Florida	289	432	160 708	137 246	130 468	116 983	13 605	8 973	2 006	355	675	412	119 617	77 000	739	669
Georgia	354	409	147 081	70 290	101 591	53 226	14 993	5 916	1 559	592	420	273	154 242	109 600	596	546
Hawaii	14	21	22 068	19 414	15 159	16 318	1 825	1 198	216	217	69	49	177 378	133 100	963	874
Idaho	15	22	6 576	8 583	5 297	6 916	468	559	86	95	48	33	111 628	86 800	447	386
Illinois	833	1 087	247 105	196 886	181 408	154 696	21 621	13 373	2 316	1 345	705	481	161 994	110 600	612	552
Indiana	204	301	66 538	58 254	52 056	47 621	5 872	4 401	903	440	281	207	127 207	95 300	542	474
Iowa	467	562	42 515	34 567	35 033	29 179	3 928	3 036	527	350	160	105	145 059	96 100	429	359
Kansas	416	555	28 608	29 541	24 514	25 953	2 831	2 300	299	223	150	96	152 749	99 200	474	368
Kentucky	275	332	52 686	41 426	39 770	33 492	4 456	3 204	637	309	153	108	103 518	76 000	555	435
Louisiana	172	231	46 967	37 369	38 249	32 584	4 477	2 460	570	67	184	145	117 048	93 700	787	679
Maine	20	21	9 024	8 174	6 458	6 891	812	537	111	9	54	38	111 801	77 900	472	484
Maryland	90	103	38 913	57 012	30 229	44 957	3 618	3 339	403	233	307	201	164 083	110 600	732	689
Massachusetts	50	85	153 977	97 878	106 622	76 635	11 968	4 686	1 846	1 062	380	248	163 652	107 200	898	814
Michigan	176	235	112 181	93 822	84 166	76 884	10 258	6 212	1 526	860	502	344	140 380	97 100	645	606
Minnesota	519	626	72 124	55 519	53 852	45 388	6 002	3 724	990	392	284	173	161 089	99 600	630	530
Mississippi	111	123	28 522	21 411	23 391	18 502	2 761	1 617	391	149	111	74	113 381	79 300	579	482
Missouri	430	544	88 301	64 685	70 564	54 287	7 123	4 614	1 190	494	280	201	136 452	98 600	572	469
Montana	100	156	8 670	7 331	7 293	6 324	760	583	114	81	35	24	102 639	77 500	468	370
Nebraska	329	392	27 766	20 182	23 263	17 634	2 659	1 620	309	203	94	63	148 970	101 900	452	342
Nevada	26	19	32 406	14 388	9 725	8 911	3 709	1 066	775	191	65	35	105 008	72 200	759	640
New Hampshire	20	45	10 724	10 032	8 997	8 327	994	548	223	165	66	42	150 342	99 500	609	646
New Jersey	66	131	70 031	94 183	59 273	78 251	5 945	5 335	654	765	562	382	194 531	130 400	1 013	879
New Mexico	69	90	15 538	11 061	12 028	9 578	1 240	782	200	34	73	45	117 932	79 300	639	517
New York...............	159	193	1 032 218	682 199	602 522	475 985	66 651	35 923	9 112	1 424	1 046	735	155 262	107 500	906	754
North Carolina	56	78	191 424	80 245	121 378	58 361	13 648	4 942	1 943	680	405	242	144 850	92 300	501	432
North Dakota	123	150	8 544	7 551	7 280	6 690	742	599	100	63	34	25	137 652	98 500	381	329
Ohio	257	289	172 732	113 772	117 027	89 705	12 787	7 951	2 308	983	571	409	134 038	95 900	532	494
Oklahoma	332	419	36 134	26 863	30 058	23 691	3 280	2 085	370	221	132	96	104 348	78 500	526	422
Oregon	43	50	22 155	22 950	16 125	17 991	1 857	1 681	363	294	143	87	114 492	74 700	565	529
Pennsylvania	217	300	243 682	172 427	184 271	136 338	20 324	10 846	3 103	664	680	469	148 019	100 800	667	610
Rhode Island	8	11	6 451	14 673	4 959	10 995	551	841	83	33	65	39	171 958	98 500	870	823
South Carolina	79	85	26 353	25 217	21 277	18 511	2 204	1 760	330	210	190	120	138 081	92 500	582	502
South Dakota	117	125	29 335	19 109	13 207	10 934	2 686	1 848	683	426	36	25	131 868	91 200	429	309
Tennessee	238	253	75 930	47 404	57 185	39 871	6 462	3 410	962	183	259	175	126 899	92 000	519	466
Texas	877	1 183	205 143	170 822	168 199	145 644	17 243	10 307	2 440	677	929	628	134 755	101 600	711	612
Utah	48	55	35 991	13 799	18 856	10 587	3 432	1 008	434	117	88	57	137 715	100 600	547	436
Vermont	22	27	6 221	6 051	5 206	5 341	511	429	104	21	30	20	132 159	91 800	512	474
Virginia................	154	178	89 893	69 599	64 890	54 672	7 392	4 485	1 205	302	383	263	152 529	109 600	553	506
Washington	84	94	44 727	39 742	35 540	32 753	4 012	2 792	745	502	241	164	112 669	83 500	650	549
West Virginia	113	180	22 268	17 445	18 011	14 825	2 261	1 551	319	176	62	45	86 835	66 400	646	519
Wisconsin	365	473	65 696	47 507	51 099	39 765	5 450	3 718	812	484	238	165	122 491	88 000	506	463
Wyoming	54	71	8 184	4 649	7 017	4 126	703	398	189	49	21	17	114 130	97 000	433	330

[1]Data are subject to copyright; see below for source citation.

Source: Insured commercial banks–For 1996, U.S. Federal Deposit Insurance Corporation, Statistics on Banking, annual and for 1990, Internet site <http://www.fdic.gov/databank/sob/his96/cb09stus.html> (accessed 11 March 98); Life insurance in force–American Council of Life Insurance, Washington, DC, Life Insurance Fact Book,biennial (copyright); Automobile insurance–National Association of Insurance Commissioners, Kansas City, MO, State Average Expenditures and Premiums for Personal Automobile Insurance, annual (copyright).

STATE AND METROPOLITAN AREA DATA BOOK

Table A–42. States — **Services**

Geographic area	Services, total — Nonfarm employment (1,000) 1996	1995	1990	Services, total — Earnings (BEA) (mil dol) 1995	1994	1990	Services, total — Establishments 1994	Net change, 1990–1994	Business services, 1994 (SIC 73) Establishments	Employees (1,000)	Health services, 1994 (SIC 80) Establishments	Employees (1,000)	Legal services, 1994 (SIC 81) Establishments	Employees (1,000)
United States	¹34 359	¹33 107	¹27 934	1 213 456	1 118 187	885 726	2 342 302	2 83 011	340 336	6 240	476 204	10 624	161 622	963
Alabama....................	406	395	316	12 942	11 917	8 917	31 376	4 444	3 746	68	6 135	170	2 131	11
Alaska....................	62	61	51	2 365	2 251	1 820	6 266	992	715	6	987	17	461	2
Arizona....................	561	520	400	16 826	14 838	11 151	36 138	5 925	5 859	105	7 812	136	2 271	13
Arkansas....................	247	237	190	6 578	6 064	4 416	19 468	2 733	2 181	43	3 976	95	1 284	5
California	3 917	3 730	3 343	174 428	160 872	137 451	283 804	20 556	43 992	828	63 112	1 003	21 492	129
Colorado	565	539	403	18 846	17 101	12 336	42 287	7 642	6 979	110	7 684	138	2 913	14
Connecticut	481	466	425	20 486	19 097	15 806	34 176	2 165	5 292	83	7 074	167	2 597	15
Delaware	102	96	85	3 148	2 890	2 322	6 822	837	1 124	21	1 299	30	308	3
District of Columbia	263	265	259	13 990	13 531	11 154	11 068	483	1 220	27	1 414	71	1 610	29
Florida	2 118	2 056	1 593	64 595	59 071	45 167	146 377	22 874	24 293	424	32 082	576	11 860	61
Georgia	903	838	635	29 631	26 474	19 233	61 015	10 474	10 434	187	12 072	263	4 051	22
Hawaii....................	166	165	154	6 248	6 040	4 974	10 359	929	1 396	23	2 411	38	795	4
Idaho	115	109	81	3 576	3 160	2 277	9 730	1 711	1 119	13	1 937	35	589	3
Illinois	1 640	1 577	1 349	61 553	56 548	44 202	103 402	12 489	17 165	350	20 117	493	7 217	49
Indiana	653	632	525	19 341	17 891	13 525	47 574	6 603	6 117	105	9 497	245	2 582	12
Iowa	359	341	289	9 099	8 353	6 436	25 718	2 775	2 648	51	4 632	132	1 493	7
Kansas	301	290	243	9 011	8 248	6 462	23 815	2 924	3 039	45	4 356	117	1 422	6
Kentucky	408	392	328	11 452	10 515	7 914	28 771	3 327	3 235	60	6 147	150	2 036	9
Louisiana	486	473	372	15 378	14 038	11 047	34 527	4 304	4 434	81	7 463	201	3 556	17
Maine	150	148	128	4 391	4 074	3 396	12 216	1 290	1 205	17	2 377	57	693	4
Maryland	715	690	623	26 635	24 849	20 310	46 654	6 581	7 602	143	9 816	195	2 991	17
Massachusetts	1 063	1 024	916	43 755	40 125	32 376	60 685	5 224	9 346	185	11 355	344	4 830	29
Michigan	1 165	1 114	942	38 627	35 358	27 749	78 559	11 054	10 227	219	16 881	380	4 913	27
Minnesota	672	645	548	21 372	19 729	14 805	44 038	7 100	6 727	124	6 814	234	2 216	17
Mississippi	247	232	161	6 782	6 212	4 016	18 060	2 471	1 744	27	3 370	94	1 426	6
Missouri	708	685	579	22 169	20 355	15 710	48 243	5 456	6 516	110	9 029	248	2 623	16
Montana	102	96	75	2 763	2 541	1 830	9 684	2 246	991	8	1 723	32	592	2
Nebraska	220	210	178	6 088	5 549	4 280	15 633	1 824	1 983	55	2 633	72	864	4
Nevada	364	347	273	12 212	11 063	7 854	13 199	2 776	2 282	30	2 604	40	979	5
New Hampshire	162	152	128	5 272	4 768	3 814	12 141	1 418	1 838	27	2 002	45	741	4
New Jersey	1 122	1 081	978	47 464	44 162	36 314	79 770	8 536	14 011	226	17 585	341	6 070	37
New Mexico.................	192	193	148	5 971	5 417	3 963	14 302	2 301	1 848	22	2 679	53	1 069	5
New York..................	2 610	2 537	2 377	115 410	108 937	92 008	165 492	9 295	25 455	451	34 910	908	12 980	107
North Carolina.............	822	760	592	24 079	21 914	15 828	58 127	8 988	8 429	150	9 879	261	3 064	16
North Dakota...............	85	81	69	2 089	1 918	1 477	6 382	809	567	7	943	35	346	1
Ohio	1 415	1 387	1 189	43 703	40 529	32 524	92 276	9 105	12 408	266	19 973	498	5 484	31
Oklahoma..................	364	344	273	9 893	9 038	7 376	28 060	3 491	3 509	55	5 774	125	2 244	10
Oregon....................	385	364	296	12 287	11 100	8 381	30 997	5 186	4 397	64	5 908	102	1 942	9
Pennsylvania	1 651	1 596	1 444	56 630	52 995	43 390	104 088	8 379	12 235	233	23 737	565	6 266	45
Rhode Island	146	144	129	4 741	4 365	3 625	9 850	707	1 366	26	2 031	49	748	4
South Carolina	373	363	294	10 503	9 513	7 208	29 137	4 283	3 616	82	5 185	117	1 926	10
South Dakota	90	88	72	2 458	2 242	1 586	7 308	1 338	667	8	1 178	35	421	1
Tennessee	656	636	486	21 614	19 528	14 163	43 288	6 004	5 653	117	8 945	223	2 413	12
Texas	2 221	2 122	1 741	77 547	70 829	54 344	155 887	23 325	23 748	496	32 275	672	11 781	66
Utah	256	239	180	7 439	6 770	4 796	14 486	2 615	2 339	56	3 255	63	742	5
Vermont	82	79	69	2 380	2 231	1 735	7 026	930	791	7	1 082	24	452	2
Virginia	911	872	732	30 824	28 148	21 630	59 528	8 753	9 555	191	10 378	230	3 524	20
Washington	649	622	504	24 443	22 309	15 591	51 553	8 923	7 258	95	9 916	193	3 135	19
West Virginia	191	183	115	4 902	4 576	3 435	13 844	1 582	1 208	14	3 013	75	941	5
Wisconsin	655	631	532	18 227	16 957	12 690	43 454	5 547	5 265	93	7 901	222	2 182	13
Wyoming	48	48	38	1 295	1 187	912	5 642	1 287	562	4	846	16	356	1

¹National totals are derived independently and differ from the sum of the states.

Source: Employment–U.S. Bureau of Labor Statistics, Employment and Earnings, monthly, May issues, compiled from data supplied by cooperating state agencies; Earnings–U.S. Bureau of Economic Analysis, Survey of Current Business, Volume 76, Number 10, October 1996; Industry data–U.S. Bureau of the Census, County Business Patterns, on CD-ROM, annual (related Internet site <http://www.census.gov/epcd/cbp/view/cbpview.html>).

Table A–43. States — **Agriculture and Mineral Industries**

Geographic area	Agriculture, 1992 (SIC 01-02) — All farms — Number of farms (1,000)	Land in farms (mil acres)	Average size of farm (acres)	Value of land and buildings[1] (mil dol)	Farms with sales of $10,000 or more — Number of farms (1,000)	Land in farms (mil acres)	Average size of farm (acres)	Value of land and buildings[1] (mil dol)	Mineral industries, 1992 (SIC 10, 12-14) — Establishments[2]	Paid employees[3] — Number (1,000)	Annual payroll Total (mil dol)	Per employee (dollars)	Production workers — Total (1,000)	Wages (mil dol)	Value added by mining[4] (mil dol)	Value of shipments[5] (mil dol)
United States	1 925	945.5	491	687 432	1 019	822.0	807	555 056	[6]30 787	[6]638.2	[6]24 198.6	37 917	[6]415.4	[6]13 832.6	[6]113 621.3	[6]162 095.4
Alabama	38	8.5	223	8 350	14	5.7	410	5 152	395	10.8	400.7	37 102	7.8	269.2	1 527.7	2 114.6
Alaska	1	.9	1 803	249	Z	.6	3 788	138	195	10.5	638.6	60 819	6.3	344.3	8 522.0	9 546.8
Arizona	7	35.0	5 173	10 984	3	32.7	10 260	9 837	252	13.7	505.5	36 898	11.2	390.3	1 821.9	2 661.9
Arkansas	44	14.1	322	12 407	21	11.3	536	9 668	360	3.3	84.6	25 636	2.5	61.0	461.4	572.9
California	78	29.0	373	63 689	40	25.8	639	52 685	1 232	34.5	1 416.2	41 049	19.4	675.6	6 038.8	7 545.2
Colorado	27	34.0	1 252	14 568	15	30.7	2 029	11 932	1 132	17.1	759.0	44 386	9.0	318.4	2 407.9	3 421.4
Connecticut	3	.4	105	2 138	1	.2	173	1 299	82	1.4	69.1	49 357	.5	19.0	79.7	98.9
Delaware	3	.6	224	1 351	2	.5	309	1 184	[7]23	7.2	[7]9.1	[7]45 500	Z	[7]1.2	[7]7.3	[7]10.0
District of Columbia	X	X	X	X	X	X	X	X	[7]	[7]	[7]	[7]	[7]	[7]	[7]	[7]
Florida	35	10.8	306	21 801	15	9.2	614	17 924	293	8.3	260.5	31 386	6.3	170.1	979.9	1 548.6
Georgia	41	10.0	246	11 437	17	7.5	431	7 547	215	8.2	249.3	30 402	6.4	177.5	804.9	1 176.0
Hawaii	5	1.6	298	3 854	2	1.5	729	3 044	7	.2	9.4	47 000	.2	8.1	27.3	33.7
Idaho	22	13.5	609	9 077	13	11.6	909	7 829	136	2.8	109.8	39 214	2.1	70.6	203.1	323.5
Illinois	78	27.3	351	41 844	56	26.0	464	39 607	858	17.5	686.8	39 246	12.7	476.3	1 999.9	2 943.6
Indiana	63	15.6	249	21 732	37	14.1	384	19 151	426	7.1	258.2	36 366	5.3	178.7	825.6	1 190.0
Iowa	97	31.3	325	38 063	77	29.9	388	36 345	187	2.0	52.7	26 350	1.4	35.4	153.4	219.8
Kansas	63	46.7	738	21 725	41	43.2	1 041	19 438	1 207	10.9	353.1	32 394	6.8	169.4	2 290.0	4 347.2
Kentucky	90	13.7	151	14 775	41	10.0	248	10 603	1 140	30.6	1 068.3	34 912	25.6	865.5	3 687.8	6 080.9
Louisiana	26	7.8	306	7 474	11	6.4	604	5 645	1 784	48.1	1 797.9	37 378	31.0	1 050.3	14 834.6	22 353.7
Maine	6	1.3	218	1 396	3	.9	340	842	22	.1	1.4	14 000	Z	1.0	5.0	6.6
Maryland	13	2.2	171	6 570	7	1.8	282	4 862	115	2.5	67.5	27 000	2.0	54.5	201.3	307.7
Massachusetts	5	.5	100	2 421	2	.3	145	1 478	84	1.2	40.5	33 750	.5	16.1	69.7	96.1
Michigan	47	10.1	217	11 517	24	8.3	352	8 999	531	8.7	289.7	33 299	6.8	213.5	1 675.9	2 523.5
Minnesota	75	25.7	342	23 319	53	23.2	438	21 005	154	7.4	279.7	37 797	6.3	234.1	748.5	1 325.0
Mississippi	32	10.2	318	7 952	12	7.5	640	5 566	449	4.3	115.9	26 953	3.2	81.5	643.6	799.9
Missouri	98	28.5	291	22 070	47	22.5	477	16 771	342	5.3	177.4	33 472	3.6	113.2	470.5	660.4
Montana	23	59.6	2 613	13 578	15	53.6	3 612	11 658	367	5.4	189.1	35 019	4.0	128.7	1 100.0	1 324.9
Nebraska	53	44.4	839	22 713	42	42.6	1 007	21 640	194	1.3	31.8	24 462	1.0	21.9	136.8	188.5
Nevada	3	9.3	3 205	2 347	1	8.3	6 081	1 902	306	12.3	489.2	39 772	10.7	414.1	1 968.3	2 591.9
New Hampshire	2	.4	158	836	1	.2	257	418	41	.3	9.6	32 000	.2	5.7	25.3	33.1
New Jersey	9	.8	93	5 590	4	.6	179	3 734	114	2.5	99.3	39 720	1.4	48.6	199.1	279.4
New Mexico	14	46.8	3 281	9 220	6	42.4	7 273	7 298	737	14.6	487.7	33 404	11.1	354.5	3 955.1	5 689.9
New York	32	7.5	231	9 130	18	6.0	332	7 012	445	7.5	301.4	40 187	3.8	1.2	476.6	616.9
North Carolina	52	8.9	172	13 950	25	7.0	281	10 118	212	4.3	126.4	29 395	3.1	80.5	322.2	508.2
North Dakota	31	39.4	1 267	13 163	25	36.8	1 449	12 194	274	4.1	161.3	39 341	3.3	125.8	859.9	1 184.8
Ohio	71	14.2	201	20 626	38	11.9	314	16 799	1 022	15.0	486.5	32 433	10.5	303.3	1 453.9	2 064.2
Oklahoma	67	32.1	480	15 754	30	26.3	889	11 851	2 742	44.5	1 678.1	37 710	20.1	614.9	6 406.9	8 341.0
Oregon	32	17.6	552	11 824	12	15.6	1 289	8 534	157	1.7	61.1	35 941	1.0	27.9	105.3	140.8
Pennsylvania	45	7.2	160	14 752	24	5.4	221	11 309	1 219	24.9	878.8	35 293	18.6	612.5	2 344.7	3 714.9
Rhode Island	1	.1	76	313	Z	Z	118	194	18	.1	3.6	36 000	.1	2.5	12.1	16.1
South Carolina	20	4.5	221	5 093	7	3.0	452	2 986	86	1.6	47.6	29 750	1.3	34.1	177.5	234.1
South Dakota	34	44.8	1 316	12 264	27	39.0	1 452	10 955	72	2.3	81.6	35 478	1.8	64.1	213.1	308.6
Tennessee	75	11.2	149	13 977	24	7.3	298	8 007	291	4.6	120.0	26 087	3.5	84.0	348.3	539.3
Texas	181	130.9	725	65 060	70	111.2	1 586	47 031	7 544	149.9	5 984.3	39 922	75.2	2 264.3	26 192.6	38 546.4
Utah	14	9.6	712	4 704	6	8.2	1 372	3 546	391	8.1	298.5	36 852	6.2	219.9	1 755.4	2 174.1
Vermont	5	1.3	235	1 730	3	1.0	328	1 219	60	.7	20.5	29 286	.5	13.5	77.7	110.8
Virginia	42	8.3	197	13 534	17	6.0	355	9 100	577	15.9	546.5	34 371	12.7	414.2	1 601.8	2 890.9
Washington	30	15.7	520	14 178	15	13.5	915	11 060	194	3.2	112.5	35 156	2.4	83.1	310.5	420.2
West Virginia	17	3.3	192	2 810	4	1.5	394	1 229	1 163	33.0	1 330.8	40 327	27.4	1 097.1	4 212.4	6 854.9
Wisconsin	68	15.5	228	14 285	46	13.4	290	12 199	167	2.3	79.2	34 435	1.6	54.6	251.2	322.7
Wyoming	9	32.9	3 772	5 242	6	29.7	5 376	4 516	718	16.0	643.5	40 219	12.5	483.9	5 965.6	8 424.1

Z Less than 500 farms, 50 production workers, or 50,000 acres.
X Not applicable.

[1] Based on reports for a sample of farms.
[2] Establishments in business at any time during the year.
[3] For pay period including March 12.
[4] Computed by subtracting cost of supplies, minerals received for preparation, purchased fuel and electric energy, contract work, and purchased machinery from the value of shipments and capital expenditures.
[5] Represents value of shipments of primary and secondary products of the industry and amount received for services performed for other establishments on a contract, fee, or other basis.
[6] Includes offshore areas not associated with a state.
[7] District of Columbia included with Delaware.

Source: Agriculture–U.S. Bureau of the Census, 1992 Census of Agriculture, Geographic Area Series, Vol. 1 AC92-A-51; Mineral industries–U.S. Bureau of the Census, 1992 Census of Mineral Industries, Subject Series, General Summary, MIC92-S-1.

Table A–44. States — Construction Industries and Manufactures

Geographic area	Construction industries, establishments with payroll, 1992 (SIC 15-17)								Manufactures, 1992 (SIC 20-39)							
	Estab-lish-ments[1]	Paid employees[2]			Construc-tion workers (1,000)	Value of con-struc-tion work (mil dol)	Net value of con-struc-tion work (mil dol)	Value added (mil dol)	Estab-lish-ments[1]	Paid employees[3]			Production workers[2]		Value added by manufac-tures (mil dol)	Value of ship-ments[4] (mil dol)
		Number (1,000)	Annual payroll Total (mil dol)	Per em-ployee (dollars)						Number (1,000)	Annual payroll Total (mil dol)	Per em-ployee (dollars)	Total (1,000)	Wages (mil dol)		
United States	**572 851**	**4 668**	**117 730**	**25 219**	**3 596**	**528 106**	**391 190**	**234 618**	**381 870**	**18 253**	**560 485**	**30 706**	**11 654**	**281 737**	**1 428 707**	**3 006 275**
Alabama	7 653	78	1 638	20 930	62	7 462	5 524	3 065	6 436	380	9 217	24 255	284	5 934	23 653	52 708
Alaska	1 676	13	473	36 497	10	1 876	1 476	922	513	16	426	26 625	12	313	1 347	3 678
Arizona	8 306	87	1 904	21 953	66	10 324	6 823	4 122	4 758	177	5 420	30 621	99	2 244	14 960	25 767
Arkansas	4 445	34	652	19 139	27	3 303	2 483	1 351	3 913	227	4 878	21 489	179	3 353	14 204	34 050
California	64 103	511	14 227	27 836	388	64 256	46 350	28 914	50 513	1 960	65 766	33 554	1 117	26 955	158 240	305 805
Colorado	9 704	84	2 046	24 419	65	10 555	7 414	4 323	5 295	184	5 926	32 207	107	2 773	15 300	29 220
Connecticut	8 828	55	1 679	30 355	41	7 143	5 352	3 399	6 283	326	12 411	38 071	171	4 733	24 677	40 778
Delaware	2 071	18	445	25 179	14	1 799	1 366	839	736	67	2 770	41 343	31	850	4 881	13 000
District of Columbia	333	7	215	30 922	5	1 018	558	558	351	13	553	42 538	4	116	1 570	2 008
Florida	34 291	275	5 710	20 800	204	30 033	21 605	12 025	16 396	474	13 018	27 464	289	5 796	33 081	64 320
Georgia	13 581	124	2 712	21 892	95	13 761	9 840	5 373	9 767	556	14 278	25 680	394	8 159	41 038	90 999
Hawaii	2 481	32	1 112	34 342	25	4 833	3 552	2 148	1 018	21	556	26 476	13	293	1 526	3 790
Idaho	3 541	22	479	21 569	17	2 261	1 710	1 014	1 838	66	1 769	26 803	46	1 022	4 465	10 557
Illinois	24 579	212	6 493	30 633	162	26 738	19 913	12 631	18 784	970	31 605	32 582	588	14 977	74 860	158 129
Indiana	13 124	116	2 940	25 343	91	11 888	9 429	5 583	9 285	619	19 114	30 879	435	11 662	49 662	104 871
Iowa	6 707	49	1 115	22 666	39	5 090	3 914	2 254	3 913	227	6 484	28 564	158	3 852	20 502	46 432
Kansas	5 940	48	1 084	22 612	38	5 255	3 944	2 231	3 464	189	5 261	27 836	126	3 045	15 156	36 095
Kentucky	7 337	64	1 364	21 384	50	6 359	4 784	2 682	4 310	277	7 524	27 162	203	4 691	25 265	60 029
Louisiana	6 404	92	2 106	22 930	75	7 545	6 298	3 805	4 048	179	5 460	30 503	126	3 308	20 509	60 940
Maine	3 993	21	453	21 126	17	1 950	1 571	979	2 200	91	2 447	26 890	67	1 589	5 458	11 611
Maryland	13 782	134	3 437	25 617	102	14 650	10 523	6 472	4 337	195	6 291	32 261	114	3 005	15 588	31 047
Massachusetts	13 447	87	2 509	28 918	64	11 384	8 249	5 074	10 145	480	16 421	34 210	273	7 085	36 519	65 702
Michigan	20 446	142	3 666	25 892	108	16 048	12 019	7 110	16 531	917	34 207	37 303	574	18 452	71 724	161 409
Minnesota	10 664	86	2 454	28 542	66	11 747	8 249	5 113	7 934	394	12 664	32 142	225	5 391	27 175	57 324
Mississippi	3 938	35	650	18 801	28	3 154	2 444	1 320	3 767	238	5 030	21 134	188	3 366	13 988	32 655
Missouri	12 828	97	2 402	24 749	76	10 764	7 956	4 773	7 846	408	11 868	29 088	260	6 049	33 995	73 746
Montana	2 561	13	294	22 009	11	1 415	1 089	609	1 375	22	544	24 727	16	364	1 421	4 137
Nebraska	4 324	30	650	21 603	23	3 315	2 575	1 427	2 028	100	2 516	25 160	72	1 555	7 952	21 816
Nevada	3 311	41	1 166	28 409	31	5 202	3 739	2 330	1 249	28	744	26 571	18	385	1 720	3 288
New Hampshire	3 319	17	412	24 039	13	1 772	1 369	815	2 332	94	2 820	30 000	60	1 470	6 493	11 260
New Jersey	19 643	131	4 009	30 517	99	16 493	12 952	8 401	13 281	574	20 616	35 916	301	7 676	46 091	86 885
New Mexico	4 001	31	610	19 749	25	2 790	2 150	1 312	1 594	39	965	24 744	27	564	4 946	9 492
New York	36 550	257	7 572	29 419	194	30 717	23 251	14 768	26 617	1 049	35 225	33 580	592	14 354	86 349	154 211
North Carolina	18 428	146	2 976	20 449	113	13 852	10 457	5 786	11 877	831	20 456	24 616	609	11 842	65 446	128 599
North Dakota	1 677	12	252	21 322	10	1 144	917	534	666	19	438	23 053	13	257	1 423	3 678
Ohio	23 352	190	4 967	26 098	145	22 014	16 264	9 436	18 292	1 046	34 904	33 369	681	19 317	86 161	184 637
Oklahoma	5 596	44	933	21 360	34	4 216	3 221	1 875	4 064	157	4 282	27 274	109	2 611	13 808	30 287
Oregon	8 631	53	1 355	25 462	41	6 141	4 538	2 721	6 865	213	6 076	28 526	144	3 453	14 444	32 215
Pennsylvania	26 222	213	5 621	26 330	166	24 008	18 001	11 183	18 102	952	29 230	30 704	609	14 769	69 733	139 251
Rhode Island	2 866	14	359	25 693	11	1 809	1 258	767	2 664	88	2 403	27 307	59	1 229	5 166	9 578
South Carolina	8 444	70	1 415	20 304	54	6 218	4 633	2 537	4 839	367	9 425	25 681	272	5 689	24 725	51 996
South Dakota	1 999	13	253	19 748	10	1 234	977	561	889	35	739	21 114	25	448	2 267	5 956
Tennessee	9 270	90	1 966	21 896	70	9 470	6 704	3 632	7 610	504	12 618	25 036	370	7 755	35 799	76 209
Texas	29 110	336	8 013	23 882	261	36 731	27 465	16 444	21 678	957	29 451	30 774	584	14 171	82 532	211 648
Utah	4 366	35	775	22 184	28	3 775	2 691	1 593	2 525	106	2 860	26 981	68	1 477	7 271	15 750
Vermont	2 544	12	241	20 299	9	1 197	863	496	1 343	45	1 289	28 644	30	659	3 379	6 386
Virginia	17 151	144	3 160	22 000	112	14 033	10 495	6 110	6 521	408	11 265	27 610	283	6 400	35 933	65 860
Washington	17 279	122	3 352	27 518	94	15 370	11 286	6 745	8 521	342	11 612	33 953	200	5 531	27 765	72 800
West Virginia	3 595	25	542	21 682	20	1 998	1 715	1 094	1 786	78	2 337	29 962	56	1 457	6 511	13 217
Wisconsin	12 714	97	2 635	27 226	76	11 079	8 491	5 096	10 087	546	16 083	29 456	368	9 143	41 174	88 067
Wyoming	1 692	11	235	21 489	9	916	743	450	577	9	225	25 000	6	146	856	2 385

[1]Establishments in business at any time during the year.
[2]Represents the average of the employment for pay periods ending nearest the 12th of March, May, August, and November.
[3]Represents the average of production workers plus all other employees for the pay period including March 12.
[4]Includes extensive duplication, since products of some industries are used as materials by others.

Source: Construction industries–U.S. Bureau of the Census, 1992 Census of Construction Industries, Geographic Area Series, United States Summary, CC92-A-10; Manufactures–U.S. Bureau of the Census, 1992 Census of Manufactures, Subject Series, General Summary, MC92-S-1.

Geographic area	Transportation, 1992 (SIC 41, 44, 45, 42, 47)[1]					Communications, 1992 (SIC 48)					Electric, gas, and sanitary services, 1992 (SIC 49)				
	Estab-lish-ments[2]	Paid employees[3]			Revenue (mil dol)	Estab-lish-ments[2]	Paid employees[3]			Revenue (mil dol)	Estab-lish-ments[2]	Paid employees[3]			Revenue (mil dol)
		Number (1,000)	Annual payroll				Number (1,000)	Annual payroll				Number (1,000)	Annual payroll		
			Total (mil dol)	Per employee (dollars)				Total (mil dol)	Per employee (dollars)				Total (mil dol)	Per employee (dollars)	
United States	183 453	3 142.7	82 637.5	26 295	292 211	39 244	1 294.2	47 057.9	36 360	230 667	20 049	915.0	39 155.2	42 792	310 961
Alabama	2 788	40.5	891.9	22 019	3 253	804	18.3	584.6	31 991	2 971	353	17.4	732.4	42 114	5 120
Alaska	962	11.3	348.6	30 742	1 345	184	3.3	127.6	38 980	671	115	1.8	100.1	55 010	572
Arizona	2 319	31.0	671.5	21 691	2 258	542	17.4	529.9	30 536	2 493	313	12.3	538.3	43 897	3 527
Arkansas	2 077	29.2	659.4	22 597	2 404	533	8.7	244.3	28 116	1 485	422	10.5	411.9	39 175	3 015
California	21 015	312.9	7 984.8	25 519	29 263	3 186	151.4	5 567.8	36 765	29 231	1 585	79.1	3 856.0	48 764	27 379
Colorado	2 694	34.3	850.2	24 768	2 785	802	26.6	1 020.0	38 380	3 521	366	13.3	509.9	38 324	4 175
Connecticut	2 344	34.0	877.7	25 824	3 347	349	19.6	739.9	37 693	3 278	214	14.2	671.6	47 145	5 477
Delaware	646	8.3	187.4	22 513	680	106	(4)	D	D	D	32	(5)	D	D	D
District of Columbia	488	4.5	109.5	24 166	489	173	9.4	477.9	50 972	2 317	43	39.3	D	D	D
Florida	10 685	146.8	3 318.0	22 608	14 649	1 979	68.6	2 390.8	34 848	12 586	718	39.3	1 615.1	41 125	11 326
Georgia	4 585	74.6	1 763.8	23 641	6 330	1 211	51.2	1 941.1	37 906	7 827	543	26.1	1 056.6	40 452	8 747
Hawaii	1 265	23.2	544.7	23 453	1 837	211	7.0	248.4	35 655	924	57	2.8	141.7	50 846	944
Idaho	1 089	9.2	181.6	19 805	755	222	3.4	93.8	27 734	646	194	3.4	129.2	38 042	1 104
Illinois	9 568	143.2	3 655.7	25 526	14 920	1 606	60.7	2 392.5	39 420	8 971	618	45.3	2 070.8	45 750	15 408
Indiana	4 131	68.7	1 666.2	24 252	7 469	887	23.4	785.0	33 534	3 650	453	22.7	879.4	38 783	7 548
Iowa	2 877	31.8	667.3	20 987	2 829	741	11.1	290.2	26 233	2 141	366	10.8	379.7	35 266	2 847
Kansas	2 173	29.0	607.3	20 970	2 174	596	14.1	468.8	33 312	2 777	339	11.6	439.4	37 766	3 430
Kentucky	2 943	42.0	1 054.1	25 077	4 122	658	12.3	377.0	30 615	2 218	419	14.5	530.8	36 634	4 486
Louisiana	3 420	55.1	1 297.9	23 558	5 502	668	16.1	507.8	31 562	3 048	641	20.2	815.9	40 473	7 937
Maine	1 303	9.2	188.1	20 398	745	226	4.6	147.6	32 066	859	145	4.7	162.9	35 016	1 483
Maryland	3 538	48.0	1 114.8	23 221	3 672	643	26.6	970.0	36 498	4 458	164	15.9	701.7	44 123	5 043
Massachusetts	4 391	59.1	1 404.0	23 767	4 667	838	33.8	1 405.5	41 552	5 640	306	19.7	924.0	46 971	9 425
Michigan	5 242	69.3	1 850.7	26 690	6 382	1 237	33.9	1 165.8	34 434	6 399	647	32.3	1 531.7	47 385	11 221
Minnesota	3 932	51.9	1 108.8	21 349	4 545	841	18.7	583.9	31 206	3 234	351	15.5	670.7	43 225	4 045
Mississippi	1 802	22.6	499.1	22 107	1 729	531	8.6	266.5	30 879	1 563	612	10.3	359.5	34 905	2 921
Missouri	4 886	68.0	1 523.5	22 389	6 205	1 016	33.6	1 144.9	34 087	4 915	436	20.4	815.7	39 952	5 544
Montana	1 031	9.6	193.7	20 081	795	249	3.5	92.6	26 697	635	238	4.0	147.9	37 311	872
Nebraska	1 774	20.8	479.2	23 087	2 194	356	10.0	312.7	31 410	1 414	143	2.3	83.9	36 066	1 855
Nevada	885	14.5	301.2	20 774	1 010	218	6.4	208.7	32 454	1 071	109	6.8	292.1	43 026	1 494
New Hampshire	790	10.7	247.9	23 133	769	176	4.1	149.7	36 577	822	125	5.0	195.3	39 381	1 880
New Jersey	7 891	127.3	3 562.0	27 973	12 402	1 257	74.8	3 390.3	45 350	7 598	400	28.2	1 379.3	48 977	11 063
New Mexico	955	13.3	289.1	21 814	794	318	5.7	158.9	27 873	928	249	7.6	276.0	36 142	2 030
New York	14 506	190.5	4 944.9	25 958	17 386	1 901	111.1	5 081.8	45 725	29 025	625	61.4	3 057.8	49 767	20 308
North Carolina	4 611	68.3	1 586.1	23 239	5 115	981	29.5	964.5	32 741	5 314	459	28.8	1 102.2	38 247	8 616
North Dakota	869	6.4	119.5	18 555	541	253	3.4	83.3	24 520	473	154	3.7	145.8	38 968	1 080
Ohio	7 051	103.4	2 585.6	25 005	8 873	1 362	46.0	1 621.4	35 229	7 624	588	46.7	1 847.8	39 526	15 155
Oklahoma	2 008	23.9	534.3	22 325	1 962	674	13.1	402.9	30 804	2 340	529	14.6	549.0	37 590	6 238
Oregon	2 859	38.2	953.0	24 946	2 952	579	12.9	421.2	32 526	2 351	288	9.0	374.2	41 760	3 104
Pennsylvania	7 882	125.5	2 858.3	22 771	9 276	1 592	53.5	1 832.1	34 276	8 540	888	52.2	2 355.9	45 115	16 743
Rhode Island	626	6.3	137.5	21 969	484	110	3.9	133.9	34 081	696	51	2.6	104.4	40 346	1 005
South Carolina	1 975	29.3	609.1	20 790	2 126	551	13.3	410.9	30 962	2 713	300	15.4	611.3	39 599	4 123
South Dakota	975	8.7	167.2	19 154	729	237	3.3	83.7	25 075	527	136	2.3	74.0	32 041	664
Tennessee	3 595	61.4	1 536.8	25 016	5 220	806	20.3	649.9	32 073	3 538	246	6.2	204.1	32 662	2 003
Texas	11 886	167.8	4 019.9	23 964	15 581	3 118	87.5	2 820.0	32 219	16 274	2 354	75.0	3 062.8	40 865	38 020
Utah	1 081	20.9	503.2	24 072	1 747	247	6.4	201.8	31 390	984	187	7.1	308.5	43 581	2 124
Vermont	584	4.7	99.1	20 988	327	151	(4)	D	D	D	81	2.3	93.4	41 112	988
Virginia	4 540	55.0	1 269.1	23 086	4 745	1 038	43.1	1 593.4	36 987	7 658	299	22.1	907.5	41 120	6 222
Washington	4 411	59.9	1 631.3	27 219	6 473	862	26.6	952.0	35 727	4 730	442	9.5	374.6	39 419	2 753
West Virginia	1 348	13.0	277.0	21 245	955	383	7.7	215.9	28 086	1 095	269	9.8	390.3	39 711	2 164
Wisconsin	4 982	66.0	1 462.1	22 162	5 374	874	19.3	606.4	31 469	3 172	324	17.9	705.6	39 418	5 126
Wyoming	538	4.7	111.6	23 936	304	161	(4)	D	D	D	113	3.4	140.4	41 575	910

D Figure withheld to avoid disclosure of information.

[1]Transportation includes passenger, water and air transportation; motor freight transportation and warehousing; and transportation services.
[2]Establishments with payroll in business at any time during the year.
[3]For pay period including March 12.
[4]1,000 - 2,499 employees.
[5]2,500 - 4,999 employees.

Source: U.S. Bureau of the Census, 1992 Census of Transportation, Communication, and Utilities, Geographic Area Series, Summary, UC92-A-1.

Table A-46. States — Wholesale and Retail Trade and Finance, Insurance, and Real Estate

Geographic area	Wholesale trade, 1992 (SIC 50,51)					Retail trade, 1992 (SIC52-59)						Finance, insurance, and real estate, 1992 (SIC 60-65, 67)				
	Estab-lish-ments[1]	Paid employees[2] Number (1,000)	Annual payroll Total (mil dol)	Per em-ployee (dollars)	Sales (mil dol)	Estab-lish-ments[1]	Paid employees[2] Number (1,000)	Annual payroll Total (mil dol)	Per em-ployee (dollars)	Sales Total (mil dol)	Sales Per capita[3] (dollars)	Estab-lish-ments[1]	Paid employees[2] Number (1,000)	Annual payroll Total (mil dol)	Per em-ployee (dollars)	Revenue (mil dol)
United States	495 457	5 791.3	173 272	29 920	3 238 520	2 671 715	18 407.5	222 868	12 107	1 949 193	7 644	2 466 656	6 509.6	211 569	32 501	1 937 681
Alabama	7 066	80.1	1 951	24 360	31 971	43 418	269.7	2 989	11 083	28 845	6 983	26 947	72.6	1 840	25 359	D
Alaska	908	8.5	290	34 079	3 600	6 733	39.5	671	16 991	5 101	8 687	4 885	D	D	D	D
Arizona	6 518	68.8	1 837	26 686	27 975	37 033	288.3	3 437	11 921	29 999	7 810	41 665	87.9	2 457	27 938	17 362
Arkansas	4 296	43.9	989	22 541	18 070	27 867	152.0	1 633	10 741	16 661	6 954	17 647	35.9	881	24 508	D
California	58 437	731.6	23 537	32 171	432 946	307 946	2 050.6	28 064	13 686	232 647	7 533	342 899	768.4	25 974	33 802	237 001
Colorado	7 554	84.0	2 478	29 501	46 872	40 515	283.5	3 488	12 306	29 274	8 451	46 973	99.0	2 841	28 710	22 166
Connecticut	6 262	77.1	3 200	41 502	72 446	35 391	240.9	3 464	14 381	28 515	8 703	40 513	150.4	5 936	39 472	D
Delaware	1 088	16.1	674	41 900	12 258	7 616	60.2	763	12 669	6 623	9 605	8 871	38.4	1 125	29 266	D
District of Columbia	499	6.6	231	35 195	3 308	5 058	46.9	642	13 694	3 637	6 203	6 656	D	D	D	D
Florida	30 137	280.9	7 485	26 645	132 562	149 615	1 102.3	13 276	12 044	121 789	9 013	171 532	365.6	9 816	26 853	80 070
Georgia	14 608	179.4	5 329	29 707	113 804	68 934	509.3	5 809	11 407	51 306	7 581	56 467	165.4	4 922	29 760	41 015
Hawaii	2 202	23.3	625	26 795	8 002	13 185	110.4	1 481	13 414	11 510	10 028	15 105	37.2	1 042	28 021	D
Idaho	2 288	24.9	528	21 219	8 881	12 626	73.9	846	11 443	7 937	7 440	10 887	17.6	407	23 077	D
Illinois	24 637	331.9	10 931	32 935	219 361	107 227	846.1	10 076	11 909	87 595	7 554	111 052	376.5	13 260	35 214	120 726
Indiana	10 264	115.7	3 052	26 368	52 395	58 801	442.1	4 772	10 795	43 365	7 673	44 410	121.0	3 172	26 205	35 164
Iowa	6 971	69.4	1 639	23 630	29 420	33 975	226.1	2 304	10 192	20 477	7 292	25 702	70.7	1 843	26 084	17 258
Kansas	5 854	61.8	1 638	26 517	34 867	28 635	185.8	2 022	10 883	18 034	7 175	23 937	59.3	1 507	25 400	D
Kentucky	5 931	70.3	1 701	24 216	31 575	40 790	261.2	2 803	10 732	26 241	6 993	26 126	62.5	1 558	24 931	16 342
Louisiana	7 347	81.3	1 994	24 536	37 287	39 590	288.8	3 096	10 718	28 635	6 700	31 195	75.2	1 843	24 492	14 771
Maine	1 974	21.9	541	24 723	6 521	17 199	90.1	1 120	12 433	10 594	8 571	10 481	23.9	673	28 119	D
Maryland	7 188	100.5	3 180	31 640	52 877	46 294	366.6	4 801	13 097	38 436	7 829	53 193	132.0	4 149	31 443	35 803
Massachusetts	10 950	141.5	5 035	35 583	86 657	63 669	469.5	5 986	12 749	49 042	8 177	56 487	216.7	8 088	37 318	D
Michigan	15 517	185.2	5 960	32 181	125 671	89 707	706.8	8 187	11 583	73 039	7 755	76 543	190.8	5 325	27 905	61 315
Minnesota	10 219	123.1	3 819	31 016	72 451	46 929	372.0	4 069	10 939	36 411	8 137	44 957	124.8	4 116	32 995	36 514
Mississippi	3 868	39.9	914	22 892	15 815	27 166	151.0	1 597	10 575	15 489	5 930	16 327	36.9	832	22 516	7 300
Missouri	11 236	129.6	3 553	27 409	68 416	56 599	391.5	4 411	11 267	38 936	7 504	47 267	130.9	3 634	27 761	31 640
Montana	1 853	16.4	343	20 915	5 884	11 490	64.4	697	10 823	6 449	7 833	8 843	13.6	302	22 188	D
Nebraska	4 035	47.1	1 076	22 869	32 489	19 166	132.2	1 308	9 897	11 837	7 380	16 232	48.5	1 284	26 459	D
Nevada	2 075	21.8	607	27 780	7 812	13 098	99.3	1 422	14 326	11 791	8 840	15 875	28.4	726	25 579	D
New Hampshire	2 104	20.5	635	31 026	8 152	14 809	97.1	1 261	12 987	11 389	10 220	11 842	28.9	841	29 148	D
New Jersey	18 444	262.7	9 629	36 652	176 022	80 374	522.4	7 613	14 574	64 945	8 314	95 437	227.9	8 121	35 633	D
New Mexico	2 515	22.6	513	22 717	6 264	17 005	112.3	1 294	11 518	11 596	7 324	12 944	25.8	591	22 889	D
New York	40 935	433.8	15 232	35 111	288 944	185 607	1 088.4	14 867	13 659	122 649	6 777	189 958	736.1	37 877	51 456	356 141
North Carolina	13 351	151.1	4 167	27 571	76 365	77 991	507.8	5 687	11 201	51 214	7 487	58 306	131.4	3 501	26 651	D
North Dakota	2 086	18.5	406	22 024	7 600	7 700	51.8	514	9 938	4 816	7 580	6 747	12.3	281	22 863	D
Ohio	19 305	260.1	7 283	28 000	127 344	106 087	837.9	9 257	11 048	80 699	7 336	93 476	248.6	6 745	27 128	70 478
Oklahoma	5 993	57.9	1 398	24 138	26 381	37 309	211.3	2 305	10 910	22 071	6 882	26 472	59.3	1 447	24 423	11 564
Oregon	6 455	72.1	2 021	28 034	42 415	33 841	226.7	2 872	12 671	24 828	8 338	30 150	65.0	1 728	26 608	D
Pennsylvania	20 230	254.4	7 485	29 422	126 370	128 237	861.6	10 043	11 657	90 607	7 558	96 571	301.2	8 992	29 853	79 082
Rhode Island	1 771	19.5	551	28 218	6 648	11 052	67.3	839	12 469	6 986	6 973	9 812	27.5	764	27 760	D
South Carolina	5 564	56.7	1 457	25 711	21 310	40 867	263.9	2 845	10 778	25 618	7 127	28 271	62.3	1 477	23 692	D
South Dakota	1 809	16.4	335	20 458	6 505	9 367	57.5	576	10 019	5 260	7 413	7 209	17.2	360	20 896	D
Tennessee	9 341	115.4	3 064	26 547	59 682	56 897	368.0	4 231	11 496	38 785	7 726	39 161	101.2	2 716	26 837	D
Texas	36 610	408.6	11 788	28 848	274 614	189 297	1 230.4	14 676	11 928	134 837	7 619	161 341	397.9	11 886	29 873	99 734
Utah	3 231	39.6	1 005	25 364	15 281	16 224	126.3	1 385	10 966	12 709	7 015	18 030	36.2	867	23 962	4 835
Vermont	1 112	11.4	307	27 034	4 523	9 043	45.9	564	12 278	4 882	8 547	6 217	12.0	309	25 667	D
Virginia	9 290	115.8	3 268	28 220	51 453	60 822	474.6	5 753	12 121	48 979	7 667	62 660	153.3	4 319	28 184	41 337
Washington	10 732	122.5	3 628	29 609	62 468	53 417	381.2	5 081	13 331	41 720	8 105	55 330	115.2	3 395	29 485	D
West Virginia	2 427	24.5	575	23 509	7 843	18 589	112.1	1 208	10 782	11 540	6 386	10 438	23.2	503	21 628	D
Wisconsin	9 383	117.6	3 223	27 398	47 598	54 469	405.0	4 350	10 740	39 195	7 845	41 362	132.8	3 733	28 111	D
Wyoming	987	7.0	165	23 531	2 546	6 439	37.3	413	11 067	3 651	7 869	5 248	6.5	152	23 262	D

D Figures withheld to avoid disclosure.

[1]Establishments in business at any time during the year.
[2]For pay period including March 12.
[3]Based on resident population estimated as of July 1, 1992.

Source: Wholesale trade–U.S. Bureau of the Census, 1992 Census of Wholesale Trade, Geographic Area Series, WC92-1-1 through 52RV; Retail trade–U.S. Bureau of the Census, 1992 Census of Retail Trade, Geographic Area Series, RC92-A-1 through 52, and 1992 Census of Retail Trade, Nonemployer Statistics Series, Summary, RC92-N-1; Finance, insurance, and real estate–U.S. Bureau of the Census, 1992 Census of Financial, Insurance, and Real Estate Industries, Geographic Area Series, FC92-A-1 through 52, and 1992 Census of Financial, Insurance, and Real Estate Industries, Nonemployer Statistics Series, Summary, FC92-N-1.

Geographic area	Firms subject to federal income tax, 1992							Tax-exempt firms, 1992				
	All establishments		Establishments with payroll					Establishments with payroll				
					Annual payroll					Annual payroll		
	Total[1] (1,000)	Receipts (mil dol)	Total[1] (1,000)	Receipts (mil dol)	Total (mil dol)	Per employee (dollars)	Paid employees[2] (1,000)	Total[1] (1,000)	Revenue (mil dol)	Total (mil dol)	Per employee (dollars)	Paid employees[2] (1,000)
United States	8 593.5	1 345 146	1 825.4	1 202 613	452 697	23 468	19 290.4	208.9	446 256	186 672	23 021	8 108.9
Alabama	98.7	14 933	23.0	13 649	5 162	20 791	248.3	2.4	5 319	2 148	21 642	99.3
Alaska	24.2	2 770	4.5	2 382	884	27 736	31.9	.9	1 028	445	25 959	17.2
Arizona	132.4	18 648	28.7	16 616	6 220	20 784	299.3	2.6	5 386	2 075	22 100	93.9
Arkansas	67.8	6 902	14.0	6 007	2 250	16 856	133.5	1.9	2 946	1 206	18 724	64.4
California	1 243.0	224 885	244.5	198 432	71 824	27 146	2 645.8	20.1	49 179	18 799	26 585	707.1
Colorado	168.2	21 229	32.9	18 810	7 183	22 514	319.1	3.3	6 301	2 401	23 004	104.4
Connecticut	123.4	21 562	27.4	19 102	7 551	27 710	272.5	3.4	7 046	3 280	26 199	125.2
Delaware	21.2	3 142	5.3	2 823	1 170	21 597	54.2	.6	1 324	588	22 385	26.3
District of Columbia	26.0	11 752	7.4	11 238	4 299	35 633	120.7	2.6	9 782	3 118	32 367	96.3
Florida	495.6	82 890	120.0	74 347	27 658	21 710	1 274.0	8.4	17 885	7 195	22 641	317.8
Georgia	207.7	34 081	46.9	30 802	11 409	22 738	501.8	3.8	9 122	3 706	22 702	163.2
Hawaii	41.6	8 027	8.5	7 291	2 654	22 501	118.0	1.0	2 081	924	24 635	37.5
Idaho	38.3	3 918	7.3	3 440	1 305	20 532	63.5	.9	1 089	447	19 948	22.4
Illinois	370.7	63 955	79.8	57 927	22 077	24 477	902.0	9.0	23 341	9 521	22 834	417.0
Indiana	164.6	19 610	34.5	17 548	6 742	19 012	354.6	5.2	9 009	3 649	20 249	180.2
Iowa	95.3	8 755	17.8	7 711	2 899	17 839	162.5	3.7	4 656	2 065	17 094	120.8
Kansas	91.0	9 589	16.9	8 460	3 168	19 557	162.0	3.0	3 693	1 611	18 670	86.3
Kentucky	103.8	11 685	21.0	10 378	3 864	18 331	210.8	2.6	4 753	1 922	19 398	99.1
Louisiana	117.1	17 943	27.1	16 067	5 912	19 942	296.5	2.6	5 587	2 338	21 234	110.1
Maine	46.7	4 246	9.0	3 597	1 367	20 088	68.1	1.7	2 068	956	21 268	45.0
Maryland	179.1	29 822	36.8	26 937	10 765	25 718	418.6	3.9	9 853	3 925	24 101	162.9
Massachusetts	246.2	43 676	46.6	38 949	15 103	27 693	545.4	7.2	16 940	7 698	25 511	301.8
Michigan	278.3	39 049	61.3	35 124	14 203	23 133	614.0	7.5	16 757	7 154	23 341	306.5
Minnesota	176.5	21 146	31.0	18 764	7 544	21 601	349.2	5.6	9 718	4 346	20 861	208.3
Mississippi	55.9	6 277	12.8	5 487	1 991	18 399	108.2	1.6	2 961	1 219	20 000	60.9
Missouri	166.6	22 388	36.4	20 339	7 699	20 612	373.5	4.4	9 484	3 996	20 507	194.9
Montana	34.3	2 629	6.9	2 197	722	16 401	44.0	1.4	1 243	524	17 862	29.3
Nebraska	59.3	6 492	11.3	5 828	2 290	19 039	120.3	1.9	2 572	1 118	19 092	58.6
Nevada	47.2	17 541	10.8	16 585	5 431	21 208	256.1	.7	1 013	382	23 168	16.5
New Hampshire	46.7	5 413	9.2	4 612	1 840	22 192	82.9	1.4	1 933	767	21 124	36.3
New Jersey	265.2	55 842	65.9	50 242	18 485	27 561	670.7	4.8	13 855	6 282	25 640	245.0
New Mexico	53.2	6 880	10.7	6 191	2 332	20 914	111.5	1.5	1 899	849	19 776	42.9
New York	617.1	115 939	133.7	103 025	38 012	28 272	1 344.5	16.3	49 030	22 980	26 376	871.3
North Carolina	196.1	24 631	42.2	22 155	8 410	19 788	425.0	4.8	9 777	4 152	22 420	185.2
North Dakota	22.2	1 795	4.2	1 576	616	18 905	32.6	1.1	1 312	585	15 922	36.7
Ohio	321.5	45 210	69.9	40 844	16 137	21 278	758.4	9.3	20 111	8 361	21 226	393.9
Oklahoma	112.1	11 169	21.2	9 607	3 641	18 539	196.4	2.5	3 935	1 620	19 495	83.1
Oregon	118.9	12 382	23.3	10 663	3 963	20 284	195.4	3.1	4 479	1 857	21 254	87.4
Pennsylvania	345.6	55 409	77.8	49 383	18 741	23 513	797.1	12.4	26 516	11 490	22 343	514.3
Rhode Island	33.3	4 196	7.6	3 664	1 413	21 935	64.4	1.1	2 217	1 003	23 458	42.7
South Carolina	90.0	12 169	21.5	10 930	4 349	18 666	233.0	2.1	4 200	1 694	22 318	75.9
South Dakota	25.2	2 076	4.8	1 790	592	17 176	34.4	1.1	1 258	552	16 823	32.8
Tennessee	148.3	22 712	32.0	20 410	7 581	20 917	362.4	3.5	7 549	3 028	21 815	138.8
Texas	597.2	94 721	123.6	84 763	32 402	22 655	1 430.2	10.9	21 692	8 614	21 668	397.5
Utah	65.4	8 389	11.7	7 491	2 667	19 253	138.5	1.0	1 784	732	20 991	34.9
Vermont	27.7	2 325	5.0	1 946	633	17 057	37.1	1.1	1 021	449	20 545	21.9
Virginia	200.8	36 436	45.9	33 606	13 138	24 990	525.7	4.7	10 782	4 191	23 764	176.4
Washington	185.1	24 125	39.5	21 448	8 091	22 801	354.9	5.0	8 837	3 778	23 383	161.6
West Virginia	44.0	4 951	9.5	4 466	1 575	18 777	83.9	1.6	2 718	1 138	19 984	57.0
Wisconsin	138.1	17 220	32.0	15 577	6 295	19 871	316.8	4.8	8 654	3 534	19 112	184.9
Wyoming	19.2	1 612	4.1	1 384	436	16 487	26.5	.7	561	257	16 675	15.4

[1]Establishments in business at any time during the year.
[2]For pay period including March 12.

Source: Establishments, receipts, and revenues–U.S. Bureau of the Census, 1992 Census of Service Industries, Nonemployer Statistics Series, Summary, SC92-N-1; Payroll and paid employees–U.S. Bureau of the Census, 1992 Economic Census CD-ROM, Report Series Disc 1G (related publication–U.S. Bureau of the Census, 1992 Census of Service Industries, Geographic Area Series, SC92-A-1 through 52).

Table A–48. States — Women- and Minority-Owned Firms

Geographic area	Firms								Sales and receipts (mil dol)							
	Women-owned		Black-owned		Hispanic-owned		American Indian- and Alaska Native-owned[1]		Women-owned		Black-owned		Hispanic-owned		American Indian- and Alaska Native-owned[1]	
	1992	1987	1992	1987	1992	1987	1992	1987	1992	1987	1992	1987	1992	1987	1992	1987
United States	5 888 883	4 114 787	620 912	424 165	771 708	422 373	606 426	376 711	642 484	278 138	32 197	19 763	72 824	24 732	99 709	34 036
Alabama....................	71 466	48 018	14 707	10 085	1 029	397	1 777	1 007	7 628	3 624	535	440	151	30	315	131
Alaska......................	19 380	13 976	739	507	766	502	3 916	5 034	1 871	829	39	14	58	27	379	196
Arizona....................	93 300	60 567	2 936	1 811	17 835	9 845	5 852	3 398	8 974	2 911	138	91	1 298	513	943	303
Arkansas..................	50 440	35 469	5 738	4 392	701	324	1 214	658	4 416	2 008	233	215	60	14	162	56
California.................	801 487	559 821	68 968	47 728	249 717	132 212	232 672	147 633	84 943	31 027	5 478	2 364	19 553	8 120	37 685	14 783
Colorado..................	121 659	89 411	4 372	2 871	13 817	9 516	5 788	3 543	10 784	4 261	295	106	1 212	394	843	230
Connecticut.............	79 931	60 924	5 714	4 061	4 502	2 235	3 485	2 051	11 078	5 320	292	226	438	176	783	D
Delaware.................	14 904	9 727	2 060	1 399	497	184	809	479	2 303	753	157	78	109	6	166	D
District of Columbia...	14 599	10 987	10 111	8 275	1 452	762	1 393	807	1 610	774	452	412	312	64	323	133
Florida....................	352 048	221 361	40 371	25 527	118 208	64 413	17 499	8 902	39 485	16 828	2 265	1 212	16 127	4 949	3 372	D
Georgia...................	143 045	88 050	38 264	21 283	5 501	1 931	8 961	4 221	22 450	5 874	1 677	1 180	772	145	1 509	469
Hawaii.....................	29 743	21 696	717	399	3 192	1 226	38 392	31 406	2 575	857	27	12	188	58	4 767	1 662
Idaho......................	29 946	18 973	152	94	1 865	974	759	513	2 339	813	25	5	126	31	103	38
Illinois....................	250 613	177 057	28 433	19 011	18 368	9 636	21 743	14 872	33 289	13 884	1 773	1 100	1 951	589	5 080	1 445
Indiana...................	125 411	89 949	8 349	5 867	2 454	1 427	3 193	1 808	16 056	8 913	711	350	310	106	634	209
Iowa.......................	71 040	53 592	1 106	703	859	475	1 011	617	6 021	2 905	76	45	129	20	184	55
Kansas....................	66 429	53 505	3 078	2 323	2 396	1 541	1 842	1 366	5 760	2 661	92	154	186	62	247	D
Kentucky.................	74 280	53 454	5 097	3 738	752	359	1 614	899	6 763	3 265	251	120	104	17	304	97
Louisiana................	76 849	55 852	20 312	15 331	4 983	2 697	4 826	2 808	11 743	2 962	774	532	701	136	572	D
Maine.....................	35 260	23 922	235	131	427	139	483	233	3 046	1 635	25	5	40	12	69	27
Maryland.................	121 777	81 891	35 758	21 678	7 289	2 931	13 697	7 954	11 333	5 509	1 242	720	570	185	1 584	711
Massachusetts..........	147 572	111 376	7 225	4 761	6 914	2 636	7 009	3 916	16 104	11 140	428	252	508	174	1 030	297
Michigan.................	193 820	133 958	19 695	13 708	5 036	2 654	7 409	4 729	17 796	7 889	1 268	701	714	126	1 263	D
Minnesota...............	124 143	88 137	2 785	1 448	1 583	751	3 168	2 024	11 812	4 991	283	125	171	29	540	172
Mississippi..............	40 879	28 976	14 067	9 667	660	308	1 765	1 178	3 452	2 062	505	532	94	12	333	D
Missouri..................	117 885	87 658	9 973	7 832	2 216	1 247	3 451	2 193	11 075	5 349	403	336	265	50	636	167
Montana..................	25 310	17 747	113	77	568	304	845	612	1 814	930	7	7	27	10	88	30
Nebraska.................	43 637	32 285	1 350	863	1 147	619	670	451	4 941	1 649	62	31	77	19	94	31
Nevada...................	32 430	18 831	1 736	1 002	3 900	1 767	2 769	1 395	3 674	1 414	113	39	484	142	408	93
New Hampshire.........	31 492	22 713	326	229	487	244	666	333	4 125	1 858	46	31	80	13	93	D
New Jersey...............	164 798	117 373	20 137	14 556	22 198	12 094	23 116	12 665	26 657	13 554	1 239	996	2 828	902	4 385	D
New Mexico..............	40 636	25 397	925	587	21 586	14 299	4 608	2 155	2 966	1 166	61	27	1 480	702	226	104
New York..................	395 944	284 912	51 312	36 289	50 601	28 254	63 053	36 257	59 950	29 970	2 268	1 886	4 732	1 556	10 853	3 218
North Carolina..........	142 516	93 532	29 221	19 487	2 802	918	6 155	3 827	14 365	6 813	893	746	419	93	762	D
North Dakota............	15 355	12 689	117	57	116	88	385	329	1 095	572	8	1	10	2	54	D
Ohio.......................	224 693	154 084	22 690	15 983	4 289	1 989	7 146	4 011	20 905	8 872	1 096	626	828	192	1 384	D
Oklahoma................	82 894	63 690	4 621	3 461	2 854	1 516	5 627	3 751	6 605	2 948	191	94	247	50	826	155
Oregon...................	87 970	58 941	1 447	848	3 538	1 598	5 414	3 340	9 327	4 279	101	34	331	110	1 069	351
Pennsylvania............	227 500	167 362	15 917	11 728	5 186	2 650	12 053	7 189	29 400	13 339	1 134	747	560	247	3 083	D
Rhode Island............	21 353	14 517	857	489	1 297	426	987	472	2 918	1 340	65	18	126	40	114	D
South Carolina..........	64 812	42 604	18 343	12 815	1 057	393	1 877	965	5 049	2 950	673	444	147	16	295	88
South Dakota............	18 215	13 374	111	63	239	109	555	375	1 681	726	10	5	35	4	114	17
Tennessee................	101 134	67 448	14 920	10 423	1 602	554	3 026	1 664	8 573	4 226	555	386	148	35	734	D
Texas.....................	414 179	298 138	50 008	35 725	155 909	94 754	38 763	22 682	35 330	13 385	2 339	1 084	11 796	4 108	5 708	1 815
Utah.......................	45 626	29 810	354	202	2 375	1 300	1 746	1 239	4 204	1 392	45	9	180	47	180	D
Vermont..................	21 033	13 802	139	98	351	118	274	111	1 568	766	7	7	33	5	74	D
Virginia...................	138 494	94 416	26 100	18 781	7 654	2 716	13 752	8 163	11 990	5 952	1 211	811	958	141	1 754	D
Washington..............	136 337	90 285	4 575	2 583	6 093	2 686	15 648	8 241	16 057	4 689	257	176	750	141	2 936	792
West Virginia............	30 644	22 549	1 093	727	313	177	712	551	2 080	1 114	42	39	48	14	136	76
Wisconsin................	99 357	69 185	3 446	2 381	1 762	894	2 486	1 451	11 511	4 667	324	191	300	74	478	D
Wyoming.................	14 617	10 796	97	81	766	584	362	233	992	524	5	4	53	22	35	D

D Figure withheld to avoid disclosure.

[1]Includes Asian- and Pacific Islander-owned.

Source: Women-owned–U.S. Bureau of the Census, 1992 Economic Census, Women-Owned Businesses, WB92-1; Black-owned–U.S. Bureau of the Census, 1992 Economic Census, Survey of Minority-Owned Business Enterprises, Black, MB92-1; Hispanic-owned–U.S. Bureau of the Census, 1992 Economic Census, Survey of Minority-Owned Business Enterprises, Hispanic, MB92-2; American Indian and Alaska Native-owned–U.S. Bureau of the Census, 1992 Economic Census, Survey of Minority-Owned Business Enterprises, Asians and Pacific Islanders, American Indians, and Alaska Natives, MB92-3RV.

Table A–49. States — State Government Employment and Finances

Geographic area	Employment (full-time equivalent) Number (1,000)		Per 10,000 population[1]		Finances Revenue (mil dol) Total[2]		Revenue General, 1995 Total[2]	Inter-governmental from federal government	Taxes	Expenditures (mil dol) Total[2]		Expenditures General, 1995 Total	Inter-governmental	Selected functions Education	Public welfare	Health and hospitals
	1995	1990	1995	1990	1995	1990				1995	1990					
United States	3 971	3 840	151	154	903 756	632 172	739 016	202 485	399 148	836 894	572 318	733 503	240 978	249 670	194 854	60 003
Alabama......................	81	79	191	196	12 280	9 077	10 583	3 194	5 078	11 542	8 119	10 490	2 620	4 401	2 291	1 303
Alaska........................	22	22	366	401	8 288	5 547	7 358	975	1 922	5 599	4 688	5 047	1 096	1 258	643	176
Arizona.......................	58	50	135	137	12 593	8 619	10 510	2 681	6 223	11 162	8 265	10 072	3 992	3 601	2 468	545
Arkansas.....................	48	43	192	182	7 368	4 545	6 467	2 068	3 392	6 616	4 223	6 071	1 586	2 352	1 519	579
California	338	325	107	109	118 303	89 275	94 252	27 527	53 269	109 231	78 867	94 007	44 893	30 027	28 513	7 782
Colorado	57	54	153	165	11 555	7 614	9 191	2 666	4 531	9 802	6 510	8 434	2 703	3 691	2 135	371
Connecticut	63	58	193	178	13 718	9 621	12 060	2 755	7 474	13 576	9 886	11 603	2 409	2 815	2 910	1 287
Delaware	22	21	307	314	3 441	2 332	3 114	554	1 595	2 980	2 128	2 709	510	920	414	201
District of Columbia	X	X	X	X	X	X	X	X	X	X	X	X	X	X	X	X
Florida	175	160	123	123	37 359	23 868	31 013	7 642	18 565	34 750	21 723	32 168	10 950	10 846	7 046	2 451
Georgia	115	112	159	173	20 284	13 197	17 123	5 162	9 487	19 154	12 213	17 771	4 850	7 341	4 590	1 241
Hawaii	51	49	436	445	5 778	4 363	5 099	1 120	2 874	6 015	3 832	5 372	144	1 645	894	522
Idaho	21	19	179	186	3 845	2 436	3 151	781	1 733	3 360	2 047	2 941	944	1 251	487	130
Illinois	141	145	119	127	34 689	24 568	29 064	7 770	16 590	32 991	22 072	28 845	7 989	8 505	8 824	2 015
Indiana	89	89	153	161	16 261	11 491	14 848	3 313	8 046	15 284	10 414	14 326	5 115	5 840	3 207	870
Iowa	53	57	187	207	9 268	6 748	8 087	2 093	4 403	8 586	6 317	7 916	2 587	3 167	1 650	713
Kansas	48	50	187	200	7 374	5 163	6 495	1 570	3 765	7 116	4 705	6 460	2 206	2 876	1 212	514
Kentucky	73	75	191	204	12 846	8 656	11 085	3 039	6 285	11 395	7 772	10 191	2 790	4 062	2 776	592
Louisiana	93	85	214	200	13 956	10 190	12 066	4 642	4 677	14 461	9 420	13 135	2 981	4 245	3 876	1 576
Maine	21	22	172	179	4 208	3 266	3 673	1 169	1 813	4 179	3 044	3 664	750	1 046	1 257	218
Maryland	81	89	161	186	16 430	12 306	13 696	3 013	8 061	15 069	11 299	12 902	3 074	3 818	2 956	1 045
Massachusetts	82	93	135	155	24 101	17 229	21 545	5 297	11 601	24 282	18 736	21 870	4 740	4 102	6 178	2 008
Michigan.....................	141	144	148	155	35 328	23 411	30 217	7 130	17 723	34 669	23 098	30 875	13 590	13 889	6 179	3 346
Minnesota	73	70	158	160	18 329	13 236	15 210	3 394	9 328	16 380	11 355	14 808	5 629	5 558	3 923	1 026
Mississippi	50	47	186	183	8 301	5 411	7 056	2 448	3 599	7 414	4 838	6 708	2 279	2 495	1 631	542
Missouri	79	74	149	145	15 586	9 344	12 516	3 758	6 752	12 482	8 326	11 400	3 462	4 285	2 888	929
Montana	18	17	208	211	3 293	2 270	2 644	861	1 214	2 988	2 007	2 565	685	981	463	154
Nebraska	30	29	181	186	4 615	3 074	4 195	1 091	2 220	4 250	2 885	4 094	1 144	1 440	916	444
Nevada	21	19	134	160	5 478	3 268	3 896	736	2 698	4 581	2 929	3 718	1 425	1 351	612	128
New Hampshire	17	16	147	145	3 270	1 948	2 674	791	918	3 096	1 972	2 718	374	557	943	160
New Jersey	125	112	157	145	32 675	22 760	25 343	5 781	13 607	32 605	21 849	26 438	7 901	7 406	6 773	1 693
New Mexico.................	42	40	251	262	6 634	4 787	5 660	1 334	2 844	6 363	4 172	5 867	1 966	2 363	879	570
New York	257	285	142	158	90 997	64 360	69 875	21 683	34 294	81 372	59 139	68 308	25 190	17 494	25 785	6 024
North Carolina	115	107	159	161	22 091	14 625	19 170	5 045	11 426	20 437	13 493	18 735	6 665	7 761	4 020	1 584
North Dakota................	16	15	257	234	2 448	1 819	2 143	660	959	2 213	1 755	2 048	437	737	438	103
Ohio	143	139	128	128	41 306	28 771	28 263	7 945	15 186	34 990	25 237	28 129	9 534	9 891	7 593	2 322
Oklahoma....................	68	65	206	208	9 160	7 223	7 724	1 982	4 416	8 990	6 515	7 566	2 449	3 371	1 656	578
Oregon.......................	52	52	166	184	12 986	8 216	9 438	3 002	4 286	11 030	6 352	9 509	2 980	3 086	2 076	837
Pennsylvania	152	127	126	107	40 015	27 388	32 772	9 117	18 262	39 394	24 531	33 633	9 031	9 677	11 111	2 916
Rhode Island................	20	21	203	205	4 156	3 062	3 386	1 141	1 490	4 265	3 014	3 544	504	885	902	335
South Carolina	78	79	213	227	12 068	8 852	9 609	2 953	4 763	11 623	7 910	9 889	2 367	3 537	2 447	1 206
South Dakota	14	13	194	192	2 099	1 507	1 766	658	694	1 880	1 344	1 774	337	515	375	107
Tennessee	84	79	161	163	12 900	9 183	11 522	3 992	5 908	13 432	8 403	12 578	3 263	4 303	3 805	1 060
Texas	268	223	143	131	49 422	31 237	40 352	12 322	20 289	44 643	26 027	40 475	11 797	16 286	10 635	3 106
Utah	42	37	215	216	6 325	4 313	5 304	1 453	2 676	5 780	3 857	5 289	1 447	2 483	924	422
Vermont	13	13	216	233	2 074	1 593	1 869	631	801	2 014	1 565	1 854	309	611	511	58
Virginia	116	117	175	188	18 993	13 609	16 251	3 296	8 784	17 040	12 632	15 664	4 297	5 979	2 804	1 586
Washington	96	91	175	187	23 576	15 095	16 765	3 923	10 196	21 200	13 567	17 555	5 340	7 273	3 730	1 368
West Virginia	35	34	189	188	6 629	4 458	5 628	1 987	2 732	6 262	4 212	5 418	1 255	1 994	1 576	215
Wisconsin	64	67	126	136	16 826	15 338	15 337	3 545	9 029	16 302	11 416	14 546	5 723	5 030	3 160	938
Wyoming	11	11	227	239	2 240	1 902	1 952	796	667	2 045	1 641	1 803	676	626	252	108

X Not applicable.

[1]Based on resident population estimated as of July 1 for 1995 and enumerated as of April 1 for 1990.
[2]Includes other items not shown separately.

Source: State government employment–For 1995, U.S. Bureau of the Census, Internet site <http://www.census.gov/govs/apes/95fstall.txt> (accessed 26 June 1997), for 1990, U.S. Bureau of the Census, Public Employment, GE90-1, September 1991; State government finances–for 1995, U.S. Bureau of the Census, Internet site <http://www.census.gov/govs/www/state.html> (released February 1997), for 1990, Government Finances: 1989-90, GF90-5, December 1991.

Table A–50. States — State General Fund, Tax Collection, and Federal Aid

Geographic area	State general fund[1] (mil dol) Resources[2] 1997, prel.	1996	Expenditures[3] 1997, prel.	1996	Balance[4] 1997, prel.	1996	State government tax collections (mil dol) Total[5] 1996	1990	1996 Sales and gross receipts Total[5]	General	Individual income	Corporation net income	Federal aid to state and local government (mil dol) Total 1996	1990	By selected function, 1996 Medicaid	Highway trust fund
United States	**410 972**	**389 031**	**390 031**	**371 421**	**18 494**	**16 259**	**418 264**	**300 721**	**205 687**	**139 279**	**133 976**	**29 316**	**[6]227 542**	**134 457**	**[6]91 990**	**[6]19 543**
Alabama	4 514	4 298	4 481	4 240	32	58	5 258	3 820	2 774	1 439	1 578	218	3 325	2 101	1 455	257
Alaska	2 498	2 347	2 436	2 347	62	–	1 519	1 546	99	–	–	326	1 051	717	199	231
Arizona	5 446	4 933	4 899	4 533	548	400	6 409	4 377	3 658	2 720	1 494	448	3 095	1 620	1 174	230
Arkansas	2 772	2 632	2 772	2 632	–	–	3 709	2 261	1 940	1 376	1 162	229	2 131	1 250	956	204
California	49 769	46 078	48 910	45 393	[7]859	[7]685	57 747	43 419	24 093	18 980	20 760	5 831	26 413	13 932	9 021	1 523
Colorado	5 048	4 758	4 534	4 408	375	369	4 820	3 069	2 037	1 322	2 274	206	2 410	1 429	777	275
Connecticut	9 582	9 111	9 320	8 861	263	250	7 830	5 268	3 932	2 445	2 614	641	3 080	1 973	1 429	311
Delaware	2 159	2 030	1 766	1 651	[7]393	[7]379	1 688	1 130	253	–	632	166	600	313	215	74
District of Columbia	X	X	X	X	X	X	X	X	X	X	X	X	2 578	1 718	390	63
Florida	16 120	14 997	15 537	14 710	583	287	19 699	13 308	15 241	11 429	–	1 008	8 442	4 576	3 382	610
Georgia	11 801	10 928	11 122	10 439	679	489	10 292	7 078	4 786	3 824	4 244	719	5 359	3 136	2 276	406
Hawaii	3 322	3 284	3 186	3 124	136	161	3 079	2 335	1 905	1 432	1 000	66	1 126	598	357	177
Idaho	1 405	1 349	1 392	1 337	13	12	1 857	1 138	852	600	655	153	887	569	268	122
Illinois	19 280	18 267	18 474	17 841	806	426	17 277	12 891	8 486	5 057	5 781	1 621	9 229	5 280	3 280	601
Indiana	9 070	8 249	7 931	7 344	745	805	8 437	6 102	3 761	2 868	3 478	894	3 657	2 423	1 654	325
Iowa	4 496	4 095	4 027	3 781	369	253	4 441	3 313	2 148	1 456	1 588	203	2 030	1 289	771	230
Kansas	4 022	3 818	3 559	3 439	463	379	3 979	2 669	1 931	1 401	1 377	255	1 700	1 021	588	208
Kentucky	6 187	5 789	5 649	5 286	284	223	6 489	4 261	3 066	1 784	2 075	285	3 355	2 044	1 541	192
Louisiana	5 913	5 311	5 913	5 090	–	318	4 906	4 087	2 559	1 622	1 160	328	4 734	2 658	2 588	256
Maine	1 816	1 723	1 769	1 682	17	13	1 897	1 561	936	658	709	71	1 389	762	642	86
Maryland	7 581	7 396	7 374	7 383	207	13	8 167	6 450	3 555	2 000	3 485	331	3 544	2 350	1 303	315
Massachusetts	19 090	18 054	17 735	16 881	[7]1 194	[7]1 172	12 455	9 369	3 888	2 610	6 707	1 228	6 813	3 857	2 546	1 005
Michigan	8 345	8 673	8 345	8 673	–	–	19 129	11 343	8 324	6 587	5 868	2 190	7 194	4 751	3 119	441
Minnesota	11 274	10 421	9 644	9 078	1 630	[7]1 343	10 243	6 829	4 492	2 900	4 136	703	3 535	2 366	1 580	242
Mississippi	2 917	2 816	2 850	2 731	67	86	3 861	2 397	2 602	1 832	742	202	2 754	1 595	1 264	182
Missouri	6 716	6 285	6 590	5 822	126	464	7 210	4 939	3 451	2 465	2 741	426	4 091	2 177	1 822	324
Montana	1 023	1 017	998	985	23	30	1 256	775	269	–	383	76	964	591	291	178
Nebraska	2 226	2 005	1 870	1 758	271	248	2 369	1 513	1 225	815	840	127	1 232	779	449	143
Nevada	1 589	1 393	1 552	1 257	108	159	2 889	1 597	2 435	1 572	–	–	876	442	264	106
New Hampshire	893	808	847	852	-1	-44	837	602	429	–	52	180	890	427	391	78
New Jersey	16 661	16 234	15 843	15 532	[7]1 108	[7]867	14 385	10 425	7 364	4 318	4 734	1 155	6 506	3 977	2 782	514
New Mexico	3 194	2 937	2 975	2 773	[7]212	[7]144	3 061	2 016	1 736	1 284	643	163	1 942	959	709	167
New York	33 330	33 331	32 897	32 679	[7]433	[7]287	34 150	28 615	11 914	6 963	17 399	2 730	24 560	15 761	12 875	980
North Carolina	11 226	10 411	10 467	9 685	319	291	11 882	7 865	5 144	2 971	4 929	939	5 227	2 942	2 591	265
North Dakota	767	699	685	651	[7]82	48	985	694	560	282	152	74	734	471	220	94
Ohio	17 504	16 645	16 404	15 858	149	251	15 649	11 436	7 604	4 991	5 903	807	8 776	5 388	3 971	687
Oklahoma	4 105	3 838	3 880	3 549	225	289	4 618	3 472	1 870	1 210	1 512	164	2 435	1 568	882	211
Oregon	4 697	4 060	3 902	3 531	794	529	4 416	2 782	591	–	2 823	300	2 797	1 708	987	214
Pennsylvania	17 058	16 347	16 548	16 279	403	156	18 295	13 220	8 758	5 701	5 214	1 504	10 117	6 125	4 333	686
Rhode Island	1 816	1 714	1 760	1 714	56	–	1 549	1 233	778	465	581	87	1 176	773	469	117
South Carolina	5 187	4 935	4 613	4 336	[7]574	[7]599	5 113	3 934	2 604	1 919	1 813	251	3 032	1 892	1 482	207
South Dakota	649	631	639	616	–	–	730	505	572	383	–	38	867	511	227	138
Tennessee	5 794	5 471	5 640	5 326	[7]153	[7]125	6 185	4 245	4 744	3 537	114	534	4 476	2 717	2 202	348
Texas	27 229	26 682	24 850	24 636	2 379	2 046	21 271	14 717	17 235	10 811	–	–	13 297	6 889	6 031	1 074
Utah	3 082	2 793	3 011	2 595	71	197	2 914	1 777	1 471	1 170	1 139	177	1 446	838	470	143
Vermont	771	707	721	702	–	–	841	687	404	183	281	45	641	377	236	81
Virginia	8 616	7 759	8 361	7 655	255	104	8 900	6 827	3 589	1 996	4 301	363	3 403	2 237	1 137	340
Washington	9 615	9 175	9 113	8 619	502	556	10 586	7 423	7 868	6 182	–	–	4 152	2 568	1 640	332
West Virginia	2 640	2 539	2 457	2 338	149	158	2 771	2 230	1 452	797	751	235	2 088	1 009	941	156
Wisconsin	9 608	8 747	9 284	8 132	[7]327	[7]582	9 586	6 558	4 030	2 708	4 151	621	3 679	2 538	1 545	283
Wyoming	551	512	499	459	52	53	626	612	274	211	–	–	708	568	114	123

– Represents zero.
X Not applicable.

[1]Data subject to copyright, see below for source citation.
[2]Includes funds budgeted, adjustments, and balances from previous year.
[3]May or may not include budget stabilization fund transfers, depending on state accounting practices.
[4]Resources less expenditures.
[5]Includes amounts not shown separately.
[6]U.S. total includes American Samoa, Guam, Northern Marianas, Puerto Rico, Virgin Islands, and undistributed data.
[7]Ending balance is held in budget stabilization fund.

Source: State general fund–National Governors Association and the National Association of State Budget Offices, Washington, DC; Fiscal Survey of the States, December 1997, semiannual, (copyright); State government tax collection–U.S. Bureau of the Census, for 1996, Internet address <http://www.census.gov/govs/www/sttax96.html>, (revised January 1998 unpublished data); for 1990, State Government Tax Collection: 1992, GF/92-1, October 1994; Federal aid to state and local government–U.S. Bureau of the Census, for 1996, Federal Expenditures by State for Fiscal Year 1996, FES/96, April 1997, (revisions January 1998, unpublished data); for 1990, Federal Expenditures by State for Fiscal Year 1995, FES/95, June 1996.

Table A–51. States — **Federal Government**

Geographic area	Nonfarm employment (1,000)			Federal earnings (BEA) (mil dol)						Federal funds and grants						
				Civilian			Military			Total		Defense, 1996		Selected object categories, 1996 (mil dol)		
	1995	1994	1990	1995	1994	1990	1995	1994	1990	1996 (mil dol)	1990 (mil dol)	Percent	Per capita[1] (dollars)	Direct payments for individuals	Grants to state and local government	Salaries and wages
United States	2 976.0[2]	3 024.0[2]	3 263.0[2]	132 706	131 277	110 383	47 079	47 324	46 544	1 394 057[3]	1 002 703[3]	16.7[3]	863[3]	749 273[3]	227 572[3]	169 731[3]
Alabama	55.2	56.9	65.5	2 696	2 612	2 265	849	858	817	23 409	17 261	17.4	956	13 616	3 325	2 898
Alaska	17.5	18.5	18.7	794	799	671	619	642	634	4 341	3 227	33.7	2 409	1 021	1 051	1 327
Arizona	43.6	44.0	46.1	1 839	1 803	1 454	758	705	696	21 819	15 072	22.2	1 092	12 269	3 095	2 523
Arkansas	21.2	21.1	22.8	885	851	704	263	251	333	12 076	8 250	8.3	398	7 984	2 131	1 037
California	308.9	325.1	362.1	13 466	14 041	11 925	6 211	6 535	7 493	157 446	115 802	21.0	1 038	80 432	26 415	18 038
Colorado	57.0	58.7	57.2	2 508	2 463	1 935	1 090	1 102	1 010	20 009	14 586	25.5	1 337	8 814	2 410	3 235
Connecticut	23.9	24.0	26.4	1 113	1 062	918	350	347	424	17 915	14 739	18.7	1 022	9 692	3 080	1 418
Delaware	5.9	5.9	6.1	237	229	202	172	162	149	3 363	2 149	13.1	609	2 096	600	411
District of Columbia	203.1	211.1	216.4	11 825	11 570	9 070	717	710	624	22 475	17 353	11.1	4 591	2 596	2 578	11 304
Florida	119.4	119.7	125.0	5 237	5 066	4 214	2 654	2 705	2 956	79 166	51 359	16.0	880	53 349	8 442	7 660
Georgia	99.0	100.6	103.6	4 018	4 021	3 292	2 082	2 059	1 619	34 731	21 149	24.2	1 142	17 933	5 359	5 904
Hawaii	31.2	31.4	33.9	1 218	1 250	1 111	1 508	1 532	1 440	8 016	5 461	40.7	2 752	3 238	1 126	2 409
Idaho	13.1	13.3	13.1	526	528	397	157	160	161	5 476	3 888	8.8	406	2 865	887	630
Illinois	102.7	102.9	115.3	4 580	4 588	3 875	1 072	1 008	1 118	51 229	36 696	6.4	277	31 744	9 232	5 440
Indiana	42.1	42.8	47.7	1 843	1 900	1 567	252	300	328	24 215	16 915	10.6	441	15 096	3 657	1 970
Iowa	20.6	20.4	20.7	830	812	672	123	123	109	13 408	9 962	4.8	227	7 687	2 030	944
Kansas	29.4	29.1	29.2	1 207	1 173	925	751	798	680	12 347	9 538	15.1	725	7 054	1 700	1 700
Kentucky	40.1	41.0	45.3	1 556	1 535	1 319	1 060	1 054	854	19 618	13 524	13.0	655	11 289	3 355	2 442
Louisiana	35.6	35.8	38.4	1 496	1 471	1 242	780	789	845	22 117	15 116	10.9	556	12 575	4 735	2 084
Maine	13.6	14.3	19.3	607	604	628	180	205	270	6 808	4 925	19.5	1 068	3 654	1 389	722
Maryland	155.6	155.5	164.3	7 289	7 073	5 770	1 300	1 260	1 175	37 040	27 118	20.1	1 471	14 491	3 545	7 324
Massachusetts	57.9	58.7	63.6	2 629	2 581	2 161	397	422	490	36 456	29 778	15.6	933	18 731	6 814	2 857
Michigan	57.7	57.5	62.2	2 407	2 357	2 030	281	329	438	39 286	29 205	5.6	228	26 183	7 196	2 778
Minnesota	33.5	33.7	35.4	1 477	1 456	1 192	193	196	182	18 857	15 073	7.6	309	10 694	3 536	1 655
Mississippi	27.3	27.5	28.6	1 119	1 075	872	648	632	536	15 184	10 066	21.9	1 222	8 191	2 754	1 571
Missouri	63.8	66.2	72.3	2 650	2 666	2 355	566	537	536	35 094	24 258	30.9	2 021	15 667	4 091	3 185
Montana	13.2	13.5	13.8	525	527	419	162	157	146	4 973	3 345	14.3	451	2 416	964	632
Nebraska	16.2	16.8	18.2	619	624	548	367	349	456	7 595	6 092	14.3	659	4 216	1 232	1 031
Nevada	13.6	13.4	12.4	617	585	421	273	253	261	7 428	4 144	14.4	665	4 201	876	850
New Hampshire	7.9	7.7	8.8	357	338	294	42	43	96	5 001	3 559	16.7	719	2 842	890	448
New Jersey	70.4	71.3	80.9	3 321	3 352	2 958	522	504	583	38 346	28 322	10.8	520	23 889	6 507	3 556
New Mexico	31.1	31.3	31.8	1 355	1 306	1 017	523	490	444	12 073	8 640	15.6	1 097	4 429	1 942	1 686
New York	145.7	146.9	168.2	6 584	6 544	5 736	979	1 083	1 074	94 667	70 493	5.6	294	54 035	24 563	7 157
North Carolina	60.8	59.3	58.8	2 460	2 317	1 818	2 900	2 833	2 140	32 771	20 172	18.0	807	19 453	5 227	4 898
North Dakota	9.3	9.5	10.5	345	337	285	325	288	288	3 570	2 910	15.5	860	1 656	734	644
Ohio	90.6	89.5	97.1	3 922	3 787	3 222	638	639	664	50 143	37 920	10.3	463	31 166	8 778	4 612
Oklahoma	43.3	44.5	51.1	1 885	1 832	1 638	930	866	781	16 685	11 804	17.7	896	9 880	2 435	2 721
Oregon	30.3	30.6	33.9	1 333	1 348	1 132	140	143	131	14 173	9 826	5.2	230	8 798	2 797	1 410
Pennsylvania	125.8	129.1	143.2	5 414	5 352	4 796	609	677	675	64 166	45 424	9.8	521	40 973	10 118	5 625
Rhode Island	10.4	10.1	11.1	433	412	379	208	217	239	5 668	4 318	13.7	784	3 266	1 176	634
South Carolina	29.9	32.1	40.3	1 228	1 287	1 258	1 183	1 327	1 499	18 401	13 664	17.9	892	10 336	3 033	2 203
South Dakota	11.1	11.3	11.5	426	418	342	164	170	205	3 872	2 863	9.7	513	1 971	867	534
Tennessee	54.2	54.8	63.6	2 548	2 523	2 244	401	422	433	27 557	18 049	8.2	427	15 497	4 477	2 702
Texas	188.2	188.5	203.2	8 076	7 875	6 762	3 939	3 790	3 442	86 493	58 237	20.3	917	45 723	13 299	11 249
Utah	31.8	32.3	40.1	1 315	1 311	1 231	250	250	239	8 193	6 511	16.4	672	3 919	1 446	1 478
Vermont	5.5	5.5	5.8	225	215	177	41	42	34	2 775	1 772	11.7	550	1 485	641	270
Virginia	181.8	184.6	189.6	8 366	8 256	6 768	5 303	5 315	4 948	50 301	36 346	43.3	3 265	18 562	3 404	12 322
Washington	69.7	70.7	74.2	3 005	2 928	2 440	1 738	1 643	1 489	29 246	20 149	21.4	1 129	14 838	4 152	4 574
West Virginia	19.1	18.0	16.9	804	748	547	92	91	72	10 059	6 609	4.7	261	6 407	2 089	815
Wisconsin	29.8	29.9	31.2	1 200	1 183	954	187	193	179	19 958	14 928	5.1	196	12 925	3 679	1 377
Wyoming	7.4	7.4	7.6	290	284	233	129	118	107	2 515	1 855	13.0	681	1 195	708	395

[1]Based on resident population estimated as of July 1, 1996.
[2]National totals are derived independently and differ from the sum of the states.
[3]U.S. total includes American Samoa, Guam, Northern Marianas, Puerto Rico, Virgin Islands, and undistributed data.

Source: Employment–Louisiana Electronic Assistance Program, Internet site <http://leap.nlu.edu/bea/wwwhome.htm> (accessed 1 August 1997); Earnings–U.S. Bureau of Economic Analysis, Survey of Current Business, Volume 76, Number 10, October 1996; Federal funds and grants–U.S. Bureau of the Census, Federal Expenditures by State for Fiscal Year 1996, issued April 1997 FES/96, and unpublished data.

Table A–52. States — Social Security, Food Stamp, and School Lunch Programs

Geographic area	Social security benefits								Federal food stamp program				National school lunch program			
	Recipients (Dec 31) (1,000)				Payments (mil dol)				Participants (Sept 30) (1,000)		Federal cost (mil dol)		Participants[2] (1,000)		Federal cost (mil dol)	
	Total		Retired workers and dependents[1]		Total		Retired workers and dependents[1]									
	1995	1990	1995	1990	1995	1990	1995	1990	1996	1990	1996	1990	1996	1990	1996	1990
United States	42 372	38 889	29 529	27 800	327 510	244 024	221 607	169 931	25 485	20 036	22 387	14 153	25 929	24 019	4 529	3 098
Alabama	776	709	481	452	5 496	4 019	3 315	2 503	509	454	440	328	563	570	95	77
Alaska	45	34	28	22	323	204	203	132	46	25	54	25	48	39	13	8
Arizona	703	591	509	440	5 435	3 701	3 823	2 681	427	317	372	239	404	331	82	47
Arkansas	503	470	318	310	3 490	2 581	2 142	1 664	274	235	224	155	320	292	55	41
California	3 984	3 665	2 866	2 695	31 116	23 293	21 644	16 661	3 143	1 955	2 556	968	2 471	2 147	624	396
Colorado	495	422	340	300	3 694	2 551	2 439	1 754	244	221	210	156	315	282	45	31
Connecticut	566	527	427	408	4 817	3 649	3 570	2 774	223	133	175	72	240	231	36	23
Delaware	122	104	88	76	973	691	681	494	58	33	47	25	68	59	10	6
District of Columbia...........	78	77	54	55	528	430	351	295	93	62	95	43	50	47	14	10
Florida......................	2 984	2 653	2 244	2 043	23 031	16 648	16 769	12 431	1 371	781	1 296	609	1 213	1 110	263	158
Georgia	1 010	884	636	572	7 269	5 066	4 485	3 224	793	536	703	382	1 021	908	167	106
Hawaii	166	149	130	117	1 243	893	949	693	130	77	196	81	147	145	22	14
Idaho	178	157	128	116	1 326	953	918	681	80	59	61	40	142	131	20	14
Illinois	1 829	1 753	1 295	1 265	14 976	11 760	10 274	8 273	1 105	1 013	1 034	835	997	932	183	131
Indiana	962	913	672	645	7 748	5 929	5 247	4 088	390	311	330	226	604	635	72	54
Iowa........................	540	524	393	388	4 177	3 292	2 914	2 355	177	170	141	109	395	392	41	31
Kansas......................	434	407	313	303	3 418	2 625	2 396	1 900	172	142	135	96	319	302	41	29
Kentucky....................	712	646	420	403	5 026	3 656	2 853	2 198	478	458	414	334	517	498	82	61
Louisiana....................	702	652	412	391	4 923	3 689	2 771	2 146	670	727	597	549	683	694	128	104
Maine	237	215	163	155	1 683	1 246	1 127	866	131	94	113	63	104	108	16	11
Maryland....................	679	609	481	442	5 300	3 875	3 618	2 706	375	255	362	203	378	347	62	40
Massachusetts	1 049	970	748	727	8 230	6 224	5 692	4 521	374	347	295	207	487	454	72	44
Michigan	1 594	1 490	1 096	1 045	13 173	10 010	8 752	6 797	935	917	773	663	772	733	117	82
Minnesota...................	713	669	521	503	5 431	4 101	3 807	2 955	295	263	221	165	542	489	59	42
Mississippi..................	495	451	290	276	3 268	2 374	1 889	1 441	457	499	376	352	417	428	89	76
Missouri.....................	968	914	664	648	7 317	5 582	4 867	3 833	554	431	480	312	583	547	80	58
Montana	152	138	104	97	1 127	846	746	574	71	57	58	41	87	84	13	10
Nebraska....................	282	268	206	200	2 138	1 664	1 500	1 192	102	95	78	59	212	191	24	18
Nevada......................	229	168	169	127	1 785	1 049	1 271	767	97	50	91	41	98	67	18	8
New Hampshire..............	186	162	135	123	1 450	1 032	1 029	761	53	31	42	20	92	91	10	6
New Jersey	1 310	1 229	966	921	11 167	8 462	8 050	6 224	541	382	511	289	549	507	97	60
New Mexico	258	219	170	149	1 793	1 243	1 157	829	235	157	199	117	194	172	42	30
New York	2 972	2 832	2 112	2 077	24 446	19 034	16 991	13 692	2 099	1 548	2 054	1 086	1 713	1 546	344	232
North Carolina...............	1 232	1 075	819	739	8 934	6 250	5 842	4 207	631	419	551	282	777	749	127	91
North Dakota................	116	113	82	82	834	653	558	456	40	39	32	25	89	94	10	8
Ohio........................	1 913	1 803	1 308	1 253	15 153	11 616	9 902	7 763	1 045	1 089	935	861	1 006	919	139	109
Oklahoma...................	575	532	393	375	4 226	3 165	2 786	2 151	354	267	308	186	376	362	66	46
Oregon	544	492	403	374	4 266	3 170	3 057	2 339	288	216	259	168	254	234	40	26
Pennsylvania................	2 332	2 237	1 694	1 641	18 795	14 677	13 080	10 351	1 124	952	983	661	1 019	990	150	102
Rhode Island................	190	181	140	137	1 478	1 150	1 067	855	91	64	78	42	60	60	13	7
South Carolina..............	625	541	404	359	4 506	3 117	2 876	2 053	358	299	299	240	463	451	83	60
South Dakota...............	136	128	95	93	959	739	648	514	49	50	41	35	108	102	15	12
Tennessee..................	926	825	588	547	6 672	4 763	4 136	3 088	638	527	542	372	623	590	93	68
Texas.......................	2 470	2 193	1 652	1 505	18 151	13 030	11 712	8 672	2 372	1 880	2 140	1 429	2 252	2 003	452	304
Utah........................	224	192	160	140	1 692	1 175	1 183	848	110	99	87	71	251	233	33	24
Vermont	98	88	68	63	738	542	500	379	56	38	44	22	52	47	7	4
Virginia	949	834	642	577	6 992	4 928	4 569	3 302	538	346	451	247	634	586	89	60
Washington	793	714	578	534	6 334	4 633	4 478	3 367	476	340	426	229	441	361	73	43
West Virginia................	384	370	231	228	2 903	2 247	1 658	1 330	300	262	252	192	206	198	33	29
Wisconsin...................	884	838	643	619	7 015	5 409	4 940	3 877	283	286	198	180	512	468	62	45
Wyoming....................	71	62	50	44	545	388	375	274	33	28	28	21	58	57	7	5

[1]Includes benefits for persons aged 72 and over not insured under regular or transitional provisions of Social Security Act.
[2]Data cover public and private elementary and secondary schools and residential child care institutions.

Source: Social security benefits–Social Security Administration, Social Security Bulletin, quarterly; Food stamp and national school lunch programs–U.S. Department of Agriculture, Food and Consumer Service, Annual Historical Review of FNS Programs, and unpublished data.

Table A–53. States — **Social Welfare Programs and Workers' Compensation**

Geographic area	Public aid recipients as percent of population[1]		Supplemental security income				Aid to families with dependent children				State unemployment insurance				Workers' compensation payments (mil dol)	
			Recipients (June) (1,000)		Annual payments (mil dol)		Recipients (Dec) (1,000)		Annual payments (mil dol)		Beneficiaries, first payments (1,000)		Benefits paid (mil dol)			
	1994	1990	1995	1990	1995	1990	1994	1990	1994	1990	1995	1994	1995	1994	1995	1990
United States	7.7	6.5	6 430	4 703	27 035	16 133	13 790	11 958	22 777	18 995	7 903	7 822	19 891	20 185	[2]40 410	35,344
Alabama	6.8	6.5	[3]164	[3]132	[3]600	[3]351	124	132	92	63	149	137	178	174	[4]516	444
Alaska	7.5	4.6	[3]37	[3]35	[3]27	[3]14	37	24	113	62	47	47	114	114	106	113
Arizona	6.5	4.7	371	343	[3]288	[3]139	198	144	268	146	74	76	150	157	386	371
Arkansas	6.6	6.3	95	75	326	187	66	73	58	57	89	81	156	146	159	229
California	11.7	9.4	1 023	845	5 391	4 278	2 682	2 023	6 113	5 107	1 224	1 311	2 964	3 261	[4]7 177	6 065
Colorado	4.7	4.3	356	337	[3]217	[3]110	115	109	158	138	71	73	179	180	584	595
Connecticut	6.4	4.7	[3]44	331	[3]181	[3]96	171	135	397	309	142	143	435	486	[4]733	694
Delaware	5.2	4.4	11	8	40	22	26	22	40	30	24	23	60	59	[4]103	75
District of Columbia	16.6	10.9	20	16	83	54	75	54	127	87	24	24	94	91	113	86
Florida	6.8	4.6	[5]329	216	[5]1 300	653	645	420	826	443	271	285	635	684	2 518	1 976
Georgia	8.2	7.1	197	158	692	415	390	320	430	333	192	188	270	252	699	735
Hawaii	6.9	5.2	18	14	82	51	65	44	163	100	48	41	180	172	326	216
Idaho	3.4	2.7	[3]16	[3]10	[3]63	[3]29	24	17	30	20	48	45	92	78	148	105
Illinois	8.3	7.1	[3]265	[3]171	[3]1 160	[3]593	713	656	932	868	338	321	1 076	1 044	1 438	1 607
Indiana	5.2	3.9	[3]88	359	[3]348	[3]174	203	164	229	174	121	106	224	217	361	350
Iowa	5.4	4.7	42	32	148	86	105	96	169	154	78	71	153	143	233	231
Kansas	4.7	4.1	37	24	141	65	82	77	124	103	59	60	137	144	[4]280	266
Kentucky	9.3	7.9	[3]161	[3]113	[3]635	[3]337	195	204	199	185	123	164	211	215	498	383
Louisiana	9.7	9.8	181	131	717	378	260	279	169	188	82	82	138	146	516	575
Maine	7.4	6.6	30	23	96	56	61	62	107	104	50	51	102	103	286	380
Maryland	5.9	5.1	[5]81	59	[5]332	185	227	198	313	304	117	119	331	325	522	505
Massachusetts	7.5	6.4	161	117	700	397	288	282	730	647	203	212	732	787	[4]773	1 235
Michigan	9.1	8.6	209	139	896	483	619	684	1 136	1 232	365	324	843	829	[4]1 585	1 205
Minnesota	5.4	4.9	[3]62	[3]39	[3]235	[3]110	169	177	379	355	116	115	328	338	[4]733	582
Mississippi	10.9	11.4	141	113	504	300	147	176	82	86	74	58	112	90	[4]218	198
Missouri	7.1	5.8	[3]112	[3]84	[3]431	[3]237	260	218	287	237	146	145	272	303	733	496
Montana	5.6	4.9	14	10	53	29	34	29	49	40	28	27	53	53	151	150
Nebraska	4.0	3.7	[3]21	[3]15	[3]76	[3]42	42	44	62	60	27	27	44	40	141	137
Nevada	3.8	2.9	20	11	79	33	41	25	48	28	55	52	143	127	365	339
New Hampshire	3.5	2.2	[3]10	[3]7	[3]39	[3]19	29	21	62	35	22	25	35	41	169	169
New Jersey	6.0	5.3	142	102	594	340	324	323	524	459	307	298	1 254	1 201	[4]972	844
New Mexico	8.7	5.8	[3]44	[3]30	[3]166	[3]90	105	67	144	66	28	28	65	62	145	228
New York	10.0	7.7	577	400	2 724	1 557	1 273	1 031	2 993	2 337	583	581	1 988	2 000	[4]2 780	1 752
North Carolina	7.2	5.6	[3]187	[3]146	[3]639	[3]403	322	255	356	257	233	190	316	262	495	480
North Dakota	3.9	3.6	[3]9	[3]8	[3]29	[3]18	15	16	26	24	15	14	30	27	71	60
Ohio	8.1	7.3	244	152	1 044	483	634	657	940	896	259	255	648	690	2 303	1 960
Oklahoma	6.2	5.6	[3]74	[3]60	[3]266	[3]158	127	129	166	135	48	48	100	106	580	369
Oregon	5.1	4.3	[3]46	[3]31	[3]183	[3]95	107	99	197	150	138	138	340	330	463	573
Pennsylvania	7.2	6.0	260	186	1 159	635	611	549	927	827	479	470	1 476	1 458	[4]2 663	2 019
Rhode Island	8.6	6.4	24	17	100	53	63	52	136	104	57	57	182	175	138	219
South Carolina	6.7	5.8	[3]110	[3]90	[3]384	[3]234	133	118	115	97	109	100	171	174	[4]353	277
South Dakota	4.4	4.2	14	10	47	26	18	19	25	22	8	8	13	12	63	56
Tennessee	9.0	7.2	177	138	648	384	281	230	216	176	168	154	256	242	400	463
Texas	6.3	5.4	[6]400	[6]288	[6]1 391	[6]755	794	673	544	431	366	375	931	975	[4]2 006	2 896
Utah	3.6	3.3	20	12	80	38	48	47	77	65	30	31	59	62	140	187
Vermont	7.0	5.7	13	10	50	31	27	25	65	51	23	23	47	50	65	61
Virginia	4.8	3.9	[3]128	[3]94	[3]471	[3]257	190	158	253	181	120	114	201	214	65	61
Washington	7.1	6.0	91	60	398	208	289	237	612	447	237	242	794	822	557	507
West Virginia	9.6	8.9	[6]66	[6]46	[6]276	[6]146	109	109	126	112	61	57	133	125	1 129	883
Wisconsin	6.5	6.6	111	84	487	288	214	236	423	441	213	192	417	376	529	389
Wyoming	4.5	3.8	[3]6	[3]3	[3]21	[3]9	15	16	21	20	13	12	29	25	75	49

[1]Total SSI and AFDC recipients as of June as a percentage of resident population estimated as of July 1 for 1994 and enumerated as of April 1 for 1990.
[2]Total includes an amount for benefits under deductible provisions not distributed by all states.
[3]Data for persons with federal SSI payments only; state has state-administered supplementation.
[4]Includes benefits under deductible provisions.
[5]Data for federal SSI payments and federally-administered state supplementation only; state also has state-administered supplementation.
[6]Data for persons with federal SSI payments only; state supplementary payments not made.

Source: Public aid recipients–Compiled by the U.S. Bureau of the Census. Data from U.S. Social Security Administration, Social Security Bulletin, quarterly, and U.S. Administration for Children and Families, Quarterly Public Assistance Statistics, annual; Supplemental security income–U.S. Social Security Administration, Social Security Bulletin, quarterly, and Annual Statistical Supplement to the Social Security Bulletin; State unemployment insurance–U.S. Employment and Training Administration, Unemployment Insurance Financial Handbook, annual; Workers' compensation payments–U.S. Social Security Administration, Social Security Bulletin, summer 1995, and prior issues, beginning 1995, Jack Schmulowitz, Baltimore, MD, unpublished data.

Geographic area	Medicare								Medicaid							
	1996		1995		1994		1990		1995		1994		1993		1990	
	Enroll-ment[1] (1,000)	Pay-ments[2] (mil dol)	Enroll-ment[1] (1,000)	Pay-ments[2] (mil dol)	Enroll-ment[1] (1,000)	Pay-ments[2] (mil dol)	Enroll-ment[1] (1,000)	Pay-ments[2] (mil dol)	Recipi-ents[3] (1,000)	Pay-ments[4] (mil dol)	Recipi-ents[3] (1,000)	Pay-ments[4] (mil dol)	Recipi-ents[3] (1,000)	Pay-ments[4] (mil dol)	Recipi-ents[3] (1,000)	Pay-ments[4] (mil dol)
United States	37 169	190 187	36 703	175 976	36 102	158 517	33 498	108 150	35 210	119 885	34 110	108 029	32 664	101 547	24 014	64 709
Alabama	651	3 349	641	3 042	630	2 717	582	1 854	539	1 455	544	1 312	522	1 192	352	609
Alaska	35	156	34	133	32	111	25	89	68	252	69	243	65	217	39	139
Arizona	614	2 950	597	2 717	577	2 483	498	1 565	494	218	510	199	404	212	X	X
Arkansas....................	427	1 749	422	1 638	416	1 455	391	1 125	353	1 376	340	1 253	339	998	264	599
California	3 690	21 688	3 633	20 406	3 562	18 938	3 279	11 751	5 017	10 521	5 008	9 988	4 834	9 650	3 624	6 507
Colorado....................	432	2 022	421	1 835	409	1 635	358	926	294	1 063	289	952	281	911	191	516
Connecticut	506	2 811	502	2 584	497	2 314	469	1 511	380	2 125	354	1 943	334	1 825	250	1 205
Delaware	103	474	100	445	98	452	88	282	79	324	75	277	69	252	41	123
District of Columbia...........	77	1 207	78	1 164	79	1 135	78	398	138	532	127	550	120	555	93	246
Florida	2 655	16 046	2 610	14 828	2 554	13 733	2 339	7 677	1 735	4 802	1 727	4 266	1 745	4 131	1 038	2 361
Georgia	849	4 444	832	4 090	811	3 629	732	2 347	1 147	3 076	1 085	2 845	955	2 441	651	2 076
Hawaii	153	612	149	580	146	532	127	262	52	258	121	338	110	293	85	191
Idaho	153	523	150	463	146	401	132	323	115	360	110	331	100	301	55	162
Illinois	1 623	7 792	1 617	7 276	1 606	6 617	1 534	4 770	1 552	5 600	1 441	4 826	1 396	4 625	1 067	2 424
Indiana	830	3 770	823	3 491	813	3 153	762	2 249	559	1 878	605	2 250	565	2 354	347	1 343
Iowa........................	475	1 642	474	1 527	472	1 407	457	1 183	304	1 036	303	982	289	896	240	620
Kansas	385	1 631	383	1 545	380	1 536	363	1 040	256	831	252	782	243	702	194	491
Kentucky....................	596	2 610	586	2 401	575	2 177	534	1 582	641	1 945	638	1 779	618	1 707	468	977
Louisiana	586	3 938	580	3 448	572	2 953	531	1 984	785	2 708	778	2 684	751	2 873	585	1 315
Maine	205	791	202	707	198	625	183	501	153	760	177	807	169	713	133	432
Maryland	610	3 005	601	2 868	591	2 707	541	2 177	414	2 019	415	1 875	445	1 721	330	1 090
Massachusetts	942	5 884	933	5 496	923	4 958	867	3 152	728	3 972	710	3 052	765	2 726	591	2 730
Michigan	1 361	6 566	1 348	6 237	1 329	5 634	1 233	4 618	1 168	3 409	1 187	3 274	1 172	3 077	1 048	2 195
Minnesota	636	2 593	631	2 378	623	2 172	588	1 314	473	2 550	426	1 982	425	1 930	380	1 410
Mississippi	402	2 016	397	1 723	390	1 477	366	1 096	520	1 266	537	1 090	504	896	433	586
Missouri	838	4 122	832	3 821	823	3 352	781	2 391	695	2 039	669	1 809	609	1 548	448	897
Montana	132	470	130	489	128	396	117	317	99	326	96	303	89	287	61	171
Nebraska	250	934	249	840	247	758	237	553	168	608	164	593	165	553	119	309
Nevada	202	1 004	192	894	182	810	141	437	105	350	95	307	88	301	47	149
New Hampshire..............	159	653	156	597	152	530	137	344	97	473	86	389	79	380	45	243
New Jersey	1 177	5 958	1 169	5 603	1 158	5 188	1 092	3 485	790	3 813	790	3 612	794	3 485	567	2 298
New Mexico	216	799	211	710	205	596	179	474	287	714	268	638	241	543	130	275
New York	2 653	14 860	2 639	13 904	2 618	12 565	2 509	9 619	3 035	22 086	2 908	18 731	2 742	17 557	2 329	11 877
North Carolina	1 049	4 689	1 025	4 276	999	3 679	892	2 326	1 084	3 175	985	2 685	898	2 452	563	1 426
North Dakota	103	438	103	412	102	373	98	257	61	297	63	284	62	273	49	194
Ohio........................	1 676	7 870	1 666	7 262	1 646	6 513	1 543	4 844	1 533	5 585	1 523	4 995	1 491	4 667	1 221	3 132
Oklahoma	492	2 472	487	2 178	479	1 793	451	1 346	394	1 055	391	974	387	1 043	273	688
Oregon	472	1 801	467	1 685	460	1 589	424	998	452	1 327	411	1 036	325	831	227	519
Pennsylvania	2 078	11 468	2 069	10 796	2 055	10 066	1 956	7 408	1 230	4 633	1 255	4 224	1 223	3 886	1 177	2 883
Rhode Island	169	867	168	772	166	703	159	489	135	673	115	685	191	710	171	442
South Carolina..............	520	2 144	508	1 926	495	1 697	442	1 126	496	1 438	486	1 396	470	1 249	317	743
South Dakota...............	117	447	117	563	116	357	110	272	74	305	72	284	70	264	49	166
Tennessee	783	4 487	770	4 083	753	3 664	692	2 231	1 466	2 772	939	1 965	909	1 977	613	1 163
Texas	2 117	12 733	2 076	11 504	2 024	9 386	1 824	6 027	2 562	6 565	2 514	6 141	2 308	5 575	1 442	2 781
Utah	191	813	187	708	182	630	160	429	160	464	157	451	148	408	108	247
Vermont	84	306	83	284	81	250	75	188	100	320	94	259	81	235	60	153
Virginia	833	3 277	817	2 979	798	2 700	722	2 140	681	1 833	643	1 723	576	1 623	379	985
Washington	699	2 826	687	2 603	671	2 277	615	1 650	639	1 461	668	1 574	633	1 537	448	952
West Virginia	331	1 373	329	1 208	325	1 100	308	844	389	1 169	367	1 107	347	1 056	250	361
Wisconsin	767	2 909	761	2 673	753	2 436	714	2 014	460	1 894	474	1 830	471	1 786	393	1 248
Wyoming....................	61	198	60	180	59	159	52	155	51	171	51	157	46	125	29	59

X Not applicable.

[1]Hospital and/or medical insurance enrollment as of September.
[2]Benefit payments for all areas represent 100% fee for service experience and actual HMO expenditures through the fiscal year and relate to the state of the provider.
[3]Persons who had payments made on their behalf at any time during the fiscal year.
[4]Payments are for fiscal year and reflect federal and state contribution payments. Data exclude disproportionate hospital share payments.

Source: U.S. Health Care Financing Administration, unpublished data.

Table A–55. States — Elections

Geographic area	Voting-age population (1,000)		Percent of voting-age population casting votes for President		Popular vote for President[1]						Votes cast for U.S. Senators[1]					
					1996			1992			1996			1994		
					Total[2] (1,000)	Percent of total		Total[2] (1,000)	Percent of total		Total[2] (1,000)	Percent of total		Total[2] (1,000)	Percent of total	
	1996	1992	1996	1992		Democratic	Republican		Democratic	Republican		Democratic	Republican		Democratic	Republican
United States	196 509	189 524	49.0	55.1	96 273	49.2	40.7	104 425	43.0	37.4	X	X	X	X	X	X
Alabama	3 218	3 080	47.7	54.8	1 534	43.2	50.1	1 688	40.9	47.6	1 499	45.7	51.9	X	X	X
Alaska	425	405	56.9	63.8	242	33.3	50.8	259	30.1	39.4	232	10.3	76.7	X	X	X
Arizona	3 094	2 812	45.4	52.9	1 404	46.5	44.3	1 487	36.5	38.5	X	X	X	1 119	39.5	53.7
Arkansas	1 860	1 774	47.5	53.6	884	53.7	36.8	951	53.2	35.4	846	47.3	52.7	X	X	X
California	23 133	22 521	43.3	49.4	10 019	51.1	38.2	11 132	46.0	32.6	X	X	X	8 503	46.8	44.8
Colorado	2 843	2 579	53.1	60.8	1 511	44.4	45.8	1 569	40.2	35.9	1 470	46.3	50.7	X	X	X
Connecticut	2 468	2 508	56.4	64.4	1 393	52.8	34.7	1 616	42.2	35.8	X	X	X	1 080	67.0	31.0
Delaware	547	521	49.5	55.6	271	51.8	36.6	290	43.4	35.2	276	60.0	38.1	199	42.5	55.8
District of Columbia...........	435	467	42.8	48.7	186	85.2	9.3	228	84.6	9.2	X	X	X	X	X	X
Florida	11 043	10 422	48.0	51.0	5 301	48.0	42.3	5 314	39.0	40.9	X	X	X	4 105	29.5	70.5
Georgia	5 396	5 006	42.6	46.4	2 299	45.8	47.0	2 321	43.5	42.9	2 259	48.8	47.6	X	X	X
Hawaii	882	866	40.8	43.1	360	56.9	31.6	373	48.0	36.7	X	X	X	357	71.8	24.2
Idaho	845	750	58.2	64.3	492	33.6	52.2	482	28.4	42.1	497	39.9	57.0	X	X	X
Illinois	8 764	8 598	49.2	58.7	4 311	54.3	36.8	5 050	48.6	34.3	4 246	55.8	41.0	X	X	X
Indiana	4 369	4 209	48.9	54.8	2 135	41.6	47.1	2 306	36.8	42.9	X	X	X	1 544	30.5	67.4
Iowa.....................	2 138	2 073	57.7	65.3	1 234	50.3	39.9	1 355	43.2	37.3	1 224	51.8	46.7	X	X	X
Kansas	1 898	1 840	56.6	62.9	1 074	36.1	54.3	1 157	33.7	38.9	[3]1 065	43.4	53.8	X	X	X
Kentucky	2 924	2 798	47.5	53.4	1 389	45.8	44.9	1 493	44.5	41.3	1 307	42.8	55.5	X	X	X
Louisiana	3 137	3 045	56.9	58.8	1 784	52.0	39.9	1 790	45.6	40.9	[4]1 700	50.2	49.8	X	X	X
Maine	939	932	64.5	72.9	606	51.6	30.8	679	38.7	30.5	607	43.9	49.2	511	36.4	60.3
Maryland.................	3 811	3 705	46.7	53.6	1 781	54.3	38.3	1 985	49.8	35.6	X	X	X	1 369	59.1	40.9
Massachusetts	4 623	4 616	55.3	60.1	2 556	61.5	28.1	2 774	47.5	29.0	2 556	52.2	44.7	2 179	58.1	41.0
Michigan	7 067	6 947	54.5	61.5	3 849	51.7	38.5	4 275	43.8	36.4	3 762	58.4	39.9	3 043	42.8	51.9
Minnesota	3 412	3 272	64.3	71.8	2 193	51.1	35.0	2 348	43.5	31.9	2 183	50.3	41.3	1 773	44.1	49.1
Mississippi	1 961	1 873	45.6	52.4	894	44.1	49.2	982	40.7	49.7	879	27.4	71.0	608	31.2	68.8
Missouri	3 980	3 851	54.2	62.1	2 158	47.5	41.2	2 392	44.1	33.9	X	X	X	1 775	35.7	59.7
Montana	647	600	62.9	68.4	407	41.3	44.1	411	37.7	35.0	407	49.6	44.7	350	37.6	62.4
Nebraska	1 208	1 164	56.0	63.4	677	35.0	53.7	738	29.4	46.6	677	41.7	56.1	579	54.8	45.0
Nevada..................	1 180	1 011	39.3	50.1	464	43.9	42.9	506	37.4	34.8	X	X	X	368	52.7	42.4
New Hampshire...............	860	838	58.0	64.2	499	49.3	39.4	538	38.8	37.5	493	46.2	49.2	X	X	X
New Jersey..............	6 005	5 964	51.2	56.1	3 076	53.7	35.9	3 344	42.9	40.6	2 883	52.7	42.6	2 055	50.3	47.0
New Mexico	1 210	1 121	46.0	50.8	556	49.2	41.9	570	46.0	37.4	552	29.8	64.7	463	54.0	46.0
New York	13 579	13 705	46.5	50.5	6 316	59.5	30.6	6 927	49.7	33.9	X	X	X	4 790	55.2	41.5
North Carolina	5 499	5 190	45.8	50.3	2 516	44.0	48.7	2 612	42.6	43.5	2 556	45.9	52.6	X	X	X
North Dakota	473	462	56.2	66.7	266	40.1	46.9	308	32.1	44.2	X	X	X	237	58.0	42.0
Ohio.....................	8 358	8 207	54.2	60.2	4 534	47.4	41.0	4 940	40.2	38.3	X	X	X	3 437	39.2	53.4
Oklahoma	2 419	2 352	49.9	59.1	1 207	40.4	48.3	1 390	34.0	42.7	1 183	40.1	56.7	982	40.0	55.2
Oregon	2 396	2 220	57.5	65.9	1 378	47.2	39.1	1 463	42.4	32.5	1 360	45.9	49.8	[5]1 190	[5]48.0	46.5
Pennsylvania	9 196	9 161	49.0	54.1	4 506	49.2	40.0	4 960	45.1	36.1	X	X	X	3 513	46.9	49.4
Rhode Island	750	768	52.0	59.0	390	59.7	26.8	453	47.0	29.1	363	63.5	35.1	345	35.5	64.5
South Carolina..............	2 777	2 669	41.4	45.1	1 151	44.0	49.8	1 203	39.9	48.0	1 161	44.0	53.4	X	X	X
South Dakota............	530	505	61.1	66.6	324	43.0	46.5	336	37.2	40.8	324	51.3	48.7	X	X	X
Tennessee	4 021	3 796	47.1	52.2	1 894	48.0	45.6	1 983	47.1	42.4	1 779	36.8	61.4	[6]1 480	42.1	[6]56.4
Texas	13 622	12 681	41.2	48.5	5 612	43.8	48.8	6 154	37.1	40.6	5 527	43.9	54.8	4 280	38.3	60.8
Utah	1 323	1 169	50.3	63.6	666	33.3	54.4	744	24.6	43.4	X	X	X	519	28.3	68.8
Vermont	441	429	58.5	67.5	258	53.4	31.1	290	46.2	30.3	X	X	X	212	40.6	50.3
Virginia	5 089	4 855	47.5	52.7	2 417	45.1	47.1	2 559	40.6	45.0	2 355	47.4	52.5	2 057	45.6	42.9
Washington	4 122	3 812	54.7	60.0	2 254	49.8	37.3	2 288	43.4	31.9	X	X	X	1 700	44.3	55.7
West Virginia	1 414	1 376	45.0	49.7	636	51.5	36.8	684	48.4	35.4	596	76.6	23.4	421	69.0	31.0
Wisconsin................	3 824	3 675	57.4	68.9	2 196	48.8	38.5	2 531	41.1	36.8	X	X	X	1 565	58.3	40.7
Wyoming................	352	329	60.2	61.0	212	36.8	49.8	201	33.8	39.3	211	42.2	54.1	202	39.3	58.9

X Not applicable.

[1]Data are subject to copyright, see below for source citation.
[2]Includes votes cast for minor parties.
[3]Kansas had elections to fill two Senate seats in 1996. Pat Roberts was elected to fill the full-term seat vacated by the retiring Nancy Kassenbaum. Sam Brownback was elected to fill the short-term seat vacated by Robert Dole, who resigned in 1996 to run for president.
[4]Louisiana holds an open-primary election with candidates from all parties running on the same ballot. Any candidate who receives a majority is elected.
[5]Special election in January 1996 to fill the unexpired term of Senator Packwood.
[6]In a special election in 1994 to fill an unexpired term, the Republican candidate received 60.4 percent of 1,465,835 total votes cast.

Source: Voting-age population–For 1996, Statistical Brief (SB/96-2) and for 1992, U.S. Bureau of the Census, Current Population Reports, P25-1117; Votes cast for president–Election Research Center, Chevy Chase, MD, America Votes, biennial, for 1996, Congressional Quarterly, Inc., Washington, DC, America Votes, biennial (copyright); Votes cast for U.S. Senators, 1994–Congressional Quarterly, Inc., Washington, DC, America Votes, biennial, for 1996, Congressional Quarterly, Inc., Washington, DC, Congressional Quarterly Weekly Report, Volume 55, No. 7, February 15, 1997 (copyright).

Table A–56. States — Composition of Congress, Governors, and State Legislatures

Geographic area	Composition of 104th Congress[1], 1997 Senate[2] Democratic	Senate[2] Republican	House of Representatives[3] Democratic	House of Representatives[3] Republican	Votes cast for Governor[4] 1996 Total[5]	1996 Percent for leading party	1994 Total[5]	1994 Percent for leading party	Composition of state legislatures[4], 1996 Lower House[6] Democratic	Lower House[6] Republican	Upper House[7] Democratic	Upper House[7] Republican	Black elected officials, 1993[4]	Hispanic public officials, 1994	Women holding state public offices[4][8], 1996
United States	46	53	197	236	X	X	X	X	2 886	2 539	998	931	7 984	5 459	80
Alabama	1	1	4	3	X	X	1 202	R-50.3	72	33	22	12	699	–	3
Alaska	–	2	–	1	X	X	213	D-41.1	16	24	7	13	3	–	1
Arizona	–	2	1	5	X	X	1 129	R-52.5	22	38	12	18	15	341	3
Arkansas	2	–	2	2	X	X	717	D-59.8	86	13	28	6	380	2	2
California	2	–	25	26	X	X	8 659	R-55.2	43	37	25	15	273	796	2
Colorado	–	2	2	4	X	X	1 116	D-55.5	24	41	15	20	20	201	3
Connecticut	2	–	3	3	X	X	1 147	R-36.2	97	54	19	17	62	26	2
Delaware	1	1	–	1	271	D-69.5	X	X	14	27	13	8	23	1	4
District of Columbia	X	X	X	X	X	X	X	X	X	X	X	X	198	1	–
Florida	1	1	8	15	X	X	4 206	D-50.8	59	61	17	23	200	64	1
Georgia	1	1	3	8	X	X	1 545	D-51.1	106	74	34	22	545	–	1
Hawaii	2	–	2	–	X	X	369	D-36.6	39	12	23	2	–	–	1
Idaho	–	2	–	2	X	X	413	R-52.3	11	59	5	30	–	2	1
Illinois	2	–	10	10	X	X	3 107	R-63.9	60	58	28	31	465	881	2
Indiana	–	2	4	6	2 110	D-51.5	X	X	50	50	19	31	72	8	4
Iowa	1	1	–	5	X	X	997	R-56.8	46	54	21	29	11	–	1
Kansas	–	2	–	4	X	X	821	R-64.1	48	77	13	27	21	7	3
Kentucky	1	1	2	4	X	X	984	D-50.9	64	36	20	18	63	–	–
Louisiana	2	–	2	5	X	X	[9]1 550	[9]R-63.5	76	28	25	14	636	12	1
Maine	–	2	1	1	X	X	511	I-35.4	81	69	19	15	1	–	–
Maryland	2	–	4	4	X	X	1 410	D-50.2	100	41	32	15	140	2	1
Massachusetts	2	–	8	2	X	X	2 164	R-70.9	134	25	34	6	30	1	–
Michigan	1	1	9	7	X	X	3 088	R-61.5	58	52	16	22	333	8	2
Minnesota	1	1	6	2	X	X	1 766	R-62.0	70	64	42	24	16	3	3
Mississippi	–	2	3	2	X	X	819	R-55.6	86	33	34	18	751	–	–
Missouri	–	2	6	3	2 143	D-57.2	X	X	88	75	19	15	185	1	[10]2
Montana	1	1	1	–	405	R-79.6	X	X	35	65	16	34	–	2	1
Nebraska	2	–	–	3	X	X	580	D-73.0	(11)	(11)	(11)	(11)	6	3	1
Nevada	2	–	–	2	X	X	371	D-53.9	25	17	9	12	10	4	1
New Hampshire	–	2	–	2	497	D-57.2	312	R-69.9	143	255	9	15	2	–	–
New Jersey	2	–	5	8	X	X	X	X	30	50	16	24	211	37	1
New Mexico	1	1	1	2	X	X	468	R-49.8	42	28	25	17	3	716	2
New York	1	1	17	14	X	X	5 204	R-48.8	96	54	26	35	299	83	1
North Carolina	–	2	4	8	2 566	D-56.0	X	X	59	61	30	20	468	–	–
North Dakota	2	–	–	1	264	R-66.2	X	X	26	72	19	30	–	–	5
Ohio	1	1	6	13	X	X	3 346	R-71.8	39	60	12	21	219	4	2
Oklahoma	–	2	1	5	X	X	995	R-46.9	65	36	33	15	123	1	3
Oregon	–	1	3	2	X	X	1 221	D-50.9	29	31	10	20	10	5	1
Pennsylvania	–	2	11	10	X	X	3 585	R-45.4	99	104	20	30	158	8	2
Rhode Island	1	1	2	–	X	X	361	R-47.4	84	16	41	9	12	1	1
South Carolina	1	1	2	4	X	X	934	R-50.4	53	70	26	20	450	–	1
South Dakota	1	1	1	–	X	X	312	R-55.4	23	47	13	22	3	–	3
Tennessee	–	2	4	5	X	X	1 487	R-54.3	61	38	18	15	168	–	1
Texas	–	2	18	12	X	X	4 396	R-53.5	82	68	14	16	472	2 215	1
Utah	–	2	1	2	672	R-75.0	X	X	20	55	9	20	–	1	2
Vermont	1	1	–	–	255	D-70.6	212	D-68.7	89	57	17	13	2	–	1
Virginia	1	1	6	5	X	X	X	X	53	46	20	20	155	–	–
Washington	1	1	2	7	2 237	D-58.0	X	X	45	53	23	26	19	14	4
West Virginia	2	–	3	–	629	R-51.6	X	X	74	25	25	9	21	–	–
Wisconsin	2	–	3	6	X	X	1 563	R-67.3	47	52	17	16	30	2	2
Wyoming	–	2	–	1	X	X	201	R-58.7	17	43	9	21	1	3	2

X Not applicable.
R Republican; D Democrat.
– Represents zero.

[1]As of beginning of second session.
[2]Oregon had one vacancy.
[3]Vermont had one Independent-Socialist Representative. California had one vacancy.
[4]Data are subject to copyright, see below for source citation. See note below for terms of state legislatures.
[5]Includes minor party and scattered votes.
[6]Status as of July 1997. Excludes one Independent each for Alaska, California, Louisiana, Massachusetts, and Virginia; two independent for New Hampshire and 5 vacancies.
[7]Status as of July 1997. Excludes one independent in Maine, one independent in California, one vacancy in Georgia, two vacancies in Mississippi, and three vacancies in Minnesota.
[8]Excludes women elected to the judiciary, women appointed to state cabinet-level positions, women elected to executive posts by the legislature, and elected members of university Board of Trustees or board of education.
[9]Results of a runoff election in November 1995.
[10]Includes one official who was appointed to an elective position.
[11]Single chamber (unicameral body) of 49 members, elected without party designation.

Note: For state legislatures: members of both houses serve 4-year terms in Alabama, Louisiana, Maryland, and Mississippi. Upper House members serve 4-year terms; Lower House members serve 2-year terms in Alaska, Arkansas, California, Colorado, Delaware, Florida, Hawaii, Illinois, Indiana, Iowa, Kansas, Kentucky, Michigan, Minnesota, Missouri, Montana, Nevada, New Jersey, New Mexico, North Dakota, Ohio, Oklahoma, Oregon, Pennsylvania, South Carolina, Tennessee, Texas, Utah, Virginia, Washington, West Virginia, Wisconsin, and Wyoming. Members of both houses serve 2-year terms in Arizona, Connecticut, Georgia, Idaho, Maine, Massachusetts, New Hampshire, New York, North Carolina, Rhode Island, South Dakota, and Vermont.

Source: Composition of Congress–U.S. Congress, Joint Committee on Printing, Congressional Directory, biennial; and unpublished data. Vote Cast for Governor–Congressional Quarterly, Inc., Washington, DC, Congressional Quarterly Weekly Report, Volume 53, No. 15, April 15, 1995, and unpublished data (copyright). Composition of State Legislatures–National Conference of State Legislatures, Denver, CO, unpublished data, (copyright); Black Elected Officials–Joint Center for Political and Economic Studies, Washington, DC, Black Elected Officials: A National Roster, annual (copyright). Hispanic Public Officials–National Association of Latino Elected and Appointed Officials,Washington, DC, National Roster of Hispanic Elected Officials, annual. Women Holding State Public Office–Center for the American Woman and Politics, Eagleton Institute of Politics, Rutgers University, New Brunswick, NJ, information releases (copyright).

Metro Areas

[MSA = Metropolitan statistical area. CMSA = Consolidated MSA. PMSA = Primary MSA. NECMA = New England county metropolitan area. All areas defined as of June 30, 1996. Table includes 245 MSAs, 17 CMSAs, and 58 PMSAs not in New England; as well as 12 NECMAs. Table excludes 10 MSAs, 1 CMSA, and 15 PMSAs in New England]

Metro-politan area code[1]	Metropolitan areas	Land area,[2] 1990 (sq miles)	Population 1997 (July 1) Total persons	Rank[3]	Per square mile[4]	1996 (July 1)	1990[5] (April 1)	1980 (April 1)	Net change, 1990–1997 Total[6]	Natural change[7]	Net inter-national migration	Percent change 1990–1997 Percent	Rank[3]	1980–1990
0040	Abilene, TX MSA	915.7	121 456	232	132.6	121 404	119 655	110 932	1 801	7 301	1 423	1.5	223	7.9
0120	Albany, GA MSA	685.5	117 674	237	171.7	117 074	112 571	112 394	5 103	6 963	227	4.5	182	.2
0160	Albany-Schenectady-Troy, NY MSA	3 222.4	876 420	54	272.0	879 051	861 623	824 729	14 797	25 517	8 127	1.7	221	4.5
0200	Albuquerque, NM MSA	5 943.5	674 837	62	113.5	668 507	589 131	[8]485 429	85 706	42 054	11 331	14.5	52	[8]21.4
0220	Alexandria, LA MSA	1 322.7	126 491	222	95.6	126 025	131 556	135 282	-5 065	4 909	660	-3.9	268	-2.8
0240	Allentown-Bethlehem-Easton, PA MSA	1 103.2	613 836	67	556.4	612 421	595 081	551 052	18 755	10 944	4 408	3.2	202	8.0
0280	Altoona, PA MSA	525.8	130 923	219	249.0	131 327	130 542	136 621	381	149	226	.3	237	-4.4
0320	Amarillo, TX MSA	1 823.9	208 165	156	114.1	206 321	187 514	173 699	20 651	11 540	3 775	11.0	73	8.0
0380	Anchorage, AK MSA	1 697.6	251 047	141	147.9	249 377	226 338	174 431	24 709	27 284	3 503	10.9	76	29.8
0450	Anniston, AL MSA	608.5	117 092	239	192.4	116 513	116 032	119 761	1 060	3 393	110	.9	228	-3.1
0460	Appleton-Oshkosh-Neenah, WI MSA	1 398.9	342 154	115	244.6	339 493	315 121	291 369	27 033	15 207	961	8.6	120	8.2
0480	Asheville, NC MSA	1 105.7	211 284	154	191.1	209 568	191 772	177 761	19 512	2 484	505	10.2	84	7.9
0500	Athens, GA MSA	591.0	138 523	209	234.4	136 932	126 262	104 672	12 261	6 738	1 200	9.7	96	20.6
0520	Atlanta, GA MSA	6 126.2	3 627 184	11	592.1	3 531 203	2 959 500	2 233 229	667 684	233 406	54 892	22.6	13	32.5
0600	Augusta-Aiken, GA-SC MSA	2 448.9	457 228	85	186.7	453 049	415 220	363 451	42 008	24 570	1 774	10.1	86	14.2
0640	Austin-San Marcos, TX MSA	4 226.0	1 071 023	42	253.4	1 040 709	846 227	585 051	224 796	74 578	21 583	26.6	8	44.6
0680	Bakersfield, CA MSA	8 141.6	628 605	64	77.2	621 719	544 981	403 089	83 624	59 828	23 106	15.3	47	35.2
0733	Bangor, ME NECMA	3 396.0	143 300	202	42.2	143 895	146 601	137 015	-3 301	2 991	225	-2.3	260	7.0
0743	Barnstable-Yarmouth, MA NECMA	395.8	205 128	158	518.3	202 339	186 605	147 925	18 523	-1 558	1 264	9.9	93	26.1
0760	Baton Rouge, LA MSA	1 586.6	570 165	71	359.4	566 114	528 261	494 151	41 904	35 822	3 217	7.9	126	6.9
0840	Beaumont-Port Arthur, TX MSA	2 154.4	374 991	105	174.1	374 440	361 218	373 211	13 773	14 850	3 657	3.8	193	-3.2
0860	Bellingham, WA MSA	2 120.1	154 249	191	72.8	152 217	127 780	106 701	26 469	6 011	3 238	20.7	20	19.8
0870	Benton Harbor, MI MSA	571.0	160 713	187	281.5	161 175	161 378	171 276	-665	5 229	711	-.4	243	-5.8
0880	Billings, MT MSA	2 635.2	125 771	223	47.7	125 514	113 419	108 035	12 352	4 934	189	10.9	77	5.0
0920	Biloxi-Gulfport-Pascagoula, MS MSA	1 784.5	343 423	114	192.4	341 166	312 368	300 176	31 055	16 772	857	9.9	92	4.1
0960	Binghamton, NY MSA	1 225.6	251 698	139	205.4	253 987	264 497	263 460	-12 799	6 602	3 982	-4.8	272	.4
1000	Birmingham, AL MSA	3 187.3	900 029	53	282.4	894 024	839 942	815 333	60 087	29 315	2 705	7.2	151	3.0
1010	Bismarck, ND MSA	3 559.6	91 044	262	25.6	90 162	83 831	79 988	7 213	3 865	388	8.6	118	4.8
1020	Bloomington, IN MSA	394.4	116 653	240	295.8	115 917	108 978	98 783	7 675	3 932	752	7.0	153	10.3
1040	Bloomington-Normal, IL MSA	1 183.6	140 797	205	119.0	139 577	129 180	119 149	11 617	6 820	684	9.0	111	8.4
1080	Boise City, ID MSA	1 644.8	383 843	103	233.4	372 816	295 851	256 881	87 992	23 260	3 893	29.7	4	15.2
1123	Boston-Worcester-Lawrence-Lowell-Brockton, MA-NH NECMA	6 450.0	5 827 654	7	903.5	5 788 380	5 685 763	5 336 242	141 891	241 159	104 750	2.5	207	6.5
1240	Brownsville-Harlingen-San Benito, TX MSA	905.6	320 801	118	354.2	313 835	260 120	209 727	60 681	41 271	21 254	23.3	12	24.0
1260	Bryan-College Station, TX MSA	585.8	133 008	216	227.1	131 494	121 862	93 588	11 146	9 465	3 024	9.1	106	30.2
1280	Buffalo-Niagara Falls, NY MSA	1 567.7	1 164 721	36	742.9	1 173 350	1 189 340	1 242 826	-24 619	27 208	7 675	-2.1	258	-4.3
1303	Burlington, VT NECMA	1 258.7	191 088	168	151.8	189 497	177 059	154 935	14 029	10 468	1 625	7.9	127	14.3
1320	Canton-Massillon, OH MSA	970.9	402 644	97	414.7	402 677	394 106	404 421	8 538	10 736	415	2.2	211	-2.6
1350	Casper, WY MSA	5 340.1	63 638	272	11.9	63 647	61 226	71 856	2 412	3 264	134	3.9	192	-14.8
1360	Cedar Rapids, IA MSA	717.5	181 704	171	253.2	179 941	168 767	169 775	12 937	9 418	1 220	7.7	135	-.6
1400	Champaign-Urbana, IL MSA	997.2	168 473	178	168.9	167 971	173 025	168 392	-4 552	9 097	1 702	-2.6	263	2.8
1440	Charleston-North Charleston, SC MSA	2 591.7	509 856	78	196.7	502 536	506 877	430 346	2 979	35 836	1 976	.6	234	17.8
1480	Charleston, WV MSA	1 249.5	253 850	137	203.2	254 390	250 454	269 595	3 396	3 720	686	1.4	225	-7.1
1520	Charlotte-Gastonia-Rock Hill, NC-SC MSA	3 378.4	1 350 243	32	399.7	1 318 718	1 162 140	971 447	188 103	63 220	9 939	16.2	40	19.6
1540	Charlottesville, VA MSA	1 177.1	146 617	198	124.6	144 599	131 373	113 568	15 244	5 420	1 396	11.6	67	15.7
1560	Chattanooga, TN-GA MSA	1 824.7	447 488	88	245.2	444 514	424 347	417 838	23 141	12 442	1 567	5.5	170	1.6
1580	Cheyenne, WY MSA	2 686.2	78 473	269	29.2	78 703	73 142	68 649	5 331	4 669	292	7.3	149	6.5
1602	Chicago-Gary-Kenosha, IL-IN-WI CMSA	6 930.5	8 642 175	3	1 247.0	8 590 176	8 239 820	8 114 844	402 355	551 711	258 603	4.9	175	1.5
1600	Chicago, IL PMSA	5 065.0	7 773 896	X	1 534.8	7 726 089	7 410 858	7 246 048	363 038	515 656	255 140	4.9	X	2.3
2960	Gary, IN PMSA	915.2	623 423	X	681.2	621 132	604 526	642 733	18 897	25 552	2 622	3.1	X	-5.9
3740	Kankakee, IL PMSA	677.5	101 984	X	150.5	101 560	96 255	102 926	5 729	3 962	541	6.0	X	-6.5
3800	Kenosha, WI PMSA	272.8	142 872	X	523.7	141 395	128 181	123 137	14 691	6 541	300	11.5	X	4.1
1620	Chico-Paradise, CA MSA	1 639.6	194 160	165	118.4	192 953	182 120	143 851	12 040	3 857	3 174	6.6	160	26.6
1642	Cincinnati-Hamilton, OH-KY-IN CMSA	3 809.6	1 934 145	23	507.7	1 919 010	1 817 569	1 726 430	116 576	87 121	6 470	6.4	163	5.3
1640	Cincinnati, OH-KY-IN PMSA	3 342.3	1 607 396	X	480.9	1 595 652	1 526 090	1 467 643	81 306	71 907	5 369	5.3	X	4.0
3200	Hamilton-Middletown, OH PMSA	467.3	326 749	X	699.2	323 358	291 479	258 787	35 270	15 214	1 101	12.1	X	12.6
1660	Clarksville-Hopkinsville, TN-KY MSA	1 260.6	197 481	162	156.7	194 103	169 439	150 220	28 042	16 941	553	16.5	38	12.8

X Not applicable.

[1]Federal Information Processing Standards (FIPS) codes for metropolitan areas defined as of June 30, 1996.
[2]Dry land and land temporarily or partially covered by water.
[3]Based on 273 metropolitan areas (245 MSAs, 17 CMSAs, and 11 NECMAs); see text for more information. When metropolitan areas share the same rank, the next lower rank is omitted.
[4]Based on 1990 land area.
[5]Includes count resolution corrections through December 1996.
[6]Includes net domestic migration, net federal movement, and residual not shown separately.
[7]Difference between the number of births and the number of deaths.
[8]1980 population based on 1990 boundaries.

Source: Land Area—U.S. Bureau of the Census, data file from Geography Division based on the TIGER/GICS computer file (related Internet site <http://www.census.gov/population/www/censusdata/density.html>); 1990–1997 Population—U.S. Bureau of the Census, "Estimates of the Population of Counties and Demographic Components of Population Change: April 1, 1990 to July 1, 1997" (CO-97-5) Internet site <http://www.census.gov/population/www/estimates/co_97_5.html> (accessed 30 March 1998); 1996 Population—U.S. Bureau of the Census, "Estimates of the Population of Counties, Annual Time Series, July 1, 1990 to July 1, 1997" (co-97-4) Internet site <http://www.census.gov/population/www/estimates/co_97_4.html> (accessed 30 March 1998); 1980 Population—U.S. Bureau of the Census, "1980–1990 Intercensal Population Estimates by County" on diskette.

Table B–1. Metro Areas — Area and Population—Con.

[MSA = Metropolitan statistical area. CMSA = Consolidated MSA. PMSA = Primary MSA. NECMA = New England county metropolitan area. All areas defined as of June 30, 1996. Table includes 245 MSAs, 17 CMSAs, and 58 PMSAs not in New England; as well as 12 NECMAs. Table excludes 10 MSAs, 1 CMSA, and 15 PMSAs in New England]

Metro-politan area code[1]	Metropolitan areas	Land area,[2] 1990 (sq miles)	1997 (July 1) Total persons	1997 (July 1) Rank[3]	1997 (July 1) Per square mile[4]	1996 (July 1)	1990[5] (April 1)	1980 (April 1)	Net change, 1990–1997 Total[6]	Net change, 1990–1997 Natural change[7]	Net change, 1990–1997 Net inter-national migration	Percent change 1990–1997 Percent	Percent change 1990–1997 Rank[3]	1980–1990
1692	Cleveland-Akron, OH CMSA	3 612.7	2 908 439	14	805.1	2 909 182	2 859 644	2 938 277	48 795	98 370	14 301	1.7	222	-2.7
0080	Akron, OH PMSA....................	905.2	682 442	X	753.9	679 586	657 575	660 328	24 867	24 451	2 164	3.8	X	-.4
1680	Cleveland-Lorain-Elyria, OH PMSA ..	2 707.5	2 225 997	X	822.2	2 229 596	2 202 069	2 277 949	23 928	73 919	12 137	1.1	X	-3.3
1720	Colorado Springs, CO MSA	2 126.7	480 041	80	225.7	472 393	397 014	309 424	83 027	38 100	1 821	20.9	19	28.3
1740	Columbia, MO MSA	685.4	128 309	221	187.2	125 943	112 379	100 376	15 930	7 113	1 110	14.2	53	12.0
1760	Columbia, SC MSA	1 457.3	503 948	79	345.8	497 671	453 932	409 953	50 016	25 546	1 977	11.0	72	10.7
1800	Columbus, GA-AL MSA	1 570.0	272 035	133	173.3	271 418	260 862	254 660	11 173	15 192	741	4.3	188	2.4
1840	Columbus, OH MSA	3 142.1	1 460 242	31	464.7	1 446 583	1 345 450	1 214 291	114 792	79 633	8 234	8.5	122	10.8
1880	Corpus Christi, TX MSA	1 527.7	387 100	101	253.4	382 754	349 894	326 228	37 206	27 593	4 060	10.6	79	7.3
1900	Cumberland, MD-WV MSA	753.1	99 122	258	131.6	100 107	101 643	107 782	-2 521	-1 095	238	-2.5	261	-5.7
1922	Dallas-Fort Worth, TX CMSA	9 104.7	4 683 013	9	514.4	4 565 324	4 037 282	3 046 136	645 731	350 476	137 762	16.0	41	32.5
1920	Dallas, TX PMSA....................	6 186.6	3 126 613	X	505.4	3 043 684	2 676 248	2 055 284	450 365	242 833	103 271	16.8	X	30.2
2800	Fort Worth-Arlington, TX PMSA	2 918.1	1 556 400	X	533.4	1 521 640	1 361 034	990 852	195 366	107 643	34 491	14.4	X	37.4
1950	Danville, VA MSA	1 014.0	108 602	248	107.1	108 958	108 728	111 789	-126	79	194	-.1	239	-2.7
1960	Davenport-Moline-Rock Island, IA-IL MSA	1 708.0	357 163	109	209.1	357 072	350 855	384 749	6 308	11 678	2 333	1.8	217	-8.8
2000	Dayton-Springfield, OH MSA	1 683.6	944 934	49	561.3	949 591	951 270	942 083	-6 336	34 724	3 257	-.7	245	1.0
2020	Daytona Beach, FL MSA	1 590.9	465 925	82	292.9	457 918	399 438	269 675	66 487	-4 817	5 986	16.6	36	48.1
2030	Decatur, AL MSA	1 275.6	141 690	204	111.1	140 579	131 556	120 401	10 134	5 267	208	7.7	133	9.3
2040	Decatur, IL MSA	580.6	114 265	242	196.8	115 310	117 206	131 375	-2 941	3 371	432	-2.5	262	-10.8
2082	Denver-Boulder-Greeley, CO CMSA	8 496.2	2 318 355	20	272.9	2 271 732	1 980 140	1 741 899	338 215	144 337	36 547	17.1	33	13.7
1125	Boulder-Longmont, CO PMSA	742.5	261 617	X	352.3	257 557	225 339	189 625	36 278	14 526	4 935	16.1	X	18.8
2080	Denver, CO PMSA	3 760.9	1 901 156	X	505.5	1 862 554	1 622 980	1 428 836	278 176	119 965	28 805	17.1	X	13.6
3060	Greeley, CO PMSA	3 992.8	155 582	X	39.0	151 621	131 821	123 438	23 761	9 846	2 807	18.0	X	6.8
2120	Des Moines, IA MSA	1 727.7	429 717	92	248.7	426 992	392 928	367 561	36 789	23 275	4 218	9.4	101	6.9
2162	Detroit-Ann Arbor-Flint, MI CMSA......	6 565.9	5 438 756	8	828.3	5 423 379	5 187 171	5 293 161	251 585	256 342	50 466	4.9	176	-2.0
0440	Ann Arbor, MI PMSA...............	2 029.1	539 415	X	265.8	530 735	490 058	454 977	49 357	27 834	5 556	10.1	X	7.7
2160	Detroit, MI PMSA..................	3 897.1	4 463 948	X	1 145.5	4 457 136	4 266 654	4 387 735	197 294	205 112	43 696	4.6	X	-2.8
2640	Flint, MI PMSA....................	639.7	435 393	X	680.6	435 508	430 459	450 449	4 934	23 396	1 214	1.1	X	-4.4
2180	Dothan, AL MSA	1 141.5	134 270	213	117.6	133 387	130 964	122 453	3 306	6 460	241	2.5	206	7.0
2190	Dover, DE MSA	590.7	122 709	226	207.7	121 752	110 993	98 219	11 716	6 808	615	10.6	80	13.0
2200	Dubuque, IA MSA	608.2	88 084	264	144.8	88 329	86 403	93 745	1 681	2 553	154	1.9	214	-7.8
2240	Duluth-Superior, MN-WI MSA	7 535.0	238 184	143	31.6	237 625	239 971	266 650	-1 787	-22	486	-.7	246	-10.0
2290	Eau Claire, WI MSA	1 648.2	143 486	201	87.1	142 804	137 543	130 932	5 943	4 528	358	4.3	187	5.0
2320	El Paso, TX MSA	1 013.1	701 576	60	692.5	685 018	591 610	479 899	109 966	87 348	62 298	18.6	26	23.3
2330	Elkhart-Goshen, IN MSA	463.8	170 725	176	368.1	168 811	156 198	137 330	14 527	10 361	1 083	9.3	103	13.7
2335	Elmira, NY MSA	408.2	93 088	260	228.0	93 596	95 195	97 656	-2 107	1 929	855	-2.2	259	-2.5
2340	Enid, OK MSA	1 058.5	56 699	273	53.6	56 878	56 735	62 820	-36	-36	206	-.1	238	-9.7
2360	Erie, PA MSA	802.0	279 401	132	348.4	280 027	275 572	279 780	3 829	9 576	1 407	1.4	224	-1.5
2400	Eugene-Springfield, OR MSA	4 554.2	311 356	123	68.4	306 529	282 912	275 226	28 444	8 599	1 933	10.1	90	2.8
2440	Evansville-Henderson, IN-KY MSA	1 467.4	288 929	129	196.9	288 004	278 990	276 252	9 939	7 399	658	3.6	196	1.0
2520	Fargo-Moorhead, ND-MN MSA	2 811.0	166 396	182	59.2	164 752	153 296	137 574	13 100	8 421	2 147	8.5	121	11.4
2560	Fayetteville, NC MSA	653.1	284 047	131	434.9	283 737	274 713	247 160	9 334	29 272	1 435	3.4	200	11.1
2580	Fayetteville-Springdale-Rogers, AR MSA	1 793.5	266 980	134	148.9	261 283	210 908	178 609	56 072	11 361	1 540	26.6	7	18.1
2620	Flagstaff, AZ-UT MSA	22 611.3	119 547	235	5.3	117 943	101 760	79 032	17 787	10 398	779	17.5	30	28.8
2650	Florence, AL MSA	1 264.1	137 288	210	108.6	136 749	131 327	135 065	5 961	2 775	292	4.5	181	-2.8
2655	Florence, SC MSA	799.2	124 379	224	155.6	123 224	114 344	110 163	10 035	4 314	258	8.8	117	3.8
2670	Fort Collins-Loveland, CO MSA	2 601.4	226 021	150	86.9	221 454	186 136	149 184	39 885	11 569	1 509	21.4	18	24.8
2700	Fort Myers-Cape Coral, FL MSA.......	803.6	387 091	102	481.7	380 919	335 113	205 266	51 978	1 004	4 689	15.5	45	63.3
2710	Fort Pierce-Port St. Lucie, FL MSA	1 128.2	295 646	128	262.1	289 731	251 071	151 196	44 575	2 048	6 387	17.8	29	66.1
2720	Fort Smith, AR-OK MSA	1 805.8	192 395	166	106.5	191 008	175 911	162 813	16 484	7 245	828	9.4	100	8.0
2750	Fort Walton Beach, FL MSA	935.8	167 580	180	179.1	165 633	143 777	109 920	23 803	10 295	714	16.6	37	30.8
2760	Fort Wayne, IN MSA	2 447.7	477 536	81	195.1	474 156	456 281	444 772	21 255	26 303	1 533	4.7	178	2.6
2840	Fresno, CA MSA	8 101.6	868 703	56	107.2	859 551	755 580	577 737	113 123	84 413	43 400	15.0	51	30.8
2880	Gadsden, AL MSA	534.8	104 313	250	195.1	102 327	99 840	103 057	4 473	727	127	4.5	183	-3.1
2900	Gainesville, FL MSA	874.3	198 326	161	226.8	197 429	181 596	151 369	16 730	9 476	3 122	9.2	104	20.0
2975	Glens Falls, NY MSA	1 705.2	122 582	227	71.9	122 409	118 539	109 649	4 043	3 213	770	3.4	198	8.1
2980	Goldsboro, NC MSA	552.6	111 981	244	202.6	111 801	104 666	97 054	7 315	4 875	444	7.0	154	7.8
2985	Grand Forks, ND-MN MSA	3 408.4	101 700	253	29.8	103 482	103 272	100 944	-1 572	5 362	554	-1.5	253	2.3

X Not applicable.

[1]Federal Information Processing Standards (FIPS) codes for metropolitan areas defined as of June 30, 1996.
[2]Dry land and land temporarily or partially covered by water.
[3]Based on 273 metropolitan areas (245 MSAs, 17 CMSAs, and 11 NECMAs); see text for more information. When metropolitan areas share the same rank, the next lower rank is omitted.
[4]Based on 1990 land area.
[5]Includes count resolution corrections through December 1996.
[6]Includes net domestic migration, net federal movement, and residual not shown separately.
[7]Difference between the number of births and the number of deaths.

Source: Land Area—U.S. Bureau of the Census, data file from Geography Division based on the TIGER/GICS computer file (related Internet site <http://www.census.gov/population/www/censusdata/density.html>); 1990–1997 Population—U.S. Bureau of the Census, "Estimates of the Population of Counties and Demographic Components of Population Change: April 1, 1990 to July 1, 1997" (CO-97-5) Internet site <http://www.census.gov/population/www/estimates/co_97_5.html> (accessed 30 March 1998); 1996 Population—U.S. Bureau of the Census, "Estimates of the Population of Counties, Annual Time Series, July 1, 1990 to July 1, 1997" (co-97-4) Internet site <http://www.census.gov/population/www/estimates/co_97_4.html> (accessed 30 March 1998); 1980 Population—U.S. Bureau of the Census, "1980–1990 Intercensal Population Estimates by County" on diskette.

Table B–1. Metro Areas — **Area and Population**—Con.

[MSA = Metropolitan statistical area. CMSA = Consolidated MSA. PMSA = Primary MSA. NECMA = New England county metropolitan area. All areas defined as of June 30, 1996. Table includes 245 MSAs, 17 CMSAs, and 58 PMSAs not in New England; as well as 12 NECMAs. Table excludes 10 MSAs, 1 CMSA, and 15 PMSAs in New England]

Metropolitan area code[1]	Metropolitan areas	Land area,[2] 1990 (sq miles)	Population						Net change, 1990–1997			Percent change		
			1997 (July 1)			1996 (July 1)	1990[5] (April 1)	1980 (April 1)	Total[6]	Natural change[7]	Net international migration	1990–1997		1980–1990
			Total persons	Rank[3]	Per square mile[4]							Percent	Rank[3]	
2995	Grand Junction, CO MSA	3 327.9	110 681	245	33.3	108 324	93 145	81 530	17 536	2 912	327	18.8	25	14.2
3000	Grand Rapids-Muskegon-Holland, MI MSA	2 758.6	1 026 295	46	372.0	1 015 273	937 891	840 824	88 404	64 009	6 851	9.4	97	11.5
3040	Great Falls, MT MSA	2 698.0	79 134	268	29.3	80 787	77 691	80 696	1 443	4 168	97	1.9	215	–3.7
3080	Green Bay, WI MSA	528.7	214 244	152	405.2	212 443	194 594	175 280	19 650	11 427	776	10.1	88	11.0
3120	Greensboro--Winston Salem--High Point, NC MSA	3 882.9	1 152 779	37	296.9	1 139 359	1 050 304	950 763	102 475	38 666	6 363	9.8	95	10.5
3150	Greenville, NC MSA	651.6	121 057	233	185.8	119 117	108 480	90 146	12 577	5 608	455	11.6	68	20.3
3160	Greenville-Spartanburg-Anderson, SC MSA	3 210.7	904 729	52	281.8	894 789	830 539	744 428	74 190	30 065	3 049	8.9	114	11.6
3240	Harrisburg-Lebanon-Carlisle, PA MSA	1 990.9	615 025	66	308.9	613 658	587 986	556 242	27 039	16 476	4 065	4.6	179	5.7
3283	Hartford, CT NECMA	1 514.9	1 105 174	39	729.5	1 106 322	1 123 678	1 051 606	–18 504	40 663	17 470	–1.6	254	6.9
3285	Hattiesburg, MS MSA	964.1	109 584	247	113.7	107 914	98 738	89 839	10 846	4 374	208	11.0	74	9.9
3290	Hickory-Morganton-Lenoir, NC MSA	1 638.7	318 368	120	194.3	314 378	292 405	270 457	25 963	10 969	1 192	8.9	116	8.1
3320	Honolulu, HI MSA	600.2	869 857	55	1 449.3	869 343	836 231	762 565	33 626	66 814	30 622	4.0	190	9.7
3350	Houma, LA MSA	2 339.9	191 227	167	81.7	189 386	182 842	176 876	8 385	11 613	405	4.6	180	3.4
3362	Houston-Galveston-Brazoria, TX CMSA	7 706.7	4 320 041	10	560.6	4 239 927	3 731 029	3 118 480	589 012	357 651	173 821	15.8	42	19.6
1145	Brazoria, TX PMSA	1 386.9	225 406	X	162.5	220 410	191 707	169 587	33 699	15 840	3 263	17.6	X	13.0
2920	Galveston-Texas City, TX PMSA	398.7	242 979	X	609.4	240 213	217 396	195 738	25 583	12 760	3 983	11.8	X	11.1
3360	Houston, TX PMSA	5 921.1	3 851 656	X	650.5	3 779 304	3 321 926	2 753 155	529 730	329 051	166 575	15.9	X	20.7
3400	Huntington-Ashland, WV-KY-OH MSA	2 159.8	315 204	122	145.9	315 973	312 529	336 410	2 675	3 263	393	.9	230	–7.1
3440	Huntsville, AL MSA	1 373.1	332 993	116	242.5	329 975	293 047	242 971	39 946	18 119	1 655	13.6	58	20.6
3480	Indianapolis, IN MSA	3 523.3	1 503 468	29	426.7	1 488 837	1 380 491	1 305 911	122 977	78 997	6 195	8.9	115	5.7
3500	Iowa City, IA MSA	614.5	102 318	252	166.5	101 589	96 119	81 717	6 199	6 306	1 256	6.4	162	17.6
3520	Jackson, MI MSA	706.6	155 346	189	219.8	154 448	149 756	151 495	5 590	5 659	299	3.7	194	–1.1
3560	Jackson, MS MSA	2 363.0	425 383	93	180.0	421 683	395 396	362 038	29 987	23 229	1 123	7.6	140	9.2
3580	Jackson, TN MSA	845.6	99 319	257	117.5	98 320	90 801	87 273	8 518	3 110	197	9.4	99	4.0
3600	Jacksonville, FL MSA	2 635.6	1 034 604	44	392.5	1 015 271	906 727	722 252	127 877	55 184	11 964	14.1	54	25.5
3605	Jacksonville, NC MSA	766.9	143 013	203	186.5	142 899	149 838	112 784	–6 825	19 025	437	–4.6	271	32.9
3610	Jamestown, NY MSA	1 062.1	140 015	207	131.8	141 110	141 895	146 925	–1 880	1 966	729	–1.3	250	–3.4
3620	Janesville-Beloit, WI MSA	720.5	150 332	194	208.6	149 958	139 510	139 420	10 822	5 946	386	7.8	132	.1
3660	Johnson City-Kingsport-Bristol, TN-VA MSA	2 865.5	460 147	84	160.6	456 957	436 047	433 638	24 100	4 264	1 135	5.5	169	.6
3680	Johnstown, PA MSA	1 762.9	237 674	144	134.8	239 138	241 280	264 506	–3 606	–919	496	–1.5	252	–8.8
3700	Jonesboro, AR MSA	710.8	76 932	270	108.2	76 099	68 956	63 239	7 976	2 909	173	11.6	69	9.0
3710	Joplin, MO MSA	1 266.3	147 127	196	116.2	145 668	134 910	127 513	12 217	4 086	425	9.1	110	5.8
3720	Kalamazoo-Battle Creek, MI MSA	1 881.8	446 699	90	237.4	444 389	429 453	420 771	17 246	19 254	1 736	4.0	190	2.1
3760	Kansas City, MO-KS MSA	5 406.8	1 709 273	24	316.1	1 688 301	1 582 874	1 449 380	126 399	79 810	11 442	8.0	125	9.2
3810	Killeen-Temple, TX MSA	2 110.9	299 740	126	142.0	298 765	255 299	214 587	44 441	29 748	2 166	17.4	32	19.0
3840	Knoxville, TN MSA	2 449.1	654 181	63	267.1	648 150	585 960	546 488	68 221	16 675	2 688	11.6	66	7.2
3850	Kokomo, IN MSA	553.5	99 981	256	180.6	100 250	96 946	103 715	3 035	3 862	303	3.1	203	–6.5
3870	La Crosse, WI-MN MSA	1 011.2	121 507	230	120.2	121 179	116 401	109 438	5 106	3 930	465	4.4	185	6.4
3880	Lafayette, LA MSA	2 593.8	372 027	106	143.4	368 149	345 053	330 786	26 974	22 343	1 060	7.8	130	4.3
3920	Lafayette, IN MSA	904.9	171 539	174	189.6	171 084	161 572	153 247	9 967	6 998	1 153	6.2	165	5.4
3960	Lake Charles, LA MSA	1 071.2	178 874	172	167.0	178 094	168 134	167 223	10 740	8 959	601	6.4	164	.5
3980	Lakeland-Winter Haven, FL MSA	1 874.9	448 646	87	239.3	441 966	405 382	321 652	43 264	12 517	5 618	10.7	78	26.0
4000	Lancaster, PA MSA	949.1	454 063	86	478.4	450 347	422 822	362 346	31 241	22 292	2 863	7.4	147	16.7
4040	Lansing-East Lansing, MI MSA	1 707.2	447 349	89	262.0	446 820	432 684	419 750	14 665	23 353	3 856	3.4	201	3.1
4080	Laredo, TX MSA	3 357.0	183 219	169	54.6	177 029	133 239	99 258	49 980	28 520	15 994	37.5	2	34.2
4100	Las Cruces, NM MSA	3 807.4	168 470	179	44.2	164 029	135 510	96 340	32 960	16 116	9 866	24.3	11	40.7
4120	Las Vegas, NV-AZ MSA	39 370.3	1 262 099	34	32.1	1 197 613	852 646	528 000	409 453	63 217	22 557	48.0	1	61.5
4150	Lawrence, KS MSA	457.0	91 093	261	199.3	89 674	81 798	67 640	9 295	4 480	874	11.4	71	20.9
4200	Lawton, OK MSA	1 069.4	113 957	243	106.6	114 954	111 486	112 456	2 471	9 630	359	2.2	209	–.9
4243	Lewiston-Auburn, ME NECMA	470.3	101 045	255	214.9	101 572	105 259	99 509	–4 214	2 239	–153	–4.0	269	5.8
4280	Lexington, KY MSA	1 920.0	444 073	91	231.3	439 719	405 936	370 900	38 137	19 809	2 450	9.4	98	9.4
4320	Lima, OH MSA	805.8	154 944	190	192.3	155 469	154 340	154 795	604	5 633	311	.4	236	–.3
4360	Lincoln, NE MSA	838.9	233 319	146	278.1	231 080	213 641	192 884	19 678	11 810	2 982	9.2	104	10.8
4400	Little Rock-North Little Rock, AR MSA	2 908.7	552 194	72	189.8	547 639	513 026	474 463	39 168	26 436	1 767	7.6	137	8.1
4420	Longview-Marshall, TX MSA	1 760.6	208 250	155	118.3	206 235	193 801	180 355	14 449	6 460	1 890	7.5	144	7.5

X Not applicable.

[1] Federal Information Processing Standards (FIPS) codes for metropolitan areas defined as of June 30, 1996.
[2] Dry land and land temporarily or partially covered by water.
[3] Based on 273 metropolitan areas (245 MSAs, 17 CMSAs, and 11 NECMAs); see text for more information. When metropolitan areas share the same rank, the next lower rank is omitted.
[4] Based on 1990 land area.
[5] Includes count resolution corrections through December 1996.
[6] Includes net domestic migration, net federal movement, and residual not shown separately.
[7] Difference between the number of births and the number of deaths.

Source: Land Area—U.S. Bureau of the Census, data file from Geography Division based on the TIGER/GICS computer file (related Internet site <http://www.census.gov/population/www/censusdata/density.html>);   1990–1997 Population—U.S. Bureau of the Census, "Estimates of the Population of Counties and Demographic Components of Population Change: April 1, 1990 to July 1, 1997" (CO-97-5) Internet site <http://www.census.gov/population/www/estimates/co_97_5.html> (accessed 30 March 1998);   1996 Population—U.S. Bureau of the Census, "Estimates of the Population of Counties, Annual Time Series, July 1, 1990 to July 1, 1997" (co-97-4) Internet site <http://www.census.gov/population/www/estimates/co_97_4.html> (accessed 30 March 1998);   1980 Population—U.S. Bureau of the Census, "1980–1990 Intercensal Population Estimates by County" on diskette.

[MSA = Metropolitan statistical area. CMSA = Consolidated MSA. PMSA = Primary MSA. NECMA = New England county metropolitan area. All areas defined as of June 30, 1996. Table includes 245 MSAs, 17 CMSAs, and 58 PMSAs not in New England; as well as 12 NECMAs. Table excludes 10 MSAs, 1 CMSA, and 15 PMSAs in New England]

Metro-politan area code[1]	Metropolitan areas	Land area,[2] 1990 (sq miles)	Population 1997 (July 1) Total persons	Rank[3]	Per square mile[4]	1996 (July 1)	1990[5] (April 1)	1980 (April 1)	Net change, 1990–1997 Total[6]	Natural change[7]	Net inter-national migration	Percent change 1990–1997 Percent	Rank[3]	1980–1990
4472	Los Angeles-Riverside-Orange, CA CMSA	33 966.0	15 608 886	2	459.5	15 426 907	14 531 529	11 497 548	1 077 357	1 487 406	1 027 717	7.4	146	26.4
4480	Los Angeles-Long Beach, CA PMSA	4 060.0	9 145 219	X	2 252.5	9 083 596	8 863 052	7 477 238	282 167	912 187	712 578	3.2	X	18.5
5945	Orange, CA PMSA	789.7	2 674 091	X	3 386.2	2 619 358	2 410 668	1 932 921	263 423	255 240	184 603	10.9	X	24.7
6780	Riverside-San Bernardino, CA PMSA	27 270.4	3 063 608	X	112.3	3 009 260	2 588 793	1 558 215	474 815	260 820	97 917	18.3	X	66.1
8735	Ventura, CA PMSA	1 845.9	725 968	X	393.3	714 693	669 016	529 174	56 952	59 159	32 619	8.5	X	26.4
4520	Louisville, KY-IN MSA	2 072.3	993 369	48	479.4	988 802	949 012	953 520	44 357	33 436	3 805	4.7	177	−.5
4600	Lubbock, TX MSA	899.6	230 672	148	256.4	231 399	222 636	211 651	8 036	15 311	2 089	3.6	195	5.2
4640	Lynchburg, VA MSA	1 790.8	207 426	157	115.8	205 578	193 928	182 207	13 498	4 338	577	7.0	155	6.4
4680	Macon, GA MSA	1 532.1	316 077	121	206.3	312 035	291 079	272 945	24 998	14 483	1 136	8.6	119	6.6
4720	Madison, WI MSA	1 202.2	397 511	98	330.7	394 487	367 085	323 545	30 426	20 031	3 171	8.3	123	13.5
4800	Mansfield, OH MSA	899.3	174 851	173	194.4	175 282	174 007	181 280	844	4 680	−21	.5	235	−4.0
4880	McAllen-Edinburg-Mission, TX MSA	1 569.1	510 922	77	325.6	494 890	383 545	283 323	127 377	73 247	41 389	33.2	3	35.4
4890	Medford-Ashland, OR MSA	2 785.4	170 960	175	61.4	168 392	146 387	132 456	24 573	3 515	1 357	16.8	35	10.5
4900	Melbourne-Titusville-Palm Bay, FL MSA	1 018.5	460 977	83	452.6	454 514	398 978	272 959	61 999	9 300	4 142	15.5	44	46.2
4920	Memphis, TN-AR-MS MSA	3 007.6	1 083 186	41	360.1	1 075 386	1 007 306	938 777	75 880	65 820	4 980	7.5	141	7.3
4940	Merced, CA MSA	1 928.9	196 123	163	101.7	193 039	178 403	134 558	17 720	21 939	10 799	9.9	93	32.6
4992	Miami-Fort Lauderdale, FL CMSA	3 153.6	3 515 358	12	1 114.7	3 478 051	3 192 725	2 643 766	322 633	134 177	218 429	10.1	87	20.8
2680	Fort Lauderdale, FL PMSA	1 208.9	1 470 758	X	1 216.6	1 440 542	1 255 531	1 018 257	215 227	27 172	55 812	17.1	X	23.3
5000	Miami, FL PMSA	1 944.7	2 044 600	X	1 051.4	2 037 509	1 937 194	1 625 509	107 406	107 005	162 617	5.5	X	19.2
5082	Milwaukee-Racine, WI CMSA	1 793.1	1 636 572	26	912.7	1 637 539	1 607 183	1 570 152	29 389	78 341	7 877	1.8	216	2.4
5080	Milwaukee-Waukesha, WI PMSA	1 460.0	1 451 179	X	994.0	1 453 050	1 432 149	1 397 020	19 030	70 088	7 314	1.3	X	2.5
6600	Racine, WI PMSA	333.1	185 393	X	556.6	184 489	175 034	173 132	10 359	8 253	563	5.9	X	1.1
5120	Minneapolis-St. Paul, MN-WI MSA	6 064.4	2 792 137	16	460.4	2 760 404	2 538 776	2 198 190	253 361	174 676	29 948	10.0	91	15.5
5160	Mobile, AL MSA	2 829.9	527 118	76	186.3	520 622	476 923	443 536	50 195	24 464	1 815	10.5	81	7.5
5170	Modesto, CA MSA	1 494.6	421 818	94	282.2	415 977	370 522	265 900	51 296	32 296	14 688	13.8	57	39.3
5200	Monroe, LA MSA	611.0	147 055	197	240.7	146 839	142 191	139 241	4 864	7 358	300	3.4	197	2.1
5240	Montgomery, AL MSA	2 007.5	319 175	119	159.0	316 566	292 517	272 687	26 658	15 541	496	9.1	108	7.3
5280	Muncie, IN MSA	393.3	117 625	238	299.1	118 274	119 659	128 587	−2 034	2 549	249	−1.7	255	−6.9
5330	Myrtle Beach, SC MSA	1 133.7	169 178	177	149.2	163 661	144 053	101 419	25 125	4 922	590	17.4	31	42.0
5345	Naples, FL MSA	2 025.5	195 731	164	96.6	188 820	152 099	85 971	43 632	5 647	8 091	28.7	5	76.9
5360	Nashville, TN MSA	4 073.1	1 134 524	38	278.5	1 114 380	985 026	850 505	149 498	51 990	7 940	15.2	49	15.8
5523	New London-Norwich, CT NECMA	666.1	252 958	138	379.8	252 948	254 957	238 409	−1 999	11 300	1 272	−.8	247	6.9
5560	New Orleans, LA MSA	3 399.4	1 307 758	33	384.7	1 308 472	1 285 262	1 304 212	22 496	65 923	10 954	1.8	220	−1.5
5602	New York-Northern New Jersey-Long Island, NY-NJ-CT-PA CMSA/NECMA	10 165.7	19 876 488	1	1 955.3	19 799 710	19 480 012	18 829 146	396 476	958 005	1 081 307	2.0	212	3.5
0875	Bergen-Passaic, NJ PMSA	419.2	1 335 393	X	3 185.6	1 327 151	1 296 244	1 292 970	39 149	49 281	72 877	3.0	X	.3
2281	Dutchess, NY PMSA	801.7	264 687	X	330.2	262 968	259 462	245 055	5 225	11 016	2 799	2.0	X	5.9
3640	Jersey City, NJ PMSA	46.7	551 451	X	11 808.4	549 257	553 099	556 972	−1 648	28 535	52 094	−.3	X	−.7
5015	Middlesex-Somerset-Hunterdon, NJ PMSA	1 045.4	1 105 522	X	1 057.5	1 090 408	1 019 858	886 383	85 664	56 885	44 876	8.4	X	15.1
5190	Monmouth-Ocean, NJ PMSA	1 108.2	1 076 971	X	971.8	1 063 268	986 296	849 211	90 675	21 436	10 731	9.2	X	16.1
5380	Nassau-Suffolk, NY PMSA	1 198.0	2 666 302	X	2 225.6	2 657 422	2 609 212	2 605 813	57 090	121 524	55 859	2.2	X	.1
5483	New Haven-Bridgeport-Stamford-Waterbury-Danbury, CT NECMA	1 231.7	1 625 515	X	1 319.7	1 623 353	1 631 864	1 568 468	−6 349	66 812	31 313	−.4	X	4.0
5600	New York, NY PMSA	1 147.5	8 611 099	X	7 504.2	8 596 656	8 546 846	8 274 961	64 253	480 976	719 649	.8	X	3.3
5640	Newark, NJ PMSA	1 577.8	1 943 494	X	1 231.8	1 937 648	1 915 694	1 963 576	27 800	88 321	79 170	1.5	X	−2.4
5660	Newburgh, NY-PA PMSA	1 363.5	366 268	X	268.6	362 168	335 613	277 874	30 655	21 000	3 439	9.1	X	20.8
8480	Trenton, NJ PMSA	226.0	329 786	X	1 459.2	329 411	325 824	307 863	3 962	12 219	8 500	1.2	X	5.8
5720	Norfolk-Virginia Beach-Newport News, VA-NC MSA	2 348.6	1 544 945	27	657.8	1 535 679	1 444 710	1 200 998	100 235	104 448	8 857	6.9	156	20.3
5790	Ocala, FL MSA	1 579.0	237 308	145	150.3	231 483	194 835	122 488	42 473	799	1 949	21.8	16	59.1
5800	Odessa-Midland, TX MSA	1 801.4	243 389	142	135.1	239 722	225 545	198 010	17 844	18 825	5 832	7.9	128	13.9
5880	Oklahoma City, OK MSA	4 247.5	1 030 504	45	242.6	1 022 327	958 839	860 969	71 665	46 289	2 423	7.5	143	11.4
5920	Omaha, NE-IA MSA	2 475.8	687 454	61	277.7	680 307	639 580	605 419	47 874	40 760	3 709	7.5	142	5.6
5960	Orlando, FL MSA	3 490.9	1 467 045	30	420.2	1 426 408	1 224 844	804 774	242 201	70 175	33 982	19.8	23	52.2
5990	Owensboro, KY MSA	462.4	91 011	263	196.8	90 726	87 189	85 949	3 822	3 064	197	4.4	186	1.4

X Not applicable.

[1]Federal Information Processing Standards (FIPS) codes for metropolitan areas defined as of June 30, 1996.
[2]Dry land and land temporarily or partially covered by water.
[3]Based on 273 metropolitan areas (245 MSAs, 17 CMSAs, and 11 NECMAs); see text for more information. When metropolitan areas share the same rank, the next lower rank is omitted.
[4]Based on 1990 land area.
[5]Includes count resolution corrections through December 1996.
[6]Includes net domestic migration, net federal movement, and residual not shown separately.
[7]Difference between the number of births and the number of deaths.

Source: Land Area—U.S. Bureau of the Census, data file from Geography Division based on the TIGER/GICS computer file (related Internet site <http://www.census.gov/population/www/censusdata/density.html>); 1990–1997 Population—U.S. Bureau of the Census, "Estimates of the Population of Counties and Demographic Components of Population Change: April 1, 1990 to July 1, 1997" (CO-97-5) Internet site <http://www.census.gov/population/www/estimates/co_97_5.html> (accessed 30 March 1998); 1996 Population—U.S. Bureau of the Census, "Estimates of the Population of Counties, Annual Time Series, July 1, 1990 to July 1, 1997" (co-97-4) Internet site <http://www.census.gov/population/www/estimates/co_97_4.html> (accessed 30 March 1998); 1980 Population—U.S. Bureau of the Census, "1980–1990 Intercensal Population Estimates by County" on diskette.

Table B–1. Metro Areas — **Area and Population**—Con.

[MSA = Metropolitan statistical area. CMSA = Consolidated MSA. PMSA = Primary MSA. NECMA = New England county metropolitan area. All areas defined as of June 30, 1996. Table includes 245 MSAs, 17 CMSAs, and 58 PMSAs not in New England; as well as 12 NECMAs. Table excludes 10 MSAs, 1 CMSA, and 15 PMSAs in New England]

Metro-politan area code[1]	Metropolitan areas	Land area,[2] 1990 (sq miles)	1997 (July 1) Total persons	Rank[3]	Per square mile[4]	1996 (July 1)	1990[5] (April 1)	1980 (April 1)	Net change, 1990–1997 Total[6]	Natural change[7]	Net inter-national migration	Percent change 1990–1997 Percent	Rank[3]	1980–1990
6015	Panama City, FL MSA	763.7	146 223	199	191.5	144 659	126 994	97 740	19 229	6 507	560	15.1	50	29.9
6020	Parkersburg-Marietta, WV-OH MSA	1 002.6	150 641	193	150.3	151 292	149 169	157 893	1 472	2 729	234	1.0	227	−5.5
6080	Pensacola, FL MSA	1 679.4	397 085	99	236.4	386 978	344 406	289 782	52 679	18 123	3 672	15.3	48	18.9
6120	Peoria-Pekin, IL MSA	1 796.5	345 954	113	192.6	346 282	339 172	365 864	6 782	12 065	1 269	2.0	213	−7.3
6162	Philadelphia-Wilmington-Atlantic City, PA-NJ-DE-MD CMSA	5 936.0	5 971 860	6	1 006.0	5 973 281	5 893 019	5 649 031	78 841	225 139	75 701	1.3	226	4.3
0560	Atlantic-Cape May, NJ PMSA	816.4	334 694	X	410.0	333 025	319 416	276 385	15 278	10 401	6 490	4.8	X	15.6
6160	Philadelphia, PA-NJ PMSA	3 855.8	4 940 653	X	1 281.4	4 949 301	4 922 257	4 781 235	18 396	182 975	62 997	.4	X	2.9
8760	Vineland-Millville-Bridgeton, NJ PMSA	489.3	140 907	X	288.0	141 230	138 053	132 866	2 854	5 443	1 294	2.1	X	3.9
9160	Wilmington-Newark, DE-MD PMSA	774.5	555 606	X	717.4	549 725	513 293	458 545	42 313	26 320	4 920	8.2	X	11.9
6200	Phoenix-Mesa, AZ MSA	14 574.0	2 839 539	15	194.8	2 753 043	2 238 498	1 600 093	601 041	179 536	49 788	26.9	6	39.9
6240	Pine Bluff, AR MSA	884.8	82 259	266	93.0	82 905	85 487	90 718	−3 228	3 011	205	−3.8	267	−5.8
6280	Pittsburgh, PA MSA	4 623.9	2 361 019	19	510.6	2 373 640	2 394 811	2 571 223	−33 792	13 573	7 211	−1.4	251	−6.9
6323	Pittsfield, MA NECMA	931.4	134 244	214	144.1	134 711	139 352	145 110	−5 108	476	846	−3.7	266	−4.0
6340	Pocatello, ID MSA	1 113.2	73 850	271	66.3	73 379	66 026	65 421	7 824	5 679	309	11.8	64	.9
6403	Portland, ME NECMA	835.6	251 438	140	300.9	249 784	243 135	215 789	8 303	7 319	1 372	3.4	198	12.7
6442	Portland-Salem, OR-WA CMSA	6 953.8	2 112 802	22	303.8	2 072 805	1 793 476	1 583 518	319 326	97 140	38 715	17.8	28	13.3
6440	Portland-Vancouver, OR-WA PMSA	5 027.7	1 787 549	X	355.5	1 753 760	1 515 452	1 333 623	272 097	82 873	31 977	18.0	X	13.6
7080	Salem, OR PMSA	1 926.1	325 253	X	168.9	319 045	278 024	249 895	47 229	14 267	6 738	17.0	X	11.3
6483	Providence-Warwick-Pawtucket, RI NECMA	941.0	904 831	51	961.6	905 806	916 270	865 771	−11 439	34 488	11 672	−1.2	249	5.8
6520	Provo-Orem, UT MSA	1 998.4	328 142	117	164.2	320 241	263 590	218 106	64 552	45 378	4 132	24.5	10	20.9
6560	Pueblo, CO MSA	2 388.8	132 901	218	55.6	130 991	123 051	125 972	9 850	3 550	419	8.0	124	−2.3
6580	Punta Gorda, FL MSA	693.7	133 681	215	192.7	131 298	110 975	58 460	22 706	−5 763	2 269	20.5	21	89.8
6640	Raleigh-Durham-Chapel Hill, NC MSA	3 491.0	1 050 054	43	300.8	1 022 413	858 485	664 788	191 569	55 514	10 959	22.3	14	29.1
6660	Rapid City, SD MSA	2 776.4	87 190	265	31.4	86 906	81 343	70 361	5 847	6 499	322	7.2	150	15.6
6680	Reading, PA MSA	859.2	354 057	111	412.1	352 099	336 523	312 509	17 534	8 387	3 291	5.2	172	7.7
6690	Redding, CA MSA	3 785.7	163 178	184	43.1	161 944	147 036	115 613	16 142	4 710	1 302	11.0	74	27.2
6720	Reno, NV MSA	6 342.5	305 792	124	48.2	298 665	254 667	193 623	51 125	17 031	8 367	20.1	22	31.5
6740	Richland-Kennewick-Pasco, WA MSA	2 945.3	182 799	170	62.1	180 302	150 033	144 469	32 766	13 535	7 147	21.8	15	3.9
6760	Richmond-Petersburg, VA MSA	2 944.8	943 264	50	320.3	934 727	865 640	761 311	77 624	39 986	6 578	9.0	113	13.7
6800	Roanoke, VA MSA	850.9	228 534	149	268.6	228 634	224 592	220 393	3 942	2 479	1 295	1.8	218	1.9
6820	Rochester, MN MSA	653.0	114 619	241	175.5	113 158	106 470	92 006	8 149	8 127	1 572	7.7	136	15.7
6840	Rochester, NY MSA	3 425.6	1 086 082	40	317.0	1 086 439	1 062 470	1 030 630	23 612	48 667	10 653	2.2	209	3.1
6880	Rockford, IL MSA	1 554.1	354 774	110	228.3	352 561	329 676	325 852	25 098	15 618	3 888	7.6	138	1.2
6895	Rocky Mount, NC MSA	1 045.4	145 571	200	139.2	143 822	133 369	123 141	12 202	5 337	519	9.1	106	8.3
6922	Sacramento-Yolo, CA CMSA	5 094.0	1 655 866	25	325.1	1 631 232	1 481 220	1 099 814	174 646	104 332	45 362	11.8	65	34.7
6920	Sacramento, CA PMSA	4 081.6	1 503 069	X	368.3	1 480 973	1 340 010	986 440	163 059	94 871	37 748	12.2	X	35.8
9270	Yolo, CA PMSA	1 012.4	152 797	X	150.9	150 259	141 210	113 374	11 587	9 461	7 614	8.2	X	24.6
6960	Saginaw-Bay City-Midland, MI MSA	1 774.5	402 949	96	227.1	402 993	399 320	421 518	3 629	17 545	1 606	.9	228	−5.3
6980	St. Cloud, MN MSA	1 752.9	161 211	185	92.0	159 820	149 509	133 348	11 702	8 487	562	7.8	129	12.1
7000	St. Joseph, MO MSA	845.0	97 111	259	114.9	97 096	97 715	101 868	−604	1 628	93	−.6	244	−4.1
7040	St. Louis, MO-IL MSA	6 393.0	2 557 806	18	400.1	2 548 410	2 492 348	2 414 061	65 458	103 337	15 833	2.6	205	3.2
7120	Salinas, CA MSA	3 321.9	361 907	108	108.9	350 018	355 660	290 444	6 247	37 429	22 684	1.8	218	22.5
7160	Salt Lake City-Ogden, UT MSA	1 617.5	1 247 554	35	771.3	1 226 277	1 072 227	910 222	175 327	120 516	13 799	16.4	39	17.8
7200	San Angelo, TX MSA	1 522.2	102 468	251	67.4	102 024	98 458	84 784	4 190	4 586	1 222	4.3	189	16.1
7240	San Antonio, TX MSA	3 326.8	1 511 386	28	454.3	1 485 811	1 324 749	1 088 881	186 637	106 213	30 642	14.1	55	21.7
7320	San Diego, CA MSA	4 204.5	2 722 650	17	647.6	2 677 203	2 498 016	1 861 846	224 634	218 627	129 997	9.0	111	34.2
7362	San Francisco-Oakland-San Jose, CA CMSA	7 368.6	6 700 753	5	909.4	6 616 009	6 277 525	5 367 900	423 228	385 053	354 028	6.7	159	16.9
5775	Oakland, CA PMSA	1 457.8	2 270 325	X	1 557.4	2 236 006	2 108 078	1 761 710	162 247	135 607	91 519	7.7	X	19.7
7360	San Francisco, CA PMSA	1 015.6	1 662 005	X	1 636.5	1 648 258	1 603 678	1 488 895	58 327	55 188	116 930	3.6	X	7.7
7400	San Jose, CA PMSA	1 291.2	1 609 037	X	1 246.2	1 588 282	1 497 577	1 295 071	111 460	132 115	107 578	7.4	X	15.6
7485	Santa Cruz-Watsonville, CA PMSA	445.7	240 488	X	539.6	237 717	229 734	188 141	10 754	15 403	11 449	4.7	X	22.1
7500	Santa Rosa, CA PMSA	1 576.2	428 609	X	271.9	421 324	388 222	299 681	40 387	16 310	10 492	10.4	X	29.5
8720	Vallejo-Fairfield-Napa, CA PMSA	1 582.1	490 289	X	309.9	484 422	450 236	334 402	40 053	30 430	16 060	8.9	X	34.6
7460	San Luis Obispo-Atascadero-Paso Robles, CA MSA	3 304.5	233 291	147	70.6	229 982	217 162	155 435	16 129	6 804	4 443	7.4	145	39.7
7480	Santa Barbara-Santa Maria-Lompoc, CA MSA	2 738.5	390 199	100	142.5	384 959	369 608	298 694	20 591	25 847	20 021	5.6	168	23.7

X Not applicable.

[1] Federal Information Processing Standards (FIPS) codes for metropolitan areas defined as of June 30, 1996.
[2] Dry land and land temporarily or partially covered by water.
[3] Based on 273 metropolitan areas (245 MSAs, 17 CMSAs, and 11 NECMAs); see text for more information. When metropolitan areas share the same rank, the next lower rank is omitted.
[4] Based on 1990 land area.
[5] Includes count resolution corrections through December 1996.
[6] Includes net domestic migration, net federal movement, and residual not shown separately.
[7] Difference between the number of births and the number of deaths.

Source: Land Area—U.S. Bureau of the Census, data file from Geography Division based on the TIGER/GICS computer file (related Internet site <http://www.census.gov/population/www/censusdata/density.html>); 1990–1997 Population—U.S. Bureau of the Census, "Estimates of the Population of Counties and Demographic Components of Population Change: April 1, 1990 to July 1, 1997" (CO-97-5) Internet site <http://www.census.gov/population/www/estimates/co_97_5.html> (accessed 30 March 1998); 1996 Population—U.S. Bureau of the Census, "Estimates of the Population of Counties, Annual Time Series, July 1, 1990 to July 1, 1997" (co-97-4) Internet site <http://www.census.gov/population/www/estimates/co_97_4.html> (accessed 30 March 1998); 1980 Population—U.S. Bureau of the Census, "1980–1990 Intercensal Population Estimates by County" on diskette.

[MSA = Metropolitan statistical area. CMSA = Consolidated MSA. PMSA = Primary MSA. NECMA = New England county metropolitan area. All areas defined as of June 30, 1996. Table includes 245 MSAs, 17 CMSAs, and 58 PMSAs not in New England; as well as 12 NECMAs. Table excludes 10 MSAs, 1 CMSA, and 15 PMSAs in New England]

Metro-politan area code[1]	Metropolitan areas	Land area,[2] 1990 (sq miles)	Population 1997 (July 1) Total persons	Rank[3]	Per square mile[4]	1996 (July 1)	1990[5] (April 1)	1980 (April 1)	Net change, 1990–1997 Total[6]	Natural change[7]	Net inter-national migration	Percent change 1990–1997 Percent	Rank[3]	1980–1990
7490	Santa Fe, NM MSA	2 018.8	140 066	206	69.4	137 161	117 043	93 118	23 023	6 494	2 587	19.7	24	25.7
7510	Sarasota-Bradenton, FL MSA	1 313.0	538 783	74	410.3	531 586	489 483	350 696	49 300	–14 073	7 784	10.1	89	39.6
7520	Savannah, GA MSA	1 361.7	284 090	130	208.6	281 175	257 899	230 728	26 191	16 099	1 453	10.2	85	11.8
7560	Scranton--Wilkes-Barre--Hazleton, PA MSA	2 232.6	621 641	65	278.4	627 150	638 524	659 387	–16 883	–7 512	2 143	–2.6	264	–3.2
7602	Seattle-Tacoma-Bremerton, WA CMSA	7 223.5	3 367 872	13	466.2	3 309 180	2 970 300	2 408 749	397 572	181 142	54 700	13.4	60	23.3
1150	Bremerton, WA PMSA	396.0	234 608	X	592.4	231 156	189 731	147 152	44 877	14 215	1 845	23.7	X	28.9
5910	Olympia, WA PMSA	727.1	200 362	X	275.6	196 709	161 238	124 264	39 124	8 246	1 774	24.3	X	29.8
7600	Seattle-Bellevue-Everett, WA PMSA	4 424.9	2 268 126	X	512.6	2 226 300	2 033 128	1 651 666	234 998	119 995	46 331	11.6	X	23.1
8200	Tacoma, WA PMSA	1 675.5	664 776	X	396.8	655 015	586 203	485 667	78 573	38 686	4 750	13.4	X	20.7
7610	Sharon, PA MSA	671.9	122 045	229	181.6	122 243	121 003	128 299	1 042	547	109	.9	230	–5.7
7620	Sheboygan, WI MSA	513.7	109 896	246	213.9	109 440	103 877	100 935	6 019	2 887	528	5.8	167	2.9
7640	Sherman-Denison, TX MSA	933.7	101 561	254	108.8	100 306	95 019	89 796	6 522	1 437	790	6.9	157	5.8
7680	Shreveport-Bossier City, LA MSA	2 316.5	378 738	104	163.5	378 898	376 330	376 789	2 408	14 707	838	.6	232	–.1
7720	Sioux City, IA-NE MSA	1 136.7	120 823	234	106.3	121 024	115 018	117 457	5 805	6 204	2 426	5.0	174	–2.1
7760	Sioux Falls, SD MSA	1 387.3	160 670	188	115.8	159 138	139 236	123 377	21 434	8 498	1 673	15.4	46	12.9
7800	South Bend, IN MSA	457.3	258 056	136	564.3	257 338	247 052	241 617	11 004	10 510	1 060	4.5	184	2.2
7840	Spokane, WA MSA	1 763.8	404 650	95	229.4	403 669	361 333	341 835	43 317	16 334	2 610	12.0	63	5.7
7880	Springfield, IL MSA	1 182.6	203 942	159	172.5	203 908	189 550	187 770	14 392	6 766	1 030	7.6	139	.9
7920	Springfield, MO MSA	1 831.6	300 980	125	164.3	296 902	264 346	228 118	36 634	10 010	843	13.9	56	15.9
8003	Springfield, MA NECMA	1 147.5	591 110	70	515.1	591 045	602 878	581 831	–11 768	16 663	7 640	–2.0	257	3.6
8050	State College, PA MSA	1 107.6	132 993	217	120.1	132 216	124 812	112 760	8 181	4 527	1 073	6.6	161	10.7
8080	Steubenville-Weirton, OH-WV MSA	581.5	136 725	212	235.1	138 214	142 523	163 734	–5 798	–1 209	–33	–4.1	270	–13.0
8120	Stockton-Lodi, CA MSA	1 399.3	542 504	73	387.7	533 005	480 628	347 342	61 876	39 567	22 026	12.9	62	38.4
8140	Sumter, SC MSA	665.5	106 589	249	160.2	106 938	101 276	88 243	5 313	6 235	199	5.2	171	14.8
8160	Syracuse, NY MSA	3 082.8	740 771	59	240.3	745 115	742 237	722 865	–1 466	31 412	6 391	–.2	240	2.7
8240	Tallahassee, FL MSA	1 183.0	260 611	135	220.3	259 713	233 609	190 329	27 002	13 941	3 359	11.6	70	22.7
8280	Tampa-St. Petersburg-Clearwater, FL MSA	2 554.5	2 227 000	21	871.8	2 198 898	2 067 959	1 613 600	159 041	9 453	29 537	7.7	134	28.2
8320	Terre Haute, IN MSA	1 017.8	148 468	195	145.9	149 364	147 585	155 476	883	2 311	432	.6	233	–5.1
8360	Texarkana, TX-Texarkana, AR MSA	1 512.0	123 380	225	81.6	123 522	120 132	113 067	3 248	3 520	439	2.7	204	6.2
8400	Toledo, OH MSA	1 364.6	611 805	68	448.3	610 624	614 128	616 864	–2 323	26 056	2 705	–.4	242	–.4
8440	Topeka, KS MSA	549.9	164 932	183	299.9	164 761	160 976	154 916	3 956	5 734	727	2.5	208	3.9
8520	Tucson, AZ MSA	9 187.0	780 150	57	84.9	767 743	666 957	531 443	113 193	36 735	16 192	17.0	34	25.5
8560	Tulsa, OK MSA	5 015.0	764 396	58	152.4	754 323	708 954	657 173	55 442	36 284	4 604	7.8	130	7.9
8600	Tuscaloosa, AL MSA	1 325.3	160 760	186	121.3	158 872	150 522	137 541	10 238	6 223	431	6.8	158	9.4
8640	Tyler, TX MSA	928.5	166 723	181	179.6	164 654	151 309	128 366	15 414	6 752	2 670	10.2	83	17.9
8680	Utica-Rome, NY MSA	2 624.6	298 878	127	113.9	301 719	316 645	320 180	–17 767	6 508	4 078	–5.6	273	–1.1
8750	Victoria, TX MSA	882.6	82 024	267	92.9	81 624	74 361	68 807	7 663	5 204	743	10.3	82	8.1
8780	Visalia-Tulare-Porterville, CA MSA	4 824.3	353 175	112	73.2	350 053	311 921	245 738	41 254	34 282	18 075	13.2	61	26.9
8800	Waco, TX MSA	1 041.9	202 983	160	194.8	201 493	189 123	170 755	13 860	8 811	2 242	7.3	148	10.8
8872	Washington-Baltimore, DC-MD-VA-WV CMSA	9 578.3	7 206 517	4	752.4	7 145 947	6 726 395	5 790 555	480 122	412 441	195 900	7.1	152	16.2
0720	Baltimore, MD PMSA	2 609.4	2 475 332	X	948.6	2 468 790	2 382 172	2 199 497	93 160	102 079	23 030	3.9	X	8.3
3180	Hagerstown, MD PMSA	458.2	128 155	X	279.7	127 287	121 393	113 086	6 762	3 049	542	5.6	X	7.3
8840	Washington, DC-MD-VA-WV PMSA	6 510.7	4 603 030	X	707.0	4 549 870	4 222 830	3 477 972	380 200	307 313	172 328	9.0	X	21.4
8920	Waterloo-Cedar Falls, IA MSA	567.4	121 502	231	214.1	122 245	123 798	137 961	–2 296	3 464	431	–1.9	256	–10.3
8940	Wausau, WI MSA	1 545.1	122 450	228	79.3	121 475	115 400	111 270	7 050	5 643	632	6.1	166	3.7
8960	West Palm Beach-Boca Raton, FL MSA	1 974.2	1 018 524	47	515.9	996 125	863 503	576 758	155 021	9 596	36 017	18.0	27	49.7
9000	Wheeling, WV-OH MSA	950.5	154 153	192	162.2	155 175	159 301	185 566	–5 148	–1 419	96	–3.2	265	–14.2
9040	Wichita, KS MSA	2 967.8	530 508	75	178.8	523 278	485 270	442 401	45 238	31 733	4 960	9.3	102	9.7
9080	Wichita Falls, TX MSA	1 537.5	137 103	211	89.2	137 608	130 351	128 348	6 752	5 096	960	5.2	173	1.6
9140	Williamsport, PA MSA	1 234.9	118 405	236	95.9	118 991	118 710	118 416	–305	2 333	393	–.3	241	.2
9200	Wilmington, NC MSA	1 053.8	213 580	153	202.7	207 099	171 269	139 248	42 311	5 976	490	24.7	9	23.0
9260	Yakima, WA MSA	4 296.1	218 318	151	50.8	216 110	188 823	172 508	29 495	18 652	11 321	15.6	43	9.5
9280	York, PA MSA	904.6	370 518	107	409.6	367 906	339 574	313 024	30 944	11 290	1 213	9.1	108	8.5
9320	Youngstown-Warren, OH MSA	1 563.6	595 215	69	380.7	597 870	600 895	644 922	–5 680	9 322	691	–.9	248	–6.8
9340	Yuba City, CA MSA	1 233.2	139 315	208	113.0	137 898	122 643	101 979	16 672	10 154	7 697	13.6	59	20.3
9360	Yuma, AZ MSA	5 514.4	130 016	220	23.6	125 404	106 895	[8]76 205	23 121	15 172	10 326	21.6	17	[8]40.3

X Not applicable.

[1]Federal Information Processing Standards (FIPS) codes for metropolitan areas defined as of June 30, 1996.
[2]Dry land and land temporarily or partially covered by water.
[3]Based on 273 metropolitan areas (245 MSAs, 17 CMSAs, and 11 NECMAs); see text for more information. When metropolitan areas share the same rank, the next lower rank is omitted.
[4]Based on 1990 land area.
[5]Includes count resolution corrections through December 1996.
[6]Includes net domestic migration, net federal movement, and residual not shown separately.
[7]Difference between the number of births and the number of deaths.
[8]1980 population based on 1990 boundaries.

Source: Land Area—U.S. Bureau of the Census, data file from Geography Division based on the TIGER/GICS computer file (related Internet site <http://www.census.gov/population/www/censusdata/density.html>);   1990–1997 Population—U.S. Bureau of the Census, "Estimates of the Population of Counties and Demographic Components of Population Change: April 1, 1990 to July 1, 1997" (CO-97-5) Internet site <http://www.census.gov/population/www/estimates/co_97_5.html> (accessed 30 March 1998);   1996 Population—U.S. Bureau of the Census, "Estimates of the Population of Counties, Annual Time Series, July 1, 1990 to July 1, 1997" (co-97-4) Internet site <http://www.census.gov/population/www/estimates/co_97_4.html> (accessed 30 March 1998);   1980 Population—U.S. Bureau of the Census, "1980–1990 Intercensal Population Estimates by County" on diskette.

[MSA = Metropolitan statistical area. CMSA = Consolidated MSA. PMSA = Primary MSA. NECMA = New England county metropolitan area. All areas defined as of June 30, 1996. Table includes 245 MSAs, 17 CMSAs, and 58 PMSAs not in New England; as well as 12 NECMAs. Table excludes 10 MSAs, 1 CMSA, and 15 PMSAs in New England]

| Metropolitan areas | Population (BEA) Projections | | | | Population characteristics, 1996 | | | | | | | | | | | | | |
| | | | | | Age, percent— | | | | | | | | | | Race, percent— | | | |
	2010 (1,000)	2005 (1,000)	2000 (1,000)	1993 estimate[1] (1,000)	Under 5 years	5 to 14 years	15 to 24 years	25 to 34 years	35 to 44 years	45 to 54 years	55 to 64 years	65 years and over Per- cent	65 years and over Rank[2]	75 years and over	White	Black	Asian or Pacific Islander	Percent Hispanic origin[3]
Abilene, TX MSA	132.2	129.4	126.8	121.4	8.2	15.3	16.4	14.3	14.5	10.9	8.0	12.4	133	5.8	90.9	6.8	1.8	17.4
Albany, GA MSA	132.2	127.4	122.8	116.1	8.0	17.1	15.8	14.6	16.3	11.3	7.5	9.3	242	3.8	51.0	48.1	.6	1.2
Albany-Schenectady-Troy, NY MSA	988.5	956.3	923.0	874.2	7.0	13.8	13.2	15.1	16.5	12.0	8.0	14.6	56	6.7	93.0	5.1	1.7	2.1
Albuquerque, NM MSA	810.2	761.5	710.5	630.0	7.6	15.0	14.4	14.7	17.4	12.4	7.8	10.7	199	4.4	89.1	3.3	1.9	38.4
Alexandria, LA MSA	134.9	131.7	128.9	125.2	7.3	16.0	14.6	14.0	15.0	12.1	8.5	12.5	130	5.5	68.8	29.9	.9	1.3
Allentown-Bethlehem-Easton, PA MSA	679.1	658.1	640.0	609.2	6.3	13.2	12.3	14.4	16.6	12.5	8.7	16.0	35	7.3	95.9	2.5	1.5	5.8
Altoona, PA MSA	141.5	137.8	134.8	131.8	5.8	14.5	11.9	12.7	16.0	12.4	9.1	17.6	20	8.3	98.6	.9	.4	.4
Amarillo, TX MSA	215.1	209.2	203.3	193.8	8.1	15.7	14.0	14.5	15.8	11.6	8.7	11.7	158	5.1	90.8	5.9	2.4	16.0
Anchorage, AK MSA	299.2	286.8	273.0	250.3	7.7	15.6	16.3	14.7	19.7	14.5	6.8	4.7	273	1.5	81.3	6.2	5.9	4.7
Anniston, AL MSA	126.0	122.6	120.0	117.0	6.5	13.7	15.0	14.1	15.9	12.4	9.2	12.9	114	5.4	79.8	19.1	.9	1.4
Appleton-Oshkosh-Neenah, WI MSA	385.2	369.0	352.8	328.6	6.7	15.1	14.2	15.5	16.7	12.1	7.7	12.0	150	5.8	96.9	.4	1.6	1.0
Asheville, NC MSA	240.6	229.0	217.6	200.9	6.2	12.8	11.7	13.8	16.2	13.0	9.4	16.9	23	7.8	91.3	7.8	.6	1.1
Athens, GA MSA	157.5	149.9	142.3	130.7	6.5	12.7	23.4	15.8	15.0	10.8	6.4	9.4	240	4.3	74.4	22.8	2.6	2.2
Atlanta, GA MSA	4 231.3	3 960.2	3 681.6	3 228.6	7.6	14.1	13.8	18.4	18.6	12.8	6.8	7.9	265	3.4	71.4	25.8	2.6	3.0
Augusta-Aiken, GA-SC MSA	538.5	511.6	485.4	443.6	7.5	15.3	14.4	16.1	16.7	12.1	7.9	9.9	225	4.0	64.8	32.9	2.0	2.1
Austin-San Marcos, TX MSA	1 250.7	1 167.6	1 076.7	932.1	8.0	14.3	17.5	17.5	17.8	10.8	6.1	8.0	264	3.5	86.6	10.0	3.0	24.3
Bakersfield, CA MSA	762.7	719.9	674.0	599.9	10.1	18.4	12.8	16.5	15.3	10.4	6.5	9.9	225	4.2	87.5	6.4	4.4	33.8
Bangor, ME NECMA	163.8	158.1	152.8	146.2	5.4	13.8	15.9	14.3	17.0	13.1	8.4	12.2	141	5.5	98.0	.4	.8	.6
Barnstable-Yarmouth, MA NECMA	235.8	224.1	212.4	192.9	5.7	12.5	8.2	13.6	16.1	11.7	9.4	22.8	7	10.7	96.7	1.9	.8	1.5
Baton Rouge, LA MSA	661.5	632.0	601.5	553.2	7.5	15.6	17.3	14.8	16.6	11.8	7.2	9.2	246	3.7	67.4	31.1	1.3	1.6
Beaumont-Port Arthur, TX MSA	400.0	392.1	385.4	372.0	6.8	15.8	12.9	13.4	15.7	12.5	9.6	13.2	96	5.6	73.0	24.6	2.1	5.1
Bellingham, WA MSA	187.1	175.1	162.6	142.2	6.3	14.5	16.2	13.4	17.5	12.2	7.4	12.4	135	6.0	93.8	.6	2.3	4.0
Benton Harbor, MI MSA	168.6	166.2	164.6	161.7	6.9	15.5	13.2	13.4	15.7	12.6	8.5	14.3	65	6.4	81.8	16.6	1.2	1.9
Billings, MT MSA	155.3	146.4	136.9	120.9	6.3	14.7	14.8	12.5	16.8	13.5	9.1	12.3	139	5.6	95.7	.6	.6	3.0
Biloxi-Gulfport-Pascagoula, MS MSA	376.7	363.5	351.1	330.5	7.8	14.8	15.1	15.3	15.4	12.1	8.8	10.7	200	4.1	77.6	19.9	2.3	1.9
Binghamton, NY MSA	275.3	271.3	268.4	264.4	7.2	14.3	12.8	15.0	15.2	12.5	8.4	14.7	55	6.7	95.8	2.0	2.1	1.4
Birmingham, AL MSA	961.8	931.0	904.5	864.6	7.0	13.4	13.4	15.6	16.9	12.1	8.6	13.0	109	5.7	70.3	28.9	.6	.6
Bismarck, ND MSA	101.2	97.4	93.6	87.3	6.3	15.6	14.0	14.0	17.6	12.3	8.3	11.8	156	5.6	96.6	.1	.5	.7
Bloomington, IN MSA	134.7	128.2	121.9	112.2	5.4	9.9	29.8	15.8	14.2	9.7	6.3	8.8	254	4.0	93.8	2.9	3.1	1.7
Bloomington-Normal, IL MSA	157.6	151.5	145.3	135.9	6.8	13.7	21.3	14.4	15.7	10.5	6.7	10.8	196	5.3	93.5	4.7	1.6	1.7
Boise City, ID MSA	436.9	411.1	383.6	334.2	7.6	15.3	16.4	13.9	16.7	12.1	7.4	10.7	202	5.0	97.3	.5	1.5	7.6
Boston-Worcester-Lawrence-Lowell-Brockton, MA-NH NECMA	6 455.6	6 217.8	5 993.4	5 699.7	6.5	13.4	12.1	17.6	17.0	12.6	7.6	13.2	96	6.3	90.7	5.7	3.4	5.1
Brownsville-Harlingen-San Benito, TX MSA	360.3	341.7	322.2	290.6	9.8	18.7	17.0	12.8	14.1	9.9	7.1	10.7	201	4.4	99.0	.4	.4	84.4
Bryan-College Station, TX MSA	170.3	159.1	147.1	128.6	7.0	12.1	33.0	15.2	12.3	8.5	4.9	7.0	268	3.2	83.1	12.0	4.6	16.5
Buffalo-Niagara Falls, NY MSA	1 271.2	1 246.5	1 224.6	1 192.4	7.0	14.0	12.1	14.8	15.4	12.0	9.1	15.7	39	6.8	86.6	11.4	1.3	2.5
Burlington, VT NECMA	222.8	211.7	200.4	183.5	6.2	14.0	16.2	16.9	17.6	13.0	6.9	9.1	249	4.1	97.2	.9	1.4	1.2
Canton-Massillon, OH MSA	425.7	417.4	411.0	401.0	6.4	14.0	12.8	13.6	16.6	12.9	8.9	14.9	49	6.5	92.2	7.0	.5	.9
Casper, WY MSA	67.8	66.3	65.2	63.0	6.5	15.2	15.3	11.7	17.1	13.2	9.6	11.4	172	4.4	97.9	.8	.6	3.7
Cedar Rapids, IA MSA	194.4	188.2	182.5	174.9	6.5	13.4	14.8	14.9	17.1	13.0	8.3	12.0	149	5.6	96.5	2.2	1.1	1.4
Champaign-Urbana, IL MSA	193.8	187.0	180.0	170.5	7.2	12.4	23.5	16.9	14.9	9.6	6.3	9.2	247	4.3	83.4	10.6	5.8	2.2
Charleston-North Charleston, SC MSA	629.6	599.0	568.5	525.6	8.3	14.9	14.8	18.1	16.3	11.5	7.1	9.1	250	3.6	67.0	31.1	1.6	1.9
Charleston, WV MSA	272.1	265.5	260.8	254.1	5.9	12.2	12.9	13.5	16.4	13.9	10.1	15.0	46	6.3	93.8	5.5	.6	.5
Charlotte-Gastonia-Rock Hill, NC-SC MSA	1 519.7	1 439.9	1 361.4	1 233.5	7.3	14.0	13.1	16.7	16.8	12.7	8.1	11.3	176	4.8	77.7	20.4	1.4	1.5
Charlottesville, VA MSA	166.5	158.4	150.5	138.4	6.4	12.2	18.0	16.8	15.9	11.4	7.7	11.5	170	5.1	81.4	15.9	2.5	1.4
Chattanooga, TN-GA MSA	508.2	487.0	467.0	435.2	6.6	13.6	13.2	14.4	16.4	13.4	9.5	13.0	106	5.7	84.4	14.4	.9	.9
Cheyenne, WY MSA	87.0	84.2	81.5	76.9	6.8	13.8	16.7	12.9	16.6	13.4	8.7	11.3	181	4.8	94.7	3.1	1.4	10.3
Chicago-Gary-Kenosha, IL-IN-WI CMSA	9 535.9	9 218.9	8 905.9	8 465.9	8.1	14.6	13.6	16.0	16.7	12.1	7.8	11.3	179	4.9	76.6	19.3	3.9	13.1
Chicago, IL PMSA	8 626.3	8 328.4	8 029.6	7 612.1	8.2	14.5	13.5	16.1	16.7	12.0	7.7	11.2	X	4.9	76.0	19.5	4.3	13.6
Gary, IN PMSA	639.2	629.6	624.5	617.3	7.0	15.4	13.8	14.4	16.7	12.6	8.5	11.7	X	4.6	78.8	20.2	.8	9.8
Kankakee, IL PMSA	112.3	108.9	105.5	100.4	7.8	16.3	13.4	13.2	15.5	11.8	8.1	13.8	X	6.3	82.6	16.3	.9	2.6
Kenosha, WI PMSA	158.1	152.0	146.2	136.2	7.1	14.7	13.9	15.0	16.2	12.6	7.9	12.5	X	5.7	93.9	5.0	.7	5.7
Chico-Paradise, CA MSA	243.5	229.2	214.0	191.1	7.2	14.7	14.5	12.4	14.6	10.5	7.7	18.6	14	8.5	92.9	1.4	3.7	9.6
Cincinnati-Hamilton, OH-KY-IN CMSA	2 117.7	2 048.0	1 982.0	1 881.3	7.4	14.7	13.9	15.4	16.3	12.0	8.1	12.1	145	5.5	87.3	11.5	1.0	.6
Cincinnati, OH-KY-IN PMSA	1 744.9	1 692.0	1 643.3	1 571.9	7.5	14.7	13.5	15.5	16.3	12.0	8.2	12.4	X	5.6	86.0	12.9	1.0	.6
Hamilton-Middletown, OH PMSA	372.8	355.8	338.7	309.4	6.9	14.6	15.9	14.9	16.7	12.3	8.1	10.6	X	4.6	93.7	5.0	1.2	.6
Clarksville-Hopkinsville, TN-KY MSA	209.9	201.8	193.9	180.2	8.8	14.0	18.3	18.2	14.8	10.3	7.0	8.7	255	3.8	76.5	20.8	2.3	4.4

X Not applicable.

[1]Latest estimate available when projections were prepared.
[2]Based on 273 metropolitan areas (245 MSAs, 17 CMSAs, and 11 NECMAs); see text for more information. When metropolitan areas share the same rank, the next lower rank is omitted.
[3]Persons of Hispanic origin may be of any race.

Source: Population Projections (BEA)—U.S. Bureau of Economic Analysis, "Regional Economic Information System (REIS) 1969-1994" on CD-ROM; Population Characteristics, 1996—U.S. Bureau of the Census, "County Population Estimates by Age, Sex, Race, and Hispanic Origin - 4/1/90 to 7/1/96" data file (related Internet site <http://www.census.gov/population/www/estimates/co_casrh.html>).

[MSA = Metropolitan statistical area. CMSA = Consolidated MSA. PMSA = Primary MSA. NECMA = New England county metropolitan area. All areas defined as of June 30, 1996. Table includes 245 MSAs, 17 CMSAs, and 58 PMSAs not in New England; as well as 12 NECMAs. Table excludes 10 MSAs, 1 CMSA, and 15 PMSAs in New England]

| Metropolitan areas | Population (BEA) | | | | Population characteristics, 1996 | | | | | | | | | | | | | |
| | Projections | | | | Age, percent— | | | | | | | | | | Race, percent— | | |
	2010 (1,000)	2005 (1,000)	2000 (1,000)	1993 estimate[1] (1,000)	Under 5 years	5 to 14 years	15 to 24 years	25 to 34 years	35 to 44 years	45 to 54 years	55 to 64 years	65 years and over Percent	65 years and over Rank[2]	75 years and over	White	Black	Asian or Pacific Islander	Percent Hispanic origin[3]
Cleveland-Akron, OH CMSA	2 985.5	2 945.1	2 920.3	2 893.9	6.7	13.7	13.1	14.6	16.4	12.4	8.7	14.3	61	6.2	82.0	16.5	1.3	2.2
Akron, OH PMSA.................	733.7	714.9	698.3	672.7	6.5	13.6	14.5	14.6	16.7	12.2	8.6	13.4	X	5.7	87.8	10.8	1.2	.7
Cleveland-Lorain-Elyria, OH PMSA ..	2 251.8	2 230.2	2 222.1	2 221.2	6.8	13.8	12.7	14.6	16.4	12.4	8.8	14.6	X	6.3	80.3	18.3	1.3	2.7
Colorado Springs, CO MSA	572.5	535.9	498.1	435.0	7.7	15.3	15.6	15.6	17.1	12.9	7.6	8.2	263	3.2	88.2	7.7	3.2	10.1
Columbia, MO MSA	145.8	138.3	130.5	119.3	6.9	12.9	23.6	16.9	16.1	9.7	5.6	8.5	258	3.9	87.5	8.6	3.6	1.3
Columbia, SC MSA	575.4	547.9	520.2	480.2	6.7	13.3	15.4	17.3	17.4	12.4	7.6	9.9	228	4.0	68.3	30.2	1.3	1.6
Columbus, GA-AL MSA	299.0	290.3	282.7	271.2	7.8	14.5	16.2	16.3	15.1	11.1	8.3	10.6	204	4.4	58.3	39.6	1.8	4.1
Columbus, OH MSA	1 677.8	1 604.4	1 530.0	1 409.2	7.1	13.7	15.3	16.9	17.1	12.0	7.5	10.4	209	4.5	84.8	13.1	1.9	1.0
Corpus Christi, TX MSA	408.1	397.3	386.9	369.3	8.6	16.9	15.0	14.3	15.8	11.3	7.9	10.3	213	4.2	94.3	4.1	1.1	56.5
Cumberland, MD-WV MSA	101.2	100.1	100.0	101.3	5.5	13.1	13.9	11.3	14.4	13.2	9.8	18.9	12	8.8	96.9	2.6	.5	.5
Dallas-Fort Worth, TX CMSA.........	5 338.1	5 056.3	4 759.8	4 279.2	8.3	14.8	14.3	17.3	17.5	12.4	7.0	8.5	259	3.5	81.8	14.2	3.4	15.1
Dallas, TX PMSA	3 538.1	3 354.4	3 161.0	2 844.1	8.3	14.7	14.4	17.5	17.7	12.4	6.8	8.2	X	3.5	80.1	15.8	3.5	16.0
Fort Worth-Arlington, TX PMSA	1 800.0	1 701.9	1 598.9	1 435.1	8.3	14.9	14.1	16.8	17.1	12.4	7.3	9.0	X	3.7	85.2	11.1	3.1	13.3
Danville, VA MSA	110.8	109.4	108.9	109.4	5.8	13.2	11.9	13.7	15.7	13.1	9.9	16.6	27	7.3	65.5	34.0	.4	.6
Davenport-Moline-Rock Island, IA-IL MSA	378.0	370.0	363.2	357.3	7.0	15.1	13.1	13.6	16.5	12.6	8.4	13.6	85	6.3	92.8	6.0	.9	5.0
Dayton-Springfield, OH MSA..........	1 036.8	1 011.3	989.5	958.9	6.7	13.9	14.1	14.5	16.4	13.0	8.6	12.8	119	5.5	84.2	14.3	1.2	.9
Daytona Beach, FL MSA	595.1	551.2	505.6	432.2	5.7	12.1	11.7	12.1	14.0	11.2	11.1	23.2	6	10.2	88.1	10.5	1.2	5.1
Decatur, AL MSA	157.3	151.5	146.2	137.7	6.9	13.9	13.5	15.2	16.2	13.4	8.9	12.1	143	5.2	86.1	12.0	.4	.8
Decatur, IL MSA	126.9	123.7	120.8	117.3	6.9	15.0	12.8	12.7	16.3	12.7	9.0	14.7	52	6.9	86.2	13.2	.6	.6
Denver-Boulder-Greeley, CO CMSA ...	2 730.7	2 570.7	2 404.2	2 146.3	7.2	14.4	13.3	15.2	18.8	14.0	7.9	9.3	243	4.0	91.2	5.2	2.8	14.0
Boulder-Longmont, CO PMSA	318.9	298.5	277.1	244.2	6.4	12.9	17.0	15.5	19.7	13.9	6.7	7.9	X	3.7	95.4	1.0	3.0	7.7
Denver, CO PMSA	2 234.8	2 104.9	1 969.9	1 761.8	7.3	14.5	12.5	15.3	18.9	14.1	8.0	9.4	X	3.9	90.1	6.2	2.9	14.2
Greeley, CO PMSA	177.0	167.3	157.2	140.2	7.5	16.1	16.7	12.9	16.0	12.7	7.6	10.5	X	4.9	97.3	.5	1.1	23.3
Des Moines, IA MSA	469.5	453.0	436.7	412.1	6.9	13.6	14.2	16.0	17.3	12.6	7.9	11.5	167	5.4	93.5	4.1	2.1	2.5
Detroit-Ann Arbor-Flint, MI CMSA.......	5 445.7	5 366.1	5 315.4	5 245.6	7.0	14.5	13.7	15.3	16.9	12.7	8.0	11.9	151	5.1	76.8	21.0	1.9	2.3
Ann Arbor, MI PMSA	598.9	573.2	547.0	509.3	6.6	13.8	17.5	16.1	18.1	12.5	6.5	8.9	X	3.9	89.0	7.3	3.3	2.9
Detroit, MI PMSA	4 408.0	4 359.1	4 336.5	4 303.8	7.0	14.5	13.3	15.3	16.8	12.7	8.1	12.4	X	5.3	75.2	22.6	1.8	2.3
Flint, MI PMSA	438.8	433.8	431.9	432.5	7.2	16.0	13.9	14.7	16.3	13.1	8.1	10.6	X	4.6	77.3	21.1	.9	2.4
Dothan, AL MSA	153.7	148.0	142.8	133.8	7.8	14.6	14.4	15.9	15.5	12.0	8.2	11.6	166	5.0	76.2	22.3	1.1	1.8
Dover, DE MSA	139.9	133.7	127.8	118.2	7.8	14.8	13.6	16.7	16.3	12.2	7.7	10.9	191	4.8	77.1	20.5	1.8	3.0
Dubuque, IA MSA	93.5	91.4	89.6	88.0	6.4	14.8	15.4	13.2	15.6	12.2	8.6	13.9	78	6.8	98.8	.5	.7	.7
Duluth-Superior, MN-WI MSA	254.6	250.3	246.9	241.7	5.4	14.3	13.6	12.0	16.9	12.0	8.9	16.9	24	8.2	96.6	.7	.8	.6
Eau Claire, WI MSA	163.0	156.7	150.5	141.1	6.4	14.8	17.1	13.2	16.3	11.3	7.5	13.3	94	6.4	97.0	.2	2.3	.6
El Paso, TX MSA	785.9	748.9	710.5	646.9	9.6	17.0	17.2	14.8	14.9	10.6	7.4	8.5	257	3.3	94.4	3.6	1.4	73.5
Elkhart-Goshen, IN MSA	188.6	181.2	173.8	161.6	8.3	15.0	13.7	15.0	16.7	12.3	7.7	11.3	179	5.1	93.9	5.0	.8	2.4
Elmira, NY MSA	100.2	98.6	97.1	95.0	7.1	15.2	12.1	14.1	15.4	12.0	8.4	15.6	42	7.0	92.6	6.1	1.0	1.8
Enid, OK MSA	60.5	59.1	57.9	56.5	6.7	15.3	12.8	13.5	14.6	12.0	9.4	15.7	41	7.6	93.0	3.7	1.2	2.4
Erie, PA MSA	296.1	289.0	283.6	279.8	6.8	15.2	14.4	13.7	16.0	11.7	7.9	14.3	63	6.3	93.1	6.0	.7	1.6
Eugene-Springfield, OR MSA	351.0	335.6	319.9	295.2	6.2	13.7	15.6	13.4	17.1	13.4	7.9	12.9	114	6.0	95.6	.9	2.4	3.4
Evansville-Henderson, IN-KY MSA	319.7	308.8	298.7	285.0	6.8	13.7	13.0	14.9	16.4	12.4	8.7	14.0	70	6.4	93.1	6.1	.6	.6
Fargo-Moorhead, ND-MN MSA........	186.0	179.1	172.1	159.9	6.3	13.8	19.5	14.8	16.7	10.9	7.2	10.9	191	5.4	97.4	.4	1.3	1.7
Fayetteville, NC MSA	331.7	318.1	305.6	284.8	9.4	16.3	17.7	18.9	14.8	10.2	6.4	6.8	271	2.3	63.1	31.9	3.1	7.6
Fayetteville-Springdale-Rogers, AR MSA	297.8	280.7	262.9	234.7	7.0	13.9	15.7	14.4	14.6	11.5	8.8	14.1	68	6.1	96.9	.9	.9	2.7
Flagstaff, AZ-UT MSA	145.4	136.3	126.7	110.9	8.3	17.2	19.8	15.1	16.6	10.5	6.1	6.4	270	2.4	68.8	1.7	1.1	11.3
Florence, AL MSA	148.4	144.2	140.7	135.3	6.3	12.7	13.7	13.8	15.3	13.4	9.9	14.8	50	6.3	86.5	13.0	.3	.5
Florence, SC MSA	141.0	134.8	128.7	119.7	6.8	15.5	14.4	14.2	16.6	12.7	8.2	11.6	165	4.7	59.9	39.6	.3	.5
Fort Collins-Loveland, CO MSA	280.0	259.7	238.4	205.1	6.7	14.5	17.1	14.2	17.8	12.8	7.1	9.9	224	4.5	96.8	.7	1.8	7.5
Fort Myers-Cape Coral, FL MSA.......	510.6	468.3	425.0	359.3	6.1	12.0	9.5	11.9	13.6	11.3	10.7	24.8	3	10.4	91.1	7.8	.9	5.9
Fort Pierce-Port St. Lucie, FL MSA	403.7	368.3	331.6	272.3	6.4	12.9	9.8	12.4	13.9	11.0	10.2	23.4	5	9.5	84.4	14.3	1.0	5.6
Fort Smith, AR-OK MSA	218.6	208.8	199.1	183.4	7.3	15.2	13.9	14.1	15.1	12.7	8.6	13.1	101	6.0	88.2	4.2	2.7	2.3
Fort Walton Beach, FL MSA	209.5	195.0	180.5	157.3	7.9	16.0	13.5	16.6	16.0	12.4	8.3	9.2	247	3.3	85.3	10.3	3.8	4.2
Fort Wayne, IN MSA	528.8	511.2	494.9	466.3	7.7	15.2	14.3	15.4	16.7	11.7	7.8	12.1	144	5.5	91.6	7.3	.9	2.2
Fresno, CA MSA	1 038.3	981.6	920.4	822.9	10.0	18.4	13.8	15.3	15.1	10.2	6.4	10.8	197	4.8	84.3	5.0	9.3	41.2
Gadsden, AL MSA.................	107.8	104.9	102.5	99.9	5.9	13.1	13.5	13.0	15.6	12.7	10.0	16.3	29	6.9	84.8	14.5	.4	.5
Gainesville, FL MSA	243.3	228.2	212.9	190.5	6.7	13.7	22.9	15.7	15.8	9.8	5.9	9.5	236	4.2	74.4	21.8	3.5	4.7
Glens Falls, NY MSA	137.1	132.9	128.7	121.9	7.1	15.0	12.1	14.8	16.1	12.4	8.1	14.4	60	6.6	97.3	2.0	.5	1.8
Goldsboro, NC MSA	123.9	119.1	114.7	107.9	7.6	15.1	13.1	17.4	16.0	12.2	8.3	10.4	210	4.1	65.5	33.1	1.2	2.1
Grand Forks, ND-MN MSA	111.7	109.2	107.0	103.4	7.0	14.6	19.2	15.3	15.1	10.1	6.7	12.0	146	6.1	95.1	1.7	1.3	2.9

X Not applicable.

[1] Latest estimate available when projections were prepared.
[2] Based on 273 metropolitan areas (245 MSAs, 17 CMSAs, and 11 NECMAs); see text for more information. When metropolitan areas share the same rank, the next lower rank is omitted.
[3] Persons of Hispanic origin may be of any race.

Source: Population Projections (BEA)—U.S. Bureau of Economic Analysis, "Regional Economic Information System (REIS) 1969-1994" on CD-ROM; Population Characteristics, 1996—U.S. Bureau of the Census, "County Population Estimates by Age, Sex, Race, and Hispanic Origin - 4/1/90 to 7/1/96" data file (related Internet site <http://www.census.gov/population/www/estimates/co_casrh.html>).

Table B–2. Metro Areas — Population Projections and Characteristics—Con.

[MSA = Metropolitan statistical area. CMSA = Consolidated MSA. PMSA = Primary MSA. NECMA = New England county metropolitan area. All areas defined as of June 30, 1996. Table includes 245 MSAs, 17 CMSAs, and 58 PMSAs not in New England; as well as 12 NECMAs. Table excludes 10 MSAs, 1 CMSA, and 15 PMSAs in New England]

Metropolitan areas	Population (BEA) Projections — 2010 (1,000)	2005 (1,000)	2000 (1,000)	1993 estimate[1] (1,000)	Under 5 years	5 to 14 years	15 to 24 years	25 to 34 years	35 to 44 years	45 to 54 years	55 to 64 years	65 years and over Percent	Rank[2]	75 years and over	White	Black	Asian or Pacific Islander	Percent Hispanic origin[3]
Grand Junction, CO MSA	125.3	118.8	112.0	100.7	6.4	15.4	12.6	11.6	16.2	13.5	9.6	14.7	54	6.4	97.9	.5	.9	9.2
Grand Rapids-Muskegon-Holland, MI MSA	1 134.5	1 088.0	1 041.0	974.2	8.0	16.3	13.7	15.7	16.4	11.3	7.1	11.5	168	5.3	90.7	7.5	1.2	3.7
Great Falls, MT MSA	84.3	83.0	82.0	80.3	7.0	14.9	14.6	13.0	15.3	13.5	9.2	12.7	124	6.0	92.9	1.6	1.1	2.0
Green Bay, WI MSA	239.3	229.3	219.4	204.5	6.9	15.1	14.8	15.9	17.4	12.0	7.1	10.8	194	5.2	95.5	.6	1.7	1.0
Greensboro--Winston Salem--High Point, NC MSA	1 303.5	1 242.8	1 184.6	1 092.0	6.6	13.1	13.2	15.6	16.4	13.2	8.9	12.9	110	5.7	79.0	19.6	1.0	1.2
Greenville, NC MSA	141.2	133.7	126.2	114.0	7.2	14.2	18.7	16.2	15.6	10.6	7.2	10.3	214	4.3	64.5	34.3	1.0	1.4
Greenville-Spartanburg-Anderson, SC MSA	1 026.5	979.0	931.8	862.2	6.3	13.0	14.4	14.7	16.0	13.5	8.8	13.3	95	5.8	81.1	17.9	.8	1.0
Harrisburg-Lebanon-Carlisle, PA MSA	702.5	674.1	646.2	605.5	6.2	13.5	12.9	14.5	17.3	12.8	8.4	14.3	61	6.6	90.8	7.6	1.5	2.2
Hartford, CT NECMA	1 273.1	1 224.2	1 177.9	1 119.6	6.7	13.7	12.1	15.5	17.1	12.7	8.0	14.1	69	6.7	88.2	9.4	2.2	8.1
Hattiesburg, MS MSA	117.1	112.9	109.0	102.2	7.5	14.3	19.4	15.1	14.4	10.6	7.5	11.3	177	5.0	73.0	26.2	.7	.9
Hickory-Morganton-Lenoir, NC MSA	358.8	342.8	327.2	302.0	6.5	13.6	12.8	14.9	16.3	14.0	9.2	12.7	122	5.4	91.2	7.7	.9	1.0
Honolulu, HI MSA	1 009.1	967.9	927.7	866.5	7.6	13.6	14.7	14.8	16.4	12.5	7.9	12.6	128	5.1	31.4	3.8	64.3	7.3
Houma, LA MSA	207.6	201.5	195.5	186.4	8.0	17.1	16.0	14.7	15.2	12.0	7.8	9.3	244	3.7	79.4	16.0	1.0	1.7
Houston-Galveston-Brazoria, TX CMSA	5 006.9	4 757.4	4 495.5	4 027.9	8.5	15.8	14.3	16.6	18.2	12.2	6.9	7.4	266	2.9	76.5	18.3	4.8	23.6
Brazoria, TX PMSA	250.7	239.9	228.8	207.2	8.1	16.8	13.5	16.1	17.6	12.5	7.6	7.9	X	3.1	89.1	8.9	1.5	20.7
Galveston-Texas City, TX PMSA	264.7	255.6	246.4	232.1	7.5	15.5	12.9	14.7	17.0	12.9	8.9	10.7	X	4.2	79.1	18.3	2.3	16.9
Houston, TX PMSA	4 491.5	4 261.8	4 020.2	3 588.6	8.6	15.8	14.5	16.7	18.3	12.2	6.8	7.2	X	2.8	75.6	18.8	5.2	24.2
Huntington-Ashland, WV-KY-OH MSA	342.5	334.7	328.9	316.4	5.7	13.0	14.8	12.7	15.4	13.9	10.0	14.5	57	6.3	97.3	2.2	.4	.5
Huntsville, AL MSA	364.7	349.8	336.0	313.7	7.2	12.8	14.6	17.9	16.0	13.4	8.7	9.5	234	3.8	77.8	19.8	1.8	1.5
Indianapolis, IN MSA	1 634.2	1 575.4	1 520.9	1 443.1	7.4	13.9	13.3	16.6	17.0	12.4	8.1	11.3	175	5.0	85.2	13.6	1.0	1.1
Iowa City, IA MSA	114.8	110.1	105.3	99.0	6.0	10.6	26.2	18.8	16.2	9.4	5.4	7.4	267	3.6	92.4	2.4	5.0	2.3
Jackson, MI MSA	165.0	161.1	157.7	152.6	6.7	14.6	12.7	15.2	17.1	12.3	8.3	13.1	102	5.9	90.6	8.4	.6	1.8
Jackson, MS MSA	473.6	455.3	437.5	407.4	7.6	14.7	15.9	16.0	16.7	11.3	7.7	10.2	217	4.5	56.1	43.3	.6	.6
Jackson, TN MSA	[4]97.9	[4]93.6	[4]89.2	[4]81.4	6.9	14.5	15.1	14.2	15.6	11.5	8.3	13.8	82	5.6	69.9	29.5	.4	.6
Jacksonville, FL MSA	1 229.7	1 153.2	1 075.4	962.4	7.8	15.8	13.2	15.5	17.0	12.0	7.5	11.1	186	4.6	75.1	22.1	2.5	3.3
Jacksonville, NC MSA	161.5	156.4	152.2	145.1	9.7	14.0	26.0	21.3	12.5	7.2	4.5	4.7	272	1.8	76.5	19.7	3.1	8.1
Jamestown, NY MSA	146.1	144.8	144.3	142.4	7.0	15.3	13.0	13.3	14.8	11.7	8.5	16.3	29	7.9	96.8	2.2	.5	3.7
Janesville-Beloit, WI MSA	157.2	153.2	149.6	144.3	6.8	15.0	13.7	14.1	16.3	13.0	8.4	12.6	127	6.0	92.9	5.9	.9	1.6
Johnson City-Kingsport-Bristol, TN-VA MSA	517.7	498.0	479.5	448.3	5.7	12.1	13.4	13.7	15.8	14.4	10.1	14.9	48	6.5	97.2	2.2	.4	.6
Johnstown, PA MSA	252.9	247.6	243.7	240.5	5.4	14.0	12.2	12.5	15.9	12.0	9.3	18.7	13	8.4	97.7	1.9	.3	.7
Jonesboro, AR MSA	(5)	(5)	(5)	(5)	7.0	14.7	18.0	14.4	14.6	12.0	8.4	11.9	151	5.5	92.9	6.1	.7	1.1
Joplin, MO MSA	168.3	160.4	152.3	139.7	6.5	14.7	13.8	13.3	15.5	12.2	8.7	15.3	44	7.1	96.4	1.1	.7	1.0
Kalamazoo-Battle Creek, MI MSA	491.6	476.7	462.8	440.2	6.9	14.7	15.2	14.2	16.5	12.2	7.8	12.4	136	5.7	88.1	9.9	1.4	2.4
Kansas City, MO-KS MSA	1 908.2	1 830.3	1 751.9	1 630.9	7.2	14.8	13.1	15.6	17.6	12.4	7.8	11.4	173	5.1	84.8	13.3	1.4	3.5
Killeen-Temple, TX MSA	314.4	302.6	290.9	269.3	9.1	15.6	19.3	17.3	14.6	9.7	6.2	8.2	262	3.6	75.5	19.7	4.1	14.9
Knoxville, TN MSA	750.4	716.2	681.8	620.3	6.3	12.5	13.8	15.0	16.4	13.3	9.2	13.4	93	5.7	92.2	6.4	1.1	.8
Kokomo, IN MSA	105.9	103.9	102.4	99.1	6.7	14.2	12.9	13.9	16.5	14.4	9.1	12.3	139	5.4	94.0	5.0	.7	1.6
La Crosse, WI-MN MSA	140.6	134.6	128.5	119.2	6.4	14.1	17.0	13.9	16.2	11.0	7.6	13.4	91	6.6	96.1	.5	3.1	.8
Lafayette, LA MSA	402.2	389.3	376.4	357.6	8.1	16.6	15.5	14.7	15.2	11.5	8.0	10.4	210	4.5	69.9	29.1	.8	1.4
Lafayette, IN MSA	188.8	182.0	175.5	165.5	6.5	12.0	23.7	15.2	14.5	10.4	6.8	10.8	195	5.0	94.2	1.8	3.7	2.0
Lake Charles, LA MSA	196.4	189.8	183.1	172.0	7.3	16.0	14.7	13.9	15.6	12.2	8.9	11.3	177	4.6	74.6	24.7	.5	1.3
Lakeland-Winter Haven, FL MSA	527.3	498.0	468.2	422.9	7.0	14.8	12.0	12.4	14.3	11.8	9.2	18.5	16	8.0	83.3	15.4	.9	5.3
Lancaster, PA MSA	517.2	495.8	474.0	438.6	7.5	15.2	13.1	14.7	16.2	12.1	7.7	13.5	87	6.5	95.4	3.0	1.5	4.7
Lansing-East Lansing, MI MSA	489.9	474.1	459.3	435.9	6.9	14.7	18.3	15.3	17.0	11.7	6.5	9.5	236	4.4	89.0	7.9	2.5	4.6
Laredo, TX MSA	206.7	194.0	179.9	156.4	11.0	18.6	18.1	14.0	13.6	9.8	6.4	8.6	256	3.7	99.1	.2	.5	94.9
Las Cruces, NM MSA	207.9	192.6	176.5	151.8	8.5	16.6	19.5	13.3	14.5	10.9	7.6	9.1	251	3.7	96.2	1.9	1.2	57.6
Las Vegas, NV-AZ MSA	1 568.4	1 419.3	1 262.2	1 010.3	7.6	14.0	12.1	15.6	16.0	13.0	9.4	12.3	138	4.7	85.6	9.1	4.2	14.1
Lawrence, KS MSA	109.2	103.3	96.9	86.4	6.0	11.5	29.0	15.5	14.9	9.4	5.4	8.3	261	3.9	89.4	4.3	3.7	3.4
Lawton, OK MSA	128.0	124.5	121.4	118.1	8.4	16.2	17.9	16.2	14.5	10.4	7.5	8.9	253	3.6	74.0	17.9	3.4	8.0
Lewiston-Auburn, ME NECMA	113.6	109.9	106.7	103.9	6.1	14.3	14.1	14.5	16.0	12.7	8.1	14.2	66	6.6	98.5	.6	.7	1.0
Lexington, KY MSA	509.6	486.1	462.8	425.9	6.6	12.4	17.5	16.4	16.9	12.1	7.7	10.3	214	4.5	88.3	10.1	1.4	1.0
Lima, OH MSA	164.8	161.6	159.1	155.9	7.1	15.5	13.4	14.2	16.0	11.7	8.2	13.9	77	6.4	90.5	8.7	.6	1.2
Lincoln, NE MSA	264.5	253.5	241.9	223.6	6.5	13.1	19.2	15.4	17.0	11.1	6.9	10.8	197	5.1	94.6	2.4	2.3	3.0
Little Rock-North Little Rock, AR MSA	630.4	602.9	576.0	532.9	7.3	14.6	15.2	15.7	16.4	12.0	7.9	10.9	193	4.8	78.0	20.8	.8	1.5
Longview-Marshall, TX MSA	225.5	218.5	211.7	199.6	7.0	16.0	13.5	12.7	15.5	12.4	9.0	13.9	76	6.5	77.4	21.7	.5	3.6

X Not applicable.

[1]Latest estimate available when projections were prepared.
[2]Based on 273 metropolitan areas (245 MSAs, 17 CMSAs, and 11 NECMAs); see text for more information. When metropolitan areas share the same rank, the next lower rank is omitted.
[3]Persons of Hispanic origin may be of any race.
[4]Excludes Chester County, which was added to the MSA on June 30, 1996.
[5]Data not available from source; new MSA effective June 30, 1996.

Source: Population Projections (BEA)—U.S. Bureau of Economic Analysis, "Regional Economic Information System (REIS) 1969-1994" on CD-ROM; Population Characteristics, 1996—U.S. Bureau of the Census, "County Population Estimates by Age, Sex, Race, and Hispanic Origin - 4/1/90 to 7/1/96" data file (related Internet site <http://www.census.gov/population/www/estimates/co_casrh.html>).

Table B–2. Metro Areas — Population Projections and Characteristics—Con.

[MSA = Metropolitan statistical area. CMSA = Consolidated MSA. PMSA = Primary MSA. NECMA = New England county metropolitan area. All areas defined as of June 30, 1996. Table includes 245 MSAs, 17 CMSAs, and 58 PMSAs not in New England; as well as 12 NECMAs. Table excludes 10 MSAs, 1 CMSA, and 15 PMSAs in New England]

Metropolitan areas	Population (BEA) Projections 2010 (1,000)	2005 (1,000)	2000 (1,000)	1993 estimate[1] (1,000)	Under 5 years	5 to 14 years	15 to 24 years	25 to 34 years	35 to 44 years	45 to 54 years	55 to 64 years	65 years and over Percent	Rank[2]	75 years and over	White	Black	Asian or Pacific Islander	Percent Hispanic origin[3]
Los Angeles-Riverside-Orange, CA CMSA	18 700.2	17 746.2	16 732.6	15 210.2	9.0	15.2	14.1	17.5	16.2	11.1	6.6	10.2	220	4.5	79.8	8.4	11.1	37.8
Los Angeles-Long Beach, CA PMSA	10 445.0	10 060.5	9 669.4	9 133.6	8.9	14.8	14.5	17.9	16.2	11.0	6.7	10.0	X	4.4	75.2	11.2	12.9	43.0
Orange, CA PMSA	3 226.2	3 046.4	2 848.9	2 515.3	8.3	13.9	14.6	17.8	16.5	12.5	6.9	9.5	X	4.3	84.8	1.8	12.8	27.9
Riverside-San Bernardino, CA PMSA	4 130.2	3 795.1	3 429.1	2 867.4	9.9	17.6	12.7	16.5	15.6	10.1	6.4	11.2	X	4.9	86.8	7.1	4.9	32.0
Ventura, CA PMSA	898.8	844.2	785.2	693.9	8.6	16.1	13.2	15.9	17.2	12.4	6.7	9.8	X	4.4	90.2	2.4	6.5	31.7
Louisville, KY-IN MSA	1 054.8	1 025.7	1 001.2	974.0	6.6	13.5	13.3	15.2	17.2	12.8	9.0	12.4	134	5.4	86.1	13.0	.8	.8
Lubbock, TX MSA	251.4	244.9	238.7	227.6	7.9	14.9	19.0	14.9	14.7	10.8	7.6	10.2	217	4.4	89.7	8.3	1.7	26.8
Lynchburg, VA MSA	227.3	219.1	211.4	200.7	6.2	12.9	13.9	14.1	15.6	13.2	9.3	14.8	51	6.8	79.7	19.5	.6	.8
Macon, GA MSA	344.5	332.2	320.9	303.0	7.5	15.1	14.1	14.1	16.1	12.5	8.3	10.6	206	4.3	60.7	38.0	1.0	1.5
Madison, WI MSA	464.7	442.5	419.8	386.4	6.3	12.5	17.7	17.5	18.7	11.5	6.4	9.4	241	4.4	93.1	3.5	3.1	2.1
Mansfield, OH MSA	182.3	179.6	177.8	175.1	6.4	14.5	13.2	13.7	16.0	13.4	9.0	13.8	81	6.1	92.5	6.8	.5	.8
McAllen-Edinburg-Mission, TX MSA	590.5	551.1	509.0	442.8	10.3	19.3	17.6	12.9	14.0	9.4	6.5	10.0	222	4.0	99.1	.3	.4	87.3
Medford-Ashland, OR MSA	192.7	183.2	173.5	158.2	6.3	14.0	12.6	11.7	16.4	14.1	9.2	15.7	39	7.2	97.2	.3	1.2	5.7
Melbourne-Titusville-Palm Bay, FL MSA	594.5	550.7	506.0	435.8	6.6	13.5	11.0	14.7	14.9	12.6	10.0	16.7	26	6.5	88.3	9.2	2.0	4.1
Memphis, TN-AR-MS MSA	1 216.8	1 168.5	1 122.2	1 042.3	8.1	15.3	14.6	16.0	16.8	11.7	7.5	10.0	222	4.3	56.8	41.9	1.1	1.1
Merced, CA MSA	239.0	226.2	212.5	192.6	11.1	20.4	13.5	15.5	14.1	9.6	6.4	9.5	234	4.0	83.8	4.8	10.3	38.3
Miami-Fort Lauderdale, FL CMSA	4 132.8	3 916.8	3 698.0	3 353.8	6.9	13.1	11.9	14.9	16.0	11.8	8.5	16.9	25	8.3	78.3	19.6	1.8	36.6
Fort Lauderdale, FL PMSA	1 763.3	1 645.7	1 526.6	1 350.8	6.4	12.2	10.6	14.6	16.1	11.5	7.8	20.8	X	10.9	80.3	17.5	1.9	10.9
Miami, FL PMSA	2 369.5	2 271.1	2 171.4	2 003.1	7.3	13.7	12.9	15.1	15.9	11.9	9.0	14.2	X	6.5	77.0	21.1	1.8	54.4
Milwaukee-Racine, WI CMSA	1 777.6	1 728.8	1 685.3	1 634.2	6.9	14.8	13.6	15.1	17.0	12.3	8.2	12.2	142	5.6	83.0	14.8	1.6	4.6
Milwaukee-Waukesha, WI PMSA	1 578.3	1 535.6	1 497.7	1 454.1	6.9	14.7	13.6	15.2	17.0	12.2	8.2	12.2	X	5.6	82.5	15.2	1.7	4.4
Racine, WI PMSA	199.3	193.1	187.6	180.2	6.9	15.6	13.2	14.9	16.9	12.7	8.1	11.8	X	5.3	86.8	12.1	.8	6.6
Minneapolis-St. Paul, MN-WI MSA	3 148.0	3 015.3	2 876.6	2 654.5	7.2	15.0	13.6	16.8	18.4	12.3	7.0	9.7	231	4.5	91.2	4.4	3.4	2.0
Mobile, AL MSA	567.7	547.3	528.9	504.9	7.5	14.7	13.9	14.6	15.7	12.2	8.6	12.7	125	5.3	70.7	28.0	.9	1.2
Modesto, CA MSA	523.0	491.5	457.4	402.4	9.8	18.5	12.4	15.3	15.4	10.9	6.6	11.1	183	5.0	90.4	1.8	6.6	26.7
Monroe, LA MSA	168.3	162.1	155.8	145.9	7.6	15.8	17.6	13.2	14.6	11.5	8.1	11.7	160	5.2	66.2	33.0	.7	1.0
Montgomery, AL MSA	353.3	339.8	327.5	307.4	7.4	14.3	15.2	15.5	16.3	11.9	8.0	11.4	174	5.0	62.4	36.7	.7	1.0
Muncie, IN MSA	126.9	124.2	122.2	119.4	5.9	11.7	21.4	12.6	14.4	12.7	8.5	12.8	116	5.8	92.4	6.6	.7	.9
Myrtle Beach, SC MSA	190.8	179.1	167.1	148.5	6.3	12.9	13.0	15.9	15.5	12.6	10.3	13.5	90	4.6	80.8	18.0	1.0	1.2
Naples, FL MSA	263.7	237.9	210.9	170.7	6.5	12.4	10.1	12.5	14.0	11.6	10.5	22.4	8	9.1	93.3	5.7	.6	17.1
Nashville, TN MSA	1 287.9	1 221.9	1 154.8	1 044.5	7.2	13.9	13.9	16.9	17.2	12.6	7.9	10.4	208	4.6	82.6	15.7	1.4	1.1
New London-Norwich, CT NECMA	282.0	271.2	261.1	248.8	7.4	14.6	12.2	16.6	16.5	12.0	7.7	12.9	113	5.9	92.1	5.3	2.0	4.1
New Orleans, LA MSA	1 427.4	1 389.6	1 354.1	1 304.0	7.4	15.1	14.9	14.7	16.6	12.1	8.1	11.1	185	4.6	62.6	35.0	2.1	4.8
New York-Northern New Jersey-Long Island, NY-NJ-CT-PA CMSA/NECMA	20 914.5	20 515.1	20 175.3	19 646.4	7.2	13.4	12.3	15.7	16.6	12.8	8.6	13.4	92	6.1	74.2	19.3	6.2	16.8
Bergen-Passaic, NJ PMSA	1 383.9	1 354.2	1 328.5	1 297.6	6.7	12.8	11.8	14.4	16.8	13.5	9.2	14.8	X	6.7	82.7	9.6	7.4	14.3
Dutchess, NY PMSA	279.6	274.3	269.8	262.9	7.3	14.0	12.9	16.1	17.3	13.2	7.7	11.7	X	5.4	87.6	9.1	3.1	4.5
Jersey City, NJ PMSA	587.4	575.0	564.9	552.8	7.2	12.7	13.2	17.7	15.9	11.6	8.6	13.0	X	5.7	75.2	15.7	8.8	38.6
Middlesex-Somerset-Hunterdon, NJ PMSA	1 276.8	1 218.0	1 156.0	1 056.8	7.1	12.9	12.7	16.5	17.9	13.3	8.2	11.5	X	4.7	84.2	7.8	7.8	8.8
Monmouth-Ocean, NJ PMSA	1 286.5	1 215.2	1 141.5	1 022.6	7.0	14.3	10.7	13.0	16.6	12.3	8.0	18.2	X	8.8	90.3	6.7	2.8	4.8
Nassau-Suffolk, NY PMSA	2 770.4	2 726.9	2 691.9	2 643.2	6.8	13.6	12.3	14.8	16.6	13.9	9.3	12.6	X	5.2	88.2	8.3	3.3	7.7
New Haven-Bridgeport-Stamford-Waterbury-Danbury, CT NECMA	1 821.4	1 756.3	1 696.0	1 628.3	6.8	13.6	11.5	15.3	16.8	13.0	8.3	14.7	X	7.0	86.5	10.9	2.5	8.9
New York, NY PMSA	8 635.7	8 599.7	8 603.7	8 572.7	7.4	13.2	12.5	16.6	16.2	12.3	8.5	13.2	X	6.1	62.1	29.0	8.4	24.7
Newark, NJ PMSA	2 049.5	2 010.9	1 979.2	1 928.6	7.2	13.9	12.3	14.9	17.2	13.2	8.4	12.9	X	5.9	73.0	22.9	3.9	11.9
Newburgh, NY-PA PMSA	443.9	419.3	392.4	352.6	8.5	16.1	12.2	15.4	17.2	12.2	7.1	11.2	X	5.0	91.0	7.2	1.5	7.9
Trenton, NJ PMSA	379.2	365.2	351.4	328.6	7.0	13.5	13.9	14.7	17.0	12.5	8.1	13.4	X	5.5	74.7	20.8	4.4	7.5
Norfolk-Virginia Beach-Newport News, VA-NC MSA	1 731.6	1 660.4	1 594.2	1 513.9	7.9	15.0	14.9	18.2	16.1	11.1	7.1	9.6	232	3.8	66.7	29.7	3.2	2.9
Ocala, FL MSA	305.4	280.1	253.8	214.1	6.4	13.8	10.3	11.5	13.6	11.7	10.6	22.1	9	8.5	84.3	14.6	.7	4.0
Odessa-Midland, TX MSA	257.4	251.3	245.5	234.5	9.5	17.6	13.2	15.0	16.0	11.2	8.3	9.2	245	3.7	91.9	6.6	1.0	30.4
Oklahoma City, OK MSA	1 144.6	1 102.0	1 060.6	995.7	7.2	15.0	15.6	14.8	16.2	12.0	8.2	10.9	190	4.8	82.3	10.8	2.2	4.6
Omaha, NE-IA MSA	758.1	730.1	701.6	658.0	7.3	15.3	14.8	15.3	17.1	12.1	7.6	10.5	207	4.6	89.4	8.5	1.5	4.3
Orlando, FL MSA	1 963.1	1 786.9	1 604.8	1 333.8	7.2	14.7	13.0	15.7	16.5	11.8	7.9	13.2	99	5.7	83.4	13.8	2.5	10.5
Owensboro, KY MSA	99.8	96.6	93.7	89.4	7.2	14.3	13.9	14.2	15.6	12.7	9.3	12.8	120	5.6	95.2	4.3	.4	.4

X Not applicable.

[1] Latest estimate available when projections were prepared.
[2] Based on 273 metropolitan areas (245 MSAs, 17 CMSAs, and 11 NECMAs); see text for more information. When metropolitan areas share the same rank, the next lower rank is omitted.
[3] Persons of Hispanic origin may be of any race.

Source: Population Projections (BEA)—U.S. Bureau of Economic Analysis, "Regional Economic Information System (REIS) 1969-1994" on CD-ROM; Population Characteristics, 1996—U.S. Bureau of the Census, "County Population Estimates by Age, Sex, Race, and Hispanic Origin - 4/1/90 to 7/1/96" data file (related Internet site <http://www.census.gov/population/www/estimates/co_casrh.html>).

[MSA = Metropolitan statistical area. CMSA = Consolidated MSA. PMSA = Primary MSA. NECMA = New England county metropolitan area. All areas defined as of June 30, 1996. Table includes 245 MSAs, 17 CMSAs, and 58 PMSAs not in New England; as well as 12 NECMAs. Table excludes 10 MSAs, 1 CMSA, and 15 PMSAs in New England]

| Metropolitan areas | Population (BEA) Projections | | | | Population characteristics, 1996 | | | | | | | | | | | | | | |
| | 2010 (1,000) | 2005 (1,000) | 2000 (1,000) | 1993 estimate[1] (1,000) | Age, percent— | | | | | | | | | | Race, percent— | | | |
					Under 5 years	5 to 14 years	15 to 24 years	25 to 34 years	35 to 44 years	45 to 54 years	55 to 64 years	65 years and over Per-cent	Rank[2]	75 years and over	White	Black	Asian or Pacific Islander	Percent Hispanic origin[3]
Panama City, FL MSA	175.5	164.8	154.1	137.2	7.3	15.9	12.7	14.9	15.8	12.8	8.7	12.0	148	4.7	84.2	12.4	2.6	2.4
Parkersburg-Marietta, WV-OH MSA.....	161.7	158.1	155.5	151.0	6.1	13.2	13.4	13.2	15.9	14.2	9.3	14.7	53	6.8	98.3	1.1	.4	.4
Pensacola, FL MSA	441.8	420.0	398.4	364.9	7.4	15.9	14.1	14.7	15.7	12.8	8.2	11.2	182	4.5	78.7	17.6	2.5	2.4
Peoria-Pekin, IL MSA	370.3	361.0	352.2	343.0	7.0	15.3	13.3	13.1	16.4	12.5	8.6	13.9	75	6.7	90.8	8.0	1.0	1.4
Philadelphia-Wilmington-Atlantic City, PA-NJ-DE-MD CMSA	6 581.9	6 388.4	6 218.3	5 941.4	7.1	14.2	12.6	15.3	16.5	12.2	8.2	13.8	80	6.2	77.6	19.4	2.7	4.7
Atlantic-Cape May, NJ PMSA	399.5	379.7	359.3	328.0	7.3	13.5	11.8	14.9	15.6	11.5	8.6	16.8	X	7.9	81.4	15.8	2.5	7.2
Philadelphia, PA-NJ PMSA	5 396.2	5 254.1	5 135.5	4 940.4	7.1	14.3	12.6	15.2	16.5	12.3	8.2	13.8	X	6.2	76.9	20.0	2.9	4.3
Vineland-Millville-Bridgeton, NJ PMSA	153.7	149.5	145.5	139.0	7.8	15.7	12.8	14.3	15.9	11.8	8.0	13.8	X	6.2	78.2	19.4	1.3	16.6
Wilmington-Newark, DE-MD PMSA ..	632.5	605.1	578.0	534.0	6.8	13.7	13.3	17.0	17.3	12.3	7.7	11.8	X	5.0	81.3	16.5	2.0	3.2
Phoenix-Mesa, AZ MSA	3 231.3	3 008.6	2 772.5	2 392.1	7.8	13.8	13.7	16.1	16.2	12.0	7.7	12.7	121	5.7	91.4	4.0	2.2	19.5
Pine Bluff, AR MSA	85.2	84.2	84.0	84.3	7.3	15.5	17.0	13.4	14.9	11.5	7.9	12.5	130	5.8	53.5	45.7	.5	.9
Pittsburgh, PA MSA	2 537.4	2 482.0	2 441.5	2 406.9	5.8	12.8	11.7	13.8	16.3	12.5	9.4	17.7	18	7.9	90.7	8.3	.9	.7
Pittsfield, MA NECMA	143.2	140.3	138.3	136.3	5.6	13.7	11.6	14.0	16.0	12.7	8.7	17.7	19	8.6	96.6	2.2	1.0	1.3
Pocatello, ID MSA	(4)	(4)	(4)	(4)	7.9	17.5	18.2	13.1	15.5	11.0	7.1	9.6	232	4.5	94.9	1.1	1.3	5.6
Portland, ME NECMA	288.6	275.3	262.4	246.1	5.7	12.8	13.7	15.5	18.0	12.8	7.8	13.7	83	6.3	98.0	.7	1.1	.8
Portland-Salem, OR-WA CMSA	2 432.1	2 299.6	2 160.3	1 944.3	6.9	14.4	13.3	14.7	17.7	13.5	7.5	12.0	146	5.8	92.4	2.7	3.9	5.6
Portland-Vancouver, OR-WA PMSA ..	2 061.5	1 948.1	1 828.9	1 644.5	6.8	14.3	13.2	14.9	18.1	13.6	7.4	11.7	X	5.6	91.8	3.0	4.3	4.7
Salem, OR PMSA	370.6	351.5	331.4	299.8	7.0	14.9	14.1	13.5	15.8	12.8	7.9	14.1	X	6.9	95.3	1.0	2.1	10.3
Providence-Warwick-Pawtucket, RI NECMA	1 012.4	978.9	949.3	914.1	6.4	13.5	12.5	16.1	16.2	11.7	7.6	15.9	36	7.6	92.5	4.8	2.2	6.3
Provo-Orem, UT MSA................	397.1	367.5	335.2	283.4	10.2	18.5	27.2	13.8	10.7	7.6	5.0	7.0	269	3.2	97.2	.2	1.8	4.0
Pueblo, CO MSA	134.9	131.8	129.1	125.7	6.6	14.9	13.3	11.8	15.2	12.6	10.3	15.4	43	6.8	96.2	2.2	.8	39.0
Punta Gorda, FL MSA	196.1	175.9	155.2	123.4	4.4	9.8	7.6	8.9	11.2	10.5	13.3	34.3	1	14.4	94.3	4.4	1.0	3.4
Raleigh-Durham-Chapel Hill, NC MSA ..	1 268.5	1 181.3	1 092.4	938.1	7.0	13.1	15.1	18.5	17.7	11.9	6.9	9.7	230	4.2	73.1	24.2	2.4	2.1
Rapid City, SD MSA	109.8	103.1	96.1	85.9	8.3	15.4	16.3	15.4	16.6	11.2	7.1	9.8	229	4.4	88.7	2.0	1.5	2.8
Reading, PA MSA	381.4	369.9	359.6	345.6	6.4	13.5	12.4	14.2	16.2	12.5	8.8	16.1	33	7.7	95.0	3.6	1.3	6.4
Redding, CA MSA	217.7	201.9	185.0	158.8	7.8	16.8	10.6	12.2	16.2	13.1	8.3	15.0	47	6.4	94.0	.8	2.4	5.0
Reno, NV MSA	348.3	329.2	309.3	274.6	7.5	13.3	12.7	16.4	17.8	12.8	8.3	11.1	184	4.4	90.2	2.5	5.2	12.1
Richland-Kennewick-Pasco, WA MSA...	222.7	207.3	190.8	166.2	8.2	17.9	13.7	14.3	16.5	12.5	7.4	9.5	236	4.1	94.5	1.9	2.7	17.1
Richmond-Petersburg, VA MSA	1 046.4	1 003.4	963.6	906.0	6.7	13.7	12.8	16.6	18.0	12.6	8.0	11.6	164	5.0	68.0	29.9	1.8	1.4
Roanoke, VA MSA	245.6	239.6	234.8	227.8	5.7	12.2	12.0	14.3	16.9	13.2	9.6	16.1	34	7.4	85.7	13.2	.9	.8
Rochester, MN MSA	134.9	129.1	122.9	112.5	7.5	15.5	12.6	16.8	17.3	13.0	7.1	10.1	221	5.0	94.5	.9	4.2	1.2
Rochester, NY MSA	1 172.9	1 149.2	1 127.5	1 089.3	7.6	14.8	12.8	15.6	16.5	12.3	7.5	12.8	116	5.9	87.8	9.9	1.8	3.7
Rockford, IL MSA	391.7	378.0	364.2	343.3	7.6	15.1	12.6	14.5	16.6	12.7	8.2	12.8	116	5.9	90.8	7.6	1.3	4.4
Rocky Mount, NC MSA...............	163.2	156.3	149.7	138.3	7.0	15.4	12.6	15.1	16.7	12.1	8.4	12.6	126	5.3	57.9	41.6	.3	1.0
Sacramento-Yolo, CA CMSA...........	2 155.4	1 997.0	1 825.9	1 576.2	8.1	15.8	12.2	15.9	17.2	11.9	7.4	11.5	171	4.8	81.9	7.0	9.7	14.4
Sacramento, CA PMSA	1 978.0	1 828.4	1 666.8	1 430.7	8.1	15.9	11.5	15.9	17.4	12.0	7.5	11.6	X	4.9	81.5	7.5	9.7	13.4
Yolo, CA PMSA	177.4	168.7	159.2	145.6	8.0	14.7	19.0	15.8	15.2	10.7	6.4	10.2	X	4.6	85.7	2.4	10.3	24.7
Saginaw-Bay City-Midland, MI MSA.....	428.0	419.7	413.4	403.1	7.0	15.5	13.6	13.9	16.5	13.1	8.0	12.5	132	5.6	88.0	10.6	.9	5.1
St. Cloud, MN MSA	178.3	171.9	165.3	155.3	6.9	16.7	19.3	14.0	14.9	10.2	7.0	11.1	187	5.3	98.3	.4	.9	.6
St. Joseph, MO MSA	106.8	104.5	102.4	98.3	6.7	14.9	13.3	13.5	15.2	11.4	8.7	16.3	28	8.0	96.2	3.1	.4	2.2
St. Louis, MO-IL MSA	2 797.5	2 713.7	2 637.2	2 528.1	7.3	15.0	13.0	15.2	16.6	12.0	8.3	12.5	128	5.7	81.0	17.6	1.2	1.3
Salinas, CA MSA	446.3	423.1	398.5	366.3	9.7	16.4	13.6	17.5	15.8	10.0	6.6	10.3	212	4.6	82.9	6.0	10.1	39.9
Salt Lake City-Ogden, UT MSA.........	1 546.8	1 441.1	1 326.5	1 154.5	9.3	17.9	17.7	15.3	14.8	10.2	6.3	8.4	260	3.7	95.0	1.2	3.0	7.3
San Angelo, TX MSA	113.0	109.4	106.0	100.2	8.0	15.3	15.7	13.8	15.1	11.0	8.1	13.0	105	6.0	93.6	4.4	1.4	30.0
San Antonio, TX MSA	1 722.5	1 636.7	1 547.6	1 407.1	8.7	15.5	15.1	14.9	15.9	11.5	7.7	10.6	203	4.4	91.3	6.6	1.6	52.1
San Diego, CA MSA	3 434.9	3 207.1	2 963.9	2 611.9	8.4	14.6	14.1	17.5	16.3	10.7	6.7	11.7	159	5.1	82.5	6.4	10.2	25.1
San Francisco-Oakland-San Jose, CA CMSA...........................	7 690.4	7 347.3	6 985.7	6 469.4	7.4	13.5	12.2	17.0	18.1	12.7	7.4	11.7	157	5.3	72.5	8.7	18.1	18.6
Oakland, CA PMSA	2 587.8	2 469.4	2 346.3	2 168.9	7.6	14.1	12.2	16.4	18.2	12.8	7.2	11.4	X	5.1	68.4	14.8	16.1	15.9
San Francisco, CA PMSA	1 808.1	1 754.9	1 701.0	1 637.7	6.1	10.8	11.2	17.4	18.5	13.3	8.4	14.2	X	6.6	67.1	7.5	24.9	17.2
San Jose, CA PMSA	1 847.8	1 764.7	1 675.5	1 543.6	8.0	13.8	13.4	18.8	17.2	12.7	7.0	9.2	X	3.9	74.3	3.8	21.2	24.8
Santa Cruz-Watsonville, CA PMSA ..	296.2	279.8	261.7	233.4	7.7	14.2	13.9	15.6	19.4	11.2	6.0	11.9	X	6.0	92.9	1.3	4.9	25.0
Santa Rosa, CA PMSA	534.0	499.8	462.2	406.3	7.6	14.9	11.0	14.3	19.0	12.3	6.7	14.3	X	6.9	93.6	1.5	3.6	13.4
Vallejo-Fairfield-Napa, CA PMSA	616.5	578.7	539.0	479.5	8.5	16.5	11.9	15.9	17.9	11.7	6.8	10.8	X	4.8	74.8	10.8	13.4	16.7
San Luis Obispo-Atascadero-Paso Robles, CA MSA	307.6	285.7	261.6	222.0	6.8	13.4	15.3	14.7	16.7	10.6	7.2	15.1	45	6.8	92.3	2.8	3.7	16.5
Santa Barbara-Santa Maria-Lompoc, CA MSA	467.9	444.9	419.7	378.0	8.0	13.6	15.8	16.2	15.5	10.9	7.1	12.9	111	6.1	90.0	3.0	5.7	32.1

X Not applicable.

[1] Latest estimate available when projections were prepared.
[2] Based on 273 metropolitan areas (245 MSAs, 17 CMSAs, and 11 NECMAs); see text for more information. When metropolitan areas share the same rank, the next lower rank is omitted.
[3] Persons of Hispanic origin may be of any race.
[4] Data not available from source; new MSA effective June 30, 1996.

Source: Population Projections (BEA)—U.S. Bureau of Economic Analysis, "Regional Economic Information System (REIS) 1969-1994" on CD-ROM; Population Characteristics, 1996—U.S. Bureau of the Census, "County Population Estimates by Age, Sex, Race, and Hispanic Origin - 4/1/90 to 7/1/96" data file (related Internet site <http://www.census.gov/population/www/estimates/co_casrh.html>).

[MSA = Metropolitan statistical area. CMSA = Consolidated MSA. PMSA = Primary MSA. NECMA = New England county metropolitan area. All areas defined as of June 30, 1996. Table includes 245 MSAs, 17 CMSAs, and 58 PMSAs not in New England; as well as 12 NECMAs. Table excludes 10 MSAs, 1 CMSA, and 15 PMSAs in New England]

| Metropolitan areas | Population (BEA) | | | | Population characteristics, 1996 | | | | | | | | | | | | | | |
| | Projections | | | | Age, percent— | | | | | | | | | | Race, percent— | | | |
	2010 (1,000)	2005 (1,000)	2000 (1,000)	1993 estimate[1] (1,000)	Under 5 years	5 to 14 years	15 to 24 years	25 to 34 years	35 to 44 years	45 to 54 years	55 to 64 years	65 years and over Per-cent	65 years and over Rank[2]	75 years and over	White	Black	Asian or Pacific Islander	Percent Hispanic origin[3]
Santa Fe, NM MSA	169.7	158.4	146.4	127.0	6.8	14.2	12.8	12.7	20.1	15.0	8.4	10.2	219	4.1	95.2	.9	1.1	45.2
Sarasota-Bradenton, FL MSA	722.5	663.1	602.0	510.5	5.2	10.5	8.6	10.7	13.0	10.8	10.3	30.9	2	15.0	92.1	6.8	.8	4.1
Savannah, GA MSA	322.0	307.9	294.3	271.6	7.7	15.3	13.8	15.8	15.8	11.7	8.1	11.7	160	4.8	61.7	36.6	1.4	1.8
Scranton--Wilkes-Barre--Hazleton, PA MSA	677.9	663.1	652.0	639.1	5.5	12.6	12.7	12.5	15.3	12.3	9.3	19.9	11	9.5	98.3	1.0	.7	.7
Seattle-Tacoma-Bremerton, WA CMSA .	4 128.5	3 861.0	3 580.4	3 188.9	7.0	13.9	13.3	16.4	18.3	13.2	7.3	10.6	204	4.8	86.0	5.0	7.7	4.0
Bremerton, WA PMSA	281.1	263.7	245.6	215.2	7.5	15.7	14.5	14.6	17.7	12.8	6.8	10.5	X	4.8	89.7	2.9	5.6	4.3
Olympia, WA PMSA	258.4	238.7	217.6	183.4	6.5	15.5	13.3	13.7	18.6	13.7	7.4	11.4	X	5.3	91.5	2.1	4.8	4.1
Seattle-Bellevue-Everett, WA PMSA	2 799.9	2 612.9	2 415.8	2 158.5	6.8	13.2	12.9	17.0	18.9	13.4	7.3	10.6	X	4.8	85.7	4.6	8.5	3.7
Tacoma, WA PMSA	789.1	745.7	701.4	631.9	7.5	15.3	14.7	15.8	16.6	12.4	7.4	10.3	X	4.7	84.2	8.0	6.3	4.7
Sharon, PA MSA	128.6	126.1	124.4	122.3	5.7	13.6	13.2	12.3	15.3	12.6	9.4	17.8	17	8.2	94.0	5.5	.4	.5
Sheboygan, WI MSA	120.0	116.1	112.3	106.1	6.3	15.2	12.8	14.3	16.6	12.2	8.2	14.5	58	7.0	96.3	.7	2.6	2.1
Sherman-Denison, TX MSA	106.4	103.7	101.2	96.1	6.5	14.4	12.7	12.2	15.0	12.7	9.6	17.0	22	8.1	90.8	7.4	.6	3.7
Shreveport-Bossier City, LA MSA	407.2	396.8	387.2	376.7	7.5	15.4	14.3	13.5	15.4	12.2	8.8	13.0	107	5.8	62.7	36.3	.7	1.4
Sioux City, IA-NE MSA	132.0	127.8	123.8	118.5	7.3	15.7	13.9	14.0	15.6	11.1	8.4	14.0	71	6.7	94.2	1.9	1.9	4.8
Sioux Falls, SD MSA	186.1	176.0	165.4	148.4	7.0	14.8	15.0	15.2	17.3	11.4	7.4	11.9	153	5.6	97.2	.7	.7	.7
South Bend, IN MSA	284.9	275.4	266.6	253.5	7.1	13.5	15.5	14.4	16.0	10.9	8.4	14.2	66	6.5	87.7	10.7	1.3	2.7
Spokane, WA MSA	456.4	437.1	417.4	390.9	6.7	14.9	14.3	14.0	16.7	12.5	7.7	13.2	98	6.4	94.5	1.6	2.3	2.6
Springfield, IL MSA	223.3	214.8	206.1	194.5	7.2	14.9	11.5	14.6	17.4	12.3	8.1	14.0	73	6.9	90.5	8.3	1.0	.9
Springfield, MO MSA	354.0	333.1	311.6	282.3	6.3	13.9	16.6	14.1	16.4	11.9	7.9	13.0	108	6.0	97.0	1.7	.8	1.0
Springfield, MA NECMA	661.0	640.9	623.1	597.6	6.6	14.3	14.3	15.5	15.9	11.6	7.5	14.4	59	6.6	90.2	7.7	1.9	9.8
State College, PA MSA	152.3	145.7	138.9	129.1	5.3	10.4	28.4	15.6	14.1	10.4	6.3	9.5	236	4.3	93.0	2.6	4.3	1.4
Steubenville-Weirton, OH-WV MSA	140.7	140.1	140.6	140.8	5.2	12.5	13.3	11.8	15.9	13.4	10.8	17.2	21	7.2	95.3	4.2	.4	.6
Stockton-Lodi, CA MSA	628.8	596.4	561.8	510.9	9.4	17.7	13.1	15.2	15.6	10.8	6.7	11.6	162	5.2	77.9	5.8	15.2	27.7
Sumter, SC MSA	123.0	117.9	112.9	106.1	7.6	15.4	15.9	17.4	15.5	11.1	7.2	9.9	227	4.1	54.1	44.6	1.1	1.5
Syracuse, NY MSA	803.4	789.6	777.4	754.8	7.6	15.2	13.8	15.3	15.7	11.7	7.7	13.0	102	5.8	91.7	6.2	1.5	1.7
Tallahassee, FL MSA	334.4	310.6	285.9	249.6	6.6	14.8	20.9	15.1	16.9	10.7	6.1	9.0	252	3.8	64.9	33.1	1.7	3.1
Tampa-St. Petersburg-Clearwater, FL MSA	2 752.3	2 579.7	2 403.1	2 136.7	6.1	12.5	10.8	13.2	15.0	11.5	9.0	21.9	10	10.4	87.9	10.2	1.6	8.6
Terre Haute, IN MSA	157.8	154.8	152.6	150.0	6.2	13.0	15.8	13.7	15.2	11.6	8.5	15.9	36	7.5	94.4	4.3	1.0	.9
Texarkana, TX-Texarkana, AR MSA	132.6	129.1	126.1	121.8	6.9	15.6	13.4	12.9	15.7	12.4	8.8	14.3	63	6.5	75.7	23.4	.4	1.8
Toledo, OH MSA	661.9	646.6	633.6	613.6	7.2	14.4	15.7	14.7	16.0	11.4	7.8	12.9	111	5.9	86.3	12.2	1.2	3.9
Topeka, KS MSA	186.5	180.2	174.0	164.2	6.7	14.5	13.4	14.2	17.1	12.5	8.5	13.1	102	6.1	88.9	9.0	1.0	6.4
Tucson, AZ MSA	889.6	842.5	793.2	709.9	7.4	13.1	14.6	15.2	16.2	11.5	8.2	13.8	79	6.1	90.5	3.7	2.3	27.9
Tulsa, OK MSA	865.4	831.0	796.9	738.3	7.2	15.0	14.0	14.2	16.7	12.6	8.6	11.6	163	5.0	83.8	8.5	1.1	2.7
Tuscaloosa, AL MSA	177.3	170.6	164.4	155.1	6.4	12.6	20.4	14.5	15.5	11.0	8.1	11.5	169	5.0	71.3	27.6	1.0	.9
Tyler, TX MSA	187.8	179.7	171.5	157.3	7.1	14.9	13.8	13.2	15.7	12.4	9.0	14.0	72	6.2	77.0	21.9	.6	7.1
Utica-Rome, NY MSA	319.2	316.7	315.9	317.5	7.0	14.6	12.6	14.5	15.0	11.9	8.1	16.2	31	7.3	93.7	5.1	1.0	2.5
Victoria, TX MSA	93.3	89.3	85.2	78.2	8.3	17.6	13.4	13.6	16.1	11.8	8.1	11.0	189	4.6	92.4	6.8	.5	38.9
Visalia-Tulare-Porterville, CA MSA	423.9	401.4	376.9	338.2	10.3	19.9	13.3	14.4	14.4	10.3	6.4	11.0	188	5.1	90.8	1.7	5.8	44.9
Waco, TX MSA	217.7	211.4	205.1	194.5	7.5	14.6	17.1	12.8	14.3	11.2	8.5	14.0	74	6.4	82.2	16.4	1.0	14.9
Washington-Baltimore, DC-MD-VA-WV CMSA	8 396.3	7 996.0	7 593.8	6 985.6	7.1	13.8	12.4	17.5	18.1	13.2	7.5	10.3	216	4.4	69.2	25.7	4.8	4.9
Baltimore, MD PMSA	2 791.0	2 692.6	2 596.7	2 443.9	7.0	14.3	12.0	16.2	17.4	12.7	8.0	12.3	X	5.3	70.1	27.2	2.4	1.7
Hagerstown, MD PMSA	150.9	143.9	136.8	126.0	6.1	13.5	12.3	15.6	16.2	12.6	8.7	15.0	X	6.9	91.7	7.1	.9	1.0
Washington, DC-MD-VA-WV PMSA .	5 454.5	5 159.5	4 860.3	4 415.6	7.1	13.6	12.6	18.3	18.6	13.5	7.2	9.1	X	3.8	68.1	25.4	6.2	6.8
Waterloo-Cedar Falls, IA MSA	125.8	124.2	123.2	124.4	6.0	14.1	17.2	12.4	16.1	12.1	8.5	13.5	89	6.3	91.4	7.4	1.1	1.1
Wausau, WI MSA	138.9	133.4	127.8	119.6	6.6	16.1	13.2	14.2	16.8	12.5	7.8	12.7	122	5.9	96.6	.1	2.8	.5
West Palm Beach-Boca Raton, FL MSA	1 259.4	1 168.1	1 073.8	931.8	6.3	11.8	9.8	13.4	14.8	10.9	8.6	24.3	4	11.8	83.9	14.4	1.5	9.8
Wheeling, WV-OH MSA	159.3	158.1	158.1	158.6	5.6	12.3	13.1	12.0	15.6	12.7	10.2	18.5	15	8.2	97.4	2.1	.4	.4
Wichita, KS MSA	580.9	560.2	539.8	504.9	7.7	15.5	13.6	15.3	16.7	11.6	7.9	11.9	153	5.3	88.5	8.1	2.3	5.3
Wichita Falls, TX MSA	134.7	133.7	133.1	130.0	7.3	14.6	15.7	14.3	14.4	11.6	9.0	13.1	100	6.0	87.7	9.4	2.0	10.0
Williamsport, PA MSA	132.1	128.5	125.4	120.9	6.4	14.5	12.5	13.6	16.2	12.3	8.6	15.8	38	7.5	96.6	2.7	.5	.7
Wilmington, NC MSA	248.7	232.3	215.7	187.4	6.3	13.4	13.1	14.5	16.3	13.0	9.7	13.6	84	5.1	79.0	20.0	.6	1.3
Yakima, WA MSA	238.6	229.1	219.4	203.7	8.7	17.2	14.4	13.6	15.0	11.6	7.3	12.3	137	6.1	91.0	1.5	1.8	29.6
York, PA MSA	401.8	388.4	376.0	353.8	6.5	13.9	12.0	14.9	17.6	13.3	8.1	13.6	86	6.2	95.1	3.9	.9	2.0
Youngstown-Warren, OH MSA	625.3	617.7	613.8	605.3	6.3	13.9	12.6	12.9	16.1	12.5	9.6	16.2	32	6.7	89.2	10.2	.5	1.5
Yuba City, CA MSA	163.2	155.1	146.5	132.4	9.7	17.8	12.3	14.3	14.4	11.7	7.8	11.9	155	5.2	83.1	2.9	11.5	17.5
Yuma, AZ MSA	156.7	148.3	139.6	124.5	8.6	15.7	15.5	14.6	13.8	10.1	8.2	13.5	88	5.4	93.1	3.4	1.8	44.8

X Not applicable.

[1]Latest estimate available when projections were prepared.
[2]Based on 273 metropolitan areas (245 MSAs, 17 CMSAs, and 11 NECMAs); see text for more information. When metropolitan areas share the same rank, the next lower rank is omitted.
[3]Persons of Hispanic origin may be of any race.

Source: Population Projections (BEA)—U.S. Bureau of Economic Analysis, "Regional Economic Information System (REIS) 1969-1994" on CD-ROM; Population Characteristics, 1996—U.S. Bureau of the Census, "County Population Estimates by Age, Sex, Race, and Hispanic Origin - 4/1/90 to 7/1/96" data file (related Internet site <http://www.census.gov/population/www/estimates/co_casrh.html>).

Table B–3. Metro Areas — Households, Births, and Deaths

[MSA = Metropolitan statistical area. CMSA = Consolidated MSA. PMSA = Primary MSA. NECMA = New England county metropolitan area. All areas defined as of June 30, 1996. Table includes 245 MSAs, 17 CMSAs, and 58 PMSAs not in New England; as well as 12 NECMAs. Table excludes 10 MSAs, 1 CMSA, and 15 PMSAs in New England]

Metropolitan areas	Households, 1997[1] Number	Households, 1997[1] Percent change, 1990–1997	Births Number 1994	Births Number 1992	Births Number 1990	Births Rate[2] 1994	Births Rate[2] 1992	Births Rate[2] 1990	Deaths Number 1994	Deaths Number 1992	Deaths Number 1990	Deaths Rate Total[2] 1994	Deaths Rate Total[2] 1992	Deaths Rate Total[2] 1990	Deaths Rate By cause,[3] 1992 Cardio-vascular diseases	Deaths Rate By cause,[3] 1992 Motor vehicle accidents
Abilene, TX MSA	44 300	2.3	2 026	2 153	2 142	16.7	17.7	17.9	1 071	1 030	1 020	8.8	8.5	8.5	379.2	6.6
Albany, GA MSA	41 600	5.7	1 847	2 025	2 075	15.9	17.6	18.4	1 000	882	884	8.6	7.7	7.9	260.0	16.5
Albany-Schenectady-Troy, NY MSA	337 300	2.1	11 543	11 829	12 539	13.1	13.6	14.6	8 210	8 186	7 860	9.3	9.4	9.1	429.9	10.0
Albuquerque, NM MSA	253 000	14.2	10 211	10 178	10 125	15.8	16.5	17.2	4 534	4 034	3 830	7.0	6.5	6.5	222.9	20.0
Alexandria, LA MSA	45 200	−1.6	1 928	2 046	2 049	15.3	15.7	15.6	1 279	1 253	1 204	10.1	9.6	9.2	401.8	17.6
Allentown-Bethlehem-Easton, PA MSA	234 200	3.7	7 415	7 808	8 184	12.1	12.9	13.8	6 119	5 907	5 591	10.0	9.8	9.4	423.4	15.2
Altoona, PA MSA	50 800	.9	1 539	1 665	1 604	11.6	12.7	12.3	1 595	1 491	1 534	12.0	11.3	11.8	561.5	18.3
Amarillo, TX MSA	78 700	9.5	3 259	3 269	3 314	16.4	17.1	17.7	1 822	1 626	1 649	9.1	8.5	8.8	365.2	21.9
Anchorage, AK MSA	91 600	10.8	4 658	4 944	4 897	18.5	20.1	21.6	939	889	790	3.7	3.6	3.5	99.8	14.3
Anniston, AL MSA	43 400	1.0	1 608	1 689	1 700	14.3	14.6	14.7	1 171	1 120	1 129	10.4	9.7	9.7	411.8	24.2
Appleton-Oshkosh-Neenah, WI MSA	126 100	9.2	4 526	4 619	4 704	13.6	14.3	14.9	2 457	2 354	2 337	7.4	7.3	7.4	319.4	10.5
Asheville, NC MSA	86 400	11.8	2 448	2 540	2 620	12.0	12.8	13.7	2 209	2 102	1 996	10.8	10.6	10.4	430.2	11.6
Athens, GA MSA	51 900	10.3	1 716	1 780	1 865	12.9	13.8	14.8	865	820	844	6.5	6.3	6.7	254.6	19.3
Atlanta, GA MSA	1 330 200	20.6	54 132	52 210	52 543	16.2	16.6	17.8	21 950	20 132	19 422	6.6	6.4	6.6	239.0	15.6
Augusta-Aiken, GA-SC MSA	166 100	11.4	6 892	7 270	7 549	15.4	16.4	18.2	3 792	3 676	3 669	8.5	8.3	8.8	349.2	16.7
Austin-San Marcos, TX MSA	403 700	23.8	15 717	14 901	14 746	16.2	16.5	17.4	5 481	5 019	4 606	5.7	5.6	5.4	203.4	18.0
Bakersfield, CA MSA	206 100	13.6	12 622	12 978	12 495	20.6	22.1	22.9	4 185	4 097	4 020	6.8	7.0	7.4	286.4	22.3
Bangor, ME NECMA	54 200	.3	1 608	1 721	1 961	11.0	11.8	13.4	1 336	1 210	1 196	9.1	8.3	8.2	338.2	15.1
Barnstable-Yarmouth, MA NECMA	85 700	10.5	2 155	2 255	2 475	11.0	11.9	13.3	2 385	2 348	2 196	12.2	12.3	11.8	504.8	13.1
Baton Rouge, LA MSA	204 100	8.3	8 890	9 238	9 094	15.9	16.9	17.2	4 001	3 799	3 774	7.2	7.0	7.1	285.2	18.9
Beaumont-Port Arthur, TX MSA	139 000	3.5	5 529	5 840	5 531	14.8	15.8	15.3	3 623	3 526	3 420	9.7	9.5	9.5	381.7	22.2
Bellingham, WA MSA	58 200	19.9	1 912	1 839	1 771	13.1	13.3	13.9	1 008	1 020	968	6.9	7.4	7.6	302.5	13.8
Benton Harbor, MI MSA	61 300	.5	2 244	2 573	2 628	13.9	15.9	16.3	1 566	1 455	1 565	9.7	9.0	9.7	390.7	13.0
Billings, MT MSA	49 900	11.7	1 597	1 725	1 693	13.0	14.6	14.9	974	899	858	7.9	7.6	7.6	273.5	14.4
Biloxi-Gulfport-Pascagoula, MS MSA	125 000	11.8	5 296	5 316	5 120	15.7	16.5	16.4	2 990	2 634	2 590	8.9	8.2	8.3	342.7	16.8
Binghamton, NY MSA	95 800	−4.8	3 135	3 516	3 848	12.0	13.2	14.5	2 442	2 447	2 462	9.3	9.2	9.3	436.3	10.5
Birmingham, AL MSA	342 900	7.2	12 459	12 647	13 310	14.2	14.8	15.8	8 836	8 390	8 462	10.0	9.8	10.1	370.3	24.4
Bismarck, ND MSA	34 600	10.3	1 197	1 209	1 215	13.6	14.1	14.5	651	623	604	7.4	7.2	7.2	309.4	10.5
Bloomington, IN MSA	42 600	8.3	1 129	1 200	1 272	9.9	10.8	11.7	673	589	571	5.9	5.3	5.2	223.3	12.7
Bloomington-Normal, IL MSA	51 800	10.7	1 907	1 809	1 821	14.0	13.6	14.1	981	919	905	7.2	6.9	7.0	288.9	11.3
Boise City, ID MSA	138 600	27.4	5 426	5 303	4 995	15.6	16.6	16.9	2 323	2 236	2 115	6.7	7.0	7.1	283.8	17.5
Boston-Worcester-Lawrence-Lowell-Brockton, MA-NH NECMA	2 170 100	2.8	81 167	84 482	89 747	14.2	14.9	15.8	49 425	48 285	48 098	8.6	8.5	8.5	340.4	8.7
Brownsville-Harlingen-San Benito, TX MSA	88 200	20.4	7 691	7 328	6 633	25.7	26.3	25.5	1 854	1 703	1 601	6.2	6.1	6.2	209.3	14.0
Bryan-College Station, TX MSA	47 100	7.7	1 921	1 860	1 880	14.7	14.9	15.4	616	586	594	4.7	4.7	4.9	182.1	17.6
Buffalo-Niagara Falls, NY MSA	458 000	−.8	15 785	16 719	17 829	13.3	14.0	15.0	12 468	12 378	12 353	10.5	10.4	10.4	494.1	12.1
Burlington, VT NECMA	71 500	10.4	2 664	2 716	2 790	14.3	15.0	15.8	1 166	1 212	1 141	6.2	6.7	6.4	279.1	7.7
Canton-Massillon, OH MSA	153 800	3.1	5 296	5 516	5 743	13.2	13.8	14.6	3 967	3 727	3 751	9.9	9.3	9.5	394.9	16.3
Casper, WY MSA	25 700	7.8	955	950	932	14.9	15.2	15.2	451	419	424	7.1	6.7	6.9	222.9	30.5
Cedar Rapids, IA MSA	70 800	8.1	2 550	2 644	2 644	14.4	15.3	15.7	1 363	1 234	1 239	7.7	7.1	7.3	276.3	6.4
Champaign-Urbana, IL MSA	62 300	−2.5	2 251	2 426	2 581	13.6	13.9	14.9	1 157	1 021	1 039	7.0	5.9	6.0	227.6	9.7
Charleston-North Charleston, SC MSA	175 100	−1.4	8 017	9 398	9 962	15.5	17.9	19.7	3 699	3 533	3 479	7.2	6.7	6.9	263.1	17.1
Charleston, WV MSA	104 000	3.6	3 515	3 178	3 158	13.8	12.6	12.6	2 806	2 612	2 585	11.0	10.3	10.3	428.7	19.0
Charlotte-Gastonia-Rock Hill, NC-SC MSA	509 500	15.6	18 454	18 648	19 300	14.6	15.4	16.6	10 274	9 698	9 285	8.1	8.0	8.0	334.7	14.0
Charlottesville, VA MSA	54 000	10.9	1 820	1 839	1 915	13.0	13.6	14.6	1 066	944	957	7.6	7.0	7.3	264.6	17.0
Chattanooga, TN-GA MSA	173 300	6.2	6 012	5 893	6 360	13.7	13.7	15.0	4 413	4 028	4 060	10.0	9.4	9.6	410.0	17.2
Cheyenne, WY MSA	30 600	8.9	1 193	1 296	1 205	15.3	17.2	16.5	546	564	525	7.0	7.5	7.2	277.2	30.5
Chicago-Gary-Kenosha, IL-IN-WI CMSA	3 105 300	4.6	147 998	149 552	151 373	17.4	17.8	18.4	72 365	69 577	69 963	8.5	8.3	8.5	342.2	11.3
Chicago, IL PMSA	2 790 900	4.5	135 468	136 483	138 326	17.7	18.1	18.7	64 633	61 962	62 514	8.5	8.2	8.4	338.7	10.6
Gary, IN PMSA	225 000	4.2	8 939	9 273	9 261	14.5	15.1	15.3	5 583	5 483	5 308	9.0	8.9	8.8	367.7	17.4
Kankakee, IL PMSA	37 200	7.4	1 565	1 628	1 705	15.5	16.4	17.7	1 022	1 019	1 005	10.1	10.3	10.4	424.0	23.2
Kenosha, WI PMSA	52 200	11.0	2 026	2 168	2 081	14.7	16.2	16.2	1 127	1 113	1 136	8.2	8.3	8.9	362.2	13.4
Chico-Paradise, CA MSA	80 000	11.6	2 483	2 610	2 644	12.9	13.8	14.5	1 984	2 038	1 988	10.3	10.8	10.9	426.1	23.3
Cincinnati-Hamilton, OH-KY-IN CMSA	722 600	6.4	27 798	28 578	29 599	14.7	15.4	16.3	16 276	15 787	15 573	8.6	8.5	8.6	350.5	13.2
Cincinnati, OH-KY-IN PMSA	605 000	5.3	23 550	24 144	25 174	14.9	15.5	16.5	14 005	13 630	13 431	8.9	8.8	8.8	363.7	12.5
Hamilton-Middletown, OH PMSA	117 600	12.5	4 248	4 434	4 425	13.4	14.6	15.2	2 271	2 157	2 142	7.2	7.1	7.3	283.2	16.8
Clarksville-Hopkinsville, TN-KY MSA	63 000	12.5	3 772	3 862	3 409	20.4	21.6	20.1	1 364	1 151	1 129	7.4	6.4	6.7	241.2	18.5

[1] As of January 1. Data subject to copyright; see below for source citation.
[2] Per 1,000 resident population estimated as of July 1 for 1994 and 1992 and enumerated as of April 1 for 1990.
[3] Per 100,000 resident population estimated as of July 1, 1992.

Source: Households, 1997—Market Statistics, New York, NY, annual (copyright); Households, 1990—U.S. Bureau of the Census, 1990 Census of Population and Housing, Summary Tape File (STF) 1C on CD-ROM; Births—U.S. National Center for Health Statistics, "Vital Statistics of the United States, Vol. I, Natality," annual and unpublished data; Deaths—U.S. National Center for Health Statistics, "Vital Statistics of the United States, Vol. II, Mortality," annual and unpublished data.

[MSA = Metropolitan statistical area. CMSA = Consolidated MSA. PMSA = Primary MSA. NECMA = New England county metropolitan area. All areas defined as of June 30, 1996. Table includes 245 MSAs, 17 CMSAs, and 58 PMSAs not in New England; as well as 12 NECMAs. Table excludes 10 MSAs, 1 CMSA, and 15 PMSAs in New England]

Metropolitan areas	Households, 1997[1]		Births						Deaths							
			Number			Rate[2]			Number			Rate				
												Total[2]			By cause,[3] 1992	
	Number	Percent change, 1990–1997	1994	1992	1990	1994	1992	1990	1994	1992	1990	1994	1992	1990	Cardio-vascular diseases	Motor vehicle accidents
Cleveland-Akron, OH CMSA	1 123 600	2.7	41 141	43 425	44 473	14.2	15.1	15.6	28 211	27 180	27 458	9.7	9.4	9.6	399.3	9.0
Akron, OH PMSA	262 200	5.2	9 326	9 604	9 807	13.9	14.4	14.9	5 838	6 063	5 804	8.7	9.1	8.8	365.0	6.7
Cleveland-Lorain-Elyria, OH PMSA ..	861 400	1.9	31 815	33 821	34 666	14.3	15.3	15.7	22 373	21 117	21 654	10.0	9.5	9.8	409.6	9.7
Colorado Springs, CO MSA	178 300	21.3	7 791	7 540	7 350	17.2	17.9	18.5	2 391	2 210	2 140	5.3	5.3	5.4	189.9	14.3
Columbia, MO MSA	48 000	14.5	1 697	1 725	1 682	14.0	14.8	15.0	723	716	673	6.0	6.1	6.0	231.0	9.4
Columbia, SC MSA	180 100	10.3	7 052	7 320	7 606	14.9	15.5	16.8	3 497	3 422	3 367	7.4	7.3	7.4	270.7	15.9
Columbus, GA-AL MSA	96 800	4.4	4 502	4 979	4 804	16.5	18.5	18.4	2 411	2 333	2 440	8.8	8.7	9.4	343.6	20.8
Columbus, OH MSA	553 700	7.8	21 867	22 071	21 894	15.4	15.9	16.3	10 922	10 386	10 209	7.7	7.5	7.6	298.6	10.0
Corpus Christi, TX MSA	130 300	9.9	6 307	6 350	6 352	16.8	17.6	18.2	2 715	2 583	2 484	7.2	7.1	7.1	279.8	16.3
Cumberland, MD-WV MSA	39 600	Z	943	1 224	1 240	9.3	12.1	12.2	1 297	1 212	1 196	12.8	11.9	11.8	548.4	13.8
Dallas-Fort Worth, TX CMSA...........	1 717 500	13.9	75 951	75 374	76 332	17.3	17.9	18.9	28 978	27 286	26 774	6.6	6.5	6.6	258.2	14.4
Dallas, TX PMSA	1 140 600	13.9	51 822	50 885	50 835	17.8	18.2	19.0	18 777	17 822	17 350	6.5	6.4	6.5	250.0	14.4
Fort Worth-Arlington, TX PMSA	576 900	13.9	24 129	24 489	25 497	16.4	17.2	18.7	10 201	9 464	9 424	7.0	6.7	6.9	274.3	14.5
Danville, VA MSA	43 800	3.5	1 354	1 343	1 501	12.3	12.3	13.8	1 300	1 332	1 260	11.8	12.2	11.6	550.4	26.6
Davenport-Moline-Rock Island, IA-IL MSA	139 800	2.6	4 772	5 146	5 223	13.4	14.4	14.9	3 374	3 223	3 133	9.4	9.0	8.9	396.5	13.5
Dayton-Springfield, OH MSA	364 200	Z	13 018	13 979	14 388	13.6	14.6	15.1	8 669	8 321	8 261	9.1	8.7	8.7	373.5	12.4
Daytona Beach, FL MSA	187 800	13.6	4 710	4 802	5 070	10.6	11.3	12.7	5 549	5 225	4 856	12.5	12.3	12.2	568.6	13.9
Decatur, AL MSA	53 200	8.1	1 933	1 920	2 005	14.1	14.1	15.2	1 223	1 183	1 172	8.9	8.7	8.9	384.0	19.9
Decatur, IL MSA	45 600	–.9	1 650	1 723	1 725	14.1	14.6	14.7	1 172	1 130	1 179	10.0	9.6	10.1	452.9	16.1
Denver-Boulder-Greeley, CO CMSA	914 600	16.5	32 842	33 925	33 062	15.0	16.2	16.7	13 979	12 862	12 321	6.4	6.2	6.2	227.6	14.1
Boulder-Longmont, CO PMSA	103 600	17.2	3 069	3 279	3 324	12.3	13.8	14.8	1 246	1 103	1 098	5.0	4.6	4.9	180.5	8.8
Denver, CO PMSA	756 100	16.4	27 514	28 360	27 536	15.3	16.6	17.0	11 796	10 840	10 375	6.6	6.3	6.4	231.1	14.3
Greeley, CO PMSA	54 900	15.7	2 259	2 286	2 202	15.6	16.8	16.7	937	919	848	6.5	6.8	6.4	265.9	21.3
Des Moines, IA MSA	167 500	9.4	6 346	6 498	6 261	15.2	16.0	15.9	3 224	2 974	3 113	7.7	7.3	7.9	296.8	13.0
Detroit-Ann Arbor-Flint, MI CMSA......	1 968 400	2.7	79 449	82 661	88 488	15.2	15.8	17.1	45 955	44 255	44 303	8.8	8.5	8.5	366.7	12.8
Ann Arbor, MI PMSA	191 000	9.1	6 916	6 929	7 248	13.5	13.7	14.8	3 176	3 109	3 012	6.2	6.2	6.1	255.7	13.7
Detroit, MI PMSA	1 612 000	2.0	65 924	68 469	73 585	15.4	15.9	17.2	39 144	37 494	37 728	9.1	8.7	8.8	379.2	12.3
Flint, MI PMSA	165 400	2.5	6 609	7 263	7 655	15.3	16.8	17.8	3 635	3 652	3 563	8.4	8.5	8.3	371.5	16.0
Dothan, AL MSA	50 400	4.1	2 005	2 129	2 186	15.1	16.0	16.7	1 176	1 084	943	8.8	8.1	7.2	337.9	15.0
Dover, DE MSA	44 300	11.7	1 895	1 908	2 041	15.9	16.5	18.4	925	931	893	7.7	8.0	8.0	304.7	39.7
Dubuque, IA MSA	32 100	4.2	1 177	1 168	1 259	13.4	13.4	14.6	873	810	842	9.9	9.3	9.7	422.5	20.6
Duluth-Superior, MN-WI MSA	95 900	.7	2 649	2 864	2 880	11.0	11.8	12.0	2 697	2 582	2 596	11.2	10.7	10.8	451.4	12.8
Eau Claire, WI MSA	52 900	5.0	1 776	1 803	1 913	12.5	12.9	13.9	1 280	1 140	1 157	9.0	8.1	8.4	337.2	12.1
El Paso, TX MSA	207 500	16.3	15 607	15 771	14 964	23.4	25.1	25.3	3 635	3 424	3 203	5.5	5.4	5.4	190.7	18.6
Elkhart-Goshen, IN MSA	62 100	9.5	2 691	2 631	2 720	16.4	16.5	17.4	1 298	1 208	1 151	7.9	7.6	7.4	334.5	16.3
Elmira, NY MSA	34 600	–1.9	1 173	1 274	1 387	12.4	13.4	14.6	947	978	970	10.0	10.3	10.2	433.0	16.8
Enid, OK MSA	22 800	1.5	747	768	839	13.2	13.6	14.8	592	579	603	10.4	10.2	10.6	419.5	19.5
Erie, PA MSA	104 100	2.5	3 933	4 104	4 211	14.0	14.7	15.3	2 702	2 552	2 617	9.6	9.2	9.5	410.1	11.8
Eugene-Springfield, OR MSA	121 300	9.5	3 570	3 647	3 877	11.9	12.5	13.7	2 545	2 382	2 211	8.5	8.2	7.8	311.9	12.0
Evansville-Henderson, IN-KY MSA	114 000	4.9	3 821	3 845	4 183	13.3	13.6	15.0	2 981	2 800	2 753	10.4	9.9	9.9	397.1	18.0
Fargo-Moorhead, ND-MN MSA........	63 600	10.1	2 210	2 259	2 225	13.6	14.3	14.5	1 093	1 070	989	6.7	6.8	6.5	282.8	13.9
Fayetteville, NC MSA	94 700	3.5	5 590	6 533	5 791	19.7	23.6	21.1	1 741	1 628	1 626	6.1	5.9	5.9	225.5	20.9
Fayetteville-Springdale-Rogers, AR MSA	102 400	26.5	3 712	3 376	3 262	15.2	15.0	15.5	2 064	1 927	1 824	8.5	8.5	8.6	344.6	21.3
Flagstaff, AZ-UT MSA	38 100	20.4	1 821	1 967	2 062	16.0	18.3	20.3	500	493	449	4.4	4.6	4.4	149.7	25.1
Florence, AL MSA	53 500	4.9	1 750	1 752	1 804	13.0	13.1	13.7	1 390	1 328	1 325	10.3	9.9	10.1	441.8	29.9
Florence, SC MSA	44 300	10.2	1 724	1 856	1 952	14.2	15.7	17.1	1 140	1 092	1 132	9.4	9.2	9.9	416.1	22.0
Fort Collins-Loveland, CO MSA	85 200	20.9	2 781	2 685	2 771	13.1	13.5	14.9	1 235	1 101	1 027	5.8	5.6	5.5	214.9	14.6
Fort Myers-Cape Coral, FL MSA......	159 700	14.0	4 312	4 229	4 534	11.7	12.0	13.5	4 374	3 984	3 771	11.9	11.3	11.3	480.7	21.5
Fort Pierce-Port St. Lucie, FL MSA	116 700	15.3	3 349	3 523	3 784	13.0	13.2	15.1	3 369	2 945	2 778	12.1	11.1	11.1	489.1	19.1
Fort Smith, AR-OK MSA.............	73 200	9.4	2 843	2 743	2 880	15.3	15.2	16.4	1 940	1 771	1 771	10.5	9.8	10.1	449.6	18.8
Fort Walton Beach, FL MSA	61 500	15.4	2 434	2 570	2 507	15.1	16.8	17.4	1 058	1 017	919	6.6	6.6	6.4	260.8	13.7
Fort Wayne, IN MSA	178 600	5.8	7 500	7 562	7 871	16.0	16.3	17.3	3 907	3 844	3 778	8.3	8.3	8.3	393.9	16.2
Fresno, CA MSA	286 800	15.0	17 520	18 149	17 394	20.9	22.5	23.0	6 230	5 806	5 521	7.4	7.2	7.3	275.2	30.0
Gadsden, AL MSA	40 000	3.4	1 334	1 352	1 345	13.1	13.5	13.5	1 249	1 112	1 140	12.2	11.1	11.4	502.5	18.0
Gainesville, FL MSA	79 800	12.0	2 483	2 561	2 745	12.9	13.5	15.1	1 357	1 238	1 206	7.0	6.5	6.6	210.0	14.3
Glens Falls, NY MSA	44 500	3.9	1 630	1 576	1 741	13.4	13.0	14.7	1 226	1 058	1 112	10.1	8.8	9.4	381.5	17.4
Goldsboro, NC MSA	41 100	11.4	1 602	1 625	1 704	14.7	15.1	16.3	922	913	904	8.5	8.5	8.6	348.3	18.6
Grand Forks, ND-MN MSA	37 900	1.5	1 552	1 593	1 693	14.9	15.4	16.4	820	830	751	7.9	8.0	7.3	344.8	10.6

Z Less than .05 percent.

[1]As of January 1. Data subject to copyright; see below for source citation.
[2]Per 1,000 resident population estimated as of July 1 for 1994 and 1992 and enumerated as of April 1 for 1990.
[3]Per 100,000 resident population estimated as of July 1, 1992.

Source: Households, 1997—Market Statistics, New York, NY, annual (copyright);   Households, 1990—U.S. Bureau of the Census, 1990 Census of Population and Housing, Summary Tape File (STF) 1C on CD-ROM;   Births—U.S. National Center for Health Statistics, "Vital Statistics of the United States, Vol. I, Natality," annual and unpublished data;   Deaths—U.S. National Center for Health Statistics, "Vital Statistics of the United States, Vol. II, Mortality," annual and unpublished data.

[MSA = Metropolitan statistical area. CMSA = Consolidated MSA. PMSA = Primary MSA. NECMA = New England county metropolitan area. All areas defined as of June 30, 1996. Table includes 245 MSAs, 17 CMSAs, and 58 PMSAs not in New England; as well as 12 NECMAs. Table excludes 10 MSAs, 1 CMSA, and 15 PMSAs in New England]

Metropolitan areas	Households, 1997[1]		Births						Deaths							
			Number			Rate[2]			Number			Rate				
												Total[2]			By cause,[3] 1992	
	Number	Percent change, 1990–1997	1994	1992	1990	1994	1992	1990	1994	1992	1990	1994	1992	1990	Cardio-vascular diseases	Motor vehicle accidents
Grand Junction, CO MSA	43 400	19.7	1 308	1 322	1 282	12.6	13.5	13.8	961	869	820	9.3	8.9	8.8	363.1	24.5
Grand Rapids-Muskegon-Holland, MI MSA	365 600	9.5	15 663	16 251	17 194	15.8	16.8	18.3	7 451	6 764	6 824	7.5	7.0	7.3	294.0	14.6
Great Falls, MT MSA	31 000	2.9	1 219	1 322	1 352	15.0	16.7	17.4	705	627	613	8.7	7.9	7.9	300.4	15.1
Green Bay, WI MSA	80 300	11.1	3 050	2 947	3 174	14.7	14.6	16.3	1 562	1 371	1 349	7.5	6.8	6.9	318.2	11.4
Greensboro–Winston Salem--High Point, NC MSA	456 200	10.0	14 914	15 193	15 516	13.4	14.1	14.8	9 925	9 611	9 158	8.9	8.9	8.7	374.5	16.0
Greenville, NC MSA	44 900	10.9	1 717	1 756	1 687	14.8	15.6	15.6	960	918	868	8.3	8.2	8.0	307.4	13.3
Greenville-Spartanburg-Anderson, SC MSA	344 700	10.2	11 630	12 071	12 589	13.3	14.2	15.2	8 052	7 251	7 197	9.2	8.5	8.7	350.4	20.9
Harrisburg-Lebanon-Carlisle, PA MSA	237 700	5.0	7 804	8 092	8 273	12.8	13.5	14.1	5 758	5 571	5 366	9.4	9.3	9.1	416.3	12.7
Hartford, CT NECMA	422 000	-.4	15 769	15 817	16 677	14.1	14.1	14.8	10 252	9 396	9 157	9.2	8.4	8.1	351.2	9.7
Hattiesburg, MS MSA	39 400	9.3	1 604	1 542	1 612	15.5	15.3	16.3	968	906	928	9.3	9.0	9.4	438.7	29.8
Hickory-Morganton-Lenoir, NC MSA	122 700	9.2	4 113	4 094	4 197	13.4	13.7	14.4	2 815	2 520	2 486	9.2	8.4	8.5	348.9	20.4
Honolulu, HI MSA	281 800	6.2	14 788	14 849	15 432	17.0	17.3	18.5	5 257	5 003	4 863	6.0	5.8	5.8	241.1	8.2
Houma, LA MSA	63 500	4.7	2 941	3 108	3 283	15.7	16.7	18.0	1 433	1 307	1 337	7.6	7.0	7.3	291.9	25.8
Houston-Galveston-Brazoria, TX CMSA	1 515 700	13.2	73 069	74 813	73 024	17.8	18.9	19.6	25 499	23 987	23 498	6.2	6.1	6.3	226.5	16.7
Brazoria, TX PMSA	74 500	16.4	3 519	3 469	3 281	16.5	17.0	17.1	1 332	1 227	1 185	6.3	6.0	6.2	211.5	25.5
Galveston-Texas City, TX PMSA	90 400	11.0	3 735	3 856	3 732	15.9	16.9	17.2	2 047	1 883	1 800	8.7	8.3	8.3	339.1	17.1
Houston, TX PMSA	1 350 800	13.2	65 815	67 488	66 011	18.0	19.1	19.9	22 120	20 877	20 513	6.0	5.9	6.2	220.1	16.2
Huntington-Ashland, WV-KY-OH MSA	122 300	2.2	3 984	3 997	3 946	12.6	12.7	12.6	3 497	3 412	3 296	11.0	10.8	10.5	467.3	22.6
Huntsville, AL MSA	127 200	14.7	4 755	4 950	4 822	14.5	16.1	16.5	2 343	2 129	2 014	7.2	6.9	6.9	309.8	19.5
Indianapolis, IN MSA	582 100	9.9	23 017	23 274	23 780	15.8	16.3	17.2	12 630	11 888	11 603	8.6	8.3	8.4	335.1	12.4
Iowa City, IA MSA	38 400	6.5	1 287	1 359	1 408	12.8	13.9	14.6	474	435	429	4.7	4.4	4.5	176.4	8.2
Jackson, MI MSA	56 400	5.1	2 060	2 188	2 398	13.5	14.4	16.0	1 370	1 291	1 299	9.0	8.5	8.7	363.4	18.5
Jackson, MS MSA	150 400	7.3	6 645	6 629	6 848	16.1	16.4	17.3	3 566	3 333	3 196	8.6	8.3	8.1	342.5	21.5
Jackson, TN MSA	37 500	9.8	1 318	1 435	1 413	13.7	15.4	15.6	1 026	936	905	10.7	10.0	10.0	442.3	16.1
Jacksonville, FL MSA	385 200	12.1	14 994	16 044	16 483	15.4	16.7	18.2	8 336	7 620	7 536	8.6	8.0	8.3	308.6	16.7
Jacksonville, NC MSA	38 100	-6.3	3 155	3 663	3 450	21.8	25.3	23.0	630	595	578	4.3	4.1	3.9	135.6	18.0
Jamestown, NY MSA	53 800	.2	1 760	1 915	1 997	12.4	13.5	14.1	1 569	1 445	1 485	11.1	10.2	10.5	481.0	21.1
Janesville-Beloit, WI MSA	56 500	8.1	2 021	2 120	2 178	13.8	14.8	15.6	1 214	1 223	1 280	8.3	8.6	9.2	367.1	9.8
Johnson City-Kingsport-Bristol, TN-VA MSA	181 200	6.2	5 227	5 304	5 316	11.6	11.9	12.2	4 794	4 517	4 364	10.6	10.2	10.0	437.9	21.4
Johnstown, PA MSA	90 800	-.8	2 578	2 741	2 843	10.7	11.4	11.8	2 909	2 699	2 590	12.1	11.2	10.7	527.1	17.4
Jonesboro, AR MSA	29 100	10.7	1 069	974	1 052	14.6	13.7	15.3	676	633	573	9.2	8.9	8.3	392.9	22.5
Joplin, MO MSA	57 900	9.2	2 071	1 994	1 938	14.6	14.5	14.4	1 571	1 458	1 487	11.1	10.6	11.0	456.2	21.8
Kalamazoo-Battle Creek, MI MSA	169 700	5.5	6 258	6 498	6 928	14.2	14.9	16.1	3 697	3 677	3 547	8.4	8.4	8.3	345.8	17.4
Kansas City, MO-KS MSA	652 800	7.3	23 812	24 969	26 157	14.4	15.5	16.5	13 776	13 201	12 946	8.3	8.2	8.2	338.5	14.0
Killeen-Temple, TX MSA	98 400	17.2	6 153	5 661	5 634	21.3	22.2	22.1	1 765	1 665	1 511	6.1	6.5	5.9	310.1	16.5
Knoxville, TN MSA	260 100	12.5	7 960	8 020	8 062	12.6	13.2	13.8	5 872	5 427	5 551	9.3	8.9	9.5	349.8	21.0
Kokomo, IN MSA	39 500	5.2	1 361	1 439	1 473	13.7	14.6	15.2	869	868	817	8.7	8.8	8.4	374.8	15.2
La Crosse, WI-MN MSA	46 200	6.2	1 576	1 632	1 688	13.1	13.8	14.5	1 069	947	1 023	8.9	8.0	8.8	327.0	16.1
Lafayette, LA MSA	132 800	9.0	5 924	6 111	6 032	16.4	17.3	17.5	2 799	2 703	2 761	7.8	7.7	8.0	316.6	20.4
Lafayette, IN MSA	62 100	8.8	2 233	2 323	2 336	13.3	14.2	14.5	1 260	1 268	1 234	7.5	7.7	7.6	330.1	12.8
Lake Charles, LA MSA	65 000	7.7	2 783	2 778	2 740	16.0	16.3	16.3	1 538	1 449	1 408	8.8	8.5	8.4	351.6	19.9
Lakeland-Winter Haven, FL MSA	175 200	12.3	6 198	6 309	6 493	14.4	15.1	16.0	4 728	4 304	4 309	11.0	10.3	10.6	431.1	26.3
Lancaster, PA MSA	162 000	7.3	6 894	6 901	7 292	15.6	15.9	17.2	3 870	3 544	3 490	8.7	8.2	8.3	362.9	12.7
Lansing-East Lansing, MI MSA	164 000	4.5	6 015	6 323	6 697	13.5	14.5	15.5	2 949	2 837	2 751	6.6	6.5	6.4	263.4	14.2
Laredo, TX MSA	45 300	31.5	4 929	4 532	3 879	29.9	30.5	29.1	802	759	738	4.9	5.1	5.5	185.5	14.8
Las Cruces, NM MSA	54 800	21.7	3 119	3 165	2 899	19.9	21.6	21.4	922	853	723	5.9	5.8	5.3	195.5	18.4
Las Vegas, NV-AZ MSA	489 400	48.1	18 153	16 437	15 397	16.8	17.0	18.1	9 455	7 992	7 067	8.7	8.3	8.3	303.2	18.8
Lawrence, KS MSA	33 300	10.5	1 112	1 051	1 071	12.8	12.5	13.1	452	429	420	5.2	5.1	5.1	200.2	10.7
Lawton, OK MSA	36 800	-2.0	2 103	2 481	2 128	18.5	20.6	19.1	822	783	708	7.2	6.5	6.4	277.5	19.9
Lewiston-Auburn, ME NECMA	39 900	-.3	1 226	1 387	1 520	11.9	13.3	14.4	1 003	990	1 000	9.7	9.5	9.5	414.7	12.5
Lexington, KY MSA	168 800	9.5	5 975	6 123	6 025	13.9	14.6	14.8	3 372	3 294	2 969	7.8	7.9	7.3	306.0	14.1
Lima, OH MSA	55 700	.6	2 135	2 236	2 533	13.7	14.3	16.4	1 475	1 412	1 386	9.5	9.1	9.0	404.8	18.6
Lincoln, NE MSA	90 100	8.9	3 127	3 070	3 103	13.8	13.9	14.5	1 623	1 499	1 504	7.2	6.8	7.0	281.6	8.6
Little Rock-North Little Rock, AR MSA	209 800	7.3	8 066	8 164	8 585	15.0	15.5	16.7	4 685	4 335	4 423	8.7	8.3	8.6	312.2	17.3
Longview-Marshall, TX MSA	76 900	6.7	2 848	2 998	2 957	14.1	15.1	15.3	2 106	1 910	1 919	10.5	9.6	9.9	404.0	25.8

[1]As of January 1. Data subject to copyright; see below for source citation.
[2]Per 1,000 resident population estimated as of July 1 for 1994 and 1992 and enumerated as of April 1 for 1990.
[3]Per 100,000 resident population estimated as of July 1, 1992.

Source: Households, 1997—Market Statistics, New York, NY, annual (copyright);   Households, 1990—U.S. Bureau of the Census, 1990 Census of Population and Housing, Summary Tape File (STF) 1C on CD-ROM;   Births—U.S. National Center for Health Statistics, "Vital Statistics of the United States, Vol. I, Natality," annual and unpublished data;   Deaths—U.S. National Center for Health Statistics, "Vital Statistics of the United States, Vol. II, Mortality," annual and unpublished data.

[MSA = Metropolitan statistical area.   CMSA = Consolidated MSA.   PMSA = Primary MSA.   NECMA = New England county metropolitan area.   All areas defined as of June 30, 1996.   Table includes 245 MSAs, 17 CMSAs, and 58 PMSAs not in New England; as well as 12 NECMAs.   Table excludes 10 MSAs, 1 CMSA, and 15 PMSAs in New England]

Metropolitan areas	Households, 1997[1]		Births						Deaths							
			Number			Rate[2]			Number			Rate				
												Total[2]			By cause,[3] 1992	
	Number	Percent change, 1990–1997	1994	1992	1990	1994	1992	1990	1994	1992	1990	1994	1992	1990	Cardio-vascular diseases	Motor vehicle accidents
Los Angeles-Riverside-Orange, CA CMSA	5 165 900	5.4	298 378	320 157	327 023	19.5	21.3	22.5	103 664	100 732	100 511	6.8	6.7	6.9	283.8	13.5
Los Angeles-Long Beach, CA PMSA	3 069 900	2.7	180 654	197 520	204 363	19.9	21.9	23.1	62 747	61 980	62 744	6.9	6.9	7.1	293.5	12.6
Orange, CA PMSA	879 600	6.4	49 417	51 889	51 262	19.3	20.8	21.3	15 369	14 827	14 717	6.0	5.9	6.1	251.6	10.7
Riverside-San Bernardino, CA PMSA	987 200	13.9	56 426	58 224	58 663	19.3	20.6	22.7	21 369	20 025	19 072	7.3	7.1	7.4	297.7	18.8
Ventura, CA PMSA	229 200	5.5	11 881	12 524	12 735	16.9	18.3	19.0	4 179	3 900	3 978	6.0	5.7	5.9	216.8	12.7
Louisville, KY-IN MSA	387 200	5.7	13 774	14 068	14 406	14.0	14.6	15.2	9 501	8 935	8 933	9.7	9.3	9.4	386.7	12.9
Lubbock, TX MSA	84 600	3.8	3 796	3 853	3 983	16.5	17.2	17.9	1 766	1 590	1 566	7.7	7.1	7.0	306.3	15.1
Lynchburg, VA MSA	78 900	8.5	2 671	2 568	2 772	13.2	12.9	14.3	1 959	1 977	1 883	9.6	9.9	9.7	412.4	17.1
Macon, GA MSA	116 400	9.3	4 764	4 831	4 991	15.5	16.2	17.1	2 812	2 637	2 537	9.2	8.8	8.7	370.0	14.4
Madison, WI MSA	156 500	9.6	4 848	5 209	5 309	12.4	13.7	14.5	2 374	2 177	2 080	6.1	5.7	5.7	242.8	11.0
Mansfield, OH MSA	67 300	2.0	2 282	2 374	2 565	13.0	13.6	14.7	1 739	1 625	1 685	9.9	9.3	9.7	424.5	13.1
McAllen-Edinburg-Mission, TX MSA	132 500	28.0	12 737	11 777	10 695	27.4	27.9	27.9	2 245	2 197	2 194	4.8	5.2	5.7	190.4	20.8
Medford-Ashland, OR MSA	66 800	16.7	2 000	1 973	2 086	12.3	12.8	14.2	1 595	1 444	1 412	9.8	9.4	9.6	343.4	17.5
Melbourne-Titusville-Palm Bay, FL MSA	184 700	14.5	5 222	5 538	5 692	11.8	13.0	14.3	4 203	3 935	3 626	9.5	9.3	9.1	360.6	16.7
Memphis, TN-AR-MS MSA	392 700	7.5	18 265	18 763	19 060	17.3	18.2	18.9	9 556	8 812	8 851	9.1	8.5	8.8	350.6	23.0
Merced, CA MSA	61 500	11.1	4 144	4 256	4 323	21.1	22.5	24.2	1 236	1 102	1 118	6.3	5.8	6.3	213.8	27.0
Miami-Fort Lauderdale, FL CMSA	1 345 900	10.2	52 415	51 115	53 269	15.4	15.5	16.7	34 245	33 659	32 630	10.1	10.2	10.2	436.7	16.2
Fort Lauderdale, FL PMSA	608 700	15.2	19 498	18 324	18 754	14.1	14.0	14.9	15 810	15 235	14 417	11.4	11.6	11.5	514.5	15.5
Miami, FL PMSA	737 200	6.5	32 917	32 791	34 515	16.4	16.4	17.8	18 435	18 424	18 213	9.2	9.2	9.4	385.5	16.6
Milwaukee-Racine, WI CMSA	614 800	2.2	24 546	25 538	26 066	15.0	15.7	16.2	14 070	13 401	13 793	8.6	8.2	8.6	350.8	8.8
Milwaukee-Waukesha, WI PMSA	547 900	1.9	21 985	22 921	23 366	15.1	15.8	16.3	12 608	11 979	12 355	8.7	8.3	8.6	352.6	8.6
Racine, WI PMSA	66 900	5.0	2 561	2 617	2 700	14.0	14.5	15.4	1 462	1 422	1 438	8.0	7.9	8.2	336.7	10.0
Minneapolis-St. Paul, MN-WI MSA	1 046 200	9.0	41 785	41 806	43 189	15.5	16.0	17.0	17 876	16 968	16 794	6.6	6.5	6.6	241.6	10.4
Mobile, AL MSA	193 500	11.2	8 109	7 998	7 996	15.9	16.2	16.8	4 648	4 325	4 374	9.1	8.7	9.2	347.5	26.9
Modesto, CA MSA	138 500	10.5	7 413	7 564	7 915	18.2	19.1	21.4	3 115	2 931	2 723	7.7	7.4	7.3	279.5	19.2
Monroe, LA MSA	52 200	3.3	2 214	2 428	2 427	15.2	16.7	17.1	1 255	1 272	1 242	8.6	8.8	8.7	344.0	25.5
Montgomery, AL MSA	116 300	10.2	4 913	5 151	5 274	15.9	17.0	18.0	2 934	2 624	2 653	9.5	8.7	9.1	341.8	18.8
Muncie, IN MSA	45 000	-.4	1 438	1 511	1 556	12.1	12.6	13.0	1 128	1 054	1 073	9.5	8.8	9.0	391.4	13.4
Myrtle Beach, SC MSA	66 900	20.0	1 887	2 206	2 320	12.4	14.5	16.1	1 484	1 288	1 159	9.7	8.5	8.0	341.6	26.4
Naples, FL MSA	78 500	27.2	2 478	2 381	2 512	13.9	14.3	16.5	1 785	1 611	1 508	10.0	9.7	9.9	388.6	27.7
Nashville, TN MSA	432 500	15.1	15 696	15 598	15 984	14.7	15.3	16.2	8 967	8 245	8 020	8.4	8.1	8.1	334.5	18.9
New London-Norwich, CT NECMA	93 200	Z	2 867	3 677	4 048	11.5	14.8	15.9	1 827	1 940	1 958	7.3	7.8	7.7	332.5	8.9
New Orleans, LA MSA	483 000	2.8	21 034	21 489	22 379	16.1	16.5	17.4	12 164	11 729	11 720	9.3	9.0	9.1	348.7	15.5
New York-Northern New Jersey-Long Island, NY-NJ-CT-PA CMSA/NECMA	7 208 400	1.1	312 040	317 210	323 964	15.8	16.2	16.6	180 511	178 628	181 306	9.1	9.1	9.3	403.0	9.9
Bergen-Passaic, NJ PMSA	474 000	2.1	19 078	18 936	18 814	14.7	14.7	14.7	11 848	11 697	11 814	9.1	9.1	9.2	395.3	8.0
Dutchess, NY PMSA	90 800	1.4	3 455	3 818	3 861	13.2	14.5	14.9	2 230	2 180	2 087	8.5	8.3	8.0	369.6	12.2
Jersey City, NJ PMSA	203 200	-2.7	9 023	9 569	9 773	16.4	17.3	17.7	5 117	5 366	5 480	9.3	9.7	9.9	375.4	8.3
Middlesex-Somerset-Hunterdon, NJ PMSA	394 500	8.1	15 852	16 015	15 819	14.8	15.4	15.5	7 798	7 631	7 391	7.3	7.3	7.2	292.0	8.7
Monmouth-Ocean, NJ PMSA	396 600	8.4	14 450	14 253	14 685	14.0	14.1	14.9	11 281	10 834	10 606	10.9	10.7	10.8	489.4	9.0
Nassau-Suffolk, NY PMSA	867 200	1.3	39 677	38 697	39 436	15.0	14.7	15.1	22 410	22 080	21 913	8.5	8.4	8.4	387.9	13.4
New Haven-Bridgeport-Stamford-Waterbury-Danbury, CT NECMA	610 500	.1	23 511	24 423	25 459	14.5	15.0	15.6	14 759	14 541	14 306	9.1	8.9	8.8	388.2	9.6
New York, NY PMSA	3 240 600	-.4	146 599	150 511	154 120	17.0	17.6	18.0	81 586	81 347	84 540	9.5	9.5	9.9	432.1	9.1
Newark, NJ PMSA	691 700	.8	30 239	30 197	31 028	15.6	15.7	16.2	17 680	17 437	17 631	9.1	9.1	9.2	358.1	11.6
Newburgh, NY-PA PMSA	121 200	8.2	5 616	5 855	5 905	15.8	16.8	17.6	2 812	2 659	2 674	7.9	7.6	8.0	348.7	10.6
Trenton, NJ PMSA	118 100	1.0	4 540	4 936	5 064	13.8	15.1	15.5	2 990	2 856	2 864	9.1	8.7	8.8	350.8	10.7
Norfolk-Virginia Beach-Newport News, VA-NC MSA	557 100	9.0	26 150	26 948	27 156	17.1	18.0	18.8	11 236	10 648	10 431	7.4	7.1	7.2	278.5	9.4
Ocala, FL MSA	94 800	21.3	2 620	2 542	2 771	11.9	12.3	14.2	2 202	2 355	2 207	12.2	11.4	11.3	504.3	28.0
Odessa-Midland, TX MSA	86 800	6.8	4 111	4 350	4 415	17.4	18.7	19.6	1 687	1 542	1 499	7.1	6.6	6.6	219.4	10.3
Oklahoma City, OK MSA	391 900	6.6	14 721	14 752	14 848	14.6	15.0	15.5	8 432	8 066	7 766	8.4	8.2	8.1	354.4	15.0
Omaha, NE-IA MSA	255 300	6.3	10 380	10 582	11 265	15.6	16.1	17.6	4 955	4 890	4 815	7.5	7.5	7.5	322.1	13.9
Orlando, FL MSA	551 600	18.6	20 442	20 008	20 326	15.0	15.4	16.6	11 017	10 092	9 613	8.1	7.7	7.8	316.2	14.3
Owensboro, KY MSA	35 100	6.2	1 237	1 292	1 274	13.7	14.6	14.6	870	830	817	9.6	9.4	9.4	409.1	16.9

Z Less than .05 percent.

[1]As of January 1.   Data subject to copyright; see below for source citation.
[2]Per 1,000 resident population estimated as of July 1 for 1994 and 1992 and enumerated as of April 1 for 1990.
[3]Per 100,000 resident population estimated as of July 1, 1992.

Source: Households, 1997—Market Statistics, New York, NY, annual (copyright);   Households, 1990—U.S. Bureau of the Census, 1990 Census of Population and Housing, Summary Tape File (STF) 1C on CD-ROM;   Births—U.S. National Center for Health Statistics, "Vital Statistics of the United States, Vol. I, Natality," annual and unpublished data;   Deaths—U.S. National Center for Health Statistics, "Vital Statistics of the United States, Vol. II, Mortality," annual and unpublished data.

[MSA = Metropolitan statistical area. CMSA = Consolidated MSA. PMSA = Primary MSA. NECMA = New England county metropolitan area. All areas defined as of June 30, 1996. Table includes 245 MSAs, 17 CMSAs, and 58 PMSAs not in New England; as well as 12 NECMAs. Table excludes 10 MSAs, 1 CMSA, and 15 PMSAs in New England]

Metropolitan areas	Households, 1997[1]		Births						Deaths							
	Number	Percent change, 1990–1997	Number			Rate[2]			Number			Total[2]			By cause,[3] 1992	
			1994	1992	1990	1994	1992	1990	1994	1992	1990	1994	1992	1990	Cardio-vascular diseases	Motor vehicle accidents
Panama City, FL MSA	55 600	13.6	1 956	2 133	2 065	14.0	16.0	16.3	1 202	1 097	1 081	8.6	8.2	8.5	299.8	20.2
Parkersburg-Marietta, WV-OH MSA.....	59 700	3.3	1 874	1 987	1 993	12.4	13.2	13.4	1 616	1 476	1 489	10.7	9.8	10.0	451.2	13.3
Pensacola, FL MSA...................	143 900	12.0	5 345	5 619	5 836	14.3	15.6	16.9	3 226	2 904	2 715	8.7	8.1	7.9	320.7	17.5
Peoria-Pekin, IL MSA	132 500	2.4	4 783	4 913	5 013	13.9	14.3	14.8	3 239	3 075	3 111	9.4	9.0	9.2	366.3	12.8
Philadelphia-Wilmington-Atlantic City, PA-NJ-DE-MD CMSA	2 198 700	1.8	88 314	92 399	97 716	14.8	15.6	16.6	59 014	57 218	56 191	9.9	9.6	9.5	385.6	12.0
Atlantic-Cape May, NJ PMSA ...	128 200	4.2	5 178	5 446	5 430	15.7	16.7	17.0	3 803	3 697	3 486	11.5	11.3	10.9	474.2	15.3
Philadelphia, PA-NJ PMSA	1 820 200	1.1	73 099	76 473	81 447	14.8	15.5	16.5	49 228	47 940	47 281	9.9	9.7	9.6	387.2	11.4
Vineland-Millville-Bridgeton, NJ PMSA	45 100	–4.3	2 109	2 241	2 323	15.2	16.1	16.8	1 475	1 372	1 324	10.6	9.9	9.6	407.9	19.4
Wilmington-Newark, DE-MD PMSA ..	205 200	8.6	7 928	8 239	8 516	14.7	15.6	16.6	4 508	4 209	4 100	8.3	8.0	8.0	310.1	13.2
Phoenix-Mesa, AZ MSA	1 057 600	24.9	44 350	42 153	42 592	17.8	18.0	19.0	20 345	18 262	16 941	8.2	7.8	7.6	298.5	16.4
Pine Bluff, AR MSA	28 900	–3.7	1 284	1 374	1 459	15.2	16.2	17.1	910	916	958	10.8	10.8	11.2	446.8	25.9
Pittsburgh, PA MSA	950 700	.4	28 667	30 627	31 287	11.9	12.7	13.1	27 388	26 602	26 745	11.4	11.1	11.2	497.0	11.8
Pittsfield, MA NECMA	53 800	–.9	1 487	1 612	1 815	10.9	11.8	13.0	1 510	1 438	1 483	11.1	10.5	10.6	448.8	19.0
Pocatello, ID MSA	25 800	10.2	1 270	1 209	1 144	17.6	17.6	17.3	437	480	412	6.1	7.0	6.2	293.2	11.7
Portland, ME NECMA	99 400	5.2	3 055	3 299	3 527	12.4	13.5	14.5	2 217	2 157	2 049	9.0	8.8	8.4	346.2	11.9
Portland-Salem, OR-WA CMSA	803 500	16.3	29 129	28 725	28 911	14.6	15.1	16.1	16 183	15 229	14 911	8.1	8.0	8.3	319.4	12.5
Portland-Vancouver, OR-WA PMSA .	686 200	16.4	24 436	24 167	24 380	14.5	15.0	16.1	13 404	12 623	12 447	8.0	7.8	8.2	306.6	12.4
Salem, OR PMSA	117 300	15.4	4 693	4 558	4 531	15.3	15.5	16.3	2 779	2 606	2 464	9.0	8.9	8.9	389.2	12.9
Providence-Warwick-Pawtucket, RI NECMA	339 800	–1.6	12 420	13 319	14 012	13.6	14.6	15.3	8 716	8 764	8 850	9.6	9.6	9.7	410.4	9.6
Provo-Orem, UT MSA	85 000	21.1	7 588	7 057	6 754	25.1	25.6	25.6	1 286	1 164	1 114	4.3	4.2	4.2	168.0	13.4
Pueblo, CO MSA	50 500	7.3	1 763	1 773	1 771	13.8	14.3	14.4	1 271	1 207	1 223	9.9	9.7	9.9	378.8	18.6
Punta Gorda, FL MSA	56 800	17.3	1 009	987	1 065	8.0	8.2	9.6	1 828	1 644	1 588	14.5	13.7	14.3	590.2	13.3
Raleigh-Durham-Chapel Hill, NC MSA ..	410 300	22.7	14 301	13 888	13 718	14.8	15.2	16.0	6 638	6 228	5 812	6.9	6.8	6.8	267.9	14.9
Rapid City, SD MSA	33 100	8.3	1 413	1 504	1 696	16.3	17.7	20.8	563	622	519	6.5	7.3	6.4	292.5	15.3
Reading, PA MSA	134 400	5.3	4 661	4 781	4 957	13.4	13.9	14.7	3 610	3 417	3 286	10.4	10.0	9.8	440.7	13.1
Redding, CA MSA	63 500	13.5	2 120	2 257	2 303	13.2	14.3	15.7	1 557	1 459	1 373	9.7	9.3	9.3	346.6	25.4
Reno, NV MSA........................	121 500	18.8	4 435	4 361	4 522	15.6	16.2	17.8	2 250	1 998	1 894	7.9	7.4	7.4	295.1	13.8
Richland-Kennewick-Pasco, WA MSA...	66 000	21.3	3 022	2 909	2 835	17.3	18.0	18.9	1 119	999	963	6.4	6.2	6.4	239.9	18.6
Richmond-Petersburg, VA MSA	363 000	9.4	13 271	13 754	14 186	14.5	15.4	16.4	7 970	7 595	7 314	8.7	8.5	8.4	335.3	14.1
Roanoke, VA MSA.....................	93 100	3.8	2 853	2 965	3 052	12.5	13.1	13.6	2 593	2 409	2 405	11.3	10.6	10.7	469.8	10.6
Rochester, MN MSA	43 100	7.6	1 729	1 754	1 862	15.3	15.9	17.5	680	691	601	6.0	6.3	5.6	250.0	8.2
Rochester, NY MSA...................	406 900	2.7	15 200	16 853	17 316	14.0	15.6	16.3	9 217	8 869	8 568	8.5	8.2	8.1	342.5	11.6
Rockford, IL MSA	134 100	7.4	5 054	5 069	5 348	14.6	14.9	16.2	3 152	2 693	2 763	9.1	7.9	8.4	316.5	17.7
Rocky Mount, NC MSA................	53 500	8.4	2 121	2 182	2 236	15.1	16.0	16.8	1 473	1 359	1 372	10.5	9.9	10.3	426.4	26.3
Sacramento-Yolo, CA CMSA......	620 900	11.6	25 298	26 463	26 622	15.9	17.0	18.0	11 863	10 791	10 893	7.5	6.9	7.4	271.1	16.5
Sacramento, CA PMSA	566 600	12.1	23 021	24 066	24 228	16.0	17.0	18.1	10 864	9 853	9 954	7.5	7.0	7.4	272.5	16.3
Yolo, CA PMSA	54 300	6.5	2 277	2 397	2 394	15.5	16.6	17.0	999	938	939	6.8	6.5	6.6	256.9	18.0
Saginaw-Bay City-Midland, MI MSA.....	151 400	2.1	5 749	6 248	6 608	14.3	15.5	16.5	3 481	3 272	3 216	8.6	8.1	8.1	357.5	17.9
St. Cloud, MN MSA	54 900	8.3	2 105	2 178	2 230	13.4	14.2	14.9	936	931	946	6.0	6.1	6.3	260.8	20.2
St. Joseph, MO MSA	37 800	–.3	1 367	1 434	1 404	14.0	14.6	14.4	1 077	1 077	1 147	11.0	11.0	11.7	489.9	28.5
St. Louis, MO-IL MSA	961 700	2.1	37 318	39 078	41 497	14.5	15.5	16.6	24 763	23 158	23 024	9.8	9.2	9.2	392.2	15.9
Salinas, CA MSA	115 000	1.8	7 081	8 204	7 921	21.3	22.3	22.3	2 244	2 157	2 250	6.7	5.9	6.3	226.7	14.1
Salt Lake City-Ogden, UT MSA........	399 700	15.0	22 567	22 449	21 918	19.2	19.9	20.4	6 372	5 998	5 624	5.4	5.3	5.2	196.4	13.2
San Angelo, TX MSA	37 300	5.3	1 492	1 526	1 657	14.8	15.4	16.8	862	849	861	8.5	8.6	8.7	368.6	22.2
San Antonio, TX MSA	518 500	13.1	25 093	24 146	24 109	17.5	17.5	18.2	10 533	10 032	9 388	7.4	7.3	7.1	280.6	13.1
San Diego, CA MSA	942 700	6.2	47 663	50 724	50 634	18.2	19.5	20.3	18 512	17 639	17 102	7.1	6.8	6.8	266.4	11.4
San Francisco-Oakland-San Jose, CA CMSA	2 458 800	5.5	99 330	103 922	107 645	15.3	16.2	17.2	47 869	46 475	46 456	7.4	7.3	7.4	280.4	10.8
Oakland, CA PMSA..................	825 100	5.8	33 844	35 439	36 914	15.5	16.5	17.7	15 808	15 178	15 368	7.3	7.1	7.4	277.6	9.6
San Francisco, CA PMSA	667 400	3.9	22 191	23 088	24 019	13.5	14.2	15.0	14 706	14 709	14 726	9.0	9.1	9.2	335.2	10.6
San Jose, CA PMSA	546 300	5.0	26 649	27 496	28 107	17.1	18.0	18.8	8 697	8 244	8 262	5.6	5.4	5.5	214.4	10.1
Santa Cruz-Watsonville, CA PMSA ..	86 600	3.6	3 681	4 040	4 319	16.5	17.4	18.8	1 721	1 634	1 669	7.3	7.1	7.3	298.7	12.9
Santa Rosa, CA PMSA	164 700	10.5	5 513	5 805	6 114	13.4	14.4	15.7	3 498	3 385	3 240	8.5	8.4	8.3	333.1	15.4
Vallejo-Fairfield-Napa, CA PMSA	168 700	9.0	7 452	8 054	8 172	15.5	17.0	18.2	3 439	3 325	3 191	7.2	7.0	7.1	263.6	14.2
San Luis Obispo-Atascadero-Paso Robles, CA MSA	87 100	8.5	2 692	2 640	3 034	12.0	12.0	14.0	1 859	1 746	1 783	8.3	7.9	8.2	341.4	10.9
Santa Barbara-Santa Maria-Lompoc, CA MSA	136 400	5.1	6 404	6 597	6 754	16.7	17.5	18.3	2 949	2 663	2 570	7.7	7.1	7.0	305.6	13.5

[1]As of January 1. Data subject to copyright; see below for source citation.
[2]Per 1,000 resident population estimated as of July 1 for 1994 and 1992 and enumerated as of April 1 for 1990.
[3]Per 100,000 resident population estimated as of July 1, 1992.

Source: Households, 1997—Market Statistics, New York, NY, annual (copyright); Households, 1990—U.S. Bureau of the Census, 1990 Census of Population and Housing, Summary Tape File (STF) 1C on CD-ROM; Births—U.S. National Center for Health Statistics, "Vital Statistics of the United States, Vol. I, Natality," annual and unpublished data; Deaths—U.S. National Center for Health Statistics, "Vital Statistics of the United States, Vol. II, Mortality," annual and unpublished data.

[MSA = Metropolitan statistical area. CMSA = Consolidated MSA. PMSA = Primary MSA. NECMA = New England county metropolitan area. All areas defined as of June 30, 1996. Table includes 245 MSAs, 17 CMSAs, and 58 PMSAs not in New England; as well as 12 NECMAs. Table excludes 10 MSAs, 1 CMSA, and 15 PMSAs in New England]

Metropolitan areas	Households, 1997[1]		Births						Deaths							
			Number			Rate[2]			Number			Rate				
												Total[2]			By cause,[3] 1992	
	Number	Percent change, 1990–1997	1994	1992	1990	1994	1992	1990	1994	1992	1990	1994	1992	1990	Cardio-vascular diseases	Motor vehicle accidents
Santa Fe, NM MSA	53 800	19.4	1 710	1 678	1 623	13.0	13.6	13.9	828	733	702	6.3	5.9	6.0	174.2	23.5
Sarasota-Bradenton, FL MSA	239 600	10.6	5 278	5 499	5 701	10.2	10.9	11.6	7 621	7 106	6 883	14.7	14.1	14.1	649.5	16.3
Savannah, GA MSA	104 800	10.4	4 584	4 680	4 797	16.6	17.5	18.6	2 325	2 265	2 292	8.4	8.5	8.9	350.5	18.7
Scranton--Wilkes-Barre--Hazleton, PA MSA	244 200	–.9	6 961	7 198	7 602	10.9	11.2	11.9	8 168	7 849	7 874	12.8	12.3	12.3	581.8	12.5
Seattle-Tacoma-Bremerton, WA CMSA	1 294 500	12.0	46 393	48 498	48 652	14.4	15.5	16.4	22 367	21 324	20 895	6.9	6.8	7.0	265.0	11.2
Bremerton, WA PMSA	85 300	23.1	3 325	3 558	3 414	15.3	16.9	18.0	1 399	1 359	1 360	6.5	6.4	7.2	235.4	14.7
Olympia, WA PMSA	75 600	21.6	2 440	2 442	2 353	13.0	13.8	14.6	1 338	1 221	1 123	7.1	6.9	7.0	278.5	14.7
Seattle-Bellevue-Everett, WA PMSA	891 700	10.2	30 856	32 241	32 320	14.2	15.2	15.9	14 922	14 309	14 071	6.8	6.7	6.9	257.8	9.8
Tacoma, WA PMSA	241 900	12.7	9 772	10 257	10 565	15.3	16.6	18.0	4 708	4 435	4 341	7.4	7.2	7.4	295.9	13.7
Sharon, PA MSA	46 600	2.2	1 450	1 423	1 471	11.9	11.7	12.2	1 384	1 358	1 387	11.3	11.1	11.5	509.1	22.1
Sheboygan, WI MSA	40 900	6.0	1 389	1 343	1 402	12.9	12.8	13.5	950	1 009	910	8.8	9.6	8.8	420.6	11.4
Sherman-Denison, TX MSA	38 500	4.5	1 202	1 325	1 448	12.3	13.9	15.2	1 108	1 113	1 096	11.4	11.6	11.5	546.4	24.1
Shreveport-Bossier City, LA MSA	142 300	1.8	5 641	6 026	6 424	14.9	16.1	17.1	3 808	3 578	3 673	10.1	9.6	9.8	378.9	20.6
Sioux City, IA-NE MSA	45 600	6.2	2 018	1 981	1 961	16.9	16.9	17.0	1 162	1 133	1 077	9.7	9.7	9.4	460.5	14.5
Sioux Falls, SD MSA	60 100	13.1	2 249	2 292	2 312	14.8	15.7	16.6	1 124	1 081	945	7.4	7.4	6.8	312.5	14.4
South Bend, IN MSA	98 700	6.9	3 646	3 818	3 900	14.3	15.2	15.8	2 365	2 256	2 387	9.3	9.0	9.7	399.7	9.6
Spokane, WA MSA	160 500	13.3	5 387	5 526	5 566	13.6	14.5	15.4	3 248	3 236	3 091	8.2	8.5	8.6	345.0	13.3
Springfield, IL MSA	82 800	8.5	2 818	2 866	2 861	13.9	14.9	15.1	1 878	1 737	1 758	9.3	9.0	9.3	398.5	10.9
Springfield, MO MSA	113 900	11.9	3 887	3 812	3 674	13.5	13.8	13.9	2 744	2 435	2 310	9.5	8.8	8.7	382.9	16.3
Springfield, MA NECMA	218 800	–.5	7 945	8 288	8 843	13.3	13.9	14.7	5 738	5 673	5 342	9.6	9.5	8.9	391.3	11.4
State College, PA MSA	45 100	5.7	1 335	1 454	1 529	10.3	11.4	12.3	782	750	733	6.0	5.9	5.9	247.4	12.6
Steubenville-Weirton, OH-WV MSA	54 400	–1.5	1 483	1 455	1 514	10.6	10.3	10.6	1 692	1 599	1 621	12.1	11.3	11.4	493.4	15.6
Stockton-Lodi, CA MSA	172 000	8.8	9 358	9 468	9 886	18.0	18.8	20.6	3 991	3 824	3 819	7.7	7.6	7.9	304.6	20.2
Sumter, SC MSA	36 100	10.3	1 670	1 771	1 906	15.7	17.1	18.8	774	786	811	7.3	7.6	8.0	370.4	25.1
Syracuse, NY MSA	275 300	.9	10 411	11 291	11 819	13.8	15.0	15.9	6 648	6 303	6 330	8.8	8.4	8.5	367.9	13.2
Tallahassee, FL MSA	101 900	15.5	3 519	3 505	3 578	13.8	14.3	15.3	1 661	1 631	1 532	6.5	6.7	6.6	241.0	23.7
Tampa-St. Petersburg-Clearwater, FL MSA	933 100	7.3	27 244	27 406	28 977	12.6	13.0	14.0	27 158	25 724	24 972	12.6	12.2	12.1	535.3	18.1
Terre Haute, IN MSA	56 800	1.7	1 974	2 025	2 052	13.2	13.6	13.9	1 729	1 603	1 686	11.6	10.8	11.4	498.8	12.8
Texarkana, TX-Texarkana, AR MSA	46 500	3.6	1 764	1 807	1 829	14.4	14.9	15.2	1 308	1 321	1 260	10.7	10.9	10.5	470.5	23.1
Toledo, OH MSA	230 600	Z	9 039	9 392	10 228	14.8	15.3	16.7	5 710	5 547	5 493	9.3	9.0	8.9	434.4	13.7
Topeka, KS MSA	65 300	2.4	2 366	2 328	2 492	14.3	14.3	15.5	1 643	1 420	1 415	10.0	8.7	8.8	361.1	10.4
Tucson, AZ MSA	303 500	15.9	11 361	11 521	11 414	15.5	16.6	17.1	6 681	5 955	5 608	9.1	8.6	8.4	335.7	19.2
Tulsa, OK MSA	296 000	6.8	10 900	11 398	11 620	14.7	15.6	16.4	6 439	5 922	5 877	8.7	8.1	8.3	353.3	18.1
Tuscaloosa, AL MSA	59 600	7.7	2 129	2 223	2 182	13.7	14.5	14.5	1 363	1 271	1 188	8.8	8.3	7.9	345.0	22.2
Tyler, TX MSA	62 300	9.7	2 472	2 341	2 349	15.5	15.1	15.5	1 524	1 423	1 360	9.5	9.2	9.0	387.5	18.7
Utica-Rome, NY MSA	110 800	–5.7	3 948	4 317	4 581	12.5	13.5	14.5	3 278	3 172	3 193	10.4	9.9	10.1	460.9	12.5
Victoria, TX MSA	28 800	9.8	1 300	1 351	1 286	16.2	17.5	17.3	593	579	555	7.4	7.5	7.5	332.9	20.7
Visalia-Tulare-Porterville, CA MSA	110 200	12.6	7 355	7 442	7 254	21.3	22.4	23.3	2 551	2 481	2 497	7.4	7.5	8.0	319.4	32.8
Waco, TX MSA	75 200	7.1	3 213	3 027	3 065	16.2	15.7	16.2	1 916	1 862	1 808	9.7	9.7	9.6	416.4	22.8
Washington-Baltimore, DC-MD-VA-WV CMSA	2 658 600	6.7	107 314	112 254	115 595	15.2	16.3	17.2	53 519	50 613	50 310	7.6	7.3	7.5	267.8	11.4
Baltimore, MD PMSA	918 600	4.4	35 563	37 864	39 899	14.5	15.6	16.7	22 876	21 852	21 682	9.3	9.0	9.1	333.6	12.1
Hagerstown, MD PMSA	47 100	5.2	1 534	1 634	1 647	12.1	13.0	13.7	1 195	1 119	1 108	9.5	8.9	9.1	380.4	16.0
Washington, DC-MD-VA-WV PMSA	1 692 900	8.1	70 217	72 756	74 035	15.7	16.7	17.5	29 448	27 642	27 520	6.6	6.4	6.5	227.8	10.9
Waterloo-Cedar Falls, IA MSA	46 900	–.1	1 606	1 653	1 703	13.0	13.3	13.8	1 240	1 131	1 143	10.0	9.1	9.2	422.1	19.3
Wausau, WI MSA	44 300	6.6	1 653	1 664	1 687	13.7	14.1	14.6	910	843	876	7.6	7.1	7.6	280.0	15.2
West Palm Beach-Boca Raton, FL MSA	420 700	15.1	12 782	12 229	12 933	13.3	13.4	15.0	11 752	10 869	10 166	12.3	11.9	11.8	528.4	17.6
Wheeling, WV-OH MSA	62 300	–.9	1 757	1 802	1 927	11.1	11.4	12.1	2 026	1 932	1 938	12.8	12.2	12.2	555.0	15.8
Wichita, KS MSA	196 700	5.4	8 341	8 737	8 719	16.5	17.5	18.0	4 033	3 912	3 838	8.0	7.8	7.9	324.5	16.2
Wichita Falls, TX MSA	51 200	6.2	2 021	1 990	2 126	15.3	15.5	16.3	1 322	1 261	1 203	10.0	9.8	9.2	444.8	13.2
Williamsport, PA MSA	45 700	1.7	1 465	1 638	1 709	12.1	13.6	14.4	1 306	1 212	1 131	10.8	10.1	9.5	433.2	12.4
Wilmington, NC MSA	83 900	23.0	2 555	2 525	2 504	13.2	13.9	14.6	1 726	1 703	1 522	8.9	9.4	8.9	389.4	18.7
Yakima, WA MSA	74 900	13.5	4 273	4 328	4 021	20.4	21.7	21.3	1 698	1 646	1 609	8.1	8.3	8.5	368.5	23.6
York, PA MSA	140 600	9.3	4 497	4 854	4 890	12.5	13.9	14.4	3 071	2 829	2 838	8.5	8.1	8.4	347.0	14.9
Youngstown-Warren, OH MSA	229 900	.8	7 691	8 057	8 221	12.8	13.3	13.7	6 561	6 336	6 285	10.9	10.5	10.5	477.9	14.7
Yuba City, CA MSA	48 900	14.0	2 469	2 620	2 632	18.3	20.1	21.5	1 106	1 032	1 013	8.2	7.9	8.3	287.4	25.4
Yuma, AZ MSA	42 000	17.3	3 003	[4]3 022	[4]2 695	23.5	[4]22.9	[4]22.3	830	[4]921	[4]853	6.5	[4]7.0	[4]7.1	[4]274.2	[4]28.0

Z Less than .05 percent.

[1]As of January 1. Data subject to copyright; see below for source citation.
[2]Per 1,000 resident population estimated as of July 1 for 1994 and 1992 and enumerated as of April 1 for 1990.
[3]Per 100,000 resident population estimated as of July 1, 1992.
[4]Includes La Paz County which is not in the MSA. In 1994, there were 219 births and 168 deaths in La Paz County.

Table B-4. Metro Areas — Infant Deaths, Physicians, Hospitals, and Education

[MSA = Metropolitan statistical area. CMSA = Consolidated MSA. PMSA = Primary MSA. NECMA = New England county metropolitan area. All areas defined as of June 30, 1996. Table includes 245 MSAs, 17 CMSAs, and 58 PMSAs not in New England; as well as 12 NECMAs. Table excludes 10 MSAs, 1 CMSA, and 15 PMSAs in New England]

Metropolitan areas	Infant deaths[1]				Physicians,[3] 1995				Community hospitals,[6] 1995				Public school enrollment[7]			
	Number		Rate[2]		Number		Per 100,000 population		Number	Beds			1994–1995		1991–1992	Percent change, 1992–1995
	1994	1990	1994	1990	Total	Office-based	Rate[4]	Rank[5]		Number	Rate[4]		Number	Rank[5]		
Abilene, TX MSA	13	23	6.4	10.7	224	202	182.3	168	2	493	401.1		24 614	200	23 490	4.8
Albany, GA MSA	22	28	11.9	13.5	213	173	182.5	166	2	590	505.6		22 751	215	22 942	−.8
Albany-Schenectady-Troy, NY MSA	69	99	6.0	7.9	2 413	1 601	273.8	56	14	3 312	375.9		132 600	57	128 618	3.1
Albuquerque, NM MSA	105	84	10.3	8.3	2 112	1 364	319.3	30	10	1 540	232.9		112 056	64	106 045	5.7
Alexandria, LA MSA	23	16	11.9	7.8	282	232	222.2	106	3	750	590.9		24 800	198	25 301	−2.0
Allentown-Bethlehem-Easton, PA MSA	58	57	7.8	7.0	1 335	1 007	217.9	113	9	2 212	361.1		89 244	72	85 477	4.4
Altoona, PA MSA	17	16	11.0	10.0	233	193	176.4	178	5	677	512.5		21 263	222	21 193	.3
Amarillo, TX MSA	36	20	11.0	6.0	487	364	237.9	86	5	957	467.6		38 656	148	36 082	7.1
Anchorage, AK MSA	34	43	7.3	8.8	NA	NA	NA	NA	6	670	266.6		47 655	127	44 749	6.5
Anniston, AL MSA	12	24	7.5	14.1	156	146	137.5	239	3	372	328.0		19 619	230	20 485	−4.2
Appleton-Oshkosh-Neenah, WI MSA	20	34	4.4	7.2	590	512	175.4	181	7	957	284.5		54 902	115	51 050	7.5
Asheville, NC MSA	23	28	9.4	10.7	576	468	277.8	54	3	780	376.2		31 389	166	29 480	6.5
Athens, GA MSA	19	27	11.1	14.5	261	226	193.5	140	2	590	437.5		19 607	231	18 434	6.4
Atlanta, GA MSA	462	600	8.5	11.4	7 937	5 755	230.7	95	43	9 706	282.1		580 442	11	520 952	11.4
Augusta-Aiken, GA-SC MSA	62	94	9.0	12.5	1 607	924	354.9	18	6	1 601	353.5		86 151	76	81 724	5.4
Austin-San Marcos, TX MSA	84	98	5.3	6.6	1 884	1 538	187.1	149	14	1 920	190.7		172 469	44	153 459	12.4
Bakersfield, CA MSA	141	129	11.2	10.3	800	616	129.8	244	10	1 396	226.6		133 702	55	125 403	6.6
Bangor, ME NECMA	8	10	5.0	5.1	316	244	217.1	116	NA	NA	NA		25 473	191	25 559	−.3
Barnstable-Yarmouth, MA NECMA	17	25	7.9	10.1	392	336	196.8	134	NA	NA	NA		30 964	168	27 958	10.8
Baton Rouge, LA MSA	96	103	10.8	11.3	1 042	835	185.0	156	11	2 062	366.1		99 382	67	98 716	.7
Beaumont-Port Arthur, TX MSA	54	45	9.8	8.1	551	485	146.5	218	10	2 011	534.8		73 922	89	72 633	1.8
Bellingham, WA MSA	9	14	4.7	7.9	262	227	175.5	180	1	196	131.3		23 572	208	21 446	9.9
Benton Harbor, MI MSA	17	41	7.6	15.6	223	195	137.9	238	4	662	409.3		29 194	176	30 197	−3.3
Billings, MT MSA	9	14	5.6	8.3	336	303	269.4	60	2	526	421.8		22 108	217	21 388	3.4
Biloxi-Gulfport-Pascagoula, MS MSA	50	43	9.4	8.4	493	416	144.2	224	7	1 234	361.0		60 797	107	58 044	4.7
Binghamton, NY MSA	25	26	8.0	6.8	534	392	207.2	129	2	718	278.6		44 996	134	44 414	1.3
Birmingham, AL MSA	141	141	11.3	10.6	3 183	1 966	358.3	17	18	5 437	612.0		146 270	52	143 501	1.9
Bismarck, ND MSA	7	3	5.8	2.5	249	198	279.2	52	3	655	734.6		16 497	255	16 398	.6
Bloomington, IN MSA	10	8	8.9	6.3	231	199	200.2	133	1	257	222.7		13 236	266	12 939	2.3
Bloomington-Normal, IL MSA	15	8	7.9	4.4	217	187	156.9	209	2	479	346.2		23 136	211	22 092	4.7
Boise City, ID MSA	29	46	5.3	9.2	647	545	179.0	173	5	916	253.5		67 408	98	60 848	10.8
Boston-Worcester-Lawrence-Lowell-Brockton, MA-NH NECMA	462	622	5.7	6.9	22 220	13 022	385.3	11	NA	NA	NA		851 089	8	799 196	6.5
Brownsville-Harlingen-San Benito, TX MSA	46	40	6.0	6.0	296	252	96.1	268	5	937	304.4		80 254	82	75 343	6.5
Bryan-College Station, TX MSA	11	9	5.7	4.8	240	198	182.6	165	2	309	235.1		19 255	237	17 593	9.4
Buffalo-Niagara Falls, NY MSA	126	149	8.0	8.4	3 486	2 103	294.9	39	18	5 174	437.7		179 241	41	175 204	2.3
Burlington, VT NECMA	15	19	5.6	6.8	836	469	443.1	9	NA	NA	NA		32 199	164	28 952	11.2
Canton-Massillon, OH MSA	42	36	7.9	6.3	692	530	172.1	188	5	1 645	409.0		68 820	96	68 308	.7
Casper, WY MSA	3	10	3.1	10.7	134	101	209.7	126	1	203	317.6		13 144	267	13 318	−1.3
Cedar Rapids, IA MSA	18	26	7.1	9.8	330	272	184.9	158	2	866	485.2		30 902	169	29 048	6.4
Champaign-Urbana, IL MSA	20	20	8.9	7.7	472	336	283.7	47	2	808	485.6		23 687	207	24 235	−2.3
Charleston-North Charleston, SC MSA	89	117	11.1	11.7	1 916	1 134	382.1	13	8	1 829	364.7		89 664	71	89 089	.6
Charleston, WV MSA	16	31	4.6	9.8	709	489	278.5	53	5	1 236	485.5		41 978	142	42 765	−1.8
Charlotte-Gastonia-Rock Hill, NC-SC MSA	171	209	9.3	10.8	2 367	1 936	183.5	163	13	3 454	267.7		204 198	34	189 817	7.6
Charlottesville, VA MSA	11	20	6.0	10.4	1 338	576	938.5	3	2	818	573.7		20 024	228	18 883	6.0
Chattanooga, TN-GA MSA	42	63	7.0	9.9	976	720	220.2	109	10	1 808	408.0		69 840	95	68 820	1.5
Cheyenne, WY MSA	9	12	7.5	10.0	149	111	189.9	146	1	178	226.8		14 862	263	14 558	2.1
Chicago-Gary-Kenosha, IL-IN-WI CMSA	1 441	1 719	9.7	11.4	24 225	15 220	283.4	48	107	29 418	344.2		1 367 708	3	1 311 160	4.3
Chicago, IL PMSA	1 306	1 593	9.6	11.5	22 954	14 134	298.7	X	95	25 784	335.5		1 212 618	X	1 157 395	4.8
Gary, IN PMSA	101	92	11.3	9.9	941	820	151.6	X	8	2 618	421.7		112 113	X	113 601	−1.3
Kankakee, IL PMSA	16	19	10.2	11.1	146	118	143.9	X	2	731	720.4		18 801	X	18 311	2.7
Kenosha, WI PMSA	18	15	8.9	7.2	184	148	131.8	X	2	285	204.2		24 176	X	21 853	10.6
Chico-Paradise, CA MSA	16	21	6.4	7.9	352	321	182.4	167	5	588	304.7		33 955	163	31 195	8.8
Cincinnati-Hamilton, OH-KY-IN CMSA	259	291	9.3	9.8	4 746	3 190	248.8	75	26	5 783	303.1		304 286	22	288 339	5.5
Cincinnati, OH-KY-IN PMSA	215	247	9.1	9.8	4 388	2 881	276.3	X	22	5 081	320.0		251 384	X	237 336	5.9
Hamilton-Middletown, OH PMSA	44	44	10.4	9.9	358	309	112.0	X	4	702	219.6		52 902	X	51 003	3.7
Clarksville-Hopkinsville, TN-KY MSA	35	25	9.3	7.3	186	162	102.5	266	2	319	175.9		29 718	173	26 450	12.4

NA Not available.
X Not applicable.

[1]Deaths of infants under 1 year old.
[2]Per 1,000 live births for the years shown.
[3]Covers active, nonfederal physicians as of December 31. Data subject to copyright; see below for source citation.
[4]Per 100,000 resident population estimated as of July 1, 1995.
[5]Based on 272 metropolitan areas (244 MSAs, 17 CMSAs, and 11 NECMAs); see text for more information. When metropolitan areas share the same rank, the next lower rank is omitted.
[6]Covers nonfederal, short-stay (average length of stay less than 30 days) hospitals except hospital units of institutions. Data subject to copyright; see below for source citation.
[7]Aggregated from school district data to county of school superintendent's location to metropolitan area.

Source: Infant Deaths—U.S. National Center for Health Statistics, "Vital Statistics of the United States, Vol. II, Mortality," annual; Physicians—American Medical Association, Chicago, IL, "Physician Characteristics and Distribution in the U.S.," annual (copyright); Community Hospitals—Healthcare InfoSource, Inc., a subsidiary of the American Hospital Association, "Hospital Statistics," 1996/97 edition (copyright); Public School Enrollment—U.S. National Center for Education Statistics, Common Core of Data (CCD) Public Agency Universe Internet data files for years shown at site <http://nces.ed.gov/ccd/pubagency.html> (accessed April 1997).

[MSA = Metropolitan statistical area. CMSA = Consolidated MSA. PMSA = Primary MSA. NECMA = New England county metropolitan area. All areas defined as of June 30, 1996. Table includes 245 MSAs, 17 CMSAs, and 58 PMSAs not in New England; as well as 12 NECMAs. Table excludes 10 MSAs, 1 CMSA, and 15 PMSAs in New England]

| Metropolitan areas | Infant deaths[1] | | | | Physicians,[3] 1995 | | | | Community hospitals,[6] 1995 | | | Public school enrollment[7] | | | |
| | Number | | Rate[2] | | Number | | Per 100,000 population | | Number | Beds | | 1994–1995 | | | Percent change, 1992–1995 |
	1994	1990	1994	1990	Total	Office-based	Rate[4]	Rank[5]		Number	Rate[4]	Number	Rank[5]	1991–1992	
Cleveland-Akron, OH CMSA	415	511	10.1	11.5	8 916	5 428	306.6	37	40	10 987	377.8	445 002	15	435 675	2.1
Akron, OH PMSA	74	75	7.9	7.6	1 512	962	223.6	X	7	2 104	311.2	108 549	X	106 051	2.4
Cleveland-Lorain-Elyria, OH PMSA	341	436	10.7	12.6	7 404	4 466	331.7	X	33	8 883	397.9	336 453	X	329 624	2.1
Colorado Springs, CO MSA	55	68	7.1	9.3	664	580	142.8	227	2	862	185.3	82 382	80	74 130	11.1
Columbia, MO MSA	8	20	4.7	11.9	949	475	769.2	4	4	979	793.5	18 721	243	17 230	8.7
Columbia, SC MSA	49	85	6.9	11.2	1 383	930	287.2	45	5	1 549	321.7	83 020	79	78 658	5.5
Columbus, GA-AL MSA	53	71	11.8	14.8	417	330	153.4	214	5	1 346	495.2	44 881	135	42 955	4.5
Columbus, OH MSA	170	216	7.8	9.9	3 489	2 234	243.2	80	14	4 316	300.9	232 718	31	221 735	5.0
Corpus Christi, TX MSA	41	51	6.5	8.0	677	563	178.2	176	8	1 545	406.6	80 129	83	78 771	1.7
Cumberland, MD-WV MSA	8	11	8.5	8.9	189	168	187.0	150	3	536	530.3	16 094	256	15 969	.8
Dallas-Fort Worth, TX CMSA	518	681	6.8	8.9	8 582	6 210	192.0	143	67	11 645	260.5	802 002	10	743 900	7.8
Dallas, TX PMSA	330	429	6.4	8.4	6 465	4 478	217.3	X	44	8 055	270.8	531 986	X	491 411	8.3
Fort Worth-Arlington, TX PMSA	188	252	7.8	9.9	2 117	1 732	141.6	X	23	3 590	240.0	270 016	X	252 489	6.9
Danville, VA MSA	22	20	16.2	13.3	139	123	126.9	246	1	306	279.3	17 610	249	18 421	–4.4
Davenport-Moline-Rock Island, IA-IL MSA	35	53	7.3	10.1	514	440	143.7	226	6	1 312	366.8	63 612	104	63 260	.6
Dayton-Springfield, OH MSA	94	126	7.2	8.8	2 016	1 449	211.7	123	12	3 439	361.3	155 496	47	157 083	–1.0
Daytona Beach, FL MSA	25	44	5.3	8.7	635	537	141.0	232	7	1 512	335.7	60 454	108	54 348	11.2
Decatur, AL MSA	15	15	7.8	7.5	150	140	108.0	262	4	530	381.6	25 111	195	24 853	1.0
Decatur, IL MSA	17	20	10.3	11.6	183	155	157.3	208	2	546	469.4	20 743	224	21 642	–4.2
Denver-Boulder-Greeley, CO CMSA	226	294	6.9	8.9	6 164	4 267	276.0	55	23	4 932	220.9	370 495	19	344 874	7.4
Boulder-Longmont, CO PMSA	17	23	5.5	6.9	638	544	250.9	X	4	451	177.4	41 140	X	38 185	7.7
Denver, CO PMSA	195	254	7.1	9.2	5 303	3 546	289.7	X	18	4 155	227.0	303 983	X	283 024	7.4
Greeley, CO PMSA	14	17	6.2	7.7	223	177	150.1	X	1	326	219.4	25 372	X	23 665	7.2
Des Moines, IA MSA	50	58	7.9	9.3	734	572	173.6	185	6	1 689	399.5	72 412	91	69 597	4.0
Detroit-Ann Arbor-Flint, MI CMSA	751	1 030	9.5	11.6	14 051	8 197	267.1	62	67	16 643	316.4	855 520	7	866 547	–1.3
Ann Arbor, MI PMSA	39	56	5.6	7.7	2 794	1 435	535.9	X	11	1 883	361.2	80 515	X	80 314	.3
Detroit, MI PMSA	616	881	9.3	12.0	10 466	6 238	243.1	X	50	13 222	307.1	693 630	X	701 493	–1.1
Flint, MI PMSA	96	93	14.5	12.1	791	524	182.2	X	6	1 538	354.2	81 375	X	84 740	–4.0
Dothan, AL MSA	20	21	10.0	9.6	277	252	207.5	128	3	647	484.8	23 294	210	23 386	–.4
Dover, DE MSA	16	29	8.4	14.2	136	116	112.2	256	1	193	159.2	24 314	203	23 296	4.4
Dubuque, IA MSA	7	16	5.9	12.7	187	164	212.2	122	2	528	599.1	12 447	268	11 955	4.1
Duluth-Superior, MN-WI MSA	19	24	7.2	8.3	499	414	208.3	127	9	1 344	561.0	39 132	146	41 233	–5.1
Eau Claire, WI MSA	13	9	7.3	4.7	321	276	225.4	102	5	854	599.7	23 704	206	22 915	3.4
El Paso, TX MSA	89	90	5.7	6.0	991	711	146.0	221	8	1 767	260.4	148 028	50	143 749	3.0
Elkhart-Goshen, IN MSA	24	27	8.9	9.9	177	156	106.1	264	2	390	233.8	29 615	174	27 752	6.7
Elmira, NY MSA	10	15	8.5	10.8	206	163	219.1	111	2	526	559.6	15 494	260	15 240	1.7
Enid, OK MSA	5	7	6.7	8.3	103	83	179.6	172	3	391	681.9	10 320	272	10 334	–.1
Erie, PA MSA	30	58	7.6	13.8	524	413	186.7	151	8	1 281	456.4	42 961	138	43 581	–1.4
Eugene-Springfield, OR MSA	26	25	7.3	6.4	550	505	181.3	169	4	582	191.8	48 355	126	47 178	2.5
Evansville-Henderson, IN-KY MSA	34	50	8.9	12.0	643	518	223.7	103	6	1 591	553.4	45 237	133	44 690	1.2
Fargo-Moorhead, ND-MN MSA	17	18	7.7	8.1	445	340	271.6	58	2	639	390.0	27 726	182	26 491	4.7
Fayetteville, NC MSA	56	52	10.0	9.0	335	262	117.6	253	2	493	173.0	49 995	124	46 097	8.5
Fayetteville-Springdale-Rogers, AR MSA	28	32	7.5	9.8	396	339	156.4	210	8	724	286.0	43 033	137	38 219	12.6
Flagstaff, AZ-UT MSA	15	23	8.2	11.2	208	189	178.7	175	3	186	159.8	21 911	219	20 521	6.8
Florence, AL MSA	10	11	5.7	6.1	213	197	157.5	207	4	943	697.3	22 094	218	21 954	.6
Florence, SC MSA	25	28	14.5	14.3	273	222	222.6	105	4	819	667.9	23 472	209	23 384	.4
Fort Collins-Loveland, CO MSA	21	17	7.6	6.1	394	328	181.3	169	3	403	185.4	35 719	154	32 902	8.6
Fort Myers-Cape Coral, FL MSA	26	31	6.0	6.8	642	564	171.1	191	5	1 468	391.2	49 413	125	44 294	11.6
Fort Pierce-Port St. Lucie, FL MSA	28	42	8.4	11.1	460	406	162.9	202	3	777	275.1	39 868	143	34 958	14.0
Fort Smith, AR-OK MSA	15	15	5.3	5.2	346	301	183.4	164	5	924	489.7	35 815	153	34 295	4.4
Fort Walton Beach, FL MSA	16	22	6.6	8.8	226	185	138.2	237	3	417	255.0	29 029	178	27 112	7.1
Fort Wayne, IN MSA	59	67	7.9	8.5	786	656	166.7	197	9	1 510	320.3	78 824	84	77 608	1.6
Fresno, CA MSA	161	138	9.2	7.9	1 469	1 114	173.2	186	13	1 671	197.1	189 382	36	179 367	5.6
Gadsden, AL MSA	14	19	10.5	14.1	153	134	150.1	217	2	538	527.6	16 548	254	17 122	–3.4
Gainesville, FL MSA	30	32	12.1	11.7	1 464	716	749.2	5	4	1 138	582.4	28 812	180	27 921	3.2
Glens Falls, NY MSA	10	13	6.1	7.5	219	184	179.0	173	2	555	453.7	22 840	213	21 782	4.9
Goldsboro, NC MSA	20	20	12.5	11.7	132	107	119.3	252	1	267	241.3	18 516	247	18 285	1.3
Grand Forks, ND-MN MSA	9	14	5.8	8.3	212	152	203.5	130	4	706	677.7	18 863	240	18 343	2.8

X Not applicable.

[1]Deaths of infants under 1 year old.
[2]Per 1,000 live births for the years shown.
[3]Covers active, nonfederal physicians as of December 31. Data subject to copyright; see below for source citation.
[4]Per 100,000 resident population estimated as of July 1, 1995.
[5]Based on 272 metropolitan areas (244 MSAs, 17 CMSAs, and 11 NECMAs); see text for more information. When metropolitan areas share the same rank, the next lower rank is omitted.
[6]Covers nonfederal, short-stay (average length of stay less than 30 days) hospitals except hospital units of institutions. Data subject to copyright; see below for source citation.
[7]Aggregated from school district data to county of school superintendent's location to metropolitan area.

Source: Infant Deaths—U.S. National Center for Health Statistics, "Vital Statistics of the United States, Vol. II, Mortality," annual; Physicians—American Medical Association, Chicago, IL, "Physician Characteristics and Distribution in the U.S.," annual (copyright); Community Hospitals—Healthcare InfoSource, Inc., a subsidiary of the American Hospital Association, "Hospital Statistics," 1996/97 edition (copyright); Public School Enrollment—U.S. National Center for Education Statistics, Common Core of Data (CCD) Public Agency Universe Internet data files for years shown at site <http://nces.ed.gov/ccd/pubagency.html> (accessed April 1997).

[MSA = Metropolitan statistical area.   CMSA = Consolidated MSA.   PMSA = Primary MSA.   NECMA = New England county metropolitan area.   All areas defined as of June 30, 1996.   Table includes 245 MSAs, 17 CMSAs, and 58 PMSAs not in New England; as well as 12 NECMAs.   Table excludes 10 MSAs, 1 CMSA, and 15 PMSAs in New England]

Metropolitan areas	Infant deaths[1]				Physicians,[3] 1995				Community hospitals,[6] 1995			Public school enrollment[7]			
	Number		Rate[2]		Number		Per 100,000 population		Number	Beds		1994–1995			Percent change, 1992–1995
	1994	1990	1994	1990	Total	Office-based	Rate[4]	Rank[5]		Number	Rate[4]	Number	Rank[5]	1991–1992	
Grand Junction, CO MSA	7	12	5.4	9.4	202	161	190.2	145	4	659	620.6	19 103	239	18 106	5.5
Grand Rapids-Muskegon-Holland, MI MSA	124	144	7.9	8.4	1 637	1 204	163.3	201	15	2 629	262.2	174 186	42	170 799	2.0
Great Falls, MT MSA	11	12	9.0	8.9	186	162	229.5	99	2	422	520.8	15 156	261	14 654	3.4
Green Bay, WI MSA	28	22	9.2	6.9	350	317	166.1	198	3	639	303.3	35 074	156	32 947	6.5
Greensboro--Winston Salem--High Point, NC MSA	148	162	9.9	10.4	2 677	1 864	238.0	85	13	3 651	324.5	170 812	45	162 924	4.8
Greenville, NC MSA	28	28	16.3	16.6	664	353	562.5	6	1	677	573.5	19 136	238	17 861	7.1
Greenville-Spartanburg-Anderson, SC MSA	87	136	7.5	10.8	1 631	1 269	184.5	161	13	2 765	312.7	142 305	53	136 685	4.1
Harrisburg-Lebanon-Carlisle, PA MSA	59	71	7.6	8.6	1 760	1 055	287.7	43	8	1 850	302.4	114 324	63	95 286	20.0
Hartford, CT NECMA	147	147	9.3	8.8	3 620	2 232	325.9	25	NA	NA	NA	183 601	38	176 830	3.8
Hattiesburg, MS MSA	26	19	16.2	11.8	247	227	232.8	93	2	718	676.7	18 855	241	18 174	3.7
Hickory-Morganton-Lenoir, NC MSA	39	45	9.5	10.7	435	385	140.0	234	6	887	285.5	50 397	123	48 337	4.3
Honolulu, HI MSA	99	103	6.7	6.7	2 287	1 690	262.6	66	12	2 100	241.2	NA	NA	NA	NA
Houma, LA MSA	30	33	10.2	10.1	227	197	120.4	251	5	672	356.5	38 633	149	37 698	2.5
Houston-Galveston-Brazoria, TX CMSA	585	603	8.0	8.3	10 976	6 841	262.7	65	61	13 522	323.7	815 486	9	769 939	5.9
Brazoria, TX PMSA	21	26	6.0	7.9	200	132	92.4	X	4	282	130.3	44 544	X	42 350	5.2
Galveston-Texas City, TX PMSA	36	28	9.6	7.5	1 190	507	500.5	X	4	1 209	508.5	61 855	X	59 064	4.7
Houston, TX PMSA	528	549	8.0	8.3	9 586	6 202	257.4	X	53	12 031	323.1	709 087	X	668 525	6.1
Huntington-Ashland, WV-KY-OH MSA	25	30	6.3	7.6	690	489	217.8	114	6	1 414	446.3	54 584	116	56 150	−2.8
Huntsville, AL MSA	43	45	9.0	9.3	567	468	172.9	187	5	1 023	312.0	51 604	122	49 139	5.0
Indianapolis, IN MSA	195	267	8.5	11.2	4 559	2 882	308.9	34	21	5 462	370.1	240 315	30	232 175	3.5
Iowa City, IA MSA	13	13	10.1	9.2	1 394	499	1 374.8	2	2	1 062	1 047.4	12 171	270	11 484	6.0
Jackson, MI MSA	16	25	7.8	10.4	148	131	96.5	267	2	394	256.8	24 533	202	24 914	−1.5
Jackson, MS MSA	59	92	8.9	13.4	1 411	888	339.0	22	10	2 518	604.9	73 273	90	71 346	2.7
Jackson, TN MSA	15	17	11.4	12.0	262	218	269.1	61	[8]2	[8]766	[8]786.8	15 945	257	15 844	.6
Jacksonville, FL MSA	108	181	7.2	11.0	2 329	1 651	237.2	88	11	3 198	325.7	169 787	46	159 695	6.3
Jacksonville, NC MSA	32	42	10.1	12.2	109	93	75.6	272	1	133	92.2	20 223	226	18 971	6.6
Jamestown, NY MSA	12	11	6.8	5.5	164	143	116.1	254	4	660	467.1	26 209	189	25 516	2.7
Janesville-Beloit, WI MSA	14	20	6.9	9.2	241	206	162.3	203	3	494	332.7	27 090	186	25 682	5.5
Johnson City-Kingsport-Bristol, TN-VA MSA	27	42	5.2	7.9	1 159	863	255.1	69	10	1 827	402.2	69 991	94	70 398	−.6
Johnstown, PA MSA	13	25	5.0	8.8	447	308	185.9	154	7	1 083	450.3	35 337	155	36 623	−3.5
Jonesboro, AR MSA	9	6	8.4	5.7	205	173	273.7	57	NA	NA	NA	12 380	269	12 267	.9
Joplin, MO MSA	21	14	10.1	7.2	204	178	142.2	229	4	759	529.0	24 565	201	24 272	1.2
Kalamazoo-Battle Creek, MI MSA	34	72	5.4	10.4	936	667	211.6	124	9	1 531	346.1	75 071	86	76 841	−2.3
Kansas City, MO-KS MSA	180	233	7.6	8.9	4 161	2 797	248.7	77	34	6 148	367.4	281 341	25	264 685	6.3
Killeen-Temple, TX MSA	38	53	6.2	9.4	688	432	235.2	91	4	784	268.0	57 310	114	50 198	14.2
Knoxville, TN MSA	40	71	5.0	8.8	1 668	1 324	260.3	68	10	2 488	388.3	99 729	66	95 191	4.8
Kokomo, IN MSA	11	18	8.1	12.2	122	108	122.2	249	4	449	449.6	17 263	251	17 736	−2.7
La Crosse, WI-MN MSA	5	7	3.2	4.1	408	317	337.4	23	3	628	519.3	18 838	242	17 778	6.0
Lafayette, LA MSA	65	64	11.0	10.6	593	468	162.3	203	11	1 485	406.5	68 634	97	67 379	1.9
Lafayette, IN MSA	16	22	7.2	9.4	292	248	171.9	190	3	534	314.3	24 184	204	23 398	3.4
Lake Charles, LA MSA	25	30	9.0	10.9	279	250	158.4	206	6	888	504.0	34 487	160	33 407	3.2
Lakeland-Winter Haven, FL MSA	63	67	10.2	10.3	620	531	142.1	230	5	1 443	330.8	71 297	92	66 841	6.7
Lancaster, PA MSA	38	72	5.5	9.9	655	524	146.3	219	5	1 046	233.7	65 343	101	62 638	4.3
Lansing-East Lansing, MI MSA	50	72	8.3	10.8	858	557	192.4	142	6	1 178	264.1	74 934	87	78 170	−4.1
Laredo, TX MSA	30	23	6.1	5.9	133	118	77.2	271	2	440	255.2	42 634	140	37 968	12.3
Las Cruces, NM MSA	17	27	5.5	9.3	178	148	111.2	257	1	221	138.1	34 789	157	31 580	10.2
Las Vegas, NV-AZ MSA	136	139	7.5	9.0	1 583	1 319	138.5	236	12	2 423	212.0	180 778	39	149 651	20.8
Lawrence, KS MSA	8	5	7.2	4.7	133	112	150.5	215	1	108	122.2	11 870	271	10 717	10.8
Lawton, OK MSA	15	15	7.1	7.0	150	121	134.6	241	2	496	445.0	23 086	212	22 264	3.7
Lewiston-Auburn, ME NECMA	12	8	9.8	5.3	224	187	217.7	115	NA	NA	NA	17 438	250	17 695	−1.5
Lexington, KY MSA	44	36	7.4	6.0	1 730	1 111	397.6	10	13	2 040	468.9	66 512	100	65 070	2.2
Lima, OH MSA	13	26	6.1	10.3	207	183	133.1	243	3	577	371.0	29 080	177	29 232	−.5
Lincoln, NE MSA	22	23	7.0	7.4	450	372	195.9	136	4	993	432.3	34 734	158	32 864	5.7
Little Rock-North Little Rock, AR MSA	75	87	9.3	10.1	2 020	1 302	372.2	16	12	2 930	539.8	88 357	74	87 436	1.1
Longview-Marshall, TX MSA	22	26	7.7	8.8	259	243	126.9	246	5	632	309.7	42 528	141	41 892	1.5

NA Not available.
X Not applicable.

[1]Deaths of infants under 1 year old.
[2]Per 1,000 live births for the years shown.
[3]Covers active, nonfederal physicians as of December 31.   Data subject to copyright; see below for source citation.
[4]Per 100,000 resident population estimated as of July 1, 1995.
[5]Based on 272 metropolitan areas (244 MSAs, 17 CMSAs, and 11 NECMAs); see text for more information.   When metropolitan areas share the same rank, the next lower rank is omitted.
[6]Covers nonfederal, short-stay (average length of stay less than 30 days) hospitals except hospital units of institutions.   Data subject to copyright; see below for source citation.
[7]Aggregated from school district data to county of school superintendent's location to metropolitan area.
[8]Excludes Chester County, which was added to the MSA on June 30, 1996.

Source: Infant Deaths—U.S. National Center for Health Statistics, "Vital Statistics of the United States, Vol. II, Mortality," annual;   Physicians—American Medical Association, Chicago, IL, "Physician Characteristics and Distribution in the U.S.," annual (copyright);   Community Hospitals—Healthcare InfoSource, Inc., a subsidiary of the American Hospital Association, "Hospital Statistics," 1996/97 edition (copyright);   Public School Enrollment—U.S. National Center for Education Statistics, Common Core of Data (CCD) Public Agency Universe Internet data files for years shown at site <http://nces.ed.gov/ccd/pubagency.html> (accessed April 1997).

[MSA = Metropolitan statistical area. CMSA = Consolidated MSA. PMSA = Primary MSA. NECMA = New England county metropolitan area. All areas defined as of June 30, 1996. Table includes 245 MSAs, 17 CMSAs, and 58 PMSAs not in New England; as well as 12 NECMAs. Table excludes 10 MSAs, 1 CMSA, and 15 PMSAs in New England]

Metropolitan areas	Infant deaths[1]				Physicians,[3] 1995				Community hospitals,[6] 1995				Public school enrollment[7]			
	Number		Rate[2]		Number		Per 100,000 population			Beds			1994–1995			Percent change, 1992–1995
	1994	1990	1994	1990	Total	Office-based	Rate[4]	Rank[5]	Number	Number	Rate[4]	Number	Rank[5]	1991–1992	
Los Angeles-Riverside-Orange, CA CMSA	2 072	2 680	6.9	8.2	36 319	26 168	236.6	89	190	39 026	254.2	2 594 815	2	2 491 776	4.1
Los Angeles-Long Beach, CA PMSA	1 254	1 634	6.9	8.0	23 840	16 681	262.6	X	114	25 546	281.4	1 473 717	X	1 441 228	2.3
Orange, CA PMSA	301	397	6.1	7.7	6 691	5 179	257.4	X	35	6 238	240.0	412 266	X	390 908	5.5
Riverside-San Bernardino, CA PMSA	460	550	8.2	9.4	4 481	3 240	150.9	X	33	5 957	200.6	588 099	X	543 410	8.2
Ventura, CA PMSA	57	99	4.8	7.8	1 307	1 068	184.9	X	8	1 285	181.8	120 733	X	116 230	3.9
Louisville, KY-IN MSA	127	131	9.2	9.1	2 857	2 016	289.6	41	15	3 883	393.6	146 639	51	145 066	1.1
Lubbock, TX MSA	22	35	5.8	8.8	810	539	349.1	20	7	1 661	715.8	42 907	139	42 359	1.3
Lynchburg, VA MSA	34	18	12.7	6.5	298	257	145.9	222	3	751	367.6	31 698	165	30 769	3.0
Macon, GA MSA	76	80	16.0	16.0	681	504	220.2	109	8	1 245	402.5	53 928	117	51 624	4.5
Madison, WI MSA	36	35	7.4	6.6	1 906	1 048	485.1	8	4	1 285	327.1	59 200	109	54 155	9.3
Mansfield, OH MSA	20	31	8.8	12.1	193	172	110.1	259	5	613	349.7	31 100	167	32 118	-3.2
McAllen-Edinburg-Mission, TX MSA	65	58	5.1	5.4	408	345	84.6	269	5	1 044	216.4	127 406	60	118 719	7.3
Medford-Ashland, OR MSA	19	18	9.5	8.6	306	273	184.7	159	3	426	257.1	27 680	183	25 934	6.7
Melbourne-Titusville-Palm Bay, FL MSA	41	32	7.9	5.6	703	618	156.1	211	5	1 118	248.3	64 595	102	58 883	9.7
Memphis, TN-AR-MS MSA	255	271	14.0	14.2	2 985	1 952	279.8	51	13	4 160	389.9	192 642	35	182 395	5.6
Merced, CA MSA	30	33	7.2	7.6	214	168	111.0	258	5	331	171.7	46 957	130	43 847	7.1
Miami-Fort Lauderdale, FL CMSA	408	511	7.8	9.6	9 730	7 265	281.3	49	47	13 111	379.0	520 870	13	474 586	9.8
Fort Lauderdale, FL PMSA	189	174	9.7	9.3	2 963	2 500	209.7	X	19	5 072	359.0	199 255	X	170 032	17.2
Miami, FL PMSA	219	337	6.7	9.8	6 767	4 765	330.7	X	28	8 039	392.9	321 615	X	304 554	5.6
Milwaukee-Racine, WI CMSA	243	248	9.9	9.5	4 600	3 120	280.6	50	25	5 297	323.1	267 488	28	254 743	5.0
Milwaukee-Waukesha, WI PMSA	218	222	9.9	9.5	4 348	2 904	298.8	X	22	4 766	327.5	237 219	X	225 035	5.4
Racine, WI PMSA	25	26	9.8	9.6	252	216	136.9	X	3	531	288.4	30 269	X	29 708	1.9
Minneapolis-St. Paul, MN-WI MSA	291	332	7.0	7.7	6 829	4 665	250.1	73	34	6 617	242.4	474 346	14	421 252	12.6
Mobile, AL MSA	84	80	10.4	10.0	1 191	808	231.8	94	10	2 121	412.8	84 606	78	85 506	-1.1
Modesto, CA MSA	63	64	8.5	8.1	633	536	154.0	213	6	1 335	324.8	87 132	75	81 718	6.6
Monroe, LA MSA	24	32	10.8	13.2	318	246	216.6	118	5	1 022	696.1	28 917	179	29 056	-.5
Montgomery, AL MSA	59	62	12.0	11.8	524	444	167.8	196	8	1 218	390.0	53 175	118	52 600	1.1
Muncie, IN MSA	10	17	7.0	10.9	289	209	243.0	81	1	408	343.1	18 057	248	18 390	-1.8
Myrtle Beach, SC MSA	23	24	12.2	10.3	225	202	142.6	228	3	498	315.5	25 253	192	24 720	2.2
Naples, FL MSA	21	19	8.5	7.6	351	280	191.9	144	1	434	237.2	25 157	193	21 855	15.1
Nashville, TN MSA	129	136	8.2	8.5	3 554	2 313	324.6	27	18	4 492	410.3	173 200	43	161 574	7.2
New London-Norwich, CT NECMA	21	37	7.3	9.1	486	362	194.2	138	NA	NA	NA	39 781	144	37 623	5.7
New Orleans, LA MSA	200	254	9.5	11.3	4 893	2 966	372.3	15	30	6 369	484.6	210 423	33	205 904	2.2
New York-Northern New Jersey-Long Island, NY-NJ-CT-PA CMSA/NECMA	2 450	3 125	7.9	9.6	75 297	42 990	380.5	14	209	78 968	399.0	2 845 213	1	2 686 376	5.9
Bergen-Passaic, NJ PMSA	131	146	6.9	7.8	4 871	3 108	372.7	X	12	5 155	394.4	175 306	X	165 145	6.2
Dutchess, NY PMSA	21	24	6.1	6.2	564	434	215.7	X	3	704	269.2	42 580	X	40 556	5.0
Jersey City, NJ PMSA	86	112	9.5	11.5	1 106	650	200.7	X	9	2 461	446.5	73 598	X	69 078	6.5
Middlesex-Somerset-Hunterdon, NJ PMSA	86	123	5.4	7.8	3 227	2 035	299.0	X	9	2 877	266.5	147 731	X	136 914	7.9
Monmouth-Ocean, NJ PMSA	86	105	6.0	7.2	2 244	1 657	213.4	X	10	3 258	309.9	155 905	X	145 398	7.2
Nassau-Suffolk, NY PMSA	242	320	6.1	8.1	10 824	6 824	407.7	X	27	9 145	344.4	410 969	X	396 952	3.5
New Haven-Bridgeport-Stamford-Waterbury-Danbury, CT NECMA	173	193	7.4	7.6	6 367	3 887	391.5	X	[8]16	[8]4 131	[8]254.0	238 107	X	224 014	6.3
New York, NY PMSA	1 263	1 701	8.6	11.0	38 438	19 337	445.3	X	84	39 205	454.2	1 198 260	X	1 125 405	6.5
Newark, NJ PMSA	291	304	9.6	9.8	6 029	3 917	311.1	X	27	9 601	495.4	291 010	X	279 412	4.2
Newburgh, NY-PA PMSA	34	41	6.1	6.9	553	421	154.0	X	6	909	253.2	62 150	X	57 613	7.9
Trenton, NJ PMSA	37	56	8.1	11.1	1 074	720	325.4	X	6	1 522	461.2	49 597	X	45 889	8.1
Norfolk-Virginia Beach-Newport News, VA-NC MSA	240	382	9.2	14.1	3 107	2 338	202.4	131	17	4 070	265.1	265 048	29	250 944	5.6
Ocala, FL MSA	23	26	8.8	9.4	288	244	127.7	245	2	535	237.2	34 020	161	30 458	11.7
Odessa-Midland, TX MSA	29	35	7.1	7.9	332	271	139.7	235	4	748	314.7	52 717	121	50 594	4.2
Oklahoma City, OK MSA	107	169	7.3	11.4	2 575	1 679	253.3	71	19	3 583	352.4	179 402	40	172 051	4.3
Omaha, NE-IA MSA	87	83	8.4	7.4	2 119	1 340	315.7	32	13	2 995	446.3	114 586	62	112 703	1.7
Orlando, FL MSA	146	155	7.1	7.6	2 550	2 076	184.0	162	13	4 609	332.6	219 880	32	200 048	9.9
Owensboro, KY MSA	6	11	4.9	8.6	160	141	176.5	177	1	356	392.7	14 647	264	13 979	4.8

X Not applicable.
NA Not available.

[1]Deaths of infants under 1 year old.
[2]Per 1,000 live births for the years shown.
[3]Covers active, nonfederal physicians as of December 31. Data subject to copyright; see below for source citation.
[4]Per 100,000 resident population estimated as of July 1, 1995.
[5]Based on 272 metropolitan areas (244 MSAs, 17 CMSAs, and 11 NECMAs); see text for more information. When metropolitan areas share the same rank, the next lower rank is omitted.
[6]Covers nonfederal, short-stay (average length of stay less than 30 days) hospitals except hospital units of institutions. Data subject to copyright; see below for source citation.
[7]Aggregated from school district data to county of school superintendent's location to metropolitan area.
[8]Data for NECMA not available. Data are for 5 Connecticut PMSAs: Bridgeport, Danbury, New Haven-Meriden, Stamford-Norwalk, and Waterbury.

Source: Infant Deaths—U.S. National Center for Health Statistics, "Vital Statistics of the United States, Vol. II, Mortality," annual; Physicians—American Medical Association, Chicago, IL, "Physician Characteristics and Distribution in the U.S.," annual (copyright); Community Hospitals—Healthcare InfoSource, Inc., a subsidiary of the American Hospital Association, "Hospital Statistics," 1996/97 edition (copyright); Public School Enrollment—U.S. National Center for Education Statistics, Common Core of Data (CCD) Public Agency Universe Internet data files for years shown at site <http://nces.ed.gov/ccd/pubagency.html> (accessed April 1997).

[MSA = Metropolitan statistical area. CMSA = Consolidated MSA. PMSA = Primary MSA. NECMA = New England county metropolitan area. All areas defined as of June 30, 1996. Table includes 245 MSAs, 17 CMSAs, and 58 PMSAs not in New England; as well as 12 NECMAs. Table excludes 10 MSAs, 1 CMSA, and 15 PMSAs in New England]

Metropolitan areas	Infant deaths[1]				Physicians,[3] 1995				Community hospitals,[6] 1995			Public school enrollment[7]			
	Number		Rate[2]		Number		Per 100,000 population		Number	Beds		1994–1995			Percent change, 1992–1995
	1994	1990	1994	1990	Total	Office–based	Rate[4]	Rank[5]		Number	Rate[4]	Number	Rank[5]	1991–1992	
Panama City, FL MSA	22	22	11.2	10.7	208	181	146.3	219	2	491	345.3	24 802	197	22 666	9.4
Parkersburg-Marietta, WV-OH MSA	19	21	10.1	10.5	204	172	134.5	242	5	794	523.5	26 243	188	26 713	–1.8
Pensacola, FL MSA	40	51	7.5	8.7	710	592	187.7	148	6	1 700	449.5	63 737	103	60 366	5.6
Peoria-Pekin, IL MSA	37	58	7.7	11.6	797	561	230.4	96	5	1 243	359.3	57 548	113	57 771	–.4
Philadelphia-Wilmington-Atlantic City, PA-NJ-DE-MD CMSA	786	1 041	8.9	10.7	19 447	11 782	325.8	26	87	21 949	367.7	863 806	6	816 458	5.8
Atlantic-Cape May, NJ PMSA	53	63	10.2	11.6	508	388	153.1	X	5	1 073	323.4	52 177	X	47 962	8.8
Philadelphia, PA-NJ PMSA	672	876	9.2	10.8	17 475	10 409	352.8	X	75	19 071	385.0	709 751	X	670 842	5.8
Vineland-Millville-Bridgeton, NJ PMSA	18	20	8.5	8.6	191	161	138.7	X	2	568	412.3	24 848	X	24 228	2.6
Wilmington-Newark, DE-MD PMSA	43	82	5.4	9.6	1 273	824	233.1	X	5	1 237	226.5	77 030	X	73 426	4.9
Phoenix-Mesa, AZ MSA	358	380	8.1	8.9	5 230	3 927	196.8	134	30	6 373	239.8	443 053	16	393 512	12.6
Pine Bluff, AR MSA	14	14	10.9	9.6	143	112	170.8	192	1	481	574.6	16 716	253	17 981	–7.0
Pittsburgh, PA MSA	240	280	8.4	8.9	7 668	4 891	320.9	29	44	12 481	522.3	332 759	21	326 100	2.0
Pittsfield, MA NECMA	6	12	4.0	6.6	391	278	289.4	42	NA	NA	NA	21 204	223	20 601	2.9
Pocatello, ID MSA	8	11	6.3	9.6	127	106	173.8	183	NA	NA	NA	15 614	259	15 429	1.2
Portland, ME NECMA	12	29	3.9	8.2	880	571	353.6	19	NA	NA	NA	37 475	151	35 317	6.1
Portland-Salem, OR-WA CMSA	188	229	6.5	7.9	4 853	3 555	239.0	84	24	4 185	206.1	333 221	20	315 776	5.5
Portland-Vancouver, OR-WA PMSA	146	193	6.0	7.9	4 414	3 167	257.1	X	20	3 634	211.6	282 729	X	265 675	6.4
Salem, OR PMSA	42	36	8.9	7.9	439	388	139.9	X	4	551	175.6	50 492	X	50 101	.8
Providence-Warwick-Pawtucket, RI NECMA	64	112	5.2	8.0	2 798	1 692	307.7	36	NA	NA	NA	135 863	54	129 855	4.6
Provo-Orem, UT MSA	41	46	5.4	6.8	357	306	114.9	255	4	539	173.5	74 023	88	70 001	5.7
Pueblo, CO MSA	15	17	8.5	9.6	287	235	221.4	108	2	510	393.5	22 750	216	22 578	.8
Punta Gorda, FL MSA	4	9	4.0	8.5	227	184	176.0	179	3	610	473.0	15 092	262	13 571	11.2
Raleigh-Durham-Chapel Hill, NC MSA	126	142	8.8	10.4	4 914	2 534	493.0	7	10	3 488	349.9	148 760	49	134 061	11.0
Rapid City, SD MSA	14	13	9.9	7.7	201	164	230.4	96	1	356	408.0	18 621	246	17 766	4.8
Reading, PA MSA	30	44	6.4	8.9	648	491	185.0	156	4	928	264.9	58 561	111	54 593	7.3
Redding, CA MSA	18	20	8.5	8.7	345	284	214.5	119	3	404	251.1	30 039	171	28 821	4.2
Reno, NV MSA	18	39	4.1	8.6	717	571	246.4	78	4	954	327.8	45 752	132	40 028	14.3
Richland-Kennewick-Pasco, WA MSA	18	30	6.0	10.6	222	193	123.7	248	4	387	215.7	37 015	152	33 654	10.0
Richmond-Petersburg, VA MSA	130	162	9.8	11.4	2 807	1 820	303.1	38	15	3 646	393.7	154 785	48	146 277	5.8
Roanoke, VA MSA	26	32	9.1	10.5	769	538	336.2	24	4	1 207	527.7	34 726	159	34 212	1.5
Rochester, MN MSA	13	12	7.5	6.4	2 147	979	1 906.3	1	3	1 294	1 148.9	20 136	227	19 285	4.4
Rochester, NY MSA	113	163	7.4	9.4	3 356	1 993	308.7	35	17	3 951	363.5	187 803	37	177 973	5.5
Rockford, IL MSA	50	46	9.9	8.6	646	530	185.1	155	6	1 075	308.0	58 597	110	56 668	3.4
Rocky Mount, NC MSA	35	22	16.5	9.8	156	147	109.3	260	3	507	355.3	25 774	190	25 142	2.5
Sacramento-Yolo, CA CMSA	190	225	7.5	8.5	3 884	2 881	241.4	83	15	3 411	212.0	285 558	24	270 355	5.6
Sacramento, CA PMSA	168	208	7.3	8.6	3 387	2 552	231.9	X	13	3 260	223.2	261 034	X	246 665	5.8
Yolo, CA PMSA	22	17	9.7	7.1	497	329	335.0	X	2	151	101.8	24 524	X	23 690	3.5
Saginaw-Bay City-Midland, MI MSA	47	67	8.2	10.1	693	493	172.1	188	6	1 607	399.1	66 990	99	70 618	–5.1
St. Cloud, MN MSA	6	19	2.9	8.5	267	238	168.1	195	5	640	403.0	30 593	170	29 295	4.4
St. Joseph, MO MSA	12	12	8.8	8.5	141	122	144.7	223	2	482	494.8	16 950	252	17 095	–.8
St. Louis, MO-IL MSA	315	396	8.4	9.5	7 259	4 439	285.8	46	41	11 057	435.3	396 412	18	381 831	3.8
Salinas, CA MSA	41	61	5.8	7.7	555	455	165.9	199	4	577	172.5	61 844	105	62 468	–1.0
Salt Lake City-Ogden, UT MSA	145	174	6.4	7.9	2 979	1 986	248.8	75	15	2 647	221.1	281 199	26	274 863	2.3
San Angelo, TX MSA	7	9	4.7	5.4	188	177	184.6	160	3	473	464.6	19 750	229	19 181	3.0
San Antonio, TX MSA	187	168	7.5	7.0	3 728	2 511	254.8	70	19	4 340	296.6	274 830	27	263 407	4.3
San Diego, CA MSA	315	367	6.6	7.2	6 555	4 752	249.6	74	24	5 735	218.3	428 360	17	405 894	5.5
San Francisco-Oakland-San Jose, CA CMSA	602	719	6.1	6.7	20 399	14 398	311.8	33	79	15 229	232.7	939 868	5	904 055	4.0
Oakland, CA PMSA	208	292	6.1	7.9	5 308	4 077	242.1	X	24	4 511	205.7	335 289	X	319 932	4.8
San Francisco, CA PMSA	121	157	5.5	6.5	8 075	5 209	490.8	X	23	4 999	303.9	177 282	X	171 290	3.5
San Jose, CA PMSA	154	154	5.8	5.5	4 643	3 176	295.1	X	14	3 608	229.3	237 335	X	231 293	2.6
Santa Cruz-Watsonville, CA PMSA	28	20	7.6	4.6	473	413	200.1	X	2	385	162.9	37 640	X	36 037	4.4
Santa Rosa, CA PMSA	29	29	5.3	4.7	971	815	233.2	X	9	896	215.2	67 233	X	63 280	6.2
Vallejo-Fairfield-Napa, CA PMSA	62	67	8.3	8.2	929	708	193.9	X	7	830	173.3	85 089	X	82 223	3.5
San Luis Obispo-Atascadero-Paso Robles, CA MSA	19	26	7.1	8.6	496	402	218.8	112	5	465	205.1	34 013	162	31 947	6.5
Santa Barbara-Santa Maria-Lompoc, CA MSA	32	45	5.0	6.7	945	794	246.1	79	8	897	233.6	58 533	112	54 908	6.6

X Not applicable.
NA Not available.

[1]Deaths of infants under 1 year old.
[2]Per 1,000 live births for the years shown.
[3]Covers active, nonfederal physicians as of December 31. Data subject to copyright; see below for source citation.
[4]Per 100,000 resident population estimated as of July 1, 1995.
[5]Based on 272 metropolitan areas (244 MSAs, 17 CMSAs, and 11 NECMAs); see text for more information. When metropolitan areas share the same rank, the next lower rank is omitted.
[6]Covers nonfederal, short-stay (average length of stay less than 30 days) hospitals except hospital units of institutions. Data subject to copyright; see below for source citation.
[7]Aggregated from school district data to county of school superintendent's location to metropolitan area.

Source: Infant Deaths—U.S. National Center for Health Statistics, "Vital Statistics of the United States, Vol. II, Mortality," annual; Physicians—American Medical Association, Chicago, IL, "Physician Characteristics and Distribution in the U.S.," annual (copyright); Community Hospitals—Healthcare InfoSource, Inc., a subsidiary of the American Hospital Association, "Hospital Statistics," 1996/97 edition (copyright); Public School Enrollment—U.S. National Center for Education Statistics, Common Core of Data (CCD) Public Agency Universe Internet data files for years shown at site <http://nces.ed.gov/ccd/pubagency.html> (accessed April 1997).

Table B–4. Metro Areas — Infant Deaths, Physicians, Hospitals, and Education—Con.

[MSA = Metropolitan statistical area. CMSA = Consolidated MSA. PMSA = Primary MSA. NECMA = New England county metropolitan area. All areas defined as of June 30, 1996. Table includes 245 MSAs, 17 CMSAs, and 58 PMSAs not in New England; as well as 12 NECMAs. Table excludes 10 MSAs, 1 CMSA, and 15 PMSAs in New England]

Metropolitan areas	Infant deaths[1] Number 1994	1990	Rate[2] 1994	1990	Physicians,[3] 1995 Number Total	Office-based	Per 100,000 population Rate[4]	Rank[5]	Community hospitals,[6] 1995 Number	Beds Number	Rate[4]	Public school enrollment[7] 1994–1995 Number	Rank[5]	1991–1992	Percent change, 1992–1995
Santa Fe, NM MSA	10	13	5.8	8.0	322	274	237.3	87	2	321	236.6	18 717	244	18 274	2.4
Sarasota-Bradenton, FL MSA	54	65	10.2	11.4	1 139	1 015	217.0	117	7	2 045	389.6	61 295	106	56 185	9.1
Savannah, GA MSA	55	57	12.0	11.9	659	486	235.7	90	4	1 270	454.1	47 046	129	44 479	5.8
Scranton--Wilkes-Barre--Hazleton, PA MSA	47	50	6.8	6.6	1 221	981	193.1	141	15	2 888	456.7	85 395	77	85 481	−.1
Seattle-Tacoma-Bremerton, WA CMSA	280	349	6.0	7.2	8 698	6 167	265.8	63	32	5 822	177.9	528 408	12	491 574	7.5
Bremerton, WA PMSA	17	24	5.1	7.0	305	269	134.7	X	1	252	111.3	40 539	X	37 754	7.4
Olympia, WA PMSA	13	16	5.3	6.8	380	318	197.2	X	2	426	221.1	36 343	X	33 674	7.9
Seattle-Bellevue-Everett, WA PMSA	183	211	5.9	6.5	6 980	4 758	316.7	X	22	4 150	188.3	335 427	X	311 780	7.6
Tacoma, WA PMSA	67	98	6.9	9.3	1 033	822	159.3	X	7	994	153.2	116 099	X	108 366	7.1
Sharon, PA MSA	15	11	10.3	7.5	172	150	140.8	233	3	607	497.0	19 466	232	19 457	Z
Sheboygan, WI MSA	11	9	7.9	6.4	133	127	122.2	249	3	320	293.9	19 455	233	18 598	4.6
Sherman-Denison, TX MSA	7	12	5.8	8.3	171	162	173.8	183	3	515	523.3	18 650	245	17 920	4.1
Shreveport-Bossier City, LA MSA	58	72	10.3	11.2	1 204	751	317.4	31	10	2 066	544.7	76 719	85	78 054	−1.7
Sioux City, IA-NE MSA	28	29	13.9	14.8	225	195	186.6	152	2	535	443.6	21 632	221	21 401	1.1
Sioux Falls, SD MSA	16	24	7.1	10.4	497	372	322.6	28	4	1 071	695.1	27 070	187	24 464	10.7
South Bend, IN MSA	33	43	9.1	11.0	515	416	200.5	132	4	827	322.0	38 771	147	37 984	2.1
Spokane, WA MSA	37	37	6.9	6.6	971	771	241.5	82	7	1 368	340.3	71 248	93	67 520	5.5
Springfield, IL MSA	27	22	9.6	7.7	778	478	383.1	12	3	1 269	624.9	44 165	136	40 303	9.6
Springfield, MO MSA	28	30	7.2	8.2	627	549	213.6	120	3	1 592	542.3	47 059	128	44 263	6.3
Springfield, MA NECMA	67	62	8.4	7.0	1 490	1 024	251.0	72	NA	NA	NA	92 691	70	89 426	3.7
State College, PA MSA	7	15	5.2	9.8	202	171	154.7	212	2	265	203.0	13 789	265	13 071	5.5
Steubenville-Weirton, OH-WV MSA	8	12	5.4	7.9	149	116	106.8	263	3	693	496.9	21 799	220	23 402	−6.8
Stockton-Lodi, CA MSA	71	86	7.6	8.7	720	593	136.9	240	6	996	189.4	103 635	65	97 990	5.8
Sumter, SC MSA	21	23	12.6	12.1	90	79	84.2	270	1	188	175.8	19 371	234	18 947	2.2
Syracuse, NY MSA	102	107	9.8	9.1	2 026	1 299	270.5	59	9	2 532	338.1	133 005	56	128 902	3.2
Tallahassee, FL MSA	38	50	10.8	14.0	548	419	212.9	121	4	910	353.6	39 694	145	38 172	4.0
Tampa-St. Petersburg-Clearwater, FL MSA	239	296	8.8	10.2	4 871	3 750	223.3	104	37	8 440	387.0	295 701	23	272 735	8.4
Terre Haute, IN MSA	17	25	8.6	12.2	255	213	170.4	193	4	627	419.1	24 643	199	24 488	.6
Texarkana, TX-Texarkana, AR MSA	10	18	5.7	9.8	229	194	186.1	153	3	766	622.5	24 092	205	23 777	1.3
Toledo, OH MSA	79	92	8.7	9.0	1 758	1 174	287.7	43	10	2 689	440.0	96 581	69	96 752	−.2
Topeka, KS MSA	13	25	5.5	10.0	433	325	262.5	67	3	684	414.7	27 172	185	26 678	1.9
Tucson, AZ MSA	87	93	7.7	8.1	2 217	1 517	293.5	40	8	1 991	263.6	119 210	61	107 464	10.9
Tulsa, OK MSA	96	97	8.8	8.3	1 411	1 104	188.9	147	14	2 634	352.7	132 315	58	127 632	3.7
Tuscaloosa, AL MSA	30	22	14.1	10.1	350	239	221.6	107	3	633	400.8	25 099	196	25 078	.1
Tyler, TX MSA	18	18	7.3	7.7	432	345	265.6	64	5	824	506.7	29 508	175	28 591	3.2
Utica-Rome, NY MSA	30	33	7.6	7.2	509	386	165.1	200	5	1 101	357.2	52 853	120	52 670	.3
Victoria, TX MSA	10	16	7.7	12.4	170	161	210.5	125	3	553	684.6	15 617	258	15 361	1.7
Visalia-Tulare-Porterville, CA MSA	52	57	7.1	7.9	376	324	108.1	261	7	650	186.9	81 126	81	76 287	6.3
Waco, TX MSA	28	22	8.7	7.2	349	271	174.5	182	3	503	251.5	37 620	150	35 072	7.3
Washington-Baltimore, DC-MD-VA-WV CMSA	991	1 161	9.2	10.0	24 801	15 312	348.9	21	68	17 967	252.8	1 095 773	4	1 022 799	7.1
Baltimore, MD PMSA	320	376	9.0	9.4	9 627	5 521	390.1	X	25	7 810	316.4	385 863	X	359 456	7.3
Hagerstown, MD PMSA	16	12	10.4	7.2	202	164	158.9	X	1	321	252.5	19 510	X	18 092	7.8
Washington, DC-MD-VA-WV PMSA	655	773	9.3	10.4	14 972	9 627	331.8	X	42	9 836	218.0	690 400	X	645 251	7.0
Waterloo-Cedar Falls, IA MSA	10	17	6.2	10.0	209	176	170.0	194	3	591	480.7	19 272	236	19 376	−.5
Wausau, WI MSA	9	16	5.4	9.5	219	190	180.9	171	1	240	198.3	19 355	235	18 510	4.6
West Palm Beach-Boca Raton, FL MSA	103	135	8.1	10.4	2 289	1 980	234.4	92	16	3 342	342.3	127 519	59	110 972	14.9
Wheeling, WV-OH MSA	13	16	7.4	8.3	356	264	227.3	100	6	1 176	750.9	22 790	214	23 472	−2.9
Wichita, KS MSA	85	103	10.2	11.8	1 169	823	229.7	98	10	2 178	427.9	89 103	73	85 456	4.3
Wichita Falls, TX MSA	18	17	8.9	8.0	263	202	193.7	139	3	443	326.3	25 131	194	23 520	6.8
Williamsport, PA MSA	15	14	10.2	8.2	233	191	194.3	137	4	509	424.5	20 442	225	20 396	.2
Wilmington, NC MSA	12	18	4.7	7.2	453	358	225.8	101	4	719	358.4	29 858	172	28 083	6.3
Yakima, WA MSA	28	45	6.6	11.2	307	253	143.8	225	4	470	220.1	45 832	131	42 197	8.6
York, PA MSA	35	32	7.8	6.5	549	398	150.5	215	3	745	204.3	53 147	119	49 669	7.0
Youngstown-Warren, OH MSA	72	91	9.4	11.1	972	690	162.1	205	8	2 103	350.6	97 256	68	99 420	−2.2
Yuba City, CA MSA	17	25	6.9	9.5	192	169	141.3	231	2	176	129.6	28 209	181	26 526	6.3
Yuma, AZ MSA	14	[8]20	4.7	[8]7.4	[9]129	[9]115	[9]94.8	[9]265	2	266	218.4	27 310	184	23 672	15.4

X Not applicable.
Z Less than .05 percent.
NA Not available.

[1]Deaths of infants under 1 year old.
[2]Per 1,000 live births for the years shown.
[3]Covers active, nonfederal physicians as of December 31. Data subject to copyright; see below for source citation.
[4]Per 100,000 resident population estimated as of July 1, 1995.
[5]Based on 272 metropolitan areas (244 MSAs, 17 CMSAs, and 11 NECMAs); see text for more information. When metropolitan areas share the same rank, the next lower rank is omitted.
[6]Covers nonfederal, short-stay (average length of stay less than 30 days) hospitals except hospital units of institutions. Data subject to copyright; see below for source citation.
[7]Aggregated from school district data to county of school superintendent's location to metropolitan area.
[8]Includes LaPaz County which is not in the MSA. In 1994, there was 1 infant death in LaPaz County.
[9]Includes LaPaz County which is not in the MSA.

Source: Infant Deaths—U.S. National Center for Health Statistics, "Vital Statistics of the United States, Vol. II, Mortality," annual; Physicians—American Medical Association, Chicago, IL, "Physician Characteristics and Distribution in the U.S.," annual (copyright); Community Hospitals—Healthcare InfoSource, Inc., a subsidiary of the American Hospital Association, "Hospital Statistics," 1996/97 edition (copyright); Public School Enrollment—U.S. National Center for Education Statistics, Common Core of Data (CCD) Public Agency Universe Internet data files for years shown at site <http://nces.ed.gov/ccd/pubagency.html> (accessed April 1997).

Table B–5. Metro Areas — Social Programs and Crime

[MSA = Metropolitan statistical area. CMSA = Consolidated MSA. PMSA = Primary MSA. NECMA = New England county metropolitan area. All areas defined as of June 30, 1996. Table includes 245 MSAs, 17 CMSAs, and 58 PMSAs not in New England; as well as 12 NECMAs. Table excludes 10 MSAs, 1 CMSA, and 15 PMSAs in New England]

Metropolitan areas	Social security program (December)						SSI[2] program recipients (December) (1,000)		Serious crimes known to police[3]						
	Beneficiaries				Payments				Number				Rate[5]		
	1994			1990 (1,000)	1994 ($1,000)	1990 ($1,000)	1995	1990	1995		1994	1990	1995	1994	1990
	Total (1,000)	Rate[1]	Retired workers (1,000)						Total	Percent violent[4]					
Abilene, TX MSA	19.6	161.3	11.4	18.7	11 883	9 799	2.6	2.2	6 377	11.5	6 426	6 038	5 135	5 129	5 046
Albany, GA MSA	16.9	144.7	9.3	15.5	9 272	7 316	5.3	3.9	9 118	9.0	9 622	10 844	7 693	8 072	9 634
Albany-Schenectady-Troy, NY MSA	156.8	177.7	104.2	149.8	103 830	86 394	17.7	13.1	33 395	9.8	34 041	32 077	3 856	3 908	3 790
Albuquerque, NM MSA	93.1	143.8	54.7	81.8	55 444	42 275	13.5	9.4	45 954	11.3	44 388	42 297	8 931	8 778	9 303
Alexandria, LA MSA	22.6	179.1	10.7	21.1	11 627	9 436	6.7	5.5	7 970	12.3	8 527	6 422	6 472	6 691	4 910
Allentown-Bethlehem-Easton, PA MSA ..	121.8	199.2	83.7	115.2	82 211	67 596	9.8	6.8	17 804	8.1	18 688	18 507	3 094	3 243	3 110
Altoona, PA MSA	23.8	179.8	15.0	23.0	14 396	11 955	4.0	2.7	1 687	6.1	3 267	3 052	1 278	2 476	2 338
Amarillo, TX MSA	29.3	147.1	17.5	26.8	18 553	14 810	2.9	1.9	14 345	10.3	14 635	14 599	7 146	7 348	7 784
Anchorage, AK MSA	15.7	62.5	8.8	12.4	9 758	6 758	3.0	1.8	18 427	13.7	18 820	13 162	7 269	7 419	5 815
Anniston, AL MSA	21.9	194.1	11.9	20.8	11 901	9 704	4.4	3.4	6 698	15.0	6 624	6 026	5 685	5 582	5 193
Appleton-Oshkosh-Neenah, WI MSA	50.7	152.6	33.1	47.6	33 920	27 566	4.3	3.4	9 997	3.2	10 779	11 877	2 938	3 219	3 769
Asheville, NC MSA	42.5	208.2	26.5	38.8	25 294	19 671	5.5	4.8	7 665	11.3	8 268	NA	3 757	4 484	NA
Athens, GA MSA	16.7	125.4	9.6	15.7	9 838	7 829	3.5	2.7	8 117	10.5	8 362	3 932	7 074	7 384	3 143
Atlanta, GA MSA	369.8	110.8	216.4	319.2	233 079	172 804	60.3	42.8	239 454	11.3	237 622	244 847	7 182	7 435	8 446
Augusta-Aiken, GA-SC MSA	66.1	147.4	36.6	58.2	38 407	29 002	13.1	10.7	21 700	12.0	20 765	26 227	4 770	4 530	6 317
Austin-San Marcos, TX MSA	97.9	101.0	57.0	85.1	60 387	45 174	14.6	11.2	59 430	9.6	58 011	72 062	6 051	6 195	8 516
Bakersfield, CA MSA.............	83.4	136.4	45.4	73.4	49 201	38 210	25.1	21.4	34 595	12.9	38 359	34 850	5 782	6 514	6 412
Bangor, ME NECMA	25.2	172.6	14.3	23.4	14 694	11 932	3.8	2.8	3 879	3.2	4 276	4 867	2 681	2 950	3 320
Barnstable-Yarmouth, MA NECMA	55.5	283.4	39.0	50.6	36 487	28 895	3.6	2.8	7 306	19.5	7 083	7 815	4 359	4 373	4 975
Baton Rouge, LA MSA	71.6	128.2	35.4	65.7	42 615	33 852	14.9	10.2	47 824	16.1	48 463	42 393	8 513	8 941	8 472
Beaumont-Port Arthur, TX MSA	67.2	179.3	36.3	63.9	43 809	36 308	8.9	6.5	23 592	11.1	24 990	27 224	6 213	6 502	7 537
Bellingham, WA MSA	22.1	151.3	14.1	19.7	14 254	11 010	2.2	1.4	8 447	5.8	7 931	6 532	5 715	5 536	5 112
Benton Harbor, MI MSA	30.9	191.8	19.3	31.3	20 255	17 809	5.0	3.7	9 326	16.3	10 070	11 975	6 521	6 718	7 420
Billings, MT MSA	20.1	163.3	12.4	18.2	12 740	10 053	1.9	1.3	NA	NA	NA	6 596	NA	NA	5 813
Biloxi-Gulfport-Pascagoula, MS MSA....	53.3	157.8	28.2	46.8	30 387	23 023	9.5	6.2	12 455	6.4	14 280	12 245	5 929	7 040	6 415
Binghamton, NY MSA	51.8	197.7	34.2	49.5	34 003	28 241	6.0	4.0	7 189	6.8	8 625	8 322	2 749	3 234	3 146
Birmingham, AL MSA	156.8	178.2	83.5	146.9	97 492	78 911	25.8	19.7	56 935	16.5	55 711	53 268	6 500	6 393	6 542
Bismarck, ND MSA	14.1	159.9	8.4	12.7	8 416	6 543	1.2	1.0	3 040	4.8	2 994	3 023	3 432	3 458	3 646
Bloomington, IN MSA	13.3	117.0	8.6	11.9	8 929	6 928	1.2	.8	4 103	14.5	4 172	2 961	6 501	6 673	2 717
Bloomington-Normal, IL MSA	17.6	129.1	11.3	16.6	11 798	9 719	1.3	.9	NA	NA	NA	[6]5 436	NA	NA	[6]4 208
Boise City, ID MSA	47.7	136.8	30.4	42.7	29 658	23 039	5.3	3.3	18 499	7.1	17 389	15 125	5 182	5 116	5 112
Boston-Worcester-Lawrence-Lowell-Brockton, MA-NH NECMA	924.4	161.3	606.8	859.3	598 841	484 717	139.1	102.0	218 203	15.0	219 764	230 507	4 145	4 273	4 923
Brownsville-Harlingen-San Benito, TX MSA	39.0	130.4	20.5	34.9	18 626	14 706	15.3	11.1	17 654	8.6	19 454	17 250	5 784	6 717	6 632
Bryan-College Station, TX MSA	11.5	87.8	6.6	10.0	6 968	5 227	1.7	1.2	8 008	8.3	8 068	7 834	6 028	6 203	6 429
Buffalo-Niagara Falls, NY MSA	238.3	200.6	150.3	230.3	160 872	135 367	30.3	21.7	59 202	15.3	60 588	62 050	5 000	5 058	5 217
Burlington, VT NECMA	23.8	127.6	14.4	20.9	14 867	11 304	3.4	2.6	8 228	2.8	7 552	NA	4 741	NA	NA
Canton-Massillon, OH MSA	76.4	190.2	46.0	74.9	50 277	42 854	7.3	5.0	16 054	12.5	18 781	16 348	4 731	5 038	4 493
Casper, WY MSA	10.9	169.7	6.7	9.3	7 216	5 489	1.2	.6	4 082	5.3	4 071	3 326	6 336	6 387	5 432
Cedar Rapids, IA MSA	28.5	161.5	19.1	26.7	19 378	15 760	2.3	1.7	1 385	5.6	1 264	8 948	2 437	2 384	5 302
Champaign-Urbana, IL MSA	19.4	117.1	11.9	18.0	11 737	9 578	2.3	1.5	NA	NA	NA	[6]9 847	NA	NA	[6]5 702
Charleston-North Charleston, SC MSA ..	68.1	131.9	37.3	58.5	38 089	28 173	14.2	10.1	36 428	13.7	34 349	35 355	6 982	6 390	6 975
Charleston, WV MSA	53.2	208.9	28.9	51.1	34 440	28 553	7.2	5.3	10 355	9.5	10 829	9 978	4 060	4 242	3 984
Charlotte-Gastonia-Rock Hill, NC-SC MSA	188.6	149.6	121.4	167.2	120 971	92 319	20.4	15.0	85 976	15.5	86 320	91 510	6 714	6 897	7 917
Charlottesville, VA MSA	20.2	143.5	13.1	17.5	12 827	9 430	2.3	1.9	5 998	7.3	5 543	5 062	4 221	4 024	3 861
Chattanooga, TN-GA MSA	79.6	181.2	47.5	72.8	50 130	39 637	12.1	9.3	19 448	12.3	19 355	27 565	5 848	4 598	6 831
Cheyenne, WY MSA	10.5	134.8	6.6	9.2	6 490	4 989	1.1	.7	3 226	4.1	3 262	3 369	4 097	4 188	4 606
Chicago-Gary-Kenosha, IL-IN-WI CMSA	1 199.1	141.1	771.0	1 144.0	830 796	691 609	201.6	131.0	NA	NA	NA	[6]558 888	NA	NA	[6]6 807
Chicago, IL PMSA	1 054.0	137.9	687.5	1 006.0	732 290	610 201	184.1	119.0	NA	NA	NA	[6]513 726	NA	NA	[6]6 934
Gary, IN PMSA	104.3	168.7	58.9	99.3	71 467	59 028	11.7	7.9	30 323	15.6	33 896	32 551	4 904	5 452	5 648
Kankakee, IL PMSA	18.5	183.0	10.6	18.0	11 958	10 144	3.1	2.2	NA	NA	NA	[6]6 375	NA	NA	[6]6 623
Kenosha, WI PMSA	22.2	161.7	14.0	20.7	15 081	12 236	2.8	1.8	4 981	7.8	6 355	6 236	3 586	4 661	4 865
Chico-Paradise, CA MSA	40.6	211.1	25.9	39.1	25 068	21 021	8.4	7.9	9 749	7.5	10 296	8 684	5 046	5 373	4 768
Cincinnati-Hamilton, OH-KY-IN CMSA ..	296.2	156.3	172.9	278.0	191 262	155 128	38.9	24.9	NA	NA	NA	NA	NA	NA	NA
Cincinnati, OH-KY-IN PMSA	250.2	158.4	147.5	236.9	161 313	132 044	33.5	21.6	NA	NA	NA	NA	NA	NA	NA
Hamilton-Middletown, OH PMSA ...	45.9	145.4	25.4	41.1	29 949	23 084	5.4	3.3	13 729	10.2	13 928	12 588	5 616	5 756	5 567
Clarksville-Hopkinsville, TN-KY MSA	22.1	119.1	12.2	19.6	12 061	9 228	4.6	3.3	9 132	13.2	8 729	7 756	4 878	4 812	4 577

NA Not available.

[1]Per 1,000 resident population estimated as of July 1, 1994.
[2]Supplemental security income.
[3]Data on serious crimes have not been adjusted for underreporting; this may affect comparability over time or among geographic areas.
[4]Includes murder and nonnegligent manslaughter, forcible rape, robbery, and aggravated assault.
[5]Per 100,000 resident population provided by the Federal Bureau of Investigation.
[6]Excludes forcible rape data for Illinois because figures furnished by the state-level Uniform Crime Reporting (UCR) Program administered by the Illinois Department of State Police were not in accordance with national UCR guidelines.

Source: Social Security—U.S. Social Security Administration, Office of Research and Statistics, "OASDI Beneficiaries by State and County (December)," annual (related Internet site <http://www.ssa.gov/statistics/ores_home.html>); Supplemental Security Income—U.S. Social Security Administration, Office of Research, Evaluation, and Statistics, "SSI Recipients by State and County - December," annual (related Internet site <http://www.ssa.gov/statistics/ores_home.html>); Serious Crimes—U.S. Federal Bureau of Investigation, unpublished data, annual.

[MSA = Metropolitan statistical area. CMSA = Consolidated MSA. PMSA = Primary MSA. NECMA = New England county metropolitan area. All areas defined as of June 30, 1996. Table includes 245 MSAs, 17 CMSAs, and 58 PMSAs not in New England; as well as 12 NECMAs. Table excludes 10 MSAs, 1 CMSA, and 15 PMSAs in New England]

Metropolitan areas	Social security program (December)						SSI[2] program recipients (December) (1,000)		Serious crimes known to police[3]						
	Beneficiaries				Payments				Number				Rate[5]		
	1994						1995		1995						
	Total (1,000)	Rate[1]	Retired workers (1,000)	1990 (1,000)	1994 ($1,000)	1990 ($1,000)	1995	1990	Total	Percent violent[4]	1994	1990	1995	1994	1990
Los Angeles-Riverside-Orange, CA CMSA	1 714.4	112.3	1 101.6	1 609.8	1 129 083	920 664	481.4	400.3	894 288	19.5	942 209	1 007 804	5 815	6 187	6 935
Los Angeles-Long Beach, CA PMSA	970.2	106.8	623.7	943.1	641 744	542 707	337.1	285.4	562 433	23.2	591 795	661 767	6 116	6 425	7 466
Orange, CA PMSA	275.2	107.3	182.2	248.6	191 551	148 856	48.6	36.4	119 418	11.0	127 945	143 775	4 672	5 061	5 964
Riverside-San Bernardino, CA PMSA	384.4	131.6	242.2	343.1	241 475	187 430	81.6	66.5	187 247	14.7	196 525	175 786	6 410	7 037	6 790
Ventura, CA PMSA	84.6	120.7	53.5	75.0	54 313	41 671	14.1	11.9	25 190	12.1	25 944	26 476	3 567	3 714	3 957
Louisville, KY-IN MSA	170.5	173.8	99.7	160.5	108 597	88 594	23.4	16.2	41 566	14.5	44 263	43 783	4 474	4 794	4 840
Lubbock, TX MSA	32.3	139.9	18.1	29.2	19 662	15 493	4.8	3.7	15 542	13.7	14 636	14 264	6 617	6 270	6 407
Lynchburg, VA MSA	37.8	186.4	23.5	36.0	23 196	18 900	4.5	3.9	6 262	13.2	6 628	6 381	3 056	3 260	3 290
Macon, GA MSA	47.5	154.6	25.7	43.2	25 500	19 916	10.8	8.4	20 888	8.8	20 455	20 455	6 313	6 720	7 036
Madison, WI MSA	48.0	123.1	31.6	44.1	32 972	26 542	6.4	4.7	16 094	6.9	16 461	19 440	4 091	4 253	5 296
Mansfield, OH MSA	32.9	188.0	19.8	31.3	21 208	17 369	3.8	2.3	8 414	14.9	8 291	8 731	5 164	5 079	5 136
McAllen-Edinburg-Mission, TX MSA	56.4	121.4	30.0	49.8	25 458	19 821	23.4	16.0	31 689	8.1	30 737	25 276	6 747	7 026	6 590
Medford-Ashland, OR MSA	33.7	207.6	22.4	30.0	21 398	16 463	2.3	1.4	10 298	7.5	9 775	7 752	6 276	6 110	5 295
Melbourne-Titusville-Palm Bay, FL MSA	96.4	217.3	64.9	77.2	61 596	42 402	6.7	3.5	24 807	13.4	27 657	29 063	5 509	6 280	7 284
Memphis, TN-AR-MS MSA	152.7	144.8	83.7	139.4	89 235	70 656	41.8	29.6	83 046	15.5	NA	NA	8 650	NA	NA
Merced, CA MSA	24.0	122.2	13.6	20.9	13 508	10 434	8.4	7.1	11 129	12.9	10 642	8 264	5 625	5 532	4 632
Miami-Fort Lauderdale, FL CMSA	576.9	169.8	392.9	546.4	369 102	308 581	130.3	91.2	364 602	13.8	372 960	365 633	10 537	11 536	11 453
Fort Lauderdale, FL PMSA	283.8	204.8	198.7	270.9	195 469	162 771	22.3	12.0	113 529	10.4	124 459	109 980	8 086	9 200	8 760
Miami, FL PMSA	293.1	145.7	194.2	275.6	173 633	145 810	108.0	79.1	251 073	15.4	248 501	255 653	12 212	13 217	13 198
Milwaukee-Racine, WI CMSA	273.4	167.0	176.8	263.5	187 378	157 135	46.8	32.3	88 116	9.9	88 130	96 742	5 337	5 312	6 019
Milwaukee-Waukesha, WI PMSA	242.2	166.5	157.0	233.2	166 017	139 083	42.4	29.2	79 174	9.8	78 757	86 876	5 394	5 334	6 066
Racine, WI PMSA	31.2	170.5	19.8	30.4	21 361	18 052	4.3	3.1	8 942	10.1	9 373	9 866	4 882	5 130	5 637
Minneapolis-St. Paul, MN-WI MSA	336.9	125.1	220.9	306.9	225 478	178 264	35.1	20.1	142 915	9.3	138 017	102 922	5 275	5 165	4 054
Mobile, AL MSA	88.3	173.4	48.6	80.4	52 090	40 789	16.8	11.4	32 418	12.6	33 039	30 745	6 279	6 647	6 578
Modesto, CA MSA	57.9	142.2	33.6	52.9	34 799	27 754	17.8	15.4	30 937	12.2	30 748	24 201	7 568	7 648	6 532
Monroe, LA MSA	21.6	148.2	11.6	20.9	12 353	10 283	5.4	4.2	10 833	12.1	10 125	9 176	7 351	6 929	6 453
Montgomery, AL MSA	49.7	160.5	27.7	45.4	28 098	22 239	13.1	9.1	17 335	11.0	17 156	15 842	5 535	5 561	5 720
Muncie, IN MSA	21.0	176.6	12.6	20.2	14 092	11 723	2.8	1.7	4 415	9.2	4 736	2 713	6 129	6 433	3 819
Myrtle Beach, SC MSA	31.1	204.1	19.8	24.4	18 650	12 341	4.2	3.2	15 242	11.7	15 262	12 966	9 946	9 854	9 001
Naples, FL MSA	45.9	257.8	32.6	36.3	32 388	21 911	1.8	1.0	10 157	12.9	9 751	9 526	5 671	5 720	6 263
Nashville, TN MSA	150.7	140.7	89.8	134.9	93 573	71 801	22.2	16.7	NA	NA	NA	51 893	NA	NA	6 262
New London-Norwich, CT NECMA	41.0	164.8	27.2	37.8	27 696	22 233	3.0	2.2	5 809	9.6	5 465	7 366	4 191	3 916	4 906
New Orleans, LA MSA	205.6	156.9	106.5	193.0	123 011	100 731	51.3	31.6	NA	NA	NA	NA	NA	NA	NA
New York-Northern New Jersey-Long Island, NY-NJ-CT-PA CMSA/NECMA	3 097.2	157.0	2 068.8	2 952.4	2 171 689	1 799 135	568.1	403.9	915 437	18.4	1 013 189	1 312 310	4 671	5 176	6 773
Bergen-Passaic, NJ PMSA	224.5	172.5	158.8	214.1	166 505	137 025	20.7	14.7	46 589	9.2	46 685	58 839	3 554	3 578	4 602
Dutchess, NY PMSA	42.9	164.3	26.6	39.1	29 435	23 173	5.1	4.3	7 592	14.3	7 489	8 915	2 942	2 872	3 436
Jersey City, NJ PMSA	81.8	148.4	52.7	80.6	53 142	46 418	21.0	15.1	35 162	16.9	36 297	42 228	6 333	6 471	7 635
Middlesex-Somerset-Hunterdon, NJ PMSA	152.0	142.2	104.5	135.1	111 186	85 032	11.4	8.2	34 635	7.5	35 993	38 823	3 224	3 402	3 807
Monmouth-Ocean, NJ PMSA	212.3	204.9	150.9	199.2	149 013	120 457	11.4	9.1	35 552	7.0	36 117	38 461	3 417	3 559	3 899
Nassau-Suffolk, NY PMSA	442.9	167.2	289.4	405.3	323 665	255 159	37.7	28.9	54 808	8.1	60 208	107 617	2 076	2 274	4 125
New Haven-Bridgeport-Stamford-Waterbury-Danbury, CT NECMA	278.2	171.0	193.6	263.2	199 206	163 487	22.5	16.1	79 314	8.1	81 095	99 877	5 130	5 236	6 377
New York, NY PMSA	1 253.7	145.5	822.4	1 229.4	852 608	733 262	383.4	268.0	482 626	24.5	573 933	758 388	5 645	6 703	8 895
Newark, NJ PMSA	300.8	155.4	200.2	286.9	213 557	176 571	40.4	29.8	113 404	17.7	108 731	127 975	5 834	5 593	6 680
Newburgh, NY-PA PMSA	52.4	147.3	32.3	46.6	34 142	26 336	6.7	4.5	10 843	10.4	11 012	12 121	3 115	3 219	3 612
Trenton, NJ PMSA	55.9	169.7	37.3	53.0	39 230	32 215	7.7	5.3	14 912	11.9	15 629	19 066	4 503	4 719	5 852
Norfolk-Virginia Beach-Newport News, VA-NC MSA	188.4	123.3	112.4	164.8	110 820	83 485	29.7	18.6	86 277	10.3	86 788	93 869	5 580	5 658	6 504
Ocala, FL MSA	66.9	304.5	46.7	55.6	41 927	30 097	5.3	3.2	14 154	17.1	13 554	14 218	6 342	6 297	7 298
Odessa-Midland, TX MSA	32.5	137.3	18.1	28.4	20 993	16 160	4.5	2.8	13 557	12.5	14 126	20 655	5 608	5 814	9 158
Oklahoma City, OK MSA	145.4	144.1	90.2	131.1	88 665	69 305	17.4	12.0	80 148	10.2	81 698	75 304	7 907	8 173	7 854
Omaha, NE-IA MSA	92.6	139.6	59.2	85.4	60 124	48 313	9.4	6.5	33 733	11.4	33 601	34 732	5 747	5 506	5 430
Orlando, FL MSA	229.0	168.0	147.7	196.1	142 891	105 951	26.8	13.9	94 664	14.2	102 603	95 762	6 848	7 599	7 823
Owensboro, KY MSA	17.2	190.0	10.2	15.9	10 528	8 402	2.5	1.7	3 869	3.2	3 620	3 052	4 256	3 998	3 500

NA Not available.

[1]Per 1,000 resident population estimated as of July 1, 1994.
[2]Supplemental security income.
[3]Data on serious crimes have not been adjusted for underreporting; this may affect comparability over time or among geographic areas.
[4]Includes murder and nonnegligent manslaughter, forcible rape, robbery, and aggravated assault.
[5]Per 100,000 resident population provided by the Federal Bureau of Investigation.

Source: Social Security—U.S. Social Security Administration, Office of Research and Statistics, "OASDI Beneficiaries by State and County (December)," annual (related Internet site <http://www.ssa.gov/statistics/ores_home.html>); Supplemental Security Income—U.S. Social Security Administration, Office of Research, Evaluation, and Statistics, "SSI Recipients by State and County - December," annual (related Internet site <http://www.ssa.gov/statistics/ores_home.html>); Serious Crimes—U.S. Federal Bureau of Investigation, unpublished data, annual.

[MSA = Metropolitan statistical area. CMSA = Consolidated MSA. PMSA = Primary MSA. NECMA = New England county metropolitan area. All areas defined as of June 30, 1996. Table includes 245 MSAs, 17 CMSAs, and 58 PMSAs not in New England; as well as 12 NECMAs. Table excludes 10 MSAs, 1 CMSA, and 15 PMSAs in New England]

Metropolitan areas	Social security program (December) Beneficiaries 1994				Payments		SSI² program recipients (December) (1,000)		Serious crimes known to police³ Number				Rate⁵		
	Total (1,000)	Rate¹	Retired workers (1,000)	1990 (1,000)	1994 ($1,000)	1990 ($1,000)	1995	1990	1995 Total	Percent violent⁴	1994	1990	1995	1994	1990
Panama City, FL MSA	23.6	168.9	14.0	20.5	13 691	10 269	3.2	2.3	8 804	10.2	8 673	8 051	6 198	6 254	6 390
Parkersburg-Marietta, WV-OH MSA	29.7	195.6	16.9	28.5	18 557	15 462	4.2	2.7	3 310	5.3	2 993	3 578	2 978	2 667	2 432
Pensacola, FL MSA	59.8	160.5	34.4	50.8	34 075	24 793	9.3	6.4	21 897	18.0	23 190	20 893	5 817	6 237	6 066
Peoria-Pekin, IL MSA	63.0	183.1	39.3	60.1	42 489	35 349	7.1	4.3	NA	NA	NA	⁶15 563	NA	NA	⁶4 605
Philadelphia-Wilmington-Atlantic City, PA-NJ-DE-MD CMSA	1 005.1	168.6	661.4	956.2	684 214	563 622	134.7	97.3	273 184	14.8	266 696	296 510	4 871	4 484	5 053
Atlantic-Cape May, NJ PMSA	65.1	197.2	44.1	62.3	43 189	35 725	6.6	5.3	26 659	8.6	25 210	32 379	8 037	7 645	10 137
Philadelphia, PA-NJ PMSA	834.0	168.4	550.2	796.1	569 748	470 918	116.3	83.5	227 782	15.6	216 748	227 458	4 607	4 390	4 645
Vineland-Millville-Bridgeton, NJ PMSA	26.2	188.4	16.5	25.5	16 917	14 304	4.4	3.5	9 076	14.7	8 861	8 708	6 505	6 330	6 308
Wilmington-Newark, DE-MD PMSA	79.9	147.8	50.6	72.3	54 360	42 675	7.3	5.0	9 667	13.3	15 877	27 965	5 023	2 933	5 448
Phoenix-Mesa, AZ MSA	399.5	160.8	260.7	343.0	262 873	195 701	37.8	22.3	224 362	8.7	204 821	190 232	8 790	8 292	8 526
Pine Bluff, AR MSA	15.2	180.4	8.0	15.0	8 184	6 897	4.3	3.4	6 319	22.3	5 585	6 233	7 426	6 393	7 291
Pittsburgh, PA MSA	513.3	213.8	314.6	498.9	344 682	290 458	54.6	40.5	54 761	12.6	65 594	38 234	2 390	2 836	1 912
Pittsfield, MA NECMA	30.2	222.1	20.4	28.9	19 789	16 514	3.5	2.9	3 109	23.5	2 999	1 360	2 794	2 668	2 825
Pocatello, ID MSA	8.9	123.9	5.3	7.9	5 547	4 271	1.2	.7	3 643	7.3	2 949	3 151	5 003	4 047	4 772
Portland, ME NECMA	42.8	173.2	27.5	40.0	26 850	21 818	4.9	3.7	11 523	5.5	11 008	13 733	4 647	4 494	5 648
Portland-Salem, OR-WA CMSA	294.0	147.8	194.5	274.5	195 086	158 027	30.3	20.4	135 514	9.7	130 426	108 143	6 893	6 634	6 051
Portland-Vancouver, OR-WA PMSA	239.8	142.6	158.4	223.1	160 510	129 641	25.2	16.4	111 966	10.9	108 778	92 180	6 752	6 533	6 101
Salem, OR PMSA	54.2	176.1	36.1	51.4	34 576	28 386	5.0	4.0	23 548	3.8	21 648	15 963	7 652	7 188	5 781
Providence-Warwick-Pawtucket, RI NECMA	174.2	190.9	120.9	167.3	113 150	94 499	22.9	16.5	38 471	8.6	37 859	49 665	4 247	4 157	5 452
Provo-Orem, UT MSA	28.2	93.4	16.3	25.3	17 926	14 001	2.8	1.9	13 634	3.2	11 636	10 565	4 582	4 015	4 008
Pueblo, CO MSA	26.6	208.3	14.1	24.2	15 116	12 182	4.9	3.2	8 798	15.9	8 400	8 722	6 724	6 433	7 088
Punta Gorda, FL MSA	46.2	366.6	34.8	35.2	30 642	20 195	1.2	.6	4 112	8.6	4 287	2 645	3 202	3 474	2 383
Raleigh-Durham-Chapel Hill, NC MSA	124.3	128.4	75.7	108.3	76 925	57 070	19.5	14.6	59 241	10.0	57 930	47 778	6 032	6 162	5 596
Rapid City, SD MSA	12.9	148.4	7.7	11.2	7 719	5 867	1.6	1.0	4 856	6.9	5 035	4 164	5 750	5 816	5 119
Reading, PA MSA	66.3	190.2	47.6	63.3	45 034	37 262	5.0	3.5	11 318	11.0	11 163	11 392	3 368	3 325	3 401
Redding, CA MSA	32.5	202.8	19.0	29.5	19 749	15 692	7.6	6.8	8 814	11.6	9 048	7 332	5 481	5 643	4 987
Reno, NV MSA	39.8	140.4	26.9	34.0	26 101	19 318	3.4	2.1	17 609	9.7	17 688	17 540	5 927	6 040	6 887
Richland-Kennewick-Pasco, WA MSA	21.3	122.0	13.4	19.7	14 520	11 664	2.0	1.4	9 408	6.9	8 575	9 299	5 381	5 130	6 198
Richmond-Petersburg, VA MSA	136.1	148.8	86.6	122.9	88 620	69 019	17.8	12.4	48 877	11.3	50 899	51 397	5 279	5 543	5 937
Roanoke, VA MSA	42.8	187.0	27.0	39.3	26 682	21 077	5.2	3.9	8 603	8.2	8 679	12 303	3 726	3 743	5 481
Rochester, MN MSA	14.9	131.3	10.1	13.0	9 633	7 298	1.2	.7	4 201	6.9	3 867	3 906	3 686	3 424	3 669
Rochester, NY MSA	183.9	169.0	121.9	173.2	124 778	102 487	24.0	16.2	48 706	7.6	47 214	52 179	4 497	4 366	4 952
Rockford, IL MSA	59.1	170.8	38.0	53.8	40 322	32 057	5.9	3.9	NA	NA	NA	⁶22 953	NA	NA	⁶6 962
Rocky Mount, NC MSA	24.0	170.4	13.0	22.0	12 790	10 024	6.2	4.9	8 702	11.4	9 532	7 525	6 145	6 766	5 693
Sacramento-Yolo, CA CMSA	220.7	139.0	134.3	197.3	134 269	104 067	56.6	47.2	112 867	11.5	116 724	98 084	7 072	7 339	6 622
Sacramento, CA PMSA	202.7	140.6	123.4	182.1	123 123	95 873	52.2	43.2	103 093	11.5	105 965	88 779	7 116	7 343	6 625
Yolo, CA PMSA	18.0	123.2	10.9	15.2	11 146	8 194	4.4	4.0	9 774	11.9	10 759	9 305	6 642	7 303	6 595
Saginaw-Bay City-Midland, MI MSA	70.9	176.0	41.1	66.0	47 024	37 896	10.5	6.6	17 737	16.5	18 854	23 116	4 557	4 737	5 789
St. Cloud, MN MSA	21.5	137.2	12.9	19.8	12 112	9 626	1.7	1.2	5 316	4.8	4 610	4 945	3 356	2 954	3 319
St. Joseph, MO MSA	19.8	202.8	12.5	19.7	12 413	10 645	2.2	1.6	5 384	6.7	5 484	4 766	5 702	5 762	4 877
St. Louis, MO-IL MSA	430.2	170.0	267.0	405.9	285 166	233 775	52.0	34.6	NA	NA	NA	NA	NA	NA	NA
Salinas, CA MSA	45.5	136.8	28.3	41.1	27 743	21 986	8.4	7.3	17 999	16.0	18 158	18 077	5 089	4 846	5 083
Salt Lake City-Ogden, UT MSA	129.1	109.6	79.9	114.0	81 350	62 871	13.1	7.9	83 844	5.7	73 288	73 543	7 132	6 210	6 859
San Angelo, TX MSA	17.0	167.9	9.9	15.8	10 032	8 119	2.4	1.9	5 231	9.2	5 339	6 421	5 071	5 183	6 522
San Antonio, TX MSA	198.1	138.3	109.8	175.0	105 883	81 565	38.2	27.5	98 074	7.2	107 146	136 973	6 697	7 478	10 340
San Diego, CA MSA	342.4	130.9	222.0	316.3	215 243	172 302	72.4	60.3	133 073	15.8	152 779	178 595	5 031	5 774	7 149
San Francisco-Oakland-San Jose, CA CMSA	832.9	128.1	537.0	779.1	557 105	450 817	201.3	172.8	330 825	13.6	385 909	378 533	5 356	5 918	6 053
Oakland, CA PMSA	278.1	127.6	174.1	260.0	184 664	149 425	69.6	61.4	108 350	12.1	154 427	143 422	5 938	7 066	6 886
San Francisco, CA PMSA	238.5	145.5	161.0	227.9	165 070	136 882	65.0	55.1	96 503	15.2	99 238	109 525	5 834	5 999	6 830
San Jose, CA PMSA	157.8	101.4	102.6	144.4	107 880	84 796	39.2	31.5	66 654	14.6	68 403	69 524	4 259	4 399	4 642
Santa Cruz-Watsonville, CA PMSA	31.6	134.1	20.1	30.7	19 887	16 790	5.7	5.3	13 663	12.9	14 916	13 719	5 786	6 347	5 972
Santa Rosa, CA PMSA	66.8	162.2	42.8	61.8	43 563	34 691	9.9	9.6	19 497	10.0	20 719	16 811	4 729	5 079	4 330
Vallejo-Fairfield-Napa, CA PMSA	60.2	125.3	36.5	54.4	36 041	28 233	11.9	10.0	26 158	14.3	28 206	25 532	5 394	5 836	5 659
San Luis Obispo-Atascadero-Paso Robles, CA MSA	40.2	179.2	26.3	36.9	25 302	20 143	5.0	4.7	9 030	17.1	9 194	8 296	4 016	4 098	3 820
Santa Barbara-Santa Maria-Lompoc, CA MSA	56.9	148.2	36.7	52.3	36 782	29 266	8.7	7.3	15 137	11.8	16 565	17 299	3 958	4 336	4 680

NA Not available.

¹Per 1,000 resident population estimated as of July 1, 1994.
²Supplemental security income.
³Data on serious crimes have not been adjusted for underreporting; this may affect comparability over time or among geographic areas.
⁴Includes murder and nonnegligent manslaughter, forcible rape, robbery, and aggravated assault.
⁵Per 100,000 resident population provided by the Federal Bureau of Investigation.
⁶Excludes forcible rape data for Illinois because figures furnished by the state-level Uniform Crime Reporting (UCR) Program administered by the Illinois Department of State Police were not in accordance with national UCR guidelines.

Source: Social Security—U.S. Social Security Administration, Office of Research and Statistics, "OASDI Beneficiaries by State and County (December)," annual (related Internet site <http://www.ssa.gov/statistics/ores_home.html>); Supplemental Security Income—U.S. Social Security Administration, Office of Research, Evaluation, and Statistics, "SSI Recipients by State and County - December," annual (related Internet site <http://www.ssa.gov/statistics/ores_home.html>); Serious Crimes—U.S. Federal Bureau of Investigation, unpublished data, annual.

Table B–5. Metro Areas — Social Programs and Crime—Con.

[MSA = Metropolitan statistical area.   CMSA = Consolidated MSA.   PMSA = Primary MSA.   NECMA = New England county metropolitan area.   All areas defined as of June 30, 1996.   Table includes 245 MSAs, 17 CMSAs, and 58 PMSAs not in New England; as well as 12 NECMAs.   Table excludes 10 MSAs, 1 CMSA, and 15 PMSAs in New England]

Metropolitan areas	Social security program (December)						SSI[2] program recipients (December) (1,000)		Serious crimes known to police[3]						
	Beneficiaries				Payments				Number				Rate[5]		
	1994			1990	1994	1990	1995	1990	1995		1994	1990	1995	1994	1990
	Total (1,000)	Rate[1]	Retired workers (1,000)	(1,000)	($1,000)	($1,000)			Total	Percent violent[4]					
Santa Fe, NM MSA	16.8	127.6	10.1	14.4	10 207	7 526	1.8	1.4	NA	NA	NA	380	NA	NA	NA
Sarasota-Bradenton, FL MSA	164.3	316.6	119.7	159.0	110 787	92 188	6.2	3.8	34 292	13.5	34 711	35 761	6 521	6 725	7 306
Savannah, GA MSA	43.8	158.4	24.6	40.5	26 766	21 310	8.1	6.5	18 127	10.6	18 362	19 522	6 443	7 222	7 565
Scranton--Wilkes-Barre--Hazleton, PA MSA	150.7	236.9	99.3	149.1	93 346	80 128	14.4	11.0	8 681	7.5	11 062	10 862	1 822	1 955	1 790
Seattle-Tacoma-Bremerton, WA CMSA	423.3	131.4	275.3	388.4	285 683	227 229	52.8	34.6	201 342	8.3	203 753	197 176	6 320	6 271	6 660
Bremerton, WA PMSA	26.6	122.7	17.0	23.4	15 173	11 421	3.0	1.9	10 038	9.2	8 307	8 451	4 481	3 794	4 454
Olympia, WA PMSA	27.8	148.2	17.6	24.6	17 918	13 838	3.0	1.8	8 614	6.5	8 723	6 783	4 526	4 756	4 268
Seattle-Bellevue-Everett, WA PMSA	283.4	130.0	188.6	262.7	197 918	158 747	33.6	22.2	135 954	7.1	141 035	141 026	6 396	6 393	6 940
Tacoma, WA PMSA	85.5	134.0	52.1	77.7	54 674	43 223	13.2	8.8	46 736	12.1	45 688	40 916	7 238	7 134	7 054
Sharon, PA MSA	26.7	218.9	16.2	26.1	17 890	15 144	2.7	1.8	2 420	9.8	3 078	2 321	2 028	2 553	1 918
Sheboygan, WI MSA	19.5	181.4	13.3	19.4	13 347	11 538	1.6	1.3	3 910	3.6	3 680	4 239	3 624	3 442	4 081
Sherman-Denison, TX MSA	19.5	200.0	12.1	18.9	11 642	9 679	2.0	1.7	5 195	9.3	5 315	6 465	5 242	5 379	6 804
Shreveport-Bossier City, LA MSA	64.4	170.5	35.6	61.2	37 242	30 681	14.9	10.8	29 098	11.6	31 963	28 507	7 643	8 470	7 691
Sioux City, IA-NE MSA	21.8	182.4	13.5	21.7	13 745	11 905	2.1	1.7	9 227	16.5	8 361	6 844	7 713	7 069	5 950
Sioux Falls, SD MSA	22.9	150.8	14.3	21.6	14 444	11 796	2.0	1.5	6 223	8.7	5 784	5 036	4 596	4 022	3 617
South Bend, IN MSA	46.1	180.7	31.4	45.3	31 490	26 938	3.9	2.5	12 625	8.5	13 343	5 777	5 914	6 330	4 082
Spokane, WA MSA	62.8	158.3	39.2	60.3	40 168	33 336	8.1	6.1	26 675	7.7	26 306	22 104	6 629	6 643	6 352
Springfield, IL MSA	35.5	175.3	21.4	33.6	22 519	18 737	4.4	2.6	NA	NA	NA	[6]9 808	NA	NA	[6]5 302
Springfield, MO MSA	49.5	171.7	29.7	44.1	29 435	22 529	5.8	4.2	14 552	6.4	15 408	14 719	4 992	5 498	5 568
Springfield, MA NECMA	107.7	180.6	70.3	102.0	67 435	56 272	20.6	13.6	20 393	16.5	22 467	23 654	4 408	5 280	4 996
State College, PA MSA	15.3	118.1	10.0	14.3	10 043	8 047	1.5	1.0	3 461	4.7	3 465	4 201	2 661	2 724	3 394
Steubenville-Weirton, OH-WV MSA	32.0	228.2	17.3	31.4	21 280	18 112	3.3	2.1	1 329	8.1	1 770	3 372	1 114	1 242	2 366
Stockton-Lodi, CA MSA	71.8	138.4	42.1	65.4	43 090	34 359	24.3	20.7	37 801	12.7	41 838	39 978	7 259	8 158	8 318
Sumter, SC MSA	15.4	144.8	8.3	13.3	8 288	6 171	4.6	3.5	6 720	17.6	6 851	6 063	6 283	6 439	5 907
Syracuse, NY MSA	127.7	169.9	82.3	120.4	84 937	70 068	16.4	11.3	27 558	8.2	26 694	29 403	3 677	3 498	3 962
Tallahassee, FL MSA	30.9	121.1	18.5	28.4	18 254	14 348	6.3	4.6	22 893	12.9	24 423	19 539	8 900	9 622	8 364
Tampa-St. Petersburg-Clearwater, FL MSA	520.8	241.2	357.4	497.8	332 558	275 645	43.9	26.9	155 775	15.7	173 365	167 137	7 118	7 954	8 086
Terre Haute, IN MSA	29.0	193.7	17.6	29.3	18 422	16 153	3.2	2.3	7 783	8.0	5 917	3 608	6 407	NA	NA
Texarkana, TX-Texarkana, AR MSA	21.8	177.8	12.3	20.9	11 783	9 671	4.3	3.3	6 399	11.4	7 298	7 822	5 131	5 833	6 511
Toledo, OH MSA	100.9	164.9	60.8	96.7	65 954	55 314	16.3	8.3	35 473	9.2	39 967	43 397	6 199	6 479	7 098
Topeka, KS MSA	27.9	168.9	17.7	26.0	17 878	14 498	3.8	2.3	15 931	9.5	NA	12 687	13 148	NA	7 881
Tucson, AZ MSA	127.1	173.0	80.8	111.2	81 843	62 132	13.0	8.6	73 376	9.0	73 139	62 875	9 785	10 064	9 428
Tulsa, OK MSA	115.5	155.4	71.0	106.1	75 762	60 327	11.7	9.1	40 272	13.7	39 600	47 508	5 386	5 323	6 701
Tuscaloosa, AL MSA	25.3	163.1	13.3	22.7	14 778	11 341	5.7	4.4	13 791	8.2	13 421	11 165	8 709	8 566	7 418
Tyler, TX MSA	28.1	175.8	17.0	26.3	17 591	14 142	3.7	2.8	10 337	10.1	12 121	11 271	6 381	7 551	7 449
Utica-Rome, NY MSA	65.4	207.5	42.0	64.2	40 898	35 136	9.4	7.1	9 656	8.0	9 246	9 024	3 120	2 895	2 896
Victoria, TX MSA	12.3	153.5	6.5	11.2	7 344	5 735	2.0	1.5	5 130	12.9	5 364	4 891	6 339	6 699	6 577
Visalia-Tulare-Porterville, CA MSA	49.7	143.7	28.0	45.0	27 914	22 205	16.2	16.0	19 429	12.3	19 396	16 755	5 632	5 759	5 372
Waco, TX MSA	33.5	169.2	19.8	32.4	19 579	16 306	4.8	3.8	13 727	13.6	13 931	14 591	6 834	6 998	7 715
Washington-Baltimore, DC-MD-VA-WV CMSA	823.8	116.9	528.7	746.2	521 414	407 905	111.2	79.7	439 524	15.0	421 938	396 767	6 196	6 003	5 898
Baltimore, MD PMSA	365.9	148.9	233.7	338.0	240 330	192 654	50.4	37.0	185 048	17.9	180 839	161 411	7 461	7 299	6 776
Hagerstown, MD PMSA	21.4	169.3	13.8	19.8	13 847	11 065	2.0	1.5	3 504	14.2	3 088	3 180	2 748	2 417	2 620
Washington, DC-MD-VA-WV PMSA	436.5	97.8	281.0	388.4	267 237	204 186	58.8	41.2	250 972	12.8	238 011	232 176	5 595	5 381	5 497
Waterloo-Cedar Falls, IA MSA	23.3	187.8	14.5	22.9	15 401	13 194	2.8	1.9	7 503	7.7	6 234	6 340	6 038	4 926	5 121
Wausau, WI MSA	19.3	160.5	12.2	17.8	12 308	9 841	2.4	1.8	2 994	3.7	3 150	3 843	2 473	2 622	3 330
West Palm Beach-Boca Raton, FL MSA	244.3	255.2	178.7	217.8	176 349	134 792	12.3	7.3	82 904	11.4	82 881	83 457	8 555	8 893	9 669
Wheeling, WV-OH MSA	36.3	230.0	21.4	35.9	23 319	20 044	3.7	2.5	2 902	9.6	2 919	2 629	1 928	1 929	1 737
Wichita, KS MSA	78.0	153.9	50.7	71.1	53 136	42 177	7.9	4.6	NA	NA	NA	32 966	NA	NA	6 793
Wichita Falls, TX MSA	22.3	168.6	13.2	21.3	13 484	11 159	2.6	1.9	7 771	11.6	9 455	11 664	5 779	7 103	8 948
Williamsport, PA MSA	23.7	196.4	15.7	23.5	15 197	13 088	2.9	1.9	3 277	6.6	3 818	3 545	2 892	3 318	2 996
Wilmington, NC MSA	37.1	191.8	22.9	30.8	23 118	16 265	5.5	3.8	13 799	8.0	13 124	11 400	7 042	6 991	6 680
Yakima, WA MSA	31.9	151.8	20.5	31.0	19 593	16 581	4.9	3.8	16 779	7.2	15 681	15 876	8 022	7 778	8 500
York, PA MSA	59.8	166.1	41.7	55.5	40 091	32 238	4.9	3.4	10 330	9.7	10 330	9 761	2 512	3 010	2 874
Youngstown-Warren, OH MSA	127.9	212.3	74.5	123.1	83 214	69 553	15.3	9.5	12 263	15.9	11 626	18 051	3 047	3 181	3 920
Yuba City, CA MSA	20.9	155.0	11.9	19.1	12 159	9 677	6.5	6.1	8 578	19.8	8 824	7 044	6 314	6 655	5 743
Yuma, AZ MSA	18.3	143.8	11.5	15.9	10 399	7 912	2.0	1.1	2 094	5.6	1 665	4 650	3 524	2 927	7 219

NA Not available.

[1] Per 1,000 resident population estimated as of July 1, 1994.
[2] Supplemental security income.
[3] Data on serious crimes have not been adjusted for underreporting; this may affect comparability over time or among geographic areas.
[4] Includes murder and nonnegligent manslaughter, forcible rape, robbery, and aggravated assault.
[5] Per 100,000 resident population provided by the Federal Bureau of Investigation.
[6] Excludes forcible rape data for Illinois because figures furnished by the state-level Uniform Crime Reporting (UCR) Program administered by the Illinois Department of State Police were not in accordance with national UCR guidelines.

Source: Social Security—U.S. Social Security Administration, Office of Research and Statistics, "OASDI Beneficiaries by State and County (December)," annual (related Internet site <http://www.ssa.gov/statistics/ores_home.html>);   Supplemental Security Income—U.S. Social Security Administration, Office of Research, Evaluation, and Statistics, "SSI Recipients by State and County - December," annual (related Internet site <http://www.ssa.gov/statistics/ores_home.html>);   Serious Crimes—U.S. Federal Bureau of Investigation, unpublished data, annual.

Table B–6. Metro Areas — Building Permits, Cost of Living, and Poverty

[MSA = Metropolitan statistical area. CMSA = Consolidated MSA. PMSA = Primary MSA. NECMA = New England county metropolitan area. All areas defined as of June 30, 1996. Table includes 245 MSAs, 17 CMSAs, and 58 PMSAs not in New England; as well as 12 NECMAs. Table excludes 10 MSAs, 1 CMSA, and 15 PMSAs in New England]

Metropolitan areas	New private housing units authorized by building permits[1]					Cost of living index,[2] Third Quarter 1996							Persons below poverty level, 1993			
				1990–1996 period									Number		Percent	
	1996	1995	1994	Total units	Percent of 1990 housing stock	Composite index (100%)	Grocery items (16%)	Housing (28%)	Utilities (8%)	Transportation (10%)	Health care (5%)	Miscellaneous goods and services (33%)	All persons	Related children 5 to 17 years	All persons	Related children 5 to 17 years
Abilene, TX MSA	372	412	449	2 086	4.2	92.4	88.9	84.0	92.2	102.6	100.0	97.0	20 652	4 967	17.6	21.4
Albany, GA MSA	956	1 161	712	4 881	11.4	92.8	98.1	76.1	105.7	96.8	88.4	101.1	29 095	8 823	25.1	34.5
Albany-Schenectady-Troy, NY MSA	2 641	2 535	2 943	19 340	5.4	NA	NA	NA	NA	NA	NA	NA	91 779	21 142	10.5	14.1
Albuquerque, NM MSA	5 755	6 581	6 505	31 305	13.0	101.9	100.0	104.2	101.6	98.2	107.0	101.1	116 224	29 869	17.9	23.6
Alexandria, LA MSA	434	332	364	1 470	2.9	92.0	87.8	88.5	93.3	93.7	76.9	99.0	29 710	8 241	24.1	31.1
Allentown-Bethlehem-Easton, PA MSA ..	2 465	2 260	2 282	16 032	6.7	103.4	107.2	101.9	118.5	98.2	94.4	102.1	55 101	11 723	9.0	11.5
Altoona, PA MSA	259	379	276	2 274	4.2	96.1	101.2	95.3	118.8	87.0	88.8	92.5	19 982	5 046	15.1	20.4
Amarillo, TX MSA	573	453	523	2 823	3.5	90.0	92.9	86.5	62.8	102.3	88.8	95.0	32 636	8 284	16.5	21.1
Anchorage, AK MSA	1 314	1 056	861	6 097	6.5	124.8	121.9	133.8	84.0	109.7	173.5	123.6	23 820	5 564	9.4	10.9
Anniston, AL MSA	312	275	269	1 610	3.4	90.9	97.6	80.3	103.9	89.4	88.8	94.2	20 320	4 480	18.0	21.8
Appleton-Oshkosh-Neenah, WI MSA	2 746	2 310	2 885	16 890	14.0	98.2	94.9	101.8	93.7	97.9	98.9	97.8	22 094	4 936	6.6	7.5
Asheville, NC MSA	1 604	1 092	1 260	8 436	9.9	104.8	96.4	107.7	116.6	105.1	85.9	106.8	27 404	5 500	13.6	16.9
Athens, GA MSA	1 891	1 517	1 176	8 234	16.2	NA	NA	NA	NA	NA	NA	NA	24 279	4 969	19.0	23.4
Atlanta, GA MSA	48 262	48 277	41 237	253 413	20.7	99.5	101.9	96.4	94.4	104.9	109.7	98.8	448 008	108 884	13.4	18.3
Augusta-Aiken, GA-SC MSA	2 227	2 096	2 615	17 198	10.4	94.0	96.9	80.2	110.5	97.3	94.9	99.1	73 468	19 275	16.6	21.9
Austin-San Marcos, TX MSA	17 077	13 765	10 785	60 974	16.5	101.3	87.6	105.4	89.2	100.0	105.5	106.9	135 873	31 668	14.3	18.4
Bakersfield, CA MSA	2 767	3 496	3 124	25 503	12.8	104.0	109.2	92.8	115.1	115.5	112.1	103.8	130 629	37 050	21.8	27.6
Bangor, ME NECMA	304	325	371	2 533	4.1	NA	NA	NA	NA	NA	NA	NA	21 932	4 978	15.2	19.1
Barnstable-Yarmouth, MA NECMA	1 564	1 634	1 666	10 098	7.5	NA	NA	NA	NA	NA	NA	NA	19 327	4 661	9.8	15.6
Baton Rouge, LA MSA	4 363	3 320	2 984	16 679	7.9	100.0	101.8	98.2	107.5	103.8	92.5	99.3	105 004	26 806	18.9	23.1
Beaumont-Port Arthur, TX MSA	680	592	834	5 102	3.4	94.6	88.2	89.8	91.7	98.9	96.7	101.0	67 370	18 032	18.0	23.6
Bellingham, WA MSA	1 288	1 348	2 220	11 612	20.8	104.8	103.0	113.1	81.8	97.4	125.7	102.5	16 994	3 480	11.8	12.7
Benton Harbor, MI MSA	698	547	604	3 910	5.6	106.7	107.4	112.7	98.8	100.4	100.2	106.0	28 406	8 355	17.6	26.1
Billings, MT MSA	547	515	542	3 126	6.4	100.9	103.7	103.9	73.9	103.8	102.5	102.5	15 547	3 401	12.6	13.8
Biloxi-Gulfport-Pascagoula, MS MSA....	2 197	2 320	2 726	11 893	9.2	94.8	97.0	86.4	109.9	90.5	97.0	97.9	63 343	16 777	18.8	25.1
Binghamton, NY MSA	209	234	262	2 286	2.1	103.8	105.8	97.3	130.7	102.8	87.8	105.1	31 332	7 433	12.1	16.3
Birmingham, AL MSA	6 699	5 998	4 860	33 761	9.7	98.4	97.3	98.5	98.6	96.3	99.5	99.3	148 031	33 740	16.8	21.9
Bismarck, ND MSA	499	515	884	4 245	12.8	99.4	108.5	95.0	87.8	94.7	103.1	102.1	9 209	2 014	10.5	10.8
Bloomington, IN MSA	879	979	1 212	6 516	15.5	97.2	103.2	97.7	86.5	95.6	94.8	97.3	14 160	1 966	14.0	13.6
Bloomington-Normal, IL MSA	1 214	1 289	1 492	8 053	16.4	NA	NA	NA	NA	NA	NA	NA	11 366	2 194	8.8	9.5
Boise City, ID MSA	4 538	4 675	6 543	32 756	28.7	103.1	101.4	108.6	67.5	100.0	116.6	106.3	39 781	8 491	11.5	11.8
Boston-Worcester-Lawrence-Lowell-Brockton, MA-NH NECMA	16 612	15 437	17 023	105 651	4.7	142.5	115.0	206.6	137.2	120.3	136.2	110.0	602 998	149 821	10.6	15.7
Brownsville-Harlingen-San Benito, TX MSA	2 532	2 025	2 235	10 440	11.8	88.2	83.5	77.0	96.4	104.0	93.3	92.8	115 790	37 148	38.5	49.4
Bryan-College Station, TX MSA	1 340	1 008	1 523	5 587	11.4	90.5	91.5	84.3	105.9	88.2	99.7	90.5	23 973	4 267	19.9	21.6
Buffalo-Niagara Falls, NY MSA	2 973	2 387	3 047	20 981	4.3	96.6	109.8	85.3	126.8	105.9	96.3	89.9	176 727	42 777	14.9	20.8
Burlington, VT NECMA	871	895	992	5 965	8.1	118.2	107.5	135.2	128.9	101.6	119.9	110.5	19 732	4 046	10.8	11.9
Canton-Massillon, OH MSA	1 230	1 228	1 323	9 005	5.7	97.1	100.9	100.1	83.5	96.6	91.2	97.3	51 341	13 079	12.8	17.8
Casper, WY MSA	172	69	87	507	1.7	NA	NA	NA	NA	NA	NA	NA	8 747	1 975	13.6	15.2
Cedar Rapids, IA MSA	1 092	1 264	1 162	7 640	11.2	98.9	95.0	103.0	100.4	100.2	94.2	97.5	16 551	3 556	9.3	11.1
Champaign-Urbana, IL MSA	654	655	987	4 275	6.2	102.8	103.5	106.1	110.6	94.9	109.2	98.9	20 515	3 867	13.3	15.3
Charleston-North Charleston, SC MSA ..	2 792	2 262	2 672	20 359	10.2	97.1	97.5	86.0	123.5	93.9	97.9	100.8	85 825	22 334	16.5	22.7
Charleston, WV MSA	518	408	548	3 294	3.0	100.4	106.2	100.3	109.8	101.0	91.6	96.9	47 408	10 727	18.5	25.3
Charlotte-Gastonia-Rock Hill, NC-SC MSA	18 458	13 777	13 831	85 796	18.1	99.0	96.5	97.6	103.6	98.6	102.6	99.8	153 127	33 519	12.1	15.1
Charlottesville, VA MSA	1 213	1 144	1 378	8 956	17.2	NA	NA	NA	NA	NA	NA	NA	17 398	3 356	13.0	15.8
Chattanooga, TN-GA MSA	2 669	2 449	2 656	14 518	8.2	93.0	96.9	86.3	88.8	88.5	88.0	99.9	73 474	16 892	16.7	21.7
Cheyenne, WY MSA	664	298	369	2 027	6.6	97.5	106.7	91.7	89.2	96.5	95.0	100.6	8 967	1 880	11.5	12.8
Chicago-Gary-Kenosha, IL-IN-WI CMSA	38 928	36 769	38 373	240 572	7.6	NA	NA	NA	NA	NA	NA	NA	1 169 550	310 437	13.7	19.8
Chicago, IL PMSA	34 086	32 425	33 375	209 011	7.3	NA	NA	NA	NA	NA	NA	NA	1 054 987	278 910	13.7	20.0
Gary, IN PMSA	3 191	3 027	3 490	20 911	9.1	NA	NA	NA	NA	NA	NA	NA	86 381	23 938	13.8	19.1
Kankakee, IL PMSA	534	533	657	3 475	9.4	NA	NA	NA	NA	NA	NA	NA	13 306	3 645	13.3	17.5
Kenosha, WI PMSA	1 117	784	851	7 175	14.0	NA	NA	NA	NA	NA	NA	NA	14 876	3 944	10.8	14.8
Chico-Paradise, CA MSA	673	728	924	7 364	9.7	NA	NA	NA	NA	NA	NA	NA	36 375	8 095	19.0	24.3
Cincinnati-Hamilton, OH-KY-IN CMSA ..	12 354	11 284	12 133	78 325	10.8	NA	NA	NA	NA	NA	NA	NA	233 089	61 890	12.3	17.3
Cincinnati, OH-KY-IN PMSA	9 548	9 069	9 694	62 815	10.3	90.4	95.9	84.0	88.0	92.1	98.5	91.8	202 055	54 015	12.8	18.1
Hamilton-Middletown, OH PMSA	2 806	2 215	2 439	15 510	14.1	NA	NA	NA	NA	NA	NA	NA	31 034	7 875	9.9	13.2
Clarksville-Hopkinsville, TN-KY MSA	2 091	2 326	2 529	13 017	21.5	94.5	93.2	95.3	92.4	96.7	89.9	95.3	28 681	7 285	16.4	22.0

NA Not available.

[1]Beginning 1994, based on a 19,000 permit-issuing place universe; earlier years based on a 17,000 permit-issuing place universe.

[2]Data are subject to copyright; see below for source citation. The index measures relative price levels for consumer goods and services in participating areas for a midmanagement standard of living. The index does not measure inflation, but compares prices at a single point in time. The average for all participating areas, both metropolitan and nonmetropolitan, equals 100, and each index is read as a percentage of the average for all places.

Source: Building Permits—U.S. Bureau of the Census, "Construction–Building Permits" on diskette, annual (related Internet site <http://www.census.gov/const/www/C40/table3.html>), and "1990 Census of Population and Housing, Summary Tape File 1C" on CD-ROM;   Cost of Living Index—ACCRA (American Chamber of Commerce Research Association), Alexandria, VA 22302-9950, "ACCRA Cost of Living Index, Third Quarter 1996" (copyright);   Poverty—U.S. Bureau of the Census, "State and County Income and Poverty Estimates - 1993," Internet site <http://www.census.gov/ftp/pub/housing/saipe/est93ALL.dat> (accessed 16 January 1998).

90   Abilene, TX—Clarksville, TN   STATE AND METROPOLITAN AREA DATA BOOK

[MSA = Metropolitan statistical area. CMSA = Consolidated MSA. PMSA = Primary MSA. NECMA = New England county metropolitan area. All areas defined as of June 30, 1996. Table includes 245 MSAs, 17 CMSAs, and 58 PMSAs not in New England; as well as 12 NECMAs. Table excludes 10 MSAs, 1 CMSA, and 15 PMSAs in New England]

Metropolitan areas	New private housing units authorized by building permits[1]					Cost of living index,[2] Third Quarter 1996							Persons below poverty level, 1993			
				1990–1996 period									Number		Percent	
				Total units	Percent of 1990 housing stock	Composite index (100%)	Grocery items (16%)	Housing (28%)	Utilities (8%)	Transportation (10%)	Health care (5%)	Miscellaneous goods and services (33%)	All persons	Related children 5 to 17 years	All persons	Related children 5 to 17 years
	1996	1995	1994													
Cleveland-Akron, OH CMSA	11 295	10 632	10 930	71 766	6.2	NA	NA	NA	NA	NA	NA	NA	426 681	111 857	14.6	21.6
Akron, OH PMSA.................	3 898	3 092	3 789	23 286	8.8	NA	NA	NA	NA	NA	NA	NA	90 906	22 444	13.5	19.1
Cleveland-Lorain-Elyria, OH PMSA ..	7 397	7 540	7 141	48 480	5.4	104.4	103.5	103.1	115.2	108.7	111.4	100.8	335 775	89 413	15.0	22.4
Colorado Springs, CO MSA	5 292	4 725	3 806	22 669	13.7	103.4	96.6	124.2	71.2	98.5	123.8	94.6	53 863	12 631	12.1	14.0
Columbia, MO MSA	1 638	1 353	1 558	9 197	20.6	94.5	102.1	83.7	81.2	99.2	102.2	100.5	15 830	2 973	14.0	15.5
Columbia, SC MSA	3 893	3 546	3 696	22 869	12.9	94.0	97.5	88.9	111.5	86.5	88.6	95.3	67 005	14 812	14.4	17.8
Columbus, GA-AL MSA	1 256	1 442	1 950	9 183	9.1	NA	NA	NA	NA	NA	NA	NA	55 181	14 787	20.9	29.1
Columbus, OH MSA	12 147	10 652	11 543	72 775	13.3	105.1	106.5	106.6	109.8	103.2	96.6	104.1	173 701	44 881	12.4	18.0
Corpus Christi, TX MSA	2 316	1 347	1 118	7 792	5.7	NA	NA	NA	NA	NA	NA	NA	85 814	24 192	22.9	29.6
Cumberland, MD-WV MSA	241	300	315	2 209	5.1	101.0	98.8	104.8	114.5	96.1	91.3	98.8	16 663	3 874	16.7	22.6
Dallas-Fort Worth, TX CMSA..........	38 808	36 657	34 036	197 538	11.6	NA	NA	NA	NA	NA	NA	NA	655 268	164 662	14.9	20.0
Dallas, TX PMSA.................	28 673	27 123	26 026	147 763	13.0	98.9	96.7	94.9	99.9	105.0	107.9	99.8	455 292	114 064	15.6	20.8
Fort Worth-Arlington, TX PMSA	10 135	9 534	8 010	49 775	8.7	92.2	86.4	76.2	119.0	100.3	95.1	99.4	199 976	50 598	13.6	18.3
Danville, VA MSA	364	366	400	2 823	6.1	NA	NA	NA	NA	NA	NA	NA	18 511	4 351	16.8	22.9
Davenport-Moline-Rock Island, IA-IL MSA	1 280	901	798	6 274	4.3	96.9	103.7	91.4	101.7	98.5	93.7	97.3	44 778	11 135	12.5	16.1
Dayton-Springfield, OH MSA	4 098	3 203	3 628	22 790	5.9	105.9	98.0	115.5	114.6	102.7	101.3	101.3	122 039	32 279	12.8	18.8
Daytona Beach, FL MSA	3 455	3 600	3 409	25 859	13.2	95.9	99.2	91.5	101.1	95.8	97.2	96.7	65 615	13 358	15.0	20.4
Decatur, AL MSA	663	508	438	3 865	7.3	93.6	98.5	84.8	89.8	99.9	91.4	98.2	19 449	4 361	14.1	17.2
Decatur, IL MSA	338	402	319	1 999	4.0	93.9	99.6	80.1	109.9	98.7	90.1	98.2	15 943	4 131	13.7	18.6
Denver-Boulder-Greeley, CO CMSA	21 531	21 432	20 585	108 761	12.6	NA	NA	NA	NA	NA	NA	NA	231 925	52 588	10.6	12.8
Boulder-Longmont, CO PMSA	2 744	3 094	2 623	17 337	18.3	109.5	98.9	137.5	77.5	104.4	121.3	97.9	20 547	3 579	8.3	8.6
Denver, CO PMSA	16 931	16 868	16 798	84 820	11.8	103.4	97.6	117.4	77.5	107.5	120.7	96.5	189 454	43 693	10.5	12.9
Greeley, CO PMSA	1 856	1 470	1 164	6 604	12.9	90.2	96.9	86.5	73.0	96.9	105.4	89.8	21 924	5 316	15.3	17.7
Des Moines, IA MSA	3 395	3 280	3 856	21 672	13.5	97.7	98.6	92.9	87.6	95.2	102.9	103.6	41 327	9 010	9.8	12.0
Detroit-Ann Arbor-Flint, MI CMSA......	26 710	24 014	23 382	147 531	7.3	NA	NA	NA	NA	NA	NA	NA	823 968	228 366	15.7	23.3
Ann Arbor, MI PMSA..............	4 881	4 078	4 091	25 378	13.5	NA	NA	NA	NA	NA	NA	NA	46 218	9 914	9.3	10.9
Detroit, MI PMSA..............	19 709	18 024	17 572	111 926	6.7	113.4	110.6	137.5	86.2	102.2	118.8	103.1	694 582	193 768	16.1	24.2
Flint, MI PMSA..............	2 120	1 912	1 719	10 227	6.0	NA	NA	NA	NA	NA	NA	NA	83 168	24 684	19.0	27.9
Dothan, AL MSA	416	509	469	3 128	5.9	93.1	99.0	87.4	99.5	92.9	81.8	95.6	23 584	5 922	17.7	23.1
Dover, DE MSA	659	941	976	5 912	14.0	102.8	110.7	94.5	112.2	98.0	105.0	104.7	15 333	3 975	13.0	17.4
Dubuque, IA MSA	331	458	441	2 787	8.7	107.6	100.0	130.0	90.8	99.3	94.2	101.0	8 901	1 995	10.2	11.3
Duluth-Superior, MN-WI MSA	692	777	811	5 331	4.6	NA	NA	NA	NA	NA	NA	NA	34 345	7 871	14.4	17.1
Eau Claire, WI MSA	964	808	746	4 881	9.1	98.8	100.5	103.4	98.9	94.8	107.4	93.5	17 290	4 070	12.4	14.7
El Paso, TX MSA	3 333	2 629	3 797	18 961	10.1	NA	NA	NA	NA	NA	NA	NA	201 749	60 352	30.2	39.6
Elkhart-Goshen, IN MSA	1 177	1 043	988	6 505	10.8	92.3	95.1	89.5	89.4	95.4	90.9	93.4	16 107	4 022	9.8	12.6
Elmira, NY MSA	114	125	124	876	2.3	112.3	108.4	122.3	141.6	106.4	92.9	103.8	12 739	3 300	13.9	18.8
Enid, OK MSA	156	112	102	551	2.1	NA	NA	NA	NA	NA	NA	NA	9 124	2 086	16.2	19.0
Erie, PA MSA	808	857	873	5 834	5.4	NA	NA	NA	NA	NA	NA	NA	38 547	9 815	13.9	18.2
Eugene-Springfield, OR MSA	2 169	2 769	1 997	12 548	10.8	108.3	93.4	131.2	73.6	105.0	115.7	104.1	44 779	8 788	15.0	16.3
Evansville-Henderson, IN-KY MSA	1 417	1 398	1 341	8 508	7.2	93.1	102.1	91.4	86.4	94.4	89.5	92.2	35 720	8 227	12.5	16.0
Fargo-Moorhead, ND-MN MSA........	1 205	1 648	1 641	10 242	14.8	96.8	101.2	96.6	90.7	91.6	103.3	102.5	18 263	3 608	11.6	12.1
Fayetteville, NC MSA	1 633	1 905	2 185	15 279	15.5	97.2	98.6	85.1	116.7	94.7	89.8	104.0	42 177	11 162	15.5	19.9
Fayetteville-Springdale-Rogers, AR MSA	2 996	3 778	4 286	20 609	23.2	93.1	99.5	84.5	86.8	90.3	85.9	101.0	26 034	5 847	10.8	13.6
Flagstaff, AZ-UT MSA................	1 477	1 418	844	6 592	14.3	111.4	105.0	131.0	96.8	112.7	110.7	101.3	23 834	6 347	21.7	24.2
Florence, AL MSA	481	422	611	3 176	5.7	94.1	96.1	85.8	98.5	97.5	95.3	98.1	19 520	4 179	14.4	18.2
Florence, SC MSA	725	574	682	4 513	10.4	NA	NA	NA	NA	NA	NA	NA	25 927	6 720	21.4	26.8
Fort Collins-Loveland, CO MSA	3 491	2 797	3 202	16 815	21.6	105.8	105.9	121.6	68.4	97.2	116.0	101.8	22 804	4 061	10.8	10.1
Fort Myers-Cape Coral, FL MSA	5 710	5 002	5 316	33 653	17.8	98.4	98.7	92.5	102.4	106.2	103.8	99.1	45 396	9 841	12.3	18.3
Fort Pierce-Port St. Lucie, FL MSA	3 260	2 791	3 250	21 550	16.8	NA	NA	NA	NA	NA	NA	NA	38 662	8 936	13.9	20.4
Fort Smith, AR-OK MSA..............	905	1 101	1 152	5 447	7.3	88.8	98.8	75.9	100.5	84.4	78.5	95.2	32 798	7 697	17.6	21.0
Fort Walton Beach, FL MSA	1 843	1 622	2 345	11 981	19.1	98.5	98.0	92.3	98.4	97.6	107.8	102.6	17 779	4 550	11.2	14.2
Fort Wayne, IN MSA	2 816	2 756	2 785	17 562	9.7	91.3	97.6	83.9	90.0	96.1	88.7	94.0	48 302	11 495	10.2	12.4
Fresno, CA MSA	3 910	4 916	5 329	37 552	14.1	107.1	106.6	99.5	112.3	119.9	113.0	107.9	228 351	68 701	27.2	36.7
Gadsden, AL MSA..................	258	323	291	1 628	3.9	92.1	98.8	80.9	100.4	92.7	90.9	96.5	18 337	4 007	17.9	22.0
Gainesville, FL MSA	1 853	1 971	1 582	10 997	13.9	100.4	101.5	97.5	117.5	101.3	105.7	97.0	37 326	7 392	20.2	23.1
Glens Falls, NY MSA	441	432	535	3 970	7.1	99.8	101.9	85.8	130.7	104.1	100.0	102.0	13 664	3 263	11.4	14.3
Goldsboro, NC MSA	466	539	576	3 268	8.3	NA	NA	NA	NA	NA	NA	NA	18 255	4 475	17.5	21.7
Grand Forks, ND-MN MSA	268	475	263	2 059	5.0	101.2	103.9	96.0	96.5	104.4	93.7	106.0	13 873	2 956	13.9	14.7

NA Not available.

[1]Beginning 1994, based on a 19,000 permit-issuing place universe; earlier years based on a 17,000 permit-issuing place universe.
[2]Data are subject to copyright; see below for source citation. The index measures relative price levels for consumer goods and services in participating areas for a midmanagement standard of living. The index does not measure inflation, but compares prices at a single point in time. The average for all participating areas, both metropolitan and nonmetropolitan, equals 100, and each index is read as a percentage of the average for all places.

Source: Building Permits—U.S. Bureau of the Census, "Construction–Building Permits" on diskette, annual (related Internet site <http://www.census.gov/const/www/C40/table3.html>), and "1990 Census of Population and Housing, Summary Tape File 1C" on CD-ROM; Cost of Living Index—ACCRA (American Chamber of Commerce Research Association), Alexandria, VA 22302-9950, "ACCRA Cost of Living Index, Third Quarter 1996" (copyright); Poverty—U.S. Bureau of the Census, "State and County Income and Poverty Estimates - 1993," Internet site <http://www.census.gov/ftp/pub/housing/saipe/est93ALL.dat> (accessed 16 January 1998).

[MSA = Metropolitan statistical area.   CMSA = Consolidated MSA.   PMSA = Primary MSA.   NECMA = New England county metropolitan area.   All areas defined as of June 30, 1996.   Table includes 245 MSAs, 17 CMSAs, and 58 PMSAs not in New England; as well as 12 NECMAs.   Table excludes 10 MSAs, 1 CMSA, and 15 PMSAs in New England]

Metropolitan areas	New private housing units authorized by building permits[1]			1990–1996 period		Cost of living index,[2] Third Quarter 1996							Persons below poverty level, 1993			
													Number		Percent	
												Miscellaneous goods and services (33%)		Related children 5 to 17 years		Related children 5 to 17 years
	1996	1995	1994	Total units	Percent of 1990 housing stock	Composite index (100%)	Grocery items (16%)	Housing (28%)	Utilities (8%)	Transportation (10%)	Health care (5%)		All persons		All persons	
Grand Junction, CO MSA	1 044	941	924	4 873	12.4	101.4	102.3	108.5	77.7	104.3	96.9	100.8	14 688	3 457	14.2	16.5
Grand Rapids-Muskegon-Holland, MI MSA	7 940	7 102	6 606	42 395	11.9	103.7	109.3	113.3	81.9	102.8	88.4	101.2	115 292	31 696	11.6	15.7
Great Falls, MT MSA	134	127	138	783	2.4	107.0	105.2	128.4	70.4	100.9	103.2	100.8	11 152	2 516	13.8	15.5
Green Bay, WI MSA	1 705	1 890	2 078	12 492	16.7	98.7	96.1	99.3	88.4	100.6	102.4	100.7	18 163	4 239	8.7	10.2
Greensboro--Winston Salem--High Point, NC MSA	9 403	8 863	7 962	51 409	11.6	100.9	94.9	107.8	110.1	100.3	87.7	98.4	124 962	25 801	11.3	14.1
Greenville, NC MSA	1 019	1 558	1 853	9 680	22.5	97.6	96.1	88.9	132.7	92.1	94.4	99.2	24 982	5 542	22.0	27.2
Greenville-Spartanburg-Anderson, SC MSA	7 661	6 072	6 256	38 734	11.5	94.2	97.8	91.3	103.8	91.0	87.9	94.6	110 274	23 546	12.7	15.6
Harrisburg-Lebanon-Carlisle, PA MSA	2 841	2 376	2 867	19 392	8.0	101.7	96.6	96.5	118.4	111.2	102.4	101.9	53 669	12 145	8.9	11.5
Hartford, CT NECMA	2 908	2 520	2 959	18 839	4.2	NA	NA	NA	NA	NA	NA	NA	107 861	30 519	9.7	16.2
Hattiesburg, MS MSA	189	185	98	655	1.7	92.4	95.9	79.2	102.7	102.4	90.7	97.1	23 260	6 053	22.9	30.6
Hickory-Morganton-Lenoir, NC MSA	2 038	1 519	1 547	10 863	8.9	NA	NA	NA	NA	NA	NA	NA	32 344	6 869	10.5	12.9
Honolulu, HI MSA	2 000	4 544	4 612	26 250	9.3	NA	NA	NA	NA	NA	NA	NA	75 992	17 476	8.9	11.7
Houma, LA MSA	834	783	687	4 517	6.8	NA	NA	NA	NA	NA	NA	NA	41 328	11 841	21.9	27.9
Houston-Galveston-Brazoria, TX CMSA	24 118	21 682	22 481	131 212	8.5	NA	NA	NA	NA	NA	NA	NA	733 796	199 136	17.8	23.9
Brazoria, TX PMSA	1 730	1 366	1 198	9 029	12.1	NA	NA	NA	NA	NA	NA	NA	25 383	6 396	12.3	14.2
Galveston-Texas City, TX PMSA	1 512	1 490	1 317	9 565	9.6	NA	NA	NA	NA	NA	NA	NA	37 516	9 732	15.9	21.0
Houston, TX PMSA	20 876	18 826	19 966	112 618	8.3	93.8	92.2	82.5	98.7	106.3	104.0	97.8	670 897	183 008	18.2	24.7
Huntington-Ashland, WV-KY-OH MSA	278	489	202	1 762	1.3	99.0	104.5	87.0	118.7	100.8	98.9	101.4	67 259	16 309	21.3	28.9
Huntsville, AL MSA	947	757	996	9 851	8.3	95.7	95.5	84.7	90.3	96.4	104.0	104.8	43 028	9 424	13.2	17.2
Indianapolis, IN MSA	13 737	13 606	11 909	75 913	13.3	94.7	99.2	97.2	87.9	95.9	93.0	91.9	173 388	42 891	11.8	16.2
Iowa City, IA MSA	907	838	1 182	6 149	16.5	NA	NA	NA	NA	NA	NA	NA	9 185	1 241	9.7	8.9
Jackson, MI MSA	716	634	621	4 178	7.2	NA	NA	NA	NA	NA	NA	NA	20 800	5 247	14.2	18.5
Jackson, MS MSA	2 893	3 089	3 443	16 124	10.6	95.5	98.7	93.6	102.9	96.3	82.2	96.1	91 399	22 818	22.3	28.2
Jackson, TN MSA	705	1 118	923	4 843	13.2	94.8	97.5	91.9	94.1	100.5	84.3	96.6	17 600	4 187	18.7	23.4
Jacksonville, FL MSA	11 290	8 590	8 560	58 754	15.3	96.0	100.2	84.9	107.7	97.2	93.0	100.9	136 910	34 589	14.0	18.1
Jacksonville, NC MSA	832	676	784	4 599	9.7	NA	NA	NA	NA	NA	NA	NA	19 371	4 565	16.4	19.2
Jamestown, NY MSA	231	225	291	1 759	2.8	NA	NA	NA	NA	NA	NA	NA	23 837	6 056	17.1	22.7
Janesville-Beloit, WI MSA	947	1 037	1 103	5 846	10.7	NA	NA	NA	NA	NA	NA	NA	16 021	4 186	11.0	14.5
Johnson City-Kingsport-Bristol, TN-VA MSA	1 841	2 072	1 968	10 735	5.8	95.3	92.3	100.8	84.8	88.5	86.4	98.0	76 206	16 441	17.0	22.4
Johnstown, PA MSA	481	432	443	2 986	2.9	NA	NA	NA	NA	NA	NA	NA	35 133	8 675	14.8	19.6
Jonesboro, AR MSA	894	401	744	3 802	13.4	87.4	96.2	78.9	78.2	82.0	88.3	94.0	12 203	2 583	16.8	19.9
Joplin, MO MSA	738	742	709	3 918	6.8	89.9	94.4	84.1	83.5	86.1	96.7	93.9	23 026	5 388	16.2	20.0
Kalamazoo-Battle Creek, MI MSA	2 089	2 128	1 973	12 008	6.8	NA	NA	NA	NA	NA	NA	NA	65 914	17 736	15.1	21.5
Kansas City, MO-KS MSA	12 344	11 183	10 862	68 376	10.3	97.5	98.3	93.3	94.8	97.8	107.7	99.4	206 211	51 512	12.4	16.3
Killeen-Temple, TX MSA	2 210	2 192	1 603	9 820	10.3	92.2	88.0	85.7	98.9	91.1	104.5	96.1	41 634	10 733	15.4	19.3
Knoxville, TN MSA	5 453	4 548	4 285	27 814	11.0	97.5	94.9	90.6	93.2	90.8	97.4	107.6	96 626	20 685	15.4	20.1
Kokomo, IN MSA	741	666	560	3 135	7.8	NA	NA	NA	NA	NA	NA	NA	11 421	2 808	11.4	14.8
La Crosse, WI-MN MSA	825	747	648	4 327	9.5	NA	NA	NA	NA	NA	NA	NA	13 003	2 818	11.0	12.5
Lafayette, LA MSA	1 774	1 411	1 556	7 729	5.6	96.7	96.1	90.0	107.4	101.7	89.5	100.0	86 052	24 082	23.8	30.5
Lafayette, IN MSA	1 449	974	1 157	7 247	12.0	NA	NA	NA	NA	NA	NA	NA	17 834	3 052	11.5	11.7
Lake Charles, LA MSA	1 344	899	811	5 680	8.6	97.5	98.0	91.3	114.8	95.8	86.4	100.8	33 225	8 750	19.1	23.7
Lakeland-Winter Haven, FL MSA	2 626	2 365	2 683	18 052	9.7	NA	NA	NA	NA	NA	NA	NA	76 333	17 840	17.9	22.6
Lancaster, PA MSA	2 083	1 923	2 433	16 977	10.9	103.2	96.7	102.5	106.8	109.6	90.7	106.7	42 291	11 450	9.6	13.5
Lansing-East Lansing, MI MSA	2 184	1 935	1 926	12 951	7.8	107.2	109.6	127.0	77.7	99.0	107.5	98.7	51 925	12 779	12.0	15.4
Laredo, TX MSA	1 299	1 900	1 820	9 923	26.7	NA	NA	NA	NA	NA	NA	NA	59 848	18 608	36.1	44.9
Las Cruces, NM MSA	890	983	1 105	6 099	12.4	98.0	97.4	99.4	90.4	96.9	96.2	99.5	46 823	13 494	30.0	38.7
Las Vegas, NV-AZ MSA	32 381	29 545	27 760	170 139	45.2	104.7	110.9	106.8	75.7	116.9	119.2	101.1	140 519	31 649	12.9	16.8
Lawrence, KS MSA	1 892	841	1 189	7 271	22.9	99.5	90.5	108.0	78.6	92.0	92.9	104.9	11 086	1 724	13.6	13.4
Lawton, OK MSA	189	263	170	1 266	2.9	92.9	95.7	86.0	87.1	94.2	92.9	98.6	19 153	5 167	17.3	22.2
Lewiston-Auburn, ME NECMA	262	296	283	1 781	4.1	NA	NA	NA	NA	NA	NA	NA	14 977	3 614	14.5	19.0
Lexington, KY MSA	4 145	4 265	3 834	23 992	14.4	97.4	97.3	94.9	82.2	96.6	100.0	103.1	67 797	14 846	16.2	20.9
Lima, OH MSA	491	439	461	3 238	5.4	NA	NA	NA	NA	NA	NA	NA	17 842	4 601	11.7	14.7
Lincoln, NE MSA	2 321	1 951	1 955	12 929	14.9	89.1	93.0	75.7	83.3	101.2	84.0	97.7	20 009	3 349	9.0	8.6
Little Rock-North Little Rock, AR MSA	2 709	3 282	2 738	16 386	7.6	86.9	96.2	80.7	101.1	93.3	72.0	85.1	81 594	19 124	15.2	18.7
Longview-Marshall, TX MSA	364	450	369	1 953	2.4	NA	NA	NA	NA	NA	NA	NA	37 210	9 295	18.6	22.7

NA Not available.

[1]Beginning 1994, based on a 19,000 permit-issuing place universe; earlier years based on a 17,000 permit-issuing place universe.
[2]Data are subject to copyright; see below for source citation.   The index measures relative price levels for consumer goods and services in participating areas for a midmanagement standard of living. The index does not measure inflation, but compares prices at a single point in time. The average for all participating areas, both metropolitan and nonmetropolitan, equals 100, and each index is read as a percentage of the average for all places.

Source: Building Permits—U.S. Bureau of the Census, "Construction–Building Permits" on diskette, annual (related Internet site <http://www.census.gov/const/www/C40/table3.html>), and "1990 Census of Population and Housing, Summary Tape File 1C" on CD-ROM;   Cost of Living Index—ACCRA (American Chamber of Commerce Research Association), Alexandria, VA 22302-9950, "ACCRA Cost of Living Index, Third Quarter 1996" (copyright);   Poverty—U.S. Bureau of the Census, "State and County Income and Poverty Estimates - 1993," Internet site <http://www.census.gov/ftp/pub/housing/saipe/est93ALL.dat> (accessed 16 January 1998).

[MSA = Metropolitan statistical area. CMSA = Consolidated MSA. PMSA = Primary MSA. NECMA = New England county metropolitan area. All areas defined as of June 30, 1996. Table includes 245 MSAs, 17 CMSAs, and 58 PMSAs not in New England; as well as 12 NECMAs. Table excludes 10 MSAs, 1 CMSA, and 15 PMSAs in New England]

Metropolitan areas	New private housing units authorized by building permits[1]					Cost of living index,[2] Third Quarter 1996							Persons below poverty level, 1993			
				1990–1996 period									Number		Percent	
	1996	1995	1994	Total units	Percent of 1990 housing stock	Composite index (100%)	Grocery items (16%)	Housing (28%)	Utilities (8%)	Transportation (10%)	Health care (5%)	Miscellaneous goods and services (33%)	All persons	Related children 5 to 17 years	All persons	Related children 5 to 17 years
Los Angeles-Riverside-Orange, CA CMSA	32 587	28 796	35 674	269 329	5.1	NA	NA	NA	NA	NA	NA	NA	3 042 667	777 295	19.9	27.3
Los Angeles-Long Beach, CA PMSA	7 731	7 763	7 754	83 684	2.6	119.7	117.1	132.0	116.0	116.2	137.5	109.1	2 164 629	551 752	23.8	33.3
Orange, CA PMSA	10 173	8 193	12 640	61 709	7.1	NA	NA	NA	NA	NA	NA	NA	323 655	74 884	12.6	16.9
Riverside-San Bernardino, CA PMSA	12 362	10 698	12 824	109 111	10.6	108.7	107.3	106.1	98.7	114.7	130.3	108.3	476 400	131 195	16.3	21.4
Ventura, CA PMSA	2 321	2 142	2 456	14 825	6.5	NA	NA	NA	NA	NA	NA	NA	77 983	19 464	11.1	14.0
Louisville, KY-IN MSA	6 497	5 630	6 280	38 839	9.9	94.0	95.0	88.0	94.9	102.1	96.0	95.7	147 246	36 062	15.0	20.5
Lubbock, TX MSA	1 136	765	832	5 068	5.5	90.5	93.0	84.5	72.2	95.9	92.9	96.8	47 276	11 261	21.0	26.0
Lynchburg, VA MSA	1 165	1 123	1 091	7 233	9.1	95.0	100.7	91.6	89.5	89.3	92.9	98.4	26 499	5 853	13.3	17.2
Macon, GA MSA	2 744	2 396	1 814	13 091	11.4	95.7	100.4	89.1	102.6	94.8	87.4	99.2	58 811	15 926	19.3	26.9
Madison, WI MSA	3 009	3 394	3 809	23 103	15.6	112.2	98.8	128.8	92.1	105.1	110.8	111.7	32 293	5 669	8.4	9.0
Mansfield, OH MSA	478	460	462	2 863	4.1	100.1	101.0	94.1	139.4	95.8	89.0	98.0	22 662	5 927	13.1	17.7
McAllen-Edinburg-Mission, TX MSA	5 339	4 510	4 640	21 415	16.7	94.5	91.1	86.5	102.5	91.5	85.8	103.4	193 584	62 857	41.1	51.8
Medford-Ashland, OR MSA	1 276	1 301	1 878	9 537	15.8	NA	NA	NA	NA	NA	NA	NA	23 391	4 922	14.4	16.3
Melbourne-Titusville-Palm Bay, FL MSA	3 301	2 764	4 007	25 684	13.9	NA	NA	NA	NA	NA	NA	NA	51 543	10 999	11.6	15.1
Memphis, TN-AR-MS MSA	9 806	9 020	7 472	51 526	13.1	95.4	102.7	95.5	78.6	99.3	92.0	95.3	228 057	61 869	21.7	30.0
Merced, CA MSA	875	782	1 066	7 463	12.8	NA	NA	NA	NA	NA	NA	NA	48 376	15 754	24.5	33.0
Miami-Fort Lauderdale, FL CMSA	20 970	27 588	27 036	150 287	10.7	NA	NA	NA	NA	NA	NA	NA	684 047	159 260	20.0	28.4
Fort Lauderdale, FL PMSA	14 419	12 870	15 726	81 990	13.0	NA	NA	NA	NA	NA	NA	NA	171 871	36 982	12.3	17.6
Miami, FL PMSA	6 551	14 718	11 310	68 297	8.9	107.7	103.6	111.5	107.1	114.1	123.4	101.9	512 176	122 278	25.4	34.8
Milwaukee-Racine, WI CMSA	7 376	7 007	7 827	54 772	8.7	NA	NA	NA	NA	NA	NA	NA	218 626	63 828	13.3	20.1
Milwaukee-Waukesha, WI PMSA	6 446	6 176	6 945	48 441	8.6	105.4	102.1	120.8	82.5	104.3	102.1	100.3	199 132	58 551	13.7	20.9
Racine, WI PMSA	930	831	882	6 331	9.5	NA	NA	NA	NA	NA	NA	NA	19 494	5 277	10.6	14.2
Minneapolis-St. Paul, MN-WI MSA	18 206	17 774	17 621	121 214	11.9	101.4	97.4	97.0	100.9	113.9	126.9	99.1	257 496	61 762	9.5	11.8
Mobile, AL MSA	4 369	4 861	5 015	19 984	9.9	93.9	99.1	77.1	101.4	104.7	93.9	100.9	111 312	29 262	21.9	29.5
Modesto, CA MSA	1 401	1 310	1 483	13 821	10.5	NA	NA	NA	NA	NA	NA	NA	70 339	20 564	17.2	22.9
Monroe, LA MSA	538	577	529	2 970	5.3	96.7	93.6	83.3	131.2	94.5	89.0	103.1	36 100	9 907	25.1	32.1
Montgomery, AL MSA	1 882	2 235	2 582	12 023	10.3	94.3	95.3	84.4	95.7	107.0	97.1	97.9	57 482	14 503	19.0	24.8
Muncie, IN MSA	273	345	329	2 366	4.8	96.5	98.7	101.0	79.3	100.7	91.2	95.5	18 803	3 734	16.4	20.0
Myrtle Beach, SC MSA	4 054	3 203	2 362	15 447	17.2	99.9	99.2	99.7	101.3	95.2	93.9	102.4	27 273	6 576	17.8	25.4
Naples, FL MSA	5 449	4 257	4 322	31 130	33.1	NA	NA	NA	NA	NA	NA	NA	23 496	5 380	13.1	20.2
Nashville, TN MSA	15 673	11 426	10 216	63 879	15.5	94.2	97.1	91.3	91.1	96.8	95.1	95.1	152 643	35 222	14.4	18.6
New London-Norwich, CT NECMA	926	805	1 126	5 843	5.6	NA	NA	NA	NA	NA	NA	NA	20 268	5 850	8.3	13.3
New Orleans, LA MSA	4 739	4 020	4 130	24 576	4.5	94.9	97.6	83.0	132.9	100.0	79.2	96.0	319 762	86 082	24.4	32.5
New York-Northern New Jersey-Long Island, NY-NJ-CT-PA CMSA/NECMA	41 241	34 418	36 252	235 545	3.1	NA	NA	NA	NA	NA	NA	NA	2 910 137	776 022	14.7	23.4
Bergen-Passaic, NJ PMSA	1 606	1 356	1 582	9 325	1.9	NA	NA	NA	NA	NA	NA	NA	109 980	25 542	8.4	12.1
Dutchess, NY PMSA	711	552	574	4 789	4.9	NA	NA	NA	NA	NA	NA	NA	20 091	4 164	8.0	9.3
Jersey City, NJ PMSA	360	294	464	2 563	1.1	NA	NA	NA	NA	NA	NA	NA	101 359	26 857	18.2	30.2
Middlesex-Somerset-Hunterdon, NJ PMSA	5 939	5 073	4 490	30 914	8.1	NA	NA	NA	NA	NA	NA	NA	62 880	13 327	5.9	7.8
Monmouth-Ocean, NJ PMSA	5 267	4 799	5 924	32 256	7.4	NA	NA	NA	NA	NA	NA	NA	78 501	17 319	7.5	9.5
Nassau-Suffolk, NY PMSA	5 445	4 098	4 662	30 859	3.3	NA	NA	NA	NA	NA	NA	NA	180 827	40 935	6.8	8.9
New Haven-Bridgeport-Stamford-Waterbury-Danbury, CT NECMA	3 718	4 285	4 293	26 906	4.1	123.0	128.0	133.1	159.6	107.4	128.2	106.5	152 121	43 791	9.3	16.0
New York, NY PMSA	11 457	7 296	6 553	53 796	1.6	234.5	144.6	465.5	173.4	123.6	206.9	132.2	1 908 994	528 283	22.1	37.1
Newark, NJ PMSA	3 507	3 946	4 807	24 885	3.4	NA	NA	NA	NA	NA	NA	NA	225 410	57 975	11.6	17.1
Newburgh, NY-PA PMSA	2 429	1 861	1 599	12 835	9.1	NA	NA	NA	NA	NA	NA	NA	40 023	10 630	11.4	15.2
Trenton, NJ PMSA	802	858	1 304	6 417	5.2	NA	NA	NA	NA	NA	NA	NA	29 951	7 199	9.3	13.1
Norfolk-Virginia Beach-Newport News, VA-NC MSA	8 314	8 648	8 887	61 115	10.9	98.5	98.0	89.5	129.2	104.1	101.5	97.0	212 663	55 665	14.1	19.7
Ocala, FL MSA	2 434	2 115	2 317	15 416	16.3	NA	NA	NA	NA	NA	NA	NA	40 375	9 693	18.4	26.0
Odessa-Midland, TX MSA	358	352	332	2 256	2.4	93.0	93.0	80.7	96.0	101.1	91.2	100.9	44 947	12 663	18.8	24.1
Oklahoma City, OK MSA	5 042	4 346	4 285	26 106	6.1	90.0	89.6	77.1	92.7	92.4	94.5	98.9	161 404	40 034	16.1	20.5
Omaha, NE-IA MSA	5 592	4 063	3 264	26 972	10.5	92.0	92.9	92.0	86.7	102.7	88.9	90.6	72 135	16 594	10.8	12.5
Orlando, FL MSA	16 084	16 014	16 654	116 071	22.1	99.4	99.6	93.4	102.6	98.8	110.2	101.7	182 401	42 352	13.4	17.3
Owensboro, KY MSA	414	528	427	2 728	7.8	92.2	100.0	86.7	69.6	94.0	91.0	98.3	14 852	3 651	16.5	21.3

NA Not available.

[1]Beginning 1994, based on a 19,000 permit-issuing place universe; earlier years based on a 17,000 permit-issuing place universe.
[2]Data are subject to copyright; see below for source citation. The index measures relative price levels for consumer goods and services in participating areas for a midmanagement standard of living. The index does not measure inflation, but compares prices at a single point in time. The average for all participating areas, both metropolitan and nonmetropolitan, equals 100, and each index is read as a percentage of the average for all places.

Source: Building Permits—U.S. Bureau of the Census, "Construction–Building Permits" on diskette, annual (related Internet site <http://www.census.gov/const/www/C40/table3.html>), and "1990 Census of Population and Housing, Summary Tape File 1C" on CD-ROM; Cost of Living Index—ACCRA (American Chamber of Commerce Research Association), Alexandria, VA 22302-9950, "ACCRA Cost of Living Index, Third Quarter 1996" (copyright); Poverty—U.S. Bureau of the Census, "State and County Income and Poverty Estimates - 1993," Internet site <http://www.census.gov/ftp/pub/housing/saipe/est93ALL.dat> (accessed 16 January 1998).

[MSA = Metropolitan statistical area.   CMSA = Consolidated MSA.   PMSA = Primary MSA.   NECMA = New England county metropolitan area.   All areas defined as of June 30, 1996.   Table includes 245 MSAs, 17 CMSAs, and 58 PMSAs not in New England; as well as 12 NECMAs.   Table excludes 10 MSAs, 1 CMSA, and 15 PMSAs in New England]

Metropolitan areas	New private housing units authorized by building permits[1]			1990–1996 period		Cost of living index,[2] Third Quarter 1996							Persons below poverty level, 1993			
													Number		Percent	
	1996	1995	1994	Total units	Percent of 1990 housing stock	Composite index (100%)	Grocery items (16%)	Housing (28%)	Utilities (8%)	Transportation (10%)	Health care (5%)	Miscellaneous goods and services (33%)	All persons	Related children 5 to 17 years	All persons	Related children 5 to 17 years
Panama City, FL MSA	998	1 044	1 019	7 294	11.1	94.7	98.7	86.6	98.1	95.6	90.4	99.2	22 820	5 729	16.3	20.9
Parkersburg-Marietta, WV-OH MSA.....	402	306	296	1 490	2.4	NA	NA	NA	NA	NA	NA	NA	24 566	5 845	16.1	21.6
Pensacola, FL MSA................	4 565	2 844	3 273	20 848	14.4	95.2	102.2	83.3	95.3	97.3	99.7	100.4	66 629	17 584	18.2	24.0
Peoria-Pekin, IL MSA	1 450	1 308	1 034	7 585	5.6	101.1	104.3	103.1	94.8	101.0	96.2	100.4	41 404	10 423	12.1	15.6
Philadelphia-Wilmington-Atlantic City, PA-NJ-DE-MD CMSA	19 537	17 732	20 141	128 087	5.4	NA	NA	NA	NA	NA	NA	NA	784 671	202 305	13.2	19.1
Atlantic-Cape May, NJ PMSA	1 712	1 222	1 776	9 585	5.0	NA	NA	NA	NA	NA	NA	NA	39 746	9 248	12.1	17.0
Philadelphia, PA-NJ PMSA	14 559	13 148	14 591	93 982	4.9	125.5	112.7	140.1	199.9	117.4	99.3	108.3	671 495	175 337	13.6	19.8
Vineland-Millville-Bridgeton, NJ PMSA	316	403	323	2 123	4.2	NA	NA	NA	NA	NA	NA	NA	21 232	5 912	15.8	22.0
Wilmington-Newark, DE-MD PMSA ..	2 950	2 959	3 451	22 397	11.1	110.1	115.8	111.0	124.1	99.2	118.2	104.8	52 198	11 808	9.8	12.4
Phoenix-Mesa, AZ MSA	39 646	37 536	34 775	187 206	18.6	103.3	104.5	97.9	106.6	118.3	117.7	99.7	411 455	104 976	16.5	22.7
Pine Bluff, AR MSA	154	144	114	871	2.6	109.5	103.1	107.9	133.6	106.4	111.4	108.7	22 533	5 670	27.6	33.0
Pittsburgh, PA MSA	5 622	5 464	6 756	41 815	4.1	109.5	103.1	107.9	133.6	106.4	111.4	108.7	314 774	74 781	13.1	19.0
Pittsfield, MA NECMA	400	281	311	2 318	3.6	NA	NA	NA	NA	NA	NA	NA	15 683	3 748	11.7	16.3
Pocatello, ID MSA	425	330	357	2 044	8.0	NA	NA	NA	NA	NA	NA	NA	8 959	2 024	12.4	11.9
Portland, ME NECMA	1 162	1 077	1 105	7 650	7.0	NA	NA	NA	NA	NA	NA	NA	27 185	5 488	11.0	13.5
Portland-Salem, OR-WA CMSA	21 633	20 443	18 918	122 032	16.8	NA	NA	NA	NA	NA	NA	NA	232 643	48 605	11.7	13.0
Portland-Vancouver, OR-WA PMSA .	18 260	18 032	17 043	105 463	17.0	109.1	99.7	121.7	89.2	112.8	124.0	104.1	189 093	38 548	11.2	12.3
Salem, OR PMSA	3 373	2 411	1 875	16 569	15.7	106.0	95.1	112.9	103.6	108.4	124.8	101.8	43 550	10 057	14.4	16.8
Providence-Warwick-Pawtucket, RI NECMA	2 214	2 095	2 316	16 097	4.3	116.0	101.5	134.9	134.3	109.7	118.6	103.9	115 416	29 413	12.8	19.1
Provo-Orem, UT MSA...............	3 955	4 395	3 765	20 996	28.8	103.9	97.3	115.5	81.9	107.4	118.6	98.9	38 825	8 289	13.0	10.5
Pueblo, CO MSA	1 193	938	657	3 841	7.6	90.0	102.0	81.8	81.5	95.0	116.7	87.1	26 379	6 370	20.7	25.2
Punta Gorda, FL MSA	1 065	973	1 586	10 798	16.7	NA	NA	NA	NA	NA	NA	NA	12 493	2 313	10.0	15.2
Raleigh-Durham-Chapel Hill, NC MSA ..	14 200	13 773	15 080	77 922	21.7	103.0	100.9	108.2	112.3	93.7	104.7	99.5	106 253	20 541	11.2	13.2
Rapid City, SD MSA	347	629	646	2 969	8.8	96.7	100.5	93.2	103.8	98.5	92.3	96.4	12 941	3 365	14.8	19.1
Reading, PA MSA	1 553	1 378	1 766	10 740	8.0	NA	NA	NA	NA	NA	NA	NA	38 787	9 253	11.2	15.8
Redding, CA MSA	710	773	968	8 381	13.8	NA	NA	NA	NA	NA	NA	NA	25 428	6 631	15.9	20.7
Reno, NV MSA	4 377	3 265	3 451	20 074	17.9	112.4	106.4	129.0	90.9	117.7	110.9	105.3	29 156	5 756	10.3	12.3
Richland-Kennewick-Pasco, WA MSA...	880	1 030	2 330	7 910	13.5	99.5	101.5	95.0	83.7	96.3	131.6	101.3	22 633	6 416	12.9	16.1
Richmond-Petersburg, VA MSA	6 147	5 929	6 504	42 798	12.0	103.0	99.4	101.9	117.7	108.4	108.3	99.7	109 983	25 722	12.1	16.2
Roanoke, VA MSA	991	906	1 047	6 383	6.7	92.5	94.4	91.1	85.2	91.8	93.6	94.4	27 299	5 979	12.0	16.4
Rochester, MN MSA	764	478	548	5 675	13.6	97.7	97.0	91.0	96.1	108.6	98.6	101.1	8 290	1 820	7.3	7.9
Rochester, NY MSA	3 107	2 888	3 501	23 382	5.5	102.2	117.0	86.9	127.9	118.9	89.2	99.5	120 569	31 583	11.2	16.1
Rockford, IL MSA	2 402	2 401	2 120	14 845	11.3	105.3	101.3	107.6	110.3	108.4	101.9	103.8	37 190	8 844	10.7	13.4
Rocky Mount, NC MSA...............	464	478	693	3 738	7.1	NA	NA	NA	NA	NA	NA	NA	26 241	6 062	18.7	22.2
Sacramento-Yolo, CA CMSA.............	8 974	8 043	9 343	70 188	11.5	NA	NA	NA	NA	NA	NA	NA	231 470	58 905	14.6	19.6
Sacramento, CA PMSA	8 174	7 327	8 688	64 326	11.6	NA	NA	NA	NA	NA	NA	NA	207 679	53 840	14.4	19.6
Yolo, CA PMSA	800	716	655	5 862	11.1	NA	NA	NA	NA	NA	NA	NA	23 791	5 065	16.6	19.8
Saginaw-Bay City-Midland, MI MSA.....	1 339	1 200	1 461	8 900	5.7	NA	NA	NA	NA	NA	NA	NA	68 354	19 478	16.9	24.0
St. Cloud, MN MSA	1 347	1 268	1 363	8 125	14.7	96.7	100.5	88.1	96.2	107.7	98.3	98.9	16 302	3 741	16.0	10.9
St. Joseph, MO MSA	342	377	279	1 895	4.6	94.1	88.2	96.4	82.5	95.1	95.2	97.4	15 755	3 795	16.2	20.3
St. Louis, MO-IL MSA	12 666	11 520	13 134	76 292	7.4	98.7	107.0	97.4	93.1	96.9	109.8	95.6	334 902	85 587	13.1	17.8
Salinas, CA MSA	1 502	1 326	1 478	8 025	6.6	143.6	112.8	212.7	100.4	128.6	160.6	111.5	52 959	14 400	16.1	21.9
Salt Lake City-Ogden, UT MSA........	12 743	10 616	8 709	55 888	15.1	96.5	102.2	96.7	76.4	96.5	105.6	96.7	117 958	28 584	9.9	9.7
San Angelo, TX MSA	476	225	262	1 765	4.4	93.0	90.3	79.9	87.4	98.8	87.0	106.3	16 903	4 257	17.2	21.9
San Antonio, TX MSA	9 642	8 279	9 296	40 469	7.9	92.2	95.2	85.1	96.0	93.0	98.3	94.5	312 418	87 085	21.9	29.9
San Diego, CA MSA —	6 848	6 633	6 943	55 868	5.9	121.9	113.4	152.2	100.9	131.0	120.0	103.4	422 935	104 347	16.3	22.8
San Francisco-Oakland-San Jose, CA CMSA —	21 432	15 695	18 039	126 671	5.2	NA	NA	NA	NA	NA	NA	NA	660 572	141 432	10.2	13.2
Oakland, CA PMSA...............	7 033	6 167	6 955	46 551	5.7	NA	NA	NA	NA	NA	NA	NA	238 415	53 903	11.0	14.3
San Francisco, CA PMSA	3 016	2 429	2 206	16 311	2.4	NA	NA	NA	NA	NA	NA	NA	160 058	28 185	9.8	12.7
San Jose, CA PMSA	7 574	3 401	3 945	30 195	5.6	NA	NA	NA	NA	NA	NA	NA	142 122	32 680	9.2	12.4
Santa Cruz-Watsonville, CA PMSA ..	507	437	515	3 421	3.7	NA	NA	NA	NA	NA	NA	NA	31 969	6 719	13.8	16.9
Santa Rosa, CA PMSA...............	1 487	1 930	2 511	15 689	9.7	NA	NA	NA	NA	NA	NA	NA	42 700	9 013	10.4	12.3
Vallejo-Fairfield-Napa, CA PMSA	1 815	1 331	1 907	14 504	8.9	NA	NA	NA	NA	NA	NA	NA	45 308	10 932	9.6	11.4
San Luis Obispo-Atascadero-Paso Robles, CA MSA	1 156	916	1 080	7 372	8.2	NA	NA	NA	NA	NA	NA	NA	27 271	5 249	12.7	14.6
Santa Barbara-Santa Maria-Lompoc, CA MSA	780	793	705	6 163	4.5	113.2	106.9	134.0	107.4	112.0	114.5	100.1	54 289	11 610	14.5	18.4

NA Not available.

[1]Beginning 1994, based on a 19,000 permit-issuing place universe; earlier years based on a 17,000 permit-issuing place universe.

[2]Data are subject to copyright; see below for source citation.   The index measures relative price levels for consumer goods and services in participating areas for a midmanagement standard of living.   The index does not measure inflation, but compares prices at a single point in time.   The average for all participating areas, both metropolitan and nonmetropolitan, equals 100, and each index is read as a percentage of the average for all places.

Source: Building Permits—U.S. Bureau of the Census, "Construction–Building Permits" on diskette, annual (related Internet site <http://www.census.gov/const/www/C40/table3.html>), and "1990 Census of Population and Housing, Summary Tape File 1C" on CD-ROM;   Cost of Living Index—ACCRA (American Chamber of Commerce Research Association), Alexandria, VA 22302-9950, "ACCRA Cost of Living Index, Third Quarter 1996" (copyright);   Poverty—U.S. Bureau of the Census, "State and County Income and Poverty Estimates - 1993," Internet site <http://www.census.gov/ftp/pub/housing/saipe/est93ALL.dat> (accessed 16 January 1998).

Table B–6. Metro Areas — Building Permits, Cost of Living, and Poverty—Con.

[MSA = Metropolitan statistical area. CMSA = Consolidated MSA. PMSA = Primary MSA. NECMA = New England county metropolitan area. All areas defined as of June 30, 1996. Table includes 245 MSAs, 17 CMSAs, and 58 PMSAs not in New England; as well as 12 NECMAs. Table excludes 10 MSAs, 1 CMSA, and 15 PMSAs in New England]

| Metropolitan areas | New private housing units authorized by building permits[1] | | | | | Cost of living index,[2] Third Quarter 1996 | | | | | | | Persons below poverty level, 1993 | | | |
| | | | | 1990–1996 period | | | | | | | | | Number | | Percent | |
	1996	1995	1994	Total units	Percent of 1990 housing stock	Composite index (100%)	Grocery items (16%)	Housing (28%)	Utilities (8%)	Transportation (10%)	Health care (5%)	Miscellaneous goods and services (33%)	All persons	Related children 5 to 17 years	All persons	Related children 5 to 17 years
Santa Fe, NM MSA	340	445	586	3 169	6.5	107.4	99.5	125.8	86.8	104.3	111.8	100.7	15 165	3 632	11.6	14.6
Sarasota-Bradenton, FL MSA	6 192	5 011	5 155	34 714	12.7	102.0	94.8	108.5	107.0	92.9	108.1	100.1	58 381	11 302	11.2	16.8
Savannah, GA MSA	2 142	2 063	1 977	12 886	12.1	NA	NA	NA	NA	NA	NA	NA	51 028	14 322	18.6	27.3
Scranton--Wilkes-Barre--Hazleton, PA MSA	1 399	1 359	1 605	10 979	4.1	97.5	104.2	97.7	100.4	93.1	90.5	96.0	78 418	17 099	12.5	16.5
Seattle-Tacoma-Bremerton, WA CMSA	24 283	21 868	23 456	170 688	13.9	NA	NA	NA	NA	NA	NA	NA	331 474	72 156	10.3	12.6
Bremerton, WA PMSA	1 769	1 554	2 000	15 059	20.3	111.1	102.9	116.8	109.8	107.6	134.3	107.3	20 621	5 160	9.5	11.7
Olympia, WA PMSA	1 996	2 228	2 092	14 665	22.1	NA	NA	NA	NA	NA	NA	NA	19 640	4 595	10.4	12.2
Seattle-Bellevue-Everett, WA PMSA	15 730	13 673	13 911	105 762	12.3	115.0	110.6	124.6	78.4	112.8	147.1	112.6	210 330	42 464	9.6	11.5
Tacoma, WA PMSA	4 788	4 413	5 453	35 202	15.4	104.6	110.6	103.3	76.2	111.5	138.4	101.8	80 883	19 937	12.9	16.1
Sharon, PA MSA	339	397	364	2 166	4.4	NA	NA	NA	NA	NA	NA	NA	17 624	4 278	14.8	19.9
Sheboygan, WI MSA	720	733	712	4 056	10.0	101.2	103.9	114.2	81.8	100.1	90.4	95.8	7 843	1 803	7.3	8.3
Sherman-Denison, TX MSA	210	209	121	852	1.9	NA	NA	NA	NA	NA	NA	NA	15 369	3 418	15.9	18.9
Shreveport-Bossier City, LA MSA	1 366	1 148	1 253	6 010	3.7	93.7	88.4	95.0	95.9	96.4	88.9	94.9	86 666	23 977	22.9	30.9
Sioux City, IA-NE MSA	427	579	876	3 415	7.5	NA	NA	NA	NA	NA	NA	NA	15 360	3 844	12.8	15.7
Sioux Falls, SD MSA	1 547	1 518	1 751	9 484	17.1	95.1	97.0	93.0	92.4	95.8	102.3	95.2	13 521	2 875	8.9	9.6
South Bend, IN MSA	1 303	1 150	1 388	9 018	9.2	92.1	91.8	89.1	97.2	92.9	96.6	92.4	30 186	7 163	12.1	16.1
Spokane, WA MSA	3 401	2 716	3 241	19 748	13.2	107.7	102.4	125.2	61.2	101.0	119.8	106.3	53 045	12 709	13.4	16.6
Springfield, IL MSA	1 131	1 201	1 549	8 947	11.0	95.6	103.8	80.8	80.8	93.0	107.8	106.2	21 591	5 011	10.6	13.4
Springfield, MO MSA	2 259	2 468	3 782	15 556	14.2	91.4	93.5	89.6	72.5	96.0	95.7	94.4	43 353	9 320	15.3	18.1
Springfield, MA NECMA	1 166	1 319	1 351	9 538	4.1	NA	NA	NA	NA	NA	NA	NA	76 428	21 854	13.2	21.0
State College, PA MSA	516	872	541	4 405	9.5	NA	NA	NA	NA	NA	NA	NA	13 787	1 911	11.8	11.1
Steubenville-Weirton, OH-WV MSA	100	102	143	780	1.3	NA	NA	NA	NA	NA	NA	NA	22 499	5 298	16.0	21.8
Stockton-Lodi, CA MSA	2 337	2 300	2 299	17 688	10.6	NA	NA	NA	NA	NA	NA	NA	96 179	28 384	18.8	25.9
Sumter, SC MSA	389	356	368	3 221	9.2	94.7	97.4	79.5	115.3	93.8	94.2	101.5	22 256	5 868	21.9	27.4
Syracuse, NY MSA	1 452	1 238	1 911	12 775	4.3	103.2	112.4	92.7	133.6	109.1	106.8	97.9	91 942	22 371	12.5	16.1
Tallahassee, FL MSA	1 926	2 881	2 253	15 992	16.6	102.3	97.5	104.2	116.6	99.2	98.1	101.3	42 345	9 480	17.3	20.2
Tampa-St. Petersburg-Clearwater, FL MSA	14 680	13 619	14 743	90 759	8.9	94.3	101.7	86.5	108.3	96.0	96.4	93.0	318 761	69 094	14.8	20.8
Terre Haute, IN MSA	512	376	447	3 106	5.0	NA	NA	NA	NA	NA	NA	NA	19 936	4 314	13.9	17.0
Texarkana, TX-Texarkana, AR MSA	652	218	251	1 925	3.8	88.6	90.8	76.0	91.1	97.6	95.8	93.9	23 508	5 977	19.3	24.0
Toledo, OH MSA	2 024	2 192	1 982	12 308	5.0	100.6	102.5	91.8	137.0	106.2	95.8	97.7	90 111	23 724	14.8	20.8
Topeka, KS MSA	785	684	809	5 121	7.4	NA	NA	NA	NA	NA	NA	NA	19 892	5 039	12.1	16.1
Tucson, AZ MSA	5 697	7 275	8 480	37 206	12.5	99.8	104.5	95.1	110.9	102.1	113.8	95.6	139 155	34 206	19.0	26.4
Tulsa, OK MSA	3 576	3 582	3 085	20 088	6.4	93.0	93.6	83.0	100.1	91.7	95.9	99.2	122 238	28 811	16.3	20.0
Tuscaloosa, AL MSA	1 054	1 413	851	6 584	11.2	101.4	97.3	98.0	104.9	97.8	94.9	107.5	28 946	6 149	19.3	23.7
Tyler, TX MSA	778	314	395	2 311	3.6	91.2	88.8	81.4	96.9	101.3	89.2	96.8	28 090	6 954	17.6	22.6
Utica-Rome, NY MSA	422	479	689	4 278	3.2	104.3	101.7	98.7	136.7	107.3	98.2	102.7	43 138	11 212	14.1	19.8
Victoria, TX MSA	174	172	202	1 130	3.9	90.8	85.0	88.0	95.4	93.1	92.2	93.9	14 510	3 974	18.1	23.2
Visalia-Tulare-Porterville, CA MSA	1 375	1 714	1 918	12 895	12.3	108.6	99.6	106.2	124.2	116.4	124.8	106.0	97 914	30 491	28.2	36.6
Waco, TX MSA	423	509	494	2 857	3.6	91.2	86.2	78.8	117.1	101.2	86.4	96.1	41 249	9 906	21.3	27.1
Washington-Baltimore, DC-MD-VA-WV CMSA	42 396	40 944	45 217	288 370	10.8	NA	NA	NA	NA	NA	NA	NA	697 974	155 682	9.9	12.9
Baltimore, MD PMSA	10 741	11 349	12 556	87 789	9.3	100.4	101.9	99.5	112.5	105.6	95.9	96.9	294 802	71 467	12.0	16.6
Hagerstown, MD PMSA	640	544	676	4 045	8.5	99.0	92.5	93.9	102.0	100.3	96.5	105.8	12 687	2 730	10.6	12.9
Washington, DC-MD-VA-WV PMSA	31 015	29 051	31 965	196 536	11.7	125.4	109.0	158.7	94.2	125.3	120.9	113.5	390 485	81 485	8.8	10.8
Waterloo-Cedar Falls, IA MSA	324	232	263	1 738	3.5	NA	NA	NA	NA	NA	NA	NA	17 131	4 102	14.1	17.6
Wausau, WI MSA	691	711	803	4 886	11.2	105.5	99.6	123.1	88.5	94.6	109.2	99.8	10 274	2 605	8.4	10.1
West Palm Beach-Boca Raton, FL MSA	9 971	10 285	11 645	66 473	14.4	107.7	101.9	108.9	117.6	105.6	110.0	107.4	118 376	25 301	12.3	18.3
Wheeling, WV-OH MSA	107	155	79	648	.9	NA	NA	NA	NA	NA	NA	NA	27 823	6 278	17.8	23.9
Wichita, KS MSA	2 895	2 712	3 038	17 893	8.8	NA	NA	NA	NA	NA	NA	NA	63 374	15 911	12.5	15.7
Wichita Falls, TX MSA	498	402	389	2 036	3.7	89.7	93.8	75.2	97.8	96.7	92.2	95.8	21 179	5 187	16.5	20.9
Williamsport, PA MSA	400	314	333	2 261	4.6	101.9	99.3	100.5	137.8	95.7	98.1	96.3	16 385	3 949	13.7	17.7
Wilmington, NC MSA	3 808	3 965	3 721	20 408	21.7	102.6	98.1	109.8	113.8	89.3	99.8	100.0	30 399	6 312	15.7	19.2
Yakima, WA MSA	719	623	904	5 175	7.3	106.8	102.0	122.4	91.3	100.1	127.1	97.8	48 617	13 829	23.0	30.2
York, PA MSA	2 132	1 976	2 447	15 819	11.7	96.8	94.4	89.4	109.4	106.2	93.0	99.2	29 707	6 478	8.2	10.1
Youngstown-Warren, OH MSA	1 604	1 551	1 567	10 720	4.4	96.3	96.8	98.2	107.0	89.0	91.9	94.7	94 917	25 173	15.6	22.7
Yuba City, CA MSA	398	495	611	5 759	12.7	NA	NA	NA	NA	NA	NA	NA	24 472	7 167	18.1	25.0
Yuma, AZ MSA	1 151	773	776	5 336	11.5	98.9	103.6	80.4	152.6	113.7	103.2	94.5	35 412	9 200	28.0	33.5

NA Not available.

[1]Beginning 1994, based on a 19,000 permit-issuing place universe; earlier years based on a 17,000 permit-issuing place universe.

[2]Data are subject to copyright; see below for source citation. The index measures relative price levels for consumer goods and services in participating areas for a midmanagement standard of living. The index does not measure inflation, but compares prices at a single point in time. The average for all participating areas, both metropolitan and nonmetropolitan, equals 100, and each index is read as a percentage of the average for all places.

Source: Building Permits—U.S. Bureau of the Census, "Construction–Building Permits" on diskette, annual (related Internet site <http://www.census.gov/const/www/C40/table3.html>), and "1990 Census of Population and Housing, Summary Tape File 1C" on CD-ROM; Cost of Living Index—ACCRA (American Chamber of Commerce Research Association), Alexandria, VA 22302-9950, "ACCRA Cost of Living Index, Third Quarter 1996" (copyright); Poverty—U.S. Bureau of the Census, "State and County Income and Poverty Estimates - 1993," Internet site <http://www.census.gov/ftp/pub/housing/saipe/est93ALL.dat> (accessed 16 January 1998).

Private Nonfarm Business Establishments and Personal Income

[MSA = Metropolitan statistical area.   CMSA = Consolidated MSA.   PMSA = Primary MSA.   NECMA = New England county metropolitan area.   All areas defined as of June 30, 1996.   Table includes 245 MSAs, 17 CMSAs, and 58 PMSAs not in New England; as well as 12 NECMAs.   Table excludes 10 MSAs, 1 CMSA, and 15 PMSAs in New England]

| Metropolitan areas | Private nonfarm business establishments | | Personal income 1994 | | | | | | | | | | | | | 1993 (mil dol) | 1990 (mil dol) |
	Total, 1995	Percent change, 1990–1995	Per capita Total (mil dol)	Percent change, 1990–1994	Per capita Dollars	Rank[2]	Transfer payments (mil dol)	Earnings Total (mil dol)	Goods-related Total[3]	Goods-related Manufacturing	Service-related Total[4]	Retail trade	FIRE[5]	Services	Government		
Abilene, TX MSA	3 528	6.4	2 264	21.0	18 572	177	432	1 637	14.7	6.9	84.1	11.1	3.9	28.3	23.8	2 158	1 871
Albany, GA MSA	2 846	5.9	2 032	27.2	17 371	225	413	1 669	D	21.1	D	9.7	3.3	24.0	22.0	1 885	1 597
Albany-Schenectady-Troy, NY MSA	20 259	.4	19 868	18.1	22 701	39	3 857	14 382	D	13.1	D	9.1	7.4	27.5	27.5	19 075	16 829
Albuquerque, NM MSA	16 817	13.9	12 839	33.4	19 890	120	2 165	9 641	18.4	10.8	81.5	10.9	5.4	20.8	20.8	11 845	9 626
Alexandria, LA MSA	2 997	4.8	2 252	22.5	17 801	208	685	1 451	15.9	9.1	83.2	10.1	4.3	32.3	24.5	2 082	1 838
Allentown-Bethlehem-Easton, PA MSA	14 490	1.9	13 353	18.8	21 826	62	2 291	8 800	D	28.8	D	9.9	5.9	27.1	10.3	12 816	11 236
Altoona, PA MSA	3 166	4.8	2 379	23.6	18 051	199	598	1 671	23.5	18.4	76.0	13.7	3.2	25.6	14.1	2 260	1 925
Amarillo, TX MSA	5 437	7.3	3 899	28.2	19 791	126	615	2 781	21.1	9.6	77.1	11.3	4.8	25.8	17.4	3 645	3 041
Anchorage, AK MSA	7 568	11.3	6 855	24.9	27 031	7	1 009	5 753	17.9	1.4	82.1	10.2	4.5	23.0	27.5	6 597	5 489
Anniston, AL MSA	2 540	10.5	1 899	20.5	16 247	253	469	1 398	24.1	20.4	74.8	10.1	2.4	15.1	36.1	1 829	1 576
Appleton-Oshkosh-Neenah, WI MSA	8 600	10.6	7 039	27.5	21 182	86	909	5 663	D	40.3	D	8.2	5.4	17.7	10.0	6 611	5 522
Asheville, NC MSA	5 937	11.0	4 023	25.7	19 768	127	725	2 847	28.4	22.2	70.0	11.4	3.9	27.9	14.8	3 833	3 199
Athens, GA MSA	3 401	12.8	2 421	26.8	18 148	196	353	1 881	D	17.6	D	10.2	3.5	19.4	30.9	2 251	1 910
Atlanta, GA MSA	97 502	18.2	78 720	29.3	23 633	27	8 132	65 240	D	12.7	D	9.4	8.5	28.3	12.1	73 325	60 882
Augusta-Aiken, GA-SC MSA	9 351	8.0	8 406	21.7	18 746	169	1 574	6 336	D	30.6	D	9.2	3.1	20.9	21.6	8 009	6 906
Austin-San Marcos, TX MSA	26 590	28.4	19 869	36.9	20 611	102	2 358	15 995	23.2	17.5	76.6	9.6	6.3	28.9	22.9	18 450	14 511
Bakersfield, CA MSA	10 469	-2.7	10 057	17.1	16 506	250	2 186	7 396	21.6	5.6	70.7	9.7	2.7	19.8	24.4	9 846	8 592
Bangor, ME NECMA	3 958	2.9	2 680	16.3	18 291	190	571	1 984	25.0	20.4	74.5	12.8	3.3	26.5	18.3	2 574	2 305
Barnstable-Yarmouth, MA NECMA	7 410	3.2	4 883	17.5	24 886	15	930	2 351	12.6	4.6	87.2	18.7	5.3	36.2	16.7	4 611	4 155
Baton Rouge, LA MSA	13 535	14.5	10 820	28.2	19 383	140	1 760	8 240	29.1	15.0	70.7	8.7	6.3	25.8	17.4	10 101	8 438
Beaumont-Port Arthur, TX MSA	8 174	5.8	7 060	23.0	18 937	161	1 440	5 036	36.3	26.6	63.6	9.9	2.8	25.8	12.7	6 699	5 742
Bellingham, WA MSA	4 993	22.8	2 790	29.4	19 191	145	460	1 929	30.6	18.4	68.5	13.7	3.7	23.7	13.4	2 630	2 157
Benton Harbor, MI MSA	3 973	4.8	3 207	24.3	19 832	124	618	2 219	43.4	38.7	55.6	9.1	3.9	20.4	10.9	3 008	2 579
Billings, MT MSA	4 479	14.3	2 520	32.1	20 524	105	405	1 869	15.3	7.1	83.4	13.1	5.8	30.9	12.9	2 391	1 907
Biloxi-Gulfport-Pascagoula, MS MSA	6 993	14.2	5 767	38.8	17 002	238	1 167	4 514	28.7	23.1	71.3	8.6	2.9	25.5	26.7	5 272	4 155
Binghamton, NY MSA	5 157	-5.0	5 099	9.9	19 469	137	1 119	3 624	D	30.7	D	9.0	4.0	23.5	9.9	5 017	4 639
Birmingham, AL MSA	22 015	8.5	18 503	24.9	21 217	85	3 021	14 327	D	12.8	D	9.0	8.2	27.2	14.2	17 457	14 812
Bismarck, ND MSA	2 823	11.0	1 701	27.2	19 312	141	292	1 241	13.7	7.0	83.8	11.3	5.1	29.3	20.4	1 611	1 337
Bloomington, IN MSA	2 815	10.4	2 002	26.0	17 595	215	259	1 603	27.2	20.1	72.8	11.5	4.1	20.8	28.7	1 894	1 589
Bloomington-Normal, IL MSA	3 410	12.6	3 002	27.2	21 815	63	349	2 510	20.8	16.1	76.9	8.0	26.0	20.2	12.4	2 748	2 360
Boise City, ID MSA	10 844	29.0	7 481	45.9	21 516	74	947	6 006	36.4	24.3	62.1	10.0	6.0	20.0	13.5	6 815	5 128
Boston-Worcester-Lawrence-Lowell-Brockton, MA-NH NECMA	153 154	2.4	149 517	16.4	26 093	10	23 350	112 114	23.0	19.0	76.8	8.9	9.1	34.4	11.8	141 685	128 494
Brownsville-Harlingen-San Benito, TX MSA	5 530	13.3	3 399	35.3	11 346	271	911	2 234	16.8	13.8	81.7	14.2	3.9	26.6	24.3	3 193	2 512
Bryan-College Station, TX MSA	2 945	21.4	1 985	30.5	15 224	260	261	1 582	14.2	7.5	85.3	11.8	4.3	21.8	40.6	1 866	1 522
Buffalo-Niagara Falls, NY MSA	27 678	.4	25 067	17.8	21 079	89	5 455	17 583	D	24.4	D	9.8	6.6	25.3	17.2	23 952	21 277
Burlington, VT NECMA	6 189	6.6	3 951	17.6	21 253	83	513	3 195	30.4	24.0	D	10.0	5.6	26.3	14.8	3 835	3 359
Canton-Massillon, OH MSA	9 923	7.9	7 835	20.0	19 471	136	1 544	5 180	42.4	35.4	57.1	10.6	3.9	21.8	10.3	7 403	6 530
Casper, WY MSA	2 545	10.9	1 458	22.3	22 819	37	208	972	32.7	5.7	66.7	10.9	4.0	22.8	14.8	1 405	1 193
Cedar Rapids, IA MSA	5 081	13.4	3 992	25.1	22 579	43	500	3 302	35.8	28.9	63.5	9.1	5.9	24.4	9.5	3 714	3 192
Champaign-Urbana, IL MSA	4 010	6.7	3 222	13.7	19 235	144	435	2 554	19.0	14.1	78.2	9.3	4.1	24.0	32.5	3 075	2 835
Charleston-North Charleston, SC MSA	12 307	6.8	9 191	17.2	17 598	214	1 734	6 838	17.7	11.3	81.7	11.6	3.9	23.8	31.7	8 912	7 844
Charleston, WV MSA	6 778	8.8	5 427	25.9	21 300	82	1 203	3 962	23.0	13.1	76.9	9.4	5.5	28.9	15.4	5 136	4 310
Charlotte-Gastonia-Rock Hill, NC-SC MSA	36 242	10.5	27 659	27.3	21 943	57	3 350	23 235	D	22.3	D	9.2	8.9	21.2	10.1	25 773	21 727
Charlottesville, VA MSA	4 205	10.0	3 265	28.8	23 204	30	389	2 234	D	12.2	D	10.0	6.8	23.7	32.3	3 105	2 535
Chattanooga, TN-GA MSA	10 865	6.2	8 735	24.1	19 890	120	1 529	6 504	27.7	22.4	71.9	11.1	7.3	24.2	18.1	8 230	7 039
Cheyenne, WY MSA	2 111	13.6	1 631	26.3	20 913	92	287	1 113	11.9	5.0	87.2	10.1	8.6	16.2	38.1	1 560	1 292
Chicago-Gary-Kenosha, IL-IN-WI CMSA	214 772	8.3	215 361	20.6	25 257	12	29 606	164 233	D	20.1	D	8.4	9.7	D	11.5	205 074	178 641
Chicago, IL PMSA	196 733	8.1	198 329	20.5	25 865	X	26 636	153 023	D	19.2	D	8.3	10.1	D	11.5	188 945	164 535
Gary, IN PMSA	12 922	10.9	12 414	19.7	20 029	X	2 116	8 521	41.6	32.3	58.2	9.2	3.2	22.1	11.0	11 764	10 373
Kankakee, IL PMSA	2 240	11.7	1 918	22.2	18 937	X	397	1 247	D	24.4	D	11.0	3.9	22.6	13.9	1 807	1 570
Kenosha, WI PMSA	2 877	13.4	2 699	24.8	19 588	X	456	1 442	38.4	31.5	61.1	11.8	3.3	20.4	15.4	2 557	2 163
Chico-Paradise, CA MSA	4 503	-2.4	3 299	19.7	17 157	232	876	1 901	15.4	8.0	82.0	14.0	5.1	32.1	19.5	3 161	2 757
Cincinnati-Hamilton, OH-KY-IN CMSA	45 228	7.9	41 447	22.4	21 881	60	6 719	29 938	D	24.8	D	10.1	6.6	D	12.0	39 188	33 873
Cincinnati, OH-KY-IN PMSA	39 395	7.6	35 266	22.0	22 301	X	5 699	26 618	D	24.4	D	10.0	6.9	D	11.7	33 356	28 911
Hamilton-Middletown, OH PMSA	5 833	9.9	6 181	24.6	19 761	X	1 021	3 320	35.7	28.4	63.9	11.2	4.5	19.8	14.8	5 832	4 962
Clarksville-Hopkinsville, TN-KY MSA	3 479	14.9	2 780	35.0	14 947	264	508	2 146	21.5	17.0	76.5	9.8	2.3	13.3	45.7	2 635	2 060

D Withheld to avoid disclosure.
X Not applicable.

[1]Based on resident population estimated as of July 1, 1994.
[2]Based on 273 metropolitan areas (245 MSAs, 17 CMSAs, and 11 NECMAs); see text for more information.   When metropolitan areas share the same rank, the next lower rank is omitted.
[3]Includes mining and construction, not shown separately.
[4]Includes agricultural services, forestry, and fisheries; transportation and public utilities; and wholesale trade, not shown separately.
[5]Finance, insurance, and real estate.

Source: Private Nonfarm Business Establishments—U.S. Bureau of the Census, "County Business Patterns" on diskette, annual (related Internet site <http://www.census.gov/epcd/cbp/view/cbpview.html>);   Personal Income—U.S. Bureau of Economic Analysis, "Regional Economic Information System (REIS) 1969-1994" on CD-ROM (related Internet site <http://www.bea.doc.gov/bea/dr1.htm>).

[MSA = Metropolitan statistical area. CMSA = Consolidated MSA. PMSA = Primary MSA. NECMA = New England county metropolitan area. All areas defined as of June 30, 1996. Table includes 245 MSAs, 17 CMSAs, and 58 PMSAs not in New England; as well as 12 NECMAs. Table excludes 10 MSAs, 1 CMSA, and 15 PMSAs in New England]

Metropolitan areas	Private nonfarm business establishments		Personal income														
			1994														
					Per capita[1]			Earnings									
												Percent, by selected industries–					
										Goods-related		Service-related					
	Total, 1995	Percent change, 1990–1995	Total (mil dol)	Percent change, 1990–1994	Dollars	Rank[2]	Transfer pay-ments (mil dol)	Total (mil dol)	Total[3]	Man-ufac-turing	Total[4]	Retail trade	FIRE[5]	Serv-ices	Gov-ern-ment	1993 (mil dol)	1990 (mil dol)
Cleveland-Akron, OH CMSA	74 265	6.3	66 444	19.7	22 921	36	11 962	48 888	32.7	27.9	67.0	8.2	6.3	27.6	12.1	62 709	55 519
Akron, OH PMSA..................	16 730	8.2	14 221	22.0	21 013	X	2 547	9 771	33.9	28.6	66.0	9.9	4.2	24.8	13.5	13 363	11 658
Cleveland-Lorain-Elyria, OH PMSA ..	57 535	5.7	52 222	19.1	23 502	X	9 415	39 117	32.4	27.7	67.3	7.7	6.8	28.3	11.7	49 346	43 861
Colorado Springs, CO MSA	11 826	23.5	8 873	33.5	19 613	128	1 511	6 533	19.3	13.4	80.6	9.9	5.0	28.5	27.8	8 208	6 644
Columbia, MO MSA	3 478	17.8	2 412	31.5	19 849	122	309	1 911	14.8	8.9	85.0	10.1	8.3	23.2	35.1	2 245	1 834
Columbia, SC MSA	12 917	10.8	9 718	23.0	19 979	117	1 594	7 681	17.5	12.2	82.0	8.6	23.1	27.1		9 182	7 898
Columbus, GA-AL MSA	5 532	3.6	4 708	23.4	17 177	231	988	3 359	D	D	D	9.8	7.9	21.4	28.5	4 503	3 814
Columbus, OH MSA	35 232	10.0	31 386	27.3	22 060	55	4 868	24 917	21.5	16.3	78.0	12.2	10.0	26.3	11.1	29 405	24 664
Corpus Christi, TX MSA	8 892	9.3	6 518	26.9	17 350	226	1 279	4 806	26.5	15.9	72.4	10.3	3.8	26.0	21.9	6 195	5 137
Cumberland, MD-WV MSA	2 367	.9	1 673	13.9	16 548	248	488	1 013	29.9	23.9	D	12.3	3.4	24.6	17.8	1 606	1 468
Dallas-Fort Worth, TX CMSA..........	116 786	12.1	102 300	26.9	23 449	29	11 203	84 162	24.2	17.0	75.7	9.7	8.0	28.4	10.2	96 436	80 619
Dallas, TX PMSA..................	82 410	12.9	70 946	28.8	24 479	X	7 217	62 013	23.4	15.9	76.5	9.0	9.2	29.7	9.6	66 679	55 091
Fort Worth-Arlington, TX PMSA	34 376	10.4	31 354	22.8	21 412	X	3 986	22 150	26.5	19.9	73.3	11.5	4.6	24.5	11.9	29 757	25 527
Danville, VA MSA	2 355	4.9	1 838	16.7	16 713	244	350	1 199	46.7	41.3	52.0	10.7	2.9	18.3	12.5	1 784	1 575
Davenport-Moline-Rock Island, IA-IL MSA	9 118	5.9	7 458	17.7	20 843	95	1 272	5 585	D	24.7	D	10.7	5.0	22.2	15.2	7 058	6 334
Dayton-Springfield, OH MSA	21 497	3.8	20 434	20.9	21 366	78	3 922	15 407	34.3	29.8	65.0	9.0	3.9	24.8	17.4	19 317	16 900
Daytona Beach, FL MSA	10 958	7.9	7 749	22.8	17 595	215	1 912	3 709	18.4	11.8	80.0	15.9	5.9	32.4	17.3	7 275	6 313
Decatur, AL MSA	3 086	11.9	2 572	26.3	18 558	179	457	1 681	D	40.0	D	10.4	3.3	14.5	13.3	2 430	2 037
Decatur, IL MSA	2 835	2.5	2 430	15.1	20 842	96	440	1 897	38.9	31.2	59.0	9.2	4.2	19.5	8.5	2 336	2 110
Denver-Boulder-Greeley, CO CMSA	70 984	20.1	53 390	30.5	24 379	20	6 180	42 213	21.0	13.1	78.5	9.2	8.1	29.2	14.5	50 477	40 913
Boulder-Longmont, CO PMSA	9 588	31.0	6 406	34.1	25 664	X	549	4 902	30.5	25.7	69.3	9.4	4.0	32.6	15.1	6 032	4 776
Denver, CO PMSA	58 068	18.3	44 425	30.0	24 731	X	5 240	35 477	19.1	11.0	80.8	9.3	8.8	29.2	14.4	41 995	34 181
Greeley, CO PMSA	3 328	21.8	2 559	30.8	17 758	X	391	1 834	31.9	20.4	59.7	8.2	4.8	19.3	13.8	2 450	1 956
Des Moines, IA MSA	12 450	10.1	9 863	26.8	23 680	26	1 248	8 177	D	12.5	D	10.3	16.8	25.0	13.2	9 240	7 777
Detroit-Ann Arbor-Flint, MI CMSA	122 795	6.2	128 545	22.7	24 459	18	19 949	96 787	D	34.0	D	8.2	5.3	24.6	11.6	118 481	104 758
Ann Arbor, MI PMSA...............	12 887	13.9	13 153	30.7	25 525	X	1 355	9 070	35.9	31.6	63.9	8.0	3.6	22.0	23.4	11 982	10 064
Detroit, MI PMSA	100 841	5.2	106 351	21.6	24 692	X	16 825	80 617	D	33.0	D	8.2	5.7	25.3	10.3	98 222	87 449
Flint, MI PMSA	9 067	7.0	9 041	24.8	20 866	X	1 768	7 099	51.0	47.6	48.9	8.2	2.9	19.2	11.2	8 276	7 245
Dothan, AL MSA	3 481	11.6	2 311	20.5	17 182	230	454	1 758	25.6	21.0	72.2	11.5	3.1	22.9	20.4	2 220	1 919
Dover, DE MSA	2 729	5.4	2 064	26.9	17 201	229	401	1 517	20.4	14.4	78.6	13.3	3.0	18.8	36.7	1 962	1 626
Dubuque, IA MSA	2 567	8.9	1 755	22.9	19 895	119	276	1 446	D	34.4	D	9.8	3.4	26.1	7.1	1 636	1 427
Duluth-Superior, MN-WI MSA	6 417	8.6	4 427	20.1	18 377	185	1 043	3 035	24.3	10.8	75.6	11.6	3.2	24.7	21.2	4 213	3 686
Eau Claire, WI MSA	3 733	10.4	2 554	22.6	18 001	200	474	1 805	24.8	18.9	73.3	16.0	3.5	23.1	17.7	2 413	2 084
El Paso, TX MSA	11 963	7.9	8 603	25.4	12 941	270	1 926	6 494	21.0	16.7	78.9	11.5	3.7	21.6	27.7	8 195	6 863
Elkhart-Goshen, IN MSA	4 993	7.7	3 410	28.7	20 795	99	403	3 435	63.0	58.5	36.8	6.6	2.5	12.9	5.3	3 134	2 651
Elmira, NY MSA	1 972	-2.5	1 785	17.7	18 891	162	443	1 171	30.0	25.3	69.4	11.1	4.2	24.3	19.0	1 703	1 517
Enid, OK MSA	1 694	6.7	1 053	16.0	18 506	182	241	692	17.9	6.8	76.8	12.7	4.2	23.4	19.1	1 014	908
Erie, PA MSA	6 508	2.9	5 397	20.5	19 254	143	1 072	3 937	39.9	35.0	60.0	10.2	5.1	23.9	11.6	5 194	4 478
Eugene-Springfield, OR MSA	9 170	11.2	5 731	26.8	19 167	147	1 032	3 934	25.5	18.6	72.5	13.1	4.5	26.0	17.0	5 361	4 519
Evansville-Henderson, IN-KY MSA	7 730	5.0	5 984	22.1	20 888	94	998	4 467	38.8	28.7	60.6	10.0	4.4	24.4	9.0	5 686	4 900
Fargo-Moorhead, ND-MN MSA........	5 157	15.3	3 152	26.7	19 496	135	489	2 418	D	8.3	D	10.7	7.4	27.5	15.9	2 915	2 487
Fayetteville, NC MSA	5 247	10.2	4 807	35.1	16 784	243	906	3 944	15.2	11.7	84.2	10.0	2.6	13.2	52.5	4 662	3 559
Fayetteville-Springdale-Rogers, AR MSA	6 774	33.5	4 609	40.0	19 008	155	704	3 652	31.2	25.5	64.2	17.5	3.7	16.6	12.1	4 218	3 293
Flagstaff, AZ-UT MSA................	3 543	47.4	1 809	37.1	15 858	254	313	1 275	D	7.8	D	15.8	2.3	27.6	31.5	1 677	1 320
Florence, AL MSA	3 437	11.8	2 358	23.2	17 380	224	471	1 586	34.4	28.2	64.0	11.1	3.4	17.7	22.1	2 220	1 915
Florence, SC MSA	3 132	5.6	2 136	25.9	17 625	213	464	1 646	31.2	25.0	67.7	12.4	5.2	22.4	17.3	2 028	1 696
Fort Collins-Loveland, CO MSA	6 765	28.5	4 284	35.6	20 169	109	517	2 889	32.8	24.1	66.7	12.7	3.7	22.4	21.1	3 982	3 158
Fort Myers-Cape Coral, FL MSA.......	10 785	5.4	8 103	23.5	22 056	56	1 566	4 171	14.9	4.3	83.5	15.3	7.2	34.9	15.3	7 629	6 563
Fort Pierce-Port St. Lucie, FL MSA	7 311	7.3	6 280	21.3	22 565	44	1 139	2 778	14.3	6.3	79.9	13.0	6.8	30.2	13.9	5 954	5 177
Fort Smith, AR-OK MSA	4 836	10.3	3 142	27.2	16 963	239	626	2 562	36.8	30.5	62.1	10.0	3.3	25.8	10.1	2 925	2 471
Fort Walton Beach, FL MSA	4 446	18.0	3 049	30.7	18 960	160	713	2 071	10.5	5.7	89.5	12.1	4.7	26.2	41.6	2 915	2 333
Fort Wayne, IN MSA	12 344	7.7	10 005	22.2	21 333	80	1 348	7 899	D	35.5	D	8.9	6.4	20.7	8.9	9 415	8 184
Fresno, CA MSA	16 840	2.3	14 276	17.5	17 105	236	3 232	9 934	16.5	9.8	74.8	10.8	5.0	23.1	19.3	14 012	12 146
Gadsden, AL MSA...................	2 133	9.5	1 708	23.2	17 008	237	394	1 099	D	33.5	D	11.2	3.6	24.0	12.1	1 607	1 386
Gainesville, FL MSA	5 071	7.9	3 747	27.9	19 407	139	694	2 854	D	6.2	D	10.7	4.9	31.4	35.5	3 529	2 931
Glens Falls, NY MSA	3 167	-4.4	2 225	17.2	18 226	192	489	1 488	29.5	22.6	69.5	12.0	4.1	26.9	14.8	2 127	1 898
Goldsboro, NC MSA	2 205	4.6	1 724	25.0	15 770	258	354	1 259	21.0	15.6	69.9	9.6	2.9	17.8	29.7	1 650	1 379
Grand Forks, ND-MN MSA	2 619	4.9	1 821	19.4	17 579	217	334	1 340	D	6.5	D	10.9	3.4	21.5	32.7	1 689	1 525

X Not applicable.
D Withheld to avoid disclosure.

[1]Based on resident population estimated as of July 1, 1994.
[2]Based on 273 metropolitan areas (245 MSAs, 17 CMSAs, and 11 NECMAs); see text for more information. When metropolitan areas share the same rank, the next lower rank is omitted.
[3]Includes mining and construction, not shown separately.
[4]Includes agricultural services, forestry, and fisheries; transportation and public utilities; and wholesale trade, not shown separately.
[5]Finance, insurance, and real estate.

Source: Private Nonfarm Business Establishments—U.S. Bureau of the Census, "County Business Patterns" on diskette, annual (related Internet site <http://www.census.gov/epcd/cbp/view/cbpview.html>);   Personal Income—U.S. Bureau of Economic Analysis, "Regional Economic Information System (REIS) 1969-1994" on CD-ROM (related Internet site <http://www.bea.doc.gov/bea/dr1.htm>).

[MSA = Metropolitan statistical area.   CMSA = Consolidated MSA.   PMSA = Primary MSA.   NECMA = New England county metropolitan area.   All areas defined as of June 30, 1996.   Table includes 245 MSAs, 17 CMSAs, and 58 PMSAs not in New England; as well as 12 NECMAs.   Table excludes 10 MSAs, 1 CMSA, and 15 PMSAs in New England]

Metropolitan areas	Private nonfarm business establishments		Personal income														
			1994														
			Per capita[1]				Transfer pay-ments (mil dol)	Earnings								
										Percent, by selected industries—						
									Goods-related		Service-related					
	Total, 1995	Percent change, 1990–1995	Total (mil dol)	Percent change, 1990–1994	Dollars	Rank[2]		Total (mil dol)	Total[3]	Man-ufac-turing	Total[4]	Retail trade	FIRE[5]	Serv-ices	Gov-ern-ment	1993 (mil dol)	1990 (mil dol)
Grand Junction, CO MSA	3 113	23.5	1 885	32.3	18 193	195	362	1 230	20.8	8.3	78.5	14.6	4.0	29.1	17.0	1 771	1 425
Grand Rapids-Muskegon-Holland, MI MSA	25 198	11.9	21 338	30.8	21 665	69	2 901	16 589	D	35.7	D	9.5	4.5	21.2	9.8	19 556	16 308
Great Falls, MT MSA	2 460	5.5	1 533	23.5	18 879	164	320	1 020	8.8	3.4	89.7	14.3	6.4	29.4	26.7	1 490	1 241
Green Bay, WI MSA	5 671	12.9	4 526	28.5	21 835	61	565	3 857	33.2	26.4	66.5	10.1	6.5	22.7	10.2	4 248	3 522
Greensboro--Winston Salem--High Point, NC MSA	30 358	7.2	24 121	24.0	21 786	67	3 185	18 541	D	31.0	D	10.2	D	22.6	9.6	22 720	19 457
Greenville, NC MSA	2 818	16.6	2 156	29.0	18 542	180	343	1 614	27.7	21.7	67.5	10.8	3.3	16.2	30.2	2 022	1 671
Greenville-Spartanburg-Anderson, SC MSA	22 635	12.6	16 279	23.3	18 673	170	2 537	12 839	D	33.9	D	11.6	4.0	19.5	11.8	15 276	13 202
Harrisburg-Lebanon-Carlisle, PA MSA	14 724	5.4	13 590	21.4	22 289	52	2 215	10 965	D	16.6	D	9.2	7.2	22.7	22.7	12 935	11 190
Hartford, CT NECMA	29 660	–2.8	29 988	10.7	26 842	9	4 552	24 451	23.4	19.0	76.1	8.4	16.7	25.8	14.3	29 138	27 085
Hattiesburg, MS MSA	2 667	12.8	1 641	30.3	18 425	255	351	1 156	19.6	12.8	79.3	13.4	5.1	24.6	24.1	1 514	1 260
Hickory-Morganton-Lenoir, NC MSA	7 516	5.0	5 862	25.7	19 175	146	857	4 711	D	48.4	D	9.5	1.8	13.8	10.9	5 494	4 663
Honolulu, HI MSA	21 004	–.8	22 145	20.0	25 329	11	3 190	17 166	12.3	4.5	87.4	12.8	7.4	27.6	26.6	21 549	18 448
Houma, LA MSA	4 140	7.6	2 834	24.5	15 132	261	631	1 813	28.8	9.6	70.6	11.0	3.4	22.8	15.7	2 624	2 276
Houston-Galveston-Brazoria, TX CMSA	97 987	11.6	92 840	27.1	22 651	40	10 292	76 151	D	14.8	D	7.9	6.0	28.3	11.0	88 264	73 025
Brazoria, TX PMSA	3 520	9.3	3 945	21.6	18 650	X	506	2 616	54.3	37.7	44.9	7.9	2.1	13.8	13.4	3 719	3 243
Galveston-Texas City, TX PMSA	4 541	6.7	4 719	24.6	20 106	X	760	2 749	26.5	19.2	73.5	9.8	6.0	18.3	28.9	4 478	3 787
Houston, TX PMSA	89 926	12.0	84 176	27.6	23 046	X	9 026	70 787	D	13.7	D	7.8	6.1	29.2	10.3	80 067	65 995
Huntington-Ashland, WV-KY-OH MSA	6 696	4.8	5 357	22.6	16 921	240	1 355	3 561	D	24.0	D	10.1	3.3	23.2	15.6	5 087	4 369
Huntsville, AL MSA	7 524	15.4	6 682	24.6	21 139	88	1 031	6 157	30.6	27.5	68.8	7.0	2.3	26.1	27.3	6 407	5 361
Indianapolis, IN MSA	39 498	12.7	33 865	27.1	23 168	31	4 574	26 960	D	22.1	D	9.6	9.0	24.2	13.6	31 817	26 638
Iowa City, IA MSA	2 413	16.2	2 155	30.4	21 546	72	186	1 766	D	8.7	D	8.4	3.0	19.2	47.8	1 986	1 652
Jackson, MI MSA	3 294	8.9	2 847	21.7	18 573	176	529	1 838	31.9	26.8	67.7	10.3	3.3	20.0	17.6	2 660	2 340
Jackson, MS MSA	10 452	5.0	7 882	29.5	19 135	150	1 224	6 158	16.8	10.9	82.7	10.6	9.3	26.6	19.6	7 281	6 086
Jackson, TN MSA	2 755	13.0	1 763	31.9	18 343	187	320	1 496	34.5	26.4	64.5	11.3	2.9	23.4	16.7	1 624	1 336
Jacksonville, FL MSA	26 135	9.1	20 348	23.7	20 936	91	3 433	15 038	D	8.7	D	10.3	12.6	27.5	18.8	19 284	16 443
Jacksonville, NC MSA	2 395	10.9	1 982	29.7	13 550	269	348	1 649	6.1	2.7	92.2	9.0	1.7	8.5	69.1	1 908	1 529
Jamestown, NY MSA	3 115	–5.9	2 477	17.9	17 419	223	625	1 630	35.0	30.4	63.7	10.8	2.7	20.7	19.4	2 387	2 100
Janesville-Beloit, WI MSA	3 214	5.7	2 991	26.5	20 483	106	472	2 123	47.3	41.7	51.1	10.1	2.7	17.5	11.3	2 784	2 365
Johnson City-Kingsport-Bristol, TN-VA MSA	9 874	10.9	7 778	21.1	17 261	228	1 542	5 524	D	34.3	D	10.7	3.0	22.5	13.5	7 450	6 421
Johnstown, PA MSA	5 465	3.0	4 187	17.6	17 466	222	1 243	2 493	24.3	15.7	74.7	13.7	5.3	27.1	15.0	3 997	3 560
Jonesboro, AR MSA	2 126	17.6	1 209	29.5	16 472	251	227	958	27.9	22.5	68.2	11.5	3.7	26.3	14.8	1 137	934
Joplin, MO MSA	3 973	10.0	2 525	29.5	17 806	206	501	1 870	33.7	28.6	65.1	11.5	2.7	20.8	9.4	2 350	1 950
Kalamazoo-Battle Creek, MI MSA	10 320	7.8	9 165	24.3	20 706	101	1 572	6 869	D	34.1	D	8.7	D	21.8	15.0	8 640	7 374
Kansas City, MO-KS MSA	45 161	8.5	37 296	22.8	22 642	41	5 157	28 864	D	15.3	D	9.3	8.6	26.9	14.9	35 103	30 369
Killeen-Temple, TX MSA	4 440	13.2	4 467	35.4	15 552	259	843	3 516	D	9.1	D	8.0	2.6	16.8	52.9	4 137	3 298
Knoxville, TN MSA	17 661	11.3	12 600	29.9	19 963	118	2 049	9 478	D	19.1	D	D	4.1	D	15.4	11 835	9 699
Kokomo, IN MSA	2 268	5.7	2 166	26.6	21 814	64	329	2 065	64.2	61.7	34.4	7.3	2.2	11.6	8.4	2 021	1 711
La Crosse, WI-MN MSA	3 289	7.2	2 412	23.1	20 084	113	386	1 822	D	20.3	D	11.1	4.1	27.6	13.7	2 276	1 959
Lafayette, LA MSA	8 906	12.5	5 982	27.2	16 551	247	1 297	4 143	30.4	12.0	69.0	10.6	3.8	27.3	13.3	5 516	4 704
Lafayette, IN MSA	3 719	8.6	3 165	26.9	18 988	157	422	2 555	37.6	32.4	61.0	8.9	4.7	18.3	22.9	2 959	2 494
Lake Charles, LA MSA	4 079	10.1	3 108	29.0	17 933	201	642	2 341	39.9	26.7	60.1	8.8	3.1	23.4	12.5	2 874	2 409
Lakeland-Winter Haven, FL MSA	9 243	2.1	7 661	23.0	17 833	205	1 578	5 019	22.5	13.8	74.4	14.9	5.0	26.4	13.1	7 114	6 229
Lancaster, PA MSA	10 568	4.4	9 656	20.2	21 811	65	1 261	6 773	40.9	31.9	57.0	10.7	4.5	20.7	8.4	9 241	8 035
Lansing-East Lansing, MI MSA	10 061	8.1	9 048	23.6	20 747	100	1 279	7 235	27.8	23.2	71.9	8.7	5.6	22.2	27.3	8 377	7 321
Laredo, TX MSA	3 755	30.3	1 841	52.4	11 287	272	410	1 436	13.4	2.4	86.6	17.4	4.3	19.4	22.8	1 685	1 208
Las Cruces, NM MSA	3 071	19.3	2 130	27.0	13 696	268	477	1 349	10.2	4.6	82.0	11.3	3.7	19.8	38.3	2 013	1 676
Las Vegas, NV-AZ MSA	24 651	28.7	24 043	46.3	22 338	51	3 628	18 020	13.5	3.4	86.5	9.9	4.8	49.6	12.3	21 546	16 433
Lawrence, KS MSA	2 334	24.5	1 478	25.7	16 791	242	193	1 016	22.9	16.3	76.6	12.6	4.5	21.8	28.6	1 392	1 175
Lawton, OK MSA	2 097	7.4	1 774	20.9	15 088	263	418	1 332	14.6	11.2	85.1	9.3	3.0	14.7	52.3	1 741	1 468
Lewiston-Auburn, ME NECMA	2 659	–4.0	1 975	14.2	19 009	154	432	1 228	27.0	21.6	D	12.4	4.8	32.3	10.9	1 885	1 729
Lexington, KY MSA	11 453	5.1	8 688	22.9	20 162	110	1 192	7 136	D	22.0	D	10.6	D	23.4	17.9	8 263	7 070
Lima, OH MSA	3 840	3.0	2 939	18.8	18 865	165	595	2 299	45.2	39.6	53.6	9.6	2.4	19.8	12.0	2 764	2 475
Lincoln, NE MSA	6 403	13.9	4 779	29.3	21 174	87	600	3 781	21.0	15.3	78.4	9.2	7.4	24.5	23.6	4 491	3 696
Little Rock-North Little Rock, AR MSA	15 122	11.0	10 743	26.8	19 988	116	1 820	8 638	18.0	12.6	81.4	10.2	7.4	26.3	20.5	10 164	8 475
Longview-Marshall, TX MSA	5 446	7.7	3 694	22.6	18 340	188	755	2 511	35.9	24.9	63.8	12.3	3.4	23.5	11.5	3 488	3 012

D Withheld to avoid disclosure.
X Not applicable.

[1]Based on resident population estimated as of July 1, 1994.
[2]Based on 273 metropolitan areas (245 MSAs, 17 CMSAs, and 11 NECMAs); see text for more information.   When metropolitan areas share the same rank, the next lower rank is omitted.
[3]Includes mining and construction, not shown separately.
[4]Includes agricultural services, forestry, and fisheries; transportation and public utilities; and wholesale trade, not shown separately.
[5]Finance, insurance, and real estate.

Source: Private Nonfarm Business Establishments—U.S. Bureau of the Census, "County Business Patterns" on diskette, annual (related Internet site <http://www.census.gov/epcd/cbp/view/cbpview.html>);   Personal Income—U.S. Bureau of Economic Analysis, "Regional Economic Information System (REIS) 1969-1994" on CD-ROM (related Internet site <http://www.bea.doc.gov/bea/dr1.htm>).

Table B–7. Metro Areas — Private Nonfarm Business Establishments and Personal Income—Con.

[MSA = Metropolitan statistical area.   CMSA = Consolidated MSA.   PMSA = Primary MSA.   NECMA = New England county metropolitan area.   All areas defined as of June 30, 1996.   Table includes 245 MSAs, 17 CMSAs, and 58 PMSAs not in New England; as well as 12 NECMAs.   Table excludes 10 MSAs, 1 CMSA, and 15 PMSAs in New England]

Metropolitan areas	Private nonfarm business establishments		Personal income														
			1994														
					Per capita[1]			Earnings									
									Percent, by selected industries–								
									Goods-related		Service-related						
	Total, 1995	Percent change, 1990–1995	Total (mil dol)	Percent change, 1990–1994	Dollars	Rank[2]	Transfer payments (mil dol)	Total (mil dol)	Total[3]	Manufacturing	Total[4]	Retail trade	FIRE[5]	Services	Government	1993 (mil dol)	1990 (mil dol)
Los Angeles-Riverside-Orange, CA CMSA	347 903	−1.6	329 646	9.3	21 542	73	53 640	249 127	21.6	16.4	78.0	9.6	7.3	34.3	13.3	324 298	301 614
Los Angeles-Long Beach, CA PMSA	214 320	−2.4	197 289	7.1	21 562	X	34 058	164 046	20.8	16.7	79.1	8.7	7.4	36.8	12.6	196 416	184 246
Orange, CA PMSA	70 783	−.7	64 893	10.5	25 516	X	7 556	47 921	24.9	19.0	74.8	10.6	9.2	31.3	10.2	62 849	58 721
Riverside-San Bernardino, CA PMSA	47 454	.1	51 565	15.9	17 741	X	9 835	27 547	20.8	11.8	77.7	13.3	4.1	26.5	21.4	49 552	44 485
Ventura, CA PMSA	15 346	.8	15 899	12.3	22 626	X	2 191	9 612	20.4	12.9	75.8	10.3	5.7	29.4	17.7	15 482	14 162
Louisville, KY-IN MSA	25 569	10.9	21 658	25.2	22 080	54	3 359	16 098	D	23.0	D	10.0	7.0	25.6	12.2	20 481	17 294
Lubbock, TX MSA	6 351	8.7	4 295	22.0	18 635	171	714	3 247	13.9	8.6	83.8	14.8	4.5	28.5	20.6	4 075	3 521
Lynchburg, VA MSA	5 103	9.2	3 819	20.2	18 824	168	618	2 669	D	35.3	D	10.0	5.8	20.8	11.3	3 629	3 178
Macon, GA MSA	7 054	5.3	5 718	21.1	18 600	174	1 141	4 252	D	D	D	9.9	6.1	21.7	27.1	5 410	4 721
Madison, WI MSA	11 413	14.7	9 537	30.4	24 435	19	1 043	7 711	19.4	13.3	80.2	9.1	9.3	23.1	27.3	8 968	7 311
Mansfield, OH MSA	4 083	6.3	3 141	16.8	17 889	203	649	2 263	D	37.2	D	10.5	4.0	18.7	12.3	2 976	2 690
McAllen-Edinburg-Mission, TX MSA	7 231	16.3	4 770	36.8	10 347	273	1 263	3 130	15.3	9.3	83.3	16.3	3.7	23.5	26.4	4 441	3 487
Medford-Ashland, OR MSA	4 738	12.7	3 067	30.8	18 888	163	610	1 965	27.8	20.1	71.6	15.9	4.4	24.7	15.0	2 848	2 345
Melbourne-Titusville-Palm Bay, FL MSA	10 739	10.2	8 678	22.2	19 567	132	1 816	5 675	28.5	23.0	71.4	10.1	3.3	35.5	16.2	8 306	7 104
Memphis, TN-AR-MS MSA	24 143	4.7	22 774	26.5	21 564	71	3 965	17 820	19.2	14.1	80.3	10.1	6.8	25.3	15.7	21 243	18 001
Merced, CA MSA	2 851	.9	2 974	15.9	15 106	262	780	1 895	21.6	16.6	65.5	10.6	3.6	15.5	23.6	2 906	2 566
Miami-Fort Lauderdale, FL CMSA	112 116	11.5	74 698	19.7	21 918	59	13 127	49 856	12.8	8.0	86.8	11.5	9.1	33.9	14.6	70 760	62 388
Fort Lauderdale, FL PMSA	46 105	15.5	34 168	21.5	24 706	X	5 428	18 746	14.9	8.7	85.0	13.3	9.2	34.3	13.8	32 207	28 114
Miami, FL PMSA	66 011	8.8	40 530	18.3	20 015	X	7 700	31 110	11.6	7.6	87.9	10.5	9.0	33.7	15.1	38 553	34 274
Milwaukee-Racine, WI CMSA	42 797	5.7	38 849	22.0	23 729	24	6 208	28 915	33.9	28.8	65.9	8.2	7.7	25.7	11.3	36 884	31 851
Milwaukee-Waukesha, WI PMSA	38 656	6.2	34 858	22.0	23 949	X	5 585	26 340	32.4	27.3	67.5	8.2	8.2	26.3	11.4	33 108	28 581
Racine, WI PMSA	4 141	1.4	3 991	22.0	21 965	X	623	2 575	49.1	43.9	50.0	8.5	2.6	20.3	11.1	3 776	3 270
Minneapolis-St. Paul, MN-WI MSA	75 083	13.8	67 831	24.3	25 231	13	8 073	54 833	D	22.5	D	9.1	9.3	25.6	12.4	63 873	54 579
Mobile, AL MSA	12 507	13.3	8 783	30.0	17 148	233	1 747	6 032	25.6	17.7	73.2	11.6	4.7	26.7	16.2	8 312	6 758
Modesto, CA MSA	7 693	−.5	7 055	16.5	17 342	227	1 504	4 502	29.2	20.5	65.8	11.8	3.5	22.9	15.1	6 869	6 054
Monroe, LA MSA	3 910	8.1	2 419	24.6	16 520	249	526	1 798	23.1	18.3	76.2	11.3	7.3	27.4	15.8	2 274	1 941
Montgomery, AL MSA	7 663	11.1	6 117	26.4	19 607	129	1 144	4 569	18.5	12.4	80.7	10.0	6.8	24.2	28.5	5 750	4 838
Muncie, IN MSA	2 753	6.0	2 300	22.1	19 292	142	411	1 717	D	29.8	D	9.6	3.0	23.1	16.3	2 175	1 883
Myrtle Beach, SC MSA	6 271	18.8	2 722	23.7	17 804	207	511	1 876	16.5	9.8	82.9	22.8	7.2	32.2	12.9	2 517	2 200
Naples, FL MSA	6 939	17.4	5 453	29.5	30 910	2	632	2 433	14.7	3.4	80.5	14.9	9.2	36.4	9.8	5 119	4 209
Nashville, TN MSA	30 715	14.7	24 643	35.9	23 037	33	3 039	20 030	D	18.4	D	10.8	6.9	31.6	11.4	22 692	18 127
New London-Norwich, CT NECMA	5 811	−.6	6 009	17.1	24 075	23	972	4 602	30.7	26.5	67.9	8.6	2.4	28.0	20.3	5 710	5 129
New Orleans, LA MSA	30 870	7.6	25 960	23.4	19 835	123	5 250	19 342	20.9	11.2	79.0	9.9	6.1	30.9	16.1	24 490	21 038
New York-Northern New Jersey-Long Island, NY-NJ-CT-PA CMSA/NECMA	555 346	1.4	571 868	16.4	29 021	3	96 590	408 855	D	12.7	D	7.0	16.0	32.3	13.7	552 201	491 234
Bergen-Passaic, NJ PMSA	43 834	1.1	40 587	12.6	31 120	X	4 847	27 556	23.6	19.2	76.4	9.2	6.9	31.2	10.2	39 375	36 035
Dutchess, NY PMSA	6 384	1.0	6 016	7.1	23 005	X	1 032	3 673	29.9	24.8	69.9	9.6	5.0	26.2	21.8	5 991	5 619
Jersey City, NJ PMSA	13 143	7.6	12 255	14.0	22 185	X	2 615	9 678	15.0	12.7	85.0	8.2	12.6	22.2	18.5	11 920	10 753
Middlesex-Somerset-Hunterdon, NJ PMSA	30 441	7.9	32 008	19.9	29 947	X	3 249	24 845	24.6	20.5	75.2	7.8	9.3	25.4	11.5	30 658	26 695
Monmouth-Ocean, NJ PMSA	27 314	8.2	27 464	20.0	26 535	X	4 134	12 698	13.3	6.6	86.3	12.3	6.0	34.3	19.5	26 472	22 892
Nassau-Suffolk, NY PMSA	85 510	.1	79 569	14.1	30 007	X	11 263	43 698	16.4	11.7	83.4	9.9	10.2	32.9	16.8	76 602	69 738
New Haven-Bridgeport-Stamford-Waterbury-Danbury, CT NECMA	48 501	−1.4	52 232	15.1	32 117	X	6 868	34 447	26.4	22.2	73.5	8.8	10.8	31.0	9.8	50 431	45 370
New York, NY PMSA	227 469	.8	247 284	17.3	28 800	X	51 437	200 025	D	8.4	D	5.2	23.3	34.6	12.9	238 919	210 790
Newark, NJ PMSA	55 783	.3	57 339	17.7	29 652	X	8 420	40 451	22.7	18.4	77.2	6.8	8.9	28.8	14.3	55 325	48 727
Newburgh, NY-PA PMSA	7 900	−.4	7 174	16.2	20 152	X	1 305	3 802	16.6	11.5	82.6	12.1	5.4	25.5	26.2	6 930	6 174
Trenton, NJ PMSA	9 067	3.5	9 941	17.8	30 179	X	1 422	7 983	19.7	16.6	80.2	6.4	6.4	32.9	25.7	9 579	8 440
Norfolk-Virginia Beach-Newport News, VA-NC MSA	32 482	4.8	29 065	19.8	19 005	156	5 253	21 334	17.4	12.1	82.4	9.0	4.2	23.1	36.5	27 908	24 258
Ocala, FL MSA	5 015	7.7	3 655	28.0	16 629	245	930	1 889	23.2	16.1	75.1	15.4	5.0	24.7	17.1	3 415	2 855
Odessa-Midland, TX MSA	7 157	5.0	4 698	20.9	19 798	125	646	3 323	35.6	7.3	64.4	9.6	3.7	19.6	13.6	4 518	3 887
Oklahoma City, OK MSA	27 748	12.8	19 170	22.1	19 031	153	3 409	14 538	20.6	12.8	78.8	10.5	5.9	25.6	23.6	18 327	15 701
Omaha, NE-IA MSA	17 881	8.8	14 922	25.9	22 514	47	2 108	11 630	D	11.8	D	9.2	9.5	27.5	15.8	14 031	11 851
Orlando, FL MSA	39 546	15.1	27 391	26.5	20 120	111	4 302	21 227	15.8	9.4	83.1	11.7	7.1	37.1	12.3	25 802	21 645
Owensboro, KY MSA	2 335	1.2	1 630	23.7	18 088	198	298	1 123	29.6	20.0	67.8	11.7	4.6	23.2	14.7	1 532	1 318

X Not applicable.
D Withheld to avoid disclosure.

[1]Based on resident population estimated as of July 1, 1994.
[2]Based on 273 metropolitan areas (245 MSAs, 17 CMSAs, and 11 NECMAs); see text for more information.   When metropolitan areas share the same rank, the next lower rank is omitted.
[3]Includes mining and construction, not shown separately.
[4]Includes agricultural services, forestry, and fisheries; transportation and public utilities; and wholesale trade, not shown separately.
[5]Finance, insurance, and real estate.

Source: Private Nonfarm Business Establishments—U.S. Bureau of the Census, "County Business Patterns" on diskette, annual (related Internet site <http://www.census.gov/epcd/cbp/view/cbpview.html>);   Personal Income—U.S. Bureau of Economic Analysis, "Regional Economic Information System (REIS) 1969-1994" on CD-ROM (related Internet site <http://www.bea.doc.gov/bea/dr1.htm>).

Private Nonfarm Business Establishments and Personal Income—Con.

[MSA = Metropolitan statistical area.   CMSA = Consolidated MSA.   PMSA = Primary MSA.   NECMA = New England county metropolitan area.   All areas defined as of June 30, 1996.   Table includes 245 MSAs, 17 CMSAs, and 58 PMSAs not in New England; as well as 12 NECMAs.   Table excludes 10 MSAs, 1 CMSA, and 15 PMSAs in New England]

Metropolitan areas	Private nonfarm business establishments		Personal income														
			1994														
					Per capita[1]			Earnings									
											Percent, by selected industries–						
									Goods-related		Service-related						
	Total, 1995	Percent change, 1990–1995	Total (mil dol)	Percent change, 1990–1994	Dollars	Rank[2]	Transfer payments (mil dol)	Total (mil dol)	Total[3]	Manufacturing	Total[4]	Retail trade	FIRE[5]	Services	Government	1993 (mil dol)	1990 (mil dol)
Panama City, FL MSA	4 158	13.9	2 496	30.8	17 840	204	596	1 652	13.7	6.1	86.3	14.7	4.8	25.6	31.2	2 360	1 909
Parkersburg-Marietta, WV-OH MSA.....	3 875	6.7	2 822	25.7	18 614	173	604	1 963	37.4	29.3	62.3	11.0	3.9	22.0	15.4	2 676	2 245
Pensacola, FL MSA.................	8 270	7.4	6 495	25.5	17 517	221	1 566	4 233	17.9	10.6	81.6	10.9	3.6	28.6	28.1	6 168	5 174
Peoria-Pekin, IL MSA...............	8 341	8.8	7 375	19.4	21 464	76	1 200	5 488	38.5	32.4	60.2	8.9	4.9	24.5	9.4	6 953	6 179
Philadelphia-Wilmington-Atlantic City, PA-NJ-DE-MD CMSA..........	148 353	1.9	149 311	18.0	25 055	14	26 127	104 525	D	18.0	D	8.8	8.6	D	13.7	143 257	126 512
Atlantic-Cape May, NJ PMSA ..	9 876	.9	8 328	15.2	25 236	X	1 466	6 428	D	3.9	D	10.0	3.0	D	17.0	8 005	7 229
Philadelphia, PA-NJ PMSA ...	119 777	.8	124 821	17.8	25 221	X	22 203	85 738	D	17.5	D	8.8	8.6	D	13.6	119 863	105 962
Vineland-Millville-Bridgeton, NJ PMSA	3 097	−2.3	2 800	17.8	20 171	X	670	1 882	31.0	25.3	67.0	9.3	5.9	19.7	21.8	2 708	2 378
Wilmington-Newark, DE-MD PMSA ..	15 603	12.5	13 362	22.1	24 685	X	1 787	10 477	34.5	28.9	65.3	8.1	12.3	23.0	11.3	12 681	10 944
Phoenix-Mesa, AZ MSA	63 148	14.9	51 938	29.1	20 999	90	8 102	37 872	23.3	16.1	75.7	11.1	8.7	28.4	13.7	47 638	40 237
Pine Bluff, AR MSA	1 697	−2.0	1 326	18.2	15 782	257	316	995	26.4	23.8	71.7	9.8	3.5	19.9	22.7	1 274	1 121
Pittsburgh, PA MSA	57 654	1.5	54 647	20.3	22 751	38	11 227	37 536	25.4	17.8	74.5	9.5	6.5	32.1	11.3	52 431	45 437
Pittsfield, MA NECMA	3 994	−3.0	3 068	13.9	22 526	46	652	1 866	29.1	23.7	70.6	12.6	4.4	36.1	10.4	2 954	2 693
Pocatello, ID MSA	1 739	10.8	1 162	31.4	16 382	252	211	758	16.4	10.0	83.3	12.4	5.8	19.1	24.9	1 103	884
Portland, ME NECMA	9 181	7.3	5 974	16.8	24 090	22	954	4 792	D	11.7	D	13.4	11.8	31.1	13.1	5 666	5 115
Portland-Salem, OR-WA CMSA	59 459	18.6	43 949	30.8	22 172	53	6 472	32 571	25.5	18.4	73.4	10.4	6.9	25.9	14.3	41 086	33 612
Portland-Vancouver, OR-WA PMSA .	51 548	19.2	38 374	31.0	22 891	X	5 412	28 821	25.9	18.9	73.2	10.3	7.1	26.4	12.7	35 878	29 292
Salem, OR PMSA	7 911	14.8	5 576	29.1	18 233	X	1 060	3 750	22.5	15.0	74.9	11.5	5.0	22.3	27.2	5 209	4 320
Providence-Warwick-Pawtucket, RI NECMA	25 246	−.3	20 000	15.1	21 929	58	4 196	13 090	26.4	21.8	73.5	9.8	7.3	31.4	14.6	19 345	17 372
Provo-Orem, UT MSA	5 665	31.7	4 203	39.4	14 444	265	622	3 077	22.8	15.7	76.8	9.4	3.1	44.3	13.1	3 887	3 015
Pueblo, CO MSA	2 954	9.4	2 186	26.5	17 117	235	662	1 306	23.0	15.2	76.0	13.6	5.2	25.0	21.7	2 051	1 728
Punta Gorda, FL MSA	2 628	5.7	2 400	23.4	18 976	159	670	892	14.1	2.7	84.7	17.6	5.7	39.5	14.6	2 241	1 945
Raleigh-Durham-Chapel Hill, NC MSA ..	28 030	19.4	22 190	32.7	22 993	34	2 451	18 439	D	19.4	D	9.6	5.6	28.2	19.3	20 778	16 725
Rapid City, SD MSA	3 056	15.1	1 657	32.8	19 135	150	270	1 308	D	8.9	D	14.4	3.8	27.7	24.4	1 574	1 248
Reading, PA MSA	7 920	3.7	7 810	19.8	22 467	48	1 292	5 514	38.0	32.4	61.0	10.6	6.2	22.4	10.4	7 437	6 516
Redding, CA MSA	4 373	−3.1	2 932	19.9	18 326	189	722	1 866	21.5	11.3	77.8	13.5	3.3	28.6	18.3	2 825	2 446
Reno, NV MSA....................	9 729	15.8	7 656	29.2	27 062	6	913	5 671	16.8	7.6	83.1	10.6	5.0	40.2	12.4	7 033	5 925
Richland-Kennewick-Pasco, WA MSA ...	4 034	20.0	3 578	41.0	20 799	98	547	2 807	13.7	7.2	81.3	8.4	2.1	45.3	16.8	3 356	2 538
Richmond-Petersburg, VA MSA	25 285	7.7	22 329	20.5	24 358	21	2 964	16 844	D	16.5	D	9.5	10.6	22.1	20.8	21 175	18 535
Roanoke, VA MSA.................	6 924	6.1	5 122	19.1	22 417	50	809	4 002	D	16.8	D	10.8	7.4	27.6	12.8	4 914	4 299
Rochester, MN MSA	2 689	15.6	2 610	22.5	23 114	32	303	2 392	26.6	22.3	72.3	7.8	2.7	45.6	9.6	2 498	2 131
Rochester, NY MSA	23 604	1.0	24 640	16.0	22 593	42	4 476	18 158	D	34.2	61.0	8.5	5.1	24.3	13.8	23 784	21 245
Rockford, IL MSA	8 694	8.8	7 225	20.4	20 838	97	1 045	5 532	45.7	40.0	53.9	8.1	4.3	20.3	8.8	6 716	5 998
Rocky Mount, NC MSA	3 111	2.6	2 505	24.2	17 932	202	470	1 946	D	30.8	D	12.3	3.9	15.1	13.5	2 361	2 018
Sacramento-Yolo, CA CMSA..........	36 797	.1	34 632	20.2	21 811	65	6 595	25 382	15.4	7.5	83.8	10.3	6.6	25.5	30.6	33 035	28 820
Sacramento, CA PMSA	33 670	.2	31 504	20.0	21 857	X	6 087	22 587	15.3	7.4	84.4	10.2	6.9	26.4	30.9	30 075	26 251
Yolo, CA PMSA	3 127	−.4	3 127	21.7	21 362	X	508	2 794	15.5	8.4	78.8	11.1	3.6	17.7	28.6	2 960	2 570
Saginaw-Bay City-Midland, MI MSA.....	9 345	8.7	8 411	23.3	20 908	93	1 509	6 014	46.1	40.8	53.7	9.2	3.2	21.1	11.2	7 836	6 824
St. Cloud, MN MSA	4 182	12.4	2 689	24.7	17 141	234	427	2 145	D	20.1	D	16.6	3.3	22.4	16.5	2 523	2 156
St. Joseph, MO MSA	2 524	7.2	1 785	17.3	18 213	193	381	1 187	D	24.1	D	10.6	2.7	22.7	14.0	1 677	1 522
St. Louis, MO-IL MSA	64 760	5.0	60 066	19.6	23 684	25	9 200	43 541	D	21.6	D	9.3	7.1	27.1	11.9	56 775	50 212
Salinas, CA MSA	8 021	−1.7	7 935	13.8	22 548	45	1 213	5 437	11.3	6.7	73.3	10.3	4.3	23.4	19.0	7 923	6 970
Salt Lake City-Ogden, UT MSA.........	29 575	21.4	21 944	33.6	18 625	172	2 956	17 667	21.5	14.0	78.2	10.5	7.3	25.7	18.5	20 400	16 429
San Angelo, TX MSA	2 562	8.5	1 843	21.8	18 209	194	363	1 234	20.3	13.5	77.8	10.9	3.5	26.4	22.8	1 756	1 513
San Antonio, TX MSA	31 274	11.9	26 542	28.3	18 466	184	5 273	19 388	13.9	7.9	85.8	11.5	8.0	26.7	25.8	25 038	20 691
San Diego, CA MSA	60 243	−.6	56 923	14.8	21 626	70	9 616	39 655	18.4	12.6	80.6	10.2	6.0	31.1	23.7	55 046	49 587
San Francisco-Oakland-San Jose, CA CMSA	182 418	1.0	184 469	18.9	28 322	4	23 615	140 532	D	18.5	D	9.1	7.7	31.7	13.6	177 172	155 119
Oakland, CA PMSA	53 920	1.6	57 899	18.7	26 530	X	8 345	38 850	21.7	13.9	78.1	10.5	6.3	29.2	17.3	55 799	48 767
San Francisco, CA PMSA	59 916	−.6	56 424	18.6	34 282	X	6 512	46 583	12.1	7.9	87.7	8.8	14.0	36.9	12.7	54 057	47 572
San Jose, CA PMSA	40 442	2.2	43 992	19.6	28 251	X	4 731	40 249	41.0	37.0	58.8	6.9	2.7	30.2	8.8	42 300	36 770
Santa Cruz-Watsonville, CA PMSA ..	6 450	−3.5	5 717	16.9	24 326	X	776	3 329	22.3	16.0	71.2	12.7	3.7	30.1	14.2	5 521	4 889
Santa Rosa, CA PMSA..........	12 169	1.5	9 979	18.3	24 327	X	1 461	5 721	25.7	15.3	72.1	12.6	7.5	27.2	14.3	9 572	8 435
Vallejo-Fairfield-Napa, CA PMSA	9 521	3.4	10 458	20.4	21 669	X	1 791	5 800	D	10.9	D	12.1	3.1	22.7	29.8	9 923	8 686
San Luis Obispo-Atascadero-Paso Robles, CA MSA...................	6 077	−.2	4 286	15.4	19 160	148	775	2 637	17.4	7.3	80.0	14.3	4.1	25.8	21.8	4 141	3 716
Santa Barbara-Santa Maria-Lompoc, CA MSA	10 157	−2.3	9 316	12.8	24 485	17	1 316	6 183	19.9	13.4	77.0	11.2	4.9	35.2	16.0	9 050	8 259

D Withheld to avoid disclosure.
X Not applicable.

[1]Based on resident population estimated as of July 1, 1994.
[2]Based on 273 metropolitan areas (245 MSAs, 17 CMSAs, and 11 NECMAs); see text for more information.   When metropolitan areas share the same rank, the next lower rank is omitted.
[3]Includes mining and construction, not shown separately.
[4]Includes agricultural services, forestry, and fisheries; transportation and public utilities; and wholesale trade, not shown separately.
[5]Finance, insurance, and real estate.

Source: Private Nonfarm Business Establishments—U.S. Bureau of the Census, "County Business Patterns" on diskette, annual (related Internet site <http://www.census.gov/epcd/cbp/view/cbpview.html>);   Personal Income—U.S. Bureau of Economic Analysis, "Regional Economic Information System (REIS) 1969-1994" on CD-ROM (related Internet site <http://www.bea.doc.gov/bea/dr1.htm>).

[MSA = Metropolitan statistical area. CMSA = Consolidated MSA. PMSA = Primary MSA. NECMA = New England county metropolitan area. All areas defined as of June 30, 1996. Table includes 245 MSAs, 17 CMSAs, and 58 PMSAs not in New England; as well as 12 NECMAs. Table excludes 10 MSAs, 1 CMSA, and 15 PMSAs in New England]

Metropolitan areas	Private nonfarm business establishments Total, 1995	Private nonfarm business establishments Percent change, 1990–1995	Personal income 1994 Total (mil dol)	Personal income 1994 Percent change, 1990–1994	Per capita[1] Dollars	Per capita[1] Rank[2]	Transfer payments (mil dol)	Earnings Total (mil dol)	Goods-related Total[3]	Goods-related Manufacturing	Service-related Total[4]	Service-related Retail trade	Service-related FIRE[5]	Service-related Services	Service-related Government	1993 (mil dol)	1990 (mil dol)
Santa Fe, NM MSA	4 643	20.8	3 081	35.4	23 572	28	334	2 331	9.1	3.2	90.8	11.5	4.7	31.7	38.7	2 866	2 276
Sarasota-Bradenton, FL MSA	15 597	7.8	14 026	22.6	27 083	5	2 547	6 220	17.0	10.7	81.0	13.6	6.9	40.4	12.0	13 161	11 443
Savannah, GA MSA	6 871	8.2	5 398	22.6	19 586	131	971	3 811	25.2	18.7	74.6	10.8	4.0	27.7	17.8	5 088	4 404
Scranton--Wilkes-Barre--Hazleton, PA MSA	14 865	-.6	12 485	17.4	19 600	130	3 201	8 090	29.0	23.0	70.8	11.2	5.2	25.7	13.4	11 988	10 633
Seattle-Tacoma-Bremerton, WA CMSA	94 354	13.4	79 941	26.2	24 785	16	11 292	60 441	24.0	17.6	75.8	9.7	6.4	28.0	17.5	76 373	63 334
Bremerton, WA PMSA	4 698	22.5	4 246	27.7	19 263	X	860	2 664	8.3	2.6	91.6	10.3	3.0	20.3	53.1	4 081	3 324
Olympia, WA PMSA	4 673	22.2	3 951	34.1	21 105	X	740	2 411	13.1	6.6	85.8	11.0	3.4	22.1	42.4	3 734	2 946
Seattle-Bellevue-Everett, WA PMSA	70 667	11.8	59 060	25.6	27 098	X	7 202	47 831	26.3	20.0	73.6	9.3	6.9	29.3	12.6	56 511	47 025
Tacoma, WA PMSA	14 316	16.2	12 684	26.4	19 871	X	2 490	7 534	18.5	10.9	81.0	11.5	5.1	24.1	28.2	12 047	10 038
Sharon, PA MSA	2 732	4.0	2 144	17.4	17 542	220	524	1 354	33.8	29.2	65.1	12.5	3.4	27.3	11.1	2 026	1 827
Sheboygan, WI MSA	2 505	9.8	2 282	26.4	21 331	81	329	1 718	53.6	48.1	45.9	7.9	4.5	16.2	9.7	2 143	1 806
Sherman-Denison, TX MSA	2 320	4.7	1 798	17.7	18 478	183	409	1 193	39.0	33.7	60.5	11.6	4.7	22.4	11.0	1 705	1 527
Shreveport-Bossier City, LA MSA	8 807	3.1	7 124	26.8	18 828	166	1 586	4 942	25.0	16.8	74.6	9.4	4.2	27.2	20.6	6 722	5 620
Sioux City, IA-NE MSA	3 293	6.6	2 404	30.0	20 200	107	412	1 790	27.8	21.2	69.9	10.2	4.9	27.3	11.0	2 229	1 849
Sioux Falls, SD MSA	5 240	15.5	3 484	38.0	22 982	35	411	2 819	D	13.1	D	11.1	9.8	27.6	9.5	3 172	2 525
South Bend, IN MSA	6 611	4.8	5 258	26.2	20 587	103	813	3 835	30.5	24.1	69.1	9.9	5.6	31.1	9.2	4 919	4 166
Spokane, WA MSA	11 260	19.1	7 746	30.8	19 564	133	1 578	5 505	21.6	14.3	77.8	11.6	6.4	27.0	18.7	7 329	5 922
Springfield, IL MSA	5 514	13.5	4 393	20.1	22 436	49	700	3 474	10.1	4.2	88.3	8.9	8.4	29.2	29.8	4 140	3 657
Springfield, MO MSA	8 772	15.5	5 441	30.0	18 826	167	898	4 132	D	16.9	D	13.0	4.7	28.9	11.9	5 081	4 186
Springfield, MA NECMA	13 422	-4.5	12 248	10.0	20 561	104	2 814	7 883	24.6	19.9	74.9	10.3	7.0	29.7	18.2	11 725	11 137
State College, PA MSA	3 082	10.0	2 292	21.1	17 659	211	336	1 837	20.9	15.5	78.6	9.8	3.5	20.3	37.1	2 211	1 893
Steubenville-Weirton, OH-WV MSA	2 818	5.7	2 474	14.6	17 643	212	669	1 651	51.2	44.2	48.6	8.2	2.1	18.0	9.7	2 347	2 159
Stockton-Lodi, CA MSA	9 595	-2.7	9 376	19.6	18 093	197	2 149	6 078	21.9	14.8	72.0	12.2	5.2	21.7	18.4	9 036	7 838
Sumter, SC MSA	1 766	.3	1 540	23.9	14 429	266	364	1 107	31.6	25.4	66.4	9.9	2.7	16.9	30.2	1 455	1 243
Syracuse, NY MSA	16 777	-3.2	15 156	14.9	20 103	112	2 947	11 092	25.0	19.4	D	9.2	6.8	D	17.6	14 650	13 187
Tallahassee, FL MSA	6 586	6.4	4 809	29.3	18 977	158	750	3 866	D	3.6	D	10.1	4.7	28.0	40.7	4 499	3 719
Tampa-St. Petersburg-Clearwater, FL MSA	57 994	5.5	46 059	23.5	21 357	79	9 332	29 004	15.4	10.0	83.9	11.8	8.7	34.8	13.7	43 231	37 291
Terre Haute, IN MSA	3 513	9.8	2 645	22.4	17 671	210	533	1 917	33.5	25.8	65.8	14.2	3.3	21.5	15.8	2 532	2 162
Texarkana, TX-Texarkana, AR MSA	2 744	5.7	2 032	16.2	16 560	246	495	1 379	22.4	16.8	76.0	13.5	3.7	26.7	19.6	1 944	1 748
Toledo, OH MSA	14 713	2.0	13 036	20.7	21 235	84	2 506	9 993	34.0	27.9	65.5	9.2	3.9	24.5	13.7	12 233	10 802
Topeka, KS MSA	4 529	1.5	3 537	18.1	21 425	77	606	2 943	D	13.8	D	10.9	7.7	24.5	23.1	3 362	2 995
Tucson, AZ MSA	17 167	11.6	13 588	33.0	18 575	175	2 686	8 640	21.2	12.7	78.5	12.0	5.0	30.2	21.6	12 380	10 213
Tulsa, OK MSA	20 996	9.3	14 897	20.5	20 048	114	2 281	11 429	29.3	18.3	70.2	9.5	6.1	26.8	9.5	14 293	12 360
Tuscaloosa, AL MSA	3 671	13.5	2 759	24.6	17 560	219	529	2 063	33.1	20.1	66.8	10.3	3.1	17.6	27.5	2 594	2 215
Tyler, TX MSA	4 637	11.4	3 179	24.2	19 994	115	540	2 277	29.1	20.6	69.3	12.9	4.8	27.4	13.0	3 020	2 560
Utica-Rome, NY MSA	6 400	-4.3	5 775	15.5	18 257	191	1 453	3 731	D	19.0	D	10.0	7.0	23.3	27.2	5 575	5 002
Victoria, TX MSA	2 128	5.1	1 602	31.0	20 172	108	254	967	25.9	13.8	73.1	13.5	5.4	25.8	15.6	1 501	1 223
Visalia-Tulare-Porterville, CA MSA	5 801	-.3	5 418	19.9	15 783	256	1 329	3 517	16.5	11.2	68.1	12.1	3.9	16.1	19.0	5 227	4 519
Waco, TX MSA	4 760	7.1	3 464	24.8	17 564	218	691	2 459	26.8	21.5	71.3	11.1	6.2	24.7	17.5	3 254	2 776
Washington-Baltimore, DC-MD-VA-WV CMSA	181 055	7.6	189 819	19.2	26 919	8	25 995	147 957	D	6.6	D	8.0	6.7	D	27.2	181 186	159 226
Baltimore, MD PMSA	60 307	6.6	59 115	16.4	24 045	X	9 473	41 110	D	12.2	D	9.2	8.6	30.5	20.5	56 450	50 776
Hagerstown, MD PMSA	3 106	6.4	2 241	14.7	17 701	X	433	1 619	D	19.4	D	12.8	3.3	24.4	17.5	2 146	1 954
Washington, DC-MD-VA-WV PMSA	117 642	8.2	128 464	20.6	28 762	X	16 089	105 229	D	4.2	D	7.4	6.1	D	30.0	122 590	106 495
Waterloo-Cedar Falls, IA MSA	3 134	4.1	2 405	22.0	19 444	138	439	1 977	D	33.4	D	9.6	4.1	21.8	15.4	2 242	1 972
Wausau, WI MSA	3 136	13.8	2 345	25.3	19 527	134	340	1 767	36.9	31.3	61.4	8.9	8.9	18.5	11.3	2 215	1 872
West Palm Beach-Boca Raton, FL MSA	32 701	16.3	31 994	26.4	33 519	1	3 954	14 395	17.0	11.0	80.0	11.6	9.7	35.2	11.3	30 415	25 319
Wheeling, WV-OH MSA	3 724	5.0	2 898	19.4	18 356	186	769	1 733	27.7	16.4	D	11.8	4.6	D	13.5	2 752	2 428
Wichita, KS MSA	13 357	7.8	10 902	20.7	21 512	75	1 661	8 452	35.2	29.1	64.3	10.1	4.7	25.4	12.1	10 547	9 032
Wichita Falls, TX MSA	3 521	-.2	2 518	19.5	19 072	152	510	1 765	24.5	15.4	74.0	9.9	3.6	23.1	26.2	2 392	2 107
Williamsport, PA MSA	2 921	.9	2 238	19.3	18 515	181	467	1 596	32.5	27.0	66.7	13.6	4.0	24.5	14.2	2 144	1 876
Wilmington, NC MSA	6 605	23.8	3 591	33.6	18 560	178	686	2 610	D	19.2	D	13.0	4.6	22.5	17.4	3 355	2 688
Yakima, WA MSA	4 710	10.0	3 688	25.7	17 759	209	482	2 405	18.3	13.1	69.8	11.2	2.9	22.5	16.2	3 558	2 935
York, PA MSA	7 760	-.4	7 757	20.7	21 680	68	1 048	5 189	41.6	34.6	58.2	11.8	3.6	20.9	9.1	7 401	6 427
Youngstown-Warren, OH MSA	13 524	2.9	11 572	19.9	19 155	149	2 662	7 681	41.7	36.3	57.9	10.6	3.8	22.5	11.1	10 919	9 654
Yuba City, CA MSA	2 409	-2.7	2 273	24.4	16 809	241	626	1 357	14.9	6.1	72.9	11.4	3.0	20.0	26.6	2 183	1 827
Yuma, AZ MSA	2 358	20.0	1 757	34.9	13 762	267	395	1 291	8.2	3.4	79.3	11.0	2.5	18.6	27.9	1 701	1 303

X Not applicable.
D Withheld to avoid disclosure.

[1]Based on resident population estimated as of July 1, 1994.
[2]Based on 273 metropolitan areas (245 MSAs, 17 CMSAs, and 11 NECMAs); see text for more information. When metropolitan areas share the same rank, the next lower rank is omitted.
[3]Includes mining and construction, not shown separately.
[4]Includes agricultural services, forestry, and fisheries; transportation and public utilities; and wholesale trade, not shown separately.
[5]Finance, insurance, and real estate.

Source: Private Nonfarm Business Establishments—U.S. Bureau of the Census, "County Business Patterns" on diskette, annual (related Internet site <http://www.census.gov/epcd/cbp/view/cbpview.html>); Personal Income—U.S. Bureau of Economic Analysis, "Regional Economic Information System (REIS) 1969-1994" on CD-ROM (related Internet site <http://www.bea.doc.gov/bea/dr1.htm>).

[MSA = Metropolitan statistical area. CMSA = Consolidated MSA. PMSA = Primary MSA. NECMA = New England county metropolitan area. All areas defined as of June 30, 1996. Table includes 245 MSAs, 17 CMSAs, and 58 PMSAs not in New England; as well as 12 NECMAs. Table excludes 10 MSAs, 1 CMSA, and 15 PMSAs in New England]

| Metropolitan areas | Personal income projections (constant (1987) dollars) | | | | | | | | Civilian labor force | | | | | | | | |
| | Total (mil dol) | | | | Per capita[2] (dollars) | | | | Total (1,000) | | | Unemployed (1,000) | | | Unemployment rate[3] | | |
	2010	2005	2000	1993 esti-mate[1]	2010	2005	2000	1993 esti-mate[1]	1996	1995	1994	1996	1995	1994	1996	1995	1994
Abilene, TX MSA	2 296	2 122	1 947	1 671	17 366	16 402	15 358	13 762	60.5	59.6	58.1	3.0	3.1	3.0	4.9	5.2	5.1
Albany, GA MSA	2 054	1 881	1 711	1 472	15 539	14 765	13 934	12 680	55.7	53.5	54.5	3.3	3.3	4.8	6.0	6.2	8.9
Albany-Schenectady-Troy, NY MSA	20 165	18 594	16 980	14 825	20 400	19 444	18 397	16 958	446.8	450.9	455.5	20.4	22.5	22.3	4.6	5.0	4.9
Albuquerque, NM MSA	14 509	12 955	11 408	9 295	17 908	17 013	16 056	14 754	345.1	340.0	333.2	18.5	13.8	14.7	5.3	4.1	4.4
Alexandria, LA MSA	2 164	1 999	1 836	1 621	16 042	15 177	14 242	12 946	59.0	58.5	57.1	4.0	3.9	4.1	6.8	6.6	7.2
Allentown-Bethlehem-Easton, PA MSA	13 547	12 474	11 426	10 034	19 948	18 954	17 853	16 470	303.7	301.4	300.8	16.6	16.8	17.6	5.5	5.6	5.8
Altoona, PA MSA	2 299	2 134	1 974	1 765	16 244	15 485	14 643	13 392	62.1	61.7	62.1	3.5	3.9	4.1	5.7	6.4	6.6
Amarillo, TX MSA	3 941	3 630	3 312	2 858	18 322	17 349	16 292	14 746	112.4	111.1	107.8	4.4	4.2	3.8	3.9	3.8	3.5
Anchorage, AK MSA	7 303	6 681	6 053	5 201	24 408	23 293	22 173	20 780	138.1	132.8	135.2	7.5	7.0	7.6	5.5	5.2	5.6
Anniston, AL MSA	1 901	1 752	1 609	1 432	15 088	14 286	13 411	12 236	52.6	53.4	52.3	3.3	4.4	4.0	6.2	8.3	7.6
Appleton-Oshkosh-Neenah, WI MSA	7 470	6 794	6 117	5 170	19 393	18 412	17 339	15 733	220.7	215.4	209.8	6.2	6.7	8.4	2.8	3.1	4.0
Asheville, NC MSA	4 461	4 025	3 595	2 970	18 541	17 576	16 523	14 784	108.6	104.8	105.1	3.7	3.9	4.0	3.4	3.7	3.8
Athens, GA MSA	2 684	2 411	2 140	1 756	17 039	16 084	15 040	13 433	71.1	67.8	66.2	2.2	2.2	2.3	3.1	3.2	3.5
Atlanta, GA MSA	91 580	81 458	71 429	57 148	21 643	20 569	19 402	17 701	1 973.2	1 880.1	1 845.8	75.1	81.3	86.6	3.8	4.3	4.7
Augusta-Aiken, GA-SC MSA	9 364	8 446	7 550	6 284	17 389	16 510	15 553	14 167	202.4	201.4	203.0	13.5	13.2	12.8	6.7	6.6	6.3
Austin-San Marcos, TX MSA	23 726	21 040	18 288	14 362	19 970	18 020	16 986	15 408	634.1	609.2	579.6	19.0	17.7	18.5	3.0	2.9	3.2
Bakersfield, CA MSA	11 619	10 448	9 256	7 640	15 234	14 513	13 733	12 735	279.0	273.2	272.8	35.5	37.8	40.1	12.7	13.8	14.7
Bangor, ME NECMA	2 757	2 529	2 307	2 021	16 831	15 996	15 099	13 826	76.7	74.9	71.7	4.1	4.5	5.6	5.3	6.1	7.8
Barnstable-Yarmouth, MA NECMA	5 298	4 797	4 288	3 557	22 466	21 405	20 188	18 441	102.7	101.1	100.5	6.0	7.1	8.3	5.8	7.1	8.3
Baton Rouge, LA MSA	11 532	10 461	9 398	7 906	17 432	16 552	15 624	14 292	287.7	278.8	275.9	16.7	17.1	20.4	5.8	6.1	7.4
Beaumont-Port Arthur, TX MSA	7 209	6 671	6 135	5 287	18 022	17 013	15 919	14 212	180.9	182.7	182.7	16.5	17.9	18.5	9.1	9.8	10.1
Bellingham, WA MSA	3 221	2 876	2 531	2 039	17 214	16 423	15 565	14 336	79.7	75.9	73.9	5.9	5.6	5.4	7.5	7.4	7.3
Benton Harbor, MI MSA	2 998	2 807	2 621	2 356	17 781	16 891	15 923	14 570	82.1	81.8	83.4	4.9	4.5	5.0	6.0	5.5	6.0
Billings, MT MSA	2 867	2 579	2 288	1 856	18 463	17 613	16 712	15 355	68.2	66.9	67.9	3.0	3.2	2.7	4.4	4.8	4.0
Biloxi-Gulfport-Pascagoula, MS MSA	5 581	5 123	4 684	4 107	14 815	14 092	13 341	12 426	161.7	162.1	165.0	8.5	10.0	9.5	5.2	6.1	5.7
Binghamton, NY MSA	4 820	4 543	4 273	3 938	17 507	16 746	15 921	14 893	121.6	123.1	127.5	5.4	6.7	8.6	4.4	5.4	6.8
Birmingham, AL MSA	18 744	17 178	15 674	13 657	19 489	18 451	17 329	15 795	448.3	439.2	432.0	14.3	18.7	17.8	3.2	4.3	4.1
Bismarck, ND MSA	1 814	1 654	1 491	1 250	17 924	16 982	15 934	14 314	52.4	49.5	47.9	1.5	1.8	2.0	2.9	3.5	4.2
Bloomington, IN MSA	2 260	2 029	1 798	1 471	16 776	15 824	14 749	13 109	60.9	61.4	60.6	1.7	2.1	2.4	2.7	3.4	3.9
Bloomington-Normal, IL MSA	2 958	2 719	2 477	2 147	18 769	17 945	17 048	15 798	79.4	78.9	77.6	2.5	2.3	2.2	3.1	2.9	2.8
Boise City, ID MSA	8 369	7 483	6 584	5 248	19 155	18 203	17 165	15 702	206.3	197.1	191.4	8.1	8.1	7.9	3.9	4.1	4.1
Boston-Worcester-Lawrence-Lowell-Brockton, MA-NH NECMA	150 064	138 237	126 459	110 615	23 246	22 232	21 100	19 407	3 069.4	3 055.1	3 045.6	130.3	156.6	174.2	4.2	5.1	5.7
Brownsville-Harlingen-San Benito, TX MSA	4 016	3 578	3 136	2 505	11 145	10 472	9 734	8 619	124.3	122.8	122.2	15.6	15.5	15.6	12.6	12.6	12.8
Bryan-College Station, TX MSA	2 451	2 162	1 870	1 466	14 390	13 586	12 712	11 400	69.5	68.8	68.6	1.7	2.1	1.8	2.5	3.0	2.7
Buffalo-Niagara Falls, NY MSA	23 883	22 300	20 706	18 628	18 788	17 890	16 908	15 622	572.3	569.0	576.3	29.2	30.8	35.1	5.1	5.4	6.1
Burlington, VT NECMA	4 371	3 955	3 541	2 999	19 617	18 683	17 667	16 344	111.1	108.6	106.7	3.9	3.6	4.1	3.5	3.3	3.8
Canton-Massillon, OH MSA	7 476	6 963	6 459	5 772	17 562	16 681	15 716	14 395	201.0	197.7	197.2	10.8	9.8	12.0	5.4	5.0	6.1
Casper, WY MSA	1 376	1 286	1 203	1 092	20 288	19 403	18 451	17 333	33.0	33.1	32.3	2.1	1.8	2.1	6.4	5.6	6.6
Cedar Rapids, IA MSA	3 845	3 554	3 264	2 881	19 779	18 883	17 886	16 470	109.4	107.0	105.8	3.2	3.0	3.3	2.9	2.8	3.1
Champaign-Urbana, IL MSA	3 218	2 965	2 707	2 376	16 605	15 857	15 041	13 933	93.3	91.6	91.6	2.9	2.7	3.2	3.1	2.9	3.5
Charleston-North Charleston, SC MSA	10 259	9 243	8 243	6 939	16 295	15 430	14 499	13 202	241.5	245.4	243.4	13.3	12.4	15.0	5.5	5.0	6.1
Charleston, WV MSA	5 193	4 805	4 452	4 002	19 085	18 097	17 070	15 751	130.3	127.0	126.3	7.1	7.2	8.4	5.4	5.7	6.6
Charlotte-Gastonia-Rock Hill, NC-SC MSA	29 888	27 014	24 201	20 083	19 667	18 761	17 777	16 281	735.2	706.7	686.6	27.0	23.8	25.0	3.7	3.4	3.6
Charlottesville, VA MSA	3 406	3 089	2 778	2 371	20 458	19 501	18 456	17 128	71.5	72.4	70.8	1.8	1.7	2.1	2.6	2.4	2.9
Chattanooga, TN-GA MSA	9 171	8 353	7 555	6 441	18 046	17 151	16 178	14 800	220.9	220.2	221.5	10.1	10.7	9.9	4.6	4.8	4.4
Cheyenne, WY MSA	1 669	1 536	1 407	1 208	19 180	18 246	17 265	15 704	39.4	39.6	38.9	1.4	1.4	1.7	3.6	3.7	4.4
Chicago-Gary-Kenosha, IL-IN-WI CMSA	217 459	200 469	183 262	160 271	22 804	21 745	20 578	18 931	4 479.2	4 462.4	4 396.3	225.2	229.5	250.4	5.0	5.1	5.7
Chicago, IL PMSA	201 375	185 462	169 300	147 707	23 344	22 269	21 084	19 404	4 051.3	4 030.7	3 971.4	203.9	203.9	223.5	5.0	5.1	5.6
Gary, IN PMSA	11 539	10 806	10 104	9 173	18 052	17 163	16 179	14 859	299.7	304.8	300.0	15.6	19.4	19.7	5.2	6.4	6.6
Kankakee, IL PMSA	1 854	1 719	1 583	1 404	16 511	15 789	15 000	13 987	51.9	51.9	50.9	3.0	3.3	3.4	5.8	6.4	6.8
Kenosha, WI PMSA	2 691	2 482	2 276	1 987	17 022	16 329	15 567	14 589	76.4	75.0	74.0	2.7	2.9	3.7	3.5	3.8	5.1
Chico-Paradise, CA MSA	3 988	3 548	3 098	2 462	16 379	15 479	14 476	12 883	82.9	82.6	83.8	7.4	8.3	8.5	9.0	10.0	10.2
Cincinnati-Hamilton, OH-KY-IN CMSA	42 040	38 671	35 320	30 465	19 852	18 882	17 820	16 194	986.2	972.1	962.5	41.7	40.9	47.4	4.2	4.2	4.9
Cincinnati, OH-KY-IN PMSA	35 486	32 705	29 942	25 911	20 337	19 327	18 220	16 484	819.6	806.6	801.6	34.8	34.3	38.8	4.2	4.3	4.8
Hamilton-Middletown, OH PMSA	6 554	5 966	5 378	4 554	17 581	16 769	15 880	14 718	166.6	165.5	161.0	6.9	6.6	8.6	4.1	4.0	5.3
Clarksville-Hopkinsville, TN-KY MSA	2 922	2 672	2 425	2 062	13 923	13 240	12 504	11 445	78.5	77.8	75.2	3.3	3.4	3.3	4.2	4.4	4.4

[1]Latest estimate available when projections were prepared.
[2]Based on resident population projected as of July 1 for 2010, 2005, and 2000 by the Bureau of Economic Analysis or estimated as of July 1, 1993 by the Bureau of the Census; 1993 estimate excludes subsequent census revisions.
[3]Civilian unemployed as a percent of total civilian labor force.

Source: Personal Income Projections—U.S. Bureau of Economic Analysis, "Regional Economic Information System (REIS) 1969-1994" on CD-ROM; Civilian Labor Force—U.S. Bureau of Labor Statistics, Local Area Unemployment Statistics–Time Series, Internet site <gopher://hopi2.bls.gov:70/11/Time%20Series/LA%20Local%20Area%20Unemployment%20Statistics/Data> for each state (accessed April 1997), BLS gopher service discontinued October 31, 1997 (related BLS Internet site <http://www.bls.gov>).

[MSA = Metropolitan statistical area. CMSA = Consolidated MSA. PMSA = Primary MSA. NECMA = New England county metropolitan area. All areas defined as of June 30, 1996. Table includes 245 MSAs, 17 CMSAs, and 58 PMSAs not in New England; as well as 12 NECMAs. Table excludes 10 MSAs, 1 CMSA, and 15 PMSAs in New England]

| Metropolitan areas | Personal income projections (constant (1987) dollars) | | | | | | | | Civilian labor force | | | | | | | | |
| | Total (mil dol) | | | | Per capita[2] (dollars) | | | | Total (1,000) | | | Unemployed (1,000) | | | Unemployment rate[3] | | |
	2010	2005	2000	1993 esti-mate[1]	2010	2005	2000	1993 esti-mate[1]	1996	1995	1994	1996	1995	1994	1996	1995	1994
Cleveland-Akron, OH CMSA	61 800	57 863	54 016	48 786	20 700	19 647	18 497	16 858	1 464.3	1 446.4	1 440.7	74.1	71.3	82.3	5.1	4.9	5.7
Akron, OH PMSA.................	14 019	12 952	11 892	10 421	19 108	18 117	17 030	15 491	359.9	354.7	352.7	16.6	15.9	18.0	4.6	4.5	5.1
Cleveland-Lorain-Elyria, OH PMSA ..	47 781	44 912	42 124	38 365	21 219	20 138	18 957	17 272	1 104.4	1 091.6	1 088.1	57.4	55.4	64.3	5.2	5.1	5.9
Colorado Springs, CO MSA	10 238	9 123	8 004	6 398	17 883	17 023	16 070	14 707	238.7	233.3	220.2	11.1	10.7	10.7	4.6	4.6	4.8
Columbia, MO MSA	2 625	2 362	2 095	1 733	18 004	17 077	16 054	14 522	78.2	76.5	72.5	1.3	1.4	1.4	1.7	1.9	2.0
Columbia, SC MSA	10 590	9 556	8 533	7 114	18 404	17 442	16 403	14 815	258.6	258.6	252.8	9.6	8.5	10.3	3.7	3.3	4.1
Columbus, GA-AL MSA	4 778	4 392	4 017	3 517	15 981	15 130	14 210	12 968	116.7	114.2	112.7	6.0	6.8	6.9	5.1	6.0	6.1
Columbus, OH MSA	32 889	29 951	27 002	22 791	19 603	18 668	17 648	16 173	794.0	782.2	770.1	24.6	24.4	29.9	3.1	3.1	3.9
Corpus Christi, TX MSA	6 879	6 317	5 753	4 928	16 857	15 899	14 870	13 345	178.9	174.6	173.9	15.0	15.9	16.1	8.4	9.1	9.2
Cumberland, MD-WV MSA	1 550	1 456	1 369	1 257	15 318	14 540	13 693	12 408	45.2	43.8	43.6	3.6	3.8	3.9	8.0	8.7	8.8
Dallas-Fort Worth, TX CMSA...........	115 240	103 833	92 360	75 836	21 588	20 535	19 404	17 722	2 597.1	2 525.2	2 469.6	103.9	119.2	131.6	4.0	4.7	5.3
Dallas, TX PMSA	79 590	71 738	63 835	52 409	22 495	21 386	20 194	18 427	1 757.9	1 708.9	1 665.0	70.9	79.4	86.7	4.0	4.6	5.2
Fort Worth-Arlington, TX PMSA	35 650	32 095	28 526	23 427	19 806	18 858	17 841	16 324	839.2	816.3	804.6	33.0	39.8	44.8	3.9	4.9	5.6
Danville, VA MSA	1 666	1 575	1 488	1 390	15 032	14 392	13 662	12 707	56.8	59.7	58.5	4.2	5.0	4.5	7.4	8.4	7.8
Davenport-Moline-Rock Island, IA-IL MSA	7 053	6 577	6 104	5 519	18 658	17 775	16 807	15 446	182.9	180.4	181.0	8.0	7.9	8.6	4.4	4.4	4.7
Dayton-Springfield, OH MSA	19 670	18 275	16 906	15 040	18 972	18 071	17 085	15 685	474.4	471.9	469.5	21.3	18.8	21.9	4.5	4.0	4.7
Daytona Beach, FL MSA	9 715	8 525	7 339	5 673	16 325	15 466	14 515	13 125	188.3	187.4	187.2	7.8	8.9	11.4	4.2	4.7	6.1
Decatur, AL MSA	2 655	2 427	2 205	1 898	16 877	16 022	15 085	13 781	69.5	69.0	67.4	3.6	4.6	4.6	5.1	6.6	6.8
Decatur, IL MSA	2 385	2 221	2 054	1 834	18 794	17 953	17 006	15 636	60.1	60.5	59.7	4.9	4.5	4.6	8.1	7.5	7.7
Denver-Boulder-Greeley, CO CMSA	60 529	54 310	48 039	39 313	22 166	21 126	19 981	18 316	1 297.0	1 298.0	1 250.1	50.1	50.0	49.1	3.9	3.9	3.9
Boulder-Longmont, CO PMSA	7 570	6 734	5 885	4 693	23 738	22 559	21 239	19 216	162.1	161.9	156.9	6.1	6.6	5.9	3.8	4.1	3.7
Denver, CO PMSA	50 134	45 028	39 885	32 743	22 434	21 392	20 247	18 585	1 054.7	1 055.3	1 018.1	40.3	39.7	39.9	3.8	3.8	3.9
Greeley, CO PMSA	2 824	2 548	2 268	1 877	15 955	15 230	14 428	13 308	80.2	80.8	75.0	3.7	3.8	3.3	4.6	4.7	4.4
Des Moines, IA MSA	9 928	9 118	8 304	7 184	21 147	20 129	19 016	17 434	257.3	250.3	249.2	7.2	6.5	7.0	2.8	2.6	2.8
Detroit-Ann Arbor-Flint, MI CMSA.......	116 634	109 357	102 322	92 546	21 418	20 379	19 250	17 643	2 636.3	2 601.1	2 609.2	117.8	130.2	149.6	4.5	5.0	5.7
Ann Arbor, MI PMSA	13 619	12 348	11 065	9 295	22 740	21 543	20 228	18 250	278.1	273.4	275.9	8.1	9.1	9.9	2.9	3.3	3.6
Detroit, MI PMSA	95 076	89 535	84 223	76 789	21 569	20 540	19 422	17 842	2 155.5	2 124.3	2 129.3	97.0	107.3	123.5	4.5	5.0	5.8
Flint, MI PMSA	7 939	7 474	7 034	6 462	18 092	17 229	16 287	14 941	202.6	203.4	204.0	12.7	13.8	16.3	6.3	6.8	8.0
Dothan, AL MSA	2 499	2 275	2 059	1 737	16 258	15 374	14 419	12 978	64.2	63.2	63.1	2.9	3.6	4.0	4.5	5.7	6.4
Dover, DE MSA	2 200	2 005	1 808	1 527	15 726	14 998	14 149	12 920	68.7	69.4	68.9	3.5	3.2	3.6	5.1	4.5	5.2
Dubuque, IA MSA	1 664	1 545	1 428	1 271	17 796	16 908	15 939	14 442	50.5	49.8	50.0	2.9	1.8	1.9	5.7	3.7	3.7
Duluth-Superior, MN-WI MSA	4 323	4 036	3 746	3 314	16 978	16 125	15 173	13 709	123.1	121.6	121.1	6.9	6.9	8.0	5.6	5.7	6.6
Eau Claire, WI MSA	2 658	2 433	2 205	1 879	16 304	15 524	14 653	13 316	79.7	76.4	75.6	3.0	2.9	3.9	3.7	3.8	5.2
El Paso, TX MSA	9 719	8 770	7 814	6 459	12 367	11 710	10 998	9 984	290.4	285.9	284.0	33.6	29.9	29.6	11.6	10.5	10.4
Elkhart-Goshen, IN MSA	3 530	3 217	2 901	2 458	18 719	17 754	16 689	15 209	94.3	97.5	93.3	3.7	3.6	2.9	3.9	3.7	3.2
Elmira, NY MSA	1 692	1 583	1 472	1 318	16 881	16 054	15 162	13 878	44.0	42.6	43.3	1.9	2.1	2.3	4.3	4.8	5.3
Enid, OK MSA	1 028	956	885	790	16 983	16 168	15 283	13 982	26.9	27.2	27.3	.9	1.0	1.1	3.4	3.8	4.1
Erie, PA MSA	5 336	4 954	4 563	4 063	18 022	17 140	16 124	14 521	139.3	139.9	137.8	8.1	8.9	9.2	5.8	6.4	6.7
Eugene-Springfield, OR MSA	6 117	5 553	4 983	4 158	17 427	16 547	15 576	14 086	159.0	154.5	155.3	9.2	7.5	8.4	5.8	4.8	5.4
Evansville-Henderson, IN-KY MSA	6 077	5 582	5 091	4 429	19 009	18 075	17 044	15 539	155.3	158.1	155.4	7.0	8.1	7.8	4.5	5.2	5.0
Fargo-Moorhead, ND-MN MSA	3 247	2 977	2 702	2 272	17 455	16 623	15 700	14 207	97.8	93.3	91.7	2.4	2.4	2.6	2.5	2.6	2.8
Fayetteville, NC MSA	5 229	4 757	4 305	3 647	15 763	14 954	14 086	12 807	112.9	110.0	108.6	5.3	5.9	5.6	4.7	5.3	5.2
Fayetteville-Springdale-Rogers, AR MSA	4 942	4 452	3 964	3 274	16 596	15 861	15 078	13 949	138.5	134.9	129.8	4.1	3.2	3.2	2.9	2.4	2.4
Flagstaff, AZ-UT MSA	2 137	1 893	1 647	1 281	14 700	13 888	13 002	11 550	61.2	60.4	55.3	5.2	4.7	5.3	8.6	7.8	9.5
Florence, AL MSA	2 337	2 154	1 978	1 732	15 751	14 935	14 058	12 804	70.1	69.7	67.3	4.3	4.6	4.5	6.2	6.6	6.6
Florence, SC MSA	2 302	2 085	1 870	1 577	16 323	15 466	14 528	13 175	60.6	61.3	61.2	5.1	3.9	4.8	8.4	6.4	7.8
Fort Collins-Loveland, CO MSA	5 063	4 474	3 882	3 072	18 081	17 227	16 285	14 979	133.1	127.8	121.0	5.1	5.0	4.4	3.8	3.9	3.6
Fort Myers-Cape Coral, FL MSA.......	10 138	8 868	7 607	5 864	19 855	18 937	17 898	16 319	170.2	170.1	167.0	6.4	7.1	8.2	3.7	4.2	4.9
Fort Pierce-Port St. Lucie, FL MSA ...	8 109	7 060	6 023	4 565	20 087	19 170	18 163	16 763	122.4	117.0	118.5	12.6	12.6	14.7	10.3	10.7	12.4
Fort Smith, AR-OK MSA	3 342	3 032	2 726	2 293	15 289	14 523	13 691	12 502	96.0	95.6	94.9	5.0	4.9	5.3	5.3	5.2	5.6
Fort Walton Beach, FL MSA	3 613	3 199	2 797	2 235	17 244	16 406	15 496	14 209	74.5	76.4	73.2	2.9	3.3	3.8	3.9	4.3	5.2
Fort Wayne, IN MSA	10 236	9 407	8 585	7 388	19 356	18 403	17 347	15 845	262.5	267.2	259.1	9.3	10.4	11.3	3.5	3.9	4.4
Fresno, CA MSA	16 672	14 979	13 247	10 868	16 057	15 260	14 393	13 207	426.5	423.3	419.4	55.9	60.3	58.4	13.1	14.3	13.9
Gadsden, AL MSA.................	1 677	1 547	1 422	1 247	15 557	14 744	13 872	12 478	49.4	48.3	47.9	2.6	3.2	3.1	5.3	6.7	6.5
Gainesville, FL MSA	4 306	3 839	3 373	2 740	17 700	16 823	15 843	14 382	100.9	100.0	99.6	2.8	2.9	3.3	2.8	2.9	3.3
Glens Falls, NY MSA	2 248	2 079	1 905	1 657	16 399	15 644	14 799	13 589	61.3	62.4	62.0	3.9	4.1	4.4	6.3	6.6	7.1
Goldsboro, NC MSA	1 815	1 660	1 510	1 286	14 650	13 941	13 167	11 914	48.3	46.5	47.1	2.3	2.4	2.4	4.8	5.1	5.2
Grand Forks, ND-MN MSA	1 790	1 659	1 528	1 316	16 021	15 195	14 277	12 722	55.1	67.0	67.1	1.9	1.9	2.2	3.4	2.8	3.2

[1]Latest estimate available when projections were prepared.

[2]Based on resident population projected as of July 1 for 2010, 2005, and 2000 by the Bureau of Economic Analysis or estimated as of July 1, 1993 by the Bureau of the Census; 1993 estimate excludes subsequent census revisions.

[3]Civilian unemployed as a percent of total civilian labor force.

Source: Personal Income Projections—U.S. Bureau of Economic Analysis, "Regional Economic Information System (REIS) 1969-1994" on CD-ROM; Civilian Labor Force—U.S. Bureau of Labor Statistics, Local Area Unemployment Statistics–Time Series, Internet site <gopher://hopi2.bls.gov:70/11/Time%20Series/LA%20%20Local%20Area%20Unemployment%20Statistics/Data> for each state (accessed April 1997), BLS gopher service discontinued October 31, 1997 (related BLS Internet site <http://www.bls.gov>).

Table B–8. Metro Areas — **Personal Income Projections and Civilian Labor Force**—Con.

[MSA = Metropolitan statistical area. CMSA = Consolidated MSA. PMSA = Primary MSA. NECMA = New England county metropolitan area. All areas defined as of June 30, 1996. Table includes 245 MSAs, 17 CMSAs, and 58 PMSAs not in New England; as well as 12 NECMAs. Table excludes 10 MSAs, 1 CMSA, and 15 PMSAs in New England]

| Metropolitan areas | Personal income projections (constant (1987) dollars) | | | | | | | | Civilian labor force | | | | | | | | |
| | Total (mil dol) | | | | Per capita[2] (dollars) | | | | Total (1,000) | | | Unemployed (1,000) | | | Unemployment rate[3] | | |
	2010	2005	2000	1993 esti-mate[1]	2010	2005	2000	1993 esti-mate[1]	1996	1995	1994	1996	1995	1994	1996	1995	1994
Grand Junction, CO MSA	2 124	1 910	1 692	1 377	16 955	16 074	15 108	13 675	54.5	53.5	50.8	2.9	3.0	2.8	5.4	5.6	5.6
Grand Rapids-Muskegon-Holland, MI MSA	21 785	19 862	17 923	15 258	19 202	18 256	17 217	15 662	555.8	538.7	534.6	22.6	21.8	24.0	4.1	4.1	4.5
Great Falls, MT MSA	1 461	1 367	1 277	1 152	17 336	16 470	15 570	14 344	37.4	36.8	36.9	1.8	2.0	1.8	4.7	5.4	4.9
Green Bay, WI MSA	4 739	4 319	3 898	3 295	19 805	18 836	17 766	16 111	130.3	126.3	121.4	4.0	4.0	5.2	3.0	3.2	4.3
Greensboro--Winston Salem--High Point, NC MSA	25 926	23 507	21 147	17 707	19 890	18 914	17 852	16 215	632.3	612.1	603.7	21.0	20.1	20.6	3.3	3.3	3.4
Greenville, NC MSA	2 406	2 166	1 931	1 574	17 040	16 203	15 300	13 806	64.8	58.7	59.3	3.2	2.9	2.7	5.0	5.0	4.6
Greenville-Spartanburg-Anderson, SC MSA	17 653	15 954	14 265	11 940	17 197	16 296	15 309	13 848	469.6	472.4	461.7	20.2	15.8	20.7	4.3	3.4	4.5
Harrisburg-Lebanon-Carlisle, PA MSA	14 038	12 836	11 650	10 070	19 983	19 042	18 028	16 631	345.3	335.8	331.5	11.6	12.7	13.0	3.4	3.8	3.9
Hartford, CT NECMA	31 250	28 731	26 190	22 853	24 546	23 469	22 234	20 412	575.5	575.6	589.9	34.9	33.8	34.6	6.1	5.9	5.9
Hattiesburg, MS MSA	1 676	1 531	1 391	1 173	14 314	13 542	12 757	11 477	49.9	49.5	47.9	2.0	2.0	2.3	4.0	4.0	4.8
Hickory-Morganton-Lenoir, NC MSA	6 256	5 686	5 125	4 294	17 436	16 586	15 662	14 220	177.6	172.3	171.0	7.1	7.2	5.7	4.0	4.2	3.3
Honolulu, HI MSA	23 350	21 435	19 537	16 863	23 140	22 146	21 060	19 460	427.3	420.8	422.3	22.6	19.3	19.6	5.3	4.6	4.6
Houma, LA MSA	2 848	2 612	2 379	2 065	13 716	12 960	12 169	11 076	83.7	80.6	79.6	3.8	4.4	5.2	4.6	5.4	6.5
Houston-Galveston-Brazoria, TX CMSA	102 419	92 984	83 478	69 264	20 456	19 545	18 569	17 196	2 250.2	2 216.8	2 191.9	122.9	131.2	145.1	5.5	5.9	6.6
Brazoria, TX PMSA	4 356	3 952	3 547	2 912	17 374	16 475	15 502	14 053	105.7	105.4	107.0	7.1	7.8	7.7	6.7	7.4	7.2
Galveston-Texas City, TX PMSA	4 927	4 524	4 119	3 508	18 612	17 700	16 718	15 114	127.3	126.0	124.8	10.3	9.5	10.5	8.1	7.6	8.4
Houston, TX PMSA	93 137	84 508	75 811	62 844	20 736	19 829	18 858	17 512	2 017.3	1 985.5	1 960.2	105.5	113.8	126.9	5.2	5.7	6.5
Huntington-Ashland, WV-KY-OH MSA	5 238	4 861	4 507	3 963	15 295	14 522	13 702	12 525	136.2	135.7	135.3	9.7	10.0	11.4	7.1	7.4	8.4
Huntsville, AL MSA	7 143	6 497	5 874	5 024	19 586	18 572	17 481	16 016	163.0	160.5	161.3	5.7	7.8	8.8	3.5	4.8	5.5
Indianapolis, IN MSA	35 042	32 003	28 993	24 805	21 443	20 314	19 063	17 189	814.9	823.9	800.7	26.4	31.8	33.1	3.2	3.9	4.1
Iowa City, IA MSA	2 126	1 943	1 757	1 513	18 519	17 649	16 688	15 286	65.3	64.6	64.5	1.9	1.8	1.7	2.9	2.7	2.6
Jackson, MI MSA	2 622	2 451	2 285	2 066	15 891	15 215	14 488	13 540	74.3	73.1	74.3	3.8	4.0	4.7	5.1	5.4	6.3
Jackson, MS MSA	8 093	7 393	6 715	5 694	17 088	16 237	15 347	13 977	220.4	216.0	211.7	7.9	8.4	9.6	3.6	3.9	4.5
Jackson, TN MSA	[4]1 712	[4]1 549	[4]1 385	[4]1 139	[4]17 487	[4]16 550	[4]15 524	[4]13 990	62.4	53.6	52.4	3.0	2.7	2.2	4.9	5.0	4.2
Jacksonville, FL MSA	23 291	20 826	18 392	15 102	18 940	18 060	17 193	15 692	511.6	502.8	494.4	18.3	18.6	23.9	3.6	3.7	4.8
Jacksonville, NC MSA	2 129	1 940	1 761	1 492	13 181	12 405	11 567	10 279	44.1	42.6	41.9	1.8	1.7	1.8	4.1	3.9	4.3
Jamestown, NY MSA	2 214	2 107	2 003	1 859	15 157	14 554	13 883	13 055	67.3	67.6	68.7	3.5	4.0	4.5	5.2	5.9	6.6
Janesville-Beloit, WI MSA	2 894	2 680	2 467	2 167	18 408	17 492	16 488	15 017	78.7	79.8	76.1	3.0	3.1	4.0	3.8	3.9	5.2
Johnson City-Kingsport-Bristol, TN-VA MSA	8 240	7 535	6 839	5 812	15 917	15 130	14 262	12 965	228.6	230.4	225.8	11.3	12.1	12.6	4.9	5.3	5.6
Johnstown, PA MSA	4 038	3 761	3 494	3 131	15 966	15 190	14 338	13 017	106.3	106.0	105.5	8.4	8.9	9.8	7.9	8.4	9.2
Jonesboro, AR MSA	(5)	(5)	(5)	(5)	(5)	(5)	(5)	(5)	41.1	39.5	38.8	1.7	1.5	1.7	4.1	3.9	4.3
Joplin, MO MSA	2 762	2 493	2 221	1 828	16 411	15 541	14 583	13 082	79.5	77.0	73.6	3.4	3.5	3.5	4.3	4.6	4.8
Kalamazoo-Battle Creek, MI MSA	9 063	8 363	7 668	6 713	18 436	17 543	16 569	15 250	223.0	223.1	226.0	9.8	10.2	10.8	4.4	4.6	4.8
Kansas City, MO-KS MSA	38 857	35 517	32 177	27 549	20 363	19 405	18 367	16 892	940.3	924.3	896.3	38.8	40.1	42.1	4.1	4.3	4.7
Killeen-Temple, TX MSA	4 753	4 330	3 910	3 255	15 119	14 309	13 441	12 088	113.0	110.6	106.1	5.5	5.4	5.7	4.8	4.9	5.4
Knoxville, TN MSA	13 692	12 414	11 137	9 228	18 246	17 334	16 335	14 877	345.9	341.4	335.9	14.6	14.7	13.7	4.2	4.3	4.1
Kokomo, IN MSA	2 013	1 884	1 758	1 569	19 009	18 137	17 171	15 831	52.3	54.8	51.6	1.9	2.3	2.8	3.6	4.2	5.5
La Crosse, WI-MN MSA	2 596	2 357	2 115	1 755	18 465	17 513	16 457	14 724	71.4	69.4	68.9	2.2	2.6	2.7	3.1	3.7	3.9
Lafayette, LA MSA	6 075	5 547	5 020	4 308	15 103	14 249	13 337	12 048	167.6	161.8	159.8	10.0	10.5	11.9	6.0	6.5	7.4
Lafayette, IN MSA	3 230	2 956	2 682	2 301	17 110	16 242	15 284	13 906	87.9	82.9	85.6	2.5	2.5	3.0	2.9	3.1	3.5
Lake Charles, LA MSA	3 149	2 883	2 620	2 241	16 035	15 191	14 307	13 030	88.8	84.8	83.2	5.5	5.5	6.7	6.2	6.5	8.0
Lakeland-Winter Haven, FL MSA	8 524	7 688	6 795	5 566	16 165	15 377	14 512	13 161	195.0	196.6	199.1	12.9	14.1	17.0	6.6	7.2	8.5
Lancaster, PA MSA	10 259	9 323	8 364	7 077	19 833	18 804	17 646	16 135	235.8	231.4	227.8	7.7	8.2	8.5	3.3	3.5	3.7
Lansing-East Lansing, MI MSA	8 941	8 231	7 528	6 513	18 251	17 362	16 391	14 942	234.6	231.3	233.8	8.6	8.5	9.5	3.7	3.7	4.1
Laredo, TX MSA	2 246	1 983	1 711	1 313	10 865	10 221	9 511	8 398	69.2	70.4	68.1	8.8	10.8	6.6	12.7	15.4	9.6
Las Cruces, NM MSA	2 608	2 298	1 993	1 567	12 545	11 931	11 290	10 325	66.3	63.1	62.4	6.7	5.4	5.4	10.2	8.6	8.6
Las Vegas, NV-AZ MSA	31 367	27 059	22 772	16 746	19 999	19 065	18 041	16 755	634.6	595.1	572.4	34.9	32.8	36.5	5.5	5.5	6.4
Lawrence, KS MSA	1 730	1 548	1 361	1 081	15 842	14 985	14 045	12 510	50.7	50.0	49.2	2.5	2.4	2.6	4.9	4.8	5.2
Lawton, OK MSA	1 836	1 691	1 550	1 364	14 346	13 581	12 764	11 553	40.9	40.8	41.7	1.9	2.2	2.7	4.6	5.4	6.4
Lewiston-Auburn, ME NECMA	1 983	1 824	1 670	1 483	17 458	16 593	15 649	14 273	58.8	57.2	55.1	3.4	3.3	4.2	5.7	5.7	7.6
Lexington, KY MSA	9 274	8 443	7 627	6 426	18 199	17 368	16 479	15 087	241.3	240.3	233.0	6.7	7.2	8.3	2.8	3.0	3.6
Lima, OH MSA	2 828	2 636	2 445	2 184	17 160	16 309	15 369	14 010	75.8	75.4	75.5	4.6	4.2	4.8	6.1	5.6	6.3
Lincoln, NE MSA	5 157	4 691	4 211	3 514	19 496	18 506	17 406	15 715	139.2	136.0	132.6	3.6	3.1	3.2	2.6	2.2	2.4
Little Rock-North Little Rock, AR MSA	11 275	10 303	9 353	7 984	17 885	17 089	16 238	14 983	298.0	294.7	289.3	11.4	10.3	11.9	3.8	3.5	4.1
Longview-Marshall, TX MSA	3 894	3 569	3 242	2 753	17 269	16 334	15 312	13 791	102.9	101.2	100.5	7.9	7.7	8.5	7.7	7.6	8.5

[1]Latest estimate available when projections were prepared.
[2]Based on resident population projected as of July 1 for 2010, 2005, and 2000 by the Bureau of Economic Analysis or estimated as of July 1, 1993 by the Bureau of the Census; 1993 estimate excludes subsequent census revisions.
[3]Civilian unemployed as a percent of total civilian labor force.
[4]Excludes Chester County, which was added to the MSA on June 30, 1996.
[5]Data not available from source; new MSA effective June 30, 1996.

Source: Personal Income Projections—U.S. Bureau of Economic Analysis, "Regional Economic Information System (REIS) 1969-1994" on CD-ROM; Civilian Labor Force—U.S. Bureau of Labor Statistics, Local Area Unemployment Statistics–Time Series, Internet site <gopher://hopi2.bls.gov:70/11/Time%20Series/LA%20%20Local%20Area%20Unemployment%20Statistics/Data> for each state (accessed April 1997), BLS gopher service discontinued October 31, 1997 (related BLS Internet site <http://www.bls.gov>).

Personal Income Projections and Civilian Labor Force—Con.

[MSA = Metropolitan statistical area. CMSA = Consolidated MSA. PMSA = Primary MSA. NECMA = New England county metropolitan area. All areas defined as of June 30, 1996. Table includes 245 MSAs, 17 CMSAs, and 58 PMSAs not in New England; as well as 12 NECMAs. Table excludes 10 MSAs, 1 CMSA, and 15 PMSAs in New England]

| Metropolitan areas | Personal income projections (constant (1987) dollars) | | | | | | | | Civilian labor force | | | | | | | | |
| | Total (mil dol) | | | | Per capita[2] (dollars) | | | | Total (1,000) | | | Unemployed (1,000) | | | Unemployment rate[3] | | |
	2010	2005	2000	1993 esti-mate[1]	2010	2005	2000	1993 esti-mate[1]	1996	1995	1994	1996	1995	1994	1996	1995	1994
Los Angeles-Riverside-Orange, CA CMSA	373 551	337 862	301 602	253 950	19 976	19 039	18 025	16 696	7 454.3	7 371.0	7 388.8	545.7	552.8	639.4	7.3	7.5	8.7
Los Angeles-Long Beach, CA PMSA	211 661	194 320	176 837	154 444	20 264	19 315	18 288	16 909	4 415.4	4 380.6	4 390.6	362.9	345.1	411.5	8.2	7.9	9.4
Orange, CA PMSA	76 689	68 694	60 478	49 134	23 771	22 549	21 228	19 534	1 343.8	1 322.8	1 333.5	55.2	67.5	76.4	4.1	5.1	5.7
Riverside-San Bernardino, CA PMSA	66 708	58 289	49 694	38 455	16 151	15 359	14 492	13 411	1 313.2	1 284.3	1 279.7	100.7	111.7	121.5	7.7	8.7	9.5
Ventura, CA PMSA	18 492	16 558	14 593	11 918	20 574	19 614	18 585	17 176	381.8	383.4	384.9	27.0	28.5	30.1	7.1	7.4	7.8
Louisville, KY-IN MSA	21 685	20 011	18 390	16 037	20 558	19 510	18 368	16 465	529.2	529.9	518.8	23.1	23.1	22.3	4.4	4.4	4.3
Lubbock, TX MSA	4 444	4 084	3 721	3 188	17 675	16 677	15 588	14 007	122.2	120.0	117.6	4.8	4.9	5.0	3.9	4.1	4.2
Lynchburg, VA MSA	3 858	3 546	3 236	2 831	16 971	16 183	15 307	14 105	102.2	106.6	104.7	3.8	3.9	4.2	3.7	3.6	4.0
Macon, GA MSA	5 926	5 419	4 925	4 231	17 203	16 312	15 348	13 963	147.1	142.0	142.2	7.0	7.1	8.3	4.8	5.0	5.8
Madison, WI MSA	10 308	9 348	8 382	6 996	22 181	21 126	19 966	18 107	257.0	248.3	242.7	4.3	4.4	5.6	1.7	1.8	2.3
Mansfield, OH MSA	2 910	2 733	2 559	2 329	15 964	15 217	14 394	13 303	84.3	84.1	85.1	5.1	5.2	6.7	6.1	6.2	7.9
McAllen-Edinburg-Mission, TX MSA	5 887	5 180	4 470	3 486	9 969	9 400	8 782	7 873	189.9	187.6	182.5	36.0	37.1	35.7	19.0	19.8	19.6
Medford-Ashland, OR MSA	3 355	3 026	2 695	2 209	17 409	16 519	15 531	13 965	85.9	82.5	82.4	7.1	5.5	5.5	8.3	6.7	6.7
Melbourne-Titusville-Palm Bay, FL MSA	10 707	9 442	8 189	6 435	18 010	17 145	16 184	14 766	197.8	200.9	207.1	10.8	13.1	15.3	5.4	6.5	7.4
Memphis, TN-AR-MS MSA	23 817	21 711	19 633	16 586	19 573	18 587	17 495	15 913	536.1	525.1	511.0	23.4	25.9	24.4	4.4	4.9	4.8
Merced, CA MSA	3 444	3 099	2 744	2 267	14 411	13 698	12 912	11 772	82.9	84.7	87.2	13.4	14.3	13.5	16.2	16.9	15.5
Miami-Fort Lauderdale, FL CMSA	82 074	74 204	66 292	55 264	19 859	18 945	17 926	16 478	1 763.3	1 751.6	1 752.6	112.6	116.5	134.0	6.4	6.7	7.6
Fort Lauderdale, FL PMSA	38 611	34 569	30 526	25 138	21 897	21 006	19 996	18 610	733.3	719.0	713.2	37.7	41.0	46.5	5.1	5.7	6.5
Miami, FL PMSA	43 463	39 635	35 766	30 125	18 343	17 452	16 471	15 039	1 030.1	1 032.6	1 039.4	74.9	75.5	87.6	7.3	7.3	8.4
Milwaukee-Racine, WI CMSA	38 884	35 852	32 855	28 833	21 874	20 738	19 495	17 643	896.4	874.2	868.0	31.6	31.2	40.8	3.5	3.6	4.7
Milwaukee-Waukesha, WI PMSA	34 885	32 163	29 473	25 865	22 103	20 945	19 679	17 788	802.3	781.7	776.3	27.6	27.1	35.5	3.4	3.5	4.6
Racine, WI PMSA	3 999	3 689	3 382	2 968	20 064	19 102	18 027	16 469	94.1	92.5	91.8	4.0	4.0	5.4	4.2	4.4	5.8
Minneapolis-St. Paul, MN-WI MSA	69 735	63 922	57 955	50 034	22 152	21 199	20 147	18 849	1 618.3	1 603.9	1 585.4	50.0	46.9	51.5	3.1	2.9	3.2
Mobile, AL MSA	9 064	8 277	7 516	6 501	15 966	15 123	14 210	12 875	258.2	254.3	248.3	13.5	17.4	16.3	5.2	6.8	6.5
Modesto, CA MSA	8 527	7 616	6 681	5 367	16 304	15 494	14 606	13 337	196.6	196.0	196.1	27.6	30.0	30.7	14.0	15.3	15.7
Monroe, LA MSA	2 580	2 349	2 120	1 775	15 328	14 492	13 605	12 165	69.2	67.3	65.5	4.4	3.9	4.6	6.4	5.8	7.0
Montgomery, AL MSA	6 336	5 784	5 251	4 491	17 933	17 022	16 033	14 610	156.0	152.6	149.5	6.3	8.6	7.3	4.0	5.6	4.9
Muncie, IN MSA	2 317	2 136	1 956	1 705	18 262	17 196	16 007	14 281	62.8	65.9	65.2	2.9	3.3	3.7	4.6	5.0	5.7
Myrtle Beach, SC MSA	3 158	2 802	2 450	1 956	16 550	15 647	14 663	13 173	92.7	90.8	85.0	5.1	4.6	6.1	5.5	5.0	7.2
Naples, FL MSA	7 323	6 300	5 286	3 896	27 772	26 481	25 063	22 824	83.1	81.5	80.6	4.8	5.7	6.6	5.8	6.9	8.2
Nashville, TN MSA	26 876	24 216	21 538	17 640	20 868	19 818	18 651	16 888	619.7	607.1	586.3	20.4	20.4	18.1	3.3	3.4	3.1
New London-Norwich, CT NECMA	6 050	5 559	5 067	4 471	21 455	20 499	19 404	17 970	132.9	131.4	131.5	7.9	7.0	6.8	5.9	5.3	5.2
New Orleans, LA MSA	25 358	23 503	21 688	19 222	17 765	16 914	16 017	14 740	612.9	605.4	601.5	39.6	38.7	44.7	6.5	6.4	7.4
New York-Northern New Jersey-Long Island, NY-NJ-CT-PA CMSA/NECMA	551 482	515 923	479 982	431 301	26 368	25 148	23 791	21 953	9 695.1	9 500.2	9 509.1	629.3	615.0	663.7	6.5	6.5	7.0
Bergen-Passaic, NJ PMSA	38 436	36 131	33 783	30 691	27 773	26 681	25 429	23 652	670.3	661.6	655.5	42.4	44.7	47.8	6.3	6.8	7.3
Dutchess, NY PMSA	5 913	5 534	5 161	4 678	21 147	20 174	19 128	17 794	117.6	115.2	117.2	5.0	5.8	8.2	4.2	5.0	7.0
Jersey City, NJ PMSA	11 927	11 126	10 325	9 325	20 304	19 350	18 278	16 868	287.5	284.3	281.5	26.5	26.5	26.3	9.2	9.3	9.3
Middlesex-Somerset-Hunterdon, NJ PMSA	34 599	31 550	28 375	23 923	27 098	25 903	24 546	22 637	613.2	599.8	587.5	27.9	28.8	30.6	4.5	4.8	5.2
Monmouth-Ocean, NJ PMSA	30 816	27 850	24 787	20 600	23 954	22 918	21 714	20 145	512.9	501.3	491.4	28.7	28.7	29.9	5.6	5.7	6.1
Nassau-Suffolk, NY PMSA	73 732	69 393	65 041	59 075	26 614	25 448	24 162	22 350	1 365.5	1 355.8	1 362.1	57.5	67.7	77.4	4.2	5.0	5.7
New Haven-Bridgeport-Stamford-Waterbury-Danbury, CT NECMA	53 121	48 924	44 699	39 597	29 165	27 856	26 356	24 318	856.8	847.8	859.1	47.3	45.0	46.5	5.5	5.3	5.4
New York, NY PMSA	229 857	217 235	204 660	187 216	26 617	25 261	23 787	21 839	3 923.2	3 792.5	3 825.6	315.0	287.0	309.9	8.0	7.6	8.1
Newark, NJ PMSA	54 601	51 304	47 932	43 188	26 641	25 513	24 218	22 393	1 009.1	1 003.9	991.5	62.0	63.2	68.8	6.1	6.3	6.9
Newburgh, NY-PA PMSA	8 050	7 285	6 493	5 472	18 136	17 374	16 546	15 519	170.0	168.4	169.5	7.4	8.5	9.5	4.4	5.1	5.6
Trenton, NJ PMSA	10 430	9 591	8 727	7 537	27 505	26 263	24 834	22 936	169.1	169.5	168.3	9.6	9.2	9.0	5.6	5.4	5.3
Norfolk-Virginia Beach-Newport News, VA-NC MSA	29 748	27 230	24 780	21 845	17 179	16 399	15 544	14 430	715.9	729.1	716.7	34.5	36.1	41.0	4.8	4.9	5.7
Ocala, FL MSA	4 655	4 067	3 483	2 670	15 241	14 520	13 725	12 468	91.3	88.4	88.9	4.4	4.8	6.3	4.9	5.4	7.1
Odessa-Midland, TX MSA	4 778	4 426	4 071	3 536	18 564	17 612	16 583	15 079	120.2	119.5	119.7	6.8	7.4	8.7	5.7	6.2	7.3
Oklahoma City, OK MSA	19 511	17 950	16 410	14 247	17 046	16 288	15 473	14 308	518.0	503.6	496.6	17.4	18.5	22.8	3.4	3.7	4.6
Omaha, NE-IA MSA	15 517	14 201	12 860	10 930	20 469	19 451	18 330	16 612	375.8	368.9	360.6	11.1	10.2	11.4	3.0	2.8	3.2
Orlando, FL MSA	35 646	30 904	26 228	20 016	18 158	17 295	16 343	15 007	776.5	751.2	743.4	29.3	33.8	42.0	3.8	4.5	5.6
Owensboro, KY MSA	1 631	1 501	1 375	1 200	16 340	15 538	14 676	13 422	47.7	49.2	47.6	2.8	2.8	2.4	5.8	5.6	5.0

[1]Latest estimate available when projections were prepared.
[2]Based on resident population projected as of July 1 for 2010, 2005, and 2000 by the Bureau of Economic Analysis or estimated as of July 1, 1993 by the Bureau of the Census; 1993 estimate excludes subsequent census revisions.
[3]Civilian unemployed as a percent of total civilian labor force.

Source: Personal Income Projections—U.S. Bureau of Economic Analysis, "Regional Economic Information System (REIS) 1969-1994" on CD-ROM; Civilian Labor Force—U.S. Bureau of Labor Statistics, Local Area Unemployment Statistics–Time Series, Internet site <gopher://hopi2.bls.gov:70/11/Time%20Series/LA%20Local%20Area%20Unemployment%20Statistics/Data> for each state (accessed April 1997), BLS gopher service discontinued October 31, 1997 (related BLS Internet site <http://www.bls.gov>).

[MSA = Metropolitan statistical area. CMSA = Consolidated MSA. PMSA = Primary MSA. NECMA = New England county metropolitan area. All areas defined as of June 30, 1996. Table includes 245 MSAs, 17 CMSAs, and 58 PMSAs not in New England; as well as 12 NECMAs. Table excludes 10 MSAs, 1 CMSA, and 15 PMSAs in New England]

| Metropolitan areas | Personal income projections (constant (1987) dollars) | | | | | | | | Civilian labor force | | | | | | | | |
| | Total (mil dol) | | | | Per capita[2] (dollars) | | | | Total (1,000) | | | Unemployed (1,000) | | | Unemployment rate[3] | | |
	2010	2005	2000	1993 esti-mate[1]	2010	2005	2000	1993 esti-mate[1]	1996	1995	1994	1996	1995	1994	1996	1995	1994
Panama City, FL MSA	2 869	2 554	2 245	1 805	16 345	15 496	14 566	13 153	64.6	63.0	63.9	3.8	4.2	5.4	5.9	6.6	8.5
Parkersburg-Marietta, WV-OH MSA	2 735	2 537	2 351	2 080	16 912	16 049	15 118	13 777	77.0	75.7	75.0	4.8	5.2	5.3	6.2	6.9	7.0
Pensacola, FL MSA	7 098	6 409	5 728	4 789	16 067	15 260	14 378	13 123	166.6	166.7	166.1	6.5	7.0	7.6	3.9	4.2	4.6
Peoria-Pekin, IL MSA	7 106	6 602	6 095	5 427	19 190	18 288	17 304	15 823	180.5	179.3	174.9	11.0	7.7	8.1	6.1	4.3	4.6
Philadelphia-Wilmington-Atlantic City, PA-NJ-DE-MD CMSA	148 635	137 662	126 811	111 611	22 582	21 549	20 393	18 785	2 987.1	2 931.2	2 940.9	169.7	178.0	185.3	5.7	6.1	6.3
Atlantic-Cape May, NJ PMSA	9 136	8 320	7 465	6 248	22 870	21 911	20 776	19 048	173.1	169.6	166.8	16.0	16.1	16.3	9.3	9.5	9.8
Philadelphia, PA-NJ PMSA	122 668	113 943	105 396	93 471	22 732	21 686	20 523	18 920	2 462.8	2 414.6	2 426.4	130.0	142.3	147.9	5.3	5.9	6.1
Vineland-Millville-Bridgeton, NJ PMSA	2 956	2 716	2 467	2 113	19 229	18 167	16 955	15 203	64.6	64.8	63.8	6.4	6.3	6.7	9.9	9.7	10.5
Wilmington-Newark, DE-MD PMSA	13 876	12 684	11 483	9 779	21 938	20 961	19 867	18 313	286.7	282.2	283.9	17.2	13.3	14.4	6.0	4.7	5.1
Phoenix-Mesa, AZ MSA	61 549	54 395	47 217	37 072	19 048	18 080	17 030	15 498	1 459.8	1 354.7	1 256.9	54.4	46.9	59.4	3.7	3.5	4.7
Pine Bluff, AR MSA	1 204	1 130	1 066	980	14 131	13 422	12 694	11 629	37.2	36.9	37.2	2.9	2.8	3.3	7.7	7.6	8.8
Pittsburgh, PA MSA	51 678	48 286	45 064	41 008	20 366	19 454	18 458	17 038	1 146.8	1 142.0	1 143.1	57.3	67.3	72.4	5.0	5.9	6.3
Pittsfield, MA NECMA	3 065	2 856	2 650	2 351	21 404	20 355	19 158	17 248	65.6	65.7	66.5	3.2	4.0	4.9	4.9	6.2	7.4
Pocatello, ID MSA	(4)	(4)	(4)	(4)	(4)	(4)	(4)	(4)	37.1	36.3	36.6	2.0	2.1	2.3	5.3	5.8	6.4
Portland, ME NECMA	6 320	5 738	5 172	4 430	21 898	20 844	19 709	18 002	140.7	132.1	126.6	4.1	4.7	6.3	2.9	3.6	5.0
Portland-Salem, OR-WA CMSA	48 223	43 480	38 672	31 876	19 828	18 907	17 901	16 394	1 167.4	1 113.6	1 094.7	54.9	43.5	48.8	4.7	3.9	4.5
Portland-Vancouver, OR-WA PMSA	42 038	37 892	33 694	27 795	20 392	19 451	18 423	16 901	1 003.8	956.3	936.6	45.5	36.1	40.4	4.5	3.8	4.3
Salem, OR PMSA	6 185	5 588	4 978	4 081	16 689	15 896	15 021	13 612	163.6	157.3	158.1	9.3	7.4	8.4	5.7	4.7	5.3
Providence-Warwick-Pawtucket, RI NECMA	20 320	18 721	17 155	15 120	20 071	19 124	18 071	16 541	456.3	446.9	458.6	23.5	31.3	32.3	5.1	7.0	7.0
Provo-Orem, UT MSA	5 391	4 691	3 983	2 964	13 576	12 765	11 882	10 459	147.6	142.4	142.6	4.3	4.1	4.5	2.9	2.9	3.1
Pueblo, CO MSA	2 101	1 955	1 808	1 605	15 577	14 835	14 004	12 765	58.2	58.0	54.8	3.4	3.4	3.2	5.9	5.9	5.8
Punta Gorda, FL MSA	3 370	2 876	2 389	1 735	17 184	16 348	15 390	14 059	44.4	44.0	44.6	1.9	2.1	2.5	4.2	4.7	5.6
Raleigh-Durham-Chapel Hill, NC MSA	26 815	23 757	20 745	16 164	21 139	20 111	18 990	17 230	579.6	550.2	537.8	13.6	14.1	14.4	2.3	2.6	2.7
Rapid City, SD MSA	1 923	1 715	1 505	1 213	17 512	16 635	15 663	14 118	45.3	44.1	43.8	1.5	1.3	1.5	3.3	3.0	3.4
Reading, PA MSA	7 700	7 124	6 553	5 787	20 189	19 259	18 222	16 744	180.1	177.2	175.5	7.8	8.5	8.5	4.3	4.8	4.9
Redding, CA MSA	3 766	3 306	2 840	2 188	17 300	16 375	15 350	13 776	72.3	72.6	73.5	7.1	8.2	8.8	9.9	11.3	11.9
Reno, NV MSA	8 547	7 735	6 916	5 718	24 539	23 497	22 361	20 822	167.2	163.0	161.3	8.1	7.8	8.4	4.8	4.8	5.2
Richland-Kennewick-Pasco, WA MSA	4 388	3 871	3 348	2 606	19 705	18 674	17 545	15 679	92.8	94.0	92.9	8.7	7.5	5.5	9.4	8.0	6.0
Richmond-Petersburg, VA MSA	22 416	20 552	18 748	16 452	21 422	20 482	19 456	18 158	489.6	507.8	497.2	18.2	19.0	21.9	3.7	3.7	4.4
Roanoke, VA MSA	4 860	4 534	4 218	3 820	19 787	18 922	17 963	16 768	127.8	130.6	127.7	3.7	3.7	4.5	2.9	2.8	3.5
Rochester, MN MSA	2 787	2 556	2 315	1 963	20 658	19 796	18 839	17 452	64.5	63.8	64.8	2.0	1.9	2.2	3.0	2.9	3.4
Rochester, NY MSA	23 531	22 048	20 547	18 468	20 062	19 186	18 224	16 954	569.7	563.7	569.8	22.7	25.7	30.0	4.0	4.6	5.3
Rockford, IL MSA	7 221	6 648	6 064	5 247	18 434	17 587	16 650	15 285	193.7	192.8	187.9	9.2	8.1	10.4	4.8	4.2	5.5
Rocky Mount, NC MSA	2 652	2 419	2 191	1 836	16 252	15 477	14 639	13 275	73.1	68.4	68.3	6.2	4.4	4.0	8.5	6.5	5.9
Sacramento-Yolo, CA CMSA	43 343	38 139	32 858	25 802	20 109	19 098	17 995	16 369	811.8	803.4	795.7	48.8	54.1	56.1	6.0	6.7	7.0
Sacramento, CA PMSA	39 916	35 052	30 125	23 536	20 180	19 171	18 074	16 450	724.9	715.9	708.6	43.3	48.1	50.2	6.0	6.7	7.1
Yolo, CA PMSA	3 427	3 086	2 733	2 266	19 317	18 294	17 164	15 564	86.9	87.5	87.1	5.5	6.0	5.9	6.3	6.9	6.8
Saginaw-Bay City-Midland, MI MSA	7 915	7 372	6 843	6 103	18 492	17 564	16 552	15 144	192.0	192.3	194.6	9.4	11.3	12.5	4.9	5.9	6.4
St. Cloud, MN MSA	2 897	2 641	2 376	1 970	16 250	15 361	14 371	12 686	93.5	91.9	90.6	4.7	3.8	3.7	5.0	4.2	4.1
St. Joseph, MO MSA	1 755	1 632	1 509	1 320	16 434	15 612	14 737	13 428	49.6	50.2	48.4	3.3	3.6	4.3	6.6	7.1	8.9
St. Louis, MO-IL MSA	59 217	54 766	50 388	44 447	19 690	18 731	17 695	16 681	1 362.8	1 334.3	1 286.2	61.3	63.3	61.4	4.5	4.7	4.8
Salinas, CA MSA	8 788	7 925	7 051	6 110	19 690	18 731	17 695	16 681	179.3	174.9	178.7	19.8	21.8	21.6	11.0	12.5	12.1
Salt Lake City-Ogden, UT MSA	26 041	23 001	19 932	15 754	16 835	15 960	15 026	13 646	642.2	625.9	628.3	20.5	20.6	22.0	3.2	3.3	3.5
San Angelo, TX MSA	1 918	1 759	1 594	1 376	16 973	16 081	15 088	13 756	50.8	50.1	49.6	1.8	2.1	2.3	3.5	4.1	4.6
San Antonio, TX MSA	29 618	26 682	23 751	19 651	17 195	16 302	15 347	13 965	732.0	719.5	698.6	31.7	31.8	31.9	4.3	4.4	4.6
San Diego, CA MSA	68 450	60 697	52 899	42 716	19 928	18 926	17 848	16 354	1 236.3	1 226.3	1 235.1	65.6	78.4	86.9	5.3	6.4	7.0
San Francisco-Oakland-San Jose, CA CMSA	197 876	180 019	161 812	137 838	25 730	24 501	23 163	21 306	3 553.3	3 484.4	3 499.2	163.4	195.9	216.8	4.6	5.6	6.2
Oakland, CA PMSA	62 999	57 101	51 145	43 379	24 345	23 124	21 798	20 000	1 142.9	1 132.8	1 136.1	56.6	65.2	69.8	5.0	5.8	6.1
San Francisco, CA PMSA	56 592	52 198	47 721	42 097	31 299	29 744	28 054	25 705	910.6	891.7	902.7	36.0	45.2	49.2	4.0	5.1	5.4
San Jose, CA PMSA	47 850	43 518	39 058	32 969	25 896	24 660	23 311	21 359	896.6	860.7	859.6	32.3	42.6	53.7	3.6	5.0	6.2
Santa Cruz-Watsonville, CA PMSA	6 579	5 924	5 240	4 271	22 213	21 173	20 023	18 297	140.2	142.6	141.6	11.6	13.0	13.7	8.3	9.1	9.7
Santa Rosa, CA PMSA	11 626	10 385	9 101	7 385	21 771	20 779	19 691	18 177	230.4	225.4	226.1	10.1	12.5	13.1	4.4	5.5	5.8
Vallejo-Fairfield-Napa, CA PMSA	12 230	10 893	9 548	7 737	19 837	18 823	17 714	16 136	232.6	231.3	233.1	16.7	17.3	17.4	7.2	7.5	7.4
San Luis Obispo-Atascadero-Paso Robles, CA MSA	5 504	4 849	4 176	3 215	17 893	16 972	15 963	14 481	103.6	102.3	101.8	5.7	6.7	7.2	5.5	6.5	7.1
Santa Barbara-Santa Maria-Lompoc, CA MSA	10 538	9 546	8 519	7 085	22 522	21 457	20 299	18 744	192.7	193.3	196.9	10.9	13.0	14.1	5.7	6.7	7.2

[1]Latest estimate available when projections were prepared.
[2]Based on resident population projected as of July 1 for 2010, 2005, and 2000 by the Bureau of Economic Analysis or estimated as of July 1, 1993 by the Bureau of the Census; 1993 estimate excludes subsequent census revisions.
[3]Civilian unemployed as a percent of total civilian labor force.
[4]Data not available from source; new MSA effective June 30, 1996.

Source: Personal Income Projections—U.S. Bureau of Economic Analysis, "Regional Economic Information System (REIS) 1969-1994" on CD-ROM; Civilian Labor Force—U.S. Bureau of Labor Statistics, Local Area Unemployment Statistics–Time Series, Internet site <gopher://hopi2.bls.gov:70/11/Time%20Series/LA%20%20Local%20Area%20Unemployment%20Statistics/Data> for each state (accessed April 1997), BLS gopher service discontinued October 31, 1997 (related BLS Internet site <http://www.bls.gov>).

[MSA = Metropolitan statistical area. CMSA = Consolidated MSA. PMSA = Primary MSA. NECMA = New England county metropolitan area. All areas defined as of June 30, 1996. Table includes 245 MSAs, 17 CMSAs, and 58 PMSAs not in New England; as well as 12 NECMAs. Table excludes 10 MSAs, 1 CMSA, and 15 PMSAs in New England]

Metropolitan areas	Personal income projections (constant (1987) dollars)								Civilian labor force								
	Total (mil dol)				Per capita[2] (dollars)				Total (1,000)			Unemployed (1,000)			Unemployment rate[3]		
	2010	2005	2000	1993 estimate[1]	2010	2005	2000	1993 estimate[1]	1996	1995	1994	1996	1995	1994	1996	1995	1994
Santa Fe, NM MSA	3 631	3 213	2 796	2 207	21 399	20 285	19 097	17 377	72.2	73.2	72.6	3.7	2.9	2.4	5.1	3.9	3.3
Sarasota-Bradenton, FL MSA	17 443	15 291	13 161	10 215	24 143	23 059	21 861	20 010	242.5	226.6	225.8	8.0	8.3	9.9	3.3	3.7	4.4
Savannah, GA MSA	5 825	5 287	4 757	3 989	18 090	17 171	16 165	14 685	130.1	126.1	125.8	6.3	6.6	7.0	4.8	5.2	5.6
Scranton--Wilkes-Barre--Hazleton, PA MSA	12 112	11 275	10 455	9 398	17 867	17 003	16 035	14 706	310.7	311.7	309.8	22.1	24.1	24.5	7.1	7.7	7.9
Seattle-Tacoma-Bremerton, WA CMSA .	91 053	81 441	71 791	59 429	22 055	21 093	20 051	18 636	1 787.4	1 732.3	1 673.5	96.1	96.7	98.3	5.4	5.6	5.9
Bremerton, WA PMSA	4 887	4 375	3 867	3 137	17 386	16 590	15 744	14 579	93.5	90.8	88.3	6.3	6.0	5.3	6.8	6.6	6.0
Olympia, WA PMSA	5 006	4 392	3 771	2 900	19 373	18 398	17 328	15 812	97.0	93.7	88.9	6.4	5.8	5.5	6.6	6.2	6.2
Seattle-Bellevue-Everett, WA PMSA	67 074	59 992	52 863	44 015	23 956	22 960	21 888	20 391	1 277.8	1 235.7	1 196.0	63.5	65.6	68.1	5.0	5.3	5.7
Tacoma, WA PMSA	14 086	12 683	11 291	9 377	17 850	17 008	16 098	14 839	319.0	312.1	300.3	19.8	19.3	19.5	6.2	6.2	6.5
Sharon, PA MSA	2 000	1 873	1 750	1 583	15 552	14 849	14 068	12 939	55.5	54.7	54.6	2.4	2.8	3.8	4.4	5.1	6.9
Sheboygan, WI MSA	2 295	2 114	1 933	1 678	19 128	18 209	17 215	15 811	61.7	61.2	59.4	1.7	1.7	2.0	2.8	2.7	3.3
Sherman-Denison, TX MSA	1 869	1 724	1 580	1 361	17 561	16 629	15 613	14 157	49.3	48.0	47.5	2.4	2.4	2.9	4.8	5.1	6.1
Shreveport-Bossier City, LA MSA......	6 938	6 418	5 911	5 245	17 039	16 174	15 266	13 924	183.1	178.0	176.1	13.2	13.0	14.4	7.2	7.3	8.2
Sioux City, IA-NE MSA	2 383	2 198	2 011	1 747	18 055	17 202	16 242	14 742	66.7	64.8	64.4	2.4	2.0	2.0	3.6	3.0	3.2
Sioux Falls, SD MSA............	3 835	3 442	3 042	2 436	20 606	19 555	18 391	16 416	93.7	89.9	88.0	2.0	1.8	2.1	2.1	2.0	2.3
South Bend, IN MSA	5 201	4 793	4 389	3 821	18 254	17 405	16 464	15 071	135.8	139.3	134.2	5.4	5.9	5.9	4.0	4.2	4.4
Spokane, WA MSA	8 095	7 387	6 673	5 719	17 736	16 900	15 988	14 630	201.6	198.1	189.0	11.7	10.6	9.3	5.8	5.4	4.9
Springfield, IL MSA	4 548	4 165	3 773	3 241	20 365	19 391	18 305	16 662	106.5	106.3	105.6	4.8	4.7	4.5	4.5	4.4	4.2
Springfield, MO MSA	6 298	5 611	4 920	3 981	17 790	16 846	15 791	14 100	170.1	163.0	153.7	5.8	5.6	5.1	3.4	3.4	3.3
Springfield, MA NECMA	12 132	11 254	10 387	9 161	18 353	17 560	16 671	15 329	287.8	289.0	292.2	12.9	16.9	20.0	4.5	5.8	6.8
State College, PA MSA............	2 532	2 296	2 054	1 714	16 622	15 756	14 788	13 275	65.1	62.6	61.8	1.9	2.1	2.2	2.9	3.4	3.6
Steubenville-Weirton, OH-WV MSA	2 199	2 084	1 981	1 836	15 628	14 878	14 092	13 042	57.5	57.5	58.5	3.6	3.8	4.8	6.3	6.7	8.3
Stockton-Lodi, CA MSA	10 656	9 605	8 536	7 102	16 946	16 105	15 194	13 901	240.8	242.9	244.5	27.0	29.8	30.8	11.2	12.3	12.6
Sumter, SC MSA	1 642	1 489	1 338	1 135	13 350	12 632	11 849	10 695	44.5	44.9	44.3	2.9	2.6	3.5	6.5	5.9	7.9
Syracuse, NY MSA	14 419	13 530	12 627	11 366	17 947	17 136	16 242	15 058	363.3	361.5	366.3	17.6	20.0	21.6	4.8	5.5	5.9
Tallahassee, FL MSA	5 801	5 121	4 443	3 485	17 348	16 488	15 540	13 964	142.1	142.5	140.2	4.4	4.2	5.3	3.1	3.0	3.8
Tampa-St. Petersburg-Clearwater, FL MSA	52 914	47 126	41 370	33 366	19 225	18 268	17 215	15 616	1 100.9	1 090.2	1 078.0	43.1	47.5	57.3	3.9	4.4	5.3
Terre Haute, IN MSA	2 575	2 401	2 230	1 976	16 317	15 513	14 612	13 175	74.2	77.2	74.9	4.8	4.8	5.0	6.5	6.2	6.7
Texarkana, TX-Texarkana, AR MSA	2 092	1 924	1 761	1 535	15 779	14 901	13 961	12 603	57.4	56.9	57.2	4.2	4.5	5.3	7.4	7.9	9.2
Toledo, OH MSA	12 401	11 528	10 669	9 541	18 736	17 829	16 838	15 550	313.5	310.5	312.1	15.1	15.1	17.2	4.8	4.9	5.5
Topeka, KS MSA	3 614	3 328	3 039	2 625	19 376	18 469	17 466	15 998	89.4	88.4	88.9	4.6	4.0	4.4	5.2	4.5	5.0
Tucson, AZ MSA	14 746	13 258	11 758	9 571	16 575	15 737	14 824	13 483	382.1	371.5	356.1	14.3	12.3	14.1	3.7	3.3	3.9
Tulsa, OK MSA	15 525	14 261	13 010	11 201	17 939	17 161	16 326	15 171	387.5	380.9	381.4	12.9	15.8	22.2	3.3	4.1	5.8
Tuscaloosa, AL MSA	2 869	2 612	2 363	2 017	16 182	15 312	14 370	13 004	77.8	76.0	74.8	2.8	3.6	3.4	3.6	4.7	4.6
Tyler, TX MSA	3 518	3 198	2 876	2 409	18 731	17 794	16 767	15 315	87.0	84.5	82.7	5.6	4.7	4.8	6.4	5.5	5.8
Utica-Rome, NY MSA	5 160	4 897	4 642	4 324	16 166	15 463	14 695	13 619	141.8	144.0	144.0	7.5	8.0	8.1	5.3	5.5	5.6
Victoria, TX MSA	1 737	1 577	1 415	1 175	18 620	17 656	16 606	15 028	41.9	42.0	42.0	2.1	2.5	2.5	5.1	6.1	5.9
Visalia-Tulare-Porterville, CA MSA......	6 139	5 532	4 912	4 044	14 482	13 783	13 032	11 959	160.6	162.0	165.3	25.5	26.9	26.4	15.9	16.6	16.0
Waco, TX MSA	3 636	3 336	3 032	2 589	16 703	15 779	14 782	13 312	100.0	99.6	97.4	4.5	4.6	4.6	4.4	4.6	4.7
Washington-Baltimore, DC-MD-VA-WV CMSA	202 139	184 234	166 382	141 541	24 075	23 041	21 910	20 262	3 916.3	3 909.3	3 867.5	172.8	182.8	182.1	4.4	4.7	4.7
Baltimore, MD PMSA	60 769	55 989	51 216	44 172	21 773	20 794	19 724	18 074	1 302.9	1 275.8	1 262.7	70.7	72.0	73.9	5.4	5.6	5.9
Hagerstown, MD PMSA	2 381	2 173	1 964	1 675	15 779	15 098	14 355	13 290	68.7	65.9	64.4	3.6	4.1	4.3	5.3	6.2	6.7
Washington, DC-MD-VA-WV PMSA .	138 989	126 072	113 202	95 694	25 482	24 435	23 291	21 672	2 544.7	2 567.7	2 540.5	98.4	106.7	103.8	3.9	4.2	4.1
Waterloo-Cedar Falls, IA MSA	2 164	2 031	1 900	1 746	17 205	16 353	15 425	14 032	68.8	67.8	68.0	3.1	3.0	3.4	4.6	4.5	4.9
Wausau, WI MSA	2 506	2 277	2 045	1 714	18 040	17 067	15 999	14 329	71.2	70.5	68.8	2.8	3.1	3.7	3.9	4.4	5.4
West Palm Beach-Boca Raton, FL MSA	39 746	34 878	30 058	23 444	31 559	29 858	27 993	25 159	466.6	451.2	455.1	31.1	32.4	40.1	6.7	7.2	8.8
Wheeling, WV-OH MSA	2 622	2 468	2 330	2 156	16 456	15 613	14 738	13 596	72.6	71.2	71.8	4.1	4.5	5.6	5.7	6.4	7.9
Wichita, KS MSA	11 353	10 445	9 525	8 156	19 543	18 646	17 646	16 154	267.0	262.2	268.0	11.5	12.3	17.1	4.3	4.7	6.4
Wichita Falls, TX MSA	2 462	2 314	2 166	1 911	18 278	17 310	16 272	14 696	66.0	64.5	63.0	3.0	3.0	3.3	4.5	4.7	5.2
Williamsport, PA MSA	2 193	2 034	1 878	1 666	16 599	15 827	14 979	13 782	57.8	57.0	57.0	3.7	4.2	4.2	6.5	7.3	7.3
Wilmington, NC MSA	4 214	3 738	3 275	2 590	16 942	16 093	15 185	13 820	105.7	99.2	99.1	5.7	6.6	7.8	5.3	6.6	7.9
Yakima, WA MSA	3 938	3 602	3 259	2 794	16 506	15 721	14 856	13 716	116.0	114.0	110.5	15.6	14.3	12.9	13.4	12.6	11.7
York, PA MSA	7 880	7 229	6 575	5 663	19 613	18 611	17 488	16 006	192.8	190.4	187.6	8.4	8.0	8.3	4.3	4.2	4.4
Youngstown-Warren, OH MSA	10 870	10 180	9 513	8 559	17 383	16 481	15 498	14 140	282.7	285.3	282.9	18.0	17.9	22.1	6.4	6.3	7.8
Yuba City, CA MSA	2 577	2 326	2 070	1 702	15 790	14 997	14 131	12 851	55.4	56.0	56.7	8.3	9.1	9.2	15.0	16.3	16.1
Yuma, AZ MSA	2 010	1 808	1 607	1 315	12 824	12 194	11 514	10 560	68.8	66.5	63.6	21.4	19.1	20.4	31.0	28.7	32.2

[1]Latest estimate available when projections were prepared.
[2]Based on resident population projected as of July 1 for 2010, 2005, and 2000 by the Bureau of Economic Analysis or estimated as of July 1, 1993 by the Bureau of the Census; 1993 estimate excludes subsequent census revisions.
[3]Civilian unemployed as a percent of total civilian labor force.

Source: Personal Income Projections—U.S. Bureau of Economic Analysis, "Regional Economic Information System (REIS) 1969-1994" on CD-ROM; Civilian Labor Force—U.S. Bureau of Labor Statistics, Local Area Unemployment Statistics–Time Series, Internet site <gopher://hopi2.bls.gov:70/11/Time%20Series/LA%20%20Local%20Area%20Unemployment%20Statistics/Data> for each state (accessed April 1997), BLS gopher service discontinued October 31, 1997 (related BLS Internet site <http://www.bls.gov>).

Table B–9. Metro Areas — Nonfarm Employment and Average Annual Pay

[MSA = Metropolitan statistical area. CMSA = Consolidated MSA. PMSA = Primary MSA. NECMA = New England county metropolitan area. All areas defined as of June 30, 1996. Table includes 245 MSAs, 17 CMSAs, and 58 PMSAs not in New England; as well as 12 NECMAs. Table excludes 10 MSAs, 1 CMSA, and 15 PMSAs in New England]

Metropolitan areas	Nonfarm employment 1996									1995 (1,000)	1994 (1,000)	Average annual pay 1996, preliminary			1995 (dollars)	1994 (dollars)
	Total (1,000)	Percent change, 1994–1996	Goods-related (1,000)		Service-related (1,000)							Dollars	Rank[5]	Percent change, 1994–1996		
			Total[1]	Man-ufac-turing	Total[2]	Trade[3]	FIRE[4]	Serv-ices	Gov-ern-ment							
Abilene, TX MSA	53.7	6.1	6.6	3.1	47.0	14.3	2.0	18.2	9.8	52.6	50.6	21 035	252	3.5	20 365	20 320
Albany, GA MSA	58.8	7.1	12.6	8.4	46.2	14.1	2.2	14.6	12.5	56.8	54.9	24 832	134	6.5	23 910	23 317
Albany-Schenectady-Troy, NY MSA	425.0	–1.2	53.9	39.4	371.0	91.9	25.7	128.8	108.5	429.1	430.2	28 719	40	5.5	27 694	27 231
Albuquerque, NM MSA	325.6	6.0	51.8	29.6	273.8	78.5	17.1	100.9	62.3	320.2	307.3	25 835	106	6.3	25 093	24 309
Alexandria, LA MSA	53.4	4.3	6.6	3.4	46.8	11.9	2.3	16.5	13.3	53.0	51.2	21 995	234	6.2	21 268	20 712
Allentown-Bethlehem-Easton, PA MSA	258.2	1.0	67.1	56.9	191.1	53.7	13.5	79.6	30.0	257.6	255.6	28 771	39	8.2	27 804	26 602
Altoona, PA MSA	56.9	.9	12.7	10.1	44.2	15.1	2.0	14.9	7.9	56.4	56.4	22 675	217	7.3	21 768	21 127
Amarillo, TX MSA	92.2	5.4	14.6	9.5	77.6	25.9	4.6	24.6	16.9	91.0	87.5	23 076	202	4.4	22 633	22 108
Anchorage, AK MSA	120.6	.4	10.8	2.0	109.9	29.7	7.1	33.5	27.8	120.5	120.1	33 501	8	–1.8	33 650	34 098
Anniston, AL MSA	NA	NA	NA	NA	NA	NA	NA	NA	NA	NA	NA	22 366	225	4.4	22 024	21 433
Appleton-Oshkosh-Neenah, WI MSA	189.3	5.3	69.8	59.1	119.5	39.8	9.3	41.3	21.8	185.3	179.7	27 107	76	6.8	26 279	25 381
Asheville, NC MSA	103.0	3.0	25.8	20.1	77.2	25.2	3.1	29.3	14.8	101.3	100.0	23 731	173	8.4	22 912	21 892
Athens, GA MSA	71.3	9.7	14.3	11.8	57.0	18.2	2.1	15.0	19.7	69.0	65.0	23 304	190	4.8	22 762	22 234
Atlanta, GA MSA	1 905.6	10.0	309.2	215.7	1 596.4	511.7	121.5	554.8	250.4	1 817.2	1 733.1	31 354	18	9.3	29 959	28 688
Augusta-Aiken, GA-SC MSA	192.9	1.3	52.4	41.3	140.4	43.0	6.3	45.2	39.6	191.1	190.5	25 976	100	4.2	25 611	24 919
Austin-San Marcos, TX MSA	538.3	11.1	101.7	73.0	436.6	115.1	28.8	150.1	125.0	516.6	484.6	28 707	42	12.1	26 922	25 618
Bakersfield, CA MSA	175.2	2.6	29.0	9.8	146.3	42.4	6.0	41.3	47.4	172.8	170.8	24 314	151	–1.1	24 659	24 591
Bangor, ME NECMA	NA	NA	NA	NA	NA	NA	NA	NA	NA	NA	NA	23 523	180	5.3	22 953	22 335
Barnstable-Yarmouth, MA NECMA	NA	NA	NA	NA	NA	NA	NA	NA	NA	NA	NA	24 154	158	8.0	23 097	22 371
Baton Rouge, LA MSA	277.7	6.1	56.0	24.3	221.8	64.0	16.7	71.2	57.4	269.0	261.7	25 995	97	6.5	25 172	24 410
Beaumont-Port Arthur, TX MSA	150.8	1.3	37.5	24.3	113.3	35.4	4.8	39.4	25.5	150.8	148.8	27 318	73	3.5	26 827	26 397
Bellingham, WA MSA	NA	NA	NA	NA	NA	NA	NA	NA	NA	NA	NA	23 307	189	8.1	22 357	21 554
Benton Harbor, MI MSA	71.2	1.7	23.1	20.9	48.1	15.9	2.6	18.3	8.4	71.0	70.0	25 864	104	4.1	25 188	24 854
Billings, MT MSA	NA	NA	NA	NA	NA	NA	NA	NA	NA	NA	NA	23 491	182	5.2	22 813	22 320
Biloxi-Gulfport-Pascagoula, MS MSA	NA	NA	NA	NA	NA	NA	NA	NA	NA	NA	NA	23 223	199	4.1	22 869	22 299
Binghamton, NY MSA	110.3	–1.8	28.6	24.8	81.7	23.3	3.9	28.7	21.2	111.3	112.3	26 904	78	4.5	26 008	25 744
Birmingham, AL MSA	449.6	4.6	80.7	52.0	368.9	109.9	32.8	127.8	68.2	442.8	430.0	28 520	45	8.6	27 337	26 252
Bismarck, ND MSA	47.1	4.2	5.0	2.5	42.1	11.8	2.3	15.0	9.8	46.3	45.2	22 617	218	6.1	22 014	21 317
Bloomington, IN MSA	63.2	3.8	13.1	9.9	50.3	14.8	2.3	12.3	19.1	61.6	60.9	23 311	188	6.5	22 590	21 880
Bloomington-Normal, IL MSA	76.3	3.5	11.1	8.7	65.2	17.4	13.5	18.3	13.2	75.4	73.7	29 962	23	7.9	29 023	27 769
Boise City, ID MSA	186.3	9.3	46.5	33.6	139.8	44.7	11.5	45.9	28.8	179.0	170.4	26 342	86	7.2	26 072	24 571
Boston-Worcester-Lawrence-Lowell-Brockton, MA-NH NECMA	NA	NA	NA	NA	NA	NA	NA	NA	NA	NA	NA	34 383	6	9.5	32 798	31 403
Brownsville-Harlingen-San Benito, TX MSA	93.6	3.4	15.6	12.6	78.1	23.6	3.6	24.9	21.8	92.0	90.5	19 056	266	6.1	18 566	17 952
Bryan-College Station, TX MSA	64.8	2.7	7.0	3.6	57.8	14.3	2.4	13.5	26.3	63.7	63.1	20 683	258	7.4	19 788	19 255
Buffalo-Niagara Falls, NY MSA	538.2	.7	110.0	89.3	428.2	129.1	28.0	158.1	87.2	539.2	534.5	27 607	66	7.1	26 749	25 780
Burlington, VT NECMA	NA	NA	NA	NA	NA	NA	NA	NA	NA	NA	NA	27 724	61	8.4	26 480	25 582
Canton-Massillon, OH MSA	177.9	4.6	55.1	46.3	122.8	44.1	5.8	48.0	19.3	175.3	170.1	25 109	125	4.9	24 644	23 945
Casper, WY MSA	29.5	2.1	5.0	1.5	24.5	8.4	1.2	8.1	5.3	29.5	28.9	23 200	200	4.7	22 621	22 152
Cedar Rapids, IA MSA	109.0	5.5	26.3	20.7	82.8	24.8	5.7	33.9	10.7	107.4	103.3	27 523	68	7.1	26 572	25 706
Champaign-Urbana, IL MSA	96.6	3.9	15.2	12.0	81.5	21.4	3.4	20.1	34.1	94.5	93.0	24 939	131	7.0	24 353	23 318
Charleston-North Charleston, SC MSA	212.3	2.7	34.2	20.5	178.1	54.2	8.5	55.7	48.7	209.0	206.8	23 167	201	4.5	22 508	22 175
Charleston, WV MSA	127.8	3.8	18.5	9.8	109.3	31.6	7.0	38.4	23.2	125.4	123.1	26 700	79	6.3	25 846	25 116
Charlotte-Gastonia-Rock Hill, NC-SC MSA	727.8	6.4	190.7	147.7	537.2	175.5	48.3	175.6	85.2	710.4	684.2	29 291	28	10.4	27 859	26 520
Charlottesville, VA MSA	78.0	5.4	12.2	8.1	65.8	16.0	3.8	19.0	24.6	75.7	74.0	25 704	110	7.7	24 708	23 860
Chattanooga, TN-GA MSA	215.8	.7	52.9	43.6	163.0	52.0	13.4	53.7	35.6	217.1	214.4	25 464	114	7.2	24 775	23 747
Cheyenne, WY MSA	NA	NA	NA	NA	NA	NA	NA	NA	NA	NA	NA	21 999	233	–.8	21 913	22 167
Chicago-Gary-Kenosha, IL-IN-WI CMSA	4 319.8	4.1	903.0	727.3	3 417.1	992.6	313.7	1 307.8	539.8	4 251.9	4 148.4	33 405	9	8.1	32 047	30 888
Chicago, IL PMSA	3 969.7	4.2	810.8	656.4	3 158.9	906.0	301.1	1 217.7	489.8	3 908.5	3 810.2	33 907	X	8.2	32 523	31 340
Gary, IN PMSA	258.2	3.4	68.3	51.3	190.0	62.8	9.3	66.8	35.8	252.1	249.8	28 504	X	6.9	27 498	26 671
Kankakee, IL PMSA	43.1	4.6	10.7	8.5	32.7	10.8	1.7	11.4	6.9	42.4	41.2	25 205	X	9.6	23 961	22 991
Kenosha, WI PMSA	48.8	3.4	13.2	11.1	35.5	13.0	1.6	11.9	7.3	48.9	47.2	26 228	X	9.3	24 933	24 001
Chico-Paradise, CA MSA	NA	NA	NA	NA	NA	NA	NA	NA	NA	NA	NA	21 021	253	3.1	20 573	20 380
Cincinnati-Hamilton, OH-KY-IN CMSA	934.2	5.0	206.2	162.3	728.0	246.0	56.5	256.8	121.1	914.0	889.9	28 878	36	7.1	27 886	26 958
Cincinnati, OH-KY-IN PMSA	822.5	4.8	178.8	141.1	643.6	215.1	52.1	231.5	101.8	803.5	785.2	29 043	X	7.1	28 057	27 106
Hamilton-Middletown, OH PMSA	111.7	6.7	27.4	21.2	84.4	30.9	4.4	25.3	19.3	110.5	104.7	27 629	X	7.1	26 601	25 804
Clarksville-Hopkinsville, TN-KY MSA	NA	NA	NA	NA	NA	NA	NA	NA	NA	NA	NA	21 511	243	8.1	20 728	19 893

NA Not available.
X Not applicable.

[1]Includes mining and construction, not shown separately.
[2]Includes transportation and public utilities, not shown separately.
[3]Wholesale and retail trade.
[4]Finance, insurance, and real estate.
[5]Based on 270 metropolitan areas (242 MSAs, 17 CMSAs, and 11 NECMAs); see text for more information. When metropolitan areas share the same rank, the next lower rank is omitted.

Source: Nonfarm Employment—U.S. Bureau of Labor Statistics, "Employment and Earnings," May 1997 (related Internet site <http://www.bls.gov>); Average Annual Pay—U.S. Bureau of Labor Statistics, Average Annual Pay News Release, for 1996 and 1995, Internet sites <http://www.bls.gov/news.release/anpay2.t01.htm> and <http://www.bls.gov/news.release/anpay2.t02.htm> (accessed 2 December 1997), for 1994, Internet site <http://stats.bls.gov/news.release/anpay2.t01.htm> and <http://stats.bls.gov/news.release/anpay2.t02.htm> (accessed 30 April 1997).

Table B–9. Metro Areas — Nonfarm Employment and Average Annual Pay—Con.

[MSA = Metropolitan statistical area. CMSA = Consolidated MSA. PMSA = Primary MSA. NECMA = New England county metropolitan area. All areas defined as of June 30, 1996. Table includes 245 MSAs, 17 CMSAs, and 58 PMSAs not in New England; as well as 12 NECMAs. Table excludes 10 MSAs, 1 CMSA, and 15 PMSAs in New England]

Metropolitan areas	Nonfarm employment											Average annual pay				
	1996											1996, preliminary				
			Goods-related (1,000)		Service-related (1,000)												
	Total (1,000)	Percent change, 1994–1996	Total[1]	Manufacturing	Total[2]	Trade[3]	FIRE[4]	Services	Government	1995 (1,000)	1994 (1,000)	Dollars	Rank[5]	Percent change, 1994–1996	1995 (dollars)	1994 (dollars)
Cleveland-Akron, OH CMSA	1 436.6	4.0	345.7	290.2	1 090.9	345.3	84.4	411.8	189.4	1 416.8	1 380.7	29 355	27	6.4	28 382	27 585
Akron, OH PMSA	317.3	4.5	77.7	64.8	239.6	78.9	12.6	86.6	46.7	312.9	303.6	28 106	X	6.6	27 090	26 357
Cleveland-Lorain-Elyria, OH PMSA ..	1 119.3	3.9	268.0	225.4	851.3	266.4	71.8	325.2	142.7	1 103.9	1 077.1	29 705	X	6.4	28 742	27 927
Colorado Springs, CO MSA	207.2	11.8	36.9	24.9	170.3	46.8	10.5	68.0	33.7	197.4	185.3	25 771	107	8.5	24 500	23 754
Columbia, MO MSA	NA	NA	NA	NA	NA	NA	NA	NA	NA	NA	NA	23 917	170	5.7	23 150	22 636
Columbia, SC MSA	271.8	5.4	39.6	25.5	232.3	63.0	19.7	65.9	71.3	264.4	257.9	24 479	147	6.9	23 647	22 901
Columbus, GA-AL MSA	111.0	5.9	26.2	21.1	84.9	25.1	7.3	28.5	20.3	108.2	104.8	22 858	208	6.4	22 257	21 478
Columbus, OH MSA	798.9	5.7	124.9	91.6	674.1	216.7	67.6	220.5	133.6	783.5	755.9	27 888	54	6.1	26 948	26 291
Corpus Christi, TX MSA	150.4	5.1	28.4	13.6	122.1	35.1	6.5	43.0	31.1	145.7	143.1	24 976	130	5.6	24 032	23 660
Cumberland, MD-WV MSA	NA	NA	NA	NA	NA	NA	NA	NA	NA	NA	NA	22 719	213	6.8	21 958	21 268
Dallas-Fort Worth, TX CMSA	2 338.8	8.0	465.8	343.3	1 873.2	588.2	161.1	670.2	280.3	2 251.8	2 165.1	31 713	16	9.2	30 339	29 050
Dallas, TX PMSA	1 659.7	8.3	321.7	236.3	1 338.1	415.5	130.5	490.8	191.1	1 597.0	1 532.5	32 996	X	9.6	31 500	30 105
Fort Worth-Arlington, TX PMSA	679.1	7.4	144.1	107.0	535.1	172.7	30.6	179.4	89.2	654.8	632.6	28 511	X	7.7	27 454	26 463
Danville, VA MSA	44.5	1.1	18.0	15.8	17.5	.6	1.4	8.6	5.8	44.4	44.0	22 169	230	4.6	21 931	21 192
Davenport-Moline-Rock Island, IA-IL MSA	173.7	3.5	38.0	29.5	135.7	47.3	8.0	45.3	26.1	170.1	167.8	26 510	81	4.2	25 861	25 434
Dayton-Springfield, OH MSA	468.2	2.9	117.4	100.1	350.9	109.1	17.7	132.5	72.5	465.7	455.2	28 659	43	7.3	27 676	26 721
Daytona Beach, FL MSA	148.4	5.5	21.3	14.0	127.1	42.8	6.7	51.0	23.0	145.7	140.7	21 121	249	6.2	20 497	19 895
Decatur, AL MSA	NA	NA	NA	NA	NA	NA	NA	NA	NA	NA	NA	24 853	105	7.1	24 133	24 133
Decatur, IL MSA	57.4	5.9	17.5	13.8	40.0	12.3	1.9	13.9	6.7	54.3	54.2	28 399	47	4.9	27 339	27 071
Denver-Boulder-Greeley, CO CMSA	NA	NA	NA	NA	NA	NA	NA	NA	NA	NA	NA	31 198	19	9.8	29 531	28 416
Boulder-Longmont, CO PMSA	150.9	6.3	36.1	29.9	114.7	33.6	5.4	46.7	25.4	146.4	142.0	30 968	X	14.9	28 441	26 948
Denver, CO PMSA	1 007.2	6.8	153.4	89.3	853.8	246.4	78.0	304.1	140.9	980.5	942.8	31 627	X	9.2	30 059	28 965
Greeley, CO PMSA	NA	NA	NA	NA	NA	NA	NA	NA	NA	NA	NA	24 527	X	7.0	23 468	22 929
Des Moines, IA MSA	267.1	5.7	36.6	25.0	230.5	70.9	36.6	75.7	34.3	261.9	252.8	27 528	67	7.9	26 376	25 509
Detroit-Ann Arbor-Flint, MI CMSA	2 493.4	5.0	633.1	543.8	1 860.3	584.1	126.4	726.2	320.2	2 442.6	2 373.8	35 072	3	7.0	34 121	32 788
Ann Arbor, MI PMSA	260.5	4.5	62.5	53.3	198.0	51.6	9.7	61.7	69.4	255.6	249.3	31 027	X	6.0	30 013	29 258
Detroit, MI PMSA	2 051.1	5.2	519.3	445.8	1 531.7	486.9	110.1	615.6	226.4	2 006.2	1 949.4	35 748	X	7.7	34 710	33 201
Flint, MI PMSA	181.8	3.8	51.3	44.7	130.6	45.6	6.6	48.9	24.4	180.8	175.1	33 294	X	.2	33 389	33 219
Dothan, AL MSA	NA	NA	NA	NA	NA	NA	NA	NA	NA	NA	NA	23 268	194	5.0	23 094	22 155
Dover, DE MSA	51.9	6.4	8.8	6.4	43.1	13.3	2.3	11.2	14.6	50.8	48.8	24 177	157	11.4	23 054	21 709
Dubuque, IA MSA	49.4	.4	13.3	11.4	36.1	12.0	1.6	16.8	3.6	50.4	49.2	24 745	137	6.3	24 053	23 277
Duluth-Superior, MN-WI MSA	108.6	5.1	17.0	8.2	91.7	27.9	3.4	30.7	23.0	106.5	103.3	24 184	155	6.5	23 217	22 712
Eau Claire, WI MSA	68.5	6.7	13.9	11.1	54.6	18.8	2.4	18.1	11.8	66.8	64.2	22 147	231	4.7	21 613	21 151
El Paso, TX MSA	235.6	2.0	55.4	44.7	180.3	56.3	8.8	51.8	50.4	235.1	231.0	21 834	236	8.0	20 971	20 221
Elkhart-Goshen, IN MSA	115.8	2.5	62.8	58.5	53.0	21.9	2.8	18.0	6.9	116.4	113.0	26 333	87	6.7	25 155	24 690
Elmira, NY MSA	42.4	3.9	10.8	9.4	31.5	10.7	1.4	10.7	7.2	41.2	40.8	24 358	149	6.5	23 749	22 880
Enid, OK MSA	23.7	.9	3.9	1.9	19.8	5.9	1.0	6.6	4.2	23.5	23.5	20 629	260	5.2	19 934	19 601
Erie, PA MSA	127.3	2.0	38.5	34.0	88.8	28.7	5.5	35.1	14.9	127.4	124.8	25 941	102	5.8	25 204	24 518
Eugene-Springfield, OR MSA	132.4	4.8	26.3	19.7	106.1	34.0	7.0	35.6	25.0	129.5	126.3	24 150	159	7.3	23 206	22 510
Evansville-Henderson, IN-KY MSA	150.6	2.5	42.3	31.8	108.3	36.7	7.3	42.2	14.8	148.9	146.9	25 319	119	6.3	24 294	23 821
Fargo-Moorhead, ND-MN MSA	91.5	5.7	12.9	7.5	78.6	26.5	5.7	27.3	13.7	89.1	86.6	22 973	206	7.4	22 077	21 397
Fayetteville, NC MSA	NA	NA	NA	NA	NA	NA	NA	NA	NA	NA	NA	22 514	220	7.6	21 557	20 928
Fayetteville-Springdale-Rogers, AR MSA	135.0	9.0	39.9	34.0	95.1	37.0	4.7	25.8	18.2	131.1	123.8	23 003	204	6.5	22 363	21 597
Flagstaff, AZ-UT MSA	NA	NA	NA	NA	NA	NA	NA	NA	NA	NA	NA	21 444	244	(6)	20 849	(6)
Florence, AL MSA	NA	NA	NA	NA	NA	NA	NA	NA	NA	NA	NA	22 801	210	4.6	22 310	21 798
Florence, SC MSA	NA	NA	NA	NA	NA	NA	NA	NA	NA	NA	NA	23 440	186	8.1	22 605	21 681
Fort Collins-Loveland, CO MSA	NA	NA	NA	NA	NA	NA	NA	NA	NA	NA	NA	26 166	91	8.0	24 983	24 221
Fort Myers-Cape Coral, FL MSA	148.5	6.3	19.1	6.7	129.4	42.5	8.3	48.7	23.4	145.4	139.7	23 246	196	6.6	22 233	21 814
Fort Pierce-Port St. Lucie, FL MSA	NA	NA	NA	NA	NA	NA	NA	NA	NA	NA	NA	23 601	177	6.0	23 015	22 275
Fort Smith, AR-OK MSA	94.1	3.9	32.3	27.7	61.9	19.5	3.1	23.4	9.6	92.6	90.6	22 016	232	4.9	21 461	20 982
Fort Walton Beach, FL MSA	NA	NA	NA	NA	NA	NA	NA	NA	NA	NA	NA	20 653	259	6.9	19 788	19 325
Fort Wayne, IN MSA	263.2	4.3	85.4	73.2	177.9	63.1	14.4	61.0	26.8	260.0	252.4	26 465	83	6.8	25 557	24 774
Fresno, CA MSA	270.7	4.5	43.6	29.9	227.0	66.0	14.1	68.2	64.9	266.9	259.0	21 704	240	2.1	21 331	21 253
Gadsden, AL MSA	NA	NA	NA	NA	NA	NA	NA	NA	NA	NA	NA	23 256	195	2.9	23 558	22 609
Gainesville, FL MSA	110.0	4.9	9.8	5.5	100.2	24.3	4.8	30.7	38.1	107.7	104.9	22 349	227	4.9	21 822	21 302
Glens Falls, NY MSA	49.5	.6	10.5	8.5	38.9	11.4	2.3	14.1	9.7	50.3	49.2	24 321	150	4.8	23 346	23 204
Goldsboro, NC MSA	NA	NA	NA	NA	NA	NA	NA	NA	NA	NA	NA	21 417	246	10.0	20 343	19 476
Grand Forks, ND-MN MSA	48.5	4.3	6.1	3.8	42.5	13.5	1.5	13.2	12.0	47.6	46.5	20 476	261	5.5	19 904	19 416

X Not applicable.
NA Not available.

[1] Includes mining and construction, not shown separately.
[2] Includes transportation and public utilities, not shown separately.
[3] Wholesale and retail trade.
[4] Finance, insurance, and real estate.
[5] Based on 270 metropolitan areas (242 MSAs, 17 CMSAs, and 11 NECMAs); see text for more information. When metropolitan areas share the same rank, the next lower rank is omitted.
[6] Data not available from source; new metropolitan area effective June 30, 1995.

Source: Nonfarm Employment—U.S. Bureau of Labor Statistics, "Employment and Earnings," May 1997 (related Internet site <http://www.bls.gov>); Average Annual Pay—U.S. Bureau of Labor Statistics, Average Annual Pay News Release, for 1996 and 1995, <http://www.bls.gov/news.release/anpay2.t01.htm> and <http://www.bls.gov/news.release/anpay2.t02.htm> (accessed 2 December 1997), for 1994, Internet site <http://stats.bls.gov/news.release/anpay2.t01.htm> and <http://stats.bls.gov/news.release/anpay2.t02.htm> (accessed 30 April 1997).

[MSA = Metropolitan statistical area.   CMSA = Consolidated MSA.   PMSA = Primary MSA.   NECMA = New England county metropolitan area.   All areas defined as of June 30, 1996.   Table includes 245 MSAs, 17 CMSAs, and 58 PMSAs not in New England; as well as 12 NECMAs.   Table excludes 10 MSAs, 1 CMSA, and 15 PMSAs in New England]

Metropolitan areas	Nonfarm employment											Average annual pay				
	1996											1996, preliminary				
			Goods-related (1,000)		Service-related (1,000)												
	Total (1,000)	Percent change, 1994–1996	Total[1]	Manufacturing	Total[2]	Trade[3]	FIRE[4]	Services	Government	1995 (1,000)	1994 (1,000)	Dollars	Rank[5]	Percent change, 1994–1996	1995 (dollars)	1994 (dollars)
Grand Junction, CO MSA	NA	NA	NA	NA	NA	NA	NA	NA	NA	NA	NA	22 715	214	(6)	22 181	(6)
Grand Rapids-Muskegon-Holland, MI MSA	534.3	7.5	175.9	152.1	358.4	132.6	21.1	133.8	52.2	519.2	497.0	28 478	46	7.7	27 298	26 431
Great Falls, MT MSA	NA	NA	NA	NA	NA	NA	NA	NA	NA	NA	NA	21 073	251	5.4	20 213	19 985
Green Bay, WI MSA	130.7	7.5	34.3	27.8	96.4	30.7	9.9	31.0	15.6	127.3	121.6	27 118	75	7.2	26 298	25 289
Greensboro--Winston Salem--High Point, NC MSA	611.8	3.8	194.8	165.9	417.0	142.0	30.8	146.6	64.7	605.4	589.5	26 130	92	8.0	25 229	24 197
Greenville, NC MSA	NA	NA	NA	NA	NA	NA	NA	NA	NA	NA	NA	23 466	184	4.3	22 635	22 490
Greenville-Spartanburg-Anderson, SC MSA	448.9	4.6	153.5	125.1	295.4	112.6	15.3	93.4	54.4	440.2	429.3	25 397	116	8.1	24 667	23 497
Harrisburg-Lebanon-Carlisle, PA MSA	344.4	4.7	58.2	45.3	286.2	76.7	25.0	90.2	71.1	336.2	328.8	27 788	60	7.0	26 856	25 982
Hartford, CT NECMA	NA	NA	NA	NA	NA	NA	NA	NA	NA	NA	NA	34 819	4	5.0	33 948	33 172
Hattiesburg, MS MSA	NA	NA	NA	NA	NA	NA	NA	NA	NA	NA	NA	21 797	238	8.6	20 867	20 063
Hickory-Morganton-Lenoir, NC MSA	NA	NA	NA	NA	NA	NA	NA	NA	NA	NA	NA	22 493	222	5.2	21 726	21 385
Honolulu, HI MSA	403.9	–1.8	30.5	12.7	373.3	101.3	29.8	120.5	88.6	408.3	411.5	28 336	48	2.2	27 936	27 736
Houma, LA MSA	68.6	8.5	15.3	6.1	53.2	16.7	2.2	14.4	12.8	65.2	63.2	24 099	161	7.4	22 969	22 431
Houston-Galveston-Brazoria, TX CMSA	1 966.0	5.3	430.0	222.5	1 536.2	454.7	102.9	561.2	285.4	1 925.0	1 866.4	32 620	11	8.5	31 107	30 059
Brazoria, TX PMSA	72.3	.4	26.7	16.5	45.6	14.0	1.8	13.5	13.5	71.5	72.0	30 781	X	6.4	29 892	28 941
Galveston-Texas City, TX PMSA	87.2	3.7	13.8	8.0	73.6	18.6	5.4	17.4	28.0	87.1	84.1	27 370	X	8.7	26 361	25 178
Houston, TX PMSA	1 806.5	5.6	389.5	198.0	1 417.0	422.1	95.7	530.3	243.9	1 766.4	1 710.3	32 895	X	8.4	31 390	30 349
Huntington-Ashland, WV-KY-OH MSA	119.0	2.9	24.8	17.5	94.2	31.3	3.8	31.5	20.6	118.0	115.6	23 929	169	2.4	23 408	23 368
Huntsville, AL MSA	167.8	3.0	44.5	38.7	123.4	33.5	4.6	43.2	38.6	165.5	162.9	31 473	17	3.6	31 233	30 389
Indianapolis, IN MSA	812.1	5.0	168.9	125.8	643.2	215.5	59.2	211.0	108.8	796.7	773.7	29 137	30	6.2	28 081	27 437
Iowa City, IA MSA	63.9	3.1	6.8	4.7	57.1	12.4	1.7	13.6	27.3	63.5	62.0	25 536	113	5.8	24 798	24 131
Jackson, MI MSA	60.1	4.3	15.1	13.0	45.2	15.4	1.9	14.1	10.2	59.1	57.6	27 640	65	4.6	26 848	26 414
Jackson, MS MSA	215.8	5.5	32.7	21.3	183.1	51.4	15.3	56.1	45.1	209.7	204.5	24 928	132	8.2	24 193	23 030
Jackson, TN MSA	NA	NA	NA	NA	NA	NA	NA	NA	NA	NA	NA	[7]24 898	X	[7]10.2	[7]23 901	[7]22 591
Jacksonville, FL MSA	495.6	7.9	64.0	36.7	431.6	124.4	51.2	154.6	66.5	482.2	459.4	26 373	85	8.5	25 256	24 315
Jacksonville, NC MSA	NA	NA	NA	NA	NA	NA	NA	NA	NA	NA	NA	17 534	270	7.4	16 951	16 332
Jamestown, NY MSA	NA	NA	NA	NA	NA	NA	NA	NA	NA	NA	NA	22 807	209	3.4	22 358	22 051
Janesville-Beloit, WI MSA	66.9	3.7	23.8	21.2	43.1	15.4	1.8	15.1	8.4	67.3	64.5	27 832	57	7.8	26 898	25 819
Johnson City-Kingsport-Bristol, TN-VA MSA	194.3	3.2	63.5	53.6	130.8	43.7	5.7	45.1	28.4	194.7	188.3	24 492	146	8.2	23 424	22 643
Johnstown, PA MSA	86.8	2.2	16.9	12.6	69.9	20.6	4.5	26.0	13.8	87.0	84.9	21 561	242	4.4	21 085	20 644
Jonesboro, AR MSA	NA	NA	NA	NA	NA	NA	NA	NA	NA	NA	NA	(8)	X	(8)	(8)	(8)
Joplin, MO MSA	NA	NA	NA	NA	NA	NA	NA	NA	NA	NA	NA	21 994	235	8.4	21 359	20 296
Kalamazoo-Battle Creek, MI MSA	206.3	2.3	57.6	50.1	148.7	45.9	10.7	51.6	33.6	205.5	201.7	28 611	44	7.9	27 259	26 517
Kansas City, MO-KS MSA	878.6	4.5	150.3	106.7	728.3	217.9	62.5	251.2	127.7	861.0	840.8	28 774	38	8.2	27 597	26 601
Killeen-Temple, TX MSA	94.3	8.4	13.7	9.9	80.6	22.5	3.9	24.6	26.2	92.1	87.0	22 432	223	7.6	21 589	20 850
Knoxville, TN MSA	315.6	3.8	67.1	48.1	248.5	81.4	13.2	84.0	55.8	313.8	304.1	25 340	118	6.9	24 567	23 711
Kokomo, IN MSA	52.4	5.6	22.8	21.2	29.6	11.5	1.5	8.4	6.9	52.1	49.6	34 779	5	4.7	33 967	33 231
La Crosse, WI-MN MSA	67.7	4.3	14.0	11.4	53.7	19.5	2.7	18.8	9.7	66.4	64.9	23 001	205	6.9	21 874	21 517
Lafayette, LA MSA	152.8	7.5	37.2	15.4	115.6	39.6	5.8	38.0	23.0	146.9	142.1	23 942	167	9.0	22 735	21 974
Lafayette, IN MSA	90.0	5.6	25.6	21.9	64.5	19.0	3.7	16.6	22.9	88.8	85.2	25 990	98	6.1	25 263	24 487
Lake Charles, LA MSA	83.7	9.1	22.6	11.5	61.1	17.8	2.7	23.3	13.0	80.3	76.7	26 059	95	5.3	25 399	24 741
Lakeland-Winter Haven, FL MSA	165.9	4.7	33.1	21.3	132.8	46.3	7.7	45.1	24.7	162.0	158.5	24 106	160	7.7	23 238	22 377
Lancaster, PA MSA	206.0	3.7	68.0	56.0	138.0	51.2	9.0	51.4	18.3	203.2	198.7	26 467	82	6.6	25 605	24 838
Lansing-East Lansing, MI MSA	228.6	3.8	37.8	29.8	190.8	50.6	13.1	54.6	66.4	225.6	220.2	29 247	29	4.4	28 149	28 026
Laredo, TX MSA	56.3	–1.1	6.6	1.4	49.5	15.3	2.1	9.7	13.9	55.5	56.9	20 388	262	8.9	19 174	18 730
Las Cruces, NM MSA	50.2	7.0	6.0	2.6	44.3	10.7	1.9	10.8	19.1	48.5	46.9	20 371	263	4.7	20 186	19 451
Las Vegas, NV-AZ MSA	591.2	16.5	81.5	21.3	509.7	120.4	28.9	268.8	61.5	544.5	507.6	27 324	72	8.2	26 263	25 247
Lawrence, KS MSA	44.1	5.0	7.2	5.2	37.1	11.6	2.0	10.1	12.2	43.6	42.0	21 198	248	4.5	20 860	20 287
Lawton, OK MSA	37.4	.8	5.3	3.7	32.1	8.8	1.8	8.2	11.5	36.7	37.1	20 916	254	3.2	20 780	20 268
Lewiston-Auburn, ME NECMA	NA	NA	NA	NA	NA	NA	NA	NA	NA	NA	NA	22 495	221	8.1	21 582	20 809
Lexington, KY MSA	259.9	6.9	56.4	44.0	203.5	59.5	10.0	69.1	54.5	251.6	243.1	25 746	109	9.5	24 501	23 510
Lima, OH MSA	76.8	2.8	23.6	20.0	53.2	18.4	2.1	19.6	10.2	76.0	74.7	25 013	128	2.7	24 694	24 359
Lincoln, NE MSA	142.9	7.5	22.8	16.7	120.2	30.6	9.3	36.0	35.3	137.3	132.9	24 018	164	6.4	23 285	22 564
Little Rock-North Little Rock, AR MSA	297.3	5.7	48.3	34.0	249.0	69.4	17.1	84.8	57.1	290.9	281.3	25 392	117	7.2	24 569	23 678
Longview-Marshall, TX MSA	84.9	4.7	25.3	18.3	59.5	21.5	3.0	19.7	11.4	83.6	81.1	23 983	165	7.1	23 080	22 397

NA Not available.
X Not applicable.

[1]Includes mining and construction, not shown separately.
[2]Includes transportation and public utilities, not shown separately.
[3]Wholesale and retail trade.
[4]Finance, insurance, and real estate.
[5]Based on 270 metropolitan areas (242 MSAs, 17 CMSAs, and 11 NECMAs); see text for more information.   When metropolitan areas share the same rank, the next lower rank is omitted.
[6]Data not available from source; new metropolitan area effective June 30, 1995.
[7]Excludes Chester County, which was added to the MSA on June 30, 1996.
[8]Data not available from source; new MSA effective June 30, 1996.

Source: Nonfarm Employment—U.S. Bureau of Labor Statistics, "Employment and Earnings," May 1997 (related Internet site <http://www.bls.gov>);   Average Annual Pay—U.S. Bureau of Labor Statistics, Average Annual Pay News Release, for 1996 and 1995, <http://www.bls.gov/news.release/anpay2.t01.htm> and <http://www.bls.gov/news.release/anpay2.t02.htm> (accessed 2 December 1997), for 1994, Internet site <http://stats.bls.gov/news.release/anpay2.t01.htm> and <http://stats.bls.gov/news.release/anpay2.t02.htm> (accessed 30 April 1997).

[MSA = Metropolitan statistical area.   CMSA = Consolidated MSA.   PMSA = Primary MSA.   NECMA = New England county metropolitan area.   All areas defined as of June 30, 1996.   Table includes 245 MSAs, 17 CMSAs, and 58 PMSAs not in New England; as well as 12 NECMAs.   Table excludes 10 MSAs, 1 CMSA, and 15 PMSAs in New England]

Metropolitan areas	Nonfarm employment											Average annual pay				
	1996											1996, preliminary				
			Goods-related (1,000)		Service-related (1,000)												
	Total (1,000)	Percent change, 1994–1996	Total[1]	Manufacturing	Total[2]	Trade[3]	FIRE[4]	Services	Government	1995 (1,000)	1994 (1,000)	Dollars	Rank[5]	Percent change, 1994–1996	1995 (dollars)	1994 (dollars)
Los Angeles-Riverside-Orange, CA CMSA	6 033.4	3.8	1 214.7	987.4	4 818.9	1 408.0	343.8	1 894.2	874.2	5 915.4	5 813.3	31 897	14	5.0	30 915	30 368
Los Angeles-Long Beach, CA PMSA	3 801.9	2.7	760.4	646.1	3 041.5	841.8	216.7	1 245.3	533.3	3 746.5	3 701.9	33 478	X	5.2	32 445	31 831
Orange, CA PMSA	1 184.2	5.1	264.8	211.8	919.5	297.3	85.6	364.1	129.9	1 151.7	1 126.8	32 179	X	6.1	30 904	30 315
Riverside-San Bernardino, CA PMSA	807.4	7.5	146.8	99.2	660.7	209.9	29.7	211.7	167.4	779.9	751.3	25 248	X	3.1	24 815	24 477
Ventura, CA PMSA	239.9	2.8	42.7	30.3	197.2	59.0	11.8	73.1	43.6	237.3	233.3	28 260	X	5.0	27 262	26 905
Louisville, KY-IN MSA	536.3	4.1	115.7	88.4	420.7	132.5	28.4	153.1	68.7	527.6	515.4	26 628	80	8.1	25 554	24 627
Lubbock, TX MSA	109.6	5.5	11.5	7.4	98.1	31.5	5.2	31.3	24.3	107.6	103.9	22 721	212	6.9	21 529	21 259
Lynchburg, VA MSA	96.3	1.9	31.3	25.7	65.0	21.4	4.1	23.2	12.6	96.1	94.5	23 934	168	7.1	23 077	22 340
Macon, GA MSA	145.4	6.4	27.6	20.2	117.8	33.9	8.2	37.8	32.7	140.8	136.6	24 766	135	6.1	23 853	23 333
Madison, WI MSA	261.9	5.3	40.6	28.7	221.4	57.1	20.1	65.2	70.3	255.2	248.7	27 191	74	6.9	26 364	25 432
Mansfield, OH MSA	79.8	3.0	25.1	22.5	54.7	18.1	2.9	19.1	10.4	79.5	77.5	24 536	143	7.1	23 584	22 908
McAllen-Edinburg-Mission, TX MSA	126.6	6.5	20.6	13.1	106.3	35.1	4.6	27.4	34.7	123.4	118.9	18 928	267	7.0	18 031	17 683
Medford-Ashland, OR MSA	65.3	5.3	12.1	9.1	53.3	19.4	3.1	17.3	10.3	63.5	62.0	22 679	216	5.3	22 112	21 541
Melbourne-Titusville-Palm Bay, FL MSA	169.6	.2	35.1	26.0	134.5	40.7	5.7	58.9	24.5	168.6	169.2	27 360	70	3.9	26 854	26 325
Memphis, TN-AR-MS MSA	544.2	8.0	85.8	62.7	458.4	139.9	28.3	151.8	77.8	534.7	503.7	27 912	53	8.0	26 915	25 840
Merced, CA MSA	NA	NA	NA	NA	NA	NA	NA	NA	NA	NA	NA	20 909	255	4.5	20 256	20 007
Miami-Fort Lauderdale, FL CMSA	1 547.8	5.0	189.0	120.2	1 358.7	417.5	110.2	505.6	215.2	1 511.3	1 474.5	28 056	52	6.9	27 161	26 239
Fort Lauderdale, FL PMSA	606.4	7.4	76.7	42.9	529.6	170.4	43.3	203.3	82.0	584.7	564.7	27 547	X	6.6	26 691	25 830
Miami, FL PMSA	941.4	3.5	112.3	77.3	829.1	247.1	66.9	302.3	133.2	926.6	909.8	28 383	X	7.2	27 453	26 488
Milwaukee-Racine, WI CMSA	893.6	3.1	232.1	200.4	661.6	193.8	59.0	268.8	98.3	883.1	866.4	28 979	35	7.7	27 830	26 909
Milwaukee-Waukesha, WI PMSA	813.7	3.2	203.9	175.2	609.8	177.4	56.7	248.1	88.9	804.0	788.8	29 079	X	7.9	27 926	26 958
Racine, WI PMSA	79.9	3.0	28.2	25.2	51.8	16.4	2.3	20.7	9.4	79.1	77.6	27 973	X	5.9	26 861	26 410
Minneapolis-St. Paul, MN-WI MSA	1 579.1	5.3	330.0	273.2	1 249.1	381.9	112.5	451.6	217.0	1 547.0	1 499.4	31 941	13	9.8	30 170	29 102
Mobile, AL MSA	213.7	5.4	43.0	27.1	170.7	57.0	9.5	57.4	33.8	208.2	202.8	24 262	153	6.9	23 318	22 687
Modesto, CA MSA	128.4	5.0	32.8	26.5	95.6	32.0	4.3	30.2	23.5	124.0	122.3	23 735	172	3.0	23 376	23 037
Monroe, LA MSA	67.0	6.3	11.8	8.2	55.2	16.7	4.5	17.5	12.7	65.9	63.0	23 389	187	6.4	22 977	21 978
Montgomery, AL MSA	154.1	5.0	26.5	17.7	127.4	36.6	8.9	39.6	36.0	150.0	146.7	24 561	145	6.6	23 798	22 984
Muncie, IN MSA	59.2	−.7	13.6	11.1	45.7	13.5	1.8	15.0	11.3	61.5	59.6	25 144	123	6.2	24 123	23 671
Myrtle Beach, SC MSA	NA	NA	NA	NA	NA	NA	NA	NA	NA	NA	NA	18 551	268	6.0	17 910	17 498
Naples, FL MSA	NA	NA	NA	NA	NA	NA	NA	NA	NA	NA	NA	23 728	175	10.0	22 747	21 568
Nashville, TN MSA	607.2	6.4	126.4	96.9	480.8	147.2	36.5	188.2	77.4	595.4	570.8	28 172	50	7.5	27 346	26 200
New London-Norwich, CT NECMA	NA	NA	NA	NA	NA	NA	NA	NA	NA	NA	NA	32 000	12	6.6	30 892	30 015
New Orleans, LA MSA	603.6	3.2	89.7	47.4	513.9	150.2	30.6	187.5	103.5	598.9	585.0	26 085	94	5.4	25 593	24 748
New York-Northern New Jersey-Long Island, NY-NJ-CT-PA CMSA/NECMA	8 893.0	2.0	1 298.3	1 010.3	7 595.3	1 867.0	846.9	2 957.0	1 377.2	8 805.5	8 720.1	40 089	1	10.3	38 047	36 357
Bergen-Passaic, NJ PMSA	626.1	2.4	127.7	106.7	498.5	173.3	34.1	186.4	70.9	618.6	611.4	36 840	X	6.2	35 746	34 675
Dutchess, NY PMSA	105.8	3.7	21.5	17.4	84.4	20.5	4.3	32.9	22.7	103.5	102.0	30 546	X	5.8	29 707	28 860
Jersey City, NJ PMSA	239.4	1.1	32.8	28.9	206.7	57.1	23.8	57.2	39.6	237.7	236.7	36 833	X	11.6	34 621	33 012
Middlesex-Somerset-Hunterdon, NJ PMSA	581.1	4.0	112.3	93.0	469.0	135.4	42.9	167.8	76.4	569.3	558.5	39 631	X	8.0	37 925	36 690
Monmouth-Ocean, NJ PMSA	354.4	3.8	38.4	21.6	316.0	96.7	17.8	117.4	63.2	347.7	341.3	29 920	X	5.6	29 033	28 338
Nassau-Suffolk, NY PMSA	1 098.2	2.2	155.4	110.6	942.9	285.4	78.7	351.6	178.4	1 092.7	1 074.5	32 993	X	7.2	31 635	30 765
New Haven-Bridgeport-Stamford-Waterbury-Danbury, CT NECMA	[6]787.1	[6]2.8	[6]170.7	[6]145.2	[6]616.5	[6]174.3	[6]55.1	[6]258.0	[6]90.1	[6]775.5	[6]765.4	39 488	X	11.1	37 546	35 535
New York, NY PMSA	3 857.7	1.4	432.7	318.5	3 424.9	673.7	504.1	1 401.1	615.5	3 820.2	3 803.2	45 028	X	12.8	42 272	39 933
Newark, NJ PMSA	930.8	1.7	165.9	135.8	765.0	186.2	69.9	286.7	141.4	927.6	915.2	38 886	X	8.3	37 224	35 910
Newburgh, NY-PA PMSA	118.3	2.1	16.3	12.1	101.9	32.5	5.3	31.0	26.5	117.3	115.9	25 594	X	4.4	25 016	24 507
Trenton, NJ PMSA	194.1	−1.0	24.6	20.5	169.5	31.9	10.9	66.9	52.5	195.4	196.0	37 598	X	6.4	36 614	35 345
Norfolk-Virginia Beach-Newport News, VA-NC MSA	646.0	4.7	107.1	67.1	538.9	153.9	29.6	187.3	136.5	630.6	617.0	24 184	155	5.2	23 544	22 988
Ocala, FL MSA	NA	NA	NA	NA	NA	NA	NA	NA	NA	NA	NA	21 677	241	6.9	21 082	20 273
Odessa-Midland, TX MSA	97.2	3.6	24.2	6.8	73.0	26.3	3.5	22.1	17.1	95.8	93.8	25 897	103	4.8	25 032	24 722
Oklahoma City, OK MSA	491.9	7.0	77.5	51.9	414.4	118.7	27.6	143.4	101.2	476.5	459.8	24 286	152	4.2	23 626	23 298
Omaha, NE-IA MSA	384.6	6.5	56.9	39.5	327.8	92.1	32.7	126.9	50.2	373.7	361.1	25 961	101	9.3	24 978	23 748
Orlando, FL MSA	748.8	9.6	91.8	51.7	657.0	186.2	44.7	305.4	81.4	714.4	683.2	25 204	121	6.7	24 450	23 630
Owensboro, KY MSA	42.0	1.9	10.3	6.9	31.8	10.8	1.8	10.4	6.7	42.5	41.2	22 209	229	6.9	21 685	20 784

X Not applicable.
NA Not available.

[1]Includes mining and construction, not shown separately.
[2]Includes transportation and public utilities, not shown separately.
[3]Wholesale and retail trade.
[4]Finance, insurance, and real estate.
[5]Based on 270 metropolitan areas (242 MSAs, 17 CMSAs, and 11 NECMAs); see text for more information.   When metropolitan areas share the same rank, the next lower rank is omitted.
[6]Data for NECMA not available.   Data are for 5 Connecticut PMSAs: Bridgeport, Danbury, New Haven-Meriden, Stamford-Norwalk, and Waterbury.

Source: Nonfarm Employment—U.S. Bureau of Labor Statistics, "Employment and Earnings," May 1997 (related Internet site <http://www.bls.gov>);   Average Annual Pay—U.S. Bureau of Labor Statistics, Average Annual Pay News Release, for 1996 and 1995, <http://www.bls.gov/news.release/anpay2.t01.htm> and <http://www.bls.gov/news.release/anpay2.t02.htm> (accessed 2 December 1997), for 1994, Internet site <http://stats.bls.gov/news.release/anpay2.t01.htm> and <http://stats.bls.gov/news.release/anpay2.t02.htm> (accessed 30 April 1997).

[MSA = Metropolitan statistical area. CMSA = Consolidated MSA. PMSA = Primary MSA. NECMA = New England county metropolitan area. All areas defined as of June 30, 1996. Table includes 245 MSAs, 17 CMSAs, and 58 PMSAs not in New England; as well as 12 NECMAs. Table excludes 10 MSAs, 1 CMSA, and 15 PMSAs in New England]

Metropolitan areas	Nonfarm employment											Average annual pay				
	1996											1996, preliminary				
			Goods-related (1,000)		Service-related (1,000)												
	Total (1,000)	Percent change, 1994–1996	Total[1]	Manufacturing	Total[2]	Trade[3]	FIRE[4]	Services	Government	1995 (1,000)	1994 (1,000)	Dollars	Rank[5]	Percent change, 1994–1996	1995 (dollars)	1994 (dollars)
Panama City, FL MSA	NA	NA	NA	NA	NA	NA	NA	NA	NA	NA	NA	21 121	249	6.4	20 491	19 858
Parkersburg-Marietta, WV-OH MSA	68.4	4.0	18.0	13.3	50.4	17.3	2.5	17.2	10.6	67.0	65.8	24 686	140	5.2	24 000	23 475
Pensacola, FL MSA	146.6	4.0	22.5	11.5	124.1	37.2	5.8	47.0	27.5	144.2	141.0	23 244	197	5.3	22 506	22 078
Peoria-Pekin, IL MSA	166.3	5.7	39.3	31.9	127.1	40.3	8.0	51.5	18.2	158.6	157.3	27 861	56	3.2	27 548	27 010
Philadelphia-Wilmington-Atlantic City, PA-NJ-DE-MD CMSA	2 738.0	2.3	471.1	367.3	2 266.9	601.0	201.3	955.6	380.5	2 700.4	2 675.2	32 625	10	8.3	31 238	30 120
Atlantic-Cape May, NJ PMSA	176.4	3.3	13.3	6.4	163.2	36.5	5.9	85.1	28.5	173.5	170.8	27 511	X	5.1	26 585	26 185
Philadelphia, PA-NJ PMSA	2 214.3	2.0	384.9	305.8	1 829.4	493.3	154.4	774.8	302.3	2 186.7	2 171.5	33 080	X	8.4	31 695	30 519
Vineland-Millville-Bridgeton, NJ PMSA	57.0	.5	14.9	12.8	42.0	11.1	3.3	12.0	12.7	57.2	56.7	27 901	X	5.6	27 104	26 430
Wilmington-Newark, DE-MD PMSA	290.3	5.1	58.0	42.3	232.3	60.1	37.7	83.7	37.0	283.0	276.2	33 223	X	10.1	31 439	30 175
Phoenix-Mesa, AZ MSA	1 309.5	14.7	251.0	153.7	1 058.5	323.8	94.8	401.6	172.5	1 224.9	1 141.9	27 826	58	8.1	26 748	25 738
Pine Bluff, AR MSA	35.8	3.5	9.1	8.0	26.8	7.5	1.4	8.4	7.7	35.3	34.6	22 738	211	4.6	22 457	21 740
Pittsburgh, PA MSA	1 058.6	1.7	185.2	133.8	873.4	257.4	61.6	365.6	123.1	1 051.0	1 041.0	29 069	33	7.2	28 051	27 121
Pittsfield, MA NECMA	NA	NA	NA	NA	NA	NA	NA	NA	NA	NA	NA	26 297	88	6.6	25 513	24 658
Pocatello, ID MSA	NA	NA	NA	NA	NA	NA	NA	NA	NA	NA	NA	26 379	84	7.9	25 359	24 455
Portland, ME NECMA	NA	NA	NA	NA	NA	NA	NA	NA	NA	NA	NA	(6)	X	(6)	(6)	(6)
Portland-Salem, OR-WA CMSA	1 007.1	9.1	218.5	159.4	788.8	246.4	69.8	270.1	149.0	964.1	922.9	29 112	31	10.2	27 649	26 427
Portland-Vancouver, OR-WA PMSA	878.8	9.6	193.6	141.5	685.3	218.8	63.4	239.6	113.4	839.6	802.1	29 940	X	10.6	28 358	27 065
Salem, OR PMSA	128.3	6.2	24.9	17.9	103.5	27.6	6.4	30.5	35.6	124.5	120.8	23 747	X	5.9	23 108	22 419
Providence-Warwick-Pawtucket, RI NECMA	NA	NA	NA	NA	NA	NA	NA	NA	NA	NA	NA	27 339	71	7.1	26 487	25 515
Provo-Orem, UT MSA	129.8	11.8	28.2	18.8	101.6	29.1	3.6	49.4	17.2	123.1	116.1	23 481	183	9.8	22 848	21 377
Pueblo, CO MSA	NA	NA	NA	NA	NA	NA	NA	NA	NA	NA	NA	22 357	226	6.1	21 869	21 066
Punta Gorda, FL MSA	NA	NA	NA	NA	NA	NA	NA	NA	NA	NA	NA	21 817	237	8.8	21 058	20 048
Raleigh-Durham-Chapel Hill, NC MSA	574.3	7.1	112.5	82.0	461.9	120.6	27.3	172.4	116.0	557.5	536.2	29 077	32	8.9	27 925	26 703
Rapid City, SD MSA	45.9	4.1	7.1	4.2	38.8	13.9	1.7	14.0	7.3	45.2	44.1	20 719	256	5.8	20 107	19 584
Reading, PA MSA	160.1	2.8	49.8	43.2	110.3	37.3	9.0	38.2	18.5	158.4	155.7	28 205	49	5.6	27 442	26 705
Redding, CA MSA	NA	NA	NA	NA	NA	NA	NA	NA	NA	NA	NA	23 856	171	1.8	23 590	23 431
Reno, NV MSA	172.6	9.1	25.4	13.0	147.2	39.2	7.5	67.4	22.4	165.8	158.2	27 679	63	8.0	26 513	25 632
Richland-Kennewick-Pasco, WA MSA	NA	NA	NA	NA	NA	NA	NA	NA	NA	NA	NA	27 864	55	3.8	27 570	26 835
Richmond-Petersburg, VA MSA	506.0	3.0	91.3	59.7	414.7	120.4	42.9	128.1	96.8	502.1	491.2	28 714	41	8.4	27 598	26 483
Roanoke, VA MSA	140.2	4.7	27.5	19.6	112.7	37.5	9.1	40.2	17.4	137.5	133.9	24 589	141	7.7	23 955	22 825
Rochester, MN MSA	70.3	3.2	12.9	10.4	57.5	14.3	2.4	31.8	7.0	68.7	68.1	30 663	21	8.5	29 107	28 262
Rochester, NY MSA	527.5	1.9	145.1	128.0	382.5	110.5	23.3	153.4	77.4	523.5	517.6	30 241	22	6.9	29 301	28 299
Rockford, IL MSA	174.3	5.6	59.4	52.7	114.9	36.7	7.3	45.3	17.2	172.1	165.1	28 093	51	6.1	27 228	26 488
Rocky Mount, NC MSA	NA	NA	NA	NA	NA	NA	NA	NA	NA	NA	NA	23 280	192	7.0	22 532	21 749
Sacramento-Yolo, CA CMSA	NA	NA	NA	NA	NA	NA	NA	NA	NA	NA	NA	29 519	25	5.1	29 214	28 092
Sacramento, CA PMSA	605.8	6.4	73.1	43.2	532.6	133.5	39.3	167.5	167.0	587.0	569.2	29 576	X	5.2	29 289	28 125
Yolo, CA PMSA	NA	NA	NA	NA	NA	NA	NA	NA	NA	NA	NA	29 053	X	4.4	28 616	27 825
Saginaw-Bay City-Midland, MI MSA	175.0	3.2	48.1	39.5	126.8	44.9	6.7	45.8	22.3	172.6	169.5	31 138	20	7.1	29 863	29 080
St. Cloud, MN MSA	83.9	5.8	19.2	15.5	64.7	25.9	2.9	20.4	12.6	82.5	79.3	22 681	215	6.7	21 685	21 253
St. Joseph, MO MSA	NA	NA	NA	NA	NA	NA	NA	NA	NA	NA	NA	23 242	198	6.1	22 279	21 911
St. Louis, MO-IL MSA	1 268.5	3.6	259.2	195.9	1 009.2	303.8	77.6	392.3	155.4	1 244.1	1 224.0	29 469	26	7.6	28 599	27 392
Salinas, CA MSA	113.7	4.9	13.7	9.4	100.0	30.4	6.1	31.4	26.8	109.2	108.4	24 851	133	5.9	24 260	23 462
Salt Lake City-Ogden, UT MSA	643.0	10.9	123.7	81.4	519.4	157.8	41.5	170.8	107.2	611.8	579.6	25 770	108	8.1	24 693	23 839
San Angelo, TX MSA	41.9	5.0	7.7	5.3	34.1	10.3	1.7	11.4	8.5	41.0	39.9	21 426	245	4.3	21 124	20 543
San Antonio, TX MSA	633.7	6.4	83.2	49.4	550.5	157.0	42.5	189.5	131.1	619.9	595.4	24 460	148	6.3	23 725	23 016
San Diego, CA MSA	999.0	4.6	160.8	116.2	838.2	234.7	56.6	319.3	189.6	978.6	955.3	28 845	37	5.8	27 842	27 261
San Francisco-Oakland-San Jose, CA CMSA	NA	NA	NA	NA	NA	NA	NA	NA	NA	NA	NA	37 966	2	10.1	36 186	34 475
Oakland, CA PMSA	915.8	4.4	162.3	113.7	753.6	208.6	51.8	266.2	168.1	897.5	877.4	34 402	X	7.0	33 180	32 157
San Francisco, CA PMSA	951.7	5.3	107.5	76.0	844.2	199.5	97.8	346.4	124.5	916.5	903.7	40 016	X	9.6	37 975	36 510
San Jose, CA PMSA	879.1	9.9	279.4	246.6	599.7	173.4	29.9	283.6	87.8	831.9	799.9	44 819	X	14.6	42 409	39 123
Santa Cruz-Watsonville, CA PMSA	NA	NA	NA	NA	NA	NA	NA	NA	NA	NA	NA	26 098	X	8.4	25 036	24 068
Santa Rosa, CA PMSA	157.2	6.9	32.1	23.3	125.2	40.4	9.4	44.4	25.0	150.3	147.0	26 876	X	6.5	26 177	25 232
Vallejo-Fairfield-Napa, CA PMSA	144.3	2.6	26.1	17.1	118.2	38.0	5.6	37.8	31.0	141.7	140.6	25 889	X	-1.1	25 453	26 181
San Luis Obispo-Atascadero-Paso Robles, CA MSA	NA	NA	NA	NA	NA	NA	NA	NA	NA	NA	NA	23 969	166	7.4	23 026	22 327
Santa Barbara-Santa Maria-Lompoc, CA MSA	146.6	2.1	23.1	16.2	123.4	35.0	7.1	46.4	29.6	144.4	143.6	26 251	89	3.4	25 805	25 390

NA Not available.
X Not applicable.

[1]Includes mining and construction, not shown separately.
[2]Includes transportation and public utilities, not shown separately.
[3]Wholesale and retail trade.
[4]Finance, insurance, and real estate.
[5]Based on 270 metropolitan areas (242 MSAs, 17 CMSAs, and 11 NECMAs); see text for more information. When metropolitan areas share the same rank, the next lower rank is omitted.
[6]Data not available from source; new MSA effective June 30, 1996.

Source: Nonfarm Employment—U.S. Bureau of Labor Statistics, "Employment and Earnings," May 1997 (related Internet site <http://www.bls.gov>); Average Annual Pay—U.S. Bureau of Labor Statistics, Average Annual Pay News Release, for 1996 and 1995, <http://www.bls.gov/news.release/anpay2.t01.htm> and <http://www.bls.gov/news.release/anpay2.t02.htm> (accessed 2 December 1997), for 1994, Internet site <http://stats.bls.gov/news.release/anpay2.t01.htm> and <http://stats.bls.gov/news.release/anpay2.t02.htm> (accessed 30 April 1997).

[MSA = Metropolitan statistical area. CMSA = Consolidated MSA. PMSA = Primary MSA. NECMA = New England county metropolitan area. All areas defined as of June 30, 1996. Table includes 245 MSAs, 17 CMSAs, and 58 PMSAs not in New England; as well as 12 NECMAs. Table excludes 10 MSAs, 1 CMSA, and 15 PMSAs in New England]

Metropolitan areas	Nonfarm employment											Average annual pay				
	1996											1996, preliminary				
			Goods-related (1,000)		Service-related (1,000)											
	Total (1,000)	Percent change, 1994–1996	Total[1]	Manufacturing	Total[2]	Trade[3]	FIRE[4]	Services	Government	1995 (1,000)	1994 (1,000)	Dollars	Rank[5]	Percent change, 1994–1996	1995 (dollars)	1994 (dollars)
Santa Fe, NM MSA	69.8	1.3	5.4	2.0	64.4	15.0	3.2	20.9	24.0	70.4	68.9	24 539	142	8.6	23 691	22 596
Sarasota-Bradenton, FL MSA	225.4	11.6	32.6	20.3	192.8	57.7	11.5	95.5	22.8	210.1	201.9	22 560	219	6.0	22 279	21 282
Savannah, GA MSA	130.1	6.0	24.6	17.0	105.8	33.7	4.2	37.8	20.8	126.2	122.7	25 084	126	8.4	23 865	23 130
Scranton--Wilkes-Barre--Hazleton, PA MSA	271.2	1.2	65.5	55.3	205.7	65.1	13.7	77.2	34.9	271.3	268.0	24 071	162	7.3	23 278	22 430
Seattle-Tacoma-Bremerton, WA CMSA	NA	NA	NA	NA	NA	NA	NA	NA	NA	NA	NA	31 792	15	10.4	30 052	28 809
Bremerton, WA PMSA	NA	NA	NA	NA	NA	NA	NA	NA	NA	NA	NA	25 954	X	3.4	25 877	25 095
Olympia, WA PMSA	NA	NA	NA	NA	NA	NA	NA	NA	NA	NA	NA	26 575	X	5.0	26 083	25 300
Seattle-Bellevue-Everett, WA PMSA	1 225.2	5.8	257.2	195.8	968.0	295.0	75.0	348.4	175.4	1 180.2	1 158.3	33 588	X	11.3	31 550	30 181
Tacoma, WA PMSA	221.3	4.2	36.7	24.2	184.6	54.9	11.3	61.5	46.9	217.2	212.4	25 548	X	7.2	24 687	23 832
Sharon, PA MSA	46.6	4.3	12.5	11.0	34.1	12.1	1.4	13.1	5.4	46.0	44.7	23 494	181	4.9	22 815	22 403
Sheboygan, WI MSA	58.2	3.2	26.0	23.7	32.2	10.8	2.3	11.2	6.2	58.1	56.4	26 020	96	6.6	24 875	24 411
Sherman-Denison, TX MSA	41.7	6.6	12.2	10.4	29.5	9.4	2.0	11.0	5.5	40.6	39.1	23 879	124	8.1	23 898	23 231
Shreveport-Bossier City, LA MSA	167.4	5.6	31.8	19.9	135.6	38.5	6.7	49.9	32.2	162.9	158.5	23 731	173	3.2	23 408	22 990
Sioux City, IA-NE MSA	64.5	4.9	16.3	12.9	48.2	16.0	2.6	18.5	7.3	63.6	61.5	23 273	193	8.9	22 443	21 367
Sioux Falls, SD MSA	98.8	7.0	18.0	13.4	80.8	25.6	10.6	28.7	9.6	96.0	92.3	23 547	178	7.1	22 739	21 979
South Bend, IN MSA	131.4	3.1	29.1	22.2	102.9	33.9	6.5	42.9	13.8	130.8	127.5	25 661	111	6.4	25 096	24 115
Spokane, WA MSA	180.6	3.3	32.6	22.0	148.0	45.6	10.4	53.8	30.1	178.5	174.8	24 536	143	7.5	23 595	22 828
Springfield, IL MSA	112.3	2.3	9.2	4.4	103.0	24.3	7.8	32.4	33.5	110.8	109.8	29 714	24	6.3	28 615	27 963
Springfield, MO MSA	155.6	6.4	30.2	23.6	125.5	44.9	6.6	44.7	18.7	151.3	146.2	22 875	207	8.0	22 111	21 183
Springfield, MA NECMA	NA	NA	NA	NA	NA	NA	NA	NA	NA	NA	NA	27 423	69	6.9	26 437	25 661
State College, PA MSA	66.1	6.1	11.3	8.7	54.8	12.6	2.0	13.7	24.4	64.1	62.3	24 730	138	4.6	24 298	23 641
Steubenville-Weirton, OH-WV MSA	50.1	.2	15.6	13.5	34.4	11.0	1.4	12.9	6.3	50.5	50.0	26 245	90	3.9	25 649	25 254
Stockton-Lodi, CA MSA	163.3	3.7	30.4	23.6	132.9	39.3	8.4	40.2	33.2	160.3	157.4	24 765	136	2.1	24 380	24 263
Sumter, SC MSA	NA	NA	NA	NA	NA	NA	NA	NA	NA	NA	NA	20 708	257	7.1	19 880	19 334
Syracuse, NY MSA	333.0	.7	61.8	49.5	271.2	78.5	18.1	97.0	59.4	332.0	330.7	27 652	64	4.0	27 267	26 577
Tallahassee, FL MSA	145.3	4.8	11.4	5.2	133.9	29.9	5.5	37.3	57.5	144.2	138.6	24 244	154	9.0	23 141	22 246
Tampa-St. Petersburg-Clearwater, FL MSA	1 021.5	6.7	135.6	87.1	885.9	256.5	71.0	382.2	131.1	993.8	957.3	25 540	112	7.5	24 650	23 767
Terre Haute, IN MSA	69.2	1.5	15.3	12.0	53.9	20.6	2.3	16.3	11.4	70.1	68.2	23 047	203	4.9	22 583	21 972
Texarkana, TX-Texarkana, AR MSA	50.1	3.9	8.3	6.1	41.8	13.0	1.7	13.2	11.7	49.2	48.2	22 390	224	5.8	21 770	21 169
Toledo, OH MSA	312.7	3.0	75.8	60.7	237.0	78.1	10.9	87.5	46.1	308.2	303.7	27 793	59	7.2	26 907	25 921
Topeka, KS MSA	100.2	3.5	14.7	10.3	85.6	21.7	6.6	27.0	23.9	98.4	96.8	25 404	115	6.4	24 904	23 912
Tucson, AZ MSA	308.1	5.7	50.1	28.6	257.9	67.0	12.2	96.8	68.5	302.7	291.5	24 705	139	10.9	23 622	22 286
Tulsa, OK MSA	361.8	5.6	76.9	55.2	284.9	86.0	20.0	108.8	41.8	350.2	342.6	26 116	93	5.3	25 338	24 805
Tuscaloosa, AL MSA	74.8	4.9	18.5	10.7	56.2	17.2	2.4	13.1	21.0	73.3	71.3	25 051	127	5.4	24 487	23 772
Tyler, TX MSA	73.3	5.9	15.5	11.4	57.7	18.8	3.8	20.8	10.9	71.9	69.2	25 295	120	6.6	24 176	23 729
Utica-Rome, NY MSA	126.3	-.6	22.9	19.9	103.4	27.2	7.7	36.8	27.8	128.3	127.1	23 677	176	3.8	23 207	22 808
Victoria, TX MSA	33.5	1.8	6.4	3.0	27.1	9.3	1.6	8.6	6.1	33.0	32.9	23 448	185	8.8	22 267	21 553
Visalia-Tulare-Porterville, CA MSA	NA	NA	NA	NA	NA	NA	NA	NA	NA	NA	NA	19 768	265	5.1	19 439	18 807
Waco, TX MSA	92.8	4.3	20.8	16.7	72.0	21.3	5.6	26.5	14.9	91.9	89.0	23 302	191	7.0	22 534	21 777
Washington-Baltimore, DC-MD-VA-WV CMSA	NA	NA	NA	NA	NA	NA	NA	NA	NA	NA	NA	34 199	7	7.1	32 816	31 920
Baltimore, MD PMSA	1 136.2	1.9	162.8	101.0	973.4	264.4	71.5	371.2	209.3	1 129.3	1 115.5	29 953	X	7.1	28 733	27 955
Hagerstown, MD PMSA	NA	NA	NA	NA	NA	NA	NA	NA	NA	NA	NA	24 388	X	6.1	23 695	22 983
Washington, DC-MD-VA-WV PMSA	2 421.8	1.9	213.3	95.8	2 208.5	466.9	130.4	902.6	596.9	2 404.7	2 376.5	36 383	X	7.2	34 910	33 947
Waterloo-Cedar Falls, IA MSA	68.9	3.8	17.0	14.5	51.9	16.4	3.2	17.9	12.3	68.3	66.4	25 170	122	4.1	24 813	24 181
Wausau, WI MSA	61.7	4.8	19.9	17.3	41.7	15.0	4.7	11.7	7.0	60.6	58.9	25 011	129	7.3	24 112	23 313
West Palm Beach-Boca Raton, FL MSA	416.4	7.8	53.6	29.3	362.8	108.8	28.8	157.3	52.5	399.1	386.1	29 057	34	9.2	27 912	26 617
Wheeling, WV-OH MSA	64.4	4.0	10.0	6.2	54.4	16.2	2.7	21.9	10.4	63.2	61.9	22 228	228	3.3	21 769	21 516
Wichita, KS MSA	264.5	4.9	77.2	62.1	187.4	61.9	11.2	70.9	33.0	255.8	252.2	27 688	62	9.5	26 388	25 291
Wichita Falls, TX MSA	58.2	6.8	11.5	8.1	46.6	13.6	2.2	15.5	12.5	56.8	54.5	21 718	239	5.3	21 264	20 624
Williamsport, PA MSA	53.1	2.3	15.1	12.8	38.0	12.6	2.3	14.1	7.1	52.3	51.9	23 526	179	5.2	23 093	22 368
Wilmington, NC MSA	NA	NA	NA	NA	NA	NA	NA	NA	NA	NA	NA	24 050	163	6.6	23 233	22 552
Yakima, WA MSA	NA	NA	NA	NA	NA	NA	NA	NA	NA	NA	NA	19 780	264	7.5	19 271	18 398
York, PA MSA	160.9	3.1	56.5	48.3	104.4	39.4	5.0	36.9	16.0	159.8	156.1	26 955	77	7.3	26 074	25 113
Youngstown-Warren, OH MSA	241.2	3.4	68.5	58.4	172.7	61.8	9.3	61.5	30.2	241.1	233.3	25 981	99	3.8	25 380	25 025
Yuba City, CA MSA	NA	NA	NA	NA	NA	NA	NA	NA	NA	NA	NA	21 374	247	1.1	21 237	21 145
Yuma, AZ MSA	NA	NA	NA	NA	NA	NA	NA	NA	NA	NA	NA	18 213	269	1.2	18 286	17 996

NA Not available.
X Not applicable.

[1]Includes mining and construction, not shown separately.
[2]Includes transportation and public utilities, not shown separately.
[3]Wholesale and retail trade.
[4]Finance, insurance, and real estate.
[5]Based on 270 metropolitan areas (242 MSAs, 17 CMSAs, and 11 NECMAs); see text for more information. When metropolitan areas share the same rank, the next lower rank is omitted.

Source: Nonfarm Employment—U.S. Bureau of Labor Statistics, "Employment and Earnings," May 1997 (related Internet site <http://www.bls.gov>);   Average Annual Pay—U.S. Bureau of Labor Statistics, Average Annual Pay News Release, for 1996 and 1995, <http://www.bls.gov/news.release/anpay2.t01.htm> and <http://www.bls.gov/news.release/anpay2.t02.htm> (accessed 2 December 1997), for 1994, Internet site <http://stats.bls.gov/news.release/anpay2.t01.htm> and <http://stats.bls.gov/news.release/anpay2.t02.htm> (accessed 30 April 1997).

Table B–10. Metro Areas — Export Sales, Banking, and Federal Funds and Grants

[MSA = Metropolitan statistical area. CMSA = Consolidated MSA. PMSA = Primary MSA. NECMA = New England county metropolitan area. All areas defined as of June 30, 1996. Table includes 245 MSAs, 17 CMSAs, and 58 PMSAs not in New England; as well as 12 NECMAs. Table excludes 10 MSAs, 1 CMSA, and 15 PMSAs in New England]

Metropolitan areas	Export sales Total (mil dol) 1996	1995	1994	Percent change 1995–1996	1994–1995	Banking,[1] 1996 Number of offices	Deposits Total (mil dol)	Percent change, 1990–1996	Federal funds and grants, 1996 Total expenditures (mil dol)	Percent change, 1990–1996	Per capita[2] Total Dollars	Rank[3]	By selected type—(dollars) Direct payments for individuals	Procurement contract awards	Salaries and wages	Grant awards
Abilene, TX MSA	NA	NA	NA	NA	NA	36	1 114.8	21.0	783.9	48.0	6 419	41	2 851	958	2 029	550
Albany, GA MSA	52.5	31.5	31.8	66.6	-1.0	22	844.7	60.1	615.7	47.1	5 249	82	2 744	395	1 341	751
Albany-Schenectady-Troy, NY MSA	1 101.0	1 061.2	831.4	3.8	27.6	270	11 400.6	20.0	6 940.7	30.6	7 900	21	2 875	818	526	3 662
Albuquerque, NM MSA	740.3	270.1	335.5	174.1	-19.5	168	4 822.1	18.5	5 087.5	37.5	7 592	25	2 570	2 958	1 178	878
Alexandria, LA MSA	21.6	18.7	16.9	15.7	10.4	43	1 082.9	21.0	723.1	28.5	5 726	57	3 160	233	672	1 609
Allentown-Bethlehem-Easton, PA MSA	1 477.2	1 492.8	1 371.1	-1.0	8.9	232	7 115.7	8.2	2 377.4	48.2	3 870	195	2 984	127	251	494
Altoona, PA MSA	80.2	74.2	46.4	8.1	59.9	57	1 397.9	31.9	616.8	39.8	4 692	116	3 468	156	320	726
Amarillo, TX MSA	NA	NA	NA	NA	NA	37	1 921.4	15.1	1 045.7	56.3	5 076	92	2 381	1 634	414	514
Anchorage, AK MSA	109.0	150.4	198.2	-27.6	-24.1	41	1 917.3	8.8	1 692.9	32.4	6 758	33	1 462	1 148	2 923	1 214
Anniston, AL MSA	NA	NA	NA	NA	NA	33	1 079.9	33.9	817.3	15.2	7 200	29	3 901	732	1 999	560
Appleton-Oshkosh-Neenah, WI MSA	608.5	593.7	507.7	2.5	16.9	84	2 612.6	23.4	1 093.8	21.0	3 212	255	1 975	682	162	367
Asheville, NC MSA	236.7	185.2	228.6	27.8	-19.0	59	1 885.4	32.8	950.6	48.0	4 526	135	3 060	192	500	763
Athens, GA MSA	NA	NA	NA	NA	NA	42	1 173.4	57.9	541.0	52.4	3 943	186	2 106	161	581	1 082
Atlanta, GA MSA	5 891.5	5 811.4	4 739.1	1.4	22.6	851	39 854.3	47.6	15 357.9	78.4	4 337	149	1 909	998	640	771
Augusta-Aiken, GA-SC MSA	443.9	405.2	326.3	9.6	24.2	109	3 112.3	57.8	3 414.2	4.5	7 527	26	2 691	3 029	1 137	662
Austin-San Marcos, TX MSA	2 743.1	2 929.2	2 128.8	-6.4	37.6	193	6 889.4	23.5	5 292.1	43.9	5 082	91	1 800	512	436	2 323
Bakersfield, CA MSA	721.3	730.5	780.4	-1.3	-6.4	88	2 482.9	2.5	3 116.1	44.0	5 004	95	2 312	849	1 075	743
Bangor, ME NECMA	NA	NA	NA	NA	NA	52	1 313.3	-15.1	653.6	47.1	4 508	136	2 794	231	517	953
Barnstable-Yarmouth, MA NECMA	NA	NA	NA	NA	NA	101	3 360.4	15.8	1 200.5	53.6	5 944	51	4 465	252	557	660
Baton Rouge, LA MSA	552.9	569.6	458.0	-2.9	24.4	163	5 384.6	47.8	2 539.4	55.7	4 476	141	2 285	168	206	1 808
Beaumont-Port Arthur, TX MSA	115.4	118.9	97.0	-3.0	22.6	63	2 978.2	3.6	1 648.8	41.8	4 388	146	3 081	463	274	544
Bellingham, WA MSA	275.4	253.5	210.7	8.6	20.4	64	1 662.6	40.0	762.0	9.4	4 997	97	2 208	1 946	244	590
Benton Harbor, MI MSA	317.2	369.3	368.8	-14.1	.1	58	1 410.2	20.7	602.4	26.3	3 732	213	2 893	104	125	593
Billings, MT MSA	NA	NA	NA	NA	NA	23	1 070.9	11.2	504.2	42.6	4 002	178	2 487	116	658	698
Biloxi-Gulfport-Pascagoula, MS MSA	119.9	281.0	281.6	-57.3	-.2	98	2 357.4	49.7	3 715.7	48.4	10 827	5	3 096	5 027	2 118	574
Binghamton, NY MSA	443.3	558.1	474.9	-20.6	17.5	66	2 120.4	-3.6	1 430.9	18.6	5 632	61	2 823	1 883	213	697
Birmingham, AL MSA	625.8	550.5	453.8	13.7	21.3	248	11 008.2	35.3	3 995.6	52.4	4 466	142	2 927	251	520	756
Bismarck, ND MSA	NA	NA	NA	NA	NA	20	655.8	-4.9	524.3	38.4	5 819	54	2 485	63	570	2 604
Bloomington, IN MSA	198.8	127.6	115.7	55.9	10.2	34	810.5	49.2	399.0	44.3	3 435	241	1 871	198	176	1 155
Bloomington-Normal, IL MSA	NA	NA	NA	NA	NA	51	1 436.9	58.2	375.1	41.1	2 696	271	1 872	58	236	349
Boise City, ID MSA	1 338.5	1 635.0	1 289.8	-18.1	26.8	92	2 994.2	51.8	1 439.8	53.6	3 864	198	2 098	247	569	939
Boston-Worcester-Lawrence-Lowell-Brockton, MA-NH NECMA	NA	NA	NA	NA	NA	1 644	93 550.5	-10.1	32 376.2	21.0	5 585	66	2 855	1 082	467	1 172
Brownsville-Harlingen-San Benito, TX MSA	2 612.6	2 245.9	2 113.4	16.3	6.3	50	1 892.0	4.9	1 104.1	75.2	3 505	235	2 060	152	208	1 066
Bryan-College Station, TX MSA	NA	NA	NA	NA	NA	21	893.9	11.0	432.3	51.4	3 277	250	1 668	200	357	1 042
Buffalo-Niagara Falls, NY MSA	2 262.2	2 295.8	1 569.7	-1.5	46.3	270	14 632.5	-1.8	5 430.1	42.3	4 620	128	3 056	227	405	923
Burlington, VT NECMA	NA	NA	NA	NA	NA	60	1 913.4	-3.4	953.2	77.1	5 002	96	2 073	1 288	647	982
Canton-Massillon, OH MSA	406.0	377.2	315.9	7.6	19.4	109	3 250.1	25.9	1 483.3	41.9	3 681	221	2 799	114	175	584
Casper, WY MSA	NA	NA	NA	NA	NA	11	2 648.8	432.2	248.9	32.6	3 896	192	2 604	116	497	662
Cedar Rapids, IA MSA	391.1	402.2	363.8	-2.8	10.6	52	1 960.6	36.5	865.0	36.1	4 821	108	2 271	1 700	289	521
Champaign-Urbana, IL MSA	214.4	103.4	89.3	107.3	15.8	59	1 981.9	35.2	642.2	4.9	3 837	205	1 910	163	407	1 302
Charleston-North Charleston, SC MSA	595.1	501.6	388.5	18.6	29.1	118	2 597.8	32.2	3 211.6	11.8	6 486	40	2 997	1 033	1 434	1 014
Charleston, WV MSA	412.2	394.4	277.6	4.5	42.1	71	2 919.8	25.6	1 672.9	62.9	6 571	36	3 340	229	530	2 457
Charlotte-Gastonia-Rock Hill, NC-SC MSA	2 291.3	2 088.0	1 782.8	9.7	17.1	406	17 334.8	48.1	4 067.1	69.7	3 079	262	2 128	151	259	530
Charlottesville, VA MSA	140.2	157.4	123.0	-10.9	27.9	52	1 445.2	48.0	599.4	46.3	4 139	169	2 355	284	466	1 024
Chattanooga, TN-GA MSA	273.5	301.0	237.3	-9.2	26.9	142	4 418.1	52.8	2 334.0	48.2	5 232	83	3 013	630	1 001	574
Cheyenne, WY MSA	NA	NA	NA	NA	NA	17	568.5	20.9	662.7	38.7	8 371	16	2 934	964	2 752	1 664
Chicago-Gary-Kenosha, IL-IN-WI CMSA	22 601.2	21 665.7	17 804.7	4.3	21.7	1 542	117 580.2	21.5	33 317.1	38.7	3 874	194	2 435	275	460	687
Chicago, IL PMSA	22 030.1	21 083.4	17 333.6	4.5	21.6	1 342	111 150.0	20.9	30 192.7	38.1	3 904	X	2 411	288	489	698
Gary, IN PMSA	303.2	310.6	267.5	-2.4	16.1	148	4 772.3	37.7	2 318.4	49.2	3 725	X	2 682	182	225	621
Kankakee, IL PMSA	113.7	137.8	86.0	-17.5	60.3	29	1 004.5	47.8	395.5	40.6	3 879	X	2 878	166	197	581
Kenosha, WI PMSA	154.3	133.9	117.7	15.2	13.8	23	653.4	-1.3	410.5	31.8	2 898	X	2 305	37	97	445
Chico-Paradise, CA MSA	78.1	70.1	77.2	11.4	-9.1	43	1 231.2	7.0	833.3	50.3	4 329	150	3 295	119	123	697
Cincinnati-Hamilton, OH-KY-IN CMSA	4 874.3	4 335.0	4 122.8	12.4	5.1	611	20 736.5	33.8	8 125.9	15.9	4 230	158	2 427	746	395	650
Cincinnati, OH-KY-IN PMSA	4 784.1	4 256.7	4 056.5	12.4	4.9	534	18 800.9	34.4	7 222.8	12.0	4 522	X	2 504	860	457	686
Hamilton-Middletown, OH PMSA	90.1	78.3	66.3	15.0	18.3	77	1 935.5	28.1	903.1	61.2	2 791	X	2 043	181	88	473
Clarksville-Hopkinsville, TN-KY MSA	NA	NA	NA	NA	NA	47	1 121.4	28.3	1 513.5	82.6	8 121	18	2 485	963	4 114	531

NA Not available.
X Not applicable.

[1]As of June 30. Covers all FDIC-insured commercial and savings banks.
[2]Based on resident population estimated as of July 1, 1996.
[3]Based on 273 metropolitan areas (245 MSAs, 17 CMSAs, and 11 NECMAs); see text for more information. When metropolitan areas share the same rank, the next lower rank is omitted.

Source: Export Sales—U.S. Department of Commerce, International Trade Administration, "Export Sales of U.S. Metropolitan Areas, 1993-1996," Internet site <http://www.ita.doc.gov/industry/otea/metro/metro.html> (accessed 9 October 1997); Banking—U.S. Federal Deposit Insurance Corporation, "Data Book: Summary of Deposits in Operating Banks and Branches," annual (related Internet site <http://www.fdic.gov/databank/index.html>); Federal Funds and Grants—U.S. Bureau of the Census, "Consolidated Federal Funds Report: County Areas," annual for fiscal year (related Internet site <http://www.census.gov/govs/www/cffr.html>).

[MSA = Metropolitan statistical area.   CMSA = Consolidated MSA.   PMSA = Primary MSA.   NECMA = New England county metropolitan area.   All areas defined as of June 30, 1996.   Table includes 245 MSAs, 17 CMSAs, and 58 PMSAs not in New England; as well as 12 NECMAs.   Table excludes 10 MSAs, 1 CMSA, and 15 PMSAs in New England]

Metropolitan areas	Export sales					Banking,[1] 1996			Federal funds and grants, 1996							
	Total (mil dol)			Percent change		Deposits			Total expend-itures (mil dol)	Percent change, 1990–1996	Per capita[2]					
											Total		By selected type—(dollars)			
	1996	1995	1994	1995–1996	1994–1995	Number of offices	Total (mil dol)	Percent change, 1990–1996			Dollars	Rank[3]	Direct pay-ments for indi-viduals	Pro-cure-ment contract awards	Sal-aries and wages	Grant awards
Cleveland-Akron, OH CMSA	7 335.4	6 638.7	5 699.6	10.5	16.5	722	29 777.4	26.9	12 850.5	35.1	4 411	144	2 908	323	386	785
Akron, OH PMSA.................	2 260.3	1 931.7	1 606.3	17.0	20.3	180	6 144.4	46.7	2 714.9	36.5	3 992	X	2 675	424	242	641
Cleveland-Lorain-Elyria, OH PMSA ..	5 075.2	4 707.0	4 093.3	7.8	15.0	542	23 633.0	22.6	10 135.6	34.7	4 538	X	2 979	292	430	829
Colorado Springs, CO MSA	857.0	954.7	900.7	−10.2	6.0	66	2 274.1	28.0	3 176.4	34.4	6 717	34	2 681	1 510	2 196	320
Columbia, MO MSA	57.9	51.1	50.2	13.2	1.9	40	1 150.4	38.8	487.7	47.5	3 881	193	2 064	257	684	850
Columbia, SC MSA	310.8	343.3	300.4	−9.5	14.3	137	4 470.2	22.7	3 078.8	44.0	6 306	45	2 595	473	1 333	1 895
Columbus, GA-AL MSA	253.2	245.4	172.8	3.2	42.0	85	2 569.3	47.4	1 783.4	41.4	6 550	37	3 073	524	2 387	559
Columbus, OH MSA	1 497.2	1 358.2	1 295.5	10.2	4.8	404	16 534.9	34.7	6 732.2	51.5	4 650	123	2 230	294	513	1 597
Corpus Christi, TX MSA	241.8	162.4	153.6	48.9	5.7	76	2 354.0	.8	1 922.7	62.4	5 006	94	2 480	845	935	717
Cumberland, MD-WV MSA	45.9	53.8	64.3	−14.7	−16.3	34	631.2	−3.2	545.8	39.2	5 425	74	3 880	414	312	798
Dallas-Fort Worth, TX CMSA	9 469.6	8 785.4	7 731.7	7.8	13.6	840	44 555.7	23.8	19 123.5	34.6	4 180	165	1 908	1 360	463	439
Dallas, TX PMSA	7 096.9	6 870.4	5 679.7	3.3	21.0	574	33 636.1	26.6	11 103.1	41.3	3 643	X	1 825	890	467	448
Fort Worth-Arlington, TX PMSA	2 372.7	1 915.0	2 052.0	23.9	−6.7	266	10 919.7	15.8	8 020.4	26.4	5 254	X	2 072	2 298	454	421
Danville, VA MSA	89.1	155.7	202.7	−42.8	−23.2	39	1 161.1	20.8	382.9	37.1	3 505	235	2 904	45	115	433
Davenport-Moline-Rock Island, IA-IL MSA	1 576.1	1 291.0	1 098.9	22.1	17.5	101	3 848.9	11.7	1 639.0	25.8	4 581	129	2 804	318	911	496
Dayton-Springfield, OH MSA	2 201.5	2 404.8	2 671.3	−8.5	−10.0	251	7 778.4	28.3	6 007.4	30.0	6 319	44	2 923	1 179	1 498	705
Daytona Beach, FL MSA	111.7	85.9	110.3	30.1	−22.2	124	5 067.2	67.4	2 200.1	52.6	4 820	109	4 080	131	149	453
Decatur, AL MSA.................	91.6	65.6	54.5	39.6	20.4	41	1 086.8	37.7	589.9	18.6	4 214	164	2 584	166	798	641
Decatur, IL MSA	NA	NA	NA	NA	NA	38	1 358.6	33.0	452.4	46.2	3 919	189	2 972	140	172	493
Denver-Boulder-Greeley, CO CMSA	NA	NA	NA	NA	NA	364	19 528.1	38.0	12 096.6	33.1	5 312	78	2 080	1 649	787	772
Boulder-Longmont, CO PMSA	NA	NA	NA	NA	NA	56	2 151.5	57.8	1 190.3	49.4	4 609	X	1 756	1 015	584	1 246
Denver, CO PMSA	1 502.9	1 385.3	1 089.8	8.5	27.1	274	16 287.3	35.2	10 480.5	30.7	5 614	X	2 140	1 852	867	734
Greeley, CO PMSA	558.8	582.9	501.8	−4.1	16.2	34	1 089.3	48.9	425.8	54.2	2 798	X	1 896	241	152	435
Des Moines, IA MSA..............	426.0	378.5	348.9	12.5	8.5	107	4 461.6	21.4	2 735.7	46.8	6 400	42	2 280	180	742	1 319
Detroit-Ann Arbor-Flint, MI CMSA	30 161.2	29 924.3	30 577.5	.8	−2.1	1 065	49 651.7	8.0	21 426.1	40.0	4 055	174	2 652	278	327	787
Ann Arbor, MI PMSA	1 311.1	1 157.9	2 075.8	13.2	−44.2	149	3 961.2	25.0	2 148.1	74.0	4 054	X	1 817	198	338	1 681
Detroit, MI PMSA	27 531.2	27 314.7	27 469.7	.8	−.6	832	42 784.1	6.3	17 617.8	35.8	4 080	X	2 746	303	343	678
Flint, MI PMSA	1 318.8	1 451.7	1 032.1	−9.2	40.7	84	2 906.4	13.5	1 660.2	51.2	3 807	X	2 734	128	156	779
Dothan, AL MSA	NA	NA	NA	NA	NA	48	1 539.5	52.9	787.0	30.5	5 920	52	3 136	288	1 871	609
Dover, DE MSA	NA	NA	NA	NA	NA	37	1 652.0	19.0	813.9	59.5	6 658	35	2 678	677	1 784	1 506
Dubuque, IA MSA	183.5	180.7	177.6	1.5	1.8	29	1 015.6	25.6	286.7	16.8	3 250	253	2 577	65	180	364
Duluth-Superior, MN-WI MSA	NA	NA	NA	NA	NA	76	1 996.6	23.2	1 106.7	35.1	4 622	127	3 085	177	508	838
Eau Claire, WI MSA	320.6	399.9	465.7	−19.8	−14.1	38	981.9	20.4	580.4	45.2	4 052	175	2 360	251	190	729
El Paso, TX MSA	5 212.7	4 120.8	3 561.3	26.5	15.7	55	3 136.3	−1.3	3 104.1	60.6	4 535	133	2 238	482	1 088	724
Elkhart-Goshen, IN MSA	367.5	501.5	460.4	−26.7	8.9	51	1 540.1	−7.6	417.7	29.9	2 472	272	1 986	119	84	273
Elmira, NY MSA	196.9	139.5	116.8	41.2	19.4	24	785.4	8.8	389.0	32.1	4 170	166	2 923	79	253	897
Enid, OK MSA	NA	NA	NA	NA	NA	19	557.1	44.6	354.8	46.1	6 191	48	3 250	1 026	1 019	807
Erie, PA MSA	321.9	490.8	285.4	−34.4	71.9	91	2 558.5	43.6	1 117.9	44.4	3 984	181	2 796	109	261	811
Eugene-Springfield, OR MSA ..	168.9	190.3	173.1	−11.3	10.0	73	2 133.8	60.3	1 149.3	51.3	3 745	212	2 656	87	282	707
Evansville-Henderson, IN-KY MSA	545.1	525.1	487.4	3.8	7.7	73	3 121.0	24.4	1 108.6	47.3	3 840	204	2 742	334	195	537
Fargo-Moorhead, ND-MN MSA	181.9	155.0	137.3	17.3	12.9	52	1 377.2	15.8	613.8	28.1	3 716	215	2 039	170	592	584
Fayetteville, NC MSA	65.4	66.6	57.9	−1.8	15.0	59	1 331.1	33.1	2 899.6	78.4	10 181	10	2 719	1 136	5 752	561
Fayetteville-Springdale-Rogers, AR MSA	801.2	669.3	433.8	19.7	54.3	80	2 943.9	64.5	876.5	53.6	3 359	246	2 486	116	253	496
Flagstaff, AZ-UT MSA.............	NA	NA	NA	NA	NA	23	501.5	29.8	471.3	44.6	3 994	179	2 015	268	831	872
Florence, AL MSA	25.2	29.5	25.7	−14.5	14.7	57	1 588.3	58.3	659.5	45.9	4 846	104	3 300	251	753	522
Florence, SC MSA	121.6	249.0	117.2	−51.2	112.4	35	936.0	43.3	474.8	65.2	3 849	201	2 600	51	235	945
Fort Collins-Loveland, CO MSA	468.1	373.9	354.5	25.2	5.5	42	1 710.6	85.5	659.7	54.9	2 975	265	1 881	163	400	525
Fort Myers-Cape Coral, FL MSA.......	NA	NA	NA	NA	NA	138	4 892.2	46.1	1 896.4	67.7	4 991	98	4 272	115	215	375
Fort Pierce-Port St. Lucie, FL MSA	107.6	114.2	92.3	−5.8	23.7	73	2 666.3	35.7	1 468.6	85.9	5 113	87	4 448	93	125	424
Fort Smith, AR-OK MSA	NA	NA	NA	NA	NA	61	1 856.7	52.7	741.0	52.3	3 870	195	2 818	126	340	577
Fort Walton Beach, FL MSA	NA	NA	NA	NA	NA	57	1 504.7	61.3	2 045.3	64.2	12 331	2	4 077	2 364	4 821	394
Fort Wayne, IN MSA	991.4	1 029.4	770.9	−3.7	33.5	123	4 554.4	−6.1	1 861.8	43.9	3 917	190	2 228	968	297	385
Fresno, CA MSA	691.8	714.4	763.4	−3.2	−6.4	138	4 340.9	13.7	3 025.4	61.6	3 511	234	2 116	122	445	798
Gadsden, AL MSA................	NA	NA	NA	NA	NA	25	851.4	32.4	450.4	48.5	4 410	145	3 428	121	163	691
Gainesville, FL MSA	88.3	91.6	65.7	−3.7	39.4	47	1 480.3	41.8	925.9	61.9	4 711	115	2 589	319	675	1 118
Glens Falls, NY MSA	NA	NA	NA	NA	NA	41	1 195.2	9.9	429.6	45.3	3 513	233	2 617	59	174	653
Goldsboro, NC MSA	NA	NA	NA	NA	NA	34	820.2	64.4	650.1	69.9	5 826	53	2 745	455	1 774	836
Grand Forks, ND-MN MSA	NA	NA	NA	NA	NA	28	808.7	5.5	583.1	34.9	5 613	64	2 102	616	1 891	852

X Not applicable.
NA Not available.

[1]As of June 30. Covers all FDIC-insured commercial and savings banks.
[2]Based on resident population estimated as of July 1, 1996.
[3]Based on 273 metropolitan areas (245 MSAs, 17 CMSAs, and 11 NECMAs); see text for more information. When metropolitan areas share the same rank, the next lower rank is omitted.

Source: Export Sales—U.S. Department of Commerce, International Trade Administration, "Export Sales of U.S. Metropolitan Areas, 1993-1996," Internet site <http://www.ita.doc.gov/industry/otea/metro/metro.html> (accessed 9 October 1997);   Banking—U.S. Federal Deposit Insurance Corporation, "Data Book: Summary of Deposits in Operating Banks and Branches," annual (related Internet site <http://www.fdic.gov/databank/index.html>);   Federal Funds and Grants—U.S. Bureau of the Census, "Consolidated Federal Funds Report: County Areas," annual for fiscal year (related Internet site <http://www.census.gov/govs/www/cffr.html>).

[MSA = Metropolitan statistical area. CMSA = Consolidated MSA. PMSA = Primary MSA. NECMA = New England county metropolitan area. All areas defined as of June 30, 1996. Table includes 245 MSAs, 17 CMSAs, and 58 PMSAs not in New England; as well as 12 NECMAs. Table excludes 10 MSAs, 1 CMSA, and 15 PMSAs in New England]

Metropolitan areas	Export sales Total (mil dol) 1996	1995	1994	Percent change 1995–1996	1994–1995	Banking,[1] 1996 Number of offices	Deposits Total (mil dol)	Percent change, 1990–1996	Federal funds and grants, 1996 Total expenditures (mil dol)	Percent change, 1990–1996	Per capita[2] Total Dollars	Rank[3]	By selected type—(dollars) Direct payments for individuals	Procurement contract awards	Salaries and wages	Grant awards
Grand Junction, CO MSA	NA	NA	NA	NA	NA	24	725.5	26.7	430.9	32.1	3 977	182	2 860	209	435	458
Grand Rapids-Muskegon-Holland, MI MSA	2 656.5	2 304.1	1 993.5	15.3	15.6	305	10 194.6	33.6	3 087.4	41.7	3 041	263	2 097	296	204	432
Great Falls, MT MSA	NA	NA	NA	NA	NA	12	526.0	-1.0	993.5	74.0	12 253	3	3 096	534	2 333	724
Green Bay, WI MSA	189.0	212.7	187.3	-11.2	13.6	56	2 458.2	56.3	644.0	36.5	3 023	264	1 931	469	242	367
Greensboro--Winston Salem--High Point, NC MSA	3 495.6	3 356.3	2 773.3	4.2	21.0	356	15 438.5	52.3	4 368.2	46.0	3 828	206	2 409	532	267	610
Greenville, NC MSA	NA	NA	NA	NA	NA	43	959.7	35.7	401.0	68.1	3 368	245	2 255	46	159	893
Greenville-Spartanburg-Anderson, SC MSA	2 720.4	2 305.3	1 745.0	18.0	32.1	240	7 037.3	64.6	3 058.8	69.3	3 411	244	2 430	305	162	506
Harrisburg-Lebanon-Carlisle, PA MSA	775.5	601.0	535.0	29.0	12.3	254	7 410.0	27.3	4 719.8	45.5	7 678	23	3 115	565	995	2 952
Hartford, CT NECMA	2 416.0	2 167.6	1 967.1	11.5	10.2	369	19 549.8	-17.3	5 645.6	21.5	5 086	88	2 844	498	373	1 282
Hattiesburg, MS MSA	NA	NA	NA	NA	NA	35	850.1	40.2	409.2	45.4	3 792	210	2 711	69	329	670
Hickory-Morganton-Lenoir, NC MSA	464.3	476.1	397.9	-2.5	19.6	96	2 928.1	71.2	974.1	62.5	3 093	260	2 291	70	130	595
Honolulu, HI MSA	265.7	228.2	215.5	16.4	5.9	199	11 369.8	-1.1	6 347.6	33.2	7 281	28	2 662	1 027	2 668	918
Houma, LA MSA	58.0	60.0	53.8	-3.4	11.7	75	1 718.0	24.2	677.7	29.8	3 569	229	2 437	246	109	773
Houston-Galveston-Brazoria, TX CMSA	NA	NA	NA	NA	NA	778	36 549.1	17.0	15 027.0	63.2	3 533	231	1 755	848	321	595
Brazoria, TX PMSA	D	D	1 761.0	D	D	37	1 132.2	26.6	551.4	50.7	2 497	X	1 803	192	96	372
Galveston-Texas City, TX PMSA	NA	NA	NA	NA	NA	49	1 602.0	18.8	1 003.3	64.0	4 169	X	2 473	828	219	633
Houston, TX PMSA	16 541.5	16 247.9	13 388.2	1.8	21.4	692	33 814.9	16.6	13 472.3	63.7	3 553	X	1 706	888	340	606
Huntington-Ashland, WV-KY-OH MSA	193.9	237.2	162.4	-18.2	46.0	80	2 402.6	7.7	1 522.6	39.1	4 808	110	3 350	147	403	901
Huntsville, AL MSA	899.1	829.0	672.1	8.5	23.3	87	3 351.2	88.5	3 470.3	-5.6	10 511	8	2 628	5 363	2 057	447
Indianapolis, IN MSA	4 012.8	3 555.9	3 003.8	12.8	18.4	462	14 523.7	13.4	6 547.9	36.6	4 388	146	2 495	412	580	884
Iowa City, IA MSA	NA	NA	NA	NA	NA	23	1 135.6	35.2	439.9	50.9	4 329	150	1 481	864	601	1 324
Jackson, MI MSA	128.1	98.5	96.3	30.1	2.3	43	833.6	21.0	519.1	39.3	3 358	247	2 572	99	144	528
Jackson, MS MSA	231.4	203.0	154.3	14.0	31.6	141	4 276.9	14.1	2 330.8	53.2	5 535	70	2 487	624	579	1 825
Jackson, TN MSA	155.2	175.3	132.5	-11.5	32.3	43	1 037.4	26.6	376.3	47.3	3 820	208	2 755	55	282	689
Jacksonville, FL MSA	677.0	604.1	500.4	12.1	20.7	204	8 468.4	13.5	5 621.6	45.2	5 573	67	2 910	548	1 580	516
Jacksonville, NC MSA	NA	NA	NA	NA	NA	23	462.9	31.2	1 469.7	39.6	10 169	11	2 096	1 620	6 044	393
Jamestown, NY MSA	241.2	256.6	209.4	-6.0	22.5	43	938.3	-13.6	600.5	42.1	4 265	155	2 955	187	150	961
Janesville-Beloit, WI MSA	107.1	80.2	76.3	33.5	5.1	38	1 236.9	31.7	467.6	21.5	3 105	259	2 304	124	108	524
Johnson City-Kingsport-Bristol, TN-VA MSA	1 566.5	1 677.5	1 580.8	-6.6	6.1	152	4 393.1	55.4	1 969.9	42.0	4 299	154	3 076	365	316	532
Johnstown, PA MSA	NA	NA	NA	NA	NA	116	2 840.3	27.9	1 246.8	47.1	5 217	84	3 699	272	279	950
Jonesboro, AR MSA	NA	NA	NA	NA	NA	34	998.3	77.3	282.2	53.7	3 706	217	2 386	95	265	812
Joplin, MO MSA	71.4	50.3	44.6	42.0	12.8	46	1 260.8	38.3	660.9	78.7	4 535	133	2 811	960	178	561
Kalamazoo-Battle Creek, MI MSA	836.1	897.3	869.0	-6.8	3.3	106	2 989.9	23.2	1 707.9	37.4	3 843	203	2 517	231	538	538
Kansas City, MO-KS MSA	3 985.1	3 350.2	2 578.6	19.0	29.9	446	18 380.5	-.7	7 880.2	35.3	4 662	122	2 559	636	829	544
Killeen-Temple, TX MSA	NA	NA	NA	NA	NA	42	1 356.1	20.1	2 630.3	68.8	8 859	15	2 356	1 096	4 947	449
Knoxville, TN MSA	764.1	633.2	689.2	20.7	-8.1	192	6 052.3	39.3	4 611.2	47.1	7 102	30	2 890	3 035	517	653
Kokomo, IN MSA	2 056.4	1 648.9	1 858.4	24.7	-11.3	35	853.7	27.2	345.3	43.7	3 433	242	2 742	50	187	417
La Crosse, WI-MN MSA	273.2	276.2	93.1	-1.1	196.8	31	959.3	16.7	396.9	31.9	3 266	251	2 273	215	220	515
Lafayette, LA MSA	164.8	192.7	148.7	-14.5	29.6	133	3 046.5	27.7	1 358.8	62.3	3 686	219	2 381	197	171	873
Lafayette, IN MSA	133.2	116.2	74.9	14.6	55.1	56	1 706.8	26.5	546.8	32.8	3 194	257	2 020	69	184	887
Lake Charles, LA MSA	48.2	64.6	55.9	-25.3	15.5	52	1 203.8	13.1	737.0	35.2	4 120	171	2 698	514	162	716
Lakeland-Winter Haven, FL MSA	241.5	237.7	199.2	1.6	19.3	108	3 499.3	17.4	1 751.2	69.1	3 971	184	3 325	45	153	431
Lancaster, PA MSA	626.2	581.5	469.3	7.7	23.9	184	4 856.0	18.4	1 421.5	58.7	3 153	258	2 299	313	182	348
Lansing-East Lansing, MI MSA	202.2	224.0	208.6	-9.7	7.4	120	3 009.5	19.3	2 537.0	44.7	5 669	60	2 266	112	335	2 933
Laredo, TX MSA	3 440.7	2 897.8	4 157.4	18.7	-30.3	17	2 548.9	4.9	565.4	83.6	3 198	256	1 644	110	340	1 097
Las Cruces, NM MSA	NA	NA	NA	NA	NA	32	780.7	28.1	935.2	29.3	5 708	58	2 339	1 352	992	1 017
Las Vegas, NV-AZ MSA	D	D	144.8	D	D	183	8 111.4	40.0	5 561.1	84.1	4 630	126	2 703	960	511	450
Lawrence, KS MSA	5.7	4.1	6.2	40.6	-34.6	26	534.2	38.7	264.3	22.7	2 940	267	1 728	160	297	734
Lawton, OK MSA	NA	NA	NA	NA	NA	17	533.5	18.0	1 056.6	27.2	9 504	14	3 137	772	4 987	598
Lewiston-Auburn, ME NECMA	NA	NA	NA	NA	NA	33	831.3	13.2	423.9	48.8	4 166	167	3 015	34	166	946
Lexington, KY MSA	1 499.9	1 235.0	1 078.6	21.5	14.5	138	4 061.7	7.7	1 825.7	49.6	4 139	169	2 326	515	489	794
Lima, OH MSA	207.3	226.0	166.2	-8.3	36.0	61	1 775.4	37.5	726.4	-24.1	4 671	119	3 324	577	206	528
Lincoln, NE MSA	225.3	208.8	207.2	7.9	.8	62	2 337.5	29.9	1 103.6	49.2	4 762	113	2 299	214	558	1 644
Little Rock-North Little Rock, AR MSA	210.4	193.6	219.0	8.7	-11.6	181	5 475.3	48.1	2 994.4	50.2	5 461	73	2 743	209	1 038	1 430
Longview-Marshall, TX MSA	144.2	121.2	97.3	19.0	24.6	45	1 758.1	-.4	760.4	38.1	3 678	222	2 851	108	151	562

NA Not available.
D Withheld to avoid disclosure.
X Not applicable.

[1]As of June 30. Covers all FDIC-insured commercial and savings banks.
[2]Based on resident population estimated as of July 1, 1996.
[3]Based on 273 metropolitan areas (245 MSAs, 17 CMSAs, and 11 NECMAs); see text for more information. When metropolitan areas share the same rank, the next lower rank is omitted.

Source: Export Sales—U.S. Department of Commerce, International Trade Administration, "Export Sales of U.S. Metropolitan Areas, 1993-1996," Internet site <http://www.ita.doc.gov/industry/otea/metro/metro.html> (accessed 9 October 1997);   Banking—U.S. Federal Deposit Insurance Corporation, "Data Book: Summary of Deposits in Operating Banks and Branches," annual (related Internet site <http://www.fdic.gov/databank/index.html>);   Federal Funds and Grants—U.S. Bureau of the Census, "Consolidated Federal Funds Report: County Areas," annual for fiscal year (related Internet site <http://www.census.gov/govs/www/cffr.html>).

Export Sales, Banking, and Federal Funds and Grants—Con.

[MSA = Metropolitan statistical area.   CMSA = Consolidated MSA.   PMSA = Primary MSA.   NECMA = New England county metropolitan area.   All areas defined as of June 30, 1996.   Table includes 245 MSAs, 17 CMSAs, and 58 PMSAs not in New England; as well as 12 NECMAs.   Table excludes 10 MSAs, 1 CMSA, and 15 PMSAs in New England]

Metropolitan areas	Export sales Total (mil dol) 1996	1995	1994	Percent change 1995–1996	1994–1995	Banking,[1] 1996 Number of offices	Deposits Total (mil dol)	Percent change, 1990–1996	Federal funds and grants, 1996 Total expend- itures (mil dol)	Percent change, 1990–1996	Per capita[2] Total Dollars	Rank[3]	By selected type— (dollars) Direct pay- ments for indi- viduals	Pro- cure- ment contract awards	Sal- aries and wages	Grant awards
Los Angeles-Riverside-Orange, CA CMSA	35 696.5	35 581.9	31 098.3	.3	14.4	2 045	120 222.7	3.8	65 386.4	28.1	4 220	162	2 160	974	369	709
Los Angeles-Long Beach, CA PMSA	24 437.9	24 731.0	22 224.8	-1.2	11.3	1 178	83 123.8	.3	40 885.5	20.9	4 479	X	2 173	1 121	333	844
Orange, CA PMSA	8 309.3	8 041.1	6 716.0	3.3	19.7	449	21 749.4	14.1	11 242.6	41.9	4 264	X	1 993	1 440	351	472
Riverside-San Bernardino, CA PMSA	1 982.1	1 856.5	1 458.9	6.8	27.3	311	11 324.8	14.1	10 221.8	42.5	3 389	X	2 269	208	368	539
Ventura, CA PMSA	967.3	953.4	698.7	1.5	36.5	107	4 024.7	2.2	3 036.4	41.7	4 248	X	2 158	611	893	580
Louisville, KY-IN MSA	2 327.1	2 199.8	1 798.8	5.8	22.3	310	12 083.6	16.0	4 347.2	50.7	4 383	148	2 718	546	455	650
Lubbock, TX MSA	189.0	258.7	165.1	-27.0	56.7	56	2 420.0	13.2	887.8	39.1	3 826	207	2 595	235	352	616
Lynchburg, VA MSA	258.8	192.1	152.5	34.7	26.0	59	1 837.0	26.2	959.1	-20.8	4 666	120	2 785	1 218	296	348
Macon, GA MSA	220.1	197.6	173.3	11.4	14.0	75	2 442.3	42.5	2 166.4	43.5	6 928	32	3 300	654	2 326	637
Madison, WI MSA	522.4	497.5	417.1	5.0	19.3	102	3 926.3	45.6	2 190.0	39.7	5 539	69	1 979	350	512	2 668
Mansfield, OH MSA	413.0	394.9	349.9	4.6	12.9	59	1 474.0	32.1	648.1	46.3	3 694	218	2 717	102	247	600
McAllen-Edinburg-Mission, TX MSA	1 579.7	1 617.1	1 826.4	-2.3	-11.5	70	3 195.7	16.7	1 611.3	75.6	3 251	252	1 907	112	226	986
Medford-Ashland, OR MSA	NA	NA	NA	NA	NA	48	1 204.1	67.5	673.5	50.0	3 994	179	2 955	193	393	447
Melbourne-Titusville-Palm Bay, FL MSA	635.0	310.1	315.9	104.8	-1.9	97	2 994.9	21.9	4 431.0	34.2	9 760	13	4 007	4 544	884	319
Memphis, TN-AR-MS MSA	3 786.1	4 163.8	2 729.5	-9.1	52.6	282	10 326.8	32.6	5 002.3	38.6	4 640	124	2 496	501	772	838
Merced, CA MSA	NA	NA	NA	NA	NA	31	734.1	-8.4	667.7	16.1	3 472	238	2 241	107	107	982
Miami-Fort Lauderdale, FL CMSA	12 545.8	11 975.5	10 773.4	4.8	11.2	712	43 952.9	40.8	14 857.3	46.0	4 228	159	3 178	112	346	580
Fort Lauderdale, FL PMSA	1 864.5	1 774.7	1 506.7	5.1	17.8	296	16 312.2	93.3	6 021.4	48.5	4 187	X	3 488	95	231	357
Miami, FL PMSA	10 681.2	10 200.8	9 266.7	4.7	10.1	416	27 640.7	21.3	8 835.8	44.3	4 256	X	2 963	123	425	734
Milwaukee-Racine, WI CMSA	4 210.4	3 842.0	3 316.7	9.6	15.8	433	20 291.6	55.7	6 320.9	32.8	3 848	202	2 570	204	350	714
Milwaukee-Waukesha, WI PMSA	3 717.2	3 506.9	2 913.5	6.0	20.4	386	18 658.5	59.9	5 733.2	32.4	3 933	X	2 594	219	380	729
Racine, WI PMSA	493.2	335.1	403.2	47.2	-16.9	47	1 633.0	19.8	587.8	36.4	3 177	X	2 380	79	112	592
Minneapolis-St. Paul, MN-WI MSA	12 384.0	11 071.8	8 863.5	11.9	24.9	526	28 665.7	21.4	10 673.3	31.7	3 860	199	1 947	475	403	848
Mobile, AL MSA	459.9	415.8	395.3	10.6	5.2	135	4 864.0	62.9	2 232.3	45.5	4 301	153	3 052	256	307	646
Modesto, CA MSA	359.6	279.2	236.7	28.8	18.0	68	2 119.8	-1.0	1 338.6	58.8	3 219	254	2 280	143	90	697
Monroe, LA MSA	134.0	167.8	107.1	-20.2	56.6	51	1 475.4	-19.2	546.4	60.9	3 709	216	2 660	54	163	804
Montgomery, AL MSA	192.9	244.1	231.0	-21.0	5.7	94	3 338.4	33.9	2 483.5	48.0	7 885	22	3 184	653	1 593	2 432
Muncie, IN MSA	137.6	158.3	107.4	-13.1	47.4	39	992.0	35.0	410.1	39.1	3 458	239	2 611	89	184	550
Myrtle Beach, SC MSA	NA	NA	NA	NA	NA	60	1 555.8	49.9	570.4	8.4	3 481	237	2 893	94	108	379
Naples, FL MSA	76.0	75.0	56.0	1.3	34.0	87	3 234.2	67.7	779.9	76.4	4 144	168	3 624	64	132	314
Nashville, TN MSA	1 445.5	1 412.3	1 310.5	2.3	7.8	330	13 193.1	41.6	5 020.2	105.8	4 494	138	2 342	459	485	1 196
New London-Norwich, CT NECMA	157.5	178.2	141.5	-11.6	26.0	75	2 623.1	-16.8	2 700.3	20.2	10 770	6	2 863	5 483	1 756	662
New Orleans, LA MSA	3 316.8	3 037.8	2 326.2	9.2	30.6	290	12 458.9	17.4	7 370.0	37.9	5 614	63	2 904	1 078	652	904
New York-Northern New Jersey-Long Island, NY-NJ-CT-PA CMSA/NECMA	D	D	48 190.3	D	D	5 058	397 302.1	-.2	95 870.5	34.8	4 831	106	2 838	386	403	1 190
Bergen-Passaic, NJ PMSA	4 499.9	4 784.0	4 387.0	-5.9	9.0	482	23 682.0	22.8	5 186.0	28.3	3 955	X	2 791	457	194	505
Dutchess, NY PMSA	D	D	980.6	D	D	76	2 170.0	5.9	915.0	47.1	3 483	X	2 483	43	236	715
Jersey City, NJ PMSA	1 140.8	1 159.9	1 351.2	-1.6	-14.2	118	8 668.5	43.7	2 676.7	49.2	4 860	X	2 579	439	844	968
Middlesex-Somerset-Hunterdon, NJ PMSA	3 628.1	3 448.1	3 035.9	5.2	13.6	317	24 437.9	104.3	3 604.2	42.9	3 303	X	2 237	276	283	497
Monmouth-Ocean, NJ PMSA	478.2	471.8	410.2	1.4	15.0	332	11 589.8	12.6	5 155.2	42.8	4 839	X	3 305	519	604	404
Nassau-Suffolk, NY PMSA	3 680.2	3 558.6	2 866.3	3.4	24.2	772	44 808.8	.8	11 991.6	11.6	4 508	X	2 829	787	359	521
New Haven-Bridgeport-Stamford-Waterbury-Danbury, CT NECMA	[4]6 978.8	[4]7 626.0	[4]6 019.6	[4]-8.5	[4]26.7	545	26 803.6	-16.6	7 968.5	25.3	4 893	X	2 877	714	323	965
New York, NY PMSA	27 970.5	27 131.1	23 543.7	3.1	15.2	1 592	218 722.2	-8.3	45 719.2	44.2	5 289	X	2 927	200	393	1 754
Newark, NJ PMSA	5 044.2	5 640.0	5 205.5	-10.6	8.3	597	28 226.1	6.1	8 457.9	23.9	4 359	X	2 710	292	424	923
Newburgh, NY-PA PMSA	153.3	148.9	152.8	2.9	-2.6	117	3 234.7	12.4	1 519.9	78.0	4 192	X	2 317	279	1 033	549
Trenton, NJ PMSA	267.8	392.5	237.5	-31.8	65.2	110	4 958.5	28.1	2 676.4	29.7	8 105	X	3 111	932	543	3 492
Norfolk-Virginia Beach-Newport News, VA-NC MSA	1 256.9	1 005.5	807.7	25.0	24.5	371	8 423.2	.6	12 525.2	5.7	8 132	17	2 859	1 446	3 435	384
Ocala, FL MSA	NA	NA	NA	NA	NA	64	2 329.7	77.0	1 104.8	71.2	4 802	111	4 204	68	123	403
Odessa-Midland, TX MSA	92.1	118.2	68.3	-22.1	73.0	43	2 238.8	3.8	694.5	72.2	2 901	269	2 170	35	142	541
Oklahoma City, OK MSA	483.9	485.8	488.6	-.4	-.6	222	8 434.3	33.5	5 737.9	41.5	5 589	65	2 753	542	1 354	928
Omaha, NE-IA MSA	608.3	425.9	393.3	42.8	8.3	172	7 429.9	42.0	3 490.9	35.8	5 121	86	2 415	497	1 030	615
Orlando, FL MSA	1 219.0	968.8	848.5	25.8	14.2	308	11 496.8	22.8	6 363.3	41.6	4 490	140	2 849	847	393	392
Owensboro, KY MSA	NA	NA	NA	NA	NA	27	831.0	29.2	350.6	69.0	3 860	199	2 710	199	157	769

X Not applicable.
NA Not available.
D Withheld to avoid disclosure.

[1]As of June 30. Covers all FDIC-insured commercial and savings banks.
[2]Based on resident population estimated as of July 1, 1996.
[3]Based on 273 metropolitan areas (245 MSAs, 17 CMSAs, and 11 NECMAs); see text for more information. When metropolitan areas share the same rank, the next lower rank is omitted.
[4]Data for NECMA not available. Data are for 5 Connecticut PMSAs: Bridgeport, Danbury, New Haven-Meriden, Stamford-Norwalk, and Waterbury.

Source: Export Sales—U.S. Department of Commerce, International Trade Administration, "Export Sales of U.S. Metropolitan Areas, 1993-1996," Internet site <http://www.ita.doc.gov/industry/otea/metro/metro.html> (accessed 9 October 1997); Banking—U.S. Federal Deposit Insurance Corporation, "Data Book: Summary of Deposits in Operating Banks and Branches," annual (related Internet site <http://www.fdic.gov/databank/index.html>);   Federal Funds and Grants—U.S. Bureau of the Census, "Consolidated Federal Funds Report: County Areas," annual for fiscal year (related Internet site <http://www.census.gov/govs/www/cffr.html>).

Export Sales, Banking, and Federal Funds and Grants—Con.

[MSA = Metropolitan statistical area.   CMSA = Consolidated MSA.   PMSA = Primary MSA.   NECMA = New England county metropolitan area.   All areas defined as of June 30, 1996.   Table includes 245 MSAs, 17 CMSAs, and 58 PMSAs not in New England; as well as 12 NECMAs.   Table excludes 10 MSAs, 1 CMSA, and 15 PMSAs in New England]

Metropolitan areas	Export sales					Banking,[1] 1996			Federal funds and grants, 1996							
	Total (mil dol)			Percent change		Deposits					Per capita[2]					
											Total		By selected type— (dollars)			
	1996	1995	1994	1995–1996	1994–1995	Number of offices	Total (mil dol)	Percent change, 1990–1996	Total expend-itures (mil dol)	Percent change, 1990–1996	Dollars	Rank[3]	Direct pay-ments for indi-viduals	Pro-cure-ment contract awards	Sal-aries and wages	Grant awards
Panama City, FL MSA	174.8	216.5	121.2	−19.3	78.7	30	714.1	36.3	1 159.1	81.6	8 014	19	3 574	702	2 293	493
Parkersburg-Marietta, WV-OH MSA	211.9	186.6	313.6	13.6	−40.5	53	1 709.6	41.3	687.9	53.0	4 538	132	3 077	101	543	798
Pensacola, FL MSA	36.8	32.2	34.0	14.4	−5.4	92	2 837.9	29.8	2 521.4	46.9	6 535	38	3 548	593	1 501	641
Peoria-Pekin, IL MSA	NA	NA	NA	NA	NA	89	2 933.0	18.8	1 274.5	42.8	3 678	222	2 708	177	339	418
Philadelphia-Wilmington-Atlantic City, PA-NJ-DE-MD CMSA	NA	NA	NA	NA	NA	1 661	87 107.6	−1.2	30 305.0	33.5	5 073	93	3 050	547	602	859
Atlantic-Cape May, NJ PMSA	NA	NA	NA	NA	NA	122	2 623.1	10.8	1 660.5	47.1	4 976	X	3 281	360	595	723
Philadelphia, PA-NJ PMSA	7 727.9	7 896.9	6 545.8	−2.1	20.6	1 325	56 696.2	−4.5	25 942.5	31.9	5 238	X	3 102	615	631	875
Vineland-Millville-Bridgeton, NJ PMSA	NA	NA	NA	NA	NA	39	1 073.1	43.1	605.1	44.0	4 451	X	3 062	148	286	948
Wilmington-Newark, DE-MD PMSA	4 551.1	4 361.1	3 720.4	4.4	17.2	175	26 715.3	4.0	2 096.8	42.1	3 806	X	2 440	152	420	783
Phoenix-Mesa, AZ MSA	7 912.1	6 780.4	5 561.1	16.7	21.9	460	23 744.4	28.9	11 588.0	37.8	4 219	163	2 486	642	403	676
Pine Bluff, AR MSA	152.8	153.7	152.5	−.5	.8	25	728.3	25.3	444.1	16.0	5 350	77	3 170	383	754	925
Pittsburgh, PA MSA	3 933.7	3 982.2	3 150.6	−1.2	26.4	769	38 268.6	23.0	13 374.9	43.2	5 621	62	3 709	668	411	816
Pittsfield, MA NECMA	175.5	151.9	112.2	15.6	35.3	52	1 951.9	.5	803.3	−7.0	5 959	50	3 457	1 589	254	652
Pocatello, ID MSA	NA	NA	NA	NA	NA	21	477.6	24.7	264.8	66.5	3 597	227	2 312	97	268	879
Portland, ME NECMA	339.2	373.1	319.5	−9.1	16.8	98	3 327.8	−18.5	1 128.4	37.8	4 494	138	2 737	189	862	684
Portland-Salem, OR-WA CMSA	9 357.3	9 043.3	6 521.8	3.5	38.7	483	17 645.5	49.0	8 042.4	42.8	3 870	195	2 270	186	459	932
Portland-Vancouver, OR-WA PMSA	9 234.3	8 931.3	6 448.8	3.4	38.5	406	15 379.9	51.4	6 331.1	42.8	3 599	X	2 213	207	498	657
Salem, OR PMSA	123.0	112.0	72.9	9.9	53.5	77	2 265.6	34.7	1 711.3	39.9	5 357	X	2 580	70	245	2 445
Providence-Warwick-Pawtucket, RI NECMA	NA	NA	NA	NA	NA	234	13 972.3	1.3	4 432.7	43.4	4 885	100	3 177	144	358	1 196
Provo-Orem, UT MSA	301.9	201.6	200.2	49.7	.7	60	1 488.3	48.6	673.7	45.8	2 107	273	1 387	88	142	482
Pueblo, CO MSA	NA	NA	NA	NA	NA	21	943.6	50.3	615.7	35.8	4 692	116	3 521	150	245	758
Punta Gorda, FL MSA	NA	NA	NA	NA	NA	36	1 441.9	51.3	715.9	73.7	5 489	72	5 043	28	87	322
Raleigh-Durham-Chapel Hill, NC MSA	2 609.8	2 093.2	1 758.7	24.7	19.0	340	9 542.5	58.2	4 750.1	52.4	4 633	125	2 018	278	453	1 869
Rapid City, SD MSA	NA	NA	NA	NA	NA	19	797.5	47.8	501.9	24.9	5 760	55	2 755	237	1 988	744
Reading, PA MSA	326.2	293.4	271.6	11.2	8.0	100	3 632.7	−14.2	1 278.6	51.9	3 629	226	2 717	137	183	579
Redding, CA MSA	53.0	41.0	28.6	29.3	43.2	33	1 215.7	15.5	786.5	72.9	4 863	103	3 257	398	309	888
Reno, NV MSA	314.6	368.2	213.7	−14.6	72.3	59	2 379.7	26.5	1 100.3	62.5	3 683	220	2 308	309	467	591
Richland-Kennewick-Pasco, WA MSA	228.1	146.6	271.6	55.6	−46.0	34	845.1	30.0	2 110.3	45.4	11 727	4	1 990	8 641	381	658
Richmond-Petersburg, VA MSA	5 609.4	5 389.3	5 260.6	4.1	2.4	309	15 171.7	38.7	4 753.5	53.8	5 083	90	2 629	327	927	1 189
Roanoke, VA MSA	238.3	231.3	195.9	3.0	18.1	95	3 187.9	7.7	1 071.7	31.4	4 678	118	3 118	465	734	342
Rochester, MN MSA	92.9	93.9	72.7	−1.1	29.2	29	828.8	17.7	397.8	56.8	3 515	232	1 869	146	417	1 025
Rochester, NY MSA	4 307.7	3 860.5	3 143.7	11.6	22.8	275	10 458.7	−23.6	4 327.4	50.3	3 977	182	2 624	238	244	856
Rockford, IL MSA	721.9	641.4	616.1	12.6	4.1	87	3 301.2	24.8	1 086.6	41.4	3 084	261	2 304	199	189	345
Rocky Mount, NC MSA	NA	NA	NA	NA	NA	46	1 264.4	39.5	524.7	51.6	3 640	225	2 521	116	192	787
Sacramento-Yolo, CA CMSA	NA	NA	NA	NA	NA	258	9 853.5	8.9	12 406.6	39.7	7 601	24	2 734	554	634	3 660
Sacramento, CA PMSA	1 908.6	1 448.3	1 087.9	31.8	33.1	231	8 844.0	8.0	11 717.6	38.0	7 905	X	2 797	567	624	3 903
Yolo, CA PMSA	NA	NA	NA	NA	NA	27	1 009.5	17.2	689.0	76.3	4 596	X	2 109	424	727	1 255
Saginaw-Bay City-Midland, MI MSA	1 254.5	1 035.6	776.8	21.1	33.3	108	2 652.0	13.3	1 430.4	37.5	3 547	230	2 627	76	217	607
St. Cloud, MN MSA	NA	NA	NA	NA	NA	51	1 725.7	40.5	465.4	41.3	2 903	268	1 890	87	419	453
St. Joseph, MO MSA	94.4	49.6	39.2	90.4	26.5	32	1 018.6	1.4	411.4	44.1	4 227	161	3 122	45	302	717
St. Louis, MO-IL MSA	4 497.4	3 997.7	3 673.3	12.5	8.8	539	29 555.0	29.7	20 294.6	48.9	7 964	20	2 842	3 708	693	699
Salinas, CA MSA	337.6	359.9	322.0	−6.2	11.8	51	2 196.2	10.5	1 649.3	16.4	4 864	102	2 633	424	1 109	677
Salt Lake City-Ogden, UT MSA	2 111.5	1 838.2	1 808.7	14.9	1.6	279	9 420.1	42.1	4 960.8	28.2	4 073	172	1 947	323	1 017	779
San Angelo, TX MSA	NA	NA	NA	NA	NA	22	938.0	17.7	487.3	38.5	4 750	114	2 730	311	1 193	476
San Antonio, TX MSA	1 050.0	771.1	656.3	36.2	17.5	203	9 801.7	16.0	8 550.5	41.1	5 338	56	2 847	513	1 701	669
San Diego, CA MSA	6 719.4	5 860.9	4 867.3	14.6	20.4	448	17 501.4	18.9	16 706.0	35.1	6 291	46	2 654	1 227	1 666	738
San Francisco-Oakland-San Jose, CA CMSA	48 103.9	43 548.3	35 966.3	10.5	21.1	1 161	85 974.5	22.4	31 882.2	25.5	4 827	107	2 420	982	615	789
Oakland, CA PMSA	7 309.2	6 372.5	5 113.2	14.7	24.6	357	20 856.3	17.1	10 379.0	23.9	4 697	X	2 464	820	630	746
San Francisco, CA PMSA	8 560.4	8 133.7	9 303.8	5.2	−12.6	362	41 398.0	25.5	8 332.4	34.8	5 033	X	2 689	522	788	1 016
San Jose, CA PMSA	29 331.3	26 822.8	19 942.7	9.4	34.5	236	16 519.6	28.9	8 538.2	17.0	5 338	X	1 926	2 197	401	807
Santa Cruz-Watsonville, CA PMSA	1 943.1	1 408.2	857.4	38.0	64.2	36	1 460.5	−2.2	740.3	45.5	3 113	X	2 258	89	107	649
Santa Rosa, CA PMSA	681.8	572.9	485.2	19.0	18.1	85	3 118.3	16.4	1 527.0	58.3	3 628	X	2 672	92	250	602
Vallejo-Fairfield-Napa, CA PMSA	278.0	238.1	264.0	16.7	−9.8	85	2 621.8	7.3	2 365.2	14.6	4 907	X	2 791	493	1 233	378
San Luis Obispo-Atascadero-Paso Robles, CA MSA	NA	NA	NA	NA	NA	56	1 605.2	24.1	788.5	51.0	3 437	240	2 670	104	147	486
Santa Barbara-Santa Maria-Lompoc, CA MSA	648.0	565.2	420.2	14.6	34.5	90	3 865.8	36.8	2 030.3	25.0	5 266	81	2 536	1 415	711	595

NA Not available.
X Not applicable.

[1]As of June 30. Covers all FDIC-insured commercial and savings banks.
[2]Based on resident population estimated as of July 1, 1996.
[3]Based on 273 metropolitan areas (245 MSAs, 17 CMSAs, and 11 NECMAs); see text for more information. When metropolitan areas share the same rank, the next lower rank is omitted.

Source: Export Sales—U.S. Department of Commerce, International Trade Administration, "Export Sales of U.S. Metropolitan Areas, 1993-1996," Internet site <http://www.ita.doc.gov/industry/otea/metro/metro.html> (accessed 9 October 1997); Banking—U.S. Federal Deposit Insurance Corporation, "Data Book: Summary of Deposits in Operating Banks and Branches," annual (related Internet site <http://www.fdic.gov/databank/index.html>); Federal Funds and Grants—U.S. Bureau of the Census, "Consolidated Federal Funds Report: County Areas," annual for fiscal year (related Internet site <http://www.census.gov/govs/www/cffr.html>).

[MSA = Metropolitan statistical area. CMSA = Consolidated MSA. PMSA = Primary MSA. NECMA = New England county metropolitan area. All areas defined as of June 30, 1996. Table includes 245 MSAs, 17 CMSAs, and 58 PMSAs not in New England; as well as 12 NECMAs. Table excludes 10 MSAs, 1 CMSA, and 15 PMSAs in New England]

Metropolitan areas	Export sales Total (mil dol) 1996	1995	1994	Percent change 1995–1996	1994–1995	Banking,[1] 1996 Deposits Number of offices	Total (mil dol)	Percent change, 1990–1996	Federal funds and grants, 1996 Total expenditures (mil dol)	Percent change, 1990–1996	Per capita[2] Total Dollars	Rank[3]	By selected type—(dollars) Direct payments for individuals	Procurement contract awards	Salaries and wages	Grant awards
Santa Fe, NM MSA	NA	NA	NA	NA	NA	42	1 232.8	41.5	1 880.0	28.3	13 700	1	2 020	8 558	483	2 632
Sarasota-Bradenton, FL MSA	180.2	182.8	187.4	-1.4	-2.5	189	7 704.9	30.1	2 942.4	56.3	5 564	68	4 932	94	187	343
Savannah, GA MSA	459.4	567.5	423.3	-19.1	34.1	70	2 474.6	23.8	1 963.4	108.5	6 947	31	2 762	986	2 503	668
Scranton--Wilkes-Barre--Hazleton, PA MSA	392.0	431.9	328.2	-9.2	31.6	241	8 081.8	-.9	3 399.1	18.1	5 412	75	3 840	405	333	796
Seattle-Tacoma-Bremerton, WA CMSA	NA	NA	NA	NA	NA	938	32 347.1	20.8	17 089.3	41.7	5 146	85	2 379	707	1 109	938
Bremerton, WA PMSA	79.9	109.8	54.6	-27.3	101.2	60	1 326.0	67.9	2 198.0	43.0	9 485	X	2 808	1 024	5 219	431
Olympia, WA PMSA	NA	NA	NA	NA	NA	56	1 101.0	73.4	1 437.7	73.4	7 294	X	2 781	59	261	4 177
Seattle-Bellevue-Everett, WA PMSA	21 391.1	17 815.4	21 753.0	20.1	-18.1	634	25 512.1	16.7	9 945.0	34.3	4 450	X	2 211	819	621	785
Tacoma, WA PMSA	1 179.7	1 098.9	774.9	7.4	41.8	188	4 407.9	26.0	3 508.6	53.2	5 338	X	2 676	412	1 573	664
Sharon, PA MSA	56.9	60.7	40.4	-6.2	50.2	44	1 337.0	13.3	549.7	56.9	4 500	137	3 613	113	124	640
Sheboygan, WI MSA	283.3	258.7	244.3	9.5	5.9	28	1 253.3	50.8	325.2	37.3	2 964	266	2 301	201	99	348
Sherman-Denison, TX MSA	147.5	90.7	36.1	62.6	151.0	30	1 130.0	25.0	382.9	34.0	3 806	209	3 172	57	137	417
Shreveport-Bossier City, LA MSA	172.6	169.1	134.6	2.1	25.6	101	3 197.4	-.1	2 011.4	24.2	5 299	80	3 109	337	1 022	818
Sioux City, IA-NE MSA	NA	NA	NA	NA	NA	38	1 229.7	33.9	480.8	34.2	3 970	185	2 561	421	374	517
Sioux Falls, SD MSA	NA	NA	NA	NA	NA	65	4 852.7	17.6	611.7	52.0	3 906	191	2 475	266	636	475
South Bend, IN MSA	494.8	389.5	160.3	27.0	142.9	56	2 125.5	5.7	1 366.5	34.6	5 302	79	2 697	1 862	236	492
Spokane, WA MSA	347.9	310.9	269.4	11.9	15.4	96	3 006.6	11.1	1 839.0	49.4	4 542	131	2 794	257	804	667
Springfield, IL MSA	35.5	35.1	29.8	1.3	17.8	75	2 915.5	44.5	2 132.0	55.6	10 444	9	2 903	86	533	6 872
Springfield, MO MSA	120.3	120.2	103.8	.1	15.8	84	2 780.3	32.4	1 065.8	57.2	3 597	227	2 571	114	408	493
Springfield, MA NECMA	530.3	512.1	434.8	3.6	17.8	170	6 609.7	-21.4	2 702.0	33.2	4 566	130	2 961	241	557	788
State College, PA MSA	NA	NA	NA	NA	NA	57	1 252.0	50.3	529.6	37.5	4 028	176	2 050	369	220	1 378
Steubenville-Weirton, OH-WV MSA	NA	NA	NA	NA	NA	54	1 144.4	7.1	645.2	24.0	4 665	121	3 807	53	138	650
Stockton-Lodi, CA MSA	357.8	355.7	320.3	.6	11.0	78	3 194.7	1.4	1 952.1	54.9	3 660	224	2 271	121	431	824
Sumter, SC MSA	NA	NA	NA	NA	NA	18	506.0	43.5	607.8	38.7	5 672	59	2 666	453	2 001	524
Syracuse, NY MSA	1 665.5	1 894.3	1 600.9	-12.1	18.3	199	7 257.5	-2.7	2 992.9	24.0	4 014	177	2 549	368	329	755
Tallahassee, FL MSA	27.2	24.2	18.7	12.4	29.4	70	2 080.7	41.6	2 562.5	73.3	9 879	12	2 271	592	344	6 664
Tampa-St. Petersburg-Clearwater, FL MSA	1 921.8	2 116.1	1 835.8	-9.2	15.3	565	24 321.6	25.7	11 885.3	47.8	5 404	76	3 988	455	450	500
Terre Haute, IN MSA	253.7	163.6	88.8	55.0	84.3	53	1 837.7	33.8	647.9	37.6	4 329	150	2 990	196	507	603
Texarkana, TX-Texarkana, AR MSA	64.1	52.2	24.6	22.7	112.0	29	1 123.4	23.4	783.7	29.0	6 324	43	3 443	843	1 264	740
Toledo, OH MSA	1 207.5	1 177.7	986.9	2.5	19.3	172	5 254.4	9.6	2 402.2	44.4	3 929	188	2 708	170	213	821
Topeka, KS MSA	130.2	133.0	125.2	-2.1	6.2	61	1 593.2	2.3	1 236.9	60.4	7 499	27	3 091	306	883	2 481
Tucson, AZ MSA	800.1	671.7	638.1	19.1	5.3	126	4 971.9	49.7	4 754.9	50.3	6 192	47	2 980	1 697	760	749
Tulsa, OK MSA	1 549.6	1 485.1	1 241.0	4.3	19.7	164	7 215.5	39.6	2 594.6	46.8	3 430	243	2 484	155	330	451
Tuscaloosa, AL MSA	NA	NA	NA	NA	NA	39	1 348.4	57.4	646.7	50.1	4 073	172	2 629	207	396	833
Tyler, TX MSA	NA	NA	NA	NA	NA	40	1 669.0	-1.3	623.9	57.1	3 781	211	2 798	262	219	489
Utica-Rome, NY MSA	278.0	238.0	269.3	16.8	-11.6	79	2 914.4	-14.1	1 537.5	13.5	5 084	89	3 304	342	445	983
Victoria, TX MSA	NA	NA	NA	NA	NA	12	960.8	-1.1	269.4	62.6	3 304	249	2 393	37	130	691
Visalia-Tulare-Porterville, CA MSA	143.7	120.6	107.7	19.2	12.0	55	1 766.4	11.6	1 174.1	58.5	3 355	248	2 014	68	139	1 109
Waco, TX MSA	NA	NA	NA	NA	NA	35	1 681.7	13.8	983.2	38.9	4 873	101	2 849	997	507	503
Washington-Baltimore, DC-MD-VA-WV CMSA	NA	NA	NA	NA	NA	1 898	64 366.4	-1.3	76 532.8	40.4	10 682	7	2 789	3 335	3 333	1 121
Baltimore, MD PMSA	2 110.4	2 209.2	1 869.0	-4.5	18.2	611	20 631.7	-14.3	14 895.0	25.7	6 020	X	2 926	997	1 007	1 081
Hagerstown, MD PMSA	NA	NA	NA	NA	NA	54	1 198.5	29.2	528.7	41.2	4 154	X	2 724	304	570	536
Washington, DC-MD-VA-WV PMSA	8 083.5	8 350.4	7 969.3	-3.2	4.8	1 233	42 536.3	5.7	61 109.1	44.5	13 392	X	2 717	4 688	4 672	1 159
Waterloo-Cedar Falls, IA MSA	200.9	194.6	149.7	3.2	30.0	29	1 127.7	28.8	456.4	.3	3 717	214	2 811	48	239	573
Wausau, WI MSA	148.9	117.3	113.6	26.9	3.3	44	1 396.0	57.3	331.0	37.1	2 717	270	2 060	69	201	366
West Palm Beach-Boca Raton, FL MSA	955.8	898.0	834.3	6.4	7.6	248	10 501.8	24.9	6 445.8	73.1	6 492	39	4 154	1 658	261	406
Wheeling, WV-OH MSA	15.1	9.0	10.8	67.5	-16.0	64	1 889.9	26.3	774.0	48.3	4 968	99	3 537	62	222	1 118
Wichita, KS MSA	1 916.8	1 727.7	1 540.6	10.9	12.1	132	4 372.4	9.9	2 444.2	20.7	4 765	112	2 510	1 030	727	474
Wichita Falls, TX MSA	77.0	80.7	65.1	-4.6	24.0	33	1 328.7	15.4	826.3	43.2	6 062	49	3 231	671	1 653	491
Williamsport, PA MSA	151.0	150.4	123.3	.4	22.0	47	1 136.9	13.8	505.5	32.5	4 245	156	2 950	228	277	636
Wilmington, NC MSA	301.7	211.7	180.7	42.6	17.2	84	2 177.3	72.9	920.6	79.6	4 453	143	3 007	431	280	714
Yakima, WA MSA	176.0	168.9	147.6	4.2	14.4	52	1 218.3	25.9	851.0	60.0	3 935	187	2 203	276	275	1 150
York, PA MSA	945.1	973.9	952.0	-3.0	2.3	123	3 663.8	.6	1 560.9	75.6	4 238	157	2 338	1 033	513	336
Youngstown-Warren, OH MSA	223.1	225.9	185.3	-1.2	21.9	169	4 389.2	10.4	2 530.8	44.8	4 228	159	3 238	77	186	719
Yuba City, CA MSA	74.0	70.5	61.5	4.9	14.7	22	715.1	18.8	660.1	46.6	4 834	105	2 776	94	1 044	754
Yuma, AZ MSA	NA	NA	NA	NA	NA	25	744.7	10.7	689.8	56.9	5 513	71	2 941	348	1 469	741

NA Not available.
X Not applicable.

[1]As of June 30. Covers all FDIC-insured commercial and savings banks.
[2]Based on resident population estimated as of July 1, 1996.
[3]Based on 273 metropolitan areas (245 MSAs, 17 CMSAs, and 11 NECMAs); see text for more information. When metropolitan areas share the same rank, the next lower rank is omitted.

Source: Export Sales—U.S. Department of Commerce, International Trade Administration, "Export Sales of U.S. Metropolitan Areas, 1993-1996," Internet site <http://www.ita.doc.gov/industry/otea/metro/metro.html> (accessed 9 October 1997); Banking—U.S. Federal Deposit Insurance Corporation, "Data Book: Summary of Deposits in Operating Banks and Branches," annual (related Internet site <http://www.fdic.gov/databank/index.html>); Federal Funds and Grants—U.S. Bureau of the Census, "Consolidated Federal Funds Report: County Areas," annual for fiscal year (related Internet site <http://www.census.gov/govs/www/cffr.html>).

TABLE C

Metro Counties

Note:

Table C presents data for metropolitan (metro) areas and their component counties defined as of June 30, 1996. Areas covered are 245 MSAs (metropolitan statistical areas), 17 CMSAs (consolidated MSAs), and 58 PMSAs (primary MSAs) located outside New England; 12 NECMAs (New England county metropolitan areas); and the 844 component counties for these areas. For a discussion of metro area and component counties concepts, see Appendix B.

Data are presented for 43 items. The MSAs, CMSAs, and NECMAs are presented in alphabetic order. PMSAs are presented alphabetically under the related CMSA. Component counties are listed under the related metro area. For an alphabetic listing of PMSAs with related CMSA, see Appendix C. For an alphabetic listing of metropolitan counties by state, see Appendix D.

FIPS metropolitan area and FIPS state/county codes are shown in the first 2 columns of Table C-1. For a discussion of geographic codes, see Appendix B.

For a more detailed listing of subjects covered in the table, see subject index.

Table C—Metro Counties

Table C–1. Metro Counties — **Population**

[MSA = Metropolitan statistical area. CMSA = Consolidated MSA. PMSA = Primary MSA. NECMA = New England county metropolitan area. All areas defined as of June 30, 1996. Table includes 245 MSAs, 17 CMSAs, and 58 PMSAs not in New England; 12 NECMAs; and 844 component counties]

Metro-politan area code[1]	State and county code[2]	Metropolitan areas and component counties	Total persons: 1997 (July 1)	Total persons: 1990[3] (April 1)	Total persons: 1980 (April 1)	Net change 1990–1997: Total[4]	Net change 1990–1997: Births	Net change 1990–1997: Deaths	Net change 1990–1997: Net inter-national migration	Net change: 1980–1990	Percent change: 1990–1997	Percent change: 1980–1990	Percent—65 years and over, 1996	Percent—Hispanic origin[5], 1996
0040	48 441	Abilene, TX MSA (Taylor)	121 456	119 655	110 932	1 801	15 099	7 798	1 423	8 723	1.5	7.9	12.4	17.4
0120		Albany, GA MSA	117 674	112 571	112 394	5 103	13 845	6 882	227	177	4.5	.2	9.3	1.2
	13 095	Dougherty	95 800	96 321	100 710	–521	12 189	6 298	211	–4 389	–.5	–4.4	9.9	1.3
	13 177	Lee	21 874	16 250	11 684	5 624	1 656	584	16	4 566	34.6	39.1	6.7	1.0
0160		Albany-Schenectady-Troy, NY MSA	876 420	861 623	824 729	14 797	84 488	58 971	8 127	36 894	1.7	4.5	14.6	2.1
	36 001	Albany	294 312	292 793	285 909	1 519	27 233	20 859	4 035	6 884	.5	2.4	15.3	2.2
	36 057	Montgomery	51 453	51 981	53 439	–528	4 907	4 666	139	–1 458	–1.0	–2.7	20.0	6.5
	36 083	Rensselaer	154 364	154 429	151 966	–65	15 210	10 557	1 287	2 463	Z	1.6	13.8	1.5
	36 091	Saratoga	196 584	181 276	153 759	15 308	19 302	9 256	1 292	27 517	8.4	17.9	10.7	1.3
	36 093	Schenectady	147 224	149 285	149 946	–2 061	15 180	11 442	1 368	–661	–1.4	–.4	17.2	2.1
	36 095	Schoharie	32 483	31 859	29 710	624	2 656	2 191	6	2 149	2.0	7.2	14.8	2.1
0200		Albuquerque, NM MSA	674 837	589 131	[6]485 429	85 706	73 984	31 930	11 331	[6]103 702	14.5	[6]21.4	10.7	38.4
	35 001	Bernalillo	526 088	480 577	420 261	45 511	59 305	26 272	10 007	60 316	9.5	14.4	10.8	38.4
	35 043	Sandoval	85 823	63 319	34 400	22 504	8 832	3 130	598	28 919	35.5	84.1	10.3	28.5
	35 061	Valencia	62 926	45 235	[6]30 768	17 691	5 847	2 528	726	[6]14 467	39.1	[6]47.0	10.4	51.4
0220	22 079	Alexandria, LA MSA (Rapides)	126 491	131 556	135 282	–5 065	14 317	9 408	660	–3 726	–3.9	–2.8	12.5	1.3
0240		Allentown-Bethlehem-Easton, PA MSA	613 836	595 081	551 052	18 755	54 530	43 586	4 408	44 029	3.2	8.0	16.0	5.8
	42 025	Carbon	58 844	56 846	53 285	1 998	4 369	5 210	67	3 561	3.5	6.7	19.2	1.2
	42 077	Lehigh	297 703	291 130	272 349	6 573	28 014	21 447	3 060	18 781	2.3	6.9	15.8	6.5
	42 095	Northampton	257 289	247 105	225 418	10 184	22 147	16 929	1 281	21 687	4.1	9.6	15.4	6.0
0280	42 013	Altoona, PA MSA (Blair)	130 923	130 542	136 621	381	11 440	11 291	226	–6 079	.3	–4.4	17.6	.4
0320		Amarillo, TX MSA	208 165	187 514	173 699	20 651	24 146	12 606	3 775	13 815	11.0	8.0	11.7	16.0
	48 375	Potter	109 243	97 841	98 637	11 402	14 895	8 341	3 128	–796	11.7	–.8	13.0	22.9
	48 381	Randall	98 922	89 673	75 062	9 249	9 251	4 265	647	14 611	10.3	19.5	10.3	8.3
0380	02 020	Anchorage, AK MSA (Anchorage)	251 047	226 338	174 431	24 709	33 955	6 671	3 503	51 907	10.9	29.8	4.7	4.7
0450	01 015	Anniston, AL MSA (Calhoun)	117 092	116 032	119 761	1 060	11 945	8 552	110	–3 729	.9	–3.1	12.9	1.4
0460		Appleton-Oshkosh-Neenah, WI MSA	342 154	315 121	291 369	27 033	33 030	17 823	961	23 752	8.6	8.2	12.0	1.0
	55 015	Calumet	38 045	34 291	30 867	3 754	3 595	1 767	–22	3 424	10.9	11.1	11.1	.6
	55 087	Outagamie	154 175	140 510	128 730	13 665	15 687	7 449	586	11 780	9.7	9.2	11.2	.9
	55 139	Winnebago	149 934	140 320	131 772	9 614	13 748	8 607	397	8 548	6.9	6.5	13.0	1.1
0480		Asheville, NC MSA	211 284	191 772	177 761	19 512	18 223	15 739	505	14 011	10.2	7.9	16.9	1.1
	37 021	Buncombe	192 784	174 819	160 934	17 965	16 780	14 304	466	13 885	10.3	8.6	16.8	1.1
	37 115	Madison	18 500	16 953	16 827	1 547	1 443	1 435	39	126	9.1	.7	17.9	.8
0500		Athens, GA MSA	138 523	126 262	104 672	12 261	12 897	6 159	1 200	21 590	9.7	20.6	9.4	2.2
	13 059	Clarke	91 042	87 594	74 498	3 448	8 517	3 971	1 005	13 096	3.9	17.6	8.9	2.6
	13 195	Madison	24 416	21 050	17 747	3 366	2 435	1 327	121	3 303	16.0	18.6	11.4	1.4
	13 219	Oconee	23 065	17 618	12 427	5 447	1 945	861	74	5 191	30.9	41.8	9.5	1.6
0520		Atlanta, GA MSA	3 627 184	2 959 500	2 233 229	667 684	389 389	155 983	54 892	726 271	22.6	32.5	7.9	3.0
	13 013	Barrow	38 966	29 721	21 354	9 245	4 343	1 986	197	8 367	31.1	39.2	11.3	1.4
	13 015	Bartow	69 181	55 915	40 760	13 266	7 567	3 622	186	15 155	23.7	37.2	10.4	1.5
	13 045	Carroll	81 402	71 422	56 346	9 980	8 687	4 430	271	15 076	14.0	26.8	10.5	1.3
	13 057	Cherokee	126 838	90 204	51 699	36 634	13 412	3 793	532	38 505	40.6	74.5	7.3	2.0
	13 063	Clayton	204 197	181 436	150 357	22 761	24 757	7 982	2 005	31 079	12.5	20.7	5.9	3.2
	13 067	Cobb	551 059	447 745	297 718	103 314	57 127	18 253	7 180	150 027	23.1	50.4	6.4	3.4
	13 077	Coweta	80 658	53 853	39 268	26 805	8 156	3 651	212	14 585	49.8	37.1	10.1	1.1
	13 089	De Kalb	587 730	546 171	483 024	41 559	67 389	28 178	18 605	63 147	7.6	13.1	8.2	4.1
	13 097	Douglas	86 653	71 120	54 573	15 533	9 024	3 537	370	16 547	21.8	30.3	7.2	1.8
	13 113	Fayette	85 047	62 415	29 043	22 632	5 604	2 665	497	33 372	36.3	114.9	7.3	2.7
	13 117	Forsyth	75 749	44 083	27 958	31 666	6 112	2 359	445	16 125	71.8	57.7	9.1	2.3
	13 121	Fulton	722 540	648 779	589 904	73 761	85 432	44 954	14 084	58 875	11.4	10.0	9.7	2.9
	13 135	Gwinnett	500 816	352 910	166 808	147 906	50 437	11 686	8 425	186 102	41.9	111.6	4.9	4.0
	13 151	Henry	98 103	58 741	36 309	39 362	9 312	3 398	566	22 432	67.0	61.8	8.4	1.3
	13 217	Newton	55 148	41 808	34 666	13 340	5 952	2 882	209	7 142	31.9	20.6	10.6	1.5
	13 223	Paulding	68 962	41 611	26 110	27 351	6 818	2 099	102	15 501	65.7	59.4	7.7	1.2
	13 227	Pickens	18 574	14 432	11 652	4 142	1 576	1 249	34	2 780	28.7	23.9	13.9	.6
	13 247	Rockdale	67 050	54 091	36 570	12 959	6 024	2 748	653	17 521	24.0	47.9	8.2	1.8
	13 255	Spalding	56 972	54 457	47 899	2 515	6 293	4 030	201	6 558	4.6	13.7	11.7	.9
	13 297	Walton	51 539	38 586	31 211	12 953	5 367	2 481	118	7 375	33.6	23.6	11.3	1.4
0600		Augusta-Aiken, GA-SC MSA	457 228	415 220	363 451	42 008	51 885	27 315	1 774	51 769	10.1	14.2	9.9	2.1
	13 073	Columbia, GA	88 812	66 031	40 118	22 781	8 219	2 719	625	25 913	34.5	64.6	5.9	2.4
	13 189	McDuffie, GA	21 588	20 119	18 546	1 469	2 305	1 521	45	1 573	7.3	8.5	11.6	.7
	13 245	Richmond, GA	193 098	189 719	181 629	3 379	24 843	13 262	692	8 090	1.8	4.5	9.7	3.0
	45 003	Aiken, SC	133 980	120 991	105 630	12 989	14 523	8 441	363	15 361	10.7	14.5	12.1	1.0
	45 037	Edgefield, SC	19 750	18 360	17 528	1 390	1 995	1 372	49	832	7.6	4.7	12.7	.5

Z Less than .05 percent.

[1]Federal Information Processing Standards (FIPS) codes for metropolitan areas defined as of June 30, 1996.
[2]FIPS codes for counties/county equivalents defined as of January 1, 1990.
[3]Includes count resolution corrections through December 1996.
[4]Includes net domestic migration, net federal movement, and residual not shown separately.
[5]Persons of Hispanic origin may be of any race.
[6]1980 population based on 1990 boundaries.

Source: 1990–1997 Population—U.S. Bureau of the Census, "Estimates of the Population of Counties and Demographic Components of Population Change: April 1, 1990 to July 1, 1997" (CO-97-5) Internet site <http://www.census.gov/population/www/estimates/co_97_5.html> (accessed 30 March 1998); 1980 Population—U.S. Bureau of the Census, "1980–1990 Intercensal Population Estimates by County," on diskette; 65 Plus and Hispanic Population—U.S. Bureau of the Census, "County Population Estimates by Age, Sex, Race, and Hispanic Origin - 4/1/90 to 7/1/96" data file (related Internet site <http: //www.census.gov/population/www/estimates/co_casrh.html>).

Table C–1. Metro Counties — **Population**—Con.

[MSA = Metropolitan statistical area. CMSA = Consolidated MSA. PMSA = Primary MSA. NECMA = New England county metropolitan area. All areas defined as of June 30, 1996. Table includes 245 MSAs, 17 CMSAs, and 58 PMSAs not in New England; 12 NECMAs; and 844 component counties]

Metro-politan area code[1]	State and county code[2]	Metropolitan areas and component counties	Total persons 1997 (July 1)	Total persons 1990[3] (April 1)	Total persons 1980 (April 1)	Net change 1990–1997 Total[4]	Births	Deaths	Net inter-national migration	1980–1990	Percent change 1990–1997	Percent change 1980–1990	65 years and over, 1996	Hispanic origin[5], 1996
0640		Austin-San Marcos, TX MSA	1 071 023	846 227	585 051	224 796	112 515	37 937	21 583	261 176	26.6	44.6	8.0	24.3
	48 021	Bastrop.......................	49 031	38 263	24 726	10 768	4 617	2 596	561	13 537	28.1	54.7	12.6	21.2
	48 055	Caldwell......................	31 625	26 392	23 637	5 233	2 941	1 833	394	2 755	19.8	11.7	13.5	42.4
	48 209	Hays.........................	86 284	65 614	40 594	20 670	6 914	2 811	920	25 020	31.5	61.6	8.4	32.6
	48 453	Travis........................	693 606	576 407	419 573	117 199	78 634	24 502	17 759	156 834	20.3	37.4	7.5	24.8
	48 491	Williamson....................	210 477	139 551	76 521	70 926	19 409	6 195	1 949	63 030	50.8	82.4	7.8	17.1
0680	06 029	Bakersfield, CA MSA (Kern)....	628 605	544 981	403 089	83 624	90 347	30 519	23 106	141 892	15.3	35.2	9.9	33.8
0733	23 019	Bangor, ME NECMA (Penobscot)......	143 300	146 601	137 015	–3 301	12 156	9 165	225	9 586	–2.3	7.0	12.2	.6
0743	25 001	Barnstable-Yarmouth, MA NECMA (Barnstable)	205 128	186 605	147 925	18 523	15 965	17 523	1 264	38 680	9.9	26.1	22.8	1.5
0760		Baton Rouge, LA MSA	570 165	528 261	494 151	41 904	65 081	29 259	3 217	34 110	7.9	6.9	9.2	1.6
	22 005	Ascension....................	69 978	58 214	50 068	11 764	7 852	3 131	107	8 146	20.2	16.3	8.3	1.9
	22 033	East Baton Rouge	394 249	380 105	366 191	14 144	46 233	21 149	2 980	13 914	3.7	3.8	9.4	1.7
	22 063	Livingston....................	85 470	70 523	58 806	14 947	8 479	3 826	77	11 717	21.2	19.9	8.7	1.1
	22 121	West Baton Rouge	20 468	19 419	19 086	1 049	2 517	1 153	53	333	5.4	1.7	9.5	1.2
0840		Beaumont-Port Arthur, TX MSA.......	374 991	361 218	373 211	13 773	40 956	26 106	3 657	–11 993	3.8	–3.2	13.2	5.1
	48 199	Hardin......................	48 403	41 320	40 721	7 083	4 568	2 784	64	599	17.1	1.5	12.2	2.1
	48 245	Jefferson....................	241 940	239 389	248 652	2 551	27 280	18 043	3 436	–9 263	1.1	–3.7	14.2	6.4
	48 361	Orange......................	84 648	80 509	83 838	4 139	9 108	5 279	157	–3 329	5.1	–4.0	11.2	3.0
0860	53 073	Bellingham, WA MSA (Whatcom)....	154 249	127 780	106 701	26 469	13 829	7 818	3 238	21 079	20.7	19.8	12.4	4.0
0870	26 021	Benton Harbor, MI MSA (Berrien)......	160 713	161 378	171 276	–665	16 707	11 478	711	–9 898	–.4	–5.8	14.3	1.9
0880	30 111	Billings, MT MSA (Yellowstone).......	125 771	113 419	108 035	12 352	12 059	7 125	189	5 384	10.9	5.0	12.3	3.0
0920		Biloxi-Gulfport-Pascagoula, MS MSA ..	343 423	312 368	300 176	31 055	37 760	20 988	857	12 192	9.9	4.1	10.7	1.9
	28 045	Hancock.....................	39 261	31 760	24 496	7 501	3 452	2 528	73	7 264	23.6	29.7	14.5	2.2
	28 047	Harrison.....................	175 611	165 365	157 665	10 246	21 082	11 555	632	7 700	6.2	4.9	10.9	2.3
	28 059	Jackson.....................	128 551	115 243	118 015	13 308	13 226	6 905	152	–2 772	11.5	–2.3	9.3	1.2
0960		Binghamton, NY MSA	251 698	264 497	263 460	–12 799	24 323	17 721	3 982	1 037	–4.8	.4	14.7	1.4
	36 007	Broome......................	198 734	212 160	213 648	–13 426	19 585	14 898	3 282	–1 488	–6.3	–.7	15.5	1.5
	36 107	Tioga.......................	52 964	52 337	49 812	627	4 738	2 823	700	2 525	1.2	5.1	11.3	.9
1000		Birmingham, AL MSA	900 029	839 942	815 333	60 087	92 297	62 982	2 705	24 609	7.2	3.0	13.0	.6
	01 009	Blount......................	45 081	39 248	36 459	5 833	4 111	2 888	262	2 789	14.9	7.6	13.6	1.1
	01 073	Jefferson....................	658 664	651 520	671 371	7 144	69 691	51 536	1 942	–19 851	1.1	–3.0	14.0	.6
	01 115	St. Clair	60 838	49 811	41 205	11 027	5 586	3 487	56	8 606	22.1	20.9	11.8	.6
	01 117	Shelby	135 446	99 363	66 298	36 083	12 909	5 071	445	33 065	36.3	49.9	7.8	.8
1010		Bismarck, ND MSA	91 044	83 831	79 988	7 213	8 529	4 664	388	3 843	8.6	4.8	11.8	.7
	38 015	Burleigh	66 647	60 131	54 811	6 516	6 355	3 172	412	5 320	10.8	9.7	11.0	.7
	38 059	Morton.....................	24 397	23 700	25 177	697	2 174	1 492	–24	–1 477	2.9	–5.9	14.0	.4
1020	18 105	Bloomington, IN MSA (Monroe)........	116 653	108 978	98 783	7 675	8 536	4 604	752	10 195	7.0	10.3	8.8	1.7
1040	17 113	Bloomington-Normal, IL MSA (McLean)..	140 797	129 180	119 149	11 617	13 644	6 824	684	10 031	9.0	8.4	10.8	1.7
1080		Boise City, ID MSA..................	383 843	295 851	256 881	87 992	39 933	16 673	3 893	38 970	29.7	15.2	10.7	7.6
	16 001	Ada	267 168	205 775	173 125	61 393	26 625	10 652	1 890	32 650	29.8	18.9	9.8	3.6
	16 027	Canyon	116 675	90 076	83 756	26 599	13 308	6 021	2 003	6 320	29.5	7.5	12.6	16.9
1123		Boston-Worcester-Lawrence-Lowell-Brockton, MA-NH NECMA	5 827 654	5 685 763	5 336 242	141 891	598 448	357 289	104 750	349 521	2.5	6.5	13.2	5.1
	25 005	Bristol, MA	515 501	506 325	474 641	9 176	51 557	34 779	–1 949	31 684	1.8	6.7	15.1	3.3
	25 009	Essex, MA	691 400	670 080	633 688	21 320	72 545	45 598	13 533	36 392	3.2	5.7	14.5	8.9
	25 017	Middlesex, MA	1 417 868	1 398 468	1 367 034	19 400	141 860	83 343	28 582	31 434	1.4	2.3	13.0	4.1
	25 021	Norfolk, MA	639 243	616 087	606 587	23 156	60 843	40 287	11 213	9 500	3.8	1.6	14.6	1.7
	25 023	Plymouth, MA	462 159	435 276	405 437	26 883	47 113	26 243	4 222	29 839	6.2	7.4	11.9	2.7
	25 025	Suffolk, MA	642 900	663 906	650 142	–21 006	74 628	44 177	38 396	13 764	–3.2	2.1	12.5	12.9
	25 027	Worcester, MA	725 540	709 705	646 352	15 835	75 138	47 167	7 288	63 353	2.2	9.8	14.2	5.7
	33 011	Hillsborough, NH	357 840	335 838	276 608	22 002	38 038	18 127	2 237	59 230	6.6	21.4	11.0	2.2
	33 015	Rockingham, NH	267 105	245 845	190 345	21 260	26 545	12 031	957	55 500	8.6	29.2	9.8	1.3
	33 017	Strafford, NH	108 098	104 233	85 408	3 865	10 181	5 537	271	18 825	3.7	22.0	11.7	1.2
1240	48 061	Brownsville-Harlingen-San Benito, TX MSA (Cameron)	320 801	260 120	209 727	60 681	54 285	13 014	21 254	50 393	23.3	24.0	10.7	84.4
1260	48 041	Bryan-College Station, TX MSA (Brazos)	133 008	121 862	93 588	11 146	13 871	4 406	3 024	28 274	9.1	30.2	7.0	16.5
1280		Buffalo-Niagara Falls, NY MSA	1 164 721	1 189 340	1 242 826	–24 619	117 788	90 580	7 675	–53 486	–2.1	–4.3	15.7	2.5
	36 029	Erie........................	944 472	968 584	1 015 472	–24 112	96 244	74 405	6 594	–46 888	–2.5	–4.6	15.7	2.9
	36 063	Niagara.....................	220 249	220 756	227 354	–507	21 544	16 175	1 081	–6 598	–.2	–2.9	15.7	1.2
1303		Burlington, VT NECMA	191 088	177 059	154 935	14 029	19 048	8 580	1 625	22 124	7.9	14.3	9.1	1.2
	50 007	Chittenden	141 387	131 761	115 534	9 626	13 727	5 798	1 491	16 227	7.3	14.0	8.3	1.4
	50 011	Franklin	43 505	39 980	34 788	3 525	4 744	2 442	72	5 192	8.8	14.9	11.5	.6
	50 013	Grand Isle	6 196	5 318	4 613	878	577	340	62	705	16.5	15.3	11.6	.6
1320		Canton-Massillon, OH MSA	402 644	394 106	404 421	8 538	39 400	28 664	415	–10 315	2.2	–2.6	14.9	.9
	39 019	Carroll.....................	28 925	26 521	25 598	2 404	2 380	1 786	8	923	9.1	3.6	14.2	.5
	39 151	Stark.......................	373 719	367 585	378 823	6 134	37 020	26 878	407	–11 238	1.7	–3.0	14.9	.9

[1]Federal Information Processing Standards (FIPS) codes for metropolitan areas defined as of June 30, 1996.
[2]FIPS codes for counties/county equivalents defined as of January 1, 1990.
[3]Includes count resolution corrections through December 1996.
[4]Includes net domestic migration, net federal movement, and residual not shown separately.
[5]Persons of Hispanic origin may be of any race.

Source: 1990–1997 Population—U.S. Bureau of the Census, "Estimates of the Population of Counties and Demographic Components of Population Change: April 1, 1990 to July 1, 1997" (CO-97-5) Internet site <http://www.census.gov/population/www/estimates/co_97_5.html> (accessed 30 March 1998); 1980 Population—U.S. Bureau of the Census, "1980–1990 Intercensal Population Estimates by County," on diskette; 65 Plus and Hispanic Population—U.S. Bureau of the Census, "County Population Estimates by Age, Sex, Race, and Hispanic Origin - 4/1/90 to 7/1/96" data file (related Internet site <http://www.census.gov/population/www/estimates/co_casrh.html>).

Table C–1. Metro Counties — **Population**—Con.

[MSA = Metropolitan statistical area.   CMSA = Consolidated MSA.   PMSA = Primary MSA.   NECMA = New England county metropolitan area.   All areas defined as of June 30, 1996   Table includes 245 MSAs, 17 CMSAs, and 58 PMSAs not in New England; 12 NECMAs; and 844 component counties]

Metro-politan area code[1]	State and county code[2]	Metropolitan areas and component counties	Total persons			Net change 1990–1997					Percent change		Percent—	
			1997 (July 1)	1990[3] (April 1)	1980 (April 1)	Total[4]	Births	Deaths	Net inter-national migration	1980–1990	1990–1997	1980–1990	65 years and over, 1996	Hispanic origin[5], 1996
1350	56 025	Casper, WY MSA (Natrona)	63 638	61 226	71 856	2 412	6 695	3 431	134	−10 630	3.9	−14.8	11.4	3.7
1360	19 113	Cedar Rapids, IA MSA (Linn)	181 704	168 767	169 775	12 937	18 978	9 560	1 220	−1 008	7.7	−.6	12.0	1.4
1400	17 019	Champaign-Urbana, IL MSA (Champaign)	168 473	173 025	168 392	−4 552	16 802	7 705	1 702	4 633	−2.6	2.8	9.2	2.2
1440		Charleston-North Charleston, SC MSA .	509 856	506 877	430 346	2 979	62 520	26 684	1 976	76 531	.6	17.8	9.1	1.9
	45 015	Berkeley	134 311	128 776	94 745	5 535	16 662	5 353	131	34 031	4.3	35.9	6.1	2.6
	45 019	Charleston	284 815	295 041	276 556	−10 226	35 775	17 438	1 735	18 485	−3.5	6.7	11.0	1.6
	45 035	Dorchester	90 730	83 060	59 045	7 670	10 083	3 893	110	24 015	9.2	40.7	7.8	1.7
1480		Charleston, WV MSA	253 850	250 454	269 595	3 396	23 695	19 975	686	−19 141	1.4	−7.1	15.0	.5
	54 039	Kanawha	203 646	207 619	231 414	−3 973	19 630	17 317	623	−23 795	−1.9	−10.3	15.9	.5
	54 079	Putnam	50 204	42 835	38 181	7 369	4 065	2 658	63	4 654	17.2	12.2	11.2	.4
1520		Charlotte-Gastonia-Rock Hill, NC-SC MSA	1 350 243	1 162 140	971 447	188 103	136 826	73 606	9 939	190 693	16.2	19.6	11.3	1.5
	37 025	Cabarrus, NC	116 001	98 935	85 895	17 066	10 748	6 750	359	13 040	17.2	15.2	13.8	.8
	37 071	Gaston, NC	183 368	175 093	162 568	8 275	19 032	12 369	683	12 525	4.7	7.7	12.6	.8
	37 109	Lincoln, NC	57 209	50 319	42 372	6 890	5 362	3 243	226	7 947	13.7	18.8	12.2	2.0
	37 119	Mecklenburg, NC	613 310	511 481	404 270	101 829	64 809	28 948	7 480	107 211	19.9	26.5	9.4	2.1
	37 159	Rowan, NC	123 527	110 605	99 186	12 922	10 959	8 997	421	11 419	11.7	11.5	15.7	1.0
	37 179	Union, NC	106 326	84 210	70 436	22 116	11 204	4 858	397	13 774	26.3	19.6	10.1	1.3
	45 091	York, SC	150 502	131 497	106 720	19 005	14 712	8 441	373	24 777	14.5	23.2	11.3	.8
1540		Charlottesville, VA MSA	146 617	131 373	113 568	15 244	13 148	7 728	1 396	17 805	11.6	15.7	11.5	1.4
	51 003	Albemarle	77 518	68 172	55 783	9 346	6 324	3 347	655	12 389	13.7	22.2	10.2	1.6
	51 065	Fluvanna	17 768	12 429	10 244	5 339	1 433	843	21	2 185	43.0	21.3	13.8	.8
	51 079	Greene	13 427	10 297	7 625	3 130	1 467	620	11	2 672	30.4	35.0	10.3	.8
	51 540	Charlottesville city	37 904	40 475	39 916	−2 571	3 924	2 918	709	559	−6.4	1.4	13.3	1.5
1560		Chattanooga, TN-GA MSA	447 488	424 347	417 838	23 141	43 715	31 273	1 567	6 509	5.5	1.6	13.0	.9
	47 065	Hamilton, TN	294 676	285 536	287 643	9 140	29 437	21 459	1 280	−2 107	3.2	−.7	13.3	1.0
	47 115	Marion, TN	26 733	24 860	24 416	1 873	2 429	2 429	26	444	7.5	1.8	12.2	.5
	13 047	Catoosa, GA	49 567	42 464	36 991	7 103	4 487	2 732	145	5 473	16.7	14.8	11.3	.8
	13 083	Dade, GA	14 664	13 147	12 318	1 517	1 448	754	14	829	11.5	6.7	11.5	.8
	13 295	Walker, GA	61 848	58 340	56 470	3 508	5 914	4 409	102	1 870	6.0	3.3	13.8	.6
1580	56 021	Cheyenne, WY MSA (Laramie)	78 473	73 142	68 649	5 331	8 733	4 064	292	4 493	7.3	6.5	11.3	10.3
1602		Chicago-Gary-Kenosha, IL-IN-WI CMSA..............................	8 642 175	8 239 820	8 114 844	402 355	1 073 073	521 362	258 603	124 976	4.9	1.5	11.3	13.1
1600		Chicago, IL PMSA	7 773 896	7 410 858	7 246 048	363 038	980 274	464 618	255 140	164 810	4.9	2.3	11.2	13.6
	17 031	Cook	5 076 786	5 105 044	5 253 628	−28 258	675 014	353 901	206 165	−148 584	−.6	−2.8	12.4	16.5
	17 037	DeKalb	83 602	77 932	74 628	5 670	7 143	3 994	766	3 304	7.3	4.4	10.7	3.8
	17 043	Du Page	870 378	781 689	658 858	88 689	101 634	35 448	24 665	122 831	11.3	18.6	8.7	5.6
	17 063	Grundy	36 253	32 337	30 582	3 916	3 388	2 020	206	1 755	12.1	5.7	13.0	3.0
	17 089	Kane	380 801	317 471	278 405	63 330	46 711	16 426	6 311	39 066	19.9	14.0	9.2	16.9
	17 093	Kendall	49 856	39 413	37 202	10 443	4 650	1 796	349	2 211	26.5	5.9	8.7	5.8
	17 097	Lake	594 799	516 418	440 388	78 381	71 500	23 353	11 452	76 030	15.2	17.3	8.4	9.4
	17 111	McHenry	236 952	183 241	147 897	53 711	25 857	9 643	2 467	35 344	29.3	23.9	9.5	4.2
	17 197	Will	444 469	357 313	324 460	87 156	44 377	18 037	2 759	32 853	24.4	10.1	8.6	7.1
2960		Gary, IN PMSA	623 423	604 526	642 733	18 897	66 238	40 686	2 622	−38 207	3.1	−5.9	11.7	9.8
	18 089	Lake	479 339	475 594	522 917	3 745	54 119	33 703	2 331	−47 323	.8	−9.0	12.2	11.5
	18 127	Porter	144 084	128 932	119 816	15 152	12 119	6 983	291	9 116	11.8	7.6	9.9	3.8
3740	17 091	Kankakee, IL PMSA (Kankakee)	101 984	96 255	102 926	5 729	11 600	7 638	541	−6 671	6.0	−6.5	13.8	2.6
3800	55 059	Kenosha, WI PMSA (Kenosha)	142 872	128 181	123 137	14 691	14 961	8 420	300	5 044	11.5	4.1	12.5	5.7
1620	06 007	Chico-Paradise, CA MSA (Butte) ...	194 160	182 120	143 851	12 040	18 482	14 625	3 174	38 269	6.6	26.6	18.6	9.6
1642		Cincinnati-Hamilton, OH-KY-IN CMSA ..	1 934 145	1 817 569	1 726 430	116 576	205 228	118 107	6 470	91 139	6.4	5.3	12.1	.6
1640		Cincinnati, OH-KY-IN PMSA	1 607 396	1 526 090	1 467 643	81 306	173 516	101 609	5 369	58 447	5.3	4.0	12.4	.6
	39 015	Brown, OH	40 243	34 966	31 920	5 277	4 022	2 615	27	3 046	15.1	9.5	13.4	.2
	39 025	Clermont, OH	173 163	150 167	128 483	22 996	18 575	8 073	573	21 684	15.3	16.9	9.0	.6
	39 061	Hamilton, OH.................	851 599	866 228	873 203	−14 629	95 420	61 578	3 798	−6 975	−1.7	−.8	13.9	.7
	39 165	Warren, OH	140 080	113 927	99 276	26 153	13 461	6 131	268	14 651	23.0	14.8	9.2	.6
	21 015	Boone, KY	76 173	57 589	45 842	18 584	7 518	2 932	242	11 747	32.3	25.6	8.2	.7
	21 037	Campbell, KY	87 422	83 866	83 317	3 556	9 260	5 968	178	549	4.2	.7	13.0	.5
	21 077	Gallatin, KY	6 771	5 393	4 842	1 378	714	405	3	551	25.6	11.4	12.3	.2
	21 081	Grant, KY	19 828	15 737	13 308	4 091	2 069	1 114	26	2 429	26.0	18.3	11.5	.3
	21 117	Kenton, KY	146 224	142 031	137 058	4 193	16 526	9 078	197	4 973	3.0	3.6	11.6	.6
	21 191	Pendleton, KY	13 859	12 036	10 989	1 823	1 361	852	8	1 047	15.1	9.5	12.2	.4
	18 029	Dearborn, IN	46 576	38 835	34 291	7 741	4 134	2 513	43	4 544	19.9	13.3	12.0	.4
3200	18 115	Ohio, IN	5 458	5 315	5 114	143	456	350	6	201	2.7	3.9	14.1	.2
	39 017	Hamilton-Middletown, OH PMSA (Butler)	326 749	291 479	258 787	35 270	31 712	16 498	1 101	32 692	12.1	12.6	10.6	.6

[1]Federal Information Processing Standards (FIPS) codes for metropolitan areas defined as of June 30, 1996.
[2]FIPS codes for counties/county equivalents defined as of January 1, 1990.
[3]Includes count resolution corrections through December 1996.
[4]Includes net domestic migration, net federal movement, and residual not shown separately.
[5]Persons of Hispanic origin may be of any race.

Source: 1990–1997 Population—U.S. Bureau of the Census, "Estimates of the Population of Counties and Demographic Components of Population Change: April 1, 1990 to July 1, 1997" (CO-97-5) Internet site <http://www.census.gov/population/www/estimates/co_97_5.html> (accessed 30 March 1998);   1980 Population—U.S. Bureau of the Census, "1980–1990 Intercensal Population Estimates by County," on diskette;   65 Plus and Hispanic Population—U.S. Bureau of the Census, "County Population Estimates by Age, Sex, Race, and Hispanic Origin - 4/1/90 to 7/1/96" data file (related Internet site <http://www.census.gov/population/www/estimates/co_casrh.html>).

Table C–1. Metro Counties — **Population**—Con.

[MSA = Metropolitan statistical area. CMSA = Consolidated MSA. PMSA = Primary MSA. NECMA = New England county metropolitan area. All areas defined as of June 30, 1996   Table includes 245 MSAs, 17 CMSAs, and 58 PMSAs not in New England; 12 NECMAs; and 844 component counties]

Metro-politan area code[1]	State and county code[2]	Metropolitan areas and component counties	Total persons 1997 (July 1)	Total persons 1990[3] (April 1)	Total persons 1980 (April 1)	Net change 1990–1997 Total[4]	Net change 1990–1997 Births	Net change 1990–1997 Deaths	Net change 1990–1997 Net international migration	Net change 1980–1990	Percent change 1990–1997	Percent change 1980–1990	Percent 65 years and over, 1996	Percent Hispanic origin[5], 1996
1660		Clarksville-Hopkinsville, TN-KY MSA ...	197 481	169 439	150 220	28 042	26 094	9 153	553	19 219	16.5	12.8	8.7	4.4
	47 125	Montgomery, TN	124 252	100 498	83 342	23 754	16 017	5 162	277	17 156	23.6	20.6	7.9	4.6
	21 047	Christian, KY	73 229	68 941	66 878	4 288	10 077	3 991	276	2 063	6.2	3.1	10.0	4.1
1692 0080		Cleveland-Akron, OH CMSA	2 908 439	2 859 644	2 938 277	48 795	304 114	205 744	14 301	−78 633	1.7	−2.7	14.3	2.2
		Akron, OH PMSA	682 442	657 575	660 328	24 867	68 181	43 730	2 164	−2 753	3.8	−.4	13.4	.7
	39 133	Portage	150 792	142 585	135 856	8 207	13 592	7 120	464	6 729	5.8	5.0	9.9	.7
	39 153	Summit	531 650	514 990	524 472	16 660	54 589	36 610	1 700	−9 482	3.2	−1.8	14.4	.7
1680		Cleveland-Lorain-Elyria, OH PMSA	2 225 997	2 202 069	2 277 949	23 928	235 933	162 014	12 137	−75 880	1.1	−3.3	14.6	2.7
	39 007	Ashtabula	103 140	99 821	104 215	3 319	10 147	7 714	76	−4 394	3.3	−4.2	15.3	1.8
	39 035	Cuyahoga	1 386 803	1 412 140	1 498 400	−25 337	153 310	113 454	11 016	−86 260	−1.8	−5.8	16.2	2.6
	39 055	Geauga	87 913	81 129	74 474	6 784	8 783	4 154	30	6 655	8.4	8.9	10.9	.4
	39 085	Lake	223 715	215 499	212 801	8 216	20 766	13 109	384	2 698	3.8	1.3	12.3	.8
	39 093	Lorain	282 465	271 126	274 909	11 339	29 976	17 127	447	−3 783	4.2	−1.4	11.9	6.6
	39 103	Medina	141 961	122 354	113 150	19 607	12 951	6 456	184	9 204	16.0	8.1	9.9	.7
1720	08 041	Colorado Springs, CO MSA (El Paso) ..	480 041	397 014	309 424	83 027	55 355	17 255	1 821	87 590	20.9	28.3	8.2	10.1
1740	29 019	Columbia, MO MSA (Boone)	128 309	112 379	100 376	15 930	12 388	5 275	1 110	12 003	14.2	12.0	8.5	1.3
1760		Columbia, SC MSA	503 948	453 932	409 953	50 016	51 346	25 800	1 977	43 979	11.0	10.7	9.9	1.6
	45 063	Lexington	200 371	167 611	140 353	32 760	19 963	9 248	557	27 258	19.5	19.4	9.5	1.1
	45 079	Richland	303 577	286 321	269 600	17 256	31 383	16 552	1 420	16 721	6.0	6.2	10.1	1.9
1800		Columbus, GA-AL MSA	272 035	260 862	254 660	11 173	33 093	17 901	741	6 202	4.3	2.4	10.6	4.1
	13 053	Chattahoochee, GA	16 320	16 934	21 732	−614	1 839	262	161	−4 798	−3.6	−22.1	1.3	15.8
	13 145	Harris, GA	22 227	17 788	15 464	4 439	1 931	1 237	13	2 324	25.0	15.0	13.4	.9
	13 215	Muscogee, GA	182 769	179 280	170 108	3 489	24 167	12 534	510	9 172	1.9	5.4	10.6	4.4
	01 113	Russell, AL	50 719	46 860	47 356	3 859	5 156	3 868	57	−496	8.2	−1.0	12.5	.9
1840		Columbus, OH MSA	1 460 242	1 345 450	1 214 291	114 792	157 504	77 871	8 234	131 159	8.5	10.8	10.4	1.0
	39 041	Delaware	87 396	66 929	53 840	20 467	7 150	3 381	318	13 089	30.6	24.3	9.4	.6
	39 045	Fairfield	121 457	103 472	93 678	17 985	10 777	6 398	164	9 794	17.4	10.5	11.6	.6
	39 049	Franklin	1 017 274	961 437	869 126	55 837	117 796	54 595	7 263	92 311	5.8	10.6	10.1	1.2
	39 089	Licking	139 411	128 300	120 981	11 111	13 290	8 477	247	7 319	8.7	6.0	12.3	.6
	39 097	Madison	41 486	37 068	33 004	4 418	3 865	2 152	136	4 064	11.9	12.3	10.3	.7
	39 129	Pickaway	53 218	48 244	43 662	4 974	4 626	2 868	106	4 582	10.3	10.5	10.2	.8
1880		Corpus Christi, TX MSA	387 100	349 894	326 228	37 206	46 917	19 324	4 060	23 666	10.6	7.3	10.3	56.5
	48 355	Nueces	317 474	291 145	268 215	26 329	38 947	15 826	3 612	22 930	9.0	8.5	10.4	57.0
	48 409	San Patricio	69 626	58 749	58 013	10 877	7 970	3 498	448	736	18.5	1.3	10.2	54.1
1900		Cumberland, MD-WV MSA	99 122	101 643	107 782	−2 521	8 042	9 137	238	−6 139	−2.5	−5.7	18.9	.5
	24 001	Allegany, MD	72 289	74 946	80 548	−2 657	6 189	7 124	207	−5 602	−3.5	−7.0	20.4	.6
	54 057	Mineral, WV	26 833	26 697	27 234	136	1 853	2 013	31	−537	.5	−2.0	14.9	.4
1922 1920		Dallas-Fort Worth, TX CMSA	4 683 013	4 037 282	3 046 136	645 731	556 319	205 843	137 762	991 146	16.0	32.5	8.5	15.1
		Dallas, TX PMSA	3 126 613	2 676 248	2 055 284	450 365	376 971	134 138	103 271	620 964	16.8	30.2	8.2	16.0
	48 085	Collin	401 352	264 036	144 576	137 316	38 657	8 686	8 197	119 460	52.0	82.6	5.4	8.2
	48 113	Dallas	2 023 140	1 852 810	1 556 419	170 330	267 816	95 779	86 671	296 391	9.2	19.0	8.4	19.9
	48 121	Denton	365 058	273 525	143 126	91 533	38 324	9 021	4 892	130 399	33.5	91.1	5.3	8.5
	48 139	Ellis	100 627	85 167	59 743	15 460	10 652	5 078	1 158	25 424	18.2	42.6	10.3	15.6
	48 213	Henderson	67 347	58 543	42 606	8 804	5 462	5 337	631	15 937	15.0	37.4	19.5	4.9
	48 231	Hunt	69 309	64 343	55 248	4 966	6 690	4 951	508	9 095	7.7	16.5	14.5	5.4
	48 257	Kaufman	63 857	52 220	39 038	11 637	6 099	4 000	731	13 182	22.3	33.8	12.0	7.7
	48 397	Rockwall	35 923	25 604	14 528	10 319	3 271	1 286	493	11 076	40.3	76.2	7.8	7.1
2800		Fort Worth-Arlington, TX PMSA	1 556 400	1 361 034	990 852	195 366	179 348	71 705	34 491	370 182	14.4	37.4	9.0	13.3
	48 221	Hood	36 205	28 981	17 714	7 224	2 808	2 336	209	11 267	24.9	63.6	16.3	5.6
	48 251	Johnson	114 052	97 165	67 649	16 887	10 453	6 052	1 182	29 516	17.4	43.6	10.6	9.5
	48 367	Parker	78 811	64 785	44 609	14 026	6 708	3 931	529	20 176	21.7	45.2	11.4	5.1
	48 439	Tarrant	1 327 332	1 170 103	860 880	157 229	159 379	59 386	32 571	309 223	13.4	35.9	8.6	14.2
1950		Danville, VA MSA	108 602	108 728	111 789	−126	9 519	9 440	194	−3 061	−.1	−2.7	16.6	.6
	51 143	Pittsylvania	57 588	55 672	[6]55 140	1 916	3 947	3 887	98	[6]532	3.4	[6]1.0	14.1	.5
	51 590	Danville city	51 014	53 056	[6]56 649	−2 042	5 572	5 553	96	[6]−3 593	−3.8	[6]−6.3	19.3	.6
1960		Davenport-Moline-Rock Island, IA-IL MSA	357 163	350 855	384 749	6 308	35 992	24 314	2 333	−33 894	1.8	−8.8	13.6	5.0
	19 163	Scott, IA	157 433	150 973	160 022	6 460	17 071	9 098	1 198	−9 049	4.3	−5.7	11.2	4.2
	17 073	Henry, IL	51 453	51 159	57 968	294	4 348	4 020	75	−6 809	.6	−11.7	16.6	2.0
	17 161	Rock Island, IL	148 277	148 723	166 759	−446	14 573	11 196	1 060	−18 036	−.3	−10.8	15.1	7.0
2000		Dayton-Springfield, OH MSA	944 934	951 270	942 083	−6 336	97 645	62 921	3 257	9 187	−.7	1.0	12.8	.9
	39 023	Clark	146 185	147 548	150 236	−1 363	14 622	11 116	253	−2 688	−.9	−1.8	14.4	.8
	39 057	Greene	139 704	136 731	129 769	2 973	12 535	7 476	710	6 962	2.2	5.4	10.0	1.2
	39 109	Miami	97 742	93 182	90 381	4 560	9 205	6 054	147	2 801	4.9	3.1	13.1	.5
	39 113	Montgomery	561 303	573 809	571 697	−12 506	61 283	38 275	2 147	2 112	−2.2	.4	13.0	1.0
2020		Daytona Beach, FL MSA	465 925	399 438	269 675	66 487	34 631	39 448	5 986	129 763	16.6	48.1	23.2	5.1
	12 035	Flagler	46 128	28 701	10 913	17 427	2 158	2 805	1 289	17 788	60.7	163.0	25.2	5.9
	12 127	Volusia	419 797	370 737	258 762	49 060	32 473	36 643	4 697	111 975	13.2	43.3	23.0	5.0

[1]Federal Information Processing Standards (FIPS) codes for metropolitan areas defined as of June 30, 1996.
[2]FIPS codes for counties/county equivalents defined as of January 1, 1990.
[3]Includes count resolution corrections through December 1996.
[4]Includes net domestic migration, net federal movement, and residual not shown separately.
[5]Persons of Hispanic origin may be of any race.
[6]1980 population based on 1990 boundaries.

Source: 1990–1997 Population—U.S. Bureau of the Census, "Estimates of the Population of Counties and Demographic Components of Population Change: April 1, 1990 to July 1, 1997" (CO-97-5) Internet site <http://www.census.gov/population/www/estimates/co_97_5.html> (accessed 30 March 1998); 1980 Population—U.S. Bureau of the Census, "1980–1990 Intercensal Population Estimates by County," on diskette; 65 Plus and Hispanic Population—U.S. Bureau of the Census, "County Population Estimates by Age, Sex, Race, and Hispanic Origin - 4/1/90 to 7/1/96" data file (related Internet site <http://www.census.gov/population/www/estimates/co_casrh.html>).

Table C–1. Metro Counties — **Population**—Con.

[MSA = Metropolitan statistical area. CMSA = Consolidated MSA. PMSA = Primary MSA. NECMA = New England county metropolitan area. All areas defined as of June 30, 1996 Table includes 245 MSAs, 17 CMSAs, and 58 PMSAs not in New England; 12 NECMAs; and 844 component counties]

Metropolitan area code[1]	State and county code[2]	Metropolitan areas and component counties	Total persons 1997 (July 1)	Total persons 1990[3] (April 1)	Total persons 1980 (April 1)	Net change 1990–1997 Total[4]	Net change 1990–1997 Births	Net change 1990–1997 Deaths	Net change 1990–1997 Net international migration	Net change 1980–1990	Percent change 1990–1997	Percent change 1980–1990	Percent 65 years and over, 1996	Percent Hispanic origin[5], 1996
2030		Decatur, AL MSA	141 690	131 556	120 401	10 134	14 094	8 827	208	11 155	7.7	9.3	12.1	.8
	01 079	Lawrence	33 386	31 513	30 170	1 873	3 352	2 095	23	1 343	5.9	4.5	12.4	.6
	01 103	Morgan	108 304	100 043	90 231	8 261	10 742	6 732	185	9 812	8.3	10.9	12.0	.8
2040	17 115	Decatur, IL MSA (Macon)	114 265	117 206	131 375	-2 941	12 093	8 722	432	-14 169	-2.5	-10.8	14.7	.6
2082		Denver-Boulder-Greeley, CO CMSA ...	2 318 355	1 980 140	1 741 899	338 215	243 261	98 924	36 547	238 241	17.1	13.7	9.3	14.0
1125	08 013	Boulder-Longmont, CO PMSA (Boulder)	261 617	225 339	189 625	36 278	23 325	8 799	4 935	35 714	16.1	18.8	7.9	7.7
2080		Denver, CO PMSA	1 901 156	1 622 980	1 428 836	278 176	203 342	83 377	28 805	194 144	17.1	13.6	9.4	14.2
	08 001	Adams	316 066	265 038	245 944	51 028	35 108	12 151	3 889	19 094	19.3	7.8	7.8	20.8
	08 005	Arapahoe	463 201	391 511	293 300	71 690	45 678	15 228	4 735	98 211	18.3	33.5	7.6	6.4
	08 031	Denver	498 985	467 610	492 686	31 375	63 615	35 321	16 338	-25 076	6.7	-5.1	14.4	25.6
	08 035	Douglas	126 248	60 391	25 153	65 857	11 421	1 575	618	35 238	109.1	140.1	4.2	3.6
	08 059	Jefferson	496 656	438 430	371 753	58 226	47 520	19 102	3 225	66 677	13.3	17.9	8.1	8.0
3060	08 123	Greeley, CO PMSA (Weld)	155 582	131 821	123 438	23 761	16 594	6 748	2 807	8 383	18.0	6.8	10.5	23.3
2120		Des Moines, IA MSA	429 717	392 928	367 561	36 789	46 338	23 063	4 218	25 367	9.4	6.9	11.5	2.5
	19 049	Dallas	35 765	29 755	29 513	6 010	3 201	2 060	238	242	20.2	.8	14.4	.9
	19 153	Polk	354 232	327 140	303 170	27 092	39 576	18 979	3 909	23 970	8.3	7.9	11.4	2.8
	19 181	Warren	39 720	36 033	34 878	3 687	3 561	2 024	71	1 155	10.2	3.3	10.7	1.1
2162		Detroit-Ann Arbor-Flint, MI CMSA	5 438 756	5 187 171	5 293 161	251 585	586 687	330 345	50 466	-105 990	4.9	-2.0	11.9	2.3
0440		Ann Arbor, MI PMSA	539 415	490 058	454 977	49 357	50 467	22 633	5 556	35 081	10.1	7.7	8.9	2.9
	26 091	Lenawee	97 998	91 476	89 948	6 522	8 967	5 850	275	1 528	7.1	1.7	12.4	7.1
	26 093	Livingston	141 914	115 645	100 289	26 269	12 414	5 345	252	15 356	22.7	15.3	8.5	1.0
	26 161	Washtenaw	299 503	282 937	264 740	16 566	29 086	11 438	5 029	18 197	5.9	6.9	7.9	2.4
2160		Detroit, MI PMSA	4 463 948	4 266 654	4 387 735	197 294	486 067	280 955	43 946	-121 081	4.6	-2.8	12.4	2.3
	26 087	Lapeer	86 893	74 768	70 038	12 125	8 065	3 756	106	4 730	16.2	6.8	9.0	2.4
	26 099	Macomb	783 451	717 400	694 600	66 051	71 951	45 000	3 332	22 800	9.2	3.3	12.9	1.3
	26 115	Monroe	142 301	133 600	134 659	8 701	12 823	7 657	321	-1 059	6.5	-.8	10.8	1.8
	26 125	Oakland	1 166 512	1 083 592	1 011 793	82 920	118 777	60 192	18 404	71 799	7.7	7.1	11.3	2.1
	26 147	St. Clair	157 704	145 607	138 802	12 097	15 222	9 680	449	6 805	8.3	4.9	12.9	2.1
	26 163	Wayne	2 127 087	2 111 687	2 337 843	15 400	259 229	154 670	21 084	-226 156	.7	-9.7	13.1	2.7
2640	26 049	Flint, MI PMSA (Genesee)	435 393	430 459	450 449	4 934	50 153	26 757	1 214	-19 990	1.1	-4.4	10.6	2.4
2180		Dothan, AL MSA....................	134 270	130 964	122 453	3 306	14 799	8 339	241	8 511	2.5	7.0	11.6	1.8
	01 045	Dale	49 107	49 633	47 821	-526	5 859	2 829	74	1 812	-1.1	3.8	9.8	3.4
	01 069	Houston	85 163	81 331	74 632	3 832	8 940	5 510	167	6 699	4.7	9.0	12.6	.8
2190	10 001	Dover, DE MSA (Kent)	122 709	110 993	98 219	11 716	13 703	6 895	615	12 774	10.6	13.0	10.9	3.0
2200	19 061	Dubuque, IA MSA (Dubuque)	88 084	86 403	93 745	1 681	8 793	6 240	154	-7 342	1.9	-7.8	13.9	.7
2240		Duluth-Superior, MN-WI MSA	238 184	239 971	266 650	-1 787	19 612	19 634	486	-26 679	-.7	-10.0	16.9	.6
	27 137	St. Louis, MN	194 989	198 213	222 229	-3 224	15 738	16 170	365	-24 016	-1.6	-10.8	17.0	.6
	55 031	Douglas, WI	43 195	41 758	44 421	1 437	3 874	3 464	121	-2 663	3.4	-6.0	16.4	.6
2290		Eau Claire, WI MSA....................	143 486	137 543	130 932	5 943	13 165	8 637	358	6 611	4.3	5.0	13.3	.6
	55 017	Chippewa	54 249	52 360	52 127	1 889	4 821	3 722	43	233	3.6	.4	14.5	.4
	55 035	Eau Claire	89 237	85 183	78 805	4 054	8 344	4 915	315	6 378	4.8	8.1	12.6	.7
2320	48 141	El Paso, TX MSA (El Paso)	701 576	591 610	479 899	109 966	112 934	25 586	62 298	111 711	18.6	23.3	8.5	73.5
2330	18 039	Elkhart-Goshen, IN MSA (Elkhart)......	170 725	156 198	137 330	14 527	19 578	9 217	1 083	18 868	9.3	13.7	11.3	2.4
2335	36 015	Elmira, NY MSA (Chemung)..........	93 088	95 195	97 656	-2 107	8 969	7 040	855	-2 461	-2.2	-2.5	15.6	1.8
2340	40 047	Enid, OK MSA (Garfield)	56 699	56 735	62 820	-36	5 578	4 466	206	-6 085	-.1	-9.7	15.7	2.4
2360	42 049	Erie, PA MSA (Erie)	279 401	275 572	279 780	3 829	28 772	19 196	1 407	-4 208	1.4	-1.5	14.3	1.6
2400	41 039	Eugene-Springfield, OR MSA (Lane) ...	311 356	282 912	275 226	28 444	26 699	18 100	1 933	7 686	10.1	2.8	12.9	3.4
2440		Evansville-Henderson, IN-KY MSA	288 929	278 990	276 252	9 939	27 989	20 590	658	2 738	3.6	1.0	14.0	.6
	18 129	Posey, IN	26 640	25 968	26 414	672	2 558	1 537	18	-446	2.6	-1.7	12.2	.5
	18 163	Vanderburgh, IN	166 837	165 058	167 515	1 779	16 710	13 421	459	-2 457	1.1	-1.5	15.8	.7
	18 173	Warrick, IN	50 831	44 920	41 474	5 911	4 532	2 545	94	3 446	13.2	8.3	10.2	.5
	21 101	Henderson, KY	44 621	43 044	40 849	1 577	4 189	3 087	87	2 195	3.7	5.4	12.7	.5
2520		Fargo-Moorhead, ND-MN MSA	166 396	153 296	137 574	13 100	16 258	7 837	2 147	15 722	8.5	11.4	10.9	1.7
	38 017	Cass, ND	114 580	102 874	88 247	11 706	11 335	5 114	1 826	14 627	11.4	16.6	10.3	1.0
	27 027	Clay, MN	51 816	50 422	49 327	1 394	4 923	2 723	321	1 095	2.8	2.2	12.2	3.2
2560	37 051	Fayetteville, NC MSA (Cumberland)....	284 047	274 713	247 160	9 334	41 639	12 367	1 435	27 553	3.4	11.1	6.3	7.6
2580		Fayetteville-Springdale-Rogers, AR MSA	266 980	210 908	178 609	56 072	26 279	14 918	1 540	32 299	26.6	18.1	14.1	2.7
	05 007	Benton	130 006	97 499	78 115	32 507	11 848	7 705	812	19 384	33.3	24.8	17.4	2.7
	05 143	Washington	136 974	113 409	100 494	23 565	14 431	7 213	728	12 915	20.8	12.9	11.1	2.6
2620		Flagstaff, AZ-UT MSA	119 547	101 760	79 032	17 787	13 986	3 588	779	22 728	17.5	28.8	6.4	11.3
	04 005	Coconino, AZ	113 719	96 591	75 008	17 128	13 408	3 268	736	21 583	17.7	28.8	6.0	11.8
	49 025	Kane, UT	5 828	5 169	4 024	659	578	320	43	1 145	12.7	28.5	13.8	2.3

[1]Federal Information Processing Standards (FIPS) codes for metropolitan areas defined as of June 30, 1996.
[2]FIPS codes for counties/county equivalents defined as of January 1, 1990.
[3]Includes count resolution corrections through December 1996.
[4]Includes net domestic migration, net federal movement, and residual not shown separately.
[5]Persons of Hispanic origin may be of any race.

Source: 1990–1997 Population—U.S. Bureau of the Census, "Estimates of the Population of Counties and Demographic Components of Population Change: April 1, 1990 to July 1, 1997" (CO-97-5) Internet site <http://www.census.gov/population/www/estimates/co_97_5.html> (accessed 30 March 1998); 1980 Population—U.S. Bureau of the Census, "1980–1990 Intercensal Population Estimates by County," on diskette; 65 Plus and Hispanic Population—U.S. Bureau of the Census, "County Population Estimates by Age, Sex, Race, and Hispanic Origin - 4/1/90 to 7/1/96" data file (related Internet site <http://www.census.gov/population/www/estimates/co_casrh.html>).

Table C–1. Metro Counties — **Population**—Con.

[MSA = Metropolitan statistical area. CMSA = Consolidated MSA. PMSA = Primary MSA. NECMA = New England county metropolitan area. All areas defined as of June 30, 1996   Table includes 245 MSAs, 17 CMSAs, and 58 PMSAs not in New England; 12 NECMAs; and 844 component counties]

Metro-politan area code[1]	State and county code[2]	Metropolitan areas and component counties	Total persons 1997 (July 1)	Total persons 1990[3] (April 1)	Total persons 1980 (April 1)	Net change 1990–1997 Total[4]	Net change 1990–1997 Births	Net change 1990–1997 Deaths	Net change 1990–1997 Net inter-national migration	Net change 1980–1990	Percent change 1990–1997	Percent change 1980–1990	Percent— 65 years and over, 1996	Percent— Hispanic origin[5], 1996
2650		Florence, AL MSA	137 288	131 327	135 065	5 961	12 883	10 108	292	−3 738	4.5	−2.8	14.8	.5
	01 033	Colbert	53 047	51 666	54 519	1 381	4 976	4 189	163	−2 853	2.7	−5.2	15.0	.5
	01 077	Lauderdale....................	84 241	79 661	80 546	4 580	7 907	5 919	129	−885	5.7	−1.1	14.7	.6
2655	45 041	Florence, SC MSA (Florence)	124 379	114 344	110 163	10 035	12 979	8 665	258	4 181	8.8	3.8	11.6	.5
2670	08 069	Fort Collins-Loveland, CO MSA (Larimer)	226 021	186 136	149 184	39 885	20 227	8 658	1 509	36 952	21.4	24.8	9.9	7.5
2700	12 071	Fort Myers-Cape Coral, FL MSA (Lee)..	387 091	335 113	205 266	51 978	31 270	30 266	4 689	129 847	15.5	63.3	24.8	5.9
2710		Fort Pierce-Port St. Lucie, FL MSA	295 646	251 196	151 196	44 575	24 952	22 904	6 387	99 875	17.8	66.1	23.4	5.6
	12 085	Martin	116 087	100 900	64 014	15 187	8 609	9 901	2 589	36 886	15.1	57.6	27.5	6.2
	12 111	St. Lucie	179 559	150 171	87 182	29 388	16 343	13 003	3 798	62 989	19.6	72.3	20.7	5.2
2720		Fort Smith, AR-OK MSA	192 395	175 911	162 813	16 484	20 632	13 387	828	13 098	9.4	8.0	13.1	2.3
	05 033	Crawford, AR..................	49 545	42 493	36 892	7 052	5 063	3 108	73	5 601	16.6	15.2	11.7	2.2
	05 131	Sebastian, AR.................	105 968	99 590	95 172	6 378	11 880	7 524	731	4 418	6.4	4.6	13.6	2.7
	40 135	Sequoyah, OK.................	36 882	33 828	30 749	3 054	3 689	2 755	24	3 079	9.0	10.0	13.4	1.2
2750	12 091	Fort Walton Beach, FL MSA (Okaloosa)	167 580	143 777	109 920	23 803	17 832	7 537	714	33 857	16.6	30.8	9.2	4.2
2760		Fort Wayne, IN MSA	477 536	456 281	444 772	21 255	54 702	28 399	1 533	11 509	4.7	2.6	12.1	2.2
	18 001	Adams	32 837	31 095	29 619	1 742	4 335	1 929	61	1 476	5.6	5.0	13.6	3.4
	18 003	Allen	312 091	300 836	294 335	11 255	36 894	18 037	1 260	6 501	3.7	2.2	11.4	2.5
	18 033	De Kalb	38 722	35 324	33 606	3 398	3 990	2 256	23	1 718	9.6	5.1	12.1	1.2
	18 069	Huntington	37 144	35 427	35 596	1 717	3 793	2 561	76	−169	4.8	−.5	14.4	1.0
	18 179	Wells	26 773	25 948	25 401	825	2 712	1 756	58	547	3.2	2.2	13.7	1.3
	18 183	Whitley	29 969	27 651	26 215	2 318	2 978	1 860	55	1 436	8.4	5.5	13.2	.6
2840		Fresno, CA MSA..................	868 703	755 580	577 737	113 123	127 529	43 116	43 400	177 843	15.0	30.8	10.8	41.2
	06 019	Fresno	754 396	667 490	514 621	86 906	113 294	37 536	37 783	152 869	13.0	29.7	10.7	41.2
	06 039	Madera	114 307	88 090	63 116	26 217	14 235	5 580	5 617	24 974	29.8	39.6	11.8	41.2
2880	01 055	Gadsden, AL MSA (Etowah)	104 313	99 840	103 057	4 473	9 649	8 922	127	−3 217	4.5	−3.1	16.3	.5
2900	12 001	Gainesville, FL MSA (Alachua)	198 326	181 596	151 369	16 730	18 784	9 308	3 122	30 227	9.2	20.0	9.5	4.7
2975		Glens Falls, NY MSA	122 582	118 539	109 649	4 043	11 525	8 312	770	8 890	3.4	8.1	14.4	1.8
	36 113	Warren	61 893	59 209	54 854	2 684	5 740	4 181	711	4 355	4.5	7.9	15.0	1.0
	36 115	Washington	60 689	59 330	54 795	1 359	5 785	4 131	59	4 535	2.3	8.3	13.7	2.5
2980	37 191	Goldsboro, NC MSA (Wayne)	111 981	104 666	97 054	7 315	11 661	6 786	444	7 612	7.0	7.8	10.4	2.1
2985		Grand Forks, ND-MN MSA	101 700	103 272	100 944	−1 572	11 317	5 955	554	2 328	−1.5	2.3	12.0	2.9
	38 035	Grand Forks, ND	69 609	70 683	66 100	−1 074	8 217	3 013	531	4 583	−1.5	6.9	9.3	2.1
	27 119	Polk, MN	32 091	32 589	34 844	−498	3 100	2 942	23	−2 255	−1.5	−6.5	18.0	4.6
2995	08 077	Grand Junction, CO MSA (Mesa)	110 681	93 145	81 530	17 536	9 575	6 663	327	11 615	18.8	14.2	14.7	9.2
3000		Grand Rapids-Muskegon-Holland, MI MSA	1 026 295	937 891	840 824	88 404	116 616	52 607	6 851	97 067	9.4	11.5	11.5	3.7
	26 005	Allegan	100 585	90 509	81 555	10 076	10 145	5 386	200	8 954	11.1	11.0	12.1	3.8
	26 081	Kent	539 425	500 631	444 506	38 794	65 500	27 460	4 983	56 125	7.7	12.6	11.3	3.5
	26 121	Muskegon	165 882	158 983	157 589	6 899	17 671	10 871	250	1 394	4.3	.9	13.6	2.7
	26 139	Ottawa	220 403	187 768	157 174	32 635	23 300	8 890	1 418	30 594	17.4	19.5	10.2	4.9
3040	30 013	Great Falls, MT MSA (Cascade)	79 134	77 691	80 696	1 443	9 263	5 095	97	−3 005	1.9	−3.7	12.7	2.0
3080	55 009	Green Bay, WI MSA (Brown)	214 244	194 594	175 280	19 650	22 054	10 627	776	19 314	10.1	11.0	10.8	1.0
3120		Greensboro--Winston-Salem--High Point, NC MSA	1 152 779	1 050 304	950 763	102 475	110 869	72 203	6 363	99 541	9.8	10.5	12.9	1.2
	37 001	Alamance	117 919	108 213	99 319	9 706	10 681	8 354	460	8 894	9.0	9.0	15.4	1.2
	37 057	Davidson	139 159	126 677	113 162	12 482	12 910	8 146	235	13 515	9.9	11.9	12.6	.8
	37 059	Davie	31 198	27 859	24 599	3 339	2 590	1 923	38	3 260	12.0	13.3	14.3	.8
	37 067	Forsyth	285 807	265 878	243 704	19 929	29 120	18 600	1 385	22 174	7.5	9.1	12.7	1.3
	37 081	Guilford	381 916	347 420	317 154	34 496	37 584	23 500	3 523	30 266	9.9	9.5	12.4	1.3
	37 151	Randolph	119 534	106 546	91 300	12 988	11 306	6 877	413	15 246	12.2	16.7	12.8	1.2
	37 169	Stokes	42 705	37 223	33 086	5 482	3 638	2 498	66	4 137	14.7	12.5	12.0	1.2
	37 197	Yadkin	34 541	30 488	28 439	4 053	3 040	2 305	243	2 049	13.3	7.2	15.6	2.2
3150	37 147	Greenville, NC MSA (Pitt)	121 057	108 480	90 146	12 577	12 374	6 766	455	18 334	11.6	20.3	10.3	1.4
3160		Greenville-Spartanburg-Anderson, SC MSA	904 729	830 539	744 428	74 190	87 044	56 979	3 049	86 111	8.9	11.6	13.3	1.0
	45 007	Anderson	158 251	145 177	133 235	13 074	14 847	10 726	222	11 942	9.0	9.0	14.5	.5
	45 021	Cherokee	48 357	44 506	40 983	3 851	4 808	3 192	34	3 523	8.7	8.6	13.9	.7
	45 045	Greenville....................	348 523	320 167	287 895	28 356	34 570	20 502	1 760	32 272	8.9	11.2	12.7	1.3
	45 077	Pickens	104 618	93 896	79 292	10 722	8 941	5 583	241	14 604	11.4	18.4	12.3	.9
	45 083	Spartanburg..................	244 980	226 793	203 023	18 187	23 878	16 976	792	23 770	8.0	11.7	13.5	.9
3240		Harrisburg-Lebanon-Carlisle, PA MSA ..	615 025	587 986	556 242	27 039	57 596	41 120	4 065	31 744	4.6	5.7	14.3	2.2
	42 041	Cumberland...................	207 852	195 257	179 625	12 595	17 000	12 830	1 086	15 632	6.5	8.7	13.8	.9
	42 043	Dauphin	245 793	237 813	232 317	7 980	25 722	17 516	2 318	5 496	3.4	2.4	14.7	3.2
	42 075	Lebanon	117 216	113 744	108 582	3 472	10 671	8 234	587	5 162	3.1	4.8	15.5	3.0
	42 099	Perry.........................	44 164	41 172	35 718	2 992	4 133	2 540	74	5 454	7.3	15.3	11.5	.6

[1]Federal Information Processing Standards (FIPS) codes for metropolitan areas defined as of June 30, 1996.
[2]FIPS codes for counties/county equivalents defined as of January 1, 1990.
[3]Includes count resolution corrections through December 1996.
[4]Includes net domestic migration, net federal movement, and residual not shown separately.
[5]Persons of Hispanic origin may be of any race.

Source: 1990–1997 Population—U.S. Bureau of the Census, "Estimates of the Population of Counties and Demographic Components of Population Change: April 1, 1990 to July 1, 1997" (CO-97-5) Internet site <http://www.census.gov/population/www/estimates/co_97_5.html> (accessed 30 March 1998); 1980 Population—U.S. Bureau of the Census, "1980–1990 Intercensal Population Estimates by County," on diskette; 65 Plus and Hispanic Population—U.S. Bureau of the Census, "County Population Estimates by Age, Sex, Race, and Hispanic Origin - 4/1/90 to 7/1/96" data file (related Internet site <http://www.census.gov/population/www/estimates/co_casrh.html>).

Table C–1. Metro Counties — **Population**—Con.

[MSA = Metropolitan statistical area. CMSA = Consolidated MSA. PMSA = Primary MSA. NECMA = New England county metropolitan area. All areas defined as of June 30, 1996 Table includes 245 MSAs, 17 CMSAs, and 58 PMSAs not in New England; 12 NECMAs; and 844 component counties]

Metropolitan area code[1]	State and county code[2]	Metropolitan areas and component counties	Total persons			Net change 1990–1997					Percent change		Percent—	
			1997 (July 1)	1990[3] (April 1)	1980 (April 1)	Total[4]	Births	Deaths	Net international migration	1980–1990	1990–1997	1980–1990	65 years and over, 1996	Hispanic origin[5], 1996
3283		Hartford, CT NECMA	1 105 174	1 123 678	1 051 606	−18 504	112 359	71 696	17 470	72 072	−1.6	6.9	14.1	8.1
	09 003	Hartford	825 141	851 783	807 766	−26 642	86 161	56 971	15 691	44 017	−3.1	5.4	14.8	10.0
	09 007	Middlesex	149 010	143 196	129 017	5 814	14 450	8 964	947	14 179	4.1	11.0	14.0	2.4
	09 013	Tolland	131 023	128 699	114 823	2 324	11 748	5 761	832	13 876	1.8	12.1	9.8	2.1
3285		Hattiesburg, MS MSA	109 584	98 738	89 839	10 846	11 316	6 942	208	8 899	11.0	9.9	11.3	.9
	28 035	Forrest	73 759	68 314	66 018	5 445	7 844	5 300	206	2 296	8.0	3.5	12.1	.9
	28 073	Lamar	35 825	30 424	23 821	5 401	3 472	1 642	2	6 603	17.8	27.7	9.7	.8
3290		Hickory-Morganton-Lenoir, NC MSA	318 368	292 405	270 457	25 963	30 339	19 370	1 192	21 948	8.9	8.1	12.7	1.0
	37 003	Alexander	30 660	27 544	24 999	3 116	2 676	1 709	69	2 545	11.3	10.2	11.6	1.1
	37 023	Burke	81 718	75 740	72 504	5 978	7 621	5 198	270	3 236	7.9	4.5	13.4	.8
	37 027	Caldwell	75 619	70 709	67 746	4 910	7 212	4 651	125	2 963	6.9	4.4	12.7	.8
	37 035	Catawba	130 371	118 412	105 208	11 959	12 830	7 812	728	13 204	10.1	12.6	12.5	1.3
3320	15 003	Honolulu, HI MSA (Honolulu)	869 857	836 231	762 565	33 626	104 362	37 548	30 622	73 666	4.0	9.7	12.6	7.3
3350		Houma, LA MSA	191 227	182 842	176 876	8 385	21 858	10 245	405	5 966	4.6	3.4	9.3	1.7
	22 057	Lafourche	88 037	85 860	82 483	2 177	9 539	4 806	182	3 377	2.5	4.1	9.9	1.7
	22 109	Terrebonne	103 190	96 982	94 393	6 208	12 319	5 439	223	2 589	6.4	2.7	8.7	1.7
3362		Houston-Galveston-Brazoria, TX CMSA	4 320 041	3 731 029	3 118 480	589 012	537 917	180 266	173 821	612 549	15.8	19.6	7.4	23.6
1145	48 039	Brazoria, TX PMSA (Brazoria)	225 406	191 707	169 587	33 699	25 048	9 208	3 263	22 120	17.6	13.0	7.9	20.7
2920	48 167	Galveston-Texas City, TX PMSA (Galveston)	242 979	217 396	195 738	25 583	27 314	14 554	3 983	21 658	11.8	11.1	10.7	16.9
3360		Houston, TX PMSA	3 851 656	3 321 926	2 753 155	529 730	485 555	156 504	166 575	568 771	15.9	20.7	7.2	24.2
	48 071	Chambers	23 545	20 088	18 538	3 457	2 019	1 130	460	1 550	17.2	8.4	9.7	7.2
	48 157	Fort Bend	321 149	225 421	130 962	95 728	29 774	7 371	10 162	94 459	42.5	72.1	5.1	22.2
	48 201	Harris	3 158 095	2 818 101	2 409 547	339 994	420 521	132 413	151 496	408 554	12.1	17.0	7.2	26.2
	48 291	Liberty	63 948	52 726	47 088	11 222	6 539	4 038	599	5 638	21.3	12.0	11.4	7.6
	48 339	Montgomery	258 127	182 201	127 222	75 926	24 161	10 097	3 418	54 979	41.7	43.2	8.8	8.7
	48 473	Waller	26 792	23 389	19 798	3 403	2 541	1 455	440	3 591	14.5	18.1	11.2	13.3
3400		Huntington-Ashland, WV-KY-OH MSA	315 204	312 529	336 410	2 675	28 536	25 273	393	−23 881	.9	−7.1	14.5	.5
	54 011	Cabell, WV	95 061	96 827	106 835	−1 766	8 720	8 576	202	−10 008	−1.8	−9.4	16.6	.5
	54 099	Wayne, WV	42 077	41 636	46 021	441	3 692	3 154	36	−4 385	1.1	−9.5	14.0	.3
	21 019	Boyd, KY	49 865	51 150	55 513	−1 285	4 403	4 236	62	−4 363	−2.5	−7.9	14.7	1.2
	21 043	Carter, KY	26 591	24 340	25 060	2 251	2 649	1 859	8	−720	9.2	−2.9	12.8	.3
	21 089	Greenup, KY	37 125	36 742	39 132	383	2 993	2 535	44	−2 390	1.0	−6.1	12.0	.2
	39 087	Lawrence, OH	64 485	61 834	63 849	2 651	6 079	4 913	41	−2 015	4.3	−3.2	13.7	.3
3440		Huntsville, AL MSA	332 993	293 047	242 971	39 946	34 486	16 367	1 655	50 076	13.6	20.6	9.5	1.5
	01 083	Limestone	60 700	54 135	46 005	6 565	5 793	3 657	60	8 130	12.1	17.7	11.6	.7
	01 089	Madison	272 293	238 912	196 966	33 381	28 693	12 710	1 595	41 946	14.0	21.3	9.1	1.7
3480		Indianapolis, IN MSA	1 503 468	1 380 491	1 305 911	122 977	169 102	90 105	6 195	74 580	8.9	5.7	11.3	1.1
	18 011	Boone	42 985	38 147	36 446	4 838	4 143	2 683	151	1 701	12.7	4.7	12.9	.9
	18 057	Hamilton	154 785	108 936	82 027	45 849	15 234	5 115	810	26 909	42.1	32.8	8.1	.9
	18 059	Hancock	53 071	45 527	43 939	7 544	4 551	2 734	27	1 588	16.6	3.6	10.4	1.0
	18 063	Hendricks	92 291	75 717	69 804	16 574	7 555	4 112	196	5 913	21.9	8.5	9.6	.6
	18 081	Johnson	106 888	88 109	77 240	18 779	9 999	5 643	136	10 869	21.3	14.1	10.5	.9
	18 095	Madison	131 840	130 669	139 336	1 171	12 551	9 786	148	−8 667	.9	−6.2	14.1	.9
	18 097	Marion	813 670	797 159	765 233	16 511	104 617	53 804	4 624	31 926	2.1	4.2	11.7	1.4
	18 109	Morgan	64 787	55 920	51 999	8 867	6 257	3 509	50	3 921	15.9	7.5	10.4	.5
	18 145	Shelby	43 151	40 307	39 887	2 844	4 195	2 719	53	420	7.1	1.1	12.3	.4
3500	19 103	Iowa City, IA MSA (Johnson)	102 318	96 119	81 717	6 199	9 646	3 340	1 256	14 402	6.4	17.6	7.4	2.3
3520	26 075	Jackson, MI MSA (Jackson)	155 346	149 756	151 495	5 590	15 747	10 088	299	−1 739	3.7	−1.1	13.1	1.8
3560		Jackson, MS MSA	425 383	395 396	362 038	29 987	48 313	25 084	1 123	33 358	7.6	9.2	10.2	.6
	28 049	Hinds	247 492	254 441	250 998	−6 949	30 411	16 779	797	3 443	−2.7	1.4	10.9	.5
	28 089	Madison	70 888	53 794	41 613	17 094	8 191	3 310	162	12 181	31.8	29.3	9.3	.6
	28 121	Rankin	107 003	87 161	69 427	19 842	9 711	4 995	164	17 734	22.8	25.5	9.0	.8
3580		Jackson, TN MSA	99 319	90 801	87 273	8 518	10 098	6 988	197	3 528	9.4	4.0	13.8	.6
	47 023	Chester	14 524	12 819	12 727	1 705	1 201	944	10	92	13.3	.7	15.2	.5
	47 113	Madison	84 795	77 982	74 546	6 813	8 897	6 044	187	3 436	8.7	4.6	13.5	.7
3600		Jacksonville, FL MSA	1 034 604	906 727	722 252	127 877	112 477	57 293	11 964	184 475	14.1	25.5	11.1	3.3
	12 019	Clay	135 179	105 986	67 052	29 193	11 756	5 803	1 827	38 934	27.5	58.1	8.3	3.5
	12 031	Duval	732 622	672 971	571 003	59 651	87 499	42 286	8 556	101 968	8.9	17.9	10.9	3.4
	12 089	Nassau	54 096	43 941	32 894	10 155	5 008	2 716	66	11 047	23.1	33.6	10.2	1.5
	12 109	St. Johns	112 707	83 829	51 303	28 878	8 214	6 488	1 515	32 526	34.4	63.4	16.5	3.0
3605	37 133	Jacksonville, NC MSA (Onslow)	143 013	149 838	112 784	−6 825	23 754	4 729	437	37 054	−4.6	32.9	4.7	8.1
3610	36 013	Jamestown, NY MSA (Chautauqua)	140 015	141 895	146 925	−1 880	13 159	11 193	729	−5 030	−1.3	−3.4	16.3	3.7
3620	55 105	Janesville-Beloit, WI MSA (Rock)	150 332	139 510	139 420	10 822	15 001	9 055	386	90	7.8	.1	12.6	1.6

[1]Federal Information Processing Standards (FIPS) codes for metropolitan areas defined as of June 30, 1996.
[2]FIPS codes for counties/county equivalents defined as of January 1, 1990.
[3]Includes count resolution corrections through December 1996.
[4]Includes net domestic migration, net federal movement, and residual not shown separately.
[5]Persons of Hispanic origin may be of any race.

Source: 1990–1997 Population—U.S. Bureau of the Census, "Estimates of the Population of Counties and Demographic Components of Population Change: April 1, 1990 to July 1, 1997" (CO-97-5) Internet site <http://www.census.gov/population/www/estimates/co_97_5.html> (accessed 30 March 1998); 1980 Population—U.S. Bureau of the Census, "1980–1990 Intercensal Population Estimates by County," on diskette; 65 Plus and Hispanic Population—U.S. Bureau of the Census, "County Population Estimates by Age, Sex, Race, and Hispanic Origin - 4/1/90 to 7/1/96" data file (related Internet site <http://www.census.gov/population/www/estimates/co_casrh.html>).

Table C–1. Metro Counties — Population—Con.

[MSA = Metropolitan statistical area. CMSA = Consolidated MSA. PMSA = Primary MSA. NECMA = New England county metropolitan area. All areas defined as of June 30, 1996 Table includes 245 MSAs, 17 CMSAs, and 58 PMSAs not in New England; 12 NECMAs; and 844 component counties]

Metro-politan area code[1]	State and county code[2]	Metropolitan areas and component counties	Total persons 1997 (July 1)	1990[3] (April 1)	1980 (April 1)	Net change 1990–1997 Total[4]	Births	Deaths	Net inter-national migration	1980–1990	Percent change 1990–1997	1980–1990	Percent— 65 years and over, 1996	Hispanic origin[5], 1996
3660		Johnson City-Kingsport-Bristol, TN-VA MSA	460 147	436 047	433 638	24 100	38 042	33 778	1 135	2 409	5.5	.6	14.9	.6
	47 019	Carter, TN	53 082	51 505	50 205	1 577	4 187	4 159	−2	1 300	3.1	2.6	15.4	.5
	47 073	Hawkins, TN	48 777	44 565	43 751	4 212	4 184	3 290	19	814	9.5	1.9	13.3	.5
	47 163	Sullivan, TN	150 684	143 596	143 968	7 088	12 969	10 734	417	−372	4.9	−.3	14.3	.6
	47 171	Unicoi, TN	17 259	16 549	16 362	710	1 352	1 432	16	187	4.3	1.1	17.5	.8
	47 179	Washington, TN	101 558	92 315	88 755	9 243	8 512	6 917	576	3 560	10.0	4.0	14.1	.8
	51 169	Scott, VA	22 688	23 204	25 068	−516	1 688	2 040	8	−1 864	−2.2	−7.4	18.1	.4
	51 191	Washington, VA	48 802	45 887	46 487	2 915	3 702	3 349	48	−600	6.4	−1.3	15.2	.4
	51 520	Bristol city, VA	17 297	18 426	19 042	−1 129	1 448	1 857	53	−616	−6.1	−3.2	20.2	.4
3680		Johnstown, PA MSA	237 674	241 280	264 506	−3 606	19 123	20 042	496	−23 226	−1.5	−8.8	18.7	.7
	42 021	Cambria	157 419	163 062	183 263	−5 643	12 779	13 971	244	−20 201	−3.5	−11.0	19.4	.8
	42 111	Somerset	80 255	78 218	81 243	2 037	6 344	6 071	252	−3 025	2.6	−3.7	17.3	.4
3700	05 031	Jonesboro, AR MSA (Craighead)	76 932	68 956	63 239	7 976	7 677	4 768	173	5 717	11.6	9.0	11.9	1.1
3710		Joplin, MO MSA	147 127	134 910	127 513	12 217	15 064	10 978	425	7 397	9.1	5.8	15.3	1.0
	29 097	Jasper	98 812	90 465	86 958	8 347	10 320	7 587	284	3 507	9.2	4.0	15.6	1.1
	29 145	Newton	48 315	44 445	40 555	3 870	4 744	3 391	141	3 890	8.7	9.6	14.5	1.0
3720		Kalamazoo-Battle Creek, MI MSA	446 699	429 453	420 771	17 246	45 947	26 693	1 736	8 682	4.0	2.1	12.4	2.4
	26 025	Calhoun	141 821	135 982	141 579	5 839	14 570	9 825	197	−5 597	4.3	−4.0	13.9	2.2
	26 077	Kalamazoo	229 192	223 411	212 378	5 781	23 325	12 176	1 208	11 033	2.6	5.2	11.2	2.1
	26 159	Van Buren	75 686	70 060	66 814	5 626	8 052	4 692	331	3 246	8.0	4.9	13.3	3.7
3760		Kansas City, MO-KS MSA	1 709 273	1 582 874	1 449 380	126 399	179 048	99 238	11 442	133 494	8.0	9.2	11.4	3.5
	29 037	Cass, MO	77 896	63 808	51 029	14 088	7 143	3 986	116	12 779	22.1	25.0	10.6	1.6
	29 047	Clay, MO	174 035	153 411	136 488	20 624	16 426	8 597	896	16 923	13.4	12.4	10.2	2.8
	29 049	Clinton, MO	18 620	16 595	15 916	2 025	1 570	1 372	18	679	12.2	4.3	15.0	1.0
	29 095	Jackson, MO	647 973	633 234	629 266	14 739	71 449	45 426	4 942	3 968	2.3	.6	12.9	3.5
	29 107	Lafayette, MO	32 524	31 107	29 931	1 417	2 941	2 847	48	1 176	4.6	3.9	16.6	.8
	29 165	Platte, MO	68 680	57 867	46 341	10 813	6 500	2 741	394	11 526	18.7	24.9	8.1	2.5
	29 177	Ray, MO	23 216	21 968	21 378	1 248	2 044	1 552	13	590	5.7	2.8	13.3	.6
	20 091	Johnson, KS	417 336	355 021	270 269	62 315	42 085	15 650	3 509	84 752	17.6	31.4	9.3	2.6
	20 103	Leavenworth, KS	70 176	64 371	54 809	5 805	6 310	3 519	41	9 562	9.0	17.4	9.4	4.4
	20 121	Miami, KS	26 190	23 466	21 618	2 724	2 344	1 834	9	1 848	11.6	8.5	13.8	1.6
	20 209	Wyandotte, KS	152 627	162 026	172 335	−9 399	20 236	11 714	1 456	−10 309	−5.8	−6.0	12.9	8.7
3810		Killeen-Temple, TX MSA	299 740	255 299	214 587	44 441	41 770	12 022	2 166	40 712	17.4	19.0	8.2	14.9
	48 027	Bell	222 302	191 073	157 820	31 229	34 781	9 907	1 849	33 253	16.3	21.1	9.0	15.8
	48 099	Coryell	77 438	64 226	56 767	13 212	6 989	2 115	317	7 459	20.6	13.1	5.9	12.2
3840		Knoxville, TN MSA	654 181	585 960	546 488	68 221	58 306	41 631	2 688	39 472	11.6	7.2	13.4	.8
	47 001	Anderson	71 429	68 250	67 346	3 179	6 095	5 128	469	904	4.7	1.3	15.4	.9
	47 009	Blount	100 377	85 969	77 770	14 408	8 329	6 207	159	8 199	16.8	10.5	14.7	.7
	47 093	Knox	365 626	335 749	319 694	29 877	33 975	23 298	1 868	16 055	8.9	5.0	12.8	.9
	47 105	Loudon	38 234	31 255	28 553	6 979	3 180	2 599	99	2 702	22.3	9.5	14.6	.4
	47 155	Sevier	62 602	51 043	41 418	11 559	5 445	3 489	89	9 625	22.6	23.2	12.6	.8
	47 173	Union	15 913	13 694	11 707	2 219	1 282	910	4	1 987	16.2	17.0	11.2	.6
3850		Kokomo, IN MSA	99 981	96 946	103 715	3 035	10 237	6 375	303	−6 769	3.1	−6.5	12.3	1.6
	18 067	Howard	83 586	80 827	86 896	2 759	8 781	5 208	283	−6 069	3.4	−7.0	11.7	1.7
	18 159	Tipton	16 395	16 119	16 819	276	1 456	1 167	20	−700	1.7	−4.2	15.0	.9
3870		La Crosse, WI-MN MSA	121 507	116 401	109 438	5 106	11 569	7 639	465	6 963	4.4	6.4	13.4	.8
	55 063	La Crosse, WI	102 279	97 904	91 056	4 375	9 702	6 255	450	6 848	4.5	7.5	12.9	.9
	27 055	Houston, MN	19 228	18 497	18 382	731	1 867	1 384	15	115	4.0	.6	16.1	.3
3880		Lafayette, LA MSA	372 027	345 053	330 786	26 974	43 089	20 746	1 060	14 267	7.8	4.3	10.4	1.4
	22 001	Acadia	57 691	55 882	56 427	1 809	6 877	4 119	40	−545	3.2	−1.0	12.5	.8
	22 055	Lafayette	184 102	164 762	150 017	19 340	20 875	8 128	732	14 745	11.7	9.8	8.7	1.8
	22 097	St. Landry	83 465	80 312	84 128	3 153	9 938	6 012	180	−3 816	3.9	−4.5	12.7	.9
	22 099	St. Martin	46 769	44 097	40 214	2 672	5 399	2 487	108	3 883	6.1	9.7	9.9	1.4
3920		Lafayette, IN MSA	171 539	161 572	153 247	9 967	16 595	9 597	1 153	8 325	6.2	5.4	10.8	2.0
	18 023	Clinton	33 232	30 974	31 545	2 258	3 425	2 575	83	−571	7.3	−1.8	15.6	1.9
	18 157	Tippecanoe	138 307	130 598	121 702	7 709	13 170	7 022	1 070	8 896	5.9	7.3	9.7	2.1
3960	22 019	Lake Charles, LA MSA (Calcasieu)	178 874	168 134	167 223	10 740	19 729	10 770	601	911	6.4	.5	11.3	1.3
3980	12 105	Lakeland-Winter Haven, FL MSA (Polk)	448 646	405 382	321 652	43 264	45 169	32 652	5 618	83 730	10.7	26.0	18.5	5.3
4000	42 071	Lancaster, PA MSA (Lancaster)	454 063	422 822	362 346	31 241	49 584	27 292	2 863	60 476	7.4	16.7	13.5	4.7
4040		Lansing-East Lansing, MI MSA	447 349	432 684	419 750	14 665	44 703	21 350	3 856	12 934	3.4	3.1	9.5	4.6
	26 037	Clinton	63 087	57 893	55 893	5 194	6 034	2 865	588	2 000	9.0	3.6	9.8	2.6
	26 045	Eaton	100 173	92 879	88 337	7 294	8 648	4 955	282	4 542	7.9	5.1	10.3	2.8
	26 065	Ingham	284 089	281 912	275 520	2 177	30 021	13 530	2 986	6 392	.8	2.3	9.2	5.6

[1]Federal Information Processing Standards (FIPS) codes for metropolitan areas defined as of June 30, 1996.
[2]FIPS codes for counties/county equivalents defined as of January 1, 1990.
[3]Includes count resolution corrections through December 1996.
[4]Includes net domestic migration, net federal movement, and residual not shown separately.
[5]Persons of Hispanic origin may be of any race.

Source: 1990–1997 Population—U.S. Bureau of the Census, "Estimates of the Population of Counties and Demographic Components of Population Change: April 1, 1990 to July 1, 1997" (CO-97-5) Internet site <http://www.census.gov/population/www/estimates/co_97_5.html> (accessed 30 March 1998); 1980 Population—U.S. Bureau of the Census, "1980–1990 Intercensal Population Estimates by County," on diskette; 65 Plus and Hispanic Population—U.S. Bureau of the Census, "County Population Estimates by Age, Sex, Race, and Hispanic Origin - 4/1/90 to 7/1/96" data file (related Internet site <http: //www.census.gov/population/www/estimates/co_casrh.html>).

Table C–1. Metro Counties — **Population**—Con.

[MSA = Metropolitan statistical area. CMSA = Consolidated MSA. PMSA = Primary MSA. NECMA = New England county metropolitan area. All areas defined as of June 30, 1996   Table includes 245 MSAs, 17 CMSAs, and 58 PMSAs not in New England; 12 NECMAs; and 844 component counties]

Metro-politan area code[1]	State and county code[2]	Metropolitan areas and component counties	Total persons			Net change					Percent change		Percent—	
						1990–1997								
			1997 (July 1)	1990[3] (April 1)	1980 (April 1)	Total[4]	Births	Deaths	Net inter-national migration	1980–1990	1990–1997	1980–1990	65 years and over, 1996	Hispanic origin[5], 1996
4080	48 479	Laredo, TX MSA (Webb)	183 219	133 239	99 258	49 980	34 250	5 730	15 994	33 981	37.5	34.2	8.6	94.9
4100	35 013	Las Cruces, NM MSA (Dona Ana)	168 470	135 510	96 340	32 960	22 393	6 277	9 866	39 170	24.3	40.7	9.1	57.6
4120		Las Vegas, NV-AZ MSA	1 262 099	852 646	528 000	409 453	127 306	64 089	22 557	324 646	48.0	61.5	12.3	14.1
	32 003	Clark, NV	1 106 047	741 368	463 087	364 679	112 806	52 453	21 816	278 281	49.2	60.1	11.3	15.1
	32 023	Nye, NV	27 168	17 781	9 048	9 387	1 795	1 470	109	8 733	52.8	96.5	12.7	9.5
	04 015	Mohave, AZ	128 884	93 497	55 865	35 387	12 705	10 166	632	37 632	37.8	67.4	20.5	6.2
4150	20 045	Lawrence, KS MSA (Douglas)	91 093	81 798	67 640	9 295	7 778	3 298	874	14 158	11.4	20.9	8.3	3.4
4200	40 031	Lawton, OK MSA (Comanche)	113 957	111 486	112 456	2 471	15 503	5 873	359	–970	2.2	–.9	8.9	8.0
4243	23 001	Lewiston-Auburn, ME NECMA (Androscoggin)	101 045	105 259	99 509	–4 214	9 592	7 353	–153	5 750	–4.0	5.8	14.2	1.0
4280		Lexington, KY MSA	444 073	405 936	370 900	38 137	44 043	24 234	2 450	35 036	9.4	9.4	10.3	1.0
	21 017	Bourbon	19 349	19 236	19 405	113	1 844	1 406	52	–169	.6	–.9	13.7	.5
	21 049	Clark	31 679	29 496	28 322	2 183	3 088	2 056	40	1 174	7.4	4.1	12.4	.4
	21 067	Fayette	239 874	225 366	204 165	14 508	24 586	12 988	1 949	21 201	6.4	10.4	9.8	1.4
	21 113	Jessamine	36 038	30 508	26 065	5 530	3 752	1 709	55	4 443	18.1	17.0	8.8	.8
	21 151	Madison	65 343	57 508	53 352	7 835	5 922	3 368	87	4 156	13.6	7.8	10.4	.4
	21 209	Scott	29 446	23 867	21 813	5 579	2 766	1 503	129	2 054	23.4	9.4	10.9	.6
	21 239	Woodford	22 344	19 955	17 778	2 389	2 085	1 204	138	2 177	12.0	12.2	10.5	.6
4320		Lima, OH MSA	154 944	154 340	154 795	604	16 224	10 591	311	–455	.4	–.3	13.9	1.2
	39 003	Allen	107 979	109 755	112 241	–1 776	11 490	7 552	259	–2 486	–1.6	–2.2	13.8	1.4
	39 011	Auglaize	46 965	44 585	42 554	2 380	4 734	3 039	52	2 031	5.3	4.8	14.1	.7
4360	31 109	Lincoln, NE MSA (Lancaster)	233 319	213 641	192 884	19 678	23 099	11 289	2 982	20 757	9.2	10.8	10.8	3.0
4400		Little Rock-North Little Rock, AR MSA ..	552 194	513 026	474 463	39 168	59 790	33 354	1 767	38 563	7.6	8.1	10.9	1.5
	05 045	Faulkner	76 595	60 006	46 192	16 589	6 878	3 491	87	13 814	27.6	29.9	10.6	1.1
	05 085	Lonoke	49 270	39 268	34 518	10 002	4 279	2 776	33	4 750	25.5	13.8	11.2	1.2
	05 119	Pulaski	350 426	349 569	340 597	857	42 216	23 025	1 591	8 972	.2	2.6	10.9	1.7
	05 125	Saline	75 903	64 183	53 156	11 720	6 417	4 062	56	11 027	18.3	20.7	10.7	1.1
4420		Longview-Marshall, TX MSA	208 250	193 801	180 355	14 449	21 256	14 796	1 890	13 446	7.5	7.5	13.9	3.6
	48 183	Gregg	113 147	104 948	99 495	8 199	12 742	7 953	1 376	5 453	7.8	5.5	13.6	4.4
	48 203	Harrison	59 687	57 483	52 265	2 204	5 403	4 337	379	5 218	3.8	10.0	13.8	2.7
	48 459	Upshur	35 416	31 370	28 595	4 046	3 111	2 506	135	2 775	12.9	9.7	15.1	2.5
4472		Los Angeles-Riverside-Orange, CA CMSA	15 608 886	14 531 529	11 497 548	1 077 357	2 222 649	735 243	1 027 717	3 033 981	7.4	26.4	10.2	37.8
4480	06 037	Los Angeles-Long Beach, CA PMSA (Los Angeles)	9 145 219	8 863 052	7 477 238	282 167	1 359 485	447 298	712 578	1 385 814	3.2	18.5	10.0	43.0
5945	06 059	Orange, CA PMSA (Orange)	2 674 091	2 410 668	1 932 921	263 423	364 550	109 310	184 603	477 747	10.9	24.7	9.5	27.9
6780		Riverside-San Bernardino, CA PMSA	3 063 608	2 588 793	1 558 215	474 815	410 032	149 212	97 917	1 030 578	18.3	66.1	11.2	32.0
	06 065	Riverside	1 447 791	1 170 413	663 199	277 378	180 063	75 812	49 268	507 214	23.7	76.5	13.5	31.7
	06 071	San Bernardino	1 615 817	1 418 380	895 016	197 437	229 969	73 400	48 649	523 364	13.9	58.5	9.2	32.3
8735	06 111	Ventura, CA PMSA (Ventura)	725 968	669 016	529 174	56 952	88 582	29 423	32 619	139 842	8.5	26.4	9.8	31.7
4520		Louisville, KY-IN MSA	993 369	949 012	953 520	44 357	100 884	67 448	3 805	–4 508	4.7	–.5	12.4	.8
	21 029	Bullitt, KY	58 005	47 567	43 346	10 438	5 584	2 170	64	4 221	21.9	9.7	6.8	.5
	21 111	Jefferson, KY	670 622	665 123	684 638	5 499	71 132	49 405	3 474	–19 515	.8	–2.9	13.4	.8
	21 185	Oldham, KY	43 248	33 263	27 795	9 985	3 408	1 407	42	5 468	30.0	19.7	6.7	.8
	18 019	Clark, IN	93 212	87 774	88 838	5 438	8 844	6 510	113	–1 064	6.2	–1.2	12.1	.8
	18 043	Floyd, IN	71 465	64 404	61 205	7 061	6 788	4 512	82	3 199	11.0	5.2	12.8	.5
	18 061	Harrison, IN	33 999	29 890	27 276	4 109	2 922	1 839	11	2 614	13.7	9.6	11.5	.6
	18 143	Scott, IN	22 818	20 991	20 422	1 827	2 206	1 605	19	569	8.7	2.8	12.0	.9
4600	48 303	Lubbock, TX MSA (Lubbock)	230 672	222 636	211 651	8 036	27 702	12 391	2 089	10 985	3.6	5.2	10.2	26.8
4640		Lynchburg, VA MSA	207 426	193 928	182 207	13 498	18 766	14 428	577	11 721	7.0	6.4	14.8	.8
	51 009	Amherst	29 965	28 578	29 122	1 387	2 585	1 941	28	–544	4.9	–1.9	13.2	1.0
	51 019	Bedford......................	55 661	45 552	34 927	10 109	4 489	2 867	191	10 625	22.2	30.4	13.2	.6
	51 031	Campbell	50 176	47 572	45 424	2 604	4 404	2 898	72	2 148	5.5	4.7	12.3	.6
	51 515	Bedford city	6 296	6 177	5 991	119	538	879	10	186	1.9	3.1	25.2	1.3
	51 680	Lynchburg city................	65 328	66 049	66 743	–721	6 750	5 843	276	–694	–1.1	–1.0	17.6	.9
4680		Macon, GA MSA.................	316 077	291 079	272 945	24 998	34 791	20 308	1 136	18 134	8.6	6.6	10.6	1.5
	13 021	Bibb.........................	155 975	150 137	150 256	5 838	18 569	12 573	487	–119	3.9	–.1	12.7	.9
	13 153	Houston	103 543	89 208	77 605	14 335	10 773	4 603	314	11 603	16.1	15.0	7.7	2.6
	13 169	Jones	22 634	20 739	16 579	1 895	1 910	1 111	5	4 160	9.1	25.1	9.5	.6
	13 225	Peach	24 053	21 189	19 151	2 864	2 512	1 325	319	2 038	13.5	10.6	9.8	2.4
	13 289	Twiggs	9 872	9 806	9 354	66	1 027	696	11	452	.7	4.8	10.8	.6
4720	55 025	Madison, WI MSA (Dane)	397 511	367 085	323 545	30 426	36 932	16 901	3 171	43 540	8.3	13.5	9.4	2.1
4800		Mansfield, OH MSA	174 851	174 007	181 280	844	17 188	12 508	–21	–7 273	.5	–4.0	13.8	.8
	39 033	Crawford	47 089	47 870	50 075	–781	4 472	3 763	20	–2 205	–1.6	–4.4	15.1	.6
	39 139	Richland	127 762	126 137	131 205	1 625	12 716	8 745	–41	–5 068	1.3	–3.9	13.3	.9
4880	48 215	McAllen-Edinburg-Mission, TX MSA (Hidalgo)	510 922	383 545	283 323	127 377	89 710	16 463	41 389	100 222	33.2	35.4	10.0	87.3

[1]Federal Information Processing Standards (FIPS) codes for metropolitan areas defined as of June 30, 1996.
[2]FIPS codes for counties/county equivalents defined as of January 1, 1990.
[3]Includes count resolution corrections through December 1996.
[4]Includes net domestic migration, net federal movement, and residual not shown separately.
[5]Persons of Hispanic origin may be of any race.

Source: 1990–1997 Population—U.S. Bureau of the Census, "Estimates of the Population of Counties and Demographic Components of Population Change: April 1, 1990 to July 1, 1997" (CO-97-5) Internet site <http://www.census.gov/population/www/estimates/co_97_5.html> (accessed 30 March 1998); 1980 Population—U.S. Bureau of the Census, "1980–1990 Intercensal Population Estimates by County," on diskette; 65 Plus and Hispanic Population—U.S. Bureau of the Census, "County Population Estimates by Age, Sex, Race, and Hispanic Origin - 4/1/90 to 7/1/96" data file (related Internet site <http://www.census.gov/population/www/estimates/co_casrh.html>).

Table C–1. Metro Counties — **Population**—Con.

[MSA = Metropolitan statistical area. CMSA = Consolidated MSA. PMSA = Primary MSA. NECMA = New England county metropolitan area. All areas defined as of June 30, 1996 Table includes 245 MSAs, 17 CMSAs, and 58 PMSAs not in New England; 12 NECMAs; and 844 component counties]

Metropolitan area code[1]	State and county code[2]	Metropolitan areas and component counties	Total persons 1997 (July 1)	Total persons 1990[3] (April 1)	Total persons 1980 (April 1)	Net change 1990–1997 Total[4]	Net change 1990–1997 Births	Net change 1990–1997 Deaths	Net change 1990–1997 Net international migration	Net change 1980–1990	Percent change 1990–1997	Percent change 1980–1990	Percent 65 years and over, 1996	Percent Hispanic origin[5], 1996
4890	41 029	Medford-Ashland, OR MSA (Jackson) ..	170 960	146 387	132 456	24 573	14 865	11 350	1 357	13 931	16.8	10.5	15.7	5.7
4900	12 009	Melbourne-Titusville-Palm Bay, FL MSA (Brevard)	460 977	398 978	272 959	61 999	38 456	29 156	4 142	126 019	15.5	46.2	16.7	4.1
4920		Memphis, TN-AR-MS MSA...........	1 083 186	1 007 306	938 777	75 880	133 707	67 887	4 980	68 529	7.5	7.3	10.0	1.1
	47 047	Fayette, TN	29 526	25 559	25 305	3 967	2 833	1 816	38	254	15.5	1.0	12.5	.7
	47 157	Shelby, TN	865 970	826 330	777 113	39 640	110 714	56 428	4 694	49 217	4.8	6.3	10.1	1.2
	47 167	Tipton, TN	45 981	37 568	32 930	8 413	4 892	2 564	32	4 638	22.4	14.1	10.6	1.0
	05 035	Crittenden, AR	49 690	49 939	49 499	–249	6 656	3 566	66	440	–.5	.9	9.8	1.2
	28 033	De Soto, MS	92 019	67 910	53 930	24 109	8 612	3 513	150	13 980	35.5	25.9	8.3	.6
4940	06 047	Merced, CA MSA (Merced)	196 123	178 403	134 558	17 720	30 511	8 572	10 799	43 845	9.9	32.6	9.5	38.3
4992		Miami-Fort Lauderdale, FL CMSA.....	3 515 358	3 192 725	2 643 766	322 633	378 313	244 136	218 429	548 959	10.1	20.8	16.9	36.6
2680	12 011	Fort Lauderdale, FL PMSA (Broward)	1 470 758	1 255 531	1 018 257	215 227	139 152	111 980	55 812	237 274	17.1	23.3	20.8	10.9
5000	12 025	Miami, FL PMSA (Dade)	2 044 600	1 937 194	1 625 509	107 406	239 161	132 156	162 617	311 685	5.5	19.2	14.2	54.4
5082		Milwaukee-Racine, WI CMSA........	1 636 572	1 607 183	1 570 152	29 389	181 012	102 671	7 877	37 031	1.8	2.4	12.2	4.6
5080		Milwaukee-Waukesha, WI PMSA	1 451 179	1 432 149	1 397 020	19 030	161 980	91 892	7 314	35 129	1.3	2.5	12.2	4.4
	55 079	Milwaukee	908 940	959 275	964 988	–50 335	115 375	67 542	6 272	–5 713	–5.2	–.6	13.5	5.9
	55 089	Ozaukee.....................	80 737	72 831	66 981	7 906	6 814	3 771	215	5 850	10.9	8.7	11.0	.9
	55 131	Washington	112 694	95 328	84 848	17 366	10 222	5 012	81	10 480	18.2	12.4	10.4	.9
	55 133	Waukesha	348 808	304 715	280 203	44 093	29 569	15 567	746	24 512	14.5	8.7	9.7	2.3
6600	55 101	Racine, WI PMSA (Racine)	185 393	175 034	173 132	10 359	19 032	10 779	563	1 902	5.9	1.1	11.8	6.6
5120		Minneapolis-St. Paul, MN-WI MSA	2 792 137	2 538 776	2 198 190	253 361	303 186	128 510	29 948	340 586	10.0	15.5	9.7	2.0
	27 003	Anoka, MN...................	286 673	243 641	195 998	43 032	30 658	7 929	1 630	47 643	17.7	24.3	5.6	1.3
	27 019	Carver, MN	63 198	47 915	37 046	15 283	7 029	1 965	300	10 869	31.9	29.3	8.5	.7
	27 025	Chisago, MN	39 439	30 521	25 717	8 918	3 624	1 961	58	4 804	29.2	18.7	12.1	.6
	27 037	Dakota, MN	334 585	275 189	194 279	59 396	37 402	9 574	2 280	80 910	21.6	41.6	6.4	2.0
	27 053	Hennepin, MN	1 053 178	1 032 431	941 411	20 747	115 803	59 052	15 519	91 020	2.0	9.7	11.4	1.8
	27 059	Isanti, MN	29 557	25 921	23 600	3 636	2 542	1 417	74	2 321	14.0	9.8	11.2	.6
	27 123	Ramsey, MN	484 354	485 783	459 784	–1 429	56 802	28 980	8 192	25 999	–.3	5.7	12.3	3.8
	27 139	Scott, MN	76 078	57 846	43 784	18 232	8 800	2 333	276	14 062	31.5	32.1	7.3	1.0
	27 141	Sherburne, MN	57 867	41 945	29 908	15 922	5 614	2 041	193	12 037	38.0	40.2	7.1	.8
	27 163	Washington, MN	191 548	145 858	113 571	45 690	17 889	5 366	937	32 287	31.3	28.4	6.4	1.8
	27 171	Wright, MN	83 156	68 710	58 681	14 446	8 760	3 474	275	10 029	21.0	17.1	9.9	.6
	55 093	Pierce, WI	35 194	32 765	31 149	2 429	3 004	1 656	106	1 616	7.4	5.2	10.9	.9
	55 109	St. Croix, WI	57 310	50 251	43 262	7 059	5 259	2 762	108	6 989	14.0	16.2	10.1	.5
5160		Mobile, AL MSA	527 118	476 923	443 536	50 195	57 980	33 516	1 815	33 387	10.5	7.5	12.7	1.2
	01 003	Baldwin.....................	128 842	98 280	78 556	30 562	10 771	7 680	107	19 724	31.1	25.1	15.4	1.5
	01 097	Mobile......................	398 276	378 643	364 980	19 633	47 209	25 836	1 708	13 663	5.2	3.7	11.8	1.1
5170	06 099	Modesto, CA MSA (Stanislaus)	421 818	370 522	265 900	51 296	54 104	21 808	14 688	104 622	13.8	39.3	11.1	26.7
5200	22 073	Monroe, LA MSA (Ouachita)	147 055	142 191	139 241	4 864	16 609	9 251	300	2 950	3.4	2.1	11.7	1.0
5240		Montgomery, AL MSA	319 175	292 517	272 687	26 658	36 082	20 541	496	19 830	9.1	7.3	11.4	1.0
	01 001	Autauga	41 306	34 222	32 259	7 084	4 174	2 321	17	1 963	20.7	6.1	10.0	1.0
	01 051	Elmore	60 272	49 210	43 390	11 062	5 877	3 514	52	5 820	22.5	13.4	11.7	.8
	01 101	Montgomery	217 597	209 085	197 038	8 512	26 031	14 706	427	12 047	4.1	6.1	11.5	1.0
5280	18 035	Muncie, IN MSA (Delaware)	117 625	119 659	128 587	–2 034	10 689	8 140	249	–8 928	–1.7	–6.9	12.8	.9
5330	45 051	Myrtle Beach, SC MSA (Horry)	169 178	144 053	101 419	25 125	14 969	10 047	590	42 634	17.4	42.0	13.5	1.2
5345	12 021	Naples, FL MSA (Collier)	195 731	152 099	85 971	43 632	17 809	12 162	8 091	66 128	28.7	76.9	22.4	17.1
5360		Nashville, TN MSA	1 134 524	985 026	850 505	149 498	114 655	62 665	7 940	134 521	15.2	15.8	10.4	1.1
	47 021	Cheatham	34 405	27 140	21 616	7 265	3 102	1 598	98	5 524	26.8	25.6	8.4	.8
	47 037	Davidson	533 689	510 786	477 811	22 903	60 653	35 344	6 179	32 975	4.5	6.9	11.4	1.4
	47 043	Dickson	41 024	35 061	30 037	5 963	4 109	2 728	51	5 024	17.0	16.7	12.6	.8
	47 147	Robertson	51 482	41 492	37 021	9 990	4 769	3 032	79	4 471	24.1	12.1	12.2	.7
	47 149	Rutherford	159 543	118 570	84 058	40 973	15 572	6 185	508	34 512	34.6	41.1	8.3	1.1
	47 165	Sumner.....................	121 836	103 281	85 790	18 555	10 677	5 968	243	17 491	18.0	20.4	10.1	.8
	47 187	Williamson	111 373	81 021	58 108	30 352	8 646	3 858	666	22 913	37.5	39.4	8.1	1.0
	47 189	Wilson	81 172	67 675	56 064	13 497	7 127	3 952	116	11 611	19.9	20.7	9.7	.9
5523	09 011	New London-Norwich, CT NECMA (New London)	252 958	254 957	238 409	–1 999	25 643	14 343	1 272	16 548	–.8	6.9	12.9	4.1
5560		New Orleans, LA MSA...............	1 307 758	1 285 262	1 304 212	22 496	152 787	86 864	10 954	–18 950	1.8	–1.5	11.1	4.8
	22 051	Jefferson	451 240	448 306	454 592	2 934	49 290	26 913	5 675	–6 286	.7	–1.4	10.6	6.9
	22 071	Orleans	469 089	496 938	557 927	–27 849	62 971	40 492	3 996	–60 989	–5.6	–10.9	13.1	3.9
	22 075	Plaquemines	25 856	25 575	26 049	281	3 056	1 385	149	–474	1.1	–1.8	8.3	2.7
	22 087	St. Bernard	66 267	66 631	64 097	–364	6 690	4 768	230	2 534	–.5	4.0	11.9	7.5
	22 089	St. Charles	47 704	42 437	37 259	5 267	5 437	2 025	194	5 178	12.4	13.9	7.6	3.0
	22 093	St. James	20 991	20 879	21 495	112	2 626	1 254	75	–616	.5	–2.9	9.9	.5
	22 095	St. John the Baptist	42 021	39 996	31 924	2 025	5 203	1 895	144	8 072	5.1	25.3	7.3	2.8
	22 103	St. Tammany	184 590	144 500	110 869	40 090	17 514	8 132	491	33 631	27.7	30.3	9.2	2.6

[1]Federal Information Processing Standards (FIPS) codes for metropolitan areas defined as of June 30, 1996.
[2]FIPS codes for counties/county equivalents defined as of January 1, 1990.
[3]Includes count resolution corrections through December 1996.
[4]Includes net domestic migration, net federal movement, and residual not shown separately.
[5]Persons of Hispanic origin may be of any race.

Source: 1990–1997 Population—U.S. Bureau of the Census, "Estimates of the Population of Counties and Demographic Components of Population Change: April 1, 1990 to July 1, 1997" (CO-97-5) Internet site <http://www.census.gov/population/www/estimates/co_97_5.html> (accessed 30 March 1998); 1980 Population—U.S. Bureau of the Census, "1980–1990 Intercensal Population Estimates by County," on diskette; 65 Plus and Hispanic Population—U.S. Bureau of the Census, "County Population Estimates by Age, Sex, Race, and Hispanic Origin - 4/1/90 to 7/1/96" data file (related Internet site <http: //www.census.gov/population/www/estimates/co_casrh.html>).

Table C–1. Metro Counties — **Population**—Con.

[MSA = Metropolitan statistical area. CMSA = Consolidated MSA. PMSA = Primary MSA. NECMA = New England county metropolitan area. All areas defined as of June 30, 1996 Table includes 245 MSAs, 17 CMSAs, and 58 PMSAs not in New England; 12 NECMAs; and 844 component counties]

Metro-politan area code[1]	State and county code[2]	Metropolitan areas and component counties	Total persons			Net change					Percent change		Percent—	
						1990–1997							65 years and over, 1996	Hispanic origin[5], 1996
			1997 (July 1)	1990[3] (April 1)	1980 (April 1)	Total[4]	Births	Deaths	Net inter-national migration	1980–1990	1990–1997	1980–1990		
5602		New York-Northern New Jersey-Long Island, NY-NJ-CT-PA CMSA/NECMA .	19 876 488	19 480 012	18 829 146	396 476	2 268 051	1 310 046	1 081 307	650 866	2.0	3.5	13.4	16.8
0875		Bergen-Passaic, NJ PMSA.........	1 335 393	1 296 244	1 292 970	39 149	135 903	86 622	72 877	3 274	3.0	.3	14.8	14.3
	34 003	Bergen	851 344	825 380	845 385	25 964	77 456	55 254	36 281	−20 005	3.1	−2.4	15.8	7.6
	34 031	Passaic	484 049	470 864	447 585	13 185	58 447	31 368	36 596	23 279	2.8	5.2	13.0	26.3
2281	36 027	Dutchess, NY PMSA (Dutchess)	264 687	259 462	245 055	5 225	26 214	15 198	2 799	14 407	2.0	5.9	11.7	4.5
3640	34 017	Jersey City, NJ PMSA (Hudson)	551 451	553 099	556 972	−1 648	66 953	38 418	52 094	−3 873	−.3	−.7	13.0	38.6
5015		Middlesex-Somerset-Hunterdon, NJ PMSA	1 105 522	1 019 858	886 383	85 664	113 458	56 573	44 876	133 475	8.4	15.1	11.5	8.8
	34 019	Hunterdon	120 578	107 802	87 361	12 776	10 537	5 241	1 272	20 441	11.9	23.4	9.8	2.1
	34 023	Middlesex...................	708 118	671 811	595 893	36 307	73 472	38 429	33 085	75 918	5.4	12.7	12.0	11.2
	34 035	Somerset...................	276 826	240 245	203 129	36 581	29 449	12 903	10 519	37 116	15.2	18.3	11.1	5.4
5190		Monmouth-Ocean, NJ PMSA	1 076 971	986 296	849 211	90 675	103 167	81 731	10 731	137 085	9.2	16.1	18.2	4.8
	34 025	Monmouth	596 250	553 093	503 173	43 157	59 130	37 452	8 649	49 920	7.8	9.9	13.3	5.2
	34 029	Ocean.....................	480 721	433 203	346 038	47 518	44 037	44 279	2 082	87 165	11.0	25.2	24.3	4.2
5380		Nassau-Suffolk, NY PMSA	2 666 302	2 609 212	2 605 813	57 090	282 658	161 134	55 859	3 399	2.2	.1	12.6	7.7
	36 059	Nassau....................	1 303 686	1 287 444	1 321 582	16 242	132 856	82 971	33 993	−34 138	1.3	−2.6	14.4	7.3
	36 103	Suffolk	1 362 616	1 321 768	1 284 231	40 848	149 802	78 163	21 866	37 537	3.1	2.9	10.9	8.1
5483		New Haven-Bridgeport-Stamford-Waterbury-Danbury, CT NECMA ..	1 625 515	1 631 864	1 568 468	−6 349	173 599	106 787	31 313	63 396	−.4	4.0	14.7	8.9
	09 001	Fairfield	833 315	827 645	807 143	5 670	90 825	51 347	22 350	20 502	.7	2.5	13.9	10.2
	09 009	New Haven	792 200	804 219	761 325	−12 019	82 774	55 440	8 963	42 894	−1.5	5.6	15.5	7.6
5600		New York, NY PMSA...........	8 611 099	8 546 846	8 274 961	64 253	1 073 590	592 614	719 649	271 885	.8	3.3	13.2	24.7
	36 005	Bronx	1 187 984	1 203 789	1 168 972	−15 805	185 135	91 961	104 645	34 817	−1.3	3.0	11.7	47.2
	36 047	Kings.....................	2 240 384	2 300 664	2 231 028	−60 280	317 799	159 795	234 195	69 636	−2.6	3.1	12.5	22.8
	36 061	New York	1 536 220	1 487 536	1 428 285	48 684	154 995	106 393	132 251	59 251	3.3	4.1	13.8	29.4
	36 079	Putnam	92 382	83 941	77 193	8 441	9 247	3 882	1 019	6 748	10.1	8.7	9.3	3.3
	36 081	Queens....................	1 975 676	1 951 598	1 891 325	24 078	234 489	133 486	196 928	60 273	1.2	3.2	14.7	21.8
	36 085	Richmond..................	402 372	378 977	352 029	23 395	45 326	24 879	9 189	26 948	6.2	7.7	11.3	9.6
	36 087	Rockland	279 860	265 475	259 530	14 385	30 714	14 602	9 836	5 945	5.4	2.3	10.2	8.0
	36 119	Westchester	896 221	874 866	866 599	21 355	95 885	57 616	31 586	8 267	2.4	1.0	14.6	11.6
5640		Newark, NJ PMSA	1 943 494	1 915 694	1 963 576	27 800	218 256	129 935	79 170	−47 882	1.5	−2.4	12.9	11.9
	34 013	Essex	750 842	777 964	851 304	−27 122	95 876	59 667	41 733	−73 340	−3.5	−8.6	12.9	15.1
	34 027	Morris	454 154	421 361	407 630	32 793	43 647	22 215	12 620	13 731	7.8	3.4	10.9	6.0
	34 037	Sussex	142 057	130 943	116 119	11 114	14 418	6 653	1 166	14 824	8.5	12.8	9.3	2.9
	34 039	Union	498 148	493 819	504 094	4 329	54 562	35 280	22 874	−10 275	.9	−2.0	15.3	16.9
	34 041	Warren	98 293	91 607	84 429	6 686	9 753	6 120	777	7 178	7.3	8.5	13.9	2.6
5660		Newburgh, NY-PA PMSA	366 268	335 613	277 874	30 655	40 349	19 349	3 439	57 739	9.1	20.8	11.2	7.9
	36 071	Orange, NY	327 160	307 647	259 603	19 513	37 446	17 503	3 326	48 044	6.3	18.5	10.7	8.5
	42 103	Pike, PA	39 108	27 966	18 271	11 142	2 903	1 846	113	9 695	39.8	53.1	15.9	3.1
8480	34 021	Trenton, NJ PMSA (Mercer)	329 786	325 824	307 863	3 962	33 904	21 685	8 500	17 961	1.2	5.8	13.4	7.5
5720		Norfolk-Virginia Beach-Newport News, VA-NC MSA	1 544 945	1 444 710	1 200 998	100 235	185 091	80 643	8 857	243 712	6.9	20.3	9.6	2.9
	51 073	Gloucester, VA	34 456	30 131	20 107	4 325	3 091	1 964	55	10 024	14.4	49.9	11.9	1.3
	51 093	Isle of Wight, VA	28 551	25 053	21 603	3 498	2 644	1 635	25	3 450	14.0	16.0	11.8	.9
	51 095	James City, VA	42 862	34 970	[6]22 339	7 892	3 445	1 807	366	[6]12 631	22.6	[6]56.5	12.3	1.5
	51 115	Mathews, VA...............	9 112	8 348	7 995	764	568	1 001	18	353	9.2	4.4	24.2	.8
	51 199	York, VA..................	57 118	42 434	35 463	14 684	3 833	1 794	223	6 971	34.6	19.7	7.8	2.3
	51 550	Chesapeake city, VA	195 616	151 982	114 486	43 634	19 757	8 536	681	37 496	28.7	32.8	8.7	1.7
	51 650	Hampton city, VA	138 555	133 811	122 617	4 744	16 551	7 478	685	11 194	3.5	9.1	9.9	2.5
	51 700	Newport News city, VA	175 839	171 439	144 903	4 400	25 219	9 908	718	26 536	2.6	18.3	9.9	3.5
	51 710	Norfolk city, VA	229 386	261 250	266 979	−31 864	35 296	16 857	1 641	−5 729	−12.2	−2.1	11.5	3.6
	51 735	Poquoson city, VA	11 450	11 005	8 726	445	814	584	48	2 279	4.0	26.1	9.1	1.3
	51 740	Portsmouth city, VA	99 503	103 910	104 577	−4 407	13 789	8 207	319	−667	−4.2	−.6	14.4	1.7
	51 800	Suffolk city, VA	61 033	52 143	47 621	8 890	5 792	4 350	129	4 522	17.0	9.5	13.3	.8
	51 810	Virginia Beach city, VA	432 545	393 089	262 199	39 456	51 948	14 472	3 965	130 890	10.0	49.9	6.4	4.0
	51 830	Williamsburg city, VA	11 800	11 409	[6]10 294	391	1 002	919	−42	[6]1 115	3.4	[6]10.8	12.2	1.8
	37 053	Currituck, NC..............	17 119	13 736	11 089	3 383	1 342	1 131	26	2 647	24.6	23.9	13.0	1.5
5790	12 083	Ocala, FL MSA (Marion)	237 308	194 835	122 488	42 473	19 418	18 619	1 949	72 347	21.8	59.1	22.1	4.0
5800		Odessa-Midland, TX MSA	243 389	225 545	198 010	17 844	30 747	11 922	5 832	27 535	7.9	13.9	9.2	30.4
	48 135	Ector	124 727	118 934	115 374	5 793	16 268	6 674	3 485	3 560	4.9	3.1	9.4	35.7
	48 329	Midland	118 662	106 611	82 636	12 051	14 479	5 248	2 347	23 975	11.3	29.0	9.1	24.8
5880		Oklahoma City, OK MSA	1 030 504	958 839	860 969	71 665	107 477	61 188	2 423	97 870	7.5	11.4	10.9	4.6
	40 017	Canadian..................	84 670	74 409	56 452	10 261	7 360	3 743	439	17 957	13.8	31.8	8.3	3.4
	40 027	Cleveland	197 164	174 253	133 173	22 911	16 335	6 870	1 289	41 080	13.1	30.8	6.8	3.5
	40 083	Logan	30 607	29 011	26 881	1 596	2 563	2 062	106	2 130	5.5	7.9	12.9	2.5
	40 087	McClain	25 816	22 795	20 291	3 021	2 244	1 574	124	2 504	13.3	12.3	12.2	3.2
	40 109	Oklahoma	630 388	599 611	568 933	30 777	73 062	42 138	362	30 678	5.1	5.4	12.1	5.4
	40 125	Pottawatomie	61 859	58 760	55 239	3 099	5 913	4 801	103	3 521	5.3	6.4	14.5	2.0

[1]Federal Information Processing Standards (FIPS) codes for metropolitan areas defined as of June 30, 1996.
[2]FIPS codes for counties/county equivalents defined as of January 1, 1990.
[3]Includes count resolution corrections through December 1996.
[4]Includes net domestic migration, net federal movement, and residual not shown separately.
[5]Persons of Hispanic origin may be of any race.
[6]1980 population based on 1990 boundaries.

Source: 1990–1997 Population—U.S. Bureau of the Census, "Estimates of the Population of Counties and Demographic Components of Population Change: April 1, 1990 to July 1, 1997" (CO-97-5) Internet site <http://www.census.gov/population/www/estimates/co_97_5.html> (accessed 30 March 1998);   1980 Population—U.S. Bureau of the Census, "1980–1990 Intercensal Population Estimates by County," on diskette;   65 Plus and Hispanic Population—U.S. Bureau of the Census, "County Population Estimates by Age, Sex, Race, and Hispanic Origin - 4/1/90 to 7/1/96" data file (related Internet site <http://www.census.gov/population/www/estimates/co_casrh.html>).

Table C–1. Metro Counties — **Population**—Con.

[MSA = Metropolitan statistical area. CMSA = Consolidated MSA. PMSA = Primary MSA. NECMA = New England county metropolitan area. All areas defined as of June 30, 1996 Table includes 245 MSAs, 17 CMSAs, and 58 PMSAs not in New England; 12 NECMAs; and 844 component counties]

Metro-politan area code[1]	State and county code[2]	Metropolitan areas and component counties	Total persons			Net change					Percent change		Percent—	
						1990–1997								
			1997 (July 1)	1990[3] (April 1)	1980 (April 1)	Total[4]	Births	Deaths	Net inter-national migration	1980–1990	1990–1997	1980–1990	65 years and over, 1996	Hispanic origin[5], 1996
5920		Omaha, NE-IA MSA	687 454	639 580	605 419	47 874	77 360	36 600	3 709	34 161	7.5	5.6	10.5	4.3
	31 025	Cass, NE	24 002	21 318	20 297	2 684	2 286	1 440	6	1 021	12.6	5.0	13.0	1.6
	31 055	Douglas, NE	441 006	416 444	397 038	24 562	50 800	25 529	3 107	19 406	5.9	4.9	11.2	4.5
	31 153	Sarpy, NE	118 571	102 583	86 015	15 988	14 005	3 025	379	16 568	15.6	19.3	4.6	5.5
	31 177	Washington, NE	18 470	16 607	15 508	1 863	1 393	1 046	2	1 099	11.2	7.1	13.3	1.1
	19 155	Pottawattamie, IA	85 405	82 628	86 561	2 777	8 876	5 560	215	-3 933	3.4	-4.5	13.2	2.7
5960		Orlando, FL MSA	1 467 045	1 224 844	804 774	242 201	146 611	76 436	33 982	420 070	19.8	52.2	13.2	10.5
	12 069	Lake	196 214	152 104	104 870	44 110	14 607	16 475	2 346	47 234	29.0	45.0	27.6	3.8
	12 095	Orange	783 974	677 491	470 865	106 483	86 092	37 546	21 898	206 626	15.7	43.9	10.8	12.3
	12 097	Osceola	142 128	107 728	49 287	34 400	14 199	7 555	4 426	58 441	31.9	118.6	13.8	15.3
	12 117	Seminole	344 729	287 521	179 752	57 208	31 713	14 860	5 312	107 769	19.9	60.0	10.4	8.4
5990	21 059	Owensboro, KY MSA (Daviess)	91 011	87 189	85 949	3 822	9 254	6 190	197	1 240	4.4	1.4	12.8	.4
6015	12 005	Panama City, FL MSA (Bay)	146 223	126 994	97 740	19 229	14 862	8 355	560	29 254	15.1	29.9	12.0	.4
6020		Parkersburg-Marietta, WV-OH MSA	150 641	149 169	157 893	1 472	13 974	11 245	234	-8 724	1.0	-5.5	14.7	.4
	54 107	Wood, WV	87 029	86 915	93 627	114	7 906	6 701	175	-6 712	.1	-7.2	15.0	.3
	39 167	Washington, OH	63 612	62 254	64 266	1 358	6 068	4 544	59	-2 012	2.2	-3.1	14.2	.4
6080		Pensacola, FL MSA	397 085	344 406	289 782	52 679	39 779	21 656	3 672	54 624	15.3	18.9	11.2	2.4
	12 033	Escambia	282 604	262 798	233 794	19 806	30 175	17 075	2 174	29 004	7.5	12.4	11.9	2.6
	12 113	Santa Rosa	114 481	81 608	55 988	32 873	9 604	4 581	1 498	25 620	40.3	45.8	9.4	2.0
6120		Peoria-Pekin, IL MSA	345 954	339 172	365 864	6 782	35 330	23 265	1 269	-26 692	2.0	-7.3	13.9	1.4
	17 143	Peoria	182 657	182 827	200 466	-170	20 245	12 572	1 118	-17 639	-.1	-8.8	14.3	1.8
	17 179	Tazewell	128 521	123 692	132 078	4 829	12 041	8 534	99	-8 386	3.9	-6.3	13.3	.9
	17 203	Woodford	34 776	32 653	33 320	2 123	3 044	2 159	52	-667	6.5	-2.0	14.2	.9
6162		Philadelphia-Wilmington-Atlantic City, PA-NJ-DE-MD CMSA	5 971 860	5 893 019	5 649 031	78 841	646 782	421 643	75 701	243 988	1.3	4.3	13.8	4.7
0560		Atlantic-Cape May, NJ PMSA	334 694	319 416	276 385	15 278	37 581	27 180	6 490	43 031	4.8	15.6	16.8	7.2
	34 001	Atlantic	236 569	224 327	194 119	12 242	28 196	17 861	5 875	30 208	5.5	15.6	15.1	9.1
	34 009	Cape May	98 125	95 089	82 266	3 036	9 385	9 319	615	12 823	3.2	15.6	21.1	2.6
6160		Philadelphia, PA-NJ PMSA	4 940 653	4 922 257	4 781 235	18 396	535 477	352 502	62 997	141 022	.4	2.9	13.8	4.3
	42 017	Bucks, PA	582 633	541 174	479 180	41 459	54 260	31 353	4 802	61 994	7.7	12.9	11.2	2.1
	42 029	Chester, PA	416 541	376 396	316 660	40 145	40 009	20 528	4 959	59 736	10.7	18.9	11.1	2.8
	42 045	Delaware, PA	543 010	547 651	555 029	-4 641	54 805	41 222	5 421	-7 378	-.8	-1.3	16.0	1.4
	42 091	Montgomery, PA	712 466	678 193	643 371	34 273	67 968	46 422	5 362	34 822	5.1	5.4	15.6	1.5
	42 101	Philadelphia, PA	1 451 372	1 585 577	1 688 210	-134 205	190 750	139 445	29 976	-102 633	-8.5	-6.1	15.6	6.8
	34 005	Burlington, NJ	417 930	395 066	362 542	22 864	39 677	22 218	3 682	32 524	5.8	9.0	11.0	4.2
	34 007	Camden, NJ	504 591	502 824	471 650	1 767	57 807	32 727	7 261	31 174	.4	6.6	12.6	9.2
	34 015	Gloucester, NJ	246 070	230 082	199 917	15 988	24 025	13 614	1 233	30 165	6.9	15.1	11.2	2.3
	34 033	Salem, NJ	66 040	65 294	64 676	746	6 176	4 973	301	618	1.1	1.0	15.3	2.9
8760	34 011	Vineland-Millville-Bridgeton, NJ PMSA (Cumberland)	140 907	138 053	132 866	2 854	15 653	10 210	1 294	5 187	2.1	3.9	13.8	16.6
9160		Wilmington-Newark, DE-MD PMSA	555 606	513 293	458 545	42 313	58 071	31 751	4 920	54 748	8.2	11.9	11.8	3.2
	10 003	New Castle, DE	474 838	441 946	398 115	32 892	50 238	27 482	4 543	43 831	7.4	11.0	12.0	3.6
	24 015	Cecil, MD	80 768	71 347	60 430	9 421	7 833	4 269	377	10 917	13.2	18.1	11.1	1.2
6200		Phoenix-Mesa, AZ MSA	2 839 539	2 238 498	1 600 093	601 041	321 403	141 867	49 788	638 405	26.9	39.9	12.7	19.5
	04 013	Maricopa	2 696 198	2 122 101	1 509 175	574 097	306 231	133 351	47 537	612 926	27.1	40.6	12.7	18.8
	04 021	Pinal	143 341	116 397	90 918	26 944	15 172	8 516	2 251	25 479	23.1	28.0	13.6	32.7
6240	05 069	Pine Bluff, AR MSA (Jefferson)	82 259	85 487	90 718	-3 228	9 751	6 740	205	-5 231	-3.8	-5.8	12.5	.9
6280		Pittsburgh, PA MSA	2 361 019	2 394 811	2 571 223	-33 792	211 793	198 220	7 211	-176 412	-1.4	-6.9	17.7	.7
	42 003	Allegheny	1 280 624	1 336 449	1 450 195	-55 825	120 115	112 063	6 211	-113 746	-4.2	-7.8	18.0	.8
	42 007	Beaver	185 682	186 093	204 441	-411	16 195	14 604	-95	-18 348	-.2	-9.0	17.5	.8
	42 019	Butler	169 197	152 013	147 912	17 184	15 368	10 785	342	4 101	11.3	2.8	14.0	.5
	42 051	Fayette	145 036	145 351	159 417	-315	12 925	13 267	296	-14 066	-.2	-8.8	18.7	.4
	42 125	Washington	205 807	204 584	217 074	1 223	16 857	17 367	141	-12 490	.6	-5.8	18.2	.8
	42 129	Westmoreland	374 673	370 321	392 184	4 352	30 333	30 134	316	-21 863	1.2	-5.6	17.7	.5
6323	25 003	Pittsfield, MA NECMA (Berkshire)	134 244	139 352	145 110	-5 108	11 371	10 895	846	-5 758	-3.7	-4.0	17.7	1.3
6340	16 005	Pocatello, ID MSA (Bannock)	73 850	66 026	65 421	7 824	8 947	3 268	309	605	11.8	.9	9.6	5.6
6403	23 005	Portland, ME NECMA (Cumberland)	251 438	243 135	215 789	8 303	23 248	15 929	1 372	27 346	3.4	12.7	13.7	.8
6442		Portland-Salem, OR-WA CMSA	2 112 802	1 793 476	1 583 518	319 326	213 096	115 956	38 715	209 958	17.8	13.3	12.0	5.6
6440		Portland-Vancouver, OR-WA PMSA	1 787 549	1 515 452	1 333 623	272 097	179 041	96 168	31 977	181 829	18.0	13.6	11.7	4.7
	41 005	Clackamas, OR	331 106	278 850	241 911	52 256	28 815	16 633	2 712	36 939	18.7	15.3	11.1	3.6
	41 009	Columbia, OR	43 751	37 557	35 646	6 194	3 595	2 470	292	1 911	16.5	5.4	12.3	2.6
	41 051	Multnomah, OR	624 619	583 887	562 647	40 732	66 587	42 739	15 362	21 240	7.0	3.8	13.4	4.6
	41 067	Washington, OR	391 335	311 554	245 860	79 781	41 768	16 345	9 211	65 694	25.6	26.7	9.9	6.3
	41 071	Yamhill, OR	80 212	65 551	55 332	14 661	7 245	4 099	1 486	10 219	22.4	18.5	12.8	8.6
	53 011	Clark, WA	316 526	238 053	192 227	78 473	31 031	13 882	2 914	45 826	33.0	23.8	10.4	3.4
7080		Salem, OR PMSA	325 253	278 024	249 895	47 229	34 055	19 788	6 738	28 129	17.0	11.3	14.1	10.3
	41 047	Marion	265 123	228 483	204 692	36 640	29 319	16 343	5 848	23 791	16.0	11.6	14.0	10.9
	41 053	Polk	60 130	49 541	45 203	10 589	4 736	3 445	890	4 338	21.4	9.6	14.4	7.8

[1]Federal Information Processing Standards (FIPS) codes for metropolitan areas defined as of June 30, 1996.
[2]FIPS codes for counties/county equivalents defined as of January 1, 1990.
[3]Includes count resolution corrections through December 1996.
[4]Includes net domestic migration, net federal movement, and residual not shown separately.
[5]Persons of Hispanic origin may be of any race.

Source: 1990–1997 Population—U.S. Bureau of the Census, "Estimates of the Population of Counties and Demographic Components of Population Change: April 1, 1990 to July 1, 1997" (CO-97-5) Internet site <http://www.census.gov/population/www/estimates/co_97_5.html> (accessed 30 March 1998); 1980 Population—U.S. Bureau of the Census, "1980–1990 Intercensal Population Estimates by County," on diskette; 65 Plus and Hispanic Population—U.S. Bureau of the Census, "County Population Estimates by Age, Sex, Race, and Hispanic Origin - 4/1/90 to 7/1/96" data file (related Internet site <http://www.census.gov/population/www/estimates/co_casrh.html>).

Table C–1. Metro Counties — **Population**—Con.

[MSA = Metropolitan statistical area. CMSA = Consolidated MSA. PMSA = Primary MSA. NECMA = New England county metropolitan area. All areas defined as of June 30, 1996 Table includes 245 MSAs, 17 CMSAs, and 58 PMSAs not in New England; 12 NECMAs; and 844 component counties]

Metro-politan area code[1]	State and county code[2]	Metropolitan areas and component counties	Total persons — 1997 (July 1)	Total persons — 1990[3] (April 1)	Total persons — 1980 (April 1)	Net change 1990–1997 Total[4]	Net change 1990–1997 Births	Net change 1990–1997 Deaths	Net change 1990–1997 Net international migration	Net change 1980–1990	Percent change 1990–1997	Percent change 1980–1990	Percent 65 years and over, 1996	Percent Hispanic origin[5], 1996
6483		Providence-Warwick-Pawtucket, RI NECMA	904 831	916 270	865 771	−11 439	90 230	55 742	11 672	50 499	−1.2	5.8	15.9	6.3
	44 001	Bristol	48 970	48 859	46 942	111	4 126	2 832	−181	1 917	.2	4.1	16.5	2.0
	44 003	Kent	161 742	161 135	154 163	607	14 840	9 635	461	6 972	.4	4.5	15.8	1.5
	44 007	Providence	574 429	596 270	571 349	−21 841	60 873	37 773	10 813	24 921	−3.7	4.4	16.5	9.1
	44 009	Washington	119 690	110 006	93 317	9 684	10 391	5 502	579	16 689	8.8	17.9	13.1	1.3
6520	49 049	Provo-Orem, UT MSA (Utah)	328 142	263 590	218 106	64 552	54 448	9 070	4 132	45 484	24.5	20.9	7.0	4.0
6560	08 101	Pueblo, CO MSA (Pueblo)	132 901	123 051	125 972	9 850	12 900	9 350	419	−2 921	8.0	−2.3	15.4	39.0
6580	12 015	Punta Gorda, FL MSA (Charlotte)	133 681	110 975	58 460	22 706	7 156	12 919	2 269	52 515	20.5	89.8	34.3	3.4
6640		Raleigh-Durham-Chapel Hill, NC MSA	1 050 054	858 485	664 788	191 569	102 679	47 165	10 959	193 697	22.3	29.1	9.7	2.1
	37 037	Chatham	44 860	38 759	33 415	6 101	4 056	2 831	674	5 344	15.7	16.0	14.8	2.4
	37 063	Durham	199 653	181 855	152 235	17 798	21 940	11 408	2 237	29 620	9.8	19.5	11.0	1.8
	37 069	Franklin	43 542	36 414	30 055	7 128	3 878	2 786	125	6 359	19.6	21.2	13.5	1.2
	37 101	Johnston	101 908	81 306	70 599	20 602	10 368	6 161	402	10 707	25.3	15.2	13.0	2.5
	37 135	Orange	108 503	93 851	77 055	14 652	8 280	4 236	1 600	16 796	15.6	21.8	9.1	2.3
	37 183	Wake	551 588	426 300	301 429	125 288	54 157	19 743	5 921	124 871	29.4	41.4	8.1	2.1
6660	46 103	Rapid City, SD MSA (Pennington)	87 190	81 343	70 361	5 847	10 644	4 145	322	10 982	7.2	15.6	9.8	2.8
6680	42 011	Reading, PA MSA (Berks)	354 057	336 523	312 509	17 534	33 831	25 444	3 291	24 014	5.2	7.7	16.1	6.4
6690	06 089	Redding, CA MSA (Shasta)	163 178	147 036	115 613	16 142	15 513	10 803	1 302	31 423	11.0	27.2	15.0	5.0
6720	32 031	Reno, NV MSA (Washoe)	305 792	254 667	193 623	51 125	32 655	15 624	8 367	61 044	20.1	31.5	11.1	12.1
6740		Richland-Kennewick-Pasco, WA MSA	182 799	150 033	144 469	32 766	21 406	7 871	7 147	5 564	21.8	3.9	9.5	17.1
	53 005	Benton	135 772	112 560	109 444	23 212	14 211	5 886	3 169	3 116	20.6	2.8	9.7	10.3
	53 021	Franklin	47 027	37 473	35 025	9 554	7 195	1 985	3 978	2 448	25.5	7.0	8.9	37.2
6760		Richmond-Petersburg, VA MSA	943 264	865 640	761 311	77 624	96 955	56 969	6 578	104 329	9.0	13.7	11.6	1.4
	51 036	Charles City	6 969	6 282	6 692	687	571	420	7	−410	10.9	−6.1	11.5	.5
	51 041	Chesterfield	242 987	209 564	141 372	33 423	23 968	7 932	1 644	68 192	15.9	48.2	6.5	1.6
	51 053	Dinwiddie	24 333	22 319	22 602	2 014	1 950	1 420	16	−283	9.0	−1.3	12.3	.7
	51 075	Goochland	17 597	14 163	11 761	3 434	1 285	931	44	2 402	24.2	20.4	11.8	.3
	51 085	Hanover	78 939	63 306	50 398	15 633	6 707	3 727	189	12 908	24.7	25.6	11.3	.7
	51 087	Henrico	243 841	217 849	180 735	25 992	24 806	14 888	2 080	37 114	11.9	20.5	13.0	1.3
	51 127	New Kent	12 261	10 445	8 781	1 816	1 086	602	21	1 664	17.4	19.0	9.6	1.0
	51 145	Powhatan	21 215	15 328	13 062	5 887	1 576	794	34	2 266	38.4	17.3	9.4	.5
	51 149	Prince George	29 741	27 394	25 733	2 347	2 854	972	−3	1 661	8.6	6.5	6.5	5.1
	51 570	Colonial Heights city	16 680	16 064	16 509	616	1 417	1 325	187	−445	3.8	−2.7	16.3	1.4
	51 670	Hopewell city	22 168	23 101	23 397	−933	2 801	1 887	29	−296	−4.0	−1.3	13.8	2.3
	51 730	Petersburg city	34 138	37 027	41 055	−2 889	4 554	3 702	182	−4 028	−7.8	−9.8	15.5	1.5
	51 760	Richmond city	192 395	202 798	219 214	−10 403	23 380	18 369	2 148	−16 416	−5.1	−7.5	15.9	1.2
6800		Roanoke, VA MSA	228 534	224 592	220 393	3 942	20 988	18 509	1 295	4 199	1.8	1.9	16.1	.8
	51 023	Botetourt	28 264	24 992	23 270	3 272	1 949	1 949	51	1 722	13.1	7.4	13.0	.8
	51 161	Roanoke	81 320	79 294	72 945	2 026	5 078	5 254	624	6 349	2.6	8.7	14.3	.8
	51 770	Roanoke city	94 153	96 509	100 220	−2 356	11 950	9 431	538	−3 711	−2.4	−3.7	18.2	.9
	51 775	Salem city	24 797	23 797	23 958	1 000	2 011	2 223	82	−161	4.2	−.7	17.4	.6
6820	27 109	Rochester, MN MSA (Olmsted)	114 619	106 470	92 006	8 149	12 920	4 793	1 572	14 464	7.7	15.7	10.1	1.2
6840		Rochester, NY MSA	1 086 082	1 062 470	1 030 630	23 612	114 971	66 304	10 653	31 840	2.2	3.1	12.8	3.7
	36 037	Genesee	61 808	60 060	59 400	1 748	6 160	4 021	807	660	2.9	1.1	14.3	.9
	36 051	Livingston	66 491	62 372	57 006	4 119	5 474	3 491	807	5 366	6.6	9.4	11.5	2.3
	36 055	Monroe	717 780	713 968	702 238	3 812	79 512	44 179	7 819	11 730	.5	1.7	12.8	4.6
	36 069	Ontario	99 976	95 101	88 909	4 875	9 698	6 424	241	6 192	5.1	7.0	13.6	1.7
	36 073	Orleans	44 734	41 846	38 496	2 888	4 324	2 795	129	3 350	6.9	8.7	12.8	3.5
	36 117	Wayne	95 293	89 123	84 581	6 170	9 803	5 394	836	4 542	6.9	5.4	11.9	2.2
6880		Rockford, IL MSA	354 774	329 676	325 852	25 098	37 022	21 404	3 888	3 824	7.6	1.2	12.8	4.4
	17 007	Boone	37 922	30 806	28 630	7 116	3 689	1 873	338	2 176	23.1	7.6	11.5	8.5
	17 141	Ogle	50 199	45 957	46 338	4 242	4 591	3 044	244	−381	9.2	−.8	14.2	3.9
	17 201	Winnebago	266 653	252 913	250 884	13 740	28 742	16 487	3 306	2 029	5.4	.8	12.8	4.0
6895		Rocky Mount, NC MSA	145 571	133 369	123 141	12 202	15 525	10 188	519	10 228	9.1	8.3	12.6	1.0
	37 065	Edgecombe	55 598	56 692	55 988	−1 094	6 715	4 485	130	704	−1.9	1.3	12.6	.6
	37 127	Nash	89 973	76 677	67 153	13 296	8 810	5 703	389	9 524	17.3	14.2	12.6	1.2
6922		Sacramento-Yolo, CA CMSA	1 655 866	1 481 220	1 099 814	174 646	187 482	83 150	45 362	381 406	11.8	34.7	11.5	14.4
6920		Sacramento, CA PMSA	1 503 069	1 340 010	986 440	163 059	170 783	75 912	37 748	353 570	12.2	35.8	11.6	13.4
	06 017	El Dorado	155 617	125 995	85 812	29 622	13 155	6 836	2 745	40 183	23.5	46.8	12.3	8.9
	06 061	Placer	221 476	172 796	117 247	48 680	19 565	10 378	2 787	55 549	28.2	47.4	12.6	10.4
	06 067	Sacramento	1 125 976	1 041 219	783 381	84 757	138 063	58 698	32 216	257 838	8.1	32.9	11.3	14.5
9270	06 113	Yolo, CA PMSA (Yolo)	152 797	141 210	113 374	11 587	16 699	7 238	7 614	27 836	8.2	24.6	10.2	24.7
6960		Saginaw-Bay City-Midland, MI MSA	402 949	399 320	421 518	3 629	42 827	25 282	1 606	−22 198	.9	−5.3	12.5	5.1
	26 017	Bay	110 423	111 723	119 881	−1 300	10 742	7 411	108	−8 158	−1.2	−6.8	14.0	3.7
	26 111	Midland	81 248	75 651	73 578	5 597	8 134	3 744	696	2 073	7.4	2.8	10.4	1.6
	26 145	Saginaw	211 278	211 946	228 059	−668	23 951	14 127	802	−16 113	−.3	−7.1	12.5	7.2
6980		St. Cloud, MN MSA	161 211	149 509	133 348	11 702	15 527	7 040	562	16 161	7.8	12.1	11.1	.6
	27 009	Benton	33 671	30 185	25 187	3 486	3 619	1 949	107	4 998	11.5	19.8	12.0	.7
	27 145	Stearns	127 540	119 324	108 161	8 216	11 908	5 091	455	11 163	6.9	10.3	10.8	.6

[1]Federal Information Processing Standards (FIPS) codes for metropolitan areas defined as of June 30, 1996.
[2]FIPS codes for counties/county equivalents defined as of January 1, 1990.
[3]Includes count resolution corrections through December 1996.
[4]Includes net domestic migration, net federal movement, and residual not shown separately.
[5]Persons of Hispanic origin may be of any race.

Source: 1990–1997 Population—U.S. Bureau of the Census, "Estimates of the Population of Counties and Demographic Components of Population Change: April 1, 1990 to July 1, 1997" (CO-97-5) Internet site <http://www.census.gov/population/www/estimates/co_97_5.html> (accessed 30 March 1998);   1980 Population—U.S. Bureau of the Census, "1980–1990 Intercensal Population Estimates by County," on diskette; 65 Plus and Hispanic Population—U.S. Bureau of the Census, "County Population Estimates by Age, Sex, Race, and Hispanic Origin - 4/1/90 to 7/1/96" data file (related Internet site <http: //www.census.gov/population/www/estimates/co_casrh.html>).

Table C–1. Metro Counties — **Population**—Con.

[MSA = Metropolitan statistical area. CMSA = Consolidated MSA. PMSA = Primary MSA. NECMA = New England county metropolitan area. All areas defined as of June 30, 1996 Table includes 245 MSAs, 17 CMSAs, and 58 PMSAs not in New England; 12 NECMAs; and 844 component counties]

Metropolitan area code[1]	State and county code[2]	Metropolitan areas and component counties	Total persons			Net change				Percent change		Percent—	
						1990–1997							
			1997 (July 1)	1990[3] (April 1)	1980 (April 1)	Total[4]	Births	Deaths	Net international migration	1980– 1990	1990– 1997	1980– 1990	65 years and over, 1996	Hispanic origin[5], 1996
7000		St. Joseph, MO MSA	97 111	97 715	101 868	−604	9 805	8 177	93	−4 153	−.6	−4.1	16.3	2.2
	29 003	Andrew...................	15 325	14 632	13 980	693	1 240	1 089	11	652	4.7	4.7	15.7	.9
	29 021	Buchanan.................	81 786	83 083	87 888	−1 297	8 565	7 088	82	−4 805	−1.6	−5.5	16.5	2.5
7040		St. Louis, MO-IL MSA	2 557 806	2 492 348	2 414 061	65 458	277 733	174 396	15 833	78 287	2.6	3.2	12.5	1.3
	29 071	Franklin, MO	90 997	80 603	71 233	10 394	8 985	5 575	422	9 370	12.9	13.2	12.1	.7
	29 099	Jefferson, MO	193 210	171 380	146 183	21 830	18 991	9 369	721	25 197	12.7	17.2	8.2	.8
	29 113	Lincoln, MO	35 181	28 892	22 193	6 289	3 394	1 897	10	6 699	21.8	30.2	11.5	1.0
	29 183	St. Charles, MO	264 275	212 751	144 107	51 524	27 283	8 907	909	68 644	24.2	47.6	6.8	1.3
	29 189	St. Louis, MO	1 003 595	993 508	974 180	10 087	101 899	66 134	7 237	19 328	1.0	2.0	12.9	1.2
	29 219	Warren, MO	23 626	19 534	14 900	4 092	2 280	1 366	22	4 634	20.9	31.1	13.9	1.0
	29 510	St. Louis city, MO	341 869	396 685	452 801	−54 816	51 594	37 988	5 554	−56 116	−13.8	−12.4	16.5	1.5
	17 027	Clinton, IL	35 367	33 944	32 617	1 423	3 110	2 186	18	1 327	4.2	4.1	13.9	1.5
	17 083	Jersey, IL	21 248	20 539	20 538	709	1 749	1 540	8	1	3.5	Z	14.0	.7
	17 119	Madison, IL	258 641	249 238	247 661	9 403	25 351	18 427	335	1 577	3.8	.6	14.1	1.4
	17 133	Monroe, IL	25 931	22 422	20 117	3 509	2 198	1 639	41	2 305	15.6	11.5	13.7	1.0
	17 163	St. Clair, IL	263 866	262 852	267 531	1 014	30 899	19 368	556	−4 679	.4	−1.7	12.9	1.9
7120	06 053	Salinas, CA MSA (Monterey)	361 907	355 660	290 444	6 247	53 940	16 511	22 684	65 216	1.8	22.5	10.3	39.9
7160		Salt Lake City-Ogden, UT MSA	1 247 554	1 072 227	910 222	175 327	166 280	45 764	13 799	162 005	16.4	17.8	8.4	7.3
	49 011	Davis...................	226 062	187 941	146 540	38 121	29 316	5 783	1 180	41 401	20.3	28.3	6.1	4.9
	49 035	Salt Lake	839 896	725 956	619 066	113 940	113 147	31 551	11 394	106 890	15.7	17.3	8.5	7.6
	49 057	Weber..................	181 596	158 330	144 616	23 266	23 817	8 430	1 225	13 714	14.7	16.1	11.0	8.8
7200	48 451	San Angelo, TX MSA (Tom Green).....	102 648	98 458	84 784	4 190	11 111	6 525	1 222	13 674	4.3	16.1	13.0	30.0
7240		San Antonio, TX MSA	1 511 386	1 324 749	1 088 881	186 637	180 726	74 513	30 642	235 868	14.1	21.7	10.6	52.1
	48 029	Bexar	1 332 547	1 185 394	988 971	147 153	165 401	65 175	28 801	196 423	12.4	19.9	10.2	54.7
	48 091	Comal	70 682	51 832	36 446	18 850	5 824	4 042	902	15 386	36.4	42.2	16.3	26.5
	48 187	Guadalupe	77 963	64 873	46 708	13 090	7 018	3 898	681	18 165	20.2	38.9	12.1	33.9
	48 493	Wilson..................	30 194	22 650	16 756	7 544	2 483	1 398	258	5 894	33.3	35.2	12.9	40.3
7320	06 073	San Diego, CA MSA (San Diego)	2 722 650	2 498 016	1 861 846	224 634	348 793	130 166	129 997	636 170	9.0	34.2	11.7	25.1
7362		San Francisco-Oakland-San Jose, CA CMSA	6 700 753	6 277 525	5 367 900	423 228	729 878	344 825	354 028	909 625	6.7	16.9	11.7	18.6
5775		Oakland, CA PMSA	2 270 325	2 108 078	1 761 710	162 247	250 170	114 563	91 519	346 368	7.7	19.7	11.4	15.9
	06 001	Alameda.................	1 371 067	1 304 346	1 105 379	66 721	158 096	71 192	63 524	198 967	5.1	18.0	11.4	17.1
	06 013	Contra Costa.............	899 258	803 732	656 331	95 526	92 074	43 371	27 995	147 401	11.9	22.5	11.4	14.0
7360		San Francisco, CA PMSA	1 662 005	1 603 678	1 488 895	58 327	161 549	106 361	116 930	114 783	3.6	7.7	14.2	17.2
	06 041	Marin...................	235 692	230 096	222 592	5 596	20 279	13 209	8 088	7 504	2.4	3.4	12.8	9.6
	06 075	San Francisco............	732 307	723 959	678 974	8 348	66 403	57 335	66 474	44 985	1.2	6.6	16.1	16.2
	06 081	San Mateo...............	694 006	649 623	587 329	44 383	74 867	35 817	42 368	62 294	6.8	10.6	12.7	20.9
7400	06 085	San Jose, CA PMSA (Santa Clara).	1 609 037	1 497 577	1 295 071	111 460	193 882	61 767	107 578	202 506	7.4	15.6	9.2	24.8
7485	06 087	Santa Cruz-Watsonville, CA PMSA (Santa Cruz)	240 488	229 734	188 141	10 754	27 704	12 301	11 449	41 593	4.7	22.1	11.9	25.0
7500	06 097	Santa Rosa, CA PMSA (Sonoma)...	428 609	388 222	299 681	40 387	41 265	24 955	10 492	88 541	10.4	29.5	14.3	13.4
8720		Vallejo-Fairfield-Napa, CA PMSA ...	490 289	450 236	334 402	40 053	55 308	24 878	16 060	115 834	8.9	34.6	10.8	16.7
	06 055	Napa	119 269	110 765	99 199	8 504	11 020	8 783	4 930	11 566	7.7	11.7	17.2	17.9
	06 095	Solano	371 020	339 471	235 203	31 549	44 288	16 095	11 130	104 268	9.3	44.3	8.8	16.3
7460	06 079	San Luis Obispo-Atascadero-Paso Robles, CA MSA (San Luis Obispo) ..	233 291	217 162	155 435	16 129	19 890	13 086	4 443	61 727	7.4	39.7	15.1	16.5
7480	06 083	Santa Barbara-Santa Maria-Lompoc, CA MSA (Santa Barbara)	390 199	369 608	298 694	20 591	46 195	20 348	20 021	70 914	5.6	23.7	12.9	32.1
7490		Santa Fe, NM MSA	140 066	117 043	93 118	23 023	12 282	5 788	2 587	23 925	19.7	25.7	10.2	45.2
	35 028	Los Alamos	18 275	18 115	17 599	160	1 507	662	202	516	.9	2.9	9.0	11.4
	35 049	Santa Fe	121 791	98 928	75 519	22 863	10 775	5 126	2 385	23 409	23.1	31.4	10.4	50.4
7510		Sarasota-Bradenton, FL MSA	538 783	489 483	350 696	49 300	39 326	53 399	7 784	138 787	10.1	39.6	30.9	4.1
	12 081	Manatee.................	237 139	211 707	148 445	25 432	20 306	21 756	4 579	63 262	12.0	42.6	28.4	5.8
	12 115	Sarasota.................	301 644	277 776	202 251	23 868	19 020	31 643	3 205	75 525	8.6	37.3	32.8	2.8
7520		Savannah, GA MSA	284 090	257 899	230 728	26 191	33 226	17 127	1 453	27 171	10.2	11.8	11.7	1.8
	13 029	Bryan	23 093	15 438	10 175	7 655	2 298	774	62	5 263	49.6	51.7	7.4	1.4
	13 051	Chatham.................	225 934	216 774	202 226	9 160	27 830	15 069	1 305	14 548	4.2	7.2	12.6	1.9
	13 103	Effingham................	35 063	25 687	18 327	9 376	3 098	1 284	86	7 360	36.5	40.2	8.1	1.1
7560		Scranton--Wilkes-Barre--Hazleton, PA MSA	621 641	638 524	659 387	−16 883	51 125	58 637	2 143	−20 863	−2.6	−3.2	19.9	.7
	42 037	Columbia	64 230	63 202	61 967	1 028	4 941	4 808	372	1 235	1.6	2.0	16.5	.7
	42 069	Lackawanna	210 464	219 097	227 908	−8 633	17 855	20 310	727	−8 811	−3.9	−3.9	20.6	.6
	42 079	Luzerne	317 560	328 149	343 079	−10 589	25 629	31 751	993	−14 930	−3.2	−4.4	20.6	.8
	42 131	Wyoming	29 387	28 076	26 433	1 311	2 700	1 768	51	1 643	4.7	6.2	13.1	.6
7602		Seattle-Tacoma-Bremerton, WA CMSA .	3 367 872	2 970 300	2 408 749	397 572	342 891	161 749	54 700	561 551	13.4	23.3	10.6	4.0
1150	53 035	Bremerton, WA PMSA (Kitsap)	234 608	189 731	147 152	44 877	24 534	10 319	1 845	42 579	23.7	28.9	10.5	4.3
5910	53 067	Olympia, WA PMSA (Thurston). ...	200 362	161 238	124 264	39 124	17 729	9 483	1 774	36 974	24.3	29.8	11.4	4.1
7600		Seattle-Bellevue-Everett, WA PMSA	2 268 126	2 033 128	1 651 666	234 998	227 959	107 964	46 331	381 462	11.6	23.1	10.6	3.7
	53 029	Island	70 664	60 195	44 048	10 469	7 409	3 319	789	16 147	17.4	36.7	13.7	4.3
	53 033	King	1 632 852	1 507 305	1 269 898	125 547	163 165	81 745	39 702	237 407	8.3	18.7	11.0	3.9
	53 061	Snohomish...............	564 610	465 628	337 720	98 982	57 385	22 900	5 840	127 908	21.3	37.9	9.3	3.1
8200	53 053	Tacoma, WA PMSA (Pierce)	664 776	586 203	485 667	78 573	72 669	33 983	4 750	100 536	13.4	20.7	10.3	4.7

Z Less than .05 percent.

[1]Federal Information Processing Standards (FIPS) codes for metropolitan areas defined as of June 30, 1996.
[2]FIPS codes for counties/county equivalents defined as of January 1, 1990.
[3]Includes count resolution corrections through December 1996.
[4]Includes net domestic migration, net federal movement, and residual not shown separately.
[5]Persons of Hispanic origin may be of any race.

Source: 1990–1997 Population—U.S. Bureau of the Census, "Estimates of the Population of Counties and Demographic Components of Population Change: April 1, 1990 to July 1, 1997" (CO-97-5) Internet site <http://www.census.gov/population/www/estimates/co_97_5.html> (accessed 30 March 1998); 1980 Population—U.S. Bureau of the Census, "1980–1990 Intercensal Population Estimates by County," on diskette; 65 Plus and Hispanic Population—U.S. Bureau of the Census, "County Population Estimates by Age, Sex, Race, and Hispanic Origin - 4/1/90 to 7/1/96" data file (related Internet site <http://www.census.gov/population/www/estimates/co_casrh.html>).

Table C-1. Metro Counties — **Population**—Con.

[MSA = Metropolitan statistical area. CMSA = Consolidated MSA. PMSA = Primary MSA. NECMA = New England county metropolitan area. All areas defined as of June 30, 1996 Table includes 245 MSAs, 17 CMSAs, and 58 PMSAs not in New England; 12 NECMAs; and 844 component counties]

Metro-politan area code[1]	State and county code[2]	Metropolitan areas and component counties	Total persons: 1997 (July 1)	Total persons: 1990[3] (April 1)	Total persons: 1980 (April 1)	Net change 1990–1997: Total[4]	Net change 1990–1997: Births	Net change 1990–1997: Deaths	Net change 1990–1997: Net inter-national migration	Net change 1980–1990	Percent change 1990–1997	Percent change 1980–1990	Percent— 65 years and over, 1996	Percent— Hispanic origin[5], 1996
7610	42 085	Sharon, PA MSA (Mercer)	122 045	121 003	128 299	1 042	10 276	9 729	109	−7 296	.9	−5.7	17.8	.5
7620	55 117	Sheboygan, WI MSA (Sheboygan)	109 896	103 877	100 935	6 019	9 854	6 967	528	2 942	5.8	2.9	14.5	2.1
7640	48 181	Sherman-Denison, TX MSA (Grayson)	101 541	95 019	89 796	6 522	9 501	8 064	790	5 223	6.9	5.8	17.0	3.7
7680		Shreveport-Bossier City, LA MSA	378 738	376 330	376 789	2 408	41 814	27 107	838	−459	.6	−.1	13.0	1.4
	22 015	Bossier	92 750	86 088	80 721	6 662	9 925	4 672	150	5 367	7.7	6.6	9.4	2.5
	22 017	Caddo	243 391	248 253	252 437	−4 862	27 787	18 686	635	−4 184	−2.0	−1.7	13.7	1.2
	22 119	Webster	42 597	41 989	43 631	608	4 102	3 749	53	−1 642	1.4	−3.8	16.8	.6
7720		Sioux City, IA-NE MSA	120 823	115 018	117 457	5 805	14 458	8 254	2 426	−2 439	5.0	−2.1	14.0	4.8
	19 193	Woodbury, IA	102 092	98 276	100 884	3 816	12 111	7 137	1 631	−2 608	3.9	−2.6	14.5	4.0
	31 043	Dakota, NE	18 731	16 742	16 573	1 989	2 347	1 117	795	169	11.9	1.0	11.2	9.6
7760		Sioux Falls, SD MSA	160 670	139 236	123 377	21 434	16 592	8 094	1 673	15 859	15.4	12.9	11.9	.7
	46 083	Lincoln	20 152	15 427	13 942	4 725	1 667	1 031	42	1 485	30.6	10.7	14.1	.2
	46 099	Minnehaha	140 518	123 809	109 435	16 709	14 925	7 063	1 631	14 374	13.5	13.1	11.6	.8
7800	18 141	South Bend, IN MSA (St. Joseph)	258 056	247 052	241 617	11 004	27 577	17 067	1 060	5 435	4.5	2.2	14.2	2.7
7840	53 063	Spokane, WA MSA (Spokane)	404 650	361 333	341 835	43 317	40 532	24 198	2 610	19 498	12.0	5.7	13.2	2.6
7880		Springfield, IL MSA	203 942	189 550	187 770	14 392	20 072	13 306	1 030	1 780	7.6	.9	14.0	.9
	17 129	Menard	12 345	11 164	11 700	1 181	1 031	871	13	−536	10.6	−4.6	15.2	.5
	17 167	Sangamon	191 597	178 386	176 070	13 211	19 041	12 435	1 017	2 316	7.4	1.3	13.9	.9
7920		Springfield, MO MSA	300 980	264 346	228 118	36 634	28 504	18 494	843	36 228	13.9	15.9	13.0	1.0
	29 043	Christian	46 960	32 644	22 402	14 316	4 137	1 933	51	10 242	43.9	45.7	11.0	.8
	29 077	Greene	225 577	207 949	185 302	17 628	21 568	14 872	769	22 647	8.5	12.2	13.4	1.1
	29 225	Webster	28 443	23 753	20 414	4 690	2 799	1 689	23	3 339	19.7	16.4	12.9	.7
8003		Springfield, MA NECMA	591 110	602 878	581 831	−11 768	58 226	41 563	7 640	21 047	−2.0	3.6	14.4	9.8
	25 013	Hampden	440 974	456 310	443 018	−15 336	47 546	33 340	6 008	13 292	−3.4	3.0	15.1	12.0
	25 015	Hampshire	150 136	146 568	138 813	3 568	10 680	8 223	1 632	7 755	2.4	5.6	12.2	3.2
8050	42 027	State College, PA MSA (Centre)	132 993	124 812	112 760	8 181	10 029	5 502	1 073	12 052	6.6	10.7	9.5	1.4
8080		Steubenville-Weirton, OH-WV MSA	136 725	142 523	163 734	−5 798	10 954	12 163	−33	−21 211	−4.1	−13.0	17.2	.6
	39 081	Jefferson, OH	76 014	80 298	91 564	−4 284	6 383	7 098	−4	−11 266	−5.3	−12.3	17.8	.6
	54 009	Brooke, WV	26 238	26 992	31 117	−754	1 975	2 205	−12	−4 125	−2.8	−13.3	16.6	.3
	54 029	Hancock, WV	34 473	35 233	41 053	−760	2 596	2 860	−17	−5 820	−2.2	−14.2	16.2	.6
8120	06 077	Stockton-Lodi, CA MSA (San Joaquin)	542 504	480 628	347 342	61 876	68 091	28 524	22 026	133 286	12.9	38.4	11.6	27.7
8140	45 085	Sumter, SC MSA (Sumter)	106 589	101 276	88 243	5 313	12 290	6 055	199	13 033	5.2	14.8	9.9	1.5
8160		Syracuse, NY MSA	740 771	742 237	722 865	−1 466	78 322	46 910	6 391	19 372	−.2	2.7	13.0	1.7
	36 011	Cayuga	82 314	82 313	79 894	1	7 836	5 706	692	2 419	Z	3.0	14.6	1.7
	36 053	Madison	71 652	69 166	65 150	2 486	6 743	4 087	610	4 016	3.6	6.2	12.0	1.0
	36 067	Onondaga	461 490	468 973	463 920	−7 483	50 708	29 793	4 424	5 053	−1.6	1.1	13.4	1.9
	36 075	Oswego	125 315	121 785	113 901	3 530	13 035	7 324	665	7 884	2.9	6.9	11.2	1.2
8240		Tallahassee, FL MSA	260 611	233 609	190 329	27 002	25 427	11 486	3 359	43 280	11.6	22.7	9.0	3.1
	12 039	Gadsden	45 441	41 116	41 674	4 325	5 278	2 912	1 414	−558	10.5	−1.3	12.1	2.9
	12 073	Leon	215 170	192 493	148 655	22 677	20 149	8 574	1 945	43 838	11.8	29.5	8.3	3.1
8280		Tampa-St. Petersburg-Clearwater, FL MSA	2 227 000	2 067 959	1 613 600	159 041	200 134	190 681	29 537	454 359	7.7	28.2	21.9	8.6
	12 053	Hernando	125 537	101 115	44 469	24 422	7 191	11 761	1 222	56 646	24.2	127.4	30.6	4.0
	12 057	Hillsborough	909 444	834 054	646 939	75 390	100 226	54 883	17 251	187 115	9.0	28.9	12.4	16.0
	12 101	Pasco	320 253	281 131	193 661	39 122	22 944	33 524	2 412	87 470	13.9	45.2	32.9	4.4
	12 103	Pinellas	871 766	851 659	728 531	20 107	69 773	90 513	8 652	123 128	2.4	16.9	26.6	3.1
8320		Terre Haute, IN MSA	148 468	147 585	155 476	883	14 610	12 299	432	−7 891	.6	−5.1	15.9	.9
	18 021	Clay	26 531	24 705	24 862	1 826	2 471	2 217	22	−157	7.4	−.6	17.1	.3
	18 165	Vermillion	16 997	16 773	18 229	224	1 555	1 643	24	−1 456	1.3	−8.0	17.5	.4
	18 167	Vigo	104 940	106 107	112 385	−1 167	10 584	8 439	386	−6 278	−1.1	−5.6	15.4	1.1
8360		Texarkana, TX-Texarkana, AR MSA	123 380	120 132	113 067	3 248	13 119	9 599	439	7 065	2.7	6.2	14.3	1.8
	48 037	Bowie, TX	83 672	81 665	75 301	2 007	8 998	6 585	351	6 364	2.5	8.5	14.7	2.0
	05 091	Miller, AR	39 708	38 467	37 766	1 241	4 121	3 014	88	701	3.2	1.9	13.4	1.5
8400		Toledo, OH MSA	611 805	614 128	616 864	−2 323	67 384	41 328	2 705	−2 736	−.4	−.4	12.9	3.9
	39 051	Fulton	41 324	38 498	37 751	2 826	4 079	2 378	83	747	7.3	2.0	13.1	5.7
	39 095	Lucas	451 325	462 361	471 741	−11 036	52 967	32 859	2 236	−9 380	−2.4	−2.0	13.5	4.0
	39 173	Wood	119 156	113 269	107 372	5 887	10 338	6 091	386	5 897	5.2	5.5	10.7	3.1
8440	20 177	Topeka, KS MSA (Shawnee)	164 932	160 976	154 916	3 956	17 000	11 266	727	6 060	2.5	3.9	13.1	6.4
8520	04 019	Tucson, AZ MSA (Pima)	780 150	666 957	531 443	113 193	83 155	46 420	16 192	135 514	17.0	25.5	13.8	27.9
8560		Tulsa, OK MSA	764 396	708 954	657 173	55 442	81 787	45 503	4 604	51 781	7.8	7.9	11.6	2.7
	40 037	Creek	66 129	60 915	59 016	5 214	6 279	4 356	45	1 899	8.6	3.2	13.0	1.4
	40 113	Osage	42 514	41 645	39 327	869	3 187	2 527	52	2 318	2.1	5.9	13.7	2.0
	40 131	Rogers	65 654	55 170	46 436	10 484	5 950	3 379	110	8 734	19.0	18.8	10.2	1.4
	40 143	Tulsa	535 896	503 341	470 593	32 555	61 629	33 012	4 383	32 748	6.5	7.0	11.6	3.1
	40 145	Wagoner	54 203	47 883	41 801	6 320	4 742	2 229	14	6 082	13.2	14.5	9.7	1.8
8600	01 025	Tuscaloosa, AL MSA (Tuscaloosa)	160 760	150 522	137 541	10 238	15 673	9 450	431	12 981	6.8	9.4	11.5	.9
8640	48 423	Tyler, TX MSA (Smith)	166 723	151 309	128 366	15 414	17 590	10 838	2 670	22 943	10.2	17.9	14.0	7.1
8680		Utica-Rome, NY MSA	298 878	316 645	320 180	−17 767	29 864	23 356	4 078	−3 535	−5.6	−1.1	16.2	2.5
	36 043	Herkimer	65 691	65 809	66 714	−118	5 888	4 913	740	−905	−.2	−1.4	17.4	.7
	36 065	Oneida	233 187	250 836	253 466	−17 649	23 976	18 443	3 338	−2 630	−7.0	−1.0	15.9	3.1

Z Less than .05 percent.

[1]Federal Information Processing Standards (FIPS) codes for metropolitan areas defined as of June 30, 1996.
[2]FIPS codes for counties/county equivalents defined as of January 1, 1990.
[3]Includes count resolution corrections through December 1996.
[4]Includes net domestic migration, net federal movement, and residual not shown separately.
[5]Persons of Hispanic origin may be of any race.

Source: 1990–1997 Population—U.S. Bureau of the Census, "Estimates of the Population of Counties and Demographic Components of Population Change: April 1, 1990 to July 1, 1997" (CO-97-5) Internet site <http://www.census.gov/population/www/estimates/co_97_5.html> (accessed 30 March 1998); 1980 Population—U.S. Bureau of the Census, "1980–1990 Intercensal Population Estimates by County," on diskette; 65 Plus and Hispanic Population—U.S. Bureau of the Census, "County Population Estimates by Age, Sex, Race, and Hispanic Origin - 4/1/90 to 7/1/96" data file (related Internet site <http: //www.census.gov/population/www/estimates/co_casrh.html>).

Table C–1. Metro Counties — **Population**—Con.

[MSA = Metropolitan statistical area. CMSA = Consolidated MSA. PMSA = Primary MSA. NECMA = New England county metropolitan area. All areas defined as of June 30, 1996 Table includes 245 MSAs, 17 CMSAs, and 58 PMSAs not in New England; 12 NECMAs; and 844 component counties]

Metropolitan area code[1]	State and county code[2]	Metropolitan areas and component counties	Total persons			Net change 1990–1997					Percent change		Percent—	
			1997 (July 1)	1990[3] (April 1)	1980 (April 1)	Total[4]	Births	Deaths	Net international migration	1980–1990	1990–1997	1980–1990	65 years and over, 1996	Hispanic origin[5], 1996
8750	48 469	Victoria, TX MSA (Victoria)	82 024	74 361	68 807	7 663	9 502	4 298	743	5 554	10.3	8.1	11.0	38.9
8780	06 107	Visalia-Tulare-Porterville, CA MSA (Tulare)	353 175	311 921	245 738	41 254	52 770	18 488	18 075	66 183	13.2	26.9	11.0	44.9
8800	48 309	Waco, TX MSA (McLennan)	202 983	189 123	170 755	13 860	22 762	13 951	2 242	18 368	7.3	10.8	14.0	14.9
8872		Washington-Baltimore, DC-MD-VA-WV CMSA.........................	7 206 517	6 726 395	5 790 555	480 122	789 582	377 141	195 900	935 840	7.1	16.2	10.3	4.9
0720		Baltimore, MD PMSA................	2 475 332	2 382 172	2 199 497	93 160	265 367	163 288	23 030	182 675	3.9	8.3	12.3	1.7
	24 003	Anne Arundel	470 028	427 239	370 775	42 789	47 308	21 583	2 928	56 464	10.0	15.2	9.5	2.1
	24 005	Baltimore	720 662	692 134	655 615	28 528	68 664	48 316	8 563	36 519	4.1	5.6	14.9	1.6
	24 013	Carroll	146 936	123 372	96 356	23 564	13 611	7 010	796	27 016	19.1	28.0	11.1	1.1
	24 025	Harford	212 560	182 132	145 930	30 428	21 437	8 767	830	36 202	16.7	24.8	9.0	2.1
	24 027	Howard	228 797	187 328	118 572	41 469	24 063	6 698	3 788	68 756	22.1	58.0	6.6	2.7
	24 035	Queen Anne's	39 093	33 953	25 508	5 140	3 159	2 145	64	8 445	15.1	33.1	14.1	.7
	24 043	Baltimore city................	657 256	736 014	786 741	−78 758	87 125	68 769	6 061	−50 727	−10.7	−6.4	14.5	1.2
3180	24 043	Hagerstown, MD PMSA (Washington)	128 155	121 393	113 086	6 762	11 571	8 522	542	8 307	5.6	7.3	15.0	1.0
8840		Washington, DC-MD-VA-WV PMSA .	4 603 030	4 222 830	3 477 972	380 200	512 644	205 331	172 328	744 858	9.0	21.4	9.1	6.8
	11 001	District of Columbia	528 964	606 900	638 432	−77 936	72 216	49 054	24 120	−31 532	−12.8	−4.9	13.9	6.9
	24 009	Calvert, MD	69 413	51 372	34 638	18 041	6 412	2 647	86	16 734	35.1	48.3	9.6	1.3
	24 017	Charles, MD	115 075	101 154	72 751	13 921	11 943	4 413	397	28 403	13.8	39.0	7.1	2.3
	24 021	Frederick, MD	183 215	150 208	114 792	33 007	18 830	7 808	1 165	35 416	22.0	30.9	10.2	1.6
	24 031	Montgomery, MD	826 766	762 207	579 053	64 559	89 287	35 108	43 485	183 154	8.5	31.6	10.8	9.4
	24 033	Prince George's, MD	770 633	723 373	665 071	47 260	93 166	33 799	20 969	58 302	6.5	8.8	7.1	4.8
	51 013	Arlington, VA	172 580	170 897	152 599	1 683	18 688	8 095	15 983	18 298	1.0	12.0	12.0	16.9
	51 043	Clarke, VA	12 910	12 101	9 965	809	1 033	907	49	2 136	6.7	21.4	15.1	.9
	51 047	Culpeper, VA	32 581	27 791	22 620	4 790	3 150	2 034	254	5 171	17.2	22.9	12.9	.9
	51 059	Fairfax, VA	914 259	818 358	[6]595 754	95 901	93 484	25 749	46 905	[6]222 604	11.7	[6]37.4	6.9	8.2
	51 061	Fauquier, VA	53 167	48 860	35 889	4 307	4 992	2 677	247	12 971	8.8	36.1	10.0	1.7
	51 099	King George, VA	16 942	13 527	10 543	3 415	1 631	780	84	2 984	25.2	28.3	9.9	1.6
	51 107	Loudoun, VA	133 493	86 129	57 427	47 364	14 168	3 429	2 204	28 702	55.0	50.0	6.5	3.4
	51 153	Prince William, VA	254 464	215 677	[6]144 636	38 787	30 712	5 544	4 880	[6]71 041	18.0	[6]49.1	3.2	6.0
	51 177	Spotsylvania, VA	81 052	57 403	[6]31 995	23 649	6 956	2 706	212	[6]25 408	41.2	[6]79.4	7.7	2.1
	51 179	Stafford, VA	87 857	61 236	40 470	26 621	7 674	2 260	253	20 766	43.5	51.3	6.3	2.8
	51 187	Warren, VA	30 008	26 142	21 200	3 866	3 183	1 837	58	4 942	14.8	23.3	14.1	1.3
	51 510	Alexandria city, VA	116 405	111 182	103 217	5 223	13 057	5 835	8 122	7 965	4.7	7.7	10.7	12.0
	51 600	Fairfax city, VA	20 365	19 894	[6]20 537	471	2 016	1 019	1 088	[6]−643	2.4	[6]−3.1	11.2	7.7
	51 610	Falls Church city, VA	9 879	9 522	9 515	357	699	493	322	7	3.7	.1	16.2	8.3
	51 630	Fredericksburg city, VA	21 088	19 027	[6]17 762	2 061	3 907	1 476	275	[6]1 265	10.8	[6]7.1	15.1	3.2
	51 683	Manassas city, VA	34 296	27 957	[6]15 505	6 339	4 412	968	958	[6]12 452	22.7	[6]80.3	5.1	7.3
	51 685	Manassas Park city, VA	8 469	6 734	6 524	1 735	1 149	212	15	210	25.8	3.2	4.1	6.4
	54 003	Berkeley, WV	69 072	59 253	46 775	9 819	6 351	4 100	171	12 478	16.6	26.7	11.8	.8
	54 037	Jefferson, WV	40 077	35 926	30 302	4 151	3 528	2 381	26	5 624	11.6	18.6	11.5	1.4
8920	19 013	Waterloo-Cedar Falls, IA MSA (Black Hawk)	121 502	123 798	137 961	−2 296	11 981	8 517	431	−14 163	−1.9	−10.3	13.5	1.1
8940	55 073	Wausau, WI MSA (Marathon)	122 450	115 400	111 270	7 050	12 180	6 537	632	4 130	6.1	3.7	12.7	.5
8960	12 099	West Palm Beach-Boca Raton, FL MSA (Palm Beach)	1 018 524	863 503	576 758	155 021	90 548	80 952	36 017	286 745	18.0	49.7	24.3	9.8
9000		Wheeling, WV-OH MSA	154 153	159 301	185 566	−5 148	12 926	14 345	96	−26 265	−3.2	−14.2	18.5	.4
	54 051	Marshall, WV	35 700	37 356	41 608	−1 656	3 043	2 921	26	−4 252	−4.4	−10.2	15.6	.6
	54 069	Ohio, WV	48 858	50 871	61 389	−2 013	4 172	4 922	72	−10 518	−4.0	−17.1	19.1	.3
	39 013	Belmont, OH	69 595	71 074	82 569	−1 479	5 711	6 502	−2	−11 495	−2.1	−13.9	19.6	.3
9040		Wichita, KS MSA	530 508	485 270	442 401	45 238	61 039	29 306	4 960	42 869	9.3	9.7	11.9	5.3
	20 015	Butler	60 235	50 580	44 782	9 655	5 228	3 316	129	5 798	19.1	12.9	13.1	2.0
	20 079	Harvey	31 594	31 028	30 531	566	2 925	2 281	130	497	1.8	1.6	16.7	7.0
	20 173	Sedgwick	438 679	403 662	367 088	35 017	52 886	23 709	4 701	36 574	8.7	10.0	11.3	5.6
9080		Wichita Falls, TX MSA	137 103	130 351	128 348	6 752	14 664	9 568	960	2 003	5.2	1.6	13.1	10.0
	48 009	Archer	8 276	7 973	7 266	303	680	481	53	707	3.8	9.7	14.6	2.9
	48 485	Wichita	128 827	122 378	121 082	6 449	13 984	9 087	907	1 296	5.3	1.1	13.0	10.4
9140	42 081	Williamsport, PA MSA (Lycoming)......	118 405	118 710	118 416	−305	11 326	8 993	393	294	−.3	.2	15.8	.7
9200		Wilmington, NC MSA	213 580	171 269	139 248	42 311	18 420	12 444	490	32 021	24.7	23.0	13.6	1.3
	37 019	Brunswick	65 938	50 985	35 777	14 953	5 276	3 991	117	15 208	29.3	42.5	15.0	1.2
	37 129	New Hanover	147 642	120 284	103 471	27 358	13 144	8 453	373	16 813	22.7	16.2	13.0	1.3
9260	53 077	Yakima, WA MSA (Yakima)	218 318	188 823	172 508	29 495	30 843	12 191	11 321	16 315	15.6	9.5	12.3	29.6
9280	42 133	York, PA MSA (York)	370 518	339 574	313 024	30 944	32 859	21 569	1 213	26 550	9.1	8.5	13.6	2.0
9320		Youngstown-Warren, OH MSA	595 215	600 895	644 922	−5 680	57 127	47 805	691	−44 027	−.9	−6.8	16.2	1.5
	39 029	Columbiana	111 644	108 276	113 572	3 368	10 277	8 271	182	−5 296	3.1	−4.7	15.4	.4
	39 099	Mahoning	257 489	264 806	289 548	−7 317	25 301	22 884	167	−24 681	−2.8	−8.5	17.6	2.7
	39 155	Trumbull	226 082	227 813	241 863	−1 731	21 549	16 650	342	−14 050	−.8	−5.8	14.9	.8
9340		Yuba City, CA MSA	139 315	122 643	101 979	16 672	17 984	7 830	7 697	20 664	13.6	20.3	11.9	17.5
	06 101	Sutter	77 754	64 415	52 246	13 339	8 816	4 154	4 809	12 169	20.7	23.3	12.3	20.0
	06 115	Yuba	61 561	58 228	49 733	3 333	9 168	3 676	2 888	8 495	5.7	17.1	11.3	14.5
9360	04 027	Yuma, AZ MSA (Yuma)	130 016	106 895	[6]76 205	23 121	21 623	6 451	10 326	[6]30 690	21.6	[6]40.3	13.5	44.8

[1]Federal Information Processing Standards (FIPS) codes for metropolitan areas defined as of June 30, 1996.
[2]FIPS codes for counties/county equivalents defined as of January 1, 1990.
[3]Includes count resolution corrections through December 1996.
[4]Includes net domestic migration, net federal movement, and residual not shown separately.
[5]Persons of Hispanic origin may be of any race.
[6]1980 population based on 1990 boundaries.

Source: 1990–1997 Population—U.S. Bureau of the Census, "Estimates of the Population of Counties and Demographic Components of Population Change: April 1, 1990 to July 1, 1997" (CO-97-5) Internet site <http://www.census.gov/population/www/estimates/co_97_5.html> (accessed 30 March 1998); 1980 Population—U.S. Bureau of the Census, "1980–1990 Intercensal Population Estimates by County," on diskette; 65 Plus and Hispanic Population—U.S. Bureau of the Census, "County Population Estimates by Age, Sex, Race, and Hispanic Origin - 4/1/90 to 7/1/96" data file (related Internet site <http://www.census.gov/population/www/estimates/co_casrh.html> data file)

Table C–2. Metro Counties — Population by Race, Poverty, Building Permits, and Labor Force

[MSA = Metropolitan statistical area. CMSA = Consolidated MSA. PMSA = Primary MSA. NECMA = New England county metropolitan area. All areas defined as of June 30, 1996. Table includes 245 MSAs, 17 CMSAs, and 58 PMSAs not in New England; 12 NECMAs; and 844 component counties]

Metropolitan areas and component counties	Population by race, 1996, percent— White	Black	Asian or Pacific Islander	Persons below poverty level, 1993 Number All persons	Related children 5 to 17 years	Percent All persons	Related children 5 to 17 years	New private housing units authorized by building permits 1996	1995	1990–1996 period Total units	Percent of 1990 housing stock	Civilian labor force, 1996 Total	Net change, 1990–1996	Unemployment Total	Rate[1]
Abilene, TX MSA (Taylor)	90.9	6.8	1.8	20 652	4 967	17.6	21.4	372	412	2 086	4.2	60 528	4 642	2 955	4.9
Albany, GA MSA	51.0	48.1	.6	29 095	8 823	25.1	34.5	956	1 161	4 881	11.4	55 713	5 083	3 349	6.0
Dougherty	45.2	53.9	.7	26 845	8 191	27.6	39.1	564	745	2 766	7.4	45 548	2 839	2 940	6.5
Lee	78.0	21.3	.4	2 250	632	12.1	13.7	392	416	2 115	38.2	10 165	2 244	409	4.0
Albany-Schenectady-Troy, NY MSA	93.0	5.1	1.7	91 779	21 142	10.5	14.1	2 641	2 535	19 340	5.4	446 825	-6 728	20 409	4.6
Albany	88.1	9.4	2.3	33 198	7 297	11.3	15.7	810	845	6 129	4.9	152 971	-5 916	5 837	3.8
Montgomery	98.1	1.1	.6	6 846	1 785	13.1	18.9	97	89	547	2.5	24 056	-561	1 929	8.0
Rensselaer	94.2	3.8	1.9	18 198	4 409	11.9	16.3	505	355	3 162	5.1	80 311	-1 595	3 925	4.9
Saratoga	97.3	1.4	1.1	14 652	3 130	7.6	8.6	890	900	6 621	8.8	100 832	3 584	4 366	4.3
Schenectady	93.3	4.8	1.7	14 677	3 476	9.8	14.2	234	293	2 531	4.0	73 418	-2 259	3 431	4.7
Schoharie	97.8	1.5	.5	4 208	1 045	13.3	17.2	105	53	350	2.4	15 237	19	921	6.0
Albuquerque, NM MSA	89.1	3.3	1.9	116 224	29 869	17.9	23.6	5 755	6 581	31 305	13.0	345 096	45 622	18 458	5.3
Bernalillo	90.5	3.7	2.2	93 580	23 258	18.0	24.0	4 344	5 204	23 954	11.9	281 408	31 055	14 974	5.3
Sandoval	76.2	2.1	1.2	11 455	3 361	14.8	19.3	1 016	947	5 409	22.9	38 101	8 638	2 115	5.6
Valencia	94.5	1.5	.8	11 189	3 250	21.0	26.8	395	430	1 942	11.6	25 587	5 929	1 369	5.4
Alexandria, LA MSA (Rapides)	68.8	29.9	.9	29 710	8 241	24.1	31.1	434	332	1 470	2.9	58 999	4 476	4 003	6.8
Allentown-Bethlehem-Easton, PA MSA	95.9	2.5	1.5	55 101	11 723	9.0	11.5	2 465	2 260	16 032	6.7	303 744	30 810	16 580	5.5
Carbon	99.2	.2	.5	6 468	1 410	10.9	14.0	170	175	1 136	4.1	26 369	2 631	1 973	7.5
Lehigh	95.2	2.9	1.7	27 323	6 118	9.2	12.5	1 176	1 046	7 150	6.0	151 344	14 375	7 809	5.2
Northampton	95.9	2.5	1.5	21 310	4 195	8.4	9.7	1 119	1 039	7 746	8.1	126 031	13 804	6 798	5.4
Altoona, PA MSA (Blair)	98.6	.9	.4	19 982	5 046	15.1	20.4	259	379	2 274	4.2	62 065	1 498	3 547	5.7
Amarillo, TX MSA	90.8	5.9	2.4	32 636	8 284	16.5	21.1	573	453	2 823	3.5	112 407	14 641	4 357	3.9
Potter	85.1	9.9	3.7	24 541	6 429	23.7	31.5	509	392	2 380	5.5	54 045	6 768	2 651	4.9
Randall	97.0	1.4	1.0	8 095	1 855	8.6	9.8	64	61	443	1.2	58 362	7 873	1 706	2.9
Anchorage, AK MSA (Anchorage)	81.3	6.2	5.9	23 820	5 564	9.4	10.9	1 314	1 056	6 097	6.5	138 105	15 126	7 548	5.5
Anniston, AL MSA (Calhoun)	79.8	19.1	.9	20 320	4 480	18.0	21.8	312	275	1 610	3.4	52 649	1 629	3 250	6.2
Appleton-Oshkosh-Neenah, WI MSA	96.9	.4	1.6	22 094	4 936	6.6	7.5	2 746	2 310	16 890	14.0	220 739	32 129	6 166	2.8
Calumet	98.6	.1	.8	2 059	482	5.5	5.7	316	257	1 380	11.1	24 810	3 452	710	2.9
Outagamie	96.4	.2	1.8	8 869	2 031	5.9	6.5	1 274	1 136	8 006	15.4	98 482	14 516	2 844	2.9
Winnebago	97.0	.8	1.7	11 166	2 423	7.7	9.4	1 156	917	7 504	13.4	97 447	14 161	2 612	2.7
Asheville, NC MSA	91.3	7.8	.6	27 404	5 500	13.6	16.9	1 604	1 092	8 436	9.9	108 582	9 084	3 705	3.4
Buncombe	90.6	8.5	.7	24 198	4 869	13.1	16.4	1 479	1 014	7 786	10.0	99 805	8 505	3 276	3.3
Madison	98.8	.8	.3	3 206	631	18.6	21.9	125	78	650	8.5	8 777	579	429	4.9
Athens, GA MSA	74.4	22.8	2.6	24 279	4 969	19.0	23.4	1 891	1 517	8 234	16.2	71 144	6 895	2 225	3.1
Clarke	66.5	29.6	3.7	18 703	3 611	22.3	28.3	1 389	1 037	5 292	14.7	46 500	2 992	1 487	3.2
Madison	89.0	10.3	.5	3 767	941	16.3	21.6	140	128	858	10.2	12 843	1 588	495	3.9
Oconee	90.3	8.7	.8	1 809	417	8.8	10.2	362	352	2 084	31.8	11 801	2 315	243	2.1
Atlanta, GA MSA	71.4	25.8	2.6	448 008	108 884	13.4	18.3	48 262	48 277	253 413	20.7	1 973 248	309 754	75 099	3.8
Barrow	85.3	13.2	1.2	5 277	1 338	15.2	20.3	520	486	1 653	14.0	18 126	2 842	702	3.9
Bartow	88.8	10.5	.4	8 102	2 002	13.0	17.4	1 282	1 273	3 749	17.2	34 457	4 530	1 833	5.3
Carroll	81.3	18.0	.5	12 010	3 021	16.0	20.9	632	483	3 501	12.6	41 098	4 244	2 073	5.0
Cherokee	96.9	2.2	.5	8 306	1 953	7.5	9.7	1 969	2 378	12 263	36.2	65 941	14 715	1 786	2.7
Clayton	69.3	26.2	4.2	27 591	6 836	14.0	18.3	1 341	1 066	8 353	11.6	115 661	12 538	5 163	4.5
Cobb	85.9	11.1	2.7	42 219	8 592	8.2	9.7	6 268	8 251	34 571	18.2	320 148	53 268	9 614	3.0
Coweta	73.8	25.6	.4	8 678	2 358	12.6	17.7	1 427	1 327	8 283	40.6	37 297	9 594	1 459	3.9
De Kalb	50.4	45.1	4.3	94 306	22 036	16.3	23.3	3 727	2 715	20 711	8.9	349 320	31 131	15 207	4.4
Douglas	89.7	9.2	.9	7 627	1 840	9.5	11.6	1 435	682	5 908	22.3	46 766	7 020	1 482	3.2
Fayette	90.9	6.4	2.6	3 033	616	3.9	3.8	1 625	1 156	7 913	35.3	43 087	9 559	1 012	2.3
Forsyth	99.4	Z	.3	4 556	944	7.9	9.5	2 967	2 803	12 111	67.8	35 185	10 314	789	2.2
Fulton	44.6	53.4	1.8	157 194	40 591	23.0	35.7	8 124	8 916	43 894	14.8	380 214	39 182	18 720	4.9
Gwinnett	89.6	5.8	4.5	25 412	5 594	5.8	6.8	9 508	9 828	49 732	36.1	283 359	67 938	7 967	2.8
Henry	86.9	12.0	.9	5 921	1 356	7.4	8.9	2 977	2 133	13 686	64.3	46 795	14 390	1 387	3.0
Newton	73.9	25.5	.4	7 624	2 042	15.8	21.9	958	798	5 200	33.6	25 415	4 571	1 142	4.5
Paulding	94.7	4.7	.3	5 078	1 274	9.0	11.7	1 631	1 597	9 114	59.8	32 091	9 921	879	2.7
Pickens	97.4	2.0	.2	2 253	549	13.8	19.4	316	279	1 758	27.5	8 908	1 212	344	3.9
Rockdale	89.0	9.3	1.5	5 527	1 317	8.8	10.6	416	908	4 028	20.2	36 536	6 340	1 111	3.0
Spalding	66.9	32.3	.7	10 611	2 928	18.6	26.1	263	241	1 954	9.4	28 952	2 170	1 431	4.9
Walton	78.3	20.9	.6	6 683	1 697	14.8	19.4	876	957	5 031	34.7	23 892	4 285	998	4.2
Augusta-Aiken, GA-SC MSA	64.8	32.9	2.0	73 468	19 275	16.6	21.9	2 227	2 096	17 198	10.4	202 419	2 304	13 488	6.7
Columbia, GA	83.6	12.5	3.6	6 167	1 604	7.7	9.1	811	758	6 154	25.9	39 720	4 978	1 645	4.1
McDuffie, GA	59.4	40.2	.2	4 397	1 197	20.7	26.8	73	92	260	3.2	9 682	118	902	9.3
Richmond, GA	51.8	45.2	2.7	41 149	11 222	21.9	31.0	741	828	5 101	6.6	81 224	-4 425	5 891	7.3
Aiken, SC	74.3	24.9	.6	18 364	4 428	13.8	17.3	527	341	4 932	10.0	62 704	1 661	4 376	7.0
Edgefield, SC	52.5	47.3	.2	3 391	824	17.4	20.9	75	77	751	10.3	9 089	-28	674	7.4

Z Less than .05 percent.

[1]Unemployment as a percent of civilian labor force.

Source: Population by Race—U.S. Bureau of the Census, "County Population Estimates by Age, Sex, Race, and Hispanic Origin - 4/1/90 to 7/1/96" data file (related Internet site <http://www.census.gov/population/www/estimates/co_casrh.html>); Poverty—U.S. Bureau of the Census, "State and County Income and Poverty Estimates - 1993," Internet site <http://www.census.gov/ftp/pub/housing/saipe/est93ALL.dat> (accessed 16 January 1998); Building Permits—U.S. Bureau of the Census, "Construction–Building Permits" on diskette, annual (related Internet site <http://www.census.gov/const/www/C40/table3.html#annual>), and "1990 Census of Population and Housing, Summary Tape File 1C" on CD-ROM; Labor Force—U.S. Bureau of Labor Statistics, Local Area Unemployment Statistics - Time Series, Internet site <gopher://hopi2.gov:70/11/Time%20Series/LA%20%20Local%20Area%20Unemployment%20Statistics/Data> for each state (accessed April 1997), BLS gopher service discontinued October 31, 1997 (related BLS Internet site <http://www.bls.gov>).

Table C–2. Metro Counties — Population by Race, Poverty, Building Permits, and Labor Force—Con.

[MSA = Metropolitan statistical area. CMSA = Consolidated MSA. PMSA = Primary MSA. NECMA = New England county metropolitan area. All areas defined as of June 30, 1996. Table includes 245 MSAs, 17 CMSAs, and 58 PMSAs not in New England; 12 NECMAs; and 844 component counties]

Metropolitan areas and component counties	Population by race, 1996, percent—			Persons below poverty level, 1993				New private housing units authorized by building permits				Civilian labor force, 1996			
				Number		Percent				1990–1996 period				Unemployment	
	White	Black	Asian or Pacific Islander	All persons	Related children 5 to 17 years	All persons	Related children 5 to 17 years	1996	1995	Total units	Percent of 1990 housing stock	Total	Net change, 1990–1996	Total	Rate[1]
Austin-San Marcos, TX MSA	86.6	10.0	3.0	135 873	31 668	14.3	18.4	17 077	13 765	60 974	16.5	634 134	156 290	19 015	3.0
Bastrop	86.4	12.4	.5	6 915	1 874	16.5	21.3	30	32	138	.8	24 468	5 958	835	3.4
Caldwell	87.9	11.3	.4	6 410	1 762	22.7	30.2	76	61	228	2.3	14 676	2 898	571	3.9
Hays	94.9	3.8	.9	11 143	2 261	16.0	17.5	607	508	1 305	5.2	45 150	11 152	1 394	3.1
Travis	83.8	11.9	3.8	94 789	21 606	14.8	20.4	11 754	9 778	46 634	17.7	434 302	99 247	13 879	3.2
Williamson	92.4	5.4	1.9	16 616	4 165	9.6	10.9	4 610	3 386	12 669	23.3	115 538	37 035	2 336	2.0
Bakersfield, CA MSA (Kern)	87.5	6.4	4.4	130 629	37 050	21.8	27.6	2 767	3 496	25 503	12.8	278 981	16 979	35 454	12.7
Bangor, ME NECMA (Penobscot)	98.0	.4	.8	21 932	4 978	15.2	19.1	304	325	2 533	4.1	76 712	1 994	4 069	5.3
Barnstable-Yarmouth, MA NECMA (Barnstable)	96.7	1.9	.8	19 327	4 661	9.8	15.6	1 564	1 634	10 098	7.5	102 662	5 154	6 000	5.8
Baton Rouge, LA MSA	67.4	31.1	1.3	105 004	26 806	18.9	23.1	4 363	3 320	16 679	7.9	287 672	29 182	16 665	5.8
Ascension	74.8	24.6	.4	11 759	3 230	18.1	21.2	705	615	1 458	6.9	31 166	4 666	2 102	6.7
East Baton Rouge	61.0	37.0	1.8	77 117	19 299	19.7	24.7	2 499	1 809	11 896	7.6	207 894	17 484	10 944	5.3
Livingston	93.4	6.1	.2	12 078	3 218	15.3	17.7	1 054	801	2 704	10.1	38 844	6 230	2 978	7.7
West Baton Rouge	61.0	38.6	.1	4 050	1 059	20.0	24.3	105	95	621	8.5	9 768	802	641	6.6
Beaumont-Port Arthur, TX MSA	73.0	24.6	2.1	67 370	18 032	18.0	23.6	680	592	5 102	3.4	180 921	10 879	16 479	9.1
Hardin	90.4	9.0	.2	6 569	1 733	14.2	17.0	15	18	145	.9	22 130	3 025	1 819	8.2
Jefferson	63.7	33.1	2.9	47 542	12 858	19.6	26.8	453	375	2 965	2.9	117 391	4 739	10 170	8.7
Orange	90.0	8.9	.8	13 259	3 441	15.6	19.0	212	199	1 992	6.2	41 400	3 115	4 490	10.8
Bellingham, WA MSA (Whatcom)	93.8	.6	2.3	16 994	3 480	11.8	12.7	1 288	1 348	11 612	20.8	79 080	11 526	5 948	7.5
Benton Harbor, MI MSA (Berrien)	81.8	16.6	1.2	28 406	8 355	17.6	26.1	698	547	3 910	5.6	82 139	1 210	4 889	6.0
Billings, MT MSA (Yellowstone)	95.7	.6	.6	15 547	3 401	12.6	13.8	547	515	3 126	6.4	68 216	6 568	2 998	4.4
Biloxi-Gulfport-Pascagoula, MS MSA	77.6	19.9	2.3	63 343	16 777	18.8	25.1	2 197	2 320	11 893	9.2	161 715	21 295	8 478	5.2
Hancock	89.5	9.4	.7	7 646	1 977	20.9	29.5	59	84	623	3.8	16 125	3 242	931	5.8
Harrison	75.7	20.7	3.3	35 005	9 243	20.2	27.8	1 397	1 586	7 225	10.7	80 588	8 358	3 957	4.9
Jackson	76.6	21.9	1.2	20 692	5 557	16.3	20.7	741	650	4 045	8.9	65 002	9 695	3 590	5.5
Binghamton, NY MSA	95.8	2.0	2.1	31 332	7 433	12.1	16.3	209	234	2 286	2.1	121 565	-10 676	5 405	4.4
Broome	95.1	2.3	2.4	25 455	5 888	12.4	17.1	142	132	1 612	1.8	96 267	-9 489	4 218	4.4
Tioga	98.3	.7	.8	5 877	1 545	10.9	13.9	67	102	674	3.3	25 298	-1 187	1 187	4.7
Birmingham, AL MSA	70.3	28.9	.6	148 031	33 740	16.8	21.9	6 699	5 998	33 761	9.7	448 257	45 471	14 348	3.2
Blount	98.2	1.4	.1	6 276	1 346	15.0	18.3	73	42	241	1.5	21 482	2 502	701	3.3
Jefferson	62.8	36.5	.6	123 089	28 049	18.6	24.5	4 164	4 131	22 760	8.3	329 422	21 504	11 349	3.4
St. Clair	89.8	9.7	.2	8 907	2 057	16.2	19.9	328	157	1 270	6.2	28 106	4 943	918	3.3
Shelby	90.8	8.3	.7	9 759	2 288	8.1	10.3	2 134	1 668	9 490	24.2	69 247	16 522	1 380	2.0
Bismarck, ND MSA	96.6	.1	.5	9 209	2 014	10.5	10.8	499	515	4 245	12.8	52 357	8 513	1 527	2.9
Burleigh	96.2	.2	.6	6 312	1 304	9.9	9.8	380	419	3 340	14.0	38 646	6 552	1 026	2.7
Morton	97.6	.1	.3	2 897	710	11.9	13.1	119	96	905	9.6	13 711	1 961	501	3.7
Bloomington, IN MSA (Monroe)	93.8	2.9	3.1	14 160	1 966	14.0	13.6	879	979	6 516	15.5	60 880	6 565	1 666	2.7
Bloomington-Normal, IL MSA (McLean)	93.5	4.7	1.6	11 366	2 194	8.8	9.5	1 214	1 289	8 053	16.4	79 366	7 626	2 489	3.1
Boise City, ID MSA	97.3	.5	1.5	39 781	8 491	11.5	11.8	4 538	4 675	32 756	28.7	206 286	52 579	8 071	3.9
Ada	97.2	.6	1.5	22 079	4 258	9.1	8.7	3 151	3 460	25 723	31.8	149 775	38 868	5 022	3.4
Canyon	97.4	.4	1.4	17 702	4 233	17.0	18.3	1 387	1 215	7 033	21.2	56 511	13 711	3 049	5.4
Boston-Worcester-Lawrence-Lowell-Brockton, MA-NH NECMA	90.7	5.7	3.4	602 998	149 821	10.6	15.7	16 612	15 437	105 651	4.7	3 069 370	-40 370	130 312	4.2
Bristol, MA	96.3	2.2	1.3	59 590	16 045	11.6	17.1	1 675	1 498	11 630	5.8	261 299	-3 712	18 287	7.0
Essex, MA	93.3	4.3	2.2	84 852	23 224	12.4	19.9	1 755	2 030	11 716	4.3	354 277	4 329	15 534	4.4
Middlesex, MA	91.2	3.5	5.2	117 548	25 845	8.5	12.2	3 405	2 852	21 244	3.9	789 907	-12 403	25 545	3.2
Norfolk, MA	93.4	2.4	4.1	39 511	8 003	6.3	8.2	1 544	1 739	10 748	4.5	347 860	3 002	11 882	3.4
Plymouth, MA	93.7	4.9	1.2	43 847	11 657	9.7	13.3	1 695	1 474	10 599	6.3	236 402	6 518	11 498	4.9
Suffolk, MA	65.6	27.2	6.7	120 961	32 849	19.4	37.7	266	262	1 672	.6	331 089	-19 092	15 056	4.5
Worcester, MA	94.7	2.8	2.3	80 065	20 205	11.3	15.8	3 108	2 738	18 731	6.7	360 469	-4 798	15 446	4.3
Hillsborough, NH	97.4	1.0	1.5	30 302	6 629	8.7	10.2	1 708	1 330	9 018	6.6	187 828	-12 761	7 470	4.0
Rockingham, NH	97.7	1.0	1.2	16 483	3 331	6.4	6.8	1 178	1 233	8 411	8.3	143 431	-413	7 207	5.0
Strafford, NH	98.0	.6	1.2	9 839	2 033	9.6	11.1	278	281	1 882	4.4	56 808	-1 040	2 387	4.2
Brownsville-Harlingen-San Benito, TX MSA (Cameron)	99.0	.4	.4	115 790	37 148	38.5	49.4	2 532	2 025	10 440	11.8	124 276	20 174	15 615	12.6
Bryan-College Station, TX MSA (Brazos)	83.1	12.0	4.6	23 973	4 267	19.9	21.6	1 340	1 008	5 587	11.4	69 463	7 885	1 715	2.5
Buffalo-Niagara Falls, NY MSA	86.6	11.4	1.3	176 727	42 777	14.9	20.8	2 973	2 387	20 981	4.3	572 250	-18 780	29 227	5.1
Erie	85.3	12.6	1.4	148 561	35 294	15.4	21.4	2 336	1 821	16 163	4.0	463 941	-17 093	22 562	4.9
Niagara	92.4	6.1	.5	28 166	7 483	12.6	18.3	637	566	4 818	5.3	108 309	-1 687	6 665	6.2
Burlington, VT NECMA	97.2	.9	1.4	19 732	4 046	10.8	11.9	871	895	5 965	8.1	111 096	10 364	3 899	3.5
Chittenden	96.9	1.1	1.8	12 899	2 253	9.8	9.7	598	651	4 394	8.4	85 336	8 299	2 540	3.0
Franklin	98.0	.3	.4	6 173	1 625	13.9	17.0	232	212	1 387	8.0	22 627	1 746	1 135	5.0
Grand Isle	98.7	.4	.3	660	168	10.9	14.9	41	32	184	4.4	3 133	319	224	7.1
Canton-Massillon, OH MSA	92.2	7.0	.5	51 341	13 079	12.8	17.8	1 230	1 228	9 005	5.7	200 972	5 105	10 797	5.4
Carroll	99.1	.5	.1	3 763	939	13.5	16.5	17	22	119	1.0	12 936	773	701	5.4
Stark	91.7	7.5	.5	47 578	12 140	12.7	17.9	1 213	1 206	8 886	6.0	188 036	4 332	10 096	5.4

[1]Unemployment as a percent of civilian labor force.

Source: Population by Race—U.S. Bureau of the Census, "County Population Estimates by Age, Sex, Race, and Hispanic Origin - 4/1/90 to 7/1/96" data file (related Internet site <http://www.census.gov/population/www/estimates/co_casrh.html>); Poverty—U.S. Bureau of the Census, "State and County Income and Poverty Estimates - 1993," Internet site <http://www.census.gov/ftp/pub/housing/saipe/est93ALL.dat> (accessed 16 January 1998); Building Permits—U.S. Bureau of the Census, "Construction–Building Permits" on diskette, annual (related Internet site <http://www.census.gov/const/www/C40/table3.html#annual>), and "1990 Census of Population and Housing, Summary Tape File 1C" on CD-ROM; Labor Force—U.S. Bureau of Labor Statistics, Local Area Unemployment Statistics - Time Series, Internet site <gopher://hopi2.gov:70/11/Time%20Series/LA%20%20Local%20Area%20Unemployment%20Statistics/Data> for each state (accessed April 1997), BLS gopher service discontinued October 31, 1997 (related BLS Internet site <http://www.bls.gov>).

[MSA = Metropolitan statistical area.   CMSA = Consolidated MSA.   PMSA = Primary MSA.   NECMA = New England county metropolitan area.   All areas defined as of June 30, 1996.   Table includes 245 MSAs, 17 CMSAs, and 58 PMSAs not in New England; 12 NECMAs; and 844 component counties]

Metropolitan areas and component counties	Population by race, 1996, percent—			Persons below poverty level, 1993				New private housing units authorized by building permits				Civilian labor force, 1996			
				Number		Percent		1990–1996 period						Unemployment	
	White	Black	Asian or Pacific Islander	All persons	Related children 5 to 17 years	All persons	Related children 5 to 17 years	1996	1995	Total units	Percent of 1990 housing stock	Total	Net change, 1990–1996	Total	Rate[1]
Casper, WY MSA (Natrona)	97.9	.8	.6	8 747	1 975	13.6	15.2	172	69	507	1.7	32 990	1 094	2 095	6.4
Cedar Rapids, IA MSA (Linn)	96.5	2.2	1.1	16 551	3 556	9.3	11.1	1 092	1 264	7 640	11.2	109 391	12 782	3 206	2.9
Champaign-Urbana, IL MSA (Champaign)	83.4	10.6	5.8	20 515	3 867	13.3	15.3	654	655	4 275	6.2	93 310	2 355	2 923	3.1
Charleston-North Charleston, SC MSA .	67.0	31.1	1.6	85 825	22 334	16.5	22.7	2 792	2 262	20 359	10.2	241 519	5 123	13 283	5.5
Berkeley	72.1	24.9	2.6	18 603	5 196	13.2	16.7	420	307	4 059	8.9	59 617	3 664	2 764	4.6
Charleston	62.4	36.3	1.2	55 674	14 443	19.3	29.5	2 053	1 706	12 900	10.4	139 554	-2 036	8 380	6.0
Dorchester	74.2	23.9	1.2	11 548	2 695	12.8	14.7	319	249	3 400	11.1	42 348	3 495	2 139	5.1
Charleston, WV MSA	93.8	5.5	.6	47 408	10 727	18.5	25.3	518	408	3 294	3.0	130 268	13 812	7 051	5.4
Kanawha	92.4	6.8	.7	41 409	9 261	19.9	27.7	96	101	891	1.0	105 421	9 002	5 712	5.4
Putnam.......................	99.2	.3	.3	5 999	1 466	12.3	16.3	422	307	2 403	14.2	24 847	4 810	1 339	5.4
Charlotte-Gastonia-Rock Hill, NC-SC MSA	77.7	20.4	1.4	153 127	33 519	12.1	15.1	18 458	13 777	85 796	18.1	735 177	83 020	26 996	3.7
Cabarrus, NC	86.0	13.1	.6	10 616	2 152	9.8	11.6	1 917	1 311	8 007	20.2	61 886	6 631	2 059	3.3
Gaston, NC	85.6	13.3	.8	23 928	5 274	13.2	16.0	779	931	6 149	8.9	101 333	6 113	5 255	5.2
Lincoln, NC	90.8	8.3	.5	5 151	1 211	9.2	12.1	406	395	2 585	12.8	31 819	3 738	1 594	5.0
Mecklenburg, NC	70.6	26.6	2.4	71 987	15 572	12.7	16.3	10 443	7 706	47 907	22.1	340 942	43 605	10 145	3.0
Rowan, NC	82.7	16.4	.6	13 571	2 900	11.7	14.5	590	581	3 623	7.8	63 523	5 152	2 273	3.6
Union, NC	82.9	16.2	.4	10 362	2 466	10.8	13.0	1 856	1 514	9 187	29.9	54 788	8 594	1 378	2.5
York, SC	78.1	20.7	.7	17 512	3 944	12.4	15.4	2 467	1 339	8 338	16.5	80 886	9 187	4 292	5.3
Charlottesville, VA MSA	81.4	15.9	2.5	17 398	3 356	13.0	15.8	1 213	1 144	8 956	17.2	71 512	3 881	1 826	2.6
Albemarle....................	85.5	11.2	3.2	5 786	1 162	8.6	10.3	682	569	5 000	19.3	36 720	1 704	809	2.2
Fluvanna	75.0	24.6	.2	1 448	368	9.3	13.5	322	364	2 167	43.0	7 982	1 610	220	2.8
Greene	92.2	7.3	.4	1 385	389	10.8	16.5	178	178	1 262	30.4	6 742	1 101	210	3.1
Charlottesville city	73.2	23.6	3.1	8 779	1 437	22.7	29.7	31	33	527	3.1	20 068	-534	587	2.9
Chattanooga, TN-GA MSA	84.4	14.4	.9	73 474	16 892	16.7	21.7	2 669	2 449	14 518	8.2	220 908	13 100	10 111	4.6
Hamilton, TN	78.4	20.2	1.2	51 744	11 699	17.7	23.2	1 661	1 526	9 799	8.0	148 695	8 355	6 417	4.3
Marion, TN...................	95.2	4.5	.2	5 035	1 227	19.0	24.3	187	152	1 246	12.4	12 388	1 097	776	6.3
Catoosa, GA	98.2	1.0	.6	5 898	1 368	12.6	16.0	572	519	1 743	10.4	23 927	2 576	1 069	4.5
Dade, GA....................	98.4	.8	.3	2 206	510	16.3	19.4	4	12	35	.7	6 645	385	321	4.8
Walker, GA	94.9	4.5	.4	8 591	2 088	14.3	18.6	245	240	1 695	7.3	29 253	687	1 528	5.2
Cheyenne, WY MSA (Laramie)	94.7	3.1	1.4	8 967	1 880	11.5	12.8	664	298	2 027	6.6	39 367	2 679	1 432	3.6
Chicago-Gary-Kenosha, IL-IN-WI CMSA	76.6	19.3	3.9	1 169 550	310 437	13.7	19.8	38 928	36 769	240 572	7.6	4 479 238	133 956	225 152	5.0
Chicago, IL PMSA	76.0	19.5	4.3	1 054 987	278 910	13.7	20.0	34 086	32 425	209 011	7.3	4 051 277	105 811	203 865	5.0
Cook........................	68.2	26.9	4.7	908 002	245 432	17.6	27.3	9 556	8 862	59 406	2.9	2 623 423	-29 336	144 722	5.5
DeKalb	94.3	2.7	2.8	6 533	985	8.7	7.9	454	516	3 435	12.6	45 768	2 523	1 952	4.3
Du Page	91.2	2.2	6.5	32 449	6 398	3.8	4.1	5 580	5 007	33 600	11.5	498 796	36 120	16 872	3.4
Grundy	99.2	.1	.5	2 009	425	5.7	5.9	340	321	2 041	16.1	17 976	979	1 200	6.7
Kane	91.4	6.6	1.8	29 430	7 635	8.4	10.5	4 714	3 705	26 155	23.5	195 795	20 130	9 660	4.9
Kendall	98.4	.6	.8	1 700	367	3.8	3.7	679	831	3 437	25.0	25 433	3 189	1 052	4.1
Lake	89.5	7.1	3.1	36 265	8 465	6.5	7.8	4 618	5 348	33 044	18.0	303 940	26 127	12 224	4.0
McHenry.....................	98.7	.2	.9	8 267	1 768	3.8	4.0	2 900	3 249	19 976	30.3	124 775	20 426	5 038	4.0
Will	86.4	11.6	1.7	30 332	7 435	7.6	8.7	5 445	4 586	27 917	22.7	215 371	25 653	11 145	5.2
Gary, IN PMSA	78.8	20.2	.8	86 381	23 938	13.8	19.1	3 191	3 027	20 911	9.1	299 695	13 210	15 565	5.2
Lake	73.0	26.0	.8	77 284	21 906	15.9	22.5	1 935	1 830	12 690	6.9	227 178	6 068	12 809	5.6
Porter	98.4	.4	1.0	9 097	2 032	6.6	7.2	1 256	1 197	8 221	17.4	72 517	7 142	2 756	3.8
Kankakee, IL PMSA (Kankakee)	82.6	16.3	.9	13 306	3 645	13.3	17.5	534	533	3 475	9.4	51 872	4 624	3 015	5.8
Kenosha, WI PMSA (Kenosha)	93.9	5.0	.7	14 876	3 944	10.8	14.8	1 117	784	7 115	14.0	76 394	10 311	2 707	3.5
Chico-Paradise, CA MSA (Butte)........	92.9	1.4	3.7	36 375	8 095	19.0	24.3	673	728	7 364	9.7	82 909	3 450	7 432	9.0
Cincinnati-Hamilton, OH-KY-IN CMSA ..	87.3	11.5	1.0	233 089	61 890	12.3	17.3	12 354	11 284	78 325	10.8	986 196	51 470	41 679	4.2
Cincinnati, OH-KY-IN PMSA	86.0	12.9	1.0	202 055	54 015	12.8	18.1	9 548	9 069	62 815	10.3	819 571	34 064	34 820	4.2
Brown, OH	98.5	1.3	.1	5 427	1 466	14.1	18.0	44	36	321	2.3	18 523	1 819	1 116	6.0
Clermont, OH	98.5	1.0	.4	15 648	4 161	9.4	12.0	1 445	1 687	9 959	18.0	88 502	8 790	3 992	4.5
Hamilton, OH.................	75.9	22.6	1.4	125 140	34 923	14.5	22.2	2 050	2 011	18 385	5.1	440 671	1 841	17 939	4.1
Warren, OH	96.7	2.4	.7	9 039	2 237	7.3	9.3	2 265	1 765	11 329	27.9	68 697	8 734	2 641	3.8
Boone, KY	98.3	.7	.8	5 686	1 304	8.3	9.4	1 523	1 489	7 880	36.7	38 082	6 055	1 560	4.1
Campbell, KY	98.4	1.0	.4	11 242	2 690	12.9	17.0	395	536	4 344	13.2	44 658	1 025	1 987	4.4
Gallatin, KY	97.9	1.8	.2	1 051	256	17.2	21.2	5	49	170	7.4	3 068	346	180	5.9
Grant, KY	99.6	.2	.2	2 892	734	15.9	19.6	219	212	923	14.1	9 100	1 328	547	6.0
Kenton, KY	96.3	3.0	.6	19 293	4 618	13.2	16.8	1 028	742	6 213	11.1	77 097	706	3 224	4.2
Pendleton, KY	99.3	.4	.1	2 264	582	17.0	21.8	4	3	31	.6	6 338	595	331	5.2
Dearborn, IN	98.8	.7	.3	3 814	929	8.7	10.4	501	491	2 902	20.0	22 172	2 772	1 162	5.2
Ohio, IN	98.9	.8	.2	559	115	10.1	10.9	69	48	358	16.6	2 663	53	141	5.3
Hamilton-Middletown, OH PMSA (Butler)	93.7	5.0	1.2	31 034	7 875	9.9	13.2	2 806	2 215	15 510	14.1	166 625	17 406	6 859	4.1

[1]Unemployment as a percent of civilian labor force.

Source: Population by Race—U.S. Bureau of the Census, "County Population Estimates by Age, Sex, Race, and Hispanic Origin - 4/1/90 to 7/1/96" data file (related Internet site <http://www.census.gov/population/www/estimates/co_casrh.html>);   Poverty—U.S. Bureau of the Census, "State and County Income and Poverty Estimates - 1993," Internet site <http://www.census.gov/ftp/pub/housing/saipe/est93ALL.dat> (accessed 16 January 1998);   Building Permits—U.S. Bureau of the Census, "Construction–Building Permits" on diskette, annual (related Internet site <http://www.census.gov/const/www/C40/table3.html#annual>), and "1990 Census of Population and Housing, Summary Tape File 1C" on CD-ROM;   Labor Force—U.S. Bureau of Labor Statistics, Local Area Unemployment Statistics - Time Series, Internet site <gopher://hopi2.gov:70/11/Time%20Series/LA%20%20Local%20Area%20Unemployment%20Statistics/Data> for each state (accessed April 1997), BLS gopher service discontinued October 31, 1997 (related BLS Internet site <http://www.bls.gov>).

Table C–2. Metro Counties — # Population by Race, Poverty, Building Permits, and Labor Force—Con.

[MSA = Metropolitan statistical area. CMSA = Consolidated MSA. PMSA = Primary MSA. NECMA = New England county metropolitan area. All areas defined as of June 30, 1996. Table includes 245 MSAs, 17 CMSAs, and 58 PMSAs not in New England; 12 NECMAs; and 844 component counties]

Metropolitan areas and component counties	Population by race, 1996, percent—			Persons below poverty level, 1993				New private housing units authorized by building permits				Civilian labor force, 1996			
				Number		Percent				1990–1996 period				Unemployment	
	White	Black	Asian or Pacific Islander	All persons	Related children 5 to 17 years	All persons	Related children 5 to 17 years	1996	1995	Total units	Percent of 1990 housing stock	Total	Net change, 1990–1996	Total	Rate[1]
Clarksville-Hopkinsville, TN-KY MSA ...	76.5	20.8	2.3	28 681	7 285	16.4	22.0	2 091	2 326	13 017	21.5	78 453	13 647	3 270	4.2
Montgomery, TN..............	78.4	18.6	2.6	16 753	4 143	14.5	19.2	1 796	2 119	11 369	30.5	54 170	13 832	2 115	3.9
Christian, KY	72.9	24.9	1.8	11 928	3 142	20.0	27.1	295	207	1 648	7.0	24 283	−185	1 155	4.8
Cleveland-Akron, OH CMSA	82.0	16.5	1.3	426 681	111 857	14.6	21.6	11 295	10 632	71 766	6.2	1 464 303	38 977	74 059	5.1
Akron, OH PMSA	87.8	10.8	1.2	90 906	22 444	13.5	19.1	3 898	3 092	23 286	8.8	359 937	26 482	16 622	4.6
Portage....................	95.8	2.9	1.0	15 157	3 433	10.6	13.0	1 043	799	5 636	10.8	81 912	6 619	3 645	4.4
Summit....................	85.6	13.0	1.2	75 749	19 011	14.3	20.8	2 855	2 293	17 650	8.3	278 025	19 863	12 977	4.7
Cleveland-Lorain-Elyria, OH PMSA .	80.3	18.3	1.3	335 775	89 413	15.0	22.4	7 397	7 540	48 480	5.4	1 104 366	12 495	57 437	5.2
Ashtabula..................	95.9	3.5	.5	17 042	4 673	16.8	23.4	320	299	1 838	4.5	46 528	865	3 333	7.2
Cuyahoga..................	71.6	26.6	1.6	256 924	69 036	18.1	29.0	2 580	2 570	18 439	3.1	678 763	−4 254	34 973	5.2
Geauga	97.9	1.4	.5	5 038	1 451	6.0	8.4	597	565	3 521	12.6	44 295	1 440	1 583	3.6
Lake	97.2	1.8	.9	16 381	3 529	7.3	8.8	1 027	1 444	7 414	8.9	122 213	3 565	5 406	4.4
Lorain	90.2	8.9	.7	32 542	8 770	11.7	15.8	1 368	1 250	8 011	8.0	140 103	4 018	8 935	6.4
Medina	98.3	.8	.7	7 848	1 954	5.8	6.9	1 505	1 412	9 257	21.4	72 464	6 861	3 207	4.4
Colorado Springs, CO MSA (El Paso) ..	88.2	7.7	3.2	53 863	12 631	12.1	14.0	5 292	4 725	22 669	13.7	238 755	47 890	11 084	4.6
Columbia, MO MSA (Boone) ...	87.5	8.6	3.6	15 830	2 973	14.0	15.5	1 638	1 353	9 197	20.6	78 157	10 947	1 320	1.7
Columbia, SC MSA	68.3	30.2	1.3	67 005	14 812	14.4	17.8	3 893	3 546	22 869	12.9	258 607	14 955	9 550	3.7
Lexington	87.7	11.4	.8	18 684	4 053	9.8	11.4	1 508	1 384	9 981	14.8	109 442	12 965	3 633	3.3
Richland	55.3	42.8	1.7	48 321	10 759	17.6	22.5	2 385	2 162	12 888	11.8	149 165	1 990	5 917	4.0
Columbus, GA-AL MSA...........	58.3	39.6	1.8	55 181	14 787	20.9	29.1	1 256	1 442	9 183	9.1	116 730	7 468	5 989	5.1
Chattahoochee, GA	63.6	31.6	4.1	1 486	419	14.7	13.3	9	10	58	1.9	2 120	−144	159	7.5
Harris, GA	70.5	28.8	.4	2 565	611	12.9	16.7	379	339	2 175	27.8	10 048	1 345	339	3.4
Muscogee, GA	56.2	41.3	2.1	40 606	11 185	22.2	32.4	639	785	5 469	7.7	80 013	3 196	4 345	5.4
Russell, AL	59.3	40.2	.3	10 524	2 572	20.4	27.3	229	308	1 481	7.5	24 549	3 071	1 146	4.7
Columbus, OH MSA...............	84.8	13.1	1.9	173 701	44 881	12.4	18.0	12 147	10 652	72 775	13.3	794 045	66 016	24 645	3.1
Delaware	96.8	2.4	.7	4 884	1 084	6.5	7.3	2 293	1 802	10 266	42.1	44 333	7 745	1 637	3.7
Fairfield	98.1	1.2	.5	9 369	2 490	8.2	10.8	820	705	5 662	14.5	61 198	7 864	2 194	3.6
Franklin	79.9	17.3	2.5	134 168	35 080	13.4	20.7	7 261	6 751	47 849	11.8	574 016	40 960	16 605	2.9
Licking	97.4	1.9	.5	15 565	3 898	11.6	15.2	1 308	988	6 138	12.3	70 498	4 890	2 652	3.8
Madison	90.4	8.8	.5	3 793	893	10.6	12.7	218	165	1 423	11.3	20 073	2 207	622	3.1
Pickaway	92.3	7.2	.3	5 922	1 436	13.0	16.1	247	241	1 437	8.8	23 927	2 350	935	3.9
Corpus Christi, TX MSA	94.3	4.1	1.1	85 814	24 192	22.9	29.6	2 316	1 347	7 792	5.7	178 864	17 827	14 975	8.4
Nueces....................	93.9	4.4	1.2	70 512	19 650	22.7	29.4	1 572	1 129	6 196	5.4	149 987	13 931	12 547	8.4
San Patricio	96.4	2.6	.6	15 302	4 542	23.8	30.4	744	218	1 596	7.2	28 877	3 896	2 428	8.4
Cumberland, MD-WV MSA	96.9	2.6	.5	16 663	3 874	16.7	22.6	241	300	2 209	5.1	45 218	953	3 630	8.0
Allegany, MD...............	96.9	2.5	.6	11 977	2 785	16.5	22.5	133	163	1 306	4.0	33 359	847	2 917	8.7
Mineral, WV...............	96.9	2.8	.3	4 686	1 089	17.2	22.9	108	137	903	8.3	11 859	106	713	6.0
Dallas-Fort Worth, TX CMSA	81.8	14.2	3.4	655 268	164 662	14.9	20.0	38 808	36 657	197 538	11.6	2 597 111	288 445	103 917	4.0
Dallas, TX PMSA	80.1	15.8	3.5	455 292	114 064	15.6	20.8	28 673	27 123	147 763	13.0	1 757 883	211 743	70 900	4.0
Collin	91.2	4.4	3.9	20 967	5 046	6.3	7.5	8 545	7 048	42 613	41.0	215 713	54 544	5 728	2.7
Dallas	74.8	20.7	3.9	358 873	92 115	18.3	25.8	13 165	15 108	77 973	9.8	1 168 301	95 460	51 687	4.4
Denton	90.6	5.3	3.5	26 890	5 225	8.4	8.8	5 767	4 114	21 895	19.5	211 508	41 700	5 975	2.8
Ellis.....................	88.6	10.5	.4	13 339	3 357	14.4	16.3	447	273	1 716	5.5	49 994	6 087	2 194	4.4
Henderson	90.8	8.5	.4	11 660	2 637	18.7	24.0	86	99	451	1.4	28 376	2 418	1 476	5.2
Hunt	87.6	11.2	.8	11 654	2 683	17.8	21.5	106	64	504	1.7	35 038	2 549	2 090	6.0
Kaufman..................	84.5	14.4	.7	9 399	2 427	16.2	19.2	137	168	963	4.8	29 839	4 507	1 205	4.0
Rockwall..................	95.0	3.6	.9	2 510	574	7.9	8.3	420	249	1 648	16.8	19 114	4 478	545	2.9
Fort Worth-Arlington, TX PMSA.....	85.2	11.1	3.1	199 976	50 598	13.6	18.3	10 135	9 534	49 775	8.7	839 228	76 702	33 017	3.9
Hood	98.3	.2	.9	3 810	832	11.9	14.2	118	173	413	2.8	15 279	1 503	736	4.8
Johnson	95.5	3.3	.7	14 711	3 781	14.1	16.8	312	268	1 791	4.8	55 039	5 265	2 464	4.5
Parker....................	97.7	1.0	.5	8 900	2 116	12.5	14.4	219	227	864	3.3	37 636	4 826	1 371	3.6
Tarrant...................	83.3	12.6	3.5	172 555	43 869	13.7	18.8	9 486	8 866	46 707	9.5	731 274	65 108	28 446	3.9
Danville, VA MSA...............	65.5	34.0	.4	18 511	4 351	16.8	22.9	364	366	2 823	6.1	56 829	572	4 231	7.4
Pittsylvania	70.5	29.2	.1	7 777	1 729	13.7	16.9	322	316	2 203	9.6	30 453	206	2 086	6.8
Danville city	60.3	38.9	.6	10 734	2 622	20.1	29.9	42	50	620	2.7	26 376	366	2 145	8.1
Davenport-Moline-Rock Island, IA-IL MSA	92.8	6.0	.9	44 778	11 135	12.5	16.1	1 280	901	6 274	4.3	182 919	6 877	8 010	4.4
Scott, IA	92.7	5.8	1.2	19 987	5 049	12.7	16.2	676	529	3 691	6.0	84 485	5 879	3 277	3.9
Henry, IL	98.1	1.5	.3	5 449	1 315	10.5	12.6	113	147	766	3.7	25 781	404	1 379	5.3
Rock Island, IL	91.1	7.8	.9	19 342	4 771	13.0	17.2	491	225	1 817	2.9	72 653	594	3 354	4.6
Dayton-Springfield, OH MSA	84.2	14.3	1.2	122 039	32 279	12.8	18.8	4 098	3 203	22 790	5.9	474 379	−2 413	21 267	4.5
Clark	89.5	9.7	.6	21 113	5 713	14.4	21.1	502	412	3 537	6.1	70 891	−314	4 006	5.7
Greene	89.9	7.8	2.0	12 636	3 098	9.3	11.8	757	944	5 917	11.8	69 310	1 309	2 693	3.9
Miami	96.9	2.1	.9	9 070	2 191	9.3	11.7	377	356	2 423	6.7	50 208	956	2 109	4.2
Montgomery	79.3	19.2	1.3	79 220	21 277	13.9	21.3	2 462	1 491	10 913	4.5	283 970	−4 364	12 459	4.4
Daytona Beach, FL MSA..............	88.1	10.5	1.2	65 615	13 358	15.0	20.4	3 455	3 600	25 859	13.2	188 251	8 559	7 841	4.2
Flagler	88.5	9.8	1.5	4 161	887	10.9	15.4	976	840	5 577	36.7	14 971	3 245	507	3.4
Volusia	88.0	10.5	1.1	61 454	12 471	15.4	20.9	2 479	2 760	20 282	11.2	173 280	5 314	7 334	4.2

[1]Unemployment as a percent of civilian labor force.

Source: Population by Race—U.S. Bureau of the Census, "County Population Estimates by Age, Sex, Race, and Hispanic Origin - 4/1/90 to 7/1/96" data file (related Internet site <http://www.census.gov/population/www/estimates/co_casrh.html>); Poverty—U.S. Bureau of the Census, "State and County Income and Poverty Estimates - 1993," Internet site <http://www.census.gov/ftp/pub/housing/saipe/est93ALL.dat> (accessed 16 January 1998); Building Permits—U.S. Bureau of the Census, "Construction–Building Permits" on diskette, annual (related Internet site <http://www.census.gov/const/www/C40/table3.html#annual>), and "1990 Census of Population and Housing, Summary Tape File 1C" on CD-ROM; Labor Force—U.S. Bureau of Labor Statistics, Local Area Unemployment Statistics - Time Series, Internet site <gopher://hopi2.gov:70/11/Time%20Series/LA%20%20Local%20Area%20Unemployment%20Statistics/Data> for each state (accessed April 1997), BLS gopher service discontinued October 31, 1997 (related BLS Internet site <http://www.bls.gov>).

[MSA = Metropolitan statistical area. CMSA = Consolidated MSA. PMSA = Primary MSA. NECMA = New England county metropolitan area. All areas defined as of June 30, 1996. Table includes 245 MSAs, 17 CMSAs, and 58 PMSAs not in New England; 12 NECMAs; and 844 component counties]

Metropolitan areas and component counties	Population by race, 1996, percent—			Persons below poverty level, 1993				New private housing units authorized by building permits				Civilian labor force, 1996			
				Number		Percent				1990–1996 period			Unemployment		
	White	Black	Asian or Pacific Islander	All persons	Related children 5 to 17 years	All persons	Related children 5 to 17 years	1996	1995	Total units	Percent of 1990 housing stock	Total	Net change, 1990–1996	Total	Rate[1]
Decatur, AL MSA	86.1	12.0	.4	19 449	4 361	14.1	17.2	663	508	3 865	7.3	69 511	4 548	3 563	5.1
Lawrence	78.0	16.4	.1	5 818	1 403	17.8	22.9	16	12	89	.7	15 714	719	1 031	6.6
Morgan	88.6	10.6	.5	13 631	2 958	12.9	15.4	647	496	3 776	9.3	53 797	3 829	2 532	4.7
Decatur, IL MSA (Macon)	86.2	13.2	.6	15 943	4 131	13.7	18.6	338	402	1 999	4.0	60 126	1 945	4 878	8.1
Denver-Boulder-Greeley, CO CMSA . . .	91.2	5.2	2.8	231 925	52 588	10.6	12.8	21 531	21 432	108 761	12.6	1 297 021	182 974	50 132	3.9
Boulder-Longmont, CO PMSA (Boulder)	95.4	1.0	3.0	20 547	3 579	8.3	8.6	2 744	3 094	17 337	18.3	162 096	28 168	6 116	3.8
Denver, CO PMSA	90.1	6.2	2.9	189 454	43 693	10.5	12.9	16 931	16 868	84 820	11.8	1 054 691	141 168	40 295	3.8
Adams	92.2	3.6	3.3	38 231	9 358	12.9	15.1	2 894	3 360	14 366	13.4	167 403	22 972	7 020	4.2
Arapahoe	89.5	6.3	3.6	29 846	6 285	6.7	7.1	3 721	3 556	18 689	11.1	263 600	38 543	8 403	3.2
Denver	81.3	14.3	3.0	89 003	21 558	18.0	29.0	1 432	786	6 176	2.6	274 043	21 842	13 506	4.9
Douglas	97.7	.8	1.0	2 490	537	2.8	2.7	5 730	4 784	24 300	109.0	58 692	23 263	1 402	2.4
Jefferson	96.4	.8	2.2	29 884	5 955	6.2	6.4	3 154	4 382	21 289	11.9	290 964	34 548	9 964	3.4
Greeley, CO PMSA (Weld)	97.7	.5	1.1	21 924	5 316	15.3	17.7	1 856	1 470	6 604	12.9	80 234	13 638	3 721	4.6
Des Moines, IA MSA	93.5	4.1	2.1	41 327	9 010	9.8	12.0	3 395	3 280	21 672	13.5	257 347	31 427	7 224	2.8
Dallas	99.3	.2	.3	2 539	535	7.8	8.0	207	195	1 441	12.2	18 815	2 702	456	2.4
Polk	92.4	5.0	2.4	36 018	7 876	10.3	13.0	2 764	2 780	18 426	13.6	215 193	25 721	6 230	2.9
Warren	99.0	.3	.5	2 770	599	7.3	7.4	424	305	1 805	13.7	23 339	3 004	538	2.3
Detroit-Ann Arbor-Flint, MI CMSA	76.8	21.0	1.9	823 968	228 366	15.7	23.3	26 710	24 014	147 531	7.3	2 636 282	62 268	117 815	4.5
Ann Arbor, MI PMSA	89.0	7.3	3.3	46 218	9 914	9.3	10.9	4 881	4 078	25 378	13.5	278 146	15 111	8 095	2.9
Lenawee	96.6	2.2	.7	11 030	2 853	11.9	14.5	387	464	2 631	7.5	45 445	1 803	2 033	4.5
Livingston	98.3	.5	.6	6 644	1 589	5.1	5.8	1 982	1 608	10 492	25.1	70 575	9 004	2 277	3.2
Washtenaw	82.1	12.1	5.4	28 544	5 472	10.4	12.4	2 512	2 006	12 255	11.0	162 126	4 304	3 785	2.3
Detroit, MI PMSA	75.2	22.6	1.8	694 582	193 768	16.1	24.2	19 709	18 024	111 926	6.7	2 155 504	43 971	96 988	4.5
Lapeer	98.2	.8	.5	7 632	2 029	9.4	11.0	572	823	3 815	14.4	41 098	3 801	2 055	5.0
Macomb	96.3	1.6	1.7	54 297	12 723	7.4	10.0	5 429	4 788	29 455	10.7	401 630	10 008	16 992	4.2
Monroe	97.1	1.9	.6	13 114	3 739	9.4	12.8	740	846	4 981	10.3	69 997	2 640	2 766	4.0
Oakland	88.7	7.8	3.1	89 110	20 579	7.8	10.1	7 554	6 975	43 127	10.0	648 164	45 114	20 985	3.2
St. Clair	96.7	2.3	.4	19 759	5 204	12.8	16.7	1 021	1 054	6 323	11.0	75 947	3 817	4 056	5.3
Wayne	55.8	42.5	1.3	510 670	149 494	24.6	38.2	4 393	3 538	24 225	2.9	918 668	−21 409	50 134	5.5
Flint, MI PMSA (Genesee)	77.3	21.1	.9	83 168	24 684	19.0	27.9	2 120	1 912	10 227	6.0	202 632	3 186	12 732	6.3
Dothan, AL MSA	76.2	22.3	1.1	23 584	5 922	17.7	23.1	416	509	3 128	5.9	64 154	3 387	2 888	4.5
Dale	79.0	18.8	1.9	8 513	2 176	17.2	22.7	72	52	440	2.3	21 075	742	1 097	5.2
Houston	74.6	24.4	.7	15 071	3 746	18.0	23.3	344	457	2 688	8.1	43 079	2 645	1 791	4.2
Dover, DE MSA (Kent)	77.1	20.5	1.8	15 333	3 975	13.0	17.4	659	941	5 912	14.0	68 735	10 485	3 524	5.1
Dubuque, IA MSA (Dubuque)	98.8	.5	.7	8 901	1 995	10.2	11.3	331	458	2 787	8.7	50 481	4 489	2 892	5.7
Duluth-Superior, MN-WI MSA	96.6	.7	.8	34 345	7 871	14.4	17.1	692	777	5 331	4.6	123 110	10 726	6 937	5.6
St. Louis, MN	96.5	.7	.7	28 136	6 198	14.3	16.5	478	591	3 965	4.2	100 740	7 676	5 747	5.7
Douglas, WI	96.7	.5	.8	6 209	1 673	14.6	20.0	214	186	1 366	6.6	22 370	3 050	1 190	5.3
Eau Claire, WI MSA	97.0	.2	2.3	17 290	4 070	12.4	14.7	964	808	4 881	9.1	79 744	9 707	2 970	3.7
Chippewa	98.9	.1	.7	6 120	1 558	11.3	13.4	316	212	1 511	7.2	29 650	3 638	1 315	4.4
Eau Claire	95.8	.3	3.3	11 170	2 512	13.1	15.7	648	596	3 370	10.3	50 094	6 069	1 655	3.3
El Paso, TX MSA (El Paso)	94.4	3.6	1.4	201 749	60 352	30.2	39.6	3 333	2 629	18 961	10.1	290 447	30 849	33 643	11.6
Elkhart-Goshen, IN MSA (Elkhart)	93.9	5.0	.8	16 107	4 022	9.8	12.6	1 177	1 043	6 505	10.8	94 340	9 719	3 695	3.9
Elmira, NY MSA (Chemung)	92.6	6.1	1.0	12 739	3 300	13.9	18.8	114	125	876	2.3	43 963	−370	1 874	4.3
Enid, OK MSA (Garfield)	93.0	3.7	1.2	9 124	2 086	16.2	19.0	156	112	551	2.1	26 868	52	915	3.4
Erie, PA MSA (Erie)	93.1	6.0	.7	38 547	9 815	13.9	18.2	808	857	5 834	5.4	139 324	6 353	8 077	5.8
Eugene-Springfield, OR MSA (Lane) . . .	95.6	.9	2.4	44 779	8 788	15.0	16.3	2 169	2 769	12 548	10.8	158 958	11 691	9 221	5.8
Evansville-Henderson, IN-KY MSA	93.1	6.1	.6	35 720	8 227	12.5	16.0	1 417	1 398	8 508	7.2	155 259	12 301	6 953	4.5
Posey, IN	98.5	1.2	.1	2 162	464	8.1	8.8	69	63	539	5.2	13 847	1 016	508	3.7
Vanderburgh, IN	90.9	8.2	.7	23 208	5 305	14.0	19.2	662	596	4 190	5.8	90 375	6 156	3 713	4.1
Warrick, IN	98.4	.9	.5	3 501	823	7.1	8.2	401	532	2 636	15.6	27 252	3 848	1 031	3.8
Henderson, KY	92.1	7.3	.4	6 849	1 635	15.4	19.4	285	207	1 143	6.4	23 785	1 281	1 701	7.2
Fargo-Moorhead, ND-MN MSA	97.2	.4	1.3	18 263	3 608	11.6	12.1	1 205	1 648	10 242	16.8	97 788	12 273	2 400	2.5
Cass, ND	97.2	.3	1.4	10 238	1 882	9.4	9.5	1 061	1 436	8 577	20.2	68 324	10 193	1 172	1.7
Clay, MN	97.1	.4	1.1	8 025	1 726	16.4	17.4	144	212	1 665	9.0	29 464	2 080	1 228	4.2
Fayetteville, NC MSA (Cumberland)	63.1	31.9	3.1	42 177	11 162	15.5	19.9	1 633	1 905	15 279	15.5	112 872	9 559	5 302	4.7
Fayetteville-Springdale-Rogers, AR MSA	96.9	.9	.9	26 034	5 847	10.8	13.6	2 996	3 778	20 609	23.2	138 463	28 606	4 075	2.9
Benton	97.9	.1	.6	11 341	2 383	9.8	11.5	1 334	1 730	9 259	22.3	63 729	14 951	1 873	2.9
Washington	96.0	1.6	1.2	14 693	3 464	11.7	15.5	1 662	2 048	11 350	24.0	74 734	13 655	2 202	2.9
Flagstaff, AZ-UT MSA	68.8	1.7	1.1	23 834	6 347	21.7	24.2	1 477	1 418	6 592	14.3	61 184	10 136	5 236	8.6
Coconino, AZ	67.3	1.7	1.1	22 937	6 127	22.0	24.8	1 359	1 332	6 014	14.0	58 615	10 087	5 057	8.6
Kane, UT	97.8	.1	.6	897	220	15.6	14.3	118	86	578	17.9	2 569	49	179	7.0

[1]Unemployment as a percent of civilian labor force.

Source: Population by Race—U.S. Bureau of the Census, "County Population Estimates by Age, Sex, Race, and Hispanic Origin - 4/1/90 to 7/1/96" data file (related Internet site <http://www.census.gov/population/www/estimates/co_casrh.html>); Poverty—U.S. Bureau of the Census, "State and County Income and Poverty Estimates - 1993," Internet site <http://www.census.gov/ftp/pub/housing/saipe/est93ALL.dat> (accessed 16 January 1998); Building Permits—U.S. Bureau of the Census, "Construction–Building Permits" on diskette, annual (related Internet site <http://www.census.gov/const/www/C40/table3.html#annual>), and "1990 Census of Population and Housing, Summary Tape File 1C" on CD-ROM; Labor Force—U.S. Bureau of Labor Statistics, Local Area Unemployment Statistics - Time Series, Internet site <gopher://hopi2.gov:70/11/Time%20Series/LA%20%20Local%20Area%20Unemployment%20Statistics/Data> for each state (accessed April 1997), BLS gopher service discontinued October 31, 1997 (related BLS Internet site <http://www.bls.gov>).

[MSA = Metropolitan statistical area. CMSA = Consolidated MSA. PMSA = Primary MSA. NECMA = New England county metropolitan area. All areas defined as of June 30, 1996. Table includes 245 MSAs, 17 CMSAs, and 58 PMSAs not in New England; 12 NECMAs; and 844 component counties]

Metropolitan areas and component counties	Population by race, 1996, percent—			Persons below poverty level, 1993				New private housing units authorized by building permits				Civilian labor force, 1996			
				Number		Percent				1990–1996 period				Unemployment	
	White	Black	Asian or Pacific Islander	All persons	Related children 5 to 17 years	All persons	Related children 5 to 17 years	1996	1995	Total units	Percent of 1990 housing stock	Total	Net change, 1990–1996	Total	Rate[1]
Florence, AL MSA	86.5	13.0	.3	19 520	4 179	14.4	18.2	481	422	3 176	5.7	70 148	8 225	4 332	6.2
Colbert	82.1	17.5	.2	8 087	1 758	15.3	19.7	263	217	1 074	4.9	26 941	2 675	1 821	6.8
Lauderdale	89.3	10.2	.3	11 433	2 421	13.9	17.3	218	205	2 102	6.3	43 207	5 550	2 511	5.8
Florence, SC MSA (Florence)	59.9	39.6	.3	25 927	6 720	21.4	26.8	725	574	4 513	10.4	60 584	4 353	5 091	8.4
Fort Collins-Loveland, CO MSA (Larimer)	96.8	.7	1.8	22 804	4 061	10.8	10.1	3 491	2 797	16 815	21.6	133 108	29 204	5 068	3.8
Fort Myers-Cape Coral, FL MSA (Lee)	91.1	7.8	.9	45 396	9 841	12.3	18.3	5 710	5 002	33 653	17.8	170 212	15 908	6 378	3.7
Fort Pierce-Port St. Lucie, FL MSA	84.4	14.3	1.0	38 662	8 936	13.9	20.4	3 260	2 791	21 550	16.8	122 440	5 356	12 578	10.3
Martin	91.8	6.9	.9	11 637	2 291	10.8	15.8	1 306	1 122	8 205	15.1	46 396	1 120	3 329	7.2
St. Lucie	79.6	19.0	1.0	27 025	6 645	15.9	22.7	1 954	1 669	13 345	18.1	76 044	4 236	9 249	12.2
Fort Smith, AR-OK MSA	88.2	4.2	2.7	32 798	7 697	17.6	21.0	905	1 101	5 447	7.3	95 987	7 116	5 043	5.3
Crawford, AR	96.4	1.0	1.2	8 459	2 066	18.0	20.7	255	184	1 719	10.3	23 641	2 726	1 193	5.0
Sebastian, AR	88.3	6.3	4.1	15 957	3 496	15.4	18.2	562	843	3 374	7.7	55 883	3 401	2 775	5.0
Sequoyah, OK	77.2	2.4	.3	8 382	2 135	23.6	28.4	88	74	354	2.5	16 463	989	1 075	6.5
Fort Walton Beach, FL MSA (Okaloosa)	85.3	10.3	3.8	17 779	4 550	11.2	14.2	1 843	1 622	11 981	19.1	74 486	8 795	2 876	3.9
Fort Wayne, IN MSA	91.6	7.3	.9	48 302	11 495	10.2	12.4	2 816	2 756	17 562	9.7	262 499	20 173	9 315	3.5
Adams	99.4	.1	.3	4 065	1 196	12.6	16.5	138	131	919	8.4	16 402	1 223	663	4.0
Allen	87.5	11.0	1.2	34 863	8 212	11.2	13.8	1 900	1 889	11 877	9.7	173 664	12 415	6 135	3.5
De Kalb	99.3	.1	.4	2 742	623	7.2	8.0	279	245	1 406	10.3	21 199	2 196	745	3.5
Huntington	98.9	.2	.5	2 903	644	8.0	8.9	180	166	1 164	8.5	20 429	1 771	793	3.9
Wells	99.6	Z	.2	1 887	412	7.1	7.8	123	137	803	8.1	14 667	1 086	488	3.3
Whitley	99.4	.1	.2	1 842	408	6.3	6.9	196	188	1 393	12.8	16 138	1 482	491	3.0
Fresno, CA MSA	84.3	5.0	9.3	228 351	68 701	27.2	36.7	3 910	4 916	37 552	14.1	426 509	57 851	55 948	13.1
Fresno	83.1	5.2	10.4	206 784	62 629	28.1	38.3	3 290	4 056	30 856	13.1	374 983	47 699	48 661	13.0
Madera	92.7	3.4	1.9	21 567	6 072	20.9	25.8	620	860	6 696	21.7	51 526	10 152	7 287	14.1
Gadsden, AL MSA (Etowah)	84.8	14.5	.4	18 337	4 007	17.9	22.0	258	323	1 628	3.9	49 366	3 162	2 600	5.3
Gainesville, FL MSA (Alachua)	74.4	21.8	3.5	37 326	7 392	20.2	23.1	1 853	1 971	10 997	13.9	100 935	7 378	2 797	2.8
Glens Falls, NY MSA	97.3	2.0	.5	13 664	3 263	11.4	14.3	441	432	3 970	7.1	61 330	1 608	3 856	6.3
Warren	98.6	.6	.7	6 703	1 589	10.9	14.0	292	258	2 465	7.8	32 137	1 116	2 219	6.9
Washington	96.0	3.5	.3	6 961	1 674	11.9	14.5	149	174	1 505	6.2	29 193	492	1 637	5.6
Goldsboro, NC MSA (Wayne)	65.5	33.1	1.2	18 255	4 475	17.5	21.7	466	539	3 268	8.3	48 342	458	2 323	4.8
Grand Forks, ND-MN MSA	95.1	1.7	1.3	13 873	2 956	13.9	14.7	268	475	2 059	5.0	55 089	–7 117	1 878	3.4
Grand Forks, ND	93.8	2.3	1.8	8 417	1 614	12.5	12.4	190	423	1 582	5.8	38 133	–4 297	911	2.4
Polk, MN	97.9	.3	.4	5 456	1 342	16.9	18.9	78	52	477	3.3	16 956	–2 820	967	5.7
Grand Junction, CO MSA (Mesa)	97.9	.5	.9	14 688	3 457	14.2	16.5	1 044	941	4 873	12.4	54 503	9 790	2 929	5.4
Grand Rapids-Muskegon-Holland, MI MSA	90.7	7.5	1.2	115 292	31 696	11.6	15.7	7 940	7 102	42 395	11.9	555 789	64 191	22 587	4.1
Allegan	97.3	1.5	.6	10 600	2 838	10.9	13.5	687	536	3 830	10.5	52 061	6 355	1 909	3.7
Kent	89.0	9.0	1.4	61 248	16 881	11.6	16.1	3 853	3 463	20 779	10.8	300 376	31 802	11 975	4.0
Muskegon	83.8	15.0	.4	29 946	8 751	18.6	26.5	945	969	5 219	8.4	79 857	6 775	4 771	6.0
Ottawa	97.4	.6	1.7	13 498	3 226	6.6	7.4	2 455	2 134	12 567	18.9	123 495	19 259	3 932	3.2
Great Falls, MT MSA (Cascade)	92.9	1.6	1.1	11 152	2 516	13.8	15.5	134	127	783	2.4	37 359	1 561	1 753	4.7
Green Bay, WI MSA (Brown)	95.5	.6	1.7	18 163	4 239	8.7	10.2	1 705	1 890	12 492	16.7	130 276	24 553	3 957	3.0
Greensboro--Winston-Salem--High Point, NC MSA	79.0	19.6	1.0	124 962	25 801	11.3	14.1	9 403	8 863	51 409	11.6	632 348	37 200	21 037	3.3
Alamance	79.4	19.6	.7	11 674	2 214	10.3	12.3	1 067	676	4 444	9.8	64 801	3 453	2 314	3.6
Davidson	89.1	10.0	.5	15 595	3 128	11.6	13.5	828	815	5 966	11.2	77 075	4 199	2 447	3.2
Davie	90.2	9.2	.3	2 610	434	8.8	8.3	268	276	1 280	11.1	16 480	773	599	3.6
Forsyth	73.5	25.3	.9	33 612	7 329	12.2	16.3	1 643	2 183	11 784	10.2	152 195	6 875	4 972	3.3
Guilford	71.2	26.7	1.6	43 223	8 972	11.9	15.2	4 451	3 921	22 169	15.1	214 765	14 640	7 252	3.4
Randolph	92.8	6.2	.5	10 155	2 097	8.9	10.7	796	685	4 302	9.9	67 716	4 764	2 351	3.5
Stokes	93.5	6.0	.3	4 372	897	10.8	12.2	203	183	567	3.7	21 884	1 469	571	2.6
Yadkin	95.5	4.3	.1	3 721	730	11.3	13.5	147	124	897	6.9	17 432	1 027	531	3.0
Greenville, NC MSA (Pitt)	64.5	34.3	1.0	24 982	5 542	22.0	27.2	1 019	1 558	9 680	22.5	64 780	7 682	3 241	5.0
Greenville-Spartanburg-Anderson, SC MSA	81.1	17.9	.8	110 274	23 546	12.7	15.6	7 661	6 072	38 734	11.5	469 616	29 121	20 231	4.3
Anderson	82.4	17.2	.3	19 828	4 256	12.9	15.6	923	856	6 040	9.9	81 013	4 866	4 009	4.9
Cherokee	78.1	21.2	.5	6 786	1 574	14.4	17.9	11	10	601	3.4	24 404	1 457	1 359	5.6
Greenville	80.4	18.6	.8	37 912	8 154	11.3	14.2	4 156	3 233	19 374	14.7	182 810	10 017	5 955	3.3
Pickens	91.1	7.7	1.1	11 549	2 048	12.1	12.8	845	530	4 046	11.3	53 968	4 789	2 815	5.2
Spartanburg	77.6	21.3	1.0	34 199	7 514	14.4	18.2	1 726	1 443	8 673	9.6	127 421	7 992	6 093	4.8
Harrisburg-Lebanon-Carlisle, PA MSA	90.8	7.6	1.5	53 669	12 145	8.9	11.5	2 841	2 376	19 392	8.0	345 336	23 558	11 621	3.4
Cumberland	96.1	2.0	1.7	11 765	2 164	6.0	6.4	1 079	859	7 292	9.5	118 385	9 698	3 391	2.9
Dauphin	81.4	16.8	1.6	28 582	6 913	11.6	16.4	1 142	899	7 395	7.2	138 340	8 455	4 806	3.5
Lebanon	98.0	.8	1.1	9 580	2 153	8.3	10.2	435	465	3 477	7.8	64 896	3 601	2 465	3.8
Perry	99.4	.2	.2	3 742	915	8.5	10.6	185	153	1 228	7.2	23 715	1 804	959	4.0

Z Less than .05 percent.

[1]Unemployment as a percent of civilian labor force.

Source: Population by Race—U.S. Bureau of the Census, "County Population Estimates by Age, Sex, Race, and Hispanic Origin - 4/1/90 to 7/1/96" data file (related Internet site <http://www.census.gov/population/www/estimates/co_casrh.html>); Poverty—U.S. Bureau of the Census, "State and County Income and Poverty Estimates - 1993," Internet site <http://www.census.gov/ftp/pub/housing/saipe/est93ALL.dat> (accessed 16 January 1998); Building Permits—U.S. Bureau of the Census, "Construction–Building Permits" on diskette, annual (related Internet site <http://www.census.gov/const/www/C40/table3.html#annual>), and "1990 Census of Population and Housing, Summary Tape File 1C" on CD-ROM; Labor Force—U.S. Bureau of Labor Statistics, Local Area Unemployment Statistics - Time Series, Internet site <gopher://hopi2.gov:70/11/Time%20Series/LA%20%20Local%20Area%20Unemployment%20Statistics/Data> for each state (accessed April 1997), BLS gopher service discontinued October 31, 1997 (related BLS Internet site <http://www.bls.gov>).

Table C–2. Metro Counties —

Table C–2. Metro Counties — **Population by Race, Poverty, Building Permits, and Labor Force**—Con.

[MSA = Metropolitan statistical area. CMSA = Consolidated MSA. PMSA = Primary MSA. NECMA = New England county metropolitan area. All areas defined as of June 30, 1996. Table includes 245 MSAs, 17 CMSAs, and 58 PMSAs not in New England; 12 NECMAs; and 844 component counties]

Metropolitan areas and component counties	Population by race, 1996, percent—			Persons below poverty level, 1993				New private housing units authorized by building permits				Civilian labor force, 1996			
				Number		Percent				1990–1996 period			Unemployment		
	White	Black	Asian or Pacific Islander	All persons	Related children 5 to 17 years	All persons	Related children 5 to 17 years	1996	1995	Total units	Percent of 1990 housing stock	Total	Net change, 1990–1996	Total	Rate[1]
Hartford, CT NECMA	88.2	9.4	2.2	107 861	30 519	9.7	16.2	2 908	2 520	18 839	4.2	575 545	–57 510	34 901	6.1
Hartford	86.1	11.4	2.3	94 118	27 427	11.2	19.3	1 810	1 485	11 819	3.5	425 755	–47 814	26 949	6.3
Middlesex	93.8	4.5	1.5	7 477	1 752	5.2	7.4	549	577	3 761	6.1	80 770	–3 490	4 726	5.9
Tolland	95.1	2.1	2.6	6 266	1 340	5.1	6.0	549	458	3 259	7.0	69 020	–6 206	3 226	4.7
Hattiesburg, MS MSA	73.0	26.2	.7	23 260	6 053	22.9	30.6	189	185	655	1.7	49 909	3 426	2 005	4.0
Forrest	66.5	32.5	.8	16 750	4 416	24.6	34.6	164	174	588	2.1	33 704	1 813	1 457	4.3
Lamar	86.5	12.8	.5	6 510	1 637	19.5	23.4	25	11	67	.6	16 205	1 613	548	3.4
Hickory-Morganton-Lenoir, NC MSA	91.2	7.7	.9	32 344	6 869	10.5	12.9	2 038	1 519	10 863	8.9	177 637	8 318	7 124	4.0
Alexander	93.2	6.3	.3	2 918	608	9.8	11.2	136	102	769	6.9	17 133	1 127	590	3.4
Burke	90.7	7.6	1.5	8 976	1 957	11.5	14.6	277	297	2 008	6.4	43 849	2 014	1 932	4.4
Caldwell	93.9	5.7	.3	8 489	1 857	11.5	14.9	385	326	2 370	8.0	41 623	1 416	1 611	3.9
Catawba	89.5	9.2	1.1	11 961	2 447	9.5	11.2	1 240	794	5 716	11.6	75 032	3 761	2 991	4.0
Honolulu, HI MSA (Honolulu)	31.4	3.8	64.3	75 992	17 476	8.9	11.7	2 000	4 544	26 250	9.3	427 341	19 606	22 602	5.3
Houma, LA MSA	79.4	16.0	1.0	41 328	11 841	21.9	27.9	834	783	4 517	6.8	83 722	8 603	3 848	4.6
Lafourche	83.2	13.6	1.0	18 510	5 125	21.2	27.2	385	356	2 011	6.4	39 299	3 599	1 697	4.3
Terrebonne	76.1	18.0	.9	22 818	6 716	22.5	28.5	449	427	2 506	7.1	44 423	5 004	2 151	4.8
Houston-Galveston-Brazoria, TX CMSA	76.5	18.3	4.8	733 796	199 136	17.8	23.9	24 118	21 682	131 212	8.5	2 250 230	228 129	122 873	5.5
Brazoria, TX PMSA (Brazoria)	89.1	8.9	1.5	25 383	6 396	12.3	14.2	1 730	1 366	9 029	12.1	105 690	7 611	7 087	6.7
Galveston-Texas City, TX PMSA (Galveston)	79.1	18.3	2.3	37 516	9 732	15.9	21.0	1 512	1 490	9 565	9.6	127 275	13 906	10 262	8.1
Houston, TX PMSA	75.6	18.8	5.2	670 897	183 008	18.2	24.7	20 876	18 826	112 618	8.3	2 017 265	206 612	105 524	5.2
Chambers	85.4	13.5	.8	2 679	611	12.3	12.4	183	145	662	8.2	10 967	1 134	579	5.3
Fort Bend	70.1	21.1	8.5	28 100	7 576	10.0	11.5	2 271	1 451	7 543	9.8	156 488	34 154	4 883	3.1
Harris	74.6	19.7	5.4	595 054	163 674	19.4	27.1	14 492	14 093	93 018	7.9	1 692 905	142 217	92 373	5.5
Liberty	83.4	15.7	.4	10 996	2 731	18.9	21.5	244	294	1 517	6.8	26 345	3 244	2 215	8.4
Montgomery	94.0	4.6	1.0	28 759	7 210	12.8	14.9	3 613	2 794	9 613	13.0	118 449	24 520	4 916	4.2
Waller	62.6	36.8	.4	5 309	1 206	22.8	24.8	73	49	265	3.0	12 111	1 343	558	4.6
Huntington-Ashland, WV-KY-OH MSA	97.3	2.2	.4	67 259	16 309	21.3	28.9	278	489	1 762	1.3	136 218	2 596	9 671	7.1
Cabell, WV	95.1	4.1	.6	20 276	4 231	21.3	28.7	80	358	775	1.8	43 743	821	2 707	6.2
Wayne, WV	99.6	Z	.1	10 189	2 537	23.7	32.3	42	1	54	.3	17 039	564	1 231	7.2
Boyd, KY	97.3	2.2	.4	8 926	2 014	17.9	23.4	49	45	267	1.2	22 336	–347	1 579	7.1
Carter, KY	99.7	.1	.1	7 269	1 883	28.3	36.7	11	11	84	.9	11 076	483	1 357	12.3
Greenup, KY	99.1	.4	.4	6 834	1 632	18.2	22.6	63	45	378	2.6	15 994	–86	1 058	6.6
Lawrence, OH	97.0	2.8	.2	13 765	4 012	21.4	31.1	33	29	204	.8	26 030	1 171	1 739	6.7
Huntsville, AL MSA	77.8	19.8	1.8	43 028	9 424	13.2	17.2	947	757	9 851	8.3	163 049	9 165	5 664	3.5
Limestone	85.4	14.0	.4	8 425	1 729	14.6	16.8	145	94	850	4.0	28 185	1 792	1 259	4.5
Madison	76.1	21.1	2.1	34 603	7 695	12.9	17.3	802	663	9 001	9.2	134 864	7 373	4 405	3.3
Indianapolis, IN MSA	85.2	13.6	1.0	173 388	42 891	11.8	16.2	13 737	13 606	75 913	13.3	814 871	87 453	26 400	3.2
Boone	99.2	.2	.3	2 724	609	6.6	7.7	471	330	2 192	15.1	23 318	3 053	543	2.3
Hamilton	97.7	.7	1.4	5 586	1 164	4.1	4.2	3 064	2 820	16 809	40.9	80 943	20 395	1 373	1.7
Hancock	99.2	.1	.5	2 871	610	5.7	6.0	634	548	3 292	20.0	28 194	4 045	802	2.8
Hendricks	98.2	1.1	.5	3 897	830	4.7	5.0	1 524	1 493	7 598	28.2	48 035	7 869	978	2.0
Johnson	98.1	.9	.8	7 804	1 639	7.9	8.6	2 201	1 455	8 392	25.2	57 304	9 660	1 405	2.5
Madison	91.1	8.3	.4	17 845	4 393	13.7	18.6	774	405	2 753	5.2	66 736	3 304	2 958	4.4
Marion	75.5	23.0	1.2	123 073	31 493	15.0	22.6	4 185	5 603	29 423	8.4	453 626	32 674	16 363	3.6
Morgan	99.5	Z	.2	5 624	1 259	9.1	10.3	678	709	3 974	19.4	33 481	4 471	1 123	3.4
Shelby	98.5	.9	.5	3 964	894	9.3	10.9	206	243	1 480	9.5	23 234	1 982	855	3.7
Iowa City, IA MSA (Johnson)	92.4	2.4	5.0	9 185	1 241	9.7	8.9	907	838	6 149	16.5	65 289	7 759	1 880	2.9
Jackson, MI MSA (Jackson)	90.6	8.4	.6	20 800	5 247	14.2	18.5	716	634	4 178	7.2	74 342	3 262	3 769	5.1
Jackson, MS MSA	56.1	43.3	.6	91 399	22 818	22.3	28.2	2 893	3 089	16 124	10.6	220 398	18 047	7 916	3.6
Hinds	46.4	52.9	.6	65 281	16 149	26.1	33.3	924	784	5 208	5.2	131 465	2 902	5 193	4.0
Madison	53.3	46.1	.5	14 345	3 946	22.4	30.7	815	1 218	6 215	29.9	33 995	7 104	1 212	3.6
Rankin	81.5	17.9	.5	11 773	2 723	12.3	14.0	1 154	1 087	4 701	14.7	54 938	8 041	1 511	2.8
Jackson, TN MSA	69.9	29.5	.4	17 600	4 187	18.7	23.4	705	1 118	4 843	13.2	62 380	18 562	3 041	4.9
Chester	87.9	11.8	.2	2 510	530	19.8	23.1	41	48	266	5.4	7 542	1 753	441	5.8
Madison	67.0	32.5	.4	15 090	3 657	18.5	23.5	664	1 070	4 577	14.4	54 838	16 809	2 600	4.7
Jacksonville, FL MSA	75.1	22.1	2.5	136 910	34 589	14.0	18.1	11 290	8 590	58 754	15.3	511 595	40 547	18 329	3.6
Clay	91.0	6.0	2.5	10 669	2 622	8.8	9.5	1 481	1 398	8 169	20.3	63 610	9 835	1 889	3.0
Duval	69.4	27.5	2.8	108 785	27 970	15.4	20.4	7 337	4 513	36 839	12.9	368 467	17 749	13 838	3.8
Nassau	87.3	11.9	.5	5 938	1 444	11.9	13.9	647	696	3 464	18.5	26 216	3 624	1 050	4.0
St. Johns	88.7	10.1	.9	11 518	2 553	11.8	15.5	1 825	1 983	10 282	25.3	53 302	9 339	1 552	2.9
Jacksonville, NC MSA (Onslow)	76.5	19.7	3.1	19 371	4 565	16.4	19.2	832	676	4 599	9.7	44 056	2 558	1 813	4.1
Jamestown, NY MSA (Chautauqua)	96.8	2.2	.5	23 837	6 056	17.1	22.7	231	225	1 759	2.8	67 301	–1 184	3 474	5.2
Janesville-Beloit, WI MSA (Rock)	92.9	5.9	.9	16 021	4 186	11.0	14.5	947	1 037	5 846	10.7	78 671	6 647	3 022	3.8

Z Less than .05 percent.

[1] Unemployment as a percent of civilian labor force.

Source: Population by Race—U.S. Bureau of the Census, "County Population Estimates by Age, Sex, Race, and Hispanic Origin - 4/1/90 to 7/1/96" data file (related Internet site <http://www.census.gov/population/www/estimates/co_casrh.html>); Poverty—U.S. Bureau of the Census, "State and County Income and Poverty Estimates - 1993," Internet site <http://www.census.gov/ftp/pub/housing/saipe/est93ALL.dat> (accessed 16 January 1998); Building Permits—U.S. Bureau of the Census, "Construction–Building Permits" on diskette, annual (related Internet site <http://www.census.gov/const/www/C40/table3.html#annual>), and "1990 Census of Population and Housing, Summary Tape File 1C" on CD-ROM; Labor Force—U.S. Bureau of Labor Statistics, Local Area Unemployment Statistics - Time Series, Internet site <gopher://hopi2.gov:70/11/Time%20Series/LA%20%20Local%20Area%20Unemployment%20Statistics/Data> for each state (accessed April 1997), BLS gopher service discontinued October 31, 1997 (related BLS Internet site <http://www.bls.gov>).

[MSA = Metropolitan statistical area. CMSA = Consolidated MSA. PMSA = Primary MSA. NECMA = New England county metropolitan area. All areas defined as of June 30, 1996. Table includes 245 MSAs, 17 CMSAs, and 58 PMSAs not in New England; 12 NECMAs; and 844 component counties]

Metropolitan areas and component counties	Population by race, 1996, percent— White	Black	Asian or Pacific Islander	Persons below poverty level, 1993 Number All persons	Related children 5 to 17 years	Percent All persons	Related children 5 to 17 years	New private housing units authorized by building permits 1996	1995	1990–1996 period Total units	Percent of 1990 housing stock	Civilian labor force, 1996 Total	Net change, 1990–1996	Unemployment Total	Rate[1]
Johnson City-Kingsport-Bristol, TN-VA MSA	97.2	2.2	.4	76 206	16 441	17.0	22.4	1 841	2 072	10 735	5.8	228 550	19 857	11 259	4.9
Carter, TN	98.5	1.0	.4	10 441	2 209	19.9	26.0	34	46	206	.9	26 163	2 217	1 447	5.5
Hawkins, TN	97.8	1.8	.2	8 781	1 975	18.4	24.1	104	108	658	3.5	23 286	2 773	1 114	4.8
Sullivan, TN	97.3	1.9	.5	23 877	5 214	16.1	21.8	748	884	3 489	5.8	75 670	6 819	3 005	4.0
Unicoi, TN	99.8	Z	.1	2 899	568	17.2	21.1	17	13	60	.8	7 982	497	520	6.5
Washington, TN	95.4	3.8	.6	15 324	3 264	16.1	21.3	541	480	2 840	7.4	51 245	5 622	1 983	3.9
Scott, VA	99.3	.7	Z	4 602	956	19.6	24.2	53	175	819	8.2	9 892	223	721	7.3
Washington, VA	98.0	1.7	.2	7 174	1 611	15.1	19.9	287	310	2 320	12.1	25 689	1 940	2 005	7.8
Bristol city, VA	93.0	6.4	.6	3 108	644	17.8	23.3	57	56	343	4.2	8 623	−234	464	5.4
Johnstown, PA MSA	97.7	1.9	.3	35 133	8 675	14.8	19.6	481	432	2 986	2.9	106 281	4 910	8 384	7.9
Cambria	96.8	2.8	.3	23 074	5 649	14.6	19.4	184	189	1 431	2.1	68 937	2 326	5 550	8.1
Somerset	99.5	.2	.2	12 059	3 026	15.1	19.9	297	243	1 555	4.4	37 344	2 584	2 834	7.6
Jonesboro, AR MSA (Craighead)	92.9	6.1	.7	12 203	2 583	16.8	19.9	894	401	3 802	13.4	41 128	4 273	1 682	4.1
Joplin, MO MSA	96.4	1.1	.7	23 026	5 388	16.2	20.0	738	742	3 918	6.8	79 464	11 944	3 435	4.3
Jasper	96.2	1.5	.7	15 771	3 716	16.6	20.7	661	683	3 542	9.0	52 847	7 959	2 115	4.0
Newton	96.9	.4	.7	7 255	1 672	15.4	18.5	77	59	376	2.0	26 617	3 985	1 320	5.0
Kalamazoo-Battle Creek, MI MSA	88.1	9.9	1.4	65 914	17 736	15.1	21.5	2 089	2 128	12 008	6.8	223 040	5 324	9 786	4.4
Calhoun	86.9	11.6	1.0	23 270	6 686	16.8	24.8	529	387	2 776	5.0	65 977	1 372	3 142	4.8
Kalamazoo	87.9	9.8	1.9	29 217	6 937	13.1	17.5	1 227	1 438	7 098	8.0	121 610	2 126	4 292	3.5
Van Buren	91.2	7.4	.4	13 427	4 113	18.0	25.9	333	303	2 134	6.8	35 453	1 826	2 352	6.6
Kansas City, MO-KS MSA	84.8	13.3	1.4	206 211	51 512	12.4	16.3	12 344	11 183	68 376	10.3	940 256	87 957	38 845	4.1
Cass, MO	97.6	1.3	.6	6 695	1 733	9.2	11.3	716	699	4 763	19.6	41 636	7 936	1 512	3.6
Clay, MO	96.5	2.0	1.0	12 653	2 772	7.6	9.1	872	785	4 894	7.8	101 450	13 954	2 977	2.9
Clinton, MO	97.1	2.4	.2	1 952	475	11.2	13.0	237	225	1 049	8.6	9 275	1 232	361	3.9
Jackson, MO	74.1	24.1	1.3	113 445	28 759	17.5	24.9	4 503	3 607	24 239	16.0	363 223	28 898	16 315	4.5
Lafayette, MO	96.1	3.3	.3	4 382	1 086	13.8	17.4	125	113	461	3.6	16 728	1 622	700	4.2
Platte, MO	95.2	2.4	1.8	4 281	964	6.5	7.7	315	230	1 840	7.6	42 232	7 948	1 096	2.6
Ray, MO	97.7	1.6	.2	2 681	680	12.1	14.3	117	128	681	7.9	11 120	778	500	4.5
Johnson, KS	95.4	2.1	2.1	18 786	3 771	4.7	4.9	4 700	4 572	25 838	17.9	238 098	26 742	7 079	3.0
Leavenworth, KS	86.2	11.3	1.9	6 374	1 458	10.4	10.3	364	468	2 670	12.6	27 608	2 014	1 495	5.4
Miami, KS	96.7	2.5	.2	2 486	550	10.1	10.7	239	222	863	9.6	12 968	779	549	4.2
Wyandotte, KS	69.2	28.6	1.4	32 476	9 264	20.8	29.1	156	134	1 078	1.6	75 918	−3 946	6 261	8.2
Killeen-Temple, TX MSA	75.5	19.7	4.1	41 634	10 733	15.4	19.3	2 210	2 192	9 820	10.3	112 998	18 268	5 468	4.8
Bell	76.0	19.3	4.2	33 424	8 756	15.8	20.9	1 924	1 853	8 233	10.8	92 108	15 310	4 468	4.9
Coryell	74.1	21.1	3.9	8 210	1 977	13.9	14.4	286	339	1 587	8.4	20 890	2 958	1 000	4.8
Knoxville, TN MSA	92.2	6.4	1.1	96 626	20 685	15.4	20.1	5 453	4 548	27 814	11.0	345 941	49 507	14 563	4.2
Anderson	94.1	4.4	1.2	11 235	2 554	15.7	20.7	274	237	2 337	8.0	36 949	4 213	1 746	4.7
Blount	95.6	3.5	.7	12 977	2 828	13.7	18.2	203	212	1 304	3.6	49 991	8 424	2 216	4.4
Knox	89.0	9.4	1.4	54 691	11 366	15.5	20.2	4 132	3 343	20 445	14.2	198 643	25 735	6 707	3.4
Loudon	98.2	1.4	.2	5 038	1 098	14.2	18.3	277	232	1 562	12.0	19 240	3 353	760	4.0
Sevier	98.7	.4	.6	9 450	2 075	16.1	20.6	434	390	1 814	7.5	33 725	6 669	2 816	8.3
Union	99.6	Z	.1	3 235	764	21.7	27.1	133	134	352	6.2	7 393	1 113	318	4.3
Kokomo, IN MSA	94.0	5.0	.7	11 421	2 808	11.4	14.8	741	666	3 135	7.8	52 254	4 114	1 897	3.6
Howard	93.0	6.0	.7	10 054	2 517	12.0	15.9	659	590	2 757	8.2	43 315	3 425	1 594	3.7
Tipton	99.5	.1	.4	1 367	291	8.2	9.2	82	76	378	5.9	8 939	689	303	3.4
La Crosse, WI-MN MSA	96.1	.5	3.1	13 003	2 818	11.0	12.5	825	747	4 327	9.5	71 442	8 743	2 212	3.1
La Crosse, WI	95.5	.6	3.6	11 290	2 398	11.4	13.0	722	638	3 762	9.8	60 562	7 554	1 805	3.0
Houston, MN	99.2	.2	.4	1 713	420	8.9	10.1	103	109	565	7.8	10 880	1 189	407	3.7
Lafayette, LA MSA	69.9	29.1	.8	86 052	24 082	23.8	30.5	1 774	1 411	7 729	5.6	167 636	18 358	9 985	6.0
Acadia	80.0	19.8	.2	15 773	4 568	27.6	34.5	195	163	675	3.1	23 258	2 074	1 824	7.8
Lafayette	74.3	24.2	1.2	32 453	8 619	18.4	23.8	1 175	894	5 420	8.0	92 411	11 933	4 186	4.5
St. Landry	56.9	42.8	.3	26 762	7 705	32.6	40.5	218	179	756	2.4	31 463	2 364	2 604	8.3
St. Martin	63.6	35.3	1.0	11 064	3 190	24.0	30.1	186	175	878	5.0	20 504	1 987	1 371	6.7
Lafayette, IN MSA	94.2	1.8	3.7	17 834	3 052	11.5	11.7	1 449	974	7 247	12.0	87 864	8 160	2 509	2.9
Clinton	99.4	.2	.2	3 382	768	10.5	12.2	192	143	626	5.2	15 958	1 474	532	3.3
Tippecanoe	93.0	2.2	4.5	14 452	2 284	11.7	11.5	1 257	831	6 621	13.8	71 906	6 686	1 977	2.7
Lake Charles, LA MSA (Calcasieu)	74.6	24.7	.5	33 225	8 750	19.1	23.7	1 344	899	5 680	8.6	88 806	12 602	5 479	6.2
Lakeland-Winter Haven, FL MSA (Polk)	83.3	15.4	.9	76 333	17 840	17.9	22.6	2 626	2 365	18 052	9.7	194 994	−5 247	12 908	6.6
Lancaster, PA MSA (Lancaster)	95.4	3.0	1.5	42 291	11 450	9.6	13.5	2 083	1 923	16 977	10.9	235 837	10 079	7 717	3.3
Lansing-East Lansing, MI MSA	89.0	7.9	2.5	51 925	12 779	12.0	15.4	2 184	1 935	12 951	7.8	234 559	1 907	8 645	3.7
Clinton	98.6	.4	.5	4 715	1 131	7.6	8.6	517	433	2 759	13.2	32 939	1 697	1 153	3.5
Eaton	94.8	3.9	.8	8 114	1 968	8.3	9.7	746	434	3 918	11.0	53 644	2 517	1 759	3.3
Ingham	84.8	10.9	3.5	39 096	9 680	14.3	19.6	921	1 068	6 274	5.8	147 976	−2 307	5 733	3.9

Z Less than .05 percent.

[1]Unemployment as a percent of civilian labor force.

Source: Population by Race—U.S. Bureau of the Census, "County Population Estimates by Age, Sex, Race, and Hispanic Origin - 4/1/90 to 7/1/96" data file (related Internet site <http://www.census.gov/population/www/estimates/co_casrh.html>);   Poverty—U.S. Bureau of the Census, "State and County Income and Poverty Estimates - 1993," Internet site <http://www.census.gov/ftp/pub/housing/saipe/est93ALL.dat> (accessed 16 January 1998);   Building Permits—U.S. Bureau of the Census, "Construction–Building Permits" on diskette, annual (related Internet site <http://www.census.gov/const/www/C40/table3.html#annual>), and "1990 Census of Population and Housing, Summary Tape File 1C" on CD-ROM;   Labor Force—U.S. Bureau of Labor Statistics, Local Area Unemployment Statistics - Time Series, Internet site <gopher://hopi2.gov:70/11/Time%20Series/LA%20%20Local%20Area%20Unemployment%20Statistics/Data> for each state (accessed April 1997), BLS gopher service discontinued October 31, 1997 (related BLS Internet site <http://www.bls.gov>).

Table C–2. Metro Counties — **Population by Race, Poverty, Building Permits, and Labor Force**—Con.

[MSA = Metropolitan statistical area. CMSA = Consolidated MSA. PMSA = Primary MSA. NECMA = New England county metropolitan area. All areas defined as of June 30, 1996. Table includes 245 MSAs, 17 CMSAs, and 58 PMSAs not in New England; 12 NECMAs; and 844 component counties]

Metropolitan areas and component counties	Population by race, 1996, percent— White	Black	Asian or Pacific Islander	Persons below poverty level, 1993 Number All persons	Related children 5 to 17 years	Percent All persons	Related children 5 to 17 years	New private housing units authorized by building permits 1996	1995	1990–1996 period Total units	Percent of 1990 housing stock	Civilian labor force, 1996 Total	Net change, 1990–1996	Unemployment Total	Rate[1]
Laredo, TX MSA (Webb)	99.1	.2	.5	59 848	18 608	36.1	44.9	1 299	1 900	9 923	26.7	69 188	13 744	8 807	12.7
Las Cruces, NM MSA (Dona Ana)	96.2	1.9	1.2	46 823	13 494	30.0	38.7	890	983	6 099	12.4	66 274	6 504	6 732	10.2
Las Vegas, NV-AZ MSA	85.6	9.1	4.2	140 519	31 649	12.9	16.8	32 381	29 545	170 139	45.2	634 599	167 056	34 858	5.5
Clark, NV	84.1	10.3	4.7	117 292	26 551	12.4	16.0	30 935	27 813	155 350	49.0	558 788	145 206	29 723	5.3
Nye, NV	93.7	2.0	1.2	2 436	507	10.7	12.6	–	–	–	–	12 812	3 735	651	5.1
Mohave, AZ	96.4	.4	.9	20 791	4 591	17.7	24.5	1 446	1 732	14 789	29.1	62 999	18 115	4 484	7.1
Lawrence, KS MSA (Douglas)	89.4	4.3	3.7	11 086	1 724	13.6	13.4	1 892	841	7 271	22.9	50 726	5 938	2 503	4.9
Lawton, OK MSA (Comanche)	74.0	17.9	3.4	19 153	5 167	17.3	22.2	189	263	1 266	2.9	40 906	-1 354	1 900	4.6
Lewiston-Auburn, ME NECMA (Androscoggin)	98.5	.6	.7	14 977	3 614	14.5	19.0	262	296	1 781	4.1	58 803	2 309	3 354	5.7
Lexington, KY MSA	88.3	10.1	1.4	67 797	14 846	16.2	20.9	4 145	4 265	23 992	14.4	241 272	15 887	6 691	2.8
Bourbon	90.9	8.9	.1	3 497	818	18.0	22.8	96	66	361	4.6	9 713	–66	331	3.4
Clark	93.8	5.7	.2	5 215	1 274	16.9	22.7	252	244	1 431	12.3	15 393	477	652	4.2
Fayette	83.9	13.8	2.2	36 337	7 715	15.8	21.4	2 425	2 382	13 111	13.4	136 711	7 848	3 366	2.5
Jessamine	95.8	3.4	.6	4 997	1 155	15.1	17.6	435	508	2 617	23.3	18 765	1 969	471	2.5
Madison	93.9	5.3	.7	11 727	2 469	20.6	24.7	395	528	3 238	15.1	33 039	2 515	1 141	3.5
Scott	92.6	6.7	.6	3 953	993	15.1	19.1	330	303	1 875	20.4	15 220	2 143	448	2.9
Woodford	92.9	6.7	.2	2 071	422	9.7	10.8	212	234	1 339	17.4	12 431	1 001	282	2.3
Lima, OH MSA	90.5	8.7	.6	17 842	4 601	11.7	14.7	491	480	3 238	5.4	75 824	89	4 596	6.1
Allen	86.7	12.4	.7	14 540	3 821	13.7	17.8	292	317	1 930	4.5	51 733	–822	3 370	6.5
Auglaize	99.2	.2	.5	3 302	780	7.1	7.9	199	163	1 308	7.7	24 091	911	1 226	5.1
Lincoln, NE MSA (Lancaster)	94.6	2.4	2.3	20 009	3 349	9.0	8.6	2 321	1 951	12 999	14.9	139 170	16 394	3 599	2.6
Little Rock-North Little Rock, AR MSA	78.0	20.8	.8	81 594	19 124	15.2	18.7	2 709	3 282	16 386	7.6	298 017	26 728	11 444	3.8
Faulkner	90.5	8.7	.5	8 262	1 555	12.3	12.1	803	668	4 621	19.8	39 069	7 149	1 801	4.6
Lonoke	89.3	9.9	.4	6 358	1 585	14.2	16.1	316	469	2 026	13.5	23 827	4 193	1 015	4.3
Pulaski	69.9	28.8	1.0	60 338	14 279	17.1	21.9	1 008	1 845	7 232	4.8	195 571	9 390	7 491	3.8
Saline	96.8	2.3	.5	6 636	1 705	9.3	11.9	582	300	2 507	10.2	39 550	5 996	1 137	2.9
Longview-Marshall, TX MSA	77.4	21.7	.5	37 210	9 295	18.6	22.7	364	450	1 953	2.4	102 874	10 013	7 940	7.7
Gregg	78.8	20.0	.7	19 084	4 672	17.5	21.5	307	372	1 527	3.4	58 350	5 074	4 221	7.2
Harrison	69.5	29.7	.4	11 806	3 124	20.5	25.0	42	61	267	1.1	28 250	2 744	2 709	9.6
Upshur	86.2	13.2	.1	6 320	1 499	19.1	22.1	15	17	159	1.2	16 274	2 195	1 010	6.2
Los Angeles-Riverside-Orange, CA CMSA	79.8	8.4	11.1	3 042 667	777 295	19.9	27.3	32 587	28 796	269 329	5.1	7 454 304	40 665	545 683	7.3
Los Angeles-Long Beach, CA PMSA (Los Angeles)	75.2	11.2	12.9	2 164 629	551 752	23.8	33.3	7 731	7 763	83 684	2.6	4 415 428	–95 584	362 867	8.2
Orange, CA PMSA (Orange)	84.8	1.8	12.8	323 655	74 884	12.6	16.9	10 173	8 193	61 709	7.1	1 343 842	14 618	55 171	4.1
Riverside-San Bernardino, CA PMSA	86.8	7.1	4.9	476 400	131 195	16.3	21.4	12 362	10 698	109 111	10.6	1 313 204	110 187	100 658	7.7
Riverside	88.6	5.8	4.5	204 353	53 647	15.0	19.7	7 540	6 806	62 500	12.9	618 055	67 284	50 626	8.2
San Bernardino	85.3	8.2	5.3	272 047	77 548	17.5	22.8	4 822	3 892	46 611	8.6	695 149	42 903	50 032	7.2
Ventura, CA PMSA (Ventura)	90.2	2.4	6.5	77 983	19 464	11.1	14.0	2 321	2 142	14 825	6.5	381 830	11 444	26 987	7.1
Louisville, KY-IN MSA	86.1	13.0	.8	147 246	36 062	15.0	20.5	6 497	5 630	38 839	9.9	529 151	27 757	23 076	4.4
Bullitt, KY	99.1	.4	.3	6 615	1 634	11.9	14.0	760	597	4 608	27.7	30 138	4 547	1 166	3.9
Jefferson, KY	81.3	17.6	.9	112 647	27 575	16.7	24.1	3 438	3 107	21 011	7.4	361 827	6 087	16 550	4.6
Oldham, KY	95.5	3.7	.5	2 702	580	7.0	6.8	520	465	3 371	30.1	21 630	4 065	567	2.6
Clark, IN	93.3	5.9	.5	10 588	2 556	11.6	15.1	798	651	4 128	11.7	50 405	4 843	2 120	4.2
Floyd, IN	95.0	4.5	.4	7 706	1 892	11.0	14.3	558	407	3 259	12.9	37 242	4 780	1 396	3.7
Harrison, IN	99.2	.4	.2	3 491	871	10.8	13.0	262	243	1 631	14.2	17 257	2 356	735	4.3
Scott, IN	99.4	.1	.3	3 497	954	15.7	21.5	161	160	831	10.3	10 652	1 079	542	5.1
Lubbock, TX MSA (Lubbock)	89.7	8.3	1.7	47 276	11 261	21.0	26.0	1 136	765	5 068	5.5	122 183	8 558	4 823	3.9
Lynchburg, VA MSA	79.7	19.5	.6	26 499	5 853	13.3	17.2	1 165	1 123	7 233	9.1	102 206	2 230	3 776	3.7
Amherst	76.9	22.3	.3	3 472	625	12.2	12.5	214	197	1 378	13.0	14 541	184	572	3.9
Bedford	90.7	8.8	.3	4 375	885	8.3	9.8	559	543	3 550	18.1	27 923	2 898	959	3.4
Campbell	83.4	16.1	.5	5 944	1 339	12.0	15.3	218	244	1 256	6.6	25 850	–56	1 005	3.9
Bedford city	75.6	23.6	.6	998	205	16.6	21.4	13	20	166	6.3	2 799	141	106	3.8
Lynchburg city	70.1	28.8	1.0	11 710	2 799	18.9	27.0	161	119	883	3.2	31 093	–937	1 134	3.6
Macon, GA MSA	60.7	38.0	1.0	58 811	15 926	19.3	26.9	2 744	2 396	13 091	11.4	147 143	10 296	7 007	4.8
Bibb	53.6	45.4	.8	35 855	9 596	23.5	33.5	1 178	1 116	5 983	9.7	72 882	3 174	3 778	5.2
Houston	73.5	24.4	1.8	12 430	3 498	12.6	18.0	1 331	1 081	5 975	17.2	48 178	5 247	1 819	3.8
Jones	70.3	29.1	.4	2 748	682	12.6	15.8	130	112	331	4.3	11 443	785	460	4.0
Peach	48.2	51.0	.5	5 554	1 490	25.2	33.1	105	84	785	10.4	10 459	952	702	6.7
Twiggs	50.0	49.9	.1	2 224	660	22.5	30.0	–	3	17	.5	4 181	138	248	5.9
Madison, WI MSA (Dane)	93.1	3.5	3.1	32 293	5 669	8.4	9.0	3 009	3 394	23 103	15.6	257 000	39 936	4 276	1.7
Mansfield, OH MSA	92.5	6.8	.5	22 662	5 927	13.1	17.7	478	460	2 863	4.1	84 280	–1 894	5 128	6.1
Crawford	99.0	.6	.3	6 359	1 642	13.3	17.7	103	71	562	2.9	22 467	–1 093	1 425	6.3
Richland	90.1	9.1	.6	16 303	4 285	13.0	17.7	375	389	2 301	4.6	61 813	–801	3 703	6.0
McAllen-Edinburg-Mission, TX MSA (Hidalgo)	99.1	.3	.4	193 584	62 857	41.1	51.8	5 339	4 510	21 415	16.7	189 906	24 147	35 996	19.0

– Represents zero.

[1]Unemployment as a percent of civilian labor force.

Source: Population by Race—U.S. Bureau of the Census, "County Population Estimates by Age, Sex, Race, and Hispanic Origin - 4/1/90 to 7/1/96" data file (related Internet site <http://www.census.gov/population/www/estimates/co_casrh.html>); Poverty—U.S. Bureau of the Census, "State and County Income and Poverty Estimates - 1993," Internet site <http://www.census.gov/ftp/pub/housing/saipe/est93ALL.dat> (accessed 16 January 1998); Building Permits—U.S. Bureau of the Census, "Construction–Building Permits" on diskette, annual (related Internet site <http://www.census.gov/const/www/C40/table3.html#annual>), and "1990 Census of Population and Housing, Summary Tape File 1C" on CD-ROM; Labor Force—U.S. Bureau of Labor Statistics, Local Area Unemployment Statistics - Time Series, Internet site <gopher://hopi2.gov:70/11/Time%20Series/LA%20%20Local%20Area%20Unemployment%20Statistics/Data> for each state (accessed April 1997), BLS gopher service discontinued October 31, 1997 (related BLS Internet site <http://www.bls.gov>).

Table C–2. Metro Counties — **Population by Race, Poverty, Building Permits, and Labor Force**—Con.

[MSA = Metropolitan statistical area.   CMSA = Consolidated MSA.   PMSA = Primary MSA.   NECMA = New England county metropolitan area.   All areas defined as of June 30, 1996.   Table includes 245 MSAs, 17 CMSAs, and 58 PMSAs not in New England; 12 NECMAs; and 844 component counties]

Metropolitan areas and component counties	Population by race, 1996, percent—			Persons below poverty level, 1993				New private housing units authorized by building permits				Civilian labor force, 1996			
				Number		Percent				1990–1996 period				Unemployment	
	White	Black	Asian or Pacific Islander	All persons	Related children 5 to 17 years	All persons	Related children 5 to 17 years	1996	1995	Total units	Percent of 1990 housing stock	Total	Net change, 1990–1996	Total	Rate[1]
Medford-Ashland, OR MSA (Jackson) ..	97.2	.3	1.2	23 391	4 922	14.4	16.3	1 276	1 301	9 537	15.8	85 922	13 720	7 096	8.3
Melbourne-Titusville-Palm Bay, FL MSA (Brevard)	88.3	9.2	2.0	51 543	10 999	11.6	15.1	3 301	2 764	25 684	13.9	197 794	–6 341	10 756	5.4
Memphis, TN-AR-MS MSA	56.8	41.9	1.1	228 057	61 869	21.7	30.0	9 806	9 020	51 526	13.1	536 131	52 326	23 399	4.4
Fayette, TN	54.0	45.8	.1	6 661	1 884	25.1	33.6	218	200	1 423	15.6	12 377	1 006	609	4.9
Shelby, TN	53.2	45.3	1.3	189 901	51 446	22.3	31.4	6 507	6 118	35 753	10.9	435 455	39 864	18 882	4.3
Tipton, TN	74.5	24.8	.4	8 267	2 363	19.4	25.7	458	524	2 164	15.4	20 279	3 516	1 027	5.1
Crittenden, AR	53.8	45.6	.4	14 125	3 973	28.0	34.8	287	352	1 607	8.5	22 611	–101	1 264	5.6
De Soto, MS	85.8	13.7	.3	9 103	2 203	11.1	13.5	2 336	1 826	10 579	43.2	45 409	8 041	1 617	3.6
Merced, CA MSA (Merced)	83.8	4.8	10.3	48 376	15 754	24.5	33.0	875	782	7 463	12.8	82 896	1 920	13 407	16.2
Miami-Fort Lauderdale, FL CMSA	78.3	19.6	1.8	684 047	159 260	20.0	28.4	20 970	27 588	150 287	10.7	1 763 342	75 719	112 625	6.4
Fort Lauderdale, FL PMSA (Broward)	80.3	17.5	1.9	171 871	36 982	12.3	17.6	14 419	12 870	81 990	13.0	733 252	69 606	37 740	5.1
Miami, FL PMSA (Dade)	77.0	21.1	1.8	512 176	122 278	25.4	34.8	6 551	14 718	68 297	8.9	1 030 090	6 113	74 885	7.3
Milwaukee-Racine, WI CMSA	83.0	14.8	1.6	218 626	63 828	13.3	20.1	7 376	7 007	54 772	8.7	896 372	65 440	31 596	3.5
Milwaukee-Waukesha, WI PMSA ...	82.5	15.2	1.7	199 132	58 551	13.7	20.9	6 446	6 176	48 441	8.6	802 274	60 907	27 639	3.4
Milwaukee	73.4	23.7	2.1	181 036	54 799	19.4	31.7	1 788	1 540	12 701	3.3	488 552	14 725	19 845	4.1
Ozaukee	98.1	.9	.8	2 073	365	2.6	2.3	485	506	4 359	16.5	46 926	5 886	1 014	2.2
Washington	99.1	.2	.5	4 288	936	3.9	4.1	878	986	8 376	24.4	51 129	1 742	1 742	2.7
Waukesha	98.1	.5	1.2	11 735	2 451	3.5	3.6	3 295	3 144	23 005	20.8	202 274	29 167	5 038	2.5
Racine, WI PMSA (Racine)	86.8	12.1	.8	19 494	5 277	10.6	14.2	930	831	6 331	9.5	94 098	4 533	3 957	4.2
Minneapolis-St. Paul, MN-WI MSA	91.2	4.4	3.4	257 496	61 762	9.5	11.8	18 206	17 774	121 214	11.9	1 618 334	149 607	50 023	3.1
Anoka, MN	96.7	.7	1.7	17 627	4 771	6.4	7.7	2 181	1 965	16 075	18.8	166 470	22 396	5 503	3.3
Carver, MN	98.1	.3	1.3	2 635	581	4.6	4.6	710	891	5 188	29.7	35 338	7 293	891	2.5
Chisago, MN	98.8	.3	.4	2 887	747	8.1	8.8	582	482	3 190	26.7	19 107	3 551	952	5.0
Dakota, MN	95.6	1.7	2.4	17 030	3 731	5.4	5.5	3 362	3 312	23 231	22.6	194 012	28 841	5 180	2.7
Hennepin, MN	86.9	7.6	4.0	123 587	28 717	11.7	16.4	3 662	3 901	25 631	5.8	642 750	30 525	19 086	3.0
Isanti, MN	98.5	.3	.6	2 663	688	9.6	10.1	266	217	1 592	16.4	14 741	1 612	749	5.1
Ramsey, MN	86.0	6.1	6.9	64 544	16 065	13.4	18.7	958	1 033	8 192	4.1	276 676	6 758	8 872	3.2
Scott, MN	97.4	.6	1.3	3 213	769	4.7	5.0	1 327	978	6 703	33.0	41 047	7 749	1 293	3.2
Sherburne, MN	98.1	.7	.7	3 408	831	6.8	6.8	989	875	4 926	32.9	28 736	6 318	1 223	4.3
Washington, MN	96.6	1.3	1.6	8 385	2 014	4.8	5.0	2 197	2 282	16 322	31.6	103 945	21 497	2 863	2.8
Wright, MN	98.9	.2	.6	5 588	1 444	7.2	7.7	1 014	912	5 375	20.4	43 485	6 220	1 810	4.2
Pierce, WI	98.7	.3	.7	2 669	597	8.1	8.7	293	303	1 376	11.9	20 511	2 431	656	3.2
St. Croix, WI	99.2	.2	.4	3 260	807	6.0	6.7	665	623	3 413	18.4	31 516	4 416	945	3.0
Mobile, AL MSA	70.7	28.0	.9	111 312	29 262	21.9	29.5	4 369	4 861	19 984	9.9	258 194	42 486	13 457	5.2
Baldwin	85.7	13.5	.3	15 778	3 820	13.6	18.0	2 691	3 103	11 650	22.9	62 587	16 232	2 813	4.5
Mobile	66.0	32.5	1.1	95 534	25 442	24.3	32.7	1 678	1 758	8 334	5.5	195 607	26 254	10 644	5.4
Modesto, CA MSA (Stanislaus)	90.4	1.8	6.6	70 339	20 564	17.2	22.9	1 401	1 310	13 821	10.5	196 624	16 076	27 596	14.0
Monroe, LA MSA (Ouachita)	66.2	33.0	.7	36 100	9 907	25.1	32.1	538	577	2 970	5.3	69 164	5 066	4 411	6.4
Montgomery, AL MSA	62.4	36.7	.7	57 482	14 503	19.0	24.8	1 882	2 235	12 023	10.3	156 041	17 051	6 287	4.0
Autauga	78.4	21.0	.4	5 862	1 507	15.2	19.0	281	259	1 597	12.5	19 964	3 222	779	3.9
Elmore	75.7	23.7	.3	8 268	1 899	15.9	18.7	491	368	1 228	6.3	26 854	4 543	1 031	3.8
Montgomery	55.8	43.2	.9	43 352	11 097	20.4	27.4	1 110	1 608	9 198	10.9	109 223	9 286	4 477	4.1
Muncie, IN MSA (Delaware)	92.4	6.6	.7	18 803	3 734	16.4	20.0	273	345	2 366	4.8	62 791	4 424	2 907	4.6
Myrtle Beach, SC MSA (Horry)	80.8	18.0	1.0	27 273	6 576	17.8	25.4	4 054	3 203	15 447	17.2	92 689	18 391	5 074	5.5
Naples, FL MSA (Collier)	93.3	5.7	.6	23 496	5 380	13.1	20.2	5 449	4 257	31 130	33.1	83 140	10 196	4 824	5.8
Nashville, TN MSA	82.6	15.7	1.4	152 643	35 222	14.4	18.6	15 673	11 426	63 879	15.5	619 699	95 917	20 360	3.3
Cheatham	97.3	2.1	.2	3 730	880	11.9	14.4	481	447	2 559	24.9	17 633	3 628	435	2.5
Davidson	73.2	24.7	1.9	93 326	21 753	18.0	26.8	4 887	3 066	18 694	8.2	305 584	31 233	9 572	3.1
Dickson	94.2	5.3	.3	6 063	1 501	15.9	20.5	304	385	1 167	8.2	19 983	2 896	898	4.5
Robertson	87.9	11.7	.2	5 958	1 334	12.8	14.8	947	815	3 846	24.3	26 101	5 004	1 316	5.0
Rutherford	88.3	9.5	2.0	16 082	3 436	11.6	12.8	4 127	3 250	16 553	36.2	84 935	20 714	2 985	3.5
Sumner	93.5	5.8	.5	12 588	2 990	11.0	13.2	1 175	1 087	6 672	16.8	65 005	10 667	2 352	3.6
Williamson	91.9	7.1	.8	6 782	1 484	6.8	7.1	2 407	1 519	9 093	30.4	57 061	14 323	1 197	2.1
Wilson	91.8	7.3	.5	8 114	1 844	10.7	12.3	1 345	857	5 295	20.2	43 397	7 452	1 605	3.7
New London-Norwich, CT NECMA (New London)	92.1	5.3	2.0	20 268	5 850	8.3	13.3	926	805	5 843	5.6	132 890	581	7 861	5.9
New Orleans, LA MSA	62.6	35.0	2.1	319 762	86 082	24.4	32.5	4 739	4 020	24 576	4.5	612 941	21 515	39 641	6.5
Jefferson	77.9	18.8	2.9	78 009	19 802	16.9	22.4	848	920	5 998	3.2	234 052	5 709	12 416	5.3
Orleans	33.9	63.5	2.4	181 550	50 345	37.9	52.9	991	276	2 227	1.0	204 989	–1 830	16 072	7.8
Plaquemines	70.7	24.9	2.6	5 611	1 538	22.1	26.6	135	116	356	3.8	10 287	117	588	5.7
St. Bernard	93.1	5.1	1.3	10 681	2 574	15.8	19.6	212	262	1 702	6.8	31 662	334	2 198	6.9
St. Charles	73.0	26.2	.6	6 850	1 838	14.8	18.1	208	215	1 505	9.4	21 925	2 220	1 492	6.8
St. James	47.6	52.3	.1	4 879	1 323	23.0	27.2	21	12	126	1.8	9 019	357	1 002	11.1
St. John the Baptist	60.6	38.6	.5	8 240	2 407	19.5	23.7	158	–	158	1.1	19 393	1 443	1 840	9.5
St. Tammany	86.9	12.0	.7	23 942	6 255	14.2	16.9	2 166	2 219	12 504	21.6	81 614	13 165	4 033	4.9

– Represents zero.

[1]Unemployment as a percent of civilian labor force.

Source: Population by Race—U.S. Bureau of the Census, "County Population Estimates by Age, Sex, Race, and Hispanic Origin - 4/1/90 to 7/1/96" data file (related Internet site <http://www.census.gov/population/www/estimates/co_casrh.html>);   Poverty—U.S. Bureau of the Census, "State and County Income and Poverty Estimates - 1993," Internet site <http://www.census.gov/ftp/pub/housing/saipe/est93ALL.dat> (accessed 16 January 1998);   Building Permits—U.S. Bureau of the Census, "Construction–Building Permits" on diskette, annual (related Internet site <http://www.census.gov/const/www/C40/table3.html#annual>), and "1990 Census of Population and Housing, Summary Tape File 1C" on CD-ROM;   Labor Force—U.S. Bureau of Labor Statistics, Local Area Unemployment Statistics - Time Series, Internet site <gopher://hopi2.gov:70/11/Time%20Series/LA%20%20Local%20Area%20Unemployment%20Statistics/Data> for each state (accessed April 1997), BLS gopher service discontinued October 31, 1997 (related BLS Internet site <http://www.bls.gov>).

[MSA = Metropolitan statistical area. CMSA = Consolidated MSA. PMSA = Primary MSA. NECMA = New England county metropolitan area. All areas defined as of June 30, 1996. Table includes 245 MSAs, 17 CMSAs, and 58 PMSAs not in New England; 12 NECMAs; and 844 component counties]

Metropolitan areas and component counties	Population by race, 1996, percent—			Persons below poverty level, 1993				New private housing units authorized by building permits				Civilian labor force, 1996			
				Number		Percent				1990–1996 period				Unemployment	
	White	Black	Asian or Pacific Islander	All persons	Related children 5 to 17 years	All persons	Related children 5 to 17 years	1996	1995	Total units	Percent of 1990 housing stock	Total	Net change, 1990–1996	Total	Rate[1]
New York-Northern New Jersey-Long Island, NY-NJ-CT-PA CMSA/NECMA .	74.2	19.3	6.2	2 910 137	776 022	14.7	23.4	41 241	34 418	235 545	3.1	9 695 106	−150 428	629 270	6.5
Bergen-Passaic, NJ PMSA.........	82.7	9.6	7.4	109 980	25 542	8.4	12.1	1 606	1 356	9 325	1.9	670 313	−10 730	42 422	6.3
Bergen......................	85.0	5.4	9.4	48 398	8 937	5.7	6.9	1 240	946	5 999	1.8	437 342	−7 631	23 169	5.3
Passaic.....................	78.5	17.4	3.7	61 582	16 605	13.3	20.4	366	410	3 326	2.0	232 971	−3 099	19 253	8.3
Dutchess, NY PMSA (Dutchess)	87.6	9.1	3.1	20 091	4 164	8.0	9.3	711	552	4 789	4.9	117 626	−16 851	4 954	4.2
Jersey City, NJ PMSA (Hudson)	75.2	15.7	8.8	101 359	26 857	18.2	30.2	360	294	2 563	1.1	287 513	329	26 488	9.2
Middlesex-Somerset-Hunterdon, NJ PMSA........................	84.2	7.8	7.8	62 880	13 327	5.9	7.8	5 939	5 073	30 914	8.1	613 185	45 176	27 894	4.5
Hunterdon...................	95.8	2.2	1.9	3 641	687	3.2	3.3	683	986	4 181	10.5	64 813	5 766	2 035	3.1
Middlesex...................	81.3	9.1	9.4	48 801	10 698	7.1	9.8	2 992	2 090	14 337	5.7	392 844	22 529	20 452	5.2
Somerset...................	86.6	6.9	6.3	10 438	1 942	4.0	4.7	2 264	1 997	12 396	13.4	155 528	16 881	5 407	3.5
Monmouth-Ocean, NJ PMSA.......	90.3	6.7	2.8	78 501	17 319	7.5	9.5	5 267	4 799	32 256	7.4	512 882	37 076	28 746	5.6
Monmouth...................	86.3	9.5	4.0	43 471	9 764	7.5	9.2	2 284	2 291	15 408	7.1	306 158	20 637	16 018	5.2
Ocean......................	95.3	3.2	1.3	35 030	7 555	7.6	9.8	2 983	2 508	16 848	7.7	206 724	16 439	12 728	6.2
Nassau-Suffolk, NY PMSA........	88.2	8.3	3.3	180 827	40 935	6.8	8.9	5 445	4 098	30 859	3.3	1 365 462	−51 251	57 467	4.2
Nassau.....................	86.0	9.6	4.3	79 236	16 492	6.0	7.7	976	860	5 003	1.1	674 308	−28 994	25 317	3.8
Suffolk.....................	90.3	7.0	2.4	101 591	24 443	7.5	9.9	4 469	3 238	25 856	5.4	691 154	−22 257	32 150	4.7
New Haven-Bridgeport-Stamford-Waterbury-Danbury, CT NECMA ..	86.5	10.9	2.5	152 121	43 791	9.3	16.0	3 718	4 285	26 906	4.1	856 759	−52 282	47 312	5.5
Fairfield...................	86.1	10.7	3.0	64 689	18 988	7.7	13.6	1 980	2 344	12 996	4.0	441 902	−23 506	21 751	4.9
New Haven	86.8	11.1	1.9	87 432	24 803	11.0	18.6	1 738	1 941	13 910	4.3	414 857	−28 776	25 561	6.2
New York, NY PMSA.............	62.1	29.0	8.4	1 908 994	528 283	22.1	37.1	11 457	7 296	53 796	1.6	3 923 183	−78 305	315 019	8.0
Bronx	52.9	42.6	3.8	394 200	122 341	33.3	52.7	885	853	7 409	1.7	449 206	−10 973	47 299	10.5
Kings......................	52.3	41.0	6.3	729 236	218 256	31.6	49.7	942	943	7 116	.8	928 089	−31 922	92 680	10.0
New York...................	63.4	26.6	9.5	336 810	80 121	22.3	45.1	3 369	1 129	9 601	1.2	782 694	2 348	57 999	7.4
Putnam....................	97.4	1.1	1.3	4 070	787	4.5	4.8	202	263	2 178	6.8	49 158	894	1 771	3.6
Queens....................	60.9	23.1	15.6	303 013	72 615	15.3	24.4	1 301	738	4 787	.6	947 398	−5 067	76 664	8.1
Richmond..................	84.6	9.0	6.2	39 824	10 068	10.0	14.2	2 155	1 472	9 496	6.8	185 941	5 434	14 491	7.8
Rockland	83.0	11.1	5.6	24 463	6 669	8.9	12.5	1 042	525	4 710	5.3	139 643	−5 583	6 063	4.3
Westchester	79.8	15.0	5.0	77 378	17 426	8.8	12.6	1 561	1 373	8 499	2.5	441 054	−33 436	18 052	4.1
Newark, NJ PMSA	73.0	22.9	3.9	225 410	57 975	11.6	17.1	3 507	3 946	24 885	3.4	1 009 078	−24 901	62 000	6.1
Essex	53.1	43.0	3.7	147 946	40 496	19.3	29.6	539	712	4 434	1.5	373 293	−21 931	28 796	7.7
Morris	90.8	3.3	5.7	17 497	3 508	4.0	4.6	1 742	2 088	12 219	7.8	249 901	3 009	10 001	4.0
Sussex	97.4	1.0	1.4	6 435	1 497	4.6	5.3	515	382	2 788	5.4	74 054	2 071	3 930	5.3
Union	75.5	20.4	3.9	47 337	11 030	9.5	13.8	267	320	2 773	1.5	262 206	−8 773	16 531	6.3
Warren	97.0	1.6	1.2	6 195	1 444	6.4	8.3	444	444	2 671	7.3	49 624	723	2 742	5.5
Newburgh, NY-PA PMSA	91.0	7.2	1.5	40 023	10 630	11.4	15.2	2 429	1 861	12 835	9.1	170 015	2 733	7 416	4.4
Orange, NY	90.1	8.0	1.6	37 048	9 996	11.7	15.7	1 968	1 435	8 649	7.8	153 299	−297	6 570	4.3
Pike, PA	98.1	1.0	.7	2 975	634	8.3	10.1	461	426	4 186	13.6	16 716	3 030	846	5.1
Trenton, NJ PMSA (Mercer)	74.7	20.8	4.4	29 951	7 199	9.3	13.1	802	858	6 417	5.2	169 090	−1 422	9 552	5.6
Norfolk-Virginia Beach-Newport News, VA-NC MSA	66.7	29.7	3.2	212 663	55 665	14.1	19.7	8 314	8 648	61 115	10.9	715 875	38 706	34 537	4.8
Gloucester, VA	86.5	12.4	.8	3 608	838	11.0	13.2	208	174	1 478	11.9	16 687	1 379	614	3.7
Isle of Wight, VA	65.2	34.2	.4	3 239	754	11.8	15.1	329	227	1 752	18.0	14 095	1 100	727	5.2
James City, VA	78.4	19.7	1.7	3 362	684	8.6	9.9	640	731	4 060	28.3	21 599	2 642	664	3.1
Mathews, VA	84.3	15.4	.2	994	189	11.2	13.9	47	61	515	10.9	4 397	224	146	3.3
York, VA	79.6	17.1	3.0	2 938	758	5.5	6.4	453	557	4 656	30.5	25 991	5 365	809	3.1
Chesapeake city, VA	67.9	30.1	1.6	18 170	5 069	10.0	13.6	1 596	1 846	14 258	25.6	96 539	16 709	3 804	3.9
Hampton city, VA	55.9	41.6	2.2	19 426	4 810	14.2	19.9	776	397	4 360	8.1	65 959	1 301	3 285	5.0
Newport News city, VA	60.4	36.2	3.0	29 193	8 290	16.2	24.8	586	833	7 471	10.7	83 101	2 411	4 335	5.2
Norfolk city, VA	54.2	41.8	3.5	56 024	14 795	25.3	40.1	213	381	1 987	2.0	87 517	−10 565	5 768	6.6
Poquoson city, VA	97.0	.8	1.9	477	105	4.1	4.3	50	31	284	7.3	6 052	194	178	2.9
Portsmouth city, VA	48.5	50.2	1.0	22 659	6 364	22.0	33.2	331	285	1 405	3.3	46 018	−893	3 396	7.4
Suffolk city, VA	51.9	47.4	.5	9 962	2 734	18.1	25.3	783	326	2 602	13.0	26 780	1 709	1 648	6.2
Virginia Beach city, VA	78.7	15.2	5.7	39 074	9 638	9.1	11.6	1 900	2 378	13 933	9.5	206 969	15 745	8 448	4.1
Williamsburg city, VA	78.6	17.5	3.6	1 589	178	19.8	22.2	51	70	250	6.3	6 135	335	468	7.6
Currituck, NC	87.7	11.2	.6	1 948	459	12.2	15.6	351	351	2 104	28.6	8 036	1 050	247	3.1
Ocala, FL MSA (Marion)	84.3	14.6	.7	40 375	9 693	18.4	26.0	2 434	2 115	15 416	16.3	91 289	8 154	4 437	4.9
Odessa-Midland, TX MSA	91.9	6.6	1.0	44 947	12 663	18.8	24.1	358	352	2 256	2.4	120 246	9 790	6 842	5.7
Ector......................	93.5	5.0	.8	27 135	7 799	21.9	28.2	71	103	604	1.2	60 260	4 341	4 134	6.9
Midland....................	90.1	8.3	1.2	17 812	4 864	15.5	19.5	287	249	1 652	3.7	59 986	5 449	2 708	4.5
Oklahoma City, OK MSA	82.3	10.8	2.2	161 404	40 034	16.1	20.5	5 042	4 346	26 106	6.1	517 969	24 304	17 356	3.4
Canadian	91.4	2.6	1.9	7 689	1 867	9.7	10.1	252	221	1 351	4.7	42 547	3 164	913	2.1
Cleveland	89.4	3.1	2.5	23 066	4 803	12.5	13.0	961	1 061	5 048	7.1	102 993	8 354	2 698	2.6
Logan	79.4	17.1	.4	5 379	1 297	18.7	21.8	13	6	56	.5	14 425	1 021	415	2.9
McClain	92.2	1.0	.2	3 443	779	13.8	14.6	121	107	615	6.6	12 274	1 048	424	3.5
Oklahoma	78.3	15.2	2.4	109 656	28 273	17.5	24.3	3 628	2 861	18 542	6.6	318 312	9 870	11 588	3.6
Pottawatomie	85.7	2.3	.7	12 171	3 015	20.5	24.5	67	90	494	2.0	27 418	847	1 318	4.8

[1]Unemployment as a percent of civilian labor force.

Source: Population by Race—U.S. Bureau of the Census, "County Population Estimates by Age, Sex, Race, and Hispanic Origin - 4/1/90 to 7/1/96" data file (related Internet site <http://www.census.gov/population/www/estimates/co_casrh.html>);   Poverty—U.S. Bureau of the Census, "State and County Income and Poverty Estimates - 1993," Internet site <http://www.census.gov/ftp/pub/housing/saipe/est93ALL.dat> (accessed 16 January 1998);   Building Permits—U.S. Bureau of the Census, "Construction–Building Permits" on diskette, annual (related Internet site <http://www.census.gov/const/www/C40/table3.html#annual>), and "1990 Census of Population and Housing, Summary Tape File 1C" on CD-ROM;   Labor Force—U.S. Bureau of Labor Statistics, Local Area Unemployment Statistics - Time Series, Internet site <gopher://hopi2.gov:70/11/Time%20Series/LA%20%20Local%20Area%20Unemployment%20Statistics/Data> for each state (accessed April 1997), BLS gopher service discontinued October 31, 1997 (related BLS Internet site <http://www.bls.gov>).

Table C–2. Metro Counties —

Population by Race, Poverty, Building Permits, and Labor Force—Con.

[MSA = Metropolitan statistical area. CMSA = Consolidated MSA. PMSA = Primary MSA. NECMA = New England county metropolitan area. All areas defined as of June 30, 1996. Table includes 245 MSAs, 17 CMSAs, and 58 PMSAs not in New England; 12 NECMAs; and 844 component counties]

| Metropolitan areas and component counties | Population by race, 1996, percent— | | | Persons below poverty level, 1993 | | | | New private housing units authorized by building permits | | | | Civilian labor force, 1996 | | | |
| | | | | Number | | Percent | | | | 1990–1996 period | | | | Unemployment | |
	White	Black	Asian or Pacific Islander	All persons	Related children 5 to 17 years	All persons	Related children 5 to 17 years	1996	1995	Total units	Percent of 1990 housing stock	Total	Net change, 1990–1996	Total	Rate[1]
Omaha, NE-IA MSA	89.4	8.5	1.5	72 135	16 594	10.8	12.5	5 592	4 063	26 972	10.5	375 831	40 379	11 093	3.0
Cass, NE	98.6	.2	.6	1 945	395	8.5	8.3	283	151	1 006	11.2	12 051	1 579	396	3.3
Douglas, NE	86.3	11.6	1.5	53 301	12 137	12.3	14.7	3 459	2 253	16 700	9.7	250 169	26 080	7 566	3.0
Sarpy, NE	91.0	5.5	3.0	5 255	1 243	4.8	4.8	1 267	1 018	6 349	17.6	56 246	7 924	1 350	2.4
Washington, NE	98.7	.6	.3	1 033	179	6.0	4.9	163	189	975	15.3	10 274	1 255	219	2.1
Pottawattamie, IA	98.6	.6	.5	10 601	2 640	12.5	16.1	420	452	1 942	5.9	47 091	3 541	1 562	3.3
Orlando, FL MSA	83.4	13.8	2.5	182 401	42 352	13.4	17.3	16 084	16 014	116 071	22.1	776 477	92 299	29 343	3.8
Lake	88.2	10.9	.6	24 565	5 146	14.1	19.4	2 635	2 253	16 191	21.4	77 361	11 079	3 490	4.5
Orange	79.1	17.5	3.0	107 632	25 896	14.7	19.9	8 679	9 684	61 335	21.7	434 114	43 386	16 303	3.8
Osceola	90.7	6.6	2.3	17 792	4 050	14.0	16.8	2 046	1 718	17 619	36.7	71 243	12 590	2 733	3.8
Seminole	87.4	9.8	2.5	32 412	7 260	9.9	11.4	2 724	2 359	20 926	17.8	193 759	25 244	6 817	3.5
Owensboro, KY MSA (Daviess)	95.2	4.3	.4	14 852	3 651	16.5	21.3	414	528	2 728	7.8	47 713	3 616	2 776	5.8
Panama City, FL MSA (Bay)	84.2	12.4	2.6	22 820	5 729	16.3	20.9	998	1 044	7 294	11.1	64 572	3 617	3 841	5.9
Parkersburg-Marietta, WV-OH MSA	98.3	1.1	.4	24 566	5 845	16.1	21.6	402	306	1 490	2.4	77 020	5 055	4 793	6.2
Wood, WV	98.5	.9	.4	15 435	3 515	17.4	23.5	359	276	1 203	3.2	44 529	2 646	2 671	6.0
Washington, OH	98.1	1.4	.4	9 131	2 330	14.4	19.2	43	30	287	1.1	32 491	2 409	2 122	6.5
Pensacola, FL MSA	78.7	17.6	2.5	66 629	17 584	18.2	24.0	4 565	2 844	20 848	14.4	166 611	6 864	6 542	3.9
Escambia	73.3	22.7	2.8	54 027	14 230	20.3	27.1	3 088	1 784	11 740	10.5	119 729	–1 106	4 872	4.1
Santa Rosa	92.6	4.6	1.8	12 602	3 354	12.6	16.2	1 477	1 060	9 108	27.7	46 882	7 970	1 670	3.6
Peoria-Pekin, IL MSA	90.8	8.0	1.0	41 404	10 423	12.1	15.6	1 450	1 308	7 585	5.6	180 519	11 973	11 049	6.1
Peoria	83.5	14.8	1.5	26 935	7 072	14.9	20.4	694	710	3 429	4.6	94 176	4 952	6 196	6.6
Tazewell	99.0	.3	.5	12 143	2 796	9.6	11.3	553	431	2 861	5.8	68 243	5 301	4 160	6.1
Woodford	99.2	.2	.4	2 326	555	6.9	7.5	203	167	1 295	10.9	18 100	1 720	693	3.8
Philadelphia-Wilmington-Atlantic City, PA-NJ-DE-MD CMSA	77.6	19.4	2.7	784 671	202 305	13.2	19.1	19 537	17 732	128 087	5.4	2 987 130	–13 239	169 666	5.7
Atlantic-Cape May, NJ PMSA	81.4	15.8	2.5	39 746	9 248	12.1	17.0	1 712	1 222	9 585	5.0	173 067	6 143	16 047	9.3
Atlantic	76.8	19.7	3.1	29 456	6 915	12.7	18.0	1 041	678	5 586	5.2	126 468	3 997	10 579	8.4
Cape May	92.3	6.4	1.0	10 290	2 333	10.6	14.7	671	544	3 999	4.7	46 599	2 146	5 468	11.7
Philadelphia, PA-NJ PMSA	76.9	20.0	2.9	671 495	175 337	13.6	19.8	14 559	13 148	93 982	4.9	2 462 759	–29 773	129 988	5.3
Bucks, PA	94.5	3.2	2.1	30 864	6 550	5.4	6.1	2 477	2 670	18 890	9.4	310 327	8 393	13 768	4.4
Chester, PA	91.2	7.1	1.5	25 472	5 705	6.4	7.9	2 290	2 657	15 482	11.1	217 708	8 551	7 218	3.3
Delaware, PA	84.9	12.5	2.5	51 539	11 712	9.5	12.8	1 083	937	5 465	2.6	275 854	–5 363	13 200	4.8
Montgomery, PA	90.3	6.4	3.2	37 159	6 651	5.3	5.8	3 371	2 827	21 106	7.9	382 036	2 952	14 708	3.8
Philadelphia, PA	53.4	42.7	3.6	404 776	111 443	26.5	42.4	674	487	3 385	.5	652 145	–51 533	45 207	6.9
Burlington, NJ	80.6	16.1	3.0	25 326	6 113	6.4	8.1	2 293	1 688	12 915	9.0	211 190	1 911	10 336	4.9
Camden, NJ	77.6	18.7	3.4	70 904	20 581	13.9	20.7	1 222	865	7 759	4.1	255 142	–740	15 353	6.0
Gloucester, NJ	88.0	9.9	1.9	18 346	4 633	7.6	9.5	1 057	878	7 944	9.6	126 547	5 932	7 856	6.2
Salem, NJ	82.2	16.5	.8	7 109	1 949	11.0	15.2	92	139	1 036	4.1	31 810	124	2 342	7.4
Vineland-Millville-Bridgeton, NJ PMSA (Cumberland)	78.2	19.4	1.3	21 232	5 912	15.8	22.0	316	403	2 123	4.2	64 605	–1 022	6 410	9.9
Wilmington-Newark, DE-MD PMSA	81.3	16.5	2.0	52 198	11 808	9.8	12.4	2 950	2 959	22 397	11.1	286 699	11 413	17 221	6.0
New Castle, DE	79.2	18.4	2.2	45 278	10 156	9.9	12.8	2 220	2 348	17 684	10.2	245 796	6 601	13 158	5.4
Cecil, MD	93.7	5.4	.6	6 920	1 652	9.0	10.6	730	611	4 713	17.0	40 903	4 812	4 063	9.9
Phoenix-Mesa, AZ MSA	91.4	4.0	2.2	411 455	104 976	16.5	22.7	39 646	37 536	187 206	18.6	1 459 788	290 829	54 408	3.7
Maricopa	91.7	4.0	2.3	379 587	95 975	16.0	22.0	38 621	36 723	182 047	19.1	1 403 167	280 054	51 094	3.6
Pinal	85.5	3.5	.6	31 868	9 001	25.7	33.2	1 025	813	5 159	9.8	56 621	10 775	3 314	5.9
Pine Bluff, AR MSA (Jefferson)	53.5	45.7	.5	22 533	5 670	27.6	33.0	154	144	871	2.6	37 227	–832	2 873	7.7
Pittsburgh, PA MSA	90.7	8.3	.9	314 774	74 781	13.1	19.0	5 622	5 464	41 815	4.1	1 146 782	32 865	57 278	5.0
Allegheny	86.0	12.5	1.4	168 717	39 879	12.8	19.6	2 031	1 951	16 319	2.8	649 971	8 058	29 156	4.5
Beaver	93.2	6.4	.3	26 054	6 274	13.7	18.8	333	373	2 809	3.7	84 471	2 531	4 187	5.0
Butler	98.8	.6	.5	14 930	3 725	9.3	12.4	1 210	1 147	8 037	13.6	82 579	8 392	4 143	5.0
Fayette	95.7	4.0	.2	33 230	8 334	22.4	30.4	309	358	2 306	3.8	56 571	1 954	4 506	8.0
Washington	95.8	3.8	.4	27 745	6 217	13.4	17.3	686	697	4 770	5.7	94 214	4 021	5 125	5.4
Westmoreland	97.2	2.2	.6	44 098	10 352	11.6	16.2	1 053	938	7 574	4.9	178 976	7 909	10 161	5.7
Pittsfield, MA NECMA (Berkshire)	96.6	2.2	1.0	15 683	3 748	11.7	16.3	400	281	2 318	3.6	65 634	–4 272	3 219	4.9
Pocatello, ID MSA (Bannock)	94.9	1.1	1.3	8 959	2 024	12.4	11.9	425	330	2 044	8.0	37 128	5 786	1 958	5.3
Portland, ME NECMA (Cumberland)	98.0	.7	1.1	27 185	5 488	11.0	13.5	1 162	1 077	7 650	7.0	140 748	6 999	4 118	2.9
Portland-Salem, OR-WA CMSA	92.4	2.7	3.9	232 643	48 605	11.7	13.0	21 633	20 443	122 032	16.8	1 167 371	182 921	54 884	4.7
Portland-Vancouver, OR-WA PMSA	91.8	3.0	4.3	189 093	38 548	11.2	12.3	18 260	18 032	105 463	17.0	1 003 750	161 341	45 543	4.5
Clackamas, OR	96.6	.5	2.2	24 049	4 848	7.7	7.8	2 972	2 970	18 748	17.2	187 790	32 433	7 399	3.9
Columbia, OR	97.5	.1	1.0	3 653	824	8.8	9.3	366	293	1 560	10.7	21 890	3 197	1 344	6.1
Multnomah, OR	86.2	6.8	5.8	92 002	17 425	15.0	17.7	4 191	2 946	19 186	7.5	365 856	39 398	18 852	5.2
Washington, OR	93.2	.8	5.4	29 477	5 938	8.1	8.5	6 874	7 106	34 446	27.6	229 478	47 565	8 864	3.9
Yamhill, OR	96.7	.6	1.4	8 976	2 030	12.6	13.1	900	802	4 773	20.6	39 529	6 994	1 930	4.9
Clark, WA	94.5	1.5	3.0	30 936	7 483	10.8	12.6	2 957	3 915	26 750	28.8	159 207	31 654	7 154	4.5
Salem, OR PMSA	95.3	1.0	2.1	43 550	10 057	14.4	16.8	3 373	2 411	16 569	15.7	163 621	21 580	9 341	5.7
Marion	95.1	1.1	2.2	36 842	8 551	14.9	17.6	2 870	2 131	14 716	16.9	134 911	17 618	7 961	5.9
Polk	96.3	.4	1.6	6 708	1 506	12.1	13.4	503	280	1 853	9.8	28 710	3 962	1 380	4.8

[1]Unemployment as a percent of civilian labor force.

Source: Population by Race—U.S. Bureau of the Census, "County Population Estimates by Age, Sex, Race, and Hispanic Origin - 4/1/90 to 7/1/96" data file (related Internet site <http://www.census.gov/population/www/estimates/co_casrh.html>);   Poverty—U.S. Bureau of the Census, "State and County Income and Poverty Estimates - 1993," Internet site <http://www.census.gov/ftp/pub/housing/saipe/est93ALL.dat> (accessed 16 January 1998);   Building Permits—U.S. Bureau of the Census, "Construction–Building Permits" on diskette, annual (related Internet site <http://www.census.gov/const/www/C40/table3.html#annual>), and "1990 Census of Population and Housing, Summary Tape File 1C" on CD-ROM;   Labor Force—U.S. Bureau of Labor Statistics, Local Area Unemployment Statistics - Time Series, Internet site <gopher://hopi2.gov:70/11/Time%20Series/LA%20Local%20Area%20Unemployment%20Statistics/Data> for each state (accessed April 1997), BLS gopher service discontinued October 31, 1997 (related BLS Internet site <http://www.bls.gov>).

[MSA = Metropolitan statistical area. CMSA = Consolidated MSA. PMSA = Primary MSA. NECMA = New England county metropolitan area. All areas defined as of June 30, 1996. Table includes 245 MSAs, 17 CMSAs, and 58 PMSAs not in New England; 12 NECMAs; and 844 component counties]

Metropolitan areas and component counties	Population by race, 1996, percent—			Persons below poverty level, 1993					New private housing units authorized by building permits				Civilian labor force, 1996			
				Number		Percent					1990–1996 period				Unemployment	
	White	Black	Asian or Pacific Islander	All persons	Related children 5 to 17 years	All persons	Related children 5 to 17 years	1996	1995	Total units	Percent of 1990 housing stock	Total	Net change, 1990– 1996	Total	Rate[1]
Providence-Warwick-Pawtucket, RI NECMA	92.5	4.8	2.2	115 416	29 413	12.8	19.1	2 214	2 095	16 097	4.3	456 318	−19 534	23 498	5.1
Bristol	98.8	.4	.7	3 212	584	6.7	7.2	89	78	822	4.4	24 806	−1 338	1 042	4.2
Kent	98.0	.7	1.0	12 265	2 603	7.4	9.2	413	491	3 349	5.1	85 368	−2 237	4 372	5.1
Providence	89.6	7.1	2.8	91 130	24 470	15.8	25.2	948	791	7 162	2.9	286 281	−17 541	15 821	5.5
Washington	96.3	1.1	1.6	8 809	1 756	7.8	8.6	764	735	4 764	9.6	59 863	1 582	2 263	3.8
Provo-Orem, UT MSA (Utah)	97.2	.2	1.8	38 825	8 289	13.0	10.5	3 955	4 395	20 996	28.8	147 606	31 218	4 328	2.9
Pueblo, CO MSA (Pueblo)	96.2	2.2	.8	26 379	6 370	20.7	25.2	1 193	938	3 841	7.6	58 150	5 795	3 418	5.9
Punta Gorda, FL MSA (Charlotte)	94.3	4.4	1.0	12 493	2 313	10.0	15.2	1 065	973	10 798	16.7	44 430	2 989	1 855	4.2
Raleigh-Durham-Chapel Hill, NC MSA	73.1	24.2	2.4	106 253	20 541	11.2	13.2	14 200	13 773	77 922	21.7	579 593	85 447	13 601	2.3
Chatham	75.9	23.4	.3	4 602	860	10.9	13.2	438	414	2 364	14.2	24 534	2 522	660	2.7
Durham	59.6	37.6	2.5	25 415	5 381	13.5	17.6	2 083	2 185	11 892	15.3	111 269	9 505	3 134	2.8
Franklin	63.1	36.4	.3	6 701	1 445	16.8	20.1	320	287	1 857	12.4	21 638	2 838	909	4.2
Johnston	81.0	18.4	.3	14 181	2 969	15.5	18.1	1 195	1 160	6 753	19.8	51 847	7 305	1 312	2.5
Orange	79.7	16.4	3.6	10 047	1 472	10.4	10.3	950	818	5 286	13.7	61 624	8 441	1 067	1.7
Wake	75.8	21.1	2.8	45 307	8 414	9.3	10.4	9 214	8 909	49 770	28.1	308 681	54 836	6 519	2.1
Rapid City, SD MSA (Pennington)	88.7	2.0	1.5	12 941	3 365	14.8	19.1	347	629	2 969	8.8	45 315	5 553	1 504	3.3
Reading, PA MSA (Berks)	95.0	3.6	1.3	38 787	9 253	11.2	15.8	1 553	1 378	10 740	8.0	180 050	3 545	7 750	4.3
Redding, CA MSA (Shasta)	94.0	.8	2.4	25 428	6 631	15.9	20.7	710	773	8 381	13.8	72 309	5 167	7 130	9.9
Reno, NV MSA (Washoe)	90.2	2.5	5.2	29 156	5 756	10.3	12.3	4 377	3 265	20 074	17.9	167 246	18 042	8 075	4.8
Richland-Kennewick-Pasco, WA MSA	94.5	1.9	2.7	22 633	6 416	12.9	16.1	880	1 030	7 910	13.5	92 760	12 967	8 738	9.4
Benton	95.4	1.2	2.6	13 129	3 453	10.0	12.0	620	864	6 896	15.4	70 618	9 796	5 995	8.5
Franklin	92.1	4.2	2.9	9 504	2 963	21.4	26.5	260	166	1 014	7.4	22 142	3 171	2 743	12.4
Richmond-Petersburg, VA MSA	68.0	29.9	1.8	109 983	25 722	12.1	16.2	6 147	5 929	42 798	12.0	489 590	19 481	18 169	3.7
Charles City	26.5	65.8	.2	963	230	14.2	19.1	49	57	359	15.5	3 513	122	172	4.9
Chesterfield	83.0	14.4	2.3	15 638	3 703	6.6	7.4	1 651	1 969	14 234	18.4	132 732	13 225	4 043	3.0
Dinwiddie	59.7	39.8	.3	2 858	652	13.1	17.1	148	151	1 264	15.8	10 844	359	455	4.2
Goochland	67.3	32.3	.3	1 351	243	8.9	10.3	192	175	1 169	22.5	8 196	803	204	2.5
Hanover	87.9	11.3	.6	3 794	726	5.3	5.7	1 023	817	6 407	27.0	41 072	4 838	909	2.2
Henrico	75.0	22.1	2.6	18 594	3 818	7.9	10.2	1 964	1 778	12 531	13.3	131 156	5 110	3 946	3.0
New Kent	76.0	22.3	.4	745	153	6.5	7.5	140	149	873	22.0	6 097	449	199	3.3
Powhatan	76.5	23.0	.3	1 115	210	6.9	7.3	311	301	1 981	40.3	9 152	1 624	228	2.5
Prince George	65.7	31.1	2.8	2 056	476	8.0	8.6	183	199	1 547	17.9	11 789	−132	444	3.8
Colonial Heights city	96.0	.8	2.9	1 278	251	7.6	9.2	39	44	588	8.9	8 772	200	351	4.0
Hopewell city	70.3	27.6	1.8	4 109	1 140	18.3	28.1	45	42	224	2.3	10 637	−838	634	6.0
Petersburg city	24.6	74.2	1.0	8 989	2 188	24.3	35.7	13	39	188	1.2	17 507	−644	1 425	8.1
Richmond city	40.7	58.0	1.1	48 493	11 932	25.3	43.0	389	208	1 433	1.5	98 123	−5 635	5 159	5.3
Roanoke, VA MSA	85.7	13.2	.9	27 299	5 979	12.0	16.4	991	906	6 383	6.7	127 836	7 611	3 693	2.9
Botetourt	94.4	5.1	.4	1 931	372	7.2	8.0	232	244	1 552	15.9	15 588	1 871	401	2.6
Roanoke	96.0	2.9	1.1	4 828	848	5.9	6.0	565	432	3 181	10.0	48 336	3 333	1 064	2.2
Roanoke city	72.3	26.6	.9	19 059	4 510	19.8	31.5	121	148	1 023	2.3	50 359	1 611	1 892	3.8
Salem city	94.2	4.8	.9	1 481	249	6.5	7.2	73	82	627	6.5	13 553	796	336	2.5
Rochester, MN MSA (Olmsted)	94.5	.9	4.2	8 290	1 820	7.3	7.9	764	478	5 675	13.6	64 477	2 902	1 960	3.0
Rochester, NY MSA	87.8	9.9	1.8	120 569	31 583	11.2	16.1	3 107	2 888	23 382	5.5	569 709	10 056	22 674	4.0
Genesee	96.2	2.0	.5	5 860	1 434	9.5	12.0	121	163	1 091	4.8	31 885	416	1 625	5.1
Livingston	95.4	3.6	.7	6 306	1 360	10.5	11.7	206	177	1 350	5.8	34 175	1 804	1 771	5.2
Monroe	84.0	13.2	2.4	84 864	22 931	11.8	18.0	2 018	1 876	15 019	5.3	381 153	2 535	13 268	3.5
Ontario	96.9	2.1	.8	9 108	2 165	9.3	11.9	372	303	2 698	6.9	52 889	1 871	2 367	4.5
Orleans	90.4	8.6	.5	5 038	1 368	11.9	15.8	79	55	721	4.4	20 950	1 157	1 166	5.6
Wayne	95.4	3.7	.6	9 393	2 325	10.0	12.3	311	314	2 503	7.1	48 657	2 273	2 477	5.1
Rockford, IL MSA	90.8	7.6	1.3	37 190	8 844	10.7	13.4	2 402	2 401	14 845	11.3	193 710	14 412	9 245	4.8
Boone	98.7	.5	.6	2 666	638	7.6	9.0	302	322	2 642	23.0	20 200	3 072	1 127	5.6
Ogle	99.2	.1	.4	3 717	791	7.6	8.0	264	368	1 988	11.0	27 011	2 319	1 186	4.4
Winnebago	88.1	10.1	1.5	30 807	7 415	11.7	15.2	1 836	1 711	10 215	10.0	146 499	9 021	6 932	4.7
Rocky Mount, NC MSA	57.9	41.6	.3	26 241	6 062	18.7	22.2	464	478	3 738	7.1	73 130	3 613	6 187	8.5
Edgecombe	43.3	56.4	.2	12 968	3 153	23.1	27.2	54	36	419	1.9	28 690	501	3 374	11.8
Nash	67.2	32.1	.4	13 273	2 909	15.7	18.5	410	442	3 319	10.7	44 440	3 112	2 813	6.3
Sacramento-Yolo, CA CMSA	81.9	7.0	9.7	231 469	58 905	14.6	19.6	8 974	8 043	70 188	11.5	811 790	45 371	48 820	6.0
Sacramento, CA PMSA	81.5	7.5	9.7	207 679	53 840	14.4	19.6	8 174	7 327	64 326	11.6	724 898	34 591	43 338	6.0
El Dorado	95.7	.5	2.6	12 406	2 823	8.5	10.0	1 464	877	8 683	14.1	73 899	8 680	4 648	6.3
Placer	95.2	.7	2.9	16 950	3 548	8.5	9.2	2 838	2 574	17 153	22.0	104 118	12 627	5 671	5.4
Sacramento	77.0	9.8	11.9	178 323	47 469	16.3	22.8	3 872	3 876	38 490	9.2	546 881	13 284	33 019	6.0
Yolo, CA PMSA (Yolo)	85.7	2.4	10.3	23 790	5 065	16.6	19.8	800	716	5 862	11.1	86 892	10 780	5 482	6.3
Saginaw-Bay City-Midland, MI MSA	88.0	10.6	.9	68 354	19 478	16.9	24.0	1 339	1 200	8 900	5.7	192 004	3 889	9 435	4.9
Bay	97.6	1.2	.5	17 469	4 478	15.5	20.6	285	340	1 951	4.4	53 806	260	2 833	5.3
Midland	97.1	1.0	1.4	9 518	2 421	12.0	15.2	324	263	2 862	9.8	40 262	2 705	1 608	4.0
Saginaw	79.6	19.1	.8	41 367	12 579	19.5	29.0	730	597	4 087	5.0	97 936	924	4 994	5.1
St. Cloud, MN MSA	98.3	.4	.9	16 302	3 741	10.6	10.9	1 347	1 268	8 125	14.7	93 460	11 202	4 668	5.0
Benton	98.6	.3	.7	3 388	861	10.4	11.8	181	141	1 419	12.3	19 469	2 659	1 005	5.2
Stearns	98.3	.5	1.0	12 914	2 880	10.6	10.7	1 166	1 127	6 706	15.3	73 991	8 543	3 663	5.0

[1]Unemployment as a percent of civilian labor force.

Source: Population by Race—U.S. Bureau of the Census, "County Population Estimates by Age, Sex, Race, and Hispanic Origin - 4/1/90 to 7/1/96" data file (related Internet site <http://www.census.gov/population/www/estimates/co_casrh.html>);   Poverty—U.S. Bureau of the Census, "State and County Income and Poverty Estimates - 1993," Internet site <http://www.census.gov/ftp/pub/housing/saipe/est93ALL.dat> (accessed 16 January 1998);   Building Permits—U.S. Bureau of the Census, "Construction–Building Permits" on diskette, annual (related Internet site <http://www.census.gov/const/www/C40/table3.html#annual>), and "1990 Census of Population and Housing, Summary Tape File 1C" on CD-ROM;   Labor Force—U.S. Bureau of Labor Statistics, Local Area Unemployment Statistics - Time Series, Internet site <gopher://hopi2.gov:70/11/Time%20Series/LA%20%20Local%20Area%20Unemployment%20Statistics/Data> for each state (accessed April 1997), BLS gopher service discontinued October 31, 1997 (related BLS Internet site <http://www.bls.gov>).

[MSA = Metropolitan statistical area. CMSA = Consolidated MSA. PMSA = Primary MSA. NECMA = New England county metropolitan area. All areas defined as of June 30, 1996. Table includes 245 MSAs, 17 CMSAs, and 58 PMSAs not in New England; 12 NECMAs; and 844 component counties]

Metropolitan areas and component counties	Population by race, 1996, percent—			Persons below poverty level, 1993				New private housing units authorized by building permits				Civilian labor force, 1996			
				Number		Percent				1990–1996 period				Unemployment	
	White	Black	Asian or Pacific Islander	All persons	Related children 5 to 17 years	All persons	Related children 5 to 17 years	1996	1995	Total units	Percent of 1990 housing stock	Total	Net change, 1990–1996	Total	Rate[1]
St. Joseph, MO MSA	96.2	3.1	.4	15 755	3 795	16.2	20.3	342	377	1 895	4.6	49 631	1 665	3 251	6.6
Andrew	99.3	.2	.2	1 797	425	11.9	13.6	23	20	150	2.6	7 918	511	400	5.1
Buchanan	95.6	3.6	.4	13 958	3 370	17.0	21.7	319	357	1 745	4.9	41 713	1 154	2 851	6.8
St. Louis, MO-IL MSA	81.0	17.6	1.2	334 902	85 587	13.1	17.8	12 666	11 520	76 292	7.4	1 362 797	79 597	61 266	4.5
Franklin, MO	98.4	1.1	.3	9 788	2 357	11.3	13.1	745	658	4 765	14.7	46 933	4 440	2 289	4.9
Jefferson, MO	98.5	.8	.4	17 143	4 498	9.3	11.4	1 554	1 318	8 282	13.1	102 167	10 302	4 403	4.3
Lincoln, MO	97.0	2.4	.3	3 867	988	12.1	14.5	98	75	558	4.5	17 082	2 661	803	4.7
St. Charles, MO	96.2	2.7	.9	15 601	3 699	6.4	7.2	3 179	3 406	19 324	24.4	147 552	25 905	4 385	3.0
St. Louis, MO	82.0	16.0	1.9	80 973	17 282	8.0	9.6	3 645	3 105	23 806	5.9	581 699	37 698	19 846	3.4
Warren, MO	96.5	3.1	.2	2 457	647	11.2	14.7	257	156	758	8.6	11 847	1 892	542	4.6
St. Louis city, MO	47.3	51.3	1.2	118 802	32 963	32.5	51.5	395	188	993	.5	172 178	−7 574	12 871	7.5
Clinton, IL	95.5	4.0	.4	2 946	668	8.7	9.5	69	91	481	3.8	17 001	558	946	5.6
Jersey, IL	99.1	.5	.2	2 413	521	11.8	12.7	112	92	775	9.4	10 325	395	634	6.1
Madison, IL	91.9	7.1	.8	30 849	7 442	12.0	15.8	1 291	1 233	8 198	8.1	126 690	2 890	7 087	5.6
Monroe, IL	99.3	.1	.4	1 264	248	5.2	5.2	226	286	1 830	20.9	12 785	872	471	3.7
St. Clair, IL	69.7	29.1	1.0	48 799	14 274	18.3	26.3	1 095	912	6 522	6.3	116 538	−442	6 989	6.0
Salinas, CA MSA (Monterey)	82.9	6.0	10.1	52 959	14 400	16.1	21.9	1 502	1 326	8 025	6.6	179 343	5 168	19 802	11.0
Salt Lake City-Ogden, UT MSA	95.0	1.2	3.0	117 958	28 584	9.9	9.7	12 743	10 616	55 888	15.1	642 237	109 866	20 519	3.2
Davis	95.8	1.4	2.2	16 694	3 966	8.0	6.7	2 605	1 908	11 517	20.6	106 833	20 389	3 442	3.2
Salt Lake	94.7	1.0	3.4	79 326	19 613	9.8	10.1	8 637	7 280	37 392	14.5	442 765	74 188	13 184	3.0
Weber	95.5	2.0	1.8	21 938	5 005	12.9	12.5	1 501	1 428	6 979	12.1	92 639	15 289	3 893	4.2
San Angelo, TX MSA (Tom Green)	93.6	4.4	1.4	16 903	4 257	17.2	21.9	476	225	1 765	4.4	50 776	4 431	1 798	3.5
San Antonio, TX MSA	91.3	6.6	1.6	312 418	87 085	21.9	29.9	9 642	8 279	40 469	7.9	731 952	100 205	31 651	4.3
Bexar	90.7	7.1	1.8	288 586	80 924	22.7	31.2	7 986	6 985	34 240	7.5	646 494	83 113	28 958	4.5
Comal	98.2	1.0	.5	7 532	1 786	12.3	16.0	1 028	885	4 459	19.4	33 727	7 974	1 124	3.3
Guadalupe	92.5	6.0	1.1	11 817	3 189	16.7	22.1	613	392	1 645	6.4	38 422	6 214	1 184	3.1
Wilson	98.4	1.2	.1	4 483	1 186	17.1	20.2	15	17	125	1.5	13 309	2 904	385	2.9
San Diego, CA MSA (San Diego)	82.5	6.4	10.2	422 935	104 347	16.3	22.8	6 848	6 633	55 868	5.9	1 236 283	34 497	65 595	5.3
San Francisco-Oakland-San Jose, CA CMSA	72.5	8.7	18.1	660 572	141 432	10.2	13.2	21 432	15 695	126 671	5.2	3 553 292	120 765	163 410	4.6
Oakland, CA PMSA	68.4	14.8	16.1	238 415	53 903	11.0	14.3	7 033	6 167	46 551	5.7	1 142 894	20 597	56 599	5.0
Alameda	62.3	18.2	18.7	160 618	35 244	12.3	16.0	3 509	2 801	20 166	4.0	684 758	1 520	33 998	5.0
Contra Costa	77.5	9.6	12.2	77 797	18 659	9.0	11.9	3 524	3 366	26 385	8.3	458 136	19 077	22 601	4.9
San Francisco, CA PMSA	67.1	7.5	24.9	160 058	28 185	9.8	12.7	3 016	2 429	16 311	2.4	910 557	8 174	36 005	4.0
Marin	90.4	3.8	5.4	14 887	2 411	6.4	7.5	742	551	3 505	3.5	130 385	−180	4 397	3.4
San Francisco	53.8	10.7	35.0	98 720	16 657	13.5	19.7	1 226	515	6 383	1.9	403 001	−2 306	18 946	4.7
San Mateo	73.5	5.4	20.6	46 451	9 117	6.9	8.7	1 048	1 363	6 423	2.6	377 171	10 660	12 662	3.4
San Jose, CA PMSA (Santa Clara)	74.3	3.8	21.2	142 122	32 680	9.2	12.4	7 574	3 401	30 195	5.6	896 635	55 999	32 328	3.6
Santa Cruz-Watsonville, CA PMSA (Santa Cruz)	92.9	1.3	4.9	31 969	6 719	13.8	16.9	507	437	3 421	3.7	140 208	3 719	11 616	8.3
Santa Rosa, CA PMSA (Sonoma)	93.6	1.5	3.6	42 700	9 013	10.4	12.3	1 487	1 930	15 689	9.7	230 410	25 079	10 146	4.4
Vallejo-Fairfield-Napa, CA PMSA	74.8	10.8	13.4	45 308	10 932	9.6	11.4	1 815	1 331	14 504	8.9	232 588	7 197	16 716	7.2
Napa	94.0	1.1	4.2	10 335	2 196	9.2	11.2	232	316	3 237	7.3	57 807	340	3 468	6.0
Solano	68.7	13.9	16.4	34 973	8 736	9.7	11.4	1 583	1 015	11 267	9.4	174 781	6 857	13 248	7.6
San Luis Obispo-Atascadero-Paso Robles, CA MSA (San Luis Obispo)	92.3	2.8	3.7	27 271	5 249	12.7	14.6	1 156	916	7 372	8.2	103 554	7 307	5 694	5.5
Santa Barbara-Santa Maria-Lompoc, CA MSA (Santa Barbara)	90.0	3.0	5.7	54 289	11 610	14.5	18.4	780	793	6 163	4.5	192 730	420	10 944	5.7
Santa Fe, NM MSA	95.2	.9	1.1	15 165	3 632	11.6	14.6	340	445	3 169	6.5	72 225	6 837	3 695	5.1
Los Alamos	95.6	.6	3.0	353	71	1.9	1.9	9	161	404	5.3	10 544	−199	315	3.0
Santa Fe	95.2	.9	.8	14 812	3 561	13.2	16.9	331	284	2 765	6.7	61 681	7 036	3 380	5.5
Sarasota-Bradenton, FL MSA	92.1	6.8	.8	58 381	11 302	11.2	16.8	6 192	5 011	34 714	12.7	242 463	23 995	8 001	3.3
Manatee	89.8	9.0	.8	29 372	6 410	12.9	20.0	2 447	2 371	14 676	12.7	106 639	11 634	3 790	3.6
Sarasota	94.0	5.1	.8	29 009	4 892	9.9	13.9	3 745	2 640	20 038	12.8	135 824	12 361	4 211	3.1
Savannah, GA MSA	61.7	36.6	1.4	51 028	14 322	18.6	27.3	2 142	2 063	12 886	12.1	130 107	9 980	6 277	4.8
Bryan	82.2	16.9	.8	2 588	713	12.8	15.2	205	271	2 132	38.4	9 585	2 462	374	3.9
Chatham	56.6	41.6	1.6	44 531	12 515	20.0	30.6	1 547	1 411	8 638	9.5	105 266	4 591	5 302	5.0
Effingham	83.1	16.3	.4	3 909	1 094	12.7	16.0	390	381	2 116	22.3	15 256	2 927	601	3.9
Scranton--Wilkes-Barre--Hazleton, PA MSA	98.3	1.0	.7	78 418	17 099	12.5	16.5	1 399	1 359	10 979	4.1	310 715	3 889	22 084	7.1
Columbia	99.0	.5	.5	6 908	1 371	11.2	13.1	205	200	1 042	4.1	32 686	1 344	2 391	7.3
Lackawanna	98.3	.8	.8	27 293	5 878	12.7	16.7	428	448	3 551	3.9	105 907	238	7 339	6.9
Luzerne	98.0	1.3	.6	40 710	8 978	12.6	17.2	654	607	5 885	4.2	157 290	1 252	11 184	7.1
Wyoming	99.0	.5	.4	3 507	872	12.0	14.7	112	104	501	4.2	14 832	1 055	1 170	7.9
Seattle-Tacoma-Bremerton, WA CMSA	86.0	5.0	7.7	331 474	72 156	10.3	12.6	24 283	21 868	170 688	13.9	1 787 435	192 712	96 068	5.4
Bremerton, WA PMSA (Kitsap)	89.7	2.9	5.6	20 621	5 160	9.5	11.7	1 769	1 554	15 059	20.3	93 532	9 324	6 337	6.8
Olympia, WA PMSA (Thurston)	91.5	2.1	4.8	19 640	4 595	10.4	12.2	1 996	2 228	14 665	22.1	97 046	16 515	6 388	6.6
Seattle-Bellevue-Everett, WA PMSA	85.7	4.6	8.5	210 330	42 464	9.6	11.5	15 730	13 673	105 762	12.3	1 277 846	123 249	63 494	5.0
Island	91.4	2.3	5.4	5 066	1 130	7.6	9.2	729	690	5 092	19.7	26 648	3 770	1 292	4.8
King	83.1	5.8	10.0	157 577	30 498	9.9	12.0	10 185	8 142	66 956	10.3	952 588	76 178	46 274	4.9
Snohomish	92.8	1.2	4.6	47 687	10 836	9.0	10.6	4 816	4 841	33 714	18.3	298 610	43 301	15 928	5.3
Tacoma, WA PMSA (Pierce)	84.2	8.0	6.3	80 883	19 937	12.9	16.1	4 788	4 413	35 202	15.4	319 011	43 624	19 849	6.2

[1]Unemployment as a percent of civilian labor force.

Source: Population by Race—U.S. Bureau of the Census, "County Population Estimates by Age, Sex, Race, and Hispanic Origin - 4/1/90 to 7/1/96" data file (related Internet site <http://www.census.gov/population/www/estimates/co_casrh.html>); Poverty—U.S. Bureau of the Census, "State and County Income and Poverty Estimates - 1993," Internet site <http://www.census.gov/ftp/pub/housing/saipe/est93ALL.dat> (accessed 16 January 1998); Building Permits—U.S. Bureau of the Census, "Construction–Building Permits" on diskette, annual (related Internet site <http://www.census.gov/const/www/C40/table3.html#annual>), and "1990 Census of Population and Housing, Summary Tape File 1C" on CD-ROM; Labor Force—U.S. Bureau of Labor Statistics, Local Area Unemployment Statistics - Time Series, Internet site <gopher://hopi2.gov:70/11/Time%20Series/LA%20%20Local%20Area%20Unemployment%20Statistics/Data> for each state (accessed April 1997), BLS gopher service discontinued October 31, 1997 (related BLS Internet site <http://www.bls.gov>).

Table C–2. Metro Counties — Population by Race, Poverty, Building Permits, and Labor Force—Con.

[MSA = Metropolitan statistical area. CMSA = Consolidated MSA. PMSA = Primary MSA. NECMA = New England county metropolitan area. All areas defined as of June 30, 1996. Table includes 245 MSAs, 17 CMSAs, and 58 PMSAs not in New England; 12 NECMAs; and 844 component counties]

Metropolitan areas and component counties	Population by race, 1996, percent—			Persons below poverty level, 1993				New private housing units authorized by building permits				Civilian labor force, 1996			
				Number		Percent				1990–1996 period				Unemployment	
	White	Black	Asian or Pacific Islander	All persons	Related children 5 to 17 years	All persons	Related children 5 to 17 years	1996	1995	Total units	Percent of 1990 housing stock	Total	Net change, 1990–1996	Total	Rate[1]
Sharon, PA MSA (Mercer)	94.0	5.5	.4	17 624	4 278	14.8	19.9	339	397	2 166	4.4	55 527	2 020	2 445	4.4
Sheboygan, WI MSA (Sheboygan)	96.3	.7	2.6	7 843	1 803	7.3	8.3	720	733	4 056	10.0	61 725	6 174	1 747	2.8
Sherman-Denison, TX MSA (Grayson)	90.8	7.4	.6	15 369	3 418	15.9	18.9	210	209	852	1.9	49 339	2 917	2 387	4.8
Shreveport-Bossier City, LA MSA	62.7	36.3	.7	86 666	23 977	22.9	30.9	1 366	1 148	6 010	3.7	183 051	15 702	13 194	7.2
Bossier	76.5	21.7	1.4	14 632	3 883	16.5	21.0	825	581	3 114	8.9	44 774	5 588	2 959	6.6
Caddo	56.9	42.3	.6	62 426	17 624	25.3	34.7	508	537	2 730	2.5	119 274	8 488	8 339	7.0
Webster	66.1	33.6	.2	9 608	2 470	22.7	29.5	33	30	166	.9	19 003	1 626	1 896	10.0
Sioux City, IA-NE MSA	94.2	1.9	1.9	15 360	3 844	12.8	15.7	427	579	3 415	7.5	66 716	7 934	2 424	3.6
Woodbury, IA	94.2	2.1	1.7	13 309	3 375	13.0	16.4	341	384	2 619	6.7	56 486	6 359	2 081	3.7
Dakota, NE	94.4	.5	3.1	2 051	469	11.4	11.9	86	195	796	12.3	10 230	1 575	343	3.4
Sioux Falls, SD MSA	97.2	.7	.7	13 521	2 875	8.9	9.6	1 547	1 518	9 484	17.1	93 735	14 675	1 988	2.1
Lincoln	99.0	.2	.4	1 173	277	6.9	7.1	213	205	945	16.2	10 361	1 983	191	1.8
Minnehaha	96.9	.8	.8	12 348	2 598	9.2	10.0	1 334	1 313	8 539	17.2	83 374	12 692	1 797	2.2
South Bend, IN MSA (St. Joseph)	87.7	10.7	1.3	30 186	7 163	12.1	16.1	1 303	1 150	9 018	9.2	135 843	11 167	5 397	4.0
Spokane, WA MSA (Spokane)	94.5	1.6	2.3	53 045	12 709	13.4	16.6	3 401	2 716	19 748	13.2	201 616	29 515	11 697	5.8
Springfield, IL MSA	90.5	8.3	1.0	21 591	5 011	10.6	13.4	1 131	1 201	8 947	11.0	106 513	731	4 751	4.5
Menard	99.5	.1	.2	1 023	245	8.5	10.0	106	114	618	13.3	6 245	383	286	4.6
Sangamon	90.0	8.8	1.0	20 568	4 766	10.7	13.6	1 025	1 087	8 329	10.8	100 268	348	4 465	4.5
Springfield, MO MSA	97.0	1.7	.8	43 353	9 320	15.3	18.1	2 259	2 468	15 556	14.2	170 065	33 158	5 775	3.4
Christian	99.0	.1	.3	4 536	1 076	11.1	12.4	732	622	2 384	18.6	24 990	7 763	962	3.8
Greene	96.4	2.1	1.0	34 337	7 066	15.9	19.0	1 408	1 752	12 775	14.5	131 345	22 770	4 199	3.2
Webster	98.4	.8	.2	4 480	1 178	17.4	21.0	119	94	397	4.4	13 730	2 625	614	4.5
Springfield, MA NECMA	90.2	7.7	1.9	76 428	21 854	13.2	21.0	1 166	1 319	9 538	4.1	287 793	−15 415	12 906	4.5
Hampden	89.0	9.6	1.2	64 892	19 735	14.6	24.0	718	878	6 195	3.4	209 534	−13 385	10 391	5.0
Hampshire	93.6	2.1	4.1	11 536	2 119	8.6	9.7	448	441	3 343	6.3	78 259	−2 030	2 515	3.2
State College, PA MSA (Centre)	93.0	2.6	4.3	13 737	1 911	11.8	11.1	516	872	4 405	9.5	65 149	4 437	1 905	2.9
Steubenville-Weirton, OH-WV MSA	95.3	4.2	.4	22 499	5 298	16.0	21.8	100	102	780	1.3	57 531	−2 678	3 612	6.3
Jefferson, OH	93.2	6.1	.4	13 437	3 344	17.1	23.9	17	28	162	.5	30 798	−1 687	2 026	6.6
Brooke, WV	98.8	.8	.3	4 011	846	15.2	19.1	16	27	222	2.0	11 515	−439	656	5.7
Hancock, WV	97.0	2.6	.3	5 051	1 108	14.3	18.9	67	47	396	2.7	15 218	−552	930	6.1
Stockton-Lodi, CA MSA (San Joaquin)	77.9	5.8	15.2	96 179	28 384	18.8	25.9	2 337	2 300	17 688	10.6	240 805	9 841	26 968	11.2
Sumter, SC MSA (Sumter)	54.1	44.6	1.1	22 256	5 868	21.9	27.4	389	356	3 221	9.2	44 478	3 784	2 888	6.5
Syracuse, NY MSA	91.7	6.2	1.5	91 942	22 371	12.5	16.1	1 452	1 238	12 775	4.3	363 324	−14 145	17 580	4.8
Cayuga	95.2	3.8	.6	10 905	2 805	13.6	17.5	150	152	1 128	3.4	37 638	−1 733	2 150	5.7
Madison	97.6	1.2	.8	7 635	1 796	11.3	13.4	110	102	1 331	5.0	34 975	−527	1 856	5.3
Onondaga	88.3	9.0	2.0	56 783	13 481	12.2	16.1	963	728	8 387	4.4	234 103	−10 846	9 597	4.1
Oswego	98.5	.6	.5	16 619	4 289	13.5	16.6	229	256	1 929	4.0	56 608	−1 039	3 977	7.0
Tallahassee, FL MSA	64.9	33.1	1.7	42 345	9 480	17.3	20.2	1 926	2 881	15 992	16.6	142 089	11 425	4 419	3.1
Gadsden	37.6	61.8	.3	12 077	3 494	29.2	34.7	120	128	1 068	7.2	18 806	816	920	4.9
Leon	70.4	27.3	2.0	30 268	5 986	14.9	16.2	1 806	2 753	14 924	18.4	123 283	10 609	3 499	2.8
Tampa-St. Petersburg-Clearwater, FL MSA	87.9	10.2	1.6	318 761	69 094	14.8	20.8	14 680	13 619	90 759	8.9	1 100 865	83 470	43 118	3.9
Hernando	94.4	4.6	.6	16 347	3 423	13.9	20.4	1 047	951	8 965	17.9	42 731	6 697	1 941	4.5
Hillsborough	82.8	14.9	1.9	148 539	35 352	17.0	22.3	8 860	7 125	43 394	11.8	494 975	42 205	18 966	3.8
Pasco	96.5	2.3	.8	43 586	8 486	14.6	21.0	2 283	2 053	13 955	9.4	121 282	12 420	5 915	4.9
Pinellas	89.1	9.0	1.7	110 289	21 833	12.8	18.7	2 490	3 490	24 445	5.3	441 877	22 148	16 296	3.7
Terre Haute, IN MSA	94.4	4.3	1.0	19 936	4 314	13.9	17.0	512	376	3 106	5.0	74 246	6 889	4 795	6.5
Clay	99.3	.5	.1	2 780	618	10.7	12.6	49	36	293	2.8	12 798	1 686	780	6.1
Vermillion	99.5	.1	.2	1 908	419	11.3	13.5	45	42	252	3.5	8 117	658	610	7.5
Vigo	92.4	5.9	1.4	15 248	3 277	15.1	18.8	418	298	2 561	5.8	53 331	4 545	3 405	6.4
Texarkana, TX-Texarkana, AR MSA	75.7	23.4	.4	23 508	5 977	19.3	24.0	652	218	1 925	3.8	57 390	2 240	4 243	7.4
Bowie, TX	76.2	22.8	.4	14 569	3 654	17.7	21.7	149	142	943	2.8	40 153	2 073	3 113	7.8
Miller, AR	74.7	24.5	.4	8 939	2 323	22.8	28.9	503	76	982	6.1	17 237	167	1 130	6.6
Toledo, OH MSA	86.3	12.2	1.2	90 111	23 724	14.8	20.8	2 024	2 192	12 308	5.0	313 509	3 388	15 088	4.8
Fulton	99.0	.3	.5	3 005	731	7.4	8.5	165	183	922	6.5	22 313	1 555	1 177	5.3
Lucas	82.2	16.2	1.3	76 592	21 097	16.7	24.9	1 122	1 178	6 865	3.6	227 279	−1 345	11 537	5.1
Wood	97.5	1.1	1.2	10 514	1 896	9.5	9.1	737	831	4 521	10.8	63 917	3 178	2 374	3.7
Topeka, KS MSA (Shawnee)	88.9	9.0	1.0	19 892	5 039	12.1	16.1	785	684	5 121	7.4	89 383	2 252	4 632	5.2
Tucson, AZ MSA (Pima)	90.5	3.7	2.3	139 155	34 206	19.0	26.4	5 697	7 275	37 206	12.5	382 095	65 580	14 269	3.7
Tulsa, OK MSA	83.8	8.5	1.1	122 238	28 811	16.3	20.0	3 576	3 582	20 088	6.4	387 547	17 929	12 866	3.3
Creek	88.3	3.3	.3	10 621	2 537	16.5	19.0	161	69	575	2.3	30 960	1 569	1 318	4.3
Osage	74.6	10.9	.2	7 457	1 844	17.7	20.8	41	44	197	1.1	19 479	471	682	3.5
Rogers	86.3	.9	.4	7 001	1 572	11.4	12.1	341	305	2 052	9.6	31 503	3 032	1 085	3.4
Tulsa	83.5	10.2	1.4	89 739	20 991	17.0	21.6	2 767	2 956	16 166	7.1	279 246	10 730	8 965	3.2
Wagoner	86.3	4.3	.4	7 420	1 867	14.2	15.7	266	208	1 098	5.7	26 359	2 127	816	3.1
Tuscaloosa, AL MSA (Tuscaloosa)	71.3	27.6	1.0	28 946	6 149	19.3	23.7	1 054	1 413	6 584	11.2	77 790	8 470	2 773	3.6
Tyler, TX MSA (Smith)	77.0	21.9	.6	28 090	6 954	17.6	22.6	778	314	2 311	3.6	86 980	11 279	5 595	6.4
Utica-Rome, NY MSA	93.7	5.1	1.0	43 138	11 212	14.1	19.8	422	479	4 278	3.2	141 844	−3 740	7 521	5.3
Herkimer	99.2	.4	.3	9 089	2 286	13.6	17.9	91	125	1 150	3.7	30 718	300	2 079	6.8
Oneida	92.1	6.4	1.2	34 049	8 926	14.2	20.3	331	354	3 128	3.1	111 126	−4 040	5 442	4.9

[1]Unemployment as a percent of civilian labor force.

Source: Population by Race—U.S. Bureau of the Census, "County Population Estimates by Age, Sex, Race, and Hispanic Origin - 4/1/90 to 7/1/96" data file (related Internet site <http://www.census.gov/population/www/estimates/co_casrh.html>); Poverty—U.S. Bureau of the Census, "State and County Income and Poverty Estimates - 1993," Internet site <http://www.census.gov/ftp/pub/housing/saipe/est93ALL.dat> (accessed 16 January 1998); Building Permits—U.S. Bureau of the Census, "Construction–Building Permits" on diskette, annual (related Internet site <http://www.census.gov/const/www/C40/table3.html#annual>), and "1990 Census of Population and Housing, Summary Tape File 1C" on CD-ROM; Labor Force—U.S. Bureau of Labor Statistics, Local Area Unemployment Statistics - Time Series, Internet site <gopher://hopi2.gov:70/11/Time%20Series/LA%20%20Local%20Area%20Unemployment%20Statistics/Data> for each state (accessed April 1997), BLS gopher service discontinued October 31, 1997 (related BLS Internet site <http://www.bls.gov>).

[MSA = Metropolitan statistical area.   CMSA = Consolidated MSA.   PMSA = Primary MSA.   NECMA = New England county metropolitan area.   All areas defined as of June 30, 1996.   Table includes 245 MSAs, 17 CMSAs, and 58 PMSAs not in New England; 12 NECMAs; and 844 component counties]

Metropolitan areas and component counties	Population by race, 1996, percent—			Persons below poverty level, 1993				New private housing units authorized by building permits				Civilian labor force, 1996			
				Number		Percent		1990–1996 period						Unemployment	
	White	Black	Asian or Pacific Islander	All persons	Related children 5 to 17 years	All persons	Related children 5 to 17 years	1996	1995	Total units	Percent of 1990 housing stock	Total	Net change, 1990–1996	Total	Rate[1]
Victoria, TX MSA (Victoria)	92.4	6.8	.5	14 510	3 974	18.1	23.2	174	172	1 130	3.9	41 909	5 616	2 120	5.1
Visalia-Tulare-Porterville, CA MSA (Tulare)	90.8	1.7	5.8	97 914	30 491	28.2	36.6	1 375	1 714	12 895	12.3	160 640	8 179	25 491	15.9
Waco, TX MSA (McLennan)	82.2	16.4	1.0	41 249	9 906	21.3	27.1	423	509	2 857	3.6	100 023	7 368	4 451	4.4
Washington-Baltimore, DC-MD-VA-WV CMSA	69.2	25.7	4.8	697 974	155 682	9.9	12.9	42 396	40 944	288 370	10.8	3 916 273	164 107	172 757	4.4
Baltimore, MD PMSA	70.1	27.2	2.4	294 802	71 467	12.0	16.6	10 741	11 349	87 789	9.3	1 302 856	56 817	70 746	5.4
Anne Arundel	82.8	14.5	2.4	30 548	6 582	6.8	8.0	3 083	3 288	23 348	14.9	250 275	19 714	10 170	4.1
Baltimore	81.8	15.0	2.9	55 142	11 091	7.7	9.9	2 355	2 545	24 473	8.7	395 437	14 264	20 664	5.2
Carroll	96.2	2.8	.8	6 266	1 299	4.6	4.8	1 205	1 362	8 506	19.5	77 389	9 240	3 222	4.2
Harford	87.5	10.3	1.8	12 270	2 884	6.0	7.2	1 872	1 597	14 300	21.5	110 261	12 599	5 890	5.3
Howard	79.8	14.3	5.6	8 286	1 706	3.8	4.2	1 726	1 799	13 030	18.0	131 329	18 651	4 054	3.1
Queen Anne's	85.3	14.0	.5	2 802	632	7.7	9.8	393	442	2 412	17.3	19 800	1 800	918	4.6
Baltimore city	33.9	64.5	1.2	179 488	47 273	25.7	38.8	107	316	1 720	.6	318 365	−19 451	25 828	8.1
Hagerstown, MD PMSA (Washington)	91.7	7.1	.9	12 687	2 730	10.6	12.9	640	544	4 045	8.5	68 748	8 053	3 612	5.3
Washington, DC-MD-VA-WV PMSA	68.1	25.4	6.2	390 485	81 485	8.8	10.8	31 015	29 051	196 536	11.7	2 544 669	99 237	98 399	3.9
District of Columbia	34.0	62.7	3.0	111 771	23 322	20.4	31.1	—	35	1 383	.5	272 167	−56 995	23 204	8.5
Calvert, MD	79.9	19.0	.8	3 822	921	6.0	6.9	814	1 210	6 554	34.5	35 620	7 187	1 442	4.0
Charles, MD	75.6	21.9	1.7	7 921	1 935	7.2	8.0	1 207	1 051	6 791	19.7	60 915	5 873	2 080	3.4
Frederick, MD	91.8	6.6	1.3	9 813	2 179	5.7	6.5	1 669	1 525	13 735	25.0	98 993	13 262	3 336	3.4
Montgomery, MD	75.0	14.4	10.3	48 412	9 637	6.0	7.2	3 062	3 682	25 313	8.6	480 289	31 961	12 562	2.6
Prince George's, MD	39.0	56.0	4.6	66 080	13 915	8.7	10.3	3 162	3 584	28 954	10.7	461 870	27 859	21 272	4.6
Arlington, VA	79.8	11.1	8.7	15 241	2 546	8.7	14.7	1 299	618	4 617	5.4	106 390	−2 092	3 355	3.2
Clarke, VA	89.6	9.9	.4	1 154	240	9.6	12.5	57	80	403	8.9	6 310	−108	187	3.0
Culpeper, VA	77.8	20.5	1.4	3 484	797	11.7	14.3	259	257	1 628	15.5	15 085	782	717	4.8
Fairfax, VA	80.6	8.3	10.8	53 093	10 798	6.0	7.1	7 898	7 226	43 295	14.1	505 477	21 722	13 632	2.7
Fauquier, VA	86.7	12.3	.8	3 618	795	7.1	8.3	305	239	2 078	11.7	26 770	229	763	2.9
King George, VA	76.4	22.2	1.2	1 396	317	8.8	10.1	96	106	1 041	19.7	8 151	1 187	326	4.0
Loudoun, VA	88.6	8.0	3.2	4 626	977	4.2	4.9	3 093	2 802	18 371	55.8	67 450	15 054	1 678	2.5
Prince William, VA	82.8	12.8	4.0	13 491	3 318	5.6	6.5	3 061	2 581	15 047	20.1	128 458	10 916	3 596	2.8
Spotsylvania, VA	86.2	12.0	1.4	4 686	1 090	6.7	7.2	1 458	1 286	8 041	39.3	37 040	5 646	1 252	3.4
Stafford, VA	90.1	7.8	1.6	4 207	934	5.6	5.7	1 418	980	8 385	40.8	40 130	7 904	1 115	2.8
Warren, VA	93.9	5.6	.4	3 186	653	11.1	13.6	185	220	1 638	14.6	14 654	604	742	5.1
Alexandria city, VA	70.9	23.3	5.5	11 663	2 159	10.2	18.8	603	251	1 644	2.8	74 022	404	2 882	3.9
Fairfax city, VA	85.0	5.3	9.5	1 460	226	7.1	8.3	98	132	381	5.0	12 261	38	179	1.5
Falls Church city, VA	89.6	3.4	6.4	543	80	5.6	6.0	5	3	64	1.4	5 753	−101	233	4.1
Fredericksburg city, VA	74.4	24.0	1.4	3 038	571	15.9	22.6	41	57	468	5.8	11 191	841	432	3.9
Manassas city, VA	83.9	11.6	4.1	2 108	437	6.7	7.3	86	201	1 378	13.5	18 551	2 094	646	3.5
Manassas Park city, VA	88.2	8.2	3.5	545	131	7.4	8.4	111	48	511	22.7	4 098	268	171	4.2
Berkeley, WV	95.4	3.8	.6	9 768	2 331	14.9	20.6	777	639	2 539	10.0	32 748	3 196	1 777	5.4
Jefferson, WV	91.8	7.6	.5	5 359	1 176	13.9	17.6	251	238	2 277	15.6	20 276	1 506	820	4.0
Waterloo-Cedar Falls, IA MSA (Black Hawk)	91.4	7.4	1.1	17 131	4 102	14.1	17.6	324	232	1 738	3.5	68 761	6 684	3 129	4.6
Wausau, WI MSA (Marathon)	96.6	.1	2.8	10 274	2 605	8.4	10.1	691	711	4 886	11.2	71 249	9 375	2 790	3.9
West Palm Beach-Boca Raton, FL MSA (Palm Beach)	83.9	14.4	1.5	118 376	25 301	12.3	18.3	9 971	10 285	66 473	14.4	466 565	35 977	31 134	6.7
Wheeling, WV-OH MSA	97.4	2.1	.4	27 823	6 278	17.8	23.9	107	155	648	.9	72 632	2 416	4 133	5.7
Marshall, WV	99.1	.5	.3	6 887	1 573	18.7	24.7	5	13	71	.5	16 611	583	1 046	6.3
Ohio, WV	95.8	3.4	.7	8 624	1 723	17.7	23.0	29	36	229	1.0	24 855	647	1 106	4.4
Belmont, OH	97.6	2.0	.2	12 312	2 982	17.4	24.0	73	106	348	1.1	31 166	1 186	1 981	6.4
Wichita, KS MSA	88.5	8.1	2.3	63 374	15 911	12.5	15.7	2 895	2 712	17 893	8.8	266 976	8 226	11 537	4.3
Butler	97.6	1.1	.4	4 930	1 176	8.9	9.6	590	432	2 098	10.5	29 385	3 313	1 138	3.9
Harvey	96.9	1.9	.8	3 089	709	10.0	11.3	80	108	579	5.9	16 107	−72	621	3.9
Sedgwick	86.7	9.5	2.7	55 355	14 026	13.1	16.9	2 225	2 172	15 076	8.9	221 484	4 985	9 778	4.4
Wichita Falls, TX MSA	87.7	9.4	2.0	21 179	5 187	16.5	20.9	498	402	2 036	3.7	66 008	5 163	2 983	4.5
Archer	99.3	.2	.1	892	206	11.1	12.5	12	8	50	1.4	4 216	362	121	2.9
Wichita	86.9	10.0	2.1	20 287	4 981	16.9	21.5	486	394	1 986	3.9	61 792	4 801	2 862	4.6
Williamsport, PA MSA (Lycoming)	96.6	2.7	.5	16 385	3 949	13.7	17.7	400	314	2 261	4.6	57 830	505	3 749	6.5
Wilmington, NC MSA	79.0	20.0	.6	30 399	6 312	15.7	19.2	3 808	3 965	20 408	21.7	105 682	15 637	5 651	5.3
Brunswick	80.7	18.5	.2	9 482	2 050	16.1	20.4	1 122	963	5 361	14.4	29 738	5 086	2 177	7.3
New Hanover	78.2	20.6	.8	20 917	4 262	15.5	18.7	2 686	3 002	15 047	26.4	75 944	10 551	3 474	4.6
Yakima, WA MSA (Yakima)	91.0	1.5	1.8	48 617	13 829	23.0	30.2	719	623	5 175	7.3	116 039	13 735	15 566	13.4
York, PA MSA (York)	95.1	3.9	.9	29 707	6 478	8.2	10.1	2 132	1 976	15 819	11.7	192 823	7 495	8 381	4.3
Youngstown-Warren, OH MSA	89.2	10.2	.5	94 917	25 173	15.6	22.7	1 604	1 551	10 720	4.4	282 722	5 070	17 971	6.4
Columbiana	98.1	1.4	.3	18 287	4 884	16.3	22.6	104	106	1 037	2.4	51 670	2 915	3 187	6.2
Mahoning	83.0	16.4	.5	45 852	12 274	17.4	26.0	903	812	5 800	5.4	119 400	931	7 897	6.6
Trumbull	92.0	7.3	.6	30 778	8 015	13.3	19.0	597	633	3 883	4.3	111 652	1 224	6 887	6.2
Yuba City, CA MSA	83.1	2.9	11.5	24 472	7 167	18.1	25.0	398	495	5 759	12.7	55 441	−1 591	8 335	15.0
Sutter	84.2	1.9	12.1	11 447	3 092	15.6	20.4	292	383	4 129	17.1	34 356	193	5 411	15.7
Yuba	81.7	4.3	10.9	13 025	4 075	21.1	30.1	106	112	1 630	7.7	21 085	−1 784	2 924	13.9
Yuma, AZ MSA (Yuma)	93.1	3.4	1.8	35 412	9 200	28.0	33.5	1 151	773	5 336	11.5	68 839	21 151	21 368	31.0

— Represents zero.

[1]Unemployment as a percent of civilian labor force.

Source: Population by Race—U.S. Bureau of the Census, "County Population Estimates by Age, Sex, Race, and Hispanic Origin - 4/1/90 to 7/1/96" data file (related Internet site <http://www.census.gov/population/www/estimates/co_casrh.html>);   Poverty—U.S. Bureau of the Census, "State and County Income and Poverty Estimates - 1993," Internet site <http://www.census.gov/ftp/pub/housing/saipe/est93ALL.dat> (accessed 16 January 1998);   Building Permits—U.S. Bureau of the Census, "Construction–Building Permits" on diskette, annual (related Internet site <http://www.census.gov/const/www/C40/table3.html#annual>), and "1990 Census of Population and Housing, Summary Tape File 1C" on CD-ROM;   Labor Force—U.S. Bureau of Labor Statistics, Local Area Unemployment Statistics - Time Series, Internet site <gopher://hopi2.gov:70/11/Time%20Series/LA%20%20Local%20Area%20Unemployment%20Statistics/Data> for each state (accessed April 1997), BLS gopher service discontinued October 31, 1997 (related BLS Internet site <http://www.bls.gov>).

[MSA = Metropolitan statistical area. CMSA = Consolidated MSA. PMSA = Primary MSA. NECMA = New England county metropolitan area. All areas defined as of June 30, 1996 Table includes 245 MSAs, 17 CMSAs, and 58 PMSAs not in New England; 12 NECMAs; and 844 component counties]

Metropolitan areas and component counties	Private nonfarm business, 1995							Personal income, 1994								
	Establishments		Employment								Earnings					
					By selected industry, percent—								By selected industry, percent—			
	Total	Net change, 1990–1995	Total	Percent change, 1990–1995	Manufacturing	Retail trade	Services	Total (mil dol)	Percent change, 1990–1994	Per capita[1] (dollars)	Total (mil dol)	Manufacturing	Retail trade	FIRE[2]	Services	Government
Abilene, TX MSA (Taylor)	3 528	212	44 958	10.6	8.1	23.7	43.4	2 264.0	21.0	18 572	1 636.6	6.9	11.1	3.9	28.3	23.8
Albany, GA MSA	2 846	158	40 733	4.1	20.5	26.1	27.8	2 032.4	27.2	17 371	1 669.5	21.1	9.7	3.3	24.0	22.0
Dougherty	2 688	89	39 697	3.7	20.4	26.2	28.0	1 735.2	25.0	17 706	1 603.4	21.7	9.7	3.4	24.4	21.5
Lee	158	69	1 036	22.3	22.2	20.7	17.8	297.2	42.1	15 645	66.1	6.7	8.0	.9	14.0	33.3
Albany-Schenectady-Troy, NY MSA	20 259	82	315 911	1.6	11.8	22.4	42.3	19 868.0	18.1	22 701	14 382.3	13.1	9.1	7.4	27.5	27.5
Albany	8 897	267	161 308	2.2	6.7	20.2	45.5	7 466.7	17.0	25 632	7 859.2	6.3	7.5	9.3	26.3	35.3
Montgomery	1 151	48	16 255	11.9	33.6	19.6	28.5	949.8	16.0	18 230	515.5	29.0	10.0	4.0	23.3	17.5
Rensselaer	2 696	–82	39 923	–3.3	14.4	20.6	46.7	3 189.3	17.7	20 405	1 569.8	14.2	10.1	4.8	34.5	18.9
Saratoga	3 778	118	44 091	10.5	15.5	32.7	29.6	4 174.3	22.1	21 640	1 819.6	17.5	14.6	6.4	23.5	21.8
Schenectady	3 198	–237	49 035	–6.6	14.8	21.8	45.5	3 545.2	16.5	23 698	2 393.5	28.2	9.2	4.8	31.6	13.1
Schoharie	539	–32	5 299	9.7	18.7	28.2	33.1	542.6	19.0	16 444	224.7	8.9	12.5	5.3	17.9	35.5
Albuquerque, NM MSA	16 817	2 057	261 824	27.0	10.9	22.8	39.0	12 839.1	33.4	19 890	9 641.3	10.8	10.9	5.4	32.6	20.8
Bernalillo	15 001	1 614	239 130	23.4	8.9	21.9	40.6	10 796.0	31.7	20 939	8 784.0	8.9	10.9	5.6	34.4	21.1
Sandoval	1 057	312	15 588	118.3	41.6	21.0	17.2	1 241.2	45.3	16 311	581.5	42.2	8.1	2.3	12.8	10.7
Valencia	759	131	7 106	36.4	9.8	34.6	33.2	801.9	40.1	14 905	275.8	5.6	17.0	3.1	16.4	29.9
Alexandria, LA MSA (Rapides)	2 997	136	43 904	15.3	7.7	23.1	47.5	2 251.8	22.5	17 801	1 451.4	9.1	10.1	4.3	32.3	24.5
Allentown-Bethlehem-Easton, PA MSA	14 490	266	239 920	2.8	25.7	19.3	33.2	13 353.1	18.8	21 826	8 800.0	28.8	9.9	5.9	27.1	10.3
Carbon	1 058	–13	12 952	–4.8	32.0	20.0	32.6	1 029.1	17.5	17 472	425.8	25.9	12.7	3.5	25.2	17.4
Lehigh	8 206	365	151 950	7.3	22.7	18.6	35.4	6 905.5	19.0	23 181	5 443.3	28.1	9.5	6.2	28.2	9.1
Northampton	5 226	–86	75 018	–3.9	30.8	20.6	28.8	5 418.5	18.9	21 249	2 930.8	30.5	10.2	5.7	25.2	11.4
Altoona, PA MSA (Blair)	3 166	144	48 490	2.3	19.6	24.6	32.4	2 379.2	23.6	18 051	1 671.2	18.4	13.7	3.2	25.6	14.1
Amarillo, TX MSA	5 437	372	75 382	15.7	15.2	25.4	33.1	3 898.9	28.2	19 791	2 781.2	9.6	11.3	4.8	25.8	17.4
Potter	3 517	–85	54 633	10.7	18.2	21.1	35.9	1 919.0	31.3	18 649	2 115.8	9.8	11.1	5.1	26.4	18.0
Randall	1 920	457	20 749	31.3	7.3	36.5	25.7	1 980.0	25.4	21 041	665.4	9.0	12.0	4.0	23.9	15.5
Anchorage, AK MSA (Anchorage)	7 568	767	98 302	14.1	2.2	23.4	33.7	6 855.1	24.9	27 031	5 753.1	1.4	10.2	4.5	23.0	27.5
Anniston, AL MSA (Calhoun)	2 540	241	38 500	15.2	29.6	24.9	26.7	1 899.3	20.5	16 247	1 398.2	20.4	10.1	2.4	15.1	36.1
Appleton-Oshkosh-Neenah, WI MSA	8 600	821	168 109	13.3	33.8	18.4	24.9	7 038.8	27.5	21 182	5 663.3	40.3	8.2	5.4	17.7	10.0
Calumet	763	146	12 791	19.7	47.3	19.3	16.0	716.7	30.1	19 422	367.1	53.5	7.2	2.0	10.5	8.7
Outagamie	3 944	774	75 256	25.0	24.8	19.0	26.8	3 200.4	28.9	21 698	2 706.3	31.7	9.6	8.5	18.2	8.6
Winnebago	3 893	–99	80 062	3.3	40.1	17.6	24.5	3 121.7	25.5	21 107	2 590.0	47.5	6.9	2.7	18.2	11.6
Asheville, NC MSA	5 937	587	88 141	11.0	22.8	23.3	35.3	4 022.8	25.7	19 768	2 847.1	22.2	11.4	3.9	27.9	14.8
Buncombe	5 671	566	86 069	11.5	22.9	23.3	35.2	3 755.9	25.8	20 204	2 738.9	22.3	11.6	4.0	28.3	14.6
Madison	266	21	2 072	–6.8	18.0	23.0	39.9	266.9	24.2	15 165	108.2	21.0	6.6	1.2	17.4	19.8
Athens, GA MSA	3 401	385	50 624	18.8	25.5	27.1	28.2	2 420.9	26.8	18 148	1 880.5	17.6	10.2	3.5	19.4	30.9
Clarke	2 642	250	44 446	16.9	25.2	28.4	28.9	1 633.5	25.1	18 089	1 622.1	18.4	10.5	3.6	19.9	33.5
Madison	324	58	2 645	43.1	36.9	12.4	22.3	371.3	27.3	16 213	115.2	7.0	8.5	1.9	14.8	15.9
Oconee	435	77	3 533	27.9	20.2	22.6	23.3	416.1	33.3	20 600	143.2	16.8	8.7	3.9	18.5	13.4
Atlanta, GA MSA	97 502	14 994	1 679 310	19.8	13.6	21.1	33.1	78 720.0	29.3	23 633	65 240.2	12.7	9.4	8.5	28.3	12.1
Barrow	658	130	7 725	9.2	37.1	27.1	16.6	565.7	33.1	16 445	276.6	31.2	12.3	3.3	14.1	13.6
Bartow	1 264	159	21 111	20.1	48.0	18.5	16.9	1 055.3	29.7	17 104	706.1	40.8	8.2	2.6	12.1	12.5
Carroll	1 615	161	27 371	7.9	39.7	20.5	21.8	1 233.9	23.9	16 109	828.7	37.1	10.5	4.0	18.4	13.4
Cherokee	1 977	571	17 959	42.1	19.4	28.6	25.0	2 155.0	43.0	19 789	669.5	12.3	12.9	5.9	20.0	15.8
Clayton	4 104	336	76 304	42.2	7.9	32.4	21.6	3 512.1	21.9	18 020	3 669.9	5.9	10.8	2.6	14.4	9.1
Cobb	15 586	2 728	237 631	28.8	11.7	24.6	33.2	12 651.4	27.9	24 860	8 688.2	12.8	12.6	7.9	25.8	11.1
Coweta	1 256	328	18 209	18.3	29.7	25.9	26.6	1 221.6	36.8	18 021	584.7	31.4	14.8	3.1	21.0	12.2
De Kalb	17 530	407	312 011	5.3	10.7	20.4	36.4	13 780.9	20.8	23 851	10 869.1	10.5	9.9	8.4	32.3	12.1
Douglas	1 694	273	20 602	29.1	9.4	33.0	35.0	1 446.5	30.1	18 103	616.0	6.4	18.0	3.9	28.7	13.8
Fayette	1 884	538	20 561	44.4	14.5	26.5	31.5	1 834.4	36.1	24 168	634.7	19.8	11.8	6.4	20.8	12.8
Forsyth	1 295	399	12 994	51.8	22.1	26.7	22.1	1 284.8	54.4	22 620	588.3	23.0	10.6	2.3	16.5	8.4
Fulton	28 205	3 729	603 247	12.7	9.9	16.3	38.0	21 589.9	28.2	31 267	27 017.1	8.9	6.8	11.6	33.6	13.0
Gwinnett	13 468	3 631	208 860	44.6	15.8	22.6	27.6	10 143.5	39.2	23 372	7 034.1	19.9	11.3	6.3	23.3	8.2
Henry	1 440	562	18 040	67.4	19.5	29.6	27.7	1 405.6	44.0	17 837	606.1	16.0	10.7	3.6	16.0	25.6
Newton	920	181	13 092	29.0	33.1	27.8	22.1	785.8	33.1	16 236	435.6	34.8	9.6	3.3	13.9	14.2
Paulding	676	210	5 662	42.9	15.2	38.7	19.7	801.1	39.0	14 382	216.5	9.3	16.5	3.3	13.8	22.1
Pickens	341	51	3 905	10.2	28.1	23.6	22.6	295.6	33.2	18 134	135.2	13.2	12.9	6.6	16.2	14.6
Rockdale	1 637	261	26 761	41.2	27.1	20.8	25.2	1 250.1	29.3	20 162	820.6	28.6	10.2	2.4	16.6	10.7
Spalding	1 153	65	18 264	12.1	37.1	24.7	23.7	941.6	23.8	16 519	550.4	27.3	13.1	4.7	21.8	19.1
Walton	799	274	9 001	31.4	38.0	21.4	19.0	765.1	36.0	17 117	292.7	27.3	11.1	3.7	13.7	18.9
Augusta-Aiken, GA-SC MSA	9 351	692	166 521	11.3	27.5	22.4	34.6	8 405.9	21.7	18 746	6 336.3	30.6	9.2	3.1	20.9	21.6
Columbia, GA	1 481	296	17 941	28.0	22.5	31.1	23.0	1 423.4	26.1	17 815	439.4	23.9	12.2	5.7	21.2	16.5
McDuffie, GA	463	10	6 780	–.7	35.1	26.3	21.1	348.4	24.6	16 435	191.5	26.9	14.9	4.4	14.1	16.4
Richmond, GA	4 606	117	82 580	6.0	16.6	23.4	43.4	3 773.5	19.0	19 253	3 259.0	17.7	10.1	3.6	25.2	31.9
Aiken, SC	2 479	240	54 793	16.0	42.2	17.9	28.4	2 570.9	22.9	19 462	2 325.1	49.6	6.9	2.0	15.7	8.7
Edgefield, SC	322	29	4 427	22.5	57.4	16.5	14.9	289.6	23.7	15 086	121.3	41.7	9.5	1.8	13.2	19.4

[1]Based on 1994 resident population estimated by the Bureau of Economic Analysis.
[2]Finance, insurance, and real estate.

Source: Private Nonfarm Business—U.S. Bureau of the Census, "County Business Patterns" on diskettes, annual (related Internet site <http://www.census.gov/epcd/cbp/view/cbpview.html>); Personal Income—U.S. Bureau of Economic Analysis, "Regional Economic Information System, 1969–1994" on CD-ROM (related Internet site <http://www.bea.doc.gov/bea/dr1.htm>).

[MSA = Metropolitan statistical area. CMSA = Consolidated MSA. PMSA = Primary MSA. NECMA = New England county metropolitan area. All areas defined as of June 30, 1996 Table includes 245 MSAs, 17 CMSAs, and 58 PMSAs not in New England; 12 NECMAs; and 844 component counties]

Metropolitan areas and component counties	Private nonfarm business, 1995							Personal income, 1994								
	Establishments		Employment								Earnings					
					By selected industry, percent—							By selected industry, percent—				
	Total	Net change, 1990–1995	Total	Percent change, 1990–1995	Manufacturing	Retail trade	Services	Total (mil dol)	Percent change, 1990–1994	Per capita[1] (dollars)	Total (mil dol)	Manufacturing	Retail trade	FIRE[2]	Services	Government
Austin-San Marcos, TX MSA	26 590	5 883	402 080	38.9	16.4	22.4	36.9	19 868.8	36.9	20 611	15 995.3	17.5	9.6	6.3	28.9	22.9
Bastrop.....................	676	170	5 330	44.9	16.7	34.4	26.1	650.4	30.4	15 267	223.0	11.8	14.9	3.1	17.0	32.2
Caldwell....................	478	38	3 606	-10.1	13.8	27.3	35.6	409.0	30.6	14 554	150.4	7.1	12.6	2.9	31.8	22.5
Hays......................	1 613	497	18 171	60.0	15.0	36.9	29.4	1 208.9	37.6	16 292	630.0	16.0	16.6	3.7	21.0	27.0
Travis....................	20 537	4 260	336 854	36.0	16.2	21.4	38.7	14 310.8	34.5	22 139	13 824.2	17.7	8.9	6.7	29.7	22.9
Williamson.................	3 286	918	38 119	67.5	19.4	22.2	26.2	3 289.8	50.9	19 049	1 167.8	19.1	13.1	4.6	25.2	18.6
Bakersfield, CA MSA (Kern)	10 469	-290	133 575	3.1	8.6	25.1	31.7	10 057.1	17.1	16 506	7 396.0	5.6	9.7	2.7	19.8	24.4
Bangor, ME NECMA (Penobscot)	3 958	110	52 579	.9	19.6	24.9	34.0	2 679.6	16.3	18 291	1 984.1	20.4	12.8	3.3	26.5	18.3
Barnstable-Yarmouth, MA NECMA (Barnstable)...............	7 410	229	59 987	-.9	5.0	35.5	38.4	4 882.6	17.5	24 886	2 350.9	4.6	18.7	5.3	36.2	16.7
Baton Rouge, LA MSA	13 535	1 715	227 204	21.9	10.3	20.8	36.3	10 819.6	28.2	19 383	8 240.0	15.0	8.7	6.3	25.8	17.4
Ascension	1 242	213	20 651	25.0	27.2	25.5	20.5	1 136.2	34.0	17 780	926.0	35.5	7.9	3.0	14.1	8.1
East Baton Rouge	10 869	1 175	189 080	19.9	7.7	20.1	39.3	8 118.7	26.1	20 486	6 680.0	11.7	8.8	7.1	28.2	18.9
Livingston.................	1 042	257	9 385	58.2	13.0	31.5	29.0	1 217.1	39.2	15 624	340.6	15.0	12.8	3.6	23.4	20.1
West Baton Rouge	382	70	8 088	28.0	24.1	13.8	14.8	347.7	26.0	17 299	293.4	26.2	5.5	1.8	9.9	10.9
Beaumont-Port Arthur, TX MSA........	8 174	450	123 128	4.5	18.7	22.6	33.5	7 059.6	23.0	18 937	5 036.4	26.6	9.9	2.8	25.8	12.7
Hardin.....................	730	122	7 266	18.2	14.3	29.6	31.1	765.7	33.4	16 792	269.6	13.4	17.2	2.9	19.3	17.2
Jefferson.................	6 045	265	96 108	3.3	16.1	21.7	36.0	4 876.9	21.2	20 078	3 956.7	23.7	9.5	2.9	28.5	12.2
Orange	1 399	63	19 754	5.8	33.1	24.4	22.1	1 417.0	23.9	16 809	810.2	45.3	9.2	2.5	15.0	13.6
Bellingham, WA MSA (Whatcom)	4 993	927	53 496	19.2	16.0	28.1	28.0	2 790.4	29.4	19 191	1 928.6	18.4	13.7	3.7	23.7	13.4
Benton Harbor, MI MSA (Berrien)	3 973	183	61 974	3.9	33.5	20.5	29.8	3 206.9	24.3	19 832	2 218.9	38.7	9.1	3.9	20.4	10.9
Billings, MT MSA (Yellowstone)	4 479	562	51 765	15.7	6.2	26.6	34.3	2 520.4	32.1	20 524	1 868.9	7.1	13.1	5.8	30.9	12.9
Biloxi-Gulfport-Pascagoula, MS MSA ...	6 993	872	114 528	30.5	22.4	22.5	38.6	5 767.1	38.8	17 002	4 513.8	23.1	8.6	2.9	25.5	26.7
Hancock....................	630	149	8 304	32.0	6.4	24.4	56.9	538.4	35.6	14 711	403.5	11.9	6.9	1.8	40.1	30.0
Harrison	4 212	585	65 058	41.8	9.0	24.6	46.7	3 038.6	38.6	17 187	2 414.1	6.9	9.9	3.7	31.5	32.1
Jackson	2 151	138	41 166	15.7	46.9	18.9	22.0	2 190.1	39.9	17 409	1 696.2	48.9	7.1	2.1	13.3	18.2
Binghamton, NY MSA	5 157	-271	92 825	-6.7	30.5	20.6	29.9	5 098.9	9.9	19 469	3 623.8	30.7	9.0	4.0	23.5	17.4
Broome....................	4 408	-237	82 685	-6.1	28.3	21.2	30.8	4 156.8	9.1	19 937	3 147.3	27.4	9.2	4.4	25.1	17.8
Tioga......................	749	-34	10 140	-11.0	48.3	15.9	22.4	942.0	13.8	17 641	476.5	52.6	7.5	1.6	13.1	14.6
Birmingham, AL MSA	22 015	1 727	417 364	15.1	13.6	20.8	33.7	18 503.4	24.9	21 217	14 326.6	12.8	9.0	8.2	27.2	14.2
Blount.....................	695	180	9 238	42.7	33.5	15.6	28.4	667.5	28.7	16 123	278.8	20.5	8.9	3.1	15.6	13.2
Jefferson	17 834	269	361 636	8.8	11.7	21.0	34.9	14 389.9	22.4	21 916	12 578.7	11.8	9.0	8.7	28.8	14.3
St. Clair	929	214	10 577	48.7	30.4	21.6	20.0	862.1	34.3	15 422	328.5	20.4	12.1	3.4	14.7	17.1
Shelby	2 557	1 064	35 913	116.1	21.9	20.2	27.3	2 584.0	36.3	21 861	1 140.6	20.3	9.0	4.4	16.8	12.2
Bismarck, ND MSA	2 823	280	36 425	15.5	6.4	24.6	42.4	1 701.4	27.2	19 312	1 241.0	7.0	11.3	5.1	29.3	20.4
Burleigh...................	2 178	219	29 796	15.2	4.9	24.7	44.0	1 302.4	27.9	20 381	1 005.4	5.3	11.0	5.4	32.0	22.0
Morton	645	61	6 629	16.9	13.0	24.0	35.0	399.0	25.2	16 489	235.6	14.2	12.6	3.7	17.4	13.7
Bloomington, IN MSA (Monroe)........	2 815	266	41 990	8.9	22.8	29.6	27.9	2 002.4	26.0	17 595	1 602.8	20.1	11.5	4.1	20.8	28.7
Bloomington-Normal, IL MSA (McLean).	3 410	382	69 224	11.9	14.5	21.1	25.0	3 001.8	27.2	21 815	2 510.5	16.1	8.0	26.0	20.2	12.4
Boise City, ID MSA.................	10 844	2 441	158 312	37.5	20.6	21.4	27.2	7 481.0	45.9	21 516	6 005.8	24.3	10.0	6.0	20.0	13.5
Ada	8 389	1 845	126 168	37.5	17.4	21.9	27.7	5 878.2	48.4	24 160	4 956.7	23.9	9.7	6.6	20.3	13.8
Canyon	2 455	596	32 144	37.5	33.2	19.8	25.1	1 602.8	37.3	15 353	1 049.1	26.2	11.6	3.1	18.4	12.1
Boston-Worcester-Lawrence-Lowell-Brockton, MA-NH NECMA	153 154	3 656	2 672 042	Z	17.2	19.3	40.4	149 517.1	16.4	26 093	112 114.3	19.0	8.9	9.1	34.4	11.8
Bristol, MA	12 001	99	183 206	.5	28.4	25.2	27.9	10 209.6	15.5	20 003	6 160.7	28.4	12.7	3.3	23.3	13.3
Essex, MA	16 763	200	251 278	-1.8	25.3	22.5	34.4	17 011.6	16.8	25 083	9 861.3	29.3	10.6	4.1	28.5	11.5
Middlesex, MA	39 745	1 303	734 997	-.9	16.6	16.6	46.9	42 090.1	16.4	29 994	31 813.8	22.6	7.8	4.5	39.6	8.9
Norfolk, MA	18 041	447	292 097	-1.5	13.8	20.6	35.9	19 401.7	17.5	30 733	11 831.5	15.4	11.9	10.4	30.7	9.2
Plymouth, MA	10 383	215	135 004	2.7	12.9	31.6	33.8	10 016.1	16.6	22 278	5 098.3	12.4	15.2	5.8	27.8	16.6
Suffolk, MA	19 136	223	511 455	.3	6.9	12.6	50.7	18 288.1	14.4	28 882	26 083.6	5.8	4.6	20.0	42.2	14.9
Worcester, MA	16 387	-22	270 856	-2.0	24.2	20.1	34.2	15 544.2	14.6	21 676	10 203.0	26.1	9.1	6.9	26.4	13.7
Hillsborough, NH	10 050	197	155 400	-.8	23.0	20.9	35.0	8 436.6	17.0	24 327	6 157.8	29.5	10.8	7.0	27.1	9.5
Rockingham, NH	8 343	867	103 207	15.8	16.1	28.8	29.4	6 379.2	20.9	25 125	3 582.5	17.6	15.7	6.0	28.1	9.3
Strafford, NH	2 305	127	34 542	6.6	30.9	21.7	28.4	2 139.9	20.3	20 131	1 321.9	29.5	11.2	6.7	20.5	20.0
Brownsville-Harlingen-San Benito, TX MSA (Cameron)	5 530	649	73 532	23.6	18.1	27.9	33.8	3 399.2	35.3	11 346	2 234.3	13.8	14.2	3.9	26.6	24.3
Bryan-College Station, TX MSA (Brazos)...................	2 945	520	38 078	27.6	8.2	31.5	36.4	1 985.2	30.5	15 224	1 581.9	7.5	11.8	4.3	21.8	40.6
Buffalo-Niagara Falls, NY MSA	27 678	97	468 160	-.3	19.7	21.6	36.5	25 067.4	17.8	21 079	17 582.7	24.4	9.8	6.6	25.3	17.2
Erie	23 014	124	401 680	.7	18.1	21.1	37.7	20 724.2	17.8	21 418	14 878.5	22.0	9.8	7.3	26.6	17.4
Niagara	4 664	-27	66 480	-6.2	28.9	24.9	29.5	4 343.2	17.7	19 599	2 704.1	37.6	9.8	2.6	18.1	16.3
Burlington, VT NECMA	6 189	385	82 823	8.8	21.8	21.6	32.1	3 951.0	17.6	21 253	3 195.0	24.0	10.0	5.6	26.3	14.8
Chittenden	5 059	419	72 237	7.9	20.9	21.1	33.5	3 118.8	17.2	22 666	2 762.6	24.3	9.7	6.0	27.5	14.0
Franklin	976	-40	10 073	15.6	29.1	24.9	21.4	717.2	19.1	16 836	403.0	23.0	12.2	3.3	18.2	19.4
Grand Isle	154	6	513	12.5	7.2	34.3	39.8	115.0	20.0	20 168	29.5	8.3	16.5	1.5	18.3	21.2
Canton-Massillon, OH MSA	9 923	725	160 096	6.5	28.9	22.3	29.1	7 835.2	20.0	19 471	5 179.8	35.4	10.6	3.9	21.8	10.3
Carroll....................	415	-7	4 570	-.5	35.2	23.3	22.9	430.6	22.3	15 489	185.5	38.3	11.5	1.6	14.4	12.0
Stark	9 508	732	155 526	6.7	28.7	22.2	29.3	7 404.6	19.9	19 767	4 994.3	35.3	10.5	3.9	22.1	10.3

Z Less than .05 percent.

[1] Based on 1994 resident population estimated by the Bureau of Economic Analysis.
[2] Finance, insurance, and real estate.

Source: Private Nonfarm Business—U.S. Bureau of the Census, "County Business Patterns" on diskettes, annual (related Internet site <http://www.census.gov/epcd/cbp/view/cbpview.html>); Personal Income—U.S. Bureau of Economic Analysis, "Regional Economic Information System, 1969–1994" on CD-ROM (related Internet site <http://www.bea.doc.gov/bea/dr1.htm>).

Table C–3. Metro Counties — Private Nonfarm Business and Personal Income—Con.

[MSA = Metropolitan statistical area. CMSA = Consolidated MSA. PMSA = Primary MSA. NECMA = New England county metropolitan area. All areas defined as of June 30, 1996. Table includes 245 MSAs, 17 CMSAs, and 58 PMSAs not in New England; 12 NECMAs; and 844 component counties]

Metropolitan areas and component counties	Establishments Total	Establishments Net change, 1990–1995	Employment Total	Employment Percent change, 1990–1995	Manufacturing	Retail trade	Services	Personal income Total (mil dol)	Percent change, 1990–1994	Per capita[1] (dollars)	Earnings Total (mil dol)	Manufacturing	Retail trade	FIRE[2]	Services	Government
Casper, WY MSA (Natrona)	2 545	251	23 306	15.9	7.0	26.4	31.7	1 458.2	22.3	22 819	972.4	5.7	10.9	4.0	22.8	14.8
Cedar Rapids, IA MSA (Linn)	5 081	599	98 757	13.5	22.7	19.2	30.8	3 991.9	25.1	22 579	3 302.1	28.9	9.1	5.9	24.4	9.5
Champaign-Urbana, IL MSA (Champaign)	4 010	251	64 027	12.1	17.1	28.2	32.3	3 221.9	13.7	19 235	2 553.6	14.1	9.3	4.1	24.0	32.5
Charleston-North Charleston, SC MSA	12 307	780	173 562	10.4	11.7	25.3	39.4	9 191.2	17.2	17 598	6 838.1	11.3	11.6	3.9	23.8	31.7
Berkeley	1 397	96	15 793	-8.9	27.0	27.5	19.9	1 909.0	15.1	13 754	830.7	31.0	9.9	1.2	12.3	26.5
Charleston	9 414	626	140 536	13.6	9.0	24.8	42.7	5 845.2	17.9	19 909	5 407.8	6.7	11.6	4.5	26.1	33.9
Dorchester	1 496	58	17 233	6.4	20.1	27.5	29.6	1 437.0	17.1	15 984	599.7	25.9	14.2	2.3	18.4	19.1
Charleston, WV MSA	6 778	548	100 788	9.2	9.6	23.9	33.7	5 427.3	25.9	21 300	3 962.2	13.1	9.4	5.5	28.9	15.4
Kanawha	5 847	369	88 894	5.3	9.7	23.1	35.2	4 550.2	23.5	22 003	3 507.2	13.4	9.1	6.0	30.4	15.9
Putnam	931	179	11 894	49.5	9.1	30.4	22.5	877.0	40.3	18 271	455.0	10.9	11.8	2.0	17.4	12.1
Charlotte-Gastonia-Rock Hill, NC-SC MSA	36 242	3 441	666 487	11.8	23.4	18.1	27.7	27 659.2	27.3	21 943	23 235.4	22.3	9.2	8.9	21.2	10.1
Cabarrus, NC	2 612	239	40 105	14.0	35.4	21.8	23.0	2 135.5	27.1	19 865	1 294.2	35.5	11.7	2.8	17.2	15.8
Gaston, NC	3 874	81	75 933	4.2	47.8	19.0	20.3	3 334.9	21.6	18 527	2 405.0	45.9	9.1	2.6	16.0	9.1
Lincoln, NC	1 135	40	16 933	13.3	48.9	17.9	14.9	992.5	26.6	17 850	477.3	45.9	9.4	2.6	11.0	14.2
Mecklenburg, NC	20 929	2 525	414 113	13.1	13.5	16.7	31.3	14 651.5	30.6	25 992	15 056.2	14.0	8.6	12.3	23.8	8.7
Rowan, NC	2 164	7	41 645	15.4	35.4	21.8	28.1	2 062.8	23.0	17 601	1 289.6	33.7	12.0	2.7	17.7	16.6
Union, NC	2 266	245	32 931	9.8	41.3	17.7	15.7	1 708.7	22.1	17 948	1 086.2	34.5	9.7	2.9	12.0	11.6
York, SC	3 262	304	44 827	10.1	29.1	22.9	24.8	2 773.4	24.4	19 628	1 626.9	30.2	11.1	2.6	20.6	12.8
Charlottesville, VA MSA	4 205	381	57 030	6.3	NA	23.6	36.5	3 264.8	28.8	23 204	2 234.1	12.2	10.0	6.8	23.7	32.3
Albemarle	893	-32	10 693	9.9	19.0	20.7	38.0	[3][2]803.7	[3]28.1	[3]24 834	[3][2]102.3	[3]12.0	[3]10.2	[3]7.1	[3]23.9	[3]33.0
Fluvanna	274	75	1 971	38.3	19.1	12.9	25.1	272.5	37.8	17 927	70.8	12.5	5.8	1.6	21.8	18.7
Greene	208	30	1 530	-21.7	NA	20.7	28.0	188.6	26.4	14 969	61.0	19.3	9.4	1.5	18.8	22.4
Charlottesville city	2 830	308	42 836	5.6	13.3	24.9	36.9	(3)	(3)	(3)	(3)	(3)	(3)	(3)	(3)	(3)
Chattanooga, TN-GA MSA	10 865	635	184 675	11.1	24.7	21.8	31.4	8 735.5	24.1	19 890	6 504.2	22.4	11.1	7.3	24.2	18.1
Hamilton, TN	8 741	406	152 426	10.0	22.0	20.9	33.4	6 538.6	24.1	22 331	5 525.5	20.3	10.8	8.1	25.6	18.2
Marion, TN	407	47	5 270	25.5	33.6	30.6	20.6	397.5	26.4	15 230	168.5	26.1	18.7	3.4	18.2	15.6
Catoosa, GA	682	121	11 386	40.0	21.2	33.7	28.8	679.5	27.3	14 612	341.6	28.1	15.2	2.7	17.2	20.5
Dade, GA	195	53	1 866	-1.8	32.8	38.1	14.0	187.0	24.0	13 454	71.7	25.1	13.7	3.5	21.6	19.2
Walker, GA	840	8	13 727	2.6	53.0	15.7	18.2	932.9	20.8	15 574	396.9	45.0	8.9	3.0	13.7	15.4
Cheyenne, WY MSA (Laramie)	2 111	252	24 689	18.3	6.4	30.0	38.7	1 631.2	26.3	20 913	1 113.1	5.0	10.1	8.6	16.2	38.1
Chicago-Gary-Kenosha, IL-IN-WI CMSA	214 772	16 541	3 833 467	5.3	19.7	18.3	34.2	215 361.0	20.6	25 257	164 233.0	20.1	8.4	9.7	D	11.5
Chicago, IL PMSA	196 733	14 695	3 519 113	4.5	19.5	18.0	34.1	198 329.5	20.5	25 865	153 023.4	19.2	8.3	10.1	D	11.5
Cook	124 980	4 650	2 374 539	.1	18.1	17.1	36.4	128 239.8	18.1	24 944	107 625.8	18.2	7.6	11.7	29.9	12.0
DeKalb	1 821	162	24 695	8.3	34.7	24.4	22.7	1 529.5	20.7	18 630	913.5	23.0	9.7	3.6	16.8	28.6
Du Page	29 412	3 400	508 351	9.1	17.0	19.3	31.4	26 682.0	22.8	31 647	20 470.9	15.6	10.6	7.2	33.2	6.9
Grundy	835	86	10 498	1.9	23.1	23.0	22.2	792.9	27.1	22 851	565.1	21.6	8.1	2.3	D	7.7
Kane	9 317	1 012	152 648	12.3	25.8	20.4	30.2	8 039.8	22.3	23 063	5 070.7	27.1	9.7	5.8	26.1	11.4
Kendall	780	137	8 663	40.7	32.4	20.6	16.3	977.7	27.5	22 170	505.1	47.6	8.2	1.7	8.0	8.8
Lake	15 967	2 712	261 383	25.6	26.4	19.8	27.8	18 443.0	29.1	32 969	11 346.7	27.1	9.1	7.2	23.5	13.5
McHenry	5 780	1 192	68 790	18.6	33.4	21.2	22.5	5 185.9	29.6	24 009	2 438.1	33.1	9.8	3.3	18.7	10.0
Will	7 841	1 344	109 546	21.5	21.0	21.2	29.6	8 438.9	26.4	21 166	4 087.4	21.2	9.2	3.7	22.9	14.3
Gary, IN PMSA	12 922	1 271	215 471	4.4	24.1	22.6	31.7	12 413.9	19.7	20 029	8 520.7	32.3	9.2	3.2	22.1	11.0
Lake	9 958	758	167 675	.3	23.6	23.2	31.7	9 394.0	18.0	19 506	6 685.1	31.5	9.4	3.4	23.0	10.8
Porter	2 964	513	47 796	22.0	25.6	20.6	31.8	3 020.0	25.3	21 852	1 835.6	35.4	8.6	2.5	18.6	11.7
Kankakee, IL PMSA (Kankakee)	2 240	235	55 258	79.1	12.9	16.2	58.6	1 918.3	22.2	18 937	1 246.6	24.0	11.0	3.9	22.6	13.9
Kenosha, WI PMSA (Kenosha)	2 877	340	43 625	21.6	22.8	26.9	27.6	2 699.3	24.8	19 588	1 442.2	31.5	11.8	3.3	20.4	15.4
Chico-Paradise, CA MSA (Butte)	4 503	-110	47 569	4.0	11.4	29.8	37.7	3 299.3	19.7	17 157	1 901.0	8.0	14.0	5.1	32.1	19.5
Cincinnati-Hamilton, OH-KY-IN CMSA	45 228	3 297	832 641	7.1	19.5	22.4	31.3	41 447.3	22.4	21 881	29 938.1	24.8	10.1	6.6	D	12.0
Cincinnati, OH-KY-IN PMSA	39 395	2 770	738 011	6.5	19.1	22.3	31.9	35 266.2	22.0	22 301	26 618.4	24.4	10.0	6.9	D	11.7
Brown, OH	525	34	6 037	-.8	21.0	21.6	28.7	595.2	27.6	15 539	195.8	23.8	11.5	2.2	20.2	22.9
Clermont, OH	2 647	208	37 699	21.5	20.8	30.6	24.2	3 019.1	26.7	18 409	1 362.8	26.0	14.2	4.2	19.3	12.9
Hamilton, OH	25 577	1 006	522 152	1.0	18.4	20.3	34.1	21 771.3	19.0	25 091	19 584.6	25.3	8.8	7.9	26.9	10.7
Warren, OH	2 422	338	39 436	36.4	30.8	27.9	23.3	2 598.2	30.4	20 507	1 189.5	27.1	14.7	2.5	20.9	14.7
Boone, KY	1 897	311	39 931	24.7	22.9	28.4	22.2	1 344.7	35.4	19 921	1 534.6	24.7	11.1	3.4	13.7	7.6
Campbell, KY	1 576	125	20 206	9.0	20.4	31.6	27.6	1 577.0	20.4	18 274	720.8	23.6	12.4	4.2	26.3	17.8
Gallatin, KY	78	4	685	-5.0	2.5	22.3	18.0	87.2	37.6	14 531	34.1	3.5	12.7	1.8	10.7	20.1
Grant, KY	389	70	3 887	27.2	13.0	43.6	19.6	268.3	33.7	14 903	99.2	13.8	23.1	5.2	14.9	21.1
Kenton, KY	3 073	416	55 238	21.4	13.5	22.5	33.5	2 972.6	24.2	20 515	1 484.2	10.0	13.8	5.1	32.7	17.7
Pendleton, KY	198	25	1 672	61.1	36.7	25.2	18.5	182.8	26.3	13 849	64.4	14.7	8.2	2.7	D	22.0
Dearborn, IN	952	239	10 581	22.4	22.1	26.6	25.3	763.2	27.1	17 626	331.7	26.2	12.3	3.8	15.8	15.8
Ohio, IN	61	-6	487	39.1	NA	25.5	51.3	86.7	27.9	15 756	16.8	5.6	14.5	.7	21.3	32.2
Hamilton-Middletown, OH PMSA (Butler)	5 833	527	94 630	11.9	22.3	22.5	26.4	6 181.1	24.6	19 761	3 319.7	28.4	11.2	4.5	19.8	14.8

NA Not available.
D Withheld to avoid disclosure.

[1]Based on 1994 resident population estimated by the Bureau of Economic Analysis.
[2]Finance, insurance, and real estate.
[3]Independent city of Charlottesville included with Albemarle County; data not available separately.

Source: Private Nonfarm Business—U.S. Bureau of the Census, "County Business Patterns" on diskettes, annual (related Internet site <http://www.census.gov/epcd/cbp/view/cbpview.html>); Personal Income—U.S. Bureau of Economic Analysis, "Regional Economic Information System, 1969–1994" on CD-ROM (related Internet site <http://www.bea.doc.gov/bea/dr1.htm>).

[MSA = Metropolitan statistical area. CMSA = Consolidated MSA. PMSA = Primary MSA. NECMA = New England county metropolitan area. All areas defined as of June 30, 1996 Table includes 245 MSAs, 17 CMSAs, and 58 PMSAs not in New England; 12 NECMAs; and 844 component counties]

Metropolitan areas and component counties	Private nonfarm business, 1995							Personal income, 1994								
	Establishments		Employment								Earnings					
					By selected industry, percent—							By selected industry, percent—				
	Total	Net change, 1990–1995	Total	Percent change, 1990–1995	Manu-fac-turing	Retail trade	Services	Total (mil dol)	Percent change, 1990–1994	Per capita[1] (dollars)	Total (mil dol)	Manu-fac-turing	Retail trade	FIRE[2]	Services	Govern-ment
Clarksville-Hopkinsville, TN-KY MSA ...	3 479	452	47 287	24.7	23.7	30.8	28.2	2 780.2	35.0	14 947	2 146.4	17.0	9.8	2.3	13.3	45.7
Montgomery, TN	2 180	370	27 712	32.9	23.0	36.0	25.4	1 838.8	39.5	15 426	817.2	21.6	17.6	3.6	19.9	20.7
Christian, KY	1 299	82	19 575	14.7	24.6	23.5	32.1	941.4	26.9	14 093	1 329.2	14.2	5.0	1.5	9.3	61.1
Cleveland-Akron, OH CMSA	74 265	4 373	1 264 855	5.4	23.6	19.6	33.0	66 443.6	19.7	22 921	48 887.6	27.9	8.2	6.3	27.6	12.1
Akron, OH PMSA	16 730	1 269	283 141	11.3	23.8	22.0	31.1	14 221.3	22.0	21 013	9 771.1	28.6	9.9	4.2	24.8	13.5
Portage	2 860	399	39 375	27.1	33.4	23.6	24.3	2 676.3	23.3	17 974	1 405.9	28.5	9.7	2.0	17.8	26.7
Summit	13 870	870	243 766	9.2	22.3	21.8	32.2	11 545.0	21.7	21 870	8 365.2	28.6	9.9	4.6	25.9	11.3
Cleveland-Lorain-Elyria, OH PMSA .	57 535	3 104	981 714	3.7	23.5	19.0	33.6	52 222.3	19.1	23 502	39 116.6	27.7	7.7	6.8	28.3	11.7
Ashtabula	2 158	183	27 840	8.6	34.8	22.8	26.2	1 714.4	21.3	16 824	931.6	34.5	11.0	2.6	18.7	14.0
Cuyahoga	38 190	1 162	709 226	1.3	20.3	17.5	36.3	35 256.6	17.7	25 126	29 606.4	24.9	7.1	7.9	31.0	11.6
Geauga	2 183	216	23 731	4.2	36.3	19.9	22.2	2 097.4	20.6	25 270	898.4	34.0	8.4	2.5	21.9	10.3
Lake	6 246	614	87 700	5.4	30.9	24.1	26.2	4 930.4	18.6	22 269	2 959.1	35.9	10.0	3.3	19.6	11.5
Lorain	5 484	378	91 279	11.1	33.7	21.5	28.0	5 394.3	23.5	19 307	3 392.7	42.2	8.8	2.6	18.8	13.1
Medina	3 274	551	41 938	29.4	25.3	24.3	26.1	2 829.3	26.5	21 257	1 328.4	26.2	11.4	7.6	21.3	12.1
Colorado Springs, CO MSA (El Paso) ..	11 826	2 251	165 390	31.1	15.0	22.2	40.5	8 873.0	33.5	19 613	6 533.2	13.4	9.9	5.0	28.5	27.8
Columbia, MO MSA (Boone)	3 478	526	56 713	23.5	10.9	22.9	41.9	2 411.7	31.5	19 849	1 910.9	8.9	10.1	8.3	23.2	35.1
Columbia, SC MSA	12 917	1 258	202 090	8.4	12.3	22.9	35.9	9 717.9	23.0	19 979	7 681.3	12.2	10.2	8.6	23.1	27.1
Lexington	4 352	682	54 281	23.1	16.7	26.1	26.6	3 766.0	27.7	20 107	1 963.6	23.1	12.4	2.9	19.7	13.4
Richland	8 565	576	147 809	3.8	10.6	21.7	39.3	5 951.9	20.3	19 899	5 717.7	8.4	9.5	10.6	24.2	31.9
Columbus, GA-AL MSA	5 532	191	NA	NA	NA	NA	NA	4 708.2	23.4	17 177	3 359.5	D	9.8	7.9	21.4	28.5
Chattahoochee, GA	47	22	(3)	NA	NA	NA	NA	241.4	23.8	15 477	468.7	D	2.4	.1	1.0	96.1
Harris, GA	274	33	3 350	34.2	41.8	11.0	28.1	353.2	24.5	17 836	93.4	17.1	15.4	2.5	30.4	18.5
Muscogee, GA	4 352	51	75 920	6.8	21.9	23.7	31.4	3 376.3	23.6	18 045	2 445.2	21.8	10.7	10.3	26.3	17.4
Russell, AL	859	85	10 253	13.7	32.9	25.5	22.4	737.3	22.2	14 289	352.2	37.2	11.8	3.0	12.7	18.1
Columbus, OH MSA	35 232	3 190	655 519	10.6	13.8	24.6	33.8	31 386.4	27.3	22 060	24 917.0	16.3	12.2	10.0	26.3	17.1
Delaware	1 902	631	26 464	59.7	23.4	19.0	32.6	1 962.0	39.3	25 614	804.8	21.1	11.1	6.1	27.9	14.0
Fairfield	2 385	309	26 302	6.1	25.1	29.3	29.1	2 239.8	29.8	19 528	889.6	26.4	13.1	5.4	18.9	19.3
Franklin	26 702	1 806	539 282	8.2	11.0	24.8	34.9	23 078.0	26.1	22 959	20 849.7	14.1	12.3	10.9	27.6	16.9
Licking	2 655	207	41 982	17.9	23.8	23.7	30.5	2 617.9	27.3	19 392	1 546.9	27.8	13.0	6.4	18.5	17.5
Madison	729	86	9 811	34.5	34.3	22.7	19.7	653.8	26.2	16 427	322.7	25.3	11.1	1.8	16.6	24.5
Pickaway	859	151	11 678	14.7	41.3	21.0	21.7	834.8	28.3	16 210	503.6	41.7	9.1	1.6	10.5	22.0
Corpus Christi, TX MSA	8 892	758	118 466	14.0	11.1	25.0	37.8	6 518.5	26.9	17 350	4 805.8	15.9	10.3	3.8	26.0	21.9
Nueces	7 943	728	109 338	15.4	10.0	24.8	38.9	5 615.7	26.5	18 063	4 364.1	15.3	10.4	3.9	27.2	21.0
San Patricio	949	30	9 128	-.8	24.5	28.1	24.9	902.8	29.5	13 932	441.7	22.1	9.2	2.6	14.8	30.1
Cumberland, MD-WV MSA	2 367	22	28 154	-3.0	20.0	29.1	31.7	1 673.1	13.9	16 548	1 013.3	23.9	12.3	3.4	24.6	17.8
Allegany, MD	1 899	-1	23 610	-2.2	18.1	29.6	32.7	1 260.8	12.3	17 061	825.0	22.9	13.0	3.7	26.8	17.3
Mineral, WV	468	23	4 544	-6.9	29.9	26.1	26.5	412.3	19.1	15 157	188.3	28.4	8.9	2.1	15.4	20.0
Dallas-Fort Worth, TX CMSA	116 786	12 643	2 066 936	15.4	16.1	19.5	33.8	102 300.3	26.9	23 449	84 162.2	17.0	9.7	8.0	28.4	10.2
Dallas, TX PMSA	82 410	9 391	1 512 583	15.4	15.3	18.2	34.2	70 946.1	28.8	24 479	62 012.6	15.9	9.0	9.2	29.7	9.6
Collin	6 875	1 790	104 583	33.0	19.8	26.0	33.0	8 628.8	38.5	26 453	4 037.0	19.7	11.1	5.6	31.2	10.7
Dallas	63 586	5 578	1 256 339	12.8	14.0	16.3	35.2	50 029.4	27.0	25 758	52 773.4	14.7	8.5	10.1	30.3	8.7
Denton	5 963	1 272	79 040	38.4	15.9	34.1	27.0	6 714.5	31.9	20 976	2 534.3	21.7	13.6	3.1	23.8	19.2
Ellis	1 712	219	22 772	24.7	39.3	18.4	23.8	1 702.6	28.8	18 527	878.3	35.6	7.6	2.4	19.6	12.3
Henderson	1 062	164	10 318	14.4	15.0	31.7	30.3	977.9	26.0	15 748	350.1	9.3	17.5	4.2	27.2	17.3
Hunt	1 225	12	18 997	-4.9	39.9	21.8	22.8	1 118.7	17.1	16 949	720.7	41.7	10.0	2.3	14.7	18.2
Kaufman	1 262	248	14 024	47.7	27.2	21.0	32.4	1 000.6	30.4	17 163	457.0	21.4	14.0	2.9	24.5	22.0
Rockwall	725	108	6 510	25.8	17.5	25.9	25.5	773.8	38.7	24 638	261.7	14.4	12.7	3.4	32.0	10.9
Fort Worth-Arlington, TX PMSA.....	34 376	3 252	554 353	15.4	18.2	23.1	32.7	31 354.3	22.8	21 412	22 149.6	19.9	11.5	4.6	24.5	11.9
Hood	764	150	6 425	43.0	4.7	39.5	34.9	663.9	28.3	21 075	195.5	3.5	18.7	5.5	27.0	19.4
Johnson	1 882	224	21 820	10.2	24.5	26.5	28.6	1 774.1	22.3	17 010	727.4	23.2	13.2	3.2	20.4	14.9
Parker	1 362	363	12 091	40.1	18.7	30.5	27.8	1 280.3	24.0	17 957	437.9	17.5	15.3	3.6	21.6	18.7
Tarrant	30 368	2 515	514 017	14.9	18.1	22.6	33.0	27 635.9	22.7	21 982	20 788.8	19.9	11.2	4.7	24.7	11.5
Danville, VA MSA	2 355	109	38 543	-1.1	41.2	20.6	21.6	1 838.4	16.7	16 713	1 198.7	41.3	10.7	2.9	18.3	12.5
Pittsylvania	899	220	11 783	40.7	42.9	15.3	18.0	[4]1 838.4	[4]16.7	[4]16 713	[4]1 198.7	[4]41.3	[4]10.7	[4]2.9	[4]18.3	[4]12.5
Danville city	1 456	-111	26 760	-12.5	40.5	23.0	23.2	(4)	(4)	(4)	(4)	(4)	(4)	(4)	(4)	(4)
Davenport-Moline-Rock Island, IA-IL MSA	9 118	505	146 659	6.8	21.3	23.5	29.7	7 457.5	17.7	20 843	5 584.7	24.7	10.7	5.0	22.2	15.2
Scott, IA	4 369	344	70 022	12.5	19.3	25.0	31.2	3 301.1	21.2	21 161	2 372.6	26.3	11.9	4.9	25.0	9.6
Henry, IL	1 130	31	12 996	8.0	35.5	25.6	17.7	923.0	13.5	17 922	374.8	17.7	14.6	4.7	14.6	18.0
Rock Island, IL	3 619	130	63 641	1.1	20.6	21.4	30.4	3 233.5	15.6	21 514	2 837.2	24.2	9.2	5.1	20.8	19.5
Dayton-Springfield, OH MSA	21 497	782	409 016	7.8	24.7	22.3	35.0	20 434.4	20.9	21 366	15 407.2	29.8	9.0	3.9	24.8	17.4
Clark	2 871	105	49 295	6.4	28.4	26.1	28.9	2 870.2	23.5	19 406	1 691.6	36.9	11.1	2.6	21.7	12.6
Greene	2 791	375	39 767	26.7	12.0	32.5	39.9	2 932.3	23.7	20 960	1 477.2	10.7	13.5	3.0	27.3	32.8
Miami	2 185	174	37 083	12.4	41.8	21.6	20.8	2 001.3	25.9	20 739	1 256.3	42.7	10.1	3.1	20.2	9.8
Montgomery	13 650	128	282 871	5.3	23.6	20.3	37.2	12 630.6	19.0	22 078	10 982.2	29.8	8.0	4.3	25.5	16.9
Daytona Beach, FL MSA	10 958	803	127 887	12.3	9.4	29.9	41.1	7 748.9	22.8	17 595	3 708.6	11.8	15.9	5.9	32.4	17.3
Flagler	744	159	7 522	24.3	21.1	27.7	28.6	594.1	41.5	15 633	216.3	17.8	12.4	11.5	26.2	17.5
Volusia	10 214	644	120 365	11.6	8.7	30.1	41.9	7 154.9	21.4	17 780	3 492.3	11.4	16.1	5.5	32.7	17.3

NA Not available.
D Withheld to avoid disclosure.

[1]Based on 1994 resident population estimated by the Bureau of Economic Analysis.
[2]Finance, insurance, and real estate.
[3]1,000–2,499 employees.
[4]Independent city of Danville included with Pittsylvania County; data not available separately.

Source: Private Nonfarm Business—U.S. Bureau of the Census, "County Business Patterns" on diskettes, annual (related Internet site <http://www.census.gov/epcd/cbp/view/cbpview.html>); Personal Income—U.S. Bureau of Economic Analysis, "Regional Economic Information System, 1969–1994" on CD-ROM (related Internet site <http://www.bea.doc.gov/bea/dr1.htm>).

[MSA = Metropolitan statistical area. CMSA = Consolidated MSA. PMSA = Primary MSA. NECMA = New England county metropolitan area. All areas defined as of June 30, 1996 Table includes 245 MSAs, 17 CMSAs, and 58 PMSAs not in New England; 12 NECMAs; and 844 component counties]

Metropolitan areas and component counties	Private nonfarm business, 1995							Personal income, 1994								
	Establishments		Employment								Earnings					
					By selected industry, percent—							By selected industry, percent—				
	Total	Net change, 1990–1995	Total	Percent change, 1990–1995	Manufacturing	Retail trade	Services	Total (mil dol)	Percent change, 1990–1994	Per capita[1] (dollars)	Total (mil dol)	Manufacturing	Retail trade	FIRE[2]	Services	Government
Decatur, AL MSA	3 086	327	47 202	15.8	35.3	21.0	25.7	2 572.1	26.3	18 558	1 681.2	40.0	10.4	3.3	14.5	13.3
Lawrence	351	31	5 352	40.3	48.2	19.8	19.9	480.3	25.7	14 823	258.2	51.2	8.7	1.0	7.1	15.4
Morgan	2 735	296	41 850	13.2	33.7	21.1	26.4	2 091.8	26.4	19 697	1 423.0	38.0	10.7	3.8	15.9	12.9
Decatur, IL MSA (Macon)	2 835	70	52 973	5.3	26.2	19.5	27.4	2 430.2	15.1	20 842	1 896.9	31.2	9.2	4.2	19.5	8.5
Denver-Boulder-Greeley, CO CMSA	70 984	11 863	1 035 244	21.9	12.4	20.3	34.9	53 389.6	30.5	24 379	42 212.9	13.1	9.2	8.1	29.2	14.5
Boulder-Longmont, CO PMSA (Boulder)	9 588	2 269	127 691	32.5	24.7	22.5	35.6	6 405.7	34.1	25 664	4 902.1	25.7	9.4	4.0	32.6	15.1
Denver, CO PMSA	58 068	8 999	859 078	19.8	10.0	20.0	35.3	44 425.0	30.0	24 731	35 476.6	11.0	9.3	8.8	29.2	14.4
Adams	6 443	804	100 183	22.4	11.8	23.6	22.5	5 297.8	31.7	18 014	3 870.6	16.0	11.7	2.3	18.2	14.8
Arapahoe	14 664	2 770	225 174	40.6	10.4	20.0	34.2	11 933.0	28.8	26 919	8 419.4	6.4	10.5	12.4	32.5	9.4
Denver	20 793	1 338	361 212	8.6	8.7	15.1	41.0	13 062.3	25.7	26 463	15 845.6	7.7	6.9	10.1	31.4	15.7
Douglas	2 603	1 258	20 571	128.4	9.8	32.7	25.4	2 506.3	68.5	28 448	700.4	6.3	12.8	4.8	31.4	14.4
Jefferson	13 565	2 829	151 938	14.1	11.3	27.5	32.8	11 625.6	29.0	24 362	6 640.7	22.6	11.6	5.5	29.9	14.4
Greeley, CO PMSA (Weld)	3 328	595	48 475	34.6	23.6	19.9	25.9	2 559.0	30.8	17 758	1 834.2	20.4	8.2	4.8	19.3	17.6
Des Moines, IA MSA	12 450	1 145	235 564	14.4	10.5	19.7	32.3	9 862.6	26.8	23 680	8 177.5	12.5	10.3	16.8	25.0	13.8
Dallas	752	140	7 620	43.3	31.1	21.0	21.7	702.4	33.0	21 881	292.3	21.2	9.5	4.8	17.4	13.2
Polk	11 008	940	221 914	13.6	9.9	19.3	32.5	8 421.2	26.2	24 346	7 662.8	12.3	10.3	17.6	25.2	14.2
Warren	690	65	6 030	13.0	7.9	32.1	36.6	739.0	28.7	19 195	222.4	6.8	13.6	3.6	26.0	12.9
Detroit-Ann Arbor-Flint, MI CMSA	122 795	7 176	2 166 866	5.6	24.6	20.4	34.0	128 544.7	22.7	24 459	96 786.7	34.0	8.2	5.3	24.6	19.3
Ann Arbor, MI PMSA	12 887	1 577	210 169	9.3	26.5	22.1	34.4	13 153.0	30.7	25 525	9 070.2	31.6	8.0	3.6	22.0	11.6
Lenawee	2 033	55	30 024	7.5	35.8	22.3	28.8	1 882.3	29.1	19 668	1 055.0	44.9	9.7	3.3	16.2	23.4
Livingston	2 938	624	34 814	25.1	24.4	24.6	26.7	3 177.3	36.6	24 611	1 217.1	28.7	11.0	8.1	19.6	14.3
Washtenaw	7 916	898	145 331	6.5	25.0	21.5	37.4	8 093.5	28.9	27 860	6 798.2	30.1	7.3	2.8	23.3	12.2
Detroit, MI PMSA	100 841	5 004	1 802 270	5.4	24.1	19.9	34.2	106 350.5	21.6	24 692	80 617.0	33.0	8.2	5.7	25.3	26.8
Lapeer	1 504	225	16 219	21.8	30.5	27.4	23.2	1 612.3	29.3	19 856	592.8	29.4	12.3	3.0	15.6	10.3
Macomb	17 909	1 312	316 640	12.5	35.1	21.3	27.9	17 850.0	22.8	24 489	13 075.3	49.2	8.7	2.4	17.4	23.2
Monroe	2 327	173	34 405	12.7	27.7	25.1	25.7	2 855.4	28.0	20 736	1 450.8	37.5	9.3	1.9	14.4	9.6
Oakland	40 440	2 868	665 004	12.2	17.3	19.8	39.0	37 016.2	25.4	32 413	27 553.9	24.5	9.2	8.0	33.0	12.7
St. Clair	3 427	530	42 996	19.3	29.3	25.8	25.1	3 059.3	23.5	20 074	1 513.3	26.1	12.2	2.8	19.6	6.9
Wayne	35 234	−104	727 006	−3.7	24.8	18.7	33.6	43 957.3	17.4	21 289	36 430.9	33.8	7.1	5.5	23.2	14.6
Flint, MI PMSA (Genesee)	9 067	595	154 427	2.1	28.5	24.0	32.1	9 041.2	24.8	20 866	7 099.5	47.6	8.2	2.9	19.2	12.7
Dothan, AL MSA	3 481	362	52 776	9.7	20.0	22.1	29.8	2 311.0	20.5	17 182	1 757.5	21.0	11.5	3.1	22.9	11.2
Dale	842	126	10 757	1.5	12.4	22.2	28.2	771.3	20.9	15 243	519.3	30.9	7.2	2.1	14.6	20.4
Houston	2 639	236	42 019	12.1	22.0	22.0	30.2	1 539.7	20.2	18 352	1 238.2	16.8	13.3	3.6	26.4	33.1
Dover, DE MSA (Kent)	2 729	141	38 068	7.1	20.0	28.3	30.5	2 064.1	26.9	17 201	1 516.8	14.4	13.3	3.0	18.8	15.0
Dubuque, IA MSA (Dubuque)	2 567	210	47 808	13.3	28.5	19.6	35.4	1 754.7	22.9	19 895	1 446.1	34.4	9.8	3.4	26.1	36.7
Duluth-Superior, MN-WI MSA	6 417	510	83 073	12.9	9.1	27.8	37.6	4 427.0	20.1	18 377	3 035.0	10.8	11.6	3.2	24.7	7.1
St. Louis, MN	5 374	451	71 110	12.8	8.1	27.2	38.7	3 707.2	19.8	18 723	2 588.7	10.2	11.6	3.4	26.2	21.2
Douglas, WI	1 043	59	11 963	13.5	14.7	31.0	30.7	719.8	21.6	16 779	446.2	13.8	11.9	2.5	16.2	21.4
Eau Claire, WI MSA	3 733	352	53 954	13.8	20.5	29.0	30.6	2 554.4	22.6	18 001	1 804.9	18.9	16.0	3.5	23.1	20.2
Chippewa	1 254	99	15 849	6.4	39.1	23.5	20.7	946.1	21.7	17 521	608.1	38.2	10.5	1.8	14.0	17.7
Eau Claire	2 479	253	38 105	17.1	12.8	31.2	34.8	1 608.2	23.1	18 296	1 196.8	9.1	18.9	4.3	27.8	15.2
El Paso, TX MSA (El Paso)	11 963	871	185 943	16.9	23.0	23.5	32.1	8 603.0	25.4	12 941	6 493.5	16.7	11.5	3.7	21.6	19.0
Elkhart-Goshen, IN MSA (Elkhart)	4 993	356	110 515	17.1	54.9	13.9	16.6	3 410.5	28.7	20 795	3 434.5	58.5	6.6	2.5	12.9	27.7
Elmira, NY MSA (Chemung)	1 972	−51	34 491	−1.2	25.0	21.5	34.4	1 785.2	17.7	18 891	1 171.0	25.3	11.1	4.2	24.3	5.3
Enid, OK MSA (Garfield)	1 694	106	19 872	15.0	12.2	25.1	31.6	1 053.0	16.0	18 506	692.1	6.8	12.7	4.2	23.4	19.0
Erie, PA MSA (Erie)	6 508	183	112 125	4.3	30.7	20.3	32.5	5 396.9	20.5	19 254	3 937.0	35.0	10.2	5.1	23.9	19.1
Eugene-Springfield, OR MSA (Lane)	9 170	923	106 351	11.3	18.7	25.2	33.5	5 731.0	26.8	19 167	3 934.3	18.6	13.1	4.5	26.0	11.6
Evansville-Henderson, IN-KY MSA	7 730	368	138 192	10.6	23.2	21.4	30.8	5 984.3	22.1	20 888	4 466.8	28.7	10.0	4.4	24.4	17.0
Posey, IN	520	38	7 405	17.8	39.6	13.7	18.0	523.1	25.6	19 890	331.3	49.2	4.9	1.6	11.7	9.0
Vanderburgh, IN	5 196	177	102 461	10.5	19.0	22.2	33.2	3 653.4	20.5	21 825	3 083.0	23.3	11.1	5.4	28.2	9.7
Warrick, IN	969	104	10 796	1.0	30.5	22.0	23.3	979.4	24.5	20 152	453.4	38.4	7.8	2.9	14.7	8.6
Henderson, KY	1 045	49	17 530	14.5	35.9	19.5	26.7	828.4	24.4	18 742	599.1	37.3	8.5	2.1	18.9	10.3
Fargo-Moorhead, ND-MN MSA	5 157	685	78 195	18.9	9.8	24.0	35.7	3 152.4	26.7	19 496	2 418.2	8.3	10.7	7.4	27.5	9.7
Cass, ND	4 056	602	64 576	21.9	10.2	22.8	33.9	2 311.9	29.1	21 055	1 974.1	8.3	10.1	8.3	28.5	15.9
Clay, MN	1 101	83	13 619	6.8	8.2	29.5	43.9	840.6	20.7	16 196	444.1	8.5	13.2	3.6	23.3	13.6
Fayetteville, NC MSA (Cumberland)	5 247	487	77 585	16.0	15.6	30.8	33.8	4 806.9	35.1	16 784	3 944.0	11.7	10.0	2.6	13.2	25.7
Fayetteville-Springdale-Rogers, AR MSA	6 774	1 699	112 324	34.4	28.7	25.5	22.8	4 609.4	40.0	19 008	3 652.3	25.5	17.5	3.7	16.6	52.5
Benton	3 063	974	53 135	38.4	30.6	28.6	19.8	2 244.1	44.2	19 463	1 672.5	28.2	25.4	3.8	14.0	12.1
Washington	3 711	725	59 189	31.1	26.9	22.6	25.5	2 365.3	36.2	18 595	1 979.8	23.1	10.9	3.6	18.8	6.8
Flagstaff, AZ-UT MSA	3 543	1 140	34 782	25.2	6.8	39.1	34.5	1 809.4	37.1	15 858	1 275.1	7.8	15.8	2.3	27.6	16.5
Coconino, AZ	3 383	1 105	33 647	25.4	7.0	38.9	34.5	1 723.0	37.1	15 910	1 230.8	8.0	15.5	2.4	27.4	31.5
Kane, UT	160	35	1 135	19.6	NA	45.6	36.5	86.3	35.7	14 885	44.2	2.3	23.3	2.2	32.7	31.7
																25.9

NA Not available.

[1]Based on 1994 resident population estimated by the Bureau of Economic Analysis.
[2]Finance, insurance, and real estate.

Source: Private Nonfarm Business—U.S. Bureau of the Census, "County Business Patterns" on diskettes, annual (related Internet site <http://www.census.gov/epcd/cbp/view/cbpview.html>); Personal Income—U.S. Bureau of Economic Analysis, "Regional Economic Information System, 1969–1994" on CD-ROM (related Internet site <http://www.bea.doc.gov/bea/dr1.htm>).

[MSA = Metropolitan statistical area. CMSA = Consolidated MSA. PMSA = Primary MSA. NECMA = New England county metropolitan area. All areas defined as of June 30, 1996 Table includes 245 MSAs, 17 CMSAs, and 58 PMSAs not in New England; 12 NECMAs; and 844 component counties]

Metropolitan areas and component counties	Private nonfarm business, 1995							Personal income, 1994								
	Establishments		Employment								Earnings					
					By selected industry, percent—							By selected industry, percent—				
	Total	Net change, 1990–1995	Total	Percent change, 1990–1995	Manufacturing	Retail trade	Services	Total (mil dol)	Percent change, 1990–1994	Per capita[1] (dollars)	Total (mil dol)	Manufacturing	Retail trade	FIRE[2]	Services	Government
Florence, AL MSA	3 437	364	49 026	15.2	31.1	22.6	26.8	2 358.4	23.2	17 380	1 586.2	28.2	11.1	3.4	17.7	22.1
Colbert	1 392	113	19 760	7.4	31.4	20.3	28.1	920.7	25.2	17 537	778.2	31.0	8.5	2.3	13.9	25.0
Lauderdale	2 045	251	29 266	21.2	30.8	24.3	25.9	1 437.8	21.9	17 281	807.9	25.5	13.6	4.5	21.3	19.3
Florence, SC MSA (Florence)	3 132	166	50 484	8.5	23.6	21.7	31.6	2 136.2	25.9	17 625	1 646.0	25.0	12.4	5.2	22.4	17.3
Fort Collins-Loveland, CO MSA (Larimer)	6 765	1 502	76 361	37.1	19.4	28.5	30.5	4 284.0	35.6	20 169	2 889.1	24.1	12.7	3.7	22.4	21.1
Fort Myers-Cape Coral, FL MSA (Lee)	10 785	552	125 854	16.4	4.7	29.2	39.9	8 103.2	23.5	22 056	4 170.9	4.3	15.3	7.2	34.9	15.3
Fort Pierce-Port St. Lucie, FL MSA	7 311	499	74 781	3.4	7.4	29.2	34.6	6 279.8	21.3	22 565	2 778.1	6.3	13.0	6.8	30.2	13.9
Martin	3 821	299	38 309	3.4	7.4	30.3	35.1	3 491.4	20.5	32 002	1 326.5	7.4	13.7	8.9	33.8	10.4
St. Lucie	3 490	200	36 472	3.4	7.4	28.1	34.0	2 788.4	22.3	16 480	1 451.6	5.3	12.3	4.9	26.9	17.0
Fort Smith, AR-OK MSA	4 836	453	84 642	20.1	34.4	17.7	28.0	3 141.5	27.2	16 963	2 561.9	30.5	10.0	3.3	25.8	10.1
Crawford, AR	880	145	11 395	20.3	34.6	17.5	19.1	646.0	32.4	13 892	363.3	25.2	10.6	2.4	14.8	12.0
Sebastian, AR	3 377	225	67 654	19.3	36.4	16.4	28.2	1 994.4	24.8	19 288	2 007.2	33.4	9.3	3.5	27.3	8.3
Sequoyah, OK	579	83	5 593	30.7	9.1	33.7	42.8	501.2	30.4	14 197	191.4	9.9	16.9	3.2	30.6	24.9
Fort Walton Beach, FL MSA (Okaloosa)	4 446	678	50 977	20.2	7.7	32.9	38.6	3 048.8	30.7	18 960	2 070.6	5.7	12.1	4.7	26.2	41.6
Fort Wayne, IN MSA	12 344	882	234 361	6.0	30.8	20.1	25.3	10 005.3	22.2	21 333	7 898.8	35.5	8.9	6.4	20.7	8.9
Adams	724	29	13 045	16.9	53.8	20.0	14.7	581.1	24.5	18 103	389.6	51.8	9.9	2.0	9.5	10.1
Allen	8 557	480	166 194	-8	22.6	21.4	27.9	6 905.8	20.6	22 443	5 867.4	30.1	8.9	7.9	23.3	8.4
De Kalb	882	100	17 384	26.7	55.6	15.2	19.0	716.8	30.6	19 116	550.5	63.1	6.5	1.5	11.8	7.9
Huntington	898	132	18 286	34.8	56.1	13.7	18.5	713.2	24.7	19 592	452.9	45.5	9.4	2.7	13.3	11.2
Wells	628	54	9 257	16.0	38.1	17.5	23.5	526.1	21.8	20 006	294.6	37.7	12.5	2.0	19.0	12.2
Whitley	655	87	10 195	40.1	39.0	21.9	21.9	562.3	27.7	19 390	343.9	50.1	8.6	2.1	13.6	12.5
Fresno, CA MSA	16 840	383	211 777	3.7	13.7	24.5	32.4	14 276.1	17.5	17 105	9 934.1	9.8	10.8	5.0	23.1	19.3
Fresno	15 122	299	194 112	2.8	13.0	24.0	33.2	12 701.5	16.9	17 406	9 002.6	9.4	10.7	5.3	23.6	19.3
Madera	1 718	84	17 665	13.9	21.3	30.0	23.7	1 574.7	22.8	15 011	931.6	14.1	11.4	1.9	18.3	20.0
Gadsden, AL MSA (Etowah)	2 133	185	34 060	9.1	30.3	23.1	28.8	1 707.7	23.2	17 008	1 098.7	33.5	11.2	3.6	24.0	12.1
Gainesville, FL MSA (Alachua)	5 071	373	71 759	17.6	8.1	28.2	44.6	3 747.5	27.9	19 407	2 854.0	6.2	10.7	4.9	31.4	35.5
Glens Falls, NY MSA	3 167	-145	42 313	7.2	21.0	22.9	38.8	2 225.4	17.2	18 226	1 488.0	22.6	12.0	4.1	26.9	18.8
Warren	2 193	-47	32 137	14.0	14.7	23.1	44.1	1 262.1	17.5	20 588	973.5	17.2	13.9	5.3	34.6	12.8
Washington	974	-98	10 176	-9.8	40.7	22.2	21.8	963.3	16.9	15 844	514.5	32.9	8.6	1.9	12.3	30.0
Goldsboro, NC MSA (Wayne)	2 205	97	35 727	7.0	27.6	22.6	29.1	1 723.7	25.0	15 770	1 259.1	15.6	9.6	2.9	17.8	29.7
Grand Forks, ND-MN MSA	2 619	123	34 628	13.1	10.7	30.2	35.8	1 821.2	19.4	17 759	1 339.9	6.5	10.9	3.4	21.5	32.7
Grand Forks, ND	1 789	119	25 630	12.6	8.1	32.1	36.1	1 268.3	24.3	17 889	1 025.3	4.6	11.2	3.4	21.5	36.0
Polk, MN	830	4	8 998	14.6	18.0	24.9	35.0	552.9	9.6	16 909	314.7	12.9	10.0	3.3	21.7	22.0
Grand Junction, CO MSA (Mesa)	3 113	593	34 086	25.3	9.8	29.3	36.5	1 884.8	32.3	18 193	1 230.1	8.3	14.6	4.0	29.1	17.0
Grand Rapids-Muskegon-Holland, MI MSA	25 198	2 674	478 087	16.4	31.7	18.8	27.6	21 337.7	30.8	21 665	16 589.1	35.7	9.5	4.5	21.2	9.8
Allegan	1 821	222	33 311	31.4	51.7	16.6	18.4	1 887.7	34.7	19 644	1 134.6	53.2	8.0	1.1	10.1	10.6
Kent	14 618	1 362	303 241	15.3	27.1	18.2	29.6	12 042.0	31.1	23 153	10 391.2	31.8	10.0	5.5	23.8	8.4
Muskegon	3 450	191	51 356	Z	30.5	24.4	27.5	2 828.2	23.0	17 309	1 845.2	33.4	10.7	3.1	21.1	15.9
Ottawa	5 309	899	90 179	26.9	40.5	18.7	24.4	4 579.7	33.8	22 308	3 218.1	43.7	7.7	3.2	16.7	10.8
Great Falls, MT MSA (Cascade)	2 460	129	25 574	6.6	4.6	31.9	39.6	1 533.0	23.5	18 879	1 020.4	3.4	14.3	6.4	29.4	26.7
Green Bay, WI MSA (Brown)	5 671	646	107 195	14.2	23.9	21.0	28.3	4 526.4	28.5	21 835	3 857.0	26.4	10.1	6.5	22.7	10.2
Greensboro--Winston-Salem--High Point, NC MSA	30 358	2 035	556 939	10.0	31.2	18.9	26.1	24 121.4	24.0	21 786	18 540.6	31.0	10.2	D	22.6	9.6
Alamance	3 112	64	56 258	11.1	40.5	19.9	23.9	2 222.0	24.1	19 577	1 562.7	36.3	11.1	5.9	22.6	8.9
Davidson	2 450	116	42 901	4.9	53.4	16.5	14.7	2 383.7	20.0	17 882	1 354.9	46.0	10.4	2.5	14.4	10.6
Davie	578	14	8 691	19.2	45.7	18.7	21.2	659.5	26.0	22 432	279.9	40.0	9.2	D	18.9	11.6
Forsyth	7 914	444	159 791	7.8	23.0	19.1	34.0	6 826.8	22.7	24 566	5 678.5	27.3	10.5	7.3	28.1	7.9
Guilford	12 739	1 001	235 023	11.4	25.3	19.5	25.5	8 729.7	25.6	23 715	7 959.3	27.2	9.9	7.2	22.2	10.4
Randolph	2 433	299	41 784	15.4	54.9	16.3	15.2	2 053.6	26.4	18 206	1 238.8	47.1	9.0	1.9	13.0	9.9
Stokes	563	58	5 166	-17.2	27.4	21.4	28.1	681.3	23.8	17 076	213.0	21.3	11.8	1.8	17.6	17.9
Yadkin	569	39	7 325	23.7	47.3	18.7	20.4	564.9	20.8	17 488	253.5	36.4	12.0	2.0	12.0	14.3
Greenville, NC MSA (Pitt)	2 818	402	45 669	30.8	20.7	25.8	33.7	2 156.4	29.0	18 542	1 614.1	21.7	10.8	3.3	16.2	30.2
Greenville-Spartanburg-Anderson, SC MSA	22 635	2 534	432 435	8.1	30.9	18.7	26.6	16 279.0	23.3	18 639	12 839.2	33.9	11.6	4.0	19.5	11.8
Anderson	3 299	117	52 726	8.3	40.2	22.3	22.7	2 641.2	21.7	17 296	1 647.7	40.3	12.7	2.7	15.3	14.4
Cherokee	901	40	17 109	-3.0	44.6	19.1	15.4	700.3	21.0	14 996	518.8	51.9	8.0	1.5	11.5	9.7
Greenville	10 748	1 879	221 686	10.5	23.6	17.1	28.6	6 932.2	23.2	20 669	6 232.3	27.7	11.6	5.6	22.9	9.9
Pickens	2 042	273	31 087	9.9	44.1	21.7	21.5	1 640.8	24.9	16 246	941.2	34.8	11.6	2.4	16.0	23.0
Spartanburg	5 645	225	109 827	4.7	35.3	19.1	27.6	4 364.5	24.2	18 369	3 499.1	39.0	11.8	2.5	17.6	11.1
Harrisburg-Lebanon-Carlisle, PA MSA	14 724	760	275 349	7.2	17.1	20.3	33.7	13 589.9	21.4	22 289	10 964.7	16.6	9.2	7.2	22.7	22.7
Cumberland	5 131	339	104 829	6.9	14.1	22.0	32.1	4 803.7	21.6	23 479	3 909.9	12.8	10.9	11.1	23.8	16.2
Dauphin	6 421	366	125 490	6.3	17.1	17.9	35.0	5 716.0	21.4	23 274	5 562.4	17.3	7.0	5.6	22.5	28.3
Lebanon	2 458	-10	39 761	10.0	24.9	22.0	35.3	2 321.1	20.5	19 941	1 278.8	26.2	12.8	2.9	21.0	18.2
Perry	714	65	5 269	17.0	15.4	30.7	22.2	749.0	23.9	17 379	213.7	10.9	14.2	2.9	16.6	22.7

Z Less than .05 percent.
D Withheld to avoid disclosure.

[1]Based on 1994 resident population estimated by the Bureau of Economic Analysis.
[2]Finance, insurance, and real estate.

Source: Private Nonfarm Business—U.S. Bureau of the Census, "County Business Patterns" on diskettes, annual (related Internet site <http://www.census.gov/epcd/cbp/view/cbpview.html>); Personal Income—U.S. Bureau of Economic Analysis, "Regional Economic Information System, 1969–1994" on CD-ROM (related Internet site <http://www.bea.doc.gov/bea/dr1.htm>).

[MSA = Metropolitan statistical area. CMSA = Consolidated MSA. PMSA = Primary MSA. NECMA = New England county metropolitan area. All areas defined as of June 30, 1996 Table includes 245 MSAs, 17 CMSAs, and 58 PMSAs not in New England; 12 NECMAs; and 844 component counties]

Metropolitan areas and component counties	Private nonfarm business, 1995							Personal income, 1994								
	Establishments		Employment								Earnings					
					By selected industry, percent—							By selected industry, percent—				
	Total	Net change, 1990–1995	Total	Percent change, 1990–1995	Manufacturing	Retail trade	Services	Total (mil dol)	Percent change, 1990–1994	Per capita[1] (dollars)	Total (mil dol)	Manufacturing	Retail trade	FIRE[2]	Services	Government
Hartford, CT NECMA	29 660	−844	520 487	−7.5	17.8	18.2	32.0	29 987.8	10.7	26 842	24 451.0	19.0	8.4	16.7	25.8	14.3
Hartford	23 161	−981	440 154	−8.0	17.2	17.5	31.7	23 113.4	10.0	27 529	20 703.5	19.1	8.2	17.8	25.5	13.1
Middlesex	4 065	145	56 104	−7.9	23.0	18.0	33.4	3 959.5	14.8	26 990	2 529.6	21.7	8.7	14.8	28.8	13.0
Tolland	2 434	−8	24 229	2.0	18.0	31.2	33.3	2 914.9	11.1	22 268	1 217.8	11.5	10.7	3.0	23.7	36.4
Hattiesburg, MS MSA	2 667	303	36 210	25.1	14.4	29.5	32.7	1 641.2	30.3	15 842	1 156.4	12.8	13.4	5.1	24.6	24.1
Forrest	2 259	215	32 395	25.7	13.5	30.0	33.9	1 121.6	27.1	15 820	915.5	13.0	11.8	5.8	22.8	27.7
Lamar	408	88	3 815	19.6	21.4	25.1	22.3	519.6	37.8	15 891	240.9	12.1	19.6	2.4	31.7	10.5
Hickory-Morganton-Lenoir, NC MSA	7 516	361	156 376	6.5	53.9	16.4	15.4	5 861.8	25.7	19 175	4 710.7	48.4	9.5	1.8	13.8	10.9
Alexander	553	31	8 639	5.3	67.5	13.7	11.7	502.6	23.3	17 095	260.7	52.6	7.7	1.5	12.5	10.5
Burke	1 442	66	30 103	.5	57.2	14.6	17.4	1 367.8	23.4	17 336	1 001.8	46.9	8.0	1.3	15.8	19.4
Caldwell	1 403	32	29 334	5.7	59.3	14.0	14.3	1 292.2	25.9	17 677	855.8	49.7	8.7	1.8	13.2	9.9
Catawba	4 118	232	88 300	9.1	49.6	18.1	15.4	2 699.2	27.3	21 715	2 592.6	48.2	10.6	2.0	13.3	8.1
Honolulu, HI MSA (Honolulu)	21 004	−172	322 339	−3.3	4.0	25.0	38.2	22 145.4	20.0	25 329	17 165.6	4.5	12.8	7.4	27.6	26.6
Houma, LA MSA	4 140	291	54 538	19.4	9.4	24.0	32.0	2 834.3	24.5	15 132	1 812.6	9.6	11.0	3.4	22.8	15.7
Lafourche	1 673	75	20 304	28.1	10.4	23.4	34.9	1 296.0	23.0	14 914	679.4	13.6	9.6	3.2	19.4	21.7
Terrebonne	2 467	216	34 234	14.8	8.8	24.4	30.2	1 538.2	25.8	15 321	1 133.2	7.1	11.7	3.5	24.8	12.1
Houston-Galveston-Brazoria, TX CMSA	97 987	10 197	1 727 913	12.6	12.5	19.1	34.8	92 839.8	27.1	22 651	76 151.1	14.8	7.9	6.0	28.3	11.0
Brazoria, TX PMSA (Brazoria)	3 520	300	56 143	7.8	27.3	22.0	21.6	3 944.6	21.6	18 650	2 615.9	37.7	7.9	2.1	13.8	13.4
Galveston-Texas City, TX PMSA (Galveston)	4 541	284	65 343	1.5	11.9	28.9	36.1	4 718.8	24.6	20 106	2 748.5	19.2	9.8	6.0	18.3	28.9
Houston, TX PMSA	89 926	9 613	1 606 427	13.3	12.0	18.6	35.2	84 176.4	27.6	23 046	70 786.7	13.7	7.8	6.1	29.2	10.3
Chambers	335	22	4 338	38.2	29.7	21.7	17.2	383.9	27.2	18 022	241.0	34.6	5.5	1.8	8.4	13.8
Fort Bend	4 036	1 373	57 448	62.8	16.7	21.7	30.2	6 029.7	37.5	21 535	2 424.6	16.4	9.2	5.0	24.9	16.2
Harris	80 034	6 784	1 475 299	10.9	11.8	18.1	35.4	71 936.1	26.0	23 623	65 692.4	13.5	7.6	6.3	29.6	9.8
Liberty	1 017	94	10 385	7.0	14.3	30.5	30.5	943.2	29.6	16 262	445.1	22.5	10.9	2.5	23.8	17.6
Montgomery	4 131	1 302	54 731	52.3	11.2	25.2	39.3	4 454.4	40.3	20 047	1 761.8	13.4	12.2	4.4	29.7	14.4
Waller	373	38	4 226	7.9	26.9	37.4	15.3	429.1	31.8	16 631	221.8	25.2	14.1	2.3	10.3	30.1
Huntington-Ashland, WV-KY-OH MSA	6 696	305	94 631	4.3	18.3	26.2	32.7	5 357.2	22.6	16 921	3 560.8	24.0	10.1	3.3	23.2	15.6
Cabell, WV	2 644	−134	40 251	4.0	14.0	27.2	37.3	1 883.1	24.6	19 454	1 431.7	16.5	11.0	4.7	31.0	15.9
Wayne, WV	758	238	10 169	69.7	21.0	17.8	33.5	578.1	21.1	13 603	278.2	15.1	8.3	1.7	12.2	32.5
Boyd, KY	1 526	24	24 785	−7.7	21.4	24.6	31.0	1 003.4	17.5	19 830	1 013.9	28.8	8.5	2.7	22.7	9.0
Carter, KY	439	68	4 006	−1.4	19.0	33.6	30.0	322.8	26.1	12 560	116.1	14.1	18.1	4.1	15.2	24.6
Greenup, KY	446	42	4 585	−10.2	23.8	26.6	17.4	591.1	16.6	15 932	287.4	40.1	8.4	2.2	13.3	12.7
Lawrence, OH	883	67	10 835	25.8	21.7	31.1	26.1	978.7	28.2	15 316	433.5	35.5	10.9	2.0	14.3	18.8
Huntsville, AL MSA	7 524	1 004	131 213	14.7	28.3	20.9	34.9	6 682.2	24.6	21 139	6 157.2	27.5	7.0	2.3	26.1	27.3
Limestone	940	115	14 881	5.9	44.6	22.5	17.6	1 003.3	28.9	17 268	933.2	36.7	5.8	.9	18.2	29.5
Madison	6 584	889	116 332	15.9	26.2	20.7	37.1	5 678.9	23.9	22 011	5 224.0	25.9	7.2	2.6	27.6	26.9
Indianapolis, IN MSA	39 498	4 447	699 534	11.0	17.7	21.3	32.3	33 865.4	27.1	23 168	26 960.1	22.1	9.6	9.0	24.2	13.6
Boone	1 136	162	11 078	23.0	16.3	25.7	28.8	1 025.7	32.5	25 077	379.3	13.7	11.3	5.8	22.4	13.3
Hamilton	4 275	1 120	56 343	43.0	13.3	21.4	26.5	4 133.8	45.6	30 780	2 385.5	13.5	9.9	23.3	19.6	7.1
Hancock	1 103	171	11 533	25.2	25.5	24.6	24.1	1 076.1	30.5	21 784	422.5	28.3	10.7	3.0	18.9	16.2
Hendricks	1 732	441	17 517	42.1	8.1	30.1	28.7	1 846.9	34.5	21 961	685.9	5.1	13.6	3.3	20.3	19.2
Johnson	2 524	459	32 446	25.8	17.3	36.2	28.7	2 134.2	31.9	21 558	913.4	21.0	17.1	5.3	24.1	14.1
Madison	2 712	133	42 875	−2.0	27.5	24.8	34.1	2 485.3	21.3	18 714	1 751.2	47.6	9.2	2.8	19.7	10.6
Marion	23 910	1 664	500 953	7.1	16.7	19.3	33.9	19 194.6	22.8	23 465	19 576.5	20.9	8.9	8.7	25.8	14.3
Morgan	1 197	202	12 080	11.7	19.5	31.4	26.0	1 135.5	29.7	18 615	370.1	20.5	14.7	3.9	20.0	17.9
Shelby	909	95	14 709	21.0	45.8	18.1	21.0	833.4	26.1	19 749	475.7	46.9	7.8	1.8	13.9	11.6
Iowa City, IA MSA (Johnson)	2 413	337	42 798	14.3	9.4	26.2	48.2	2 154.6	30.4	21 546	1 766.3	8.7	8.4	3.0	19.2	47.8
Jackson, MI MSA (Jackson)	3 294	270	51 488	12.7	27.6	24.3	28.0	2 847.2	21.7	18 573	1 838.2	26.8	10.3	3.3	20.0	17.6
Jackson, MS MSA	10 452	496	181 391	15.5	11.6	19.9	38.2	7 881.8	29.5	19 135	6 158.2	10.9	10.6	9.3	26.6	19.6
Hinds	6 870	−328	128 653	8.1	10.3	18.5	42.1	4 937.6	23.6	19 601	4 536.9	9.1	9.9	9.8	28.8	21.1
Madison	1 463	394	18 838	40.7	11.0	35.6	29.4	1 122.5	40.6	17 621	537.8	14.0	18.4	9.4	23.1	13.1
Rankin	2 119	430	33 900	37.4	16.8	16.9	28.2	1 821.7	40.8	18 917	1 083.5	17.0	9.6	7.0	19.4	16.6
Jackson, TN MSA	2 755	317	48 841	26.5	26.2	22.7	32.6	1 762.8	31.9	18 343	1 496.0	26.4	11.3	2.9	23.4	16.7
Chester	230	41	3 380	50.4	32.6	22.1	23.5	174.4	33.6	12 918	92.1	29.5	13.1	2.6	17.8	15.9
Madison	2 525	276	45 461	25.0	25.7	22.7	33.3	1 588.4	31.8	19 230	1 404.0	26.2	11.1	2.9	23.7	16.8
Jacksonville, FL MSA	26 135	2 189	414 068	15.1	8.7	21.9	35.0	20 347.8	23.7	20 936	15 038.5	8.7	10.3	12.6	27.5	18.8
Clay	2 499	278	26 781	15.9	5.8	37.8	33.1	2 238.7	25.3	18 594	767.8	5.6	20.1	3.7	32.7	15.7
Duval	19 860	1 127	348 695	14.3	8.7	19.7	34.9	14 553.8	20.9	20 685	12 947.5	8.4	9.3	14.0	26.8	19.0
Nassau	1 061	149	11 481	26.3	18.3	27.2	33.5	1 035.4	34.3	20 874	456.6	20.2	11.4	2.8	21.5	23.1
St. Johns	2 715	635	27 111	15.7	7.8	32.8	38.4	2 519.9	36.4	25 635	866.6	10.4	15.2	4.3	37.4	15.5
Jacksonville, NC MSA (Onslow)	2 395	236	25 042	12.8	10.4	39.6	28.7	1 982.4	29.7	13 550	1 649.3	2.7	9.0	1.7	8.5	69.1
Jamestown, NY MSA (Chautauqua)	3 115	−194	45 197	−4.9	31.4	22.6	30.3	2 477.0	17.9	17 419	1 630.2	30.4	10.8	2.7	20.7	19.4
Janesville-Beloit, WI MSA (Rock)	3 214	173	57 960	9.7	33.8	21.5	26.4	2 990.6	26.5	20 483	2 122.5	41.7	10.1	2.7	17.5	11.3

[1]Based on 1994 resident population estimated by the Bureau of Economic Analysis.
[2]Finance, insurance, and real estate.

Source: Private Nonfarm Business—U.S. Bureau of the Census, "County Business Patterns" on diskettes, annual (related Internet site <http://www.census.gov/epcd/cbp/view/cbpview.html>); Personal Income—U.S. Bureau of Economic Analysis, "Regional Economic Information System, 1969–1994" on CD-ROM (related Internet site <http://www.bea.doc.gov/bea/dr1.htm>).

Table C–3. Metro Counties — **Private Nonfarm Business and Personal Income—Con.**

[MSA = Metropolitan statistical area. CMSA = Consolidated MSA. PMSA = Primary MSA. NECMA = New England county metropolitan area. All areas defined as of June 30, 1996 Table includes 245 MSAs, 17 CMSAs, and 58 PMSAs not in New England; 12 NECMAs; and 844 component counties]

Metropolitan areas and component counties	Private nonfarm business, 1995							Personal income, 1994								
	Establishments		Employment								Earnings					
					By selected industry, percent—							By selected industry, percent—				
	Total	Net change, 1990–1995	Total	Percent change, 1990–1995	Manufacturing	Retail trade	Services	Total (mil dol)	Percent change, 1990–1994	Per capita[1] (dollars)	Total (mil dol)	Manufacturing	Retail trade	FIRE[2]	Services	Government
Johnson City-Kingsport-Bristol, TN-VA MSA	9 874	972	169 168	14.0	33.4	22.6	27.3	7 777.9	21.1	17 261	5 524.4	34.3	10.7	3.0	22.5	13.5
Carter, TN	761	56	10 346	12.2	30.6	23.0	29.4	725.0	20.8	13 731	293.5	28.5	12.8	3.7	22.8	16.8
Hawkins, TN	571	44	10 686	13.6	61.6	16.8	12.0	718.1	21.6	15 246	388.0	58.7	7.4	.7	8.3	14.0
Sullivan, TN	3 621	365	67 742	11.9	33.1	22.0	26.9	2 792.7	19.0	18 908	2 351.2	40.1	9.5	2.6	23.5	8.4
Unicoi, TN	264	22	3 608	-5.4	52.1	16.9	20.1	263.3	19.6	15 766	129.5	42.7	7.3	1.7	13.9	16.0
Washington, TN	2 583	211	45 412	17.5	24.1	23.5	36.2	1 811.8	27.0	18 601	1 432.8	20.3	12.2	2.8	28.7	19.9
Scott, VA	325	-8	3 304	-4.3	25.1	31.8	25.5	335.1	16.6	14 442	112.4	25.6	17.6	4.2	14.9	21.7
Washington, VA	1 081	424	13 287	71.6	17.9	28.4	29.5	31 132.0	319.4	317 230	3816.9	332.5	311.8	35.3	317.4	314.0
Bristol city, VA	668	-142	14 783	-5.1	56.5	20.8	11.4	(3)	(3)	(3)	(3)	(3)	(3)	(3)	(3)	(3)
Johnstown, PA MSA	5 465	157	70 436	2.4	18.7	23.4	32.7	4 186.7	17.6	17 466	2 493.2	15.7	13.7	5.3	27.1	15.0
Cambria	3 568	83	48 933	-.9	16.2	23.6	36.3	2 826.8	17.3	17 591	1 696.7	14.4	13.3	6.4	29.4	15.7
Somerset	1 897	74	21 503	10.6	24.4	23.1	24.7	1 359.9	18.3	17 214	796.5	18.6	14.7	3.0	22.2	13.6
Jonesboro, AR MSA (Craighead)	2 126	318	30 689	18.3	24.5	22.8	31.2	1 209.0	29.5	16 472	958.1	22.5	11.5	3.7	26.3	14.8
Joplin, MO MSA	3 973	362	64 109	27.1	27.5	20.2	28.4	2 524.9	29.5	17 806	1 869.7	28.6	11.5	2.7	20.8	9.4
Jasper	3 103	304	51 714	33.5	24.4	20.4	30.9	1 734.2	31.2	18 274	1 445.0	26.6	11.2	2.7	21.3	9.6
Newton	870	58	12 395	5.9	40.4	19.1	18.4	790.8	25.9	16 860	424.6	35.2	12.4	2.4	19.1	8.9
Kalamazoo-Battle Creek, MI MSA	10 320	749	183 177	13.1	27.5	21.6	32.3	9 164.6	24.3	20 706	6 868.7	34.1	8.7	D	21.8	15.0
Calhoun	3 068	157	58 742	13.0	31.2	21.6	31.0	2 748.7	24.6	19 633	2 189.7	37.8	9.3	5.2	16.9	17.6
Kalamazoo	5 865	498	109 215	12.8	24.8	21.0	34.3	5 186.1	23.7	22 667	4 077.7	33.2	8.0	7.5	25.6	12.7
Van Buren	1 387	94	15 220	15.5	32.3	26.5	23.1	1 229.8	25.8	16 664	601.4	26.3	10.7	D	13.7	21.1
Kansas City, MO-KS MSA	45 161	3 522	762 798	9.9	15.0	19.6	34.5	37 296.0	22.8	22 642	28 864.3	15.3	9.3	8.6	26.9	14.9
Cass, MO	1 489	258	12 448	38.4	11.4	31.2	29.2	1 305.8	26.9	18 288	393.4	9.0	16.5	4.4	21.4	18.2
Clay, MO	4 406	538	72 541	20.6	22.6	23.1	29.6	3 481.3	22.0	21 319	2 462.8	31.7	13.0	3.6	18.2	10.8
Clinton, MO	403	53	3 060	18.8	6.9	26.9	38.3	310.5	24.3	17 845	97.6	3.7	12.9	12.4	25.6	17.6
Jackson, MO	17 831	298	336 450	3.1	14.8	18.5	37.9	13 924.0	19.2	21 938	13 386.5	14.5	8.4	10.3	30.3	14.7
Lafayette, MO	757	66	6 755	14.7	19.5	27.5	29.4	568.7	18.3	17 828	228.4	13.2	12.9	4.9	19.3	20.0
Platte, MO	1 585	264	28 113	19.7	8.9	15.0	30.2	1 530.5	28.5	23 619	963.1	8.3	6.7	5.1	22.1	8.0
Ray, MO	406	51	2 873	25.3	8.1	31.0	28.7	358.2	20.6	16 282	103.8	8.6	11.8	3.9	16.2	24.9
Johnson, KS	13 622	2 021	218 049	22.6	11.4	21.4	31.8	11 737.6	28.4	29 867	7 575.0	10.4	11.0	10.9	30.1	9.5
Leavenworth, KS	1 003	82	13 589	14.8	12.1	23.7	43.2	1 125.4	26.3	16 334	767.2	5.8	6.4	3.1	16.6	58.6
Miami, KS	536	60	5 402	11.1	12.4	23.8	39.4	444.6	21.5	17 999	165.0	9.7	11.0	5.0	19.5	30.1
Wyandotte, KS	3 123	-169	63 518	-9.0	23.7	12.9	32.1	2 509.4	15.0	16 179	2 721.5	25.0	5.6	2.1	16.1	22.0
Killeen-Temple, TX MSA	4 440	517	68 558	25.2	14.0	25.8	41.0	4 466.6	35.4	15 552	3 515.9	9.1	8.0	2.6	16.8	52.9
Bell	3 751	423	63 009	25.7	14.2	24.7	42.1	3 632.1	35.7	16 854	3 231.1	9.5	7.8	2.5	17.0	52.8
Coryell	689	94	5 549	19.3	11.4	37.3	28.0	834.5	34.2	11 638	284.8	4.8	10.7	3.4	15.3	53.9
Knoxville, TN MSA	17 661	1 796	272 723	16.0	16.7	25.5	35.1	12 600.5	29.9	19 963	9 477.5	19.1	D	4.1	D	15.4
Anderson	1 678	133	36 541	11.4	22.3	16.7	47.4	1 412.6	27.1	19 840	1 433.6	34.9	D	1.9	D	12.6
Blount	1 947	224	27 858	22.0	23.6	27.7	26.5	1 668.4	27.5	17 636	916.3	32.1	14.9	3.1	18.3	13.7
Knox	10 916	740	175 189	14.1	13.5	25.6	35.5	7 702.6	29.7	21 546	6 094.6	13.3	11.5	4.6	32.6	16.8
Loudon	675	145	8 473	12.4	38.2	19.7	19.5	626.4	37.2	17 846	309.5	34.4	8.3	3.7	19.0	13.5
Sevier	2 273	504	22 646	32.1	11.6	40.6	31.0	1 011.7	34.8	17 384	654.1	11.4	27.6	5.7	33.5	11.5
Union	172	50	2 016	57.6	62.3	9.6	7.8	178.7	31.1	12 239	69.5	37.1	7.4	12.1	10.1	15.4
Kokomo, IN MSA	2 268	123	46 376	14.9	44.1	21.5	22.8	2 166.1	26.6	21 814	2 065.1	61.7	7.3	2.2	11.6	8.4
Howard	1 944	108	42 992	13.8	45.3	21.4	22.5	1 831.7	27.4	22 069	1 937.0	64.3	7.0	2.1	11.4	7.6
Tipton	324	15	3 384	29.9	27.6	22.4	26.5	334.4	22.4	20 513	128.1	21.3	12.3	3.7	13.7	20.5
La Crosse, WI-MN MSA	3 289	222	56 669	11.2	19.6	25.6	32.1	2 412.1	23.1	20 084	1 821.6	20.3	11.1	4.1	27.6	13.7
La Crosse, WI	2 884	198	52 800	10.2	20.1	26.1	31.5	2 067.0	24.0	20 465	1 694.3	20.8	11.2	4.1	28.0	13.4
Houston, MN	405	24	3 869	27.0	13.5	18.8	41.1	345.2	18.1	18 071	127.2	12.6	8.6	3.0	21.6	17.9
Lafayette, LA MSA	8 906	992	121 360	17.6	11.1	23.5	32.0	5 981.7	27.2	16 551	4 143.1	12.0	10.6	3.8	27.3	13.3
Acadia	916	67	11 324	21.8	26.1	21.2	25.8	798.2	27.1	14 027	343.9	14.1	9.9	3.6	24.3	18.8
Lafayette	5 963	803	84 937	19.9	4.8	23.8	34.2	3 421.6	27.9	19 375	2 957.5	7.1	10.5	3.8	30.2	11.0
St. Landry	1 473	51	16 036	13.6	16.7	24.4	34.1	1 196.2	26.3	14 552	576.8	24.7	11.3	4.1	21.6	20.3
St. Martin	554	71	9 063	1.4	41.9	22.0	14.7	565.7	24.7	12 378	264.9	35.8	10.5	3.5	12.2	16.7
Lafayette, IN MSA	3 719	293	66 197	16.3	31.7	24.0	25.5	3 165.3	26.9	18 988	2 555.3	32.4	8.9	4.7	18.3	22.9
Clinton	727	33	10 617	27.5	44.9	17.4	20.5	599.4	26.8	18 557	336.4	46.9	8.1	2.4	11.4	13.3
Tippecanoe	2 992	260	55 580	14.4	29.1	25.2	26.4	2 565.9	27.0	19 091	2 218.9	30.2	9.1	5.0	19.4	24.4
Lake Charles, LA MSA (Calcasieu)	4 079	374	62 872	23.7	16.9	22.4	34.6	3 107.8	29.0	17 933	2 340.9	26.7	8.8	3.1	23.4	12.5
Lakeland-Winter Haven, FL MSA (Polk)	9 243	188	151 270	12.2	13.9	24.6	34.2	7 661.2	23.0	17 833	5 019.4	13.8	14.9	5.0	26.4	13.1
Lancaster, PA MSA (Lancaster)	10 568	445	190 302	2.4	29.7	21.5	26.8	9 655.6	20.2	21 811	6 772.5	31.9	10.7	4.5	20.7	8.4
Lansing-East Lansing, MI MSA	10 061	758	160 021	7.9	19.3	26.0	33.3	9 047.6	23.6	20 747	7 235.4	23.2	8.7	5.6	22.2	27.3
Clinton	1 089	162	11 948	27.9	25.3	27.9	23.1	1 165.8	26.9	19 142	394.5	22.5	12.6	2.5	19.0	19.0
Eaton	1 713	-82	20 600	-18.7	20.3	36.1	24.4	1 964.6	23.7	20 296	796.9	16.2	11.2	11.4	17.6	23.8
Ingham	7 259	678	127 473	12.2	18.6	24.2	35.7	5 917.2	22.9	21 254	6 044.0	24.1	8.1	5.0	23.0	28.3

D Withheld to avoid disclosure.

[1]Based on 1994 resident population estimated by the Bureau of Economic Analysis.
[2]Finance, insurance, and real estate.
[3]Independent city of Bristol included with Washington County; data not available separately.

Source: Private Nonfarm Business—U.S. Bureau of the Census, "County Business Patterns" on diskettes, annual (related Internet site <http://www.census.gov/epcd/cbp/view/cbpview.html>);
Personal Income—U.S. Bureau of Economic Analysis, "Regional Economic Information System, 1969–1994" on CD-ROM (related Internet site <http://www.bea.doc.gov/bea/dr1.htm>).

[MSA = Metropolitan statistical area. CMSA = Consolidated MSA. PMSA = Primary MSA. NECMA = New England county metropolitan area. All areas defined as of June 30, 1996 Table includes 245 MSAs, 17 CMSAs, and 58 PMSAs not in New England; 12 NECMAs; and 844 component counties]

| Metropolitan areas and component counties | Private nonfarm business, 1995 | | | | | | | Personal income, 1994 | | | | | | | | |
| | Establishments | | Employment | | | | | | | | Earnings | | | | | |
	Total	Net change, 1990–1995	Total	Percent change, 1990–1995	Manufacturing	Retail trade	Services	Total (mil dol)	Percent change, 1990–1994	Per capita[1] (dollars)	Total (mil dol)	Manufacturing	Retail trade	FIRE[2]	Services	Government
Laredo, TX MSA (Webb)	3 755	874	42 538	31.9	3.3	32.4	26.4	1 840.8	52.4	11 287	1 436.2	2.4	17.4	4.3	19.4	22.8
Las Cruces, NM MSA (Dona Ana)	3 071	497	32 071	22.8	8.1	33.2	32.3	2 129.7	27.0	13 696	1 349.5	4.6	11.3	3.7	19.8	38.3
Las Vegas, NV-AZ MSA	24 651	5 493	481 837	31.6	4.0	18.8	51.9	24 042.9	46.3	22 338	18 019.7	3.4	9.9	4.8	49.6	12.3
Clark, NV	21 289	4 984	449 215	34.5	3.4	18.0	53.6	21 807.6	47.2	23 244	16 739.4	3.1	9.6	4.9	50.6	12.1
Nye, NV	364	70	3 943	−54.9	3.4	19.1	32.6	389.9	34.9	17 805	372.7	1.1	4.9	1.4	58.1	11.9
Mohave, AZ	2 998	439	28 679	22.9	13.1	32.3	28.1	1 845.3	38.6	15 881	907.7	9.5	17.5	4.8	28.3	16.4
Lawrence, KS MSA (Douglas)	2 334	460	30 088	17.5	17.4	30.3	32.6	1 477.6	25.7	16 791	1 016.4	16.3	12.6	4.5	21.8	28.6
Lawton, OK MSA (Comanche)	2 097	145	26 485	15.1	13.5	31.8	36.1	1 774.4	20.9	15 088	1 331.6	11.2	9.3	3.0	14.7	52.3
Lewiston-Auburn, ME NECMA (Androscoggin)	2 659	−111	39 431	2.6	23.9	20.5	36.2	1 975.0	14.2	19 009	1 227.7	21.6	12.4	4.8	32.3	10.9
Lexington, KY MSA	11 453	560	195 872	12.6	21.3	22.9	33.9	8 687.9	22.9	20 162	7 136.3	22.0	10.6	D	23.4	17.9
Bourbon	387	4	5 046	18.5	29.9	23.5	16.6	337.6	19.5	17 581	186.6	21.9	7.6	4.3	13.4	12.0
Clark	655	36	9 287	8.4	34.7	24.0	18.1	531.9	23.1	17 449	304.5	28.1	11.5	2.2	16.4	12.1
Fayette	7 454	210	132 372	7.6	13.5	23.3	38.9	5 283.2	20.6	22 236	4 735.5	14.2	11.5	5.9	28.0	20.3
Jessamine	719	90	8 791	18.2	24.8	21.5	27.5	547.1	25.2	16 281	262.2	20.4	13.2	D	17.8	15.2
Madison	1 199	78	17 911	17.9	28.9	29.3	30.2	962.0	29.8	15 516	634.0	26.2	12.5	2.8	19.5	25.9
Scott	559	117	15 117	67.5	52.6	15.8	20.9	518.8	34.6	19 357	648.2	65.2	5.0	.9	9.3	4.9
Woodford	480	25	7 348	14.1	50.7	16.4	18.5	507.4	23.3	23 936	365.4	36.1	5.0	2.1	10.8	6.2
Lima, OH MSA	3 840	113	65 503	3.3	29.2	21.9	30.1	2 939.2	18.8	18 865	2 298.6	39.6	9.6	2.4	19.8	12.0
Allen	2 839	78	47 845	1.4	22.8	23.0	33.8	2 054.4	18.8	18 813	1 712.4	35.8	10.2	2.5	22.2	12.3
Auglaize	1 001	35	17 658	8.8	46.4	18.7	20.1	884.8	18.7	18 987	586.2	50.7	7.9	2.2	12.6	11.1
Lincoln, NE MSA (Lancaster)	6 403	779	108 537	15.9	15.9	22.2	36.0	4 778.9	29.3	21 174	3 780.6	15.3	9.2	7.4	24.5	23.6
Little Rock-North Little Rock, AR MSA ..	15 122	1 497	251 372	16.8	13.8	20.4	39.1	10 743.4	26.8	19 988	8 638.0	12.6	10.2	7.4	26.3	20.5
Faulkner	1 431	296	23 762	32.4	32.5	21.6	29.0	1 150.2	38.6	16 598	692.9	28.8	11.2	2.6	24.0	18.0
Lonoke	792	155	7 468	24.2	31.4	26.4	21.1	742.7	37.6	16 841	283.8	22.1	11.3	2.8	12.9	14.6
Pulaski	11 748	765	207 814	13.8	10.9	19.5	41.3	7 693.7	23.7	21 795	7 255.4	10.1	9.7	8.3	27.3	21.0
Saline	1 151	281	12 328	41.6	16.1	28.8	32.1	1 156.8	30.2	16 269	405.9	21.8	15.8	3.1	20.1	21.0
Longview-Marshall, TX MSA	5 446	389	70 873	9.2	23.9	23.9	28.4	3 693.8	22.6	18 340	2 511.1	24.9	12.3	3.4	23.5	11.5
Gregg	3 980	298	54 064	11.0	24.1	23.5	28.7	2 221.5	22.4	20 232	1 634.1	18.6	13.8	3.7	25.3	11.3
Harrison	1 028	50	12 581	2.6	25.9	23.6	26.1	954.5	21.0	16 429	686.8	41.9	7.6	2.8	19.7	10.3
Upshur	438	41	4 228	7.6	15.4	31.1	31.8	517.8	26.8	15 455	190.2	17.4	15.4	2.6	21.3	17.1
Los Angeles-Riverside-Orange, CA CMSA	347 903	−5 610	5 517 431	−6.6	18.3	18.6	37.0	329 646.0	9.3	21 542	249 126.8	16.4	9.6	7.3	34.3	13.3
Los Angeles-Long Beach, CA PMSA (Los Angeles)	214 320	−5 305	3 494 193	−9.2	18.8	16.7	39.2	197 289.1	7.1	21 562	164 046.3	16.7	8.7	7.4	36.8	12.6
Orange, CA PMSA (Orange)	70 783	−472	1 151 819	−3.3	19.2	19.0	32.9	64 892.7	10.5	25 516	47 920.9	19.0	10.6	9.2	31.3	10.2
Riverside-San Bernardino, CA PMSA	47 454	44	669 661	.6	15.1	26.6	33.0	51 564.8	15.9	17 741	27 547.0	11.8	13.3	4.1	26.5	21.4
Riverside	22 752	329	297 865	2.0	13.8	27.5	34.2	25 086.8	17.5	18 543	12 140.1	11.3	13.3	4.6	27.6	21.1
San Bernardino	24 702	−285	371 796	−.5	16.1	25.9	32.1	26 477.9	14.4	17 043	15 406.9	12.3	13.4	3.7	25.6	21.6
Ventura, CA PMSA (Ventura)	15 346	123	201 758	−1.7	16.6	23.3	34.6	15 899.4	12.3	22 626	9 612.5	12.9	10.3	5.7	29.4	17.7
Louisville, KY-IN MSA	25 569	2 505	464 298	15.5	19.0	21.6	32.1	21 658.3	25.2	22 080	16 097.6	23.0	10.0	7.0	25.6	12.2
Bullitt, KY	755	205	8 944	56.8	29.5	32.8	18.3	832.8	36.7	15 196	253.6	31.5	12.9	2.7	13.1	18.1
Jefferson, KY	19 102	1 378	377 188	12.7	17.4	20.6	33.5	15 795.0	23.7	23 494	13 308.9	22.8	9.6	7.8	26.9	11.1
Oldham, KY	742	137	7 704	26.8	14.8	23.8	29.5	976.9	29.2	24 545	341.5	10.4	9.8	2.4	23.2	19.0
Clark, IN	2 314	338	35 410	18.6	19.4	29.1	27.0	1 721.4	25.9	18 937	1 122.8	21.3	13.8	2.5	19.5	15.9
Floyd, IN	1 605	279	22 233	33.4	31.8	17.3	29.8	1 424.6	29.8	20 616	695.0	27.8	9.6	4.8	20.4	18.3
Harrison, IN	617	81	7 062	36.6	32.3	27.9	19.8	555.5	30.0	17 415	210.1	26.9	13.0	3.0	15.7	17.5
Scott, IN	434	87	5 757	46.7	43.4	26.6	19.6	352.1	32.8	15 934	165.7	41.0	12.4	2.7	15.4	17.0
Lubbock, TX MSA (Lubbock)	6 351	510	84 865	9.4	9.6	27.8	36.6	4 295.3	22.0	18 635	3 247.0	8.6	14.8	4.5	28.5	20.6
Lynchburg, VA MSA...............	5 103	431	86 455	6.6	29.8	18.5	32.1	3 819.5	20.2	18 824	2 669.1	35.3	10.0	5.8	20.8	11.3
Amherst	561	69	6 426	−17.2	27.3	24.3	23.9	456.0	19.3	19 343	250.8	21.9	9.8	1.6	14.9	31.0
Bedford....................	635	243	5 274	36.6	27.9	14.8	23.1	[3]1 116.0	[3]25.8	[3]19 208	[3]365.9	[3]31.6	[3]9.4	[3]2.2	[3]20.2	[3]14.5
Campbell	886	185	13 155	17.6	42.0	19.2	14.3	[4]2 247.5	[4]17.7	[4]19 493	[4]2 052.5	[4]37.7	[4]10.1	[4]6.9	[4]21.7	[4]8.3
Bedford city	552	−77	6 241	−13.4	38.0	20.3	28.3	(3)	(3)	(3)	(3)	(3)	(3)	(3)	(3)	(3)
Lynchburg city	2 469	11	55 359	8.3	26.4	17.8	38.5	(4)	(4)	(4)	(4)	(4)	(4)	(4)	(4)	(4)
Macon, GA MSA.................	7 054	355	112 150	16.9	17.4	25.0	34.5	5 717.8	21.1	18 600	4 252.2	D	9.9	6.1	21.7	27.1
Bibb......................	4 509	90	79 810	14.5	17.7	22.5	35.7	3 103.2	20.6	20 047	2 620.8	21.6	10.5	7.9	26.4	15.1
Houston	1 834	182	23 204	28.8	9.9	35.4	36.6	1 715.1	22.9	17 447	1 267.7	9.6	9.2	3.4	14.6	53.9
Jones	190	43	1 766	48.9	15.6	17.0	31.4	388.6	21.4	17 908	81.6	7.4	9.1	3.5	21.0	18.7
Peach	435	26	5 763	5.4	47.2	26.2	13.2	382.2	15.8	16 835	205.8	41.4	10.0	3.2	9.9	22.9
Twiggs	86	14	1 607	3.4	5.2	4.7	20.7	128.7	26.8	13 000	76.3	D	1.8	.7	6.5	12.5
Madison, WI MSA (Dane)	11 413	1 460	198 563	19.7	15.4	23.2	33.5	9 536.9	30.4	24 435	7 710.8	13.3	9.1	9.3	23.1	27.3
Mansfield, OH MSA	4 083	242	69 774	5.2	32.2	22.1	28.5	3 141.2	16.8	17 889	2 262.9	37.2	10.5	4.0	18.7	12.3
Crawford	1 008	31	16 321	5.7	43.8	15.5	26.4	829.5	19.4	17 463	495.1	43.4	8.2	3.5	17.8	11.2
Richland	3 075	211	53 453	5.1	28.6	24.1	29.1	2 311.7	15.9	18 046	1 767.8	35.5	11.1	4.2	19.0	12.6
McAllen-Edinburg-Mission, TX MSA (Hidalgo)	7 231	1 015	90 975	20.5	13.3	32.8	27.4	4 769.8	36.8	10 347	3 130.3	9.3	16.3	3.7	23.5	26.4

D Withheld to avoid disclosure.

[1]Based on 1994 resident population estimated by the Bureau of Economic Analysis.
[2]Finance, insurance, and real estate.
[3]Independent city of Bedford included with Bedford County; data not available separately.
[4]Independent city of Lynchburg include with Campbell County; data not available separately.

Source: Private Nonfarm Business—U.S. Bureau of the Census, "County Business Patterns" on diskettes, annual (related Internet site <http://www.census.gov/epcd/cbp/view/cbpview.html>); Personal Income—U.S. Bureau of Economic Analysis, "Regional Economic Information System, 1969–1994" on CD-ROM (related Internet site <http://www.bea.doc.gov/bea/dr1.htm>).

Table C-3. Metro Counties — **Private Nonfarm Business and Personal Income**—Con.

[MSA = Metropolitan statistical area. CMSA = Consolidated MSA. PMSA = Primary MSA. NECMA = New England county metropolitan area. All areas defined as of June 30, 1996 Table includes 245 MSAs, 17 CMSAs, and 58 PMSAs not in New England; 12 NECMAs; and 844 component counties]

Metropolitan areas and component counties	Private nonfarm business, 1995							Personal income, 1994								
	Establishments		Employment								Earnings					
					By selected industry, percent—								By selected industry, percent—			
	Total	Net change, 1990–1995	Total	Percent change, 1990–1995	Manufacturing	Retail trade	Services	Total (mil dol)	Percent change, 1990–1994	Per capita[1] (dollars)	Total (mil dol)	Manufacturing	Retail trade	FIRE[2]	Services	Government
Medford-Ashland, OR MSA (Jackson) ..	4 738	533	54 582	15.4	19.6	25.7	30.7	3 067.5	30.8	18 888	1 964.9	20.1	15.9	4.4	24.7	15.0
Melbourne-Titusville-Palm Bay, FL MSA (Brevard).....................	10 739	995	145 351	6.3	16.5	24.7	40.9	8 677.9	22.2	19 567	5 674.6	23.0	10.1	3.3	35.5	16.2
Memphis, TN-AR-MS MSA............	24 143	1 090	457 245	11.6	14.5	20.2	33.7	22 774.1	26.5	21 564	17 820.0	14.1	10.1	6.8	25.3	15.7
Fayette, TN	332	44	4 438	14.6	51.1	13.2	16.2	433.7	37.2	16 365	178.3	33.5	7.6	4.3	11.5	18.0
Shelby, TN...................	20 766	646	406 899	10.3	12.5	19.8	34.9	19 375.3	25.3	22 592	16 210.7	12.7	10.1	7.1	25.9	16.1
Tipton, TN	661	106	7 981	27.1	36.7	22.2	19.7	670.1	32.1	15 918	277.7	28.8	10.9	3.9	19.2	14.3
Crittenden, AR	914	14	13 961	12.8	17.5	35.0	23.7	779.8	23.6	15 628	427.4	16.1	13.4	3.5	23.7	14.3
De Soto, MS	1 470	280	23 966	30.9	33.1	19.8	26.3	1 515.2	39.4	18 940	725.9	34.0	10.2	3.2	18.1	8.7
Merced, CA MSA (Merced)	2 851	25	34 198	.6	22.3	25.3	27.8	2 974.3	15.9	15 106	1 894.6	16.6	10.6	3.6	15.5	23.6
Miami-Fort Lauderdale, FL CMSA......	112 116	11 528	1 331 101	9.0	8.8	22.3	37.4	74 698.0	19.7	21 918	49 855.6	8.0	11.5	9.1	33.9	14.6
Fort Lauderdale, FL PMSA (Broward).................	46 105	6 190	526 178	14.1	7.5	25.2	38.8	34 167.9	21.5	24 706	18 745.7	8.7	13.3	9.2	34.3	13.8
Miami, FL PMSA (Dade)	66 011	5 338	804 923	6.0	9.6	20.4	36.4	40 530.0	18.3	20 015	31 109.9	7.6	10.5	9.0	33.7	15.1
Milwaukee-Racine, WI CMSA	42 797	2 311	812 075	7.1	25.5	17.7	33.2	38 848.7	22.0	23 729	28 915.0	28.8	8.2	7.7	25.7	11.3
Milwaukee-Waukesha, WI PMSA ...	38 656	2 253	738 744	7.7	24.5	17.5	33.6	34 857.7	22.0	23 949	26 340.2	27.3	8.2	8.2	26.3	11.4
Milwaukee	22 057	–112	474 292	.9	21.5	17.0	38.2	20 869.5	17.2	22 247	17 631.0	25.0	8.1	9.3	29.0	12.7
Ozaukee....................	2 489	432	32 562	21.3	38.4	19.2	25.5	2 357.4	29.4	30 224	1 080.4	39.9	8.8	4.3	20.7	10.0
Washington	2 712	499	40 593	25.9	36.8	19.1	22.5	2 454.2	31.7	22 893	1 243.1	35.5	9.0	5.1	16.7	12.6
Waukesha	11 398	1 434	191 297	22.1	27.1	18.2	26.0	9 176.6	29.6	27 624	6 385.6	29.9	8.2	6.4	21.4	7.8
Racine, WI PMSA (Racine)	4 141	58	73 331	1.7	36.0	19.3	29.1	3 991.0	22.0	21 965	2 574.8	43.9	8.5	2.6	20.3	11.1
Minneapolis-St. Paul, MN-WI MSA	75 083	9 085	1 400 789	11.6	19.2	19.4	35.0	67 831.1	24.3	25 231	54 833.0	22.5	9.1	9.3	25.6	12.4
Anoka, MN	5 456	973	80 651	18.2	28.8	25.4	27.8	5 268.2	27.3	19 490	2 949.8	35.1	11.4	2.4	20.7	12.8
Carver, MN	1 314	277	24 195	47.9	44.3	14.6	26.9	1 334.7	36.4	23 623	837.3	46.3	6.2	2.4	17.5	10.4
Chisago, MN	872	221	8 342	16.5	23.3	25.6	36.3	624.5	33.1	17 640	279.2	23.5	12.1	3.0	24.0	16.4
Dakota, MN	7 106	1 280	117 207	25.5	20.3	24.7	29.2	7 472.8	28.1	24 215	4 124.3	24.8	10.4	6.4	19.3	12.1
Hennepin, MN	36 725	3 518	765 277	8.6	15.7	17.4	37.1	31 019.1	21.3	29 528	30 854.6	17.5	9.0	12.0	28.2	10.7
Isanti, MN	561	93	6 349	18.4	24.1	23.5	35.0	487.5	26.6	17 537	244.0	21.2	9.2	2.4	26.7	20.7
Ramsey, MN	12 926	864	279 169	4.4	21.3	18.0	37.9	12 061.5	20.7	24 951	11 298.9	29.7	7.2	7.7	25.1	15.5
Scott, MN	1 689	257	23 534	39.0	21.9	19.4	36.0	1 450.4	37.0	21 487	789.8	24.3	9.5	2.0	27.3	11.6
Sherburne, MN	918	194	9 744	25.1	26.7	25.5	19.7	856.3	35.9	17 024	403.5	14.8	11.2	2.7	15.3	19.5
Washington, MN	3 531	815	43 196	27.1	21.4	29.9	25.9	4 008.7	33.9	23 105	1 585.2	28.5	12.2	6.6	18.6	16.1
Wright, MN	1 806	344	18 654	35.0	19.6	28.1	28.3	1 428.2	31.1	18 694	628.2	17.0	13.9	3.2	18.9	16.6
Pierce, WI	817	60	7 370	.3	19.8	30.1	25.4	631.0	25.4	18 451	250.9	11.7	9.0	3.3	15.9	34.1
St. Croix, WI	1 362	189	17 101	34.3	32.8	25.1	22.5	1 188.2	28.2	22 004	587.4	34.1	12.0	2.7	19.0	13.0
Mobile, AL MSA	12 507	1 473	183 669	22.6	16.3	23.3	34.3	8 783.2	30.0	17 148	6 032.4	17.7	11.6	4.7	26.7	16.2
Baldwin.....................	3 238	854	34 395	47.2	16.5	30.8	31.0	2 142.1	43.0	18 514	888.9	14.9	17.1	5.8	23.0	18.5
Mobile.....................	9 269	619	149 274	18.0	16.2	21.6	35.0	6 641.1	26.3	16 749	5 143.5	18.2	10.7	4.5	27.4	15.8
Modesto, CA MSA (Stanislaus)	7 693	–39	103 226	Z	21.5	24.7	29.4	7 054.8	16.5	17 342	4 501.7	20.5	11.8	3.5	22.9	15.1
Monroe, LA MSA (Ouachita)	3 910	293	56 471	15.7	15.2	24.8	32.4	2 418.5	24.6	16 520	1 798.0	18.3	11.3	7.3	27.4	15.8
Montgomery, AL MSA	7 663	767	117 566	12.7	16.4	24.0	33.7	6 117.4	26.4	19 607	4 568.7	12.4	10.0	6.8	24.2	28.5
Autauga	691	106	7 898	19.0	27.6	30.4	23.2	649.3	31.9	16 953	262.3	32.5	14.2	4.1	16.3	14.1
Elmore	957	214	8 961	17.3	30.0	27.9	20.3	889.1	31.0	16 019	305.8	20.1	14.4	2.7	16.2	27.3
Montgomery	6 015	447	100 707	11.9	14.4	23.1	35.8	4 579.0	24.9	20 985	4 000.6	10.5	9.3	7.3	25.3	29.5
Muncie, IN MSA (Delaware)	2 753	156	49 968	13.0	23.1	23.4	25.6	2 299.6	22.1	19 292	1 717.5	29.8	9.6	3.0	23.1	16.3
Myrtle Beach, SC MSA (Horry)	6 271	993	68 314	24.2	9.3	36.3	32.2	2 722.3	23.7	17 804	1 876.3	9.8	22.8	7.2	32.2	12.9
Naples, FL MSA (Collier)	6 939	1 026	71 444	17.5	3.6	30.1	39.0	5 452.5	29.5	30 910	2 433.2	3.4	14.9	9.2	36.4	9.8
Nashville, TN MSA	30 715	3 941	563 326	21.1	17.8	21.4	35.5	24 642.7	35.9	23 037	20 029.9	18.4	10.8	6.9	31.6	11.4
Cheatham	401	116	5 305	44.2	47.7	16.9	18.2	502.4	35.8	16 153	191.8	40.9	8.8	1.4	18.5	14.0
Davidson	18 717	1 637	371 515	14.4	11.5	20.7	39.8	13 342.3	32.5	25 308	13 570.9	12.5	11.0	8.0	35.0	11.3
Dickson	786	117	11 282	34.5	35.0	26.0	22.3	658.3	32.3	17 368	366.3	29.5	15.8	3.2	22.4	12.3
Robertson	868	256	11 934	28.7	39.0	22.3	23.5	812.2	37.1	17 579	349.4	34.6	11.5	1.8	12.9	16.3
Rutherford	2 887	544	62 523	35.6	30.4	20.9	25.4	2 774.0	45.3	19 716	2 350.3	40.9	6.9	3.9	19.9	12.3
Sumner.....................	2 356	307	33 313	33.8	36.6	19.0	27.7	2 236.5	32.5	19 687	1 093.2	34.5	9.3	2.9	22.2	13.8
Williamson..................	3 209	763	47 441	48.8	15.4	26.9	32.5	2 838.1	49.4	28 990	1 411.9	10.9	13.2	9.5	36.2	8.4
Wilson	1 491	201	20 013	23.8	29.6	26.5	25.2	1 479.0	34.5	19 694	696.2	26.5	15.1	2.8	27.7	9.6
New London-Norwich, CT NECMA (New London)	5 811	–37	98 665	4.2	25.1	20.0	40.6	6 009.1	17.1	24 075	4 601.8	26.5	8.6	2.4	28.0	20.3
New Orleans, LA MSA...............	30 870	2 186	503 996	10.3	9.3	23.2	40.2	25 960.0	23.4	19 835	19 342.4	11.2	9.9	6.1	30.9	16.1
Jefferson	12 694	1 135	196 152	13.0	8.5	25.3	37.3	9 209.3	20.7	20 169	5 882.2	9.9	13.5	6.8	31.3	10.7
Orleans.....................	10 862	–121	209 110	2.5	6.6	21.0	46.7	10 054.3	22.8	20 769	9 748.4	6.8	8.2	6.9	35.5	19.5
Plaquemines	736	7	11 158	–6.1	17.4	9.9	23.1	428.4	17.7	16 801	617.1	16.5	3.7	1.1	10.0	15.1
St. Bernard	1 091	41	12 789	13.6	13.6	32.9	33.0	1 080.9	22.8	16 133	450.1	28.8	11.7	3.5	21.4	14.8
St. Charles	769	192	17 128	27.0	25.4	12.4	25.1	854.1	25.2	18 689	791.7	40.5	3.5	1.1	8.4	9.8
St. James	305	11	6 718	29.6	55.4	10.5	15.1	334.7	21.1	15 940	283.6	58.9	3.3	1.8	7.0	13.4
St. John the Baptist	601	67	10 451	26.9	24.2	21.9	25.2	659.3	20.3	15 810	356.7	35.6	8.2	2.7	16.3	12.3
St. Tammany.................	3 812	854	40 490	39.0	5.8	31.5	42.0	3 338.9	35.1	19 970	1 212.6	5.5	14.6	5.1	30.4	21.8

Z Less than .05 percent.

[1] Based on 1994 resident population estimated by the Bureau of Economic Analysis.
[2] Finance, insurance, and real estate.

Source: Private Nonfarm Business—U.S. Bureau of the Census, "County Business Patterns" on diskettes, annual (related Internet site <http://www.census.gov/epcd/cbp/view/cbpview.html>); Personal Income—U.S. Bureau of Economic Analysis, "Regional Economic Information System, 1969–1994" on CD-ROM (related Internet site <http://www.bea.doc.gov/bea/dr1.htm>).

[MSA = Metropolitan statistical area.   CMSA = Consolidated MSA.   PMSA = Primary MSA.   NECMA = New England county metropolitan area.   All areas defined as of June 30, 1996   Table includes 245 MSAs, 17 CMSAs, and 58 PMSAs not in New England; 12 NECMAs; and 844 component counties]

Metropolitan areas and component counties	Private nonfarm business, 1995							Personal income, 1994								
	Establishments		Employment								Earnings					
					By selected industry, percent—								By selected industry, percent—			
	Total	Net change, 1990–1995	Total	Percent change, 1990–1995	Manufacturing	Retail trade	Services	Total (mil dol)	Percent change, 1990–1994	Per capita[1] (dollars)	Total (mil dol)	Manufacturing	Retail trade	FIRE[2]	Services	Government
New York-Northern New Jersey-Long Island, NY-NJ-CT-PA CMSA/NECMA .	555 346	7 433	7 871 827	–4.1	14.0	16.5	38.8	571 868.1	16.4	29 021	408 855.2	12.7	7.0	16.0	32.3	13.7
Bergen-Passaic, NJ PMSA.........	43 834	457	584 655	–5.7	20.1	18.8	31.4	40 586.5	12.6	31 120	27 556.2	19.2	9.2	6.9	31.2	10.2
Bergen......................	32 034	566	424 051	–3.5	18.1	18.6	31.7	30 033.1	12.7	35 652	20 231.3	16.5	9.0	7.3	33.4	8.7
Passaic....................	11 800	–109	160 604	–11.1	25.5	19.1	30.5	10 553.4	12.4	22 853	7 325.0	26.7	9.9	5.9	25.2	14.1
Dutchess, NY PMSA (Dutchess)	6 384	65	80 182	–18.0	15.5	23.1	43.6	6 015.8	7.1	23 005	3 672.7	24.8	9.6	5.0	26.2	21.8
Jersey City, NJ PMSA (Hudson)	13 143	932	215 395	5.4	15.5	16.2	27.3	12 255.0	14.0	22 185	9 677.8	12.7	8.2	12.6	22.2	18.5
Middlesex-Somerset-Hunterdon, NJ PMSA...............	30 441	2 227	517 374	6.3	19.5	17.5	30.7	32 007.6	19.9	29 947	24 845.0	20.5	7.8	9.3	25.4	11.5
Hunterdon	3 488	260	36 010	11.6	24.9	23.3	29.5	3 783.2	25.1	32 840	1 895.0	18.9	11.5	7.4	30.2	13.5
Middlesex..................	18 178	997	333 722	4.6	19.7	17.7	30.0	18 427.1	16.5	26 594	15 395.7	22.2	8.2	9.2	24.2	13.1
Somerset	8 775	970	147 642	9.2	17.7	15.7	32.7	9 797.3	24.7	37 581	7 554.4	17.4	6.3	10.1	26.7	7.7
Monmouth-Ocean, NJ PMSA......	27 314	2 068	284 142	3.4	9.3	28.3	38.0	27 463.9	20.0	26 535	12 697.5	6.6	12.3	6.0	34.3	19.5
Monmouth	17 362	1 347	187 447	2.0	10.5	26.3	37.5	16 681.2	18.2	28 835	8 668.3	6.9	11.0	6.3	34.8	18.7
Ocean.....................	9 952	721	96 695	6.2	6.9	32.1	38.8	10 782.6	22.8	23 620	4 029.2	5.9	15.3	5.2	33.3	21.4
Nassau-Suffolk, NY PMSA	85 510	80	982 503	–4.4	12.3	21.3	38.2	79 569.0	14.1	30 007	43 697.7	11.7	9.9	10.2	32.9	16.8
Nassau....................	46 240	–996	522 215	–8.7	8.8	22.1	40.7	45 102.1	12.3	34 630	24 375.7	9.0	10.1	12.4	37.2	13.5
Suffolk	39 270	1 076	460 288	1.0	16.2	20.3	35.5	34 467.0	16.6	25 544	19 322.0	15.1	9.6	7.3	27.5	21.0
New Haven-Bridgeport-Stamford-Waterbury-Danbury, CT NECMA ..	48 501	–668	713 566	–3.7	20.3	18.7	36.8	52 231.9	15.1	32 117	34 447.2	22.2	8.8	10.8	31.0	9.8
Fairfield	27 650	182	399 276	–2.9	20.5	18.4	35.5	32 098.6	16.9	38 682	21 135.7	23.6	8.4	13.6	29.7	7.9
New Haven	20 851	–850	314 290	–4.7	20.1	19.0	38.4	20 133.3	12.5	25 277	13 311.5	20.0	9.4	6.2	33.0	12.9
New York, NY PMSA	227 469	1 826	3 403 246	–6.3	10.1	13.2	43.7	247 284.5	17.3	28 800	200 025.3	8.4	5.2	23.3	34.6	12.9
Bronx	13 555	504	196 713	1.7	8.0	13.7	56.6	20 490.8	15.7	17 193	7 570.0	6.0	7.3	5.1	48.9	14.8
Kings......................	34 154	402	403 635	.7	12.3	14.3	49.3	45 710.6	15.0	20 119	14 701.0	10.2	8.3	8.9	41.0	11.4
New York	99 779	–91	1 819 093	–9.7	8.7	10.7	43.4	80 154.3	21.3	53 188	135 607.8	7.0	3.8	30.2	33.8	13.2
Putnam	2 119	25	15 309	–6.7	11.0	22.1	37.9	2 319.3	15.2	26 001	670.3	11.5	10.6	6.5	30.5	21.2
Queens....................	33 947	237	421 561	–7.3	12.3	16.2	35.0	47 729.7	14.0	24 294	17 467.5	9.6	8.4	8.1	31.4	9.4
Richmond..................	6 766	226	77 792	8.8	3.3	22.3	51.5	9 949.2	19.2	25 017	2 782.6	3.4	10.7	9.8	46.5	9.6
Rockland	7 853	171	92 059	4.9	15.6	18.2	44.6	7 751.4	15.9	28 197	4 138.9	17.2	7.9	7.9	28.7	18.6
Westchester	29 296	352	376 884	–4.3	13.5	17.2	40.7	33 179.2	17.0	37 326	17 087.1	15.5	8.0	10.9	32.2	14.0
Newark, NJ PMSA	55 783	171	840 341	–4.4	18.3	14.7	34.3	57 338.8	17.7	29 652	40 450.8	18.4	6.8	8.9	28.8	14.3
Essex	19 635	–586	333 646	–5.8	14.3	12.6	37.8	21 289.0	16.9	27 818	16 010.1	13.3	5.6	11.2	30.1	19.1
Morris	15 992	1 270	239 512	2.6	17.0	16.5	34.5	15 978.2	21.3	36 438	11 676.2	19.3	7.3	9.9	29.4	10.2
Sussex	3 306	177	25 894	4.6	10.0	24.0	38.0	3 345.5	19.0	24 190	1 160.9	8.6	12.0	6.9	30.7	21.4
Union	14 164	–853	211 279	–10.9	25.7	14.0	29.3	14 511.1	14.6	29 244	10 363.5	24.7	7.0	5.2	27.1	10.5
Warren	2 686	163	30 010	2.3	28.9	21.4	27.0	2 215.0	17.7	23 218	1 240.0	32.6	10.2	2.3	20.6	14.5
Newburgh, NY-PA PMSA	7 900	–30	86 779	–3.5	13.9	28.2	32.1	7 174.1	16.2	20 152	3 802.3	11.5	12.1	5.4	25.5	26.2
Orange, NY	7 250	–45	82 009	–2.2	14.4	27.9	32.0	6 566.2	15.5	20 487	3 591.6	11.8	11.9	5.4	25.2	26.5
Pike, PA	650	15	4 770	–21.1	6.2	33.4	33.9	607.8	23.7	17 122	210.7	7.1	15.6	6.2	30.7	21.1
Trenton, NJ PMSA (Mercer)	9 067	305	163 644	3.6	19.6	15.6	43.5	9 941.1	17.8	30 179	7 982.6	16.6	6.4	6.4	32.9	25.7
Norfolk-Virginia Beach-Newport News, VA-NC MSA	32 482	1 481	497 959	4.8	NA	25.5	37.6	29 065.1	19.8	19 005	21 334.2	12.1	9.0	4.2	23.1	36.5
Gloucester, VA	738	106	5 931	18.1	5.0	35.4	31.0	578.6	19.6	17 693	185.6	4.9	15.2	3.8	24.5	27.2
Isle of Wight, VA	484	27	7 943	17.4	53.2	15.2	13.6	518.6	25.3	19 138	369.3	62.9	4.3	5.6	6.3	7.9
James City, VA	990	648	12 346	92.0	6.0	28.8	49.7	[3]1 216.0	[3]29.2	[3]23 565	[3]875.6	[3]13.7	[3]14.1	[3]5.4	[3]35.7	[3]22.5
Mathews, VA	186	–10	966	–.1	15.9	31.0	26.6	183.7	16.2	20 646	36.9	14.8	16.9	2.7	18.6	22.8
York, VA...................	974	243	10 924	68.6	5.3	35.0	35.9	[4]1 363.3	[4]29.3	[4]21 368	[4]467.6	[4]8.1	[4]10.2	[4]2.0	[4]18.7	[4]39.7
Chesapeake city, VA	3 948	643	56 605	28.5	7.6	30.0	31.5	3 367.3	29.7	18 645	1 687.5	9.3	13.7	3.7	21.7	22.3
Hampton city, VA	2 390	–67	41 620	3.1	9.0	32.7	41.4	2 369.8	16.9	16 976	1 939.9	6.3	10.8	2.5	22.1	47.6
Newport News city, VA	3 768	180	72 736	–4.4	35.0	16.9	32.5	3 172.0	19.8	17 751	2 884.3	38.3	7.2	3.4	21.7	19.3
Norfolk city, VA	5 559	–455	112 562	–2.3	11.9	19.5	39.4	4 318.7	11.4	17 890	6 582.5	7.5	5.4	4.4	20.2	49.1
Poquoson city, VA	175	13	1 268	13.5	NA	37.5	33.9	(4)	(4)	(4)	(4)	(4)	(4)	(4)	(4)	(4)
Portsmouth city, VA	1 706	–98	26 832	3.1	7.7	19.5	51.0	1 755.3	14.4	16 959	1 467.5	5.0	5.3	1.8	19.7	56.2
Suffolk city, VA	1 100	30	13 937	8.6	17.2	27.1	29.7	1 009.6	21.7	18 390	504.1	17.5	9.4	2.5	21.1	18.8
Virginia Beach city, VA	9 491	708	119 643	5.6	4.5	30.8	38.2	8 949.0	19.4	20 797	4 257.6	3.0	13.0	6.1	30.5	30.2
Williamsburg city, VA...........	654	–546	12 977	–32.1	10.2	30.1	50.9	(3)	(3)	(3)	(3)	(3)	(3)	(3)	(3)	(3)
Currituck, NC	319	59	1 669	9.5	2.5	41.1	20.0	263.1	31.4	16 652	76.0	2.1	18.8	3.7	12.7	28.4
Ocala, FL MSA (Marion)	5 015	357	61 146	19.0	15.3	28.8	31.3	3 655.1	28.0	16 629	1 888.6	16.1	15.4	5.0	24.7	17.1
Odessa-Midland, TX MSA	7 157	339	80 439	12.0	7.8	22.4	31.8	4 698.1	20.9	19 798	3 322.9	7.3	9.6	3.7	19.6	13.6
Ector.....................	2 928	–382	35 069	.4	10.3	25.4	31.4	1 933.9	16.2	15 710	1 375.3	11.9	12.3	3.1	20.7	16.6
Midland...................	4 229	721	45 370	23.0	5.8	20.0	32.1	2 764.2	24.3	24 205	1 947.6	4.2	7.6	4.2	18.9	11.5
Oklahoma City, OK MSA	27 748	3 138	388 482	16.0	13.6	23.4	37.0	19 169.9	22.1	19 031	14 537.6	12.9	10.5	5.9	25.6	23.6
Canadian	1 388	166	12 113	15.8	9.0	34.5	29.5	1 426.0	26.4	17 781	630.2	27.2	11.4	2.8	16.1	19.7
Cleveland..................	3 624	776	38 646	33.7	11.1	32.9	34.6	3 268.8	26.7	17 351	1 336.4	7.6	12.8	4.0	22.7	34.6
Logan	470	38	4 231	21.5	9.2	29.6	43.5	489.4	22.1	16 424	176.6	4.6	10.6	3.0	25.7	24.5
McClain	403	80	3 772	39.7	19.3	35.3	19.5	389.8	25.5	15 908	155.0	11.8	17.4	3.7	15.8	20.1
Oklahoma	20 580	2 031	313 106	14.3	13.7	21.2	37.8	12 685.1	20.5	20 335	11 764.8	12.5	10.0	6.5	26.6	22.9
Pottawatomie	1 283	47	16 614	8.2	20.9	29.8	34.7	910.7	20.2	15 028	474.6	24.1	14.6	2.8	24.6	16.8

NA Not available.

[1]Based on 1994 resident population estimated by the Bureau of Economic Analysis.
[2]Finance, insurance, and real estate.
[3]Independent city of Williamsburg included with James City County; data not available separately.
[4]Independent city of Poquoson included with York County; data not available separately.

Source: Private Nonfarm Business—U.S. Bureau of the Census, "County Business Patterns" on diskettes, annual (related Internet site <http://www.census.gov/epcd/cbp/view/cbpview.html>); Personal Income—U.S. Bureau of Economic Analysis, "Regional Economic Information System, 1969–1994" on CD-ROM (related Internet site <http://www.bea.doc.gov/bea/dr1.htm>).

[MSA = Metropolitan statistical area. CMSA = Consolidated MSA. PMSA = Primary MSA. NECMA = New England county metropolitan area. All areas defined as of June 30, 1996 Table includes 245 MSAs, 17 CMSAs, and 58 PMSAs not in New England; 12 NECMAs; and 844 component counties]

Metropolitan areas and component counties	Private nonfarm business, 1995							Personal income, 1994								
	Establishments		Employment								Earnings					
					By selected industry, percent—							By selected industry, percent—				
	Total	Net change, 1990–1995	Total	Percent change, 1990–1995	Man-ufac-turing	Retail trade	Services	Total (mil dol)	Percent change, 1990–1994	Per capita[1] (dollars)	Total (mil dol)	Man-ufac-turing	Retail trade	FIRE[2]	Services	Govern-ment
Omaha, NE-IA MSA	17 881	1 445	330 067	13.6	11.9	19.7	38.2	14 922.2	25.9	22 514	11 630.3	11.8	9.2	9.5	27.5	15.8
Cass, NE	447	63	3 253	25.3	12.1	31.9	23.6	443.2	29.0	19 700	142.2	9.5	10.0	4.0	12.8	17.4
Douglas, NE	13 377	927	275 647	14.7	11.2	17.9	39.6	10 574.3	26.7	24 574	9 393.0	12.4	9.1	11.1	29.3	12.5
Sarpy, NE	1 819	390	22 680	2.3	10.5	27.2	35.0	1 997.2	23.9	18 289	1 061.3	4.6	7.1	2.2	16.9	42.7
Washington, NE	428	37	4 711	37.2	16.2	24.7	35.3	373.1	25.2	21 441	186.0	7.4	8.1	2.6	19.0	31.3
Pottawattamie, IA	1 810	28	23 776	7.6	20.0	31.4	27.8	1 534.4	22.8	18 398	847.8	15.3	13.1	3.7	24.5	15.9
Orlando, FL MSA	39 546	5 182	630 319	15.5	8.2	22.8	42.9	27 391.2	26.5	20 120	21 227.2	9.4	11.7	7.1	37.1	12.3
Lake	3 887	369	44 500	19.4	8.7	26.5	37.4	3 170.5	26.8	18 274	1 357.5	9.7	13.9	5.5	31.8	14.3
Orange	23 539	2 834	436 522	12.6	8.6	19.7	45.8	15 108.5	24.5	20 469	15 408.6	9.3	10.4	7.5	38.7	12.0
Osceola	2 712	434	38 414	16.6	4.2	36.8	39.5	2 049.8	29.3	16 256	1 173.2	7.0	16.9	5.4	40.8	14.5
Seminole	9 408	1 545	110 883	26.1	8.2	28.8	34.7	7 062.4	30.2	21 818	3 287.9	10.5	15.4	6.5	30.6	12.0
Owensboro, KY MSA (Daviess)	2 335	28	37 253	8.1	21.3	21.6	32.2	1 629.8	23.7	18 088	1 123.0	20.0	11.7	4.6	23.2	14.7
Panama City, FL MSA (Bay)	4 158	509	48 470	23.2	7.3	33.6	33.8	2 495.9	30.8	17 840	1 652.4	6.1	14.7	4.8	25.6	31.2
Parkersburg-Marietta, WV-OH MSA	3 875	244	57 495	11.8	22.7	24.1	31.5	2 821.9	25.7	18 614	1 963.2	29.3	11.0	3.9	22.0	15.4
Wood, WV	2 301	218	36 237	11.3	21.3	25.4	33.7	1 722.6	27.4	19 575	1 250.3	29.1	11.2	4.3	21.6	17.2
Washington, OH	1 574	26	21 258	12.8	25.1	22.0	27.7	1 099.3	23.1	17 285	712.9	29.6	10.7	3.1	22.7	12.2
Pensacola, FL MSA	8 270	570	117 887	17.6	9.4	25.1	41.8	6 495.3	25.5	17 517	4 233.1	10.6	10.9	3.6	28.6	28.1
Escambia	6 544	278	100 900	16.9	8.9	24.8	42.7	4 800.2	21.4	17 661	3 570.0	10.5	11.0	3.7	29.0	28.3
Santa Rosa	1 726	292	16 987	22.1	12.6	26.9	36.5	1 695.0	38.8	17 121	663.2	11.1	10.3	2.6	26.3	27.0
Peoria-Pekin, IL MSA	8 341	678	150 861	13.0	24.0	20.3	33.3	7 374.9	19.4	21 464	5 488.0	32.4	8.9	4.9	24.5	9.4
Peoria	5 046	399	104 260	15.0	25.2	18.1	37.3	4 027.9	19.3	21 987	3 177.6	21.4	9.9	6.5	34.0	10.3
Tazewell	2 663	203	39 518	6.4	20.9	25.4	23.2	2 658.6	18.4	21 033	2 051.4	50.9	7.2	2.7	10.9	7.3
Woodford	632	76	7 083	23.8	23.8	23.9	30.2	688.4	23.2	20 246	259.0	20.4	10.4	2.7	16.3	14.9
Philadelphia-Wilmington-Atlantic City, PA-NJ-DE-MD CMSA	148 353	2 730	NA	NA	NA	NA	NA	149 310.5	18.0	25 055	104 525.4	18.0	8.8	8.6	D	13.7
Atlantic-Cape May, NJ PMSA	9 876	86	NA	NA	NA	NA	NA	8 327.9	15.2	25 236	6 427.8	3.9	10.0	3.0	D	17.0
Atlantic	6 055	1	115 881	-2.6	5.1	18.0	61.9	5 980.9	14.8	25 758	5 306.5	4.2	8.0	2.7	57.4	15.0
Cape May	3 821	85	(3)	NA	NA	NA	NA	2 347.0	16.3	23 998	1 121.4	2.3	19.4	4.6	D	26.7
Philadelphia, PA-NJ PMSA	119 777	988	2 009 033	-.2	15.0	NA	NA	124 821.1	17.8	25 221	85 738.2	17.5	8.8	8.6	D	13.6
Bucks, PA	15 934	1 094	211 829	2.2	20.3	23.4	33.8	14 651.3	20.0	25 831	7 851.3	21.1	12.8	5.4	28.5	11.1
Chester, PA	10 562	434	153 875	-3.9	15.9	19.0	38.5	12 654.3	29.1	31 851	7 440.4	20.8	8.7	11.4	28.6	9.2
Delaware, PA	13 225	-77	204 898	2.8	14.6	19.9	42.9	14 391.4	16.6	26 243	8 005.5	19.5	11.4	7.9	32.3	9.8
Montgomery, PA	25 391	893	451 540	4.7	18.2	16.5	38.6	23 887.2	19.3	34 110	17 569.4	25.7	8.1	9.5	30.2	6.9
Philadelphia, PA	26 239	-2 127	594 043	-3.0	10.4	15.4	49.4	30 788.8	11.7	20 200	27 574.0	10.6	6.2	9.5	39.8	18.8
Burlington, NJ	9 497	432	137 050	-2.6	14.3	23.3	34.6	10 003.7	19.5	25 084	6 041.3	14.4	11.4	5.6	28.4	18.2
Camden, NJ	12 447	-109	171 861	-5.2	14.3	22.1	39.4	11 851.3	16.7	23 394	7 446.0	14.8	9.9	6.6	33.1	16.9
Gloucester, NJ	5 216	377	65 559	4.0	18.8	27.0	27.2	5 156.6	21.0	21 352	2 763.3	21.8	13.0	2.6	21.1	17.0
Salem, NJ	1 266	71	18 378	-1.8	21.0	NA	NA	1 436.4	17.2	22 167	1 047.1	24.6	6.5	2.1	D	12.9
Vineland-Millville-Bridgeton, NJ PMSA (Cumberland)	3 097	-73	47 555	-5.5	30.7	18.4	24.1	2 799.8	17.8	20 171	1 882.0	25.3	9.3	5.9	19.7	21.8
Wilmington-Newark, DE-MD PMSA	15 603	1 729	259 691	3.0	19.2	18.9	31.6	13 361.7	22.1	24 685	10 477.4	28.9	8.1	12.3	23.0	11.3
New Castle, DE	14 096	1 639	242 619	3.1	19.3	18.1	31.7	11 888.9	22.7	25 606	9 807.7	29.7	7.8	13.0	23.2	10.4
Cecil, MD	1 507	90	17 072	2.5	18.7	29.8	29.8	1 472.8	17.7	19 128	669.8	17.1	12.5	2.9	20.5	25.2
Phoenix-Mesa, AZ MSA	63 148	8 166	1 061 788	22.4	14.3	21.1	34.0	51 937.9	29.1	20 999	37 872.3	16.1	11.1	8.7	28.4	13.7
Maricopa	61 372	8 029	1 035 214	22.1	14.2	21.0	34.2	50 133.7	29.0	21 364	36 674.3	16.2	11.1	8.9	28.8	13.3
Pinal	1 776	137	26 574	35.9	18.6	25.6	27.2	1 804.2	31.8	14 240	1 198.0	13.3	9.4	1.5	13.8	27.0
Pine Bluff, AR MSA (Jefferson)	1 697	-34	26 416	8.8	26.9	23.9	31.2	1 325.7	18.2	15 782	995.0	23.8	9.8	3.5	19.9	22.7
Pittsburgh, PA MSA	57 654	876	962 531	3.3	14.2	21.1	39.2	54 647.4	20.3	22 751	37 536.3	17.8	9.5	6.5	32.1	11.3
Allegheny	34 506	-58	654 009	1.0	10.8	19.3	43.6	33 638.3	19.0	25 470	26 474.3	15.5	8.5	8.0	35.5	10.5
Beaver	3 316	53	47 150	11.3	23.8	24.4	29.9	3 461.2	21.3	18 381	1 768.0	23.3	10.7	2.7	24.3	13.3
Butler	3 730	277	52 124	16.7	23.8	24.9	25.8	3 230.7	25.5	19 955	1 931.1	29.9	10.3	2.9	18.1	14.3
Fayette	3 045	142	35 088	5.6	13.3	32.5	31.3	2 395.3	20.9	16 350	1 093.1	15.3	17.0	3.4	26.8	15.2
Washington	4 591	114	60 471	3.0	19.9	22.0	32.9	4 241.1	21.3	20 380	2 248.6	23.0	11.0	2.5	25.8	13.1
Westmoreland	8 466	348	113 689	7.9	22.1	24.1	29.2	7 680.9	22.7	20 401	4 021.2	22.8	12.3	3.2	25.3	12.2
Pittsfield, MA NECMA (Berkshire)	3 994	-125	52 756	-8.0	19.0	25.6	39.7	3 068.0	13.9	22 526	1 866.2	23.7	12.6	4.4	36.1	10.4
Pocatello, ID MSA (Bannock)	1 739	169	21 031	15.2	16.0	29.7	29.6	1 161.5	31.4	16 382	758.2	10.0	12.4	5.8	19.1	24.9
Portland, ME NECMA (Cumberland)	9 181	624	128 876	3.8	12.0	24.1	36.0	5 974.4	16.8	24 090	4 791.6	11.7	13.4	11.8	31.1	13.1
Portland-Salem, OR-WA CMSA	59 459	9 319	838 219	19.0	18.5	20.9	31.7	43 949.4	30.8	22 172	32 571.3	18.4	10.4	6.9	25.9	14.3
Portland-Vancouver, OR-WA PMSA	51 548	8 301	744 082	18.4	18.8	20.4	31.5	38 373.7	31.0	22 891	28 820.9	18.9	10.3	7.1	26.4	12.7
Clackamas, OR	8 409	1 398	106 947	25.1	21.4	25.2	25.6	7 354.1	32.7	23 708	3 775.5	17.4	13.4	5.8	23.6	11.0
Columbia, OR	805	129	7 848	-8.6	42.1	21.9	15.6	737.5	24.8	18 033	306.6	28.5	10.5	2.3	12.3	17.3
Multnomah, OR	22 627	2 634	367 961	11.6	13.6	17.6	35.4	14 568.2	26.3	23 816	14 495.1	13.9	9.2	9.1	29.2	14.6
Washington, OR	11 110	2 254	156 073	27.3	24.2	21.5	28.3	8 438.5	33.9	23 505	6 164.4	28.3	10.9	5.3	24.4	6.7
Yamhill, OR	1 782	331	21 542	24.6	24.1	21.9	31.7	1 330.3	30.4	18 248	761.6	28.2	12.2	3.9	19.2	14.4
Clark, WA	6 815	1 555	83 711	28.9	24.1	22.5	28.9	5 945.1	38.1	21 104	3 317.7	22.1	10.2	4.9	24.1	16.1
Salem, OR PMSA	7 911	1 018	94 137	24.4	15.9	24.8	33.2	5 575.7	29.1	18 233	3 750.3	15.0	11.5	5.0	22.3	27.2
Marion	6 840	901	84 783	25.6	15.1	24.9	33.9	4 622.7	28.9	18 483	3 386.8	14.0	11.5	5.3	22.6	28.0
Polk	1 071	117	9 354	14.2	23.1	23.8	27.4	953.0	29.8	17 109	363.5	24.4	11.1	2.3	19.9	19.5

NA Not available.
D Withheld to avoid disclosure.

[1]Based on 1994 resident population estimated by the Bureau of Economic Analysis.
[2]Finance, insurance, and real estate.
[3]10,000–24,999 employees.

Source: Private Nonfarm Business—U.S. Bureau of the Census, "County Business Patterns" on diskettes, annual (related Internet site <http://www.census.gov/epcd/cbp/view/cbpview.html>); Personal Income—U.S. Bureau of Economic Analysis, "Regional Economic Information System, 1969–1994" on CD-ROM (related Internet site <http://www.bea.doc.gov/bea/dr1.htm>).

[MSA = Metropolitan statistical area. CMSA = Consolidated MSA. PMSA = Primary MSA. NECMA = New England county metropolitan area. All areas defined as of June 30, 1996 Table includes 245 MSAs, 17 CMSAs, and 58 PMSAs not in New England; 12 NECMAs; and 844 component counties]

Metropolitan areas and component counties	Private nonfarm business, 1995							Personal income, 1994								
	Establishments		Employment								Earnings					
					By selected industry, percent—							By selected industry, percent—				
	Total	Net change, 1990–1995	Total	Percent change, 1990–1995	Manufacturing	Retail trade	Services	Total (mil dol)	Percent change, 1990–1994	Per capita[1] (dollars)	Total (mil dol)	Manufacturing	Retail trade	FIRE[2]	Services	Government
Providence-Warwick-Pawtucket, RI NECMA	25 246	–68	356 127	–2.9	23.2	19.6	37.2	19 999.6	15.1	21 929	13 090.2	21.8	9.8	7.3	31.4	14.6
Bristol	1 050	4	12 327	3.7	24.0	22.0	39.9	1 273.5	16.1	25 990	391.7	23.3	11.2	4.2	32.3	15.1
Kent	4 762	85	63 863	1.3	20.5	27.9	28.6	3 667.5	15.3	22 528	2 059.7	23.6	14.5	7.6	26.2	14.7
Providence	16 276	–346	248 929	–4.0	23.8	16.3	39.8	12 434.0	13.9	21 266	9 296.8	21.0	8.3	8.0	33.7	13.6
Washington	3 158	189	31 008	–4.2	23.7	28.6	32.2	2 624.5	20.6	22 723	1 342.0	23.9	12.6	3.4	23.5	21.7
Provo-Orem, UT MSA (Utah)	5 665	1 364	106 584	33.0	14.4	19.1	49.2	4 203.1	39.4	14 444	3 076.8	15.7	9.4	3.1	44.3	13.1
Pueblo, CO MSA (Pueblo)	2 954	253	40 168	17.8	12.0	29.0	38.8	2 185.8	26.5	17 117	1 306.0	15.2	15.2	5.2	25.0	21.7
Punta Gorda, FL MSA (Charlotte)	2 628	141	28 141	19.0	2.8	32.8	44.8	2 400.5	23.4	18 976	891.6	2.7	17.6	5.7	39.5	14.6
Raleigh-Durham-Chapel Hill, NC MSA	28 030	4 546	475 038	19.6	18.4	19.6	37.9	22 190.2	32.7	22 993	18 438.7	19.4	9.6	5.6	28.2	19.3
Chatham	860	114	12 658	23.6	55.9	14.4	13.9	865.0	26.3	20 744	438.6	42.8	8.9	1.4	13.3	10.1
Durham	5 366	673	143 278	24.0	27.6	13.3	45.3	4 310.5	25.6	22 415	5 543.1	34.6	5.5	3.7	36.5	11.0
Franklin	637	62	6 796	–5.4	34.2	21.0	24.5	623.4	30.3	15 430	228.6	25.5	14.1	1.6	18.4	20.3
Johnston	2 186	236	25 392	16.0	32.9	23.1	22.4	1 674.1	34.8	18 417	845.3	26.6	13.3	2.6	13.7	14.8
Orange	2 484	365	31 041	12.9	5.2	30.9	45.1	2 440.0	33.2	23 106	1 596.7	7.0	9.4	7.9	16.8	50.0
Wake	16 497	3 096	255 873	19.0	11.1	21.6	35.9	12 277.2	35.6	24 843	9 786.3	11.0	11.6	6.9	27.5	19.8
Rapid City, SD MSA (Pennington)	3 056	402	37 007	25.4	12.4	28.9	34.2	1 657.1	32.8	19 135	1 308.2	8.9	14.4	3.8	27.7	24.4
Reading, PA MSA (Berks)	7 920	283	139 980	2.0	30.4	21.5	26.7	7 809.6	19.8	22 467	5 513.6	32.4	10.6	6.2	22.4	10.4
Redding, CA MSA (Shasta)	4 373	–141	41 572	–2.6	10.0	28.3	36.0	2 932.1	19.9	18 326	1 865.6	11.3	13.5	3.3	28.6	18.3
Reno, NV MSA (Washoe)	9 729	1 331	144 052	11.6	8.4	18.9	46.3	7 655.9	29.2	27 062	5 671.2	7.6	10.6	5.0	40.2	12.4
Richland-Kennewick-Pasco, WA MSA	4 034	672	64 835	31.1	11.0	18.9	37.0	3 577.5	41.0	20 799	2 806.6	7.2	8.4	2.1	45.3	16.8
Benton	3 036	614	52 981	40.4	8.6	18.4	39.5	2 851.5	42.6	22 053	2 242.7	7.3	7.9	2.3	52.1	16.3
Franklin	998	58	11 854	1.2	21.9	20.9	26.1	726.1	35.0	17 004	563.9	6.9	10.4	1.5	18.1	18.6
Richmond-Petersburg, VA MSA	25 285	1 802	422 873	8.6	15.2	21.1	NA	22 328.7	20.5	24 358	16 844.1	16.5	9.5	10.6	22.1	20.8
Charles City	71	23	1 297	391.3	34.1	9.3	NA	111.5	20.3	16 647	28.6	15.4	5.3	.3	18.5	28.3
Chesterfield	5 052	628	68 875	7.5	11.7	29.7	26.5	5 623.8	23.8	24 262	2 807.3	18.9	12.8	5.8	20.3	18.7
Dinwiddie	270	64	3 810	160.2	6.1	42.8	13.2	[3]1 533.4	[3]19.9	[3]18 746	[3]778.3	[3]11.6	[3]19.3	[3]4.0	[3]18.8	[3]28.0
Goochland	360	42	2 434	7.3	NA	18.8	32.8	435.5	32.7	27 391	129.9	4.5	9.3	9.3	19.3	22.0
Hanover	2 295	327	28 234	16.1	14.1	20.6	22.0	1 578.6	24.7	22 078	946.1	16.8	11.0	3.3	17.3	8.9
Henrico	5 805	582	102 505	20.9	10.9	22.8	30.2	6 120.1	18.7	26 655	4 287.6	14.3	13.5	18.0	25.5	8.0
New Kent	262	42	1 678	18.7	14.7	15.8	33.6	230.0	26.2	20 356	58.5	8.2	12.2	2.4	25.1	21.7
Powhatan	337	59	1 758	19.9	6.6	20.5	17.7	308.7	28.0	17 055	111.3	4.3	6.6	2.5	11.1	41.0
Prince George	308	102	5 520	26.3	12.8	27.9	39.0	[4]874.8	[4]13.7	[4]17 889	[4]802.1	[4]23.6	[4]7.4	[4]1.2	[4]10.3	[4]44.5
Colonial Heights city	592	85	6 986	3.9	7.4	58.2	24.1	(3)	(3)	(3)	(3)	(3)	(3)	(3)	(3)	(3)
Hopewell city	487	–	7 260	2.1	34.8	20.0	28.1	(4)	(4)	(4)	(4)	(4)	(4)	(4)	(4)	(4)
Petersburg city	976	–72	13 104	–2.2	22.0	22.7	36.9	(3)	(3)	(3)	(3)	(3)	(3)	(3)	(3)	(3)
Richmond city	8 470	–80	179 412	1.0	18.5	15.0	38.5	5 512.3	17.8	27 411	6 894.5	17.0	4.6	11.1	23.2	27.4
Roanoke, VA MSA	6 924	400	122 828	6.2	17.1	21.7	31.8	5 122.2	19.1	22 417	4 001.7	16.8	10.8	7.4	27.6	12.8
Botetourt	506	115	5 254	63.0	21.6	21.9	17.5	496.1	24.6	18 652	182.1	14.7	10.3	2.1	13.7	14.3
Roanoke	1 754	328	25 058	30.4	13.1	23.3	34.0	[5]2 528.1	[5]18.0	[5]24 009	[5]1 610.7	[5]22.9	[5]8.9	[5]7.6	[5]26.1	[5]15.3
Roanoke city	3 737	–69	72 317	.2	13.9	21.9	32.9	2 097.9	19.3	21 718	2 209.0	12.6	12.3	7.7	29.9	10.9
Salem city	927	26	20 199	–4.0	32.5	18.6	28.9	(5)	(5)	(5)	(5)	(5)	(5)	(5)	(5)	(5)
Rochester, MN MSA (Olmsted)	2 689	363	61 291	2.1	15.6	20.1	50.8	2 609.6	22.5	23 114	2 392.4	22.3	7.8	2.7	45.6	9.6
Rochester, NY MSA	23 604	235	454 112	1.3	29.5	18.7	34.7	24 639.9	16.0	22 593	18 157.9	34.2	8.5	5.1	24.3	13.8
Genesee	1 298	–22	16 256	–5.2	26.5	22.4	31.2	1 145.6	14.6	18 688	652.5	24.2	9.6	2.6	18.0	24.4
Livingston	1 193	100	11 727	–6.0	20.7	32.3	26.9	1 175.8	18.3	18 089	556.9	14.6	12.1	2.6	15.7	37.0
Monroe	16 415	–89	365 112	.6	30.0	16.9	35.9	17 664.0	15.1	24 300	14 578.1	37.1	7.9	5.7	25.8	10.6
Ontario	2 382	59	32 841	6.7	21.3	27.2	33.3	2 109.9	19.0	21 355	1 169.4	20.0	13.0	3.4	23.4	22.1
Orleans	693	35	7 024	1.7	34.2	28.3	23.6	722.8	15.8	15 852	345.9	18.0	8.7	3.7	13.6	39.1
Wayne	1 623	152	21 152	17.3	38.9	21.2	25.4	1 821.9	21.1	19 590	855.0	31.6	9.7	2.0	16.2	24.8
Rockford, IL MSA	8 694	703	157 040	9.5	33.6	18.1	28.5	7 224.6	20.4	20 838	5 531.9	40.0	8.1	4.3	20.3	8.8
Boone	681	120	11 620	21.6	52.5	14.8	16.5	682.4	23.0	19 609	514.7	65.4	6.4	1.7	8.2	6.5
Ogle	1 001	72	14 664	10.3	39.2	14.4	15.9	893.6	19.2	18 312	541.4	34.3	7.4	2.5	14.4	12.0
Winnebago	7 012	511	130 756	8.4	31.3	18.8	30.9	5 648.6	20.3	21 469	4 475.8	37.8	8.4	4.8	22.4	8.7
Rocky Mount, NC MSA	3 111	79	58 541	2.5	37.9	20.5	21.4	2 505.1	24.2	17 932	1 945.9	30.8	12.3	3.9	15.1	13.5
Edgecombe	1 012	229	22 343	27.8	46.1	12.5	15.7	913.6	23.7	16 285	685.6	27.1	6.1	1.5	12.2	17.4
Nash	2 099	–150	36 198	–8.7	32.8	25.5	24.4	1 591.5	24.4	19 038	1 260.3	32.7	15.8	5.2	16.6	11.3
Sacramento-Yolo, CA CMSA	36 797	44	511 365	11.0	9.2	23.9	38.5	34 631.5	20.2	21 811	25 381.7	7.5	10.2	6.6	25.5	30.6
Sacramento, CA PMSA	33 670	55	463 577	11.2	8.8	23.7	40.0	31 504.1	20.0	21 857	22 587.5	7.4	10.2	6.9	26.4	30.9
El Dorado	3 460	57	28 876	13.2	7.5	29.8	40.6	3 080.4	24.2	21 274	1 219.6	7.0	15.0	4.3	31.0	18.8
Placer	5 760	223	61 887	15.8	13.8	27.7	32.9	4 760.8	27.1	23 984	2 689.3	14.3	14.7	5.3	25.4	13.4
Sacramento	24 450	–225	372 814	10.3	8.0	22.6	41.1	23 662.8	18.2	21 549	18 678.6	6.4	9.3	7.3	26.3	34.2
Yolo, CA PMSA (Yolo)	3 127	–11	47 788	9.6	13.0	25.6	24.2	3 127.5	21.7	21 362	2 794.3	8.4	11.1	3.6	17.7	28.6
Saginaw-Bay City-Midland, MI MSA	9 345	751	149 742	5.4	27.2	25.6	28.6	8 411.3	23.3	20 908	6 014.3	40.8	9.2	3.2	21.1	11.2
Bay	2 577	218	32 941	7.7	21.5	30.1	28.4	2 267.3	23.5	20 280	1 260.8	30.8	11.6	3.6	22.4	15.2
Midland	1 786	275	33 060	3.3	36.7	18.7	29.1	1 983.0	24.8	25 038	1 395.6	51.1	6.0	2.3	20.9	8.2
Saginaw	4 982	258	83 741	5.3	25.6	26.6	28.4	4 161.0	22.4	19 692	3 357.8	40.3	9.7	3.5	20.7	11.0
St. Cloud, MN MSA	4 182	461	73 284	24.5	21.4	29.1	29.3	2 689.4	24.7	17 141	2 144.6	20.1	16.6	3.3	22.4	16.5
Benton	512	–34	8 195	10.3	34.9	24.0	17.6	553.1	27.2	17 018	321.7	29.5	14.8	1.7	16.5	9.5
Stearns	3 670	495	65 089	26.6	19.6	29.7	30.7	2 136.4	24.1	17 173	1 822.8	18.5	16.9	3.6	23.4	17.7

NA Not available.

[1]Based on 1994 resident population estimated by the Bureau of Economic Analysis.
[2]Finance, insurance, and real estate.
[3]Independent cities of Colonial Heights and Petersburg included with Dinwiddie County; data not available separately.
[4]Independent city of Hopewell included with Prince George County; data not available separately.
[5]Independent city of Salem included with Roanoke County; data not available separately.

Source: Private Nonfarm Business—U.S. Bureau of the Census, "County Business Patterns" on diskettes, annual (related Internet site <http://www.census.gov/epcd/cbp/view/cbpview.html>); Personal Income—U.S. Bureau of Economic Analysis, "Regional Economic Information System, 1969–1994" on CD-ROM (related Internet site <http://www.bea.doc.gov/bea/dr1.htm>).

[MSA = Metropolitan statistical area. CMSA = Consolidated MSA. PMSA = Primary MSA. NECMA = New England county metropolitan area. All areas defined as of June 30, 1996 Table includes 245 MSAs, 17 CMSAs, and 58 PMSAs not in New England; 12 NECMAs; and 844 component counties]

Metropolitan areas and component counties	Private nonfarm business, 1995							Personal income, 1994								
	Establishments		Employment								Earnings					
					By selected industry, percent—							By selected industry, percent—				
	Total	Net change, 1990–1995	Total	Percent change, 1990–1995	Manufacturing	Retail trade	Services	Total (mil dol)	Percent change, 1990–1994	Per capita[1] (dollars)	Total (mil dol)	Manufacturing	Retail trade	FIRE[2]	Services	Government
St. Joseph, MO MSA	2 524	169	36 515	3.5	22.0	22.4	32.6	1 784.9	17.3	18 213	1 187.4	24.1	10.6	D	22.7	14.0
Andrew	231	31	1 620	10.6	NA	32.4	32.3	251.6	18.2	16 773	63.5	3.2	16.6	D	17.5	21.3
Buchanan	2 293	138	34 895	3.2	23.0	21.9	32.6	1 533.3	17.1	18 474	1 123.9	25.3	10.2	5.0	23.0	13.6
St. Louis, MO-IL MSA	64 760	3 057	1 121 180	2.8	18.1	19.7	35.4	60 066.0	19.6	23 684	43 540.9	21.6	9.3	7.1	27.1	11.9
Franklin, MO	2 223	232	29 475	17.0	35.3	22.0	20.8	1 568.9	23.3	18 264	829.4	34.0	13.0	3.3	16.8	10.6
Jefferson, MO	3 086	251	30 475	16.0	17.9	28.2	30.0	3 052.7	23.9	16 636	1 047.0	17.6	14.3	3.4	22.0	16.2
Lincoln, MO	660	100	5 691	35.6	15.8	28.5	24.4	513.1	21.9	16 134	172.8	10.5	13.9	3.8	16.1	20.3
St. Charles, MO	5 306	735	68 426	17.4	16.0	29.1	32.5	4 993.9	27.8	20 869	2 306.3	23.6	15.9	3.6	24.3	10.5
St. Louis, MO	29 630	56	528 032	–5.6	18.1	20.1	33.2	29 783.7	18.6	29 633	21 922.4	22.7	9.2	8.2	28.6	7.4
Warren, MO	497	90	5 863	40.2	39.6	23.4	15.5	363.6	23.4	16 680	155.7	39.6	10.8	4.2	13.3	11.3
St. Louis city, MO	10 665	787	284 665	10.5	16.6	12.3	43.2	8 118.1	17.2	22 048	10 524.8	19.3	6.3	8.4	28.4	15.5
Clinton, IL	751	10	8 875	27.8	15.4	21.1	34.8	697.6	23.2	20 047	385.5	8.0	12.6	2.5	18.5	15.4
Jersey, IL	382	37	3 844	15.0	3.7	29.4	48.7	353.8	19.3	16 849	116.9	5.1	16.5	2.9	24.6	24.2
Madison, IL	5 771	417	80 855	5.2	26.0	22.4	31.1	5 237.3	18.2	20 530	3 122.7	31.6	9.5	4.4	21.6	13.5
Monroe, IL	550	81	4 966	9.9	4.0	28.5	32.4	485.5	21.4	20 062	156.9	4.3	16.3	4.9	23.7	16.8
St. Clair, IL	5 239	261	70 013	10.1	10.7	27.8	39.0	4 897.7	19.1	18 454	2 800.5	10.1	11.2	3.3	26.8	29.2
Salinas, CA MSA (Monterey)	8 021	–139	93 457	6.3	8.0	25.4	37.7	7 934.8	13.8	22 548	5 437.2	6.7	10.3	4.3	23.4	19.0
Salt Lake City-Ogden, UT MSA	29 575	5 218	513 615	29.2	15.6	20.8	33.7	21 943.5	33.6	18 625	17 666.6	14.0	10.5	7.3	25.7	18.5
Davis	3 504	875	44 817	31.3	17.0	30.2	26.7	3 498.1	33.5	16 587	2 127.2	14.0	11.3	3.2	19.7	35.4
Salt Lake	22 507	3 876	408 445	28.7	13.7	19.4	34.8	15 369.9	34.6	19 326	13 515.0	13.1	10.3	8.4	26.7	14.6
Weber	3 564	467	60 353	30.8	27.4	23.4	31.0	3 075.5	28.8	17 881	2 024.5	20.0	10.8	4.0	25.3	26.6
San Angelo, TX MSA (Tom Green)	2 562	200	31 846	8.1	16.3	27.0	30.3	1 842.7	21.8	18 209	1 234.4	13.5	10.9	3.5	26.4	22.8
San Antonio, TX MSA	31 274	3 338	517 319	20.7	9.7	24.1	38.7	26 541.6	28.3	18 466	19 388.1	7.9	11.5	8.0	26.7	25.8
Bexar	28 091	2 850	479 745	20.0	8.5	23.7	39.7	23 701.6	27.7	18 515	18 198.7	6.8	11.3	8.3	27.1	26.4
Comal	1 697	317	18 395	23.4	17.4	33.9	26.0	1 256.4	34.6	20 664	551.3	16.1	19.6	3.0	24.1	13.6
Guadalupe	1 133	102	16 775	38.5	36.0	23.4	24.3	1 185.6	30.2	16 794	525.5	35.7	11.4	2.8	17.0	17.8
Wilson	353	69	2 404	39.8	7.9	32.5	33.7	398.0	35.7	15 426	112.6	4.6	13.8	3.4	19.0	27.0
San Diego, CA MSA (San Diego)	60 243	–338	844 451	–2.7	14.4	22.7	38.5	56 922.9	14.8	21 626	39 654.8	12.6	10.2	6.0	31.1	23.7
San Francisco-Oakland-San Jose, CA CMSA	182 418	1 813	2 793 963	–.4	17.2	18.4	37.0	184 469.4	18.9	28 322	140 532.1	18.5	9.1	7.7	31.7	13.6
Oakland, CA PMSA	53 920	834	796 199	2.8	14.6	19.4	35.4	57 899.3	18.7	26 530	38 850.3	13.9	10.5	6.3	29.2	17.3
Alameda	33 460	652	525 644	4.0	16.8	18.2	35.8	33 146.4	17.7	25 120	25 443.7	14.1	10.3	4.3	29.6	20.0
Contra Costa	20 460	182	270 555	.6	10.3	21.8	34.7	24 752.9	20.1	28 686	13 406.6	13.4	10.8	10.0	28.5	12.4
San Francisco, CA PMSA	59 916	–385	874 742	–3.5	9.1	17.8	40.6	56 424.4	18.6	34 282	46 582.6	7.9	8.8	14.0	36.9	12.7
Marin	9 646	193	91 503	2.5	5.6	25.3	42.9	9 512.8	19.2	40 480	4 586.0	4.9	12.3	12.1	43.8	10.4
San Francisco	30 668	–1 481	484 846	–6.8	7.5	15.8	44.2	24 790.3	18.8	33 742	27 515.6	5.9	7.4	17.4	37.7	15.4
San Mateo	19 602	903	298 393	.3	12.7	18.6	33.9	22 121.3	18.1	32 714	14 481.0	12.6	10.3	8.2	33.3	8.1
San Jose, CA PMSA (Santa Clara)	40 442	1 102	800 482	–1.1	29.4	15.3	35.5	43 992.5	19.6	28 251	40 249.4	37.0	6.9	2.7	30.2	8.8
Santa Cruz-Watsonville, CA PMSA (Santa Cruz)	6 450	–234	70 010	–3.6	18.4	26.3	34.3	5 716.5	16.9	24 326	3 329.1	16.0	12.7	3.7	30.1	14.2
Santa Rosa, CA PMSA (Sonoma)	12 169	179	131 326	.6	16.3	24.1	33.5	9 979.1	18.3	24 327	5 720.9	15.3	12.6	7.5	27.2	14.3
Vallejo-Fairfield-Napa, CA PMSA	9 521	317	121 204	8.1	13.5	27.0	37.6	10 457.6	20.4	21 669	5 799.8	10.9	12.1	3.1	22.7	29.8
Napa	3 274	25	39 386	9.6	20.3	20.7	40.2	2 995.6	18.6	26 049	1 654.2	18.0	10.6	3.6	30.1	15.8
Solano	6 247	292	81 818	7.4	10.2	30.0	36.4	7 462.0	21.1	20 299	4 145.6	8.0	12.8	2.9	19.7	35.4
San Luis Obispo-Atascadero-Paso Robles, CA MSA (San Luis Obispo)	6 077	–12	60 590	–.5	10.0	31.1	36.1	4 286.1	15.4	19 160	2 637.1	7.3	14.3	4.1	25.8	21.8
Santa Barbara-Santa Maria-Lompoc, CA MSA (Santa Barbara)	10 157	–239	119 638	–7.1	13.6	25.3	38.1	9 316.5	12.8	24 485	6 183.3	13.4	11.2	4.9	35.2	16.0
Santa Fe, NM MSA	4 643	801	45 786	19.5	4.1	28.8	45.5	3 080.9	35.4	23 572	2 330.6	3.2	11.5	4.7	31.7	38.7
Los Alamos	433	19	6 222	12.2	1.0	17.6	68.7	551.2	16.6	29 796	713.8	.3	2.7	1.5	25.3	67.7
Santa Fe	4 210	782	39 564	20.8	4.5	30.5	41.9	2 529.7	40.3	22 546	1 616.8	4.5	15.4	6.1	34.5	25.9
Sarasota-Bradenton, FL MSA	15 597	1 127	197 979	18.3	10.8	26.4	44.6	14 026.1	22.6	27 083	6 219.9	10.7	13.6	6.9	40.4	12.0
Manatee	5 149	824	88 504	37.2	12.2	24.2	50.4	5 194.2	27.7	23 034	2 614.5	15.0	11.8	4.1	41.6	11.4
Sarasota	10 448	303	109 475	6.4	9.7	28.2	39.9	8 831.9	19.7	30 205	3 605.4	7.6	15.0	9.0	39.4	12.4
Savannah, GA MSA	6 871	520	102 938	11.7	15.5	25.9	32.4	5 397.8	22.6	19 586	3 811.1	18.7	10.8	4.0	27.7	17.8
Bryan	302	70	2 631	32.4	15.7	38.9	21.6	288.6	41.5	14 503	82.4	15.7	15.8	4.8	17.9	28.0
Chatham	6 221	362	96 308	9.9	14.5	25.4	33.3	4 634.8	20.7	20 581	3 565.7	17.9	10.7	4.1	28.8	17.5
Effingham	348	88	3 999	58.4	37.6	28.2	17.9	474.4	31.3	15 553	163.0	38.7	9.1	2.2	9.7	19.9
Scranton--Wilkes-Barre--Hazleton, PA MSA	14 865	–88	242 155	2.0	24.9	22.0	31.8	12 485.1	17.4	19 600	8 090.2	23.0	11.2	5.2	25.7	13.4
Columbia	1 463	–3	23 498	3.4	38.9	23.2	21.3	1 121.8	21.4	17 556	721.5	33.2	12.6	2.7	19.9	16.2
Lackawanna	5 231	–19	89 378	1.6	22.8	21.2	35.0	4 361.5	16.5	20 192	2 895.7	22.8	11.0	6.0	29.8	11.9
Luzerne	7 539	–92	120 902	1.9	22.9	21.5	32.4	6 495.2	17.3	19 821	4 147.8	19.7	11.2	5.3	24.7	14.2
Wyoming	632	26	8 377	3.9	34.9	21.3	18.1	506.5	18.0	17 228	325.2	43.1	9.3	2.0	14.4	10.1
Seattle-Tacoma-Bremerton, WA CMSA	94 354	11 162	1 299 725	6.3	17.2	21.0	33.8	79 940.6	26.2	24 785	60 440.6	17.6	9.7	6.4	28.0	17.5
Bremerton, WA PMSA (Kitsap)	4 698	863	43 735	21.5	4.1	34.0	40.3	4 245.7	27.7	19 263	2 664.3	2.6	10.3	3.0	20.3	53.1
Olympia, WA PMSA (Thurston)	4 673	850	44 585	11.4	9.0	31.5	35.9	3 950.9	34.1	21 105	2 411.4	6.6	11.0	3.4	22.1	42.4
Seattle-Bellevue-Everett, WA PMSA	70 667	7 455	1 032 836	4.1	18.9	19.5	32.8	59 060.1	25.6	27 098	47 831.0	20.0	9.3	6.9	29.3	12.6
Island	1 401	254	9 422	19.2	7.8	33.5	36.2	1 248.9	26.8	18 447	626.5	3.2	9.6	3.2	15.2	55.9
King	56 521	5 396	862 946	2.7	17.1	18.6	34.2	46 506.9	24.8	29 296	40 237.8	17.2	9.1	7.4	31.7	11.9
Snohomish	12 745	1 805	160 468	11.3	29.1	23.4	24.5	11 304.3	28.9	21 561	6 966.7	37.8	10.6	4.4	17.1	12.9
Tacoma, WA PMSA (Pierce)	14 316	1 994	178 569	16.0	12.6	24.1	37.7	12 683.9	26.4	19 871	7 533.9	10.9	11.5	5.1	24.1	28.2

D Withheld to avoid disclosure.
NA Not available.

[1]Based on 1994 resident population estimated by the Bureau of Economic Analysis.
[2]Finance, insurance, and real estate.

Source: Private Nonfarm Business—U.S. Bureau of the Census, "County Business Patterns" on diskettes, annual (related Internet site <http://www.census.gov/epcd/cbp/view/cbpview.html>); Personal Income—U.S. Bureau of Economic Analysis, "Regional Economic Information System, 1969–1994" on CD-ROM (related Internet site <http://www.bea.doc.gov/bea/dr1.htm>).

[MSA = Metropolitan statistical area.   CMSA = Consolidated MSA.   PMSA = Primary MSA.   NECMA = New England county metropolitan area.   All areas defined as of June 30, 1996   Table includes 245 MSAs, 17 CMSAs, and 58 PMSAs not in New England; 12 NECMAs; and 844 component counties]

Metropolitan areas and component counties	Private nonfarm business, 1995							Personal income, 1994								
	Establishments		Employment								Earnings					
	Total	Net change, 1990–1995	Total	Percent change, 1990–1995	Manufacturing	Retail trade	Services	Total (mil dol)	Percent change, 1990–1994	Per capita[1] (dollars)	Total (mil dol)	Manufacturing	Retail trade	FIRE[2]	Services	Government
Sharon, PA MSA (Mercer)	2 732	106	41 169	7.9	26.4	25.1	32.6	2 143.6	17.4	17 542	1 353.6	29.2	12.5	3.4	27.3	11.1
Sheboygan, WI MSA (Sheboygan)	2 505	223	51 026	15.1	45.1	16.1	22.8	2 282.4	26.4	21 331	1 718.4	44.3	7.9	4.5	16.2	9.7
Sherman-Denison, TX MSA (Grayson)	2 320	105	33 597	8.5	28.4	24.4	29.4	1 797.9	17.7	18 478	1 192.7	33.7	11.6	4.7	22.4	11.0
Shreveport-Bossier City, LA MSA	8 807	266	138 540	14.4	14.4	20.4	39.8	7 124.4	26.8	18 828	4 941.8	16.8	9.4	4.2	27.2	20.6
Bossier	1 697	158	21 926	22.0	10.3	30.3	34.3	1 588.7	34.3	17 770	900.3	7.1	11.9	3.4	21.0	39.3
Caddo	6 292	85	105 946	12.7	14.1	18.3	42.3	4 893.7	25.4	19 829	3 720.5	17.7	8.7	4.4	29.4	16.7
Webster	818	23	10 668	17.0	26.4	21.1	25.9	642.1	20.3	15 215	321.0	33.2	11.3	3.5	18.4	14.0
Sioux City, IA-NE MSA	3 293	204	56 843	5.7	24.7	21.3	30.2	2 403.8	30.0	20 200	1 790.2	21.2	10.2	4.9	27.3	11.0
Woodbury, IA	2 842	161	45 325	6.5	17.1	23.7	35.1	2 099.0	30.0	20 741	1 492.9	15.6	10.7	4.6	30.7	11.7
Dakota, NE	451	43	11 518	2.5	54.9	12.0	11.0	304.8	30.1	17 123	297.4	48.7	7.5	6.1	10.3	7.3
Sioux Falls, SD MSA	5 240	705	87 398	24.5	13.0	23.0	33.6	3 484.1	38.0	22 982	2 819.4	13.1	11.1	9.8	27.6	9.5
Lincoln	378	33	2 967	6.2	19.8	24.5	28.5	367.2	41.9	21 602	168.9	10.8	10.1	2.2	15.7	8.9
Minnehaha	4 862	672	84 431	25.2	12.8	22.9	33.8	3 116.8	37.6	23 156	2 650.5	13.2	11.1	10.3	28.3	9.6
South Bend, IN MSA (St. Joseph)	6 611	304	117 353	12.5	20.3	21.7	35.6	5 257.8	26.2	20 587	3 834.8	24.1	9.9	5.6	31.1	9.2
Spokane, WA MSA (Spokane)	11 260	1 806	154 255	22.2	13.4	23.1	36.0	7 745.5	30.8	19 564	5 505.0	14.3	11.6	6.4	27.0	18.7
Springfield, IL MSA	5 514	654	79 708	13.7	5.8	23.3	43.1	4 393.0	20.1	22 436	3 473.5	4.2	8.9	8.4	29.2	29.8
Menard	266	24	1 473	14.0	NA	32.2	24.8	237.8	23.8	19 983	73.3	1.4	9.3	3.9	14.0	20.4
Sangamon	5 248	630	78 235	13.7	5.9	23.1	43.4	4 155.2	19.9	22 595	3 400.2	4.2	8.9	8.5	29.6	30.0
Springfield, MO MSA	8 772	1 177	132 563	18.9	19.0	23.0	32.7	5 440.6	30.0	18 826	4 132.5	16.9	13.0	4.7	28.9	11.9
Christian	962	286	8 353	47.6	31.3	22.5	20.0	656.8	43.2	16 178	269.4	21.0	14.5	3.9	14.7	12.2
Greene	7 269	816	119 485	16.7	17.6	23.0	34.2	4 422.3	28.4	19 884	3 712.3	16.2	12.9	4.8	30.6	11.7
Webster	541	75	4 725	36.9	32.8	24.2	17.5	361.5	27.5	13 904	150.7	27.5	12.8	3.1	12.9	16.2
Springfield, MA NECMA	13 422	-633	216 133	-6.9	19.4	21.1	36.7	12 248.3	10.0	20 561	7 883.4	19.9	10.3	7.0	29.7	18.2
Hampden	10 207	-644	172 641	-8.6	21.0	20.4	34.2	9 323.5	8.9	20 881	6 211.9	21.8	10.2	8.0	28.8	15.9
Hampshire	3 215	11	43 492	.6	13.4	24.1	46.5	2 924.8	13.7	19 603	1 671.5	12.8	10.5	2.9	33.1	27.0
State College, PA MSA (Centre)	3 082	280	42 753	6.8	20.4	26.5	31.2	2 292.1	21.1	17 659	1 836.6	15.5	9.8	3.5	20.3	37.1
Steubenville-Weirton, OH-WV MSA	2 818	151	45 047	.5	34.4	19.7	30.9	2 473.6	14.6	17 643	1 657.0	44.2	8.2	2.1	18.0	9.7
Jefferson, OH	1 686	51	21 939	-.7	19.7	25.3	35.2	1 360.9	14.0	17 292	792.2	29.3	10.9	2.8	21.1	12.5
Brooke, WV	418	34	6 656	-52.9	29.5	17.4	39.1	433.6	15.5	16 241	282.2	47.4	7.8	1.5	13.5	9.3
Hancock, WV	714	66	16 452	91.8	55.9	13.2	21.8	679.1	15.1	19 514	582.6	63.0	4.7	1.6	16.0	6.2
Stockton-Lodi, CA MSA (San Joaquin)	9 595	-269	127 288	-.2	18.3	23.3	31.1	9 376.0	19.6	18 093	6 078.2	14.8	12.2	5.2	21.7	18.4
Sumter, SC MSA (Sumter)	1 766	6	34 461	22.6	34.9	20.0	28.1	1 539.6	23.9	14 429	1 107.4	25.4	9.9	2.7	16.9	30.2
Syracuse, NY MSA	16 777	-546	283 895	-2.1	17.5	21.6	35.3	15 155.9	14.9	20 103	11 092.1	19.4	9.2	6.8	D	17.6
Cayuga	1 571	19	19 075	2.2	22.7	24.2	33.8	1 416.0	15.3	17 040	731.4	19.5	10.1	3.3	25.3	24.1
Madison	1 398	24	16 141	10.2	19.2	28.5	37.3	1 332.0	19.1	18 578	615.2	12.3	12.4	3.0	27.9	23.0
Onondaga	11 780	-650	223 633	-3.7	16.3	20.0	36.3	10 206.1	13.4	21 564	8 510.0	19.1	8.9	8.1	26.9	15.4
Oswego	2 028	61	25 046	2.7	22.9	29.4	26.2	2 201.8	19.5	17 502	1 235.4	24.5	9.5	1.9	D	26.3
Tallahassee, FL MSA	6 586	399	88 752	17.3	5.2	27.9	44.0	4 808.9	29.3	18 977	3 866.4	3.6	10.1	4.7	28.0	40.7
Gadsden	597	-35	9 055	-12.7	16.0	18.0	47.2	617.9	27.8	14 403	322.9	10.2	9.4	2.1	10.7	41.0
Leon	5 989	434	79 697	22.1	4.0	29.0	43.6	4 191.0	29.5	19 910	3 543.6	3.0	10.1	4.9	29.6	40.7
Tampa-St. Petersburg-Clearwater, FL MSA	57 994	3 048	863 046	12.3	9.8	22.1	42.5	46 058.9	23.5	21 357	29 004.2	10.0	11.8	8.7	34.8	13.7
Hernando	2 118	186	21 273	24.4	9.1	35.3	30.3	1 872.7	26.8	16 061	664.5	6.3	16.0	5.3	32.8	19.3
Hillsborough	24 734	1 492	431 933	15.4	8.1	18.8	43.6	17 632.0	24.0	20 167	15 130.5	8.0	10.2	9.7	33.2	14.7
Pasco	5 537	281	59 735	14.4	6.6	23.0	40.6	5 051.2	24.0	16 922	1 792.0	6.0	15.8	5.0	36.1	16.3
Pinellas	25 605	1 089	350 105	7.8	12.6	23.6	42.1	21 503.0	22.7	24 796	11 417.1	13.6	13.1	8.2	36.9	11.8
Terre Haute, IN MSA	3 513	313	57 411	14.6	21.8	30.9	29.0	2 645.3	22.4	17 671	1 916.7	25.8	14.2	3.3	21.5	15.8
Clay	548	96	6 535	41.6	38.3	23.5	19.5	435.1	29.5	16 865	229.0	32.0	12.6	2.6	11.5	13.2
Vermillion	283	8	4 099	33.1	38.0	26.3	17.6	288.4	19.8	17 169	182.7	47.1	9.3	1.6	9.1	12.8
Vigo	2 682	209	46 777	10.3	18.0	32.3	31.4	1 921.7	21.2	17 943	1 505.0	22.3	15.0	3.6	24.6	16.6
Texarkana, TX-Texarkana, AR MSA	2 744	147	38 077	8.7	17.0	26.3	33.3	2 032.0	16.2	16 560	1 378.8	16.8	13.5	3.7	26.7	19.6
Bowie, TX	1 985	72	27 887	16.3	14.8	26.2	36.8	1 473.8	15.9	17 629	949.5	11.3	14.3	4.1	28.2	23.8
Miller, AR	759	75	10 190	-7.6	23.3	26.9	23.7	558.2	17.0	14 275	429.3	29.2	11.7	2.9	23.3	10.4
Toledo, OH MSA	14 713	285	269 712	6.0	22.9	22.0	34.8	13 035.9	20.7	21 235	9 992.9	27.9	9.2	3.9	24.5	13.7
Fulton	1 091	91	19 168	32.6	54.6	13.4	14.6	791.7	24.3	19 743	573.7	49.6	7.6	1.9	11.4	10.4
Lucas	11 135	86	210 338	4.4	18.1	22.6	38.9	9 866.4	20.0	21 561	7 888.6	25.3	9.4	4.4	27.1	12.3
Wood	2 487	108	40 206	4.5	32.9	22.8	22.8	2 377.9	22.6	20 464	1 530.6	32.9	9.2	2.2	15.9	22.2
Topeka, KS MSA (Shawnee)	4 529	69	75 290	6.0	13.3	24.7	38.5	3 537.3	18.1	21 425	2 942.6	13.8	10.9	7.7	24.5	23.1
Tucson, AZ MSA (Pima)	17 167	1 779	247 225	17.6	11.3	25.1	39.0	13 587.9	33.0	18 575	8 640.2	12.7	12.0	5.0	30.2	21.6
Tulsa, OK MSA	20 996	1 791	311 291	9.1	16.3	19.4	33.5	14 897.5	20.5	20 048	11 428.8	18.3	9.5	6.1	26.8	9.5
Creek	1 194	153	13 645	29.5	29.7	20.6	24.0	959.8	20.1	15 067	463.8	24.9	9.7	3.5	24.3	14.5
Osage	563	171	5 088	42.0	21.6	25.1	34.0	607.7	21.3	14 300	213.3	14.5	7.9	2.5	14.1	21.0
Rogers	1 092	189	13 374	44.1	29.4	21.0	28.5	1 037.6	27.7	17 094	495.0	34.7	9.3	3.0	18.3	16.3
Tulsa	17 508	1 071	273 399	6.4	14.6	19.1	34.4	11 521.7	19.9	21 963	10 061.8	17.3	9.5	6.5	27.6	8.5
Wagoner	639	207	5 785	17.2	32.8	23.1	25.1	770.7	20.2	14 935	194.9	15.5	11.2	2.7	27.6	16.4
Tuscaloosa, AL MSA (Tuscaloosa)	3 671	438	59 308	22.2	17.6	25.9	31.9	2 758.7	24.6	17 560	2 062.9	20.1	10.3	3.1	17.6	27.5
Tyler, TX MSA (Smith)	4 637	474	63 437	20.0	19.5	22.9	35.8	3 179.0	24.2	19 994	2 276.8	20.6	12.9	4.8	27.4	13.0
Utica-Rome, NY MSA	6 400	-290	103 904	5.8	20.4	21.7	33.0	5 774.7	15.5	18 257	3 731.1	19.0	10.0	7.0	23.3	27.2
Herkimer	1 211	-26	14 265	7.8	36.3	23.2	26.7	1 105.4	18.7	16 548	519.2	33.5	11.2	3.1	15.0	23.2
Oneida	5 189	-264	89 639	5.5	17.9	21.5	34.0	4 669.3	14.7	18 715	3 211.9	16.6	9.8	7.6	24.6	27.8

NA Not available.
D Withheld to avoid disclosure.

[1]Based on 1994 resident population estimated by the Bureau of Economic Analysis.
[2]Finance, insurance, and real estate.

Source: Private Nonfarm Business—U.S. Bureau of the Census, "County Business Patterns" on diskettes, annual (related Internet site <http://www.census.gov/epcd/cbp/view/cbpview.html>);
Personal Income—U.S. Bureau of Economic Analysis, "Regional Economic Information System, 1969–1994" on CD-ROM (related Internet site <http://www.bea.doc.gov/bea/dr1.htm>).

Table C–3. Metro Counties — **Private Nonfarm Business and Personal Income**—Con.

[MSA = Metropolitan statistical area. CMSA = Consolidated MSA. PMSA = Primary MSA. NECMA = New England county metropolitan area. All areas defined as of June 30, 1996 Table includes 245 MSAs, 17 CMSAs, and 58 PMSAs not in New England; 12 NECMAs; and 844 component counties]

Metropolitan areas and component counties	Private nonfarm business, 1995							Personal income, 1994								
	Establishments		Employment								Earnings					
					By selected industry, percent—							By selected industry, percent—				
	Total	Net change, 1990–1995	Total	Percent change, 1990–1995	Manufacturing	Retail trade	Services	Total (mil dol)	Percent change, 1990–1994	Per capita[1] (dollars)	Total (mil dol)	Manufacturing	Retail trade	FIRE[2]	Services	Government
Victoria, TX MSA (Victoria)	2 128	103	25 784	14.2	11.1	28.0	33.8	1 601.7	31.0	20 172	966.7	13.8	13.5	5.4	25.8	15.6
Visalia-Tulare-Porterville, CA MSA (Tulare)	5 801	–15	73 018	10.3	17.0	25.3	29.7	5 418.3	19.9	15 783	3 516.6	11.2	12.1	3.9	16.1	19.0
Waco, TX MSA (McLennan)	4 760	316	82 519	16.3	20.8	19.5	37.1	3 463.7	24.8	17 564	2 458.6	21.5	11.1	6.2	24.7	17.5
Washington-Baltimore, DC-MD-VA-WV CMSA	181 055	12 823	2 885 144	2.3	7.6	20.6	45.8	189 819.5	19.2	26 919	147 957.4	6.6	8.0	6.7	D	27.2
Baltimore, MD PMSA	60 307	3 728	942 438	1.1	11.9	21.3	38.9	59 115.0	16.4	24 045	41 110.1	12.2	9.2	8.6	30.5	20.5
Anne Arundel	11 420	1 138	155 704	6.8	11.7	27.3	31.8	11 077.0	18.7	24 281	7 238.1	10.8	10.5	3.9	21.6	33.6
Baltimore	19 198	806	300 961	–.4	12.8	23.7	36.6	18 653.0	13.8	26 205	11 476.5	16.0	11.9	7.4	30.3	16.1
Carroll	3 715	374	38 664	3.6	16.8	26.4	30.0	3 147.8	23.5	23 078	1 197.2	16.8	12.3	3.5	21.7	15.2
Harford	4 376	623	46 572	18.4	10.9	33.4	31.0	4 260.3	19.1	21 091	1 820.3	7.6	14.0	3.5	21.4	33.0
Howard	6 374	990	97 851	8.4	7.6	19.7	37.9	6 223.4	22.6	29 218	3 625.5	7.8	10.0	7.8	34.1	11.0
Queen Anne's	993	218	7 655	26.3	10.4	37.0	22.5	827.2	14.6	22 915	262.3	7.0	17.9	3.5	20.3	17.6
Baltimore city	14 231	–421	295 031	–5.2	11.9	13.4	48.2	14 926.2	13.7	21 232	15 490.2	11.3	5.5	13.0	36.0	18.8
Hagerstown, MD PMSA (Washington)	3 106	188	48 714	12.2	19.7	21.7	29.7	2 241.0	14.7	17 701	1 618.6	19.4	12.8	3.3	24.4	17.5
Washington, DC-MD-VA-WV PMSA	117 642	8 907	1 893 992	2.6	5.1	20.2	49.6	128 463.6	20.6	28 762	105 228.7	4.2	7.4	6.1	D	30.0
District of Columbia	19 451	–136	413 757	–3.1	3.0	12.6	69.6	17 400.6	17.0	30 683	33 049.4	2.3	2.8	4.7	40.1	43.1
Calvert, MD	1 269	217	12 682	31.5	3.8	29.3	30.6	1 345.0	26.2	21 624	496.9	3.3	12.6	2.5	D	15.4
Charles, MD	2 334	330	26 833	19.3	5.4	40.3	26.7	2 347.7	20.2	21 479	1 025.2	5.1	18.9	4.6	22.4	27.2
Frederick, MD	4 241	587	57 817	16.7	13.1	24.0	30.3	3 711.7	25.9	21 668	1 939.2	11.3	11.9	8.5	27.5	17.7
Montgomery, MD	23 494	1 430	342 624	–2.5	5.5	19.6	46.6	28 525.6	18.1	35 537	17 814.1	4.9	8.3	8.4	42.3	21.1
Prince George's, MD	13 789	235	233 595	–6.7	4.9	26.0	38.4	17 204.5	15.6	22 646	10 628.8	4.4	13.4	4.5	26.7	29.6
Arlington, VA	5 041	346	111 363	8.9	4.2	15.9	55.4	6 176.7	19.6	35 376	8 163.3	2.4	4.9	3.9	35.5	39.3
Clarke, VA	277	19	3 044	29.1	37.3	15.5	30.4	276.7	23.7	22 680	108.2	31.8	6.7	4.3	21.8	12.0
Culpeper, VA	788	95	9 665	22.1	19.4	25.5	30.9	593.9	19.4	19 863	316.2	17.4	9.5	6.3	23.7	17.5
Fairfax, VA	23 464	3 963	372 035	14.0	3.5	19.9	49.4	[3]30 561.0	[3]24.3	[3]33 528	[3]19 852.7	[3]4.6	[3]8.6	[3]8.6	[3]39.8	[3]17.3
Fauquier, VA	1 381	112	10 859	–3.2	8.4	25.5	33.7	1 416.2	22.6	27 553	470.5	4.3	11.4	5.5	27.6	24.8
King George, VA	336	68	3 151	1.0	7.8	14.1	56.8	322.2	29.7	19 411	302.2	2.8	3.2	.9	25.3	57.6
Loudoun, VA	3 198	633	39 966	17.0	9.6	20.6	35.5	2 938.2	37.2	27 180	1 816.8	5.8	8.9	4.1	28.2	19.2
Prince William, VA	4 202	577	50 056	11.5	4.7	36.3	33.2	[4]5 999.5	[4]23.6	[4]21 542	[4]2 773.4	[4]10.6	[4]15.4	[4]3.4	[4]22.4	[4]23.9
Spotsylvania, VA	492	72	5 581	47.1	12.6	39.5	18.5	[5]1 836.4	[5]29.4	[5]20 987	[5]994.4	[5]10.8	[5]17.7	[5]4.9	[5]28.2	[5]15.2
Stafford, VA	1 797	773	19 666	78.8	7.3	27.7	25.7	1 426.3	35.0	18 356	496.6	2.4	9.4	9.0	18.8	27.8
Warren, VA	683	23	5 872	–.9	14.0	27.5	36.9	512.2	20.4	17 785	185.2	13.5	14.6	3.6	26.7	17.6
Alexandria city, VA	4 296	235	69 906	–2.3	3.9	20.7	51.6	3 988.4	17.8	35 327	3 827.1	3.2	8.2	6.5	41.1	28.8
Fairfax city, VA	1 401	–485	28 287	–11.4	.7	23.0	58.0	(3)	(3)	(3)	(3)	(3)	(3)	(3)	(3)	(3)
Falls Church city, VA	624	–196	12 904	.5	NA	12.0	59.3	(3)	(3)	(3)	(3)	(3)	(3)	(3)	(3)	(3)
Fredericksburg city, VA	1 517	–374	18 057	–20.5	8.8	35.3	36.7	(5)	(5)	(5)	(5)	(5)	(5)	(5)	(5)	(5)
Manassas city, VA	1 290	76	17 961	–2.2	19.4	29.2	25.7	(4)	(4)	(4)	(4)	(4)	(4)	(4)	(4)	(4)
Manassas Park city, VA	190	43	2 439	63.0	6.9	10.7	14.3	(4)	(4)	(4)	(4)	(4)	(4)	(4)	(4)	(4)
Berkeley, WV	1 325	186	18 006	17.7	20.2	28.5	31.5	1 138.5	29.5	17 382	690.8	15.2	10.3	3.6	21.0	26.9
Jefferson, WV	762	78	7 866	.9	21.3	26.5	33.0	742.4	29.8	19 086	277.8	17.1	9.9	3.7	29.6	24.3
Waterloo-Cedar Falls, IA MSA (Black Hawk)	3 134	123	54 088	14.8	26.8	24.2	30.4	2 405.2	22.0	19 444	1 976.5	33.4	9.6	4.1	21.8	15.4
Wausau, WI MSA (Marathon)	3 136	381	54 944	18.9	29.4	20.0	23.1	2 345.2	25.3	19 527	1 767.1	31.3	8.9	8.9	18.5	11.3
West Palm Beach-Boca Raton, FL MSA (Palm Beach)	32 701	4 590	379 154	14.1	9.1	24.2	40.1	31 994.1	26.4	33 519	14 395.4	11.0	11.6	9.7	35.2	11.3
Wheeling, WV-OH MSA	3 724	179	48 969	4.3	9.3	26.1	40.9	2 898.4	19.4	18 356	1 733.1	16.4	11.8	4.6	D	13.5
Marshall, WV	552	60	7 471	7.4	7.7	30.1	30.6	606.2	19.7	16 251	435.2	34.1	7.5	1.5	D	11.8
Ohio, WV	1 611	12	24 436	3.1	8.2	18.5	50.5	1 127.0	21.8	22 541	739.6	8.9	10.5	5.8	41.7	13.2
Belmont, OH	1 561	107	17 062	4.7	11.6	35.3	31.6	1 165.2	16.9	16 504	558.4	12.5	16.8	5.4	22.7	15.3
Wichita, KS MSA	13 357	972	225 119	1.5	26.2	20.2	30.1	10 902.4	20.7	21 512	8 451.6	29.1	10.1	4.7	25.4	12.1
Butler	1 113	132	10 100	11.9	17.2	29.6	26.4	1 094.1	29.4	19 642	432.7	15.0	11.9	4.0	19.8	22.8
Harvey	791	33	11 254	5.8	26.4	18.7	40.4	636.4	25.6	20 074	395.3	26.0	8.7	2.6	29.6	10.5
Sedgwick	11 453	807	203 765	.9	26.6	19.9	29.7	9 172.0	19.4	21 869	7 623.5	30.1	10.0	4.8	25.5	11.6
Wichita Falls, TX MSA	3 521	–6	46 832	13.5	17.0	23.7	37.4	2 517.6	19.5	19 072	1 764.7	15.4	9.9	3.6	23.1	26.2
Archer	148	–20	746	1.2	4.8	18.5	22.7	141.7	9.5	17 942	68.6	.1	4.4	1.9	19.4	15.0
Wichita	3 373	14	46 086	13.7	17.2	23.7	37.6	2 375.8	20.2	19 144	1 696.2	16.1	10.2	3.7	23.2	26.7
Williamsport, PA MSA (Lycoming)	2 921	26	44 913	–2.8	29.5	22.9	28.4	2 238.5	19.3	18 515	1 595.8	27.0	13.6	4.0	24.5	14.2
Wilmington, NC MSA	6 605	1 268	77 250	17.5	14.1	27.4	31.3	3 591.4	33.6	18 560	2 610.0	19.2	13.0	4.6	22.5	17.4
Brunswick	1 461	306	14 256	44.7	17.5	24.0	22.9	905.6	33.1	15 506	537.6	18.2	11.5	4.6	14.7	15.6
New Hanover	5 144	962	62 994	12.7	13.3	28.1	33.3	2 685.8	33.8	19 880	2 072.4	19.5	13.4	4.6	24.6	17.9
Yakima, WA MSA (Yakima)	4 710	429	56 692	12.4	16.6	24.8	30.6	3 688.5	25.7	17 759	2 405.3	13.1	11.2	2.9	22.5	16.2
York, PA MSA (York)	7 760	–31	146 495	3.0	32.5	21.1	24.7	7 757.1	20.7	21 680	5 188.7	34.6	11.8	3.6	20.9	9.1
Youngstown-Warren, OH MSA	13 524	379	210 064	1.7	27.1	24.2	30.3	11 571.7	19.9	19 155	7 681.3	36.3	10.6	3.8	22.5	11.1
Columbiana	2 410	116	29 343	8.1	30.8	25.0	27.9	1 809.1	19.0	16 239	893.7	29.8	12.3	3.4	21.4	13.5
Mahoning	6 598	190	95 450	3.2	14.2	25.9	36.9	5 074.4	19.5	19 228	3 082.6	14.3	13.0	5.8	31.0	14.1
Trumbull	4 516	73	85 271	–2.0	40.4	22.1	23.6	4 688.2	20.6	20 490	3 704.9	56.2	8.3	2.2	15.6	8.1
Yuba City, CA MSA	2 409	–67	23 041	–3.1	11.0	30.1	33.3	2 272.6	24.4	16 809	1 356.7	6.1	11.4	3.0	20.0	26.6
Sutter	1 584	31	14 635	–2.1	8.6	31.5	33.0	1 391.0	27.2	19 003	746.3	7.1	13.9	3.5	22.0	15.0
Yuba	825	–98	8 406	–4.9	15.0	27.7	33.8	881.6	20.2	14 219	610.4	4.9	8.5	2.4	17.6	40.9
Yuma, AZ MSA (Yuma)	2 358	393	30 257	32.2	8.5	32.1	30.8	1 757.4	34.9	13 762	1 291.1	3.4	11.0	2.5	18.6	27.9

D Withheld to avoid disclosure.
NA Not available.

[1]Based on 1994 resident population estimated by the Bureau of Economic Analysis.
[2]Finance, insurance, and real estate.
[3]Independent cities of Fairfax and Falls Church included with Fairfax County; data not available separately.
[4]Independent cities of Manassas and Manassas Park included with Prince William County; data not available separately.
[5]Independent city of Fredericksburg included with Spotsylvania County; data not available separately.

Source: Private Nonfarm Business—U.S. Bureau of the Census, "County Business Patterns" on diskettes, annual (related Internet site <http://www.census.gov/epcd/cbp/view/cbpview.html>); Personal Income—U.S. Bureau of Economic Analysis, "Regional Economic Information System, 1969–1994" on CD-ROM (related Internet site <http://www.bea.doc.gov/bea/dr1.htm>).

Central Cities

Note:

Table D presents data for metropolitan (metro) areas and their central cities defined as of June 30, 1996. Areas covered are 245 MSAs (metropolitan statistical areas), 17 CMSAs (consolidated MSAs), and 11 NECMAs (New England county metropolitan areas); and the 538 central cities. For a discussion of metro area and central city concepts, see Appendix B.

Data are presented for 3 population items. The MSAs, CMSAs, and NECMAs are presented in alphabetic order with central cities listed alphabetically under the related metro areas. For an alphabetic listing of central cities by state, see Appendix E.

FIPS metropolitan area codes and FIPS state/place codes are shown in the first 2 columns to the left of the area name. For a discussion of geographic codes, see Appendix B.

Table D. Central Cities — **Population**

[MSA = Metropolitan statistical area. CMSA = Consolidated MSA. NECMA = New England county metropolitan area. All areas defined as of June 30, 1996. Table includes 245 MSAs and 17 CMSAs not in New England, 11 NECMAS, and 538 central cities. "(part)" following a central city indicates that only part of the city is located within and central to the MSA/CMSA. "(remainder)" following a central city indicates that only the portion of the consolidated city minus the semi-independent places is the central city.]

Metro-politan area code[1]	State and place code[2]	Metropolitan areas and central cities	1996 (July 1)	1990[3] (April 1)	Percent change, 1990–1996
0040		Abilene, TX MSA	122 130	119 655	2.1
	48 01000	Abilene (part)	107 591	105 910	1.6
0120		Albany, GA MSA	117 286	112 571	4.2
	13 01052	Albany	78 591	78 804	-.3
0160		Albany-Schenectady-Troy, NY MSA	878 527	861 623	2.0
	36 01000	Albany	103 564	100 031	3.5
	36 65255	Saratoga Springs	25 118	25 001	.5
	36 65508	Schenectady	62 893	65 566	-4.1
	36 75484	Troy	52 518	54 269	-3.2
0200		Albuquerque, NM MSA	670 092	589 131	13.7
	35 02000	Albuquerque	419 681	384 915	9.0
0220		Alexandria, LA MSA	126 290	131 556	-4.0
	22 00975	Alexandria	46 051	49 049	-6.1
0240		Allentown-Bethlehem-Easton, PA MSA	614 304	595 081	3.2
	42 02000	Allentown	102 211	105 301	-2.9
	42 06088	Bethlehem	70 245	71 427	-1.7
0280		Altoona, PA MSA	131 450	130 542	.7
	42 02184	Altoona	50 101	51 881	-3.4
0320		Amarillo, TX MSA	206 015	187 514	9.9
	48 03000	Amarillo	169 588	157 571	7.6
0380		Anchorage, AK MSA	250 505	226 338	10.7
	02 03000	Anchorage	250 505	226 338	10.7
0450		Anniston, AL MSA	113 511	116 032	-2.2
	01 01852	Anniston	25 774	26 638	-3.2
0460		Appleton-Oshkosh-Neenah, WI MSA	340 564	315 121	8.1
	55 02375	Appleton	65 862	65 695	.3
	55 55750	Neenah	23 936	23 219	3.1
	55 60500	Oshkosh	57 957	55 006	5.4
0480		Asheville, NC MSA	210 042	191 772	9.5
	37 02140	Asheville	64 067	63 379	1.1
0500		Athens, GA MSA	137 204	126 262	8.7
	13 03440	Athens-Clarke County (remainder)	89 405	86 522	3.3
0520		Atlanta, GA MSA	3 541 230	2 959 500	19.7
	13 04000	Atlanta	401 907	393 929	2.0
0600		Augusta-Aiken, GA-SC MSA	453 612	415 220	9.2
	45 00550	Aiken, SC	22 834	20 386	12.0
	13 04196	Augusta, GA	41 783	44 639	-6.4
0640		Austin-San Marcos, TX MSA	1 041 330	846 227	23.1
	48 05000	Austin	541 278	472 020	14.7
	48 65600	San Marcos	34 994	28 738	21.8
0680		Bakersfield, CA MSA	622 729	544 981	14.3
	06 03526	Bakersfield	205 508	176 264	16.6
0733		Bangor, ME NECMA	144 989	146 601	-1.1
	23 02795	Bangor	31 649	33 181	-4.6
0743		Barnstable-Yarmouth, MA NECMA	201 970	186 605	8.2
	25 03600	Barnstable	43 699	40 949	6.7
	25 82525	Yarmouth town	22 335	21 174	5.5
0760		Baton Rouge, LA MSA	567 388	528 261	7.4
	22 05000	Baton Rouge	215 882	219 531	-1.7
0840		Beaumont-Port Arthur, TX MSA	375 795	361 218	4.0
	48 07000	Beaumont	111 224	114 323	-2.7
	48 58820	Port Arthur	57 701	58 551	-1.5
0860		Bellingham, WA MSA	152 512	127 780	19.4
	53 05280	Bellingham	61 043	52 179	17.0
0870		Benton Harbor, MI MSA	161 434	161 378	Z
	26 07520	Benton Harbor	11 824	12 818	-7.8
0880		Billings, MT MSA	125 966	113 419	11.1
	30 06550	Billings	91 195	81 125	12.4
0920		Biloxi-Gulfport-Pascagoula, MS MSA	343 184	312 368	9.9
	28 06220	Biloxi	48 414	46 319	4.5
	28 29700	Gulfport	64 829	64 045	1.2
	28 55360	Pascagoula	27 026	25 899	4.4
0960		Binghamton, NY MSA	254 053	264 497	-3.9
	36 06607	Binghamton	48 294	53 008	-8.9
1000		Birmingham, AL MSA	894 702	839 942	6.5
	01 07000	Birmingham	258 543	265 347	-2.6
1010		Bismarck, ND MSA	90 103	83 831	7.5
	38 07200	Bismarck	53 514	49 272	8.6
1020		Bloomington, IN MSA	116 176	108 978	6.6
	18 05860	Bloomington	66 479	62 015	7.2
1040		Bloomington-Normal, IL MSA	139 133	129 180	7.7
	17 06613	Bloomington	57 365	51 889	10.6
	17 53234	Normal	42 655	40 023	6.6
1080		Boise City, ID MSA	372 587	295 851	25.9
	16 08830	Boise City	152 737	126 685	20.6
	16 56260	Nampa	37 558	28 365	32.4
1123		Boston-Worcester-Lawrence-Lowell-Brockton, MA-NH NECMA	5 796 488	5 685 763	1.9
	25 02690	Attleboro, MA	39 070	38 383	1.8
	25 07000	Boston, MA	558 394	574 283	-2.8
	25 09000	Brockton, MA	92 324	92 788	-.5
	25 11000	Cambridge, MA	93 707	95 802	-2.2
	25 23000	Fall River, MA	90 865	92 703	-2.0
	25 23875	Fitchburg, MA	39 843	41 194	-3.3
	25 26150	Gloucester, MA	29 267	28 716	1.9
	25 34550	Lawrence, MA	68 807	70 207	-2.0
	25 35075	Leominster, MA	39 263	38 145	2.9
	25 37000	Lowell, MA	100 973	103 439	-2.4
	25 37490	Lynn, MA	80 563	81 245	-.8
	33 45140	Manchester, NH	100 967	99 332	1.6
	33 50260	Nashua, NH	81 094	79 662	1.8
	25 45000	New Bedford, MA	96 903	99 922	-3.0
	33 62900	Portsmouth, NH	25 034	25 925	-3.4
	33 65140	Rochester, NH	27 704	26 630	4.0
	25 72600	Waltham, MA	57 214	57 878	-1.1
	25 82000	Worcester, MA	166 350	169 759	-2.0
1240		Brownsville-Harlingen-San Benito, TX MSA	315 015	260 120	21.1
	48 10768	Brownsville	132 091	107 027	23.4
	48 32372	Harlingen	56 893	48 746	16.7
	48 65036	San Benito	23 047	20 125	14.5
1260		Bryan-College Station, TX MSA	131 904	121 862	8.2
	48 10912	Bryan	58 247	55 002	5.9
	48 15976	College Station	58 757	52 443	12.0
1280		Buffalo-Niagara Falls, NY MSA	1 175 240	1 189 340	-1.2
	36 11000	Buffalo	310 548	328 175	-5.4
	36 51055	Niagara Falls	58 357	61 840	-5.6
1303		Burlington, VT NECMA	190 548	177 059	7.6
	50 10675	Burlington	39 004	39 127	-.3
1320		Canton-Massillon, OH MSA	402 928	394 106	2.2
	39 12000	Canton	81 079	84 161	-3.7
	39 48244	Massillon	30 671	30 969	-1.0
1350		Casper, WY MSA	63 875	61 226	4.3
	56 13150	Casper	48 800	46 765	4.4
1360		Cedar Rapids, IA MSA	179 411	168 767	6.3
	19 12000	Cedar Rapids	113 482	108 772	4.3
1400		Champaign-Urbana, IL MSA	167 392	173 025	-3.3
	17 12385	Champaign	64 002	63 502	.8
	17 77005	Urbana	33 179	36 383	-8.8
1440		Charleston-North Charleston, SC MSA	495 143	506 877	-2.3
	45 13330	Charleston	71 052	79 925	-11.1
	45 50875	North Charleston	59 923	70 304	-14.8
1480		Charleston, WV MSA	254 575	250 454	1.6
	54 14600	Charleston	56 098	57 287	-2.1
1520		Charlotte-Gastonia-Rock Hill, NC-SC MSA	1 321 068	1 162 140	13.7
	37 12000	Charlotte, NC	441 297	419 539	5.2
	37 14100	Concord, NC	32 944	29 591	11.3
	37 25580	Gastonia, NC	56 575	54 725	3.4
	37 35200	Kannapolis, NC	35 631	31 592	12.8
	45 61405	Rock Hill, SC	44 061	41 610	5.9
1540		Charlottesville, VA MSA	144 815	131 373	10.2
	51 14968	Charlottesville	40 767	40 475	.7
1560		Chattanooga, TN-GA MSA	446 096	424 347	5.1
	47 14000	Chattanooga, TN	150 425	152 393	-1.3
1580		Cheyenne, WY MSA	79 175	73 142	8.2
	56 13900	Cheyenne	53 729	50 008	7.4

Z Less than .05 percent.

[1]Federal Information Processing Standards (FIPS) codes for metropolitan areas defined as of June 30, 1996.
[2]FIPS state and place codes.
[3]Includes count resolution corrections through December 1994.

Source: Metropolitan Area Population—U.S. Bureau of the Census, "Estimates of the Population of Counties and Demographic Components of Population Change: Annual Time Series, July 1, 1990 to July 1, 1996," (CO-96-8) data file (related Internet site <http://www.census.gov/population/estimates/county.html>); Central City Population—U.S. Bureau of the Census, unpublished data file (related Internet site <http://www.census.gov/population/www/estimates/cityplace.html>).

[MSA = Metropolitan statistical area. CMSA = Consolidated MSA. NECMA = New England county metropolitan area. All areas defined as of June 30, 1996. Table includes 245 MSAs and 17 CMSAs not in New England, 11 NECMAS, and 538 central cities. "(part)" following a central city indicates that only part of the city is located within and central to the MSA/CMSA. "(remainder)" following a central city indicates that only the portion of the consolidated city minus the semi-independent places is the central city.]

Metropolitan area code[1]	State and place code[2]	Metropolitan areas and central cities	1996 (July 1)	1990[3] (April 1)	Percent change, 1990–1996	Metropolitan area code[1]	State and place code[2]	Metropolitan areas and central cities	1996 (July 1)	1990[3] (April 1)	Percent change, 1990–1996
1602		Chicago-Gary-Kenosha, IL-IN-WI CMSA	8 599 774	8 239 820	4.4	2120	19 21000	Des Moines, IA MSA	427 436	392 928	8.8
	17 03012	Aurora, IL	116 405	99 672	16.8			Des Moines	193 422	193 189	.1
	17 14000	Chicago, IL	2 721 547	2 783 726	-2.2	2162		Detroit-Ann Arbor-Flint, MI CMSA	5 284 171	5 187 171	1.9
	17 19161	DeKalb, IL	35 554	35 076	1.4		26 03000	Ann Arbor	108 758	109 608	-.8
	18 19486	East Chicago, IN	31 761	33 892	-6.3		26 21000	Dearborn	91 418	89 286	2.4
	17 23074	Elgin, IL	86 034	77 010	11.7		26 22000	Detroit	1 000 272	1 027 974	-2.7
	17 24582	Evanston, IL	71 593	73 233	-2.2		26 29000	Flint	134 881	140 925	-4.3
	18 27000	Gary, IN	110 975	116 646	-4.9		26 65440	Pontiac	70 471	71 136	-.9
	17 38570	Joliet, IL	86 749	77 217	12.3		26 65820	Port Huron	32 873	33 694	-2.4
	17 38934	Kankakee, IL	27 217	27 541	-1.2	2180		Dothan, AL MSA	132 945	130 964	1.5
	55 39225	Kenosha, WI	86 888	80 426	8.0		01 21184	Dothan (part)	55 941	54 140	3.3
	17 53559	North Chicago, IL	31 665	34 978	-9.5	2190		Dover, DE MSA	122 244	110 993	10.1
1620		Chico-Paradise, CA MSA	192 507	182 120	5.7		10 21200	Dover	30 414	27 630	10.1
	06 13014	Chico	45 965	39 970	15.0	2200		Dubuque, IA MSA	88 201	86 403	2.1
	06 55520	Paradise	25 630	25 401	.9		19 22395	Dubuque	57 312	57 538	-.4
1642		Cincinnati-Hamilton, OH-KY-IN CMSA	1 920 931	1 817 569	5.7	2240		Duluth-Superior, MN-WI MSA	239 465	239 971	-.2
	39 15000	Cincinnati, OH	345 818	364 114	-5.0		27 17000	Duluth, MN	83 699	85 493	-2.1
	39 33012	Hamilton, OH	61 833	61 436	.6		55 78650	Superior, WI	27 396	27 134	1.0
	39 49840	Middletown, OH	48 023	46 022	4.3	2290		Eau Claire, WI MSA	143 245	137 543	4.1
1660		Clarksville-Hopkinsville, TN-KY MSA	186 368	169 439	10.0		55 22300	Eau Claire	58 872	56 806	3.6
	47 15160	Clarksville, TN	94 879	75 542	25.6	2320		El Paso, TX MSA	684 446	591 610	15.7
	21 37918	Hopkinsville, KY	28 317	29 818	-5.0		48 24000	El Paso	599 865	515 342	16.4
1692		Cleveland-Akron, OH CMSA	2 913 430	2 859 644	1.9	2330		Elkhart-Goshen, IN MSA	168 941	156 198	8.2
	39 01000	Akron	216 882	223 019	-2.8		18 20728	Elkhart	44 224	44 661	-1.0
	39 16000	Cleveland	498 246	505 616	-1.5		18 28386	Goshen	24 930	23 794	4.8
	39 25256	Elyria	56 729	56 746	-Z	2335		Elmira, NY MSA	93 282	95 195	-2.0
	39 39872	Kent	27 072	28 835	-6.1		36 24229	Elmira	32 009	33 724	-5.1
	39 44856	Lorain	69 800	71 245	-2.0	2340		Enid, OK MSA	57 312	56 735	1.0
1720		Colorado Springs, CO MSA	472 924	397 014	19.1		40 23950	Enid	45 724	45 309	.9
	08 16000	Colorado Springs	345 127	280 430	23.1	2360		Erie, PA MSA	280 570	275 572	1.8
1740		Columbia, MO MSA	125 676	112 379	11.8		42 24000	Erie	105 270	108 718	-3.2
	29 15670	Columbia	76 756	69 133	11.0	2400		Eugene-Springfield, OR MSA	306 862	282 912	8.5
1760		Columbia, SC MSA	488 207	453 932	7.6		41 23850	Eugene	123 718	112 733	9.7
	45 16000	Columbia	112 773	110 734	1.8		41 69600	Springfield	49 430	44 664	10.7
1800		Columbus, GA-AL MSA	272 273	260 862	4.4	2440		Evansville-Henderson, IN-KY MSA	288 735	278 990	3.5
	13 19007	Columbus (remainder), GA	182 828	178 683	2.3		18 22000	Evansville, IN	123 456	126 272	-2.2
1840		Columbus, OH MSA	1 447 646	1 345 450	7.6		21 35866	Henderson, KY	26 456	25 945	2.0
	39 18000	Columbus	657 053	632 945	3.8	2520		Fargo-Moorhead, ND-MN MSA	165 191	153 296	7.8
	39 41720	Lancaster	35 442	34 507	2.7		38 25700	Fargo, ND	83 778	74 084	13.1
	39 54040	Newark	48 856	44 396	10.0		27 43864	Moorhead, MN	33 343	32 295	3.2
1880		Corpus Christi, TX MSA	384 056	349 894	9.8	2560		Fayetteville, NC MSA	284 800	274 713	3.7
	48 17000	Corpus Christi (part)	280 253	257 453	8.9		37 22920	Fayetteville	79 631	75 850	5.0
1900		Cumberland, MD-WV MSA	100 600	101 643	-1.0	2580		Fayetteville-Springdale-Rogers, AR MSA	260 940	210 908	23.7
	24 21325	Cumberland, MD	22 341	23 712	-5.8		05 23290	Fayetteville	52 360	42 247	23.9
1922		Dallas-Fort Worth, TX CMSA	4 574 561	4 037 282	13.3		05 60410	Rogers	35 355	24 692	43.2
	48 04000	Arlington	294 816	261 717	12.6		05 66080	Springdale	38 572	29 945	28.8
	48 19000	Dallas	1 053 292	1 007 618	4.5	2620		Flagstaff, AZ-UT MSA	118 011	101 760	16.0
	48 19972	Denton	73 483	66 270	10.9		04 23620	Flagstaff, AZ	55 094	45 857	20.1
	48 27000	Fort Worth	479 716	447 619	7.2	2650		Florence, AL MSA	136 083	131 327	3.6
	48 37000	Irving	176 993	155 037	14.2		01 26896	Florence	38 999	36 426	7.1
1950		Danville, VA MSA	109 246	108 728	.5	2655		Florence, SC MSA	123 365	114 344	7.9
	51 21344	Danville	53 472	53 056	.8		45 25810	Florence	30 168	29 913	.9
1960		Davenport-Moline-Rock Island, IA-IL MSA	357 800	350 855	2.0	2670		Fort Collins-Loveland, CO MSA	221 725	186 136	19.1
	19 19000	Davenport, IA	97 010	95 333	1.8		08 27425	Fort Collins	104 196	87 491	19.1
	17 49867	Moline, IL	42 757	43 080	-.7		08 46465	Loveland	44 923	37 357	20.3
	17 65078	Rock Island, IL	39 679	40 630	-2.3	2700		Fort Myers-Cape Coral, FL MSA	380 001	335 113	13.4
2000		Dayton-Springfield, OH MSA	950 661	951 270	-.1		12 10275	Cape Coral	88 053	74 991	17.4
	39 21000	Dayton	172 947	182 005	-5.0		12 24125	Fort Myers	45 917	44 947	2.2
	39 25914	Fairborn	30 529	31 300	-2.5	2710		Fort Pierce-Port St. Lucie, FL MSA	287 255	251 071	14.4
	39 74118	Springfield	67 460	70 487	-4.3		12 24300	Fort Pierce	36 876	36 830	.1
2020		Daytona Beach, FL MSA	456 464	399 438	14.3		12 58715	Port St. Lucie	75 532	55 761	35.5
	12 16525	Daytona Beach	65 203	61 991	5.2	2720		Fort Smith, AR-OK MSA	191 482	175 911	8.9
2030		Decatur, AL MSA	139 979	131 556	6.4		05 24550	Fort Smith, AR	75 776	72 798	4.1
	01 20104	Decatur (part)	53 545	49 862	7.4	2750		Fort Walton Beach, FL MSA	165 873	143 777	15.4
2040		Decatur, IL MSA	115 416	117 206	-1.5		12 24475	Fort Walton Beach	21 933	21 407	2.5
	17 18823	Decatur	81 369	83 900	-3.0	2760		Fort Wayne, IN MSA	475 299	456 281	4.2
2082		Denver-Boulder-Greeley, CO CMSA	2 277 401	1 980 140	15.0		18 25000	Fort Wayne	184 783	191 839	-3.7
	08 07850	Boulder	90 928	85 127	6.8						
	08 20000	Denver	497 840	467 610	6.5						
	08 32155	Greeley	68 593	60 454	13.5						
	08 45970	Longmont	58 318	51 976	12.2						

Z Less than .05 percent.

[1]Federal Information Processing Standards (FIPS) codes for metropolitan areas defined as of June 30, 1996.
[2]FIPS state and place codes.
[3]Includes count resolution corrections through December 1994.

Source: Metropolitan Area Population—U.S. Bureau of the Census, "Estimates of the Population of Counties and Demographic Components of Population Change: Annual Time Series, July 1, 1990 to July 1, 1996," (CO-96-8) data file (related Internet site <http://www.census.gov/population/estimates/county.html>);   Central City Population—U.S. Bureau of the Census, unpublished data file (related Internet site <http://www.census.gov/population/www/estimates/cityplace.html>).

Table D. Central Cities — **Population**—Con.

[MSA = Metropolitan statistical area. CMSA = Consolidated MSA. NECMA = New England county metropolitan area. All areas defined as of June 30, 1996. Table includes 245 MSAs and 17 CMSAs not in New England, 11 NECMAS, and 538 central cities. "(part)" following a central city indicates that only part of the city is located within and central to the MSA/CMSA. "(remainder)" following a central city indicates that only the portion of the consolidated city minus the semi-independent places is the central city.]

Metro-politan area code[1]	State and place code[2]	Metropolitan areas and central cities	1996 (July 1)	1990[3] (April 1)	Percent change, 1990–1996	Metro-politan area code[1]	State and place code[2]	Metropolitan areas and central cities	1996 (July 1)	1990[3] (April 1)	Percent change, 1990–1996
2840		Fresno, CA MSA	861 753	755 580	14.1	3520		Jackson, MI MSA	154 563	149 756	3.2
	06 27000	Fresno	396 011	354 091	11.8		26 41420	Jackson	35 899	37 425	–4.1
	06 45022	Madera	35 648	29 283	21.7	3560		Jackson, MS MSA	421 068	395 396	6.5
2880		Gadsden, AL MSA	102 129	99 840	2.3		28 36000	Jackson	192 923	202 062	–4.5
	01 28696	Gadsden	41 155	42 523	–3.2	3580		Jackson, TN MSA	98 489	90 801	8.5
2900		Gainesville, FL MSA	196 525	181 596	8.2		47 37640	Jackson	50 406	49 115	2.6
	12 25175	Gainesville	87 295	85 075	2.6	3600		Jacksonville, FL MSA	1 008 633	906 727	11.2
2975		Glens Falls, NY MSA	122 267	118 539	3.1		12 35006	Jacksonville (remainder)	679 792	635 230	7.0
	36 29333	Glens Falls	14 772	15 023	–1.7	3605		Jacksonville, NC MSA	144 533	149 838	–3.5
2980		Goldsboro, NC MSA	111 581	104 666	6.6		37 34200	Jacksonville	69 889	78 031	–10.4
	37 26880	Goldsboro	40 801	40 709	.2	3610		Jamestown, NY MSA	140 800	141 895	–.8
2985		Grand Forks, ND-MN MSA	103 883	103 272	.6		36 38264	Jamestown	33 154	34 681	–4.4
	38 32060	Grand Forks, ND	50 675	49 417	2.5	3620		Janesville-Beloit, WI MSA	150 584	139 510	7.9
2995		Grand Junction, CO MSA	108 371	93 145	16.3		55 06500	Beloit	35 836	35 571	.7
	08 31660	Grand Junction	34 540	32 893	5.0		55 37825	Janesville	58 960	52 210	12.9
3000		Grand Rapids-Muskegon-Holland, MI MSA	1 015 099	937 891	8.2	3660		Johnson City-Kingsport-Bristol, TN-VA MSA	458 229	436 047	5.1
	26 34000	Grand Rapids	188 242	189 126	–.5		47 08540	Bristol, TN	23 275	23 421	–.6
	26 38640	Holland	33 247	30 745	8.1		51 09816	Bristol, VA	17 957	18 426	–2.5
	26 56320	Muskegon	39 518	39 809	–.7		47 38320	Johnson City, TN	55 542	50 354	10.3
3040		Great Falls, MT MSA	81 087	77 691	4.4		47 39560	Kingsport, TN	41 335	40 457	2.2
	30 32800	Great Falls	57 758	55 125	4.8	3680		Johnstown, PA MSA	239 017	241 280	–.9
3080		Green Bay, WI MSA	213 072	194 594	9.5		42 38288	Johnstown	26 149	28 124	–7.0
	55 31000	Green Bay	102 076	96 466	5.8	3700		Jonesboro, AR MSA	76 155	68 956	10.4
3120		Greensboro--Winston-Salem--High Point, NC MSA	1 141 238	1 050 304	8.7		05 35710	Jonesboro	52 656	46 535	13.2
	37 09060	Burlington	40 402	39 498	2.3	3710		Joplin, MO MSA	145 716	134 910	8.0
	37 28000	Greensboro	195 426	183 894	6.3		29 37592	Joplin	43 698	40 866	6.9
	37 31410	High Point	74 417	69 428	7.2	3720		Kalamazoo-Battle Creek, MI MSA	444 428	429 453	3.5
	37 75000	Winston-Salem	153 541	150 958	1.7		26 05920	Battle Creek	53 430	53 516	–.2
3150		Greenville, NC MSA	119 064	108 480	9.8		26 42160	Kalamazoo	77 460	80 277	–3.5
	37 28080	Greenville	54 602	46 305	17.9	3760		Kansas City, MO-KS MSA	1 690 343	1 582 874	6.8
3160		Greenville-Spartanburg-Anderson, SC MSA	896 679	830 539	8.0		20 36000	Kansas City, KS	142 654	151 521	–5.9
	45 01360	Anderson	26 429	26 385	.2		29 38000	Kansas City, MO	441 259	434 829	1.5
	45 30850	Greenville	57 064	58 256	–2.0		20 39000	Leavenworth, KS	39 431	38 495	2.4
	45 68290	Spartanburg	42 136	43 479	–3.1		20 52575	Olathe, KS	78 666	63 402	24.1
3240		Harrisburg-Lebanon-Carlisle, PA MSA	614 755	587 986	4.6	3810		Killeen-Temple, TX MSA	296 896	255 299	16.3
	42 11272	Carlisle	18 039	18 419	–2.1		48 39148	Killeen	78 022	63 535	22.8
	42 32800	Harrisburg	50 886	52 376	–2.8		48 72176	Temple	51 394	46 150	11.4
	42 42168	Lebanon	23 791	24 800	–4.1	3840		Knoxville, TN MSA	649 277	585 960	10.8
3283		Hartford, CT NECMA	1 110 102	1 123 678	–1.2		47 40000	Knoxville	167 535	169 761	–1.3
	09 37000	Hartford	133 086	139 739	–4.8		47 55120	Oak Ridge (part)	24 703	24 743	–.2
	09 47290	Middletown	43 243	42 762	1.1	3850		Kokomo, IN MSA	100 579	96 946	3.7
3285		Hattiesburg, MS MSA	107 897	98 738	9.3		18 40392	Kokomo	45 785	44 996	1.8
	28 31020	Hattiesburg	47 803	45 325	5.5	3870		La Crosse, WI-MN MSA	121 544	116 401	4.4
3290		Hickory-Morganton-Lenoir, NC MSA	314 965	292 405	7.7		55 40775	La Crosse, WI	50 212	51 140	–1.8
	37 31060	Hickory	30 523	28 474	7.2	3880		Lafayette, LA MSA	368 635	345 053	6.8
	37 37760	Lenoir	16 373	16 337	.2		22 40735	Lafayette	104 899	101 852	3.0
	37 44400	Morganton	14 927	15 085	–1.0	3920		Lafayette, IN MSA	171 200	161 572	6.0
3320		Honolulu, HI MSA	871 766	836 231	4.2		18 40788	Lafayette	44 344	44 622	–.6
	15 17000	Honolulu	423 475	377 059	12.3	3960		Lake Charles, LA MSA	178 881	168 134	6.4
3350		Houma, LA MSA	189 869	182 842	3.8		22 41155	Lake Charles	71 445	70 580	1.2
	22 36255	Houma	30 148	30 495	–1.1	3980		Lakeland-Winter Haven, FL MSA	440 954	405 382	8.8
3362		Houston-Galveston-Brazoria, TX CMSA	4 253 428	3 731 029	14.0		12 38250	Lakeland	73 157	70 576	3.7
	48 06128	Baytown	68 156	63 843	6.8		12 78275	Winter Haven	25 484	24 725	3.1
	48 16432	Conroe	33 748	27 675	21.9	4000		Lancaster, PA MSA	450 834	422 822	6.6
	48 28068	Galveston	60 048	59 067	1.7		42 41216	Lancaster	53 597	55 551	–3.5
	48 35000	Houston	1 744 058	1 637 859	6.5	4040		Lansing-East Lansing, MI MSA	447 538	432 684	3.4
	48 72392	Texas City	42 368	40 822	3.8		26 24120	East Lansing	48 192	50 677	–4.9
3400		Huntington-Ashland, WV-KY-OH MSA	316 641	312 529	1.3		26 46000	Lansing	125 736	127 321	–1.2
	21 02368	Ashland, KY	22 918	23 622	–3.0	4080		Laredo, TX MSA	176 792	133 239	32.7
	54 39460	Huntington, WV	53 941	54 844	–1.6		48 41464	Laredo	164 899	122 899	34.2
3440		Huntsville, AL MSA	330 153	293 047	12.7	4100		Las Cruces, NM MSA	163 849	135 510	20.9
	01 37000	Huntsville	170 424	159 880	6.6		35 39380	Las Cruces	74 779	62 360	19.9
3480		Indianapolis, IN MSA	1 492 297	1 380 491	8.1	4120		Las Vegas, NV-AZ MSA	1 201 073	852 646	40.9
	18 01468	Anderson	59 131	59 518	–.7		32 40000	Las Vegas, NV	376 906	258 204	46.0
	18 36003	Indianapolis (remainder)	746 737	731 278	2.1	4150		Lawrence, KS MSA	89 899	81 798	9.9
3500		Iowa City, IA MSA	101 609	96 119	5.7		20 38900	Lawrence	71 887	65 608	9.6
	19 38595	Iowa City	60 923	59 735	2.0						

[1]Federal Information Processing Standards (FIPS) codes for metropolitan areas defined as of June 30, 1996.
[2]FIPS state and place codes.
[3]Includes count resolution corrections through December 1994.

Source: Metropolitan Area Population—U.S. Bureau of the Census, "Estimates of the Population of Counties and Demographic Components of Population Change: Annual Time Series, July 1, 1990 to July 1, 1996," (CO-96-8) data file (related Internet site <http://www.census.gov/population/estimates/county.html>); Central City Population—U.S. Bureau of the Census, unpublished data file (related Internet site <http://www.census.gov/population/www/estimates/cityplace.html>).

Table D. Central Cities — **Population**—Con.

[MSA = Metropolitan statistical area. CMSA = Consolidated MSA. NECMA = New England county metropolitan area. All areas defined as of June 30, 1996. Table includes 245 MSAs and 17 CMSAs not in New England, 11 NECMAs, and 538 central cities. "(part)" following a central city indicates that only part of the city is located within and central to the MSA/CMSA. "(remainder)" following a central city indicates that only the portion of the consolidated city minus the semi-independent places is the central city.]

Metro-politan area code[1]	State and place code[2]	Metropolitan areas and central cities	1996 (July 1)	1990[3] (April 1)	Percent change, 1990–1996
4200	40 41850	Lawton, OK MSA / Lawton	111 171 / 82 582	111 486 / 80 561	-.3 / 2.5
4243	23 02060 / 23 38740	Lewiston-Auburn, ME NECMA / Auburn / Lewiston	101 754 / 22 997 / 36 830	105 259 / 24 309 / 39 757	-3.3 / -5.4 / -7.4
4280	21 46027	Lexington, KY MSA / Lexington-Fayette	441 073 / 239 942	405 936 / 225 366	8.7 / 6.5
4320	39 43554	Lima, OH MSA / Lima	155 499 / 42 913	154 340 / 45 553	.8 / -5.8
4360	31 28000	Lincoln, NE MSA / Lincoln	231 765 / 209 192	213 641 / 191 972	8.5 / 9.0
4400		Little Rock-North Little Rock, AR MSA	548 352	513 026	6.9
	05 15190	Conway	35 827	26 481	35.3
	05 34750	Jacksonville	29 191	29 101	.3
	05 41000	Little Rock	175 752	175 727	Z
	05 50450	North Little Rock	60 468	61 829	-2.2
4420		Longview-Marshall, TX MSA	206 732	193 801	6.7
	48 43888	Longview	74 572	70 311	6.1
	48 46776	Marshall	24 147	23 682	2.0
4472		Los Angeles-Riverside-Orange County, CA CMSA	15 495 155	14 531 529	6.6
	06 02000	Anaheim	288 945	266 406	8.5
	06 33182	Hemet	51 350	43 366	18.4
	06 36770	Irvine	127 873	110 330	15.9
	06 40130	Lancaster	115 675	97 300	18.9
	06 43000	Long Beach	421 904	429 321	-1.7
	06 44000	Los Angeles	3 553 638	3 485 557	2.0
	06 55184	Palm Desert	27 916	23 252	20.1
	06 55254	Palm Springs	43 347	40 144	8.0
	06 56000	Pasadena	134 116	131 586	1.9
	06 62000	Riverside	255 069	226 546	12.6
	06 65000	San Bernardino	183 474	170 036	7.9
	06 65042	San Buenaventura (Ventura)	97 205	92 557	5.0
	06 69000	Santa Ana	302 419	293 827	2.9
	06 78120	Temecula	39 315	27 099	45.1
4520		Louisville, KY-IN MSA	991 765	949 012	4.5
	21 48000	Louisville, KY	260 689	269 555	-3.3
	18 52326	New Albany, IN	38 224	36 322	5.2
4600		Lubbock, TX MSA	232 035	222 636	4.2
	48 45000	Lubbock	193 565	186 206	4.0
4640		Lynchburg, VA MSA	205 559	193 928	6.0
	51 47672	Lynchburg	67 250	66 049	1.8
4680		Macon, GA MSA	312 689	291 079	7.4
	13 49000	Macon	113 352	107 365	5.6
4720		Madison, WI MSA	395 366	367 085	7.7
	55 48000	Madison	197 630	190 766	3.6
4800		Mansfield, OH MSA	175 441	174 007	.8
	39 47138	Mansfield	50 906	50 627	.6
4880		McAllen-Edinburg-Mission, TX MSA	495 594	383 545	29.2
	48 22660	Edinburg	37 742	31 091	21.4
	48 45384	McAllen	103 352	84 021	23.0
	48 48768	Mission	37 777	28 653	31.8
4890		Medford-Ashland, OR MSA	168 609	146 387	15.2
	41 03050	Ashland	17 678	16 252	8.8
	41 47000	Medford	56 067	47 021	19.2
4900		Melbourne-Titusville-Palm Bay, FL MSA	453 998	398 978	13.8
	12 43975	Melbourne	67 631	60 034	12.7
	12 54000	Palm Bay	74 982	62 543	19.9
	12 71900	Titusville	41 543	39 394	5.5
4920		Memphis, TN-AR-MS MSA	1 078 151	1 007 306	7.0
	47 48000	Memphis, TN	596 725	618 652	-3.5
	05 74540	West Memphis, AR	26 894	28 259	-4.8
4940		Merced, CA MSA	192 311	178 403	7.8
	06 46898	Merced	58 099	56 155	3.5
4992		Miami-Fort Lauderdale, FL CMSA	3 514 403	3 192 725	10.1
	12 24000	Fort Lauderdale	151 805	149 238	1.7
	12 45000	Miami	365 127	358 648	1.8
	12 45025	Miami Beach	94 540	92 639	2.1
5082		Milwaukee-Racine, WI CMSA	1 642 658	1 607 183	2.2
	55 53000	Milwaukee	590 503	628 088	-6.0
	55 66000	Racine	82 572	84 298	-2.0
	55 84250	Waukesha	60 197	56 894	5.8
5120		Minneapolis-St. Paul, MN-WI MSA	2 765 116	2 538 776	8.9
	27 43000	Minneapolis, MN	358 785	368 383	-2.6
	27 58000	St. Paul, MN	259 606	272 235	-4.6
5160		Mobile, AL MSA	518 975	476 923	8.8
	01 50000	Mobile	202 581	196 263	3.2
5170		Modesto, CA MSA	415 786	370 522	12.2
	06 48354	Modesto	178 559	164 746	8.4
	06 80812	Turlock	48 994	42 224	16.0
5200		Monroe, LA MSA	147 302	142 191	3.6
	22 51410	Monroe	54 588	54 909	-.6
5240		Montgomery, AL MSA	314 955	292 517	7.7
	01 51000	Montgomery	196 363	190 350	3.2
5280		Muncie, IN MSA	118 600	119 659	-.9
	18 51876	Muncie	69 058	71 170	-3.0
5330		Myrtle Beach, SC MSA	163 856	144 053	13.7
	45 49075	Myrtle Beach	25 456	24 848	2.4
5345		Naples, FL MSA	188 187	152 099	23.7
	12 47625	Naples	19 777	19 505	1.4
5360		Nashville, TN MSA	1 117 178	985 026	13.4
	47 51560	Murfreesboro	53 966	44 922	20.1
	47 52006	Nashville-Davidson (remainder)	511 263	488 366	4.7
5523		New London-Norwich, CT NECMA	250 735	254 957	-1.7
	09 52280	New London	25 038	28 540	-12.3
	09 56200	Norwich	35 869	37 391	-4.1
5560		New Orleans, LA MSA	1 312 890	1 285 262	2.1
	22 55000	New Orleans	476 625	496 938	-4.1
	22 70805	Slidell	25 846	24 124	7.1
5602		New York-Northern New Jersey-Long Island, NY-NJ-CT-PA CMSA	19 846 588	19 462 450	2.0
	34 03580	Bayonne, NJ	60 499	61 464	-1.6
	09 08000	Bridgeport, CT	137 990	141 686	-2.6
	09 18430	Danbury, CT	65 506	65 585	-.1
	34 18130	Dover, NJ	83 776	76 388	9.7
	34 36000	Jersey City, NJ	229 039	228 517	.2
	09 46450	Meriden, CT	57 189	59 479	-3.9
	09 52000	New Haven, CT	124 665	130 474	-4.5
	36 51000	New York, NY	7 380 906	7 322 564	.8
	34 51000	Newark, NJ	268 510	275 221	-2.4
	36 50034	Newburgh, NY	26 248	26 454	-.8
	09 55990	Norwalk, CT	77 977	78 331	-.5
	36 59641	Poughkeepsie, NY	27 808	28 844	-3.6
	09 73000	Stamford, CT	110 056	108 056	1.9
	34 74000	Trenton, NJ	85 437	88 675	-3.7
	09 80000	Waterbury, CT	106 412	108 961	-2.3
	36 81677	White Plains, NY	49 653	48 718	1.9
5720		Norfolk-Virginia Beach-Newport News, VA-NC MSA	1 540 252	1 444 710	6.6
	51 35000	Hampton, VA	138 757	133 811	3.7
	51 56000	Newport News, VA	176 122	171 439	2.7
	51 57000	Norfolk, VA	233 430	261 250	-10.6
	51 64000	Portsmouth, VA	101 308	103 910	-2.5
	51 76432	Suffolk, VA	58 901	52 143	13.0
	51 82000	Virginia Beach, VA	430 385	393 089	9.5
5790		Ocala, FL MSA	230 068	194 835	18.1
	12 50750	Ocala	44 975	42 045	7.0
5800		Odessa-Midland, TX MSA	239 414	225 545	6.1
	48 48072	Midland (part)	96 980	89 443	8.4
	48 53388	Odessa	90 883	89 699	1.3
5880		Oklahoma City, OK MSA	1 026 657	958 839	7.1
	40 52500	Norman	90 228	80 071	12.7
	40 55000	Oklahoma City	469 852	444 724	5.7
	40 66800	Shawnee	26 833	26 017	3.1
5920		Omaha, NE-IA MSA	681 698	639 580	6.6
	19 16860	Council Bluffs, IA	55 569	54 315	2.3
	31 37000	Omaha, NE	364 253	342 862	6.2
5960		Orlando, FL MSA	1 417 291	1 224 844	15.7
	12 53000	Orlando	173 902	164 674	5.6
5990		Owensboro, KY MSA	90 818	87 189	4.2
	21 58620	Owensboro	54 350	53 577	1.4
6015		Panama City, FL MSA	144 637	126 994	13.9
	12 54700	Panama City	35 986	34 396	4.6

Z Less than .05 percent.

[1]Federal Information Processing Standards (FIPS) codes for metropolitan areas defined as of June 30, 1996.
[2]FIPS state and place codes.
[3]Includes count resolution corrections through December 1994.

Source: Metropolitan Area Population—U.S. Bureau of the Census, "Estimates of the Population of Counties and Demographic Components of Population Change: Annual Time Series, July 1, 1990 to July 1, 1996," (CO-96-8) data file (related Internet site <http://www.census.gov/population/estimates/county.html>); Central City Population—U.S. Bureau of the Census, unpublished data file (related Internet site <http://www.census.gov/population/www/estimates/cityplace.html>).

[MSA = Metropolitan statistical area. CMSA = Consolidated MSA. NECMA = New England county metropolitan area. All areas defined as of June 30, 1996. Table includes 245 MSAs and 17 CMSAs not in New England, 11 NECMAS, and 538 central cities. "(part)" following a central city indicates that only part of the city is located within and central to the MSA/CMSA. "(remainder)" following a central city indicates that only the portion of the consolidated city minus the semi-independent places is the central city.]

Metropolitan area code[1]	State and place code[2]	Metropolitan areas and central cities	1996 (July 1)	1990[3] (April 1)	Percent change, 1990–1996
6020		Parkersburg-Marietta, WV-OH MSA....	151 597	149 169	1.6
	39 47628	Marietta, OH	15 092	15 026	.4
	54 62140	Parkersburg, WV	32 766	33 862	-3.2
6080		Pensacola, FL MSA	385 820	344 406	12.0
	12 55925	Pensacola	59 162	59 198	-.1
6120		Peoria-Pekin, IL MSA	346 501	339 172	2.2
	17 58447	Pekin	32 433	32 254	.6
	17 59000	Peoria	112 306	113 513	-1.1
6162		Philadelphia-Wilmington-Atlantic City, PA-NJ-DE-MD CMSA	5 973 463	5 893 019	1.4
	34 02080	Atlantic City, NJ	38 361	37 986	1.0
	34 07600	Bridgeton, NJ	18 493	18 942	-2.4
	34 10000	Camden, NJ	84 844	87 492	-3.0
	34 46680	Millville, NJ	26 366	25 992	1.4
	10 50670	Newark, DE	27 870	26 463	5.3
	42 60000	Philadelphia, PA	1 478 002	1 585 577	-6.8
	34 76070	Vineland, NJ	55 906	54 780	2.1
	10 77580	Wilmington, DE	69 490	71 529	-2.9
6200		Phoenix-Mesa, AZ MSA	2 746 703	2 238 498	22.7
	04 46000	Mesa	344 764	289 199	19.2
	04 55000	Phoenix	1 159 014	984 310	17.7
	04 65000	Scottsdale	179 012	130 075	37.6
	04 73000	Tempe	162 701	141 993	14.6
6240		Pine Bluff, AR MSA	83 007	85 487	-2.9
	05 55310	Pine Bluff	54 165	57 140	-5.2
6280		Pittsburgh, PA MSA	2 379 411	2 394 811	-.6
	42 61000	Pittsburgh	350 363	369 879	-5.3
6323		Pittsfield, MA NECMA	134 788	139 352	-3.3
	25 53960	Pittsfield	46 315	48 622	-4.7
6340		Pocatello, ID MSA	73 608	66 026	11.5
	16 64090	Pocatello (part)	51 296	46 062	11.4
6403		Portland, ME NECMA	251 087	243 135	3.3
	23 60545	Portland	63 123	64 157	-1.6
6442		Portland-Salem, OR-WA CMSA	2 078 357	1 793 476	15.9
	41 59000	Portland, OR	480 824	463 634	3.7
	41 64900	Salem, OR	122 566	107 793	13.7
	53 74060	Vancouver, WA	59 982	54 651	9.8
6483		Providence-Warwick-Pawtucket, RI NECMA	907 479	916 270	-1.0
	44 54640	Pawtucket	69 068	72 644	-4.9
	44 59000	Providence	152 558	160 728	-5.1
	44 74300	Warwick	84 514	85 427	-1.1
	44 80780	Woonsocket	41 817	43 877	-4.7
6520		Provo-Orem, UT MSA	319 694	263 590	21.3
	49 57300	Orem	79 736	67 561	18.0
	49 62470	Provo	99 606	86 835	14.7
6560		Pueblo, CO MSA	131 217	123 051	6.6
	08 62000	Pueblo	99 406	98 640	.8
6580		Punta Gorda, FL MSA	130 426	110 975	17.5
	12 59200	Punta Gorda	12 552	10 637	18.0
6640		Raleigh-Durham-Chapel Hill, NC MSA	1 025 253	858 485	19.4
	37 11800	Chapel Hill	44 244	38 711	14.3
	37 19000	Durham	149 799	138 894	7.9
	37 55000	Raleigh	243 835	212 092	15.0
6660		Rapid City, SD MSA	87 145	81 343	7.1
	46 52980	Rapid City	57 642	54 523	5.7
6680		Reading, PA MSA	352 353	336 523	4.7
	42 63624	Reading	75 723	78 380	-3.4
6690		Redding, CA MSA	161 740	147 036	10.0
	06 59920	Redding	76 616	66 462	15.3
6720		Reno, NV MSA	298 787	254 667	17.3
	32 60600	Reno	155 499	133 850	16.2
6740		Richland-Kennewick-Pasco, WA MSA	179 949	150 033	19.9
	53 35275	Kennewick	51 184	42 148	21.4
	53 53545	Pasco	23 910	20 337	17.6
	53 58235	Richland	37 445	32 315	15.9
6760		Richmond-Petersburg, VA MSA	935 174	865 640	8.0
	51 61832	Petersburg	38 234	37 027	3.3
	51 67000	Richmond	198 267	202 798	-2.2
6800		Roanoke, VA MSA	229 105	224 592	2.0
	51 68000	Roanoke	95 548	96 509	-1.0

Metropolitan area code[1]	State and place code[2]	Metropolitan areas and central cities	1996 (July 1)	1990[3] (April 1)	Percent change, 1990–1996
6820		Rochester, MN MSA	113 182	106 470	6.3
	27 54880	Rochester	75 638	70 729	6.9
6840		Rochester, NY MSA	1 088 037	1 062 470	2.4
	36 63000	Rochester	221 594	230 356	-3.8
6880		Rockford, IL MSA	352 369	329 676	6.9
	17 65000	Rockford	143 531	141 787	1.2
6895		Rocky Mount, NC MSA	144 157	133 369	8.1
	37 57500	Rocky Mount	52 635	49 438	6.5
6922		Sacramento-Yolo, CA CMSA	1 632 133	1 481 220	10.2
	06 18100	Davis	52 321	46 322	13.0
	06 64000	Sacramento	376 243	369 365	1.9
	06 86328	Woodland	42 229	40 230	5.0
6960		Saginaw-Bay City-Midland, MI MSA....	403 301	399 320	1.0
	26 06020	Bay City	36 548	38 936	-6.1
	26 53780	Midland	39 849	38 053	4.7
	26 70520	Saginaw	65 014	69 512	-6.5
6980		St. Cloud, MN MSA	160 326	149 509	7.2
	27 56896	St. Cloud (part)	44 801	43 566	2.8
7000		St. Joseph, MO MSA	97 336	97 715	-.4
	29 64550	St. Joseph	70 208	71 852	-2.3
7040		St. Louis, MO-IL MSA	2 548 238	2 492 348	2.2
	17 01114	Alton, IL	31 562	33 064	-4.5
	17 04845	Belleville, IL	41 608	42 806	-2.8
	17 22255	East St. Louis, IL	38 595	40 944	-5.7
	17 30926	Granite City, IL	31 449	32 766	-4.0
	29 64082	St. Charles, MO	56 525	50 634	11.6
	29 65000	St. Louis, MO	351 565	396 685	-11.4
7120		Salinas, CA MSA	339 047	355 660	-4.7
	06 48872	Monterey	27 722	31 954	-13.2
	06 64224	Salinas	111 757	108 777	2.7
7160		Salt Lake City-Ogden, UT MSA	1 217 842	1 072 227	13.6
	49 13850	Clearfield	22 153	21 435	3.3
	49 55980	Ogden	65 720	63 943	2.8
	49 67000	Salt Lake City	172 575	159 928	7.9
7200		San Angelo, TX MSA	102 580	98 458	4.2
	48 64472	San Angelo	88 098	84 462	4.3
7240		San Antonio, TX MSA	1 490 111	1 324 749	12.5
	48 50820	New Braunfels	33 906	27 334	24.0
	48 65000	San Antonio	1 067 816	959 295	11.3
7320		San Diego, CA MSA	2 655 463	2 498 016	6.3
	06 16378	Coronado	25 701	26 540	-3.2
	06 22804	Escondido	116 184	108 648	6.9
	06 66000	San Diego	1 171 121	1 110 623	5.4
7362		San Francisco-Oakland-San Jose, CA CMSA	6 605 428	6 249 881	5.7
	06 00562	Alameda	76 042	73 979	2.8
	06 06000	Berkeley	103 243	102 724	.5
	06 23182	Fairfield	85 610	78 650	8.8
	06 29504	Gilroy	34 396	31 487	9.2
	06 50258	Napa	65 030	61 865	5.1
	06 53000	Oakland	367 230	372 242	-1.3
	06 55282	Palo Alto	58 304	55 900	4.3
	06 56784	Petaluma	48 455	43 166	12.3
	06 67000	San Francisco	735 315	723 959	1.6
	06 68000	San Jose	838 744	782 224	7.2
	06 69084	Santa Clara	98 726	93 613	5.5
	06 69112	Santa Cruz	51 155	49 711	2.9
	06 70098	Santa Rosa	121 879	113 261	7.6
	06 77000	Sunnyvale	125 156	117 324	6.7
	06 81666	Vallejo	109 593	109 199	.4
	06 83668	Watsonville	32 752	31 099	5.3
7460		San Luis Obispo-Atascadero-Paso Robles, CA MSA	229 437	217 162	5.7
	06 03064	Atascadero	24 263	23 138	4.9
	06 22300	El Paso de Robles (Paso Robles)....	20 187	18 583	8.6
	06 68154	San Luis Obispo	42 433	41 958	1.1
7480		Santa Barbara-Santa Maria-Lompoc, CA MSA	385 573	369 608	4.3
	06 42524	Lompoc	40 925	37 649	8.7
	06 69070	Santa Barbara	86 154	85 571	.7
	06 69196	Santa Maria	67 012	61 552	8.9
7490		Santa Fe, NM MSA	137 223	117 043	17.2
	35 70500	Santa Fe	66 522	56 537	17.7
7510		Sarasota-Bradenton, FL MSA	528 803	489 483	8.0
	12 07950	Bradenton	47 219	43 769	7.9
	12 64175	Sarasota	50 891	50 897	-Z

Z Less than .05 percent.

[1]Federal Information Processing Standards (FIPS) codes for metropolitan areas defined as of June 30, 1996.
[2]FIPS state and place codes.
[3]Includes count resolution corrections through December 1994.

Source: Metropolitan Area Population—U.S. Bureau of the Census, "Estimates of the Population of Counties and Demographic Components of Population Change: Annual Time Series, July 1, 1990 to July 1, 1996," (CO-96-8) data file (related Internet site <http://www.census.gov/population/estimates/county.html>); Central City Population—U.S. Bureau of the Census, unpublished data file (related Internet site <http://www.census.gov/population/www/estimates/cityplace.html>).

[MSA = Metropolitan statistical area. CMSA = Consolidated MSA. NECMA = New England county metropolitan area. All areas defined as of June 30, 1996. Table includes 245 MSAs and 17 CMSAs not in New England, 11 NECMAS, and 538 central cities. "(part)" following a central city indicates that only part of the city is located within and central to the MSA/CMSA. "(remainder)" following a central city indicates that only the portion of the consolidated city minus the semi-independent places is the central city.]

Metro-politan area code[1]	State and place code[2]	Metropolitan areas and central cities	1996 (July 1)	1990[3] (April 1)	Percent change, 1990–1996
7520		Savannah, GA MSA	282 610	257 899	9.6
	13 69000	Savannah	136 262	137 812	−1.1
7560		Scranton--Wilkes-Barre--Hazleton, PA MSA	628 073	638 524	−1.6
	42 69000	Scranton	77 189	81 805	−5.6
	42 85152	Wilkes-Barre	44 407	47 523	−6.6
7602		Seattle-Tacoma-Bremerton, WA CMSA	3 320 829	2 970 300	11.8
	53 05210	Bellevue	92 267	86 872	6.2
	53 07695	Bremerton	41 580	38 142	9.0
	53 22640	Everett	81 028	70 937	14.2
	53 51300	Olympia	39 006	33 729	15.6
	53 63000	Seattle	524 704	516 259	1.6
	53 70000	Tacoma	179 114	176 664	1.4
7610		Sharon, PA MSA	122 155	121 003	1.0
	42 69720	Sharon	16 766	17 533	−4.4
7620		Sheboygan, WI MSA	109 705	103 877	5.6
	55 72975	Sheboygan	49 987	49 587	.8
7640		Sherman-Denison, TX MSA	100 589	95 019	5.9
	48 19900	Denison	22 136	21 505	2.9
	48 67496	Sherman	33 155	31 584	5.0
7680		Shreveport-Bossier City, LA MSA......	379 596	376 330	.9
	22 08920	Bossier City	55 686	52 721	5.6
	22 70000	Shreveport	191 558	198 525	−3.5
7720		Sioux City, IA-NE MSA	121 108	115 018	5.3
	19 73335	Sioux City, IA	83 791	80 505	4.1
7760		Sioux Falls, SD MSA	156 598	139 236	12.5
	46 59020	Sioux Falls	113 223	100 836	12.3
7800		South Bend, IN MSA	257 740	247 052	4.3
	18 71000	South Bend	102 100	105 511	−3.2
7840		Spokane, WA MSA	404 920	361 333	12.1
	53 67000	Spokane	186 562	177 165	5.3
7880		Springfield, IL MSA	204 130	189 550	7.7
	17 72000	Springfield	112 921	105 417	7.1
7920		Springfield, MO MSA	296 345	264 346	12.1
	29 70000	Springfield	143 407	140 494	2.1
8003		Springfield, MA NECMA	591 804	602 878	−1.8
	25 30840	Holyoke	41 461	43 704	−5.1
	25 46330	Northhampton	28 838	29 289	−1.5
	25 67000	Springfield	149 948	156 983	−4.5
	25 76030	Westfield	37 539	38 372	−2.2
8050		State College, PA MSA.............	131 489	124 812	5.3
	42 73808	State College	39 400	38 981	1.1
8080		Steubenville-Weirton, OH-WV MSA ...	138 315	142 523	−3.0
	39 74608	Steubenville, OH	20 966	22 125	−5.2
	54 85156	Weirton, WV	21 731	22 124	−1.8
8120		Stockton-Lodi, CA MSA	533 392	480 628	11.0
	06 42202	Lodi	54 585	51 874	5.2
	06 75000	Stockton	232 660	210 943	10.3
8140		Sumter, SC MSA	107 161	101 276	5.8
	45 70405	Sumter	38 565	40 977	−5.9
8160		Syracuse, NY MSA	745 691	742 237	.5
	36 03078	Auburn	29 774	31 258	−4.7
	36 73000	Syracuse	155 865	163 860	−4.9
8240		Tallahassee, FL MSA	259 380	233 609	11.0
	12 70600	Tallahassee	136 812	124 773	9.6
8280		Tampa-St. Petersburg-Clearwater, FL MSA	2 199 231	2 067 959	6.3
	12 12875	Clearwater....................	100 132	98 669	1.5
	12 63000	St. Petersburg	235 988	240 318	−1.8
	12 71000	Tampa	285 206	280 015	1.9
8320		Terre Haute, IN MSA	149 671	147 585	1.4
	18 75428	Terre Haute	54 585	57 475	−5.0
8360		Texarkana, TX-Texarkana, AR MSA ...	123 919	120 132	3.2
	05 68810	Texarkana, AR	22 918	22 631	1.3
	48 72368	Texarkana, TX	32 462	32 294	.5
8400		Toledo, OH MSA	611 417	614 128	−.4
	39 07972	Bowling Green	28 307	28 303	Z
	39 77000	Toledo	317 606	332 943	−4.6
8440		Topeka, KS MSA	164 938	160 976	2.5
	20 71000	Topeka........................	119 658	119 883	−.2
8520		Tucson, AZ MSA	767 873	666 957	15.1
	04 77000	Tucson	449 002	411 480	9.1
8560		Tulsa, OK MSA	756 493	708 954	6.7
	40 75000	Tulsa	378 491	367 302	3.0
8600		Tuscaloosa, AL MSA	158 779	150 522	5.5
	01 77256	Tuscaloosa	82 379	77 759	5.9
8640		Tyler, TX MSA	165 002	151 309	9.0
	48 74144	Tyler	82 185	75 450	8.9
8680		Utica-Rome, NY MSA	302 405	316 645	−4.5
	36 63418	Rome	40 979	44 350	−7.6
	36 76540	Utica	61 368	68 637	−10.6
8750		Victoria, TX MSA	81 541	74 361	9.7
	48 75428	Victoria	61 059	55 076	10.9
8780		Visalia-Tulare-Porterville, CA MSA.....	349 922	311 921	12.2
	06 58240	Porterville	34 518	29 521	16.9
	06 80644	Tulare	39 927	33 249	20.1
	06 82954	Visalia	87 787	75 659	16.0
8800		Waco, TX MSA	201 775	189 123	6.7
	48 76000	Waco	108 412	103 590	4.7
8872		Washington-Baltimore, DC-MD-VA-WV CMSA	7 164 519	6 726 395	6.5
	24 01600	Annapolis, MD	33 234	33 195	.1
	51 03000	Arlington, VA	175 334	170 897	2.6
	24 04000	Baltimore, MD	675 401	736 014	−8.2
	24 30325	Frederick, MD	46 227	40 186	15.0
	51 29744	Fredericksburg, VA	22 586	19 027	18.7
	24 36075	Hagerstown, MD	34 633	35 306	−1.9
	11 50000	Washington, DC	543 213	606 900	−10.5
8920		Waterloo-Cedar Falls, IA MSA	122 806	123 798	−.8
	19 11755	Cedar Falls	34 884	34 298	1.7
	19 82425	Waterloo	65 022	66 467	−2.2
8940		Wausau, WI MSA	121 791	115 400	5.5
	55 84475	Wausau	36 809	37 060	−.7
8960		West Palm Beach-Boca Raton, FL MSA	992 840	863 503	15.0
	12 07300	Boca Raton	68 507	61 486	11.4
	12 76600	West Palm Beach	79 305	67 764	17.0
9000		Wheeling, WV-OH MSA	155 808	159 301	−2.2
	54 86452	Wheeling, WV..................	33 311	34 882	−4.5
9040		Wichita, KS MSA	512 965	485 270	5.7
	20 79000	Wichita	320 395	304 017	5.4
9080		Wichita Falls, TX MSA	136 311	130 351	4.6
	48 79000	Wichita Falls	100 138	96 259	4.0
9140		Williamsport, PA MSA	119 083	118 710	.3
	42 85312	Williamsport	30 537	31 933	−4.4
9200		Wilmington, NC MSA	206 738	171 269	20.7
	37 74440	Wilmington	62 192	55 530	12.0
9260		Yakima, WA MSA	216 234	188 823	14.5
	53 80010	Yakima	65 110	58 427	11.4
9280		York, PA MSA	368 332	339 574	8.5
	42 87048	York	40 779	42 192	−3.3
9320		Youngstown-Warren, OH MSA	598 582	600 895	−.4
	39 80892	Warren	48 347	50 793	−4.8
	39 88000	Youngstown	87 405	95 732	−8.7
9340		Yuba City, CA MSA	136 555	122 643	11.3
	06 86972	Yuba City	32 433	27 385	18.4
9360		Yuma, AZ MSA	125 142	106 895	17.1
	04 85540	Yuma	60 519	56 966	6.2

Z Less than .05 percent.

[1]Federal Information Processing Standards (FIPS) codes for metropolitan areas defined as of June 30, 1996.
[2]FIPS state and place codes.
[3]Includes count resolution corrections through December 1994.

Source: Metropolitan Area Population—U.S. Bureau of the Census, "Estimates of the Population of Counties and Demographic Components of Population Change: Annual Time Series, July 1, 1990 to July 1, 1996," (CO-96-8) data file (related Internet site <http://www.census.gov/population/estimates/county.html>);   Central City Population—U.S. Bureau of the Census, unpublished data file (related Internet site <http://www.census.gov/population/www/estimates/cityplace.html>).

Appendixes

Appendixes

Appendix A.
Source Notes and Explanations

This appendix presents general notes on population and economic censuses followed by source notes and explanations of the data items presented in table sets A through D of this publication. These table sets vary in both geographic and data coverage.

Each table set begins with information on the number of data items and tables, as well as specific geographic coverage. For each table, the table number and title are given followed by a brief listing of the data items on that table, the source citation for these items, and related definitions and other explanatory text on the source.

General Notes

POPULATION

Population estimates. The Census Bureau develops estimates with a demographic procedure called a "component change" method. A major assumption underlying this approach is that the components that constitute population change can be represented by administrative data in a statistical model. In order to build the model, Census Bureau demographers estimated each component of population change separately. For the population residing in households, the components of change are births, deaths, and net migration, including net immigration from abroad. For the nonhousehold population, change is represented by net change in the population in group quarters. To develop population estimates, the Census Bureau uses a component change procedure called the Tax Return method (formerly called the Administrative Records method). Each component in the model is represented with data that are symptomatic of some aspect of population change. For example, birth certificates are symptomatic of additions to the population resulting from births; therefore, these data are used to estimate the birth component for a state.

The estimates used as a base for data and the annual changes implied by the figures are subject to estimation error. Variations from actual population levels are inherent in the estimating procedures, stemming from the fact that the correlation between the data series and population is not perfect. The data series being used to reflect population change are all affected to some degree by factors other than population movements and, in addition, are part of reporting systems that are subject to administrative alteration.

Population data for 1997 and revised population data for 1990 through 1996 were released in late December of 1997 for states and mid-March of 1998 for counties. These population data were processed and used in Tables A-1, B-1, and C-1 of this publication. Population figures used to calculate rates or describe various population characteristics (e.g., race) in table sets A through C, as well as those in Table D, are those released in the previous annual cycle.

Decennial censuses. The population statistics for 1980 and 1990 are based on results from the censuses of population and housing, conducted by the Bureau of the Census as of April 1 in each of those years. As provided by Article 1, Section 2, of the U.S. Constitution, adopted in 1787, a census has been taken every 10 years commencing with 1790. The original purposes of the census were to apportion the seats in the U.S. House of Representatives based on the population of each state and to derive an equitable tax on each state for the payment of the Revolutionary War debt. Through the years, the nation's needs and interests have become more complex, and the content of the decennial census has changed accordingly. Presently, census data not only are used to apportion seats in the House and to aid legislators in the realignment of legislative district boundaries but also are used in the distribution of billions of federal dollars each year. These data are vital to state and local governments and to private firms for such functions as market analysis, site selection, and environmental impact studies. Persons enumerated in the census were counted as inhabitants of their usual place of residence, which generally means the place where a person lives and sleeps most of the time. This place is not necessarily the same as the legal residence, voting residence, or domicile. In the vast majority of cases, however, the use of these different bases of classification would produce substantially the same statistics, although appreciable differences may exist for a few areas.

The implementation of this usual-residence practice has resulted in the establishment of residence rules for certain categories of persons whose usual place of residence is not immediately apparent (e.g., college students were counted at their college residence). As in the above example, persons were not always counted as residents of the place where they happened to be staying on census day. However, persons without a usual place of residence were counted where they were enumerated.

For detailed discussions of the background, purposes, planning, and procedures used for the 1990 Census of Population and Housing, as well as a facsimile of the questionnaires and descriptions of the data products resulting from the census, see U.S. Bureau of the Census, *1990 Census of Population and Housing Guide, Part A, Text* (CPH-R-1A).

ECONOMIC CENSUSES

Title 13 of the United States Code (Sections 131, 191, and 224) directs the Census Bureau to take the economic censuses every 5 years, covering years ending in "2" and "7." The 1992 Economic Census consist of the following eight censuses:

Census of Retail Trade
Census of Wholesale Trade
Census of Service Industries
Census of Financial, Insurance, and Real Estate Industries
Census of Transportation, Communication, and Utilities
Census of Manufactures
Census of Mineral Industries
Census of Construction Industries

Special programs also cover enterprise statistics and minority-owned and women-owned businesses. (The Census of Agriculture and the Census of Governments are conducted separately.)

The economic censuses have been taken together as an integrated program at 5-year intervals since 1967, and before that for 1963, 1958, and 1954. Prior to that time, the individual censuses were taken separately at varying intervals.

The economic censuses trace their beginnings to the 1810 decennial census, when questions on manufacturing were included with those for population. Coverage of economic activities was expanded for 1840 and subsequent censuses to include mining and some commercial activities. In 1902, Congress established a permanent Bureau of the Census and directed that a census of manufactures be taken every 5 years. The 1905 manufactures census was the first time a census was taken apart from the regular decennial population census.

The first census of business was taken in 1930. Initially it covered retail and wholesale trade and construction industries, but it was broadened in 1933 to include some of the service trades.

The 1954 economic censuses were the first to be fully integrated—providing comparable census data across economic sectors, using consistent time periods, concepts, definitions, classifications, and reporting units. These were the first censuses to be taken by mail, using lists of firms provided by the administrative records of other federal agencies. Since 1963, administrative records have also been used to provide basic statistics for very small firms, reducing or eliminating the need to send them census questionnaires. The Enterprise Statistics Program, which publishes combined data from the economic censuses, was made possible with the implementation of the integrated census program in 1954.

The range of industries covered in the economic censuses has continued to expand. The census of construction industries began on a regular basis in 1967, and the scope of service industries was broadened in 1967, 1977, and 1987. The census of transportation began in 1963. The survey of minority-owned business enterprises was first conducted as a special project in 1969 and was incorporated into the economic censuses in 1972 along with the survey of women-owned businesses.

The 1992 Economic Census covers more of the economy than any previous census. New for 1992 are data on communication, utilities, financial, insurance, and real estate, as well as, coverage of more transportation industries. The economic, agriculture, and governments censuses now collectively cover nearly 98 percent of all economic activity.

Among other changes, new 1992 definitions affect the boundaries of about a third of all metropolitan areas. Also, the Survey of Women-Owned Businesses has now been expanded to include all corporations.

The core data from the economic censuses and surveys are collected and published in terms of "establishments"; for example, the sales of sporting goods stores in Cleveland, the production of fertilizer plants in Florida, or the employment in electronic repair shops. An establishment, as defined for census and survey purposes, is a business or industrial unit at a single geographic location that produces or distributes goods or performs services, for example, a single store or factory.

Because different establishments within the same company can be located in different geographic areas or be engaged in different kinds of business, the Census Bureau obtains separate reports for each establishment. This yields more precise information than if the company were simply to file a single report.

When more than one economic activity is conducted at a single location, each activity under separate ownership is regarded as a separate establishment. Thus, a leased department within a department store is classified as a separate establishment.

Establishments functioning primarily to manage service or support the activities of their companies' operating establishments (for example, separate administrative offices or warehouses) are identified as auxiliaries, and statistics are published in a separate report.

Establishments responding to the establishment survey are classified into industries on the basis of their principal product or activity (determined by annual sales volume) in accordance with the *1987 Standard Industrial Classification (SIC) Manual*. This is the system of industrial classification developed by experts on classification in government and private industry under the guidance of the Office of Information and Regulatory Affairs, Office of Management and Budget. This classification system is used by government agencies as well as many organizations outside the government. The SIC is a classification structure for the entire national economy.

The structure provides data on a division and industry code basis, according to the level of industrial detail. For example, manufacturing is a major industrial division, food and kindred products (code 20) is one of its major groups. One of the ways this group is further divided is into meat products (code 201) and meat packing plants (code 2011).

Periodically, the SIC is revised to reflect changes in the industrial composition of the economy. The 1987 edition of this manual represents revisions from the 1972 edition and its 1977 supplement. For more information on these revisions, see Appendix A of the 1987 SIC Manual.

More information about the scope, coverage, classification system, data items, and publications for each of the economic censuses and related surveys is published in the *Guide to the Economic Censuses and Related Statistics*. More information on the methodology, procedures, and history of the censuses is published in the *History of the 1992 Economic Censuses*.

In accordance with federal law governing census reports, no data are published that would disclose the operations of an individual establishment or business. However, the number of establishments in a kind-of-business classification is not considered a disclosure, so this information may be given even though other information is withheld.

Table A—States

Table A consists of 56 tables with 869 items of data for each state, the United States as a whole, and the District of Columbia. These tables are numbered A-1 through A-56.

A number of the statistics in tables A-1 through A-56 are also presented for metropolitan areas in tables B-1 through B-10 and for metropolitan area component counties in tables C-1 through C-3.

Table A-1. Area and Population

Area, total, land, and water, 1990;
Population, 1997, 1995, 1990, and 1980;
   Rank and per square mile of land area, 1997 and 1990;
Population change, net change, net migration, and percent change, 1990-1997;
Percent change 1980-1990.

Source: Area–U.S. Bureau of the Census, 1990 Census of Population and Housing, series CPH-2; and unpublished data from the TIGER/Geographic Identification Code Scheme (TIGER/GICS) computer file. Population—U.S. Bureau of the Census, *1990 Census of Population and Housing, Population and Housing Unit Counts*, (CPH-2); *Current Population Reports*, series P25, No. 1127; and *ST-97-1 Estimates of the Population of States: Annual Time Series, July 1,1990, to July 1, 1997*, release date, December 31, 1997, Internet site <http://www.census.gov/population/estimates/

state/ST9097T1.txt> (accessed 31 December 1997). Population change—*ST-97-3, Estimates of the Population of States: Annual Time Series, July 1, 1990, to July 1, 1997, and Demographic Components of Population Change, Annual Time Series July 1, 1990, to July 1, 1997*, release date: December 31, 1997; Internet site <http://www.census.gov/population/estimates/state/STCOM97R2.txt> (accessed 4 February 1998).

The Census Bureau provides measurements for both land area and total water area for the 1990 census. Area was calculated from the specific set of boundaries recorded for the entity in the Census Bureau's geographic database.

Land area measurement may disagree with the information displayed on census maps and in the TIGER file because, for area measurement purposes, features identified as "intermittent water" and "glacier" are reported as land area. TIGER is an acronym for the new digital (computer-readable) geographic database that automates the mapping and related geographic activities required to support the Census Bureau's census and survey programs; TIGER stands for Topologically Integrated Geographic Encoding and Referencing system.

The water figure includes inland, coastal, Great Lakes, and territorial water. "Inland water" consists of any lake, reservoir, pond, or similar body of water that is recorded in the Census Bureau's geographic database. It also includes any river, creek, canal, stream, or similar feature that is recorded in that database as a two-dimensional feature (rather than as a single line). The portions of the oceans and related large embayments (such as the Chesapeake Bay and Puget Sound), the Gulf of Mexico, and the Caribbean Sea that belong to the United States and its possessions are considered to be "coastal" and "territorial" waters; the Great Lakes are treated as a separate water entity. Rivers and bays that empty into these bodies of water are treated as "inland water" from the point beyond which they are narrower than one nautical mile across. Identification of land and inland, coastal, and territorial waters is for statistical purposes and does not necessarily reflect legal definitions thereof.

The accuracy of any area measurement figure is limited by the inaccuracy inherent in (1) the location and shape of the various boundary features in the database, and (2) rounding affecting the last digit in all operations that compute and/or sum the area measurements.

Population data for 1997 and revised population data for 1990 through 1996 were released in late December of 1997 for states. These population data were processed and used in Table A-1 of this publication. Population figures used to calculate rates or describe various population characteristics (e.g., race) in Tables A-2 through A-56 are those released in the previous annual cycle.

Figures on total persons for 1990 and 1980 are based on a complete, or 100-percent count of population as of April 1 for year shown.

Persons per square mile is the average number of inhabitants per square mile of land area. These figures are derived by dividing the total number of residents by the number of square miles of land area in the specified geographic area. To determine population per square kilometer, multiply the population per square mile by .3861.

Rank numbers are assigned on the basis of population size, with each area placed in descending order, largest to smallest. Where ties occur—two or more areas with identical populations—the same rank is assigned to each of the tied areas. In such cases, the following rank number is omitted so that the lowest rank is usually equal to the number of areas ranked. Population ranks for 1990, used April 1 corrected data and 1996 July 1 data, respectively.

The Census Bureau estimates the number of foreign immigrants who move into a county during the estimate interval. The county estimates are based on the national estimate of foreign migration developed by the Census Bureau. Estimates include emigration from the United States and the immigration of refugees, legal immigrants, undocumented immigrants, net movement from Puerto Rico, and federal and civilian citizen movement from abroad. The national estimate of the number of undocumented immigrants is allocated to states by using the distribution of the foreign-born population who arrived between 1985 and 1990 and were enumerated as residents in the 1990 census. Legal immigrants and refugees are distributed to counties on the basis of county of intended residence as reported to the Immigration and Naturalization Service.

Estimated net domestic migration is based on individual federal income tax returns. The Census Bureau determines the status of the filer by noting the address, used as a proxy for place of residence, on tax returns filed in the prior year and in the estimate year. The filers are categorized in each county into: (1) inmigrants (INS), (2) outmigrants (OUTS), and (3) nonmigrants (NONMOVERS). The Census Bureau derives a net migration rate for each county based on the difference between the inmigration and outmigration of tax filers and his or her dependents. This rate is used to produce the estimate. If this figure is preceded by a minus sign (-), the figure indicates net outmigration; otherwise, the figure represents net inmigration.

For further discussion of the methodology and guidance in the selection of a particular series, see sources.

Table A-2. Population by Residence and Projections

Metropolitan and nonmetropolitan area population;
   total, 1994 and 1990 and percent change 1990-1994;
Projections, series A and B, 2000, 2005, and 2010.

Source: Metropolitan areas—U.S. Bureau of the Census, 1990 Census of Population and Housing, Supplementary Reports, *Metropolitan Areas as Defined by the Office of Management and Budget, June 30, 1993*, (1990-CPH-S-1-1); 1990 Census of Population and Housing, Population and Housing Unit Counts (CPH-2-1); Current Population Reports, P25-1127 and Population Paper Listings PPL-27.

Projections—U.S. Bureau of the Census, Population Paper Listings, *Population Projections for States by Age, Sex, Race, and Hispanic Origin: 1995 to 2025*, PPL-47, October 1996.

Data for metropolitan areas refer to 253 metropolitan statistical areas and 18 consolidated metropolitan statistical areas defined by the U.S. Office of Management and Budget as of June 30, 1995; nonmetropolitan is the area outside metropolitan areas.

The population projections are the results of using the cohort-component method. This method requires separate assumptions for each of the components of population change: births, deaths, internal migration, and international migration. Series A is a modified linear trend of the patterns of state-to-state migration observed from 1975-76 through 1993-94. Series B is the economic model, which uses the Bureau of Economic Analysis employment projections.

Table A-3. Population by Age Group and Sex

Population, by age, 1996, and percent of population under 18 and 65 years and over, 1996, 1990, and 1980;
Males per 100 females, 1996.

Source: Age—U.S. Bureau of the Census, Press release CB97-64; Population for computation—U.S. Bureau of the Census, 1990 Census of Population and Housing, Population and Housing Unit Counts, (CPH-2); Sex—U.S. Bureau of the Census, Internet site <http:// www.census.gov/population/ estimates/state/96agesex.txt> (accessed 21 July 1997).

For 1996, age represents the number of completed years from birth to July 1; for 1990, data show completed years from birth to April 1.

The method used to produce age and sex population estimates is an updated version of a component procedure that has been modified to estimate state populations by single year of age and sex. The component procedures apply only to the population under 65 years of age. For each individual age, the estimating procedure follows the standard demographic formula of $P^1 = P^0 + B - D + M$, where P^1 is the population on the estimate date; P^0 is the population on the census date; B and D are the births and deaths occurring during the estimate period (between the census and the estimate date); and M is the net migration (including net immigration from abroad) occurring during the estimate period. The population estimates for ages 65 and over are derived using changes in medicare enrollment.

Table A-4. Series A Population Projections by Age Group

Population projections by age, 2000 and 2005 and percent of population in 2000—under 18 and 65 years and over.

Source: U.S. Bureau of the Census, Population Paper Listings, *Population Projections for States by Age, Sex, Race, and Hispanic Origin: 1995 to 2025,* PPL-47, October 1996.

The projections for age were prepared using a cohort component method whereby each component of population change—births, deaths, internal migration, and international migration—is projected separately for each birth cohort by sex and race. Series A is the preferred series model and uses state-to-state migration observed from 1975-76 through 1993-94. The source also contains a description of the process by which the cohort-component method is then applied to produce the projections.

Table A-5. Population by Race

White, Black, Asian and Pacific Islander, and American Indian, Eskimo, and Aleut, 1990, 1996, and 2000 projections;
Percent of total, White, Black, Asian and Pacific Islander, and American Indian, Eskimo, and Aleut, 1996.

Source: Race—U.S. Bureau of the Census, *Estimates of the Population of States by Race and Hispanic Origin: July 1, 1996;* Internet site <http://www.census.gov/population/estimates/state/srh/srhus96.txt> (accessed 04 March 1998). Projection—U.S. Bureau of the Census, Population Paper Listings, *Population Projections for States by Age, Sex, Race, and Hispanic Origin: 1995 to 2025,* PPL-47, October 1996.

The White population includes persons who indicated their race as "White" or reported entries such as Canadian, German, Italian, Lebanese, near Eastern, Arab, or Polish.

The Black population includes persons who indicated their race as "Black or Negro" or indicated their race as African American, Afro-American, Black Puerto Rican, Jamaican, Nigerian, West Indian, or Haitian.

The American Indian, Eskimo, and Aleut population includes persons who indicated their race as Indian (American) or who did not indicate a specific race category but reported the name of an Indian tribe, as well as persons who indicated their race as Eskimo or Aleut.

The Asian and Pacific Islander population includes persons who indicated their race as Chinese, Filipino, Japanese, Asian Indian, Korean, Vietnamese, Hawaiian, Samoan, and Guamanian, as well as persons who provided write-in entries of such Asian and Pacific Islander groups as Cambodian, Laotian, Pakistani, and Fiji Islander. Also, persons who did not classify themselves in one of the specific race categories but wrote in an entry indicating one of the specific categories were classified accordingly.

The projections for race were prepared using a cohort component method whereby each component of population change— births, deaths, internal migration, and international migration— is projected separately for each birth cohort by sex and race. Series A is the preferred series

model and uses state-to-state migration observed from 1975-76 through 1993-94. The source also contains a description of the process by which the cohort-component method is then applied to produce the projections.

For a detailed description of methodology and data accuracy, see source.

Table A-6. Hispanic Origin, Immigrants Admitted, and Households

Hispanic origin and non-Hispanic White, 1990, 1996, and 2000 projections;
Percent of total, Hispanic origin, and non-Hispanic White, 1996;
Immigrants admitted, 1995, 1994, and 1990;
Households, number, percent change, and persons per household, 1996 and 1990

Source: Hispanic origin—U.S. Bureau of the Census, *Estimates of the Population of the States by Race and Hispanic Origin: July 1, 1996;* Internet site <http://www.census.gov/population/estimates/state/srh/srhus96.txt> (accessed 04 March 1998); Projections—U.S. Bureau of the Census, Population Paper Listings, *Population Projections for States by Age, Sex, Race, and Hispanic Origin: 1995 to 2025,* PPL-47, October 1996; Immigrants—U.S. Immigration and Naturalization Service, *Statistical Yearbook,* annual; Households— U.S. Bureau of the Census, *Estimates of Housing Units and Households of States: 1990 and 1996,* Population Paper Listings PPL-73.

Persons of Hispanic origin may be of any race.

Immigrants are identified as aliens (new arrivals and persons adjusting their status) who are admitted for legal permanent residence in the United States. Immigration statistics are prepared from entry visas and change of immigration status forms. Data are shown by state of intended residence.

Households consist of all the persons who occupy a "housing unit;" that is, a house, an apartment or other group of rooms, or single room that constitutes "separate living quarters." A household includes the related family members and all the unrelated persons, if any, such as lodgers, foster children, wards, or employees who share the housing unit. A person living alone or a group of unrelated persons sharing the same housing unit is also counted as a household. The method used to prepare the estimates of households by state is based on national trends and state trends in the adult population (18 years and over) per household and on estimates of the adult population for states.

Persons per household represents the number of persons in households divided by the number of households (or householders).

For a detailed description of methodology and data accuracy, see source.

Table A-7. Live Births and Birth Rates

Births and birth rates, 1996, preliminary, 1990, and 1980; Percent of births to teenage mothers, to unmarried women, and with low birth weight, 1996, preliminary and 1990; Births by race—White, Black, and Hispanic, 1996, preliminary

Source: 1996, preliminary—U.S. National Center for Health Statistics, *Monthly Vital Statistics Report, Births and Deaths: United States, 1996;* Vol. 46, No. 1, Supplement 2, September 11, 1997; 1990 and 1980—U.S. National Center of Health Statistics, *Vital Statistics of the United States*, Vol. 1, *Natality,* annual.

Through the National Vital Statistics System, the National Center for Health Statistics (NCHS) collects and publishes data on births and deaths in the United States. The Division of Vital Statistics obtains information on births and deaths from the registration offices of all states, New York City, and the District of Columbia.

In most areas, practically all births are registered. The most recent test of the completeness of birth registration, conducted on a sample of births from 1964 to 1968, showed that 99.3 percent of all births in the United States during that period were registered.

Birth statistics are limited to events occurring during the year. The data are by place of residence and exclude events occurring to nonresidents of the United States. Births that occur outside the United States are excluded.

Birth rates represent the number of births per 1,000 resident population estimated as of July 1 for 1996 and enumerated as of April 1 for 1980 and 1990 (decennial census years).

For California, Connecticut, Maryland, Michigan, Montana, Nevada, New York, Ohio, and Texas, marital status is inferred from a comparison of the child's and parents' surname on the birth certificate.

Table A-8. Deaths and Death Rates

Deaths and death rates, 1996, preliminary, 1990, and 1980;
Infant death, number and rate, 1995, 1990, 1980; White, and Black, 1995.

Source: 1996 preliminary—U.S. National Center for Health Statistics, *Monthly Vital Statistics Report, Births and Deaths: United States, 1996,* Vol. 46, No.1, Supplement 2, September 11, 1997. 1990 and 1980—*Vital Statistics of the United States*, Vol. II, *Mortality,* annual. Infant deaths—U.S. National Center for Health Statistics, *Monthly Vital Statistics Report, Report of Final Mortality Statistics, 1995*, Vol. 45, No. 11, Supplement 2, June 12, 1997.

Through the National Vital Statistics System, the National Center for Health Statistics (NCHS) collects and publishes data on deaths in the United States. The Division of Vital Statistics obtains information on deaths from the registration offices of all states, New York City, and the District of Columbia.

In most areas, practically all deaths are registered. The most recent test of the completeness of birth registration, conducted on a sample of births from 1964 to 1968, showed that 99.3 percent of all births in the United States during that period were registered. No comparable information is available for deaths, but it is generally believed that death registration in the United States is at least as complete as birth registration.

Death statistics are limited to events occurring during the year. The data are by place of residence and exclude events occurring to nonresidents of the United States. Deaths that occur outside the United States are excluded.

Death rates represent the number of deaths per 1,000 resident population estimated as of July 1 for 1996 and enumerated as of April 1 for 1980 and 1990 (decennial census years).

Table A-9. Death Rates by Cause: 1994

Death rates by cause, 1994.

Source: U.S. National Center for Health Statistics, *Monthly Vital Statistics Report, Advance Report of Final Mortality Statistics, 1994*, Vol. 45, Number 3, Supplement, September 30, 1996.

Mortality statistics by cause of death are compiled in accordance with World Health Organization regulations, which specify that member nations classify causes of death according to the International Classification of Diseases (ICD). Data for all years are based upon the ninth revision of the ICD, which was employed beginning in 1979.

Table A-10. Community Hospitals

Total, beds, patients admitted, average daily census, personnel, outpatient visits, average cost per day, and average cost per stay, 1995 and 1990.

Source: American Hospital Association, Chicago, IL, *Hospital Statistics, 1996-97* and prior years (copyright).

Statistics for hospitals were compiled by the American Hospital Association (AHA) from surveys of all hospitals in the United States and its outlying areas. Unregistered hospitals, as well as those registered by the AHA, are included. Hospitals were asked to report data for a full year ending September 30.

Community hospitals are defined as a nonfederal short-term (average length of stay less than 30 days) general or other special hospital, excluding psychiatric and tuberculosis hospitals and hospital units of institutions, whose service and facilities are available to the public. Institutions and services commonly referred to as convalescent and resting homes, nursing homes, infirmaries, old-age homes, and sanatoriums are excluded almost entirely.

Data for beds are based on the average number of beds in the facilities over the reporting period. The average daily census includes inpatients receiving care each day; it excludes newborns. Personnel figures include full-time and full-time equivalents of part-time personnel (calculated on the basis that two part-time persons equal one full-time person) but exclude medical and dental interns, residents, and other trainees. Outpatient visits include visits by patients who are not lodged in the hospital while receiving medical, dental, or other services. Total cost per patient is based on total hospital expenses (payroll, employee benefits, professional fees, supplies, etc.) Data have been adjusted for outpatients visits.

Table A-11. Physicians, Nurses, Health Insurance, and AIDS

Physicians, number and rate, 1995, 1992, and 1990;
Nurses, number and rate, 1995 and 1992;
Persons not covered by health insurance, number and percent, 1995 and 1990;
AIDS cases reported, total and percent, 1981-96.

Source: Physicians—American Medical Association, Chicago, IL, *Physician Characteristics and Distribution in the U.S.*, annual (copyright). Nurses—U.S. Department of Health and Human Services, Health Resources and Services Administration, unpublished data. Persons not covered by health insurance—U.S. Bureau of the Census, *Health Insurance Coverage: 1995 - Table 2*, published 26 September 1996, Internet site <http://www.census.gov/hhes/hltins/cover95/c95tab2.html>. AIDS cases—U.S. Centers for Disease Control and Prevention, Atlanta, GA, unpublished data.

The number of physicians is based on information contained in the American Medical Association (AMA) Physician Masterfile. The file has been maintained by the AMA since 1906 and includes information on every physician in the country and on those graduates of American medical schools who are temporarily practicing overseas. The file also includes members and nonmembers of the AMA and graduates of foreign medical schools who are in the United States and meet U.S. educational standards for primary recognition as physicians. Thus, all physicians comprising the total manpower pool are included on the file. However, these data do not include federal physicians and nonfederal physicians who are temporarily in foreign locations. These data also exclude doctors of osteopathy and physicians with addresses unknown.

Masterfile data are obtained from both AMA surveys and inputs from physicians, other organizations, and institutions. Primary sources are as follows: medical schools, hospitals, medical societies, national boards, state licensing agencies, Educational Commission for Foreign Medical Graduates, Surgeon General of the U.S. Government, American Board of Medical Specialties, and physicians. The file utilizes data from primary sources only. For details, see source.

All rates are per 100,000 civilian population estimated as of July 1 for year shown by the U.S. Bureau of the Census.

Data for nurses are based on a survey conducted by the Division of Nursing, Bureau of Health Professions. The data represent the number of registered nurses employed in nursing as of December 31 of year shown.

Data on notifiable diseases are compiled by the Public Health Service (PHS) at its Centers for Disease Control and Prevention in Atlanta, Georgia. The list of diseases is revised annually and includes those which, by mutual agreement of the states and PHS, are communicable diseases of national importance.

Acquired Immune Deficiency syndrome (AIDS) data are based on a survey of state budget analysts, commissioners of health and AIDS coordinators, and other state agencies with AIDS programs.

Table A-12. Public School Fall Enrollment

Public school enrollment, fall—total, kindergarten through grade 8, grades 9-12; and total enrollment rate, 1994, preliminary, 1993, 1990, and 1980.

Source: U.S. National Center for Education Statistics (NCES), *Digest of Education Statistics*, annual.

The National Center for Education Statistics defines a school as "a division of the school system consisting of a group of pupils composed of one or more grade groups, organized as one unit with one or more teachers to give instruction of a defined type, and housed in a school plant of one or more buildings. More than one school may be housed in a school plant, as is the case when the elementary and secondary programs are housed in the same school plant, i.e., combined elementary and secondary schools."

Public schools are schools controlled and operated by publicly elected or appointed officials and derive primary support from public funds.

Data are from the National Center for Education Statisticsand are based on censuses of elementary and secondary schools and are subject to nonsampling error. For a discussion of the methodological details, see the source.

Table A-13. Public Elementary and Secondary Schools

Revenue—total and by source of funds, 1993-1994 and total 1990-1991;
Expenditures—total and per capita, 1993-1994 and 1990-1991, current, 1993-1994;
Teachers, total and average salary, 1994-1995.

Source: Revenue and expenditures—U.S. National Center for Education Statistics, *Digest of Education Statistics*, annual; Teachers—National Education Association, Washington, DC, *Estimates of School Statistics, 1995-96 (table5).*, (Copyright by the National Education Association. All rights reserved.)

Revenue includes gifts, tuition, and fees from patrons. Expenditures are charges incurred, whether paid or unpaid, which are presumed to benefit the current fiscal year. For elementary and secondary schools, these include all charges for current outlays plus capital outlays and interest on school debt.

Current expenditures include expenditures for operating local public schools, excluding capital outlay and interest on school debt. These expenditures include items such as salaries for school personnel, fixed charges, student transportation, school books and materials, and energy costs.

Data for public school teachers cover the school year ending in June of year shown.

Data from the National Education Association on classroom teachers' salaries are revised periodically by the Association. Teachers at the elementary and secondary school levels, as presented here, include grades kindergarten through 6 and 7 through 12, respectively.

Average salary is the arithmetic mean of the salaries of elementary and secondary school teachers. This figure is the average gross salary before deductions for social security, retirement, health insurance, etc.

Table A-14. Educational Attainment and Institutions of Higher Education

Public high school graduates—total, 1996, est., 1995, 1990, 1980;
Percent of population by educational attainment and dropouts, 1990;
Institutions of higher education—total, 1994, 1993, and 1990.

Source: Public high school graduates and institutions of higher education—U.S. National Center for Education Statistics (NCES), *Digest of Education Statistics*, annual; Education attainment by degree—U.S. Bureau of the Census, 1990 Census of Population, CPH-L-96.

Data for public high school graduates include graduates of regular day school programs but exclude other programs and persons receiving high school equivalency certificates. The data also exclude graduates of subcollegiate departments of institutions of higher education, federal schools for Indians and on federal installations, and residential schools for exceptional children. The national total includes estimates for nonresponding states.

Education attainment by degree is based on a sample of the census that was conducted by the Bureau of the Census as of April 1, 1990. Persons whose education was received in a foreign school system or an ungraded school were instructed to report the approximate equivalent in the regular American school system. Persons who were currently attending or did not finish the highest grade were tabulated as having completed the previous grade or year.

A dropout is a person 16 to 19 years old who is not in regular school and who has not completed the 12th grade or received a general equivalency degree.

Higher education is identified by NCES as "the study beyond secondary school at an institution that offers programs terminating in an associate, baccalaureate, or higher degrees." The data shown are based upon censuses of institutions listed in U.S. National Center for Education Statistics, *Education Directory: Colleges and Universities* and are subject to nonsampling error. See the sources for methodological details.

Total for institutions of higher education includes military academies not distributed by state.

Table A-15. Institutions of Higher Education

Fall enrollment—total, public, and private, 1994, 1993, and 1990;
Public institutions current funds revenue—total, tuition and fees, state and federal appropriations, 1993-1994, and total 1990-1991;
Public institutions current funds expenditures—total and education and general, 1993-1994 and total, 1990-1991.

Source: U.S. National Center for Education Statistics, *Digest of Education Statistics*, annual.

Higher education is identified by NCES as "the study beyond secondary school at an institution that offers programs terminating in an associate, baccalaureate, or higher degrees." The data shown are based upon censuses of institutions listed in U.S. National Center for Education Statistics, *Education Directory: Colleges and Universities* and are subject to nonsampling error. See the sources for methodological details.

Current funds revenue is money received during the current fiscal year from revenue which can be used to pay obligations currently due and surpluses reappropriated for the current fiscal year.

Tuition and fees are identified as a payment or charge for instruction or compensation for services, privileges, or use of equipment, books, or other goods.

Federal appropriations are budget authorities provided through the congressional appropriation process that permit federal agencies to incur obligations and to make payments.

Current funds expenditures are money spent to meet current operating costs, including salaries, wages, utilities, student services, public services, research libraries, scholarships and fellowships, auxiliary enterprises, hospitals, and independent operations. Excludes loans, capital expenditures, and investments.

Table A-16. Crimes and Crime Rates

Number of offenses known to police—total, 1995, 1994, and 1990, and violent, 1995;
Offenses per 100,000 population—total, 1995, 1994, and 1990 and by type, 1995.

Source: U.S. Federal Bureau of Investigation, *Crime in the United States*, annual (related Internet site <http://www.fbi.gov/publish.htm>).

Through the voluntary contribution of crime statistics by law enforcement agencies across the United States, the Uniform Crime Reporting (UCR) Program provides periodic assessments of crime in the nation as measured by offenses coming to the attention of the law enforcement community. The Committee of Uniform Crime Records of the International Association of Chiefs of Police initiated this voluntary national data-collection effort in 1930. UCR Program contributors compile and submit their crime data in one of two means: either directly to the FBI or through the state UCR Programs.

Users of these data are cautioned about comparing data between areas based on these respective Crime Index figures. Assessing criminality and law enforcement's responses from area to area should encompass many elements (i.e., population density and urbanization; population composition; stability of population; modes of transportation; commuting patterns and highway systems; economic conditions; cultural conditions; family conditions; climate; effective strength and emphasis of law enforcement agencies; attitudes of citizenry toward crime; and crime reporting practices). These elements may have a significant impact on crime reporting.

Not all law enforcement agencies provide data for all 12 months of the year. Data are as reported to the FBI.

Seven offenses, because of their seriousness, frequency of occurrence, and likelihood of being reported to police, were initially selected to serve as an index for evaluating fluctuations in the volume of crime. These crimes, known as the Crime Index offenses, were murder and nonnegligent manslaughter, forcible rape, robbery, aggravated assault, burglary, larceny-theft, and motor vehicle theft. By congressional mandate, arson was added as the eighth Index offense in 1979. Only the Modified Index includes arson; which is not shown in this table.

Rates are based on resident population enumerated as of April 1 for decennial census years and estimated as of July 1 for other years. Population figures used for these rates are from the FBI.

Violent crimes include four crime categories: (1) Murder and nonnegligent manslaughter, as defined in the UCR Program, is the willful (nonnegligent) killing of one human being by another. This offense excludes deaths caused by negligence, suicide, or accident; justifiable homicides; and attempts to murder or assaults to murder. (2) Forcible rape is the carnal knowledge of a female forcibly and against her will. Assaults or attempts to commit rape by force or threat of force are also included; however, statutory rape (without force) and other sex offenses are excluded. (3) Robbery is the taking or attempting to take anything of value from the care, custody, or control of a person or persons by force or threat of force or violence and/or by putting the victim in fear. (4) Aggravated assault is an unlawful attack by one person upon another for the purpose of inflicting severe or aggravated bodily injury. This type of assault is usually accompanied by the use of a weapon or by means likely to produce death or great bodily harm. Attempts are included since an injury does not necessarily have to result when a gun, knife, or other weapon is used, which could and probably would result in a serious personal injury if the crime were successfully completed.

Property crimes include four crime categories: (1) Burglary is the unlawful entry of a structure to commit a felony or theft. (2) Larceny-theft is the unlawful taking, carrying, leading, or riding away of property from the possession or constructive possession of another. It includes crimes such as shoplifting, pocket picking, purse snatching, thefts from motor vehicles, thefts of motor vehicle parts and accessories, bicycle thefts, etc., in which no use of force, violence, or fraud occurs. This crime category does not include embezzlement, "con" games, forgery, worthless checks, and motor vehicle theft. (3) Motor vehicle theft is the theft or attempted theft of a motor vehicle. This definition excludes the taking of a motor vehicle for temporary use by those persons having lawful access. (4) Arson is any willful or malicious burning or attempt to burn, with or without intent to defraud, a dwelling house, public building, motor vehicle or aircraft, personal property of another, etc. Only fires determined through investigation to have been willfully or maliciously set are classified as arson. Fires of suspicious or unknown origins are excluded.

Table A-17. Law Enforcement

State and local government employment, police protection and corrections—number, 1995-1990 and rate, 1995;
Prisoners under jurisdiction of federal and state authorities—number, 1995 and 1990, and percent change, 1990-1995, and rate, 1995;
Prisoners executed—number, 1995, and period 1977 to 1995;
Prisoners under death sentence—number, 1995 and 1990.

Source: Employment—U.S. Bureau of the Census, Census of Governments, *Public Employment 1990,* series GE, No. 1 and Internet site <http://www.census.gov/govs/apes/95stlus.txt>(accessed 26 June 1997). Prisoners—U.S. Bureau of Justice Statistics, *Prisoners*, annual; Capital punishment—U.S. Bureau of Justice Statistics, *Capital Punishment*, annual (related Internet site <http://www.ojp.usdoj.gov/bjs/correct.htm>).

Data for police protection employment cover all activities concerned with the enforcement of law and order, including coroners' offices, police-training academies, investigation bureaus, and local jails, "lockups," or other detention facilities not intended to serve as correctional facilities.

Data for corrections employment cover all activities pertaining to the confinement and correction of adults and minors accused or convicted of criminal offenses. Any pardon, probation, and parole activities also are included here.

The number for police protection and corrections shown is full-time-equivalent employment. This is a computed statistic representing the number of full-time employees that could have been employed at the same total payroll cost if all personnel were engaged on a full-time basis at the average monthly pay applying to full-time workers.

Data for prisoners under federal and state jurisdiction were collected by the Bureau of Justice Statistics. Adults convicted of criminal activity may be given a prison or jail sentence. The data represent all persons under the jurisdiction of federal and state authorities rather than those in custody of those authorities.

Data on number of executions are for persons executed under crime authority. Fifty-six persons were executed in 1995, bringing to 313 the total executed since 1977. The increase in the pace of executions comes as many inmates on death row neared the end of a series of appeals and as the courts became increasingly reluctant to sanction a lengthy appeals process in capital-punishment cases.

Data on persons under sentence of death are collected annually for the Bureau of Justice Statistics as part of the National Prisoner Statistics Program. Data are obtained from the departments of corrections in each of the 50 states and the District of Columbia. The following states and the District of Columbia did not have the death penalty as of December 31, 1995: Alaska, Hawaii, Iowa, Maine, Massachusetts, Michigan, Minnesota, North Dakota, Rhode Island, Vermont, West Virginia, and Wisconsin. The data exclude prisoners under sentence of death who remained within local correctional systems pending exhaustion of the appellate process or who had not been committed to prison.

Table A-18. Housing Starts, Sales, Vacancy Rates, and Ownership

Housing starts—number and percent single family units, 1996 and number, 1995, 1994, and 1990;
Existing home sales—number, 1997-1995, and 1990;
Vacancy rates—rental and homeowner, 1996 and 1990;
Homeownership rates—1996, 1995, and 1990.

Source: Housing starts—National Association of Home Builders, Economic Division, Washington, DC. Data provided by Econometria Forcasting Service; Existing home sales—National Association of REALTORS, Washington, DC, *Real Estate Outlook: Market Trends & Insights*, (copyright). Vacancy and homeownership rates—U.S. Bureau of the Census, *Housing Vacancy Survey Annual Statistics: 1996*, Internet site <http://www.census.gov/hhes/www/housing/hvs/annual96> (accessed 15 September 1997).

Data for housing starts were supplied to the National Association of Home Builders by Econometria Forcasting Service For details about data, please contact source.

Existing home sales data are from the National Association of REALTORS. See source for detail of statistics presented (copyright).

Vacancy rates and homeownership rates are based on data obtained from two surveys conducted by the Bureau of the Census: the Current Population Survey/Housing Vacancy Survey (CPS/HVS). Beginning in 1994, new weighting procedures based on the 1990 decennial census were implemented. In addition, the survey data collection procedures became totally computerized. Caution should be used when comparing current data with 1990 data shown here.

A housing unit is vacant if no one is living in it at the time of the interview, unless its occupants are only temporarily absent. In addition, a vacant unit may be one which is owned entirely by persons who have a usual residence elsewhere.

Rental vacancy rate is the proportion of the rental inventory which is vacant for rent. The homeowner vacancy rate is the proportion of the homeowner inventory which is vacant for sale.

The proportion of owner households to occupied households is termed the homeownership rate. It is computed by dividing the number of owner households by the number of occupied households.

Table A-19. Civilian Labor Force and Employment

Civilian noninstitutional population, 1996, 1995, and 1990, male and female, 1996;
Civilian labor force—number and employed, 1996, 1995, and 1990, male and female, 1996.

Source: Civilian noninstitutional population, civilian labor force, and employed for 1996 and 1995—U.S. Bureau of Labor Statistics, Internet site <http://stats.bls.gov/news.release/srgune.t01.htm> (accessed 08 July 1997). Male, female, and 1990 data—U.S. Bureau of Labor Statistics, unpublished data; related publication, *Employment and Earnings*, monthly, May 1997.

Data are based on the Current Population Survey (CPS) and are annual averages of monthly figures. The survey was redesigned in the early 1990s. Some concepts and definitions were revised plus the questionnaire and collection methodology. As a result, the 1990 data are not strictly comparable to later data.

The civilian noninstitutional population includes persons 16 years of age and older residing in the 50 states and the District of Columbia who are not inmates of institutions (e.g., penal and mental facilities, homes for the aged) and those who are not on active duty in the Armed Forces.

The civilian labor force comprises all civilians classified as employed or unemployed in accordance with the criteria described below.

The civilian employed are all civilians who did any work as paid employees or in their own business during the survey week or who worked 15 hours or more as unpaid workers in an enterprise operated by a family member.

Persons temporarily absent from a job because of illness, bad weather, a strike, or personal reasons also are counted as employed whether they were paid by their employer or were seeking other jobs.

Each employed person is counted only once, even if he or she holds more than one job.

The unemployed are all civilians who did not work during the survey week, who were available for work during the survey week (except for temporary illness), and who made specific efforts to find a job in the prior 4 weeks. Persons waiting to be recalled to a job from which they had been laid off also are counted as unemployed.

Table A-20. Civilian Labor Force and Unemployment

Employment/population ratio—male and female, 1996; Unemployment—total, rate, and participation rate, male and female, 1996; total and rate, 1995 and 1990.

Source: Male, female and 1990 data—U.S. Bureau of Labor Statistics, unpublished data; related publication, *Employment and Earnings,* monthly, May 1997. Unemployment total for 1995 and 1996 data—U.S. Bureau of Labor Statistics, Internet site <http://stats.bls.gov/news.release/srgune.t01.htm> (accessed 08 July 1997).

Employment/population ratio is civilian employment as a percentage of civilian noninstitutional population.

The unemployed are all civilians who did not work during the survey week, who were available for work during the survey week (except for temporary illness), and who made specific efforts to find a job in the prior 4 weeks. Persons waiting to be recalled to a job from which they have been laid off also are counted as unemployed.

For details on how the data were derived, see the source. See text for A-19 for information on the Current Population Survey.

Table A-21. Employment and Average Annual Pay by Industry

Employment—by private industries and government, 1996; Average annual pay—by private industries and government, 1996, preliminary

Source: Employment (except wholesale and retail)—U.S. Bureau of Labor Statistics, *Employment and Earnings,* monthly, May issues; Wholesale and retail employment—U.S. Bureau of Labor Statistics, Internet site <http://www.bls.gov/cgi-bin/dsrv> (accessed 10 October 1997); Annual average pay—U.S. Bureau of Labor Statistics, Internet site <http://stats.bls.gov/pub/news.release/annpay.t04.htm> (accessed 11 September 1997).

Data for employment and average annual pay, by industries and government, were obtained from an establishment survey conducted in cooperation with state agencies.

The survey gathers information on nonfarm wage and salary employment, average weekly hours, average hourly earnings, and average weekly earnings from a sample of over 340,000 establishments. Data refer to persons on establishment payrolls who received pay for any part of the pay period that included the 12th of the month. See the source for methodological details. Industry statistics are classified in accordance with the *1987 Standard Industrial Classification Manual.*

Average annual pay was computed by dividing total annual payrolls of employers covered by unemployment insurance programs by average monthly employment for these employers. Included in the annual payroll data are bonuses, the cash value of meals and lodging when supplied, and tips and other gratuities. Average annual pay only approximates annual earnings because an individual may not be employed by the same employer all year or may work for more than one employer.

Table A-22. Employment, Average Annual Pay, and Union Membership

Employment—1996 and 1990;
Average annual pay—1996 preliminary and 1990;
Labor union membership—union members, workers covered by union, 1996 and 1985 and percent of workers, 1996 and 1985.

Source: Employment—U.S. Bureau of Labor Statistics, *Employment and Earnings*, monthly, May issues; Average annual pay, 1990—U.S. Bureau of Labor Statistics, USDL 92-631, October 1992; Average annual pay, 1996—U.S. Bureau of Labor Statistics, *State and Industry Average Annual Pay for 1995 and 1996 Percent Change in Pay for All Covered Workers*, (related Internet site <http://stats.bls.gov/news.release/annpay.t04.htm>); Union members—The Bureau of National Affairs, Inc., Washington, DC, *Union Membership and Earnings Data Book: Compilations from the Current Population Survey, 1997 edition, (copyright by BNA PLUS)*, authored by Barry Hirsh and David Macpherson of Florida State University (related Internet site <http://www.bna.com/bnaplus>).

See text for A-21 for discussion of employment and average annual pay.

Union membership data are based on the Current Population Survey and represent annual averages of monthly figures for wage and salary workers in agriculture and nonagriculture. Data represent union members by place of residence and exclude unemployed members. See source for details.

Table A-23. Personal Income

Personal income and personal income per capita—current and constant (1992) dollars, 1996, preliminary, 1995, 1990 and percent change, constant (1992) dollars, 1990-1996;
Percent distribution, constant (1992) dollars, 1996 and 1990.

Source: 1996 and 1995—U.S. Bureau of Economic Analysis, *Survey of Current Business*, Volume 77, Number 5, May 1997; 1990—U.S. Bureau of Economic Analysis, *Survey of Current Business*, Volume 76, Number 10, October 1996.

Personal income is defined as the income received by, or on behalf of, all residents of the state. It consists of the income received by persons from all sources; that is, from participation in production, from both government and business transfer payments, and from government interest (which is treated like a transfer payment).

Persons consists of individuals, nonprofit institutions that primarily serve individuals, private noninsured welfare funds, and private trust funds.

Personal income is defined as the sum of wage and salary disbursements, other labor income, proprietors' income with inventory valuation and capital consumption adjustments, personal dividend income, personal interest income, and transfer payment to persons, less personal contributions for social insurance.

Per capita income shown in this table is calculated as the personal income of the residents of the state divided by the population of state as of July 1 for 1996, 1995, and 1990 and as of July 1 for 1990. The personal consumption expenditure deflator from the National Income and Product Accounts was used to convert current dollar figures into constant (1992) dollars.

Table A-24. Household and Family Income and Poverty

Median household income—Current and constant (1995) dollars, 1995, 1994, and 1990;
Median income for 4-person family—current and constant (1995) dollars, 1995 and 1990;
Persons below poverty level—number and percent, 1995, 1994, and 1990, children, 1995.

Source: Median household income—U.S. Bureau of the Census, Current Population Report, P60-193; Median income for 4-person family—U.S. Bureau of the Census, Housing and Household Economic Statistics Division, Internet site <http://www.census.gov/hhes/income/4person.html> (accessed 03 July 1997); Persons below poverty level—U.S. Bureau of the Census, *Current Population Reports*, P-60-194; Poverty Thresholds: 1995 chart—Internet site <http://www.census.gov/hhes/poverty/theshld/thres95.html> (accessed 19 November 1997)

Median household income data are based on the Current Population Survey (CPS). The CPS is designed to collect reliable data on income primarily at the national level and secondarily at the regional level. When the income data are tabulated by state, the estimates are considered less reliable and, therefore, particular caution should be used when trying to interpret the results.

Median family income is based on total money income received in the previous calendar year by all family members 15 years old and over, tabulated for all families. Family income differs from household income by excluding income received by household members not related to the householder, persons living alone, and others in nonfamily households.

Families and persons were classified as below poverty level if their total family income or unrelated individual income was less than the poverty threshold specified for the applicable family size, age of householder, and number of related children under 18 present (see table below for poverty level thresholds).

Poverty status is determined for all families (and, by implication, all family members). For persons not in families, poverty status is determined by their income in relation to the appropriate poverty threshold. Thus, two unrelated individuals living together may not have the same poverty status. The poverty thresholds are updated every year to reflect changes in the Consumer Price Index. See source for more details.

Poverty Thresholds 1995, by Size of Family

Size of family	Weighted average thresholds
1 person (unrelated individual)	7,763
Under 65 years old	7,929
65 years old and over	7,309
2 persons.......................................	9,933
Householder under 65 years old................	10,259
Householder 65 years old and over	9,219
3 persons.......................................	12,158
4 persons.......................................	15,569
5 persons	18,408
6 persons.......................................	20,804
7 persons	23,502
8 persons.......................................	26,237
9 persons	31,280

Table A-25. Energy Consumption

Energy consumption—total, 1994, 1993, and 1990, per capita, 1994, and percent change, 1990-1994;
By end-use sector and selected sources, 1994.

Source: U.S. Energy Information Administration, *State Energy Data Report 1994* DOE/EIA-0214(94).

Energy consumption data are estimated using the State Energy Data System, which is maintained by the Energy Information Administration. This system generates data by principal energy sources and major end-use sectors by using existing data surveys that report consumption directly from sales on distribution surveys at the state level. Small quantities of other energy sources for which consistent historical data are not available, such as solar energy obtained by the use of thermal and photovoltaic collectors; wind energy; and geothermal, biomass, and waste energy other than that consumed at the electric utilities, are excluded in these figures.

End-use sectors include residential, commercial, industrial, and transportation. Figures for the residential sector represent energy consumed by private household establishments primarily for space heating, air-conditioning, cooking, and clothes drying. Data for the commercial sector cover energy consumed by nonmanufacturing business establishments, such as hotels and other service enterprises, and health, social, and educational institutions, and energy consumed by federal, state, and local governments. Statistics for the industrial sector include energy consumed in manufacturing, construction, mining, and agricultural establishments. Figures for the transportation sector cover energy consumed to move people and commodities in both the public and private sectors, including military, railroad, vessel bunkering, and marine uses, as well as pipeline transmission of natural gas.

Petroleum consumption refers to the sum of all refined petroleum products supplied. For each refined petroleum product, the amount supplied is calculated by adding production and imports, then subtracting changes in primary stocks and exports. Hydroelectric consumption includes industrial and electric production and net imports of electricity.

Petroleum is a generic term applied to oil and oil products in all forms, such as crude oil, lease condensate, unfinished oils, petroleum products, natural gas plant liquids, and nonhydrocarbon compounds blended into a finished petroleum product. Natural gas is a mixture of hydrocarbons existing in the gaseous phase or in solution with crude oil in underground reservoirs. Coal is a black or brownish-black solid combustible substance formed by the partial decomposition of vegetable matter without access to air. The rank of coal, which includes anthracite, bituminous coal, and lignite, is based on fixed carbon, volatile matter, and heating value. Hydroelectric power is the production of electricity from the kinetic energy of falling water. Nuclear electric power is electricity generated by an electric power plant whose turbines are driven by steam generated in a reactor by heat from the fissioning of nuclear fuel.

Table A-26. Energy Expenditures

Energy expenditures, current and constant (1992) dollars—total, 1994, 1993, and 1990, per capita, 1994 and percent change, 1990-1994;
By end-use sector and selected sources, 1994.

Source: U.S. Energy Information Administration, *State Energy Price and Expenditure Report*, DOE/EIA-0376(94).

Energy expenditure data are derived by multiplying price estimates for the various sources by the consumption estimates, adjusting to remove process fuel and intermediate product consumption.

The expenditures shown represent consumer expenditures; that is, they represent the money spent directly by consumers to purchase energy. They vary widely by state because of differences in population, climate, amount and type of industry, fuel consumed, and other factors. Data presented by end-use sector and selected sources have the same coverage as those for consumption data above.

Table A-27. Electric and Gas Utilities

Electric utility industry—sales to customers and revenue from sales, total, 1995 and 1990, and residential, 1995;
Net generation, total, 1995 and 1990, and percent from coal and nuclear, 1995;
Net summer capability, total, 1995 and 1990.
Gas utility industry—sales to customer and revenue from sales, total, 1995 and 1990.

Source: Electric utility industry—U.S. Energy Information Administration, *Electric Power Annual, Electric Sales and Revenue 1995*, and *Inventory of Power Plants in the United States*, annual. Gas utility industry—American Gas Association, Arlington, VA, *Gas Facts*, annual (copyright).

Electric utility is identified as a corporation, person, agency, authority, or other legal entity or instrumentality that owns and/or operates facilities within the United States, its territories, or Puerto Rico for the generation, transmission, distribution, or sale of electric energy primarily for use by the public. Electric utilities are regulated by local, state, and federal authorities.

Sales to customers is the amount of kilowatthours sold in a given period of time; usually grouped by classes of service, such as residential, commercial, industrial, and other. Other sales include sales for public street and highway lighting, sales to public authorities, sales to railroads and railways, and interdepartmental sales.

The revenue associated with sales to ultimate consumers is the operating revenue reported by the utility. Operating revenue includes energy charges, demand charges, consumer service charges, environmental surcharges, fuel adjustments, and other miscellaneous charges.

Net generation is the gross generation minus plant use from all electric utility owned plants. The energy required for pumping at a pumped-storage plant is regarded as plant use and must be deducted from the gross generation.

Net summer capability is the steady hourly output, which generating equipment is expected to supply to system load exclusive of auxiliary power, as demonstrated by tests at the time of summer peak demand.

The gas utility industry consists of the companies engaged in natural gas transmission and distribution. The data shown are based mainly on figures provided by individual gas companies through the "Uniform Statistical Report." For nonreporting companies (representing approximately 6 percent of the industry), data are estimated.

Table A-28. Motor Vehicle Registrations, Highway Mileage, and Gasoline Tax

Motor vehicle registration—Total, automobile and truck, 1995 and 1990 and per 1,000 population, 1995;
Motorcycle registration—1995;
Highway mileage—total, interstate, other arterial, collector, and local, 1995;
State gasoline tax rate—1995.

Source: U.S. Federal Highway Administration, *Highway Statistics*, annual.

Vehicle registration data are collected by the Federal Highway Administration (FHWA) from state motor vehicle registration agencies. Accordingly, registration practices and dates do vary; data presented here are as near to a calendar-year basis as possible.

Total highway mileage includes roads and streets in the functional systems which are assigned to groups according to the character of service they are intended to provide. The functional systems are (1) arterial highways that generally handle the long trips, (2) collectors facilities that collect and disperse traffic between the arterials and the lower systems, and (3) local roads and streets that primarily serve direct access to residential areas.

The Interstate System connects, as directly as practicable, the nation's principal metropolitan areas, cities, and industrial centers; serves the national defense; and connects at suitable border points with routes of continental importance.

Arterial highways include those roads which generally handle the long trips. Collectors collect and disperse traffic between the arterials and the bottom system. Local roads and streets serve the residential areas, individual farms, and other local areas.

State motor-fuel taxes and related receipts include the revenues from state taxes on all motor vehicle fuels and related receipts in connection with motor-fuel taxation and administration. In most states, however, the tax on special fuels (fuels other than gasoline and gasohol) is applicable only to the gallonage used on the highways. For the few states that apply the tax to all fuel sold, the revenue and refunds covering the nonhighway portion of these special fuels are excluded.

Table A-29. Driver Licenses and Traffic Fatalities

Driver licenses, traffic fatalities, and traffic fatality rate—1995 and 1990;
Persons killed in alcohol-related crashes—number, percent, and by BAC level, 1995 and 1990;
Vehicles involved in fatal crashes—total and large trucks, 1995.

Source: Driver licenses—U.S. Federal Highway Administration, *Highway Statistics,* annual; Traffic fatalities and persons killed in alcohol-related crashes—U.S. Department of Transportation, National Highway Traffic Safety Administration, *Traffic Safety Facts 1995*. Vehicles involved in fatal crashes—National Highway Traffic Safety Administration, *Traffic Safety Facts 1995, Large Trucks.*

Each state and the District of Columbia administers its own driver licensing system. Since 1954 all states have required drivers to be licensed, and since 1959 all states have required examination prior to licensing. Tests of knowledge of state driving laws and practices, vision, and driving proficiency are now required for new licensees.

The National Highway Traffic Safety Administration (NHTSA) has a cooperative agreement with an agency in each state's government to provide information on all qualifying fatal crashes in the state. These agreements are managed by regional contracting Officer's Technical Representatives located in the 10 NHTSA regional offices.

Traffic fatality rate is per 100 million vehicle miles traveled.

A fatal crash involves a motor vehicle in transport on a trafficway in which at least one person dies within 30 days of the crash.

The Blood Alcohol Concentration (BAC) is measured as a percentage of weight of alcohol in the blood (grams/deciliter). A positive BAC level (0.01 g/dl and higher) indicates that alcohol was consumed by the person tested. A BAC level of 0.10 g/dl or more indicates that the person was intoxicated.

NHTSA defines a fatal crash as alcohol related if either a driver or a nonmotorist (usually a pedestrian) had a measurable or estimated blood alcohol concentration (BAC) of 0.01 grams per deciliter (g/dl) or above.

Large trucks involved in fatal crashes are those of 10,000 pounds gross vehicle weight or greater, including single unit trucks and truck tractors.

Table A-30. Business Failures and Starts, Patents, and Bankruptcies

Business failures—total, 1996, preliminary, 1995, 1994, and 1990;
New business starts—total, 1995, 1994, 1993, and 1990, and employment, 1995, 1994, and 1990;
Patents—total, 1996 and 1990;
Bankruptcy cases—Total, 1995 and 1990.

Source: Business failures—The Dun and Bradstreet Corporation, Murray Hill, NJ, *Business Failure Record* (copyright). Business starts—The Dun and Bradstreet Corporation, Murray Hill, NJ, *A Decade of Business Starts, Historical Statistics (by State) 1985-1996* (copyright); Patents—U.S. Patent and Trademark Office, *Patent Counts by Country/State and Year All Patents, All Types January 1, 1977– December 31, 1996,* (related Internet site <http://www.uspto.gov/web/offices/ac/ido/oeipl/tafsctall.pdf>); Bankruptcy cases—Administrative Office of the U.S. Courts, unpublished data; (related Internet site <http://www.uscourts.gov/PressReleases/bkpr.html>).

Business failure statistics include businesses that ceased operations following assignment; bankruptcy; ceased operations with losses to creditors after such actions as foreclosure or attachment; voluntarily withdrew leaving unpaid debts; were involved in court actions such as receivership, reorganization, or arrangement; or voluntarily compromised with creditors.

Business starts and employment consist of newly opened active establishments. They do not include changes in ownership of previously operating businesses, mergers, or changes in business name, location, or legal type.

Business starts and employment is based on true competitive activity in the marketplace rather than state legal filings to record new incorporations, which may or may not indicate the birth of an active business enterprise. The source, Dun and Bradstreet, tracks business starts by tabulating new entries into the company's credit database of more than 10 million businesses, and considers a business to be new if it reports a birthdate within the past 36 months.

Patents includes only U.S. patents granted to residents of the United States. Includes utility, design, plant, and reissues.

Table A-31. Private Nonfarm Establishments, Employment, and Payroll

Establishments—total, 1994 and 1990, employment size class, 1994 and net change, 1990-1994;
Employment—total, 1994 and 1990, employment size class, 1994;
Annual payroll—1994 and 1990.

Source: Establishments, employment, and annual payroll, 1994 and 1990—U.S. Bureau of the Census, *County Business Patterns*, on diskette, annual; Employment-size class, 1994—U.S. Bureau of the Census, *County Business Patterns*, CD-ROM, annual; (Related publications: U.S. Bureau of the Census, *County Business Patterns*, annual, one publication for each state, DC, and US.)

Figures for private nonfarm establishments are published in County Business Patterns (CBP), an annual report series. The data were obtained from censuses and surveys conducted by the Bureau of the Census and administrative records from the Internal Revenue Service (IRS).

Industry classifications are based on the *1987 Standard Industrial Classification (SIC) Manual*. The 1987 edition of the manual represents major revisions from the 1972 edition and its 1977 supplement. For more information on these revisions, see Appendix A of the 1987 SIC manual.

An establishment is a single physical location at which business is conducted or where services or industrial operations are performed. It is not necessarily identical with a company or enterprise, which may consist of one establishment or more. Establishment counts represent the number of locations determined to be active anytime during the year.

Paid employment consists of full- or part-time employees, including salaried officers and executives of corporations, who were on the payroll in the pay period including March 12. Included are employees on paid sick leave, holidays, and vacations; not included are proprietors and partners of unincorporated businesses.

Total annual payroll includes all forms of compensation, such as salaries, wages, commissions, bonuses, vacation allowances, sick-leave pay, and the value of payments in kind (e.g., free meals and lodging), paid during the year to all employees. Tips and gratuities received by employees from patrons and reported to employers are included. Also included are amounts paid to officers and executives of corporations of unincorporated businesses; however, it does not include profit or other compensation of proprietors or partners. Payroll is reported before deductions for social security, income tax, insurance, union dues, etc. The definition of payroll is the same as that used by the IRS on form 941.

Table A-32. Exports, Foreign Investment, and International Visitor Travel Impact

Merchandise exports—total, 1996, 1995, and 1991, percent change, 1991-1996, percent to Canada and Mexico, 1996;
Foreign direct investment—Gross book value of property, 1994 and 1990, employment, 1994 and 1990 and percent of business, 1994;
International visitor travel impact—expenditures, employment, and payroll generated, 1994 and 1990.

Source: Exports—U.S. International Trade Administration, Office of Trade and Economic Analysis, Internet site <http://www.ita.doc.gov/industry/otea/state> (accessed 08 September 1997); Foreign direct investment—U.S. Bureau of Economic Analysis, *Survey of Current Business*, May 1995, and *Foreign Direct Investment in the United States, Operations of U.S. Affiliates of Foreign Companies*, annual; and *Foreign Direct Investment in the United States, 1992 Benchmark Survey*; International visitor travel impact—U.S. International Trade Administration/Tourism Industries, *Impact of International Spending on State Economies, 1994*, Internet site <http://tinet.doc.gov/imp/imp_tab.htm> (accessed 30 January 1997), and unpublished data.

State export values are from the U.S. Census Bureau's Exporter Location (EL) series. The EL series allocates exports to states according to the location of the exporter of record. The exporter of record is not necessarily the entity that produced the merchandise. The EL series tracks the sale of origin of exports and cannot be compared with the long-standing and widely-used Origin of Movement (OM) state export series.

All export statistics were provided by the U.S. Census Bureau under contract with the International Trade Administration. Statistics exclude exports not allocated or reported by state. For additional information, contact the source.

U.S. affiliates is a U.S. business enterprise in which one foreign owner (individual, branch, partnership, association, trust corporation, or government) has a direct or indirect voting interest of 10 percent or more. Universe estimates are based on a sample survey of nonbank affiliates with assets, sales, or net income of $10 million or more.

Gross book value of property includes property, plant, and equipment.

Impact of international visitors on state economies is provided by U.S. International Trade Administration, Tourism Industries, and includes data on expenditures of international visitors and generated employment and payroll. Data are gathered from the Inflight Survey. For more information on data collection, contact source.

Table A-33. Farms and Farm Earnings

Farms—number and land in farms, 1996, 1995, and 1990, average acreage per farm, 1996 and 1990;
Value of farm land and buildings—total , 1996, 1995, and 1990 and average value per acre, 1996 and 1990;
Farm earnings—1995, 1994, and 1990.

Source: Farms and acreage—U.S. Department of Agriculture, National Agricultural Statistics Service, *Farms and Land in Farms, Final Estimates 1988-1992*, and *Farms and Land in Farms*, July releases; Value of farm land and buildings—U.S. Department of Agriculture, Economic Research Service, *AREI Updates, Number 17: Agricultural Land Values,* annual; Farm earnings—U.S. Bureau of Economic Analysis, *Survey of Current Business*, Volume 76, Number 10, October 1996.

Data presented for farms are from the U.S. Department of Agriculture. Over time, the definitions of a farm have varied. The current definition covers any place as of June 1 from which $1,000 or more of agricultural products would have been sold during the census year.

Land in farms consists primarily of agricultural land used for crops, pasture, and grazing. It also includes land not actually under cultivation or not used for pasture or grazing, provided it was part of the farm operator's total operation. Rent-free land is included as part of the farm only if the operator has sole use of it. Land that is used for pasture or grazing on a per-head basis and neither owned nor leased by the farm operator is not included, except for grazing lands that are controlled by grazing associations and leased on a per-acre basis.

Value of land and buildings is estimated by multiplying the number of acres of farmland by the average value per acre of land and buildings. Per acre values are based on data from the census of agriculture. For intercensal years, estimates are based on surveys conducted by the U.S. Department of Agriculture.

Farm earnings include the income of farm workers (wages and salaries and other labor income) and farm proprietors. The estimation of farm proprietors' income starts with the computation of the realized net income of all farms, which is derived as farm gross receipts less production expenses. This measure is then modified to reflect current production through a change-in-inventory adjustment and to exclude the income of corporate farms and salaries paid to corporate officers. Farm proprietors' income includes only the income of sole proprietorships and partnerships. Therefore, an adjustment is made to exclude the net farm income of corporate farms, including the salaries of officers of corporate farms.

Table A-34. Farm Finances and Income

Balance sheet of farming sector, assets and debt—1995, 1994, and 1990;
Farm income—Gross farm income, farm marketing cash receipts, and net farm income, 1995, 1994, and 1990, crops as percent of total, 1995.

Source: U.S. Department of Agriculture, Economic Research Service, *Farm Business Economic Report*, annual.

Figures on assets, debt, and farm income include farm operator households. The farm household accounts affect both the income and expenses in net farm income. The imputed rental value of farm-operator dwellings is included as income. The expenses for these dwellings are included in repair and operation, interest, taxes, capital consumption, and other miscellaneous expenses.

Gross income comprises cash receipts from farm marketings of crops and livestock, federal payments made directly to farmers for farm-related activities, rental value of farm homes, values of farm products consumed in farm homes, and other farm-related income, such as machine hire and customer work. Farm marketings represent quantities of agricultural products sold by farmers multiplied by prices received per unit of production at the local market.

In the net farm income accounts, Commodity Credit Corporation loans are counted as sales at the time the loan is made, and the quantities under loan are not counted in inventory calculations. Net farm income data are after inventory adjustment and include income and expenses related to the farm operator's dwelling.

Table A-35. Construction

Employment—1996, 1995, and 1990;
Earnings—1995, 1994, and 1990;
Establishment—1994 and net change, 1990-1994;
Contracts and new private housing units authorized—1996, 1995, and 1990.

Source: Employment—U.S. Bureau of Labor Statistics, *Employment and Earnings*, monthly, May issue, compiled from data supplied by cooperating state agencies; Earnings—U.S. Bureau of Economic Analysis, *Survey of Current Business*, Volume 76 Number 10, October 1996; Establishments—U.S. Bureau of the Census, *County Business Patterns* on diskette, annual; Contracts—F.W. Dodge, McGraw-Hill,

Inc., New York, NY, (copyright); New private housing units authorized—U.S. Bureau of the Census, Construction Reports, series C40, annual, from source diskette state file.

The term construction includes new work, additions, alterations, reconstruction, installation, and repairs. Three broad types of construction are covered: (1) building construction by general contractors or by operative builders, (2) heavy construction other than building by general contractors, and (3) special trade contractors and construction activity by other special trade contractors.

Industry classifications are based on the *1987 Standard Industrial Classification (SIC) Manual*. The 1987 edition of the manual represents major revisions from the 1972 edition and its 1977 supplement. For more information on these revisions, see Appendix A of the 1987 SIC manual.

Data for employment were obtained from an establishment survey conducted in cooperation with state agencies. The survey gathers information on nonfarm wage and salary employment, average weekly hours, average hourly earnings, and average weekly earnings from a sample of over 340,000 establishments. Data refer to persons on establishment payrolls who received pay for any part of the pay period that included the 12th of the month. See the source for methodological details. Industry statistics are classified in accordance with the *1987 Standard Industrial Classification Manual*.

Total earnings cover wage and salary disbursements, other labor income, and proprietors' income. Wage and salary disbursements are defined as monetary remuneration of employees, including corporate officers; commissions, tips, and bonuses; and pay-in-kind that represents income to the recipient. Other labor income consists of employer contributions to privately administered pension and welfare funds and a few small items, such as directors' fees, compensation of prison inmates, and miscellaneous judicial fees. Proprietors' income is the monetary income and income in-kind of proprietorships and partnerships, including the independent professions, and of tax-exempt cooperatives.

Figures for private nonfarm establishments are published in County Business Patterns (CBP), an annual report series. The data were obtained from surveys and censuses conducted by the Bureau of the Census and administrative records from the Internal Revenue Service (IRS).

An establishment is a single physical location at which business is conducted or where services or industrial operations are performed. It is not necessarily identical with a company or enterprise, which may consist of one establishment or more. Establishment counts represent the number of locations determined to be active anytime during the year.

Construction contracts represent value of construction in states in which work was actually done, new structures and additions, and major alterations to existing structures.

Data presented are for the number of new housing units authorized by building permits in the United States. For

1996 and 1995, the data were based on the 19,000 permit-issuing place universe; 1990 is based on the 17,000 permit-issuing universe. The 19,000 permit-issuing places in the universe account for a major portion of new residential housing units started in the United States.

The data relate to new private housing units intended for occupancy on a housekeeping basis. They exclude mobile homes (trailers), hotels, motels, and group residential structures, such as nursing homes and college dormitories. They also exclude conversions of and alterations to existing buildings.

A housing unit consists of a room or group of rooms intended for occupancy as separate living quarters by a family, by a group of unrelated persons living together, or by a person living alone.

Table A-36. Manufactures

Employment—1996, 1995, and 1990;
Earnings—1995, 1994, and 1990;
Establishments—1994 and net change, 1990-1994;
Average hourly earnings of production workers—1996, 1995, and 1990;
Value of shipments—1995, 1994, 1990.

Source: Employment and average hourly earnings—Bureau of Labor Statistics *Employment and Earnings*, monthly, May issues, compiled from data supplied by cooperating state agencies; Earnings—Bureau of Economic Analysis, *Survey of Current Business*, Volume 76, Number 10, October 1996; Establishments—U.S. Bureau of the Census, *County Business Patterns* on diskette, annual; Value of shipments—U.S. Bureau of the Census, *Annual Survey of Manufactures*, M95(AS)-3 and M91(AS)-3.

Manufacturing covers establishments primarily engaged in the mechanical or chemical transformation of substances or materials into new products. The assembly of component parts of products also is considered to be manufacturing if the resulting product is neither a structure nor other fixed improvement. These activities are usually carried on in plants, factories, or mills that characteristically use power-driven machines and materials-handling equipment.

Industry classifications are based on the *1987 Standard Industrial Classification (SIC) Manual*. The 1987 edition of the manual represents major revisions from the 1972 edition and its 1977 supplement. For more information on these revisions, see Appendix A of the 1987 SIC manual.

Data for employment were obtained from an establishment survey conducted in cooperation with state agencies. The survey gathers information on nonfarm wage and salary employment, average weekly hours, average hourly earnings, and average weekly earnings from a sample of over 340,000 establishments. Data refer to persons on establishment payrolls who received pay for any part of the pay period that included the 12th of the month. See the source for methodological details. Industry statistics are classified in accordance with the 1987 SIC Manual.

Total earnings cover wage and salary disbursements, other labor income, and proprietors' income. Wage and salary disbursements are defined as monetary remuneration of employees, including corporate officers; commissions, tips, and bonuses; and pay-in-kind that represents income to the recipient. Other labor income consists of employer contributions to privately administered pension and welfare funds and a few small items such as directors' fees, compensation of prison inmates, and miscellaneous judicial fees. Proprietors' income is the monetary income and income-in-kind of proprietorships and partnerships, including the independent professions, and of tax-exempt cooperatives.

Figures for private nonfarm establishments are published in County Business Patterns (CBP), an annual report series. The data were obtained from surveys and censuses conducted by the Bureau of the Census and administrative records from the Internal Revenue Service (IRS).

An establishment is a single physical location at which business is conducted or where services or industrial operations are performed. It is not necessarily identical with a company or enterprise, which may consist of one establishment or more. Establishment counts represent the number of locations determined to be active anytime during the year.

Average hourly earnings data are collected from the same establishment survey as the nonagricultural employment statistics and are presented on a "gross basis". They not only reflect changes in basic hourly and incentive wage rates but also such variable factors as premium pay for overtime and late-shift work and changes in output of workers paid on an incentive plan. They also reflect shifts in the number of employees between relatively high-paid and low-paid work and changes in workers' earnings in individual establishments. Averages for groups and divisions further reflect changes in average hourly earnings for individual industries. Averages of hourly earnings differ from wage rates. Earnings are the actual return to the worker for a stated period of time; rates are the amount stipulated for a given unit of work or time.

The source of data for value of shipments is the Annual Survey of Manufactures. This survey is conducted to collect data for the years between the census years for the more general measures of manufacturing activity covered in detail by the censuses. The annual survey data are estimates derived from a scientifically selected sample of establishments.

Value of shipments covers the received or receivable net selling values, f.o.b. plant (exclusive of freight and taxes), of all products shipped, both primary and secondary, as well as all miscellaneous receipts, such as receipts for contract work performed for others, installation and repair, sales of scrap, and sales of products bought and resold without further processing. Included are all items made by

or for the establishments from materials owned by it, whether sold, transferred to other plants of the same company, or shipped on consignment. The net selling value of products made in one plant on a contract basis from materials owned by another was reported by the plant providing the material.

Table A-37. Transportation

Employment—1996, 1995, and 1990;
Earnings—1995, 1994, and 1990;
Establishments, 1994 and net change, 1990-1994;
Commodity transportation—commodity shipment and percent going out of state, value and weight, 1993.

Source: Employment—Bureau of Labor Statistics, *Employment and Earnings*, monthly, May issues, complied from data supplied by cooperating state agencies; Earnings—Bureau of Economic Analysis, *Survey of Current Business*, Volume 76, Number 10, October 1996; Establishments—U.S. Bureau of the Census, County Business Patterns on diskette, annual; Commodity transportation—U.S. Department of Transportation, Bureau of Transportation Statistics, Commodity Flow Survey, (related Internet site, <http://www.bts.gov/ntda/cfs/cfsfutr.htm>).

Industry classifications are based on the *1987 Standard Industrial Classification (SIC) Manual*. The 1987 edition of the manual represents major revisions from the 1972 edition and its 1977 supplement. For more information on these revisions, see Appendix A of the 1987 SIC manual.

Data for employment were obtained from an establishment survey conducted in cooperation with state agencies. The survey gathers information on nonfarm wage and salary employment, average weekly hours, average hourly earnings, and average weekly earnings from a sample of over 340,000 establishments. Data refer to persons on establishment payrolls who received pay for any part of the pay period that included the 12th of the month. See the source for methodological details.

Total earnings cover wage and salary disbursements, other labor income, and proprietors' income. Wage and salary disbursements are defined as monetary remuneration of employees, including corporate officers; commissions, tips, and bonuses; and pay-in-kind that represents income to the recipient. Other labor income consists of employer contributions to privately administered pension and welfare funds and a few small items, such as directors' fees, compensation of prison inmates, and miscellaneous judicial fees. Proprietors' income is the monetary income and income-in-kind of proprietorships and partnerships, including the independent professions, and of tax-exempt cooperatives.

Figures for private nonfarm establishments are published in County Business Patterns (CBP), an annual report series. The data were obtained from surveys and censuses conducted by the Bureau of the Census and administrative records from the Internal Revenue Service (IRS).

An establishment is a single physical location at which business is conducted or where services or industrial operations are performed. It is not necessarily identical with a company or enterprise, which may consist of one establishment or more. Establishment counts represent the number of locations determined to be active anytime during the year.

Commodity shipping data are provided from the Department of Transportation/Department of Commerce, Commodity Flow Survey (CFS) Program, 1993 Commodity Flow Survey. This survey is designed to provide data on the flow of goods and materials by mode of transport. A sample of 200,000 establishments engaging in mining, manufacturing, wholesale, auxiliary establishments (warehouses) of multiestablishment companies, and some selected activities in retail and service was used to collect data for the commodity survey.

Previous CFS surveys reported only the principal mode of shipment while the 1993 survey reported all modes (for-hire truck, private truck, rail, inland water, deep sea water, pipeline, air, parcel delivery or Postal Service, other mode, and unknown). For a detailed summary for each state, see source at Internet site <http://www.bts.gov/ntda/cfs/desc.html>.

Table A-38. Wholesale and Retail Trade and Shopping Centers

Employment—1996, 1995, and 1990;
Earnings—1995, 1994, and 1990;
Establishment—1994 and net change, 1990-1994;
Shopping centers—total retail sales and sales per square foot, 1996 and 1990.

Source: Employment—U.S. Bureau of Labor Statistics, *Employment and Earnings*, monthly, May issues; compiled from data supplied by cooperating state agencies; Earnings—U.S. Bureau of Economic Analysis, *Survey of Current Business*, Volume 76, Number 10, October 1996; Establishments—U.S. Bureau of the Census, County Business Patterns on diskette, annual; Shopping centers—National Research Bureau, Chicago, IL, data for 1996 published by International Council of Shopping Centers in *Shopping Centers Today*, April issue (copyright—Interactive Market Systems, Inc.); data for 1990 published by Monitor Publishing, Clearwater, FL, in *Monitor Magazine,* November/December 1991 (copyright).

Industry classifications are based on the *1987 Standard Industrial Classification (SIC) Manual.* The 1987 edition of the manual represents major revisions from the 1972 edition and its 1977 supplement. For more information on these revisions, see Appendix A of the 1987 SIC manual.

Data for employment were obtained from an establishment survey conducted in cooperation with state agencies. The survey gathers information on nonfarm wage and salary employment, average weekly hours, average hourly earnings, and average weekly earnings from a sample of over 340,000 establishments. Data refer to persons on establishment payrolls who received pay for any part of the pay period that included the 12th of the month. See the source for methodological details.

Total earnings cover wage and salary disbursements, other labor income, and proprietors' income. Wage and salary disbursements are defined as monetary remuneration of employees, including corporate officers; commissions, tips, and bonuses; and pay-in-kind that represents income to the recipient. Other labor income consists of employer contributions to privately administered pension and welfare funds and a few small items, such as directors' fees, compensation of prison inmates, and miscellaneous judicial fees. Proprietors' income is the monetary income and income-in-kind of proprietorships and partnerships, including the independent professions, and of tax-exempt cooperatives.

Figures for private nonfarm establishments are published in County Business Patterns (CBP), an annual report series. The data were obtained from surveys and censuses conducted by the Bureau of the Census and administrative records from the Internal Revenue Service (IRS).

An establishment is a single physical location at which business is conducted or where services or industrial operations are performed. It is not necessarily identical with a company or enterprise, which may consist of one establishment or more. Establishment counts represent the number of locations determined to be active anytime during the year and cover only establishments with payroll.

A shopping center is a group of architecturally unified commercial establishments built on a site which is planned, developed, owned, and managed as an operating unit. It is related in its location, size, and type of shops to the trade area that the unit serves. The unit provides on-site parking in definite relationship to the types and total size of the stores. The database attempts to include all centers with three or more stores. Estimates are based on a sample of data available on shopping center properties, for details, contact source.

Table A-39. Retail Sales

Retail sales—total, 1995, 1994, and 1990, sales per household, 1995, and percent change, 1994-1995;
Food stores, general merchandise stores, department stores, automotive dealers, and eating and drinking places, 1995 and 1994.

Source: Market Statistics, New York, NY, annual (copyright).

Data are estimates from Market Statistics.

Industry classifications are based on the *1987 Standard Industrial Classification (SIC) Manual.* The 1987 edition of the manual represents major revisions from the 1972 edition and its 1977 supplement. For more information on these revisions, see Appendix A of the 1987 SIC manual.

Sales per household are based on number of households estimated as of July 1 for years shown by source.

The food stores group includes establishments primarily selling food for home preparation and consumption. These include grocery stores; meat and fish (seafood) markets; fruit and vegetable markets; candy, nut, and confectionery stores; dairy products; retail bakeries; and miscellaneous stores.

The general merchandise stores group includes retail stores which sell a number of lines of merchandise, such as dry goods, apparel and accessories, furniture and homefurnishings, small wares, hardware, and food.

The department stores group includes retail stores carrying a general line of apparel, such as suits, coats, and dresses and furnishings, homefurnishings, and housewares.

The automotive dealers group includes retail dealers selling new and used automobiles, boats, recreational vehicles, utility trailers, and motorcycles including mopeds; as well as those selling new automobile parts and accessories. Also included are automobile repair shops maintained by establishments engaged in the sale of new automobiles. Gasoline service stations (SIC 554) are excluded.

The eating and drinking places group includes retail establishments selling prepared foods and drinks for consumption on the premises and lunch counters and refreshment stands selling prepared foods and drinks for immediate consumption.

Table A-40. Finance, Insurance, and Real Estate

Employment, 1996, 1995, and 1990;
Earnings, 1995, 1994, and 1990;
Establishments, 1994 and net change, 1990-1994;
Insured saving institutions—number and assets, 1996 and 1990;
Credit unions—number and assets, 1995 and 1990.

Source: Employment—U.S. Bureau of Labor Statistics, *Employment and Earnings*, monthly, May issues; compiled from data supplied by cooperating state agencies; Earnings—U.S. Bureau of Economic Analysis, *Survey of Current Business*, Volume 76, Number 10, October 1996; Establishments—U.S. Bureau of the Census, County Business Patterns, on diskette, annual; Insured savings institutions—U.S. Federal Deposit Insurance Corporation, *Statistics on Banking*, annual, Internet site <http://www.fdic/gov/databank/sob/hist96/si12.html> (accessed 21 August 1997); Credit unions—National Credit Union Administration, *Annual Report of the National Credit Union Administration*, and unpublished data.

Finance, insurance, and real estate (FIRE) includes establishments operating primarily in the fields of finance, insurance, and real estate. Finance includes depository institutions, nondepository credit institutions, holding (but not predominantly operating) companies, other investment companies, brokers and dealers in securities and commodity contracts, and security and commodity exchanges.

Insurance covers carriers of all types of insurance and insurance agents and brokers. Real estate includes owners, lessors, lessees, buyers, sellers, agents, and developers of real estate.

Industry classifications are based on the *1987 Standard Industrial Classification (SIC) Manual*. The 1987 edition of the manual represents major revisions from the 1972 edition and its 1977 supplement. For more information on these revisions, see Appendix A of the 1987 SIC manual.

Data for employment were obtained from an establishment survey conducted in cooperation with state agencies. The survey gathers information on nonfarm wage and salary employment, average weekly hours, average hourly earnings, and average weekly earnings from a sample of over 340,000 establishments. Data refer to persons on establishment payrolls who received pay for any part of the pay period that included the 12th of the month. See the source for methodological details. Industry statistics are classified in accordance with the 1987 SIC Manual.

Total earnings cover wage and salary disbursements, other labor income, and proprietors' income. Wage and salary disbursements are defined as monetary remuneration of employees, including corporate officers; commissions, tips, and bonuses; and pay-in-kind that represents income to the recipient. Other labor income consists of employer contributions to privately administered pension and welfare funds and a few small items, such as directors' fees, compensation of prison inmates, and miscellaneous judicial fees. Proprietors' income is the monetary income and income-in-kind of proprietorships and partnerships, including the independent professions, and of tax-exempt cooperatives.

Figures for private nonfarm establishments are published in County Business Patterns (CBP), an annual report series. The data were obtained from surveys and censuses conducted by the Bureau of the Census and administrative records from the Internal Revenue Service (IRS).

An establishment is a single physical location at which business is conducted or where services or industrial operations are performed. It is not necessarily identical with a company or enterprise, which may consist of one establishment or more. Establishment counts represent the number of locations determined to be active anytime during the year.

Insured savings institutions consist of savings and loan associations and savings banks insured by Savings Association Insurance Fund (SAIF) and Banking Insurance Fund (BIF). Institutions placed in Resolution Trust Corporation (RTC) are excluded.

Credit union statistics include federally charted credit unions under the supervision of the National Credit Union Administration (NCUA) and state charted credit unions supervised by the respective state supervisory authorities.

Table A-41. Commercial Banks and Insurance

Insured commercial banks—number, asset, deposits, equity, and net income, 1996 and 1990;

Life insurance in force—total value and average per household, 1996 and 1990;
Automobile insurance—average expenditure per insured vehicle, 1995 and 1991.

Source: Insured commercial banks—U.S. Federal Deposit Insurance Corporation, *Statistics on Banking*, annual; Life insurance in force—American Council of Life Insurance, Washington, DC, *Life Insurance Fact Book*, biennial (copyright); Automobile insurance—National Association of Insurance commissioners, Kansas, MO, *State Average Expenditures and Premiums for Personal Automobile Insurance*, annual (copyright).

The category of FDIC-insured commercial banks includes all commercial banks insured by the Federal Deposit Insurance Corporation (FDIC) either through the Bank Insurance Fund (BIF) or through the Savings Association Insurance Fund (SAIF). These institutions are regulated by and submit financial data to one of the three federal commercial bank regulators (the Board of Governors of the Federal Reserve System, the Federal Deposit Insurance Corporation, or the Office of the Comptroller of the Currency).

The structure and financial data source used for insured commercial banks is the FDIC's Financial Time Series (FTS) database. The primary sources of FTS financial data are the Federal Financial Institutions Examination Council (FFIEC) *Call Reports* and the OTS *Thrift Financial Reports* submitted by all FDIC insured depository institutions. The primary source data are updated continuously as a result of corrections and amendments. Thus, the data represent the industry as of April 1997.

Life insurance data were compiled by the Data Collection Unit of American Council of Life Insurance. It covers life insurance with life insurance companies only. These data represent all life insurance in force on lives of U.S. residents whether issued by U.S. or foreign companies.

Households consist of all the persons who occupy a "housing unit," that is, a house, an apartment or other group of rooms, or a single room that constitutes "separate living quarters."

Automobile insurance is published by the National Association of Insurance Commissioners in the publication *State Average Expenditures and Premiums for Personal Automobile Insurance,* annual (copyright). The average expenditures for automobile insurance in a state are affected by a number of factors, including the underlying rate structure, the coverages purchased, the deductibles and limits selected, the types of vehicles insured, and the distribution of drives characteristics.

Table A-42. Services

Employment—1996, 1995, and 1990;
Earnings—1995, 1994, and 1990;
Establishments—1994 and net change, 1990-1994;
Business, health, and legal services—establishments and employees, 1994.

Source: Employment—U.S. Bureau of Labor Statistics, *Employment and Earnings*, monthly and May issues, compiled from data supplied by cooperating state agencies; Earnings—U.S. Bureau of Economic Analysis, *Survey of Current Business*, Volume 76, Number 10, October 1996; Establishments and industry data—U.S. Bureau of the Census, County Business Patterns, on CD-ROM, annual.

Services include establishments primarily engaged in providing a wide variety of services for individuals, business and government establishments, and other organizations.

Industry classifications are based on the *1987 Standard Industrial Classification (SIC) Manual.* The 1987 edition of the manual represents major revisions from the 1972 edition and its 1977 supplement. For more information on these revisions, see Appendix A of the 1987 SIC manual.

Data for employment were obtained from an establishment survey conducted in cooperation with state agencies. The survey gathers information on nonfarm wage and salary employment, average weekly hours, average hourly earnings, and average weekly earnings from a sample of over 390,000 establishments. Data refer to persons on establishment payrolls who received pay for any part of the pay period that included the 12th of the month. See the source for methodological details. Industry statistics are classified in accordance with the 1987 SIC Manual.

Total earnings cover wage and salary disbursements, other labor income, and proprietors' income. Wage and salary disbursements are defined as monetary remuneration of employees, including corporate officers; commissions, tips, and bonuses; and pay-in-kind that represents income to the recipient. Other labor income consists of employer contributions to privately administered pension and welfare funds and a few small items, such as directors' fees, compensation of prison inmates, and miscellaneous judicial fees. Proprietors' income is the monetary income and income-in-kind of proprietorships and partnerships, including the independent professions, and of tax-exempt cooperatives.

Figures for private nonfarm establishments are published in County Business Patterns (CBP), an annual report series. The data were obtained from surveys and censuses conducted by the Bureau of the Census and administrative records from the Internal Revenue Service (IRS).

An establishment is a single physical location at which business is conducted or where services or industrial operations are performed. It is not necessarily identical with a company or enterprise, which may consist of one establishment or more. Establishment counts represent the number of locations determined to be active anytime during the year.

Business services include establishments primarily engaged in providing services, not elsewhere classified, to business establishments on a contract or fee basis. These include advertising agencies, adjustment and collection services, direct mail advertising, photocopying, and building cleaning and maintenance to name a few.

Health services include establishments primarily engaged in furnishing medical, surgical, and other health services to persons. Associations or groups, such as HMOs, providing medical or health services to members are included, but those which limit their services to the provision of insurance against hospitalization or medical costs are classified in Insurance, Major Group 63. Hospices are also included here and are classified according to the primary service provided. Individual practitioners, group clinics in which a group of practitioners is associated for the purpose of carrying on their profession, and clinics which provide the same services through practitioners that are employees are included in this service group.

Legal services include establishments which are headed by members of the bar and engaged in offering legal advice or legal services. Nonprofit legal services are classified here. Associations of lawyers formed solely for the sharing of expenses and not for the purpose of jointly practicing their profession are also included.

Table A-43. Agriculture and Mineral Industries

Agriculture, 1992:
  All farms and farms with sales of $10,000 or more— number, land in farms, size, and value;
Mineral industries, 1992:
  Establishments;
  Paid employees—number and payroll;
  Production workers—total and wages;
  Value added by mining;
  Value of shipments.

Source: Agriculture—U.S. Bureau of the Census, 1992 Census of Agriculture, Vol. 1, AC92-A-51; Mineral Industries—U.S. Bureau of the Census, *1992 Census of Mineral Industries*, see Subject Series, *General Summary*, MIC92-S-1.

The 1992 Census of Agriculture is the 24th taken by the Bureau of the Census. For a detailed explanation of the census coverage and methodology for the 1992 Census of Agriculture, see the source. For a discussion of the scope and history of the economic censuses, as well as census disclosure rules, see General Note, Economic Censuses.

Over time, the definitions of a farm have varied. The current definition covers any place as of June 1 from which $1,000 or more of agricultural products were produced and sold, or normally would have been sold, during the census year.

Land in farms consists primarily of agricultural land used for crops, pasture, and grazing. It also includes woodland and wasteland not actually under cultivation or not used for pasture or grazing, provided it was part of the farm operator's total operation. Land in farms includes acres set aside under annual commodity acreage programs as well as acres in the Conservation Reserve Programs for places meeting the farm definition. Land in farms is an operating

unit concept and includes land owned and operated as well as land rented from others. All grazing land used under government permits on a per-head basis was included as "land in farms" provided it was part of a farm or ranch.

Value of land and buildings is based on reports for a sample farm.

The 1992 Census of Mineral Industries is taken by the Bureau of the Census. For a detailed explanation of the census coverage and methodology for the 1992 Census of Mineral Industries, see the source. For a discussion of the scope and history of the economic censuses, as well as census disclosure rules, see General Note, Economic Censuses.

Industry classifications are based on the *1987 Standard Industrial Classification (SIC) Manual.* The 1987 edition of the manual represents major revisions from the 1972 edition and its 1977 supplement. For more information on these revisions, see Appendix A of the 1987 SIC manual.

The 1992 Census of Mineral Industries covers all establishments with one paid employee or more primarily engaged in mining as defined in the *1987 Standard Industrial Classification (SIC) Manual.* A mineral establishment is defined as a single physical location where mineral operations are conducted.

Mining is defined in the broad sense to include the extraction of minerals occurring naturally: solids, such as coal and ores; liquids, such as crude petroleum; and gases, such as natural gas. The term "mining" is used in the broad sense to include quarrying, well operation, milling (crushing, screening, washing, flotation, etc.), and preparations needed to make minerals marketable.

Number of establishments includes all establishments in business at any time during the year.

Employees include all full-time and part-time employees on the payrolls of mining establishments during any part of the pay period which included the 12th of the month. Included are all persons on paid sick leave, paid holidays, and paid vacation during these pay periods. Also included are employees working for miners paid on a per ton, car, or yard basis.

Production workers include employees (up through the working-supervisor level) engaged in manual work.

Payroll includes the gross earnings of all employees on the payroll of mining establishments paid in the calendar year 1992. It includes all forms of compensation such as salaries; wages; commissions; payments received on a ton, car, or yard basis; dismissal pay; vacation and sick leave pay; employee contributions to pension plans; and compensation in kind, prior to such deductions as employees' social security contributions, withholding taxes, group insurance, union dues, and savings bonds.

Value added in mining is derived by subtracting the cost of supplies, minerals received for preparation, purchased machinery installed, purchased fuel, purchased electricity, and contract work from the sum of the value of shipments and total capital expenditures.

The amounts shown as value of shipments for each industry and state are the net selling values, f.o.b. mine or plant after discounts and allowances, excluding freight charges and excise taxes.

Table A-44. Construction Industries and Manufactures

Construction industries, 1992:
  Establishments;
  Employees—number and payroll;
  Construction workers;
  Value of construction work;
  Net value of construction work;
  Value added;
Manufactures, 1992:
  Establishments;
  Employees—number and payroll;
  Production workers total and wages;
  Value added by manufactures;
  Value of shipments.

Source: Construction Industries—U.S. Bureau of the Census, 1992 Census of Construction Industries, Geographic Area Series, *United States Summary,* CC92-A-10; Manufactures—U.S. Bureau of the Census, 1992 Census of Manufactures, Subject Series, *General Summary,* MC92-S-1.

Industry classifications are based on the *1987 Standard Industrial Classification (SIC) Manual.* The 1987 edition of the manual represents major revisions from the 1972 edition and its 1977 supplement. For more information on these revisions, see Appendix A of the 1987 SIC manual.

The 1992 Census of Construction Industries is taken by the Bureau of the Census. For a detailed explanation of the census coverage and methodology for the 1992 Census of Construction Industries, see the source. For a discussion of the scope and history of the economic censuses, as well as census disclosure rules, General, Economic Censuses.

Statistics for construction industries were obtained from the 1992 Census of Construction Industries. The census covers all employer establishments (establishments with payroll) primarily engaged in contract construction— building construction by general contractors or operative builders, heavy construction general contractors, and construction by other special trade contractors.

Prior to 1992, this census also included one industry classified in the Real Estate area, SIC 6552, Land Subdividers and Developers, Except Cemeteries. This industry is covered in the 1992 Census of Financial, Insurance, and Real Estate Industries.

An establishment is defined as a single physical location where construction is performed. A company, on the other hand, is defined as a business organization consisting of one or more establishments under common ownership or control. Establishments include all establishments with a payroll in operation at any time during the year.

Employees include all full-time and part-time employees on the payrolls of construction establishments during any part of the pay period which included the 12th of March, May, August, and November. Included are all persons on paid sick leave, paid holidays, and paid vacation during these pay periods. Officers of corporations are included, but proprietors and partners of unincorporated firms are not. Paid employees represents the average of the employment for pay periods ending nearest the 12th of March, May, August, and November.   .

Payroll includes the gross earnings of all employees on the payroll of construction establishments paid in the calendar year of 1992. It includes all forms of compensation, such as salaries; wages; commissions; dismissal pay; vacation and sick leave pay; employee contributions to pension plans; and compensation in kind, prior to such deductions as employees' social security contributions, withholding taxes, group insurance, union dues, and savings bonds.

Construction employees include all workers up through the working-supervisor level directly engaged in construction operations.

Value of construction work includes all value of construction work performed by general contractors and special trades contractors. Included is new construction, additions and alterations or reconstruction, maintenance, and repair construction work. Also included is the value of any construction work done by the reporting establishments for themselves.

Net value of construction work is derived for each establishment by subtracting the costs for construction work subcontracted out to others from the value of construction work done.

Added value is equal to dollar value of business done, less costs for construction work subcontracted out to others and cost of materials, components, supplies, and fuels.

The 1992 Census of Manufactures is taken by the Bureau of the Census. For a detailed explanation of the census coverage and methodology for the 1992 Census of Manufactures, see the source. For a discussion of the scope and history of the economic censuses, as well as census disclosure rules, see General Note, Economic Censuses.

The 1992 Census of Manufactures covers all establishments with one paid employee or more primarily engaged in manufacturing. The SIC Manual defines manufacturing as the mechanical or chemical transformation of substances or materials into new products. The assembly of component parts of products also is considered to be manufacturing if the resulting product is neither a structure nor other fixed improvement. These activities are usually carried on in plants, factories, or mills that characteristically use power-driven machines and materials-handling equipment.

An establishment is defined as a single physical location where manufacturing is performed. A company, on the other hand, is defined as a business organization consisting of one or more establishments under common ownership or control. Total establishments include all establishments in operation at any time during the year.

Paid employees include all full-time and part-time employees on the payrolls of operating manufacturing establishments during any part of the pay period which included the 12th of the month(s) specified on the reporting form. Included are all persons on paid sick leave, paid holidays, and paid vacations during these pay periods. Officers of corporations are included as employees; proprietors and partners of unincorporated firms are excluded. Paid employees is the average number of production workers plus the number of other employees in mid-March.

The number of production workers is the average for the payroll periods including the 12th of March, May, August, and November.

Payroll includes the gross earnings of all employees on the payroll of operating manufacturing establishments paid in the calendar year 1992. It includes all forms of compensation, such as salaries, wages, commissions, dismissal pay, bonuses, vacation and sick leave pay, and compensation of any kind, prior to such deductions as employees' social security contributions, withholding taxes, group insurance, union dues, and savings bonds. The total includes salaries of officers of corporations; it excludes payments to proprietors or partners of unincorporated concerns. Also excluded are payments to members of Armed Forces and pensioners carried on the active payroll of manufacturing establishments.

The census definition of payrolls is identical to that recommended to all federal statistical agencies by the Office of Management and Budget. It should be noted that this definition does not include employers' social security contributions or other nonpayroll labor costs, such as employees' pension plans, group insurance premiums, and workers' compensation.

Production workers includes workers (up through the line-supervisor level) engaged in fabricating, processing, assembling, inspecting, receiving, storing, handling, packing, warehousing, shipping (but not delivering), maintenance, repair, janitorial and guard services, product development, auxiliary production for plant's own use (e.g., power plant), recordkeeping, and other services closely associated with these production operations at the establishment. Employees above the working-supervisor level are excluded from this item.

Value added by manufacture is a measure of manufacturing activity derived by subtracting the cost of materials, supplies, containers, fuel, purchased electricity, and contract work from the value of shipments (products manufactured plus receipts for services rendered). The result of this calculation is adjusted by the addition of value added by merchandising operations (i.e., the difference between the sales value and the cost of merchandise sold without further manufacture, processing, or assembly) plus the net change in finished goods and work-in-process between the beginning- and end-of-year inventories. Value added avoids the duplication in the figures for value of shipments that results from the use of products of some establishments as materials by others. Value added is considered to be the best value measure available for comparing the relative economic importance of manufacturing among industries and geographic areas.

Value of shipments covers the received or receivable net selling values, free on board plant (exclusive of freight and taxes), of all products shipped, both primary and secondary, as well as miscellaneous receipts, such as receipts for contract work performed for others, installation and repair, sales of scrap, and sales of products bought and resold without further processing. Included are all items made by or for the establishment from materials owned by it, whether sold, transferred to other plants of the same company, or shipped on consignment. The net selling value of products made in one plant on a contract basis from materials owned by another was reported by the plant providing the materials. In the case of multiunit companies, the manufacturer was requested to report the value of products transferred to other establishments of the same company at full economic or commercial value, including not only the direct cost of production but also a reasonable proportion of all other costs (including company overhead) and profit.

Table A-45. Transportation, Communications, and Utilities

Transportation, communications, and utilities, 1992:
  Establishments;
  Paid employees—number and payroll;
  Revenue.

Source: U.S. Bureau of the Census, 1992 Census of Transportation, Communications, and Utilities, Geographic Area Series, *Summary*, UC92-A-1.

The 1992 Census of Transportation, Communications, and Utilities is taken by the Bureau of the Census. For a detailed explanation of the census coverage and methodology for the 1992 Census of Transportation, Communications, and Utilities, see the source. For a discussion of the scope and history of the economic censuses, as well as census disclosure rules, see General Note, Economic Censuses.

The 1992 Census of Transportation, Communications, and Utilities covers transportation, communications, and utilities except for SIC Major Group 43, United States Postal Service. It includes establishments primarily engaged in rendering a wide variety of services to individuals, business and government establishments, and other organizations. The 1987 Census of Transportation did not include railroad transportation (SIC 40), passenger transportation (SIC 41), air transportation, (SIC 45), pipelines, except natural gas (SIC 46), communications (SIC 48), and electric, gas and sanitary services (SIC 49).

Transportation data on this table include passenger, water, and air transportation; motor freight transportation and warehousing; and transportation services.

Communications includes establishments furnishing point-to-point communications services, whether intended to be received aurally or visually, and radio and television broadcasting.

Utilities data include establishments engaged in generation, transmission, and/or distribution of electricity or gas or steam. Such establishments may be combinations of any of the above three services and also include other types of services, such as transportation, communications, and refrigeration. Water and irrigation systems and sanitary systems engaging in the collection and disposal of garbage, sewage, and other wastes by means of destroying or processing materials, are also included.

An establishment is defined as a single physical location at which business is conducted. It is not necessarily identical with a company or enterprise, which may consist of one establishment or more. The count of establishments represents those in business at any time during the year.

Paid employees include all full-time and part-time employees during any part of the pay period which included the 12th of the month(s) specified on the reporting form. Included are all persons on paid sick leave, paid holidays, and paid vacations during these pay periods. Officers of corporations are included as employees; proprietors and partners of unincorporated firms are excluded. The definition of paid employees is the same as that used by IRS on form 941.

Payroll includes all forms of compensation, such as salaries, wages, commissions, dismissal pay, bonuses, vacation and sick leave pay, and compensation of any kind, prior to such deductions as employees' social security contributions, withholding taxes, group insurance, union dues, and savings bonds. The total includes salaries of officers of corporations; it excludes payments to proprietors or partners of unincorporated concerns. The definition of paid employees is the same as that used by IRS on form 941.

Revenue is the basic dollar volume measure for transportation, communications, and utilities establishments covered by the census. Revenue includes gross revenue from customers or clients for services rendered, from the use of facilities, and from merchandise sold in 1992, whether or not payment was received in 1992.

Revenues includes the total value of service contracts, amounts received for work subcontracted to others and from repair services provided to others, and dues and assessments from members and affiliates. Revenues are net after deductions for refunds and allowances for merchandise returned by customers.

Revenues do not include sales, occupancy, admissions, or other taxes collected directly from customers and paid directly by the firm to a local, state, or federal tax agency, nor do they include income from such sources as contributions, gifts, and grants; dividends, interest, and investments; or sale or rental of real estate.

Table A-46. Wholesale and Retail Trade and Finance, Insurance, and Real Estate

Wholesale trade, 1992:
  Establishments;
  Employees—number and payroll;
  Sales;
Retail trade, 1992:
  Establishments;
  Employees—number and payroll;
  Sales;
Finance, insurance, and real estate, 1992:
  Establishments;
  Employees—number and payroll;
  Revenue.

Source: Wholesale trade—U.S. Bureau of the Census, 1992 Census of Wholesale Trade, Geographic Area Series, WC92-1-1 through 52RV; Retail Trade—U.S. Bureau of the Census, 1992 Census of Retail Trade, Geographic Area Series, RC92-A-1 through 52; and 1992 Census of Retail Trade, Nonemployer Statistics Series, *Summary*, RC92-N-1; Financial, Insurance, and Real Estate—U.S. Bureau of the Census, 1992 Census of Financial, Insurance, and Real Estate Industries, Geographic Area Series, FC92-A-1 through 52, and U.S. Bureau of the Census, 1992 Census of Financial, Insurance, and Real Estate Industries, Nonemployer Statistics Series, *Summary*, FC92-N-1.

Industry classifications are based on the *1987 Standard Industrial Classification (SIC) Manual*. The 1987 edition of the manual represents major revisions from the 1972 edition and its 1977 supplement. For more information on these revisions, see Appendix A of the 1987 SIC manual.

The 1992 Census of Wholesale Trade is taken by the Bureau of the Census. For a detailed explanation of the census coverage and methodology for the 1992 Census of Wholesale Trade, see the source. For a discussion of the scope and history of the economic censuses, as well as census disclosure rules, see General Note, Economic Censuses.

The 1992 Census of Wholesale Trade covers all establishments with one or more paid employees primarily engaged in selling merchandise to retailers; to industrial, commercial, institutional, farm, or professional users; or to other wholesalers. Companies selling products to which they have title, as well as to those acting as agents or brokers in buying merchandise for or selling merchandise to others, are included. The census excluded governmental organizations classified in the covered industries except for wholesale liquor establishments operated by state and local governments.

An establishment is defined as a single physical location at which business is conducted. It is not necessarily identical with a company or enterprise, which may consist of one establishment or more. The count of establishments represents those in business at any time during the year.

Paid employees for pay period including March 12 consists of the full-time and part-time employees, including salaried officers and executives of corporations, who were on the payroll in the pay period including March 12, 1987. Included are employees on paid sick leave, paid holidays, and paid vacations. Proprietors and partners of unincorporated businesses are not included. The definition of paid employees is the same as that used on IRS form 941.

Annual payroll includes all forms of compensation, such as salaries, wages, commissions, bonuses, vacation allowances, sick-leave pay, and the value of payments in kind (e.g., free meals and lodgings) paid during the year to all employees. For corporations, it includes amounts paid to officers and executives; for unincorporated businesses, it does not include profit or other compensation of proprietors or partners. Payroll is reported before deductions for social security, income tax, insurance, union dues, etc. This definition of payroll is the same as that used by the IRS on form 941.

Sales include merchandise sold for cash or credit at wholesale and retail by establishments primarily engaged in wholesale trade; receipts from rental or leasing of vehicles, equipment, instruments, tools, etc.; receipts for delivery, installation, maintenance, repair, alteration, storage, and other services; and gasoline, liquor, tobacco, and other excise taxes that are paid by the manufacturer and passed on to the wholesaler.

Sales are net after deductions for refunds and allowances for merchandise returned by customers. Trade-in allowances are not deducted from total sales. Total sales do not include carrying or other credit charges; sales (or other) taxes collected from customers and forwarded to taxing authorities; and nonoperating income from such sources as investments, rental or sale of real estate, etc.

Sales do not include wholesale sales made by manufacturers, retailers, service establishments, or other businesses whose primary activity is other than wholesale trade. They do include receipts other than from the sale of merchandise at wholesale, e.g., service receipts, retail sales, etc., by establishments primarily engaged in wholesale trade. Sales figures include sales of all establishments in business at any time during the year.

The 1992 Census of Retail Trade is taken by the Bureau of the Census. For a detailed explanation of the census coverage and methodology for the 1992 Census of Retail Trade, see the source. For a discussion of the scope and history of the economic censuses, as well as census disclosure rules, see General Note, Economic Censuses.

The 1992 Census of Retail Trade covered retail trade as defined in the *1987 Standard Industrial Classification (SIC) Manual*. It included all establishments primarily engaged in selling merchandise for personal or household consumption and rendering services incidental to the sale of the goods. The census excluded governmental organizations classified in the covered industries except for liquor stores operated by state and local governments. Data for direct sellers (SIC 5963) with no paid employees and post

exchanges, ship stores, and similar establishments operated on military posts by agencies of the federal government are not included. Establishments that are auxiliary (primary function is providing a service, such as warehouses) to retail establishments within the same organization are not included.

An establishment is defined as a single physical location at which business is conducted. It is not necessarily identical with a company or enterprise, which may consist of one establishment or more. The count of establishments represents those in business at any time during the year.

Paid employees for pay period including March 12 consists of the full-time and part-time employees, including salaried officers and executives of corporations, who were on the payroll in the pay period including March 12, 1987. Included are employees on paid sick leave, paid holidays, and paid vacations. Proprietors and partners of unincorporated businesses are not included. The definition of paid employees is the same as that used on IRS form 941.

Annual payroll includes all forms of compensation, such as salaries, wages, commissions, bonuses, vacation allowances, sick-leave pay, and the value of payments in kind (e.g., free meals and lodgings) paid during the year to all employees. For corporations, it includes amounts paid to officers and executives; for unincorporated businesses, it does not include profit or other compensation of proprietors or partners. Payroll is reported before deductions for social security, income tax, insurance, union dues, etc. This definition of payroll is the same as that used by the IRS on form 941.

Sales includes merchandise sold for cash or credit at wholesale and retail by establishments primarily engaged in wholesale trade; receipts from rental or leasing of vehicles, equipment, instruments, tools, etc.; receipts for delivery, installation, maintenance, repair, alteration, storage, and other services; and gasoline, liquor, tobacco, and other excise taxes that are paid by the manufacturer and passed on to the wholesaler.

Sales are net after deductions for refunds and allowances for merchandise returned by customers. Trade-in allowances are not deducted from total sales. Total sales do not include carrying or other credit charges; sales (or other) taxes collected from customers and forwarded to taxing authorities; and nonoperating income from such sources as investments, rental or sale of real estate, etc.

Sales does not include sales made by manufacturers, wholesalers, service establishments, or other businesses whose primary activity is other than retail trade. They do include receipts other than from the sale of merchandise at retail, e.g., service receipts, industrial users, and sales to other retailers by establishments primarily engaged in retail trade. Sales figures include sales of all establishments in business at any time during the year.

The 1992 Census of Financial, Insurance, and Real Estate (FIRE) Industries is taken by the Bureau of the Census. For a detailed explanation of the census coverage and methodology for the 1992 Census of Financial, Insurance, and Real Estate, see the source. For a discussion of the scope and history of the economic censuses, as well as census disclosure rules, see General Note, Economic Censuses.

The 1992 Census of Financial, Insurance, and Real Estate (FIRE) Industries, covered financial, insurance, and real estate industries as defined in Division H of the *1987 Standard Industrial Classification (SIC) Manual*. It included establishments in the following classifications: depository institutions; nondepository credit institutions; security and commodity brokers, dealers, exchanges, and services; insurance carriers; insurance agents, brokers, and service; real estate; and holding and other investment offices.

An establishment is defined as a single physical location at which business is conducted. It is not necessarily identical with a company or enterprise, which may consist of one establishment or more. The count of establishments represents those in business at any time during the year.

Paid employees for pay period including March 12 consists of the full-time and part-time employees, including salaried officers and executives of corporations, who were on the payroll in the pay period including March 12, 1992. Included are employees on paid sick leave, paid holidays, and paid vacations. Proprietors and partners of unincorporated businesses are not included. The definition of paid employees is the same as that used on IRS form 941.

Annual payroll includes all forms of compensation, such as salaries, wages, commissions, bonuses, vacation allowances, sick-leave pay, and the value of payments in kind (e.g., free meals and lodgings) paid during the year to all employees. For corporations, it includes amounts paid to officers and executives; for unincorporated businesses, it does not include profit or other compensation of proprietors or partners. Payroll is reported before deductions for social security, income tax, insurance, union dues, etc. This definition of payroll is the same as that used by the IRS on form 941.

Revenue is the basic dollar volume measure for financial, insurance, and real estate establishments covered by the census. It includes revenue from all business activities whether or not payment was received in 1992, including net premiums earned by insurance carriers, commissions and fees from all sources, rents, net investment income, interest, dividends, and royalties. Rental revenue from leasing property marketed under operating leases is included, as well as interest earned from property marketed in 1992 under capital, finance, or full payout leases. Revenue also includes the total value of service contracts, amounts received for work contracts, amounts received for work subcontracted to others and dues and assessments from members and affiliates.

Revenues do not include sales and other taxes collected from customers and remitted directly by the firm to a local, state, or federal tax agency.

Table A-47. Service Industries

Taxable service firms, 1992:
    Establishments— number and receipts;

Establishments with payroll—number, receipts, and payroll;
    Paid employees;
Tax-exempt firms, 1992:
    Establishments with payroll—number, revenue, and payroll;
    Paid employees.

Source: Establishments, receipts, and revenue—U.S. Bureau of the Census, 1992 Census of Service Industries, Nonemployer Statistics Series, *Summary*, SC92-N-1; Payroll and paid employees—U.S. Bureau of the Census, 1992 Economic Census CD-ROM, Report Series Disc 1G. Related publications: U.S. Bureau of the Census, 1992 Census of Service Industries, Geographic Area Series. (SC87-A-1 through SC87-A-52).

Industry classifications are based on the *1987 Standard Industrial Classification (SIC) Manual*. The 1987 edition of the manual represents major revisions from the 1972 edition and its 1977 supplement. For more information on these revisions, see Appendix A of the 1987 SIC manual.

The 1992 Census of Service Industries is taken by the Bureau of the Census. For a detailed explanation of the census coverage and methodology for the 1992 Census of Service Industries, see the source. For a discussion of the scope and history of the economic censuses, as well as census disclosure rules, see General Note, Economic Censuses.

The 1992 Census of Service Industries included establishments primarily engaged in rendering a wide variety of services to individuals, business and government establishments, and other organizations except elementary and secondary schools (SIC 821); colleges, universities, professional schools, and junior colleges (SIC 822); labor unions and similar labor organizations (SIC 863); political organizations (SIC 865); religious organizations (SIC 866); and private households (SIC 881). The census also excluded governmental establishments classified in the covered industries, except for government-operated hospitals which were included.

An establishment is defined as a single physical location at which business is conducted. It is not necessarily identical with a company or enterprise, which may consist of one establishment or more. The count of establishments represents those in business at any time during the year.

Receipts represent the basic dollar volume measure for service establishments of firms subject to federal income tax. They include receipts from customers or clients for services rendered, from the use of facilities, and from merchandise sold during 1992 whether or not payment was received in 1992, except for health practitioners and legal, architectural, engineering, and surveying services, which reported on a cash basis (payments received in 1992 regardless of when services were rendered). Gasoline, liquor, tobacco, and other excise taxes, which are paid by the manufacturer or wholesaler and included in the cost of goods purchased by the service establishment are also included.

Receipts are net after deductions for refunds and allowances for merchandise returned by customers. Receipts do not include sales, occupancy, admissions, or other taxes collected from customers and remitted directly by the firm to a local, state, or federal tax agency; nor do they include income from such sources as contributions, gifts, and grants; dividends, interest, and investments; or sale or rental of real estate.

Receipts do not include service receipts of manufacturers, wholesalers, retail establishments, or other businesses whose primary activity is other than service. They do, however, include receipts other than from services rendered (e.g., sale of merchandise to individuals or other businesses) by establishments primarily engaged in performing services and classified in the service industries.

Annual payroll includes all forms of compensation, such as salaries, wages, commissions, bonuses, vacation allowances, sick-leave pay, and the value of payments in kind (e.g., free meals and lodgings) paid during the year to all employees. For corporations, it includes amounts paid to officers and executives; for unincorporated businesses, it does not include profit or other compensation of proprietors or partners. Payroll is reported before deductions for social security, income tax, insurance, union dues, etc. This definition of payroll is the same as that used by the IRS on form 941.

Paid employees for pay period including March 12 consists of the full-time and part-time employees, including salaried officers and executives of corporations, who were on the payroll in the pay period including March 12, 1992. Included are employees on paid sick leave, paid holidays, and paid vacations. Proprietors and partners of unincorporated businesses are not included. The definition of paid employees is the same as that used on IRS form 941.

Revenue is the basic dollar volume measure for firms exempt from federal income tax. It includes revenue from customers or clients for services rendered and merchandise sold during 1992, whether or not payment was received in 1992. Also included are income from interest, dividends, and gross contributions, gifts, grants (whether or not restricted for use in operations), rents, royalties, dues and assessments from members and affiliates, and receipts from fundraising activities. Receipts from taxable business activities of firms exempt from federal income tax (unrelated business income) are also included in revenue.

Revenues do not include sales, admissions, or other taxes collected by the organization from customers or clients and paid directly to a local, state, or federal tax agency; income from the sale of real estate, investments or other assets (except inventory held for resale); gross receipts of departments, concessions, etc., that are operated by others; and amounts transferred to operating funds from capital or reserve funds.

Table A-48. Women- and Minority-Owned Firms

Women- and minority-owned firms, 1992 and 1987:
  Number;
  Sales and receipts.

Source: Women-owned—U.S. Bureau of the Census, 1992 Economic Census, *Women-Owned Businesses*, WB92-1 and 1987 Economic Census, *Women-Owned Businesses*, WB87-1; Black-owned—U.S. Bureau of the Census, 1992 Economic Census, Survey of Minority-Owned Business Enterprises, *Black*, MB92-1 and 1987 Economic Census, Survey of Minority-Owned Business Enterprises, *Black,* MB87-1; Hispanic-owned—U.S. Bureau of the Census, 1992 Economic Census, Survey of Minority-Owned Business Enterprises, *Hispanic*, MB92-1, and 1987 Economic Census, Survey of Minority-Owned Business Enterprises, *Hispanic*, MB87-4; Asian, Indian and Alaska Native-owned—U.S. Bureau of the Census, 1992 Economic Census, Survey of Minority-Owned Business Enterprises, *Summary*, MB92-4 and 1987 Economic Census, Survey of Minority-Owned Business Enterprises, *Asian and Pacific Islanders and American Indian*, MB87-4.

The 1992 Economic Census, Women-Owned Businesses and the 1992 Economic Census, Minority-Owned Businesses, are taken by the Bureau of the Census. For a detailed explanation of the census coverage and methodology for the 1992 Economic Census, Women-Owned Businesses, and the 1992 Economic Census, Minority-Owned Businesses, see the source. For a discussion of the scope and history of the economic censuses, as well as census disclosure rules, see General Note, Economic Censuses.

Industry classifications are based on the *1987 Standard Industrial Classification (SIC) Manual*. The 1987 edition of the manual represents major revisions from the 1972 edition and its 1977 supplement. For more information on these revisions, see Appendix A of the 1987 SIC manual.

For 1987, classification for firm data was based on the 1972 SIC manual. The SIC structure was changed to better reflect industry trends. These changes limit the comparability of data between 1987 and 1992

The 1992 Economic Census of Women-Owned Businesses and the 1992 Survey of Minority-Owned Business Enterprises (SMOBE) provide basic economic data on businesses owned by women, Blacks, persons of Hispanic or Latin American ancestry, and persons of Asian, Pacific Islander, American Indian, or Alaska Native descent. The survey is based on the entire firm rather than on establishments of a firm. The published data cover number of firms, gross receipts, number of paid employees, and annual payroll.

For companies with more than one major type of activity, payroll data were used for determining the most significant business, and the entire company was classified to that category. Payroll data are used in preference to receipts because it is believed to be the most meaningful economic measure common to all businesses.

A firm may operate one place of business or more, such as a chain of restaurants, or have no fixed business location, such as the firm represented by a self-employed carpenter or salesperson. A firm contrasts with an establishment, which is a single physical location at which business is conducted. Most of the other economic censuses are conducted on an establishment basis rather than a firm basis.

A firm is classified as women-owned using the gender codes obtained from the SSA for individual proprietors or from information reported for the majority of owners of partnerships and corporations.

Data for minority-owned firms were obtained from a sample of firms identified as possibly minority-owned based on race and ethnic codes from social security records and by matching surnames of owners to lists of minority surnames from the most recent population census of the United States.

The race categories used in this survey are the same as those defined by the Office of Management and Budget (OMB) in their circular No. A-46, dated May 12, 1977.

Receipts include the gross value of all products sold, services rendered, or other receipts from customers during the year, less returns and allowances. Value for sales and services is given whether or not payment was actually received during the year and, therefore, does not indicate a cash flow. Although receipts data were supposed to cover calendar year 1992, fiscal year reporting was permitted if it did not produce great differences. No adjustments are made for the costs of doing business. Due to the nature of the banking, real estate, and insurance industries and educational and social services, receipts may not be a good indicator of financial worth or size.

Table A-49. State Government Employment and Finances

Employment, 1995 and 1990;
Finances—revenue and expenditures;
   Total, 1995 and 1990;
   General, 1995.

Source: State Government Employment—for 1995, U.S. Bureau of the Census, Internet site <http://www.census.gov/govs/www/apes95.html> (accessed 26 June 1997); for 1990, U.S. Bureau of the Census, *Public Employment: 1990*, GE-90-1, September 1991; State Government Finances—for 1995, Internet file <http://www.census.gov/govs/www/state.html> (released February 1997); for 1990, U.S. Bureau of the Census, *Government Finances, 1989-90*, GF/90-5, December 1991.

Data for state governments are as of October and are based upon complete censuses of all state departments, agencies, and institutions.

Full-time equivalent employment is a computed statistic representing the number of full-time employees that could have been employed if the reported number of hours worked by part-time employees had been worked by full-time employees. This statistic is calculated separately for each function of a government by dividing the "part-time hours paid" by the standard number of hours for full-time employees in the particular government and then adding the resulting quotient to the number of full-time employees.

Employment per 10,000 population is based on estimated resident population as of July 1.

The financial statistics relate to governmental fiscal years that ended June 30 of the year shown or at some date within the 12 previous months. The following governments are exceptions and are included as though they were part of the June 30 group: Alabama and its school districts, Michigan, and the District of Columbia, ending September 30; New York, ending March 31; and Texas and its school districts, ending August 31.

Revenue includes all amounts of money received by a government from external sources during its fiscal year (i.e., those originating "outside the government") net of refunds and other correcting transactions, other than issuance of debt, sale of investments, and agency or private trust transactions. Under this definition, revenue excludes amounts transferred from other funds or agencies of the same government.

Revenue comprises amounts received by all agencies, boards, commissions, or other organizations categorized as dependent on the government concerned. Stated in terms of the accounting procedures from which these data originate, revenue covers receipts from all accounting funds of a government, other than intragovernmental service (revolving), agency, and private trust funds.

General revenue comprises all revenue except that classified as liquor store, utility, or insurance trust revenue. Generally, the basis for this distinction is not the fund or administrative unit established to account for and control a particular activity, but rather the nature of the revenue source involved. Within general revenue are four main categories: taxes, intergovernmental revenue, current charges, and miscellaneous general revenue.

Intergovernmental revenue comprises monies from other governments, including grants, shared taxes, and contingent loans and advances for support of particular functions or for general financial support; any significant and identifiable amounts received as reimbursement for performance of governmental services for other governments; and any other form of revenue representing the sharing by other governments in the financing of activities administered by the receiving government. All intergovernmental revenue is reported in the general government sector, even if it is used to support activities in other sectors (such as utilities).

Intergovernmental revenue excludes any amounts received from other governments for sale of property, commodities, and utility services. It also excludes amounts received from other governments as the employer share or for support of public employee retirement or other insurance trust funds of the recipient government, which are treated as insurance trust revenue.

Intergovernmental revenue from the federal government represents all intergovernmental revenue received by a government directly from the federal government.

Taxes consist of compulsory contributions exacted by government for public purposes. However, this category excludes employer and employee payments for retirement and social insurance purposes, which are classified as insurance trust revenue, and special assessments to pay capital improvements. Tax revenue comprises gross amounts collected (including interest and penalties) minus amounts refunded during the same period. It consists of all taxes itself or relies on another government to act as its collection agent.

Government expenditures includes all amounts of money paid out by a government during the fiscal year—net of recoveries and other correcting transactions—other than for retirement of debt, purchase of investment securities, extension of loans, and agency or private trust transactions. Under this definition, expenditures relates to external payments of a government and excludes amounts transferred to funds or agencies of the same government.

Expenditures includes payments from all sources of funds, including not only current revenues but also proceeds from borrowing and prior-year fund balances. Expenditures includes amounts spent by all agencies, boards, commissions, or other organizations categories as dependent on the government concerned. Expenditures covers outlays of all accounting funds of a government other than intragovernmental service, agency, and private trust funds.

General expenditures comprises all expenditures except that classified as liquor store, utility, or insurance trust expenditures. General government expenditures are classified by function, character, and object.

Intergovernmental expenditure categories include those to state governments, local governments (n.e.c.), general purpose governments (county, municipal, or township), independent school districts, special districts, and the federal government.

Education includes all activities associated with the operation of elementary and secondary schools. It also includes state government degree granting institutions which provide academic training above grade 12. Services associated with the operation of schools, such as transportation, food service, special education programs, instructional employees, and other employees (e.g. school superintendents, administrative personnel, clerical and secretarial staffs, etc.) are included.

Public welfare includes the administration of various public assistance programs for the needy, operation of homes for the elderly, and indigent care institutions. Also, it includes programs which provide payments for medical care and services for the needy.

Health and hospitals include the administration of public health programs, community and visiting nurse services, immunization programs, drug abuse rehabilitation programs, health out-patient clinics, and environmental and pollution control activities. This category also includes government operated medical care facilities for inpatient care. The employees and payroll of private corporations which lease and operate government owned facilities are excluded.

Table A-50. State General Fund, Tax Collection, and Federal Aid

State general fund—resources, expenditures, and balances, 1997, preliminary and 1996;
State government tax collection—total, 1996 and 1990;
    Sales and gross receipts, total and general, 1996;
    Individual income, and corporation net income, 1996;
Federal aid to state and local governments—total, 1996 and 1990; and by selected function, medicaid and highway trust fund, 1996

Source: State general fund—National Governors' Association and National Association of State Budget Offices, Washington, DC, *Fiscal Survey of The States*, April 1997, semi-annual (copyright); Tax Collection—U.S. Bureau of the Census, for 1996, Internet site <http://www.census.gov/govs/www/sttax96.html>, (Revised May 22, 1997); for 1990, *State Government Tax Collection: 1992*, GF/92-1, October 1994; Federal Aid to State and Local Governments—U.S. Bureau of the Census, for 1996, *Federal Expenditures by State for Fiscal Year 1996*, FES/96, April 1997; for 1990, *Federal Expenditures by State for Fiscal Year 1995*, FES/95, June 1996.

State general funds support most ongoing broad-based state services, as opposed to long-term state capital projects, and are available for appropriation to support any governmental activity. These funds exclude special funds earmarked for particular purposes, such as highway trust funds, which are supported by fuel taxes and motor license fees.

Resources include funds budgeted, adjustments, and balances from previous year. Expenditures may or may not include budget stabilization fund transfers, depending on state accounting practices. See source for details.

Taxes are compulsory contributions exacted by government for public purposes including interest, penalties, and local shares of state-imposed taxes. Excluded are amounts paid under protest and amounts refunded during the same period. It consists of all taxes imposed by a government whether the government collects the taxes itself or relies on another government to act as its collection agent.

Sales and gross receipts taxes are taxes on goods and services, measured on the basis of the volume or value of their transfer, upon gross receipts or gross income therefrom, or as an amount per unit sold; and related taxes based upon use, storage, production, importation, or consumption of goods and service.

General sales and gross receipts taxes are applicable with only specified exceptions to sales of all types of goods and services or to all gross receipts, whether at a single rate or at classified rates; and sales use taxes.

Individual income tax includes tax on individuals measured by net income and tax on special types of income (e.g. interest, dividends, income from intangible property, etc.).

Corporation net income tax includes taxes on corporations and unincorporated businesses, measured by net income, whether on corporations in general or on specific kinds of corporations, such as financial institutions.

All amounts of federal government grants and other payments to state and local governments represent actual cash outlays made during the fiscal year. Each federal government executive department and agency provides annual data on grants and other payments to governmental units pursuant to OMB Circular A-11. The data are collected from federal agencies by the Census Bureau.

Federal government aid to state and local governments includes the following: direct cash grants to state or local government units; payments for grants-in-kind, such as purchases of commodities distributed to state or local government institutions (e.g., school programs); payments to nongovernment entities when such payments result in cash or in-kind services passed on to state and local governments; payments to regional commissions and organizations that are redistributed to the state or local level; federal government payments to state or local governments for research and development that is an integral part of the provision of public services; and shared revenues.

Table A-51. Federal Government

Employment, 1995, 1994, and 1990;
Earnings—civilian and military, 1995, 1994, and 1990;
Federal funds and grants—total, 1996 and 1990, and defense, 1996;
Selected object categories, 1996.

Source: Federal government employment—U.S. Bureau of Economic Analysis, Regional Economic Measurement Division, Louisiana Electronic Assistance Program, Internet site <http://leap.nlu.edu/bea/WWWHOME.htm> (accessed 1 August 1997); Federal earnings—U.S. Bureau of Economic Analysis, *Survey of Current Business*, Volume 76, Number 10, October 1996; Federal funds and grants—U.S. Bureau of the Census, *Federal Expenditures by State for Fiscal Year 1996*, issued April 1997, FES/96, and unpublished data.

Data for federal government employment are taken from the Regional Economic Measurement Division of the Bureau of Economic Analysis, Regional Economics Data Tables. It contains full-time and part-time estimates on employment by industry.

Total earnings cover wage and salary disbursements, other labor income, and proprietors' income. Wage and salary disbursements are defined as monetary remuneration of employees, including corporate officers; commissions, tips, and bonuses; and pay-in-kind that represents income to the recipient. They are measured before such deductions as social security contributions and union dues. All disbursements in the current period are covered. Pay-in-kind represents allowances for food, clothing, and lodging paid in kind to employees, which represents income to

them, valued at the cost to the employer. Other labor income consists of employer contributions to privately administered pension and welfare funds and a few small items, such as directors' fees, compensation of prison inmates, and miscellaneous judicial fees. Proprietors' income is the monetary income and income-in-kind of proprietorships and partnerships, including the independent professions, and of tax-exempt cooperatives.

Total federal funds and grants includes federal government expenditures for grants to state and local governments, salaries and wages, procurement, direct payment for individuals, and other programs for which data are available by state. Data for these items come from a variety of sources within the federal government and represent actual expenditures of the federal government during the fiscal year.

The Defense Department data are computed from Defense Department grants to state and local governments, salaries and wages, retired military pay, procurement, and research grants.

Per capita for defense is based on resident population estimated as of July 1.

Direct payment for individuals data are compiled from amounts reported by the Federal Agencies for the Federal Assistance Award Data System (FAADS). The FAADS is a quarterly report of financial assistance awards made by each federal agency. Coverage includes grants, direct payments to individuals and others, insurance, and loans. The Office of Management and Budget selected the Census Bureau as executive agent responsible for operating the FAADS.

All amounts of federal government grants to state and local governments represent actual cash outlays made during the fiscal year. This includes direct cash grants to state and local government units; payments for grants-in-kind, such as purchases of commodities distributed to state and local government institutions; payments to nongovernment entities when such payments result in cash or in-kind services passed on to state or local governments; payments to regional commissions and organizations that are redistributed to the state or local level; federal government payments to state and local governments for research and development that is an integral part of the provision of public service; and federal revenues shared with state and local governments.

Salaries and wages data are provided by the Department of Defense, Department of Transportation (United States Coast Guard, Office of Personnel Management (OPM), and the United States Postal Service. For detailed description, see the source.

Table A-52. Social Security, Food Stamp, and School Lunch Programs

Social security benefits—recipients and payments—total and retired workers and dependents, 1995 and 1990;
Federal food stamp program—participants and federal

cost, 1996 and 1990;
National school lunch program—participants and federal
cost, 1996 and 1990.

Source: Social security benefits—U.S. Social Security
Administration, *Social Security Bulletin*, quarterly; Federal
Food Stamp Program and National School Lunch Program—
U.S. Department of Agriculture (USDA), Food and Con-
sumer Service, *Annual Historical Review of FNS Pro-
grams*, unpublished data.

The old-age, survivors, and disability insurance program
(OASDI) provides monthly benefits for retired and disabled
workers and their dependents and to survivors of insured
workers. To be eligible for benefits, a worker must have had
a specified period of employment in which OASDI taxes
were paid. A worker becomes eligible for full retirement
benefits at age 65, although reduced benefits may be
obtained up to 3 years earlier; the worker's spouse is under
the same limitations. Survivor benefits are payable to
widows, widowers, and other dependents of deceased
insured workers.

Number of recipients in current-payment status is as of
December. Data for number of recipients are based on a
10-percent sample of administrative records. A person
eligible to receive more than one type of benefit is generally
classified or counted only once as a retired-worker beneficiary.

Data for retired workers and dependents include benefits for persons aged 72 and over not insured under
regular or transitional provisions of Social Security Act.

The Food Stamp Program is designed to help low
income households buy a more nutritious diet. Under the
program, single persons and those living in households
meeting the nationwide standard for income and assets
may receive coupons redeemable for food at most retail
food stores. The monthly amount of coupons a unit receives
is determined by household size and income. Households
without income receive the determined monthly cost of a
nutritionally adequate diet for their household size. This
amount is updated to account for food price increases.
Households with income receive the difference between
the amount of a nutritionally adequate diet and 30 percent
of their income, after certain allowable deductions. Food
stamp costs are for years ending September 30. These
costs are for benefits only and exclude administrative
expenditures. Data on persons are average monthly number participating in year ending September 30.

Data on pupils participating in the National School Lunch
Program are for the month in which the highest number of
children participated nationwide. The National School Lunch
Program covers public and private elementary and secondary schools and residential child care institutions. National
School Lunch Program costs include federal cash reimbursements at rates set by law for each meal served but do
not include the value of USDA donated commodities utilized in this program.

Table A-53. Social Welfare Programs and Workers' Compensation

Public aid recipients as percent of population—percent,
1994 and 1990;
Supplemental security income—recipients and annual payments, 1995 and 1990;
Aid to families with dependent children—recipients and
annual payments, 1994 and 1990;
State unemployment insurance—beneficiaries, first payments and benefits paid, 1995 and 1994;
Workers' compensation payments—1995 and 1990.

Source: Public aid recipients—Compiled by the U.S. Bureau
of the Census. Data from U.S. Social Security Administration, *Social Security Bulletin*, quarterly, and U.S. Administration for Children and Families, *Quarterly Public Assistance Statistics*, annual; Supplemental Security Income—U.S.
Social Security Administration, *Social Security Bulletin*,
quarterly, and *Annual Statistical Supplement to the Social
Security Bulletin;*. State unemployment insurance—U.S.
Employment and Training Administration, *Unemployment
Insurance Financial Handbook*, annual; Workers' Compensation payments—U.S. Social Security Administration, *Social
Security Bulletin*, summer 1995, and prior issues. Beginning 1995, Jack Schmulowitz, Baltimore, MD, and unpub-
lished data.

Public aid recipients is defined as total federal Supplemental Security Income (SSI) and Aid to Families with
Dependent Children (AFDC) recipients as of June as a
percentage of resident population estimated as of July 1 for
1994 and enumerated as of April 1 for 1990.

Under the direction of the Social Security Administration,
the Supplemental Security Income (SSI) program provides
cash payments in accordance with nationwide eligibility
requirements to persons with limited income and resources
who are aged, blind, or disabled.

The data cover persons with federal SSI payments
and/or federally administered state supplementation. States
have the option to supplement the federal SSI payment for
all or selected categories of recipients. The data are for
persons with federal SSI payments only for the following
states: New Hampshire, Connecticut, Indiana, Illinois, Minnesota, Missouri, North Dakota, Nebraska, Virginia, North
Carolina, South Carolina, Kentucky, Alabama, Oklahoma,
Idaho, Wyoming, Colorado, New Mexico, Arizona, Oregon,
and Alaska; these states have state-administered supplementation. Data for MD and FL cover federal SSI payments
and federally-administered state supplementation only; state
also has state-administered supplementation. Data for TX
and WV cover federal SSI payments only; no state supplementary payments are made.

The data for recipients of Aid to Families With Dependent Children (AFDC) are as of December. These data
include the children and one or both parents, or one
caretaker relative other than a parent, in families where the
needs of such adults were considered in determining the
amount of assistance.

Unemployment insurance is presently administered by the U.S. Employment and Training Administration and each state's employment security agency. By agreement with the U.S. Secretary of Labor, state agencies also administer unemployment compensation for eligible ex-service members and federal employees, unemployment assistance under the Disaster Relief Act of 1970, and workers assistance and relocation allowances under the Trade Act. Under state unemployment insurance laws, benefits related to the individual's past earnings are paid to unemployed eligible workers. State laws vary concerning the length of time benefits are paid and their amount. In most states, benefits are payable for 26 weeks and, during periods of high unemployment, extended benefits are payable under a federal-state program to those who have exhausted their regular state benefits. The basic benefit can vary among states by over 100 percent. Some states also supplement the basic benefit with allowances for dependents. About 93 percent of wage and salary workers are covered by unemployment insurance.

Workers' compensation provides protection to workers disabled from work-related injury or illness. The program includes protection under the laws of 50 states, the District of Columbia, and two federal programs (the Federal Employees Compensation Act and the Longshoremen's and Harbor Workers' Compensation Act).

Cash benefits are payable under workers' compensation to replace lost wages during periods of temporary or permanent total disability and to provide compensation for partial disabilities, such as those resulting from loss of body members. Cash benefits are also payable to survivors of workers who die because of work-related causes. In addition, workers' compensation pays for medical care and hospitalization in connection with these workplace disabilities. (Medical benefits may be paid even if no cash award is paid.)

The range in the amount of benefits paid reflects a number of influences, such as variation in state benefit formulas and maximum benefits, the differences in methods of administration, extent of litigation, occupational distribution and incidence of disability, and, most important, the size of the labor force.

Table A-54. Medicare and Medicaid

Medicare—enrollment and payments, 1996, 1995, 1994, and 1990;
Medicaid—recipients and payment, 1995, 1994, 1993, and 1990.

Source: U.S. Health Care Financing Administration, unpublished data.

Since July 1966, the federal medicare program has provided two coordinated plans for nearly all people age 65 and over: (1) a hospital insurance plan which covers hospital and related services and (2) a voluntary, supplementary medical insurance plan, financed partially by monthly premiums paid by participants, which partly covers physicians' and related medical services. Such insurance also applies, since July 1973, to disabled beneficiaries of any age after 24 months of entitlement to cash benefits under the social security or railroad retirement programs and to persons with end stage renal disease.

Enrollment data include hospital and/or medical insurance enrollment as of July 1. Payments data for states are for the calendar year and represent reimbursements.

Under medicaid, all states offer basic health services to certain poor people, such as individuals who are pregnant, aged, disabled or blind and families with dependent children. Medicaid eligibility is automatic for almost all cash welfare recipients in all states. Thirty-nine states also extend medicaid to certain other persons who qualify, except for incomes above regular eligibility levels; these persons include those who have medical expenses which, when subtracted from their income, spend down to a state's "medically needy" level, or who otherwise meet the higher "medically needy" income restrictions. Within federal guidelines, each state determines its own medicaid eligibility criteria and the health services to be provided under medicaid. The cost of providing medicaid services is jointly shared by the federal government and the states.

Table A-55. Elections

Voting age population—total, 1996 and 1992;
Percent of voting-age population casting votes for President, 1996 and 1992;
Popular votes for President and votes cast for U.S. Senator, 1996 and 1992.

Source: Voting age population—for 1992, U.S. Bureau of the Census, *Current Population Reports*, P25-1117, for 1996, Statistical Brief (SB/96-2); Popular vote for president—for 1992, Election Research Center, Chevy Chase, MD, *America Votes*, biennial, for 1996, Congressional Quarterly, Inc., Washington, DC, *America Votes*, biennial, (copyright); Votes cast for U.S. Senators—For 1994, Congressional Quarterly, Inc., Washington, DC, *America Votes*, biennial; for 1996, Congressional Quarterly, Inc., Washington, DC, *Congressional Quarterly Weekly Report*, Volume 55, No. 7, February 15, 1997 (copyright).

The voting-age population relates to persons 18 years old and over in all states and the District of Columbia. The figures include Armed Forces personnel stationed in each state, aliens, and the institutional population.

The Constitution specifies how the President and Vice President are selected. Each state elects, by popular vote, a group of electors equal in number to its total of members of Congress. The 23rd Amendment, adopted in 1961, grants the District of Columbia three presidential electors, a number equal to that of the least populous state. A majority vote of all electors is necessary to elect the President and Vice President. If no candidate receives a majority, the

House of Representatives, with each state having one vote, is empowered to elect the President and Vice President, again, with a majority of votes required.

The Senate is composed of 100 members, two from each state, who are elected to serve for a term of 6 years. One-third of the Senate is elected every 2 years. Senators were originally chosen by the state legislatures. The 17th Amendment to the Constitution, adopted in 1913, prescribed that Senators be elected by popular vote.

The percentage of votes cast for the leading party represents the percentage of the total votes cast for the party with a majority or plurality.

Table A-56. Composition of Congress, Governors, and State Legislatures

Composition of 104th Congress—Senate and House of Representative, 1997;
Votes cast for governor—1996 and 1994;
Composition of state legislatures, 1996;
Number of elected public officials, Black, 1993, Hispanic, 1994, women, 1996.

Source: Composition of Congress—U.S. Congress, Joint Committee on Printing, *Congressional Directory*, biennial, and unpublished data; Votes cast for governor—Congressional Quarterly, Inc., Washington, DC, *Congressional Quarterly Weekly Report*, Volume 53, No. 15, April 15, 1995, and unpublished data (copyright); Composition of state legislatures—National Conference of State Legislatures, Denver, CO, unpublished data (copyright); Black elected officials—Joint Center for Political and Economic Studies, Washington, DC, *Black Elected Officials: A National Roster*, annual (copyright); Hispanic public officials—National Association of Latino Elected Officials, Washington, DC: *A National Roster of Hispanic Elected Officials*, annual; Women holding state public office—Center for the American Woman and Politics, Eagleton Institute of Politics, Rutgers University, New Brunswick, NJ, information releases (copyright).

Except as noted, votes cast for Senators and members of the U.S. House of Representatives exclude elections to fill vacancies of unexpired terms.

In each state, totals for votes cast for Representatives represent the sum of votes cast in each Congressional District or votes cast for Representatives at Large in states where only one member is elected. In all years, there are numerous districts within the state where either the Republican or Democratic party had no candidate. In some states, the Republican and Democratic vote includes votes cast for the party candidate by endorsing parties.

Votes cast for governor represents total votes cast, including scattered votes.

Data shown for composition of state legislatures reflect election results in year shown for most states and to odd-year elections the previous years in a few states. The figures reflect the immediate results of elections, including holdover members in partial renewal situations. The data

do not reflect vacancies and independent members. Lower House refers to the body consisting of State Representatives; Upper House, of U.S. Senators.

As of January 1993, no Black elected officials had been identified in Hawaii, Idaho, Montana, North Dakota, or Utah. The total includes U.S. and state legislatures and elected state administrators; city and county offices which include county commissioners and councilmen, mayors, vice mayors, aldermen, regional officials and others; law enforcement officials, such as judges, magistrates, constables, marshals, sheriffs, justices of peace, and others; and members of state education agencies, college boards, school boards, and other.

Hispanic elected officials includes U.S. Representatives; state executives and legislators; county and municipal officials; judicial and law enforcement officials; and education and school boards.

Statistics for number of women holding state and local public offices cover women in statewide elective executive offices and state legislatures, county commissions, mayoralties, townships, and local councils.

Table B—Metro Areas

Table B consists of 10 tables (B-1 through B-10) with 159 data items for 332 metropolitan areas (MAs): 245 metropolitan statistical areas (MSAs), 17 consolidated metropolitan statistical areas (CMSAs), 58 primary metropolitan statistical areas (PMSAs), and 12 New England county metropolitan areas (NECMAs). Excluded from this publication are the 21 New England MAs defined in terms of cities and towns: 10 MSAs, 1 CMSA, and 15 PMSAs. All areas are defined as of June 30, 1996.

The MSAs, CMSAs, and 11 of the 12 NECMAs are presented alphabetically in each of the 10 tables. The PMSAs and the New Haven-Bridgeport-Stamford-Waterbury-Danbury, CT NECMA, which is treated as a substitute for the 5 CT PMSAs in the New York-Northern New Jersey-Long Island, NY-NJ-CT-PA CMSA/NECMA, are listed under their related CMSA. For an alphabetic listing of these PMSAs with related CMSA, see Appendix C.

Table B-1 includes a column listing the Federal Information Processing Standards (FIPS) codes for these MAs. This code is given to facilitate cross-reference with other publications, such as the *County and City Data Book,* and to provide necessary information for access to, and interchange of, data available in electronic format.

All summaries, including historical data, are presented for the areas as currently defined. Where possible, the original figures have been retabulated to reflect the status of metropolitan area boundaries as of June 30, 1996. For more information on these areas, see Appendix B, Geographic Concepts and Codes.

Table B-1. Area and Population

Land area—1990;
Population—total, rank, and per square mile, 1997;

Total, 1996, 1990, and 1980;
Net change—1990-1997;
Percent change—percent and rank, 1990-1997;
Percent change, 1980-1990.

Source: Land area—U.S. Bureau of the Census, data file from Geography Division based on the TIGER/Geographic Identification Code Scheme (TIGER/GICS) computer file (related Internet site <http://www.census.gov/population/www/censusdata/density.html>).1990-1997 population—U.S. Bureau of the Census, *Estimates of the Population of Counties and Demographic Components of Population Change: April 1, 1990, to July 1, 1997* (CO-97-5), Internet site <http://www.census.gov/population/www/estimates/co_97_5.html> (accessed 30 March 1998); 1996 population—U.S. Bureau of the Census, *Estimates of the Population of Counties, Annual Time Series, July 1, 1990, to July 1, 1997,* (CO-97-4), Internet site <http://www.census.gov/population/www/estimates/co_97_4.html> (accessed 30 March 1998); 1980 population—U.S. Bureau of the Census, 1980-1990 *Intercensal Population Estimates by County* on diskette.

TIGER is an acronym for the new digital (computer-readable) geographic database that automates the mapping and related geographic activities required to support the Census Bureau's census and survey programs. The Census Bureau developed the Topologically Integrated Geographic Encoding and Referencing (TIGER) System to automate the geographic support processes needed to meet the major geographic needs of the 1990 census.

Land area was calculated from the specific set of boundaries recorded for the entity (in this case, counties, which were then aggregated to metropolitan totals) in the Census Bureau's geographic database.

Land area measurements may disagree with the information displayed on census maps and in the TIGER file because, for area measurement purposes, features identified as "intermittent water" and "glacier" are reported as land area.

The accuracy of any area measurement figure is limited by the inaccuracy inherent in (1) the location and shape of the various boundary features in the database, and (2) rounding affecting the last digit in all operations that compute and/or sum the area measurements. Identification of land is for statistical purposes and does not necessarily reflect legal definitions.

The count of total persons is based on resident population estimated as of July 1 for 1997 and 1996, and enumerated as of April 1 for 1990 and 1980.

Population data for 1997 and revised population data for 1990 through 1996 were released in mid-March of 1998 for counties. These population data were processed and used in Table B-1 of this publication. Population figures used to calculate rates or describe various population characteristics (e.g., race) in Tables B-2 through B-10 are those released in the previous annual cycle.

The estimated population is a computed number of persons living in an area (resident population) as of July 1. County estimates are calculated using a demographic components-of-change model that incorporates information on natural change (births and deaths) and net migration (net domestic migration and net movement from abroad) in the area since the reference date. Additional information on the methodology used to produce these population estimates is available on Internet site <http://www.census.gov/population/www/methoddep.html>.

The April 1 census population is a count of the number of persons residing in an area (resident population) as reported in the census of population, or as subsequently revised. Revisions to an area's census population count may occur as the result of (1) post-census corrections of political boundaries, geographic misallocations, or documented under enumerations or over enumerations, and (2) geographic boundary updates made after the census, resulting from annexations, deannexations, new incorporations, governmental mergers, and so forth. The closing date to include these two forms of revisions for 1990 in this set of estimates was December 1994.

Rank numbers are assigned on the basis of population size, with each area placed in descending order, largest to smallest. Where ties occur—two or more areas with identical populations—the same rank is assigned to each of the tied areas. In such cases, the following rank number is omitted so that the lowest rank is usually equal to the number of areas ranked. The 273 areas ranked include the 17 CMSAs, 245 MSAs, and 11 of the 12 NECMAs. The 58 PMSAs and the New Haven-Bridgeport-Stamford-Waterbury-Danbury, CT NECMA, which is used as a PMSA substitute in the New York-Northern New Jersey-Long Island, NY-NJ-CT-PA CMSA/NECMA, are not ranked.

Population per square mile is the average number of inhabitants per square mile of land area. These figures are derived by dividing the total number of residents by the number of square miles of land area in the specified geographic area. To determine population per square kilometer, multiply the population per square mile by .3861.

Net change represents the increase or decrease between the two years shown.

Natural change is the difference between the number of births and the number of deaths.

Net international migration is the difference between migration to an area from outside the United States (immigration) and migration from the area to outside the United States (emigration) during the period. More specifically, net international migration consists of (1) legal immigration to the United States as reported by the Immigration and Naturalization Service, (2) an estimate of net undocumented immigration from abroad, (3) an estimate of emigration from the United States, and (4) net movement between Puerto Rico and the United States.

Percent change represents the increase or decrease between the two years shown as a percentage of the beginning population.

Table B-2. Population Projections and Characteristics

Population projections—totals, 2010, 2005, 2000, and 1993, estimate.
Population characteristics, 1996—age, percent;
  65 years and over, percent and rank;
  Race, percent—White, Black, and Asian or Pacific Islander;
  Hispanic origin.

Source: Population Projections (BEA)—U.S. Bureau of Economic Analysis, *Regional Economic Information System (REIS) 1969-1994* on CD-ROM; Population characteristics, 1996—U.S. Bureau of the Census, *County Population Estimates by Age, Sex, Race, and Hispanic Origin - 4/1/90 to 7/1/96* data file (related Internet site <http://www.census.gov/population/www/estimates/co_casrh.html>).

The methodology utilized for generating these projections involved several steps and phases. National projections for employment, earnings, total personal income, and population were prepared first and used as the framework for the state projections. Of these, employment projections were the first prepared and were the basis for the projections of the other three variables. Then, the state projections were used as the framework for the projections for metropolitan areas.

For each area that is in only one state, projections were prepared for the area as a whole. For each area that is in more than one state, projections were prepared for each part of the area that is in a different state, and the projections for these parts were then summed to yield projections for the area as a whole.

The preparation of the projections for metropolitan areas had two phases. In the first phase, preliminary projections were derived from a mathematical model, which projected historical trends in area shares of state economic activity and population. In the second phase, the preliminary projections were revised on the basis of the judgments of reviewers knowledgeable about regional economic and demographic trends. In particular, the preliminary projections were revised to account for special economic factors (such as plant closures, strikes, or planned new facilities) that are not easily reflected in mathematical models.

The latest population estimate available when these projections were prepared was 1993.

These data are estimates of the resident population of the counties in the United States, by age (five-year age groups from under 5 years to 85 years and over), sex (male, female), race (White; Black; American Indian, Eskimo, and Aleut; Asian and Pacific Islander) and Hispanic origin for July 1. The estimates are consistent with: (1) the estimates of the population of states by age, sex, race, and Hispanic origin: July 1, 1990, to July 1, 1996 (available under separate cover as PE-57) and (2) the July 1, 1990, to 1996 postcensal estimates of the total population of counties released as the Department of Commerce Press Release, CB96-39.

The county estimates included here are developed in a two-step procedure. First a set of state estimates by age, sex, race, and Hispanic origin (with the same categories as given above) are developed. The county detail estimates are produced in the second step using a ratio method. The ratio method is a mathematical technique for adjusting data to sum to a predetermined total.

These data were developed as part of an ongoing project to produce postcensal population estimates of counties by age, sex, race, and Hispanic origin. Though the method employed produces estimates which are fully disaggregated with respect to these characteristics, the limitations of the methodology are such that these data may not be accurate for each individual cell. Although no measures of error exist, it is believed that aggregating the individual cells to larger groups (as has been done here) reduces the level of error.

Table B-3. Households, Births, and Deaths

Households—number, 1997 and percent change, 1990-97;
Births—number and rate, 1994, 1992, and 1990;
Deaths—number and rate, 1994, 1992, and 1990;
Deaths rate by cause, cardiovascular diseases and motor vehicle accidents, 1992.

Source: Households, 1997—Market Statistics, New York, NY, annual (copyright); Households, 1990—U.S. Bureau of the Census, 1990 Census of Population and Housing, Summary Tape File (STF) 1C on CD-ROM; Births—U.S. National Center for Health Statistics, *Vital Statistics of the United States*, Vol. I, *Natality*, annual, and unpublished data; Deaths—U.S. National Center for Health Statistics, *Vital Statistics of the United States*, Vol. II, *Mortality*, annual, and unpublished data.

A household comprises all persons who occupy a housing unit. A housing unit is a house, an apartment, a group of rooms, or a single room that constitutes separate living quarters. Counts of households and occupied housing units are always identical in complete-count data.

Household data for 1997 are estimates as of January 1 prepared by Market Statistics. For methodology, see source. Household data for 1990 are complete counts from the 1990 Census of Population and Housing. See General Note, Population, for a discussion of the decennial censuses.

The National Center for Health Statistics (NCHS) collects and publishes data on births and deaths in the United States. The Division of Vital Statistics obtains information on births and deaths from the registration offices of all states, the District of Columbia, and New York City on computer tapes through the Vital Statistics Cooperative Program.

In most areas, practically all births and deaths are registered. The most recent test of the completeness of birth registration, conducted on a sample of births from 1964 to 1968, showed that 99.3 percent of all births in the

United States during that period were registered. No comparable information is available for deaths, but it is generally believed that death registration in the United States is at least as complete as birth registration.

Birth and death statistics are limited to events occurring during the year. The data are by place of residence and exclude events occurring to nonresidents of the United States. Births or deaths that occur outside the United States are excluded.

Birth and death rates represent the number of births or deaths per 1,000 resident population estimated as of July 1 for 1994 and 1992 and enumerated as of April 1 for 1990. Death rates by cause represent the number of deaths from the specified cause per 100,000 resident population estimated as of July 1, 1992.

Table B-4. Infant Deaths, Physicians, Hospitals, and Education

Infant deaths—number and rate, 1994 and 1990;

Physicians—number and office-based and per 100,000 population, rate and rank, 1995;

Community hospitals—number, 1995 and beds, number and rate, 1995;

Education—public school enrollment, number and rate, 1994-1995, number, 1991-1992, and percent change, 1992-1995.

Source: Infant deaths—U.S. National Center for Health Statistics, *Vital Statistics of the United States,* Vol. II, *Mortality,* annual; Physicians—American Medical Association (AMA), Chicago, IL, *Physician Characteristics and Distribution in the U.S.,* annual (copyright); Community hospitals— Healthcare InfoSource, Inc., a subsidiary of the American Hospital Association, *Hospital Statistics,* 1996/97 edition (copyright); Public school enrollment—U.S. National Center for Education Statistics, Common Core of Data (CCD) Public Agency Universe Internet data files for years shown at site <http://nces.ed.gov/ccd/pubagency.html> (accessed April 1997).

Infant deaths represents the number of deaths of infants under 1 year of age. The infant death rate represents these deaths per 1,000 live births.

The number of physicians covers active, nonfederal physicians, as of December 31 of the year shown. The figures are based on information contained in the *AMA Physician Masterfile.* The file has been maintained by the AMA since 1906 and includes information on every physician in the country and on those graduates of American medical schools who are temporarily practicing overseas. The file also includes members and nonmembers of the AMA and graduates of foreign medical schools who are in the United States and meet U.S. education standards for primary recognition as physicians. Thus, all physicians comprising the total manpower pool are included on the file. However, this publication excludes data for all federal physicians and nonfederal physicians who are temporarily in foreign locations.

Masterfile data are obtained from AMA surveys and inputs from physicians, other organizations, and institutions. Primary sources are as follows: medical schools, hospitals, medical societies, national boards, state licensing agencies, Educational Commission for Foreign Medical Graduates, Surgeon General of the U.S. Government, American Board of Medical Specialties, and physicians. For details, see the source.

Data for office-based practice cover all physicians rendering patient care (or patient services by pathologists) in solo, partnership, group practice, or other arrangements, and those in industry, insurance companies, health departments, laboratories, etc.

Physician rate is per 100,000 resident population estimated as of July 1, 1995. Rank is based on 272 metropolitan areas (244 MSAs, 17 CMSAs, and 11 NECMAs). For a discussion of ranks, see Guide to Tabular Presentation.

Data for community hospitals are subject to copyright, see source citation.

Community hospitals statistics were compiled by the American Hospital Association (AHA) from surveys of all hospitals in the United States and its outlying areas. AHA surveys include unregistered hospitals, as well as those registered by the AHA. Hospitals were asked to report data for a full year ending September 30.

Community hospitals are defined as nonfederal, short-term (average length of stay less than 30 days), general or other special hospitals whose facilities and services are available to the public; psychiatric and tuberculosis hospitals and hospital units of institutions are excluded.

Data for beds are based on the average number of beds in the facilities over the reporting period. Rate is per 100,000 resident population estimated as of July 1, 1995.

Data for public school enrollment are for all public elementary and secondary schools in operation during the year shown. These data are from the Common Core of Data (CCD) which is the National Center for Education Statistics (NCES) primary database on elementary and secondary public education in the United States. The CCD, collected annually, is a comprehensive, national statistical database of all public elementary and secondary schools and school districts that contains data that are comparable across all states.

The CCD is based on a set of surveys sent to state education departments. Most of the data are obtained from administrative records maintained by the State Education Agencies (SEAs). Statistical information is also collected annually from public elementary and secondary schools (approximately 87,000), public school districts (approximately 16,000), and the 50 states, the District of Columbia, and outlying areas. The SEAs compile CCD requested data into prescribed format and transmit the information to NCES.

The data presented here were compiled from the school district files. Data were placed in counties based on the location of the superintendent of school districts. County data were then aggregated to metropolitan areas (MAs).

For this reason these data should be considered estimates of public school enrollment within the MAs. See Table C for a listing of counties within these MAs.

Public school enrollment represents enrollment at all levels taught in a public school system, from prekindergarten through grade 12.

Table B-5. Social Programs and Crime

Social security program—beneficiaries, total, 1994 and 1990, rate and retired workers, 1994, payment— total, 1994 and 1990;
SSI program recipients—total, 1995 and 1990;
Serious crimes known to police—number and rate, 1995, 1994, and 1990, percent of violent offenses, 1995.

Source: Social security—U.S. Social Security Administration, office of Research and Statistics, *OASDI Beneficiaries by State and County (December)*, annual (related Internet site <http://www.ssa.gov/statistics/ores_home.html>); Supplemental Security Income—U.S. Social Security Administration, Office of Research, Evaluation, and Statistics, *SSI Recipients by State and County, December*, annual (related Internet site <http://www.ssa.gov/statistics/ores_home.html>); Serious crime—U.S. Federal Bureau of Investigation, unpublished data, annual.

The old-age, survivors, and disability insurance program (OASDI) provides monthly benefits for retired and disabled workers and their dependents and to survivors of insured workers. To be eligible for benefits, a worker must have had a specified period of employment in which OASDI taxes were paid. A worker becomes eligible for full retirement benefits at age 65, although reduced benefits may be obtained up to 3 years earlier; the worker's spouse is under the same limitations. Survivor benefits are payable to widows, widowers, and other dependents of deceased insured workers.

Data show number of recipients in current-payment status as of December. Data are for the number of recipients based on a 10-percent sample of administrative records. A person eligible to receive more than one type of benefit is generally classified or counted only once as a retired-worker beneficiary.

Retired workers include benefits for persons aged 72 and over not insured under regular or transitional provisions of the Social Security Act.

The Supplemental Security Income (SSI) program is a cash assistance program for low income, aged, blind, or disabled persons in the 50 states, the District of Columbia, and the Northern Mariana Islands. The states and other jurisdictions have the option of supplementing their SSI payments and may choose to have them administered by the federal government. When a state chooses federal administration, the Social Security Administration maintains the payment records and issues the federal payment and the state supplement in one check. The data presented here are for federally-administered payments only. State-administered supplementation payments are not included.

The data are drawn from the Supplemental Security Record, the principal administrative data file for the SSI program. The amount of payments is not shown for counties with less than four recipients. Suppressed data are included in the state and national totals.

Through the voluntary contribution of crime statistics by law enforcement agencies across the United States, the Uniform Crime Reporting (UCR) Program provides periodic assessments of crime in the nation as measured by offenses coming to the attention of the law enforcement community. The Committee on Uniform Crime Records of the International Association of Chiefs of Police initiated this voluntary national data-collection effort in 1930. UCR Program contributors compile and submit their crime data in one of two means: either directly to the FBI or through the state UCR Programs.

Users of these data are cautioned about comparing data between areas based on their respective Crime Index figures. Assessing criminality and law enforcement's responses from area to area should encompass many elements (i.e., population density and urbanization; population composition; stability of populations, modes of transportation, commuting patterns, and highway systems; economic conditions; cultural conditions; family conditions; climate; effective strength and emphasis of law enforcement agencies; attitudes of citizenry towards crime; and crime reporting practices). These elements may have a significant impact on crime reporting.

Data for serious crimes known to police have not been adjusted for underreporting; this may affect comparability over time or among geographic areas.

Seven offenses, because of their seriousness, frequency of occurrence, and likelihood of being reported to police, were initially selected to serve as an index for evaluating fluctuations in the volume of crime. These crimes, known as the Crime Index offenses, are murder and nonnegligent manslaughter, forcible rape, robbery, aggravated assault, burglary, larceny-theft, and motor vehicle theft. By congressional mandate, arson was added as the eighth Index offense in 1979. Totals shown here exclude arson.

Violent offenses include four crime categories: (1) Murder and nonnegligent manslaughter, as defined in the UCR Program, is the willful (nonnegligent) killing of one human being by another. This offense excludes deaths caused by negligence, suicide, or accident; justifiable homicides; and attempts to murder or assaults to murder; (2) Forcible rape is the carnal knowledge of a female forcibly and against her will. Assaults or attempts to commit rape by force or threat of force are also included; however, statutory rape (without force) and other sex offenses are excluded;. (3) Robbery is the taking or attempting to take anything of value from the care, custody, or control of a person or persons by force or threat of force or violence and/or by putting the victim in fear; and (4) Aggravated assault is an unlawful attack by one person upon another for the purpose of inflicting severe or aggravated bodily injury. This type of assault is usually accompanied by the use of a weapon or by means likely to produce death or great bodily harm. Attempts are included since an injury does not necessarily have to result when a gun, knife, or other weapon is used, which could and probably would result in a serious personal injury if the crime were successfully completed.

Property offenses include three crime categories: (1) Burglary is the unlawful entry of a structure to commit a felony or theft; (2) Larceny-theft is the unlawful taking, carrying, leading, or riding away of property from the possession or constructive possession of another. It includes crimes, such as shoplifting, pocket picking, purse snatching, thefts from motor vehicles, thefts of motor vehicle parts and accessories, bicycle thefts, etc., in which no use of force, violence, or fraud occurs. This crime category does not include embezzlement, con games, forgery, worthless checks, and motor vehicle theft, and (3) Motor vehicle theft is the theft or attempted theft of a motor vehicle. This definition excludes the taking of a motor vehicle for temporary use by those persons having lawful access.

The rates were based on population estimates provided by the FBI for years shown.

Table B-6. Building Permits, Cost of Living, and Poverty

New private housing units authorized by building permits—1996, 1995, and 1994, total units, 1990-1996 and percent of 1990 housing stock;
Cost of living index—composite index and component indexes, 1996;
Persons below poverty level—number and percent, all persons and related children 5 to 17 years, 1993.

Source: Building permits—U.S. Bureau of the Census, Construction—Building Permits, on diskette, annual (related Internet site <http://www.census.gov/const/www/C40/table3.html>) and 1990 Census of Population and Housing, Summary Tape File 1C on CD-ROM; Cost of living index—ACCRA (American Chamber of Commerce Research Association), Alexandria, VA 22302-9950, *ACCRA Cost of Living Index, Third Quarter 1996* (copyright); Poverty—U.S. Bureau of the Census, *State and County Income and Poverty Estimates - 1993*, Internet site <http://www.census.gov/ftp/pub/housing/saipe/est93ALL.dat> (accessed 16 January 1998).

Building permits data presented are for the number of new housing units authorized by building permits in the United States. For 1996, 1995, and 1994, the data were based on a 19,000 permit-issuing place universe; prior to 1994, data were based on a 17,000 permit-issuing universe.

The building permits data relate to new private housing units intended for occupancy on a housekeeping basis. They exclude mobile homes (trailers), hotels, motels, and group residential structures, such as nursing homes and college dormitories. They also exclude conversions of and alterations to existing buildings.

Building permits data are based on reports submitted by local building permit officials in response to a Census Bureau mail survey. They are obtained using Form C-404, *Report of New Privately Owned Residential Building or Zoning Permits Issued.* Data are collected from individual permit offices, most of which are municipalities; the remainder are counties, townships, or New England and Middle Atlantic-type towns. When a report is not received, missing data are either (1) obtained from the Survey of Use of Permits, which is used to collect information on housing starts, or (2) imputed.

The number of new housing units authorized by metropolitan area (MA) is obtained by directly cumulating the data for the permit-issuing places to counties and the counties to MAs. Although not subject to sampling variability, data are subject to various nonsampling errors. Explicit measures of their effects generally are not available, but it is believed that most of the significant response and operational errors were detected and corrected in the course of the Census Bureau's review of the data for reasonableness and consistency.

The portion of residential construction measurable from building permits records is inherently limited since such records obviously do not reflect construction activity outside of areas subject to local permits requirements. For the nation as a whole, less than 5 percent of all privately owned housing units are constructed in areas not requiring building permits. However, this proportion varies greatly from state to state and among MAs. Any attempt to use these figures for inter-area comparisons of construction volume must, at best, be made cautiously and with broad reservations.

Data presented are for the number of new housing units authorized by building permits in the United States. For 1996, 1995, and 1994, the data were based on a 19,000 permit-issuing place universe; prior to 1994, data were based on a 17,000 permit-issuing universe.

When these numbers are related to the housing stock in 1990, they provide a general indication of the amount of new housing stock that may have been added to the housing inventory. Since not all permits become actual housing starts and starts lag the permit stage of construction, these numbers do not represent total new construction, but should provide a general indicator on construction activity and the local real estate market.

The American Chamber of Commerce Research Association (ACCRA) produces the *ACCRA Cost of Living Index* to provide a useful and reasonably accurate measure of living costs differences among urban areas. Items on which the Index is based have been carefully chosen to reflect the different categories of consumer expenditures. Weights assigned to relative costs are based on government survey data on expenditure patterns for midmanagement households. All items are priced in each place at a specified time and according to standardized specifications.

The ACCRA Cost of Living Index measures relative price levels for consumer goods and services in participating areas. The average for all participating places, both metropolitan and nonmetropolitan, equals 100, and each participant's index is read as a percentage of the average for all places.

The index does not measure inflation (price change over time). Because each quarterly report is a separate comparison of prices at a single point in time and because both the number and the mix of participants may change from one quarter to the next, index data from different quarters cannot be compared.

The index reflects cost differentials for a midmanagement standard of living. Operationally, this standard of living is set by the weighting structure. Homeownership costs, for example, are more heavily weighted than they would be if the index were structured to reflect a clerical worker standard of living or average costs for all urban consumers. Weights for component indexes shown here are as follows: grocery items - 16%; housing - 28%; utilities - 8%; transportation - 10%; health care - 5%; and miscellaneous goods and services - 33%. For specific items included in component indexes, see source.

Because the number of items priced is limited, it is not valid to treat percentage differences between areas as exact measures. Since judgment sampling is used in this survey, no confidence interval can be determined. Small differences, however, should not be construed as significant—or even as indicating correctly which area is the more expensive.

Areas included in this survey are those where chamber of commerce or similar organizations volunteer to participate. The number of respondents varies from quarter to quarter, and ACCRA makes a continuing effort to expand coverage of metropolitan areas. Any metropolitan area not represented in this report is absent because its chamber of commerce opted not to participate.

The estimates of poverty presented here originate from the Small Area Income and Poverty Estimates Program at the Census Bureau. The main objective of this program is to provide updated income and poverty statistics that are needed in the administration of federal programs and in the allocation of federal funds to local jurisdictions.

The program currently makes estimates for the following key statistics: median household income, number of people below the poverty level, number of children under age 5 below the poverty level (for states only), number of related children ages 5 to 17 years in families below the poverty level, and number of people under age 18 years below the poverty level.

The estimates are not direct counts from enumerations or administrative records, or direct estimates from sample surveys. Currently available data from these sources are not adequate to provide postcensal estimates for all counties. Instead, the estimates are based on modeled relations between current income and poverty levels and income tax and program data available for counties and states for years following the decennial census.

All estimates were obtained by combining results from the Census Bureau's March 1994 Current Population Survey with aggregate data from federal individual income tax records, food stamps program participants statistics, 1994 population estimates, and 1990 census figures. For more information on the background of this program, the data inputs, the estimation models, the precision and uncertainty of the estimates, and other related topics, see Internet site <http://www.census.gov/hhes/www/saipe93.html>.

All of the tabulations for 1993 mark the first time the Census Bureau has issued county-level income and poverty estimates in noncensus years. County-level data were aggregated to metropolitan areas.

Table B-7. Private Nonfarm Business Establishments and Personal Income

Private nonfarm establishments—total, 1995 and percent change, 1990-1995;
Personal income—total, 1994, 1993, and 1990;
   Percent change, 1990-1994;
   Per capita, dollar and rank, 1994;
   Transfer payments, 1994;
   Earnings by selected industries, 1994.

Source: Private nonfarm business establishments—U.S. Bureau of the Census, County Business Patterns, on diskette, annual (related Internet site <http://www.census.gov/epcd/cbp/view/ cbpview.html>); Personal income—U.S. Bureau of Economic Analysis, Regional Economic Information System (REIS) 1969-1994 on CD-ROM (related Internet site <http://www.bea.doc.gov/bea/dr1.htm>).

Figures for private nonfarm establishments are published in County Business Patterns (CBP), an annual report series. Basic data items are extracted from the Standard Statistical Establishment List, a file of all known single and multiestablishment companies maintained and updated by the Bureau of the Census from various Census Bureau programs, such as the annual Company Organization Survey, the Annual Survey of Manufactures, and Current Business Surveys, as well as from administrative records of the Internal Revenue Service and the Social Security Administration.

An establishment is a single physical location at which business is conducted or where services or industrial operations are performed. It is not necessarily identical with a company or enterprise, which may consist of one establishment or more. All activities carried on at a location generally are grouped together and classified on the basis of the major reported activity, and all data for the establishment are included in that classification. Establishment counts represent the number of locations with paid employees any time during the year.

Total personal income is defined as the income received by, or on behalf of, all the residents of the area. It consists of the income received by persons from all sources—that is, from participation in production, from both government and business transfer payments, and from government interest.

Personal income is measured as the sum of wage and salary disbursements, other labor income, proprietors' income, rental income of persons, personal dividend income, personal interest income, and transfer payments, less personal contributions for social insurance. Personal contributions for social insurance are included in earnings by type and industry but excluded from personal income.

Per capita personal income is computed by dividing the total personal income by population estimates provided by the Bureau of the Census. It is based on resident population estimated as of July 1, 1994. For a discussion of ranks, see Guide to Tabular Presentation.

Transfer payments are income for which services are not currently rendered. They consist of both government and business transfer payments. Government transfer payments include payments under the following programs: federal old-age, survivors, disability, and health insurance; unemployment insurance; railroad and government retirement; federal and state government-insured workers' compensation; veterans benefits, including veterans life insurance; food stamps; black lung; Supplemental Security Income; and Aid to Families with Dependent Children. Government payments to nonprofit institutions, other than for work under research and development contracts, are also included. The principal business transfers are corporate gifts to nonprofit institutions and consumer bad debts.

Earnings cover wage and salary disbursements, other labor income, and proprietors' income. Wage and salary income consists of monetary remuneration of employees, including corporate officers; commissions, tips, and bonuses; and receipts in-kind that represent income to the recipients. Retroactive wages are counted when paid rather than when earned. Other labor income includes employer contributions to private pension and welfare funds, employers' payments for privately administered workers' compensation insurance, and directors' fees. Proprietors' income is the monetary income and income in-kind of proprietorships and partnerships, including the independent professions, and of tax-exempt cooperatives.

Earnings are presented for selected industry groups and industries. Goods related industries include—mining (SIC 10, 12-14), construction (SIC 15-17), and manufacturing (SIC 20-39). Service related industries include—agricultural services, forestry, and fisheries (SIC 07-09); transportation and public utilities (SIC 40-49); wholesale trade (SIC 50-51); retail trade (SIC 52-59); financial, insurance, and real estate (FIRE) (SIC 60-65, 67); services (SIC 70, 72-73, 75-76, 78-84, 86-89); and government (SIC 91-97).

Government includes the executive, legislative, judicial, administrative, and regulatory activities of federal, state, and local governments.

Table B-8. Personal Income Projections and Civilian Labor Force

Personal income projection (constant 1987 dollars)—total and per capita, 2010; 2005, 2000, and 1993 estimate; Civilian labor force—total, unemployment, and unemployment rate, 1996, 1995, and 1994.

Source: Personal income projections—U.S. Bureau of Economic Analysis, *Regional Economic Information System (REIS) 1969-1994* on CD-ROM; Civilian labor force—U.S. Bureau of Labor Statistics, *Local Area Unemployment Statistics—Time Series,* Internet site <gopher://hopi2.bls.gov:70/11/Time%20Series/LA%20%20Local%20Area%20Unemployment%20Statistics/Data> for each state (accessed April 1997), BLS gopher service discontinued October 31, 1997 (related BLS Internet site <http://www.bls.gov>).

The methodology utilized for generating these projections involved several steps and phases. National projections for employment, earnings, total personal income, and population were prepared first and used as the framework for the state projections. Of these, employment projections were the first prepared and were the basis for the projections of the other three variables. Then, the state projections were used as the framework for the projections for metropolitan areas.

For each area that is in only one state, projections were prepared for the area as a whole. For each area that is in more than one state, projections were prepared for each part of the area that is in a different state, and the projections for these parts were then summed to yield projections for the area as a whole.

The preparation of the projections for metropolitan areas had two phases. In the first phase, preliminary projections were derived from a mathematical model, which projected historical trends in area shares of state economic activity and population. In the second phase, the preliminary projections were revised on the basis of the judgments of reviewers knowledgeable about regional economic and demographic trends. In particular, the preliminary projections were revised to account for special economic factors (such as plant closures, strikes, or planned new facilities) that are not easily reflected in mathematical models.

1993 was the latest personal income estimate available when these projections were made.

Civilian labor force estimates are the product of a federal-state cooperative program in which state employment security agencies prepare labor force and unemployment estimates under concepts, definitions, and technical procedures established by the Bureau of Labor Statistics (BLS).

The national unemployment statistics published monthly by BLS are obtained from the Current Population Survey (CPS), a Census Bureau survey of households. The size of the CPS is sufficiently large to obtain reliable annual average unemployment estimates for all states and the District of Columbia. County estimates, which are controlled to the CPS-based state totals, are then derived through the use of statistics derived from state unemployment insurance operations, as well as adjustments based on data from the CPS, decennial census, and other sources.

The civilian labor force comprises all civilians 16 years old and over classified as employed or unemployed. Employed persons are (a) all civilians who, during the survey week, did any work at all as paid employees, in their own business, profession, or on their own farm, or who worked

15 hours or more as unpaid workers in an enterprise operated by a member of the family, and (b) all those who were not working but who had jobs or businesses from which they were temporarily absent because of illness, bad weather, vacation, child-care problems, maternity or paternity leave, labor-management disputes, job training, or other family or personal reasons, whether or not they were paid for the time off or were seeking other jobs. Each person is counted only once, even if he or she holds more than one job.

Unemployed persons are all persons who had no employment during the reference week, were available for work, except for temporary illness, and had made specific efforts to find employment some time during the 4-week period ending with the reference week. Persons who were waiting to be recalled to a job from which they had been laid off need not have been looking for work to be classified as unemployed.

The unemployment rate for all civilian workers represents the number of unemployed as a percent of the civilian labor force.

An explanation of the technical procedures used to develop local area labor force and unemployment estimates appears in the Explanatory Note in the BLS periodical *Employment and Earnings,* May issue. A more detailed description of the estimation procedure is contained in the BLS document, *Manual for Developing Local Area Unemployment Statistics.*

Table B-9. Nonfarm Employment and Average Annual Pay

Nonfarm employment—total, 1996, 1995, and 1994;
   Percent change, 1994-1996;
   By selected industries, 1996;
Average annual pay—1996 preliminary, 1995, and 1994;
   Rank—1996, and percent change, 1994-1996.

Source: Employment—U.S. Bureau of Labor Statistics, *Employment and Earnings*, May 1997, related Internet site <http://www.bls.gov>; Average annual pay—U.S. Bureau of Labor Statistics, Average Annual Pay News Release, for 1996 and 1995, Internet site <http://www.bls.gov/news.release/anpay2.t01.htm> and Internet site <http://www.bls.gov/news.release/anpay2.t02.htm> (accessed 2 December 1997), for 1994 Internet site <http://stats.bls.gov/news.release/anpay2.t01.htm> and Internet site <http://stats.bls.gov/news.release/anpay2.t02.htm> (accessed 30 April 1997).

Employment and wage data are derived from the Covered Employment and Wages program, commonly called the ES-202 program, a cooperative endeavor of the Bureau of Labor Statistics (BLS) and the employment security agencies of the 50 states, the District of Columbia, Puerto Rico, and the Virgin Islands (SESAs). The ES-202 program is a comprehensive and accurate source of employment and wage data by industry at the national, state, and county levels. It provides a virtual census of nonagricultural employees and their wages. In addition, about 47 percent of all workers in agriculture industries are covered.

BLS summarizes employment and wage data for workers covered by state unemployment insurance (UI) laws and for civilian workers covered by the program of Unemployment Compensation for Federal Employees (UCFE) using data compiled from quarterly contribution reports submitted to the SESAs by employers. In addition to the quarterly contribution report, employers who operate multiple establishments within a state complete a questionnaire, called the Multiple Worksite Report, which provides detailed information on the location and industry of each of their establishments.

The ES-202 program is an employer reported measure and, therefore, associated with filled jobs, whether full or part time, and place of work. If a person holds two jobs, the person would be counted twice in the ES-202 data. The ES-202 program, by definition, measures employment covered by unemployment insurance laws. In excluding approximately 9 million self-employed jobs and others, it differs significantly from those programs that include that employment.

Major exclusions from UI coverage included most agricultural workers on small farms, all members of the Armed Forces, elected officials in most states, most employees of railroads, some domestic workers, most student workers at schools, and employees of certain small nonprofit organizations.

The ES-202 data are coded according to the Standard Industrial Classification (SIC) system, which is the statistical classification standard underlying all establishment-based federal economic statistics classified by industry. ES-202 data for the period from 1988 forward are coded according to the 1987 SIC Manual.

Employment data, except those for the federal government, refer to persons on establishment payrolls who received pay for any part of the pay period which includes the 12th of the month. For federal government establishments, employment figures represent the number of persons who occupied positions on the last day of the calendar month. Intermittent workers are counted if they performed any service during the month. Workers are reported in the area where their jobs are physically located.

The data exclude proprietors, the self-employed, unpaid volunteer or family workers, farm workers, and domestic workers. Salaried officers of corporations are included. Government employment covers only civilian employees; military personnel are excluded. Employees of the Central Intelligence Agency and the National Security Agency also are excluded.

Persons on establishment payrolls who are on paid sick leave (when pay is received directly from the firm), on paid holiday, on paid vacation, or who work during a part of the pay period even though they are unemployed or on strike during the rest of the period are counted as employed. Persons on the payroll of more than one firm during the period are counted each time they are reported. Workers are counted even though, in the latter months of the year, their wages may not be subject to the unemployment insurance tax. Not counted as employed are persons who are on layoff, on leave without pay, on strike for the entire period, or who were hired but have not yet reported.

Average annual pay data are another product of the ES-202 program. Data for 1996 are preliminary and subject to revision.

Average annual pay was computed by dividing total annual pay of employees covered by unemployment insurance programs by the average monthly number of these employers. Included in the annual payroll data are bonuses, the cash value of meals and lodging when supplied, and tips and other gratuities and, in some states, employer contributions to certain deferred compensation plans, such as 401(k) plans, and stock options.

Average annual pay is affected by the ratio of full-time to part-time workers as well as the number of individuals in high-paying and low-paying occupations. When comparing average annual pay levels between metropolitan areas, these factors should be taken into consideration. Average annual pay only approximates annual earnings because an individual may not be employed by the same employer all year or may work for more than one employer. Year-to-year changes in average annual pay can result from a change in the proportion of employment in high- and low-wage jobs, as well as from changes in the level of average annual pay.

Table B-10. Export Sales, Banking, and Federal Funds and Grants

Export sales—total, 1996, 1995, and 1994;
  Percent change—1995-1996 and 1994-1995;
Banking—Number of offices and total deposits, 1996,
  percent change, 1990-1996;
Federal funds and grants—total expenditures, 1996, per-
  cent change, 1990-1996;
    Per capita—total, dollar and rank, 1996;
    By selected type, 1996—direct payment for individual,
    procurement contract awards, salaries and wages, and
    grant awards.

Source: Export sales—U.S. Department of Commerce, International Trade Administration, *Export Sales of U.S. Metropolitan Areas, 1993-1996*, Internet site <http://www.ita.doc. gov/industry/otea/metro/metro.html> (accessed 9 October 1997); Banking—U.S. Federal Deposit Insurance Corporation, *Data Book: Summary of Deposits in Operating Banks and Branches*, annual (related Internet site <http://www.fdic. gov/databank/index.html>); Federal funds and grants—U.S. Bureau of the Census, *Consolidated Federal Funds Report: County Areas*, annual for fiscal year (related Internet site <http://www.census.gov/govs/www/cffr.html>).

Merchandise export sales are from the U.S. Census Bureau's Exporter Location (EL) series. The EL series, which the Census Bureau began issuing in 1993, allocates exports to states and localities based on the location of the

exporter of record. The exporter of record is not necessarily the entity that produced the merchandise; hence, the EL series does not furnish complete and reliable data on the production origin of U.S. exports. All figures in the series are on an f.a.s. basis (free alongside ship) and include both domestic exports and re-exports.

Metropolitan export numbers were tabulated by matching five-digit ZIP Codes entered by businesses on U.S. export declarations with the five-digit ZIP Codes specified for each metropolitan area (MA) in the Census Bureau's *City Reference File*. The matching process sometimes necessitated compromises. For instance, the boundaries of five-digit ZIP Codes sometimes cross from a MA into nearby rural areas. In such cases, the ZIP Code was assigned to the MA. In cases where two or more adjacent MAs share the same five-digit ZIP Code, exports for that ZIP Code were assigned to a catch-all "crossover" category, which accounted for 2.2, 2.3, and 2.6 percent of total exports for 1994, 1995, and 1996, respectively. If a five-digit ZIP Code could not be assigned due to faulty reporting by exporters, exports were assigned to an "unknown" category, which accounted for 6.9, 6.4, and 7.1 percent of the total exports for 1994, 1995, and 1996, respectively.

The EL statistics are different from, and cannot be compared with, the long-standing and widely-used Origin of Movement (OM) state export series, which allocates exports to states based on the location where the product began its journey to the port of exit. The EL and OM series are based on different methodologies, measure entirely different dimensions of subnational export activity, and are intended for different purposes.

The Federal Deposit Insurance Corporation (FDIC) conducts an annual survey of banking office deposits as of June 30 for all FDIC-insured commercial banks, savings banks, and U.S. branches of foreign banks. Data presented here exclude U.S. branches of foreign banks. Total deposit figures for unit banks (which do not have branch offices) were obtained from the June 30 *Reports of Condition*. Where recordkeeping by banks did not permit accurate separation of individual office figures across county lines, the reporting banks were required to estimate the allocation of deposits among offices.

The number of banking offices in any given area includes every location at which deposit business is transacted. Banking offices include all offices and facilities that actually hold deposits and exclude consumer installment loan offices, computer centers, and other nondeposit installations, such as some automated teller machines (ATMs).

Federal expenditures and obligations data were prepared by the Bureau of the Census in accordance with the Consolidated Federal Funds Report (CFFR) Amendment of 1986 (P.L. 99-547). The CFFR Act specified that the following reporting systems and agencies be used as data sources: Federal Assistance Award Data System (FAADS), Federal Procurement Data System, Office of Personnel Management (OPM), Department of Defense (DOD), U.S. Postal Service, Internal Revenue Service, U.S. Coast

Guard, Public Health Service, National Oceanic and Atmospheric Administration, and Federal Bureau of Investigation (FBI). In addition to these, several other federal agencies were requested to provide data, usually for selected programs. Selected data were obtained from the information on payments to state and local governments reported by federal agencies for the Census Bureau's Federal Aid to States survey.

Per capita items are based on resident population estimated as of July 1, 1996.

Most data covering direct payments for individuals were taken from information reported for the FAADS. The two object areas of direct payments for individuals are (1) direct payments for retirement and disability benefits and (2) all other direct payments for individuals. Most data represent actual expenditures during the fiscal years. For exceptions, see the source.

Data covering procurement were provided by the United States Postal Service (USPS) for Postal Service procurement and the General Services Administration, Federal Procurement Data Center (FPDC) for procurement actions of all other federal agencies, including DOD. Amounts provided by the USPS represent actual outlays for contractual commitments while amounts provided by the FPDC represent the value of obligations for contract actions and do not reflect actual federal government expenditures. In general, only current-year contract actions are reported for data provided by the FPDC; however, multiple-year obligations may be reported for contract actions of less than 3 years' duration.

Amounts reported for salaries and wages were obtained from five sources: OPM, DOD, USPS, FBI, and Department of Transportation (DOT). DOD provided information on military payrolls; data covering civilian employees of DOD were obtained from OPM. Amounts reported by DOD represent estimates of fiscal year outlays by state and county. Data for Postal Service employees were provided by the USPS and were based upon place of employment (postal facility). Amounts represent actual outlays during the fiscal year but with the national total distributed among the states and counties on an estimated basis. Salaries and wages for employees of the FBI were obtained separately from that agency. For uniformed employees of the U.S. Coast Guard, these data were reported by DOT. Data on salaries and wages for all other federal government employees (except for employees of the Central Intelligence Agency, Defense Intelligence, and the National Security Agency) were obtained from OPM. National totals represent actual expenditures during the fiscal year.

The principal source of grants data was the information submitted for the FAADS. The Bureau of the Census is the Executive Agent for the Office of Management and Budget and is responsible for the operation of the FAADS reporting systems. The FAADS data represent the federal obligations incurred at the time the grant is awarded. The amounts reported do not represent actual expenditures since obligations in one time period may not result in outlays during the same time period. Moreover, initial amounts obligated may be adjusted at a later date, either through enhancements or deobligations. All grant awards were reported by state, county, and city of the initial recipient. For many grants, this recipient is the state government even though the grant monies are subsequently distributed to county, municipal, or township governments. These "pass-through" grants generally appear in the CFFR at the state capital city (and in the associated county). No attempt is made in the CFFR to assign the dollar amounts for these pass-through programs to locations other than the state capital.

Table C—Metro Counties

Table C consists of 3 tables (C-1 through C-3) with 43 data items for the same 332 MAs presented in Table B (245 MSAs, 17 CMSAs, 58 PMSAs, and 12 NECMAs) and their 844 component counties. All areas are defined as of June 30, 1996.

The MSAs, CMSAs, and 11 of the 12 NECMAs are presented alphabetically in each of the 3 tables. The PMSAs and the New Haven-Bridgeport-Stamford-Waterbury-Danbury, CT NECMA, which is treated as a substitute for the 5 CT PMSAs in the New York-Northern New Jersey-Long Island, NY-NJ-CT-PA CMSA/ NECMA, are listed under their related CMSA. For an alphabetic listing of these PMSAs with related CMSAs, see Appendix C. Component counties are listed alphabetically under each MA; for MAs in more than one state, the counties in the first state of the MA title are listed first, followed by the counties in the next state, and so on.

Table C-1 includes two columns listing the FIPS (Federal Information Processing Standards) codes for these areas. The first column is the FIPS MA code; the second, the FIPS state and county code. These codes are given to facilitate cross reference with other publications, such as the *County and City Data Book*, and to provide necessary information for access to, and interchange of, data available in electronic format. For more information on these areas and codes, see Appendix B, *Geographic Concepts and Codes*.

Table C-1. Population

Total persons—1997, 1990, and 1980;
Net change—total, births, deaths, and net international migration, 1990-1997, and 1980-1990;
Percent change—1990-1997 and 1980-1990;
Percent—65 years and over and Hispanic origin, 1996.

Source: 1990-1997 population—U.S. Bureau of the Census, *Estimates of the Population of Counties and Demographic Components of Population Change: April 1, 1990, to July 1, 1997* (CO-97-5), Internet site <http://www.census.gov/population/www/estimates/co_97_5.html>, (accessed 30 March 1998); 1980 population—U.S. Bureau of the Census, *1980-1990 Intercensal Population Estimates by County*, on diskette; 65 plus and Hispanic population—U.S. Bureau of the Census, *County Population Estimates* *by Age, Sex, Race, and Hispanic Origin - 4/1/90 to 7/1/96* data file (related Internet site <http://www.census.gov/population/www/estimates/co_casrh.html>).

For a discussion on the decennial census and population estimates see General Note, Population.

The count of total persons is based on resident population estimated as of July 1 for 1997 and enumerated as of April 1 for 1990 and 1980.

Population data for 1997 and revised population data for 1990 through 1996 were released in mid-March of 1998 for counties. These population data were processed and used in Table C-1 of this publication. Population figures used to calculate rates or describe various population characteristics (e.g., race) in Tables C-1 through C-3 are those released in the previous annual cycle.

The estimated population is a computed number of persons living in an area (resident population) as of July 1. County estimates are calculated using a demographic components-of-change model that incorporates information on natural change (births and deaths) and net migration (net domestic migration and net movement from abroad) in the area since the reference date. Additional information on the methodology used to produce these population estimates is available on our Internet site at <http://wwww.census.gov/population/www/methoddep.html>.

The April 1 census population is a count of the number of persons residing in an area (resident population) as reported in the census of population, or as subsequently revised. Revisions to an area's census population count may occur as the result of (1) post-census corrections of political boundaries, geographic misallocations, or documented under-enumerations or over enumerations, and (2) geographic boundary updates made after the census, resulting from annexations, deannexations, new incorporations, governmental mergers, and so forth. The closing date to include these two forms of revisions for 1990 in this set of estimates was December 1994.

Net change represents the increase or decrease between the two years shown.

Births is the number of live births occurring to the residents of an area during the period as reported from the Census Bureau's Federal-State Cooperative Program for Population Estimates (FSCPE) and the National Center for Health Statistics (NCHS).

Deaths is the number of deaths occurring within the resident population of an area during the period as reported by the Census Bureau's FSCPE and NCHS.

Net international migration is the difference between migration to an area from outside the United States (immigration) and migration from the area to outside the United States (emigration) during the period. More specifically, net international migration consists of (1) legal immigration to the United States as reported by the Immigration and Naturalization Service, (2) an estimate of net undocumented immigration from abroad, (3) an estimate of emigration from the United States, and (4) net movement between Puerto Rico and the United States.

Percent change represents the increase or decrease between the two years shown as a percentage of the beginning population.

These data are estimates of the resident population of the counties in the United States, by age (five-year age groups from under 5 to 85 and over), sex (male, female), race (White; Black; American Indian, Eskimo, and Aleut; Asian and Pacific Islander) and Hispanic origin for July 1. The estimates are consistent with: (1) the estimates of the population of states by age, sex, race, and Hispanic origin: July 1, 1990, to July 1, 1996 (available under separate cover as PE-57) and (2) the July 1, 1990, to 1996 postcensal estimates of the total population of counties released as the Department of Commerce Press Release, CB96-39.

The county estimates included here were developed in a two-step procedure. First a set of state estimates by age, sex, race, and Hispanic origin (with the same categories as given above) are developed. The county detail estimates are produced in the second step using a ratio method. The ratio method is a mathematical technique for adjusting data to sum to a predetermined total.

These data were developed as part of an ongoing project to produce postcensal population estimates of counties by age, sex, race, and Hispanic origin. Though the method employed produces estimates which are fully disaggregated with respect to these characteristics, the limitations of the methodology are such that these data may not be accurate for each individual cell. Although no measures of error exist, it is believed that aggregating the individual cells to larger groups (as has been done here) reduces the level of error.

Table C-2. Population by Race, Poverty, Building Permits, and Labor Force

Population by race, percent—White, Black, and Asian or Pacific Islander, 1996;
Persons below poverty level—number and percent, all persons and related children 5 to 17 years, 1993;
New private housing units authorized by building permits—total, 1996 and 1995;
   Total units and percent of 1980 housing stock, 1990-1996;
Civilian labor force—total, 1996;
   Net change, 1990-1996;
   Unemployment, total and rate, 1996.

Source: Population by race—U.S. Bureau of the Census, *County Population Estimates by Age, Sex, Race, and Hispanic Origin - 4/1/90 to 7/1/96* data file; related Internet site <http://www.census.gov/population/www/estimates/co_casrh.html>; Poverty—U.S. Bureau of the Census, *State and County Income and Poverty Estimates - 1993*, Internet site <http://www.census.gov/ftp/pub/housing/saipe/est93ALL.dat> (accessed 16 January 1998); Building permits—U.S. Bureau of the Census, Construction—Building Permits on diskette, annual (related Internet site <http://www.census.gov/const/www/C40/Table3.htmlannual>) and 1990 Census of

Population and Housing, Summary Tape File 1C on CD-ROM; Civilian Labor Force—U.S. Bureau of Labor Statistics, Local Area Unemployment Statistics - Time Series, Internet site <gopher://hopi2.bls.gov:70/11/Time%20Series/LA%20%20Local%20Area%20Unemployment%20Statis tics/Data> for each state (accessed April 1997), BLS gopher service discontinued October 31, 1997 (related BLS Internet site <http://www.bls.gov>).

These data are estimates of the resident population of the counties in the United States, by age (five-year age groups from under 5 to 85 and over), sex (male, female), race (White; Black; American Indian, Eskimo, and Aleut; Asian and Pacific Islander) and Hispanic origin for July 1. The estimates are consistent with: (1) the estimates of the population of states by age, sex, race, and Hispanic origin: July 1, 1990, to July 1, 1996, (available under separate cover as PE-57) and (2) the July 1, 1990, to 1996 postcensal estimates of the total population of counties released as the Department of Commerce Press Release, CB96-39.

The county estimates included here were developed in a two-step procedure. First a set of state estimates by age, sex, race, and Hispanic origin (with the same categories as given above) are developed. The county detail estimates are produced in the second step using a ratio method. The ratio method is a mathematical technique for adjusting data to sum to a predetermined total.

These data were developed as part of an ongoing project to produce postcensal population estimates of counties by age, sex, race, and Hispanic origin. Though the method employed produces estimates which are fully disaggregated with respect to these characteristics, the limitations of the methodology are such that these data may not be accurate for each individual cell. Although no measures of error exist, it is believed that aggregating the individual cells to larger groups (as has been done here) reduces the level of error.

The estimates of poverty presented here originate from the Small Area Income and Poverty Estimates Program at the Census Bureau. The main objective of this program is to provide updated income and poverty statistics that are needed in the administration of federal programs and in the allocation of federal funds to local jurisdictions.

The program currently makes estimates for the following key statistics: median household income, number of people below the poverty level, number of children under age 5 below the poverty level (for states only), number of related children ages 5 to 17 years in families below the poverty level, and number of people under age 18 years below the poverty level.

The estimates are not direct counts from enumerations or administrative records or direct estimates from sample surveys. Currently available data from these sources are not adequate to provide postcensal estimates for all counties. Instead, the estimates are based on modeled relations between current income and poverty levels and income tax and program data available for counties and states for years following the decennial census.

All estimates were obtained by combining results from the Census Bureau's March 1994 Current Population Survey with aggregate data from federal individual income tax records, food stamps program participants statistics, 1994 estimates and 1990 census figures. For more information on the background of this program, the data inputs, the estimation models, the precision and uncertainty of the estimates, and other related topics, see the Internet site <http://www.census.gov/hhes/www/saipe93.html>.

All of the tabulations for 1993 mark the first time the Census Bureau has issued county-level income and poverty estimates in noncensus years. County-level data were aggregated to metropolitan areas.

Building permits data presented are for the number of new housing units authorized by building permits in the United States. For 1996, 1995, and 1994, the data were based on a 19,000 permit-issuing place universe; prior to 1994, data were based on a 17,000 permit-issuing universe.

The building permits data relate to new private housing units intended for occupancy on a housekeeping basis. They exclude mobile homes (trailers), hotels, motels, and group residential structures, such as nursing homes and college dormitories. They also exclude conversions of and alterations to existing buildings.

Data are based upon reports submitted by local building permit officials in response to a Census Bureau mail survey. They are obtained using Form C-404, Report of New Privately Owned Residential Building or Zoning Permits Issued. Data are collected from individual permit offices, most of which are municipalities; the remainder are counties, townships, or New England and Middle Atlantic-type towns. When a report is not received, missing data are either (1) obtained for the Survey of Use of Permits which is used to collect information on housing starts, or (2) imputed.

The number of new housing units authorized by metropolitan area (MA) is obtained by directly cumulating the data for the permit-issuing places to counties and the counties to MAs. Although not subject to sampling variability, data are subject to various nonsampling errors. Explicit measures of their effects generally are not available, but it is believed that most of the significant response and operational errors were detected and corrected in the course of the Census Bureau's review of the data for reasonableness and consistency.

The portion of residential construction measurable from building permits records is inherently limited since such records obviously do not reflect construction activity outside of areas subject to local permits requirements. For the nation as a whole, less than 5 percent of all privately owned housing units are constructed in areas not requiring building permits. However, this proportion varies greatly from state to state and among MAs. Any attempt to use these figures for inter-area comparisons of construction volume must, at best, be made cautiously and with broad reservations.

When these numbers are related to the housing stock in 1990, they provide a general indication of the amount of new housing stock that may have been added to the housing inventory. Since not all permits become actual housing starts and starts lag the permit stage of construction, these numbers do not represent total new construction, but should provide a general indicator on construction activity and the local real estate market.

Civilian labor force estimates are the product of a federal-state cooperative program in which state employment security agencies prepare labor force and unemployment estimates under concepts, definitions, and technical procedures established by the Bureau of Labor Statistics (BLS).

The national unemployment statistics published monthly by BLS are obtained from the Current Population Survey (CPS), a Bureau of the Census survey of households. The size of the CPS is sufficiently large to obtain reliable annual average unemployment estimates for all states and the District of Columbia. County estimates, which are controlled to the CPS-based state totals, are then derived through the use of statistics derived from state unemployment insurance operations, as well as adjustments based on data from the CPS, decennial census, and other sources.

The civilian labor force comprises all civilians 16 years old and over classified as employed or unemployed. Employed persons are (a) all civilians who, during the survey week, did any work at all as paid employees, in their own business, profession, or on their own farm, or who worked 15 hours or more as unpaid workers in an enterprise operated by a member of the family, and (b) all those who were not working but who had jobs or businesses from which they were temporarily absent because of illness, bad weather, vacation, child-care problems, maternity or paternity leave, labor-management disputes, job training, or other family or personal reasons, whether or not they were paid for the time off or were seeking other jobs. Each person is counted only once, even if he or she holds more than one job.

Unemployed persons are all persons who had no employment during the reference week, were available for work, except for temporary illness, and had made specific efforts to find employment some time during the 4-week period ending with the reference week. Persons who were waiting to be recalled to a job from which they had been laid off need not have been looking for work to be classified as unemployed.

The unemployment rate for all civilian workers represents the number of unemployed as a percent of the civilian labor force.

An explanation of the technical procedures used to develop local area labor force and unemployment estimates appears in the Explanatory Note in the BLS periodical *Employment and Earnings*, May issue. A more detailed description of the estimation procedure is contained in the BLS document, *Manual for Developing Local Area Unemployment Statistics*.

Table C-3. Private Nonfarm Business and Personal Income

Private nonfarm business—establishments, total, 1995 and net change, 1990-1995;
  Employment, total 1995, percent change, 1990-1995, and by selected industry, percent, 1995;
Personal income—total, 1994, percent change, 1990-1994, and per capita, 1994;
  Earnings, total and by selected industry, percent, 1994.

Source: Private nonfarm business—U.S. Bureau of the Census, County Business Patterns on diskette, annual (related Internet site <http://www.census.gov/epcd/cbp/view/cbpview.html>); Personal income—U.S. Bureau of Economic Analysis, *Regional Economic Information System, 1969-1994* on CD-ROM (related Internet site <http://www.bea.doc.gov/bea/dr1.html>).

Figures for private nonfarm establishments are published in County Business Patterns (CBP), an annual report series. Basic data items are extracted from the Standard Statistical Establishment List, a file of all known single and multiestablishment companies maintained and updated by the Bureau of the Census from various Census Bureau programs, such as the annual Company Organization Survey, the Annual Survey of Manufactures, and Current Business Surveys, as well as from administrative records of the Internal Revenue Service and the Social Security Administration.

Industry classifications are based on the 1987 edition of the *Standard Industrial Classification (SIC) Manual. The* 1987 edition of the manual represents revisions from the 1972 edition and its 1977 supplement. For more information on these revisions, see Appendix A of the 1987 SIC manual.

An establishment is a single physical location at which business is conducted or where services or industrial operations are performed. It is not necessarily identical with a company or enterprise, which may consist of one establishment or more. All activities carried on at a location generally are grouped together and classified on the basis of the major reported activity, and all data for the establishment are included in that classification. Establishment counts represent the number of locations determined to be active any time during the year.

Paid employment consists of full- and part-time employees, including salaried officers and executives of corporations, who are on the payroll in the pay period including March 12. Included are employees on paid sick leave, holidays, and vacations; not included are proprietors and partners of unincorporated businesses.

Total personal income is defined as the income received by, or on behalf of, all the residents of the area. It consists of the income received by persons from all sources; that is, from participation in production, from both government and business transfer payments, and from government interest.

Personal income is measured as the sum of wage and salary disbursements, other labor income, proprietors' income, rental income of persons, personal dividend income, personal interest income, and transfer payments, less personal contributions for social insurance. Personal contributions for social insurance are included in earnings by type and industry but excluded from personal income.

Per capita personal income is computed by dividing the total personal income by population estimates provided by the Bureau of the Census. It is based on resident population estimated as of July 1, 1994.

Earnings cover wage and salary disbursements, other labor income, and proprietors' income. Wage and salary income consists of monetary remuneration of employees, including corporate officers; commissions, tips, and bonuses; and receipts in-kind that represent income to the recipients. Retroactive wages are counted when paid rather than when earned. Other labor income includes employer contributions to private pension and welfare funds, employers' payments for privately administered workers' compensation insurance, and directors' fees. Proprietors' income is the monetary income and income in-kind of proprietorships and partnerships, including the independent professions, and of tax-exempt cooperatives.

Earnings are presented for selected industry groups and industries. Goods related industries include—mining (SIC 10, 12-14), construction (SIC 15-17), and manufacturing (SIC 20-39). Service related industries include—agricultural services, forestry, and fisheries (SIC 07-09); transportation and public utilities (SIC 40-49); wholesale trade (SIC 50-51); retail trade (SIC 52-59); financial, insurance, and real estate (FIRE) (SIC 60-65, 67); services (SIC 70, 72-73, 75-76, 78-84, 86-89); and government (SIC 91-97).

Government includes the executive, legislative, judicial, administrative and regulatory activities of federal, state, and local governments.

Table D—Central Cities

Table D features 3 data items for 273 (245 MSAs, 17 CMSAs, and 11 NECMAs) of the 332 metropolitan areas (MAs) presented in Tables B and C and their 538 central cities. Central cities are not defined for PMSAs; therefore, the 58 PMSAs and 1 NECMA used as a PMSA substitute (New Haven-Bridgeport-Stamford-Waterbury-Danbury, CT NECMA) are not included in this table. MAs and central cities presented in Table D have been defined as of June 30, 1996.

The MSAs, CMSAs, and NECMAs are presented alphabetically in this table. Central cities are listed in alphabetic order of the city name.

Table D includes two columns to the left of the area name listing the FIPS (Federal Information Processing Standards) codes for these areas. The first column is the FIPS MA code; the second, the FIPS state and place code. These codes are given to facilitate cross-reference with other publications, such as the *County and City Data Book,* and to provide necessary information for access to, and interchange of, data available in electronic format. For more information on these areas and codes, see Appendix B, *Geographic Concepts and Codes.*

Table D. Population

Population—1996, 1990, and percent change 1990-1996.

Source: Metropolitan area population—U.S. Bureau of the Census, *Estimates of the Population of Counties and Demographic Components of Population Change: Annual Time Series, July 1, 1990, to July 1, 1996,* (CO-96-8) data file (related Internet site <http://www.census.gov/population/estimates/county.html>;) Central city population—U.S. Bureau of the Census, unpublished data file (related Internet site <http://www.census.gov/ population/ www/ estimates/ cityplace.html>).

For a discussion on the decennial census and population estimates see General Note, Population

The count of total persons is based on resident population estimated as of July 1 for 1996 and enumerated as of April 1 for 1990.

The estimated population is a computed number of persons living in an area (resident population) as of July 1. The estimated population at the place level is calculated by using the change in the number of housing units (from April 1, 1990, to the estimated date) at the place level to distribute population change separately computed for the county level. County estimates are calculated using a demographic components-of-change model that incorporates information on natural change (births and deaths) and net migration (net domestic migration and net movement from abroad) in the area since the reference date. Additional information on the methodology used to produce these population estimates is available on our Internet site at <http://www.census.gov/population/www/methoddep.html>.

The April 1 census population is a count of the number of persons residing in an area (resident population) as reported in the census of population, or as subsequently revised. Revisions to an area's census population count may occur as the result of (1) post-census corrections of political boundaries, geographic misallocations, or documented under enumerations or over enumerations, and (2) geographic boundary updates made after the census, resulting from annexations, deannexations, new incorporations, governmental mergers, and so forth. The closing date to include these two forms of revisions for 1990 in this set of estimates was December 1994.

Percent change represents the increase or decrease between the two years shown as a percentage of the beginning population.

Appendix B.
Geographic Concepts and Codes

Geographic Concepts

STATES

States are the major political units of the United States. The District of Columbia is treated as a state equivalent in this publication. Tables A-1 through A-56 present data for the United States, the 50 states, and the District of Columbia.

For census purposes, states are often grouped into geographic regions and divisions. These areas are delineated on the state map on the inside of the front cover.

METROPOLITAN AREAS

The U.S. Office of Management and Budget (OMB) defines metropolitan areas (MAs) according to published standards that are applied to Census Bureau data. The general concept of an MA is one of a large population nucleus, together with adjacent communities that have a high degree of economic and social integration with that nucleus. Some MAs are defined around two or more nuclei.

The major purpose of MAs is to enable all federal agencies to use the same geographic definitions in tabulating and publishing data for metropolitan areas. The definitions are designed to serve a wide variety of statistical and analytical purposes; adoption of the area for any specific purpose should be judged in terms of appropriateness for that purpose. While the definitions have been developed for statistical use by federal agencies, state and local governments as well as private business firms have often found the definitions helpful in presenting data for metropolitan areas.

MAs are defined in terms of counties because these are the smallest geographical units for which a wide range of statistical data can be obtained. In New England, however, these areas are defined in terms of cities and towns because these subcounty units are of greater local significance. OMB has also defined county-based MAs for New England called New England county metropolitan areas (NECMAs) for use with county-based data.

The standards for establishing metropolitan statistical areas (MSAs), consolidated metropolitan statistical areas (CMSAs), and primary metropolitan statistical areas (PMSAs) are divided into 16 numbered sections, which are presented at the end of this appendix. Each section deals with a different specific aspect of the definition and identification process. The standards for defining NECMAs are presented at the end of the 16 numbered sections.

Metropolitan areas presented in tables B-1 through B-10, C-1 through C-3, and D of this publication are those county-based MAs defined as of June 30, 1996. A map showing MAs appears on pages xii and xiii and a map showing NECMAs appears on page xiv.

Users who want to become more familiar with the MA standards and how they are applied may contact the Population Division, U.S. Bureau of the Census, by e-mail at pop@census.gov or by telephone at 301-457-2419. Current MA definitions and related updates are available through the Subjects A to Z area of the Census Bureau's Internet site <http://www.census.gov/>. Copies of the MA Wall Map may be ordered through the Products and Services Staff, Geography Division, U.S. Bureau of the Census, at 301-457-1128.

Historical development. In 1910, the Bureau of the Census introduced "metropolitan districts" as an area classification. This marked the first use by the Bureau of the Census of a unit for reporting population data for large cities, together with their suburbs. Originally, only cities of at least 200,000 population were designated as the core of a metropolitan district. By 1940, the concept had been expanded to apply to a city of 50,000 or more inhabitants. The metropolitan district was generally defined to include contiguous minor civil divisions (MCDs) and incorporated places having a population density of at least 150 persons per square mile; therefore, the boundaries did not necessarily follow county lines.

A major limitation of the metropolitan district concept, from the standpoint of statistical presentation, was that not many data items beyond those available from the census of population and housing were available for MCDs and smaller places. The applicability of the metropolitan district concept also was limited because other generally similar area classifications were in use (e.g., the industrial areas of the census of manufactures and the labor market areas of the Labor Department's Employment and Training Administration), which were defined in different ways.

The standard metropolitan area (SMA) concept was developed in 1949 by the Bureau of the Budget (now OMB), with the advice of the newly established Federal Committee on Standard Metropolitan Areas, to overcome the above difficulties. It was designed so that a wide variety of statistical data on metropolitan areas might be presented for a uniform set of geographic areas. The SMAs consisted of one or more contiguous counties containing at least one city of 50,000 or more inhabitants. Additional counties had to meet certain criteria of metropolitan character and of social and economic integration with the central county in order to be included in an SMA.

Changes in the official criteria have been made at the time of each census since 1950. None of these changes have involved significant deviations from the basic metropolitan concept. Several modifications have been made in the rules for determining how large a city must be to have a metropolitan area defined. Criteria changes also have been made to reflect changing national conditions. For example, the 1949 rule specified that a county must have less than 25 percent of its workers engaged in agriculture. However, with a rapidly decreasing proportion of the population engaged in farming, this requirement has been eliminated because practically no counties are still affected by it. In 1959, the designation "standard metropolitan area" was changed to "standard metropolitan statistical area" (SMSA) to emphasize the nature and purpose of the areas. The SMSA designation was changed to the current MSA/CMSA/PMSA designations in June 1983.

Currently defined MAs are based on application of 1990 standards which appeared in the Federal Register on March 30, 1990, to 1990 decennial census data and to subsequent Census Bureau population estimates and special census data. Current MA definitions were announced by OMB effective June 30, 1996.

Special MA Notes. As of the June 30, 1996, OMB announcement, there are 255 MSAs, 18 CMSAs, 73 PMSAs, and 12 NECMAs in the United States. In addition, there are 3 MSAs, 1 CMSA, and 3 PMSAs in Puerto Rico not covered in this publication. This publication also excludes the 10 MSAs, 1 CMSA, and 15 PMSAs defined in terms of cities and towns in New England.

Included are 332 MAs: 245 MSAs, 17 CMSAs, and 58 PMSAs located outside New England, as well as the 12 NECMAs. Ten of the 12 NECMAs substitute for the 10 New England MSAs; one NECMA substitutes for the Boston-Worcester-Lawrence, MA-NH-ME-CT CMSA, which is composed of 10 PMSAs; and the last NECMA substitutes for the 5 PMSAs in the Connecticut portion of the New York-Northern New Jersey-Long Island, NY-NJ-CT-PA CMSA. For this reason, this CMSA is listed as CMSA/NECMA in this publication to alert users to this substitution.

Every state now has at least one MA; New Jersey and the District of Columbia are wholly included in MAs.

Data for the St. Louis, MO-IL MSA in this publication exclude that part of Sullivan city in Crawford County, MO. Crawford County is not part of the MSA; however, all of Sullivan city is in the MSA pursuant to P.L. 100-202, Section 530, effective December 22, 1987.

COUNTIES

The primary political divisions of most states are termed "counties," which are the basic building blocks for most metropolitan areas. In Louisiana, these divisions are known

as "parishes." In Alaska, which has no counties, the county equivalents are the organized "boroughs" and the "census areas" that are delineated for statistical purposes by the State of Alaska and the Census Bureau. In four states (Maryland, Missouri, Nevada, and Virginia), there are one or more cities that are independent of any county organization and thus constitute primary divisions of their states. These cities are known as "independent cities" and are treated as equivalent to counties for statistical purposes. The District of Columbia has no primary divisions and the entire area is considered equivalent to a county for statistical purposes.

Tables C-1 through C-3 present data for the 332 metropolitan areas described above (245 MSAs, 17 CMSAs, 58 PMSAs, and 12 NECMAs) and their 844 component counties defined as of June 30, 1996.

CENTRAL CITIES

In each MSA and CMSA, the largest place and, in some cases, additional places are designated as "central cities" under section 4 of the Official Standards for Metropolitan Areas, presented at the end of this appendix. The largest central city and, in some cases, up to two additional central cities are included in the title of the MA; there are also central cities that are not included in an MA title.

An MA central city does not include any part of that city that extends beyond the MA boundary. In eight instances, only part of a city qualifies as central, because another part of the city extends beyond the MA boundary. These central cities include only that area within the MA and are listed with the word "(part)" in their name.

Five central cities include the word "(remainder)" in their name. These cities are the "remainder" of a consolidated city. A consolidated city is an incorporated place that has combined its governmental functions with a county or subcounty entity but contains one or more other incorporated places that continue to function as local governments within the consolidated government. The "consolidated city (remainder)" is the portion of the consolidated government minus the semi-independent incorporated places.

Table D presents population data for the 273 metropolitan areas described above (245 MSAs, 17 CMSAs, and 11 NECMAs used as MSA/CMSA substitutes) and their 538 central cities defined as of June 30, 1996.

Geographic Codes

STATES

Each state and equivalent is assigned a two-digit Federal Information Processing Standards (FIPS) code in alphabetic order by state name; codes range from 01 for Alabama to 56 for Wyoming. These codes are published by the National Institute of Standards and Technology (NIST), U.S. Department of Commerce, in FIPS Publication 5-2 (issued May 28, 1987) and related updates which can be ewed at Internet site <http://www.itl.nist.gov/div897/pubs>. Each state and equivalent area is also assigned a two-letter FIPS/United States Postal Service (USPS) code. These two codes are included in the CD-ROM version of tables A-1 through A-56 of this publication.

METROPOLITAN AREAS

Each metropolitan area (MSA/CMSA/PMSA/NECMA) is assigned a four-digit FIPS code, in alphabetic order nation-wide. If the fourth digit of this code is a "2," it identifies the area as a CMSA. If the fourth digit is a "3," it identifies the area as a NECMA. These codes are published by NIST in FIPS Publication 8-6 (issued March 1995) and related updates which can be viewed at Internet site <http://www.itl.nist.gov/div897/pubs>. These codes appear on tables B-1, C-1, and D in this publication and are also included in the CD-ROM version of tables B-1 through B-10, C-1 through C-3, and D of this publication.

COUNTIES

Each county and county equivalent is assigned a three-digit FIPS code that is unique within state. These codes are assigned in alphabetic order of county or county equivalent within state, except for independent cities, which follow the listing of counties. In most states, the codes begin with 001 and generally continue in increments of two; the county codes for independent cities are assigned in alphabetic sequence beginning with 510 and generally continuing in increments of 10. These codes are published by NIST in FIPS Publication 6-4 (issued August 31, 1990) and related updates which can be viewed at Internet site <http://www.itl.nist.gov/div897/pubs>. For a county code to be unique for the nation, it is combined with its two-digit FIPS state code. These five-digit codes appear next to the county name on table C-1 and are included in tables C-1 through C-3 on the CD-ROM version of this publication.

CENTRAL CITIES

Each place, including independent cities, consolidated cities, and "consolidated city (remainder)," is assigned a five-digit FIPS code that is unique within state. These codes are assigned in alphabetic order within state. These codes are published by NIST in FIPS Publication 55-DC3 (issued December 28, 1994) and related updates which can be viewed at Internet site <http://www.itl.nist.gov/div897/pubs>. For a place code to be unique for the nation, the five-digit FIPS place code is combined with the two-digit FIPS state code. The seven-digit code appears next to the name of the central cities on table D of this publication and in table D on the CD-ROM version of this publication.

Official Standards for Metropolitan Areas

BASIC STANDARDS

Sections 1 through 7 apply to all states except the six New England States.[1] (They also apply to Puerto Rico, which is not included in this publication.)

Section 1. Population Size Requirements for Qualification

Each metropolitan statistical area must include:

A. A city of 50,000 or more population, or[2]

B. A Census Bureau defined urbanized area of at least 50,000 population, provided that the component county/counties of the MSA have a total population of at least 100,000.[3]

Section 2. Central Counties

The central county/counties of the MSA are:

A. Those counties that include a central city (see Section 4) of the MSA, or at least 50 percent of the population of such a city, provided the city is located in a qualifier urbanized area; and

B. Those counties in which at least 50 percent of the population lives in the qualifier urbanized area(s).

Section 3. Outlying Counties

A. An outlying county is included in an MSA if any of the six following conditions is met:

(1) At least 50 percent of the employed workers residing in the county commute to the central county/counties, and either

(a) The population density of the county is at least 25 persons per square mile, or

(b) At least 10 percent, or at least 5,000, of the population lives in the qualifier urbanized area(s);

(2) From 40 to 50 percent of the employed workers commute to the central county/counties, and either

(a) The population density is at least 35 persons per square mile, or

---

[1]Those provisions of sections 1 through 7 that are applicable to New England are specified in the standards relating to New England (sections 11 through 15).

[2]An MSA designated on the basis of census data according to standards in effect at the time of designation will not be disqualified on the basis of lacking a city of at least 50,000 population.

[3]An MSA designated on the basis of census data according to standards in effect at the time of designation is not disqualified on the basis of lacking an urbanized area of at least 50,000 or a total MSA population of at least 100,000.

(b) At least 10 percent, or at least 5,000, of the population lives in the qualifier urbanized area(s);

(3) From 25 to 40 percent of the employed workers commute to the central county/counties and either the population density is at least 50 persons per square mile or any two of the following conditions exist:

(a) Population density is at least 35 persons per square mile,

(b) At least 35 percent of the population is urban,

(c) At least 10 percent or at least 5,000 of the population lives in the qualifier urbanized area(s);

(4) From 15 to 25 percent of the employed workers commute to the central county/counties,[4] the population density of the county is at least 50 persons per square mile, and any two of the following conditions also exist:

(a) Population density is at least 60 persons per square mile,

(b) At least 35 percent of the population is urban,

(c) Population growth between the last two decennial censuses is at least 20 percent,

(d) At least 10 percent, or at least 5,000, of the population lives in the qualifier urbanized area(s);

(5) From 15 to 25 percent of the employed workers commute to the central county/counties,[4] the population density of the county is less than 50 persons per square mile, and any of two of the following conditions also exist:

(a) At least 35 percent of the population is urban,

(b) Population growth between the last two decennial censuses is at least 20 percent,

(c) At least 10 percent, or at least 5,000, of the population lives in the qualifier urbanized area(s);

(6) At least 2,500 of the population lives in a central city of the MSA located in the qualifier urbanized area(s).[5]

B. If a county qualifies on the basis of commuting to the central county/counties of two different MSAs, it is assigned to the area to which commuting is greater,

unless the relevant commuting percentages are within 5 points of each other, in which case local opinion about the most appropriate assignment will be considered.

C. If a county qualifies as a central county under section 2 and also qualifies as an outlying county of another metropolitan area under section 3A on the basis of commuting to (or from) another central county, both counties become central counties of a single merged MSA.

Section 4. Central Cities

The central city/cities of the MSA are:

A. The city with the largest population in the MSA;

B. Each additional city with a population of at least 250,000 or with at least 100,000 persons working within its limits;

C. Each additional city with a population of at least 25,000, an employment/residence ratio of at least 0.75, and at least 40 percent of its employed residents working in the city;

D. Each additional city of 15,000 to 24,999 population that is at least one-third as large as the largest central city, has an employment/residence ratio of at least 0.75, and has at least 40 percent of its employed residents working in the city;

E. The largest city in a secondary noncontiguous urbanized area, provided it has at least 15,000 population, an employment/ residence ratio of at least 0.75, and has at least 40 percent of its employed residents working in the city;

F. Each additional city in a secondary noncontiguous urbanized area that is at least one-third as large as the largest central city of that urbanized area, that has at least 15,000 population and an employment/residence ratio of at least 0.75, and has at least 40 percent of its employed residents working in the city.

Section 5. Combining Adjacent Metropolitan Statistical Areas

Two adjacent MSAs defined in sections 1 through 4 are combined as a single MSA provided:

A. The total population of the combination is at least 1 million, and:

(1) The commuting interchange between the two MSAs is equal to:

(a) At least 15 percent of the employed workers residing in the smaller MSA, or

(b) At least 10 percent of the employed workers residing in the smaller MSA, and

---

[4]Also accepted as meeting this commuting requirements are: (a) the number of persons working in the county who lives in the central county/counties is equal to at least 15 percent of the number of employed workers living in the county; or (b) the sum of the number of workers commuting to and from the central county/counties is equal to at least 20 percent of the number of employed workers living in the county.

[5]See section 4 for the standards for identifying central cities.

(i) The urbanized area of a central city of one MSA is contiguous with the urbanized area of a central city of the other MSA, or

(ii) A central city in one MSA is included in the same urbanized area as a central city in the other MSA; and

(2) At least 60 percent of the population of each MSA is urban.

B. The total population of the combination is less than one million and:

(1) Their largest central cities are within 25 miles of each other or their urbanized areas are contiguous; and

(2) There is definite evidence that the two areas are closely integrated with each other economically and socially; and

(3) Local opinion in both areas supports the combination.

Section 6. Levels

A. Each MSA defined by sections 1 through 5 is categorized in one of the following levels based on total population:

Level A—MSAs of 1 million or more;

Level B—MSAs of 250,000 to 999,999;

Level C—MSAs of 100,000 to 249,999;

Level D—MSAs of less than 100,000.

B. Areas assigned to Level B, C, or D are designated as MSAs. Areas assigned to Level A are not finally designated or titled until they have been reviewed under sections 8 and 9.

Section 7. Titles of Metropolitan Statistical Areas (MSAs)

A. The title of an MSA assigned to Level B, C, or D includes the name of the largest central city, and up to two additional city names, as follows:

(1) The name of each additional city with a population of at least 250,000;

(2) The names of additional cities qualified as central cities by section 4, provided each is at least one-third as large as the largest central city; and

(3) The names of other central cities (up to the maximum of two additional names) if local opinion supports the resulting title.

B. An area title that includes the names of more than one city begins with the name of the largest city and lists the other cities in order of their population according to the most recent national census.[6]

C. In addition to city names, the title contains the name of each state in which the MSA is located.

STANDARDS FOR PRIMARY AND CONSOLIDATED METROPOLITAN STATISTICAL AREAS (PMSAs and CMSAs)

Sections 8 through 10 apply to Level A metropolitan statistical areas outside New England.

Section 8. Qualification as a Primary Metropolitan Statistical Areas (PMSAs)

Within a Level A MSA:

A. Any county or group of counties that was designated as an SMSA on January 1, 1980, will be designated a PMSA, unless local opinion does not support its continued separate designation for statistical purposes.

B. Any additional county/counties for which local opinion strongly supports separate designation will be considered for identification as a PMSA, provided one county is included that has:

(1) At least 100,000 population;

(2) At least 60 percent of its population urban;

(3) Less than 35 percent of its resident workers working outside the county; and

(4) Less than 2,500 population of the largest central city of the Level A MSA.

C. A set of two or more contiguous counties for which local opinion strongly supports separate designation, and that may include a county or counties that also could qualify as a PMSA under section 8B also will be considered for designation as a PMSA, provided:

(1) Each county meets requirements 1, 2, and 4 of section 8B, and has less than 50 percent of its resident workers working outside the county;

(2) Each county in the set has a commuting interchange of at least 20 percent with the other counties in the set; and

(3) The set of two or more contiguous counties has less than 35 percent of its resident workers working outside its area.

---

[6]The largest central city included in an existing metropolitan area title will not be resequenced in or displaced from that title until both its population and the number of persons working within its limits are exceeded by those of another city qualifying for the area title.

D. Each county in the interim Level A MSA, not included within a central core under sections 8A through C, is assigned to the contiguous PMSA to whose central core commuting is greatest, providing this commuting is:

(1) At least 15 percent of the county's resident workers;

(2) At least 5 percentage points higher than the commuting flow to any other PMSA central core that exceeds 15 percent; and

(3) Larger than the flow to the county containing the Level A MSAs largest central city.

E. If a county has qualifying commuting ties to two or more PMSA central cores and the relevant values are within 5 percentage points of each other, local opinion is considered before the county is assigned to any PMSA.

F. The interim PMSA definitions resulting from these procedures (including possible alternative definitions, where appropriate) are submitted to local opinion. Final definitions of PMSAs are made based on these standards, and a review of local opinion.

G. If any primary metropolitan statical area or areas have been recognized under sections 8A through F, the balance of the Level A metropolitan statistical area, which includes its largest central city, also is recognized as a primary metropolitan statistical area.[7]

Section 9. Levels and Titles of Primary Metropolitan Statistical Areas

A. PMSAs are categorized in one of four levels according to total population, following the standards of section 6A.

B. PMSAs are titled in either of two ways:

(1) Using the names of up to three cities in the primary metropolitan statistical area that have qualified as central cities of the Level A MSA under section 4, following the standards of section 7 for selection and sequencing; or

(2) Using the names of up to three counties in the PMSA, sequenced in order from largest to smallest population.

C. Local opinion on the most appropriate title is considered.

Section 10. Designation and Titles of Consolidated Metropolitan Statistical Areas

A. A Level A metropolitan statistical area in which two or more primary metropolitan statistical areas are identified by section 8 is designated a consolidated metropolitan statistical area. If no primary metropolitan statistical areas are defined, the Level A area remains a metropolitan statistical area, and is titled according to section 7.

B. Consolidated metropolitan statistical areas are titled according to the following guidelines. Local opinion is always sought before determining the title of a consolidated metropolitan statistical area.

(1) The title of each area includes up to three names, the first of which is the name of the largest central city in the area. A change in the first-named city in the title is not made until both its population and the number of persons working within its limits are exceeded by those of another city in the consolidated area.

(2) The preferred basis for determining the two remaining names is:

(a) The first city (or county) name that appears in the title of the remaining primary metropolitan statistical area with the largest total population; and

(b) The first city (or county) name that appears in the title of the primary metropolitan statistical area with the next largest total population.

(3) A regional designation may be substituted for the second and/or third names in the title if there is strong local support and the proposed designation is unambiguous and suitable for inclusion in a national standard.

STANDARDS FOR NEW ENGLAND

In the six New England States, Connecticut, Maine, Massachusetts, New Hampshire, Rhode Island, and Vermont, the cities and towns are administratively more important than the counties, and a wide range of data are compiled locally for these entities. Therefore, the cities and towns are the units used to define metropolitan areas in these states. The New England standards are based primarily on population density and commuting. As a basis for measuring commuting, a central core is first defined for each New England urbanized area.

In New England, there is an alternative county-based definition of MSAs known as the New England County Metropolitan Areas (NECMAs). (See end of this appendix for NECMA definition.)

Section 11. New England Central Cores

A central core is determined in each New England urbanized area through the definition of two zones.

---

[7]If section 8G would result in the balance of the Level A metropolitan statistical area including a noncontiguous county, this county is added to the contiguous PMSA to which the county has the greatest commuting.

A. Zone A comprises:

(1) The largest city in the urbanized area;

(2) Each additional place in the urbanized area or in a contiguous urbanized area that qualifies as a central city under section 4, provided at least 15 percent of its resident employed workers work in the largest city in the urbanized area;[8]

(3) Each additional city or town at least 50 percent of whose population lives in the urbanized area or a contiguous urbanized area, provided at least 15 percent of its resident employed workers work in the largest city in the urbanized area plus any additional central cities qualified by section 11A(2).[8]

B. Zone B comprises each city or town that has:

(1) At least 50 percent of its population living in the urbanized area or in a contiguous urbanized area, and

(2) At least 15 percent of its resident employed workers working in Zone A.[8]

C. The central core comprises Zone A, Zone B, and any city or town that is physically surrounded by Zones A or B, except that cities or towns that are not contiguous with the main portion of the central core are not included.

D. If a city or town qualifies under section 11A through C for more than one central core, it is assigned to the core to which commuting is greatest, unless the relevant commuting percentages are within 5 points of each other, in which case local opinion as to the most appropriate assignment is also considered.

Section 12. Outlying Cities and Towns

A. A city or town contiguous to a central core as defined by section 11 is included in its metropolitan statistical area if:

(1) It has a population density of at least 60 persons per square mile and at least 30 percent of its resident employed workers work in the central core; or

(2) It has a population density of at least 100 persons per square mile and at least 15 percent of the employed workers living in the city or town work in the central core.[9]

B. If a city or town has the qualifying level of commuting to two different central cores, it is assigned to the metropolitan statistical area to which commuting is greater unless the relevant commuting percentages are within 5 points of each other, in which case local opinion as to the most appropriate assignment will also be considered.

C. If a city or town has the qualifying level of commuting to a central core, but has greater commuting to a non-metropolitan city or town, it will not be assigned to any metropolitan statistical area unless the relevant commuting percentages are within 5 points of each other, in which case local opinion as to the most appropriate assignment will also be considered.

Section 13. Applicability of Basic Standards to New England Metropolitan Statistical Areas

A. An area defined by sections 11 and 12 qualifies as an metropolitan statistical area if it contains a city of at least 50,000 population or has a total population of at least 75,000.[10]

B. The area's central cities are determined according to the standards of section 4.

C. Two adjacent New England metropolitan statistical areas are combined as a single metropolitan statistical area provided the conditions of section 5A are met. Section 5B is not applied in New England.

D. Each New England metropolitan statistical area defined by section 13A through C is categorized in one of the four levels specified in section 6A. Areas assigned to Level B, C, or D are designated as metropolitan statistical areas. Areas assigned to Level A are not finally designated until they have been reviewed under sections 14 and 15.

E. New England metropolitan statistical areas are titled according to the standards of section 7.

Section 14. Qualification for Designation of Primary Metropolitan Statistical Areas (PMSAs)

The following are qualifications within a Level A metropolitan statistical area in New England:

A. Any group of cities and towns that was recognized as a standard metropolitan statistical area on January 1, 1980, will be recognized as a primary metropolitan statistical area, unless local opinion does not support its continued separate recognition for statistical purposes.

---

[8]Also accepted as meeting this commuting requirement are (a) the number of persons working in the subject city or town who lives in the specified city or area is equal to at least 15 percent of the employed workers living in the subject city or town; or (b) the sum of the number of workers commuting to and from the specified city or area is equal to at least 20 percent of the employed workers living in the subject city or town.

[9]This commuting requirement is also considered to have been met if: (a) the number of persons working in the city or town who live in the central core is equal to at least 15 percent of the employed workers living

in the city or town, or (b) the sum of the number of workers commuting to and from the central core is equal to at least 20 percent of the employed workers living in the city or town.

[10]A New England metropolitan statistical area designated on the basis of census data according to standards in effect at the time of designation is not disqualified on the basis of lacking a total population of at least 75,000.

B. Any additional group of cities and/or towns for which local opinion strongly supports separate recognition will be considered for designation as a primary metropolitan statistical area, if:

  (1) The total population of the group is at least 75,000;

  (2) It includes at least one city with a population of 15,000 or more, an employment/resident ratio of at least 0.75, and at least 40 percent of its employed residence working in the city;

  (3) It contains a core of communities, each of which has at least 50 percent of its population living in the urbanized area and which together have less than 40 percent of their resident workers commuting to jobs outside the core; and

  (4) Each community in the core also has:

    (a) At least 5 percent of its resident workers working in the component core city identified in section 14B(2), or at least 10 percent working in the component core city or in places already qualified for this core; this percentage also must be greater than that to any other core or to the largest city of the Level A MSA; and

    (b) At least 20 percent commuting interchange with the component core city together with other cities and towns already qualified for the core; this interchange also must be greater than with any other core or with the largest city of the Level A MSA.

C. Contiguous component central cores may be merged as a single core if:

  (1) Section 14B would qualify the component core city of one core for inclusion in the other core; and

  (2) There is substantial local support for treating the two as a single core.

D. Each city or town in the interim Level A MSA not included in a core under sections 14A through C is assigned to the contiguous PMSA to whose core its commuting is greatest, if:

  (1) This commuting is at least 15 percent of the place's resident workers; and

  (2) The commuting interchange with the core is greater than with the Level A MSAs largest city.

E. If a city or town has qualifying commuting ties to two or more cores and the relevant values are within 5 percentage points of each other, local opinion is considered before the place is assigned to any PMSA.

F. The interim PMSA definitions resulting from these procedures (including possible alternative definitions, where appropriate) are submitted to local opinion. Final definitions of PMSAs are made based on these standards, and a review of local opinion.

G. If any primary metropolitan statistical area or areas have been recognized under sections 14A through F, the balance of the Level A metropolitan statistical area, which includes its largest city, also is recognized as a primary metropolitan statistical area.[11]

Section 15. Levels and Titles of Primary Metropolitan Statistical Areas and Consolidated Metropolitan Statistical Areas in New England

A. New England primary metropolitan statistical areas are categorized in one of four levels according to total population, following section 6A.

B. New England primary metropolitan statistical areas are titled using the names of up to three cities in the primary area that have qualified as central cities under section 4, following the standards of section 7 for selection and sequencing.

C. Each Level A metropolitan statistical area in New England in which primary metropolitan statistical areas have been identified and supported by local opinion (according to section 14) is designated a consolidated metropolitan statistical area. Titles of New England consolidated metropolitan statistical areas are determined following the standards of section 10. A Level A metropolitan statistical area in which no primary metropolitan statistical areas have been defined is designated a metropolitan statistical area and is titled according to the standards of section 7.

Section 16. Intercensal Metropolitan Area Changes

A. Definitions

  (1) A Census Count is a special census conducted by the U.S. Bureau of the Census or a decennial census count updated to reflect annexations and boundary changes since the census.

  (2) A Census Bureau Estimate is a population estimate issued by the U.S. Bureau of the Census for an intercensal year.

B. Qualifications for Designation of a Metropolitan Statistical Area.

  The qualifications for designation are as follows:

  (1) A city reaches 50,000 population according to a Census Count or Census Bureau Estimate.

---

[11]If section 14G results in the balance of the Level A metropolitan statistical area including a noncontiguous city or town, this place is added to the contiguous primary metropolitan statistical area to which it has the greatest commuting.

(2) A nonmetropolitan county containing an urbanized area (UA) defined by the Bureau of the Census at the most recent decennial census reaches 100,000 population according to a Census Count or Census Bureau Estimate. If the potential metropolitan statistical area centered on the UA consists of two or more counties, their total population must reach 100,000. In New England, the cities and towns qualifying for the potential metropolitan statistical area must reach a total population of 75,000.

(3) The Census Bureau defines a new urbanized area based on a Census Count after the decennial census, and the potential metropolitan statistical area containing the urbanized area meets the population requirements of section 16B(2).

   If a metropolitan statistical area is qualified inter- censally by a Census Bureau Estimate, the qualification must be confirmed by the next decennial census, or the area is disqualified.

C. Addition of Counties

Counties are not added to metropolitan statistical areas between censuses, except as follows:

(1) If a central city located in a qualifier urbanized area extends into a county not included in the metropolitan statistical area and the population of the portion of the city in the county reaches 2,500 according to a Census Count, then the county qualifies as an outlying county and is added to the metropolitan statistical area.

(2) If a metropolitan statistical area qualified intercensally under section 16B meets the requirements of section 5B for combination with a metropolitan statistical area already recognized, that combination may take place and thereby alter the definition of the existing metropolitan statistical area.

D. Qualification for Designation of a Central City

A Census Count serves to qualify a central city (section 4) that has failed to qualify solely because its population was smaller than required—for example, it did not qualify as the largest city of the metropolitan statistical area (section 4A), or was below 250,000 (4B), below 25,000 (4C), or below 15,000 (4D-F). If qualification requires comparison with the population of another city, comparison is made with the latest available Census Bureau Estimate or Census Count of the population of the other city.

E. Area Titles

The title of a metropolitan statistical area, primary metropolitan statistical area, or consolidated metropolitan statistical area may be altered to include the name of a place that has newly qualified as a central city on the basis described in section 16D, and that also meets the requirements of section 7. Such a change is made by adding the new name at the end of the existing title, but cannot be made if the title already contains three names. Names in area titles are not resequenced except on the basis of a decennial census.

F. Other aspects of the metropolitan area definitions are not subject to change between censuses.

General Procedures for Defining New England County Metropolitan Areas (NECMAs)

The New England County Metropolitan Areas (NECMAs) provide an alternative to the official city-and-town-based metropolitan statistical area in that region for the convenience of data users who desire a county-defined set of areas.

The NECMA for a metropolitan statistical area includes:

1. The county containing the first-named city in the metropolitan statistical area title. In some cases, this county will contain the first-named city of one or more additional metropolitan statistical areas.

2. Each other county which has at least half of its population in the metropolitan statistical area(s) whose first-named cities are in the county identified in step 1.

The NECMA for a consolidated metropolitan statistical area also is defined by the above rules, except that the New England portion of the consolidated metropolitan statistical area which includes New York City is used as the basis for defining a separate NECMA. No NECMAs are defined for individual primary metropolitan statistical areas.

The central cities of a NECMA are those cities in the NECMA that qualify as central cities of a metropolitan statistical area or consolidated metropolitan statistical area; some central cities may not be included in any NECMA title.

The title of the NECMA includes each city in the NECMA that is the first-named title city of a metropolitan area, in descending order of metropolitan statistical area (or primary metropolitan statistical area) total population. Other cities that appear in metropolitan area titles are included only if the resulting NECMA title would consist of no more than three names.

Appendix C.
Alphabetic Listing of PMSAs With CMSAs

[PMSA=Primary metropolitan statistical area. CMSA=Consolidated MSA. Based on areas defined as of June 30, 1997. Includes one NECMA (New England county metropolitan area) used as a substitute for the 4 New England PMSAs in the New York CMSA. Excludes PMSAs and CMSA not included in the data tables of this book]

PMSA code	PMSA name	CMSA code	CMSA name
0080	Akron, OH	1692	Cleveland-Akron, OH
0440	Ann Arbor, MI	2162	Detroit-Ann Arbor-Flint, MI
0560	Atlantic-Cape May, NJ	6162	Philadelphia-Wilmington-Atlantic City, PA-NJ-DE-MD
0720	Baltimore, MD	8872	Washington-Baltimore, DC-MD-VA-WV
0875	Bergen-Passaic, NJ	5602	New York-Northern New Jersey-Long Island, NY-NJ-CT
1125	Boulder-Longmont, CO	2082	Denver-Boulder-Greeley, CO
1145	Brazoria, TX	3362	Houston-Galveston-Brazoria, TX
1150	Bremerton, WA	7602	Seattle-Tacoma-Bremerton, WA
1600	Chicago, IL	1602	Chicago-Gary-Kenosha, IL-IN-WI
1640	Cincinnati, OH-KY-IN	1642	Cincinnati-Hamilton, OH-KY-IN
1680	Cleveland-Lorain-Elyria, OH	1692	Cleveland-Akron, OH
1920	Dallas, TX	1922	Dallas-Fort Worth, TX
2080	Denver, CO	2082	Denver-Boulder-Greeley, CO
2160	Detroit, MI	2162	Detroit-Ann Arbor-Flint, MI
2281	Dutchess County, NY	5602	New York-Northern New Jersey-Long Island, NY-NJ-CT
2640	Flint, MI	2162	Detroit-Ann Arbor-Flint, MI
2680	Fort Lauderdale, FL	4992	Miami-Fort Lauderdale, FL
2800	Fort Worth-Arlington, TX	1922	Dallas-Fort Worth, TX
2920	Galveston-Texas City, TX	3362	Houston-Galveston-Brazoria, TX
2960	Gary, IN	1602	Chicago-Gary-Kenosha, IL-IN-WI
3060	Greeley, CO	2082	Denver-Boulder-Greeley, CO
3180	Hagerstown, MD	8872	Washington-Baltimore, DC-MD-VA-WV
3200	Hamilton-Middletown, OH	1642	Cincinnati-Hamilton, OH-KY-IN
3360	Houston, TX	3362	Houston-Galveston-Brazoria, TX
3640	Jersey City, NJ	5602	New York-Northern New Jersey-Long Island, NY-NJ-CT
3740	Kankakee, IL	1602	Chicago-Gary-Kenosha, IL-IN-WI
3800	Kenosha, WI	1602	Chicago-Gary-Kenosha, IL-IN-WI
4480	Los Angeles-Long Beach, CA	4472	Los Angeles-Riverside-Orange County, CA
5000	Miami, FL	4992	Miami-Fort Lauderdale, FL
5015	Middlesex-Somerset-Hunterdon, NJ	5602	New York-Northern New Jersey-Long Island, NY-NJ-CT
5080	Milwaukee-Waukesha, WI	5082	Milwaukee-Racine, WI
5190	Monmouth-Ocean, NJ	5602	New York-Northern New Jersey-Long Island, NY-NJ-CT
5380	Nassau-Suffolk, NY	5602	New York-Northern New Jersey-Long Island, NY-NJ-CT
5483	New Haven-Bridgeport-Stamford- Waterbury-Danbury, CT NECMA	5602	New York-Northern New Jersey-Long Island, NY-NJ-CT
5600	New York, NY	5602	New York-Northern New Jersey-Long Island, NY-NJ-CT
5640	Newark, NJ	5602	New York-Northern New Jersey-Long Island, NY-NJ-CT
5660	Newburgh, NY-PA	5602	New York-Northern New Jersey-Long Island, NY-NJ-CT
5775	Oakland, CA	7362	San Francisco-Oakland-San Jose, CA
5910	Olympia, WA	7602	Seattle-Tacoma-Bremerton, WA
5945	Orange County, CA	4472	Los Angeles-Riverside-Orange County, CA
6160	Philadelphia, PA-NJ	6162	Philadelphia-Wilmington-Atlantic City, PA-NJ-DE-MD
6440	Portland-Vancouver, OR-WA	6442	Portland-Salem, OR-WA
6600	Racine, WI	5082	Milwaukee-Racine, WI
6780	Riverside-San Bernardino, CA	4472	Los Angeles-Riverside-Orange County, CA
6920	Sacramento, CA	6922	Sacramento-Yolo, CA

[PMSA=Primary metropolitan statistical area. CMSA=Consolidated MSA. Based on areas defined as of June 30, 1997. Includes one NECMA (New England county metropolitan area) used as a substitute for the 4 New England PMSAs in the New York CMSA. Excludes PMSAs and CMSA not included in the data tables of this book]

PMSA code	PMSA name	CMSA code	CMSA name
7080	Salem, OR	6442	Portland-Salem, OR-WA
7360	San Francisco, CA	7362	San Francisco-Oakland-San Jose, CA
7400	San Jose, CA	7362	San Francisco-Oakland-San Jose, CA
7485	Santa Cruz-Watsonville, CA	7362	San Francisco-Oakland-San Jose, CA
7500	Santa Rosa, CA	7362	San Francisco-Oakland-San Jose, CA
7600	Seattle-Bellevue-Everett, WA	7602	Seattle-Tacoma-Bremerton, WA
8200	Tacoma, WA	7602	Seattle-Tacoma-Bremerton, WA
8480	Trenton, NJ	5602	New York-Northern New Jersey-Long Island, NY-NJ-CT
8720	Vallejo-Fairfield-Napa, CA	7362	San Francisco-Oakland-San Jose, CA
8735	Ventura, CA	4472	Los Angeles-Riverside-Orange County, CA
8760	Vineland-Millville-Bridgeton, NJ	6162	Philadelphia-Wilmington-Atlantic City, PA-NJ-DE-MD
8840	Washington, DC-MD-VA-WV	8872	Washington-Baltimore, DC-MD-VA-WV
9160	Wilmington-Newark, DE-MD	6162	Philadelphia-Wilmington-Atlantic City, PA-NJ-DE-MD
9270	Yolo, CA	6922	Sacramento-Yolo, CA

Appendix D.
Component Counties of Metropolitan Areas by State

[Lists the 844 counties comprising the 332 metropolitan areas (MAs) in this publication. Based on areas defined as of June 30, 1997. MA names corresponding to the MSA/CMSA/NECMA codes in this appendix can be found in Table B. Metro Areas, pp 60-65, or Table C. Metro Counties, pp. 122-137. MSA = Metropolitan statistical area. CMSA = Consolidated MSA. NECMA = New England county metropolitan area]

State/county code	State and component counties	MSA/CMSA/NECMA code
01	**ALABAMA**	
001	Autauga	5240
003	Baldwin	5160
009	Blount	1000
015	Calhoun	0450
033	Colbert	2650
045	Dale	2180
051	Elmore	5240
055	Etowah	2880
069	Houston	2180
073	Jefferson	1000
077	Lauderdale	2650
079	Lawrence	2030
083	Limestone	3440
089	Madison	3440
097	Mobile	5160
101	Montgomery	5240
103	Morgan	2030
113	Russell	1800
115	St. Clair	1000
117	Shelby	1000
125	Tuscaloosa	8600
02	**ALASKA**	
020	Anchorage	0380
04	**ARIZONA**	
005	Coconino	2620
013	Maricopa	6200
015	Mohave	4120
019	Pima	8520
021	Pinal	6200
027	Yuma	9360
05	**ARKANSAS**	
007	Benton	2580
031	Craighead	3700
033	Crawford	2720
035	Crittenden	4920
045	Faulkner	4400
069	Jefferson	6240
085	Lonoke	4400
091	Miller	8360
119	Pulaski	4400
125	Saline	4400
131	Sebastian	2720
143	Washington	2580
06	**CALIFORNIA**	
001	Alameda	7362
007	Butte	1620
013	Contra Costa	7362
017	El Dorado	6922
019	Fresno	2840
029	Kern	0680

State/county code	State and component counties	MSA/CMSA/NECMA code
06	**CALIFORNIA—Con.**	
037	Los Angeles	4472
039	Madera	2840
041	Marin	7362
047	Merced	4940
053	Monterey	7120
055	Napa	7362
059	Orange	4472
061	Placer	6922
065	Riverside	4472
067	Sacramento	6922
071	San Bernardino	4472
073	San Diego	7320
075	San Francisco	7362
077	San Joaquin	8120
079	San Luis Obispo	7460
081	San Mateo	7362
083	Santa Barbara	7480
085	Santa Clara	7362
087	Santa Cruz	7362
089	Shasta	6690
095	Solano	7362
097	Sonoma	7362
099	Stanislaus	5170
101	Sutter	9340
107	Tulare	8780
111	Ventura	4472
113	Yolo	6922
115	Yuba	9340
08	**COLORADO**	
001	Adams	2082
005	Arapahoe	2082
013	Boulder	2082
031	Denver	2082
035	Douglas	2082
041	El Paso	1720
059	Jefferson	2082
069	Larimer	2670
077	Mesa	2995
101	Pueblo	6560
123	Weld	2082
09	**CONNECTICUT**	
001	Fairfield	5602
003	Hartford	3283
007	Middlesex	3283
009	New Haven	5602
011	New London	5523
013	Tolland	3283
10	**DELAWARE**	
001	Kent	2190
003	New Castle	6162

State/county code	State and component counties	MSA/CMSA/NECMA code
11	**DISTRICT OF COLUMBIA**	
001	District of Columbia	8872
12	**FLORIDA**	
001	Alachua	2900
005	Bay	6015
009	Brevard	4900
011	Broward	4992
015	Charlotte	6580
019	Clay	3600
021	Collier	5345
025	Dade	4992
031	Duval	3600
033	Escambia	6080
035	Flagler	2020
039	Gadsden	8240
053	Hernando	8280
057	Hillsborough	8280
069	Lake	5960
071	Lee	2700
073	Leon	8240
081	Manatee	7510
083	Marion	5790
085	Martin	2710
089	Nassau	3600
091	Okaloosa	2750
095	Orange	5960
097	Osceola	5960
099	Palm Beach	8960
101	Pasco	8280
103	Pinellas	8280
105	Polk	3980
109	St. Johns	3600
111	St. Lucie	2710
113	Santa Rosa	6080
115	Sarasota	7510
117	Seminole	5960
127	Volusia	2020
13	**GEORGIA**	
013	Barrow	0520
015	Bartow	0520
021	Bibb	4680
029	Bryan	7520
045	Carroll	0520
047	Catoosa	1560
051	Chatham	7520
053	Chattahoochee	1800
057	Cherokee	0520
059	Clarke	0500
063	Clayton	0520
067	Cobb	0520
073	Columbia	0600
077	Coweta	0520

[Lists the 844 counties comprising the 332 metropolitan areas (MAs) in this publication. Based on areas defined as of June 30, 1997. MA names corresponding to the MSA/CMSA/NECMA codes in this appendix can be found in Table B. Metro Areas, pp 60-65, or Table C. Metro Counties, pp. 122-137. MSA = Metropolitan statistical area. CMSA = Consolidated MSA. NECMA = New England county metropolitan area]

State/county code	State and component counties	MSA/CMSA/NECMA code	State/county code	State and component counties	MSA/CMSA/NECMA code	State/county code	State and component counties	MSA/CMSA/NECMA code
13	**GEORGIA—Con.**		**18**	**INDIANA**		**21**	**KENTUCKY—Con.**	
083	Dade	1560	001	Adams	2760	043	Carter	3400
089	De Kalb	0520	003	Allen	2760	047	Christian	1660
095	Dougherty	0120	011	Boone	3480	049	Clark	4280
097	Douglas	0520	019	Clark	4520	059	Daviess	5990
103	Effingham	7520	021	Clay	8320			
						067	Fayette	4280
113	Fayette	0520	023	Clinton	3920	077	Gallatin	1642
117	Forsyth	0520	029	Dearborn	1642	081	Grant	1642
121	Fulton	0520	033	De Kalb	2760	089	Greenup	3400
135	Gwinnett	0520	035	Delaware	5280	101	Henderson	2440
145	Harris	1800	039	Elkhart	2330	111	Jefferson	4520
151	Henry	0520	043	Floyd	4520	113	Jessamine	4280
153	Houston	4680	057	Hamilton	3480	117	Kenton	1642
169	Jones	4680	059	Hancock	3480	151	Madison	4280
177	Lee	0120	061	Harrison	4520	185	Oldham	4520
189	McDuffie	0600	063	Hendricks	3480	191	Pendleton	1642
195	Madison	0500				209	Scott	4280
			067	Howard	3850	239	Woodford	4280
215	Muscogee	1800	069	Huntington	2760			
217	Newton	0520	081	Johnson	3480	**22**	**LOUISIANA**	
219	Oconee	0500	089	Lake	1602			
223	Paulding	0520	095	Madison	3480	001	Acadia	3880
225	Peach	4680				005	Ascension	0760
			097	Marion	3480	015	Bossier	7680
227	Pickens	0520	105	Monroe	1020	017	Caddo	7680
245	Richmond	0600	109	Morgan	3480	019	Calcasieu	3960
247	Rockdale	0520	115	Ohio	1642			
255	Spalding	0520	127	Porter	1602	033	East Baton Rouge	0760
289	Twiggs	4680				051	Jefferson	5560
295	Walker	1560	129	Posey	2440	055	Lafayette	3880
297	Walton	0520	141	St. Joseph	7800	057	Lafourche	3350
			143	Scott	4520	063	Livingston	0760
15	**HAWAII**		145	Shelby	3480			
			157	Tippecanoe	3920	071	Orleans	5560
003	Honolulu	3320				073	Ouachita	5200
			159	Tipton	3850	075	Plaquemines	5560
16	**IDAHO**		163	Vanderburgh	2440	079	Rapides	0220
			165	Vermillion	8320	087	St. Bernard	5560
001	Ada	1080	167	Vigo	8320			
005	Bannock	6340	173	Warrick	2440	089	St. Charles	5560
027	Canyon	1080	179	Wells	2760	093	St. James	5560
			183	Whitley	2760	095	St. John the Baptist	5560
17	**ILLINOIS**					097	St. Landry	3880
			19	**IOWA**		099	St. Martin	3880
007	Boone	6880						
019	Champaign	1400	013	Black Hawk	8920	103	St. Tammany	5560
027	Clinton	7040	049	Dallas	2120	109	Terrebonne	3350
031	Cook	1602	061	Dubuque	2200	119	Webster	7680
037	DeKalb	1602	103	Johnson	3500	121	West Baton Rouge	0760
			113	Linn	1360			
043	Du Page	1602				**23**	**MAINE**	
063	Grundy	1602	153	Polk	2120			
073	Henry	1960	155	Pottawattamie	5920	001	Androscoggin	4243
083	Jersey	7040	163	Scott	1960	005	Cumberland	6403
089	Kane	1602	181	Warren	2120	019	Penobscot	0733
			193	Woodbury	7720			
091	Kankakee	1602				**24**	**MARYLAND**	
093	Kendall	1602	**20**	**KANSAS**				
097	Lake	1602				001	Allegany	1900
111	McHenry	1602	015	Butler	9040	003	Anne Arundel	8872
113	McLean	1040	045	Douglas	4150	005	Baltimore	8872
			079	Harvey	9040	009	Calvert	8872
115	Macon	2040	091	Johnson	3760	013	Carroll	8872
119	Madison	7040	103	Leavenworth	3760			
129	Menard	7880				015	Cecil	6162
133	Monroe	7040	121	Miami	3760	017	Charles	8872
141	Ogle	6880	173	Sedgwick	9040	021	Frederick	8872
			177	Shawnee	8440	025	Harford	8872
143	Peoria	6120	209	Wyandotte	3760	027	Howard	8872
161	Rock Island	1960						
163	St. Clair	7040	**21**	**KENTUCKY**		031	Montgomery	8872
167	Sangamon	7880				033	Prince George's	8872
179	Tazewell	6120	015	Boone	1642	035	Queen Anne's	8872
			017	Bourbon	4280	043	Washington	8872
197	Will	1602	019	Boyd	3400	510	Baltimore city	8872
201	Winnebago	6880	029	Bullitt	4520			
203	Woodford	6120	037	Campbell	1642			

[Lists the 844 counties comprising the 332 metropolitan areas (MAs) in this publication. Based on areas defined as of June 30, 1997. MA names corresponding to the MSA/CMSA/NECMA codes in this appendix can be found in Table B. Metro Areas, pp 60-65, or Table C. Metro Counties, pp. 122-137. MSA = Metropolitan statistical area. CMSA = Consolidated MSA. NECMA = New England county metropolitan area]

State/county code	State and component counties	MSA/CMSA/NECMA code
25	**MASSACHUSETTS**	
001	Barnstable	0743
003	Berkshire	6323
005	Bristol	1123
009	Essex	1123
013	Hampden	8003
015	Hampshire	8003
017	Middlesex	1123
021	Norfolk	1123
023	Plymouth	1123
025	Suffolk	1123
027	Worcester	1123
26	**MICHIGAN**	
005	Allegan	3000
017	Bay	6960
021	Berrien	0870
025	Calhoun	3720
037	Clinton	4040
045	Eaton	4040
049	Genesee	2162
065	Ingham	4040
075	Jackson	3520
077	Kalamazoo	3720
081	Kent	3000
087	Lapeer	2162
091	Lenawee	2162
093	Livingston	2162
099	Macomb	2162
111	Midland	6960
115	Monroe	2162
121	Muskegon	3000
125	Oakland	2162
139	Ottawa	3000
145	Saginaw	6960
147	St. Clair	2162
159	Van Buren	3720
161	Washtenaw	2162
163	Wayne	2162
27	**MINNESOTA**	
003	Anoka	5120
009	Benton	6980
019	Carver	5120
025	Chisago	5120
027	Clay	2520
037	Dakota	5120
053	Hennepin	5120
055	Houston	3870
059	Isanti	5120
109	Olmsted	6820
119	Polk	2985
123	Ramsey	5120
137	St. Louis	2240
139	Scott	5120
141	Sherburne	5120
145	Stearns	6980
163	Washington	5120
171	Wright	5120
28	**MISSISSIPPI**	
033	De Soto	4920
035	Forrest	3285
045	Hancock	0920
047	Harrison	0920
049	Hinds	3560

State/county code	State and component counties	MSA/CMSA/NECMA code
28	**MISSISSIPPI—Con.**	
059	Jackson	0920
073	Lamar	3285
089	Madison	3560
121	Rankin	3560
29	**MISSOURI**	
003	Andrew	7000
019	Boone	1740
021	Buchanan	7000
037	Cass	3760
043	Christian	7920
047	Clay	3760
049	Clinton	3760
071	Franklin	7040
077	Greene	7920
095	Jackson	3760
097	Jasper	3710
099	Jefferson	7040
107	Lafayette	3760
113	Lincoln	7040
145	Newton	3710
165	Platte	3760
177	Ray	3760
183	St. Charles	7040
189	St. Louis	7040
219	Warren	7040
225	Webster	7920
510	St. Louis city	7040
30	**MONTANA**	
013	Cascade	3040
111	Yellowstone	0880
31	**NEBRASKA**	
025	Cass	5920
043	Dakota	7720
055	Douglas	5920
109	Lancaster	4360
153	Sarpy	5920
177	Washington	5920
32	**NEVADA**	
003	Clark	4120
023	Nye	4120
031	Washoe	6720
33	**NEW HAMPSHIRE**	
011	Hillsborough	1123
015	Rockingham	1123
017	Strafford	1123
34	**NEW JERSEY**	
001	Atlantic	6162
003	Bergen	5602
005	Burlington	6162
007	Camden	6162
009	Cape May	6162
011	Cumberland	6162
013	Essex	5602
015	Gloucester	6162
017	Hudson	5602
019	Hunterdon	5602
021	Mercer	5602
023	Middlesex	5602
025	Monmouth	5602
027	Morris	5602
029	Ocean	5602

State/county code	State and component counties	MSA/CMSA/NECMA code
34	**NEW JERSEY—Con.**	
031	Passaic	5602
033	Salem	6162
035	Somerset	5602
037	Sussex	5602
039	Union	5602
041	Warren	5602
35	**NEW MEXICO**	
001	Bernalillo	0200
013	Dona Ana	4100
028	Los Alamos	7490
043	Sandoval	0200
049	Santa Fe	7490
061	Valencia	0200
36	**NEW YORK**	
001	Albany	0160
005	Bronx	5602
007	Broome	0960
011	Cayuga	8160
013	Chautauqua	3610
015	Chemung	2335
027	Dutchess	5602
029	Erie	1280
037	Genesee	6840
043	Herkimer	8680
047	Kings	5602
051	Livingston	6840
053	Madison	8160
055	Monroe	6840
057	Montgomery	0160
059	Nassau	5602
061	New York	5602
063	Niagara	1280
065	Oneida	8680
067	Onondaga	8160
069	Ontario	6840
071	Orange	5602
073	Orleans	6840
075	Oswego	8160
079	Putnam	5602
081	Queens	5602
083	Rensselaer	0160
085	Richmond	5602
087	Rockland	5602
091	Saratoga	0160
093	Schenectady	0160
095	Schoharie	0160
103	Suffolk	5602
107	Tioga	0960
113	Warren	2975
115	Washington	2975
117	Wayne	6840
119	Westchester	5602
37	**NORTH CAROLINA**	
001	Alamance	3120
003	Alexander	3290
019	Brunswick	9200
021	Buncombe	0480
023	Burke	3290
025	Cabarrus	1520
027	Caldwell	3290
035	Catawba	3290
037	Chatham	6640
051	Cumberland	2560

[Lists the 844 counties comprising the 332 metropolitan areas (MAs) in this publication. Based on areas defined as of June 30, 1997. MA names corresponding to the MSA/CMSA/NECMA codes in this appendix can be found in Table B. Metro Areas, pp 60-65, or Table C. Metro Counties, pp. 122-137. MSA = Metropolitan statistical area. CMSA = Consolidated MSA. NECMA = New England county metropolitan area]

State/county code	State and component counties	MSA/CMSA/NECMA code	State/county code	State and component counties	MSA/CMSA/NECMA code	State/county code	State and component counties	MSA/CMSA/NECMA code
37	**NORTH CAROLINA—Con.**		**39**	**OHIO—Con.**		**42**	**PENNSYLVANIA—Con.**	
053	Currituck	5720	151	Stark	1320	129	Westmoreland	6280
057	Davidson	3120	153	Summit	1692	131	Wyoming	7560
059	Davie	3120	155	Trumbull	9320	133	York	9280
063	Durham	6640						
065	Edgecombe	6895	165	Warren	1642	**44**	**RHODE ISLAND**	
			167	Washington	6020			
067	Forsyth	3120	173	Wood	8400	001	Bristol	6483
069	Franklin	6640				003	Kent	6483
071	Gaston	1520	**40**	**OKLAHOMA**		007	Providence	6483
081	Guilford	3120				009	Washington	6483
101	Johnston	6640	017	Canadian	5880			
			027	Cleveland	5880	**45**	**SOUTH CAROLINA**	
109	Lincoln	1520	031	Comanche	4200			
115	Madison	0480	037	Creek	8560	003	Aiken	0600
119	Mecklenburg	1520	047	Garfield	2340	007	Anderson	3160
127	Nash	6895				015	Berkeley	1440
129	New Hanover	9200	083	Logan	5880	019	Charleston	1440
			087	McClain	5880	021	Cherokee	3160
133	Onslow	3605	109	Oklahoma	5880			
135	Orange	6640	113	Osage	8560	035	Dorchester	1440
147	Pitt	3150	125	Pottawatomie	5880	037	Edgefield	0600
151	Randolph	3120				041	Florence	2655
159	Rowan	1520	131	Rogers	8560	045	Greenville	3160
			135	Sequoyah	2720	051	Horry	5330
169	Stokes	3120	143	Tulsa	8560			
179	Union	1520	145	Wagoner	8560	063	Lexington	1760
183	Wake	6640				077	Pickens	3160
191	Wayne	2980	**41**	**OREGON**		079	Richland	1760
197	Yadkin	3120				083	Spartanburg	3160
			005	Clackamas	6442	085	Sumter	8140
38	**NORTH DAKOTA**		009	Columbia	6442	091	York	1520
			029	Jackson	4890			
015	Burleigh	1010	039	Lane	2400	**46**	**SOUTH DAKOTA**	
017	Cass	2520	047	Marion	6442			
035	Grand Forks	2985				083	Lincoln	7760
059	Morton	1010	051	Multnomah	6442	099	Minnehaha	7760
			053	Polk	6442	103	Pennington	6660
39	**OHIO**		067	Washington	6442			
			071	Yamhill	6442	**47**	**TENNESSEE**	
003	Allen	4320						
007	Ashtabula	1692	**42**	**PENNSYLVANIA**		001	Anderson	3840
011	Auglaize	4320				009	Blount	3840
013	Belmont	9000	003	Allegheny	6280	019	Carter	3660
015	Brown	1642	007	Beaver	6280	021	Cheatham	5360
			011	Berks	6680	023	Chester	3580
017	Butler	1642	013	Blair	0280			
019	Carroll	1320	017	Bucks	6162	037	Davidson	5360
023	Clark	2000				043	Dickson	5360
025	Clermont	1642	019	Butler	6280	047	Fayette	4920
029	Columbiana	9320	021	Cambria	3680	065	Hamilton	1560
			025	Carbon	0240	073	Hawkins	3660
033	Crawford	4800	027	Centre	8050			
035	Cuyahoga	1692	029	Chester	6162	093	Knox	3840
041	Delaware	1840				105	Loudon	3840
045	Fairfield	1840	037	Columbia	7560	113	Madison	3580
049	Franklin	1840	041	Cumberland	3240	115	Marion	1560
			043	Dauphin	3240	125	Montgomery	1660
051	Fulton	8400	045	Delaware	6162			
055	Geauga	1692	049	Erie	2360	147	Robertson	5360
057	Greene	2000				149	Rutherford	5360
061	Hamilton	1642	051	Fayette	6280	155	Sevier	3840
081	Jefferson	8080	069	Lackawanna	7560	157	Shelby	4920
			071	Lancaster	4000	163	Sullivan	3660
085	Lake	1692	075	Lebanon	3240			
087	Lawrence	3400	077	Lehigh	0240	165	Sumner	5360
089	Licking	1840				167	Tipton	4920
093	Lorain	1692	079	Luzerne	7560	171	Unicoi	3660
095	Lucas	8400	081	Lycoming	9140	173	Union	3840
			085	Mercer	7610	179	Washington	3660
097	Madison	1840	091	Montgomery	6162	187	Williamson	5360
099	Mahoning	9320	095	Northampton	0240	189	Wilson	5360
103	Medina	1692						
109	Miami	2000	099	Perry	3240	**48**	**TEXAS**	
113	Montgomery	2000	101	Philadelphia	6162			
129	Pickaway	1840	103	Pike	5602	009	Archer	9080
133	Portage	1692	111	Somerset	3680	021	Bastrop	0640
139	Richland	4800	125	Washington	6280	027	Bell	3810
						029	Bexar	7240

[Lists the 844 counties comprising the 332 metropolitan areas (MAs) in this publication. Based on areas defined as of June 30, 1997. MA names corresponding to the MSA/CMSA/NECMA codes in this appendix can be found in Table B. Metro Areas, pp 60-65, or Table C. Metro Counties, pp. 122-137. MSA = Metropolitan statistical area. CMSA = Consolidated MSA. NECMA = New England county metropolitan area]

State/county code	State and component counties	MSA/CMSA/NECMA code	State/county code	State and component counties	MSA/CMSA/NECMA code	State/county code	State and component counties	MSA/CMSA/NECMA code
48	**TEXAS—Con.**		**50**	**VERMONT**		**51**	**VIRGINIA—Con.**	
037	Bowie	8360	007	Chittenden	1303	735	Poquoson city	5720
039	Brazoria	3362	011	Franklin	1303	740	Portsmouth city	5720
041	Brazos	1260	013	Grand Isle	1303	760	Richmond city	6760
055	Caldwell	0640				770	Roanoke city	6800
061	Cameron	1240				775	Salem city	6800
			51	**VIRGINIA**				
071	Chambers	3362				800	Suffolk city	5720
085	Collin	1922	003	Albemarle	1540	810	Virginia Beach city	5720
091	Comal	7240	009	Amherst	4640	830	Williamsburg city	5720
099	Coryell	3810	013	Arlington	8872			
113	Dallas	1922	019	Bedford	4640	**53**	**WASHINGTON**	
			023	Botetourt	6800			
121	Denton	1922				005	Benton	6740
135	Ector	5800	031	Campbell	4640	011	Clark	6442
139	Ellis	1922	036	Charles City	6760	021	Franklin	6740
141	El Paso	2320	041	Chesterfield	6760	029	Island	7602
157	Fort Bend	3362	043	Clarke	8872	033	King	7602
			047	Culpeper	8872			
167	Galveston	3362				035	Kitsap	7602
181	Grayson	7640	053	Dinwiddie	6760	053	Pierce	7602
183	Gregg	4420	059	Fairfax	8872	061	Snohomish	7602
187	Guadalupe	7240	061	Fauquier	8872	063	Spokane	7840
199	Hardin	0840	065	Fluvanna	1540	067	Thurston	7602
			073	Gloucester	5720	073	Whatcom	0860
201	Harris	3362				077	Yakima	9260
203	Harrison	4420	075	Goochland	6760			
209	Hays	0640	079	Greene	1540	**54**	**WEST VIRGINIA**	
213	Henderson	1922	085	Hanover	6760			
215	Hidalgo	4880	087	Henrico	6760	003	Berkeley	8872
			093	Isle of Wight	5720	009	Brooke	8080
221	Hood	1922				011	Cabell	3400
231	Hunt	1922	095	James City	5720	029	Hancock	8080
245	Jefferson	0840	099	King George	8872	037	Jefferson	8872
251	Johnson	1922	107	Loudoun	8872			
257	Kaufman	1922	115	Mathews	5720	039	Kanawha	1480
			127	New Kent	6760	051	Marshall	9000
291	Liberty	3362				057	Mineral	1900
303	Lubbock	4600	143	Pittsylvania	1950	069	Ohio	9000
309	McLennan	8800	145	Powhatan	6760	079	Putnam	1480
329	Midland	5800	149	Prince George	6760	099	Wayne	3400
339	Montgomery	3362	153	Prince William	8872	107	Wood	6020
			161	Roanoke	6800			
355	Nueces	1880				**55**	**WISCONSIN**	
361	Orange	0840	169	Scott	3660			
367	Parker	1922	177	Spotsylvania	8872	009	Brown	3080
375	Potter	0320	179	Stafford	8872	015	Calumet	0460
381	Randall	0320	187	Warren	8872	017	Chippewa	2290
			191	Washington	3660	025	Dane	4720
397	Rockwall	1922				031	Douglas	2240
409	San Patricio	1880	199	York	5720			
423	Smith	8640	510	Alexandria city	8872	035	Eau Claire	2290
439	Tarrant	1922	515	Bedford city	4640	059	Kenosha	1602
441	Taylor	0040	520	Bristol city	3660	063	La Crosse	3870
			540	Charlottesville city	1540	073	Marathon	8940
451	Tom Green	7200				079	Milwaukee	5082
453	Travis	0640	550	Chesapeake city	5720	087	Outagamie	0460
459	Upshur	4420	570	Colonial Heights city	6760	089	Ozaukee	5082
469	Victoria	8750	590	Danville city	1950	093	Pierce	5120
473	Waller	3362	600	Fairfax city	8872	101	Racine	5082
			610	Falls Church city	8872	105	Rock	3620
479	Webb	4080						
485	Wichita	9080	630	Fredericksburg city	8872	109	St. Croix	5120
491	Williamson	0640	650	Hampton city	5720	117	Sheboygan	7620
493	Wilson	7240	670	Hopewell city	6760	131	Washington	5082
			680	Lynchburg city	4640	133	Waukesha	5082
49	**UTAH**		683	Manassas city	8872	139	Winnebago	0460
011	Davis	7160	685	Manassas Park city	8872	**56**	**WYOMING**	
025	Kane	2620	700	Newport News city	5720			
035	Salt Lake	7160	710	Norfolk city	5720	021	Laramie	1580
049	Utah	6520	730	Petersburg city	6760	025	Natrona	1350
057	Weber	7160						

[Lists of the 538 central cities of metropolitan areas (MAs) in this publication. Based on areas defined as of June 30, 1997. MA names corresponding to the MSA/CMSA/NECMA codes in this appendix can be found in Table B. Metro Areas, pp. 60-65, or Table D. Central Cities, pp. 172-182. MSA = Metropolitan statistical area. CMSA = Consolidated MSA. NECMA = New England county metropolitan area]

State/ city code	State and component cities	MSA/ CMSA/ NECMA code	State/ city code	State and component cities	MSA/ CMSA/ NECMA code	State/ city code	State and component cities	MSA/ CMSA/ NECMA code
01	**ALABAMA**		**06**	**CALIFORNIA**—Con.		**06**	**CALIFORNIA**—Con.	
01852	Anniston	0450	22300	El Paso de Robles (Paso Robles)	7460	78120	Temecula	4472
07000	Birmingham	1000	22804	Escondido	7320	80644	Tulare	8780
20104	Decatur (part)	2030	23182	Fairfield	7362	80812	Turlock	5170
21184	Dothan (part)	2180	27000	Fresno	2840	81666	Vallejo	7362
26896	Florence	2650	29504	Gilroy	7362			
						82954	Visalia	8780
28696	Gadsden	2880				83668	Watsonville	7362
37000	Huntsville	3440	33182	Hemet	4472	86328	Woodland	6922
50000	Mobile	5160	36770	Irvine	4472	86972	Yuba City	9340
51000	Montgomery	5240	40130	Lancaster	4472			
77256	Tuscaloosa	8600	42202	Lodi	8120	**08**	**COLORADO**	
			42524	Lompoc	7480	07850	Boulder	2082
02	**ALASKA**					16000	Colorado Springs	1720
			43000	Long Beach	4472	20000	Denver	2082
03000	Anchorage	0380	44000	Los Angeles	4472	27425	Fort Collins	2670
			45022	Madera	2840	31660	Grand Junction	2995
04	**ARIZONA**		46898	Merced	4940			
			48354	Modesto	5170	32155	Greeley	2082
23620	Flagstaff	2620				45970	Longmont	2082
46000	Mesa	6200	48872	Monterey	7120	46465	Loveland	2670
55000	Phoenix	6200	50258	Napa	7362	62000	Pueblo	6560
65000	Scottsdale	6200	53000	Oakland	7362			
73000	Tempe	6200	55184	Palm Desert	4472	**09**	**CONNECTICUT**	
77000	Tucson	8520	55254	Palm Springs	4472	08000	Bridgeport	5602
85540	Yuma	9360				18430	Danbury	5602
			55282	Palo Alto	7362	37000	Hartford	3283
05	**ARKANSAS**		55520	Paradise town	1620	46450	Meriden	5602
			56000	Pasadena	4472	47290	Middletown	3283
15190	Conway	4400	56784	Petaluma	7362			
23290	Fayetteville	2580	58240	Porterville	8780	52000	New Haven	5602
24550	Fort Smith	2720				52280	New London	5523
34750	Jacksonville	4400	59920	Redding	6690	55990	Norwalk	5602
35710	Jonesboro	3700	62000	Riverside	4472	56200	Norwich	5523
			64000	Sacramento	6922	73000	Stamford	5602
41000	Little Rock	4400	64224	Salinas	7120	80000	Waterbury	5602
50450	North Little Rock	4400	65000	San Bernardino	4472			
55310	Pine Bluff	6240				**10**	**DELAWARE**	
60410	Rogers	2580	65042	San Buenaventura (Ventura)	4472	21200	Dover	2190
66080	Springdale	2580	66000	San Diego	7320	50670	Newark	6162
			67000	San Francisco	7362	77580	Wilmington	6162
68810	Texarkana	8360	68000	San Jose	7362			
74540	West Memphis	4920	68154	San Luis Obispo	7460	**11**	**DISTRICT OF COLUMBIA**	
06	**CALIFORNIA**					50000	Washington	8872
00562	Alameda	7362	69000	Santa Ana	4472			
02000	Anaheim	4472	69070	Santa Barbara	7480	**12**	**FLORIDA**	
03064	Atascadero	7460	69084	Santa Clara	7362	07300	Boca Raton	8960
03526	Bakersfield	0680	69112	Santa Cruz	7362	07950	Bradenton	7510
06000	Berkeley	7362	69196	Santa Maria	7480	10275	Cape Coral	2700
						12875	Clearwater	8280
13014	Chico	1620	70098	Santa Rosa	7362	16525	Daytona Beach	2020
16378	Coronado	7320	75000	Stockton	8120			
18100	Davis	6922	77000	Sunnyvale	7362			

[Lists of the 538 central cities of metropolitan areas (MAs) in this publication. Based on areas defined as of June 30, 1997. MA names corresponding to the MSA/CMSA/NECMA codes in this appendix can be found in Table B. Metro Areas, pp. 60-65, or Table D. Central Cities, pp. 172-182. MSA = Metropolitan statistical area. CMSA = Consolidated MSA. NECMA = New England county metropolitan area]

State/ city code	State and component cities	MSA/ CMSA/ NECMA code	State/ city code	State and component cities	MSA/ CMSA/ NECMA code	State/ city code	State and component cities	MSA/ CMSA/ NECMA code
12	**FLORIDA—Con.**		**17**	**ILLINOIS—Con.**		**24**	**MARYLAND—Con.**	
24000	Fort Lauderdale	4992	72000	Springfield	7880	30325	Frederick	8872
24125	Fort Myers	2700	77005	Urbana	1400	36075	Hagerstown	8872
24300	Fort Pierce	2710	**18**	**INDIANA**		**25**	**MASSACHUSETTS**	
24475	Fort Walton Beach	2750	01468	Anderson	3480	02690	Attleboro	1123
25175	Gainesville	2900	05860	Bloomington	1020	03600	Barnstable	0743
			19486	East Chicago	1602	07000	Boston	1123
35006	Jacksonville (remainder)	3600	20728	Elkhart	2330	09000	Brockton	1123
38250	Lakeland	3980	22000	Evansville	2440	11000	Cambridge	1123
43975	Melbourne	4900						
45000	Miami	4992	25000	Fort Wayne	2760	23000	Fall River	1123
45025	Miami Beach	4992	27000	Gary	1602	23875	Fitchburg	1123
			28386	Goshen	2330	26150	Gloucester	1123
47625	Naples	5345	36010	Indianapolis (remainder)	3480	30840	Holyoke	8003
50750	Ocala	5790	40392	Kokomo	3850	34550	Lawrence	1123
53000	Orlando	5960						
54000	Palm Bay	4900	40788	Lafayette	3920	35075	Leominster	1123
54700	Panama City	6015	51876	Muncie	5280	37000	Lowell	1123
			52326	New Albany	4520	37490	Lynn	1123
55925	Pensacola	6080	71000	South Bend	7800	45000	New Bedford	1123
58725	Port St. Lucie	2710	75428	Terre Haute	8320	46330	Northampton	8003
59200	Punta Gorda	6580	**19**	**IOWA**				
63000	St. Petersburg	8280	11755	Cedar Falls	8920	53960	Pittsfield	6323
64175	Sarasota	7510	12000	Cedar Rapids	1360	67000	Springfield	8003
			16860	Council Bluffs	5920	72600	Waltham	1123
70600	Tallahassee	8240	19000	Davenport	1960	76030	Westfield	8003
71000	Tampa	8280	21000	Des Moines	2120	82000	Worcester	1123
71900	Titusville	4900				82525	Yarmouth town	0743
76600	West Palm Beach	8960	22395	Dubuque	2200			
78275	Winter Haven	3980	38595	Iowa City	3500	**26**	**MICHIGAN**	
			73335	Sioux City	7720	03000	Ann Arbor	2162
13	**GEORGIA**		82425	Waterloo	8920	05920	Battle Creek	3720
01052	Albany	0120				06020	Bay City	6960
03440	Athens-Clarke County (remainder)	0500	**20**	**KANSAS**		07520	Benton Harbor	0870
04000	Atlanta	0520	36000	Kansas City	3760	21000	Dearborn	2162
04196	Augusta	0600	38900	Lawrence	4150			
19030	Columbus (remainder)	1800	39000	Leavenworth	3760	22000	Detroit	2162
49000	Macon	4680	52575	Olathe	3760	24120	East Lansing	4040
69000	Savannah	7520	71000	Topeka	8440	29000	Flint	2162
			79000	Wichita	9040	34000	Grand Rapids	3000
15	**HAWAII**					38640	Holland	3000
17000	Honolulu (CDP)	3320	**21**	**KENTUCKY**				
			02368	Ashland	3400	41420	Jackson	3520
16	**IDAHO**		35866	Henderson	2440	42160	Kalamazoo	3720
08830	Boise City	1080	37918	Hopkinsville	1660	46000	Lansing	4040
56260	Nampa	1080	46027	Lexington-Fayette	4280	53780	Midland	6960
64090	Pocatello (part)	6340	48000	Louisville	4520	56320	Muskegon	3000
			58620	Owensboro	5990			
17	**ILLINOIS**					65440	Pontiac	2162
01114	Alton	7040	**22**	**LOUISIANA**		65820	Port Huron	2162
03012	Aurora	1602	00975	Alexandria	0220	70520	Saginaw	6960
04845	Belleville	7040	05000	Baton Rouge	0760			
06613	Bloomington	1040	08920	Bossier City	7680	**27**	**MINNESOTA**	
12385	Champaign	1400	36255	Houma	3350	17000	Duluth	2240
			40735	Lafayette	3880	43000	Minneapolis	5120
14000	Chicago	1602				43864	Moorhead	2520
18823	Decatur	2040	41155	Lake Charles	3960	54880	Rochester	6820
19161	De Kalb	1602	51410	Monroe	5200	56896	St. Cloud (part)	6980
22255	East St. Louis	7040	55000	New Orleans	5560	58000	St. Paul	5120
23074	Elgin	1602	70000	Shreveport	7680			
			70805	Slidell	5560	**28**	**MISSISSIPPI**	
24582	Evanston	1602				06220	Biloxi	0920
30926	Granite City	7040	**23**	**MAINE**		29000	Gulfport	0920
38570	Joliet	1602	02060	Auburn	4243	31020	Hattiesburg	3285
38934	Kankakee	1602	02795	Bangor	0733	36000	Jackson	3560
49867	Moline	1960	38740	Lewiston	4243	55360	Pascagoula	0920
			60545	Portland	6403			
53234	Normal town	1040				**29**	**MISSOURI**	
53559	North Chicago	1602	**24**	**MARYLAND**		15670	Columbia	1740
58447	Pekin	6120	01600	Annapolis	8872	37592	Joplin	3710
59000	Peoria	6120	04000	Baltimore	8872	38000	Kansas City	3760
65000	Rockford	6880	21325	Cumberland	1900	64082	St. Charles	7040
65078	Rock Island	1960				64550	St. Joseph	7000

State/ city code	State and component cities	MSA/ CMSA/ NECMA code	State/ city code	State and component cities	MSA/ CMSA/ NECMA code	State/ city code	State and component cities	MSA/ CMSA/ NECMA code
29	**MISSOURI—Con.**		**37**	**NORTH CAROLINA—Con.**		**42**	**PENNSYLVANIA—Con.**	
65000	St. Louis	7040	25580	Gastonia	1520	32800	Harrisburg	3240
70000	Springfield	7920	26880	Goldsboro	2980	38288	Johnstown	3680
			28000	Greensboro	3120	41216	Lancaster	4000
30	**MONTANA**		28080	Greenville	3150	42168	Lebanon	3240
			31060	Hickory	3290	60000	Philadelphia	6162
06550	Billings	0880	31400	High Point	3120			
32800	Great Falls	3040				61000	Pittsburgh	6280
			34200	Jacksonville	3605	63624	Reading	6680
31	**NEBRASKA**		35200	Kannapolis	1520	69000	Scranton	7560
			37760	Lenoir	3290	69720	Sharon	7610
28000	Lincoln	4360	44400	Morganton	3290	73808	State College borough	8050
37000	Omaha	5920						
			55000	Raleigh	6640	85152	Wilkes-Barre	7560
32	**NEVADA**		57500	Rocky Mount	6895	85312	Williamsport	9140
			74440	Wilmington	9200	87048	York	9280
40000	Las Vegas	4120	75000	Winston-Salem	3120			
60600	Reno	6720				**44**	**RHODE ISLAND**	
			38	**NORTH DAKOTA**		54640	Pawtucket	6483
33	**NEW HAMPSHIRE**		07200	Bismarck	1010	59000	Providence	6483
			25700	Fargo	2520	74300	Warwick	6483
45140	Manchester	1123	32060	Grand Forks	2985	80780	Woonsocket	6483
50260	Nashua	1123						
62900	Portsmouth	1123	**39**	**OHIO**		**45**	**SOUTH CAROLINA**	
65140	Rochester	1123	01000	Akron	1692	00550	Aiken	0600
			07972	Bowling Green	8400	01360	Anderson	3160
34	**NEW JERSEY**		12000	Canton	1320	13330	Charleston	1440
02080	Atlantic City	6162	15000	Cincinnati	1642	16000	Columbia	1760
03580	Bayonne	5602	16000	Cleveland	1692	25810	Florence	2655
07600	Bridgeton	6162						
10000	Camden	6162	18000	Columbus	1840	30850	Greenville	3160
18130	Dover township	5602	21000	Dayton	2000	49075	Myrtle Beach	5330
			25256	Elyria	1692	50875	North Charleston	1440
36000	Jersey City	5602	25914	Fairborn	2000	61405	Rock Hill	1520
46680	Millville	6162	33012	Hamilton	1642	68290	Spartanburg	3160
51000	Newark	5602				70405	Sumter	8140
74000	Trenton	5602	39872	Kent	1692			
76070	Vineland	6162	41720	Lancaster	1840	**46**	**SOUTH DAKOTA**	
			43554	Lima	4320	52980	Rapid City	6660
35	**NEW MEXICO**		44856	Lorain	1692	59020	Sioux Falls	7760
02000	Albuquerque	0200	47138	Mansfield	4800			
39380	Las Cruces	4100				**47**	**TENNESSEE**	
70500	Santa Fe	7490	47628	Marietta	6020	08540	Bristol	3660
			48244	Massillon	1320	14000	Chattanooga	1560
36	**NEW YORK**		49840	Middletown	1642	15160	Clarksville	1660
01000	Albany	0160	54040	Newark	1840	37640	Jackson	3580
03078	Auburn	8160	74118	Springfield	2000	38320	Johnson City	3660
06607	Binghamton	0960						
11000	Buffalo	1280	74608	Steubenville	8080	39560	Kingsport	3660
24229	Elmira	2335	77000	Toledo	8400	40000	Knoxville	3840
			80892	Warren	9320	48000	Memphis	4920
29333	Glens Falls	2975	88000	Youngstown	9320	51560	Murfreesboro	5360
38264	Jamestown	3610				52006	Nashville-Davidson	
50034	Newburgh	5602	**40**	**OKLAHOMA**			(remainder)	5360
51000	New York	5602	23950	Enid	2340	55120	Oak Ridge (part)	3840
51055	Niagara Falls	1280	41850	Lawton	4200			
			52500	Norman	5880	**48**	**TEXAS**	
59641	Poughkeepsie	5602	55000	Oklahoma City	5880	01000	Abilene (part)	0040
63000	Rochester	6840	66800	Shawnee	5880	03000	Amarillo	0320
63418	Rome	8680	75000	Tulsa	8560	04000	Arlington	1922
65255	Saratoga Springs	0160				05000	Austin	0640
65508	Schenectady	0160	**41**	**OREGON**		06128	Baytown	3362
			03050	Ashland	4890			
73000	Syracuse	8160	23850	Eugene	2400	07000	Beaumont	0840
75484	Troy	0160	47000	Medford	4890	10768	Brownsville	1240
76540	Utica	8680	59000	Portland	6442	10912	Bryan	1260
81677	White Plains	5602	64900	Salem	6442	15976	College Station	1260
			69600	Springfield	2400	16432	Conroe	3362
37	**NORTH CAROLINA**							
02140	Asheville	0480	**42**	**PENNSYLVANIA**		17000	Corpus Christi (part)	1880
09060	Burlington	3120	02000	Allentown	0240	19000	Dallas	1922
11800	Chapel Hill town	6640	02184	Altoona	0280	19900	Denison	7640
12000	Charlotte	1520	06086	Bethlehem	0240	19972	Denton	1922
14100	Concord	1520	11272	Carlisle borough	3240	22660	Edinburg	4880
			24000	Erie	2360	24000	El Paso	2320
19000	Durham	6640						
22920	Fayetteville	2560						

[Lists of the 538 central cities of metropolitan areas (MAs) in this publication. Based on areas defined as of June 30, 1997. MA names corresponding to the MSA/CMSA/NECMA codes in this appendix can be found in Table B. Metro Areas, pp. 60-65, or Table D. Central Cities, pp. 172-182. MSA = Metropolitan statistical area. CMSA = Consolidated MSA. NECMA = New England county metropolitan area]

State/city code	State and component cities	MSA/CMSA/NECMA code	State/city code	State and component cities	MSA/CMSA/NECMA code	State/city code	State and component cities	MSA/CMSA/NECMA code
48	**TEXAS**—Con.		**49**	**UTAH**—Con.		**53**	**WASHINGTON**—Con.	
27000	Fort Worth	1922	57300	Orem	6520	67000	Spokane	7840
28068	Galveston	3362	62470	Provo	6520	70000	Tacoma	7602
32372	Harlingen	1240	67000	Salt Lake City	7160	74060	Vancouver	6442
35000	Houston	3362				80010	Yakima	9260
37000	Irving	1922	**50**	**VERMONT**				
39148	Killeen	3810				**54**	**WEST VIRGINIA**	
			10675	Burlington	1303			
41464	Laredo	4080				14600	Charleston	1480
43888	Longview	4420	**51**	**VIRGINIA**		39460	Huntington	3400
45000	Lubbock	4600				62140	Parkersburg	6020
45384	McAllen	4880	03000	Arlington (CDP)	8872	85156	Weirton	8080
46776	Marshall	4420	09816	Bristol	3660	86452	Wheeling	9000
			14968	Charlottesville	1540			
48072	Midland (part)	5800	21344	Danville	1950	**55**	**WISCONSIN**	
48768	Mission	4880	29744	Fredericksburg	8872	02375	Appleton	0460
50820	New Braunfels	7240				06500	Beloit	3620
53388	Odessa	5800	35000	Hampton	5720	22300	Eau Claire	2290
58820	Port Arthur	0840	47672	Lynchburg	4640	31000	Green Bay	3080
			56000	Newport News	5720	37825	Janesville	3620
64472	San Angelo	7200	57000	Norfolk	5720			
65000	San Antonio	7240	61832	Petersburg	6760	39225	Kenosha	1602
65036	San Benito	1240				40775	La Crosse	3870
65600	San Marcos	0640	64000	Portsmouth	5720	48000	Madison	4720
67496	Sherman	7640	67000	Richmond	6760	53000	Milwaukee	5082
			68000	Roanoke	6800	55750	Neenah	0460
72176	Temple	3810	76432	Suffolk	5720			
72368	Texarkana	8360	82000	Virginia Beach	5720	60500	Oshkosh	0460
72392	Texas City	3362				66000	Racine	5082
74144	Tyler	8640	**53**	**WASHINGTON**		72975	Sheboygan	7620
			05210	Bellevue	7602	78650	Superior	2240
75428	Victoria	8750	05280	Bellingham	0860	84250	Waukesha	5082
76000	Waco	8800	07695	Bremerton	7602	84475	Wausau	8940
79000	Wichita Falls	9080	22640	Everett	7602			
			35275	Kennewick	6740	**56**	**WYOMING**	
49	**UTAH**		51300	Olympia	7602			
			53545	Pasco	6740	13150	Casper	1350
13850	Clearfield	7160	58235	Richland	6740	13900	Cheyenne	1580
55980	Ogden	7160	63000	Seattle	7602			

Subject Index

Note:

This index lists table and page
locations for the subjects covered
in the four data tables of this publication.
It is one alphabetic presentation of
subjects. If a subject is not covered for
a specific table (geography), the
corresponding references are blank.

Subject Index

	Table A. States		Table B. Metro Areas		Table C. Metro Counties		Table D. Central Cities	
	Page	Table	Page	Table	Page	Table	Page	Table
A								
Accidents and fatalities	10,30	A-9,29						
Acreage, farm	34,44	A-33,43						
Age groups........................	4,5	A-3,4	66-65	B-2	122-137	C-1		
Aggravated assault..................	17	A-16						
Agriculture	34,35,44	A-33,34,43						
AIDS (acquired immune deficiency syndrome)	10,12	A-9,11						
Aid to families with dependent children .	54	A-53						
Aid to state and local governments.....	51	A-50						
Alcohol-related crashes	30	A-29						
Alzheimer's disease, deaths...........	10	A-9						
American Indian, Alaska native-owned businesses......................	47	A-48						
American Indian, Eskimo, and Aleut population........................	6	A-5						
Apportionment, U.S. House of Representatives	57	A-56						
Area...............................	2	A-1						
Asian or Pacific Islander population	6	A-5	66-71	B-2	138-153	C-2		
Assaults	17	A-16						
Automobile:								
Dealers	40	A-39						
Fatalities	30	A-29						
Insurance	42	A-41						
Mileage	29	A-28						
Registrations	29	A-28						
Average annual pay by industry........	22,23	A-21,22	108-113	B-9				
B								
Balance sheet of farming sector	35	A-34						
Banking............................	41,42	A-40,41	114-119	B-10				
Bankruptcy	31	A-30						
Births and birth rates	8	A-7	72-77	B-3	122-137	C-1		
Black population	6	A-5	66-71	B-2	138-153	C-2		
Births............................	8	A-7						
Elected officials	57	A-56						
Infant mortality rates...............	9	A-8						
Owned firms.....................	49	A-48						
Building permits.....................	36	A-35	90-95	B-6	138-153	C-2		
Buildings, farms.....................	34	A-33						
Burglary...........................	17	A-16						
Business starts	31	A-30						
Business failures....................	31	A-30						
Business services establishments	43	A-42						
C								
Cancer, deaths	10	A-9						
Capital punishment..................	18	A-17						
Cardiovascular disease, deaths........	10	A-9	72-77	B-3				
Cerebrovascular disease, deaths.......	10	A-9						

	Table A. States		Table B. Metro Areas		Table C. Metro Counties		Table D. Central Cities	
	Page	Table	Page	Table	Page	Table	Page	Table
Highway:								
Accidents and fatalities	10,30	A-9,29						
Federal aid.......................	51	A-50						
Gasoline taxes....................	29	A-28						
Mileage..........................	29	A-28						
Hispanic origin......................	7,8	A-6,7	66-71	B-2	122-137	C-1		
Births..........................	8	A-7						
Elected officials	57	A-56						
Owned firms.....................	49	A-48						
HIV (human immunodeficiency virus) ...	10	A-9						
Homeownership rates	19	A-18						
Home sales	19	A-18						
Hospitals, community	11	A-10	78-83	B-4				
Beds	11	A-10	78-83	B-4				
Cost............................	11	A-10						
Patients.........................	11	A-10						
Personnel	11	A-10						
Visits	11	A-10						
Households	7	A-6	72-77	B-3				
Median income	25	A-24						
House of Representatives.............	57	A-56						
Housing...........................	19	A-18						
Cost of living index			90-95	B-6				
New units authorized	36	A-35	90-95	B-6	138-153	C-2		
Starts...........................	19	A-18						
Hydroelectric power	26	A-25						
I								
Immigrants	7	A-6						
Incorporations, new business	31	A-30						
Income:								
Banking.........................	42	A-41						
Family	25	A-24						
Farm	35	A-34						
Median	25	A-24						
Per capita.......................	24	A-23						
Personal	24	A-23						
Poverty status	25	A-24						
Projections			102-107	B-8				
Infant deaths and death rates..........	9	A-8	78-83	B-4				
Low birth weight	8	A-7						
Influenza, deaths...................	10	A-9						
Insurance:.........................	12	A-11						
Automobile	42	A-41						
Health	12	A-11						
Life.............................	42	A-41						
Insured savings institutions...........	41	A-40						
Intergovernmental revenue	50	A-49						
International visitor travel impact	33	A-32						
Interstate highway mileage	29	A-28						
J								
Job growth	31	A-30						
L								
Labor force, civilian.................	20,21	A-19,20	102-107	B-8	138-153	C-2		
Land area	2	A-1	60-65	B-1				
Farmland........................	34,44	A-33,43						
Foreign direct investments	33	A-32						
Larceny-theft	17	A-16						
Legal services	43	A-42						
Licenses	30	A-29						
Life insurance	42	A-41						

	Table A. States		Table B. Metro Areas		Table C. Metro Counties		Table D. Central Cities	
	Page	Table	Page	Table	Page	Table	Page	Table

	Table A. States		Table B. Metro Areas		Table C. Metro Counties		Table D. Central Cities	
	Page	Table	Page	Table	Page	Table	Page	Table

	Table A. States		Table B. Metro Areas		Table C. Metro Counties		Table D. Central Cities	
	Page	Table	Page	Table	Page	Table	Page	Table
Transportation, communications, and public utilities	22,46	A-21,45						
Average annual pay	22	A-21						
Earnings	38	A-37						
Employment	46	A-45						
Establishments	46	A-45						
Payroll	46	A-45						
Revenue	46	A-45						
Travel	33	A-32						
Trucks	29,30	A-28,29						
U								
Unemployment	21	A-20	102-107	B-8	138-153	C-2		
Unemployment insurance	54	A-53						
Union membership,	23	A-22						
Universities and colleges	15,16	A-14,15						
Utilities	46	A-45						
Cost of living index			90-95	B-6				
V								
Vacancy rates	19	A-18						
Vehicle registrations	29	A-28						
Violent crime	17	A-16	84-89	B-5				
Vital statistics	8-10	A-7-9	72-83	B-3,4	122-137	C-1		
Voter participation	56,57	A-55,56						
Votes:								
Congressional	56,57	A-55,56						
Gubernatorial	57	A-56						
Presidential	56	A-55						
Voting-age population	56	A-55						
W								
Wages (see Payroll and Salaries)	14,22,23,32, 33,44-48	A-13,21,22, 31,32,43-47	108-113	B-9				
Welfare programs (see also individual programs)	52-54	A-51-53	84-89	B-5				
White population	6,7	A-5,6	66-71	B-2	138-153	C-2		
Births	8	A-7						
Infant mortality rates	9	A-8						
Labor force	20	A-19						
Prisoners, sentence of death	18	A-17						
Wholesale trade:								
Average annual pay	22	A-21						
Earnings	39	A-38						
Employment	39,47	A-38,46						
Establishments	39,47	A-38,46						
Sales	47	A-46						
Women:	49	A-48						
Births	8	A-7						
Labor force	20	A-19						
Owned firms	49	A-48						
Public officials	57	A-56						
Workers' compensation	54	A-53						

USA Counties 1998

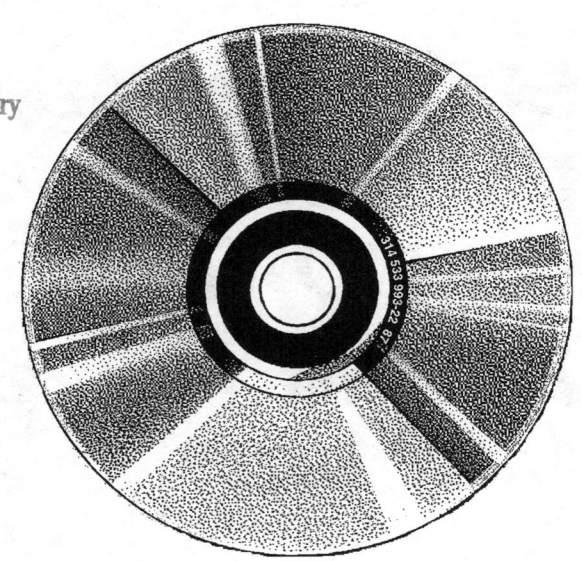

New for 1998—

- Fully integrated mapping software.

- Over 1,500 new or updated items, including 1997 population and 1990-1996 population estimates by age, sex, race, and Hispanic origin.

4th release of this popular CD-ROM, featuring—

- over 5,000 data items for every county in the Nation;

- State and U.S. totals to aid in data analysis;

- Windows software for browsing, copying, and printing the data and documentation; and

- database files that can be directly retrieved in many software packages (Visual dBASE, MS Access, FoxPro).

Price: $150.

For more information call:
Statistical Compendia Branch
Bureau of the Census
Washington, DC 20233
Telephone: 301-457-1166

To order these specials—

Mail to: U.S. Department of Commerce
Bureau of the Census
P.O. Box 277943
Atlanta, GA 30384-7943

Phone: For faster service on
orders being charged,
call 301-457-4100

for every problem there is a solution
for every question there is an answer
and for government information there is NTIS

Visit the NTIS Web site at www.ntis.gov for the latest U.S. government information products

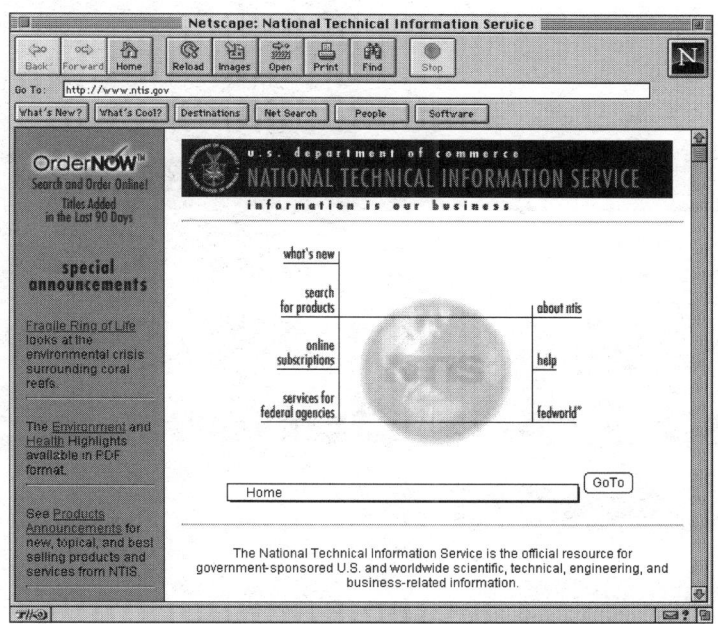

Have you seen the new NTIS Web site lately? There are now nearly 400,000 product listings on the site! We have added a number of new features to make the site easier to use -- and a guided tour to help you get the most out of your visit.

Use the NTIS Web site to find U.S. government information on business, environment, health and safety, science and technology, and more. Search or browse collections on army manuals and publications, databases, computer products, multimedia/training products, subscriptions, custom bibliographies, and technical reports on the site.

U.S. DEPARTMENT OF COMMERCE
Technology Administration
National Techncial Information Service
Springfield, VA 22161   (703) 605-6000

SPECIAL FEATURES

Search for Products
Search nearly 400,000 listings by keyword or use the advanced search to narrow your selection. And, discover other ways to locate product information on our site.

Help
Review our frequently asked questions, take a tour of the site, or quickly navigate the site with our site map.

About NTIS
All the basic facts about NTIS.

Online Subscriptions
Learn more about online subscription products like World News Connection®, Export Administration Regulations Electronic Marketplace, and the Davis-Bacon Wage Determination Database.

What's New
Keep track of what's happening at NTIS plus changes to our Web site.

Services for Federal Agencies
NTIS can help your agency become more efficient, improve customer service, and reduce overall costs.

FedWorld®
A comprehensive central access point for locating and acquiring government information.

ORDER FORM

NTIS Web Site — http://www.ntis.gov

SHIP TO ADDRESS (please print or type)

CUSTOMER MASTER NUMBER (IF KNOWN)

DATE

ATTENTION/NAME

ORGANIZATION

DIVISION / ROOM NUMBER

STREET ADDRESS

CITY

STATE

ZIP CODE

PROVINCE / TERRITORY

INTERNATIONAL POSTAL CODE

COUNTRY

PHONE NUMBER
(   )

FAX NUMBER
(   )

CONTACT NAME

INTERNET E-MAIL ADDRESS

METHOD OF PAYMENT (please print or type)

❑ VISA   ❑ MasterCard   ❑ American Express   ❑ Discover

CREDIT CARD NUMBER

EXPIRATION DATE

CARDHOLDER'S NAME

❑ NTIS Deposit Account Number:

❑ Check / Money Order enclosed for $ (PAYABLE TO NTIS IN U.S. DOLLARS)

ORDER BY PHONE (ELIMINATE MAIL TIME)
8:00 a.m. - 8:00 p.m., Eastern Time, M – F.
Sales Desk: 1-800-553-NTIS (6847)
(703) 605-6000

TDD: (703) 605-6043

CUSTOMER SERVICE: (703) 605-6050

ORDER BY FAX
24 hours/7 days a week: (703) 321-8547
To verify receipt of fax call: (703) 605-6090
7:00 a.m. – 5:00 p.m., Eastern Time, M – F.

ORDER BY MAIL
National Technical Information Service
5285 Port Royal Road
Springfield, VA 22161

RUSH SERVICE: available for an additional fee.

NTIS ORDERNOW® ONLINE
Order the most recent additions to the NTIS collection
at NTIS Web site **http://www.ntis.gov/ordernow**.

ORDER VIA E-MAIL
Order via E-mail 24 hours a day.
orders@ntis.fedworld.gov
If concerned about Internet security, you may register
your credit card at NTIS. Simply call (703) 605-6070.

BILL ME
(U.S., Canada, and Mexico only.)
NTIS will gladly bill your order, for an additional
fee of $10.00. A request to be billed must be on a
purchase order or company letterhead. An authorizing
signature, contact name, and telephone number
should be included with this request. Requests may
be mailed or faxed.

PRODUCT SELECTION (please print or type)

NTIS PRODUCT NUMBER	INTERNAL CUSTOMER ROUTING (OPTIONAL) UP TO 8 CHARACTERS	UNIT PRICE	QUANTITY						INTERNATIONAL AIRMAIL FEES (SEE BELOW)	TOTAL PRICE
			PAPER COPY	MICRO-FICHE	MAGNETIC TAPE ★	DISKETTE	CD-ROM	OTHER		
		$							$	$
		$							$	$
		$							$	$
		$							$	$
		$							$	$
		$							$	$

★ CIRCLE REQUIREMENTS	3480 CARTRIDGE	1600 BPI	6250 BPI	LABELING		FORMAT	
				STANDARD	NONLABELED	EBCDIC	ASCII

TOTAL	$	
HANDLING FEE PER TOTAL ORDER Outside North America–$10.00	$	5.00
	$	
GRAND TOTAL	$	

PLEASE NOTE
Unless microfiche or other is specified, paper copy will be sent.
Please call the Sales Desk at 1-800-553-NTIS (6847) for information on multiple copy discounts available for certain
documents.

Out-Of-Print Surcharge
A 25% out-of-print surcharge will be added to titles acquired by NTIS more than three years prior to the current calendar year.

International Airmail Fees
All regular prepaid orders are shipped "air-to-surface" unless airmail is requested. Airmail service is available for an
additional fee. Canada and Mexico add $4 *per item*. Other countries add $8 *per item*.

Thank you for your order!